[illegible]

hermeneia

Hermeneia
—A Critical
and Historical
Commentary
on the Bible

Odes of Solomon

A Commentary

by Michael Lattke

Translated by
Marianne Ehrhardt

Edited by
Harold W. Attridge

Fortress
Press

Minneapolis

Odes of Solomon
A Commentary

Cover and interior design by Kenneth Hiebert
Typesetting and page composition by
The HK Scriptorium

Library of Congress Cataloging-in-Publication Data

Lattke, Michael.
[Oden Salomos. English]
Odes of Solomon : a commentary / by Michael Lattke ; translation by Marianne Ehrhardt ; edited by Harold Attridge.
p. cm.
Includes bibliographical references and index.
ISBN 978-0-8006-6056-7 (alk. paper)
1. Odes of Solomon—Criticism, interpretation, etc. I. Attridge, Harold W. II. Title.
BS1830.O4L37313 2009
229'.912—dc22
2009015700

The paper used in this publication meets the minimum requirements of American National Standard for Information Sciences—Permanence of paper for Printed Library Materials, ANSI Z329.48–1984.

Manufactured in the U.S.A.

13 12 11 10 09 1 2 3 4 5 6 7 8 9 10

Dedicated to I.P.
with thanks.

The Author

Michael Lattke, born May 12, 1942 in Stettin (Szczecin), is Emeritus Professor of New Testament and Early Christianity at The University of Queensland, Australia. After his study of Catholic and Protestant theology in Bonn and Tübingen he studied oriental languages, especially Coptic and Syriac, at the University of Munich (1975–80). He received the Dipl.-Theol. at the University of Tübingen (1968), his Dr. theol. at the University of Freiburg im Breisgau (1974), the Dr. theol. habil. (Habilitation) at the University of Augsburg (1979), and a D. Litt. at The University of Queensland (1992). Before he settled in Brisbane (1981), he was a Research Fellow at the Institute for New Testament Textual Research at the University of Münster/Westphalia (1971–73) and a Research Assistant and Tutor in Biblical Studies and Hermeneutics at the University of Augsburg (1974–80). Since 1994 he has been a Fellow of the Australian Academy of the Humanities. In 2003 the Australian Government awarded him a Centenary Medal for his contribution to the field of early Christian studies, and in 2007 he was presented with a Festschrift, edited by Pauline Allen, Majella Franzmann, and Rick Strelan. This Festschrift also contains a comprehensive bibliography of Lattke's work, compiled by David Luckensmeyer. He is the author of *Einheit im Wort: Die spezifische Bedeutung von ἀγάπη, ἀγαπᾶν und φιλεῖν im Johannesevangelium* (1975), *Die Oden Salomos in ihrer Bedeutung für Neues Testament und Gnosis* (4 vols. in 5; 1979–98), *Register zu Rudolf Bultmanns Glauben und Verstehen,* vols. 1–4 (1984), *Hymnus: Materialien zu einer Geschichte der antiken Hymnologie* (1991), *Oden Salomos* (1995), and *Oden Salomos: Text, Übersetzung, Kommentar* (3 vols.; 1999–2005). He is currently writing a commentary on the *Apology of Aristides* for the series Kommentar zu frühchristlichen Apologeten, published by Herder.

Contents
Odes of Solomon

The name *Hermeneia,* Greek ἑρμηνεία, has been chosen as the title of the commentary series to which this volume belongs. The word *Hermeneia* has a rich background in the history of biblical interpretation as a term used in the ancient Greek-speaking world for the detailed, systematic exposition of a scriptural work. It is hoped that the series, like its name, will carry forward this old and venerable tradition. A second, entirely practical reason for selecting the name lies in the desire to avoid a long descriptive title and its inevitable acronym, or worse, an unpronounceable abbreviation.

The series is designed to be a critical and historical commentary to the Bible without arbitrary limits in size or scope. It will utilize the full range of philological and historical tools, including textual criticism (often slighted in modern commentaries), the methods of the history of tradition (including genre and prosodic analysis), and the history of religion.

Hermeneia is designed for the serious student of the Bible. It will make full use of ancient Semitic and classical languages; at the same time, English translations of all comparative materials—Greek, Latin, Canaanite, or Akkadian—will be supplied alongside the citation of the source in its original language. Insofar as possible, the aim is to provide the student or scholar with full critical discussion of each problem of interpretation and with the primary data upon which the discussion is based.

Hermeneia is designed to be international and interconfessional in the selection of authors; its editorial boards were formed with this end in view. Occasionally the series will offer translations of distinguished commentaries which originally appeared in languages other than English. Published volumes of the series will be revised continually, and eventually, new commentaries will replace older works in order to preserve the currency of the series. Commentaries are also being assigned for important literary works in the categories of apocryphal and pseudepigraphical works relating to the Old and New Testaments, including some of Essene or Gnostic authorship.

The editors of *Hermeneia* impose no systematic-theological perspective upon the series (directly, or indirectly by selection of authors). It is expected that authors will struggle to lay bare the ancient meaning of a biblical work or pericope. In this way the text's human relevance should become transparent, as is always the case in competent historical discourse. However, the series eschews for itself homiletical translation of the Bible.

The editors are heavily indebted to Fortress Press for its energy and courage in taking up an expensive, long-term project, the rewards of which will accrue chiefly to the field of biblical scholarship.

The editor responsible for this volume is Harold W. Attridge, Lillian Claus Professor of New Testament and Dean at Yale Divinity School.

Peter Machinist	*Helmut Koester*
For the Old Testament	For the New Testament
Editorial Board	Editorial Board

Editor's Note

The surviving manuscripts of the *Odes of Solomon* (see Introduction, sec. 2) have no headings that describe them formally or thematically. The headings assigned in this commentary are meant to highlight the more important formal and thematic aspects of each Ode. No attempt has been made to give headings to the individual stanzas (see Introduction, sec. 10.3.8), which, in the main, follow Franzmann's analyses and are denoted by Roman numbers.

The translation of each Ode (in the case of Odes preserved in two languages there are two separate translations) is followed by a general introduction. The first note to this introduction lists the manuscripts in which the Ode is found together with references to the editions of Charlesworth, Franzmann, and Lattke; other editions and translations are referred to in the commentary.

The commentary is arranged by stanzas or verse groups. At a suitable place in each Ode the commentary proper is interrupted by an excursus, which, generally, considers parallel passages in other Odes. With the exception of *Ode* 3, where excursuses 2 and 3 are to be found, the number of an excursus is the number of its Ode. There are nine tables, associated with *Odes* 3, 4, 6, 20 (two tables), 21, 29, 33, and 39.

Where quotations from foreign languages have been translated into English, they are generally shown by being placed in quotation marks.

The front endpapers show pages 28b–29a, and the back endpapers pages 29b–30a, of Codex Harris (abbreviated H; John Rylands Library Cod. Syr. 9), a Syriac manuscript from the thirteenth to fifteenth century containing the *Odes* and the *Psalms of Solomon*. The lighter ink on p. 29a (red in the original) reads "*Ode* 40"; that on pp. 29b–30a, "*Ode* 41" and "*Ode* 42," respectively. Photos courtesy of the University Librarian and Director, John Rylands Library, Manchester.

Preface

It was in April 1994, before I had even completed the preparatory work on my German commentary on the *Odes of Solomon,* that Helmut Koester approached me on behalf of the editorial board to ask whether I would be willing to contribute a volume to the Hermeneia series of commentaries. It took another eight years and much correspondence with Harry Attridge, Eldon Epp, and Helmut Koester on technical questions until the contracts between the publisher Fortress Press and the author and the translator, Marianne Ehrhardt, were finalized. I am grateful to the three of them for their tenacity and perseverance.

This volume, which is a translation of the manuscript that forms the basis of my three-volume German commentary, could not exist without the mental and manual labor of Marianne, the daughter of Edith and Arnold Ehrhardt, and the financial support of the Australian Research Council. I am also grateful to the Swiss editors, Othmar Keel and Max Küchler, who generously gave me permission, some years ago now, to translate my German manuscript into English.

Irmtraud Petersson not only read the German manuscript attentively and critically, but was also most helpful and supportive in the work on the English version. In 1982 I dedicated one of my first articles on the *Odes of Solomon* to I.P.; I now dedicate this Hermeneia commentary to her as the culmination of many years of research that we experienced together.

Michael Lattke

Reference Codes

1. Abbreviations

A	Codex Askew
AAAp	Richard Adelbert Lipsius, ed., *Acta apostolorum apocrypha* (3 vols.; Leipzig, 1891–1903; repr., Darmstadt: Wissenschaftliche Buchgesellschaft, 1959; repr., 1972).
AB	Anchor Bible
Abh.	Abhandlung(en)
Abt.	Abteilung(en)
Act. John	*Acts of John*
Act. Mart.	*Acts of Martyrs*
Act. Pet.	*Acts of Peter*
Act. Thom.	*Acts of Thomas*
AELAC	Association pour l'étude de la littérature apocryphe chrétienne
AGJU	Arbeiten zur Geschichte des antiken Judentums und des Urchristentums
AGSU	Arbeiten zur Geschichte des Spätjudentums und (des) Urchristentums
AJT	*American Journal of Theology*
AMRG	Arbeitsmaterialien zur Religionsgeschichte
ANF	Ante-Nicene Fathers
ANTT	Arbeiten zur neutestamentlichen Textforschung
APAT	Emil Kautzsch, ed., *Die Apokryphen und Pseudepigraphen des Alten Testaments* (2 vols.; 2nd ed.; Darmstadt: Wissenschaftliche Buchgesellschaft, 1962).
Aph.	*ʾapʿel*
Apoc. Adam	*Apocalypse of Adam*
Apoc. Mos.	*Apocalypse of Moses*
APOT	Robert Henry Charles, ed., *The Apocrypha and Pseudepigrapha of the Old Testament in English* (2 vols.; Oxford: Clarendon, 1913; repr., 1973).
ARW	*Archiv für Religionswissenschaft*
Asc. Isa.	*Ascension of Isaiah*
AtAbh	Alttestamentliche Abhandlungen
ATD	Das Alte Testament Deutsch
ATDA	Das Alte Testament Deutsch: Apokryphen
AThANT	Abhandlungen zur Theologie des Alten und Neuen Testaments
Athenagoras	
Leg.	*Legatio pro Christianis*
Aufl.	Auflage(n)
Ausg.	Ausgabe(n)
ausgew.	ausgewählt
BAWGR	Bibliothek der Alten Welt, Griechische Reihe
BBB	Bonner biblische Beiträge
B.C.E.	Before Common Era
BDAG	*A Greek-English Lexicon of the New Testament and Other Early Christian Literature (*3rd ed., rev. and ed. Frederick William Danker based on Walter Bauer's *Griechisch-deutsches Wörterbuch zu den Schriften des Neuen Testaments und der frühchristlichen Literatur,* 6th ed., ed. Kurt Aland and Barbara Aland, with Viktor Reichmann and on previous English editions by William F. Arndt, F. Wilbur Gingrich, and Frederick W. Danker [Chicago/London: University of Chicago Press, 2000]).
BDF	Friedrich Blass and Albert Debrunner, *A Grammar of the New Testament and Other Early Christian Literature* (trans. Robert W. Funk; Chicago/London: University of Chicago Press, 1961).
BDR	Friedrich Blass and Albert Debrunner, *Grammatik des neutestamentlichen Griechisch* (ed. Friedrich Rehkopf; 14th ed.; Göttingen: Vandenhoeck & Ruprecht, 1975).
Beih.	Beiheft(e)
BeO	*Bibbia e oriente*
BEThL	Bibliotheca ephemeridum theologicarum lovaniensium
BFCTh	Beiträge zur Förderung christlicher Theologie, 2. Reihe: Sammlung wissenschaftlicher Monographien
BG	*Codex Berolinensis Gnosticus* 8502
BHH	Bo Reicke and Leonhard Rost, eds., *Biblisch-Historisches Handwörterbuch: Landeskunde, Geschichte, Religion, Kultur, Literatur* (4 vols.; Göttingen: Vandenhoeck & Ruprecht, 1962–79).
BHS	*Biblia hebraica stuttgartensia* (Stuttgart: Deutsche Bibelstiftung, 1967–77).
BHTh	Beiträge zur historischen Theologie

Bib	*Biblica*
BK	*Bibel und Kirche*
BKAT	Biblischer Kommentar: Altes Testament
BKV	Bibliothek der Kirchenväter
BO	*Bibliotheca orientalis*
BSO(A)S	*Bulletin of the School of Oriental (and African) Studies*
BSV	*Biblia sacra iuxta Vulgatam versionem*
BU	Biblische Untersuchungen
BZAW	Beihefte zur *Zeitschrift für die alttestamentliche Wissenschaft*
BZNW	Beihefte zur *Zeitschrift für die neutestamentliche Wissenschaft und die Kunde der älteren Kirche*
ℭ	Coptic Version (Codex Askew [A])
c.	century
ca.	circa
CBB	Lothar Coenen, Erich Beyreuther, and Hans Bietenhard, eds., *Theologisches Begriffslexikon zum Neuen Testament* (Studien-Ausgabe in 2 vols.; 4th ed.; Wuppertal: Brockhaus, 1977).
CBQ	*Catholic Biblical Quarterly*
CChr.SL	Corpus Christianorum, Series Latina
C.E.	Common Era
chap(s).	chapter(s)
CKNTG	*Computer-Konkordanz zum Novum Testamentum Graece von Nestle–Aland, 26. Auflage und zum Greek New Testament, 3rd Edition*, ed. Institut für neutestamentliche Textforschung and Rechenzentrum der Universität Münster, esp. Horst Bachmann and Wolfgang A. Slaby (Berlin/New York: de Gruyter, 1980).
Clement of Alexandria	
Exc. ex Theod.	*Excerpta ex Theodoto*
Paed.	*Paedagogus*
Strom.	*Stromata*
col(s).	column(s)
Colloquium	*Colloquium: The Australian and New Zealand Theological Review*
ConNT	Conjectanea Neotestamentica
Corp. Herm.	*Corpus Hermeticum*
corr.	corrected, correction
CRINT	Compendia rerum iudaicarum ad Novum Testamentum
CStS	Collected Studies Series
DACL	*Dictionnaire d'archéologie chrétienne et de liturgie* (11 vols.; Paris: Letouzey et Ané, 1907).
Diogn.	*Epistle to Diognetus*
Diss.	Dissertation
DNP	Hubert Cancik and Helmuth Schneider, eds., *Der Neue Pauly: Enzyklopädie der Antike* (Stuttgart: J. B. Metzler, 1996–).
DNTB	Craig A. Evans and Stanley E. Porter, eds., *Dictionary of New Testament Background* (Downers Grove, Ill.: InterVarsity, 2000).
DSS	Dead Sea Scrolls
ed.	edited by, editor, edition
EDNT	Horst Balz and Gerhard Schneider, eds., *Exegetical Dictionary of the New Testament* (3 vols.; Grand Rapids: Eerdmans, 1990–93)
EKKNT	Evangelisch-katholischer Kommentar zum Neuen Testament
EKL	*Evangelisches Kirchenlexikon* (Göttingen: Vandenhoeck & Ruprecht, 1986).
EPRO	Études préliminaires aux religions orientales dans l'empire Romain
ERE	*Encyclopaedia of Religion and Ethics* (Edinburgh: T&T Clark, 1908–26).
Eshtaph.	*ʾeštapʿal*
esp.	especially
EstEcl	*Estudios eclesiásticos*
ET	English Translation
et al.	and others
etc.	et cetera
Ethpa.	*ʾetpaʿʿal*
Ethpalp.	*ʾetpalpal*
Ethpe.	*ʾetpʿel*
Ettaph.	*ʾettapʿal*
EWNT	Horst Balz and Gerhard Schneider, eds., *Exegetisches Wörterbuch zum Neuen Testament* (3 vols.; Stuttgart: Kohlhammer, 1980–83; 2nd ed., 1992).
Exp	*Expositor*
ExpT	*Expository Times*
fasc.	fascicle
FontChr	Fontes Christiani
frg(s).	fragment(s)
FRLANT	Forschungen zur Religion und Literatur des Alten und Neuen Testaments
FS	Festschrift
FVS	Hermann Diels and Walther Kranz, eds., *Die Fragmente der Vorsokratiker* (3 vols.; 6th ed.; 16th printing, Dublin/Zurich: Weidmann, 1972 [vols. 1–2]; 14th printing, 1973 [vol. 3]).
G, OG	Greek (Old Greek)
𝔊/𝔊*	Greek Version (*Papyrus Bodmer* XI)/Greek original

GCS	Die griechischen christlichen Schriftsteller der ersten Jahrhunderte
Ger.	German
GGA	*Göttingische gelehrte Anzeigen*
GNT	Grundrisse zum Neuen Testament
Gos. Pet.	*Gospel of Peter*
Gos. Phil.	*Gospel of Philip*
Gos. Thom.	*Gospel of Thomas*
H	Codex Harris
HAT	Handbuch zum Alten Testament
HAW	Handbuch der Altertums-wissenschaft
HB	Hebrew Bible
Hermas	
Sim.	*Similitude*
Hermeneia	Hermeneia: A Critical and Historical Commentary on the Bible
Hippolytus	
Elench.	*Elenchus*
HNT	Handbuch zum Neuen Testament
HR	*History of Religions*
HRWG	Hubert Cancik, Burkhard Gladigow, and Matthias Laubscher, eds., *Handbuch religionswissenschaftlicher Grundbegriffe* (Stuttgart: Kohlhammer, 1988–2001).
HSM	Harvard Semitic Monographs
HThKNT	Herders theologischer Kommentar zum Neuen Testament
HTR	*Harvard Theological Review*
HTS	Harvard Theological Studies
HWP	Joachim Ritter, ed., *Historisches Wörterbuch der Philosophie* (Basel: Schwabe, 1971–2001).
ibid.	ibidem
ICC	International Critical Commentary
IDB	George A. Buttrick, ed., *Interpreter's Dictionary of the Bible* (New York: Abingdon, 1962).
IDBSup	Keith Crim, ed., *Interpreter's Dictionary of the Bible: Supplementary Volume* (Nashville: Abingdon, 1976).
idem, eadem	the same
i.e.	id est
IG	*Inscriptiones graecae* (Berlin, 1924–).
Ignatius	
Eph.	*Letter to the Ephesians*
Magn.	*Letter to the Magnesians*
Phld.	*Letter to the Philadelphians*
Rom.	*Letter to the Romans*
Trall.	*Letter to the Trallians*

impr.	imprint
ITQ	*Irish Theological Quarterly*
JAC	*Jahrbuch für Antike und Christentum*
JBL	*Journal of Biblical Literature*
JECS	*Journal of Early Christian Studies*
Jg.	Jahrgang, Jahrgänge
JJS	*Journal of Jewish Studies*
Jos. Asen.	*Joseph and Aseneth*
JSHRZ	Jüdische Schriften aus hellenistisch-römischer Zeit
JSJ	*Journal for the Study of Judaism in the Persian, Hellenistic, and Roman Period*
JSNT	*Journal for the Study of the New Testament*
JSNTSup	Journal for the Study of the New Testament Supplement Series
JSOTSup	Journal for the Study of the Old Testament Supplement Series
JSPSup	Journal for the Study of the Pseudepigrapha Supplement Series
JSS	*Journal of Semitic Studies*
JTS	*Journal of Theological Studies*
Justin	
Dial.	*Dialogue with Trypho*
Kairos	*Kairos: Zeitschrift für Religionswissenschaft und Theologie.* From N.F. 30/31 (1988/89): *Zeitschrift für Judaistik und Religionswissenschaft*
KAV	Kommentar zu den apostolischen Vätern
KEK	Kritisch-Exegetischer Kommentar über das Neue Testament
KIT	Kleine Texte für Vorlesungen und Übungen
KP	*Der Kleine Pauly: Lexikon der Antike* (Stuttgart: Alfred Druckenmüller, 1969).
KTA	Kröners Taschenausgabe
κτλ.	καὶ τὰ λοιπά (*see* etc.)
KWCO	Julius Aßfalg, ed., *Kleines Wörterbuch des Christlichen Orients* (Wiesbaden: Harrassowitz, 1975)
𝔏	Latin Version (Lactantius; cf. *Ode* 19)
l(l).	line(s)
LACL	Siegmar Döpp and Wilhelm Geerlings, eds., *Lexikon der antiken christlichen Literatur* (3rd ed.; Freiburg, Basel, Vienna: Herder, 2002).
Lat.	Latin
LCI	Engelbert Kirschbaum, ed., *Lexikon der christlichen Ikonographie* (Rome: Herder, 1968).

LCL	Loeb Classical Library
LD	Lectio divina
LEH	Johan Lust, Erik Eynikel, and Katrin Hauspie, eds., *A Greek-English Lexicon of the Septuagint* (rev. ed.; Stuttgart: Deutsche Bibelgesellschaft, 2003).
Lfg./Lief.	Lieferung(en)
lit.	literal(ly)
Log.	Logion
LSJ	Henry George Liddell and Robert Scott, *Greek-English Lexicon* (9th. ed.; 1940; rev. Henry Stuart Jones; repr., with a supplement, Oxford: Clarendon, 1968)
LSJRevSup	Henry George Liddell and Robert Scott, *Greek-English Lexicon Revised Supplement* (ed. P. G. W. Glare, with the assistance of A. A. Thompson; Oxford: Clarendon, 1996).
LThK[2–3]	*Lexikon für Theologie und Kirche* (Freiburg: Herder; 2nd ed., 1957–65; 3rd ed., 1993–2001).
LXX	Septuagint
MEL[9]	*Meyers enzyklopädisches Lexikon* (32 vols.; Mannheim/Vienna/Zurich: Bibliographisches Inst., 1971–81).
MLAA	Oliver Schütze, ed., *Metzler Lexikon antiker Autoren* (Darmstadt: Wissenschaftliche Buchgesellschaft, 1997).
MPTh	*Monatsschrift für Pastoraltheologie zur Vertiefung des gesamten pfarramtlichen Wirkens*
MS(S).	manuscript(s)
MT	Masoretic Text
Mus	*Muséon*
N	Codex Nitriensis
n(n).	note(s)
NA[27]	Nestle–Aland: *Novum Testamentum Graece* post Eberhard et Erwin Nestle editione vicesima septima revisa communiter ediderunt Barbara et Kurt Aland et al. (Stuttgart: Deutsche Bibelgesellschaft, 1993).
Nag Hammadi Writings	
Disc. 8–9	*Discourse on the Eighth and Ninth*
Gos. Thom.	*Gospel of Thomas*
Orig. World	*On the Origin of the World*
Paraph. Shem	*Paraphrase of Shem*
2 Treat. Seth	*Second Treatise of the Great Seth*
Teach. Silv.	*Teachings of Silvanus*
Testim. Truth	*Testimony of Truth*
Treat. Res.	*Treatise on Resurrection*
Tri. Trac.	*Tripartite Tractate*
NedThT	*Nederlands theologisch tijdschrift*
N.F.	Neue Folge
NHC	Nag Hammadi Codex/Codices
NHD	Hans-Martin Schenke, Hans-Gebhard Bethge, and Ursula Ulrike Kaiser, eds., *Nag Hammadi Deutsch* (2 vols.; GCS N.F. 8, 12; Koptisch-Gnostische Schriften II–III; Berlin/New York: de Gruyter, 2001–3).
NHLE	James M. Robinson, ed., *The Nag Hammadi Library in English* (3rd ed.; Leiden: Brill, 1988).
NHMS	Nag Hammadi and Manichaean Studies
NHS	Nag Hammadi Studies
NKZ	*Neue kirchliche Zeitschrift*
no(s).	number(s)
N.R.	Neue Reihe
N.S., n.s.	Neue Serie (new series)
NovT	*Novum Testamentum*
NovTSup	*Novum Testamentum*, Supplements
NRSV	New Revised Standard Version
NT	New Testament
NTAbh	Neutestamentliche Abhandlungen
NTApo[2]	Edgar Hennecke, ed., *Neutestamentliche Apokryphen in deutscher Übersetzung* (2nd ed.; Tübingen: Mohr Siebeck, 1924)
NTApo[3–5]	Edgar Hennecke, *Neutestamentliche Apokryphen in deutscher Übersetzung* (ed. Wilhelm Schneemelcher; 2 vols.; Tübingen: Mohr Siebeck; 3rd ed., 1959–64; 4th ed., 1968–71; 5th ed., 1987–89).
NTApoc	Edgar Hennecke, *New Testament Apocrypha* (ed. Wilhelm Schneemelcher; English translation ed. R. McL. Wilson; 2 vols.; rev. ed.; Philadelphia: Westminster, 1965).
NTD	Das Neue Testament Deutsch
NTF	Neutestamentliche Forschungen
NTGr	Institut für neutestamentliche Textforschung (Barbara Aland et al., ed.), *Novum Testamentum graecum: Editio critica maior* (Stuttgart: Deutsche Bibelgesellschaft, 1997–).
NTOA	Novum Testamentum et orbis antiquus
NTS	*New Testament Studies*
NTSy	*The New Testament in Syriac* (London: British and Foreign Bible Society, 1962)
OBO	Orbis biblicus et orientalis

OCD	Nicholas G. L. Hammond and Howard H. Scullard, eds., *The Oxford Classical Dictionary* (2nd ed.; Oxford: Clarendon, 1970).
Odes Sol.	*Odes of Solomon*
OECT	Oxford Early Christian Texts
OLZ	*Orientalistische Literaturzeitung*
OrChr	*Oriens christianus: Hefte für die Kunde des christlichen Orients*
OrChrA	Orientalia Christiana Analecta
OrChrP	*Orientalia Christiana Periodica*
Origen	
Cels.	*Contra Celsum*
De princ.	*De principiis*
OT	Old Testament
OTP	James H. Charlesworth, ed., *The Old Testament Pseudepigrapha* (2 vols.; Garden City, N.Y.: Doubleday, 1983–85).
OTSy	The Peshiṭta Institute, ed., *The Old Testament in Syriac according to the Peshiṭta Version* (Leiden: Brill, 1972–).
P.	*Papyrus*
p(p).	page(s)
Pa.	*paʿʿel*
Palp.	*palpel*
Pap.	Papyrus
Par.	*parʿel*
par., parr.	parallel(s)
ParO	*Parole de l'Orient*
ParPass	*Parola del passato: Rivista di studi classici/antichi*
Pe.	*pʿal* (*pʿel*, *pʿol*); Beyer uses *qal* instead of *pʿal* (see Beyer, *ATTM*, 461)
PG	Migne, J.-P., ed., *Patrologiae cursus completus, Series graeca* (162 vols.; Paris: 1857–86).
PGM, *PGrM*	Karl Preisendanz, ed., *Papyri graecae magicae* (new ed. Albert Henrichs; 2 vols.; Stuttgart: Teubner, 1973–74)
Philo	
Det. pot. ins.	*Quod deterius potiori insidiari soleat*
Deus imm.	*Quod Deus sit immutabilis*
Poster. C.	*De posteritate Caini*
pl(s).	plate(s)
Porphyry	
Marc.	*Ad Marcellam*
prev.	previously
Protev. Jac.	*Protevangelium Jacobi*
ps.-, Ps.-	pseudo-, Pseudo-
pt.	part
PTMS	Princeton Theological Monograph Series
PTS	Patristische Texte und Studien
PVTG	Pseudepigrapha Veteris Testamenti graece
PW	A. F. Pauly, *Real-Encyclopädie der classischen Altertumswissenschaft* (1893–1919; new ed. G. Wissowa; 49 vols.; Munich: A. Druckenmüller, 1980).
QL	Qumran Literature
RAC	*Reallexikon für Antike und Christentum*
RB	*Revue biblique*
RE	*Realencyklopädie für protestantische Theologie und Kirche* (1896–1913, ed. J. J. Herzog; 3rd printing ed. Albert Hauck; Graz: Akademische Druck- und Verlagsanstalt, 1969–71).
repr.	reprint(ed)
rev.	revised, revision
RevQ	*Revue de Qumran*
RevSém	*Revue sémitique*
RGG$^{1-4}$	*Religion in Geschichte und Gegenwart* (1st ed., ed. F. M. Schiele, 1909–13; 2nd ed., ed. Hermann Gunkel, 1927–31; 3rd ed., ed. Kurt Galling, 1957–65; 4th ed., ed. Hans Dieter Betz; Tübingen: Mohr Siebeck, 1998–2005).
RNT	Regensburger Neues Testament
RQ	*Römische Quartalschrift für christliche Altertumskunde und Kirchengeschichte*
RQSup	*Römische Quartalschrift für christliche Altertumskunde und Kirchengeschichte* –Supplementheft
RThPh	*Revue de théologie et de philosophie*
s/s*	Syriac Version (Codex Harris [H] and Codex Nitriensis [N])
SANT	Studien zum Alten und Neuen Testament
Saph.	*sap̄ʿel*
SAQ	Sammlung ausgewählter kirchen- und dogmengeschichtlicher Quellenschriften
SBB	Stuttgarter biblische Beiträge
SBL	Society of Biblical Literature
SBLDS	SBL Dissertation Series
SBLPS	SBL Pseudepigrapha Series
SBLSCS	SBL Septuagint and Cognate Studies
SBLTT	SBL Texts and Translations
SBS	Stuttgarter Bibelstudien
SC	Sources chrétiennes
SCHNT	Studia ad corpus hellenisticum Novi Testamenti
sec.	section
Shaph.	*šap̄ʿel*

SHAW.PH	Sitzungsberichte der Heidelberger Akademie der Wissenschaften: Philosophisch-historische Klasse
SJT	*Scottish Journal of Theology*
SNTSMS	Society for New Testament Studies Monograph Series
Sophocles	
Ant.	*Antigone*
SPAW.PH	Sitzungsberichte der preussischen Akademie der Wissenschaften: Philosophisch-historische Klasse
SPB	Studia Post-Biblica
SSA	Schriften der Sektion für Altertumswissenschaft
StPatr	*Studia Patristica*
Str-B	[Hermann L. Strack and] Paul Billerbeck, *Kommentar zum Neuen Testament aus Talmud und Midrasch* (6 vols.; Munich: C. H. Beck, 1926–61).
SUNT	Studien zur Umwelt des Neuen Testaments
s.vv.	sub voce(s)
Syr.	Syriac
T. Abr.	*Testament of Abraham*
TDNT	Gerhard Kittel and Gerhard Friedrich, eds., *Theological Dictionary of the New Testament* (trans. and ed. Geoffrey W. Bromiley; 10 vols.; Grand Rapids: Eerdmans, 1964–76).
TDOT	G. Johannes Botterweck et al., eds., *Theological Dictionary of the Old Testament* (trans. David E. Green et al.; Grand Rapids: Eerdmans, 1974–).
Tertullian	
Praescr. haer.	*De praescriptione haereticorum*
TextsS	Texts and Studies
ThBü	Theologische Bücherei: Neudrucke und Berichte aus dem 20. Jahrhundert
Theophaneia	Theophaneia: Beiträge zur Religions- und Kirchengeschichte des Altertums
ThGl	*Theologie und Glaube*
ThGL	*Θησαυρὸς τῆς ἑλληνικῆς γλώσσης – Thesaurus graecae linguae* (9 vols.; Graz: Akademische Druck- und Verlagsanstalt, 1954 = 3rd ed., Paris, 1831–65).
ThH	Théologie historique
ThHKNT	Theologischer Handkommentar zum Neuen Testament
ThLZ	*Theologische Literaturzeitung*
ThR	*Theologische Rundschau*
ThStK	*Theologische Studien und Kritiken: Zeitschrift für das gesamte Gebiet der Theologie*
ThWAT	G. Johannes Botterweck, Helmer Ringgren, and Heinz-Josef Fabry, eds., *Theologisches Wörterbuch zum Alten Testament* (Stuttgart: Kohlhammer, 1973–2000; vol. 9.1, 2001).
ThWNT	Gerhard Kittel and Gerhard Friedrich, eds., *Theologisches Wörterbuch zum Neuen Testament* (10 vols.; Stuttgart: Kohlhammer, 1933–79).
trans.	translated, translator, translation
TRE	Gerhard Krause and Gerhard Müller, eds., *Theologische Realenzyklopädie* (Berlin/New York: de Gruyter, 1977–2007).
TRev	*Theologische Revue*
t.t.	technical term(s)
TU	Texte und Untersuchungen zur Geschichte der altchristlichen Literatur
UTB	Uni-Taschenbücher
UUÅ	Uppsala universitets årsskrift
v(v).	verse(s)
VC	*Vigiliae christianae*
Vg	Vulgate
viz.	videlicet
VL	Vetus Latina
v.l.	*varia lectio*
vol., vols.	volume(s)
VT	*Vetus Testamentum*
VTG	Septuaginta (LXX): Vetus Testamentum graecum
VTSup	*Vetus Testamentum*, Supplements
WMANT	Wissenschaftliche Monographien zum Alten und Neuen Testament
WUNT	Wissenschaftliche Untersuchungen zum Neuen Testament
ZAC	*Zeitschrift für antikes Christentum/Journal of Ancient Christianity*
ZAW	*Zeitschrift für die alttestamentliche Wissenschaft*
ZDMG	*Zeitschrift der deutschen morgenländischen Gesellschaft*
ZKG	*Zeitschrift für Kirchengeschichte*
ZKTh	*Zeitschrift für katholische Theologie*
ZNW	*Zeitschrift für die neutestamentliche Wissenschaft und die Kunde der älteren Kirche*
ZRGG	*Zeitschrift für Religions- und Geistesgeschichte*
ZThK	*Zeitschrift für Theologie und Kirche*
ZWTh	*Zeitschrift für wissenschaftliche Theologie*

2. Syriac Conjugations

Pe.	*pʿal* (*pʿel*, *pʿol*)
Ethpe.	*ʾetp̄ʿel*
Pa.	*paʿʿel*
Ethpa.	*ʾetpaʿʿal*
Aph.	*ʾap̄ʿel*
Ettaph.	*ʾettap̄ʿal*
Shaph.	*šap̄ʿel*
Eshtaph.	*ʾeštap̄ʿal*
Palp.	*palpel*
Ethpalp.	*ʾetpalpal*
Par.	*parʿel*
Saph.	*sap̄ʿel*

3. Transcription of Syriac[1]

ܐ	ʾ (emission of breath, if not just etymological); finally *-ā*, *-ē*, rarely *-ẹ̄*; internally *-ẹ̄-*, very rarely *-a-*
ܒ	*b/ḇ*
ܓ	*g/ḡ*
ܕ	*d/ḏ*
ܗ	*h*
ܘ	*w*; without vowel *-u-*, plus initial *ʾu-* "and"; every short and long *o* (= *ọ*) and *u* (without ܘ in *kol/kull-*, *meṭṭol/meṭṭull-*)
ܙ	*z*
ܚ	*ḥ*
ܛ	*ṭ*
ܝ ܝ	*y*; without vowel *-i-*, plus initial *ʾi-* (also ܐܝ); finally *-ī*; internally *-ī-*, *-ẹ̄-* (rarely without ܝ), *-ē-*, *-i-*
ܟ ܟ	*k/ḵ*
ܠ	*l*
ܡ ܡ	*m*
ܢ ܢ	*n*
ܣ	*s*
ܥ	ʿ (flow of breath compressed)
ܦ	*p/p̄* (also *p/f*), *p̌* (Greek π)
ܨ	*ṣ* (= *ts*)
ܩ	*q* (also *ḳ*)
ܪ	*r*
ܫ	*š* (English *sh*)
ܬ	*t/ṯ*

Syriac Vowels

Ptọ̄ḥọ̄	*a* (very rarely + ܐ [see above])
Zqọ̄p̄ọ̄	*ā* (finally + ܐ; West Syriac > *ọ̄*)
Rḇọ̄ṣọ̄	*e* (always closed); *ē* (open; finally + ܐ, internally + ܝ)
Ḥḇọ̄ṣọ̄	*i* (instead of mute [-]*y*- and in loan/foreign words, + ܝ), *ī* (+ ܝ), *ẹ̄* (closed; with or without ܐ, if not < *ay*, otherwise + ܝ; West Syriac > *ī*)
ʿṣọ̄ṣọ̄	*o*, *ō* (West Syriac > *u*, *ū*), *u*, *ū* (all of them almost always + ܘ)

4. Transcription of Coptic[2]

ⲁ	*a*
ⲃ	*b*
ⲅ	*g*
ⲇ	*d*
ⲉ	*e*
ⲍ	*z*
ⲏ	*ē*
ⲑ	*th*
ⲓ, ⲉⲓ	*i*, *y* (= Germ. *j*)
ⲕ	*k*
ⲗ	*l*
ⲙ	*m*
ⲛ	*n*
ⲝ	*ks*
ⲟ	*o*
ⲡ	*p*
ⲣ	*r*
ⲥ	*s*
ⲧ	*t*
ⲩ, ⲟⲩ	*u*, *w*
ⲫ	*ph*
ⲭ	*kh*
ⲯ	*ps*
ⲱ	*ō*
ϣ	*š*
ϥ	*f*
ϩ	*h*
ϫ	*č*
ϭ	*c*
ϯ	*ti*
ⲛ̄	*ᵉn* (e.g.)
ⲙⲛ̄	*mᵉn* (e.g.)

1 Cf. Klaus Beyer in Lattke, 3:XIII–XIV.

2 Cf. Lattke, 1:271–72; 2:285–86; 3:XII. Lambdin's transcription of ϫ is *j*, but Till's transcription *č* is to be preferred.

5. Short Titles of Commentaries, Dictionaries, Grammars, Studies, and Articles Often Cited

Abbott
Edwin A. Abbott, *Light on the Gospel from an Ancient Poet* (Diatessarica 9; Cambridge: Cambridge University Press, 1912).

Abbott and Connolly
Edwin A. Abbott and Richard H. Connolly, "The Original Language of the Odes of Solomon," *JTS* 15 (1913–14) 44–47.

Abramowski
Rudolf Abramowski, "Der Christus der Salomooden," *ZNW* 35 (1936) 44–69.

Abramowski, "Sprache"
Luise Abramowski, "Sprache und Abfassungszeit der Oden Salomos," *OrChr* 68 (1984) 80–90.

Adam, *Psalmen des Thomas*
Alfred Adam, *Die Psalmen des Thomas und das Perlenlied als Zeugnisse vorchristlicher Gnosis* (BZNW 24; Berlin: de Gruyter, 1959).

Adam, "Sprache"
Alfred Adam, "Die ursprüngliche Sprache der Salomo-Oden," *ZNW* 52 (1961) 141–56.

Aland, *Synopsis*
Kurt Aland, ed., *Synopsis of the Four Gospels* (8th ed.; Stuttgart: German Bible Society, 1987).

Aland, "Welche Rolle"
Barbara Aland, "Welche Rolle spielen Textkritik und Textgeschichte für das Verständnis des Neuen Testaments? Frühe Leserperspektiven," *NTS* 52 (2006) 303–18.

Aland and Juckel, *Briefe*
Barbara Aland and Andreas Juckel, eds., *Das Neue Testament in syrischer Überlieferung II: Die paulinischen Briefe* (3 vols.; ANTT 14, 23, 32; Berlin/New York: de Gruyter, 1991–2002).

Alegre, "Salvación"
Xavier Alegre, "El concepto de salvación en las Odas de Salomon: Contribución al estudio de una soteriología gnostizante y sus posibles relaciones con el cuarto evangelio" (Dr. theol. diss., Münster University, 1977).

Amstutz
Joseph Amstutz, *ΑΠΛΟΤΗΣ: Eine begriffsgeschichtliche Studie zum jüdisch-christlichen Griechisch* (Theophaneia 19; Bonn: Hanstein, 1968).

Arvedson, *Mysterium*
Tomas Arvedson, *Das Mysterium Christi: Eine Studie zu Mt 11.25-30* (Arbeiten und Mitteilungen aus dem neutestamentlichen Seminar zu Uppsala 7; Uppsala: Wretmans, 1937).

Attridge, *Nag Hammadi Codex I*
Harold W. Attridge, ed., *Nag Hammadi Codex I (The Jung Codex)* (2 vols.; NHS 22, 23; Leiden: Brill, 1985).

Attridge and MacRae, "Gospel of Truth"
Harold W. Attridge and George W. MacRae, "The Gospel of Truth: [NHC] I,*3*:16.31–43.24," in Attridge, *Nag Hammadi Codex I,* 1:55–117; 2:39–135.

Attridge and Pagels, "Tripartite Tractate"
Harold W. Attridge and Elaine H. Pagels, "The Tripartite Tractate: [NHC] I,*5*:51.1–138.27," in Attridge, *Nag Hammadi Codex I,* 1:159–337; 2:217–497.

Aune, "Christian Prophecy"
"The *Odes of Solomon* and Early Christian Prophecy," *NTS* 28 (1982) 435–60.

Azar
Éphrem Azar, *Les Odes de Salomon* (Paris: Cerf, 1996).

Baars, "Psalms"
Willem Baars, "Psalms of Solomon," in *OTSy*, pt. 4 fasc. 6 (1972).

Barnes, "Hymn Book"
W. E. Barnes, "An Ancient Christian Hymn Book," *Exp*, 7th Ser., 10 (1910) 52–63.

Barth
Jakob Barth, "Zur Textkritik der syrischen Oden Salomos," *RevSém* 19 (1911) 261–65.

Bauckham, "Parable"
Richard Bauckham, "The Parable of the Vine: Rediscovering a Lost Parable of Jesus," *NTS* 33 (1987) 84–101.

Bauer
Walter Bauer, "Die Oden Salomos," *NTApo* (^{3}1964 = ^{4}1971) 2:576–625.

Bauer, *Oden*
Walter Bauer, ed., *Die Oden Salomos* (KlT 64; Berlin: de Gruyter, 1933).

Bauer and Aland
Walter Bauer, *Griechisch-deutsches Wörterbuch zu den Schriften des Neuen Testaments und der frühchristlichen Literatur* (ed. Kurt Aland and Barbara Aland; 6th ed.; Berlin/New York: de Gruyter, 1988).

Bauer and Paulsen
Walter Bauer and Henning Paulsen, *Die Briefe des Ignatius von Antiochia und der Brief des Polykarp von Smyrna* (HNT 18: Die Apostolischen Väter 2; 2nd ed.; Tübingen: Mohr Siebeck, 1985).

Becker, *Reden*
Heinz Becker, *Die Reden des Johannesevangeliums und der Stil der gnostischen Offenbarungsrede* (ed. Rudolf Bultmann; FRLANT 68 = N.F. 50; Göttingen: Vandenhoeck & Ruprecht, 1956).

Berger and Nord
Klaus Berger and Christiane Nord, *Das Neue Testament und frühchristliche Schriften* (Frankfurt am Main/Leipzig: Insel, 1999).

Bernard
John Henry Bernard, *The Odes of Solomon* (TextsS 8.3; Cambridge: Cambridge University Press, 1912; repr., Nendeln/Liechtenstein: Kraus Reprint, 1967).

Beskow and Hidal
Per Beskow and Sten Hidal, *Salomos oden: Den äldsta kristna sångboken översatt och kommenterad* (Stockholm: Proprius, 1980).

Betz, *Lukian*
Hans Dieter Betz, *Lukian von Samosata und das Neue Testament: Religionsgeschichtliche und paränetische Parallelen. Ein Beitrag zum Corpus Hellenisticum Novi Testamenti* (TU 76 = V. Reihe, Bd. 21; Berlin: Akademie-Verlag, 1961).

Beyer, *ATTM*
Klaus Beyer, *Die aramäischen Texte vom Toten Meer samt den Inschriften aus Palästina, dem Testament Levis aus der Kairoer Genisa, der Fastenrolle und den alten talmudischen Zitaten* (2 vols.; Göttingen: Vandenhoeck & Ruprecht, 1984–2004).

Beyer, *ATTM.E*
Klaus Beyer, *Die aramäischen Texte vom Toten Meer samt den Inschriften aus Palästina, dem Testament Levis aus der Kairoer Genisa, der Fastenrolle und den alten talmudischen Zitaten*: *Ergänzungsband* (Göttingen: Vandenhoeck & Ruprecht, 1994).

Beyer, *Syntax*
Klaus Beyer, *Semitische Syntax im Neuen Testament*, vol. 1: *Satzlehre, Teil 1* (SUNT 1; 2nd ed.; Göttingen: Vandenhoeck & Ruprecht, 1968).

Bieder, *Höllenfahrt*
Werner Bieder, *Die Vorstellung von der Höllenfahrt Jesu Christi: Beitrag zur Entstehungsgeschichte der Vorstellung vom sog. Descensus ad inferos* (AThANT 19; Zurich: Zwingli, 1949).

Blaszczak
Gerald R. Blaszczak, *A Formcritical Study of Selected Odes of Solomon* (HSM 36; Atlanta: Scholars Press, 1985).

Bousset, *Gnosis*
Wilhelm Bousset, *Hauptprobleme der Gnosis* (Göttingen: Vandenhoeck & Ruprecht, 1907; repr., 1973).

Bousset, *Kyrios Christos*
Wilhelm Bousset, *Kyrios Christos: A History of the Belief in Christ from the Beginnings of Christianity to Irenaeus* (Nashville/New York: Abingdon, 1970), ET of *Kyrios Christos: Geschichte des Christusglaubens von den Anfängen des Christentums bis Irenaeus* (2nd ed.; Göttingen: Vandenhoeck & Ruprecht, 1921; 5th repr., 1965).

Bousset, *Offenbarung*
Wilhelm Bousset, *Die Offenbarung Johannis* (Göttingen: Vandenhoeck & Ruprecht, 1906; repr., 1966).

Brandenburger, *Fleisch*
Egon Brandenburger, *Fleisch und Geist: Paulus und die dualistische Weisheit* (WMANT 29; Neukirchen-Vluyn: Neukirchener Verlag, 1968)

Brenton
Sir Lancelot Charles Lee Brenton, *The Septuagint with Apocrypha: Greek and English* (London: Samuel Bagster & Sons, 1851; repr., Peabody, Mass: Hendrickson, 1986; 2nd printing 1987).

Brock
Sebastian P. Brock, "The Gates/Bars of Sheol Revisited," in William L. Petersen, Johan S. Vos, and Henk J. de Jonge, eds., *Sayings of Jesus: Canonical and Non-Canonical. Essays in Honour of Tjitze Baarda* (NovTSup 89; Leiden: Brill, 1997) 7–24.

Brockelmann, *Grammatik*
Carl Brockelmann, *Syrische Grammatik mit Paradigmen, Literatur, Chrestomathie und Glossar* (Porta linguarum orientalium 5; 6th ed.; Leipzig: Harrassowitz, 1951).

Brockelmann, *Grundriss*
Carl Brockelmann, *Grundriss der vergleichenden Grammatik der semitischen Sprachen* (2 vols.; Berlin: Reuther & Reichard, 1908–13; repr., Hildesheim: Olms, 1982).

Brockelmann, *Lexicon*
Karl [Carl] Brockelmann, *Lexicon Syriacum* (2nd ed.; Halle, 1928; repr., Hildesheim: Olms, 1966).

Brox, *Hirt*
Norbert Brox, *Der Hirt des Hermas* (KAV 7; Göttingen: Vandenhoeck & Ruprecht, 1991).

Brox, *Irenäus*
Norbert Brox, *Irenäus von Lyon, Epideixis, Adversus haereses – Darlegung der apostolischen Verkündigung, Gegen die Häresien* (5 vols.; FontChr 8.1–5; Freiburg: Herder, 1993–2001).

Brox, *Petrusbrief*
Norbert Brox, *Der erste Petrusbrief* (EKKNT 21; Zurich: Benziger; Neukirchen-Vluyn: Neukirchener Verlag, 1979).

Bultmann, "Bedeutung"
Rudolf Bultmann, "Die Bedeutung der neuerschlossenen mandäischen und manichäischen Quellen für das Verständnis des Johannesevangeliums," *ZNW* 24 (1925) 100–46; also in Bultmann, *Exegetica*, 55–104.

Bultmann, *Exegetica*
Rudolf Bultmann, *Exegetica: Aufsätze zur Erforschung des Neuen Testaments* (ed. Erich Dinkler; Tübingen: Mohr Siebeck, 1967).

Bultmann, *John; Das Evangelium*
Rudolf Bultmann, *The Gospel of John: A Commentary* (ed. G. R. Beasley-Murray; trans. R. W. N. Hoare and J. K. Riches; Philadelphia: Westminster, 1971), ET of *Das Evangelium des Johannes* (KEK, 2. Abt.; Göttingen: Vandenhoeck & Ruprecht, 1941; repr., 1964; *Ergänzungsheft*: Neubearbeitung 1957).

Bultmann, "Psalmbuch"
Rudolf Bultmann, "Ein jüdisch-christliches Psalmbuch aus dem ersten Jahrhundert," *MPTh* 7 (1910) 23–29.

Bultmann, "Untersuchungen"
Rudolf Bultmann, "Untersuchungen zum Johannesevangelium (Teil A. Ἀλήθεια)," *ZNW* 27 (1928) 113–63; also in Bultmann, *Exegetica*, 124–73.

Burkitt
Francis Crawford Burkitt, "A New MS of the Odes of Solomon," *JTS* 13 (1911–12) 372–85.

Buschmann
Gerd Buschmann, *Das Martyrium des Polykarp* (KAV 6; Göttingen: Vandenhoeck & Ruprecht, 1998).

Cameron, "Crux"
Peter Cameron, "The Crux in Ode of Solomon 19:6: A New Solution," *JTS* n.s. 42 (1991) 588–96.

Cameron, "Sanctuary"
Peter Cameron, "The 'Sanctuary' in the Fourth *Ode of Solomon*," in William Horbury, ed., *Templum amicitiae: Essays on the Second Temple Presented to Ernst Bammel* (JSNTSup 48; Sheffield: JSOT Press, 1991) 450–63.

Carmignac, "Affinités"
Jean Carmignac, "Les affinités qumrâniennes de la onzième Ode de Salomon," *RevQ* 3 (1961) 71–102.

Carmignac, "Auteur"
Jean Carmignac, "Un Qumrânien converti au Christianisme: l'auteur des Odes de Salomon," in Hans Bardtke, ed., *Qumran-Probleme: Vorträge des Leipziger Symposions über Qumran-Probleme vom 9. bis 14. Oktober 1961* (SSA 42; Berlin: Akademie-Verlag, 1963) 75–108.

Charlesworth
James H. Charlesworth, ed. and trans., *The Odes of Solomon* (Oxford: Clarendon, 1973; rev. repr., SBLTT 13; SBLPS 7; Missoula, Mont.: Scholars Press, 1977).

Charlesworth, *Manuscripts*
James H. Charlesworth, ed., *Papyri and Leather Manuscripts of the Odes of Solomon* (Dickerson Series of Facsimiles of Manuscripts Important for Christian Origins 1; Durham, N.C.: International Center for the Study of Ancient Near Eastern Civilizations and Christian Origins, Duke University, 1981).

Charlesworth, "Mer Morte"
James H. Charlesworth, "Les Odes de Salomon et les manuscrits de la mer Morte," *RB* 77 (1970) 522–49.

Charlesworth, "Odes"
James H. Charlesworth, "Odes of Solomon," *DNTB* (2000) 749–52.

Charlesworth, "Paronomasia"
James H. Charlesworth, "Paronomasia and Assonance in the Syriac Text of the *Odes of Solomon*," *Semitics* 1 (1970) 12–26; rev. and repr. in *Reflections* 1:147–65.

Charlesworth, *Reflections*
James H. Charlesworth, *Critical Reflections on the Odes of Solomon*, vol. 1: *Literary Setting, Textual Studies, Gnosticism, the Dead Sea Scrolls and the Gospel of John* (JSPSup 22; Sheffield: Sheffield Academic Press, 1998).

Charlesworth, "Wisdom Texts"
James H. Charlesworth, "The *Odes of Solomon* and the Jewish Wisdom Texts," in Charlotte Hempel, Armin Lange, and Hermann Lichtenberger, eds., *The Wisdom Texts from Qumran and the Development of Sapiential Thought* (BEThL 159; Leuven: Peeters, 2001) 323–49.

Christ, *Sophia*
Felix Christ, *Jesus Sophia: Die Sophia-Christologie bei den Synoptikern* (AThANT 57; Zurich: Zwingli, 1970).

Clarke
William Kemp Lowther Clarke, "The First Epistle of St Peter and the Odes of Solomon," *JTS* 15 (1913–14) 47–52.

Colpe, "Gnosis"
Carsten Colpe, "Gnosis II (Gnostizismus)," *RAC* 11 (1981) 537–659.

Colpe, *Schule*
Carsten Colpe, *Die religionsgeschichtliche Schule: Darstellung und Kritik ihres Bildes vom gnostischen Erlösermythus* (FRLANT 78 = N.F. 60; Göttingen: Vandenhoeck & Ruprecht, 1961).

Colpe, "Überlieferung"
Carsten Colpe, "Heidnische, jüdische und christliche Überlieferung in den Schriften aus Nag Hammadi X," *JAC* 25 (1982) 65–101.

Colpe and Holzhausen
Carsten Colpe and Jens Holzhausen, eds., *Das Corpus Hermeticum Deutsch* (Stuttgart-Bad Cannstatt: Frommann-Holzboog, 1997).

Connolly, "Greek"
Richard Hugh Connolly, "Greek the Original Language of the Odes of Solomon," *JTS* 14 (1912–13) 530–38.

Connolly, "Odes"
Richard Hugh Connolly, "The Odes of Solomon: Jewish or Christian?" *JTS* 13 (1911–12) 298–309.

Crum
Walter E. Crum, *A Coptic Dictionary* (Oxford: Clarendon, 1939; repr., 1962, 1972).

Dibelius
Martin Dibelius, *Die Formgeschichte des Evangeliums* (2nd repr. of the 3rd ed.; with *Nachtrag* by Gerhard Iber; ed. Günther Bornkamm; 5th ed.; Tübingen: Mohr Siebeck, 1966).

Dibelius, *Aufsätze*
Martin Dibelius, *Aufsätze zur Apostelgeschichte* (ed. Heinrich Greeven; 4th ed.; Göttingen: Vandenhoeck & Ruprecht, 1961).

Dibelius, *Jakobus*
Martin Dibelius, *Der Brief des Jakobus* (KEK 15; ed. Heinrich Greeven; 11th ed.; Göttingen: Vandenhoeck & Ruprecht, 1964).

Dibelius, *Pastoralbriefe*
Martin Dibelius, *Die Pastoralbriefe* (HNT 13; ed. Hans Conzelmann; 4th ed.; Tübingen: Mohr Siebeck, 1966).

Dibelius, *Urchristentum*
Martin Dibelius, *Botschaft und Geschichte: Gesammelte Aufsätze*, vol. 2: *Zum Urchristentum und zur hellenistischen Religionsgeschichte* (ed. Günther Bornkamm and Heinz Kraft; Tübingen: Mohr Siebeck, 1956).

Diettrich
Gustav Diettrich, *Die Oden Salomos unter Berücksichtigung der überlieferten Stichengliederung* (Neue Studien zur Geschichte der Theologie und der Kirche 9; Berlin: Trowitzsch, 1911; repr., Aalen: Scientia, 1973).

Diettrich, "Liedersammlung"
Gustav Diettrich, "Eine jüdisch-christliche Liedersammlung (aus dem apostolischen Zeitalter)," in *Die Reformation: Deutsche evangelische Kirchenzeitung für die Gemeinde* 9 (1910) 306–10, 370–76, 513–18, 533–36.

Dinkler, *Signum*
Erich Dinkler, *Signum crucis: Aufsätze zum Neuen Testament und zur Christlichen Archäologie* (Tübingen: Mohr Siebeck, 1967).

Dobschütz, "*ΚΥΡΙΟΣ ΙΗΣΟΥΣ*"
Ernst von Dobschütz, "*ΚΥΡΙΟΣ ΙΗΣΟΥΣ*," *ZNW* 30 (1931) 97–123.

Dodd, *Interpretation*
Charles Harold Dodd, *The Interpretation of the Fourth Gospel* (Cambridge: Cambridge University Press, 1953; 1st paperback ed., 1968).

Dörrie, "Platonismus"
Heinrich Dörrie, "Was ist 'spätantiker Platonismus'? Überlegung zur Grenzziehung zwischen Platonismus und Christentum," *ThR* N.F. 36 (1971) 285–302.

Drijvers, "Ode 19"
Han J. W. Drijvers, "The 19th Ode of Solomon: Its Interpretation and Place in Syrian Christianity," *JTS* n.s. 31 (1980) 337–55.

Drijvers, "Ode 23"
H. J. W. Drijvers, "Kerygma und Logos in den Oden Salomos dargestellt am Beispiel der 23. Ode," in Adolf Martin Ritter, ed., *Kerygma und Logos: Beiträge zu den geistesgeschichtlichen Beziehungen zwischen Antike und Christentum. Festschrift für Carl Andresen zum 70. Geburtstag* (Göttingen: Vandenhoeck & Ruprecht, 1979) 153–72.

Drijvers, "Odes"
H. J. W. Drijvers, "Odes of Solomon and Psalms of Mani: Christians and Manichaeans in Third-Century Syria," in Roelof van den Broek and Maarten J. Vermaseren, eds., *Studies in Gnosticism and Hellenistic Religions presented to Gilles Quispel on the Occasion of his 65th Birthday* (EPRO 91; Leiden: Brill, 1981) 117–30.

Drijvers, "Polemik"
H. J. W. Drijvers, "Die Oden Salomos und die Polemik mit den Markioniten im syrischen Christentum," in *Symposium Syriacum 1976 célebré du 13 au 17 septembre 1976 au Centre Culturel "Les Fontaines" de Chantilly, France* (OrChrA 205; Rome: Pontificium Institutum Orientalium Studiorum, 1978) 39–55.

Drijvers, "Salomoschriften"
Hendrik J. W. Drijvers, "Salomo/Salomoschriften III: Sapientia Salomonis, Psalmen Salomos und Oden Salomos," *TRE* 29 (1998) 730–32.

Drower and Macuch
Ethel Stefana Drower and Rudolf Macuch, *A Mandaic Dictionary* (Oxford: Clarendon, 1963).

Duensing, "Oden"
Hugo Duensing, "Zur vierundzwanzigsten der Oden Salomos," *ZNW* 12 (1911) 86–87.

Dunn
James D. G. Dunn, "*ΚΥΡΙΟΣ* in Acts," in Christof Landmesser, Hans-Joachim Eckstein, and Hermann Lichtenberger, eds., *Jesus Christus als die Mitte der Schrift: Studien zur Hermeneutik des Evangeliums* (BZNW 86; Berlin/New York de Gruyter, 1997) 363–78.

Ebeling
Gerhard Ebeling, "Jesus und Glaube," *ZThK* 55 (1958) 64–110.

Ehrman
Bart D. Ehrman, ed. and trans., *The Apostolic Fathers* (2 vols.; LCL 24–25; Cambridge, Mass./London: Harvard University Press, 2003).

Eissfeldt
Otto Eissfeldt, *The Old Testament: An Introduction including the Apocrypha and Pseudepigrapha, and Also the Works of Similar Type from Qumran. The History of the Formation of the Old Testament* (trans. Peter R. Ackroyd; Oxford: Blackwell, 1974).

Emerton
John Adney Emerton, "The Odes of Solomon," in H. F. D. Sparks, ed., *The Apocryphal Old Testament* (Oxford: Clarendon, 1984) 683–731.

Emerton, "Notes"
John Adney Emerton, "Notes on Some Passages in the Odes of Solomon," *JTS* n.s. 28 (1977) 507–19.

Emerton, "Problems"
John Adney Emerton, "Some Problems of Text and Language in the Odes of Solomon," *JTS* n.s. 18 (1967) 372–406.

Emerton, *Wisdom*
John Adney Emerton, *The Peshitta of the Wisdom of Solomon* (SPB 2; Leiden: Brill, 1959).

Emerton and Gordon
John Adney Emerton and Robert P. Gordon, "A Problem in the Odes of Solomon xxiii. 20," *JTS* n.s. 32 (1981) 443–47.

Engelbrecht, "God's Milk"
Edward Engelbrecht, "God's Milk: An Orthodox Confession of the Eucharist," *JECS* 7 (1999) 509–26.

Fanourgakis
Vassilios [Basileios] D. Fanourgakis, *Αἱ Ὠδαὶ Σολομῶντος: Συμβολὴ εἰς τὴν ἔρευναν τῆς ὑμνογραφίας τῆς ἀρχαϊκῆς ἐκκλησίας*

(Analekta Blatadon[Vlatadon] 29; Thessaloniki: Patriarchal Institute for Patristic Studies, 1979).

Fischer
Joseph A. Fischer, *Die Apostolischen Väter* (Munich: Kösel, 1956; 9th ed.; Darmstadt: Wissenschaftliche Buchgesellschaft, 1986).

Frankenberg
Wilhelm Frankenberg, *Das Verständnis der Oden Salomos* (BZAW 21; Gießen: Töpelmann, 1911).

Franzmann
Majella Franzmann, *The Odes of Solomon: An Analysis of the Poetical Structure and Form* (NTOA 20; Fribourg: Academic Press; Göttingen: Vandenhoeck & Ruprecht, 1991).

Franzmann, "Background"
Majella Franzmann, "Background and Parallels of the Imagery of the Coptic, Greek and Syriac *Odes of Solomon*," unpublished manuscript resulting from an Australian Research Council research project (University of Queensland, 1990).

Franzmann, "Man of Rest"
Majella Franzmann, "The Odes of Solomon, Man of Rest," *OrChrP* 51 (1985) 408–21.

Franzmann, "Note"
Majella Franzmann, "'Wipe the harlotry from your faces': A Brief Note on Ode of Solomon 13,3," *ZNW* 77 (1986) 282–83.

Franzmann, "Parable"
Majella Franzmann, "The Parable of the Vine in *Odes of Solomon* 38. 17–19? A Response to Richard Bauckham," *NTS* 35 (1989) 604–8.

Franzmann, "Strangers"
Majella Franzmann, "Strangers from Above: An Investigation of the Motif of Strangeness in the Odes of Solomon and Some Gnostic Texts," *Mus* 103 (1990) 27–41.

Franzmann, "Study"
Majella Franzmann, "A Study of the Odes of Solomon with Reference to the French Scholarship 1909-1980," in Lattke, *Bedeutung*, 3:371–425 and passim.

Frisk
Hjalmar Frisk, *Griechisches etymologisches Wörterbuch* (3 vols.; Heidelberg: Winter, 1954–72).

Funk, *Jakobus*
Wolf-Peter Funk, *Die zweite Apokalypse des Jakobus aus Nag-Hammadi-Codex V* (TU 119; Berlin: Akademie-Verlag, 1976).

Galling
Kurt Galling, ed., *Biblisches Reallexikon* (HAT, Erste Reihe 1; Tübingen: 2nd ed.; Mohr Siebeck, 1977).

Gemünden, *Vegetationsmetaphorik*
Petra von Gemünden, *Vegetationsmetaphorik im Neuen Testament und seiner Umwelt: Eine Bildfelduntersuchung* (NTOA 18; Fribourg: Academic Press; Göttingen: Vandenhoeck & Ruprecht, 1993).

Georges
Karl Ernst Georges, *Ausführliches Lateinisch-Deutsches Handwörterbuch* (ed. Heinrich Georges; 2 vols.; 14th ed.; Hannover: Hahnsche Buchhandlung, 1976).

Georgi
Dieter Georgi, *Weisheit Salomos* (JSHRZ 3.4; Gütersloh: Mohn, 1980).

Gero, "Spirit"
Stephen Gero, "The Spirit as a Dove at the Baptism of Jesus," *NovT* 18 (1976) 17–35.

Gesenius
Wilhelm Gesenius, *Hebräisches und aramäisches Handwörterbuch über das Alte Testament* (ed. Frants Buhl; 17th ed.; Berlin: Springer, 1915 = repr., 1962).

Goodspeed
Edgar J. Goodspeed, ed., *Die ältesten Apologeten: Texte mit kurzen Einleitungen* (Göttingen: Vandenhoeck & Ruprecht, 1914; repr., 1984).

Goppelt, *Der Erste Petrusbrief*
Leonhard Goppelt, *Der Erste Petrusbrief* (ed. Ferdinand Hahn; 1st ed. of this *Neubearbeitung*; KEK 12.1; 8th ed.; Göttingen: Vandenhoeck & Ruprecht, 1978).

Gräßer
Erich Gräßer, *An die Hebräer* (3 vols.; EKKNT 17.1–3; Zurich: Benziger; Neukirchen-Vluyn: Neukirchener Verlag, 1990–97).

Grese, *Corpus*
William C. Grese, *Corpus Hermeticum XIII and Early Christian Literature* (SCHNT 5; Leiden: Brill, 1979).

Greßmann
Hugo Greßmann, "Die Oden Salomos," *NTApo*[2] (1924) 437–72.

Greßmann, "Ode 23"
Hugo Greßmann, "Ode Salomos 23," SPAW.PH (1923) 616–24.

Greßmann, "Oden"
Hugo Greßmann, "Die Oden Salomos," *Die Christliche Welt: Evangelisches Gemeindeblatt für Gebildete aller Stände* 25 (1911) 633–35, 650–52, 674–77, 703–5.

Greßmann, "Oden Salomos"
Hugo Greßmann, "Die Oden Salomos," *Internationale Wochenschrift für Wissenschaft, Kunst und Technik* 5 (1911) 1–20.

Greßmann, "Referate"
Hugo Greßmann, "Referate [on Harris, Frankenberg, and Grimme]," *Deutsche Literaturzeitung* 32 (1911) 2896–902.

Greßmann, "Taufe"
Hugo Greßmann, "Die Sage von der Taufe Jesu und die vorderasiatische Taubengöttin," *ARW* 20 (1920–21) 1–40, 323–59.

Grimme
Hubert Grimme, *Die Oden Salomos syrisch-hebräisch-deutsch: Ein kritischer Versuch* (Heidelberg: Winter, 1911).

Grimme, "Handschrift"
Hubert Grimme, "Zur Handschrift N der Oden Salomos," *OLZ* 15 (1912) 492–96.

Grimme, "Ode 19"
Hubert Grimme, "Die 19. Ode Salomos," *ThGl* 3 (1911) 11–18.

Gschwind, *Niederfahrt*
Karl Gschwind, *Die Niederfahrt Christi in die Unterwelt: Ein Beitrag zur Exegese des Neuen Testamentes und zur Geschichte des Taufsymbols* (NTAbh 2.3–5; Münster: Aschendorff, 1911).

Gunkel
Hermann Gunkel, "Die Oden Salomos," *ZNW* 11 (1910) 291–328.

Gunkel, *Aufsätze*
Hermann Gunkel, *Reden und Aufsätze* (Göttingen: Vandenhoeck & Ruprecht, 1913), esp. 163–92 ("Die Oden Salomos," first publ. in *Deutsche Rundschau* 39 [1913] 25–47).

Gunkel, *Psalmen*
Hermann Gunkel, *Die Psalmen* (4th ed.; Göttingen: Vandenhoeck & Ruprecht, 1926 = 5th ed., 1968).

Gunkel and Begrich, *Einleitung*
Hermann Gunkel and Joachim Begrich, *Einleitung in die Psalmen: Die Gattungen der religiösen Lyrik Israels* (Göttingen: Vandenhoeck & Ruprecht, 1933; 3rd ed., 1975; 4th ed., 1985 [mit einem Stellenregister von Walter Beyerlin]), ET: *Introduction to the Psalms: The Genres of the Religious Lyric of Israel* (trans. James M. Nogalski; Macon, Ga.: Mercer University Press, 1998).

Hahn, *Theologie*
Ferdinand Hahn, *Theologie des Neuen Testaments* (2 vols.; Tübingen: Mohr Siebeck, 2002).

Hannah, "*Ascension of Isaiah*"
Darrell D. Hannah, "The *Ascension of Isaiah* and Docetic Christology," *VC* 53 (1999) 165–96.

Harnack
Adolf Harnack, *Ein jüdisch-christliches Psalmbuch aus dem ersten Jahrhundert [The Odes . . . of Solomon, now first published from the Syriac version by J. Rendel Harris, 1909]. Aus dem Syrischen übersetzt von Johannes Flemming* (TU 35.4; Leipzig: Hinrichs, 1910).

Harnack, *Pistis Sophia*
Adolf Harnack, *Über das gnostische Buch Pistis Sophia. Brod und Wasser: Die eucharistischen Elemente bei Justin. Zwei Untersuchungen* (TU 7.2; Leipzig: Hinrichs, 1891).

Harris
James Rendel Harris, *The Odes and Psalms of Solomon, Now First Published from the Syriac Version* (Cambridge: Cambridge University Press, 1909; 2nd ed., 1911).

Harris, "Thirty-eighth Ode"
James Rendel Harris, "The Thirty-eighth Ode of Solomon," *Exp* 8th Ser. 2 (1911) 28–37.

Harris, "Two Flood-Hymns"
James Rendel Harris, "Two Flood-Hymns of the Early Church," *Exp* 8th Ser. 2 (1911) 405–17.

Harris and Mingana
James Rendel Harris and Alphonse Mingana, *The Odes and Psalms of Solomon* (2 vols.; Manchester: Manchester University Press, 1916–20).

Hatch and Redpath
Edwin Hatch and Henry A. Redpath, *A Concordance to the Septuagint and the Other Greek Versions of the Old Testament (Including the Apocryphal Books)* (2 vols.; Oxford: Clarendon, 1897; repr., Graz: Akademische Druck- und Verlagsanstalt, 1954).

Hilgenfeld, *Die Ketzergeschichte*
Adolf Hilgenfeld, *Die Ketzergeschichte des Urchristentums urkundlich dargestellt* (Leipzig: Fues, 1884; repr., Darmstadt: Wissenschaftliche Buchgesellschaft, 1966).

Holm-Nielsen
Svend Holm-Nielsen, *Die Psalmen Salomos* (JSHRZ 4.2; Gütersloh: Mohn, 1977).

Hübner
Hans Hübner, *Die Weisheit Salomons – Liber Sapientiae Salomonis* (ATDA 4; Göttingen: Vandenhoeck & Ruprecht, 1999).

Jennings and Gantillon
William Jennings, *Lexicon to the Syriac New Testament (Peshiṭta) with Copious References, Dictions, Names of Persons and Places and Some Various Readings Found in the Curetonian, Sinaitic Palimpsest, Philoxenian & Other MSS* (rev. Ulric Gantillon; Oxford: Clarendon, 1926 = repr., 1962).

Jervell, *Apostelgeschichte*
Jacob Jervell, *Die Apostelgeschichte* (KEK 3; Göttingen: Vandenhoeck & Ruprecht, 1998).

Jervell, *Imago Dei*
Jacob Jervell, *Imago Dei: Gen 1,26 f. im Spätjudentum, in der Gnosis und in den paulinischen Briefen* (FRLANT 76 = N.F. 58; Göttingen: Vandenhoeck & Ruprecht, 1960).

Jonas, *Gnosis*
Hans Jonas, *Gnosis und spätantiker Geist,* vol. 1: *Die mythologische Gnosis. Mit einer Einleitung: Zur Geschichte und Methodologie der Forschung* (3rd ed.; Göttingen: Vandenhoeck & Ruprecht, 1964).

Kaegi
Adolf Kaegi, *Benselers griechisch-deutsches Schulwörterbuch* (12th ed.; Leipzig/Berlin: Teubner, 1904).

Käsemann, "Gottesgerechtigkeit"
Ernst Käsemann, "Gottesgerechtigkeit bei Paulus," *ZThK* 58 (1961) 367–78.

Käsemann, *Leib*
Ernst Käsemann, *Leib und Leib Christi: Eine Untersuchung zur paulinischen Begrifflichkeit* (BHTh 9; Tübingen: Mohr Siebeck, 1933).

Käsemann, *Romans*
Ernst Käsemann, *Commentary on Romans* (London: SCM, 1980), ET of *An die Römer* (HNT 8a; 4th ed.; Tübingen: Mohr Siebeck, 1980).

Käsemann, *Testament; Wille*
Ernst Käsemann, *The Testament of Jesus According to John 17* (trans. Gerhard Krodel; Philadelphia: Fortress, 1968), ET of *Jesu letzter Wille nach Johannes 17* (3rd ed.; Tübingen: Mohr Siebeck, 1971).

Käsemann, *Wandering People; Gottesvolk*
Ernst Käsemann, *The Wandering People of God: An Investigation of the Letter to the Hebrews* (trans. Roy A. Harrisville and Irving L. Sandberg; Minneapolis: Augsburg, 1984), ET of *Das wandernde Gottesvolk: Eine Untersuchung zum Hebräerbrief* (FRLANT 55 = N.F. 37; Göttingen: Vandenhoeck & Ruprecht, 1939 = 4th ed., 1961).

Kiraz
George Anton Kiraz, *A Computer-Generated Concordance to the Syriac New Testament according to the British and Foreign Bible Society's Edition* (6 vols.; Leiden: Brill, 1993).

Kittel
Gerhard Kittel, *Die Oden Salomos – überarbeitet oder einheitlich?* (Beiträge zur Wissenschaft vom Alten Testament 16; Leipzig: Hinrichs, 1914).

Kittel, "Handschrift"
Gerhard Kittel, "Eine zweite Handschrift der Oden Salomos," *ZNW* 14 (1913) 79–93.

[Gisela] Kittel, "Das leere Grab"
Gisela Kittel, "Das leere Grab als Zeichen für das überwundene Totenreich," *ZThK* 96 (1999) 458–79.

Klauck, *4. Makkabäerbuch*
Hans-Josef Klauck, *4. Makkabäerbuch* (JSHRZ 3.6; Gütersloh: Mohn, 1989).

Klauck, *Herrenmahl*
Hans-Josef Klauck, *Herrenmahl und hellenistischer Kult: Eine religionsgeschichtliche Untersuchung zum ersten Korintherbrief* (NTAbh N.F. 15; Münster: Aschendorff, 1982).

Klein, *Wörterbuch*
Otto Klein, *Syrisch-griechisches Wörterbuch zu den vier kanonischen Evangelien nebst einleitenden Untersuchungen* (BZAW 28; Gießen: Töpelmann, 1916).

Kleinert, "Stellung"
Paul Kleinert, "Zur religionsgeschichtlichen Stellung der Oden Salomos," *ThStK* 84 (1911) 569–611.

Klijn
Albertus Frederick Johannes Klijn, Review of Lattke, *Bedeutung*, vols. 1–2, in *VC* 34 (1980) 302–4.

Klijn, "Review of Testuz"
Albertus Frederick Johannes Klijn, Review of Testuz in *NedThT* 14 (1959–60) 447–48.

Kluge
Friedrich Kluge, *Etymologisches Wörterbuch der deutschen Sprache* (ed. Elmar Seebold; 22nd ed.; Berlin/New York: de Gruyter, 1989).

Koehler and Baumgartner
Ludwig Koehler and Walter Baumgartner, *Hebräisches und aramäisches Lexikon zum Alten Testament* (ed. Walter Baumgartner, Johann Jakob Stamm, and Benedikt Hartmann; 5 vols.; Leiden: Brill, 1967–95).

Kraft, *Clavis*
Heinrich Kraft, *Clavis patrum apostolicorum* (Darmstadt: Wissenschaftliche Buchgesellschaft, 1963).

Kraft, *Offenbarung*
Heinrich Kraft, *Die Offenbarung des Johannes* (HNT 16a; Tübingen: Mohr Siebeck, 1974).

Kragerud, *Pistis Sophia*
Alv Kragerud, *Die Hymnen der Pistis Sophia* (Oslo: Universitetsforlaget, 1967).

Kraus, *Psalmen*
Hans-Joachim Kraus, *Psalmen* (2 vols.; BKAT 15.1–2; Neukirchen-Vluyn: Neukirchener Verlag, 1961 = 3rd ed., 1966).

Kraus, *Theologie*
Hans-Joachim Kraus, *Theologie der Psalmen* (BKAT 15.3; Neukirchen-Vluyn: Neukirchener Verlag, 1979).

Kroll, *Hölle*
Josef Kroll, *Gott und die Hölle: Der Mythos vom Descensuskampfe* (Studien der Bibliothek Warburg 20; Leipzig/Berlin: Teubner, 1932; repr., Darmstadt: Wissenschaftliche Buchgesellschaft, 1963).

Kroll, *Hymnodik*
Josef Kroll, *Die christliche Hymnodik bis zu Klemens von Alexandreia* (1921; 2nd ed.; Libelli 240; Darmstadt: Wissenschaftliche Buchgesellschaft, 1968).

Kruse, "Die 24. Ode"
Heinz Kruse, "Die 24. Ode Salomos," *OrChr* 74 (1990) 25–43.

Labourt and Batiffol
Jean Labourt and Pierre Batiffol, *Les Odes de Salomon: Une œuvre chrétienne des environs de l'an 100–120* (Paris: Gabalda, 1911).

Lake
Kirsopp Lake, ed. and trans., *The Apostolic Fathers* (2 vols., LCL 24–25; Cambridge, Mass.: Harvard University Press; London: Heinemann, 1913; repr., 1976–77).

Lambdin
Thomas O. Lambdin, *Introduction to Sahidic Coptic* (Macon, Ga.: Mercer University Press, 1983).

Lampe
Geoffrey William Hugo Lampe, *A Patristic Greek Lexicon* (Oxford: Clarendon, 1961; repr., 1976).

Lattke
Michael Lattke, *Oden Salomos: Text, Übersetzung, Kommentar* (3 vols.; NTOA 41.1–3; Fribourg: Academic Press; Göttingen: Vandenhoeck & Ruprecht, 1999–2005).

Lattke, *Bedeutung*
Michael Lattke, *Die Oden Salomos in ihrer*

Bedeutung für Neues Testament und Gnosis (5 vols.; OBO 25.1/1a–4; Fribourg: Academic Press; Göttingen: Vandenhoeck & Ruprecht, 1979–98).

Lattke, "Bildersprache"
Michael Lattke, "Zur Bildersprache der Oden Salomos," *Symbolon: Jahrbuch für Symbolforschung* N.F. 6 (1982) 95–110.

Lattke, "Dating"
Michael Lattke, "Dating the *Odes of Solomon*," *Antichthon* 27 (1993) 45–59.

Lattke, *Einheit*
Michael Lattke, *Einheit im Wort: Die spezifische Bedeutung von ἀγάπη, ἀγαπᾶν und φιλεῖν im Johannesevangelium* (SANT 41; Munich: Kösel, 1975).

Lattke, *Hymnus*
Michael Lattke, *Hymnus: Materialien zu einer Geschichte der antiken Hymnologie* (NTOA 19; Fribourg: Academic Press; Göttingen: Vandenhoeck & Ruprecht, 1991).

Lattke, "Messias-Stellen"
Michael Lattke, "Die Messias-Stellen der Oden Salomos," in Ciliers Breytenbach and Henning Paulsen, eds., *Anfänge der Christologie: Festschrift für Ferdinand Hahn zum 65. Geburtstag* (Göttingen: Vandenhoeck & Ruprecht, 1991) 429–45.

Lattke, "Ode 13"
Michael Lattke, "Salomo-Ode 13 im Spiegel-Bild der Werke von Ephraem Syrus," *Mus* 102 (1989) 255–66.

Lattke, *Oden*
Michael Lattke, *Oden Salomos* (FontChr 19; Freiburg: Herder, 1995).

Lattke, "Psalms"
Michael Lattke, "Psalms of Solomon," *DNTB* (2000) 853–57.

Lattke, "Salomoschriften"
Michael Lattke, "Salomoschriften I–III: Weisheit Salomos, Psalmen Salomos, Oden Salomos," *RGG*^{4} 7 (2004) 805–9.

Lattke, "Textvariante"
Michael Lattke, "Eine übersehene Textvariante in den Oden Salomos (OdSal 36,1a)," *ZAC* 8 (2004) 346–49.

Lattke, "Wörter"
Michael Lattke, "Die griechischen Wörter im syrischen Text der *Oden Salomos*," in *A Festschrift for Dr. Sebastian P. Brock* (special issue *ARAM Periodical* 5:1–2; Leuven: Peeters, 1993) 285–302.

Leroy, *Rätsel*
Herbert Leroy, *Rätsel und Missverständnis: Ein Beitrag zur Formgeschichte des Johannesevangeliums* (BBB 30; Bonn: Hanstein, 1968).

Lewy, *Sobria*
Hans Lewy, *Sobria ebrietas: Untersuchungen zur Geschichte der antiken Mystik* (BZNW 9; Gießen: Töpelmann, 1929).

Lidzbarski, *Johannesbuch*
Mark Lidzbarski, *Das Johannesbuch der Mandäer: Einleitung, Übersetzung, Kommentar* (Gießen: Töpelmann, 1915).

Lidzbarski, *Liturgien*
Mark Lidzbarski, *Mandäische Liturgien* (Abhandlungen der königlichen Gesellschaft der Wissenschaften zu Göttingen, Philosophisch-historische Klasse, N.F. 17.1; Berlin, 1920; repr., Göttingen: Vandenhoeck & Ruprecht, 1970).

Lindemann
Andreas Lindemann, *Die Clemensbriefe* (HNT 17; Tübingen: Mohr Siebeck, 1992).

Lindemann and Paulsen
Andreas Lindemann and Henning Paulsen, eds., *Die Apostolischen Väter* (Tübingen: Mohr Siebeck, 1992).

Lohse, *Texte*
Eduard Lohse, ed., *Die Texte aus Qumran: Hebräisch und deutsch mit masoretischer Punktation, Übersetzung, Einführung und Anmerkungen* (Darmstadt: Wissenschaftliche Buchgesellschaft, 1964).

Lona
Horacio E. Lona, *Der erste Clemensbrief* (KAV 2; Göttingen: Vandenhoeck & Ruprecht, 1998).

Luz, *Matthäus*
Ulrich Luz, *Das Evangelium nach Matthäus* (4 vols.; EKKNT 1.1–4; Zurich/Düsseldorf: Benziger; Neukirchen-Vluyn: Neukirchener Verlag, 1985–2002).

Maier, *Qumran-Essener*
Johann Maier, *Die Qumran-Essener: Die Texte vom Toten Meer* (3 vols.; UTB 1862, 1863, 1916; Munich/Basel: Reinhardt, 1995–96).

Marcovich, *Apologiae*
Miroslav Marcovich, *Iustini Martyris Apologiae pro Christianis* (PTS 38; Berlin/New York: de Gruyter, 1994; repr., 2005).

Marcovich, *Dialogus*
Miroslav Marcovich, *Iustini Martyris Dialogus cum Tryphone* (PTS 47; Berlin/New York: de Gruyter, 1997; repr., 2005).

Margoliouth, *Supplement*
Jessie Payne Margoliouth, *Supplement to the Thesaurus Syriacus of R. Payne Smith* (Oxford: Clarendon, 1927; repr., Hildesheim/New York: Olms, 1981).

Martikainen
Jouko Martikainen, *Gerechtigkeit und Güte Gottes: Studien zur Theologie von Ephraem dem Syrer und Philoxenos von Mabbug* (Göttinger Orientforschungen, I. Reihe: Syriaca 20; Wiesbaden: Harrassowitz, 1981).

Massaux, *Influence*
Édouard Massaux, *The Influence of the Gospel of Saint Matthew on Christian Literature before Saint Irenaeus*, vol. 2: *The Later Christian Writings* (trans. Norman J. Belval and Suzanne Hecht; ed., with introduction and addenda, Arthur J. Bellinzoni; New Gospel Studies 5.2; Leuven: Peeters; Macon, Ga.: Mercer University Press, 1992).

Mayer, *Index*
Günter Mayer, *Index Philoneus* (Berlin/New York: de Gruyter, 1974).

McNeil
Brian McNeil, "The Provenance of the Odes of Solomon: A Study in Jewish and Christian Symbolism" (Ph.D. Diss., Cambridge, 1977–78).

McNeil, "Le Christ"
Brian McNeil, "Le Christ en vérité est Un," *Irénikon* 51, no. 2 (1978) 198–202.

McNeil, "Martyrdom"
Brian McNeil, "Suffering and Martyrdom in the Odes of Solomon," in William Horbury and Brian McNeil, eds., *Suffering and Martyrdom in the New Testament: Studies presented to Geoffrey M. Styler* (Cambridge: Cambridge University Press, 1981) 136–42.

McNeil, "Scriptures"
Brian McNeil, "The Odes of Solomon and the Scriptures," *OrChr* 67 (1983) 104–22.

McNeil, "Source"
Brian McNeil, "A Liturgical Source in Acts of Peter 38," *VC* 33 (1979) 342–46.

McNeil, "Sufferings"
Brian McNeil, "The Odes of Solomon and the Sufferings of Christ," in *Symposium Syriacum 1976 célebré du 13 au 17 septembre 1976 au Centre Culturel "Les Fontaines" de Chantilly, France* (OrChrA 205; Rome: Pontificium Institutum Orientalium Studiorum, 1978) 31–38.

Meeks, "Image"
Wayne A. Meeks, "The Image of the Androgyne: Some Uses of a Symbol in Earliest Christianity," *HR* 13 (1973) 165–208.

Menge and Güthling
Hermann Menge and Otto Güthling, *Enzyklopädisches Wörterbuch der griechischen und deutschen Sprache,* vol. 1: *Griechisch-Deutsch* (17th ed.; Berlin-Schöneberg: Langenscheidt, 1962).

Michel and Bauernfeind
Otto Michel and Otto Bauernfeind, eds., *Flavius Josephus, De Bello Judaico – Der Jüdische Krieg*, vol. 1: *Buch I–III* (Munich: Kösel; 2nd ed.; Darmstadt: Wissenschaftliche Buchgesellschaft, 1962).

Muraoka
Takamitsu Muraoka, *Classical Syriac: A Basic Grammar with a Chrestomathy* (With a Select Bibliography Compiled by S. P. Brock; Porta linguarum orientalium n.s. 19; Wiesbaden: Harrassowitz, 1997).

Murray, "Rock"
Robert Murray, "The Rock and the House on the Rock: A chapter in the ecclesiological symbolism of Aphraates and Ephrem," *OrChrP* 30 (1964) 315–62.

Murray, *Symbols*
Robert Murray, *Symbols of Church and Kingdom: A Study in Early Syriac Tradition* (London/New York: Cambridge University Press, 1975).

Nagel, *Thomaspsalmen*
Peter Nagel, *Die Thomaspsalmen des koptisch-manichäischen Psalmenbuches* (Quellen: Ausgewählte Texte aus der Geschichte der christlichen Kirche N.F. 1; Berlin: Evangelische Verlagsanstalt, 1980).

Newbold, "Bardaisan"
William R. Newbold, "Bardaisan and the Odes of Solomon," *JBL* 30 (1911) 161–204.

Niederwimmer
Kurt Niederwimmer, *The Didache: A Commentary* (trans. Linda M. Maloney; Hermeneia; Minneapolis: Fortess, 1998), ET of *Die Didache* (KAV 1; Göttingen: Vandenhoeck & Ruprecht, 1989).

Nock and Festugière
Arthur Darby Nock and André-Jean Festugière, eds., *Corpus Hermeticum* (4 vols.; Paris: Belles Lettres, 1946–54; repr., 1972–73).

Nöldeke
Theodor Nöldeke, *Compendious Syriac Grammar* (trans. Peter D. Daniels; Winona Lake, Ind.: Eisenbrauns, 2001).

Norden, *Theos*
Eduard Norden, *Agnostos Theos: Untersuchungen zur Formengeschichte religiöser Rede* (4th ed.; Darmstadt: Wissenschaftliche Buchgesellschaft, 1956).

Oberlinner, *Pastoralbriefe*
Lorenz Oberlinner, *Die Pastoralbriefe* (3 vols.; HThKNT 11.2.1–3; Freiburg: Herder, 1994–96).

Omodeo
Adolfo Omodeo, "Le Odi di Salomone," *ParPass* 1 (1946) 84–118.

Paulsen, *Studien*
Henning Paulsen, *Studien zur Theologie des Ignatius von Antiochien* (Forschungen zur Kirchen- und Dogmengeschichte 29; Göttingen: Vandenhoeck & Ruprecht, 1978).

Payne Smith
R. Payne Smith, ed., *Thesaurus Syriacus* (2 vols.; Oxford: Clarendon, 1879–1901; repr., Hildesheim/New York: Olms, 1981).

Payne Smith, *Dictionary*
Jessie Payne Margoliouth, ed., *A Compendious Syriac Dictionary* (Oxford: Clarendon Press, 1903; repr., 1957, 1967).

Peel, *Rheginos*
Malcolm Lee Peel, *The Epistle to Rheginos: A Valentinian Letter on the Resurrection* (New Testament Library; London: SCM, 1969).

Peterson, *Studien*
Erik Peterson, *Frühkirche, Judentum und Gnosis: Studien und Untersuchungen* (Freiburg: Herder, 1959).

Philonenko, "Conjecture"
Marc Philonenko, "Conjecture sur un verset de la onzième Ode de Salomon," *ZNW* 53 (1962) 264.

Pierre
Marie-Joseph Pierre, *Les Odes de Salomon: Texte présenté et traduit avec la collaboration de Jean-Marie Martin* (Apocryphes 4; Turnhout: Brepols, 1994).

Pierre, "Odes de Salomon"
Marie-Joseph Pierre, "Odes de Salomon," in François Bovon and Pierre Geoltrain, eds., *Écrits apocryphes chrétiens* (2 vols.; Bibliothèque de la Pléiade; Paris: Gallimard, 1997, 2005) 1:671–743.

Plöger
Otto Plöger, *Sprüche Salomos (Proverbia)* (BKAT 17; Neukirchen-Vluyn: Neukirchener Verlag, 1984).

Plooij, "Boom"
Daniel Plooij, "De Boom der Bitterheid," *Theologisch tijdschrift* 46 (1911–12) 294–303.

Plooij, "Descensus"
Daniel Plooij, "Der Descensus ad inferos in Aphrahat und den Oden Salomos," *ZNW* 14 (1913) 222–31.

Poirier, "Descensus"
Paul-Hubert Poirier, "La *Prôtennoia Trimorphe* (NH XIII,1) et le vocabulaire du *Descensus ad inferos*," *Mus* 96 (1983) 193–204.

Pokorný, "Epheser"
Petr Pokorný, "Epheserbrief und gnostische Mysterien," *ZNW* 53 (1962) 160–94.

Praechter, *Grundriss*
Karl Praechter, *Friedrich Ueberwegs Grundriss der Geschichte der Philosophie*, vol. 1: *Die Philosophie des Altertums* (Basel/Stuttgart: Schwabe, 1967).

Prostmeier
Ferdinand R. Prostmeier, *Der Barnabasbrief* (KAV 8; Göttingen: Vandenhoeck & Ruprecht, 1999).

Quasten
Johannes Quasten, *Patrology*, vol. 1: *The Beginnings of Patristic Literature* (Utrecht/Antwerp: Spectrum, 1950; repr., 1966).

Quasten, "Hirte"
Johannes Quasten, "Der gute Hirte in frühchristlicher Totenliturgie und Grabeskunst," in *Miscellanea G. Mercati*, vol. 1: *Bibbia – Letteratura cristiana antica* (Studi e testi 121; Vatican City: Biblioteca Apostolica Vaticana, 1946) 373–406.

Quispel, *Makarius*
Gilles Quispel, *Makarius, das Thomasevangelium und das Lied von der Perle* (NovTSup 15; Leiden: Brill, 1967).

Rahlfs
Alfred Rahlfs, ed., *Septuaginta. Id est Vetus Testamentum graece iuxta LXX interpretes* (2 vols.; Stuttgart: Württembergische Bibelanstalt, 1935 = 8th ed., 1965; many reprints).

Reitzenstein, *Das iranische Erlösungsmysterium*
Richard Reitzenstein, *Das iranische Erlösungsmysterium: Religionsgeschichtliche Untersuchungen* (Bonn: Marcus & Weber, 1921).

Reitzenstein, *Das mandäische Buch*
Richard Reitzenstein, *Das mandäische Buch des Herrn der Größe und die Evangelienüberlieferung* (SHAW.PH 1919, 12. Abh.; Heidelberg: Winter, 1919).

Reitzenstein, *Poimandres*
Richard Reitzenstein, *Poimandres: Studien zur griechisch-ägyptischen und frühchristlichen Literatur* (Leipzig, 1904; repr., Darmstadt: Wissenschaftliche Buchgesellschaft, 1966).

Reitzenstein, "Weltuntergangsvorstellungen"
Richard Reitzenstein, "Weltuntergangsvorstellungen: Eine Studie zur vergleichenden Religionsgeschichte," *Kyrkohistorisk årsskrift* 24 (1924; Uppsala/Stockholm, 1925) 129–212.

Reitzenstein and Schaeder, *Studien*
Richard Reitzenstein and Hans Heinrich Schaeder, *Studien zum antiken Synkretismus aus Iran und Griechenland* (Studien der Bibliothek Warburg 7; Leipzig/Berlin: Teubner, 1926; repr., Darmstadt: Wissenschaftliche Buchgesellschaft, 1965).

Rengstorf
Karl Heinrich Rengstorf, ed., *A Complete Concordance to Flavius Josephus* (Study edition in 2 vols.; Leiden: Brill, 2002).

Richter, *Studien*
Georg Richter, *Studien zum Johannesevangelium* (ed. Josef Hainz; BU 13; Regensburg: Pustet, 1977).

Richter, *Untersuchungen*
Siegfried Richter, *Exegetisch-literarkritische Untersuchungen von Herakleidespsalmen des koptisch-manichäischen Psalmenbuches* (Arbeiten zum spätantiken und koptischen Ägypten 5; Altenberge: Oros, 1994).

Robinson and Brockington
Theodore H. Robinson and Leonard Herbert Brockington, *Paradigms and Exercises in Syriac Grammar* (4th ed.; Oxford: Clarendon, 1962; repr., 1978).

Röhrich, *Lexikon*
Lutz Röhrich, *Lexikon der sprichwörtlichen Redensarten* (Herder Spektrum 4800; 5 vols.; Freiburg: Herder, 1994 [= 4th ed., 1991]; repr., 1999).

Roloff
Jürgen Roloff, *Der erste Brief an Timotheus* (EKKNT 15; Zurich: Benziger; Neukirchen-Vluyn: Neukirchener Verlag, 1988).

Rudolph, *Gnosis*
Kurt Rudolph, *Die Gnosis: Wesen und Geschichte einer spätantiken Religion* (UTB 1577; 3rd ed.; Göttingen: Vandenhoeck & Ruprecht, 1990).

Rudolph, *Mandäer*
Kurt Rudolph, *Die Mandäer*, vol. 2: *Der Kult* (FRLANT 75 = N.F. 57; Göttingen: Vandenhoeck & Ruprecht, 1961).

Rudolph, "Verfasser"
Kurt Rudolph, "War der Verfasser der *Oden Salomos* ein 'Qumran-Christ'? Ein Beitrag zur Diskussion um die Anfänge der Gnosis," *RevQ* 4 (1964) 523–55.

Sauer, *Sirach*
Georg Sauer, *Jesus Sirach (Ben Sira)* (JSHRZ 3.5; Gütersloh: Mohn, 1981).

Schenke
Hans-Martin Schenke, *Der Gott 'Mensch' in der Gnosis: Ein religionsgeschichtlicher Beitrag zur Diskussion über die paulinische Anschauung von der Kirche als Leib Christi* (Göttingen: Vandenhoeck & Ruprecht, 1962).

Schenke, "Evangelium Veritatis"
Hans-Martin Schenke, "'Evangelium Veritatis' (NHC I,3/XII,2," *NHD* 1 (2001) 27–44.

Schenke, *Herkunft*
Hans-Martin Schenke, *Die Herkunft des sogenannten Evangelium Veritatis* (Göttingen: Vandenhoeck & Ruprecht, 1959).

Schille
Gottfried Schille, *Frühchristliche Hymnen* (Berlin: Evangelische Verlagsanstalt, 1965).

Schlier, *Christus*
Heinrich Schlier, *Christus und die Kirche im Epheserbrief* (BHTh 6; Tübingen: Mohr Siebeck, 1930).

Schlier, *Epheser*
Heinrich Schlier, *Der Brief an die Epheser* (Düsseldorf: Patmos, 1957; 5th ed., 1965; 7th ed., 1971).

Schlier, *Galater*
Heinrich Schlier, *Der Brief an die Galater* (KEK 7; 4th ed.; Göttingen: Vandenhoeck & Ruprecht, 1965).

Schlier, *Untersuchungen*
Heinrich Schlier, *Religionsgeschichtliche Untersuchungen zu den Ignatiusbriefen* (BZNW 8; Gießen: Töpelmann, 1929).

Schmidt and MacDermot, *Jeu*
Carl Schmidt, ed., and Violet MacDermot, trans., *The Books of Jeu and the Untitled Text in the Bruce Codex* (NHS 13; Leiden: Brill, 1978).

Schmidt and MacDermot, *Pistis Sophia*
Carl Schmidt, ed., and Violet MacDermot, trans., *Pistis Sophia* (NHS 9; Leiden: Brill, 1978).

Schmidt and Schubart, *Acta Pauli*
Carl Schmidt and Wilhelm Schubart, eds., *ΠΡΑΞΕΙΣ ΠΑΥΛΟΥ – Acta Pauli: Nach dem Papyrus der Hamburger Staats- und Universitäts-Bibliothek* (Veröffentlichungen aus der Hamburger Staats- und Universitäts-Bibliothek, Neue Folge der Veröffentlichungen aus der Hamburger Stadtbibliothek 2; Glückstadt/Hamburg: Augustin, 1936).

Schmidt, Till, and Schenke, *Schriften*
Carl Schmidt, Walter C. Till, and Hans-Martin Schenke, eds., *Koptisch-gnostische Schriften*, vol. 1: *Die Pistis Sophia. Die beiden Bücher des Jeû. Unbekanntes altgnostisches Werk* (GCS; 4th ed.; Berlin: Akademie-Verlag, 1981).

Schmidt and Wajnberg, *Gespräche*
Carl Schmidt and Isaak Wajnberg, *Gespräche Jesu mit seinen Jüngern nach der Auferstehung: Ein katholisch-apostolisches Sendschreiben des 2. Jahrhunderts* (Leipzig, 1919; repr., Hildesheim: Olms, 1967).

Schnackenburg, *Epheser*
Rudolf Schnackenburg, *Der Brief an die Epheser* (EKKNT 10; Zurich: Benziger; Neukirchen-Vluyn: Neukirchener Verlag, 1982).

Schnackenburg, *Gospel; Johannesevangelium*
Rudolf Schnackenburg, *The Gospel According to St. John* (3 vols.; London: Burns & Oates; New York: Herder & Herder, 1968), ET of *Das Johannesevangelium* (4 vols.; HThKNT 4.1–4; Freiburg: Herder, 1965–84).

Schnackenburg, *Johannesbriefe*
Rudolf Schnackenburg, *Die Johannesbriefe* (HThKNT 13.3; 3rd ed.; Freiburg: Herder, 1965).

Schoedel, *Ignatius*
William R. Schoedel, *Ignatius of Antioch: A Commentary on the Letters of Ignatius of Antioch* (Hermeneia; Philadelphia: Fortress, 1985).

Schoedel, "Readings"
William R. Schoedel, "Some Readings in the Greek Ode of Solomon (Ode XI)," *JTS* n.s. 33 (1982) 175–82.

Schrage, *1 Korinther*
Wolfgang Schrage, *Der erste Brief an die Korinther* (4 vols.; EKKNT 7.1–4; Zurich/Düsseldorf: Benziger; Neukirchen-Vluyn: Neukirchener Verlag, 1991–2001).

Schroer and Staubli, *Körpersymbolik*
Silvia Schroer and Thomas Staubli, *Die Körpersymbolik der Bibel* (Darmstadt: Wissenschaftliche Buchgesellschaft, 1998).

Schultheß
Friedrich Schultheß, "Textkritische Bemerkungen zu den syrischen Oden Salomos," *ZNW* 11 (1910) 249–58.

Schulz
Siegfried Schulz, "Salomo-Oden," *RGG*[3] 5 (1961) 1339–42.

Schürmann, *Lukasevangelium*
Heinz Schürmann, *Das Lukasevangelium* (2 vols.; HThKNT 3.1–2; Freiburg: Herder, 1969–94).

Schweizer, *Ego eimi*
Eduard Schweizer, *Ego eimi: Die religionsgeschichtliche Herkunft und theologische Bedeutung der johanneischen Bildreden, zugleich ein Beitrag zur Quellenfrage des vierten Evangeliums* (FRLANT 56 = N.F. 38; Göttingen: Vandenhoeck & Ruprecht, 1939; 2nd ed., 1965).

Schweizer, *Kolosser*
Eduard Schweizer, *Der Brief an die Kolosser* (EKKNT 12; Zurich: Benziger; Neukirchen-Vluyn: Neukirchener Verlag, 1976).

Segal, *Point*
Judah Benzion Segal, *The Diacritical Point and the Accents in Syriac* (London Oriental Series 2; London et al.: Geoffrey Cumberlege & Oxford University Press, 1953).
Seitz, "Antecedents"
Oscar J. F. Seitz, "Antecedents and Signification of the Term δίψυχος," *JBL* 66 (1947) 211–19.
Spicq
Ceslas Spicq, *Notes de lexicographie néo-testamentaire* (3 vols.; OBO 22.1–3; Fribourg: Academic Press; Göttingen: Vandenhoeck & Ruprecht, 1978–82).
Spitta
Friedrich Spitta, "Zum Verständnis der Oden Salomos," *ZNW* 11 (1910) 193–203, 259–90.
Staerk
Willy Staerk, "Kritische Bemerkungen zu den Oden Salomos," *ZWTh* n.s. 17 (1910) 289–306.
Stählin
Otto Stählin, *Des Clemens von Alexandreia ausgewählte Schriften* (5 vols.; BKV 7, 8, 17, 19, 20; Munich: Kösel-Pustet, 1934–38).
Stenger, *Christushymnus*
Werner Stenger, *Der Christushymnus 1 Tim 3,16: Eine strukturanalytische Untersuchung* (Regensburger Studien zur Theologie 6; Frankfurt/Main: P. Lang; Bern: H. Lang, 1977).
Stölten
Willy Stölten, "Gnostische Parallelen zu den Oden Salomos," *ZNW* 13 (1912) 29–58.
Strecker, *Johannesbriefe*
Georg Strecker, *Die Johannesbriefe* (KEK 14; Göttingen: Vandenhoeck & Ruprecht, 1989).
Strelan, *Paul*
Rick Strelan, *Paul, Artemis, and the Jews in Ephesus* (BZNW 80; Berlin/New York: de Gruyter, 1996).
Strelan, *Acts*
Rick Strelan, *Strange Acts: Studies in the Cultural World of the Acts of the Apostles* (BZNW 126; Berlin/New York: de Gruyter, 2004).
Stroker, *Sayings*
William D. Stroker, *Extracanonical Sayings of Jesus* (SBL Resources for Biblical Study 18; Atlanta: Scholars Press, 1989).
Testuz
Michel Testuz, ed., *Papyrus Bodmer X–XII* (Cologny-Genève: Bibliothèque Bodmer, 1959).
Theiler, *Neuplatonismus*
Willy Theiler, *Die Vorbereitung des Neuplatonismus* (Berlin/Zurich: Weidmann, 1934; repr., 1964).
Theobald, *Fleischwerdung*
Michael Theobald, *Die Fleischwerdung des Logos: Studien zum Verhältnis des Johannesprologs zum Corpus des Evangeliums und zu 1 Joh* (NTAbh N.F. 20; Münster: Aschendorff, 1988).
Till
Walter C. Till, *Koptische Grammatik (Saïdischer Dialekt) mit Bibliographie, Lesestücken und Wörterverzeichnissen* (Lehrbücher für das Studium der orientalischen und afrikanischen Sprachen 1; 4th ed.; Leipzig: VEB Verlag Enzyklopädie, 1970).
Tosato, "Battesimo"
Angelo Tosato, "Il battesimo di Gesù e le *Odi di Salomone*," *BeO* 18 (1976) 261–69.
Tosato, "Zeloti"
Angelo Tosato, "Gesù e gli zeloti alla luce delle *Odi di Salomone*," *BeO* 19 (1977) 145–53.
Trafton
Joseph L. Trafton, *The Syriac Version of the Psalms of Solomon: A Critical Evaluation* (with a supplement: *The Psalms of Solomon: Syriac and Greek Texts*; SBLSCS 11; Atlanta: Scholars Press, 1985).
Tröger, *Gnosis*
Karl-Wolfgang Tröger, *Die Gnosis: Heilslehre und Ketzerglaube* (Herder Spektrum 4953; Freiburg: Herder, 2001).
Tsakonas
Basileios G. Tsakonas, *Αἱ Ὠδαὶ Σολομῶντος (Εἰσαγωγή - Κείμενον - Ἑρμηνεία)* (repr. from: *Θεολογία* [*Theologia*] 44 [1973] 389–416, 583–605; 45 [1974] 129–49, 309–46, 511–58, 608–46).
Uhlig, *Henochbuch*
Siegbert Uhlig, *Das äthiopische Henochbuch* (JSHRZ 5.6; Gütersloh: Mohn, 1984).
Ungnad and Staerk
Arthur Ungnad and Willy Staerk, *Die Oden Salomos* (KlT 64; Bonn: Marcus & Weber, 1910).
Urner-Astholz, "Spiegel"
Hildegard Urner-Astholz, "Spiegel und Spiegelbild," in Erich Dinkler, ed., *Zeit und Geschichte: Dankesgabe an Rudolf Bultmann zum 80. Geburtstag* (Tübingen: Mohr Siebeck, 1964) 643–70.
van Unnik
Willem Cornelis van Unnik, *Sparsa Collecta*, vol. 3 (NovTSup 31; Leiden: Brill, 1983).
van Unnik, "De ἀφθονία van God"
Willem Cornelis van Unnik, "De ἀφθονία van God in de oudchristelijke literatuur," *Mededelingen der Koninklijke Nederlandse Akademie van Wetenschappen, Afdeling Letterkunde* n.s. 36, no. 2 (1973) 3–55.
van Unnik, "Note"
Willem Cornelis van Unnik, "A Note on *Ode of Solomon* xxxiv 4," *JTS* 37 (1936) 172–75.
Vermes
Geza Vermes, *The Dead Sea Scrolls in English* (3rd ed.; London: Penguin Books, 1987; repr., 1990).
Vielhauer, *Aufsätze*
Philipp Vielhauer, *Aufsätze zum Neuen Testament*, vol. 1 (ThBü 31; Munich: Kaiser, 1965).
Vielhauer, *Oikodome*
Philipp Vielhauer, *Oikodome: Aufsätze zum Neuen Testament*, vol. 2 (ed. Günter Klein; ThBü 65; Munich: Kaiser, 1979).
Vinzent
Markus Vinzent, "Ertragen und Ausharren – die Lebenslehre des Barnabasbriefes," *ZNW* 86 (1995) 74–93.

Vogl
August Vogl, "Oden Salomos 17, 22, 24, 42: Übersetzung und Kommentar," ed. Brian McNeil, *OrChr* 62 (1978) 60–76.
Völker, *Quellen*
Walther Völker, *Quellen zur Geschichte der christlichen Gnosis* (SAQ, N.F. 5; Tübingen: Mohr Siebeck, 1932).
Vööbus
Arthur Vööbus, "Neues Licht zur Frage der Originalsprache der Oden Salomos," *Mus* 75 (1962) 275–90.
Wagner, "Lobaufruf"
Andreas Wagner, "Der Lobaufruf im israelitischen Hymnus als indirekter Sprechakt," in idem, ed., *Studien zur hebräischen Grammatik* (OBO 156; Fribourg: Academic Press; Göttingen: Vandenhoeck & Ruprecht, 1997) 143–54.
Weinreich, *Wunder*
Otto Weinreich, *Gebet und Wunder: Zwei Abhandlungen zur Religions- und Literaturgeschichte* (originally in *Genethliakon* [Tübinger Beiträge zur Altertumswissenschaft 5; Stuttgart: Kohlhammer, 1929], 169–464; repr., Darmstadt: Wissenschaftliche Buchgesellschaft, 1968).
Weiß, *Korintherbrief*
Johannes Weiß, *Der erste Korintherbrief* (KEK 5; 9th ed.; Göttingen: Vandenhoeck & Ruprecht, 1910; repr., 1970).
Wellhausen
Julius Wellhausen, Review of Harris and Harnack in *GGA* 172 (1910) 629–42.
Wengst
Klaus Wengst, *Didache (Apostellehre), Barnabasbrief, Zweiter Klemensbrief, Schrift an Diognet* (Schriften des Urchristentums 2; Darmstadt: Wissenschaftliche Buchgesellschaft, 1984).
Westendorf
Wolfhart Westendorf, *Koptisches Handwörterbuch* (Heidelberg: Winter, 1977).
Westermann, *Genesis*
Claus Westermann, *Genesis* (2 vols.; BKAT 1.1–2; Neukirchen-Vluyn: Neukirchener Verlag, 1974–81).
Westermann, *Jesaja*
Claus Westermann, *Das Buch Jesaja: Kapitel 40–66* (ATD 19; 3rd ed.; Göttingen: Vandenhoeck & Ruprecht, 1976).
Wetter, *Sohn Gottes*
Gillis Petersson Wetter, *"Der Sohn Gottes": Eine Untersuchung über den Charakter und die Tendenz des Johannes-Evangeliums. Zugleich ein Beitrag zur Kenntnis der Heilandsgestalten der Antike* (FRLANT 26 = N.F. 9; Göttingen: Vandenhoeck & Ruprecht, 1916).
Whittaker and Louis
John Whittaker, ed., and Pierre Louis, trans. *Alcinoos, Enseignement des doctrines de Platon* (Collection des universités de France, Association G. Budé; Paris: Les Belles Lettres, 1990).
Widengren
Geo Widengren, Review of Lattke, *Bedeutung*, vols. 1–2 and 1a, in *TRev* 78 (1982) 16–20.
Wilckens, *Weisheit*
Ulrich Wilckens, *Weisheit und Torheit: Eine exegetisch-religionsgeschichtliche Untersuchung zu 1. Kor. 1 und 2* (BHTh 26; Tübingen: Mohr Siebeck, 1959).
Windisch, *Barnabasbrief*
Hans Windisch, *Der Barnabasbrief* (HNT, Ergänzungs-Band: Die Apostolischen Väter III; Tübingen: Mohr Siebeck, 1920).
Wolff, *Hosea*
Hans Walter Wolff, *Dodekapropheton 1: Hosea* (BKAT 14.1; 2nd ed.; Neukirchen-Vluyn: Neukirchener Verlag, 1965).
Worrell
William H. Worrell, "The Odes of Solomon and the Pistis Sophia," *JTS* 13 (1911–12) 29–46.
Wray, *Rest*
Judith Hoch Wray, *Rest as a Theological Metaphor in the Epistle to the Hebrews and the Gospel of Truth: Early Christian Homiletics of Rest* (SBLDS 166; Atlanta: Scholars Press, 1998).
Zahn
Theodor Zahn, "Die Oden Salomos," *NKZ* 21 (1910) 667–701, 747–77.
Zahn, *Geschichte*
Theodor Zahn, *Geschichte des neutestamentlichen Kanons*, vol. 2: *Urkunden und Belege zum ersten und dritten Band. Erste Hälfte* (Erlangen/Leipzig: Deichert, 1890; repr., Hildesheim/New York: Olms, 1975).
Ziegler, *Dulcedo*
Joseph Ziegler, *Dulcedo Dei: Ein Beitrag zur Theologie der griechischen und lateinischen Bibel* (AtAbh 13.2; Münster: Aschendorff, 1937).
Zimmerli, *Ezechiel*
Walther Zimmerli, *Ezechiel* (2 vols.; BKAT 13.1–2; Neukirchen-Vluyn: Neukirchener Verlag, 1969).
Zintzen, *Mittelplatonismus*
Clemens Zintzen, ed., *Der Mittelplatonismus* (Wege der Forschung 70; Darmstadt: Wissenschaftliche Buchgesellschaft, 1981).

These enigmatic texts were discovered more than two hundred years ago, and the research publications to which they have given rise amount, by now, to a smallish library, so it seems opportune to give a short overview of the introductory problems[1] together with an equally short history of the research into the *Odes of Solomon* as a summary of my own years of research. This makes some repetition unavoidable.

1. Early Testimonies

1.1. Lists of Canonical Works[2]

Both of the lists of canonical works to be discussed clearly treat the *Psalms of Solomon* and the *Odes of Solomon* as a single book in which the *Odes* follow the *Psalms* (*P* + *O*).

1.1.1. The Stichometria of Patriarch Nicephorus (Mid-Ninth Century C.E.)[3]

Nicephorus (Nikephoros) was patriarch of Constantinople from 806 to 815. He died in 828. The chronology, compiled in 850, to which the stichometric list is appended, has been, probably erroneously, attributed to him. The stichometry lists, between the *θεῖαι γραφαὶ ἐκκλησιαζόμεναι καὶ κεκανονισμέναι* ("divine writings accepted by the church and canonized") of the Old and New Testaments[4] and the *ἀπόκρυφα* ("apocrypha") of both,[5] those works *ὅσαι ἀντιλέγονται καὶ οὐκ ἐκκλησιάζονται τῆς παλαιᾶς* ("those of the Old [Testament] that are spoken against and not accepted by the church"):

1. *Μακκαβαϊκὰ γ'* (1–2 Macc + *3 Macc* [?]),
2. *Σοφία Σολομῶντος* (Wis),
3. *Σοφία Ἰησοῦ Σιράχ* (Sir),
4. *Ψαλμοὶ καὶ ᾠδαὶ Σολομῶντος* (*Pss. Sol.* + *Odes Sol.*),
5. *Ἐσθήρ* (Esth),
6. *Ἰουδίθ* (Jdt),
7. *Σωσάννα* (Sus),
8. *Τωβὴτ ὁ καὶ Τωβίας* (Tob).

These are followed by *ὅσαι τῆς νέας ἀντιλέγονται* ("those of the New [Testament] that are spoken against"):

1. *Ἀποκάλυψις Ἰωάννου* (Rev),
2. *Ἀποκάλυψις Πέτρου* (*Apoc. Pet.*),
3. *Βαρνάβα ἐπιστολή* (*Barn.*),
4. *Εὐαγγέλιον κατὰ Ἑβραίους* (*Gos. Heb.*).

1.1.2. The Synopsis of Pseudo-Athanasius (Sixth–Seventh Century C.E.)[6]

Theodor Zahn again critically examines this so-called synopsis by an anonymous compiler. This spurious list, which is dependent on earlier lists, on the 39th

1 A much longer, and still unsurpassed, introduction is the one by J. Rendel Harris and Alphonse Mingana, *The Odes and Psalms of Solomon* (2 vols.; Manchester: Manchester University Press, 1916–20) 2:1–205. My introduction is based on Michael Lattke, "Die Oden Salomos: Einleitungsfragen und Forschungsgeschichte," *ZNW* 98 (2007) 277–307.

2 See Michael Lattke, *Die Oden Salomos in ihrer Bedeutung für Neues Testament und Gnosis*, vol. 3: *Forschungsgeschichtliche Bibliographie 1799–1984 mit kritischen Anmerkungen. Mit einem Beitrag von Majella Franzmann: A Study of the Odes of Solomon with Reference to the French Scholarship 1909–1980* (OBO 25/3; Freiburg Schweiz: Universitätsverlag; Göttingen: Vandenhoeck & Ruprecht, 1986) 2–4.

3 See Theodor Zahn, *Geschichte des neutestamentlichen Kanons*, vol. 2: *Urkunden und Belege zum ersten und dritten Band. Erste Hälfte* (Erlangen/Leipzig: Deichert, 1890; repr. Hildesheim/New York: Olms, 1975) 297–301.

4 OT: Genesis, Exodus, Leviticus, Numbers, Deuteronomy, Joshua, Judges + Ruth, 1–4 Kingdoms, 1–2 Chronicles, 1–2 Esdras, Psalms, Proverbs, Ecclesiastes (Qoheleth), Canticles, Job, Isaiah, Jeremiah, 1 Baruch, Ezekiel, Daniel, Dodekapropheton.
NT: Matthew, Mark, Luke, John, Acts, fourteen Pauline epistles (Romans–Hebrews), seven Catholic epistles (James, 1–2 Peter, 1–3 John, Jude).

5 Among the works listed for the OT are *1 Enoch*, *Testament of the Twelve Patriarchs*, *Prayer of Joseph*, *Testament of Moses*, *Assumption of Moses*, *Apocalypse of Abraham*, *Apocalypse of Elijah*, and 1 Baruch; those of the New according to the stichometry are *Acts of Paul*, *Acts of Peter*, *Acts of John*, *Acts of Thomas*, *Gospel of Thomas*, *Didache*, *1–2 Clement*, Letters of Ignatius, Polycarp *Letter to the Philippians*, *The Shepherd of Hermas*.

6 See Zahn, *Geschichte*, 302–18.

Festal Letter of Athanasius, and on Epiphanias, jumbles up the sections ἀντιλεγόμενα ("antilegomena") and ἀπόκρυφα ("apocrypha"). It cannot have originated before the sixth century, probably even later. The relevant passage, corrected and somewhat abridged, runs as follows:

> *Τὰ μὲν οὖν ἀντιλεγόμενα τῆς παλαιᾶς . . . ἔστι σοφία Σολομῶντος καὶ σοφία Ἰησοῦ υἱοῦ Σιρὰχ καὶ Ἐσθὴρ καὶ Ἰουδὶθ καὶ Τοβίτ. σὺν ἐκείνοις δὲ καὶ ταῦτα ἠρίσμηνται· Μακκαβαϊκὰ βιβλία δ' πολεμικά, Ψαλμοὶ καὶ ᾠδαὶ Σολομῶντος, Σωσάννα.*
>
> The antilegomena of the Old [Testament] . . . are: Wis, Sir, Esth, Jdt, Tob. To these are added: 1–2 Macc + *3–4 Macc, Ps. Sol.* + *Odes Sol.*, Sus.

Except for one Book of Maccabees (probably *4 Macc*) these are the same antilegomena as those listed in the stichometry attributed to Patriarch Nicephorus. The sequence (and thus the implied importance), however, has changed. The *Psalms* and *Odes of Solomon* are not yet in the fourth place but in the seventh.

1.2. Codex Askew (Fourth–Fifth Century C.E.)[7]

This Coptic-Gnostic codex also witnesses, indirectly, to a manuscript in which the *Odes of Solomon* followed the *Psalms of Solomon* (*P* + *O*). This is confirmed by the fact that the passage quoted from *Ode* 19 is nowhere to be found in the text of *Ode* 19 as preserved in the two Syriac manuscripts. That leads to the conclusion that this *Ode* 19 is in fact the first of the *Odes of Solomon* following on from the eighteen *Psalms of Solomon*. Perhaps the title of this collection of eighteen *Psalms* and forty-two (?) *Odes* may even have been *Odes of Solomon*.[8] Whether this collection existed in a Coptic translation will be considered later (see 2.2 below). The point here is that the unique manuscript of the *Pistis Sophia* witnesses both to the title *Odes* and to the authorial pseudonym Solomon.

1.3. Lactantius (Early Fourth Century C.E.)[9]

The only conclusion that can be drawn from Lactantius's Latin quotation (see sec. 2.3. below) of *Ode* 19:6–7 is that he used a collection of the *Odes of Solomon* in numerical order. Whether there was a version in Latin cannot be determined. If the *Psalms of Solomon* also formed part of the collection under a joint title, the eighteen *Psalms of Solomon* would have to have followed the forty-two *Odes* (*O*[+*P*?]), as they do in the Syriac manuscripts (see 2.4 below). This is speculation; what is important is that this church father used a collection that was arranged and numbered in a way opposite to that quoted in the *Pistis Sophia* and attested to by the lists of canonical works. Lactantius wrote the seven books of his *Divinae institutiones* between 304 and 311 and an "Epitoṃe" of the larger work after 313. In the main work he introduces the quotation from *Ode* 19 with the words *Solomon in ode undeuicesima ita dicit* ("Solomon in his nineteenth Ode said"), while in the "Epitome" he says: *apud Solomonem ita scriptum est* ("as it is written according to Solomon"). He doubts neither the (prophetically inspired) authorship of the *Odes of Solomon* nor their place in the canon of his OT.

1.4. *P. Bodmer* XI (Third–Fourth Century C.E.)[10]

This Greek papyrus contains only the text of *Ode* 11 (see 2.1 below). The codex from which it was extracted for publication is an early collection ("Sammelcodex")[11] comprising a unique selection of OT Psalms, NT epistles, NT Apocrypha, and early patristic writings bound up in the fourth century in a small volume, some parts

7 See Lattke, *Bedeutung*, vol. 1: *Ausführliche Handschriftenbeschreibung, Edition mit deutscher Parallel-Übersetzung, Hermeneutischer Anhang zur gnostischen Interpretation der Oden Salomos in der Pistis Sophia* (OBO 25/1; Fribourg, Suisse: Editions Universitaires; Göttingen: Vandenhoeck & Ruprecht, 1979) 24–31.

8 Cf. Michael Lattke, "Titel, Überschriften und Unterschriften der sogenannten *Oden* und *Psalmen Salomos*," in Hans-Gebhard Bethge, Stephen Emmel, Karen L. King, and Imke Schletterer, eds., *For the Children, Perfect Instruction: Studies in Honor of Hans-Martin Schenke on the Occasion of the Berliner Arbeitskreis für koptisch-gnostische Schriften's Thirtieth Year* (Leiden/Boston: Brill, 2002) 439–47.

9 See Lattke, *Bedeutung*, 3:5–6.

10 See Lattke, *Bedeutung*, 1:1–23.

11 See Barbara Aland, "Welche Rolle spielen Textkritik und Textgeschichte für das Verständnis des Neuen Testaments? Frühe Leserperspektiven," *NTS* 52 (2006) 303–18, esp. 305–10.

of which, including our papyrus, have been paleographically dated as probably originating as early as the third century. The heading makes it clear that the text of *Ode* 11 was copied from a collection bearing the title *Odes of Solomon*. Nothing else can be certainly said about that collection regarding its age or its remaining contents. The possibility that it also contained the *Psalms of Solomon* (whether *O* + *P* or *P* + *O*) must be kept open.

2. Manuscripts and Quotations of the *Odes of Solomon*

2.1. The Greek *P. Bodmer* XI (*Ode* 11)[12]

The earliest witness to the text of the *Odes of Solomon* is the Greek text of *Ode* 11, which is slightly fuller than the same Ode in the Syriac manuscript (see 2.4 below). The papyrus held by the Bibliotheca Bodmeriana probably dates back to the third century, which means that the text from which it was copied was even earlier (second–third century C.E.). If this immediate predecessor was *not* 𝔊*, and that is very likely, then there must have been at least one even earlier text in the late second or early third century.[13] If the lines that are only preserved in Greek already formed part of 𝔊*, and were not added in the course of the Greek textual tradition, that still does not resolve the question whether 𝔊* was a translation of 𝔖* or vice versa. If the lines in question appeared in 𝔖* (whether that was the original or a translation), then they must have been deleted at some point in the Syriac textual history. However, this verges on preempting the discussion about the original language of the Odes.

2.2. Coptic Quotations in the *Pistis Sophia*[14]

The Coptic-Gnostic work *Pistis Sophia*, preserved only in the parchment Codex Askew (A; London, British Museum, MS. Add. 5114), is a translation from Greek, dating back to the second half of the third century, and includes a more or less complete Coptic text of five Odes (1:1–5; 5:1–11; 6:8–18; 22:1–12; 25:1–12), which in places still reflects the Greek. It can, therefore, be assumed that the author took the quotations from the Odes, as well as other Scripture passages, from sources written in Greek. Whether there was ever a Coptic version of the *Odes of Solomon* as a whole is not very important. If there was not, the Greek quotations from the Odes will have been translated ad hoc and simultaneously interpreted in a Gnostic fashion.[15] The *Pistis Sophia* is thus the first known attempt at commentary on some of the Odes. The first modern commentator was Friedrich Münter in 1812, and, until 1909, commentary was limited to the Coptic text of five of the Odes (see 9.1 below). Because of the early attestations the work on the *Odes* was linked, even before the discovery of the Syriac manuscripts, to work on the quite unrelated *Psalms of Solomon* (see 9.2 below).

2.3. Latin Quotation in Lactantius (*Ode* 19:6-7)[16]

It is likely that Lactantius himself translated into Latin the Greek of the quotation from *Ode* 19, which appears twice in his works. So around or even before 300 C.E. there was a numbered collection of the Odes in Greek (see 1.3 above). The topic of *Div. inst.* 4.12 is not Mariology but Christology. The Scripture quotations[17] are chosen to show that *Christus bis adveniat in terram, semel ut unum deum gentibus nuntiet, deinde rursus ut regnet* ("Christ should twice come to the earth, once to announce to the nations the one God, then again to reign" [ANF, 7:111]). The utterances of the prophets, made centuries ago, are to serve as *firmum testimonium* ("strong testimony") for the first advent of Emmanuel (= *nobiscum deus* ["God with us"]) or the *filius hominis* ("Son of man"). And Solomon is among the prophets.

2.4. Syriac Manuscripts

The two surviving Syriac manuscripts are more or less incomplete at both ends. Neither contains the complete text of the *Odes of Solomon*, and the *Psalms of Solomon*. For, unlike the Greek tradition of the *Psalms of Solomon*, both manuscripts contain the *Odes of Solomon*

12 See Lattke, *Bedeutung*, 1:10–23.

13 The asterisk (*) after 𝔊 and 𝔖 marks the "textual starting-point of tradition" in the relevant language; see B. Aland, "Welche Rolle," 304.

14 See Lattke, *Bedeutung*, 1:24–31.

15 Ibid., 1:207–25.

16 Ibid., 3:5–6.

17 In addition to the passage from *Ode* 19 and Isa 7:14 the quotations are: Ps 84:12, 109:1; Isa 9:6, 45:1-3, 45:8, 63:10-11; Dan 7:13-14; 1 Tim 6:15.

as well as the *Psalms of Solomon*. So each of the Syriac manuscripts contained sixty poems.[18] Contrary to the evidence of the lists of canonical books (see 1.1 above) and Codex Askew (see 1.2 above), the *Psalms* follow the *Odes* (*O* + *P*) and they are numbered in sequence, so that *Psalm* 1 has the number 43 in both manuscripts. Codex H also heads most of the surviving poems with the same title ܙܡܝܪܬܐ (*zmīrtā*).[19] In the branch of the Syriac tradition represented by N and H, the collective title for these pseudo-Solomonic works, of forty-two *Odes* and eighteen *Psalms*, was most probably ܙܡܝܪ̈ܬܐ ܕܫܠܝܡܘܢ (*zmīrāṯā ḏa-šlēmōn*), that is, *Odes of Solomon*. The same can be assumed for the texts from which N and H were copied. Whether the same can be assumed for the other manuscript used in H (see 2.4.3 below) or for the two additional witnesses to the Syriac *Psalms of Solomon*, which are headed ܡܙܡܘܪܐ (*mazmōrā*) = "psalm" (see 2.4.4 below), is more doubtful.

2.4.1. Codex Nitriensis (N; Ninth–Tenth Century C.E.)[20]

In this parchment codex from the Nitrian desert (London, British Museum, MS. Add. 14538) the text of the Odes begins only partway through *Ode* 17:7 and continues to the end of *Ode* 42 (149ʳ, 149ᵛ, 150ʳ, 150ᵛ, 151ʳ). Continuing from there (starting on 151ᵛ and bearing the next following number) in the same hand is the text of *Psalm of Solomon* 1 (= no. 43) and further, unfortunately very fragmentary, passages from the *Psalms of Solomon*.[21] The fact that this is a manuscript containing nos. 17–42 of the *Odes of Solomon* was recognized by F. C. Burkitt[22] only after the publication of Codex H (see 2.4.2 below).

2.4.2. Codex Harris (H; Thirteenth–Fifteenth Century C.E.)[23]

This manuscript on paper from Mesopotamia (Manchester, John Rylands Library, Cod. Syr. 9) begins partway through *Ode* 3.[24] The surviving leaves have been paginated from 1a/1b to 56a/56b. At p. 31b line 5 the Hallelujah after *Ode* 42:20 is immediately followed by the *Psalms of Solomon*, continuing, without interruption, on the same line and with the heading and numbering ܙܡܝܪܬܐ ܕܡ ܘܬܠܬ (*zmīrtā ḏ-m[īm] ʾu-ṯlāṯ*) = *Ode* 43. The first words of *Psalm of Solomon* 17:34 are the last in this incomplete manuscript.[25]

2.4.3. Another Syriac Codex in H

Apart from the manuscripts that were copied directly for N and H, there was at least one other Syriac manuscript, as evidenced by marks in the marginalia of H (*Ode* 17:11; 28:17).[26] These alternative readings, only one of them identical with N, clearly show that H, when completed, was compared to one (or more) manuscript(s) of the Odes that was/were not identical with the text copied nor with N. One could in fact speak of a revision of H. It would be only a little pointed to say that the calligraphy of H is inversely proportional to the accuracy of its copying.[27]

2.4.4. Another Two Syriac Manuscripts of the (*Odes* and) *Psalms of Solomon*[28]

It is quite possible that other collections of the *Odes* and *Psalms of Solomon* (*O* + *P*) did not bear the title *Odes of Solomon* but the alternative *Psalms of Solomon*.[29] This can be concluded from two Syriac manuscripts in which the prayer *Ps. Sol.* 16:6–13 is explicitly headed *Psalm of*

18 On the importance of the number 60 in the history of the canon, see Zahn, *Geschichte*, 292–93.

19 The translation "ode" for ܙܡܝܪܬܐ (*zmīrtā*) is a convention, like "psalm" for ܡܙܡܘܪܐ (*mazmōrā*).

20 See Lattke, *Bedeutung*, 1:32–51.

21 See Willem Baars, "Psalms of Solomon," in *OTSy* pt. 4 fasc. 6 (1972) iii–v.

22 Francis Crawford Burkitt, "A New MS of the Odes of Solomon," *JTS* 13 (1911–12) 372–85. Because of the name of its finder, manuscript N was for some time called manuscript B.

23 See Lattke, *Bedeutung*, 1:52–77.

24 We do not know how many lines of *Ode* 3 are missing. Thus, the Syriac text of the first two Odes is completely unknown. However, the Coptic-Gnostic *Pistis Sophia* contains at least part of *Ode* 1, which it quotes under the number 19 (see 1.2 and 2.2 above).

25 Baars, "Psalms," ii–iii.

26 See Lattke, *Bedeutung*, 1:62.

27 Ibid., 1:64–66.

28 Baars, "Psalms," v–vi.

29 See Lattke, *Bedeutung*, 1:34. In the "Index to the 60 canonical books" (seventh century C.E.), the *Psalms of Solomon* are among the ἀπόκρυφα ("apocrypha") of the Old and New Testaments; see Zahn, *Geschichte*, 292. It is not impossible that this listing refers to a collection of *Psalms* and *Odes of Solomon* totalling sixty.

Solomon and in one case also provided with the number 58 (Cambridge University Library, Add. 2012, fols. 104^b–105^a).[30] The original of this fragment must have come from an *O+P* collection, although that cannot be said with certainty of the other (Woodbrooke, Selly Oak Colleges Library, Mingana Syr. MS. 331, fol. 13^{a-b}). The two manuscripts, both in the Serta script, have been dated to the fourteenth (Cambridge) and sixteenth (Woodbrooke) centuries C.E.

3. Authorship

3.1. Anonymous Authorship

We do not know whether the *Odes of Solomon* are the work of a single person. Their unity, which has been almost universally accepted since 1914,[31] at least suggests that the poems originated in one religious community. The title Odes may have been added only after the collection was complete, even, perhaps, not until it was necessary to distinguish it in a compendium of the pseudo-Solomonic *Psalms* and *Odes*.[32] That they were written using the pseudonym "Solomon" is hardly likely. Attributing them to Bardesanes[33] or to Apollos, the disciple of John,[34] is as speculative as suggesting that the author was a Qumranic Jew converted to Christianity.[35] The only conclusion possible is that the author(s) will probably never lose their anonymity. All the early testimonies to and quotations of the Odes ascribe them to the same pseudonymous "Solomon," who is supposed to have been responsible also for the *Psalms of Solomon*.[36]

3.2. The Pseudonym Solomon[37]

The pseudepigraphic name Solomon was the main and perhaps the only reason why the *Odes of Solomon* were not assigned to the ἀντιλεγόμενα ("antilegomena") or ἀπόκρυφα ("apocrypha") of the *New* Testament. The title *Ode(s) of Solomon* is ancient. The two words Ode and "Solomon" are used by Lactantius (see 1.3 and 2.3 above), who clearly considers the collection part of his Old Testament. In addition, the heading of *Ode* 11 in the Greek *P. Bodmer* XI (see 1.4 and 2.1 above), the earliest manuscript and the oldest (direct) witness, is ᾠδὴ Σολομῶντος ("*Ode of Solomon*"). But why should the poems be called Odes, whether at the time of composition or shortly thereafter? They could just as well have been called *Psalms*, like the pseudepigraphical *Psalms of Solomon*. If that title was considered already spoken for, they might still have been called *Hymns* (cf. Col 3:16 and Eph 5:19). And why were they attributed to the king and poet Solomon[38]—and that no later than the end of the second century, that is, the point in time when the original from which *P. Bodmer* XI was copied must already have existed? It seems simplistic to rely completely on

30 Cf. Harris and Mingana, 1:xi.
31 See Gerhard Kittel, *Die Oden Salomos – überarbeitet oder einheitlich?* (Beiträge zur Wissenschaft vom Alten Testament 16; Leipzig: Hinrichs, 1914).
32 Whether there was ever a collection limited to the *Odes of Solomon* (i.e., without the *Psalms of Solomon*) is unknown.
33 See William R. Newbold, "Bardaisan and the Odes of Solomon," *JBL* 30 (1911) 161–204; Martin Sprengling, "Bardesanes and the Odes of Solomon," *AJT* 15 (1911) 459–61.
34 See Preserved Smith, "The Disciples of John and the Odes of Solomon," *The Monist: A Quarterly Magazine Devoted to the Philosophy of Science* 25 (1915) 161–99.
35 See Jean Carmignac, "Un Qumrânien converti au Christianisme: l'auteur des Odes de Salomon," in Hans Bardtke, ed., *Qumran-Probleme: Vorträge des Leipziger Symposions über Qumran-Probleme vom 9. bis 14. Oktober 1961* (SSA 42; Berlin: Akademie-Verlag, 1963) 75–108.
36 On the *Psalms of Solomon*, see Michael Lattke, "Psalms of Solomon," *DNTB* (2000) 853–57; idem, "Salomoschriften I-III: Weisheit Salomos, Psalmen Salomos, Oden Salomos," *RGG*[4] 7 (2004) 805–9.
37 See Majella Franzmann, *The Odes of Solomon: An Analysis of the Poetical Structure and Form* (NTOA 20; Fribourg: Academic Press; Göttingen: Vandenhoeck & Ruprecht, 1991) 5–7; idem, "A Study of the Odes of Solomon with Reference to the French Scholarship 1909–1980," in Lattke, *Bedeutung*, 3:371–425, esp. 404–5; Michael Lattke, "Dating the *Odes of Solomon*," *Antichthon* 27 (1993) 45–59, esp. 48–49, reprinted in idem, *Bedeutung*, vol. 4: [*Ausgewählte Studien und Vorträge*] (Fribourg: Academic Press; Göttingen: Vandenhoeck & Ruprecht, 1998) 118–19. The subtitle of Lattke, *Bedeutung*, vol. 4 was accidentally omitted in press.
38 Among the works attributed to Solomon are Psalms 72 (LXX Ps 71) and 127 (LXX Ps 126), Proverbs, Ecclesiastes (Qohelet), Canticle, Wisdom, *Psalms of*

the statement in 3 Kgdms 5:12 (cf. 1 Kgs 5:12 in the MT), although the number of lines (κῶλα) in the *Odes of Solomon* comes close to 1,005 (not 5,000 as the Septuagint suggests): καὶ ἐλάλησεν Σαλωμων τρισχιλίας παραβολάς [cf. 3,000 משלים], καὶ ἦσαν ᾠδαὶ αὐτοῦ πεντακισχίλιαι [cf. 1,005 שירים] ("and Solomon spoke three thousand proverbs, and his songs [odes] were five thousand").[39] So conceptual reasons have also been adduced to explain the pseudonym: "Recent discussion focuses on the Wisdom of Solomon (Drijvers 1987), 1 Chr 22:9–10 and 2 Sam 12:25 (Franzmann 1985; 1987, 324–6)."[40] Some years ago the question "How old is the allegory that Christ (Messiah) is the true Solomon?" was proposed as a research topic.[41] The allegory can be found in the *Expositiones in Psalmos* of Athanasius (fourth century C.E.): οὗτος γάρ ἐστιν ἀληθὴς Σαλομὼν ὁ εἰρηναῖος ("For he [viz., Christ] is the true Solomon, the man of peace").[42] If this allegorical comparison were as old as the title *Odes of Solomon*, then the pseudonym might be intended christologically. In other words, the *Odes of Solomon* would actually be the "*Odes* of Christ" or the "*Odes* of the Messiah." For that name (Syriac: ܡܫܝܚܐ [*mšīḥā*]) occurs seven times in the *Odes of Solomon,* while the name "Jesus" does not occur even once.[43] Up to now, however, there is unfortunately *no* evidence that the allegory can be traced back to the second century.[44] So this problem of antique pseudepigraphy remains open and unresolved, like so many comparable ones.

4. Date of Composition[45]

4.1. A Firm *terminus ante quem* (Second/Third Century C.E.)
P. Bodmer XI, together with early testimonies and citations, gives the assurance that a *Greek* version of the *Odes of Solomon* was in circulation no later than the end of the second/beginning of the third century C.E. If the passage in Ephrem's *Madrāšā de Paradiso* (7.21: "and nothing is idle there") is an allusion to *Ode* 11:23a, there must have been a *Syriac* version of this Ode, or even of the complete collection of *Odes* (and *Psalms* [?]) *of Solomon* before 373 C.E. For the historical and critical exegesis of the *Odes of Solomon*, we will be looking for texts that may have had a direct or indirect influence on the author(s) (see 7.2–4 below). Now we are scrutinizing the Odes themselves for terms, statements, metaphors, and images that might show the influence of the *Odes of Solomon* on other texts and traditions in the second and third centuries, not in order to trace their later influence but to date them more precisely. If such traces of the *Odes of Solomon* can be shown to be probable, then there is also the opposite possibility that various texts and traditions of the second century C.E. found their way into our poems. It is, however, easier to follow one

Solomon, and the *Odes of Solomon*. In ancient Judaism, Solomon was praised but also quite sharply criticized; see Michael Lattke, "Salomo II. Antikes Judentum," *RGG*[4] 7 (2004) 803–4.

39 Alfred Rahlfs, ed., *Septuaginta. Id est Vetus Testamentum graece iuxta LXX interpretes* (2 vols.; Stuttgart: Württembergische Bibelanstalt, 1935; 8th ed., 1965; many reprints) 1:637; Sir Lancelot Charles Lee Brenton, *The Septuagint with Apocrypha: Greek and English* (London: Samuel Bagster & Sons, 1851; repr. Peabody, Mass.: Hendrickson, 1986; 2nd printing 1987) 449; *BHS*, p. 568.

40 Franzmann, 5. Cf. H. J. W. Drijvers, "Solomon as Teacher: Early Syriac Didactic Poetry," OrChrA 229 (1987 [*Symposium Syriacum* 1984]) 123–34; Majella Franzmann, "The Odes of Solomon, Man of Rest," *OrChrP* 51 (1985) 408–21; eadem, "Portrait of a Poet: Reflections on 'the Poet' in the *Odes of Solomon*," in Edgar W. Conrad and Edward G. Newing, eds., *Perspectives on Language and Text: Essays and Poems in Honor of F. I. Andersen's Sixtieth Birthday July 28, 1985* (Winona Lake, Ind.: Eisenbrauns, 1987) 315–26.

41 Michael Lattke, "Wie alt ist die Allegorie, daß Christus (Messias) der wahre Salomo sei? Eine wissenschaftliche Anfrage," *ZNW* 82 (1991) 279, reprinted in idem, *Bedeutung*, 4:111.

42 *PG* 27:324A.

43 See Michael Lattke, "Die Messias-Stellen der *Oden Salomos*," in Cilliers Breytenbach and Henning Paulsen, eds., *Anfänge der Christologie: Festschrift für Ferdinand Hahn zum 65. Geburtstag* (Göttingen: Vandenhoeck & Ruprecht, 1991) 429–45, reprinted in Lattke, *Bedeutung*, 4:89–106.

44 See Roman Hanig, "Christus als 'wahrer Salomo' in der frühen Kirche," *ZNW* 84 (1993) 111–34, a very full answer to Lattke's "Wissenschaftliche Anfrage" of 1991 (n. 41 above).

45 See Lattke, "Dating," 49–58 = idem, *Bedeutung*, 4:119–30; idem, *Oden Salomos* (FontChr 19; Freiburg: Herder, 1995) 20–35.

collection of texts that may have been used by a number of different people. We will now attempt, in a series of steps, to shift the accepted date of origin backward from the early third to the early second century C.E.

4.2. Probable Date of Origin (First Quarter of the Second Century C.E.)

4.2.1. End of the Second Century C.E.

To begin with there is a text from the first half of the third century. In chap. 2 of the *Untitled Text* in the Coptic-Gnostic Codex Bruce we find:

> The second *place* (τόπος) came into existence which will be called *demiurge* (δημιουργός) and father and *logos* (λόγος) and *source* (πηγή) and *understanding* (*mind*) (νοῦς) and man and *eternal* (ἀίδιος) and *infinite* (ἀπέραντος). . . . And the stretching out of his hands is the manifestation of the *cross* (σταυρός). The stretching out of the *cross* (σταυρός) is the *ennead* (ἐννεάς) on the right side and on the left. The sprouting of the *cross* (σταυρός) is the incomprehensible man.[46]

Also in the early third century, the African Minucius Felix concludes his remarks on the cross with the words *crucis signum est, et cum homo porrectis manibus deum pura mente veneratur* ("and it is the sign of a cross when a man adores God with a pure mind, with hands outstretched" [*Octavius* 29.8; ANF 4:191]).[47] In much the same period, perhaps even in the late second century, Tertullian, in an attack on the Jews, says *Nos uero non attollimus tantum, sed etiam expandimus, et dominica passione modula<ta>, tum et orantes confitemur Christo* ("We, however, not only raise, but even expand them [that is, our hands]; and, taking our model from the Lord's passion, even in prayer we confess to Christ" [*De oratione* 14; cf. CChr.SL 1.265.6–8 Diercks; ANF 3:685]).

This symbolism is not to be found in Justin in the second century, who defines the σχῆμα ("symbol") of the cross in the cosmos as τὸ μέγιστον σύμβολον τῆς ἰσχύος καὶ ἀρχῆς αὐτοῦ ("the greatest symbol of his [i.e., Christ's] might and ruling power") (*1 Apol.* 55.2).[48] "Since there is no other text of the first and second centuries containing this symbolism, *Ode* 27 which is almost identical with the opening lines of *Ode* 42 might have been known to Tertullian and/or Minucius Felix"[49] as well as to the unknown gnostic author of the *Untitled Text*. The still unresolved question whether Tertullian borrowed his symbolism from Minucius Felix or vice versa is of no importance in this context.

4.2.2. Second Half of the Second Century C.E.

We now come to Montanus, who was probably acquainted with the *Odes of Solomon*.[50] Since Montanism was a "Restauration urchristlicher Gedanken und Formen,"[51] the Odes may even have had some influence on Montanus and Montanism. Among the Odes that may have had such influence are *Ode* 4:3 and 6:1–2 (cf. the terms καρδία ["heart"] and λύρα ["lyre"] in Epiphanius *Haer.* 48.4).[52] "The opening of *Ode* 4 speaks about God's

46 Carl Schmidt, ed., and Violet MacDermot, trans., *The Books of Jeu and the Untitled Text in the Bruce Codex* (NHS 13; Leiden: Brill, 1978) 226–27.

47 Bernhard Kytzler, *M. Minucius Felix, Octavius* (Ger.–Lat.; Munich: Kösel, 1965) 166–69.

48 Edgar J. Goodspeed, ed., *Die ältesten Apologeten: Texte mit kurzen Einleitungen* (Göttingen: Vandenhoeck & Ruprecht, 1914; rep. 1984) 66; Miroslav Marcovich, *Iustini Martyris Apologiae pro Christianis* (PTS 38; Berlin/New York: de Gruyter, 1994; repr. 2005) 110; ANF 1:181. On the symbol of outstretched hands, cf. also Justin *Dial.* 40.3; 91.1–3; esp. 91.3 (διά τε τοῦ τύπου τῆς ἐκτάσεως τῶν χειρῶν τοῦ Μωϋσέως ["by means of the type of the stretching out of Moses' hands"]), Goodspeed, pp. 137, 205; Miroslav Marcovich, *Iustini Martyris Dialogus cum Tryphone* (PTS 47; Berlin/New York: de Gruyter, 1997; repr. 2005) 137, 228; ANF 1:245. Moses' hands are seen as a symbol of victory.

49 Lattke, "Dating," 50 = idem, *Bedeutung*, 4:120.

50 It is unlikely that the *Odes of Solomon* are Montanist; see Frederick Cornwallis Conybeare, "The *Odes of Solomon* Montanist," *ZNW* 12 (1911) 70–75; Samuel Andreas Fries, "Die *Oden Salomos*: Montanistische Lieder aus dem 2. Jahrhundert," *ZNW* 12 (1911) 108–25. Kroll, with reason, disputed this assertion in 1922; see Josef Kroll, *Die christliche Hymnodik bis zu Klemens von Alexandreia* (Libelli 240; 1921; 2nd ed.; Darmstadt: Wissenschaftliche Buchgesellschaft, 1968) 84.

51 Kurt Aland, "Montanismus," *RGG*[3] 4 (1960) 1117–18. More details on the "(Neue) Prophetie" are found in the article of Christoph Markschies, "Montanismus," RGG[4] 5 (2002) 1471–73.

52 Karl Holl, ed., *Epiphanius II: Panarion haer. 34–64* (ed. Jürgen Dummer; GCS; 2nd ed.; Berlin: Akademie-Verlag, 1980) 224–25; cf. Nathanael Bonwetsch, *Texte zur Geschichte des Montanismus*

holy place and has also been connected with Montanism."[53] In the *Doctrina patrum de incarnatione verbi* 41.14 (seventh century C.E.; ed. Franz Diekamp [1907] 306.7–10),[54] there is a quotation from Montanus (ἐκ τῶν ᾠδῶν ["from the Odes"]) that affirms the single φύσις ("nature") and ἐνέργεια ("action") of Christ before and after the incarnation (41.14).[55] If we compare this saying with *Ode* 41:15a, it is quite possible that Montanus's christological statement was an early commentary on this difficult passage.[56] "If Montanus' knowledge and use of the Odes is highly probable, the *terminus ad quem* of the *Odes* is with the same probability mid-second century."[57] The expression ἐκ τῶν ᾠδῶν ("from the Odes"), however, suggests that the *Odes of Solomon* were already called Odes and that a Greek version was in circulation.

4.2.3. Mid-Second Century C.E.

Three points that support this step backward in the dating emerge from early Valentinianism. Ptolemy compares Flora to καλὴ γῆ καὶ ἀγαθή ("a beautiful and good land") that reveals τὸν καρπόν ("the fruit") of the "seeds" (Epiphanius *Haer.* 33.7.10).[58] "This simile (ὡς) reminds us of *Ode* 11:12b: ἐγενόμην ὡς ⟦ἡ⟧ γῆ θάλλουσα καὶ γελῶσα τοῖς καρποῖς αὐτῆς. 'I became like the earth, sprouting and laughing by its fruits' (Franzmann, [p.] 88)."[59] However, the imagery of both the *Odes of Solomon* and Ptolemy may have been inspired by Matt 13:8: ἄλλα δὲ ἔπεσεν ἐπὶ τὴν γῆν τὴν καλὴν καὶ ἐδίδου καρπόν ("Other seeds fell on good soil and brought forth grain"). In Heracleon's commentary on John 4:21 (frg. 20),[60] there is the phrase πατὴρ τῆς ἀληθείας ("Father of Truth"), which, like *2 Clem.* 3:1 and 20:5, may have its source in *Ode* 41:9. The gnostic Marcus (Markos), another disciple of Valentinus, says, according to Irenaeus (*Haer.* 1.15.2): Ἀγνοίας δὲ λύσις ἡ ἐπίγνωσις αὐτοῦ ἐγίνετο ("The knowledge of the Father was removal of ignorance").[61] "This antithetical parallelism is also found in *Ode* 7:21: 'For ignorance was destroyed, because the knowledge of the Lord came' (Franzmann, [p.] 55)."[62]

4.2.4. First Half of the Second Century C.E.

We now reach a quotation from Valentinus's own works, preserved by Clement of Alexandria (*Strom.* 6.52.3–4):

> ἤδη δὲ καὶ τῶν τὴν κοινότητα πρεσβευόντων ὁ κορυφαῖος Οὐαλεντῖνος ἐν τῇ Περὶ φίλων ὁμιλίᾳ κατὰ λέξιν γράφει· »Πολλὰ τῶν γεγραμμένων ἐν

(KIT 129; Bonn: Marcus & Weber, 1914) 17 ll. 8–12; Adolf Hilgenfeld, *Die Ketzergeschichte des Urchristentums urkundlich dargestellt* (Leipzig: Fues, 1884; repr. Darmstadt: Wissenschaftliche Buchgesellschaft, 1966) 591–92; Theofried Baumeister, "Montanus," *LACL*³ (2002) 508–9.

53 Lattke, "Dating," 52 = idem, *Bedeutung*, 4:122.

54 Franz Diekamp, ed., *Doctrina patrum de incarnatione verbi*, 2nd ed., with corrections and additions of Vasileios D. Phanourgakis, ed. Euangelos K. Chrysos (Münster: Aschendorff, 1981) 306.

55 See Nathanael Bonwetsch, *Texte zur Geschichte des Montanismus* (KIT 129; Bonn: Marcus & Weber, 1914) 32 ll.13–16; Hilgenfeld, *Die Ketzergeschichte*, 591.

56 For other passages in the Odes that may have left traces in Montanism, see Lattke, *Oden*, 25.

57 Lattke, "Dating," 52 = idem, *Bedeutung*, 4:123.

58 For the Greek text in full (ἐάν γε ὡς καλὴ γῆ καὶ ἀγαθὴ γονίμων σπερμάτων τυχοῦσα τὸν δι᾽ αὐτῶν καρπὸν ἀναδείξῃς), see Karl Holl, ed., *Epiphanius I: Ancoratus und Panarion haer. 1–33* (GCS 25; Leipzig: Hinrichs, 1915), on this passage; Gilles Quispel, *Ptolémée, Lettre à Flora: Analyse, texte critique, traduction, commentaire et index grec* (SC, série annexe de textes non chrétiens, 24 *bis*; 2nd ed.; Paris: Cerf, 1966) 72; and Walther Völker, *Quellen zur Geschichte der christlichen Gnosis* (SAQ, N.F. 5; Tübingen: Mohr Siebeck, 1932) 93. Cf. the German translation by Hans Leisegang, *Die Gnosis* (KTA 32; Leipzig: Kröner, 1924; 5th ed., Stuttgart: Kröner, 1985) 308: "wenn du wie ein schönes und gutes Stück Land, das keimkräftige Samen erhalten hat, die durch sie erzeugte Frucht ans Licht gebracht hast."

59 Lattke, "Dating," 53 = idem, *Bedeutung*, 4:123.

60 Alan England Brooke, *The Fragments of Heracleon: Newly Edited from the MSS. with an Introduction and Notes* (TextsS 1.4; Cambridge: Cambridge University Press, 1891; repr. Nendeln/Liechtenstein: Kraus Reprint, 1967) 77.16–17.

61 Norbert Brox, *Irenäus von Lyon, Epideixis, Adversus haereses – Darlegung der apostolischen Verkündigung, Gegen die Häresien* (5 vols.; FontChr 8.1–5; Freiburg: Herder, 1993–2001) 1:244–45. Cf. also *Corp. Herm.* 13.8 according to Walter Bauer ("Die Oden Salomos," *NTApo*² [³1964 = ⁴1971] 576–625) 586: "Es kam zu uns die Erkenntnis (γνῶσις) Gottes; durch ihr Kommen wurde die Unkenntnis (ἄγνοια) vertrieben."

62 Lattke, "Dating," 53. As in the case of Montanism, there are other relics of Valentinianism in which traces of the *Odes* may be found; see Lattke, "Dating," 55 = idem, *Bedeutung*, 4:127; idem, *Oden*, 29.

> ταῖς δημοσίαις βίβλοις εὑρίσκεται γεγραμμένα ἐν τῇ ἐκκλησίᾳ τοῦ θεοῦ· τὰ γὰρ κοινὰ ταῦτά ἐστι τὰ ἀπὸ καρδίας ῥήματα, νόμος ὁ γραπτὸς ἐν καρδίᾳ· οὗτός ἐστιν ὁ λαὸς ὁ τοῦ ἠγαπημένου, ὁ φιλούμενος καὶ φιλῶν αὐτόν.«[63]
>
> And even Valentinus, the head of those who cultivate the community, writes in the homily *On Friends* as follows: "Much of what has been written in books used by the public is found as written in God's *Ekklesia*. For the common things are: the words from the heart, [and] the law written in the heart [cf. Rom 2:15]. This is the Beloved One's people that is loved and loves him."[64]

The last sentence of this fragment may allude to passages in Johannine and Pauline works. "But at the same time the statement 'This is the Beloved One's people that is loved and loves him' sounds like a summary of *Ode* 3."[65] We do not know when or where Clement found this homily. And we do not know when Valentinus wrote it, whether in Egypt (before 135 C.E.) or in Rome (between 136 and 165 C.E.) or perhaps even later than that. "[B]ut if it is true that the statement of Valentinos is a reflection of *Ode* 3 the *terminus ad quem* of this book of poems moves back from the mid-second century (provided the Montanist allusions are true) to the first half of the second century."[66]

4.2.5. First Quarter of the Second Century C.E.[67]

As previously remarked, the theological phrase πατὴρ τῆς ἀληθείας ("Father of Truth") in *2 Clem.* 3:1 and 20:5 may derive from *Ode* 41:9. The date for the *Mahnrede* (*2 Clement*), which is included among the so-called Apostolic Fathers and which regularly uses Gnostic terminology, is generally thought to lie sometime between 130 and 150 C.E.[68] The connection in thought and word between *2 Clement* and the *Odes of Solomon* is not limited to the passage cited and is supported also by two passages in the *Epistle of Barnabas*, which was written "around 130 or so."[69] *Barn.* 5:5–7 considers the question why παντὸς τοῦ κόσμου κύριος ("the Lord of the entire world") ὑπέμεινεν παθεῖν περὶ τῆς ψυχῆς ἡμῶν . . . ὑπὸ χειρὸς ἀνθρώπων ("allowed himself to suffer for our sake . . . by the hand of humans"). Part of the answer is, ἵνα τοῖς πατράσιν τὴν ἐπαγγελίαν ἀποδῷ καὶ αὐτὸς ἑαυτῷ τὸν λαὸν τὸν καινὸν ἑτοιμάζων ἐπιδείξῃ ἐπὶ τῆς γῆς ὤν, ὅτι τὴν ἀνάστασιν αὐτὸς ποιήσας κρινεῖ ("in order to redeem the promise given to the fathers, and to show, while he was on earth preparing a new people for himself, that he is to execute judgment after raising the dead").[70] This may be an allusion to Rom 15:8: εἰς τὸ βεβαιῶσαι τὰς ἐπαγγελίας τῶν πατέρων ("in order to confirm the promises given to the patriarchs"). But this quotation from Paul does not cover all the explanation, so it is probable that the words of *Ode* 31:8–13 have also left traces; there the "I" speaks of condemnation, endurance, suffering, my people, and the promise to the forefathers.[71] *Barn.* 11:9–10 even refers to ἕτερος προφήτης ("another prophet") as its source. But the quotation in 11:10 is a "prophetic saying of uncertain origin."[72] The influence of Gen 3:22–24 and Ezek 47:1–12 on the content is obvi-

63 Otto Stählin, ed., *Clemens Alexandrinus*, vol. 2: *Stromata I–VI*; 4th ed. with supplements by Ursula Treu (GCS; Berlin: Akademie-Verlag, 1985) 458; cf. Hilgenfeld, *Die Ketzergeschichte*, 300–301.

64 See Lattke, "Dating," 53–54 = idem, *Bedeutung*, 4:124–25.

65 Lattke, "Dating," 54 = idem, *Bedeutung*, 4:125.

66 Lattke, "Dating," 55 = idem, *Bedeutung*, 4:126.

67 Hermann Jordan, in his *Geschichte der altchristlichen Literatur* (Leipzig: Quelle & Meyer, 1911) 458–59, already suggested a date around 125 C.E. for these Greek products of early Christian poetry. Adolf Harnack, too, was prepared to "leave open the first decades of the 2nd century" for their date of origin (see Harnack, review of Harris and Mingana in *ThLZ* 46 [1921] 6–7; cf. Lattke, *Bedeutung*, 3:181).

68 Cf. Klaus Wengst, *Didache (Apostellehre), Barnabasbrief, Zweiter Klemensbrief, Schrift an Diognet* (Schriften des Urchristentums 2; Darmstadt: Wissenschaftliche Buchgesellschaft, 1984) 203–80, esp. 214 and 227; cf. θεὸς τῆς ἀληθείας ("God of Truth") in *2 Clem.* 19:1 and εὐλογητὸς ὁ θεὸς τῆς ἀληθείας – *benedictus Deus veritatis* ("blessed be/is the God of Truth") already in 1 Esdr LXX [= 3 Ezra Vulgata] 4:40.

69 Bart D. Ehrman, *The Apostolic Fathers* (2 vols.; LCL 24–25; Cambridge, Mass./London: Harvard University Press, 2003) 2:7.

70 See Ehrman, 2:26–27. On the *Epistle of Barnabas*, see already Harris and Mingana, 2:49–53.

71 See Lattke, "Dating," 56 = idem, *Bedeutung*, 4:128; idem, *Oden*, 31.

72 BDAG, *s.v.* ὡραῖος, 2.

ous. But the wording points to *Ode* 11:16c (lines found only in 𝔊): ἐθεασάμην δένδρα ὡραῖα καὶ καρποφόρα ("I saw beautiful and fruitbearing trees"). "If Barnabas found the phrase δένδρα ὡραῖα in the paradisology of *Ode* 11, the question must be asked whether his reference to ἕτερος προφήτης (*Barn.* 11:9) had the author of the Greek *Ode* in mind."[73] Confirming the date for the *Odes of Solomon* as the first quarter of the second century C.E., we will demonstrate later (see sec. 7 below) that their origin can be most suitably placed in the overlap of early Judaism, early Gnosticism, and early Christianity.

5. Language of Composition

5.1. Greek or Syriac?

The language in which the *Odes of Solomon* were originally written was clearly neither Latin nor Coptic. The quotations in the *Pistis Sophia* (see 2.2 above) and in Lactantius's *magnum opus* (see 2.3 above) are without doubt translated from the Greek. That, however, has not decided the question whether the original language was Greek. A thorough examination of Hubert Grimme's[74] work leads to the conclusion that his attempt at a Hebrew retroversion from the Syriac of the Odes is a failure.[75] Equally unconvincing is Jean Carmignac's suggestion, made a half century later, that both the Greek and the Syriac texts derive from a Hebrew original of the late first century C.E.[76] The publication of *P. Bodmer* XI (see 1.4 and 2.1 above) rekindled the debate about Greek or Syriac as the original language.[77] The following questions need to be considered: "Had an original Greek version been expanded at a rather early stage?"[78] "Was a shorter Greek original text translated into Syriac? Or was an original Syriac version (which must then have been composed well before the third century) translated into Greek and later expanded in its Greek form?"[79] In addition to these issues, there is also the question of when and why the order of the two sections of the pseudo-Solomonic collection of *Psalms* and *Odes* (or *Odes* and *Psalms*) was reversed (see sections 1 and 2 above).

5.2. Greek Words in the Syriac Text of the *Odes of Solomon*[80]

It must be emphasized that the occurrence of Greek paronyms and loanwords in an ancient Syriac text is not enough evidence to declare Greek its original language. This is true of the *Odes of Solomon*, where fourteen Greek words are used in 𝔖 in addition to γάρ/ܓܝܪ (*gēr*) and δέ/ܕܝܢ (*dēn*). Only two of them, παράδεισος ("paradise") and πρόσωπον ("face, person") are also found in the Greek of *Ode* 11. In one other instance (5:5) the Coptic quotation confirms the use of ἀήρ ("air").

5.3. The Greek and Syriac Texts of *Ode* 11

A comparison of the Greek text of *P. Bodmer* XI with the Syriac of Codex H (Codex N does not contain *Ode* 11) does not permit a final decision as to the original language of the *Odes of Solomon*. The commentary should be consulted for the detailed discussion, but it must be emphasized here that neither of the manuscripts is the original of the Greek (𝔊*) or Syriac (𝔖*), whichever is in the original or translated language. The refutation of Arthur Vööbus and Luise Abramowski, on the one hand, and those of James H. Charlesworth and John Adney Emerton, on the other, strengthen the case for a Greek original, at least slightly.[81]

73 See Lattke, "Dating," 57 = idem, *Bedeutung*, 4:129. Between *The Epistle of Barnabas* and the *Odes of Solomon* there are more connections than are mentioned here.

74 Hubert Grimme, *Die Oden Salomos syrisch-hebräisch-deutsch: Ein kritischer Versuch* (Heidelberg: Winter, 1911).

75 See Lattke, *Bedeutung*, 3:98–107.

76 Jean Carmignac, "Les affinités qumrâniennes de la onzième Ode de Salomon," *RevQ* 3 (1961) 71–102.

77 See Franzmann, "Study," 412–14; Lattke, *Oden*, 16–18.

78 See Lattke, "Dating," 47 = idem, *Bedeutung*, 4:116. *Ode* 11 in Greek includes a number of lines that have no equivalent in Syriac.

79 See Lattke, "Dating," 47 = idem, *Bedeutung*, 4:116.

80 See Michael Lattke, "Die griechischen Wörter im syrischen Text der *Oden Salomos*," in *A Festschrift for Dr. Sebastian P. Brock* (*ARAM Periodical*, special issue, 5:1–2; Leuven: Peeters, 1993) 285–302, reprinted in Lattke, *Bedeutung*, 4:133–50.

81 See Arthur Vööbus, "Neues Licht zur Frage der Originalsprache der Oden Salomos," *Mus* 75 (1962) 275–90; Luise Abramowski, "Sprache und Abfassungszeit der Oden Salomos," *OrChr* 68 (1984) 80–90; James H. Charlesworth, "Paronomasia and Assonance in the Syriac Text of the *Odes of Solomon*," *Semitics* 1 (1970) 12–26; reprinted in idem, *Critical Reflections on the Odes of Solomon*,

5.4. Pointers to a Greek Original

As is the case for most ancient texts, the original manuscript of the *Odes of Solomon* is probably lost for good. The commentary to date on the totality of the manuscript tradition in Greek, Coptic, Latin, and Syriac has delivered no cogent argument for a Syriac original, but has provided various pointers to the conclusion that a Greek original (𝔊*) was translated into Syriac (𝔖*). How many lost (and variant) copies there were between 𝔊* and *P. Bodmer* XI, or between 𝔊* and the Greek originals of the *Pistis Sophia* quotations, is quite unknown.[82] And we know even less of the number of (variant) copies there were between 𝔖* and the two Syriac manuscripts. H and N are twigs on the same branch of the Syriac tradition, but there is no telling at what point it branched off, or when the predecessors of the known manuscripts branched off from it in their turn. Erecting a stemma, even if only as "a working hypothesis,"[83] is a risky business.

6. Area of Origin

6.1. Unknown Place of Origin

We know as little about the exact place of origin of the *Odes of Solomon* as about their authorship (see 3.1 above). The quest for the place of origin (or, better, the sphere or milieu of origin) of the individual *Odes of Solomon* is more closely linked to their original language than to their era. This place of origin need not be the same as the place where the collection was compiled and edited. The sphere of origin cannot be limited to the area in which the manuscripts were found or to that in which their influence can be traced, that is, the Greek-Syriac East (as far as Mesopotamia) and the Greek-Coptic South (Egypt), to say nothing of Lactantius in Greek-Latin Bithynia, even though there is a report from there of a *carmen Christo quasi deo* ("song to Christ as if to a god") as early as the first years of the second century C.E.[84]

6.2. Suggested Places and Communities

The places of origin suggested in the course of discovery and research on the *Odes of Solomon* are always related to the supposed original language and date of origin. "In early work, Egypt was considered as a possible place of origin, though the majority of scholars opted for Syria."[85] H. J. W. Drijvers's late dating of the "42 Odes originally composed in Syriac" necessitates a decision for the linguistic area of Syriac, namely, the "Edessene milieu of ca. 200 C.E."[86] The early date and probable Greek original that are suggested here, however, mean that it is necessary to consider a number of places around the (eastern rather than western) Mediterranean. These include Egypt (e.g., Alexandria) and Asia Minor (e.g., Ephesus), but especially bilingual Syria (e.g., Antioch). Links between the epistles of Ignatius and the *Odes of Solomon* do not mandate Antioch as the place of origin but do strongly suggest Syria as the area. The relationship of the *Odes of Solomon* to the Gospel of John does not help to define the place of origin more precisely. Even the connection between our Odes and

vol. 1: *Literary Setting, Textual Studies, Gnosticism, the Dead Sea Scrolls and the Gospel of John* (JSPSup 22; Sheffield: Sheffield Academic Press, 1998); John Adney Emerton, "Some Problems of Text and Language in the Odes of Solomon," *JTS* n.s. 18 (1967) 372–406, and "Notes on Some Passages in the Odes of Solomon," *JTS* n.s. 28 (1977) 507–19; cf. Lattke, *Bedeutung*, 3:285, 327.

82 Whether there was ever a Coptic translation of the whole Greek collection of the (*Psalms* and) *Odes of Solomon* is unknown.

83 James H. Charlesworth, ed. and trans., *The Odes of Solomon* (Oxford: Clarendon, 1973; rev. repr. SBLTT 13; SBLPS 7; Missoula, Mont.: Scholars Press, 1977) 14, at the end of his "Introduction to the text" (1–14). I do not agree with Charlesworth (p. 14) that "both Syriac manuscripts are closer to the autograph than either the Coptic or Greek."

84 Pliny the Younger *Ep.* 10.96.7; cf. Michael Lattke, *Hymnus: Materialien zu einer Geschichte der antiken Hymnologie* (NTOA 19; Fribourg: Academic Press; Göttingen: Vandenhoeck & Ruprecht, 1991) 87.

85 Franzmann, 2.

86 See Hendrik J. W. Drijvers, "Salomo/Salomoschriften III. Sapientia Salomonis, Psalmen Salomos und Oden Salomos," *TRE* 29 (1998) 730–32. In his earlier work, Drijvers even dated the *Odes of Solomon* as late as the latter part of the third century C.E.; see his "*Odes of Solomon* and *Psalms* of Mani: Christians and Manichaeans in Third-Century Syria," in Roelof van den Broek and Maarten J. Vermaseren, eds., *Studies in Gnosticism and Hellenistic Religions presented to Gilles Quispel on*

some of the Qumranic writings[87] does not lead to one single conclusion, since the Essenes were not confined to Qumran. Even the "major arguments for each of the four religious milieux (scil. Judaism, Christianity, Gnosticism, Qumran)"[88] that Majella Franzmann has drawn from her work on the French research into the *Odes of Solomon* do not make it possible to decide on one particular place.

7. The *Odes of Solomon* and Their Place in Antique Religion and Literature

We have endeavored to show that the date of the texts that are the subject of this commentary belongs to the first quarter of the second century C.E. (see 4.2.5 above). At that date the title *Odes of Solomon*, which is conventionally applied to this collection of poems, may be an anachronism. Moreover, their total may not have been forty-two, which could explain the existence of *Ode* 27, an Ode that is almost identical with the first lines of *Ode* 42.[89] In the index of early Christian literary history, the *Odes of Solomon*, in the widest sense, should be entered "among the New Testament rather than the Old Testament apocrypha and pseudepigrapha."[90] They are a unique collection of religious poems or songs "characterized by a particularly large overlap or mixture of Judaism, Gnosticism and Christianity."[91] Any links to the *Κήρυγμα Πέτρου* (*Kerygma of Peter*), belonging to the "decades from 100 to 120 C.E.,"[92] which cannot yet "be regarded as an Apology in the sense of the later Greek apologists of the 2nd century,"[93] are not to be discerned among the few surviving fragments of that sermon. On the other hand, the well-established closeness between the *Odes of Solomon* and the epistles of Ignatius should be emphasized.[94] The many parallels among them do not lead to any conclusion as to their literary dependence either way,[95] but they may contribute to the discussion about the date for Ignatius's epistles, which has recently begun again, and may lend their weight to counter the arguments for a late date.[96] Before considering the separate parts of the mixture or overlap mentioned previously, we will place the *Odes of Solomon* on the hymnological line of development.[97]

7.1. The *Odes of Solomon* within Ancient Hymnology

In the first place it should be noted that Philo consistently describes the Old Testament Psalms as *ὕμνοι* ("hymns").[98] This peremptory imposition of terminology may be explanation enough for the labeling of the *Odes of Solomon* with all sorts of hymnological descriptions and especially as a "hymn book" or "book of psalms."[99] The fact, which is more important than the label, is that not all Old Testament Psalms[100] nor yet all the *Odes of Solomon*—not to mention the *Psalms of Solomon*[101]—have a

the Occasion of his 65th Birthday (EPRO 91; Leiden: Brill, 1981) 117–30, esp. 129–30.

87 See Franzmann, 2.

88 See Franzmann, "Study," 407–10.

89 In the final editing of the *Psalms* and *Odes of Solomon* (or *Odes* and *Psalms of Solomon*), it may have been necessary to achieve a total of sixty; see Zahn, *Geschichte*, 292–93.

90 See Michael Lattke, "Bestandsaufnahme frühchristlicher Literaturgeschichte," in idem, *Bedeutung*, 4:208. On the "neglected interdependence of canonical and extracanonical writings in the history of early Christian literature," see idem, "Entwicklungslinien frühchristlicher Literaturgeschichte," in idem, *Bedeutung*, 4:222–24.

91 Michael Lattke, "Bestandsaufnahme frühchristlicher Literaturgeschichte," in idem, *Bedeutung*, 4:208. This was an era "when Judaism, Gnosticism and Christianity partly overlapped like three nonconcentric circles"; cf. Lattke, *Oden*, 18.

92 Henning Paulsen, "Das Kerygma Petri und die urchristliche Apologetik," *ZKG* 88 (1977) 13.

93 Wilhelm Schneemelcher, "Das Kerygma Petri," *NTApo*[5] 2 (1989) 37; *NTApoc*, 2:36.

94 See Lattke, *Oden*, 33.

95 See Henning Paulsen, *Studien zur Theologie des Ignatius von Antiochien* (Forschungen zur Kirchen- und Dogmengeschichte 29; Göttingen: Vandenhoeck & Ruprecht, 1978) 31. I am not willing to go so far as to say, with Harris and Mingana (2:45), "Ignatius knew the Odes."

96 See Ehrman, 1:209–13.

97 On the term "Entwicklungslinie" ("line of development," sometimes translated by "trajectory"), see Lattke, *Bedeutung*, 4:210.

98 See Lattke, *Hymnus*, 129.

99 Ibid., 251.

100 Ibid., 97–100.

101 Ibid., 116–17.

hymnic character. On the question why the *Odes of Solomon* were composed at all, reference should no longer be made to the previously quoted passages about Solomon or to the [pseudo?]-Solomonic writings (see 3.2 above), but to the New Testament. Just as 1 Cor 5:9 and Col 4:16 explain the production of the apocryphal letter of the Corinthians to Paul (*3 Corinthians*) and Paul's apocryphal Epistle to the Laodiceans, so passages like Col 3:16 and Eph 5:19 explain the composition of Odes, even though they may have been collected only later and ascribed to a pseudonym.[102]

7.2. Jewish Influence

The *Odes of Solomon* originated in an era when early Christianity was still largely embedded among the varieties of early Judaism[103] and—perhaps partly for that reason—was to some extent under the influence of a mythically Platonizing (early) Gnosticism. This influence can also be traced, incidentally, in some Jewish writings of the Hellenistic-Roman period. Hellenistic Jews, Gnostics, and Christians all in their own way made use of the same corpus of Greek writings, the Septuagint (LXX), still in process of being canonically stabilized. The intertextuality between the Greek Old Testament and the *Odes of Solomon* is largely concentrated on the use of passages from Genesis, Exodus, Isaiah, Psalms, and Proverbs. Sirach and Wisdom are the main sources among the extracanonical books related to the Old Testament, which in later usage are called Apocrypha. At the same time the *Odes of Solomon* cannot be counted among the Wisdom literature.[104] Among the texts from the Dead Sea (Qumran) the main influences come from 1QH (*Thanksgiving Hymns*) and 1QS (*Rule of the Community*).

7.3. Gnostic Tinge

We may begin with a quotation from the second edition of Helmut Koester's standard work, which is even more considered and magisterial than the original:

> The *Odes of Solomon* may indeed not deserve the title of a "Gnostic Hymnbook," but the Gnostic origin and character of a considerable portion of its imagery and metaphorical language cannot be doubted. . . . This early Christian hymnal may simply be a witness for the way in which Gnosticism very deeply affected the piety and spirituality of Christianity in general.[105]

The fact that the *Odes of Solomon* were used, quoted, and Gnostically interpreted by Gnostics in the third century C.E. (see 1.2, 2.2, and 4.2.1 above) does not make it a Gnostic collection of poems. On the other hand, there is no denying the parallels with passages in the Nag Hammadi tractates, especially with the *Gospel of Truth*. And the Platonism of the second century, developing from Middle to Neo-Platonism, in its blending with Gnosticism, has also left some traces on the *Odes of Solomon*.

7.4. Christian Whole

There can be no doubt that the *Odes of Solomon* were assembled in the early Christian era and circulated among Christians in later times. Even though some of the Odes can find a fitting place in early Judaism and others have a more pronounced Gnostic tinge, the influence of the writings that were to find a place in the canon of the New Testament is felt nearly throughout.[106] The dependence of the *Odes of Solomon* on—or their relation to—the Johannine corpus (especially John

102 See Lattke, "Dating," 57–58 = idem, *Bedeutung*, 4:129–30; idem, *Oden*, 34–35.

103 On the terms "late Judaism," "early Judaism," and "middle Judaism," see Lattke, "Dating," 47 = idem, *Bedeutung*, 4:116; idem, *Oden*, 12.

104 See, in addition to some publications of Drijvers, James H. Charlesworth, "The Odes of Solomon and the Jewish Wisdom Texts," in Charlotte Hempel, Armin Lange, and Hermann Lichtenberger, eds., *The Wisdom Texts from Qumran and the Development of Sapiential Thought* (BEThL 159; Leuven: Peeters, 2001) 323–49.

105 Helmut Koester, *Introduction to the New Testament*, vol. 2: *History and Literature of Early Christianity* (2nd ed.; Berlin/New York: de Gruyter, 2000) 223–24; cf. 1st ed. (Philadelphia: Fortress; Berlin/New York: de Gruyter, 1982) 218. On earlier opinions concerning the Gnostic character of the *Odes of Solomon*, see Lattke, *Oden*, p. 34.

106 See Michael Lattke, "Die Bedeutung der apokryphen *Salomo-Oden* für die neutestamentliche Wissenschaft," in Peter Slater and Donald Wiebe, eds., *Traditions in Contact and Change: Selected Proceedings of the XIVth Congress of the International Association for the History of Religions (Winnipeg, Man., August 15–20, 1980)* (Editions SR 3; Waterloo, Ont.: Wilfrid Laurier University Press, 1983) 267–83, 704–7, repr. and corr. in Lattke, *Bedeutung*, 4:49–66.

and 1 John) has always been highlighted.[107] But it only became clear with the completion of this commentary that in addition to "the pseudo- and deutero-Pauline letters (especially Colossians, Ephesians, and 1 Timothy), Hebrews, and the letters ascribed to Peter (1 Peter),"[108] all seven of the authentic Pauline epistles, the Synoptic Gospels (especially Matthew), and possibly Revelation had all exerted a quite surprising influence in the shaping of the *Odes of Solomon*. This observation urges caution in putting the date of the Odes too close to the turn from the first to the second century C.E.

8. Literary Forms and Devices in the *Odes of Solomon*

8.1. Predominance of Soteriology

The following inventory of literary forms and devices in the *Odes of Solomon* is meant to help users of this commentary identify the speakers and appreciate the variety of expression in the predominantly mythological and soteriological discourse, whose wealth of imagery and metaphors gives the *Odes of Solomon* their unique character in *Formgeschichte* and the history of religion(s). The predominance of soteriology is seen most clearly in the number and differentiation of the statements of salvation (see "Statements of salvation, grouped," below).[109] Among the most common theologico-soteriological terms are faith, fruit, grace, holiness, imperishability, joy, life, light, love, redemption, rest, salvation, strength, truth, understanding (*gnōsis*), and word. The theologico-christological terms Father, God, Lord, Messiah, Most High, Redeemer, Savior, Son, and Spirit also occur often. There are relatively many instances of instruction and reciprocal statements, but ethical or hortatory ones are few.

8.2. Symbols and Abbreviations

*	Forms and/or passages in which the first-person speaker (the speaking "I," occasionally the "we" of the group) expressly appears as one of the redeemed or to-be-redeemed, one of the praying, petitioning, accepting/receiving, instructing, or praising persons (or assemblies of persons).
**	Forms and/or passages in which the speaking "I" (never a "we") expressly appears as one who invites, redeems, creates, elects, summons, is sent, reveals, or promises.
***	Forms and/or passages in which the speaking "I" unites the previous characteristics (* and **), especially as the redeemed Redeemer or the redeeming Redeemed One.
I/M	Images and metaphors.
R	Reciprocal statements.
S	Simile as stylistic device.

8.3. Alphabetical List of Literary Forms and Devices

Address
  See Invocation; Testimony of salvation as a first-person address

Admonition
  13 [I/M]
  See also Summons

Benediction
  6:13; 9:8b [3rd person plural, I/M; myth or historical allusion in 9:8-11a?]; 11:18; 12:13 [final]; 30:7 [I/M]; 32:1 [indirect]; 33:11a [indirect]

Calamity
  See Statement of calamity, malediction

Call to salvation
  20:7-8 [I/M]; 30:1-3 [with indicative justification]
  See also Summons; Imperative of salvation

Confession of faith
  *29:6a [messianic]

Confidence
  See Expression of confidence in salvation

Description of
– detail
  *1:2-3 [I/M]; *5:5-6 [I/M, mythological or historical allusion?]; 6:8b-10 [mythological, unlikely to be historical]; 6:11-12, 14-17; 33:2 [Gnostic-dualistic]; 33:3 [Gnostic-dualistic]; 33:4 [Gnostic-

107 See Lattke, *Oden*, 33, with additional references.
108 See Lattke, "Dating," 57 = idem, *Bedeutung*, 4:129.
109 See Lattke, *Oden*, 36–88.

[I/M]; 23:4 [Gnostic]; 30:1-3 [with indicative justification]; 31:6-7 [invitation]; **33:9-10 [with **promise of salvation, dualistic]; **33:13a [esoteric-predestinarian]; 34:6 [with statement of salvation]; 39:8 [I/M, Gnostic]
See also Call to salvation; Summons

Instruction
3:6 [with *statement of confidence in salvation]; 3:8-9 [R, esoteric, promise of salvation]; 3:10; 4:1-2 [I/M]; 4:3a-b [I/M]; 4:7 [R]; 4:7-8, 11, 12, 14; 6:3-5; 6:4 [with formulaic statement]; *6:6-7a [group, Gnostic and hymnic]; 7:7 [formulaic, Gnostic]; 7:11 [formulaic, Gnostic]; 18:9-10 [Gnostic-dualistic]; 18:11-12 [partly I/M, Gnostic-dualistic]; 18:13-15 [Gnostic-dualistic]; 20:3 [S]; 20:4; 23:1-3 [I/M, with rhetorical questions]; 26:12-13 [I/M, S]; *27 [I/M]; *28:3 [with *statement of salvation, I/M]; *28:4-5 [with *statement of salvation, I/M]; *28:6-7 [with *statement of salvation, I/M]; 28:19; 34:1-3 [I/M, Gnostic-dualistic]; 34:4-5b [Gnostic-dualistic]; 34:5c [Gnostic-dualistic]; 41:11b-12, 13-14; 41:15-16a [with *statement of salvation by the group]; *42:1-2 [I/M]
See also Doctrine of creation

Introduction
– of persons and detail
*5:4; 6:8a
– of the image
*13:1a [I/M, group]; 39:1 [I/M]
– of the similes
**42:7b [I/M]
– to the Ode [liturgical?]
42:1-2 [I/M; self-description]
– to the speech within the speech
33:5; **42:15a-b

Introductory
– benediction
11:18
– metaphorical address
*12:1-3 [S]; *19:1
– question
*38:10a
– self-description
*20:1-2

– simile
*1:1 [I/M]; *6:1-2 [I/M, R]; 7:1; *14:1 [I/M]; *15:1–2a [I/M]; *16:1 [I/M]; *28:1 [I/M]; *28:2 [I/M]; *40:1 [I/M]
– summons
8:1-2 [partly I/M]; **9:1-2 [R]; **33:6–7 [speech within the speech]

Invocation
*1:4 [I/M]; 1:5 [I/M]; 4:3c-4 [I/M, responsive]; 4:5 [formulaic]; *4:9 [group]; *4:13 [group]; *5:1-3 [with *petition and *expression of confidence in salvation]; *14:1-2 [I/M, S]
See also Petition

Litany
See Poem, hymnic [38:19-21]

Malediction
See Statement of calamity, malediction

Myth
*5:5-6 [I/M, myth or historical allusion?]; 5:8-9 [past occurrence, myth or historical allusion?]; 6:8b-10 [I/M, river]; 7:13-14 [I/M, Gnostic]; 7:15 [Gnostic]; 9:8-11a [benediction, I/M, myth or historical allusion?] ; *10:1-2; **10:3; ***10:4; ***10:5-6; 12:4 [poem]; 12:5-7 [I/M, S]; 12:8-11 [I/M]; 12:12 [I/M]; ***15:6-9; **15:9 [I/M, conqueror of death]; *17:3-4b [statement of salvation]; *17:4c-5 [statement of salvation]; *17:7-8a [statement of salvation]; **17:8b-10 [statement of salvation]; **17:11 [statement of salvation]; **17:12-13 [statement of salvation]; **17:14-15 [statement of salvation]; 19:6-7bα, 7bβ-9, 10aα; 22 [Gnostic-dualistic]; 23:5-22 [metaphorical narrative]; 24:1-2 [I/M, dove]; 24:5-12 [Gnostic-dualistic]; 24:13-14 [Gnostic-dualistic]; *28:10 [statement of salvation]; *29:4 [I/M]; *29:5-6 [with *confession of faith, myth or historical allusion?]; ***29:7-9 [I/M, myth or historical allusion?]; *29:10 [I/M, S, myth or historical allusion?]; 31:1-2 [I/M, Gnostic-dualistic]; **31:8-9 [adversaries, myth or historical allusion?]; 33:1 [I/M, ascent and descent, Gnostic-dualistic]; 33:2 [I/M, description of detail, Gnostic-dualistic]; 33:3 [I/M, description of detail, Gnostic-dualistic]; 33:4 [I/M, description of detail, Gnostic-dualistic]; *38:6-7 [Gnostic-

dualistic, hardly historical]; *38:8-9 [I/M, Gnostic-dualistic, hardly historical]; *38:10-11 [Gnostic-dualistic, hardly historical]; 41:8-16a [partly *]; *42:10 [statement of salvation]; *42:11 [statement of salvation]; *42:12-13 [statement of salvation]; **42:14 [statement of salvation]; *42:15c-18 [with *petition of the group and *expression of confidence in salvation]
See also Images and metaphors; Simile

Personal account of the persecuted and redeemed
*28:8-9; *28:11-12; *28:13-14 [I/M, S, with description of the enemy]; *28:16 [with description of the enemy]; *28:17-18 [preexistence of the persecuted]; *29:11 [doxological, with messianic justification?]; **31:8-9 [about adversaries, myth or historical allusion?]
See also Self-description

Petition
*4:10 [I/M]; *14:1-2 [I/M, S, with *expression of confidence in salvation]; *14:3-5 [with *expression of confidence in salvation]; *14:7-8 [I/M, with *statement of goal]; *14:9c-10 [group, with *expression of confidence in salvation]; *18:4-5; *18:7 [group, Gnostic dualism]; *42:15c-18 [group, with *expression of confidence in salvation, myth]
See also Expression of confidence in salvation [18:6]; Invocation

Poem
12:4 [mythological]; 19:10-11; 26:5-7 [hymnic]; 26:8-11; 38:19-21 [I/M, hymnic]

Proclamation, prophecy
7:16b-17, 18-19; 7:20-21[with perfective cause]; 7:22-23b, 23c-e

Promise of salvation
3:8-9 [instruction, R, esoteric]; 8:6-7 [I/M, predestinarian]; **8:14; **8:20c-21 [with **statement of salvation, R]; 8:22-23 [with invitation and imperatives of salvation, R]; **9:6a; 9:6-7, 11b-12; 13:1b-4 [with imperatives of salvation]; 20:9 [I/M]; **31:12-13 [with **self-description]; **33:8 [dualistic]; **33:9-10a [dualistic, with **imperatives of salvation]; **33:10b-11a [with **self-description]; **33:11b [with **self-description]; **33:13b-c [esoteric]; 39:5-6 [I/M]; 40:5 [statement of future salvation]; 41:1-2a [hymnic summons, esoteric]; **42:3-4; **42:5-7a [with **statement of salvation]

Prophecy
See Proclamation, prophecy

Question
*38:10a
See also Rhetorical questions

Reciprocal statements
*3:2c-3; *3:7; 3:8-9; 4:7; *5:15; 6:2; **8:10-11; **8:20c-21; 8:22-23; **9:1-2; 18:9-10

Report
See Description of detail, events, paradise, prayer, spring of salvation; Doxological description; Doxological self-description; Myth; Personal account; Self-description; Testimony of salvation

Responsive doxology of the group
See Doxology of the group, responsive

Responsive invocation
See Invocation

Rhetorical questions
3:4 [Wisdom]; 4:6 [I/M, introductory]; 8:19; 23:1-3 [instruction, I/M]; 26:8, 9-10, 11

Self-description
*16:2-4 [hymnic, formal]; *16:5-7 [hymnic, content]; *17:6; *20:1-2; *21:6-7 [hymnic, I/M]; *21:8-9 [hymnic, I/M]; ***22:1-5 [I/M]; *26:1-4 [hymnic, proclamation]; *27 [with *instruction]; *28:8; **31:10-11 [I/M, S]; **31:12-13 [with **promise of salvation]; **33:10b-11a [with **promise of salvation]; **33:11b [with **promise of salvation]; *35:5 [existence and actions in heaven]; *36:2c-3a [existence and actions in heaven]; *36:3b [existence and actions in heaven]; *36:4 [existence and actions in heaven]; *36:6 [existence and actions in heaven]; *36:7 [existence and actions in heaven]; *36:8 [existence and actions in heaven]; *40:3-4 [hymnic]; *41:8 [I/M]; *41:9-10 [I/M]; *42:1-2 [with *instruction]
See also Personal account of the persecuted and redeemed

Simile
*1:1 [I/M]; *5:12; *6:1-2 [I/M]; 7:1; *7:6; *11:12b-13; *12:1-3; 12:5-7; *14:1-2 [I/M]; *14:9a-b; *15:1-2a [I/M]; *15:7; *16:1 [I/M]; 18:11-12; 19:10; 20:3; *25:5-6; 26:12-13; *28:1 [I/M]; *28:2 [I/M]; *28:13-14; *29:2-3; *29:10; **31:10-11; *35:4-5; *38:1a; *40:1 [I/M]; *40:2; **42:8-9
See also Images and metaphors; Myth

Speech within the speech
11:18-24 [I/M]; **33:6-13 [I/M]; 38:10b-14; *42:15c-18

Statement of calamity, malediction
5:7 [malediction]; 22:11a-b [with statement of salvation]; 22:11c-12 [with statement of salvation]; 24:3-4 [apocalyptic events]; 35:3 [I/M, apocalyptic motifs]; 39:2-3 [description of detail]

Statements of salvation, grouped
See also Call to salvation; Expression of confidence in salvation; Imperative of salvation; Promise of salvation; Testimony of salvation

Statement of salvation
6:18 [esoteric]; 7:12 [esoteric]; 8:3-5 [with imperatives of salvation]; 9:3-4 [messianic]; 22:11a-b [with statement of calamity]; 22:11c-12 [with statement of calamity]; 31:4b-5 [on the justified mediator]; 34:6 [and imperatives of salvation, esoteric]; 40:5 [future, see: Promise of salvation]; 40:6

*Statement of salvation
*5:10–12 [with *expression of confidence in salvation in 5:12; I/M, S, cf. *Ode* 1:1]; *5:15; *7:3; *7:4 [Gnostic identification]; *7:5; *7:10; *15:3-5 [Gnostic]; *35:6

**Statement of salvation
**8:17; **8:20c-21 [with **promise of salvation, R]; **42:5-7a [with **promise of salvation]; **42:19-20

Statement of salvation [I/M]
9:8-11a [with imperative of salvation]; 15:10 [esoteric, about Gnostic believers]; 32 [based on eternal Truth personified]; 38:17; 38:18; 39:7; 39:13 [with indirect doxology]

*Statement of salvation [I/M]
*3:2c-3 [with reflection, R]; *3:5; *3:7 [with *expression of confidence in salvation, I/M, R]; *7:2; *15:2b-c [Gnostic]; *15:6; *15:8; *17:1-2; *18:1-3; *21:1-2 [already in the heights]; *21:3 [dualism]; *21:4 [about members, himself such a "member"?]; *21:5; *21:6-7 [with hymnic self-description]; *22:6-7; *22:8-10; *25:1-2; *25:3-4; *25:5-6; *25:7; *25:8-9; *25:10-12 [Gnostic-dualistic]; *28:3 [with *instruction of the redeemed]; *28:4-5 [with *instruction of the redeemed]; *28:6-7 [and *instruction of the redeemed]; *35:1-2; *35:7 [Gnostic ascent, liturgical *Sitz im Leben/Sitz im Text*?]; *36:1-2b; *38:1b-4; *38:5; *38:15 [Gnostic-dualistic]; *38:16

**Statement of salvation [I/M]
**8:15–16; **42:7b

*Statement of salvation [R]
*5:15

*Statement of salvation [S]
*7:6 [Gnostic identity];*15:7; *29:2–3

*Statement of salvation [I/M, S]
*1:1; *5:10–12 [5:12 I/M, S, cf. *Ode* 1:1: with *expression of confidence in salvation]; *6:1-2; *25:5-6 [Gnostic-dualistic]; *35:4-5; *38:1a [ascent?]

*Statement of salvation [mythological]
*17:3–4b; *17:4c–5; *17:7–8a; *28:10; *42:10; *42:11; *42:12–13

**Statement of salvation [mythological]
**17:8b-10; **17:11; **17:12-13; **17:14-15; **42:14

*Statement of salvation by the group
*41:3-4 [Messianic and hymnic]; *41:11a; *41:11b-12 [with instruction]

Summons
8:1-2 [partly I/M]; 8:22-23 [with imperatives and promises of salvation]; **9:1-2 [R]; **33:6-7 [to return, dualistic]; 41:1-2a [hymnic summons with promise of salvation, esoteric]

See also Admonition; Call to salvation; Doxology [7:25]; Exhortation; Exhortation by the group; Imperative of salvation; Introductory summons

Testimony of salvation
*25 [as a first-person address]; *29:4 [I/M, mythological, metaphorical]; *29:5-6 [with *confession of faith, mythological or historical?]; ***29:7-9 [I/M, mythological or historical?]; *29:10 [I/M, S, mythological or historical?]

Transition
38:16c

Verdict with reasoned judgment
**33:12 [I/M, future, esoteric]

9. Editions and Translations of the *Odes of Solomon* up to 1909

Based on the annotated bibliographies covering publications up to 1997,[110] those editions of the *Odes of Solomon* that have played an important role in the research on the Odes, whether internationally or limited to a smaller linguistic area, will be introduced and briefly described. Studies of details or individual problems in the Odes will not be noticed here, but are considered and listed in the commentary. There was no commentary, as such, before the appearance of my German three-volume work (1999–2005), but several editions and translations of the *Odes of Solomon* with commenting introductions and annotations had preceded it.

9.1. The Coptic *Odes of Solomon* in the *Pistis Sophia*

The history of research on the *Odes of Solomon* between 1799 and the first publication of the Syriac text in 1909 consists of work on the Coptic quotations in the *Pistis Sophia* and also includes discussion of the *Psalms of Solomon*.

9.1.1. Woide (1799)[111]

In an appendix to the edition of Codex Alexandrinus, Charles Godfrey Woide for the first time printed the Coptic text, with a Latin translation, of the five *Odes of Solomon* quoted in the *Pistis Sophia* (see 1.2 and 2.2 above).[112]

9.1.2. Münter (1812)[113]

In a program for a diocesan synod, the Danish bishop Friedrich Münter circulated the first steps in research and criticism of the *Odes of Solomon*,[114] which Woide had published and which were now officially designated as Gnostic.

9.1.3. Petermann/Schwartze (1853)[115]

This *editio princeps*[116] of the *Pistis Sophia*, with a Latin translation, was used by Carl Schmidt[117] and also consulted by Lattke[118] for his edition of the *Odes of Solomon*. "Petermann's promise, in his Foreword (p. VII) to write on the Gnostic character of the *Pistis Sophia* remained unfulfilled."[119]

9.1.4. Harnack (1891)[120]

In his work on the Gnostic *Pistis Sophia*, Harnack also considers the *Odes of Solomon* in the chapter on the *Pistis Sophia* and the Old Testament.[121] Harnack's observations mark the true beginning of critical research on the *Odes of Solomon*. It has not been possible up to the present to

110 See Lattke, *Bedeutung*, vol. 3 (containing Franzmann, "Study"); idem, "Forschungsgeschichtliche Bibliographie 1985–1997 mit Ergänzungen bis 1984," in Lattke, *Bedeutung*, 4:233–53.
111 See Lattke, *Bedeutung*, 3:1–2, 14–19.
112 Charles Godfrey Woide, *Appendix ad editionem Novi Testamenti Graeci e codice MS. Alexandrino* (Oxford: Clarendon, 1799) 148–51.
113 See Lattke, *Bedeutung*, 3:7–10, 14–19; 4:247.
114 Friedrich Münter, *Odae Gnosticae Salomoni tributae: Thebaice et Latine, praefatione et adnotationibus philologicis illustratae* (Copenhagen: Schultz, 1812).
115 See Lattke, *Bedeutung*, 3:11, 14–19.
116 Julius Heinrich Petermann, ed., and Moritz Gotthilf Schwartze, trans., *Pistis Sophia: Opus gnosticum Valentino adiudicatum e codice manuscripto coptico Londinensi* (Berlin: Dümmler, 1851–53).
117 Carl Schmidt, ed., *Pistis Sophia: Neu herausgegeben mit Einleitung nebst griechischem und koptischem Wort- und Namensregister* (Coptica 2; Copenhagen: Nordisk, 1925).
118 Lattke, *Bedeutung*, 1:24–31, 79, 84–95, 134–41, 148–53, 187–205.
119 Ibid., 3:11.
120 See ibid., 3:11–26.
121 Adolf Harnack, *Über das gnostische Buch Pistis Sophia. Brod und Wasser: Die eucharistischen Elemente bei Justin. Zwei Untersuchungen* (TU 7.2; Leipzig: Hinrichs, 1891) 1–114, esp. 31–49.

verify his suggestion "that they were published as Solomonic poems by their author; i.e., they are true pseudepigrapha."[122]

9.2. Greek *Psalms of Solomon*

9.2.1. Ryle/James (1891)[123]

There is an appendix to this critical edition of the Greek *Psalms of Solomon*, "The *Odes* of the *Pistis Sophia*,"[124] in which the first Greek back-translation of the Coptic quotations from the *Odes of Solomon* is presented, together with critical notes, and account is taken of the more important differences between the Latin translations of Woide and Schwartze.

9.2.2. Von Gebhardt (1895)[125]

This is still the most important critical edition of the *Psalms of Solomon*,[126] taking into account more manuscripts than the previous one. It is the basis[127] for the edition by Joseph Viteau and François Martin.[128] It is of only marginal interest in connection with the *Odes of Solomon*.

10. Editions and Translations of the *Odes of Solomon* since 1909

The discovery of two Syriac manuscripts (see 2.4 above) created a totally new situation, which led to a flood of publications. Half a century later, a decade after the Qumran finds, the situation changed again, quite dramatically, with the *editio princeps* of *P. Bodmer* XI (see 2.1 above). This Greek papyrus, on which Barbara Aland has published a recent article,[129] rekindled the debate on the origin and original language of the *Odes of Solomon*.[130] It is possible to distinguish three phases, post 1909, in the still-continuing research on the *Odes of Solomon*. In the first (1909–59) there are the editions and translations based on the Syriac and Coptic texts. The second (1959–61) is especially concerned with *Ode* 11. And the third (1961 to the present) is based on the Greek, Coptic, and Syriac texts for its editions and translations.

10.1. Editions and Translations Based on the Syriac and Coptic Texts

10.1.1. Harris (1909; 2nd ed., revised and enlarged, with facsimile, 1911)[131]

The *editio princeps* and also the second edition[132] were superseded almost at once, since they could not take account of Burkitt's identification of Codex N in 1912. The division of the verses, which was adopted by a number of publications before 1920, was later much revised.[133]

122 See Lattke, *Bedeutung*, 3:21.

123 See ibid., 3:27–30.

124 See Herbert Edward Ryle and Montague Rhodes James, eds., Ψαλμοὶ Σολομῶντος: *Psalms of the Pharisees, commonly called the Psalms of Solomon. The text newly revised from all the MSS* (Cambridge: Cambridge University Press, 1891) 155–61.

125 See Lattke, *Bedeutung*, 3:33–39.

126 Oscar von Gebhardt, ed., Ψαλμοὶ Σολομῶντος: *Die Psalmen Salomon's zum ersten Male mit Benutzung der Athoshandschriften und des Codex Casanatensis herausgegeben* (TU 13.2; Leipzig: Hinrichs, 1895).

127 See Svend Holm-Nielsen, *Die Psalmen Salomos* (JSHRZ 4.2; Gütersloh: Mohn, 1977) 52–53.

128 Joseph Viteau and François Martin, *Les Psaumes de Salomon: Introduction, texte grec et traduction, avec les principales variantes de la version Syriaque* (Documents pour l'étude de la Bible; Paris: Letouzey et Ané, 1911). Martin was responsible for the Syriac variants. Cf. Franzmann, "Study," 121: "In chapter six of the monograph (pp. 160–191), the authors suggest a connection between the *Odes* and the *Psalms of Solomon*, indicating common ideas and points of resemblance (p. 178) and noting the addition of the *Odes* to the *Psalms* (pp. 190–191)."

129 Barbara Aland, "Welche Rolle," esp. 309.

130 See Lattke, "Dating," 46–47 = idem, *Bedeutung*, 4:115–16.

131 See Lattke, *Bedeutung*, 3:32–47, 109.

132 James Rendel Harris, *The Odes and Psalms of Solomon, Now First Published from the Syriac Version* (Cambridge: Cambridge University Press, 1909; 2nd ed., revised and enlarged, with a facsimile, 1911). The facsimile shows only a minute portion of Codex H (*Odes Sol.* 24:13-14; 27; 28:1-4). The complete facsimile of Codex H was first published in the first volume of Harris and Mingana's edition; see also James H. Charlesworth, ed., *Papyri and Leather Manuscripts of the Odes of Solomon* (Dickerson Series of Facsimiles of Manuscripts Important for Christian Origins 1; Durham, N.C.: International Center for the Study of Ancient Near Eastern Civilizations and Christian Origins, Duke University, 1981) 27–89.

133 See the table comparing Harris with Harris and Mingana in Lattke, *Bedeutung*, 3:44–45.

10.1.2. Harnack and Flemming (1910)[134] and Ungnad and Staerk (1910)[135]

Very soon after the *editio princeps* of the *Odes of Solomon*, two German translations of Codex H appeared. Of the two, the translation by the Old Testament scholar Willy Staerk (with text-critical annotations by the expert on the Middle East Ungnad)[136] was much less influential than that of the chief librarian Johannes Flemming, which Harnack used as the basis for his hastily produced publication.[137] Harnack's hypothesis of interpolations has not been accepted. A decade later he himself no longer doubted the literary unity of the *Odes of Solomon*, but remained skeptical of an early date.[138]

10.1.3. Frankenberg (1911)[139] and Grimme (1911)[140]

Although the Greek back-translation of the minimally amended Syriac text of Codex H by Wilhelm Frankenberg,[141] acting on a suggestion by Julius Wellhausen,[142] continues to be useful, his commentary adds little to the understanding of the *Odes of Solomon*. The Hebrew back-translation by the Semitic scholar Hubert Grimme[143] is more an original work than a critical engagement with the text and can best be described as speculative. Grimme, for his part, described not only Frankenberg and Gustav Diettrich but even Jean Labourt and Pierre Batiffol as "typical cases . . . of most eccentric interpretation."[144]

10.1.4. Diettrich (1911)[145]

Gustav Diettrich had already published some preliminary comments on the *Odes of Solomon* in 1910.[146] These expositions were integrated into his translation, which is still important for its introductions and detailed comments.[147] In this commentary Diettrich's expositions will often be found occupying an antithetical position.

10.1.5. Labourt and Batiffol (1911)[148]

This collaboration is composed largely of previously published material; the French translation of the *Odes of Solomon* in the first part is by Jean Labourt, and the very important and influential introduction in the second part is by the historian of dogma Pierre Batiffol.[149] Although it was announced in the title of the second part ("Introduction et commentaire"), there is no commentary; there are, however, some important comments on the text. The suggested date (100–120 C.E.) and place of composition (Syria in the wider sense, not merely Antioch) should be considered very seriously.

134 See Lattke, *Bedeutung*, 3:49–56.

135 Ibid., 3:75–77.

136 Arthur Ungnad and Willy Staerk, *Die Oden Salomos* (KlT 64; Bonn: Marcus & Weber, 1910). Staerk expressed his views more fully elsewhere; see Willy Staerk, "Kritische Bemerkungen zu den Oden Salomos," *ZWTh* N.S. 17 (1910) 289–306.

137 Adolf Harnack, *Ein jüdisch-christliches Psalmbuch aus dem ersten Jahrhundert [The Odes . . . of Solomon, now first published from the Syriac version by J. Rendel Harris, 1909]. Aus dem Syrischen übersetzt von Johannes Flemming* (TU 35.4; Leipzig: Hinrichs, 1910).

138 See Adolf von Harnack, review of Harris and Mingana in *ThLZ* 46 (1921) 6–7; cf. Lattke, *Bedeutung*, 3:181.

139 See Lattke, *Bedeutung*, 3:92–93.

140 See ibid., 3:98–107.

141 Wilhelm Frankenberg, *Das Verständnis der Oden Salomos* (BZAW 21; Gießen: Töpelmann, 1911).

142 On Julius Wellhausen, review of Harris and Harnack in *GGA* 172 (1910) 629–42, see Lattke, *Bedeutung*, 3:78–79.

143 On Grimme, see 5.1 above.

144 Hubert Grimme, "Zu den Oden Salomos," *TRev* 10 (1911) 601.

145 See Lattke, *Bedeutung*, 3:59, 91.

146 Gustav Diettrich, "Eine jüdisch-christliche Liedersammlung (aus dem apostolischen Zeitalter)," in *Die Reformation: Deutsche evangelische Kirchenzeitung für die Gemeinde* 9 (1910) 306–10, 370–76, 513–18, 533–36.

147 Gustav Diettrich, *Die Oden Salomos unter Berücksichtigung der überlieferten Stichengliederung* (Neue Studien zur Geschichte der Theologie und der Kirche 9; Berlin: Trowitzsch, 1911; repr. Aalen: Scientia, 1973).

148 See Franzmann, "Study," 65, 86, 112–13.

149 Jean Labourt and Pierre Batiffol, *Les Odes de Salomon: Une œuvre chrétienne des environs de l'an 100–120* (Paris: Gabalda, 1911).

10.1.6. Bruston (1912)[150]

A second French translation came from a Protestant source.[151] Although Charles Bruston published corrections to his translation,[152] it is hardly usable, since the verses are not numbered. For that reason it is almost never quoted.

10.1.7. Bernard (1912)[153]

This is not an edition but an English translation based on Harris's *editio princeps* and the variant readings of Codex N.[154] Bernard's thesis that the *Odes of Solomon* are hymns of the newly baptized, his late date (second half of the second century C.E.), and his advocacy of Syriac or Aramaic as the language of composition may not convince, but any commentary can only profit from the scholarly annotations to the translation.

10.1.8. Tondelli (1914)[155]

The first Italian translation is based on both of the Syriac manuscripts.[156] Some two decades later Tondelli summarized his own contributions and dated the *Odes of Solomon* ca. 120 C.E.[157] However, Italian speakers of today will probably prefer the later translation by Mario Erbetta (see 10.3.4 below).

10.1.9. Harris and Mingana (1916–20)[158]

The introduction[159] and notes[160] of what was for decades the definitive edition, although there are hardly any published reviews, are still basic to any work on the *Odes of Solomon*. The edition of the texts that were then available,[161] and consequently also the translation,[162] have now been superseded by the work of Charlesworth, Franzmann, and Lattke, "which nowadays form the scholarly basis for further studies."[163]

10.1.10. Greßmann (1924)[164] and Bauer (1933)[165]

Hugo Greßmann's translation, with its short introductions, was influential especially in German-speaking countries.[166] What is notable is that the *Odes of Solomon* now appear in their proper place among the New Testament Apocrypha. Even more influential, and not only among German speakers, was Walter Bauer's edition[167] based on Harris and Mingana. If *P. Bodmer* XI had not been discovered, both Bauer's German translation and his edition with its text-critical comments would still be considered valid (but see 10.3.1 below).

10.2. Editions and Translations Based on the Greek (*Ode* 11)[168]

Two works should be noted particularly, because the *editio princeps* of *P. Bodmer* XI begins a new chapter in the exciting story of research on the *Odes of Solomon*, and at the same time there was a renewed attempt at a back-translation into Hebrew.

150 See Franzmann, "Study," 87, 133–34, 147–48.

151 Charles Bruston, *Les plus anciens cantiques chrétiens: Traduits sur la seconde édition du texte syriaque avec une introduction et des notes* (Geneva: Jeheber; Paris: Fischbacher, 1912) 40–83. Bruston knew already the translation of Labourt (p. 7). Franzmann's note on this work ("Study," 133) is not quite accurate, since she does not mention Bruston's translation.

152 Charles Bruston, "Rectifications à la traduction des plus anciens cantiques chrétiens I–II," *Revue de théologie et des questions religieuses* 21 (1912) 440–42, 536–37; idem, "Rectifications à la traduction des plus anciens cantiques chrétiens III–XII," *Revue de théologie et des questions religieuses* 22 (1913) 54–64, 367–75.

153 See Lattke, *Bedeutung*, 3:130–33.

154 John Henry Bernard, ed., *The Odes of Solomon* (TextsS 8.3; Cambridge: Cambridge University Press, 1912; repr. Nendeln/Liechtenstein: Kraus Reprint, 1967).

155 See Lattke, *Bedeutung*, 3:161, 370.

156 Leone Tondelli, *Le Odi di Salomone: Cantici cristiani degli inizi del II secolo. Versione dal siriaco, introduzione e note* (Prefazione del Angelo Mercati; Rome: Ferrari, 1914) 137–268.

157 See Leone Tondelli, "I Salmi e le Odi di Salomone," *Enciclopedia italiana di scienze, lettere ed arti* 30 (1936) 550–51.

158 See Lattke, *Bedeutung*, 3:173–78.

159 Harris and Mingana, 2:1–205.

160 Harris and Mingana, 2:207–409.

161 The first volume of Harris and Mingana contains, besides the facsimile of Codex H, the critical edition of the Coptic and Syriac *Odes of Solomon* and of the Syriac *Psalms of Solomon*. The frontispiece is the facsimile of the first page of Codex N (*Odes Sol.* 17:7–21:7).

162 Harris and Mingana, 2:215–405.

163 See Lattke, "Dating," 48 = idem, *Bedeutung*, 4:117–18; idem, *Oden*, 13. The commentary mentioned in *Oden* (13 n. 20) has been replaced by Lattke, *Bedeutung*, vol. 4.

164 See Lattke, *Bedeutung*, 3:191.

165 See ibid., 3:208.

166 Hugo Greßmann, "Die Oden Salomos," *NTApo*² (1924) 437–72.

167 Walter Bauer, ed., *Die Oden Salomos* (KlT 64; Berlin: de Gruyter, 1933).

168 The complete facsimile of the Greek *Ode* 11 was published only later; see Michael Lattke, *Bedeutung*,

10.2.1. Testuz (1959)[169]

Without the exemplary *editio princeps* of the relevant part of *P. Bodmer* X–XII,[170] the detailed physical and text-critical description of *P. Bodmer* XI[171] would have been much more difficult. Papyrologists will continue to use this edition because it also includes the apocryphal correspondence between Paul and the Corinthians (*3 Corinthians*) and part of a liturgical hymn.[172]

10.2.2. Carmignac (1961)[173]

Jean Carmignac sets out to find the Hebrew substratum of the *Odes of Solomon*, presenting a Hebrew back-translation of *Ode* 11 with detailed notes, ending with a critical postscript on Grimme's back-translation (see 10.1.3 above).[174] A discussion of Carmignac's untenable theory will be found in the commentary on *Ode* 11.

10.3. Editions and Translations Based on the Greek, Coptic, and Syriac Versions of the *Odes of Solomon*

The last part of this section is thoroughly international. To give non-Anglophone readers easier access to the text itself, we will list also French, German, Italian, Japanese, Modern Greek, and Spanish translations, all of which have more or less detailed introductions and annotations.[175]

10.3.1. Bauer (1964)[176]

I will begin with Walter Bauer, whose edition of 1933 (see 10.1.10), now superseded, was discussed above. His new translation replaced, in the third and fourth editions of the *Neutestamentliche Apokryphen*, the earlier one by Greßmann (see 10.1.10).[177] This faithful and precise translation remained influential for more than a quarter century and was still used by Klaus Berger and Christiane Nord in their own translation of the *Odes of Solomon*.[178]

10.3.2. Charlesworth (1973; 2nd ed., 1977)[179]

The influence of Charlesworth's edition and translation is felt well beyond the English speaking countries.[180] Even Berger and Nord used his edition of the Syriac text as their "basic text."[181] Charlesworth's later English translation spread its influence even further.[182] Contemporaneously, both Emerton (see 10.3.7 below) and Charlesworth were placing the *Odes of Solomon* with the Old Testament rather than with the New. This move can be sustained only if it is argued that the Old Testament in Hebrew, but especially in its Greek (LXX) incarnation, was also used by Christians and that some of the Old Testament Apocrypha and Pseudepigrapha have

vol. 1a: *Der syrische Text der Edition in Esṭrangelā, Faksimile des griechischen Papyrus Bodmer XI* (OBO 25.1a; Fribourg: Academic Press; Göttingen: Vandenhoeck & Ruprecht, 1980) 59–64; Charlesworth, *Manuscripts*, 7–12.

169 See Lattke, *Bedeutung*, 3:250.

170 Michel Testuz, *Papyrus Bodmer X–XII* (Cologny-Genève: Bibliothèque Bodmer, 1959) 46, 49–69.

171 See Lattke, *Bedeutung*, 1:1–23.

172 Addition to Lattke, *Hymnus*, 261–67; cf. B. Aland, "Welche Rolle," 309–10 n. 28.

173 See Franzmann, "Study," 255–56.

174 See Carmignac, "Affinités," 76–79.

175 The Dutch translation by Arent Jan Wensinck, "De Oden van Salomo: Een oudchristelijk psalmboek" (*Theologische studiën* 29 [1911] 1–60, esp. 3–51), is outdated; see Lattke, *Bedeutung*, 3:121–22. The later Dutch translation, probably published in 1942, by H. J. E. Westerman Holstijn, *Oden van Salomo: Zangen van rust in den Heere. Een bundel lyriek uit de tweede eeuw uit het Grieksch vertaald en metrisch bewerkt* (Zutphen: Ruys, n.d.), is a good deal too free; see Lattke, *Bedeutung*, 3:221.

176 See Lattke, *Bedeutung*, 3:269.

177 Bauer, 578–625. The English translation of the third edition (*NTApoc*) included a justification for omitting a translation of Bauer; in the fifth edition of the *Neutestamentliche Apokryphen in deutscher Übersetzung* (ed. Wilhelm Schneemelcher; Tübingen: Mohr Siebeck, 1987–89), the "Anhang: Dichtungen" has been dropped without explanation or any hint of a revised translation.

178 Klaus Berger and Christiane Nord, *Das Neue Testament und frühchristliche Schriften* (Frankfurt am Main/Leipzig: Insel, 1999) 933–71. The *Odes of Solomon* receive their proper place as Christian texts of the early second century C.E. in this collection.

179 See Lattke, *Bedeutung*, 3:305–6, 326–27.

180 Charlesworth.

181 Cf. Berger and Nord, 934.

182 James H. Charlesworth, "Odes of Solomon (Late First to Early-Second Century A.D.): A New Translation and Introduction," *OTP*, 2:725–71.

Christian origins or, at least, have their proper home in Christian tradition.

10.3.3. Tsakonas (1974)[183] and Fanourgakis (1979)[184]

Basileios Tsakonas's Modern Greek translation[185] is intended to be easier for the contemporary reader, while Basileios Fanourgakis's dissertation attempts to reconstruct the original Greek.[186] Unlike Frankenberg (see 10.1.3 above), from whose back-translation the new one, with a more native feeling for the Greek language, often differs, Fanourgakis was able to follow the guidelines offered by the bilingual text of *Ode* 11.

10.3.4. Erbetta (1975)[187]

This new Italian translation of the *Odes of Solomon*[188] in the appendix to the first part of *Gli Apocrifi del Nuovo Testamento*, vol. I/1–2: *Vangeli* may be expected to supersede Tondelli's (see 10.1.8 above). Although ultimately indebted to Harris and Mingana, the translation is based most directly on Bauer's minor edition[189] and his revised German translation (see 10.3.1 above). It is noteworthy that, unlike Emerton (see 10.3.7 below) and Charlesworth,[190] Mario Erbetta places these Christian, if not wholly orthodox, Odes among the New Testament Apocrypha.

10.3.5. Lattke (1979)[191]

Later German translations[192] have superseded this preliminary one by Lattke.[193] However, the concordance, containing the first complete facsimile of Codex N, that was published at the same time, has not been superseded, although it is in need of some corrections.[194]

10.3.6. Beskow and Hidal (1980),[195] Peral and Alegre (1982),[196] Onuki (1982)[197]

The first Swedish translation of the *Odes of Solomon* (Beskow and Hidal)[198] was quickly followed by the first Spanish one (Peral and Alegre).[199] In the latter work the Odes are treated as Old Testament Apocrypha because of their Jewish-Christian features. The introduction and notes are by the New Testament scholar Xavier Alegre, who some years before authored a regrettably still unpublished dissertation on the Gnosticizing soteriology of the *Odes of Solomon*.[200]

---

183 See Lattke, *Bedeutung*, 3:314.

184 See ibid., 3:337–38.

185 Basileios [Vassilios] G. Tsakonas, *Αἵ Ὠδαὶ Σολομῶντος (Εἰσαγωγή - Κείμενον - Ἑρμηνεία)* (repr. from: *Θεολογία* [*Theologia*] 44 [1973] 389–416, 583–605; 45 [1974] 129–49, 309–46, 511–58, 608–46). English summaries are found in *Θεολογία* (*Theologia*) 44 (1973) 827, and 45 (1974) 882.

186 Basileios [Vassilios] D. Fanourgakis, *Αἱ Ὠδαὶ Σολομῶντος: Συμβολὴ εἰς τὴν ἔρευναν τῆς ὑμνογραφίας τῆς ἀρχαϊκῆς ἐκκλησίας* (Analekta Blatadon [Vlatadon] 29; Thessaloniki: Patriarchal Institute for Patristic Studies, 1979) 139–75. An English summary is found on pp. 177–78.

187 See Lattke, *Bedeutung*, 3:317–18.

188 Mario Erbetta, "Le Odi di Salomone (II SEC.)," in idem, ed., *Gli Apocrifi del Nuovo Testamento* 1/1 (Turin: Marietti, 1975) 608–58.

189 Bauer, *Oden*.

190 James H. Charlesworth, "Odes of Solomon (Late First to Early-Second Century A.D.): A New Translation and Introduction," *OTP*, 2:725–71.

191 See Lattke, *Bedeutung*, 3:338–39.

192 Lattke, *Oden*, 92–216, and especially Lattke's three-volume translation and commentary (see 10.3.10 below).

193 Lattke, *Bedeutung*, 1:79–185.

194 Lattke, *Bedeutung*, vol. 2: *Vollständige Wortkonkordanz zur handschriftlichen, griechischen, koptischen, lateinischen und syrischen Überlieferung der Oden Salomos. Mit einem Faksimile des Kodex N* (OBO 25.2; Fribourg: Academic Press; Göttingen: Vandenhoeck & Ruprecht, 1979) 195–201; see also Charlesworth, *Manuscripts*, 21–26.

195 See Lattke, *Bedeutung*, 3:341.

196 See ibid., 4:177, 237.

197 See ibid., 3:357.

198 Per Beskow and Sten Hidal, *Salomos oden: Den äldsta kristna sångboken översatt och kommenterad* (Stockholm: Proprius, 1980) 9–56. The music for *Ode* 27 (p. 41) is by the New Testament scholar René Kieffer.

199 Antonio Peral and Xavier Alegre, "Odas de Salomon," in Alejandro Díez Macho, ed., with contributions by Maria Angeles Navarro, Alfonso de la Fuente, and Antonio Piñero, *Apócrifos del Antiguo Testamento* (3 vols.; Madrid: Ediciones Cristiandad, 1982) 3:59–100. The translation of *Ode* 1 is by Antonio Piñero (p. 71).

200 Xavier Alegre, "El concepto de salvación en las Odas de Salomon: Contribución al estudio de una soteriología gnostizante y sus posibles relaciones con el cuarto evangelio" (Dr. theol. diss., Münster University, 1977); see Lattke, *Bedeutung*, 3:326.

The first and only Japanese translation[201] is based on the editions of Harris and Mingana, Charlesworth (1973), and Lattke (1979) as well as various German and French translations.[202] Takashi Onuki considers the *Odes of Solomon*, in their current form, a New Testament apocryphon that may have been based on an earlier Old Testament one. He thus resurrects and modifies Harnack's theory of a reworking of earlier material.

10.3.7. Emerton (1984)[203]

H. F. D. Sparks, the editor of *The Apocryphal Old Testament*, with an eye to Robert Harry Charles's *APOT* and Montague Rhodes James's *The Apocryphal New Testament*,[204] was well aware that including the *Odes of Solomon* in his collection of translations would be problematic.[205] My English translation of the Odes is indebted to Emerton's translation as much as to the translations of Harris and Mingana, Charlesworth, and Franzmann.

10.3.8. Franzmann (1991)[206]

Emerton's translation was already available to Franzmann. The main aim of her book, which is practically identical to her Ph.D. thesis of 1990,[207] was an analysis of the poetical structure and form of the *Odes of Solomon*, which had never been done before. Her work includes also an edition and English translation of the Coptic, Greek, and Syriac texts. Franzmann's division of the individual Odes into stanzas[208] and her work on vocabulary, syntax, and imagery have been very important and valuable for this commentary.

10.3.9. Pierre (1994)[209] and Azar (1996)[210]

Two new French translations appeared independently of each other and almost simultaneously. Marie-Joseph Pierre's translation,[211] in spite of the subtitle of this scholarly little work, does not contain the Syriac text; Ephrem Azar's,[212] on the other hand, has a vocalized version of the Syriac text.[213] Both scholars would date the *Odes of Solomon* to the early part of the second century C.E. Pierre leans toward Syriac for the original language of the Odes, but is finally undecided.[214] The Iraqi Dominican Azar, whose mother tongue is Aramaic, comes down strongly on the side of Syriac. This decision should be firmly rejected (see 5.4 above).

---

201 Takashi Onuki, "Solomon no shoka (Odes of Solomon)," in Sasagu Arai, ed., *Seishyo Gaiten Giten [Biblical Apocrypha and Pseudepigrapha]*, Hoi [supplementary vol.] 2 (Tokyo: Kyobunkwan, 1982) 277–390 (introduction and trans.), 497–557 (notes).

202 See also Lattke, *Bedeutung*, 3:366, on Takashi Onuki, *Gemeinde und Welt im Johannesevangelium: Ein Beitrag zur Frage nach der theologischen und pragmatischen Funktion des johanneischen "Dualismus"* (WMANT 56; Neukirchen-Vluyn: Neukirchener Verlag, 1984).

203 See Lattke, *Bedeutung*, 3:364.

204 Montague Rhodes James, *The Apocryphal New Testament* (Oxford: Clarendon, 1924; repr. and corr. 1953; many reprints). The *Odes of Solomon* are not included even as an appendix.

205 John Adney Emerton, "The Odes of Solomon," in Hadley Frederick Davis Sparks, ed., *The Apocryphal Old Testament* (Oxford: Clarendon, 1984) 683–731; see editor's preface, pp. xiv–xvii.

206 See Lattke, *Bedeutung*, 4:246.

207 Majella Franzmann, "An Analysis of the Poetical Structure and Form of the *Odes of Solomon*" (Ph.D. diss., University of Queensland, 1990).

208 On the terms "stanza," "poem," and other technical poetic terms, see Wilfred G. E. Watson, *Classical Hebrew Poetry: A Guide to Its Techniques* (JSOTSup 26; Sheffield: JSOT Press, 1984) 11–14; cf. Lattke, "Messias-Stellen," 432–33 = idem, *Bedeutung*, 4:92–94.

209 See Michael Lattke, review of Pierre in *ThLZ* 121 (1996) 256–57, reprinted in Lattke, *Bedeutung*, 4:183–84.

210 See Lattke, *Bedeutung*, 4:250.

211 Marie-Joseph Pierre, *Les Odes de Salomon: Texte présenté et traduit avec la collaboration de Jean-Marie Martin* (Apocryphes 4; Turnhout: Brepols, 1994) 57–198. Three years later, her translation, with revised notes, was reprinted. See Marie-Joseph Pierre, "Odes de Salomon," in François Bovon and Pierre Geoltrain, eds., *Écrits apocryphes chrétiens* (2 vols.; Bibliothèque de la Pléiade; Paris: Gallimard, 1997–2005) 1:671–743. Here too the *Odes of Solomon* are found in their proper place among the Christian Apocrypha.

212 Éphrem Azar, *Les Odes de Salomon* (Paris: Cerf, 1996) 85–169.

213 Ibid., 171–250.

214 Pierre, 48.

10.3.10. Lattke (1999–2005)

This complete historical-critical and theological commentary on the *Odes of Solomon* appeared in the space of seven years.[215] The manuscript for those three volumes forms the basis for the present English commentary, slowly translated by Marianne Ehrhardt. For the third volume, the Heidelberg Semitic scholar Klaus Beyer contributed the revised transcription of the Syriac Odes in the first two volumes (*Odes* 3–14; *Odes* 15–28) that finally disposed of the mixture of transcription and transliteration that had been used in those two volumes as well as in various preliminary studies for this wide-ranging piece of research.[216] Like any translation of an ancient text, Lattke's final German rendering can only serve as a bridge for understanding the text itself. Because the *Odes of Solomon* are not as accessible as biblical texts, it was necessary to include a critical edition of the manuscript remains of the *Odes of Solomon* with the commentary. The concordance[217] gives access to the German translation but also to the Coptic, Greek, Latin, and Syriac texts.

215 Michael Lattke, *Oden Salomos: Text, Übersetzung, Kommentar* (3 vols.; NTOA 41.1-3; Fribourg: Academic Press; Göttingen: Vandenhoeck & Ruprecht, 1999-2005); cf. idem, "Druckfehler, Ergänzungen und Verbesserungen im Kommentar zu den *Oden Salomos*," http://espace.library.uq.edu.au/view.php?pid=UQ:13861.

216 Lattke, *Bedeutung*, vols. 1–4, esp. vol. 4. This fourth volume was originally intended for the commentary, but was ultimately used for the collected publication of some important preliminary studies. Also Max Küchler's NTOA series proved better suited for the publication of the commentary than Othmar Keel's OBO.

217 Lattke, 3:343–75; cf. *Bedeutung*, vol. 2, above.

Commentary

1

Ode 1: The Wreath of Truth

(I) 1a The Lord is on my head like a wreath
1b and I will not flee from him.
(II) 2a They have plaited for me the wreath of truth,
2b and it has caused thy branches to sprout in me.
3a For it is not like a wreath
3b that is dry, that does not sprout,
4a but thou art alive on my head,
4b and thou hast sprouted upon me.
(III) 5a Thy fruits are full and ripe;
5b they are full of thy salvation.

Introduction

Ode 1,[1] a "metaphorical address of the redeemed,"[2] survives only in Coptic translation. The *Pistis Sophia*, a Gnostic work translated from Greek, quotes a text "prophesied and spoken by Solomon in his 19th *Ode*,"[3] which is not the whole or part of *Ode* 19 as it appears in the two Syriac manuscripts H and N. The quotation, which may be only a fragment, must have originated in a collection containing the eighteen *Psalms of Solomon*, and at least twenty-five, perhaps all forty-two, of the *Odes* numbered consecutively in that order. Thus, the reference "in his 19th *Ode*," a fortunate instance of precision that is unfortunately never repeated, must refer to *Ode* 1. This is made more certain by the fact that in the Syriac manuscripts *Ps. Sol.* 1 is given as "*zmīrtā* 43" (H) and "Nr 43" (N).

Interpretation

■ **1** Since no parallel translation of this Ode is available to compare with its Coptic version of the Greek, it is difficult to decide which Greek word the Coptic ϫⲟⲉⲓⲥ (*čoïs*) represents.[4] Of the words that need to be considered, *κύριος* always goes with ܡܪܝܐ (*māryā*) (11:6b, 11a, 13, 15-18), *ὕψιστος* with ܡܪܝܡܐ (*mrayymā*) (11:2a, 9), while *θεός* is once ܡܪܝܐ (11:1d) and once ܐܠܗܐ (*ʾallāhā*) (11:9). In the Coptic quotations ⲛⲟⲩⲧⲉ (*nute*) parallels ܡܪܝܐ once (5:11a) while the other occurrence of ⲛⲟⲩⲧⲉ is in a verse that differs greatly from the Syriac (5:1b). Coptic ⲡⲉⲧϫⲟⲥⲉ (*petčose*), derived from ϫⲓⲥⲉ (*čise*), corresponds to ܡܪܝܡܐ (6:12).

What about ϫⲟⲉⲓⲥ then? There is no Syriac parallel for it here, but in *Ode* 5:10-11, which is the context for the quotation of "*Ode* 19" (= *Ode* 1; see above), the word refers unmistakably to the "Lord" (ϫⲟⲉⲓⲥ; Syriac ܡܪܝܐ) as "God" (ⲛⲟⲩⲧⲉ; Syriac also ܡܪܝܐ) and "Savior" (ℭ uses the Greek loanword *σωτήρ*; 𝔖 ܦܘܪܩܢܐ [*purqānā*], "salvation"). In the Coptic expansion of 6:13b the meaning of the genitive of ϫⲟⲉⲓⲥ qualifying "the water" is also given by the context; the Lord is the Most High of 6:12 (ⲡⲉⲧϫⲟⲥⲉ, Syriac ܡܪܝܡܐ).

In its five remaining occurrences, ϫⲟⲉⲓⲥ corresponds to ܡܪܝܐ (5:1a, 10a; 6:18a) and also to ܡܪܝܡܐ (5:2a) and to ܐܠܗܐ (25:1b). If the word "Most High" can be excluded, it is still doubtful whether "God" (*θεός*, ܐܠܗܐ) or "Lord" (*κύριος*, ܡܪܝܐ) was in the copy text or original. The latter is the more likely.

This still does not solve the problem whether "the Lord" of *Ode* 1 is "the Most High God" or the "Kyrios Christos." The use of the parallel metaphor "like a

1 Ms.: A, 54^{v}a (ℭ). Ed./trans.: Charlesworth, 17–18; Franzmann, 15–17; Lattke, 1:1-8.

2 See Lattke, *Oden*, 39.

3 See Lattke, *Bedeutung*, 1:193 and 216–17. The Coptic text and an English translation of Ode (not *Ps. Sol.*!) 19 [= 1] can also be found in Carl Schmidt, ed., and Violet MacDermot, trans., *Pistis Sophia* (NHS 9; Leiden: Brill, 1978) 117; in the index of "references" (802–6), "Psalms of Solomon" should be corrected to also read "Odes of Solomon" (804).

4 For a complete overview of the uses of "Lord" in the *Odes*, see Table 9, "'Lord' Used of God and the Christ/Messiah in the *Odes of Solomon*," which can be found in the commentary on 39:13.

wreath,"[5] which in 5:12a refers to "the Lord" (5:1, 10-11, 15) as the "Most High" (5:2a), does not require the conclusion that "the Lord" is identical in the two Odes. According to 17:1a the "Lord Messiah" (17:16) was crowned by his "God," who is also his "Lord" (17:2a), and his wreath is as alive as his redemption is imperishable.

There are, then, two possible interpretations. The more likely makes the "Lord" of stanza I the Kyrios (Son, Messiah), subordinate to the Most High. In this case the speaking "I" may be an individual or a group. If, however, in the less likely interpretation, the "Lord" represents κύριος, the normal "title of God,"[6] the "I" could also be the redeemed Redeemer of *Ode* 17. In that case, the poem at the head of the collection would introduce the Revealer, rather than the poet, as the "I" crowned by God.

The phrase "on my head," which forms part of the introductory adverbial clause (cf. 5:12a), means no more than "on me," as the parallelism of 4a and 4b indicates. "Head" as *pars pro toto* describes the person as a being that walks upright (cf. 5:7; 20:8; 24:1a; 28:4; 35:1; 42:20), a description that incidentally argues against the interpretation of the speaking "I" as a group.

In the course of this explication, it will be necessary to determine what meaning to give to the comparison used here.[7] Is the introductory comparison of the Lord with the Wreath of Truth (2a) (and Truth itself can also be called a wreath [9:8-11; see also 20:7]) an individual metaphor, or is it an allegory leading to further comparisons? Perhaps they are not mutually exclusive. In any case, the image is of a real wreath, not a symbolic one like the heavenly reward in *2 Clem.* 7:3 (cf. already Paul in 1 Cor 9:25).

According to Isa 28:5 (LXX), the Lord will be ὁ στέφανος τῆς ἐλπίδος ὁ πλακεὶς τῆς δόξης τῷ καταλειφθέντι μου λαῷ ("the crown of hope, the woven crown of glory, to the remnant of the people").[8]

The followers of Mithras acknowledge *their* Lord as their *corona* ("wreath").[9] This must have been common knowledge, like other uses of the wreath in religious, political, and private life in antiquity.[10] "The crowning of a successful poet with laurel"[11] was also part of life in antiquity. So, in a paradoxical way, anyone who saw a connection of the wreath with admired poets would glimpse something of the claims of the poetic "I" in the introductory image and comparison of the declaration of salvation.

A reference to the bridal crown[12] or the crown of martyrdom in Judaism or Christianity is not to be found, although this wreath is also supernatural.[13] Quite unlikely is any connection with "Eastern baptismal rites," and even less likely with the "crowning of Solomon, spoken of in Cant. iii 11."[14]

The "introductory confessional statement"[15] negating a future possibility in 1b (Future I: "I will not escape

5 Charlesworth follows Harris and Mingana in translating ⲕⲗⲟⲙ by "crown."

6 Walter E. Crum, *A Coptic Dictionary* (Oxford: Clarendon, 1939; repr. 1962, 1972) 787, *s.v.* ϫⲟⲉⲓⲥ.

7 The stylistic device of comparison ("as," or "as . . . as") expressed here by ⲛⲑⲉ + genitive, also occurs elsewhere in the imagery of the *Odes* (5:12; 6:1-2; 11:12-13; 12:2; 14:1; 18:11; 19:10; 26:12-13; 28:1-2; 29:10; 31:11; 38:1; 40:1-2; 42:7-9).

8 Rahlfs, 2:600; Brenton, 861. The variant readings πλεκεις (BS*) and του λαου (B*S, plus μου/αὐτοῦ [Q/L]) do not change the basic description "crown/wreath of hope."

9 Cf. Tertullian *Cor.* 15.4; Karl Baus, *Der Kranz in Antike und Christentum: Eine religionsgeschichtliche Untersuchung mit besonderer Berücksichtigung Tertullians: Mit 23 Abbildungen auf 16 Tafeln* (Theophaneia 2; Bonn: Hanstein, 1940; repr. 1965) 166–67.

10 Cf. Walter Grundmann, "στέφανος, στεφανόω," *ThWNT* 7 (1964) 617–22; cf. *TDNT* 7:617–24.

11 See John Boardman, Jasper Griffin, and Oswyn Murray, eds., *The Oxford History of Greece and the Hellenistic World* (Oxford/New York: Oxford University Press, 1991) 3.

12 See Crum, 104–5, *s.v.* ⲕⲗⲟⲙ.

13 Cf. *Hermas, Sim.* 68 (VIII.2).1; Ehrman, 2:360–61; Norbert Brox, *Der Hirt des Hermas* (KAV 7; Göttingen: Vandenhoeck & Ruprecht, 1991) 357.

14 Bernard, 45–46.

15 Franzmann, 16. This description of the form of utterance is as farfetched as Carsten Colpe's description of *Ode* 1 as a "doxology" ("Heidnische, jüdische und christliche Überlieferung in den Schriften aus Nag Hammadi X," *JAC* 25 [1982] 65–101, esp. 77–78).

from/flee from him/it")[16] becomes clearer by comparison with 5:10-15 and 20:7-9 where the image of the wreath is associated with a stress on unity. Instead of the compound ⲣ-ⲡⲉϥ-ⲃⲟⲗ,[17] the positive ⲡⲱⲧ is elsewhere used for "to flee" (25:1b; Syriac ܥܪܩ [ʿrq]). The pronoun can equally well be interpreted as ["from] him," that is, the Lord, or ["from] it," that is, the wreath. As will be shown, the image and the transcendence compared to it have a tendency to merge.

■ **2-4** The Coptic expression in 2a ("they have plaited")[18] parallels the colloquial English impersonal usage, so that asking "who" is unnecessary. "The 3rd person pl. often represents an unspecified subject. . . . Such expressions are often used to substitute for the passive voice which is not found in Coptic."[19] If the Greek original had a passive form of πλέκειν or ὑφαίνειν,[20] it could be compared with a statement in the theological passive in 17:1: "I was crowned by my God."

The wreath, which is compared with the Lord, is now more narrowly defined as the Wreath of Truth. The Greek loanword ἀλήθεια, derived from the Greek original, corresponds to the Syriac ܫܪܪܐ (*šrārā*), one of the commonest and most important ideas in the whole collection. The genitive of this abstract noun endues the image of the wreath with an existence in the beyond. This truth is not a concept in philosophical logic, epistemology, or ontology (ἀλήθεια—the *ens* unveiled), but a theological concept in a mythological ideology that is already important in the New Testament and early Christian writings.[21]

Excursus 1: "Truth" in the *Odes of Solomon*

The Syriac root ܫܪ (*šr[r]*) gives rise to a number of related words found in the *Odes of Solomon*. The noun ܫܪܪܐ (*šrārā*), whose basic meaning is "truth" in the sense of "steadfastness," occurs thirty-four times—it would be thirty-five times if the Syriac of 1:2a had been found.[22]

The adjective ܫܪܝܪܐ (*šrīrā*) and the Ethpa. each occur four times. In 11:5a the Greek ἐστηρίχθην (aorist pass. of στηρίζω) corresponds exactly to the idiomatic use of the Syriac Ethpa. perfect ܐܫܬܪܪܬ (*ʾeštarreṯ*). In the same verse ܫܘܥܐ ܕܫܪܪܐ (*šūʿā ḏa-šrārā*) corresponds just as idiomatically to the Greek στερεὰ πέτρα (and note the slight variation ܫܪܝܪܬܐ ܟܐܦܐ [*kēp̄ā šarrīrtā*] of this Syriac *hapax legomenon*, which occurs in 31:11b translated as "true," that is, genuine, rock). "To be made fast" soteriologically is the meaning of the Ethpa. in its other occurrences also (36:8b; 38:16a; 40:5b).

In 9:11a it is difficult to interpret the adjective in relation to ܩܝܡܐ (*qyāmā*) (cf. perhaps Heb 3:14). Understanding it as a property of the kingship of the Most High (18:3c), and of that Word which *is* the mouth of the Lord (that is, his speaking) and also the ground of his recognition (12:13a-c), is much easier (see Excursuses 7 and 12).

---

16 MacDermot follows the translation of 1b by Harris and Mingana ("And I shall not be without Him"). Charlesworth even changes "not" to "never."

17 See Wolfhart Westendorf, *Koptisches Handwörterbuch* (Heidelberg: Winter, 1977) 23.

18 Edwin A. Abbott's suggestion, "But perhaps THEY . . . is preferable here, so as to suggest divine agency," is as speculative as so much else in his very full discussion of "The Crown" (*Light on the Gospel from an Ancient Poet* [Diatessarica 9; Cambridge: Cambridge University Press, 1912] 16 n. 1).

19 See Walter C. Till, *Koptische Grammatik (Saïdischer Dialekt) mit Bibliographie, Lesestücken und Wörterverzeichnissen* (Lehrbücher für das Studium der orientalischen und afrikanischen Sprachen 1; 4th ed.; Leipzig: VEB Verlag Enzyklopädie, 1970) §326.

20 See Crum, 572, *s.v.* ϣⲱⲛⲧ.

21 See, e.g., Rudolf Bultmann, "Untersuchungen zum Johannesevangelium (Teil A. Ἀλήθεια)," *ZNW* 27 (1928) 113–63, reprinted in idem, *Exegetica: Aufsätze zur Erforschung des Neuen Testaments* (ed. Erich Dinkler; Tübingen: Mohr Siebeck, 1967) 124–73; Rudolf Schnackenburg, *The Gospel according to St. John* (3 vols.; London/New York: Burns & Oates/Herder and Herder, 1968) 1:543–58, ET of *Das Johannesevangelium* (4 vols.; HThKNT 4.1–4; Freiburg: Herder, 1965–84) 1:265–81, esp. 274–75; BDAG, *s.v.* ἀλήθεια. Pierre (p. 59), in saying "Investi d'une royauté qui n'est pas de ce monde, témoin de la «vérité» (v. 2), le chantre s'identifie ainsi au vrai Salomon, le Fils de David et le Roi-Messie, l'oint du Dieu-vérité, ce qui doit être le sens de la pseudonymie salomonienne des *Odes*," is somewhat wide of the mark.

22 Cf. R. Payne Smith, ed., *Thesaurus Syriacus* (2 vols.; Oxford: Clarendon, 1879–1901; repr. Hildesheim/New York: Olms, 1981) 2:4297–305, esp. 4303–4; Jessie Payne Margoliouth, *Supplement to the Thesaurus Syriacus of R. Payne Smith* (Oxford: Clarendon, 1927; repr. Hildesheim/New York: Olms, 1981) 336; Karl [= Carl] Brockelmann, *Lexicon Syriacum* (2nd ed.; Halle: Niemeyer, 1928; repr. Hildesheim:

"Word" (always *peṯgāmā* in this context), "recognize," and "recognition" are important in the context of "Truth" throughout. Hearing the "Word of Truth" corresponds in synthetic parallelism to the accepting reception of the knowledge of the Most High (8:8; cf. 15:4b and especially the phrase "to recognize in truth" in 8:12 and 12:13b). The plural "Words of Truth" was used in 12:1a (H) because it seemed to fit the imagery of 12:1b–2 better (but see the commentary on those verses).

A key passage is 32:2, where the Word is said to be of that Truth which is of itself (H has "from/out of itself").[23] *Ode* 32:2 provides the theological reason and a semantic visualization. This unshakable reliability comes out even more forcefully in personification as the present and future Truth (38:4c). If "Truth" in 12:12b modifies "Word" (and not the child of man, that is, man himself), then the Truth of the Word is equated to Love (see Excursus 2).

Truth is not a transcendent concept, but in this dualistic and mythological topography it is an attribute of the height (17:7d). Therefore, there can be a Father of Truth (41:9a), a Son of Truth from the Father the Most High (23:18b), and also the leading Light of Truth (38:1). Since the rest and glory of paradise is also established in the height (20:7-8), the welcome is followed by a promise of well-being in the Truth (20:9c). However, ܒܫܪܪܐ (*ba-šrārā*) may mean simply "really, truly" in this passage, as it does elsewhere (cf. 8:12; 12:13b; 39:10b; 41:15a).[24]

Truth, seen dualistically, is the opposite of falsehood (18:6b), as Light is opposed to Darkness in the parallelism of 18:6a. This also means that there are those in whom Truth is not and who are therefore destroyed and rejected (24:10b, 12b). Contempt is submerged by the Truth of the Lord (31:2c).

On the other hand, Truth is the place or means of salvation (25:10a; cf. the parallel of "righteousness" in 25:10b). Those who accept the Truth of his faith are made to live, that is, are redeemed in the beyond, by the truth of the messianic name (41:16a). Truth has a path of salvation (11:3b). On her ways it is necessary to be wise (33:8c). The thought of Truth is a certain guide (17:5a). Indeed Truth, personified and speaking, is herself a guide (38:1b, 10-14a, 15d) since she is on the right way (38:7c).

Whoever is in the mind of the Most High (18:14a) can speak the Truth inspired by the Most High (18:15). Whether in reference to the whole collection or to individual Odes, the prayer of 14:7a, "Teach me the odes of thy Truth," is important for the understanding of the "I" that speaks in these poems or songs.[25]

The concept of the Wreath of Truth may again be referred to in 9:8a, where Truth is equated with an eternal wreath, but for 2b it is necessary to refer to 20:7–8. The growing of the twigs is made clearer by the image of the wreath from the Tree of Paradise. As 3 will explicate by antithesis, this wreath is a healthy, living wreath, whose truth may be said to consist in its growing and flourishing. It is a wreath filled with sap and vigor.

With ⲛⲉⲕⲕⲗⲁⲇⲟⲥ (from Greek κλάδοι, "branches") as the "subject of the causative infinitive,"[26] the "I" of the Ode turns, for the first time, to the Lord as "Thou." Because of this personal address, the third person pronoun ("he" in ℭ) must refer to the wreath that is being described. Since the introductory comparison of 1a likens the Lord to a wreath, this imagery carries over into the prayer addressed to him in 4 and 5. The

Olms, 1966) 802–3; Ludwig Koehler and Walter Baumgartner, *Hebräisches und aramäisches Lexikon zum Alten Testament* (ed. Walter Baumgartner, Johann Jakob Stamm, and Benedikt Hartmann; 5 vols.; Leiden: Brill, 1967–95) 1528–29.

23 See Theodor Nöldeke, *Compendious Syriac Grammar* (trans. Peter D. Daniels; Winona Lake, Ind.: Eisenbrauns, 2001) §223.

24 On ἐν ἀληθείᾳ, see BDAG, *s.v.* ἀλήθεια, 3.

25 See Lattke, *Bedeutung*, 2:96–97, *s.v.* ܫܪܪ. See also the "Überblick" of Bultmann, "Untersuchungen," 159–61 (= idem, *Exegetica*, 170–72), who sees in the *Odes of Solomon* texts "die, wenn auch ursprünglich griechisch verfaßt, den orientalischen Wahrheitsbegriff deutlich zeigen, in dem sowohl der semitische Sinn von Festigkeit, wie der iranisch-gnostische Sinn von Leben, Licht und göttliches Wesen verbunden sind, und zwar mit der speziellen Wendung, daß diese 'Wahrheit' in der Offenbarung vorliegt. Es fällt dadurch also ein Licht nach rückwärts und zeigt, daß die an den Platonismus anknüpfende Entwicklung des griechischen Sprachgebrauchs im Corpus Hermeticum und der übrigen Gnosis auf orientalischen Einflüssen beruht" (159–60 and 170, respectively).

26 See Till §335. Translations of Coptic ϯ ⲟⲩⲱ (Crum, 475) in 2-4 include "sprout" (MacDermot; Franzmann); "bud" (Harris and Mingana [in 2b and 3b]; Emerton); "blossom" (Harris and Mingana [in 4b]; Charlesworth).

expression "thy branches" and the parallel "thy fruits" in 5a invite allegorical interpretations and bring to mind the address of the Ἐγώ in John 15:1-11 (which, however, has κλῆμα ["tendril"] not κλάδος, although καρπός ["fruit"] corresponds to καρποί as a loanword in ℭ). Ignatius *Trall.* 11.2 proves that κλάδοι (τοῦ σταυροῦ, "of the cross") and καρπός were used in a transferred sense about the members of the head (i.e., Χριστός, ἐν τῷ πάθει αὐτοῦ, "Christ, by his suffering") and their imperishable deeds.[27] The question is whether the basic image has also been expanded in *Ode* 1 (see below on 5a–b).

Is v. 3 a "monocolon" that concludes the first strophe (2-3) of stanza II? And is the position of 3 really "central . . . in the ode, not only by its placement, but primarily by the contrast between its negative descriptions (dry, not sprouting) and those of 2b (branches sprouting) and 4a–b (alive and sprouting)"[28]? No, it seems to me, first, that this negative comparison, expressed by the present II of ⲉⲓⲛⲉ (*ine*) is a bicolon with 3b consisting of a circumstantial clause and a relative clause containing a negative *praesens consuetudinis*.[29] Second, the connection with 4 is made by the use of the adversative conjunction ἀλλά, a Greek loanword that, in its home language, is also often used "as the contrary to a preceding οὐ."[30]

The eschatological picture in 1 Pet 5:4 (κομιεῖσθε τὸν ἀμαράντινον τῆς δόξης στέφανον, "you will obtain/win the unfading crown of glory"), which probably dates to the last decades of the first century C.E., is likely to have influenced the comparison in 3. A postscript can be found early in the third century in Minucius Felix *Oct.* 38.4, where he argues against wreaths for the dead, saying in hope of the resurrection: *nec adnectimus arescentem coronam, sed a deo aeternis floribus vividam sustinemus* ("we do not bind to us a withering garland, but we wear one living with eternal flowers from God" [ANF 4:197]).[31]

In 4 the Lord is directly addressed in prayer as "thou." Both the verbs (one in the present I and one in the perfect I) refer to the vitality and growth of the wreath. The parallelism of the adverbial phrases "on my head" (preposition + possessive article + ⲁⲡⲉ) and "on me" (preposition + pronominal suffix) was noted already in connection with 1a. In the address of this prayer it becomes clear how close the comparison instituted in 1a was meant to be: in a certain sense the Lord *is* the Wreath of Truth (2a).

■ **5** The concluding prayer, which may be called a "confessional statement,"[32] again addresses the Lord as the Wreath. In 5a the Greek loanword καρποί, prefixed by the possessive article, is described as "full" and "ripe"[33] by two verbs, both in the present I. If these "fruits" do not refer to redeemed persons,[34] these further descriptions remain within the frame of the image. Almost all the statements in stanzas II and III, after all, are designed to make the picture of the wreath as vivid as possible.[35]

The circumstantial clause of 5b, however, passes beyond the metaphorical realm, its last word ⲟⲩϫⲁï (*učaï*), especially with the possessive article ⲡⲉⲕ (*pek*) with its reference to the Lord, giving the whole stanza an unmistakable soteriological cast. Thus, the Lord

27 See Ehrman, 1:266–67.

28 Franzmann, 17.

29 This invalidates the conclusion that "[t]here is internal parallelism by the doubling of the *Umstandssatz* form" (Franzmann, 17; cf. Till §§328–34 on the "*Umstandssatz*," §462 on the "*Relativpronomen*").

30 See BDF and BDR §448.

31 See Bernhard Kytzler, *M. Minucius Felix, Octavius* (Ger.–Lat.; Munich: Kösel, 1965) 204–7.

32 Franzmann, 17.

33 So MacDermot's and Franzmann's translations; other translations include "perfect" (Harris and Mingana; Emerton) and "complete" (Charlesworth).

34 See Michael Lattke, *Einheit im Wort: Die spezifische Bedeutung von* ἀγάπη, ἀγαπᾶν *und* φιλεῖν *im Johannesevangelium* (SANT 41; Munich: Kösel, 1975) 187–88, on John 15:6.

35 According to Harris and Mingana (2:215), a monocolon may have been lost between 4b and 5a. The postulated text is that of 4:4 ("Never wilt thou be barren nor unfruitful"). It is, however, difficult to imagine the process suggested in the text-critical emendation: "We suggest, then, that the verse has dropped out of the first Ode, and having been written on the margin has been wrongly restored to the fourth Ode."

himself becomes a στέφανος ἄφθαρτος, "imperishable wreath" (1 Cor 9:25), στέφανος τῆς ζωῆς, "crown of life" (Jas 1:12; Rev 2:10), or στέφανος τῆς ἀφθαρσίας, "crown of immortality" (*Mart. Pol.* 17.1 [ca. 156 C.E.])[36] whose "fruits"—and perhaps its "twigs" (2b)—are the ones filled with the σωτηρία of the beyond.[37]

Since the redeemed "I" is not included in the closing prayer, it may be that stanza III was spoken by a group, responding in the third person to the address of the "I." The "twigs" and "fruit" may stand for members of an esoteric group or for a mythological worthy, but the question remains as to the "I" of this Ode. If the soteriological interpretation adumbrated above is correct, it must be an outstanding personage, very close to the Lord.

That there is no "Halleluja" at the end of this Ode leads to no conclusion about its original length. The "Halleluja" found in the Syriac of *Odes* 6, 22, and 25 is also omitted in the Coptic *Pistis Sophia* and *Ode* 5 is not quoted in full.

36 Ehrman, 1:390–91.

37 See Crum, 512, *s.v.* ⲟⲩϫⲁⲓ.

3

Ode 3: Metaphors of Love and *Gnōsis*

(I) 1 . . . I am putting on.
2a And his members are with him
2b and on them I hang.
(II) 2c And he loves me.
3a For I should not have known to love the Lord,
3b if he did not love me.
4a Who is able to understand love,
4b except one who is loved?
5a I love the Beloved,
5b and my soul loves him.
5c And where his rest is,
5d I am also.
(III) 6a Nor shall I be a stranger,
6b because there is no jealousy with the Most High and Merciful Lord.
7a I have been united,
7b because the lover has found him, the Beloved,
7c because I must love him, the Son,
7d so that I become a son.
(IV) 8a For he who is joined to him who does not die
8b will also be immortal.
9a And one who chooses life
9b will be living.
(V) 10a This is the Spirit of the Lord, without falsehood,
10b who teaches humankind to know his ways.
(VI) 11 Be wise, and understand, and be vigilant.
Hallelujah.

Introduction

Ode 3 is incompletely preserved in one Syriac manuscript.[1] Since the whole of *Ode* 2 is still missing, nothing can be said about its length and content. But the beginning of *Ode* 3 has also not been preserved. That means, first, that the counting of the fragmentary first line as a colon (most likely bicolon) is entirely arbitrary; and, secondly, that the equally arbitrarily numbered stanza I can be interpreted only in light of the remainder of the Ode.

In the present state of textual criticism, it is possible to state, "The centrality of the motif of love is clear from the frequency with which the root ܪܚܡ (x 10) and its synonym ܚܒ (x 2; synonymity is indicated in the parallelism of 5a–b) occur."[2]

The use of *gnōsis* in the heading for this Ode is justified by the stress on knowledge in 3a, 10b, and 11, which is closely connected with the "Unity of Redemption"[3] expressed in the imagery of love.

Interpretation

■ **1-2b** It is impossible to decide what the masculine active participle of the Aph. of ܠܒܫ (*lḇeš* [found only in this line]), combined with the enclitic form of the first person pronoun, referred to. Similarly unclear is the possibility of a causative shade of meaning. Even the aspect and tense[4] are uncertain. By comparison with the occurrences of the Pe. (4:6, 8; 7:4; 13:3; 15:8; 20:7; 21:3; 23:1, 3; 33:12; 39:8) and the noun ܠܒܘܫܐ (*lḇūšā* [8:9];

1 Ms.: H, 1a–b (s). Ed./trans.: Charlesworth, 18–20; Franzmann, 18–23; Lattke, 1:9–25 and 3:XV.

2 Franzmann, 20.

3 Lattke, "Bildersprache," 103–4 = idem, *Bedeutung*, 4:30.

4 See Carl Brockelmann, *Syrische Grammatik mit*

Greek ἔνδυμα in 11:11; Coptic ϣⲧⲏⲛ [*šᵉtēn*] in 25:8), it can be said with fair certainty that the expression here is also used in a transferred sense.

The word ܗܕܡܐ (*haddāmē* ["members"; cf. μέλη in the Coptic of 6:16]), found only in the plural, is also used metaphorically in 2a, as in 17:15; 18:2; 21:4; perhaps 6:2, probably not in 6:16. Other occurrences, however, have the literal meaning of limbs of a body (8:16; 26:4; 40:3).

Assuming that the genitive suffix on "members" and the suffix on the preposition "with" refer to the same person, it is still uncertain whether this person is the "Lord" (3a, 6b, 10a) or the "Beloved" (5a, 7b) or the "Son" (7c).

The preposition ܒ (*b-*) in 2b expresses a sense of belonging that could be translated as well with "among" as with "in." The "I" that "hangs" or "depends" (Pe. masculine passive participle of the *hapax legomenon* ܬܠܐ [*tlā*]) is most probably the same as the "I" of stanzas II and III, clearly distinguished from the Lord and the Son (and from the 'stranger' of 6a). The image of 2a-b is illuminated by the statement of salvation of the "redeemed" in 21:4a: "and I had members with/by me."

Stanza II consists of three short strophes, a declaration of salvation followed by a reflection (2c-3), a rhetorical question of Wisdom (4), and another metaphorical declaration of salvation (5).

Excursus 2: "Love" and "To Love" in the *Odes of Solomon*

As a supplement to material[5] collected and published in 1975, the twenty-five occurrences of words derived from the roots ܚܒ (*ḥb[b]*) and ܪܚܡ (*rḥm*) will be considered philologically and arranged by import.

Most senses are more or less metaphorical in a soteriological and/or theological context.

First, the few exceptions: 3:4 puts into the form of a rhetorical question the common experience that only one who is loved (masculine active participle of the Ethpe. of *rḥm* in its only occurrence) can understand love (*reḥmṯā*). *Ode* 7:1b refers in a literal sense to the erotic joy in the beloved (*rḥīmā*). 20:5a-c, in a rare ethical context, lists the three anthropological aspects: kidneys (reins), bowels (plural *raḥmē*, elsewhere always translated as "love"), and soul, in parallelism. V. 38:11a mentions the beloved (*ḥabbīḇā*) and his bride; 40:1b employs the image of the woman who loves (feminine active participle of *rḥem*) her suckling child.

Whether 19:7a and 11a are meant to be taken literally or "Mariologically" will be discussed in the commentary on that Ode.

In these two last-named instances, it already appears that the roots *ḥb[b]* and *rḥm* and their derivatives are treated very much as synonyms. Unfortunately there are hardly any Greek equivalents to discuss: only the Latin translation *miseratio* (19:7a; Syriac *raḥmē*) and one occurrence of ἀγάπη (11:2c; Syriac *ḥubbā*) are to be found. It is possible to conclude, from 3:2c-3b, that there is hardly a shade of meaning between the Aph. *ʾaḥḥeḇ* and the Pe. *rḥem*; both translate as "to love." *Ode* 14:3a, 6b, and 9a shows that *ḥubbā* (ἀγάπη) is synonymous with *raḥmē* (3a, 9a), which may, however, also often have the meaning of "sympathy."[6] So the meanings can be listed as follows (with frequencies in brackets):

"Love"	ἀγάπη (1); *ḥubbā* (17); *raḥmē* (7 or 6); *reḥmṯā* (2)
"beloved"	*ḥabbīḇā* (3); *rḥīmā* (3)
"to love"	*ʾaḥḥeḇ* (5); *rḥem* (10); cf. *ʾeṯrḥem* (1, see above)[7]

Exceptions are two *hapax legomena*: *rāḥmūṯā* ("friendship" in 12:9a, probably φιλία in 𝔊) and *mraḥḥmānā*[8] ("compassionate" as one of the attributes of the Most High Lord in 3:6b).

The most important occurrences that have not so far been discussed can best be classified according to the grammatical subject or object of the statements.

Beginning with the utterances in which the "I" does *not* include itself, two didactic statements come into view: "his [viz., the Word's] truth is love" (12:12b); "love is of the elect" (23:3a). On the one

Paradigmen, Literatur, Chrestomathie und Glossar (Porta linguarum orientalium 5; 6th ed.; Leipzig: Harrassowitz, 1951) §211.

5 Lattke, *Einheit*, 54–62 ("Religionsgeschichtlicher Exkurs zu 'lieben' im Johannesevangelium").

6 But cf. Rudolf Bultmann, "ἔλεος, κτλ.," *ThWNT* 2 (1935) 477; *TDNT* 2:480–81 on the Hebrew term רחמים: "*Love* is a better rendering."

7 The two Greek verbs ἀγαπᾶν and φιλεῖν, which were already used interchangeably in the Gospel of John (see Lattke, *Einheit*, 11), were certainly found in the Greek version of the *Odes of Solomon*, but it is impossible to say whether the alternation in the Syriac mirrors the Greek.

8 Cf. Payne Smith, 2:3884.

hand, the Lord is to be praised "in his love" (7:19a), in which the hearers are to remain (8:22b) as "beloved in the Beloved" (8:22c). On the other hand, "your love" shall grow (8:1b), the listeners are called upon to "love his [*viz.*, the Lord's] holiness" (13:3b), and an indirect doxology declares or demands "a new hymn for the Lord from those who love him" (41:16b).

Among the utterances in which the speaking "I" expressly includes itself (the "we" of the group occurs just twice) the first to be noticed are those few where the "I" is unmistakably the Redeemer and Revealer. As the redeemed Redeemer, he is the one who loves in 17:12b ("and I gave my intercession by my own love"); 42:7b ("and I laid upon them the yoke of my love"); and 42:9b ("and so is my love with those who have faith in me"). In the opposite direction, he is the one who is loved by the redeemed in 8:13 ("love me in love, you who love") and 42:4 ("and I will be with those who love me"). The two cases of "we" (41:2b and 6b), however, refer to the love of the Lord, that is, God ("in his love").

In the other cases, "I" is the redeemed speaker whom the Lord, probably always God or the Most High, loves (cf. 11:2c; 18:1a) or who remains in the Lord's love (3:2c; 6:2b; 11:2c; 14:3a, 6b, 9a; 16:2b, 7; 18:1a; 29:3a; 40:4b). In the other direction, the "I" fixes its love on the Lord (5:1b; 16:3a). The reciprocity of this love achieves full expression in 3:3a-b: "for I should not have known to love the Lord, if he did not love me." Whether the Beloved, whom the speaking "I" loves (3:5a–b) or who found the loving "I" (3:7b) is the same as the Son whom "I love" (3:7c), or is the loving Lord, is discussed in the next section.

■ **2c-5** The short monocolon 2c could also be the second hemistich of 2b. But this declaration of salvation is better taken as an "introductory confessional statement" of stanza II, because it introduces the theme of love and also forms, with the last words of 3b, an *inclusio* for the first strophe.[9] Additionally, there is the coordinating use of ܓܝܪ (*gēr*) in 3a, "placed by analogy with Greek γάρ."[10]

The masculine active participle of the Aph. linked to the direct object ("me") "indicates in the first place a condition without reference to a precise time . . . , then a continuous or momentary present . . . , but also the future."[11] In 3 it becomes clear that the subject of 2c is the Lord.

The reflection on mutual love in 3 brings to mind a similar Johannine statement, ἡμεῖς ἀγαπῶμεν [τὸν θεόν ℵ et al.], ὅτι αὐτὸς πρῶτος ἠγάπησεν ἡμᾶς, "We love [God], because he first loved us" (1 John 4:19), though the speaker here transmutes "we" into "I."[12] The somewhat chiastic bicolon 3, with the complicated syntax of the conditional clause of unreality, by coupling ܗܘܝܬ (*-wēṯ*) and ܗܘܐ (*-wā*) respectively to the two active participles ܝܕܥ (*yāḏaʿ*) and ܪܚܡ (*rāḥem*), transfers the "state" of mutual love "unmistakably into the past" and thus achieves an "expression of the continuance" of this love.[13] The masculine active participle of ܝܕܥ (*ʾiḏaʿ*) loses some of its technical sense by being attached with ܠ (*l-*) to the infinitive *merḥam*, but nevertheless belongs to the Gnostic vocabulary of the Odes.

The rhetorical question in 4 is neither a simple repetition of 3, nor is it constructed in parallelism.[14] It is in fact the foundation in wisdom for 3. The infinitive of ܦܪܫ (*praš*) expresses a distinction leading to separation (cf. 22:8). The use of ܐܠܐ (*ʾellā* = *ʾen* + negation *lā*) makes the relative clause of 4b into a real condition. The two words from the root *rḥm* in 3 are joined by two more in this verse.

In the third strophe of stanza II (5) there are two more words from this root, reinforcing the wordplay. In the first place, however, the repetition of the masculine active participle *maḥḥeḇ* refers back, verbally, to the theme of 2c. The enclitic subject has become "I" (5a). The parallelism of "soul" (5b) and "I" (5a; 5d) shows that "soul" is not to be interpreted in an anthropological dualism.[15]

Who is the "beloved" of 5a-b? Is he the same as the Lord in 3? Is he also identical with the "beloved" of 7b? In stanza III there is also the Son who is to be loved (7c). The Son, however, is certainly neither the Lord Most

9 Franzmann, 20–21.

10 Brockelmann, *Grammatik* §165; cf. Lattke, "Wörter," 287 = idem, *Bedeutung*, 4:136.

11 Brockelmann, *Grammatik* §211; cf. Nöldeke §269–77.

12 On the erotic imagery and bridal mysticism, see Michael Lattke, "Zur Bildersprache der Oden Salomos," *Symbolon: Jahrbuch für Symbolforschung* N.F. 6 (1982) 95–110, here 103–4 = *Bedeutung*, 4:29–30.

13 See Nöldeke §277.

14 Contra Franzmann, 21.

15 If "soul" means the *essential* "I," this statement would have to be changed.

High (6b) nor the Lord, whose Spirit is referred to later on (10a).

Since ܡܪܝܐ (*māryā* ["Lord," probably equivalent to Greek κύριος]) is not used here expressly of the Lord Messiah (cf. 17:16; 24:1; 29:6a; 39:11), it must be assumed that the Lord of *Ode* 3 is the same throughout, in 3a, 6b, and 10a, namely, the Most High and Merciful Lord (6b).

Even taking into consideration 8:22, it is necessary to conclude that the Beloved is the Lord, distinguished from the messianic ἠγαπημένος (Eph 1:6)[16] or ἀγαπητός (*Asc. Isa.* 1:7)[17] of whose rest the "I" now speaks (5c–d).

Excursus 3: "Rest" and "To Rest" in the *Odes of Solomon*

The *Odes of Solomon* offer only a small selection of words derived from the root ܢܘܚ (*nwḥ*) and all its differentiated uses, especially in the translation of Greek concepts.[18] "Rest" and "to rest" are technical, more or less abstract terms of the Gnostic understanding of salvation.[19] In the *Odes of Solomon* this meaning takes on the coloration of their imagery. The New Testament use of ἀναπαύειν, ἀνάπαυσις, καταπαύειν, and κατάπαυσις, which is partly dependent on the LXX (see esp. the negative pledge of Ps 94:11b LXX: Εἰ εἰσελεύσονται εἰς τὴν κατάπαυσίν μου, "They shall not enter into my rest"), influenced the Gnostic understanding of salvation, which can indeed be traced back to some New Testament passages (Matt 11:28-29; Heb 3-4).[20]

As the usage in 26:3a and 12b shows, the nouns ܢܝܚܐ (*nyāḥā*) and ܢܝܚܘܬܐ (*nīḥūṯā*), each of which occurs four times, are used as synonyms. The noun ܢܝܚܬܐ (*nyāḥtā*) is a *hapax legomenon* in H and text-critically a variant of the synonym *nīḥūṯā* of N (35:1a).

The only verbs that occur are the Ethpe. (*ʾettnīḥ* [8 times]) and the Aph. (*ʾanīḥ* [5 times]). For the latter, there is in one place a Greek equivalent ἀνεζωοποίησεν (11:12a) that is, however, a variant, to be discussed later. In the other cases, there is no way, especially where the Ethpe. occurs, to discover whether the Greek version used only a verb or whether it had a combination of a noun like ἀνάπαυσις or κατάπαυσις with a verb meaning "to find" or "to enter into" (26:10a, 12a; 28:3a; 30:2b, 7; 35:6b).

An attempt to classify these uses must begin with the statement 16:12b, "and he rested from his works," which is quite unlike any of the others and yet indicates God's Sabbath rest as the anthropomorphic

16 Cf. Heinrich Schlier, *Der Brief an die Epheser* (Düsseldorf: Patmos, 1957; 5th ed., 1965; 7th ed., 1971) 56–57.

17 Cf. Albert-Marie Denis, ed., *Apocalypsis Henochi Graece, edidit M. Black* (PVTG 3; Leiden: Brill, 1970) 45–246, here 107.

18 See Payne Smith, 2:2310–18.

19 See, e.g., Ernst Käsemann, *The Wandering People of God: An Investigation of the Letter to the Hebrews* (trans. Roy A. Harrisville and Irving L. Sandberg; Minneapolis: Augsburg, 1984) 67–75, ET of *Das wandernde Gottesvolk: Eine Untersuchung zum Hebräerbrief* (FRLANT 55 = N.F. 37; Göttingen: Vandenhoeck & Ruprecht, 1939; 4th ed., 1961) 40–45; Philipp Vielhauer, *Aufsätze zum Neuen Testament*, vol. 1 (ThBü 31; Munich: Kaiser, 1965) 215–34; Malcolm Lee Peel, *The Epistle to Rheginos: A Valentinian Letter on the Resurrection* (New Testament Library; London: SCM, 1969) 53–55; Otfried Hofius, *Katapausis: Die Vorstellung vom endzeitlichen Ruheort im Hebräerbrief* (WUNT 11; Tübingen: Mohr Siebeck, 1970) 75–90; Mark Pierce, "Themes in the 'Odes of Solomon' and Other Early Christian Writings and Their Baptismal Significance," *Ephemerides liturgicae* 98 (1984) 50–51; Jan Helderman, *Die Anapausis im Evangelium Veritatis: Eine vergleichende Untersuchung des valentinianisch-gnostischen Heilsgutes der Ruhe im Evangelium Veritatis und in anderen Schriften der Nag Hammadi-Bibliothek* (NHS 18; Leiden: Brill, 1984) *passim*; Franzmann, "Man of Rest," 411–18; Harold W. Attridge, *The Epistle to the Hebrews* (Hermeneia; Philadelphia: Fortress Press, 1989) 126–28; Hans-Friedrich Weiß, *Der Brief an die Hebräer* (KEK 13; 15th ed.; Göttingen: Vandenhoeck & Ruprecht, 1991) 268–73; Judith Hoch Wray, *Rest as a Theological Metaphor in the Epistle to the Hebrews and the Gospel of Truth: Early Christian Homiletics of Rest* (SBLDS 166; Atlanta: Scholars Press, 1998). "Love" and "rest" are juxtaposed in *Act. Thom.* 35 (see Rudolf Bultmann, "Die Bedeutung der neuerschlossenen mandäischen Quellen für das Verständnis des Johannesevangeliums," *ZNW* 24 (1925) 100–146, esp. 132 = *Exegetica*, 89), which may have been influenced by the *Odes of Solomon*.

20 Rahlfs, 2:104; Brenton, 756; cf. Peter Fiedler, "ἀνάπαυσις, ἀναπαύω," *EWNT* 1 (1980) 207–8; *EDNT* 1:87; Otfried Hofius, "κατάπαυσις, καταπαύω," *EWNT* 2 (1981) 655–56; *EDNT* 2:265–66.

foundation of so many images of salvation: καὶ κατέπαυσεν . . . ἀπὸ πάντων τῶν ἔργων αὐτοῦ (Gen 2:2; cf. Exod 20:11; Heb 4:4).

Two other occurrences are atypical. In 6:14a the servants who have received the drink proffered by the Most High "refreshed dry lips" (lit. "pacified"; the Coptic text has κτο, lit. "turned"). In 7:15b the everlasting Father of *gnōsis* (7:7) or the Father of the Aeons (7:11) is "pleased by the Son,"[21] which anthropomorphically and mythologically expresses a calming effect.

So the question with whose rest the remaining statements are principally concerned can easily be answered. Generally it is the rest of God, the Lord, the Most High. Even where there is a secondary sense of the rest of another Lord (cf. 25:12b; 35:1a, 6b), the rest of the Redeemer is clearly the eternal rest of God (25:12b), which can be found only in paradise, a nonexistent theological "site" (20:8b). Paradise begins with *gnōsis* (26:12a), where it is possible and proper to take one's rest on the Most High (26:10a), where the "Odes of His Rest" are never ending (26:3b), and where the singers stand in his peace/rest (26:12b). This "site" probably includes the image of the spring of the Lord of *Ode* 30. One of the imperative invitations to salvation, followed by its justification in the indicative, says: "And rest upon the spring of the Lord, because it is beautiful and fresh and gives rest to the soul" (30:2b, 3). And the Ode concludes with the blessing: "Blessed are those who have drunk from it, and have been at rest by it" (30:7).

The remaining passages include the speaking "I" in their image. This occurs only once in the form of a direct address looking toward the future: ". . . and let thy rest, Lord, abide near me" (14:6a).

The dominant aspect of these statements of salvation is the perfective (11:12a; 28:3a [rest as a direct consequence of faith]; 35:1a, 6b [rest in the *plērōma*]; 36:1a [resting of the Spirit of the Lord]; 37:4 [rest by the grace of the Lord]; 38:4a [Truth gave me rest]). Since the "I" is already at rest, it can state in a timeless and existential fashion: "and where his rest is, I am also" (3:5c-d).

■ **6-7** Stanza III, made up of two strophes and framed by the antithetical *inclusio* of 6a and 7d, is centered on 7a-b, "which emphasises the motif of the unity of the Lord/Beloved and the 'I.'"[22]

The declaration of salvation to come in 6a, reminiscent of the promise in Eph 2:19 (οὐκέτι ἐστὲ ξένοι, "you are no longer strangers"), is didactically explained by the theologoumenon, found in several of the *Odes of Solomon*, that God does not envy. The confidence of the "I" that it will not be a stranger receives no illumination by comparison with the other occurrences of *nuḵrāyā* (6:3; 20:6) and *ʾaḵsnāyā* (17:6, the Greek loanword ξένος), but can best be explained by the positive certainty expressed in 7d, that it is also a son. A Gnostic-christological variation on this soteriological theme is to be found in *Gos. Phil.* 53.3-4: "He [*viz.*, Christ] ransomed those who were strangers and made them his own."[23]

The Greek ἀφθονία (in 11:6b) or ἄφθονος, ἀφθόνως[24] is equivalent to *layt ḥsāmā* (3:6b) or *d-lā ḥsāmā* (7:3; 11:6; 15:6; 17:12; 20:7; 23:4). The possible translation "plentiful," which comes under consideration in other contexts (see *4 Macc* 3:10), cannot here be preferred to "without envy." The six other uses of this word are not sufficient to illuminate the usage here with the causal conjunction ("For there is no envy . . ."). Even the LXX and the New Testament are no great help, although it is possible to refer to Wis 2:24a: φθόνῳ δὲ διαβόλου θάνατος εἰσῆλθεν εἰς τὸν κόσμον ("but through the devil's envy death entered the world").[25] This concept is in no sense a correction of the Old Testament idea of the "jealousy" of God[26] but is rather an early Christian-Gnostic reception of two Platonic

21 See Payne Smith, 2:2313.

22 Franzmann, 21.

23 *NHLE*, 142; cf. Majella Franzmann, "Strangers from Above: An Investigation of the Motif of Strangeness in the Odes of Solomon and Some Gnostic Texts," *Mus* 103 (1990) 32–36.

24 Willem Cornelis van Unnik, "De ἀφθονία van God in de oudchristelijke literatuur," *Mededelingen der Koninklijke Nederlandse Akademie van Wetenschappen, Afdeling Letterkunde* N.S. 36.2 (1973) 5–13.

25 Rahlfs, 2:348. "Envy as an actual category, determining Fate and the world, is known to Greek and Hellenistic thought in general. . . . In Gnosticism Envy became an anti-creative power" (Dieter Georgi, *Weisheit Salomos* [JSHRZ 3.4; Gütersloh: Mohn, 1980] 409).

26 Martin Rehm, "Eifer Gottes, Eifersucht Gottes," *LThK*[2] 3 (1959) 732; cf. E. Reuter, "קנא *qnʾ*," *ThWAT* 7 (1993) 51–62; *TDOT* 13:47–58.

aphorisms, "which had become commonplace among Platonists and the educated public in general."[27]

Later Gnostic and anti-Gnostic uses of ἀφθονία and ἄφθονος can certainly illuminate the *Odes of Solomon*,[28] but it will suffice here to quote the two passages from Plato:

1. φθόνος γὰρ ἔξω θείου χοροῦ ἵσταται ("for jealousy is excluded from the celestial band") (*Phaedr.* 247a [LCL 1:474/75]).
2. Λέγωμεν δὴ δι' ἥν τινα αἰτίαν γένεσιν καὶ τὸ πᾶν τόδε ὁ ξυνιστὰς ξυνέστησεν. ἀγαθὸς ἦν, ἀγαθῷ δὲ οὐδεὶς περὶ οὐδενὸς οὐδέποτε ἐγγίγνεται φθόνος ("Let us now state the Cause wherefore He that constructed it constructed Becoming and the All. He was good, and in him that is good no envy ariseth ever concerning anything") (*Tim.* 29d–e [LCL 7:54/55]).[29]

Verse 6b is not a direct quotation, probably not even an intentional allusion. These passages were commonplaces among the educated, and therefore the users could quote them without being conscious of the Platonic context or accepting the edifice of Platonic philosophy.[30] The *Odes of Solomon*, unlike the "Lehrgebäude des Platonismus" ("edifice of Platonism"), stress above all "redemption and salvation—σωτηρία."[31] The "I" will not be a stranger because its Lord is not an envious and self-seeking God but a merciful one.

While ܡܪܝܡܐ (*mrayymā*), which corresponds to ὕψιστος (cf. 11:2, 9) as a description of God, is one of the commonest words in the *Odes of Solomon*, the adjective "merciful" in 6b is a *hapax legomenon* (see above, Excursus 2). The "predication of God as ἐλεήμων" is not to be found in the New Testament,[32] but it is "not rare" in the LXX (e.g., Exod 22:26; 34:6; Ps 85:15; 102:8; *Ps. Sol.* 5:2; 2 Macc 1:24; 11:9).[33]

The perfective statement of salvation in 7a makes use of a word whose primary meaning is "to mix" (cf. 19:4), which is used in later Syriac writings "of the body of Christ mixed with our bodies."[34] Here the Ethpe. perfect refers to the union between the loving and beloved Lord and the loving "I" that has already taken place (7b); this can, however, hardly be described as a "physically" sacramental "marriage to the Beloved."[35] The word translated as "found" in this verse is the same as the one translated as "be able" in v. 4.

The final bicolon, introduced by a third repetition of the causal conjunction, now paradoxically transfers the reason from the past into the future (7c) and at the same time brings in the wholly new concept of the love that the "I" bears the Son. Since the Son is not identical here with the Beloved or with the Lord,[36] the partial

27 Heinrich Dörrie, "Was ist 'spätantiker Platonismus'? Überlegungen zur Grenzziehung zwischen Platonismus und Christentum," *ThR* N.F. 36 (1971) 294, quoted in Willem Cornelis van Unnik's article, p. 46.

28 See van Unnik, ἀφθονία, *passim*; on H. J. W. Drijvers, "Die Oden Salomos und die Polemik mit den Markioniten im syrischen Christentum," in *Symposium Syriacum, 1976: Célébré du 13 au 17 septembre 1976 au Centre Culturel Les Fontaines de Chantilly, France* (OrChrA 205; Rome: Pontificium Institutum Orientalium Studiorum, 1978) 39–55, cf. Lattke, *Bedeutung*, 3:330. Cf., e.g., *Tri. Trac.* 70, 25–28: ". . . and since there is no envy [φθόνος] on the part of the Father toward those who came forth from him . . ." (*NHLE*, 70); *Gos. Truth* 18, 38–40: "the Father was not jealous [φθονεῖ]. What jealousy [φθόνος] indeed (could there be) between himself and his members [μέλη]?" (*NHLE*, 41).

29 Cf. Gunther Eigler, ed., *Platon Werke in 8 Bänden* (OG/Germ.; Darmstadt: Wissenschaftliche Buchgesellschaft, 1971–1983) 7:36–39, where Klaus Widdra remarks: "The common idea of the jealousy of the gods is here—as in Phdr. 247a7—firmly contradicted."

30 Cf. Dörrie, "Platonismus," 294–95 and *passim*.

31 Ibid., 301.

32 Only the Son is described as ἐλεήμων . . . καὶ πιστὸς ἀρχιερεὺς τὰ πρὸς τὸν θεόν in Heb 2:17.

33 Bultmann, "Bedeutung," 482.

34 Payne Smith, 2:2059: *de corpore Christi nostris corporibus immixto*.

35 Greßmann, 438.

36 Contra Franzmann, 22.

parallelism between 7b and 7c is only in the words, not in their meaning.

So the subsidiary reason for the union between the "I" and the Lord is that the "I" is to love the Son (7c) of the Father, the Most High (see 7:15; 19:2; 23:18, 22; 36:3; 41:13), that is, the Son of God as Redeemer (42:15; cf. 42:18), with the purpose, as shown by the final particle ܕ (*d-*), of also becoming a son (7d), that is, one of the sons of the Lord (cf. 31:4; 41:2).[37]

This betokens more than the prophetic statement in the LXX, *κληθήσονται υἱοὶ θεοῦ ζῶντος* (Hos 2:1), which Paul quotes in Rom 9:26 ("they shall be called children of the living God") and to which the Sermon on the Mount alludes (Matt 5:9; see also Luke 6:35; 20:36). It also implies more than Paul's epistles, which more than once refer to becoming children of God (Rom 8:14–17; Gal 3:26; 4:4–7). This absolute use of "Son" and the "I"'s appropriation of this title lie on a line of development of a "Gnostic set of ideas and vocabulary" that, despite all its differences, has "unmistakable connections" with the "Johannine Christology of the Son."[38]

■ **8-9** The promise of salvation, which is the teaching of stanza IV, is, as in stanza V, no longer couched in the first person. The parallel bicola, 8 and 9, each of which is constructed with internal parallelism,[39] therefore, and in spite of the particle ܓܝܪ (*gēr*) in 8a, do more than merely justify the soteriological and metaphorical statements of the "I" of stanzas I–III. They promise salvation in general through the concept of "immortality" and "life."

All the same, there is a connection in 8a with the preceding metaphors of love through the use of the Ethpa. masculine active participle, a *hapax legomenon* from the root ܢܩܦ (*nqp*). The words from this root belong, on the one hand, to the accepted terminology of discipleship as following the Lord (cf. Greek ἀκολουθεῖν κτλ.) and the later christological teaching of the two natures but also, on the other hand, to the language of sexuality and love.[40] The metaphorical use of this word, which probably here corresponds to a form of κολλᾶσθαι, in this context is reminiscent of the saying in 1 Cor 6:17 with its "somatic reference":[41] ὁ δὲ κολλώμενος τῷ κυρίῳ ἓν πνεῦμά ἐστιν ("But anyone united to the Lord becomes one spirit with him").

As Table 1 demonstrates, words from the roots ܚܝܐ (*ḥyʾ*) and ܡܘܬ (*mwt*)/ܡܝܬ (*myt*) are very commonly found together (see esp. 3:8-9; 5:3, 14; 6:15, 18; 11:7, 16; 15:9-10; 22:8-10; 28:6-7; 31:7; 38:3; 42:5, 14-17).

Table 1: "Life" and "Death," "To Live" and "To Die," "Living/Immortal"

Key:	*	to live (cf. ⲚⲞⲨϨⲘ [*nuhᵉm*]; ܚܝܐ [*ḥyā*])	•	to die (ⲘⲞⲨ [*mu*], ܡܝܬ [*mīṯ*])
	**	alive (ἀθάνατος, ⲞⲚϨ [*onᵉh*], ܚܝܐ [*ḥayyā*])	••	immortal (ἀθάνατος, ܕܠܐ ܡܘܬܐ [*d-lā mawtā*])
	***	life (ζωή, ⲰⲚϨ [*ōnᵉh*], ܚܝ̈ܐ [*ḥayyē*])	•••	death (ܡܘܬܐ [*mawtā*])
	****	give life (ܐܚܝ [*ʾaḥḥī*])	••••	dead, the dead (ⲔⲰⲰⲤ [*kōōs*], ⲘⲞⲞⲨⲦ [*mowt*], ܡܝܬ [*mīṯ*], ܡܝ̈ܬܐ [*mīṯē*])
	*****	midwife (ܚܝܬܐ [*ḥayytā*])		

1:4a **	alive on my head		
		3:8a •	he who joins him who does not die . . .
		3:8b ••	. . . will also be immortal

continued . . .

37 Emerton (692 n. 3) suggests a translation of 7c-d similar to ours, while Harris and Mingana (2:216) differ considerably: "In order that I may love Him, that is the Son, I shall become a son."

38 Schnackenburg, *Gospel*, 2:172–86, esp. 181–82 (= *Johannesevangelium*, 2:150–68, esp. 162, 166).

39 Franzmann, 22.

40 Payne Smith, 2:2457–62, esp. 2458.

41 Wolfgang Schrage, *Der erste Brief an die Korinther* (4 vols.; EKKNT 7.1–4; Zurich: Benziger; Neukirchen/Vluyn: Neukirchener Verlag, 1991–2001) 2:26–29.

Table 1: "Life" and "Death," "To Live" and "To Die," "Living/Immortal" (*cont.*)

3:9a ***	one who chooses life . . .		
3:9b **	. . . will be living		
5:3b *	I shall live by it (from grace [3a]) (𝔖)		
		5:14b •	I shall not die
		6:15 •	that they might not die (ℭ)
		6:15 •••	from death they seized (𝔖)
6:18b *	they lived by . . .		
6:18b **	. . . the living water (𝔖)		
8:2a ***	the holy life (ethical)		
8:16c *	might live by holy milk		
8:22d *	are kept in him who lives (22e: || saved ones in him who was saved)		
9:4a ***	in the will of the Lord is your life		
9:4b ***	and his mind is eternal life		
10:2a ***	God's [immortal] life in me	10:2a ••	immortal [life]
10:6b ***	they walked in my life and were saved		
11:6b ***	living spring (𝔊) of the Lord		
11:7a **	I drank living . . .	11:7a •	. . . water that does not die (𝔖)
		11:7a••	I drank immortal water (𝔊)
		11:16f ••	from immortal earth (𝔊)
11:16h ***	the earth of their eternal life (𝔊)		
		15:9a •••	Death was destroyed (6c: salvation) (9b: || Sheol brought to nothing)
15:10a ***	[immortal] life (= sun/Lord)	15:10a ••	immortal [life] (cf. 10b: life was known)
17:1b **	my crown is living (cf. 1:4) (2b: || my salvation)		
17:14a *	they lived (14b: || were saved)		
		18:8a •••	God is without falsehood and death
19:9a *****	she did not seek a midwife		
19:9b ****	he (who?) gave her life		
		22:8b ••••	the dead (in graves [a])
		22:9a ••••	dead bones
22:10b ***	you gave energy for life		
		24:4b •	creeping things died
24:8b ***	the completion of their corruption was life		
26:9a ***	who leads his soul to life (9b: || he himself might be saved) [cannot educate himself to life / cannot save himself]		
28:6a ***	life embraced me . . .	28:6a ••	. . . without death
		28:7b •	the Spirit in me (7a) cannot die . . .
28:7c ***	. . . because she is life (N)		
28:7c **	. . . because she lives (H)		
		28:17a •••	they sought my death

Table 1: "Life" and "Death," "To Live" and "To Die," "Living/Immortal" (*cont.*)

<table>
<tr><td></td><td></td><td>29:4b •••</td><td>from the mouth of Death
(4a: || Sheol)</td></tr>
<tr><td>30:1a **</td><td>water from the living spring of the Lord
(rest [2])</td><td></td><td></td></tr>
<tr><td>31:7b ***</td><td>take [immortal] life</td><td>31:7b ••</td><td>immortal [life]</td></tr>
<tr><td>34:6b *</td><td>believe and [you will] live and be redeemed</td><td></td><td></td></tr>
<tr><td>38:3b ***</td><td>[immortal] life
(3a: || salvation)</td><td>38:3b ••</td><td>immortal [life]</td></tr>
<tr><td></td><td></td><td>38:8b •••</td><td>supposed sweetness of Death</td></tr>
<tr><td>38:16a *</td><td>I lived and was saved</td><td></td><td></td></tr>
<tr><td>40:6a ***</td><td>gain (of salvation [5b]) is [immortal] life</td><td>40:6a ••</td><td>immortal [life]</td></tr>
<tr><td>41:3a *</td><td>We live (H)</td><td></td><td></td></tr>
<tr><td>41:3b ***</td><td>life we receive by his Messiah</td><td></td><td></td></tr>
<tr><td>41:11b ****</td><td>the savior who gives life</td><td></td><td></td></tr>
<tr><td>41:16a ****</td><td>that he might give life to souls forever</td><td></td><td></td></tr>
<tr><td></td><td></td><td>42:5a •</td><td>my persecutors died</td></tr>
<tr><td>42:5c **</td><td>I (the savior) am living</td><td></td><td></td></tr>
<tr><td></td><td></td><td>42:11b •••</td><td>Death
(11a: || Sheol)</td></tr>
<tr><td>42:14a**</td><td>congregation of living . . .</td><td>42:14a •••</td><td>. . . among its dead</td></tr>
<tr><td>42:14b **</td><td>spoke with living lips</td><td></td><td></td></tr>
<tr><td></td><td></td><td>42:15a •</td><td>they who had died</td></tr>
<tr><td></td><td></td><td>42:17b •••</td><td>our death does not come near you</td></tr>
</table>

The New Testament expression "eternal life" (ζωὴ αἰώνιος),[42] which is especially Johannine, occurs only twice in the *Odes* (9:4; 11:16h; but cf. 6:18 and 41:16), but the somewhat pleonastic phrase "immortal life" is typical for the *Odes of Solomon* and occurs a number of times (10:2; 15:10; 28:6; 31:7; 38:3; 40:6). This expression refers not to the life of an allegedly immortal soul but to the life of God, which does not exist in this world, marked as it is by mortality, death, and killing (cf., e.g., 22:8-9; 28:17; 42:5, 11, 14-17). It is impossible to describe this life of God, except by negative contrast.

Positive statements are possible only in a soteriological framework, either in metaphors—in descriptions such as the embrace of life (28:6), paradise as immortal earth (11:16), or the water or spring of life (6:18; 11:6-7; 31:1; cf. the sacred milk in 8:16)—or else mythologically in describing the annihilation of Death or of his realm (15:9-10; 29:4; 42:11-17).

After God and his Spirit have been negatively described as immortal (18:8; 28:7) the Redeemer is the first to share this immortality (10:2; 42:5) since he has himself been redeemed (cf. 8:22e; 17:1-2).

Thereafter, God's life, immortal life, becomes the impossible possibility and the signifier of human salvation (8:22; 10:6; 17:14; 26:9; 38:3, 16; 40:6; see Excursus 5), partly by the mythological mediation of the Redeemer (10:6; 17:14; 41:3 [Messiah]; 41:11; 42:14), but also directly by election (3:9), by grace and hope (5:3, 14; 6:15), by the deposit of salvation (8:22), by predestination (9:4; cf. 19:9 and 24:8), by knowledge

42 See Franzmann, 410, although she includes 11:7, which refers to the living, immortal water.

(11:7-8; 15:10), by the raising of the dead (22:8-10), by the "embrace" (28:6-7), by acceptance and faith (30:1, 7; 34:6).

The next question is whether the relative clause "who does not die" (in 𝔊 probably τῷ ἀθανάτῳ), which is the indirect object, refers to the Lord God or to the Son. If the causal function of 8 is strongly emphasized and its reference limited to 7c-d, the clause can only refer to the Son, who, as the Redeemed, partakes of God's immortal life (cf. *Diogn.* 9.2, which uses ἀθάνατος among its descriptions of God's υἱός). In that case, 9a would also refer to the Son (on this possibility, see John 11:25, ἐγώ εἰμι ἡ ἀνάστασις καὶ ἡ ζωή· ὁ πιστεύων εἰς ἐμὲ κἂν ἀποθάνῃ ζήσεται ["I am the resurrection and the life. Those who believe in me, even though they die, will live"] and also 14:19, ὅτι ἐγὼ ζῶ καὶ ὑμεῖς ζήσετε ["because I live, you also will live"]).[43] But if 8a and 9a refer to two different concepts, 7a-b, 7c-d, 8, and 9 might constitute a chiastic structure in the form A (God), B (Son), B' (Son), A' (God). This seems very complicated and unlikely.

It is more likely that both 8a and 9a refer to the immortal God and his immortal life.[44] This interpretation is in harmony with the other *Odes*, as well as fitting the content and structure of *Ode* 3.

The basic meaning of the root ܨܒܐ (*ṣbʾ*) is "to will," the Ethpe. masculine active participle of which is combined with the preposition ܒ (*b-*) in 9a (cf. 8:17) and translated "to choose." This choosing is meant not as a philosophical or theological act of free will, but, like the Greek verb εὐδοκέω, as the cheerful acquiescence in the soteriological goodwill.[45] The two parallel statements of 8b and 9b with their near identical content are given a turn toward the future by use of the imperfect ܢܗܘܐ (*nehwē*), but in this passage probably without a modal sense.[46] This future of course refers didactically to the participial statements in 8a and 9a, which themselves may be considered timeless.

■ **10** The instruction continues, perhaps actually inspired by 1 Cor 6:17 (quoted above), but very differently, since the topic is *God*'s ܪܘܚܐ (*rūḥā* ["Spirit"]; in 𝔊 surely πνεῦμα). The word ܕܓܠܘܬܐ (*daggālūṯā* ["false(hood)," also translated as "lie"]), is part of the dualistic vocabulary of the *Odes* and is parallel to darkness (18:6) and death (18:8), whose opposites are light and life. The opposite of "falsehood" or "lie" is "truth" in the theological and soteriological sense (see Excursus 1).

Again God is negatively defined, in contrast to humankind, as ὁ ἀψευδὴς θεός (Titus 1:2). The expression ὁ ἀψευδὴς καὶ ἀληθινὸς θεός ("God, who does not lie and is true"), found in *Mart. Pol.* 14.2,[47] also belongs squarely in Jewish and early Christian

43 On the term "life," see Johannes Lindblom, *Om lifvets idé hos Paulus och Johannes samt i de s.k. Salomos oden* (UUÅ 1910; Uppsala: Lundequist, 1911) 42–57, 179–87; Eduard Schweizer, *Ego eimi: Die religionsgeschichtliche Herkunft und theologische Bedeutung der johanneischen Bildreden, zugleich ein Beitrag zur Quellenfrage des vierten Evangeliums* (FRLANT 56 = N.F. 38; Göttingen: Vandenhoeck & Ruprecht, 1939; 2nd ed., 1965) 137 and 178 (index); Franz Mußner, *ΖΩΗ: Die Anschauung vom "Leben" im vierten Evangelium, unter Berücksichtigung der Johannesbriefe; Ein Beitrag zur biblischen Theologie* (Münchener theologische Studien, Historische Abteilung 5; Munich: Zink, 1952) 41–42 (and see Lattke, *Bedeutung*, 3:232); Schnackenburg, *Gospel*, 2:353–56 (*Johannesevangelium*, 1:439–40).

44 Harris and Mingana's emendation (2:216–18) of the manuscript's "life" to "the Living One [= Christ]" influenced many later users, e.g., Schweizer, *Ego eimi*, 137 n. 2. One should not, however, ignore their final remark concerning 9: "it is even possible that the reading of the MS. may be right" (Harris and Mingana, 2:217).

45 Charlesworth (19) and Franzmann (19) agree on translating 9a as follows: "And he who delights in the Life." Harris and Mingana (2:216) have "And He that hath pleasure in the Living One," while Emerton (692) has "And he who takes pleasure in life," although in a footnote he remarks that with a different pointing "life" could be read as "the living one."

46 Nöldeke §266.

47 The LCL translations by Kirsopp Lake (*The Apostolic Fathers* [2 vols.; Cambridge, Mass.: Harvard University Press; London: Heinemann, 1912; repr., 1976–77] 2:333) and Ehrman (1:387) are rather freer and also differ from each other.

thought. And in *Hermas, Man.* 28 (III).1 it is said of God *καὶ οὐδὲν παρ' αὐτῷ ψεῦδος* ("and there is no lie in him").[48]

The phrase beginning with ܕܠܐ (*d-lā*), "without," can refer to either the Spirit or the Lord. If ܕ (*d-*) is meant, or read, as a relative particle, the translation probably should be "this is the Lord's Spirit, without falsehood" (in which case, cf. *τὸ πνεῦμα τῆς ἀληθείας*, "the Spirit of truth" in John 14:17 and 15:26).

The Semitic-Syriac idiom "the sons of men" should be translated as "humankind" in 10b. There is only one passage where a distinction is made between male and female human beings (33:6); 10b is intended inclusively. This statement about the teaching of the Spirit, which is not limited to the future but is quite general, carries a reminder of the Johannine prediction of the Paraclete in John 14:26: *ἐκεῖνος ὑμᾶς διδάξει πάντα κτλ.* ("he will teach you all things, etc."). But this refers to the ways of the Lord, that is, God, which are not as the ways of humans.

Verse 10b consists of two subordinate clauses. The first hemistich forms the connection with "Spirit" in 10a and is a relative clause made up of the feminine active participle of the Pa. ܐܠܦ (*ʾallep̄* ["to teach"]; cf. 14:7) and the direct object "humankind." This is followed by a final dependent form, translated as an infinitive, whose modal third masculine plural imperfect of Pe. ܝܕܥ (*ʾidaʿ*) governs "his ways" as the object.

The term "to know" and its derivatives belong among the many words that give the *Odes* their Gnostic tinge (see Excursus 7). But the plural "ways" occurs only here and in the discourse of the Virgin "Grace" (33:7, 8, 13), and it should be clearly distinguished from the Gnostic and Gnosticizing use of the singular "way" (cf., e.g., 7:13; 11:3; 12:6; 15:6; 17:8; 22:7; 24:13; 38:7; 39:7, 13).

Behind the expression "his ways" lie the manifold uses of "way" in the Hebrew Bible and the LXX,[49] among whose high points is the passage in Isa 55:6-13, esp. vv. 8-9:

> (8) *οὐ γάρ εἰσιν αἱ βουλαί μου ὥσπερ αἱ βουλαὶ ὑμῶν*
> *οὐδὲ ὥσπερ αἱ ὁδοὶ ὑμῶν αἱ ὁδοί μου, λέγει κύριος·*
> (9) *ἀλλ' ὡς ἀπέχει ὁ οὐρανὸς ἀπὸ τῆς γῆς,*
> *οὕτως ἀπέχει ἡ ὁδός μου ἀπὸ τῶν ὁδῶν ὑμῶν*
> *καὶ τὰ διανοήματα ὑμῶν ἀπὸ τῆς διανοίας μου.*
> (8) For my counsels are not as your counsels,
> nor are my ways as your ways, saith the Lord.
> (9) But as the heaven is distant from the earth,
> so is my way distant from your ways,
> and your thoughts from my mind.[50]

Although the ways of the Lord demand a "walk" determined by the Spirit of God and faith (cf. the ethical phrase "holy life" in *Ode* 8:2), already in the LXX "the *ὁδοὶ κυρίου* are not directly equated with the *νόμος*."[51] That this is true also here is underlined by the final monocolon.[52]

■ **11** From the text it is not clear whether the speaker of these three imperatives, addressed to a number of people, is the speaking "I" of stanzas I–III or a group "we." Both possibilities can be considered, especially if this and other Odes were used in a liturgical context.[53]

In order to distinguish these imperatives of wisdom and Gnosticism from ethical or homiletical ones, they can be called "imperatives of salvation." The invitation to *gnōsis* given by the central Pe. imperative ܕܥ (*daʿ*) includes unmediated redemption. Whoever knows in *gnōsis* is saved.

48 Ehrman, 2:240–41; cf. Norbert Brox, *Der Hirt des Hermas* (KAV 7; Göttingen: Vandenhoeck & Ruprecht, 1991) 197, mentioning 1 John 2:27.

49 See Klaus Koch et al., "דֶּרֶךְ *dæræk*," *ThWAT* 2 (1977) 288–312, esp. 309; *TDOT* 3:270–91, esp. 290–91.

50 Rahlfs, 2:641; Brenton, 891.

51 Wilhelm Michaelis, "*ὁδός, κτλ.*," *ThWNT* 5 (1954) 50–53, esp. 51; cf. *TDNT* 5:50–53, esp. 52.

52 On 3:10–11, see David Edward Aune, "The *Odes of Solomon* and Early Christian Prophecy," *NTS* 28 (1982) 438; and also idem, "The Form and Function of the Proclamations to the Seven Churches (Revelation 2–3)," *NTS* 36 (1990) 193, where these verses are placed beside Rev 2:7, 11, 17, 29; 3:6, 13, 22; and 1 Cor 14:37–38 as the only early Christian "examples of the prophetic signature."

53 On "Hallelujah" as the "ending of the *Ode*," see Lattke, *Bedeutung*, 1:59.

The first Ethpa. occurs as an imperative ܐܬܚܟܡܘ (ʾeṯḥakkam) only here (cf. 38:15)[54] and does not carry the negative connotation of prying or any sexual overtones.[55] The third Ethpa. imperative ܐܬܬܥܝܪܘ (ʾettʿīr) is a *hapax legomenon* (but cf. "watchfulness" in 8:2) and carries the meaning of awaking, arising, and soberness.[56] Although the verbs are not synonymous, they belong to the pairs of words with "associated elements"[57] and complement each other.[58]

54 See Lattke, 3:373, *s.v.* "Weisheit."
55 Payne Smith, 1:1266.
56 Ibid., 2:2842.
57 Franzmann, 398, 401.
58 Grimme (125) excludes 3:11 as one of the allegedly prosaic additions; for a comprehensive treatment of this, see Lattke, *Bedeutung*, 3:98–107, esp. 104. Schlier considers *Ode* 3 in his chapter on "the celestial syzygy." See Heinrich Schlier, *Christus und die Kirche im Epheserbrief* (BHTh 6; Tübingen: Mohr Siebeck, 1930) 60–75, esp. 69–70. It is possible that the Deutero-Pauline Ephesians influenced the *Odes of Solomon*, if the date of the composition of Ephesians between 80 and 90 C.E. can be established; see Udo Schnelle, *Einleitung in das Neue Testament* (UTB 1830; Göttingen: Vandenhoeck & Ruprecht, 1994) 352.

4

Ode 4: A Prayer in the Form of a Dialogue Containing Various Teachings

(I) 1a No one changes thy holy place, my God,
1b and there is none who can change it and remove it to another place,
2a because there is no power over it/him.
2b For thy sanctuary thou didst design
2c even before thou madest the places.
3a The older one shall not be changed
3b by ones that are less than it.
(II) 3c Thou gavest thy heart, Lord, to thy believers.
4a Never wilt thou cease
4b nor wilt thou be without fruits.
(III) 5a For one hour of thy faithfulness
5b is more than all days and years.
(IV) 6a For who, after he has clothed himself with thy grace,
6b will be rejected/condemned?
7a Because thy seal is known,
7b thy creatures are also known to it.
8a And thy powers/hosts possess it,
8b and the elect archangels are clothed in it.
(V) 9a And thou gavest us thy fellowship.
9b Not that thou hast need of us,
9c but we need thee.
(VI) 10a Sprinkle on us thy droplets,
10b and open thy abundant springs
10c which let flow milk and honey for us.
(VII) 11a For there is no regret with thee,
11b that thou shouldst regret anything thou promisedst,
12 and the end was apparent to thee.
(VIII) 13a For what thou gavest,
13b thou gavest freely,
13c so that thou wilt not draw back
13d nor take them [viz. the gifts] away.
(IX) 14a For all was manifest to thee as God,
14b and was fixed before thee from the beginning.
(X) 15 And thou, O Lord, hast made all.
Hallelujah.

Introduction

Ode 4 is preserved in only one Syriac manuscript.[1] Right at the start this puzzling *Ode* raises two questions. Is *Ode* 4 really "the most important in the whole collection on account of the historical detail with which it appears to commence," which is "the Temple at Jerusalem," "a real temple"?[2] And if it does *not* concern the temple "or indeed anything physical at all," is *Ode* 4 still "a poetic unity" whose single subject is "the sacred place or sanctuary of vv. 1-2"?[3]

As the heading implies, these ten stanzas of varying length present a content that is poetically mixed rather than strictly coherent.[4] It will be necessary to examine each of the instructions and prayers, not only for its connection to the remainder of this Ode, but in the context of the collection as a whole. Since the term "temple" is not used here (it occurs only in 6:8), it may be assumed that the speaking "I" or "We" did not intend a reference to the actual temple in Jerusalem.

Only the first strophe, indeed only the first line of the first stanza, suggests an "I" as speaker, by its use of the phrase "my God."[5] Stanzas V (= 4:9) and VI (= 4:10) are clearly spoken by a "We," but the other stanzas may have either a singular or a plural speaker, which offers a good deal of freedom in the practical use of the Ode.

Interpretation

■ **1-3b** Stanza I, with its sometimes metaphorical teaching, is formed by the *inclusio* of 1 and 3 and consists of two strophes (1-2; 3), with 2a forming the conclusion that justifies 1a-b. The God addressed in 1a is at once clearly and radically contrasted with a human "no one" (negative particle + *status absolutus* of "man"). The statement of 1b takes up this opposition, by a parallel use of a word with the root ܚܠܦ (*ḥlp*), but also expands it by the antithetical repetition of ܐܬܪܐ (*ʾaṯrā*)[6] and especially by the generalizing negation ܠܐ (*lā*) + the relative particle ܕ (*d-*) + two imperfects with a modal coloring.[7]

This negation warrants closer examination. It corresponds in general to the Latin construction *ne . . . quidem*.[8] Harris and Mingana felt, correctly, that something is wrong with the Syriac text at this point.[9] A word seems to have been omitted after ܘܠܐ (*w-lā*), which has been replaced in our translation by "there is none." In Greek, too, a construction like οὐδείς (1a) . . . οὐδέ [τις/τι ἐστίν] ὅς/ὅ (1b) would be elliptical without the insertion of the words supplied here in brackets (cf. 11:23; 16:18; 34:2 the construction with ܠܝܬ ܡܕܡ ܕ [*layt meddem d-*], though without a following imperfect). So 1b could be translated as ". . . and there is nothing which . . . ," which would provide a more logical connection to 2a. Thus, Syriac leaves open what Greek

1 Ms.: H, 1b–2a (ܣ). Ed./trans.: Charlesworth, 21–25; Franzmann, 24–30; Lattke, 1:27–47 and 3:XV–XVI.
2 Harris and Mingana, 2:221.
3 Peter Cameron, "The 'Sanctuary' in the Fourth *Ode of Solomon*," in William Horbury, ed., *Templum amicitiae: Essays on the Second Temple presented to Ernst Bammel* (JSNTSup 48; Sheffield: JSOT Press, 1991) 450–63, esp. 454, 462.
4 See already Harris and Mingana, 2:223: "apparent discontinuity." Abbott (77–98, esp. 77) squeezes the rambling sequence of themes ("subjects") into a near allegorical design that is supposed to "correspond fairly to . . . events in, or associations with, the life of Abraham."
5 Although even in ancient Syriac manuscripts the unpronounced suffix "my," "which one was in the habit of so often writing—apparently without cause—was in some cases attached parasitically to words ending in a consonant" (Nöldeke §50.B). On the transcription of ܐܠܗܐ as *ʾallāhā*, with the rare secondary duplication of the consonant following *a*, see Brockelmann, *Grammatik* §69a, n. 1; Nöldeke §21.A; Takamitsu Muraoka differs; see *Classical Syriac: A Basic Grammar with a Chrestomathy* (With a Select Bibliography Compiled by S. P. Brock; Porta linguarum orientalium n.s. 19; Wiesbaden: Harrassowitz, 1997) §7.E.
6 This word corresponds to Greek τόπος (11:18, 23) and Coptic ⲙⲁ (22:6), although Coptic texts often use the Greek loanword τόπος instead.
7 See Nöldeke §266; Theodore H. Robinson and Leonard Herbert Brockington, *Paradigms and Exercises in Syriac Grammar* (4th ed.; Oxford: Clarendon, 1962; repr. 1978) 16.
8 Payne Smith, 2:1869; cf. Karl Ernst Georges, *Ausführliches Lateinisch-Deutsches Handwörterbuch* (ed. Heinrich Georges; 2 vols.; 14th ed.; Hannover: Hahnsche Buchhandlung, 1976) 2:1113.
9 Harris and Mingana, 2:218, 220.

would have been forced by its grammar to express more precisely.[10]

In 1a and 1b the Shaph. of ܚܠܦ (*ḥlap̄*) is used, while in 3a it is the Eshtaph. There can be no doubt that the meaning is "to change," but the Greek equivalent can only be conjectured.[11] Like other forms derived from this root, the Shaph. can have a positive connotation (17:13) or a negative one (24:14, "perverted"). The negative connotation is also implicit here. God's "holy place" will be changeless unto the farthest future;[12] none will or can ever change it (imperfect + accusative suffix in 1bα), not even in accordance with the parallel word ܣܝܡ, ܣܡ (*sām*), whose specific meaning of "to transfer" is inferred from the context (1bβ).

God's "holy place" cannot be displaced and it cannot be removed to any place,[13] since God's "holy place" is not the same as the created heavens (cf. the *hapax legomenon* in 16:11) but is mythologically and metaphorically the absolutely transcendent "height" (cf., e.g., 17:7; 22:1; 36:2), which corresponds to the commonly occurring ܡܪܝܡܐ (*mrayymā*, cf. ὕψιστος in 11:2, 9) as an epithet for God, the Lord.[14]

The adjective ܩܕܝܫܐ (*qaddīšā*), which is used also of the thought of the Lord (9:3), the power of the Most High (32:3), the Father of the Redeemer (31:5), and God's Spirit (6:7; 11:2; 14:8; 23:22; cf. also 19:2), by its use in 1a emphasizes the otherworldliness of this "place,"[15] which is something totally different from any celestial or earthly places whatever (1b, 2c).[16] In this sense, "place" (the Greek surely τόπος) is used only here and does not refer to the holy of holies in the temple (cf. Lev 6:9, 19, 23; 7:6; 10:13, 17),[17] or to paradise (11:16, 18, 23, 24; 20:7) as the holy dwelling (22:12 Coptic) or dwelling of the "saints" so-called (22:12 Syriac; cf. 7:16 and 23:1). Neither is this "place of God" to be identified in religious polemic as "a person united with God in love,"[18] nor yet as "the society of the predestinate" like the temple in 6:8.[19]

Nor is the term as used here connected to the idiosyncratic "designation of God as a *place*" by Philo and the rabbis.[20] A direct influence of John 14:2-3 can probably be ruled out, since the "place" in the Father's house is to be prepared in the future. This Johannine saying may, however, have influenced *1 Clem.* 5:4, 7, according to which Peter went "to the place of glory that he deserved" (εἰς τὸν ὀφειλόμενον τόπον τῆς δόξης) and Paul was taken up "to the holy place" (εἰς τὸν ἅγιον τόπον).[21] If the community in which the *Odes* originated possessed a copy of *1 Clement*, it is possible that the latter expression was taken up and given a radically new theological meaning.

It is hard to tell whether Exod 33:21 (καὶ εἶπεν κύριος Ἰδοὺ τόπος παρ᾽ ἐμοί , "And the Lord said, Behold, there is a place by me"),[22] so often discussed by the later church fathers,[23] played a part here. In any

10 This also eliminates the alternative to the addition, namely, that the ܕ (*d-*) "preceding the Imperfects . . . should be omitted" (Jakob Barth, "Zur Textkritik der syrischen Oden Salomos," *RevSém* 19 [1911] 260).

11 Payne Smith, 1:1286.

12 On the masculine active participle in 1a, see Nöldeke §270.

13 See Cameron, "Sanctuary," 457.

14 See Lattke, 3:359, *s.v.* "höchst, Höchster." See now also Max Küchler, "'Niemand verändert Deinen heiligen Ort . . .': Zum antik-jüdischen Hintergrund der erste[n] Stanza von Od Sal 4," in Pauline Allen, Majella Franzmann, and Rick Strelan, eds., *"I Sowed Fruits into Hearts" (Odes Sol. 17:13): Festschrift for Professor Michael Lattke* (Early Christian Studies 12; Strathfield, NSW: St. Pauls, 2007) 107–15.

15 See Michael Lattke, "Heiligkeit III. Neues Testament," *TRE* 14 (1985) 704.

16 So there is no justification for changing the Syriac to "No one changeth thy place, my holy God" (Harris and Mingana, 2:220).

17 See Payne Smith, 1:425.

18 Staerk, 297.

19 Alfred Loisy, "La mention du temple dans les Odes de Salomon," *ZNW* 12 (1911) 129. As a parallel to 4:1-3, Richard Hugh Connolly (review of Bernard in *JTS* 14 [1912–13] 311–13, esp. 313), suggests *2 Clem.* 14, which deals with the spiritual and preexistent "church of life" (ἐκκλησία τῆς ζωῆς) as the "body of Christ" (*2 Clem.* 14:1-2; cf. Lake, 1:150-51; Ehrman, 1:186–87). Whether this passage is actually a parallel can be doubted.

20 Helmut Köster, "τόπος," *ThWNT* 8 (1969) 201; *TDNT* 8:200.

21 Lake, 1:16–17; Ehrman, 1:44–45.

22 Rahlfs, 1:145; Brenton, 116.

23 See Geoffrey William Hugo Lampe, *A Patristic Greek Lexicon* (Oxford: Clarendon, 1961; repr., 1976) 1397, A.10.

case what *Ode* 4 has to say can really be understood only by reference to the later Gnostic use of the plural, and occasionally the singular, of "place" (Coptic ⲙⲁ, Greek τόπος), as recorded, for instance, in the *Pistis Sophia*, the two *Books of Jeû*, and the *Untitled Text*,[24] but also in the writings from Nag Hammadi.[25]

The teaching of 2a, with its causal conjunction, justifies the declaration of 1a-b. In the successively higher terrestrial and celestial "spheres of being,"[26] which are pictured as lying below the Height of the Most High, there is no higher "power" (Greek must be ἐξουσία, as in 22:4)[27] than this. This term includes secular government (cf., e.g., Luke 23:7; Rom 13:1-3), religious authority (cf. Acts 9:14; 26:10, 12), and any of the "ranks of spiritual powers"[28] "taken mainly from the theories of angels in Jewish apocalypticism."[29]

The translation of the preposition ܥܠ (*ʿal*), which basically means *super*,[30] with its suffix, is intentionally ambiguous. According to the ideas of antique cosmology there is no higher power above God's holy place (*it*); according to radical theological opinion there is also nothing that has power over *him*.

This is now justified, following the "genuine Syriac" causal particle ܓܝܪ (*gēr*),[31] because God, who is here addressed, has anthropomorphically designed/determined his *sanctuarium*[32] and thus established his planned and intentional preexistence (2b). Although ܩܘܕܫܐ (*qudšā*) can also mean "holiness" (19:2; 23:22 H), here it is a synonym for the "holy place" (1a) and is translated as "sanctuary."[33]

The commonly used verb ܥܒܕ (*ʿbad*, "to do," "to make," "to perform," cf. Greek ποιέω) as used in 2c belongs to the vocabulary of creation (cf. 4:15; 7:9, 12; 12:10; 15:7; 29:2; 36:5). The imperfect of the verb, governed by the compound conjunction "(even) before," removes the dependent clause into a future seen from a vantage point lying in the far distant past.[34] The plural "places" comprises all the multiplicity of creation, "any place."[35] In the technical aspect of poetry, 2b and 2c correspond chiastically, with the order object-verb/verb-object.[36]

The second strophe (3a-b) is hardly a "concluding confessional formula."[37] The prohibitive statement, formed by the third person imperfect Eshtaph. of ܚܠܦ (*ḥlap̄*), continues the instruction with something of a summing up of what has gone before, but also adds that the created "places" are not only spatially below but also "lesser" than the older place. Hence "lesser" implies "lower, inferior, less perfect."[38] The use of ܩܫܝܫܐ (*qaššīšā*; cf. 28:17) may be intended as a play on words with ܩܕܝܫܐ (*qaddīšā*, 1a), if the idea of a spelling mistake that needs emendation (suggested by Barth)[39] is not accepted.

■ **3c-4** That stanzas II, V, and VIII are closely connected is clear from the use of the second person singular

24 Carl Schmidt, Walter C. Till, and Hans-Martin Schenke, eds., *Koptisch-gnostische Schriften*, vol. 1: *Die Pistis Sophia. Die beiden Bücher des Jeû. Unbekanntes altgnostisches Werk* (GCS; 4th ed.; Berlin: Akademie-Verlag, 1981) *passim*, esp. 264, ll. 5–6; 335, ll. 11–13; 358, ll. 19–21.

25 Cf. *NHLE*, 188 (*Orig. World* 125,7-11); and Folker Siegert, *Nag-Hammadi-Register: Wörterbuch zur Erfassung der Begriffe in koptisch-gnostischen Schriften von Nag-Hammadi mit einem deutschen Index* (WUNT 26; Tübingen: Mohr Siebeck, 1982) 36 (ⲙⲁ), 313 (τόπος).

26 Schlier, *Epheser*, 87.

27 See Payne Smith, 2:4179.

28 Johannes Weiß, *Der erste Korintherbrief* (KEK 5; 9th ed.; Göttingen: Vandenhoeck & Ruprecht, 1910; repr., 1970) 359, on 1 Cor 15:24.

29 Schlier, *Epheser*, 87, on Eph 1:21 and Col 1:16.

30 Payne Smith, 2:2886.

31 Nöldeke §155.C.

32 Payne Smith, 2:3502.

33 Joachim Jeremias agrees, although he refers confusingly to the "restoration to its proper place" (*Golgotha* [*ΑΓΓΕΛΟΣ: Archiv für neutestamentliche Zeitgeschichte und Kulturkunde*, Beih. 1; Leipzig: Pfeiffer, 1926] 25).

34 See Nöldeke §267.

35 Cameron, "Sanctuary," 457.

36 Franzmann, 27.

37 Ibid.

38 Harris and Mingana, 2:220, on this *hapax legomenon*.

39 Barth, 261.

Pe. perfect of ܝܗܒ (*yab*), from the similarity of their structure, and from the responsive form in which "13a acts rather like a final summary about the giving of the Lord."[40] In consequence, it is also clear that 3c is not "the second half of a couplet" continuing and summing up the preceding verses,[41] but the first monocolon of a new stanza, bringing in new ideas and images.

The "Lord" addressed here (3c; cf. 15) is identical with the "God" addressed in the invocations elsewhere in the Ode (1a, 14a). "Lord" and "God" represent κύριος and θεός, the words used for God in the Greek Bible, which sometimes couples them in the expression κύριος ὁ θεός.[42] The statement in 3c is unique in early Jewish and Christian writings. Even the Dead Sea Scrolls offer no parallel.[43]

Without doubt the Old Testament occurrences of the phrase "the *leḇ* ["heart"] of Yahweh (26 times: 8 times in Jeremiah, 5 times in the Deuteronomistic History, 4 times in Job)," which "probably trace their origin to J's [the Yahwist's] fondness of an anthropomorphism"[44] (cf. Ps 33:11), are behind this concept. But even in the Old Testament the statement is "unparalleled that Yahweh's eyes and *leḇ* dwell (*hāyāh*) in the Jerusalem Temple (1 Kgs 9:3; 2 Chr 7:16)."[45] If this statement on the heart as "the center of decision" of Yahweh is called "an unsurpassable expression of Israel's election,"[46] then it must be acknowledged that this verse trumps it. As the temple was once the holiest place in Israel, it is now the faithful elect to whom the Lord has given his heart (see also the statement on "giving" the "soul" in 9:2).

Excursus 4: "Heart" in the *Odes of Solomon*

The term "heart" is used throughout and only for ܠܒܐ (*lebbā*) or καρδία (11:1). The Coptic ϩⲏⲧ (*hēt*) in 6:14 is part of a text preserved only in Coptic; it was often used to translate καρδία, but also for νοῦς, διάνοια, and ψυχή.[47]

Here, as also in the Old and New Testaments, "heart" usually means "the inner person, the seat of understanding, knowledge, and will" rather than "as in the Greek understanding" "an organ in the physiological sense" and the "location of mental and spiritual feeling."[48] It is the center[49] of the person and, in a twice-transferred sense, also of the Lord (4:13; 16:19; 30:5), of the Most High (28:19), of the Father of Truth (41:10).[50]

Very noticeable about the thirty or so occurrences of "heart" is its repeated association with the term "lips."[51] *Ode* 7:23a–b also belongs to this cluster, since the "sounds" or "notes" (*hapax legomenon* ܢܥܡܬܐ [*neʿmāṯā*]) are also "voices" produced by the lips. Since the lips may function, as it were, as a speaking tube for the hymns of the heart (16:2; 21:8; 40:2), the redeemed "I" can even say, "And I spoke with/by the lips of my heart" (37:2).

"Heart" and "lips" can be parallels, as when the purity of both is spoken of in connection with the true sacrifice (20:4), or when the spring of the Lord is said to flow from his lips and its name to come from his heart (30:5). The lips reveal the fruits of love, which strengthen the heart (16:2).[52] As one can open one's mouth (7:24; 8:4; 16:5; 31:3; 36:7), one's ears (9:1), and one's eyes (13:1), so one can also open one's heart (8:1). The mythological speech of the Redeemer, whose mouth is directed by the Lord (10:1a), and whose heart is opened by the light of the Lord (10:1b), also finds its place

40 Franzmann, 28.
41 Cameron, "Sanctuary," 457–58.
42 See Edwin Hatch and Henry A. Redpath, *A Concordance to the Septuagint and the Other Greek Versions of the Old Testament (Including the Apocryphal Books)* (2 vols.; Oxford: Clarendon, 1897; repr. Graz: Akademische Druck- und Verlagsanstalt, 1954) 630–48, 800–839; Alfred Schmoller, *Handkonkordanz zum griechischen Neuen Testament* (Stuttgart: Deutsche Bibelgesellschaft, 1989) 299–301.
43 On the "*leḇ* of Yahweh," which "functions as the norm for human conduct" (Heinz-Josef Fabry, "לֵב *leḇ*," *ThWAT* 4 [1984] 450; *TDOT* 7:435), cf. 1QH iv.13, 18, 21, 24; vi.7; CD i.11.
44 Heinz-Josef Fabry, "לֵב *leḇ*," *ThWAT* 4 (1984) 448; *TDOT* 7:434.
45 Heinz-Josef Fabry, "לֵב *leḇ*," *ThWAT* 4 (1984) 449; *TDOT* 7:435.
46 Heinz-Josef Fabry, "לֵב *leḇ*," *ThWAT* 4 (1984) 448–9; *TDOT* 7:436.
47 Crum, 714.
48 Alexander Sand, "καρδία," *EWNT* 2 (1981) 616; *EDNT* 2:250.
49 Brockelmann, *Lexikon*, 354.
50 See Silvia Schroer and Thomas Staubli, *Die Körpersymbolik der Bibel* (Darmstadt: Wissenschaftliche Buchgesellschaft, 1998) 45–60 ("A heart with understanding").
51 See *Odes* 8:1; 16:2; 20:4; 21:8; 30:5; 37:2; 40:2; cf. 6:14. This term, always used in the plural, is found by itself only four times (11:6; 12:2; 38:20; 42:14).
52 The expression καρπὸς χειλέων ("fruit of the lips" [Hos 14:3; Heb 13:15; cf. *Ps. Sol.* 15:3 and 1QS x.8])

here (cf. the parallelism of mouth and heart of the Exalted One in 36:7).

Since the heart is the center of personal life, its joy can be compared to the unborn child leaping in its mother's womb (28:2). Joy comes from the heart (32:1; cf. 6:14), as does the haughtiness of folly (24:11). If the heart is circumcised by the Holy Spirit of the Most High (11:1), the whole person is redeemed (11:2-3a). In other metaphors, redemption occurs because the Redeemer leaves tracks of light on the hearts of his chosen (10:6), or sows his fruits in their hearts (17:13). This may be compared to the imagery of salvation, whereby the wings of the Spirit are over the heart of the redeemed (28:1).

When "heart" and "limbs" are used in parallelism, they denote the totality of the person (18:1-2; 26:4). If the parallel is between "countenance" and "heart" (41:6), this personal totality is doubly expressed (see Excursus 8).

In a number of verses it is clear that the "heart" of God, and the human heart also, is understood to be the organ of thought (cf. 41:10), or the "heart of understanding" (38:14). The creator has mythologically willed and molded mind and heart (8:20). A "simple heart" is shown by its "right thoughts" (34:1). The creative word of the Lord is in parallelism with "the thought of his heart" (16:19). The Father of Truth begat the preexistent Redeemer[53] by "the thought of his heart" (41:10). The parallel of "heart" and "Spirit of the Most High" (28:19) shows that the metaphor even transcends the bounds of human thought and wisdom. This is true also of 4:3c. As the heart of the singing "I" is with the Lord only by the mediation of hymn and ode (26:2), so reciprocally the heart of the Lord is with his faithful by the gift of his superhuman grace.

The parallel in 9:2 has already been mentioned, where the object of the reciprocal "giving"[54] is the "soul," that is, the "self." Other things that may be given by the Lord or the Most High, however he is described, include "fellowship" (4:9), "judgment" (5:3 Coptic),[55] "praises" (6:7; cf. 41:4 and the inverse statement 29:11), "drink" (6:12), "a mouth" (7:24; 12:4), "a wreath" (9:10), "life" (15:10), "the way" (17:8),[56] "the mixture" (19:5), "power" (22:4), "energy for life" (22:10), "a scepter" (29:8), "a spring" (30:5), "fruits" (37:3), and "rest" (37:4).

The masculine active participle ܡܗܝܡܢܐ (*mhaymnā*), from the loanword ܗܝܡܢ (*haymen*),[57] corresponds to Greek πιστός (11:22; 22:7) and occurs in the *Odes* only in the plural (4:3; 11:22; 15:10; 22:7; 42:9). Considering the context in which the verb "to believe" (*haymen*: 28:3; 29:6; 34:6) or the noun "belief" (ܗܝܡܢܘܬܐ [*haymānūṯā*]: 8:11; 16:4; 39:5, 13; 41:1; 42:19; on 4:5 see below) is used, it can be stated that the "believers" in 3c who find rest are Gnostics who have already been or will be redeemed (cf. esp. 15:10).

Bicolon 4, beginning with a negated adverb of time (cf. only 12:6), would still be hard to understand even if the formulaic invocation of stanza III gave the immediate reason for the *parallelismus membrorum*. Does the Pe. imperfect of ܒܛܠ (*bṭel*) refer to the "being" of the Lord or to the "giving"? Everywhere else this verb "to cease"[58] whose Ethpa. means to be "destroyed" (15:9) or "frustrated" (23:19 H) is defined by its context (16:13; 23:19 N; 42:14); but even 4b does not help here, unless ܒܛܠ (*bṭel*) should be translated as "to lie fallow," which would introduce a parallel between this description of the Lord and the description of paradise in 11:23b-c.[59]

The question already arose at 1:5 whether the "fruit"[60] in the plural is a metaphor for the members of an esoteric circle or a mythological being. This question will come up again (cf. 8:2; 14:6-7; 37:3; 38:17).

The following features of some of the other occurrences are unlikely to play a role here. As the earth or a

is not to be found in the *Odes* (cf. discussion on 8:1-2).

53 This Redeemer takes to heart (literally "placed upon my heart") the faith of his people (42:19 N).

54 Lattke, 3:355, *s.v.* "geben."

55 For the Syriac reading, see Lattke, 3:364, *s.v.* "nehmen."

56 This is spoken by the redeemed Redeemer, who in his turn gives his people "*gnōsis* without envy" and "comfort" by his love (17:12).

57 "From הֶאֱמִין" (Brockelmann, *Grammatik*, §180.D).

58 Koehler and Baumgartner, 5:1679.

59 See Cameron, "Sanctuary," 458. The problematic nature of the verb in 4a can be seen from the wide variety of translations, e.g., Harris and Mingana: "Thou wilt never fail" (2:219); Charlesworth: "Never wilt Thou be idle" (22; also Franzmann, 25); Emerton: "Thou wilt never be ineffectual" (692).

60 In addition to 1:5 (and 4:4), see 7:1; 8:2; 11:1, 12, 16e (Greek); 11:23; 12:2; 14:6, 7; 16:2; 17:13; 37:3; 38:17. The singular occurs only in 10:2. The Greek text of 11:1 and 11:23 has καρποφορέω. The "fruit imagery" of the "*Odes of Solomon*, which, because of

tree bears fruit (11:12, 16e), even in paradise (11:23), so joy of the lovers (7:1) or the heart circumcised by grace (11:1) will bear fruit. The Lord enables the Redeemer to speak the "fruit of his peace" (10:2); the redeemed Redeemer also sowed his fruits in the hearts of those who are his limbs and whose head he is (17:13–15). The Gnostic says that the lips of his mouth manifest the fruits of his truth (12:2), and the singer of hymns declares that his heart—or the love of the Lord, which strengthens it—*continually* brings up fruit to his lips (16:2).

The difference between this last-mentioned verse, which can be considered a verbal parallel, and 4b is that 16:2 concerns the fruits of the speaking "I" whereas 4:4b speaks of the fruits of the Lord. If the interpretation is limited to its context in stanza II, the question is whether the connection between 3c and 4b is that the "faithful" (i.e., the Gnostics) continually bear fruits of the Lord or whether they may even *be* those fruits.

■ **5** The formulaic invocation resembles Ps 83:11a LXX: *ὅτι κρείσσων ἡμέρα μία ἐν ταῖς αὐλαῖς σου ὑπὲρ χιλιάδας* ("For one day in thy courts is better than thousands").[61] "But the significant thing is that in the *Ode* the word *haimānûthâ* [*sic*] is substituted for the reference to the temple."[62] So the temple is being trumped again (see above 3c), in this case by a word derived from the same root as the term "faithful." This play on words is the sole connection between stanzas II and III.

Although ܗܝܡܢܘܬܐ (*haymānūṯā*) is translated as "faith" elsewhere (8:11; 16:4; 39:5, 13; 41:1; 42:19), in this verse the term "faithfulness"[63] is preferred, a term that equally denotes steadfastness. "Hours" and "years" are *hapax legomena*, and the plural "days" occurs only here in the sense of duration. Because of this quantitative aspect of time, the Pa. feminine participle of ܝܬܪ (*ʾiṯar*) is translated by "more" and not "better" (28:19; cf. also "stronger" in 23:9).

■ **6-8** This stanza is formed by the *inclusio* made up of two forms of the Pe. ܠܒܫ (*lḇeš*) and consists of two strophes (6, 7-8) that show very little connection. The conjunction "because" (7a) does not answer the rhetorical question in 6, but gives the reason for the reciprocal statement of 7b, which commences the rhetorical device of merismus, the "enumeration by . . . parts"[64] of the created beings (7b-8). Whether it is possible to divide these beings into earthly creatures, on the one hand, and celestial powers and archangels, on the other,[65] will have to be considered.

The sequence of ܓܝܪ (*gēr*, 6a) and ܘ (*w-*, 6b) in the antithetical parallelism of the first bicolon occurs quite commonly without actually performing its expected explanatory function.[66] The Pe. imperfect of the verb ܠܒܫ (*lḇeš*, "to don, to put on, to dress oneself") in a metaphorical sense is clearly used modally and refers not only to the future. Its meaning is rooted in the New Testament image of "putting on grace" (Rom 13:14; 1 Cor 15:53; Gal 3:27; Eph 4:24; Col 3:10; cf. already 2 Chr 6:41 [with *σωτηρία* as the object]). How widespread this transferred meaning of *ἐνδύω* or *ἐνδύομαι* was can be seen from table 2 as well as, for example, *The Shepherd of Hermas*, where the object of the verb is most commonly *πίστις*.[67]

their Jewish-Christian-Gnostic background, occupy a unique position," is discussed by Petra von Gemünden in her chapter on the "plant imagery in Gnosticism" (*Vegetationsmetaphorik im Neuen Testament und seiner Umwelt: Eine Bildfelduntersuchung* [NTOA 18; Freiburg: Universitätsverlag; Göttingen: Vandenhoeck & Ruprecht, 1993] 376–405, esp. 402).

61 Rahlfs, 2:92; Brenton, 749; cf. Charlesworth, 23.

62 Cameron, "Sanctuary," 458.

63 Emerton, 692; cf. Diettrich, 10 ("Treue"). But Harris and Mingana (2:219), Charlesworth (22), Franzmann (25), and even Emerton (692 n. 4) use "faith."

64 Georges, 2:894.

65 Franzmann, 28.

66 See Lattke, "Wörter," 289 = idem, *Bedeutung*, 4:138.

67 See Heinrich Kraft, *Clavis patrum apostolicorum* (Darmstadt: Wissenschaftliche Buchgesellschaft, 1963) 153.

Table 2: The Objects of "to Don, to Put On, to Dress Oneself" and "to Put Off, to Doff" Used Metaphorically

*	put on (ܠܒܫ [*lḇeš*])	•	put off (ἀποδύομαι, ܫܠܚ [*šlaḥ*])
**	put on (ܐܠܒܫ [*ʾalbeš*])		
***	raiment, garment (ἔνδυμα, ϣⲧⲏⲛ [*šᵉtēn*], ܠܒܘܫܐ [*lḇūšā*])		

3:1 **	?		
4:6a *	Grace (χάρις, cf. 11:1)		
4:8b *	Seal (cf. 7a)		
7:4c *	The Lord (?), cf. Rom 13:14, etc.		
[8:9b ***	Garment || Flesh, 9a]		
		11:10b •	Folly (ἀφροσύνη)
[11:11a ***	Garment || Light, 11b]		
13:3b *	Holiness of the Lord		
15:8a *	Incorruption (by his name, cf. 1 Cor 15:33)	15:8b •	Corruption (by his grace)
20:7a *	Grace || into Paradise, 7b		
21:3b *	Light	21:3a •	Darkness
23:1b *	Joy		
23:3b *	Love		
[25:8b ***	Garments of skin, cf. Gen 3:21]		
33:12a *	Judge, Virgin "Grace"		
39:8a *	Name of the Most High || *gnōsis*		

The connection with the noun "grace" is characteristic of the *Odes of Solomon* (4:6; 20:7; cf. 33:12a). The Greek equivalent of Syriac feminine ܛܝܒܘܬܐ (*ṭaybūṯā*) is χάρις (11:1). This fundamental term in the Judeo-Christian tradition occurs more than twenty times in the *Odes of Solomon*. Grace is given (29:2 N; cf. 24:13) and received freely (5:3; 20:9). Grace is related to election (23:2) and redemption (6:6; 9:5; 15:8; 25:4; 29:5; 31:7; 34:6; 37:4; 41:3 H). The redeemed know grace (23:4 N), and thus can speak it (31:3), sing it (7:22), or manifest it (7:25), since the personified Grace of God speaks soteriologically (33:1, 10). The closest parallel to the expression and substance of 4:6 also is found in *Ode* 33 at 12a: "and those who have put me on will not be oppressed." This stunning parallel also answers the rhetorical question of 4:6 with the term "incorruption" (33:12b; cf. ἀφθαρσία in 1 Cor 15:53). One of the elect who puts on the Grace of God like a new garment will no longer be oppressed by corruption.

The Ethpe. imperfect of ܛܠܡ (*ṭlam*) cannot here mean "to lack" or "to be deprived of,"[68] since it is not followed by a phrase beginning with the preposition

68 Cameron, "Sanctuary," 459.

ܡܢ (*men*), which would represent the Greek "genitive of separation,"[69] as found for instance in Wis 18:4.[70] So the German translation "unterdrückt werden" ("to be oppressed") is as correct as the English "to be injured."[71]

There has been much speculation on the meaning of the masc. ܚܬܡܐ (*ḥāṯmā*) in the second strophe (7a; replaced in 7b, 8a, and 8b by ܠ [*l-*] + suffix). The "seal" of 23:8–9 belongs to the letter, but here there is no hint as to its meaning or connections, whether it be baptism, circumcision, the Spirit, or a sign of the cross or of a name.[72] Because the terms "Spirit" and "name" occur more than twenty times each in the *Odes*, and "sign" occurs six times, this verse cannot simply be interpreted in terms of 15:8 (see Table 2 above), 23:22 (name of the Father, etc., on the letter; but cf. 2 Tim 2:18) or 39:8 (see Table 2 above).

Since the *inclusio* establishes a connection between 6 and 7-8, "seal" is probably to be understood as a general metaphor for "that which confirms or authenticates,"[73] whose specific meaning is given in the context by the term "grace": "It might be better to understand the word as referring to some kind of . . . guarantee of God's grace."[74] In that case it is possible to point to verses in the New Testament in which σφραγίζω (John 3:33; 6:27; 2 Cor 1:22; Eph 1:13; 4:30) or σφράγις (Rom 4:11; 1 Cor 9:2) occurs. Beyond that it is possible that in Gnosticism the Seal, both here and in 8:15c, "denotes the likeness of the human being, which is his original consubstantiality with God."[75]

In one of the reciprocal statements characteristic for the *Odes*, 7a justifies the strange teaching in 7b, addressed to the second person singular, that the seal of the Lord's grace, in a quasi-personified form, knows the creatures of the Lord. The double statement of mutual nonacknowledgment (18:9-10) is less instructive here than the positive statements of creation and salvation in mutual knowledge of *Ode* 7, which may be called the Ode of *gnōsis* (see Excursus 7). As the Creator knows his creatures from everlasting (7:9), so his own will know their Creator (7:12b). The passage 8:14-15 is also to some extent a parallel, though the transitive verb "to seal" derives from the root ܛܒܥ (*ṭbʿ*):[76] "and I placed my seal on their faces" (8:15c).

One of the direct objects of "to know" in the *Odes of Solomon* is grace (19:23; perhaps 24:14). The verbs "to put on" and "to know" are used together of "the Name of the Most High" (39:8), which has led to an equation of "name" and "seal" in the *Odes of Solomon* as "a token of recognition of ownership (taking possession) and of protection in a wider sense."[77] Even though the context of *Ode* 4 does not point to this equation, the definition of the Seal of Grace may be accepted here also.

The Pe. singular masculine passive participle of ܝܕܥ (*ʾidaʿ*) in 7a is expanded by the parallel participles ܐܚܝܕܝܢ (*ʾaḥīḏīn*) and ܠܒܝܫܝܢ (*lḇīšīn*) in 8a and 8b. To know the Seal of Grace means to possess it and to be clothed by it. This passage differs from 16:13 in that the "creatures" (pl.) in 7b are not the stars but "individual" earthly and even heavenly "beings."[78] For the "powers" (8a, Greek surely δυνάμεις) are not the "heavenly bodies" (cf.

69 BDF and BDR, §180 (*genitivus separationis*).

70 See Payne Smith, 1:1477; *OTSy*, pt. 2 fasc. 5, on Wis 18:4.

71 Harris and Mingana, 2:219. Charlesworth (22), Emerton (692) and Franzmann (25) all use "be rejected." For our idiomatic translation of 6a-b (literally: "For who will put on thy grace and be oppressed/rejected?"), see Klaus Beyer, *Semitische Syntax im Neuen Testament*, vol. 1: *Satzlehre, Teil 1* (SUNT 1; 2nd ed.; Göttingen: Vandenhoeck & Ruprecht, 1968) 276–77, 281.

72 See Lattke, *Bedeutung*, 3:92 on Franz Joseph Dölger, *Sphragis: Eine altchristliche Taufbezeichnung in ihren Beziehungen zur profanen und religiösen Kultur des Altertums* (Studien zur Geschichte und Kultur des Altertums 5.3–4; Paderborn: Schöningh, 1911); Lattke, *Bedeutung*, 3:158 on Wilhelm Heitmüller, "*ΣΦΡΑΓΙΣ*," in *Neutestamentliche Studien Georg Henrici zu seinem 70. Geburtstag (14. März 1914)* (Leipzig: Hinrichs, 1914) 40–59.

73 BDAG, *s.v.* σφραγίς, 4.

74 Cameron, "Sanctuary," 459.

75 On this theory, see Hans-Martin Schenke, *Die Herkunft des sogenannten Evangelium Veritatis* (Göttingen: Vandenhoeck & Ruprecht, 1959) 39; and earlier Jacob Jervell, *Imago Dei: Gen 1,26f. im Spätjudentum, in der Gnosis und in den paulinischen Briefen* (FRLANT 76 = N.F. 58; Göttingen: Vandenhoeck & Ruprecht, 1960) 168.

76 Payne Smith, 1:1427.

77 Heitmüller, "*ΣΦΡΑΓΙΣ*" (n. 72 above).

78 Walter Bauer, *Griechisch-deutsches Wörterbuch zu den Schriften des Neuen Testaments und der frühchristlichen Literatur* (ed. Kurt Aland and Barbara Aland;

16:14)[79] but the "hosts" made up of individual "angels" among whom "select archangels" (8b, literally "great angels") stand out as a chosen "species" (cf. 8:20c).[80]

The three terms—"creatures," "powers," and "archangels"—which appear as a tapering cone of meaning from the encompassing to the encompassed, occur in a similar combination in the prayer in *Mart. Pol.* 14:1-3, which must stem from a tradition going back to New Testament formulae (cf. Rom 8:38; 1 Cor 15:24; Eph 1:21; 1 Pet 3:22): *κύριε . . . δι᾽ οὗ τὴν περὶ σοῦ ἐπίγνωσιν εἰλήφαμεν, ὁ θεὸς ἀγγέλων καὶ δυνάμεων καὶ πάσης κτίσεως παντός* "Lord . . . God of angels, of powers, and of all creation" (cf. Ps 58:6 LXX; Jdt 9:12, 14).[81]

■ **9** In this renewed invocatory response (cf. 3c) the "we" to whom the Lord has given his "fellowship" (Greek most probably *κοινωνία*) are heard for the first time. The abstract noun ("fellowship") from the root ܫܬܦ (*štp*, cf. *šawtep̄*), which was no longer used in the Pe. form, expresses "a two-sided relation" in Syriac as well.[82] Its only other occurrence is in the first person account of the redeemed (21:5). Both times ܫܘܬܦܘܬܐ (*šawtāp̄ūṯā*)[83] means more than an ecclesiological *μετουσία* or a sacramental *εὐχαριστία*.[84] It is a term that is used for marital companionship and coitus,[85] and it indicates, especially in conjunction with the verb "to give" (cf. 4:3, 13), that "close relationship"[86] which the Lord grants for the redemption of his faithful and blessed elect.

The repeated Pa. passive participle of ܚܣܪ (*ḥsar*) in the antithetical parallelism of 9b-c expresses a lack. Although the construction with the preposition ܡܢ (*men*) is known in Syriac,[87] it is more likely to represent a Greek expression containing a verb like *(προσ)δέομαι*,[88] *χρῄζω*,[89] or *ὑστερέω*,[90] or an analogous adjective or participle, together with the genitive of "what is needed."[91]

The first half of the parallelism (9b) picks up the widely accepted Greek teaching that God is without need.[92] Anyone who knew the plays of Euripides would be likely to have been aware of the famous lines from his play on Herakles/Hercules (1345–46; LCL 9:444–45):

> *δεῖται γὰρ ὁ θεός, εἴπερ ἔστ᾽ ὀρθῶς θεός,*
> *οὐδενός· ἀοιδῶν οἵδε δύστηνοι λόγοι.*

> A god, if he is truly a god, needs nothing.
> These are the wretched tales of the poets.

"Beginning with the Eleatic philosophers the idea that God has need of nothing is repeated in all the schools of Greek philosophy, right through to the neo-Pythagoreans and neo-Platonists."[93] In Plato's *Timaeus* (33d–34b) it is not only the world (*ὁ κόσμος*) that has become a blessed god (*εὐδαίμονα θεόν*) and therefore "self-sufficing rather than in need of other things" (*αὔταρκες ὂν . . . μᾶλλον ἢ προσδεὲς ἄλλων*); the ever-existing God also "established" (*κατέστησε*) the "Heaven . . . needing none other beside (*οὐρανόν . . . οὐδενὸς ἑτέρου προσδεόμενον*)."[94] Philo goes a step further, declaring, *δεῖται γὰρ οὐδενὸς οὔτε ὁ πλήρης θεὸς οὔτε ἡ ἄκρα καὶ παντελὴς ἐπιστήμη* ("For neither God, Who is full, nor supreme and consummate knowledge, need anything" [*Det. pot. ins.* 54]).[95]

6th ed.; Berlin/New York: de Gruyter, 1988), *s.v.* *δύναμις*, 6.

79 BDAG, *s.v.* *δύναμις*, 4.

80 Bauer and Aland, *s.v.* *ἀρχάγγελος*.

81 *Mart. Pol.* 14.1; cf. Ehrman, 1:387; Andreas Lindemann and Henning Paulsen, eds., *Die Apostolischen Väter* (Tübingen: Mohr Siebeck, 1992) 274.

82 Friedrich Hauck, "*κοινός, κτλ.*," *ThWNT* 3 (1938) 798; *TDNT* 3:798.

83 Cameron ("Sanctuary," 460), whose transcription "*shawthāphûthâ*" is questionable, sees this word as the high point ("culmination") of "the progression of ideas . . . from v. 1 onwards."

84 Payne Smith, 2:4355.

85 Brockelmann, *Lexicon*, 767.

86 BDAG, *s.v.* *κοινωνία*, 1.

87 Cf. Payne Smith, 1:1339 on "Ephr. . . . ii. 320."

88 BDAG, *s.v.* *προσδέομαι*.

89 BDAG, *s.v.* *χρῄζω*.

90 BDAG, *s.v.* *ὑστερέω*.

91 BDAG, *s.v.* *προσδέομαι*; cf. Heinrich Greeven, "*δέομαι, κτλ.*," *ThWNT* 2 (1935) 41–42, on Acts 17:25; cf. *TDNT* 2:41–42.

92 Martin Dibelius, *Aufsätze zur Apostelgeschichte* (ed. Heinrich Greeven; 4th ed.; Göttingen: Vandenhoeck & Ruprecht, 1961) 42.

93 Ibid., 43.

94 LCL 7:62–65; cf. Eduard Norden, *Agnostos Theos: Untersuchungen zur Formengeschichte religiöser Rede* (4th ed.; Darmstadt: Wissenschaftliche Buchgesellschaft, 1956) 14.

95 LCL 2:238–39. Cf. also *Det. pot. ins.* 55, where it

If "the emphasis on God's lack of need" is not found "in the canonical books of the Old Testament,"[96] yet the theologoumenon is to be found in 2 Macc 14:35 (σὺ κύριε τῶν ὅλων ἀπροσδεὴς ὑπάρχων) and *3 Macc.* 2:9 (the Creator ἀπροσδεεῖ). In the New Testament, it is unique to Acts 17:25, where it is said that the Creator and Lord is not προσδεόμενός τινος ("needing anything").

These occurrences, as well as the present verse, form the foundation of several statements in those "primitive Christian writings that are contemporary or nearly contemporary with the later writings in the New Testament."[97] Most of them are found in the so-called Apologists. Some of them refer not only to God's lack of need but also to the neediness of humankind, though not in the invocatory form of 9c.

In a fragment "from the Kerygma of Peter" in Clement of Alexandria, God is called ἀνεπιδεής, οὗ τὰ πάντα ἐπιδέεται ("needing nothing, whom all things need" [*Strom.* 6.39.3; ANF 2:489]).[98] Aristides *Apology* (1.4; ANF 10:264) declares that "He [*viz.* God] requires not aught from any, but all living creatures stand in need of him."[99]

Justin in his First *Apology* (10.1; ANF 1:165) claims, "we have received by tradition that God does not need (δέεσθαι) the material offerings which men can give, seeing, indeed, that He Himself is the provider of all things."[100] In Tatian's *To the Greeks* (4.2; ANF 2:66) God is πάντων ἀνενδεής ("He who is in want of nothing").[101] *Diogn.* 3.4 is aimed against both Jews and Greeks:

> ὁ γὰρ ποιήσας τὸν οὐρανὸν καὶ τὴν γῆν καὶ πάντα τὰ ἐν αὐτοῖς καὶ πᾶσιν ἡμῖν χορηγῶν, ὧν προσδεόμεθα, οὐδενὸς ἂν αὐτὸς προσδέοιτο τούτων, ὧν τοῖς οἰομένοις διδόναι παρέχει αὐτός.
>
> For the one who made heaven and earth and all that is in them, and who supplies all of us with what we need, is himself in need of none of the things that he himself provides to those who suppose that they are giving them.[102]

Finally, Theophilus of Antioch in *To Autolycus* (2.10) imputes Greek thought to the prophets when, in accordance with his own theology of the Logos, he has them teaching that God is always ἀνενδεής ("lacking

---

is said of "the deity" (τὸ θεῖον) that it is not "in need of anything" (ἐνδεὲς ὄν): "Nay, He constantly and unceasingly benefits (ὠφελεῖ) the universe." And similarly in *Poster. C.* 4, Philo says, τὸ δὲ ὂν οὐδενὸς χρεῖον ("But the Existing Being is in need of nothing" [LCL 2:330–31]). The nature of this being is described in *Deus imm.* 56, etc., as ἀπροσδεᾶ ("needing nothing" [LCL 3:38–39 modified]).

96 Dibelius, *Aufsätze*, 43.

97 Ibid., 44–45.

98 Otto Stählin, ed., *Clemens Alexandrinus*, vol. 2: *Stromata I–VI* (4th ed. with supplements by Ursula Treu; GCS; Berlin: Akademie, 1985) 451; idem, trans., *Des Clemens von Alexandreia ausgewählte Schriften* (5 vols.; BKV 7, 8, 17, 19, 20; Munich: Kösel-Pustet, 1934–38) 4:264; cf. Dibelius, *Aufsätze*, 43 n. 1.

99 Cf. J. Rendel Harris and J. Armitage Robinson, *The Apology of Aristides* (TextsS 1.1; 2nd ed.; Cambridge: Cambridge University Press, 1893; repr., Nendeln/Liechtenstein: Kraus, 1967) 35; Goodspeed, 3. Cf. also *Apol.* 13.4 (Goodspeed, 17): *Deus vere non eget* ("God is not in need" [ANF 10:274; cf. Harris and Robinson, 47]).

100 Cf. Goodspeed, 31; Marcovich, *Apologiae*, 45. Similarly Athenagoras *Leg.* 13.1: "the Framer and Father of this universe does not need (δεῖται) blood . . . , forasmuch as He . . . need[s] nothing either within or without (ἀνενδεὴς καὶ ἀπροσδεής)" (ANF 2:134–35; Goodspeed, 327; cf. also his comment on the Greek poets: ἀνεπιδεὲς γὰρ καὶ κρεῖττον ἐπιθυμίας τὸ θεῖον ("for the Deity is in want of nought, and is superior to carnal desire") (*Leg.* 29.2; ANF 2:145; Goodspeed, 351).

101 Goodspeed, 271.

102 Ehrman, 2:136–37; cf. Klaus Wengst, *Didache (Apostellehre), Barnabasbrief, zweiter Klemensbrief, Schrift an Diognet* (Schriften des Urchristentums 2; Darmstadt: Wissenschaftliche Buchgesellschaft, 1984) 316–17. In his long note to this passage, Wengst does not mention *Ode* 4:9.

nothing") and has made the world (κόσμος) for humankind to bring them to the knowledge of God: ὁ γὰρ γενητὸς καὶ προσδεής ἐστιν, ὁ δὲ ἀγένητος οὐδένος προσδεῖται ("For he who is created has needs, but he who is uncreated lacks nothing").[103] So the theological argument of 9 runs as follows: the experience of redemption (9a) demonstrates that humans, existentially, have need of God (9c), a God whose nature is conceived of so radically that he has need of nothing and nobody (9b), since he is himself "no-thing" and "no-body."

■ **10** The two parallel Pe. masculine singular imperatives, ܪܣ (*ras*) in 10a and ܦܬܚ (*ptaḥ*) in 10b, are at once metaphorical petitions and, by their immediate context, "confident assertions."[104] The relative clause in 10c (with the only occurrence of the Aph. of ܪܕܐ [*rdā*, "to (let) flow"; masculine plural participle absolute]) refers, in the first place, to the plural of ܡܒܘܥܐ (*mabbūʿā*) in 10b, but by parallelism can also be brought into relation with the paronomasiac plural of ܪܣܝܣܐ (*rsīsā*) in 10a. Whether these "droplets" of mizzling rain point to "what comes from above," while the "springs" refer to "what comes from below,"[105] depends as much on the intended meaning as on the origin of the imagery.

The expression "milk and honey" is reminiscent of "the well-known feature of the Promised Land."[106] In this connection, Deut 11:8-17[107] is more important than, for example, Exod 3:8, 17; Jer 11:5; or Ezek 20:6, since this exhortation to keep the whole of the law and to serve God in love promises not only "a land flowing with milk and honey" (γῆν ῥέουσαν γάλα καὶ μέλι [11:9]) but also a land that "shall drink water of the rain of heaven" (ἐκ τοῦ ὑετοῦ τοῦ οὐρανοῦ πίεται ὕδωρ [11:11]; note also the emphasis on rain in 11:14, 17).[108]

It must be noted, however, that although 10c comes close to the Syriac text of Deut 11:9,[109] the word for "rain" in Deut 11:11, 14, and 17 is ܡܛܪܐ (*meṭrā*). "Rain" as a whole is sometimes distinguished from the separate "drops."[110] Both words can also be used as parallels, together with other synonyms (cf. esp. Deut 32:2). And the Syriac version of Zech 10:1 shows that the rain (ܡܛܪܐ [*meṭrā*]) is composed of drops (ܪܣܝ̈ܣܐ [*rsīsē*]).[111]

Now the "drops" of 10a are certainly metaphorical, as in the expression "drops of grace" (ܪܣܝ̈ܣܐ ܕܛܝܒܘܬܐ [*rsīsē ḏ-ṭaybūṯā*]).[112] In fact, the only other occurrence of the term in the *Odes of Solomon* with the singular meaning of "sprinkling" is in *Ode* 35:1a, where it is also a metaphorical declaration of salvation.

The "springs" of "milk and honey" also are metaphorical. On the one hand, they are distanced from their original biblical connection with the [promised] land, while, on the other hand, there is no clear indication yet of the later "offering of milk and honey to the newly baptised."[113] "Spring," meaning "source" of a river or a flowing water, is found only in the imagery of the comparisons in 26:13 (with the adjective ܥܬܝܪܐ [*ʿattīrā*], which is also used here in 10b!) and 40:2. In 40:1-2 the connection with the words "milk" and "honey" in their literal meanings should be noted. Elsewhere this word, derived from the root ܢܒܥ (*nbʿ*), refers to the living spring of the Lord (11:6; 30:1-2), whose water is sweeter than honey (30:1, 4). Of the sometimes enigmatic "milk" passages (cf. esp. 8:16; 19:1, 3, 4) only one is of interest here, because it calls "milk" the "dew of the Lord" (35:5).

What is the petition that the speaking "we" of stanza VI has clothed in such metaphors? Even if the connections with the "Paradise *Ode* 11" is not as emphatic, and it is not quite so obvious "that the subject of the entire *Ode* is the sacred place, its origin conceived by God in the beginning, and its final end manifest to him" and therefore "the 'rains' and the 'milk and honey' of v. 10 are simply another way of describing the sacred place,"[114] it can be stated that what is prayed for is the

103 Robert M. Grant, ed. and trans., *Theophilus of Antioch, Ad Autolycum* (OECT; Oxford: Clarendon, 1970) 38–39; cf. ANF 2:98.
104 Cameron, "Sanctuary," 460.
105 Franzmann, 29.
106 Alois Stenzel, "Milch," *LThK*² 7 (1962) 412.
107 Cameron, "Sanctuary," 461.
108 Rahlfs, 1:306–7; Brenton, 246–47.
109 *OTSy*, pt. 1 fasc. 2 [+ pt. 2 fasc. 1b], on Deut 11:9 (. . . ܕܪܕܝܢ̈ܐ . . .).
110 Payne Smith, 2:2079, 3938.
111 *OTSy*, pt. 3 fasc. 4, on Zech 10:1.
112 Payne Smith, 2:3939.
113 Alois Stenzel, "Milch," *LThK*² 7 (1962) 412, contra Bernard, 53.
114 Cameron, "Sanctuary," 461.

promised blessing of God in the form of grace and blessing "from above."

■ **11-12** God is didactically addressed as the Lord who is without any need of repentance. This certainty, which is only loosely connected, by the particle ܓܝܪ (*gēr*), with the confiding petitions of stanza VI, belongs to a biblical tradition that joins this lack of a need for repentance with the lack of falsehood, which distinguishes God from humans (cf. 1 Kgdms 15:29 [οὐχ ὡς ἄνθρωπός ἐστιν τοῦ μετανοῆσαι αὐτός]; Num 23:19; Ps 109:4 LXX [οὐ μεταμεληθήσεται]; Rom 11:29 [ἀμεταμέλητα κτλ.]; Heb 6:13-18 [ἀδύνατον ψεύσασθαι θεόν]). At the same time, there are passages in which the word of God expresses repentance toward all people or toward an individual (cf., e.g., Gen 6:6; 1 Sam 15:11; Jer 18:10). The "theme of the repentance of Yhwh" in the Old Testament shows, indeed, "a clear progression," but also a dialectic, as follows: "Note that while the affirmative use of *nḥm* is associated with a specific situation (regret at having created mankind, or having made Saul king), its use in negation is absolute: ultimately, Yahweh does not change his mind."[115]

The subjunctive clause 11b repeats paronomasiacally the dogmatism of 11a. Both ܬܘܬܐ (*twāṯā*) and the modal imperfect of the Ethpe. ܐܬܘܐ (*ʾeṯwī*)[116] are *hapax legomena*, forms of the verb ܬܘܐ (*twā*). The lack of repentance is now complemented by a reference to the divine promises. The Eshtaph., which is derived from the root ܝܕܥ (*ydʾ* [not found as a Pe.]), has as one of its meanings "to promise";[117] its only other occurrence is in 31:13, where it is found together with ܫܘܕܝܐ (*šūḏāyā*), a *hapax legomenon* from the same root, which is often used to translate ἐπαγγελία.[118] It is hardly possible to make a connection between the statements in 11 and that in 31:12-13. They will have to be accepted simply as justifications for the preceding petitions for divine blessings.

There is also "a semantic connection . . . by the motif of the generosity of the Lord"[119] with stanza VIII. This connection, however, is interrupted by the placing of the teaching in 12, which is itself logically continued by 14a in stanza IX.[120] Verse 14b provides some similarity with the formulaic "from beginning to end" (cf. 6:4; 7:14; 11:4 [τέλος]; 26:7). There is no real distinction between Syriac ܚܪܬܐ (*ḥarṯā*; cf. only in 14:4) and ܐܚܪܝܬܐ (*ḥrāytā*).[121]

If 12, appended merely by ܘ (*w-*), refers to 11 at all, then it is simply in the sense of "all's well that ends well." God does not repent of his promises, because his eschatological omniscience has already manifested and revealed to him their positive results (cf. Rom 6:22).[122]

■ **13** This renewed invocation, which, like stanzas II and V, sounds like a response and serves as a "final summary about the giving of the Lord,"[123] interrupts the connection between 12 and 14, as mentioned above. The antecedent relative clause 13a corresponds in its construction to Greek καὶ ὃ γὰρ ἔδωκας/δέδωκας. The combination of these two words, conjunction and particle, is common in the New Testament.[124] In the Syriac of the *Odes of Solomon*, the pairing of ܘ (*w-*) and ܓܝܪ (*gēr*) is found only here and in 9:9 (but note *ʾāp̄ lā ḡēr* in 28:16 and 38:14).

The main clause, 13b, which is also the central statement of stanza VIII, should be taken as an independent colon.[125] It is enclosed between 13a and the twofold negating wish expressed in 13c-d by imperfects. The verb "to give" corresponds to the verb "to take," which here (and in 14:3) connotes "to dispossess." More commonly ܢܣܒ (*nsaḇ*) is used for "to accept" or "to receive." The adverb ܡܓܢ (*maggān*), which occurs also in 5:3 (Syriac) together with the term "grace," is used in Rom 3:24 (Syriac) to translate δωρεάν.

The compound adverb ܡܟܝܠ (*mekkēl*), made up of ܡܢ (*men*) and ܟܝܠ (*kēl*), which in 8:5 is translated as "now," when combined with the negative particle, means "no longer, no more, not again."[126] The *hapax legomenon* ܢܬܦ (*nṯap̄*), whose basic meaning is "to draw, to pull"

115 Horacio Simian-Yofre, "נחם *nḥm*," *ThWAT* 5 (1986) 374; *TDOT* 9:344. Harris and Mingana (2:219) do use "repentance" and "repent" in 11a-b.

116 Payne Smith, 2:4397.

117 Payne Smith, *Dictionary*, 186.

118 Payne Smith, 1:1552.

119 Franzmann, 29.

120 Franzmann, 30: "the logical flow."

121 See Payne Smith, 1:127, 129.

122 See Payne Smith, *Dictionary*, 69.

123 Franzmann, 28.

124 Cf. BDAG, *s.v.* γάρ, 1b.

125 See Lattke, *Bedeutung*, 1:74; contra Franzmann, 26.

126 Payne Smith, *Dictionary*, 271.

(ἕλκω),[127] reinforces the meaning of ܢܣܒ (*nsab*), which, as a transitive verb, refers to the feminine plural pronoun standing for a word like ܡܘܗܒܬܐ (*mawhbātā*). The term "gift" or "favor" (χάρισμα; Ger. *Gnadengabe*) is elsewhere found only in the singular (11:9; 15:7; 35:6).

■ **14** The address resumes, in the form of a didactic statement that takes up the explicit reference to God in 1, and expands the eschatological declaration of 12 into a teaching on the omniscience and purposive providence of God. Here again, the justifying particle ܓܝܪ (*gēr*) does not act as a strong conjunction but merely emphasizes the first word,[128] which corresponds to the use of Greek πάντα (as in 11:22).

Verse 14b differs from statements that emphasize the *coram Deo* (Rom 14:22), or from "assertions and oaths which call upon God, as the One who sees all,"[129] in speaking of predestination from the protological perspective of God himself.[130] The metaphorical use of the preposition ܩܕܡ (*qdām*) in, as it were, a spatial sense, with the suffix of the second masculine singular personal pronoun, has no parallel elsewhere in the *Odes of Solomon*. By "subjoining" ܗܘܐ (-*wā*) to the masculine passive participle of the Aph. of ܬܩܢ (*tqen*), "the Part., properly expressing only a condition, is distinctly referred to the past."[131] The Aph. ܐܬܩܢ (ʾ*atqen*), which is scarcely differentiated from the Pa., is used to translate a number of Greek verbs, often ones belonging to the language of creation.[132] So God is really the *conditor universi* (ܡܬܩܢ ܟܠ [*matqen kol*]),[133] who, according to 16:11-12, not only fixes the stars but also orders the whole of creation (ܒܪܝܬܐ [*brītā*]).

The concern here is not God's own holy "place" (1-2b)[134] but the "places" of 2c, the "foundation of the world" (41:15), which has always been (cf. ܒܪܫܝܬ [*b-rēšīt*] in Gen 1:1), like the Logos in John 1:1 (ἐν ἀρχῇ).

■ **15** The final colon is a continuation in form and content of 14b and can also be taken as a "confessional statement."[135] With the emphatic placement of "thou" at the beginning, and the repetition of "Lord"[136] from 3c, this confessional statement marvels at the definitively biblical "Creator and Lord of all."[137] The choice of words in this address by the speaking "I" or "we" corresponds to the revelatory speech of the Lord in Isa 44:24 (Syriac):[138] ܐܢܐ ܡܪܝܐ ܕܥܒܕܬ ܟܠ (ʾ*enā māryā d-ʿebdet kol*), "I am the Lord, who has made all things."[139] Such passages from the Old Testament as well as Pauline statements, molded by affirmations of Hellenistic hymnody (e.g., Rom 11:36 [ἐξ αὐτοῦ καὶ δι᾽αὐτοῦ καὶ εἰς αὐτὸν τὰ πάντα]; 1 Cor 8:6 [εἷς θεὸς ὁ πατὴρ ἐξ οὗ τὰ πάντα]) influenced the language of the *Odes of Solomon*.

"God" can be designated as the Creator of all things—and, in antiquity, can be addressed as such—because no thing and no one can produce the unnumbered "places" (2c), and even the infinite universe itself is neither God nor Lord. This statement of creation cannot be applied unconditionally to every phenomenon in the world. But it properly applies to the inexplicable secret that is "man" as an individual, experiencing being, capable of redemption (cf. 7:9, 12; 12:10; 15:7; 36:5).

127 See Payne Smith, 2:2483.
128 See Lattke, "Wörter," 287 = idem, *Bedeutung*, 4:136.
129 BDAG, *s.v.* ἐνώπιον, 2b.
130 The statement that *As. Mos.* 1:14 "records the idea that Moses was pre-existent" (Charlesworth, 25 n. 22) is only partly correct. In the Latin translation of this first-century C.E. Jewish writing, Moses says: *Itaque excogitavit et invenit me qui ab initio orbis terrarum praeparatus sum ut sim arbiter testamenti illius* ("Therefore, he [viz. the Lord of the world] has devised and invented me, I who have been prepared from the beginning of the world to be the mediator of his covenant") (Johannes Tromp, *The Assumption of Moses: A Critical Edition with Commentary* [SVTP 10; Leiden: Brill, 1993] 6–7). The commentary on this passage notes, correctly, "the issue here is not Moses' preexistence" (ibid., 143).
131 Nöldeke §277.
132 See Payne Smith, 2:4483–90, esp. 4484–86.
133 Payne Smith, 2:4485.
134 As Franzmann thinks (p. 30).
135 Ibid.
136 Emerton (p. 693), perhaps erroneously, substitutes "God" for "Lord."
137 Bo Reicke, "πᾶς, ἅπας," *ThWNT* 5 (1954) 888; *TDNT* 5:889–90.
138 *OTSy*, pt. 3 fasc. 1, on Isa 44:24.
139 Reicke, "πᾶς," *ThWNT* 5:893; *TDNT* 5:894.

5

Ode 5: My Hope, My Deliverance

Syriac (𝔰)

(I) 1a I thank/praise thee, Lord,
1b because I love thee.
2a Most High, do not leave me,
2b because thou art my hope.
3a Freely I received thy grace;
3b I shall live by it.

(II) 4a If my persecutors come,
4b let them not see me.
5a A cloud of darkness shall fall on their eyes
5b and an air of fog shall darken them.
6a And they shall have no light to see by
6b so that they cannot seize me.
7a Let their counsel become tumors,
7b and what they have cleverly devised will fall on their own heads.

(III) 8a For if they devised a counsel,
8b it did not succeed for them.
9a If they prepared with malicious intention,
9b they were found incapable of acting.

(IV) 10a For my hope is in the Lord
10b and I shall not fear.
11a And because the Lord is my salvation
11b I shall not fear.
12a And he is like a wreath on my head
12b and I shall not be shaken.
13a Even if everything were to be shaken
13b I stand firmly.
14a And if all that is seen should perish
14b I shall not die.
15a Because the Lord is with me
15b I am also with him.
Hallelujah.

Coptic (ℭ)

(I) 1a I shall give thee praise/thanks, Lord,
1b for thou art my God.
2a Leave me not, Lord,
2b for thou art my hope.
3a Thou didst give me thy justice freely,
3b and by means of thee I was saved.

(II) 4a May my persecutors fall
4b and let them not see me.
5a May a cloud of darkness cover their eyes
5b and may a fog of the air darken them.
6a And let them not see the day,

6b **lest they seize me.**
7a **Let their schemes become powerless**
    erless
7b **and let what they have schemed**
    come upon them.
(III) **8a** **They have thought of a scheme**
8b **and it has not happened for**
    them.
8c **And they have been defeated,**
    although they have power.
9a **And what they prepared mali-**
    ciously
9b **has fallen on them.**
(IV) **10a** **My hope is in the Lord**
10b **and I will not fear.**
11a **For thou art my God, my Savior.**
...

Introduction

Ode 5 is preserved in one Syriac manuscript and incompletely in the Coptic *Pistis Sophia*.[1] This quadripartite Ode, in which the speaking "I" (1-6, 10-15) is distinguished from the Lord (1a, 10-12, 15) and the Highest (2a), is the first that is known in two languages. The incomplete Coptic quotation, which ends at 11a, begins the sequence of five quotations in the *Pistis Sophia*.[2]

It is necessary to take into account in this commentary the quotations from the *Odes*, probably translations from a Greek original, as well as their Gnostic interpretations in the context of the Coptic *Pistis Sophia*, which is also likely to have been originally Greek. On the one hand, it is to be expected that the mythology, hymnology, and exegetical solutions (ⲃⲱⲗ) of the *Pistis Sophia* would have influenced the quotations of the *Odes*,[3] but, on the other hand, the Coptic version clearly helps in the reading of the Syriac (e.g., "Lord" = "God," 1a-b) and intensifies the quest for the original language of the *Odes* (see on 3b below).

The title for the Ode as a whole refers to content rather than form. It is justifiable, since stanzas I and IV open and close it positively with their profound certainty of salvation, while stanzas II and III, despite their negative descriptions of past and future disaster, finally display a hope of triumph. In this sense the crude classification of *Ode* 5 as a "song of trust"[4] or as "a pledge of praise and a castigation,"[5] which at least brings out the contrast of good and ill fortune, can be refined by attention to the literary forms of the subsections.[6]

Interpretation

■ **1-3** The speaking "I" expresses its hope and reliance on salvation by the poetic device of *parallelismus membrorum* in all three bicola and by the alternation of I-statements (1a-b, 3a-b) and you-statements (2a-b).[7] The vocatives at the end of 1a and the beginning (𝔖)/end (ℭ) of 2a are also in parallel. So vv. 1a and 2a are not merely "linked"[8] but serve to establish the identity of the Lord as the Most High. The different reading of 1b in ℭ makes it even clearer to readers and listeners that the Lord indeed stands for God, who is praised as "the light" and "the light on high" in the hymn of the *Pistis Sophia*.[9]

1 Mss.: Codex H, 2a–b (𝔖); Codex A, 53ʳa–53ᵛa (ℭ). Ed./trans.: Charlesworth, 25–28; Franzmann, 31–39; Lattke, 1:49–69 and 3:XVI–XVII.
2 See Lattke, *Bedeutung*, 1:207–25, esp. 210, 217–20.
3 Ibid., 1:212–16.
4 Otto Eissfeldt, *The Old Testament: An Introduction including the Apocrypha and Pseudepigrapha, and Also the Works of Similar Type from Qumran. The History of the Formation of the Old Testament* (trans. Peter R. Ackroyd; Oxford: Blackwell, 1974) §93 n. 2.
5 Colpe, "Überlieferung," 77.
6 Lattke, *Oden*, 41.
7 In the Coptic version, four you-statements (1b-3a) are framed by two I-statements (1a, 3b).

The speaking "I" of the Syriac Ode identifies itself in 1a as of masculine gender by the use of the Aph. singular masculine participle of ܐܘܕܝ (ʾawdī; cf. the root ܝܕܥ [ydʿ] which is not used in the Pe.). Its gender is unstated in the Coptic and would not have been specified in Greek either. The main problem of 1a, however, is the proper translation of the verb. If "to praise" in the sense of δοξάζω can be excluded,[10] it is also unlikely that it means "to confess" in the sense of ὁμολογέω, because of the following construction with ܠ (l-) + 2nd masculine singular suffix.[11]

So the meanings have been narrowed down to "to give thanks" (εὐχαριστέω + dative) and "to praise" (ἐξομολογέομαι + dative), the latter having arisen from the meanings "confess" and "profess."[12] In both cases ܠ (l-) as preposition would be the "sign of the dative."[13] The Coptic use of ⲟⲩⲱⲛϩ̄ ⲉⲃⲟⲗ (wōnᵉh ebol + first singular pronominal suffix) with future I tense and the preposition ⲛ̄- or ⲛⲁ⸗ denoting the dative serves to exclude "to give thanks" as a possible meaning[14] and, in view of the quotation of Isa 45:23 in Rom 14:11 (ἐξομολογήσεται τῷ θεῷ), strongly suggests "to praise" in the sense of ἐξομολογέομαι.[15] Although ܐܘܕܝ + ܠ (ʾawdī + l-) is the customary translation of εὐχαριστέω + dative,[16] this verse suggests rather the combination "to give thanks and praise," as in Matt 11:25 (ἐξομολογοῦμαί σοι, πάτερ, ܡܘܕܐ ܐܢܐ ܠܟ ܐܒܝ [mawdē-nā lāk̲ ʾāb̲]).

If the context of ℭ most strongly expresses the *praise* aspect, as in a hymn,[17] then 𝔖 stresses a grateful and laudatory *thanks*. Verse 1a is not, however, an actual "doxology"[18] or an "opening doxology."[19]

The justification for 1a is found in 1b, with its conjunctions that correspond to ὅτι. As in 16:3 (𝔖) a connection is established between the love of the speaking "I" for the Lord and its liturgical expression (see Excursus 2). The gender determination by the use of a participle in Syriac was discussed at 1a. Greek would have used a more ambiguous verb form (ἀγαπῶ or φιλῶ, though probably not ἐρῶ or στέργω)[20] in place of the singular masculine participle of the Pe. ܪܚܡ (rḥem). The decided difference between ℭ ("for thou art my God") and 𝔖 ("because I love thee"), which is found again in the first four words of 11a (ℭ), cannot be explained by the context of the *Pistis Sophia*.[21] The variant may be regarded as an early theological commentary, on the justification recorded in the Syriac, or as a witness for a

8 Franzmann, 35.
9 See Lattke, *Bedeutung,* 1:84–85, 218.
10 Contra Frankenberg, 7.
11 Cf. Heb 13:15, where the Greek dative is also expressed in Syriac by the preposition ܠ (l-). In most cases ὁμολογέω κτλ. is translated by ܐܘܕܝ (ʾawdī) + preposition ܒ (b-) (Matt 10:32; Luke 12:8; John 9:22; Acts 23:8; Rom 10:9-10; 1 John 1:9; 2:23; 4:15; Rev 3:5) or by ܐܘܕܝ + ܕ (d-), which corresponds to Greek ὅτι (John 1:20; 1 John 4:2-3; 2 John 7). Occasionally the latter construction is also used for ἐξομολογέομαι ὅτι (Phil 2:11 referring to Isa 45:23 LXX, where the Syriac is closer to the Hebrew than to the Greek).
12 BDAG, *s.v.* ἐξομολογέω, 4; cf. Richard Reitzenstein, *Das iranische Erlösungsmysterium: Religionsgeschichtliche Untersuchungen* (Bonn: Marcus & Weber, 1921) 252.
13 Jessie Payne Smith, ed., *A Compendious Syriac Dictionary* (Oxford: Clarendon, 1903; repr. 1957, 1967) 232.
14 Crum, 487.
15 See Harris and Mingana, 2:230: "It should, however, be noted that if the Coptic is a translation from the Greek, it is certain that we have here the rendering of the Greek ἐξομολογήσομαι exactly as in Gen. xxix.35 and elsewhere. There is, therefore, no difference between the Coptic and the Syriac" (cf. also Ps 17:50 LXX in Rom 15:9). Their translation of 1a 𝔖 is, however, "I will give thanks unto thee, O Lord."
16 Cf. John 11:41; Acts 28:15; Rom 1:8; 1 Cor 1:4, 14; 14:18; Phil 1:3; Phlm 4; Eph 1:16; Col 1:3; 1 Thess 1:2; 2 Thess 1:3; 2:13; Rev 11:17; also Rom 14:6; 16:4; Eph 5:20; Col 1:12; 3:17; 1 Thess 2:13; 5:18.
17 See, e.g., Bauer, *Oden*, 11, "Praise with thanksgiving."
18 See Thomas Söding, "Doxologie I. Biblisch," *LThK*³ 3 (1995) 354.
19 Contra Franzmann, 35.
20 See Lattke, *Einheit,* 16.
21 Neither the speculations nor the text-critical notes of W. H. Worrell ("The Odes of Solomon and the Pistis Sophia," *JTS* 13 [1911–12] 32, 35–36), help to explain these differences; cf. Lattke, *Bedeutung,* 3:122.

different reading in the Greek (ὅτι [σὺ] εἶ θεός μου). That there were such differences between 𝔊 and 𝔖 is confirmed by *Ode* 11.

In another passage, the redeemed "I" declares that its salvation occurs because Truth personified "did not abandon me" (38:4a; cf. 17:11b), but the "I" of *Ode* 5 𝔖 justifies its negatory petition in 2a (Pe. second singular masculine imperfect of ܫܒܩ [*šḇaq*] + first singular accusative suffix with preceding negation) with the statement in 2b that the Most High whom it addresses is "my hope."[22] Since this hope is uniquely directed to God the Lord, that is, to no-thing and no-body in this world (5:10; 40:1; cf. already Ps 145:5b LXX: ἡ ἐλπὶς αὐτοῦ ἐπὶ κύριον τὸν θεὸν αὐτοῦ ["whose hope is in the Lord his God"][23]), the indirect object can in a similarly transcendent fashion be equated with the "Principle of Hope"[24] which is a fundamental "characteristic of [human] existence."[25] In the deutero- and pseudo-Pauline epistles there is a comparable equation of ἐλπίς ("hope") with the μυστήριον . . . , ὅ ἐστιν Χριστὸς ἐν ὑμῖν ("mystery, . . . which is Christ in you") in Col 1:26-27 or the κύριος Χριστὸς Ἰησοῦς ("Lord Christ Jesus") in 1 Tim 1:1-2.

While the New Testament "concept of hope is essentially determined by the Old Testament,"[26] the terms "hope" (ἐλπίς, ܣܒܪܐ [*sabrā*], *Odes* 5:2, 10; 29:1; 40:1) and "to hope" (ܣܒܪ [*sabbar* = ἐλπίζω], *Ode* 42:5) play only a minor part in the *Odes of Solomon*. But the people of the *Odes of Solomon* belonged to the Hellenistic culture and would have known, perhaps through the plays of Sophocles (*Ant.* 615–17), that "ἐλπίς is an ambiguous concept"[27]: ἁ γὰρ δὴ πολύπλαγκτος ἐλπὶς πολλοῖς μὲν ὄνασις ἀνδρῶν, πολλοῖς δ' ἀπάτα κουφονόων ἐρώτων ("For widely wandering hope brings profit to many men, but to many the deception of thoughtless longings" [LCL 2:60–61]). But set against this ambiguity was the conviction, derived from a mixture of Neo-Platonism and "faith in mystery religions," that "ἐλπίς with πίστις, ἀλήθεια and ἔρως [are] the four στοιχεῖα which constitute a genuine life."[28]

Τέσσαρα στοιχεῖα μάλιστα κεκρατύνθω περὶ θεοῦ· πίστις, ἀλήθεια, ἔρως, ἐλπὶς. . . . ἐλπίσι γὰρ ἀγαθαῖς οἱ ἀγαθοὶ τῶν φαύλων ὑπερέχουσι.

Four basic principles are the most important in relation to God: Faith, Truth, Love and Hope. . . . For it is by good hopes that the Good are superior to the Bad." (Porphyry *Marc.* 24.9–14)[29]

This philosophical-ethical tradition, which finds expression at the end of the third century C.E., flows from sources similar to those for the equally formulaic uses of πίστις, ἀγάπη, and ἐλπίς in the New Testament (1 Cor 13:3; 1 Thess 1:3; 5:8; Col 1:4-5; Heb 10:22-24).[30]

For Hellenistic Jews it was evident that the Law of the Lord (νόμος κυρίου)—not God himself[31]—is hope (ἐλπίς) "for all who keep his ways" (*T. Jud.* 26:1).[32] And it was apparent to the hearers and readers of Philo of Alexandria that "he who does not hope in God (ἐπὶ θεὸν ἐλπίζῃ) is not truly human."[33]

22 The fact that ℭ repeats the vocative "Lord" (2a; cf. 1a) instead of using "Most High" is offset by the address "light on high" in the hymn of the *Pistis Sophia* (cf. Lattke, *Bedeutung*, 1:84–85, 218).

23 Rahlfs, 2:160; Brenton, 785.

24 Ernst Bloch, *Das Prinzip Hoffnung*.

25 See *MEL*[9], 30:770, *s.v.* "Existential."

26 Rudolf Bultmann, "ἐλπίς, κτλ.," *ThWNT* 2 (1935) 527; *TDNT* 2:530.

27 Bultmann, "ἐλπίς, κτλ.," *ThWNT* 2:516; *TDNT* 2:519.

28 Bultmann, "ἐλπίς, κτλ.," *ThWNT* 2:517; *TDNT* 2:521.

29 Translated from Walter Pötscher, *Porphyrios, Πρὸς Μαρκέλλαν* (Philosophia antiqua 15; Leiden: Brill, 1969) 28–29.

30 For a discussion "whether Porphyry depends on Paul" or the "possibility of a common source," see Pötscher, *Porphyrios*, 89–95.

31 Contra Bultmann, "ἐλπίς, κτλ.," *ThWNT* 2:526; *TDNT* 2:529.

32 Jürgen Becker, *Die Testamente der zwölf Patriarchen* (JSHRZ 3.1; Gütersloh: Mohn, 1974) 78; cf. *OTP* 1:802. Robert H. Charles (*The Greek Versions of the Testaments of the Twelve Patriarchs* [3rd ed.; Oxford: Clarendon, 1908; repr., Darmstadt: Wissenschaftliche Buchgesellschaft, 1966] 104–5) shows text-critical variants.

33 Bultmann, "ἐλπίς, κτλ.," *ThWNT* 2:526, with references; cf. *TDNT* 5:529–30.

As already noted at 4:13, 3a ܣ is reminiscent of Rom 3:24 (δωρεὰν τῇ αὐτοῦ χάριτι). If χάριν was found in the Greek original of the *Pistis Sophia* and misread as κρίσιν, this would explain the Coptic ϩⲁⲡ (*hap*).[34] On the other hand, the "substitution" of the forensic term "justice"[35] for "grace," a term that occurs very commonly in the *Odes of Solomon* (see on 4:6 above), may be an intentional theological "interpretation."[36] And the same may be true for the contrast between the Syriac first person statement ("I received") and the Coptic second person theological statement ("thou didst give"). In actual content the gracious giving corresponds to the grateful receiving.[37]

That the confident assertion of future salvation of 3b ܣ is found in ℭ as a statement about the past, by use of the perfect I tense,[38] is unsurprising, since it belongs to the emphasis on redemption as already achieved in the *Pistis Sophia* myth of salvation.[39] The reading ⲛⲟⲩϩⲙ̄ (*nuh*ᵉ*m*), used occasionally to translate σῴζεσθαι,[40] may be very important in the quest for the original language of the *Odes of Solomon*. The Syriac translations of the New Testament often use forms of ܚܝܐ (*ḥyā*)[41] to translate the passive of σῴζω ("be saved, attain salvation").[42] So it is quite possible that the Greek word here was σωθήσομαι. The Coptic translation, using ⲛⲟⲩϩⲙ̄ ⲉⲃⲟⲗ, transformed this future tense into a perfect I, while the Syriac correctly and idiomatically used the imperfect of "to live" (cf. 6:18 and Table 1). *Ode* 11 unfortunately offers no examples to study the use of ܚܝܐ (*ḥyā*) and the Ethpe. of ܦܪܩ (*praq*, ʾ*eṯpreq*). In other relevant passages (8:22d; 17:14a; 34:6b; 38:16a), forms of "to live" occur in close proximity to forms of "to be saved" (see Excursus 5 below at 11a).

■ **4-7** The following four bicola, which can be divided into three sections (4, 5-6, 7),[43] are concerned with events in the future, even though the translation of the imperfects (in ܣ) or optatives (in ℭ) can be very difficult.[44] These difficulties arise, in part, from the fact that the "persecutors" in these and other passages (cf. 23:20; 28:8; 42:5, 7) never become tangible. It is also unclear whether these future events are purely mythological or connected with some unidentified historical situation. The extremely mythologizing context of the *Pistis Sophia* is of no help in elucidating or resolving this uncertainty;[45] there both the hymn and the quotation from the *Odes of Solomon* are weighted with mythology.

The question whether the introduction of the persecutors by the indeterminate "I" (4), the detailed description (5-6), and the final malediction (7) contain reminiscences of an actual historical episode of persecution or are only the mythological expression of a Gnostic-dualistic position is transformed by the recognition that this text is shaped by specific linguistic elements dating back to the "Confessions of Jeremiah" (cf. the term רדפי [*rōdĕpay*] in Jer 15:15; 17:18; 20:11) and the "Individual Laments" among the Psalms.[46] In them similar "connotations" of the nominalized masculine plural participle of the root *rdp* with suffix meaning "my persecutors" (from Hebrew רדף [*rādap*]; Syriac ܪܕܦ [*rḏap̄*]) can already be found: "the assumed innocence of the persecuted, the unidentified persecutors and their vaguely described persecutions."[47]

34 See Crum, 694.
35 BDAG, *s.v.* κρίσις, 3.
36 Alv Kragerud, *Die Hymnen der Pistis Sophia* (Oslo: Universitetsforlaget, 1967) 138; cf. Lattke, *Bedeutung*, 1:218.
37 This equivalence is to be distinguished from the indicative-imperative sequence in Matt 10:8 (δωρεὰν ἐλάβετε, δωρεὰν δότε, "You received without paying, give without pay").
38 Till §313.
39 See Lattke, *Bedeutung*, 1:219.
40 See Crum, 243.
41 Payne Smith, 1:1251.
42 BDAG, *s.v.* σῴζω, 2b.
43 Franzmann, 35–36.
44 Literal trans. of 4a-b (ܣ): "Let my persecutors come, but they will not see me." For the idiomatic translation given above see Beyer, *Syntax*, 271–81; cf. Lattke, 3:XVII.
45 See Lattke, *Bedeutung*, 1:84–87, 188–91.
46 Cf. Ps 7:1; 31:16; 69:27; 71:11; 119:150, 157, 161; 143:3 (Christian Frevel, "רָדַף *rāḏap̄*," *ThWAT* 7 [1993] 370; *TDOT* 13:349).
47 Christian Frevel, "רָדַף *rāḏap̄*," *ThWAT* 7 (1993) 371; *TDOT* 13:349–50.

It does not necessarily follow from the use of the optatives in ȼ (4a, 5a-b, 7a-b) that a Greek original would also have had optatives.[48] The first person of the Coptic "Injunctive (also called the Optative)" "corresponds to the cohortative," but the third person acts more like the "jussive," a "subjunctive used imperatively."[49]

The Syriac, except in the relative clause 7bα, which acts as the subject of that colon,[50] uses only imperfects (third plural and singular). In a main clause, this verb form is used for "any reference to the future or the slightest modal colouring."[51] As "the proper form for a wish, request, summons, or command," the first imperfect of the Pe. ܐܬܐ (*ʾetā*) in 4a can be taken as a "mocking request,"[52] but also as a defiant challenge or an ironic invitation from the "I" in the certainty that the persecutors are unable to see it. In this sense of a present certainty directed toward the future and carrying a somewhat negative desire, the verb ܚܙܐ (*ḥzā*) occurs only here in 4b (with 1st singular accusative suffix) and in the first relative clause of 6a.[53]

The bicolon 6a-b is (see below) the central statement of stanza II;[54] but in the background of vv. 5-6 there is undoubtedly a biblical statement, perhaps the imperative of Ps 68:24a LXX (σκοτισθήτωσαν οἱ ὀφθαλμοὶ αὐτῶν τοῦ μὴ βλέπειν "Let their eyes be darkened that they should not see").[55] The term "cloud," whose equivalents in ܣ (ܥܢܢܐ [*ʿnānā*]) and ȼ (ⲕⲗⲟⲟⲗⲉ) are regularly used to translate νεφέλη,[56] is used in the *Odes of Solomon* not only to intensify a negative metaphor such as "darkness" but also in positive metaphors such as "cloud of peace" (35:1) and "cloud of dew" (36:7). The word used for "darkness" (ܥܡܛܢܐ [*ʿamṭānā*]) occurs only here; in all other cases darkness is ܚܫܘܟܐ (*ḥeššōḵā* = σκότος in 11:19; see Excursus 10).[57] Both words are used to translate σκότος, although the *hapax legomenon* used here is also often equated with the rarer γνόφος.[58] In ȼ also the word used for "darkness" is ⲕⲣⲙ̄ⲧⲥ̄ (*krᵉmtᵉs*), with connotations of "mist" or "fog," rather than the commoner ⲕⲁⲕⲉ, which is usually equivalent to σκότος or σκοτία.[59]

Since darkness is not only the opposite of light but can be understood as taking the form of a dark cloud, it can fall on (ܣ) or cover (ȼ) the eyes, "overshadowing" them (cf. Mark 9:7 par., ἐπισκιάζω).[60] In English and German, light, shadows, and darkness can "fall" on a thing or a person. The eyes of the persecutors, as *pars pro toto*, represent the face, seen in the parallelism of "eyes" and "face" in other passages (cf. 11:14; 13:1-2). Both expressions represent their bearers, which is strikingly illustrated by a parallel from *Apoc. Adam* (83:7-8): ⲁⲩⲱ ⲟⲩⲛ̄ ⲟⲩⲕⲗⲟⲟⲗⲉ ⲛ̄ⲕⲁⲕⲉ ⲛ̄ⲛⲏⲩ ⲉϫⲱⲟⲩ ("and a cloud of darkness will come upon them").[61]

Verse 5b partly repeats and partly carries on logically and radically the malediction of 5a. Both versions

48 Contra Frankenberg, 7, who includes the causative infinitives in 4b and 6a: ελθοιεν, ορωιεν (4), επιπεσοι, αμβλυνοι (5), μη γενοιτο (6), παχυνθειη, επιστρεψαιτο (7) [*sic*].

49 Thomas O. Lambdin, *Introduction to Sahidic Coptic* (Macon, GA: Mercer University Press, 1983) 135; *MEL*[9], 31:1395.

50 Franzmann, 35.

51 Nöldeke §266.

52 Ibid.

53 On the Coptic construction with ⲛ̄ϭⲓ (*ᵉnci*) in 4a and 7a, see Till §391: "when the nominative subject follows its verb (including a causative infinitive), the verb receives the pronoun that agrees with the nominative and the subject itself is preceded by the particle ⲛ̄ϭⲓ. . . . This idiom is extremely common."

54 Franzmann, 35.

55 Rahlfs, 2:71; Brenton, 738; see also *OTSy* pt. 2 fasc. 3, on Ps 69:24a.

56 Payne Smith, 2:2924; Crum, 104.

57 See Lattke, 3:354.

58 See Payne Smith, 1:1402; 2:2911. In early Christian writings γνόφος occurs only in Heb 12:18 for "darkness" (BDAG, *s.v.* γνόφος). This series of synonyms, γνόφῳ καὶ ζόφῳ καὶ θυέλλῃ, is clearly dependent on the similar series at the end of Deut 4:11 LXX (σκότος, γνόφος, θύελλα), which is closer to the Hebrew than Exod 10:22 or Deut 5:22(19). That this dependence was recognized quite early is shown by the variant readings correcting ζόφῳ in Heb 12:18 to σκότῳ or σκότει. The commoner word for "darkness" in the *Odes of Solomon*, ܚܫܘܟܐ (*ḥeššōḵā*), is used in the biblical translation for חֹשֶׁךְ (*ḥōšeḵ*) or σκότος (Deut 4:11; cf. *OTSy* pt. 1 fasc. 2, on that verse) as well as for γνόφος (Heb 12:18).

59 Crum, 101, 116; Westendorf, 68. Schmidt and MacDermot, *Pistis Sophia* (p. 114) prefer "smoke" to "darkness."

60 Crum, 659.

61 George W. MacRae, "The Apocalypse of Adam," in Douglas M. Parrott, ed., *Nag Hammadi Codices V, 2-5 and VI with Papyrus Berolinensis 8502, 1 and*

use the Greek word ἀήρ, which would surely also have appeared in the Greek version. But unlike 5a the sequence of words is reversed: 𝔖 has "air of fog" while ℭ uses "fog of the air." The "expressions are influenced by the theophanic language of Ps 18:12 (17:12 LXX) and 2 Sam (2 Kgdms LXX) 22:12, where in addition to σκότος the expression ἐν νεφέλαις ἀέρων (or ἀέρος) is found."[62] Whether 𝔊 had the complete phrase ὁμίχλη τοῦ ἀέρος with a genitive remains in the realm of speculation.[63] It is also uncertain whether the verb forms of ܢܚܫܟ (*ʾaḥšek*, Aph.) and ⲣ̄ⲕⲁⲕⲉ represent a future, subjunctive, or optative of σκοτίζω (cf. Rom 1:21; 11:10).[64]

The central bicolon 6a-b draws the conclusion of the elaborate bicolon 5 and repeats the prohibition of 4b in a variant form (final conjunction ܕ [*d*-] + imperfect), which needs to be translated as an infinitive. "Light" must be taken primarily as "daylight" (cf. 6:17), which is clearly and correctly stated in the Coptic version (6a). The opposition between darkness and light, which also plays an important part in Gnostic-dualistic terminology (see Excursus 10), is thus a familiar event. Dualism does come into play, however, in the contrast between the "I" and his persecutors (4a), who are prevented from "seizing" him in the negative final clause (6b; on ܐܚܕ [*ʾeḥad*], cf. 42:3, where, in the context, it refers to the persecutors of 5a). In ℭ, ⲁⲙⲁϩⲧⲉ (*amahte*) is in the negative future III, which expresses even more clearly that the impotence of the persecutors "is expected with certainty."[65]

The final curse on the persecutors shows a new and malevolent complexion. In fact, the chiastically parallel bicolon 7a-b could almost be the beginning of stanza III. But the *inclusio* formed by the diametrically opposite terms ܐܬܐ (*ʾeṯā*) and ܗܦܟ (*hp̄ak*) in vv. 4a and 7b and the regular change[66] from the imperfect (stanza II) to the perfect (stanza III) put this malediction, according to its form, into stanza II, where its content forms a bridge to stanza III.[67]

The feminine ܬܪܥܝܬܐ (*tarʿīṯā*), translated as "counsel," which includes the intentionality of the Coptic ϣⲟϫⲛⲉ (*šočne*),[68] is a synonym of the commoner ܡܚܫܒܬܐ (*maḥšaḇṯā*) and equally of the rarer ܪܥܝܢܐ (*reʿyānā*), which is derived from ܪܥܐ (*rʿā*), as is the word used here and in 8a (see Excursus 9).[69] These synonyms are only rarely used in a negative sense (cf., besides 5:7-8 relating to the persecutors, 23:19 and 24:10; also perhaps 29:8, but esp. 28:14 and finally 38:13). The mind of the nearly intangible persecutors, their cunning plans and wicked schemes,[70] and in the end even the bodily organs of the spirit ("heart and brain") are threatened by something that can be interpreted as a swelling, callosity, or tumor.[71]

The literary source of the predictive curse in 7a is to be found in the threat of Ps 7:17a (ἐπιστρέψει ὁ πόνος αὐτοῦ εἰς κεφαλὴν αὐτοῦ, "his trouble shall return on his own head"), since "the echoes of the Psalmist's vocabulary" are especially frequent in *Ode* 5: "the idea that the schemes of the opponents will rebound on them is found also in the Psalms"[72] (in addition to Ps 7:17, see Pss 9:16; 35:8 [LXX 34:8]; 54:7 [LXX 53:7]). The word "heads," found again in the plural only in 22:5 ("seven-headed dragon"), is elsewhere used only in the singular

4 (NHS 11; Leiden: Brill, 1979) 188–89; cf. *NHLE*, 285.

62 Lattke, *Oden*, 101.

63 See Lattke, "Wörter," 287 = idem, *Bedeutung*, 4:135; Payne Smith, 2:2995.

64 Payne Smith, 1:1401; Crum, 101, 116.

65 Till §§308–9; on the numerous possible equivalent verbs in Greek, see Crum, 9–10.

66 Though 7bα has an Ethpa. perfect, as noted above.

67 See Franzmann, 36; but the chiasmus is A B || B' A', not "A B C || C' B' A'."

68 See Westendorf, 342 "plan, intention, scheme."

69 Payne Smith, 2:3942.

70 On the Ethpa. of ܚܟܡ (*ḥkam*), used *malo sensu*, see Payne Smith, 1:1266; on σοφίζομαι, see BDAG, *s.v.* σοφίζω, 2.

71 See Payne Smith, 2:2765: *tumor, apostema*, φλεγμονή, φλέγμα, πώροσις. Harris and Mingana's (2:231) translation of this plural by "thick darkness" and their remarks relating apparently to it and not to v. 5—especially that this word "must be registered in any future Syriac dictionary"—must clearly be reconsidered.

72 Bauer, 582. Hermann Gunkel and Joachim Begrich (*Einleitung in die Psalmen: Die Gattungen der religiösen Lyrik Israels* [4th ed; Göttingen: Vandenhoeck & Ruprecht, 1985] 6; ET: *Introduction to the Psalms: The Genres of the Religious Lyric of Israel* [trans. James M. Nogalski; Macon, Ga.: Mercer University Press, 1998]) also emphasize for *Ode* 5, among others, the "influence of older literary forms" on the *Odes of Solomon*, which "were composed in the 2nd century A.D. by a 'Gnostically' inclined Christian of Jewish ancestry."

and represents, of course, the persons of the persecutors as a whole, which the Coptic version sets out correctly.

This curse is the opposite of Matt 5:44 and Rom 12:14 which express "solidarity with God's creatures above the abyss of earthly enmity."[73]

■ **8-9** The two parallel bicola of stanza III—though ℭ offers an additional colon (8c, on which see below)—are closely connected with stanza II, picking up the key term "counsel, schemes" from 7a. Because of the parallelism of vv. 8 and 9 (rather than of 8a and 8b, 9a and 9b),[74] even the colorless-sounding colon 8a must be taken negatively.[75] But here also the past events remain quite unclear (see on stanza II above). Even the outlines of the speaker cannot be seen. All that can be deduced from this poetic tale in the third person perfect (𝔖) is a hostile and finally unsuccessful conspiracy of the "persecutors" (cf. 4a).

While the identification of the Greek verb used in 8a must remain speculative,[76] it is clear that the (untranslatable) clause 8b, in both languages, must represent a Greek construction like οὐκ ἐγένετο αὐτοῖς.[77] So the Syriac combination ܗܘܬ (*hwāṯ*, feminine like *tarʿīṯā*) with ܠ (*l-*) is not used for "to have," as it would normally be; it means "become," "occur" (+ dative). But it cannot be interpreted as "to be granted," in contrast to Matt 18:19 and John 15:7 (cf. Mark 11:24).[78] The negation, which in ℭ is expressed by the negative perfect I, makes it necessary to consider rather a nonconvertibility, a nonsuccessfulness.

As already mentioned, 8c is found only in ℭ. This may mean that a Gnostic gloss made its way from the Coptic *Pistis Sophia* context into the quoted Ode because of the key word "power" (ϭοм [*com*]).[79] But it is equally possible, even probable, that this extra colon was already in the Greek text used for the Coptic translation. The Greek version of *Ode* 11 (*P. Bodmer* XI), which may, of course, be quite different from that in the manuscript used by the Coptic translator, also records verses that are not represented in 𝔖, viz., 11:16c-h, 22b. The impersonal construction with the use of the perfect I in the main clause ("they defeated them" = "they were defeated")[80] is continued by a concessional *Umstandssatz* expressing simultaneity,[81] which refers to the third plural personal suffix[82] of the preposition ε- (*stat. pronominalis* ερο⸗), and admits that the persecutors were powerful,[83] although they were defeated.

The vague story of past occurrences moves forward in 9a with the use in ℭ of the Greek loanword κακῶς, which corresponds exactly to the *hapax legomenon* ܒܝܫܐܝܬ (*bīšāʾīt*) in 𝔖, from plotting to the actual preparation for the evil deed or deeds.[84] The marked difference between the Syriac and the Coptic of 9b may be explained by the fact that 8c does not occur in 𝔖, which made it necessary to enhance the parallelism between

73 Ernst Käsemann, *An die Römer* (HNT 8a; 4th ed.; Tübingen: Mohr Siebeck, 1980) 335 (ET, *Commentary on Romans* [London: SCM, 1980] 347 [translator disagrees]). Despite superficial similarities, this malediction on the foe is not identical with the cry of Matt 27:25 ("his blood be on us and on our children"), which "has caused calamitous misunderstandings" (Joachim Gnilka, *Das Matthäusevangelium* [2 vols.; HThKNT 1.1–2; Freiburg: Herder, 1986–88] 2:458–59) in so much later history.

74 Contra Franzmann, 36.

75 See Payne Smith, 1:1395 (ܐܬܚܫܒ ܬܪܥܝܬܐ ܒܝܫܬܐ, *pessimam sententiam excogitavit* [*Act. Mart.* 1.246]). The *Odes of Solomon* may have influenced the Syriac *Acts of Martyrs*.

76 See Payne Smith, 1:1395, on the Ethpa. of ܚܫܒ (*ḥšaḇ*), and Crum, 162, on the stat. pron. of мокмεк.

77 Frankenberg, 7. Literal trans. of 8a-9b (𝔖): "For they have devised a plan, and it was not [came to nothing] for them. They prepared themselves maliciously, and were found to be impotent." For the idiomatic translation given above, see again Lattke, 3:XVII.

78 Commentaries on the verses mentioned hardly discuss these expressions.

79 See Lattke, *Bedeutung*, 1:86–87, 188–89.

80 The Greek original of ϫρο ερο⸗ (Crum, 783) may have been καταγωνίζομαι (BDAG, *s.v.* καταγωνίζομαι, "conquer, defeat, overcome").

81 See Till §§329, 425. The following translation is so free that it may be called erroneous: "And the powerful have been overwhelmed" (Franzmann, 34). Better are, e.g., ". . . although they were powerful" (Worrell, 36); and "Powerful as they were, . . ." (Harris and Mingana, 2:230).

82 In my concordance (Lattke, *Bedeutung*, 2:40) two headwords were left incomplete and need to be amended: "–c (3. sing. f.)," "–oγ (3. plur.)."

83 Crum, 815, 820.

84 On the Ethpa. of ܥܬܕ (*ʿṯaḏ*), see Payne Smith, 2:3009; for the possible Greek equivalent of coвтε see Crum, 323.

vv. 9a-b and 8a-b. Thus, the text of ℭ "appears to be the original form," since the colon (or even bicolon) 8c is parallel to 8a-b while 9a-b becomes parallel to 7b.[85]

The singulars in the English translation ("what," "has") are plurals in the Coptic original. In 𝔖 the use of the Ethpe. of ܐܫܟܚ (*ʾeškaḥ* ["to find"]) here contrasts with that in 8:23, where the redeemed are "found incorrupted in all aeons/eternity." The adjective ܣܪܝܩܐ (*srīqā*), which is also used as a noun, probably corresponds to μάταιος (11:8; cf. also 17:3 and 18:12).

Even if stanza III "seems to be historical, rather than general or indefinite,"[86] the linguistic form follows the literary pattern of Ps 20:12 LXX (ὅτι ἔκλιναν εἰς σὲ κακά, διελογίσαντο βουλήν, ἣν οὐ μὴ δύνωνται στῆσαι, "For they intended evils against thee; they imagined a device which they shall by no means be able to perform"),[87] and perhaps also of *4 Esdras* 7:22-24, "a poetic indictment of the wicked,"[88] esp. 7:22b-23a ("they devised for themselves vain thoughts, and proposed to themselves wicked frauds").

■ **10-15** The speaking "I" reappears, as does the Lord, who is not, however, directly addressed, as he was in stanza I, but is one of the main soteriological themes of stanza IV in company with the speaker's consistent trust in salvation. Formally stanza IV is subdivided into three strophes, whose highly parallel bicola become successively fewer (10-12 [3]; 13-14 [2]; 15 [1]).[89]

The incomplete Coptic version should be divided like the Syriac as far as it is preserved, rather than being separated into stanzas IV (10a-b) and V (11a), as Franzmann does.[90] There is a mistake in the quotation of this Ode in the *Pistis Sophia*. Instead of continuing with the text of 5:11b-15, which both the hymn and the myth of the main work presuppose, the copy has *Ode* 1:1-5. The reason for this *felix confusio*, without which there would be no trace of *Ode* 1 (= *Ode* 19 in a collection of the eighteen *Psalms* and forty-two *Odes of Solomon*), may be found in the wording of 5:12a, which is very close to that of 1:1a.[91]

The text of Ps 145:5b LXX quoted at 2b is even more relevant to v. 10a, where ℭ actually uses the Greek loan word ἐλπίς ("hope"). The two prepositions ܥܠ (*ʿal*) in 𝔖 and ϩⲛ̄ (*hᵉn*) in ℭ refer, like ἐπί,[92] to position in their basic meaning but in a metaphorical sense can mean founded or resting "on."[93]

The statement of future confidence, which most probably reflects an absolute use of φοβέομαι,[94] is quite radical in its hope for the coming rescue from existential fear and bases this not-fear on the trust that no-thing and no-body in this world but God alone (ℭ) is the Lord who is the ultimate "Savior" (ℭ) and also "salvation" (𝔖). The Greek loanword σωτήρ in the *Pistis Sophia* may derive from the LXX or be part of the transition from the hymn to the quotation;[95] the core meaning of ܦܘܪܩܢܐ (*purqānā*, masculine) most probably represents the Greek noun σωτηρία (11:3).

Excursus 5: "Save," "Salvation," and "Savior" in the *Odes of Solomon*

This excursus, unlike my essay "Sammlung durchs Wort: Erlöser, Erlösung und Erlöste im Johannesevangelium,"[96] which was in a sense a summary of my *Einheit im Wort*, will not deal with all the

85 Worrell, 36.
86 Ibid., 35.
87 Rahlfs, 2:19; Brenton, 709.
88 Michael Edward Stone, *Fourth Ezra: A Commentary on the Book of Fourth Ezra* (ed. Frank Moore Cross; Hermeneia; Minneapolis: Fortress, 1990) 191–92.
89 See the detailed discussion in Franzmann, 36–37.
90 Ibid., 39.
91 See Lattke, *Bedeutung*, 1:216–17, 219–20. I am not prepared to assert that the "Library of the Gnostic" would have contained one "book" in which the "Psalms of Solomon" and the "Odes of Solomon" were preceded by the "Psalms of David" (as Alv Kragerud, *Pistis Sophia*, 100–101, suggests). It would have been a very voluminous papyrus or parchment codex.
92 BDAG, *s.v.* ἐπί.
93 Nöldeke §250.
94 BDAG, *s.v.* φοβέω, 1.
95 See Lattke, *Bedeutung*, 1:190–91: ⲡⲁⲛⲟⲩⲧⲉ ⲁⲩⲱ ⲡⲁⲥⲱⲧⲏⲣ ⲕⲁⲧⲁ ⲡϫⲓⲥⲉ—"my God and my Savior according to the height."
96 Michael Lattke, "Sammlung durchs Wort: Erlöser, Erlösung und Erlöste im Johannesevangelium," *BK* 30 (1975) 118–22.

statements of salvation[97] in the *Odes of Solomon*,[98] but mainly with the occurrences of the Greek words σωτήρ and σωτηρία,[99] the Coptic verb ⲛⲟⲩϩⲙ̄ (*nuh^e^m*),[100] and especially the words derived from the Semitic root ܦܪܩ (*prq*).[101] The commonest of these derivatives are the Ethpe. ܐܬܦܪܩ (*ʾetpreq*), with the soteriological meanings *salvatus, redemptus, liberatus est*,[102] and the noun ܦܘܪܩܢܐ (*purqānā*), which corresponds to σωτηρία at 11:3. The noun ܦܪܘܩܐ (*pārōqā*), which occurs twice, probably equates to Greek σωτήρ (41:11; 42:18), which is found as a loanword in ℭ (5:11). In this verse, however, 𝔖 uses the more usual noun. This need be no surprise, since metonymically σωτηρία stands for σωτήρ. The Pe. ܦܪܩ (*praq*) is rare, occurring twice in the perfect (24:4; unspecified 38:2) and once each as an imperfect (31:12) and a passive participle (8:22).

The Coptic ⲛⲟⲩϩⲙ̄ (25:4; cf. 25:2) corresponds to the Pe. ܦܪܩ (*prq*).[103] In a single case, ⲛⲟⲩϩⲙ̄ ⲉⲃⲟⲗ corresponds to the Ethpa. ܐܬܦܠܛ (*ʾetpallaṭ*) and signifies an already accomplished liberation or freeing from bonds. In the two remaining occurrences of ⲛⲟⲩϩⲙ̄ ⲉⲃⲟⲗ (5:3) and ⲛⲟⲩϩⲙ̄ (6:18), 𝔖 uses ܚܝܐ (*ḥyā*). The reason for this variation may be that the Greek text did not use ζάω but the passive of σῴζω, for which Syriac translations of the New Testament often substitute "to live," making a stronger soteriological point. At the end of this linguistic survey the unique use of the Ethpa. ܐܬܦܪܩ (*ʾetparraq*) to describe a movement from one place to another may be mentioned (35:7c). The context (35:2) serves to relate this movement to the salvation of the speaker.

The frequent translation of this group of words by "to save" and the like does not mean exclusion of the word groups "deliver, deliverer, deliverance," "redeem, redeemer, redemption."[104] Since the usage in the *Odes of Solomon* is limited to theological and soteriological meanings, the term "salvation" with its connotations of "away from" (Ger. *von-her*) and "toward" (Ger. *auf-hin*) seems more helpful in defining the specific place in religious history of this text, which, despite its Jewish-Gnostic-Christian syncretism, is relatively unitary, rather than striving for a general understanding of a whole class of so-called *Erlösungsreligionen* ("redemptive faiths").[105]

97 See the inventory of "salvation motifs" in Hamilton Hess, "Salvation motifs in the Odes of Solomon," *StPatr* 20 [1989] 184. He excludes the material discussed here because "[t]he noun 'salvation' (ܦܘܪܩܢܐ), which occurs sixteen times in the Odes, and the verb to save or 'redeem' (ܦܪܩ), which occurs seventeen times, are not included in the listings because they are simply generic to the complete range of the divine saving activity." Juan Peter Miranda's overgeneralized statement, "Salvation is understood purely Gnostically," can be accepted only partially (*Der Vater, der mich gesandt hat: Religionsgeschichtliche Untersuchungen zu den johanneischen Sendungsformeln. Zugleich ein Beitrag zur johanneischen Christologie und Ekklesiologie* (Europäische Hochschulschriften, Reihe 23: Theologie 7; Bern/Frankfurt: Lang, 1972). See more fully Lattke, *Bedeutung*, 3:302–3.

98 See Lattke, *Oden*, 84–86.

99 BDAG, *s.vv.* σωτήρ and σωτηρία. Other Greek words that may be behind the Coptic or Syriac text will be considered in the appropriate places.

100 Crum, 243–44.

101 Payne Smith, 2:3293–94; Koehler and Baumgartner, 3:915–16. In the Old Testament the rare occurrences of פרק (cf. Friedrich Reiterer, "פָּרַק *pāraq*," *ThWAT* 6 [1989] 770; *TDOT* 12:112) are not translated by σῴζειν etc. (cf. Hatch and Redpath, 1328–32). Where the LXX uses words beginning σω- they normally represent words derived from a root *yšʿ*, which in Syriac is used only for the name Jesus (ܝܫܘܥ [*Yeššūʿ*]). It would be a worthwhile piece of research to establish how consistently the Syriac Bible translations represent *yšʿ*-derived words by *prq*-derived words.

102 Brockelmann, *Lexicon*, 606.

103 ⲥⲱⲧⲉ in 22:8 may also be translated by "save." The Syriac of this verse has the *hapax legomenon* ܓܒܝ (*gabbī*), "elect."

104 See Werner Foerster and Georg Fohrer, "σῴζω, κτλ.," *ThWNT* 7 (1964) 966–1024; *TDNT* 7:965–1024.

105 Cf. Carsten Colpe, "Erlösungsreligion," *HRWG* 2 (1990) 323–29. "Salvation" ("redemption"), according to Benjamin Wisner Bacon ("The Odes of the Lord's Rest," *Exp* 8th Ser., 1 [1911] 206–7), and especially Rudolf Abramowski ("Der Christus der Salomooden," *ZNW* 35 [1936] 44–69), is the dominant theme of the *Odes of Solomon* (cf. Lattke, "Bildersprache," 103, 106–7 = *Bedeutung*, 4:28, 33–34). Walter Rebell even calls it an "enthusiastic consciousness of salvation" (*Neutestamentliche Apokrypen und Apostolische Väter* [Munich: Kaiser, 1992] 80). Cf. the collection of "redeemer" parallels in Jack Thomas Sanders, *The New Testament Christological Hymns: Their Historical Religious Background* (SNTSMS 15; Cambridge: Cambridge University Press, 1971) 101–4. For a critique of the specific interpretation of "salvation" as the central theme of the *Odes of Solomon* by Leonhard Goppelt (*Christentum und Judentum im ersten und zweiten Jahrhundert: Ein Aufriß der Urgeschichte der Kirche*

In attempting to put in order these statements, which are distributed fairly evenly through more than half of the *Odes of Solomon*, a beginning can be made with the ones in which God as Redeemer or cause of redemption is contrasted with human beings, who are or are to be redeemed and who are spoken of in the third person (singular or plural). This immediately brings up two statements of salvation (19:11; 26:9) that do not fit into the picture. If 19:11a does not need emendation, the statement "she [viz., the mother] loved in/with salvation" remains difficult, even if it is accepted that "salvation" and parallel terms like "revelation" are not causally connected to the female subject. In 26:9 the rhetorical question implies that it is impossible to save oneself. At the same time, the term "life" is introduced as a parallel or even a synonym, and that also has an explanatory function in the two remaining statements of this group. In 6:18, the eternal "redemption" (ℭ and most probably 𝔊 also) is mediated by the water of life (ℭ)/the living water (𝔖). The redemption that the Lord established in 40:5 can be inscribed on the credit side (as a surplus) in the form of "immortal life," whose recipients are "incorruptible" (40:6).

In a second group of statements, those who are to receive salvation are addressed in the second person plural. Some of these statements belong to the wider class of "imperatives of salvation." The injunctions "listen to me" (33:10), "believe and live" (34:6b), are parallel to "and be saved,"[106] and there is the invitation to the redeemed to "abide" in the redeemed Redeemer (8:22). The last of the imperatives of salvation combines the paired invitations "be strong and be redeemed" with the key term "grace" (9:5), which also informs the promise of salvation in 33:11a and the statement of salvation in 34:6a (see below on 25:4, where ℭ uses the Greek loanword χάρις). The statement that the victory, written in God's book and semipersonified, "wills that you are to be saved" (9:12) is both singular and puzzling.

One example of the previous group (33:10-11) also belongs among the statements in which the speaking "I" is the active subject of redemption. Grace personified is the speaker in this case, but in general the redeeming "I" is to be identified as the redeemed Redeemer. In these utterances the redeemed appear as the object (third person) of his activity (10:6; 17:4; 31:12) and the soteriological verb "to live" (17:14) as well as the Redeemer's own "life" (10:6) again qualify redemption. The description of the "people" that is to be saved (31:12) as "seed/offspring" is likely to have influenced the term "new nation" in *Barn.* 5:7 (λαὸν τὸν καινόν).[107]

Before turning to the large number of cases in which the speaking "I" reveals itself as saved or as a recipient of salvation, it will be necessary to look at a number of "we" statements. Among these, the strong hand of the Lord, who is addressed as God, may "set our salvation to victory" (18:7). But also the "Savior," once brought low and then raised up, distinguished both from the "Most High" and the "Father," may be the one "who gives life and does not reject our souls" (41:11-13). In its context the bicolon (42:18) "may we also be saved with thee, because thou art our Savior" summarizes both the "away from," or rather "out of," aspect of salvation and also the myth of the redeemed Redeemer.

The final group needs subdivision. First comes the smaller number of cases in which the redeemed "I" itself plays the part of the Redeemer. In other words the redeemed Redeemer not only occurs in the third person, but takes the stage himself as the speaking "I." Just as 7:16a, which has not yet been discussed, speaks quite clearly near the end of the first half of that Ode about the redemption of the Son by the Creator-Father (and see on 8:22 above), so the "I" of 15:6-9 and 17:2-4 shows unmistakably the "identity of *salvator* and *salvandus*"[108] which is so hotly contested in the history of religion. Salvation is here characterized, on the one hand, by departure and liberation, and almost identified, on the other, with justification and imperishability.

In the remaining instances of this kind it must be noted (1) that the redeemed "I" may differ from case

[BFCThM 55; Gütersloh: Mohn, 1954] 195–96), see Lattke, *Bedeutung*, 3:235–36. Readers of Spanish may refer to the (thus far unpublished) dissertation by Xavier Alegre, "El concepto de salvación en las Odas de Salomon: Contribución al estudio de una soteriología gnostizante y sus posibles relaciones con el cuarto evangelio" (Dr. theol. diss., Münster University, 1977); cf. Lattke, *Bedeutung*, 3:326. See also A. Peral and X. Alegre, "Odas de Salomon," in Alejandro Díez Macho, ed., with contributions by Maria Angeles Navarro, Alfonso de la Fuente, and Antonio Piñero, *Apócrifos del Antiguo Testamento* (3 vols.; Madrid: Ediciones Cristiandad, 1982) 3:64 ("La salvación es el tema central de los OdSl").

106 Cf. the idiomatic translation of 34:6b: "Believe, then you shall live and be saved."

107 Cf. Lattke, *Oden*, 31. See also Introduction 4.2.5 above.

108 Carsten Colpe, *Die religionsgeschichtliche Schule: Darstellung und Kritik ihres Bildes vom gnostischen Erlösermythus* (FRLANT 78 = N.F. 60; Göttingen: Vandenhoeck & Ruprecht, 1961) 180–81, on which cf. Lattke, *Bedeutung*, 3:256.

to case; (2) that the "I" need not be identical with the author of any given Ode; and (3) that this means that hearers and readers can identify with this redeemed "I." Some utterances in this final group use ܠ (*l-*) to express salvation as a "*product* or *result*,"[109] "and his circumcision [of the heart] was salvation for me" (11:3 ܣ; cf. ἐγένετό μοι εἰς σωτηρίαν ἡ περιτομὴ αὐτοῦ in 𝔊). In 38:3 Codex N lets the speaking "I" say, "she [i.e., Truth personified] became for me a haven of salvation." The reading in Codex H belongs to the Syriac expressions that avoid the use of a preposition and treat "salvation" as the "predicative nominative,"[110] in a similar way to the Greek, and have it refer to the subject "cloud of peace" (35:1-2) and paradoxically to "oppression" (28:10).

The remaining instances are difficult to classify. To start with, some express redemption in the form of a verb; there is the confident expression of salvation to come in 14:5 ("and because of thy name I will be saved from the Evil One") reminiscent of the first and last petitions of the Lord's Prayer (cf. Matt 6:9, 13). Comparison with the Syriac translation of Matt 6:13 shows that the Greek of *Ode* 14 need not have used any form of ῥύομαι, which in the Lord's Prayer is translated as the Pa. ܦܨܝ (*paṣṣī*).[111] If "countenance" (πρόσωπον) represents the entire person, the statement of salvation couched in direct address, "it [i.e., the Lord's countenance] saved me by thy grace," is not difficult to interpret (25:4; on the key word "grace," see 9:5; 33:11; 34:6). *Ode* 38:2 is out of the picture (ܦܪܩ [*praq*] in the sense of "keep away"), so the last of the statements that treat redemption as a verb makes it parallel to the other two high points "established/made fast" and "lived" (38:16; see on 40:5 above).

The noun "salvation" is twice employed by the speaking "I." In the first case it says that the Lord "cast my bonds from me" and as a "helper lifted me up to his compassion and his salvation" (21:1-2). In the second, the "I" addresses God directly, mentioning freedom from "my chains" and declaring "thou wert the right hand of salvation and *my* helper" (25:1-2, where ℭ uses the verb form ⲛⲟⲩϩⲙ̄).

This completes the circuit to the text under consideration. The problem in 5:3 (ܣ "I shall live"; ℭ "I have been saved") has already been considered. The final "I"-statement is 5:11a, where the Coptic quotation ends abruptly with the Greek loanword σωτήρ and the Syriac text metonymically describes the Lord as "my salvation."

The confident expression of the statement of salvation (10-12) shows the influence of Ps 146:5b (Ps 145:5b LXX; cf. on 2b above), but also of other verses in the Psalms, e.g., Ps 26:1 LXX: Κύριος φωτισμός μου καὶ σωτήρ μου· τίνα φοβηθήσομαι; ("The Lord is my light and my Savior; whom shall I fear?").[112] The Syriac translation of Ps 27:1a from the Hebrew is closer to the Syriac of this *Ode*,[113] while σωτήρ in ℭ betrays the influence of the LXX.

Although 12a is nearly identical with 1:1a, the first colon of the *Odes of Solomon* that has been preserved, the contrast between the simile of the Lord as a wreath with the nearly apocalyptic motif of being "disturbed" (cf. 24:3; 35:3) makes a proper interpretation difficult. Comparison with the Psalms quoted above might suggest that the simile depicts a crown of light (cf. Hebrew אוֹר, Syriac ܢܘܗܪܐ, Greek φωτισμός). More probably, though, considering the parallelism between "salvation" and "wreath" (5:11-12; 17:1-2),[114] the reference is to the soteriological "crown of life," which may or may not also be a martyr's crown.[115] The following strophes reinforce this opinion.

The speaking "I" in its consciousness of salvation positions itself in 13 against cataclysm and convulsion by the use of the Ethpe./Ettaph. ܐܬܬܙܝܥ (*ʾettzīʿ*), which connects 12b to 13a and corresponds to a passive form of σαλεύω or σείω[116] (cf. 31:10-11 where the Redeemer speaks similarly of himself). The masculine "I" emphasizes this claim by placing the personal pronoun at the beginning, even though it recurs enclitically attached to the adjective ܩܝܡ (*qayyām*),[117] from the root ܩܘܡ (*qwm*, *qām*), which means *durans, permanens, reliquus, vivus*.[118] The formulation of vv. 12-13 is also likely to have been influenced by a Psalm, viz., Ps 29:7b LXX: Οὐ μὴ σαλευθῶ εἰς τὸν αἰῶνα ("I shall never be moved").[119]

109 Carl Brockelmann, *Grundriss der vergleichenden Grammatik der semitischen Sprachen* (2 vols.; Berlin: Reuther & Reichard, 1908–13; repr., Hildesheim: Olms, 1982) 2:382.
110 BDF and BDR §145.
111 See Payne Smith, 2:3206.
112 Rahlfs, 2:24; Brenton, 712.
113 See *OTSy* pt 2 fasc 3, on Ps 27:1a (ܦܘܪܩܢ and ܐܚܘܝ).
114 On this "word-pair," see Franzmann, 37, 405.
115 See Payne Smith, 1:1732 (ܟܠܝܠܐ ܕܚܝܐ [*klīlā d-ḥayyē*]).
116 Payne Smith, 1:1106; BDAG, *s.vv.* σαλεύω and σείω.
117 See Nöldeke §312 B and C.
118 Brockelmann, *Lexicon*, 654.

The Syriac of Ps 30:7b after all has ܐܙܘܥ,[120] which is derived from ܙܥ (*zāʿ*).

Verse 14a-b rephrases the assurance of salvation of 13a-b. These bicola are a very close parallel; indeed, they use identical words in several places (a redundant ܘ [*w-*] + conditional conjunction ܐܢ [*ʾen*]; ܡܕܡ [*meddem*]; the first person singular pronoun ܐܢܐ [*ʾena*] placed emphatically at the beginning). The imperfect of ܐܒܕ (*ʾebad*), a verb that belongs among the words expressing misfortune (see Excursus 28), is parallel to the imperfect of the verb "to be disturbed." The affirmative statement of 13a corresponds to the negation of the future "I shall die" in 14a. The universalizing terms "everything" (13a) and "all that is seen" (14a) explain each other and refer to the infinite world, in part knowable and able to be experienced but in part able to be investigated only in principle, together with all its material phenomena and its laws.

The concluding statement of salvation exhibits the reciprocity characteristic of the *Odes*[121] and is a strophe in its own right.[122] It opens with the dependent clause 15a, in which the speaking "I" declares the reason for the emphatically placed main clause. That is also the reason why the particle ܘ (*w-*), which is so often used redundantly, should be translated by "also" rather than "and" in 15b. The direct *address* of the two Psalms, which acted as models,[123] becomes, in the mouth of the speaking "I," a *declaration* of his unity with the Lord. A parallel content is found in *2 Apoc. Jas.* 63, 19–21: ϫⲉ ϯⲟⲛ̄ϩ ⲁⲛⲟⲕ ϩⲣⲁϊ ϩⲏⲧⲕ̄· ϥⲟⲛ̄ϩ ⲛ̄ϩⲏⲧ ⲛ̄ϭⲓ ⲡⲉⲕϩⲙⲟⲧ ("Because I am alive in you, your grace is alive in me").[124]

When this nonmystical union with the Lord of All, whether ordered or chaotic and of humankind redeemed by liberation from all other powers is proclaimed, the quintessential hope (2b, 10a) reaches its goal, not to become "as gods"[125] or to achieve "the deification of the human soul"[126] in any "theosophical sense,"[127] but to be truly human.

119 Rahlfs, 2:27; Brenton, 714.

120 See *OTSy* pt 2 fasc 3, on Ps 30:7b.

121 Cf. 3:2c-3, 7-9; 4:7; 8:10-11, 20c-23; 9:1-2; 18:9-10.

122 As Franzmann (p. 32) correctly observes, although her translation and division of 15a-b is inconsistent. The bicolon can certainly be described as a "confessional statement" and its content related to 1a-2a (Franzmann, 37).

123 Psalm 22:4b LXX (*οὐ φοβηθήσομαι κακά, ὅτι σὺ μετ᾽ ἐμοῦ εἶ*, "I will not be afraid of evils: for thou art with me") and Ps 72:23a LXX (*καὶ ἐγὼ διὰ παντὸς μετὰ σοῦ*, "Yet I am continually with thee"); Rahlfs, 2:21, 77; Brenton, 710, 741.

124 *NHLE*, 276; Wolf-Peter Funk, *Die zweite Apokalypse des Jakobus aus Nag-Hammadi-Codex V* (TU 119; Berlin: Akademie, 1976) 48–49. See n. 1 in Funk's commentary (p. 188): "It is quite clear from the parallelism that 'Grace' is identified with God and therefore simply means 'the Divine'. . . . The reciprocal formula—long ago deracinated from its mystical origin—has many variations. In addition to 'Christ' and the 'Spirit' one may find God himself *Gos. Truth* 42,26–28; *Odes Sol.* 5:15; the 'name of the Father' *Gos. Truth* 38,29–32."

125 Cf., in contrast, the following quotation from Hermann Hesse, *Der Steppenwolf* (Suhrkamp Taschenbuch 175; 2nd ed.; Frankfurt am Main: Suhrkamp, 1975) 72: "Gottwerden (Becoming a god [my trans.]) bedeutet: seine Seele so erweitert haben, daß sie das All wieder zu umfassen vermag" (means the expansion of the soul until it is able once more to embrace the All [trans. Basil Creighton]).

126 Georg Beer, "Pseudepigraphen des AT.s," *RE* 24 (1913) 377.

127 Georg Beer, "Salomo-Oden," PW, 2. Reihe, 1.2 (1920) 2000.

6

Ode 6: Spirit and *Gnōsis* of the Lord, Myth of the River, Parable of the Water of Life

Syriac (s)

(I) 1a As the wind blows through the cithara
1b and the strings speak,
2a so the Spirit of the Lord speaks in my members,
2b and I speak by/in his love.

(II) 3a For he destroys what is alien,
3b and everything is of the Lord.
4a For so it was from the beginning
4b and until the end,
5a that there should be nothing opposing
5b and nothing standing against him.

(III) 6a The Lord increased his knowledge,
6b and he was zealous that those might be known
6c that were added to us by his grace.
7a And he gave us his praise for his name:
7b our spirits praise his holy Spirit.

(IV) 8a A rivulet issued forth and became a great and wide river,
8b and it flooded everything and shattered and carried it to the temple.
9a And the restraints of men could not restrain it,
9b not even the skills of those who restrain water.
10 For it spread over the face of all the earth and inundated everything.

(V) 11a And all the thirsty upon the earth drank,
11b and thirst was stilled and quenched,
12 for from the Most High the drink was offered.

(VI) 13a Blessed, therefore, are the ministers of that drink,
13b those who have been entrusted with his water.
14a They have revived the parched lips
14b and raised up the will that was paralyzed,
15 and the souls that were near to expiring they held back from death,
16 and limbs that had fallen, they straightened and set upright.
17 They gave strength to their coming and light to their eyes.

(VII) 18a Because everyone knew them by/in the Lord
18b they also lived because of the ever-living water.
Hallelujah

Coptic (ℭ)

(IV) 8a An emanation came forth and became a great, broad river.
8b It dragged everything along and turned toward the temple.
9a They could not restrain it by fortifications and constructions,
9b and the skills of those who dam up water could not halt it.
10 It was brought over the whole earth, and took hold of everything.
(V) 11a They drank who were on the dry sand:
11b their thirst was stilled and quenched,
12 when they were offered the drink from the Most High.
(VI) 13a Blessed are the ministers of that drink,
13b to whom has been entrusted the water of the Lord.
14a They have revived the lips that were parched,
14b and those who were drained received joy of heart.
15 They have taken hold of souls that were expiring, that they might not die.
16 They have set upright limbs that had fallen.
17 They have given strength to their openness and light to their eyes.
(VII) 18a For they all have known themselves in the Lord,
18b and they were saved by water of eternal life.

Introduction

Ode 6 is preserved in one Syriac manuscript and incompletely in the Coptic *Pistis Sophia*.[1] Since Harnack's work[2] there has hardly been another Ode so discussed and theorized about as this "Temple-*Ode,*" which could be so called because of the *hapax legomenon* in 8.[3] Such a title, however, would be misleading, since the term "temple" in 8a may be difficult to interpret but is hardly the core of the Ode. Since the form of the Ode cannot

1 Mss.: Codex H, 2b–3b (ܣ); Codex A, 61ᵛa–b (ℭ). Ed. and trans.: Charlesworth, 28–33; Franzmann, 40–50; Lattke, 1:71–93 and 3:XVII–XVIII.

2 Harnack, 76, 98, 101, 123.

3 The influence of Harnack (p. 29, etc.), who partly agrees with Harris (pp. 54–58), can be seen here, as in reference to *Ode* 4, when Harris and Mingana (2:235) remark on *Ode* 6: "This is the second of the 'Temple' Odes, if we do not get rid of the reference to the Temple in the text: by means of the ingenious suggestion made by Professor Torrey that the words 'and it carried away the Temple' might be a perversion of an original Aramaic expression 'and there was none to restrain'. We do not propose, however, to alter the text at this point, it is intelligible as it stands." As to Charles Cutler Torrey's emendation, see Lattke, *Bedeutung*, 3:82–83, on Benjamin Wisner Bacon, "The Odes of the Lord's Rest," *Exp* 8th Ser., 1 (1911) 193–209.

be reduced to a common denominator, such as "didactic poem,"[4] the chosen title again reflects its content.[5] The title also highlights the three recognizably different sections (1-7, 8-10, 11-18) of the Ode, which neither divides "into four stanzas" for (Jewish) "responsorial chanting by Prophet and congregation" according to the use of the Therapeutae,[6] nor into "two distinct sub-odes (1-7, 8-18)"[7] or into "the two halves . . . that which concerns the spirit (1-7) and that which concerns the water."[8]

The general discussion at the beginning of the commentary on *Ode* 5, on the relationship of the Coptic text (and its Greek original) to the Syriac, applies equally to this Ode. The "hermeneutic circle for *Ode* 6:8-18" is of importance in the Gnostic habit of the *Pistis Sophia* of "quoting the words of the prophets . . . to legitimate the author's own statement,"[9] but plays no great part for the commentary on *Ode* 6 itself. The fact that the Coptic quotes only 8-18, the two most closely connected sections, should not cause any literary-critical doubts[10] about an original lack of connection between 1-7 and 8-18. The seven existing stanzas[11] of the Syriac text need to be considered as a unit. But this somewhat loose unity[12] is not produced by the various micro-sections or by the speaker or speakers, but only by the content. An audience is simply missing. A masculine speaking "I" distinct from the Lord and his Spirit is evident only in stanza I (2b). And only in stanza III is there an inclusive group of speakers (6c-7), who are again distinguished from the Lord and his Spirit. If the "Lord" of this *Ode* (2a, 3b, 6a, 13a) is identical with the "Most High" (12), as the Coptic explicitly states (13b ϲ), then the "I" (2b) may be the celestial revealer. However, the "we"-passage (6c-7b) would rather suggest that the "I" is an outstanding member of the group. This does not imply any specific identification of the speaker and even less of the poet(s) himself/themselves.

Interpretation

■ **1-2** Harris and Mingana's primary conjecture for the word that has crumbled away in 1a is "hand,"[13] but they also accept ܪܘܚܐ (*rūḥā*) as a possibility and suggest "spirit" as a translation of this term.[14] This is a possible but somewhat unlikely interpretation. The alternative translation of ܪܘܚܐ (*rūḥā*) as "(breath of) wind" (as in 29:10), espoused by Greßmann, Charlesworth, and Brian McNeil,[15] to name only three prominent exponents, is preferable, since in this introductory simile, where the "so" section may even include an element of reciprocity, the "as" section is meant metaphorically.[16] At the same time, there is a play on words with the term in 2a that describes the divine spiritual power, less a paronomasia[17] than an exploitation of two differing meanings of the same word, an onomatopoeic "primary word" in Semitic languages.[18]

The Pa. ܗܠܟ (*hallek*, feminine active participle) is used only here in a transferred sense and could also be translated as "to blow" or "to flow." In this metaphor of the cithara, marked by the use of the Greek loanword[19] and, apart from the lyre, the best-known Greco-Roman

---

4 Colpe, "Überlieferung," 77.
5 Abbott's (pp. 118–37) extremely speculative title "The River of the Spirit of God" is worth mentioning among the many titles applied to this *Ode* over the years.
6 Diettrich (14–15), referring to Philo of Alexandria.
7 Franzmann, 45.
8 Bauer, 583.
9 Lattke, *Bedeutung*, 1:220–22.
10 As suggested by Bauer, 583, in the form of a question.
11 I do not follow Franzmann's (p. 48) division into six stanzas, because I consider 18a-b to be an independent statement of salvation (see on stanzas VI and VII below).
12 Kittel's statement (p. 30) is still important, even if one does not agree with all the details of his summary: "It is not difficult, after our preliminary studies, to demonstrate the unity of this mixture of styles."
13 Harris and Mingana, 2:232.
14 Ibid., 2:234; cf. earlier William Emery Barnes, "An Ancient Christian Hymn Book," *Exp* 7th Ser., 10 (1910) 57.
15 Greßmann, 441; Charlesworth, 30–31; Brian McNeil, "The Spirit and the Church in Syriac Theology," *ITQ* 49 (1982) 93.
16 Cf. 1:1; 14:1, 15:1; 28:1; 40:1; and see Lattke, "Bildersprache," 101–2 = idem, *Bedeutung*, 4:26–28.
17 Charlesworth, 31.
18 Koehler and Baumgartner, 1117–21.
19 Lattke, "Wörter," 291 = idem, *Bedeutung*, 4:139; on Helmut Giesel, *Studien zur Symbolik der Musikinstrumente im Schrifttum der alten und mittelalterlichen*

stringed instrument,[20] the power of the wind is enough to move the strings (*hapax legomenon* ܡܢܢܐ [*mennē*]) to "speak." Passages such as Isa 16:11; Ignatius *Eph.* 4:1; or *Phld.* 1:2[21] offer parallels for the musicological vocabulary (κιθάρα, χορδαί) but not for the intended metaphor. Richard Hugh Connolly's question, "Why is the Greek word for harp always used in the Syriac version, and the Semitic word avoided?"[22] is still a cogent argument for Greek, not Hebrew, as the original language of the *Odes of Solomon*.

The paronomasiac repetition of ܡܠܠ (*mallel*, feminine singular active participle) would also be a transferred use if the speaking "I" of 2a referred to his own bodily limbs, and thus to himself, in parallelism with 2b. If, however, the "members" belong to the group[23] and the active participle "denotes the continuing as well as the momentary present,"[24] the verb "to speak" would bear its literal meaning. It is not necessary to invoke "inspiration"[25] and "prophecy"[26] to do justice to the elevated theological claim of the speaking "I." The Spirit of God speaks as little as God himself. But in the "limbs"—that is, in the utterances of the members of the group—there is a spiritual power that is totally different from the *skillful* power of rhetoric (cf. Mark 13:11), which is transcendentally revealing only because no-thing and no-one in this world can possess or rule it.

Using a third form of ܡܠܠ (*mallel*, masculine singular active participle) and with the third occurrence of the rather indeterminate preposition ܒ (*b-*), which might also be translated instrumentally as "through," the speaking "I" of 2b makes a personal declaration, which removes his discourse, literally understood, from any human concerns into the realm of divine love. Since ܪܘܚܐ in 2a is to be taken as a feminine,[27] the masculine possessive suffix to "love" (cf. ἀγάπη in 11:2) must refer to "the Lord" in 2a (see Excursus 2).[28]

This "enthusiastic"—in the full original sense of the word—personal declaration at the end of stanza I is not to be understood as an introduction to the further content of this Ode, but only as a claim to salvation and declaration of revelation of one of the first person speakers of the *Odes of Solomon*.[29]

■ **3-5** In didactic form and with a weakly justifying ܓܝܪ (*gēr*), v. 3a, which will be further interpreted by 5a-b, is contrasted with the double statement in 2a-b, which emphasizes the unity of the "Lord" and the "Spirit."

Kirche (von den Anfängen bis zum 13. Jahrhundert) (Kölner Beiträge zur Musikforschung 94; Regensburg: Bosse, 1978) 123–24, see Lattke, *Bedeutung*, 3:331.

20 See Ulrich Klein, "Kithara," *KP* 3 (1969) 1581; Martha Maas, "Kithara," *The New Grove Dictionary of Music and Musicians* 13 (2nd ed., 2001) 638–40.

21 See Martin Sprengling, "Bardesanes and the *Odes of Solomon*," *AJT* 15 (1911) 459.

22 Richard Hugh Connolly, "Greek the Original Language of the Odes of Solomon," *JTS* 14 (1912–13) 536. The Semitic word is ܟܢܪܐ (*kennārā*), the Syriac form of כִּנּוֹר. Edwin A. Abbott (*The Fourfold Gospel: The Beginning* [Diatessarica 10, Section 2; Cambridge: Cambridge University Press, 1914] 394) repeats the question (with arguments in favor of "Hebrew *nebhel*"); on the debate between Connolly and Abbott about the original language of the *Odes*, see Lattke, *Bedeutung*, 3:154–56.

23 Cf. 3:2; 6:16 (?); 17:15; 18:2; 21:4; 26:4 (?).

24 Nöldeke §269.

25 Diettrich, 16.

26 Charlesworth, 31.

27 On the use of ܪܘܚܐ as a masculine, from the late fourth century onward, see Sebastian P. Brock, *The Holy Spirit in the Syrian Baptismal Tradition* (Syrian Churches Series 9; Poona: Anita Printers, 1979) 3–4 (and more detail in Lattke, *Bedeutung*, 3:336).

28 Charlesworth (p. 31) says, correctly, "There is nothing uniquely Montanist about this passage." But Montanus and his disciples may have known the *Odes of Solomon* (see Introduction, 4.2.2). Montanus, who spoke in the name of Father, Son, and Paraclete, likened the human being to a lyre over which God flies like a plectrum; the human sleeps and God watches. The Lord changes the hearts of mankind and gives them a [new] heart; cf. Epiphanius *Haer.* 48.4: Μοντανός φησιν· ἰδού, ὁ ἄνθρωπος ὡσεὶ λύρα, κἀγὼ ἐφίπταμαι ὡσεὶ πλῆκτρον. ὁ ἄνθρωπος κοιμᾶται, κἀγὼ γρηγορῶ. ἰδού, κύριός ἐστιν ὁ ἐξιστάνων καρδίας ἀνθρώπων καὶ διδοὺς καρδίαν ἀνθρώποις (Nathanael Bonwetsch, *Texte zur Geschichte des Montanismus* [KIT 129; Bonn: Marcus & Weber, 1914] 17; cf. Hilgenfeld, *Die Ketzergeschichte*, 591). There is a different emphasis in *Disc. 8–9* 60,27–32: "Therefore my mind wants to sing a hymn to you daily. I am the instrument of your spirit; Mind is your plectrum. And your counsel plucks me" (*NHLE*, 326).

29 "Enthusiasm" and "enthusiastic" have progressively declined from their original meaning of "possession by a god, etc." [1608] to the current "rapturous

First, it is necessary to hark back to 3:6a, where the "I," speaking in the unity of love, explicitly denies the possibility of being a stranger. In the dualism of the *Odes of Solomon* (cf. 24:10), the Lord, who according to 3b possesses the limitless All made up of limited parts (in 𝔊 τὸ πᾶν or τὰ πάντα), has always annihilated anything inimically alien and will continue to do so (masculine singular active participle of ܐܘܒܕ [*ʾawbed*], Aph. of ܐܒܕ [*ʾebad*]).[30] The translation "what is alien" in this chiastic antithetically parallel bicolon assumes that ܡܕܡ (*meddem*) is accompanied by an attributive adjective. It is also possible that *meddem* "in apposition to a noun" corresponds to Greek τις or τι. In that case, it would be translated as "some/any stranger."[31] However, the parallelism between *meddem* (3a) and *kol meddem* = "all" (3b) strongly suggests the first translation.

The ܓܝܪ (*gēr*) in 4a is a somewhat stronger justification, and it is followed in 4b, and commonly elsewhere, by ܘ (*w-*).[32] This formulaic statement in 4a-b (cf. 7:14; 11:4) is only the first half of the tetracolon 4-5; it should not be described as "confessional" nor taken as a monocolon.[33] "The text can better be split up into two lines."[34]

The ܡܕܡ (*meddem*), negated by ܠܐ (*lā*), which appears twice in 5a-b, clearly completes the *inclusio* begun with 3a-b. The imperfects, which are governed by the conjunction ܕ (*d-*) at the beginning of 5a, are formed with "fossil connections" of the root *qbl*[35] and are "semantically equivalent,"[36] forming a synonymous parallelism (cf. the dualistic statements with "against" of 8:19 and 25:3, 11).

■ **6-7** This instruction, uttered by the whole group, turns to those who are *not* alien (3a) but "Gnostics," known and giving praise now and in the future. What the speaking "we" utter didactically (6a-7a) and finish with the description of a doxology (7b)[37] contains poetically a large number of words derived from the same roots (ܝܕܥ, ܫܡ, ܫܒܚ). The Gnosticizing expression "his knowledge," which is the direct object of the Aph. of ܣܓܝ (*sgī*) or ܣܓܐ (*sgā*), may be an objective genitive (cf. *Corp. Herm.* 1:31: "Holy is God, who wills to be known and is known by His own" (ἅγιος ὁ θεός, ὃς γνωσθῆναι βούλεται καὶ γινώσκεται τοῖς ἰδίοις).[38] Considering 6b-c, however, it is more likely to be a subjective genitive, denoting the *gnōsis* granted and increased by the Lord (in 𝔊 γνῶσις, or even the nontechnical σύνεσις; cf. 11:4 and Excursus 7).[39] For to those who were seeking *gnōsis*, whether Jews, Christians, or Jewish Christians, such *gnōsis* comes from "the Lord," that is, from no-thing and no-body in this world and new members are added to the movement *sola gratia* (χάριτι)—not by any rite or operation of law—"given" by him (6c). The *hapax legomenon* ܛܢ (*ṭan*) may represent a Greek verb like ζηλόω (6b).[40]

The term ܬܫܒܘܚܬܐ (*tešbuḥtā*), used as an accusative in 7a, can hardly be translated as "glory" (δόξα); it must be taken together with the indirect object "for his name"[41] and translated as "laud/praise" as a reference to the hymnological meaning of the Syriac noun.[42] In this case, the parallelism with 7b makes an objective genitive more likely than a subjective genitive ("his hymn"

intensity of feeling, etc." [1916] (*Oxford English Dictionary*). The Platonic connection with divination (*Timaeus* 71e [LCL 7:186–87]) is not found in the *Odes of Solomon*.

30 On this passage, see Franzmann, 31. The accuracy of her note, "This is summed up in the subsequent image of the knowledge of the Lord which goes out as a stream and destroys everything (6:8-10) but which is a restoring drink for those who belong to the Lord (6:11-18)," may be questioned.

31 See Nöldeke §219.

32 See Lattke, "Wörter," 289 = idem, *Bedeutung*, 4:138.

33 Contra Franzmann, 46.

34 A. F. J. Klijn, review of Lattke, *Bedeutung*, vols. 1–2, in *VC* 34 (1980) 303, correcting Lattke, *Bedeutung*, 1:90–91.

35 See Brockelmann, *Grammatik*, 32; idem, *Lexicon*, 640–43.

36 Franzmann, 46.

37 See ibid.: "It is a description of a doxology rather than a doxology per se." It is not, however, a "confessional formula."

38 Arthur Darby Nock and André-Jean Festugière, eds., *Corpus Hermeticum* (4 vols.; Paris: Belles Lettres, 1946–54; repr. 1972–73) 1:18.

39 Instead of "increased" it would be possible to use "multiplied" or "made great" here and in 12:3 (Lattke, *Bedeutung*, 1:91, 115; Lattke, 3:372); but cf. Klijn, 303: "This translation (viz., 'Gross machte seine Erkenntnis der Herr') is not quite wrong but the verb *ʾsgy* could better have been rendered by the word 'to multiply,' in agreement with 12:3."

40 See Payne Smith, 2:1488.

41 See Bauer, 583.

42 This meaning for the feminine noun is found in the following cases, the asterisk denoting the

or similar). God, who exercises his power of redemption from every being and every thing, by his anthropomorphic name, "the Lord," is declared also to be the source of the gift of words for his praise.

The doxological statement, 7b, which is set apart from the rest of stanza III, though thematically closely connected, and which offers "a word-play by the double use of ܪܘܚܐ,"[43] forms the conclusion of the first part of the Ode. The Syriac offers a play on words with "Holy Spirit"[44] and the plural, found only here, "spirits" in the anthropological sense (*rūḥā*/*πνεῦμα* as the site of knowledge and vehicle of glorification; cf. 40:4). This play is reminiscent of the similar wordplay in stanza I ("wind" [1a] and "Spirit" [2a]).

■ **8-10** If Harnack were right, the interpretation of the second part of this Ode would be simple: "The magnificent description that follows is not 'Gnostic' but . . . [is meant] to describe the vigorous and inexorable spread of the knowledge of God throughout the world. Baptism is not under consideration nor is there anything 'mythological' about it."[45] Unfortunately it is not so simple: stanza IV in fact is one of the most enigmatic passages of the *Odes of Solomon*.

This Gnosticizing text is filled with metaphors, which the mythological "solution" (ⲃⲱⲗ) in the *Pistis Sophia* interprets gnostically in reference to the "emanation of light," perhaps because of an allegorical identification of the "temple" with the "First Mystery" Jesus.[46] The text has indeed no reference to baptism;[47] however, it is a self-contained mythos of a symbolic river, connected to part 3 (stanzas V–VII) only by thc catchwords "drink" (12-13), "his [i.e., the Lord's] water" (13), and "living water" (18).

Neither the introductory outline (8a), which cannot be understood to refer immediately to the "knowledge" or "*gnōsis*" of 6a[48] or the "spirit" of 2a and 7b,[49] and even less to the "praise" of 7a, nor yet the subsequent descriptive details (8b-10) can be interpreted historically as referring to some specific river and/or temple. Historical references and literal descriptions of hydraulic engineering or actual places can only be seen fragmentarily in the light of the self-praise of Wisdom in Sirach 24. This chapter, "The Eulogy of Wisdom" (*αἴνεσις σοφίας*, the heading in the text), to which Harris and Mingana already referred, contains many related terms, ideas, and statements as shown in the following table.[50]

Table 3: Ecclesiasticus, or The Wisdom of Jesus Son of Sirach 24, and the *Odes of Solomon*

Verse	Terms, Statements, Ideas	Passages in the Odes
2a	ἐν ἐκκλησίᾳ ὑψίστου	6:12; 12:4; 12:11
3a	ἀπὸ στόματος ὑψίστου ἐξῆλθον	12:3; 12:11 (cf. 30:5)
3b	κατεκάλυψα γῆν	6:10-11
6a	ἐν πάσῃ τῇ γῇ	6:10
7a	ἀνάπαυσιν ἐζήτησα	30:2; 30:7 (etc.)
8a	ὁ κτίστης ἁπάντων	6:3

occurrence of "name" in the context: 10:4; *14:5; 21:9; 26:1, 5; 29:11; *31:3; 40:2c. The plural, meaning "hymns," occurs as follows: 13:2; 16:1, 2, 4; 40:2b; 41:4. Actual doxologies are found in: *16:20; 17:16; *18:16; *20:10. Cf. also 39:13 with variant wording. In place of an excursus, see Lattke, *Hymnus*, 251–53.

43 Franzmann, 46.

44 Cf. 11:2; 14:8; 19:2, 4; 23:22.

45 Harnack, 32.

46 See Lattke, *Bedeutung*, 1:220–22; Pierre, 70.

47 Contra Robert Alexander Aytoun, "The Mysteries of Baptism by Moses bar Kepha Compared with the *Odes of Solomon*," *Exp* 8th Ser., 1 (1911) 341; Erik Peterson, *Frühkirche, Judentum und Gnosis: Studien und Untersuchungen* (Freiburg: Herder, 1959) 326; Mark Pierce, "Themes in the 'Odes of Solomon' and Other Early Christian Writings and Their Baptismal Character," *Ephemerides liturgicae* 98 (1984) 49.

48 See Harnack, 32; Greßmann, 441; Franzmann, 47.

49 See Abbott, 118.

50 Harris and Mingana, 2:239, 276, 367–68. Cf. also J. Rendel Harris, *The Origin of the Prologue to St*

Table 3: Ecclesiasticus, or The Wisdom of Jesus Son of Sirach 24, and the *Odes of Solomon* (*cont.*)

8b	*κατέπαυσεν τὴν σκηνήν μου*	12:12; 30:2; 30:7 (see above)
9	*. . . ἀπ᾿ ἀρχῆς ἔκτισέν με, καὶ ἕως αἰῶνος οὐ μὴ ἐκλίπω*	6:4; 11:4
10b	*ἐν Σιων*	
11a	*ἐν πόλει*	
11b	*καὶ ἐν Ιερουσαλημ*	6:8b (the temple)
17a	*ἐβλάστησα χάριν*	6:6c; 11:1
18	*ἐγὼ μήτηρ τῆς . . . γνώσεως* (*pauci*)	6:6
19a	*προσέλθετε πρός με*	30:2
20a	*ὑπὲρ τὸ μέλι γλυκύ*	30:4a
20b	*ὑπὲρ μέλιτος κηρίον*	30:4b
21b	*οἱ πίνοντές με*	6:11-14; 30:2; 30:7
22b	*ἐν ἐμοί*	6:2; 6:18; 12:3
23a	*θεοῦ ὑψίστου*	6:12; 12:4; 12:11 (see above)
26a	*σύνεσιν*	6:6a; 11:4
27a	*ὡς φῶς* ("like a river [ܐܝܟ ܢܗܪܐ]" in 𝔖)	6:8a; 11:16g; 26:13a
30	*Κἀγὼ ὡς διῶρυξ ἀπὸ ποταμοῦ καὶ ὡς ὑδραγωγὸς ἐξῆλθον εἰς παράδεισον*	6:8a; 11:16g
31c	*ἐγένετό μοι ἡ διῶρυξ εἰς ποταμόν*	6:8a (see above)
34b	*τοῖς ἐκζητοῦσιν αὐτήν*	26:13b

It may be assumed that Sirach 24 was known to the author(s) of the *Odes of Solomon* and also to at least some of his/their listeners or readers. Such people would also know the programmatic declaration, Sir 24:33, perhaps even in the original Greek:

> *ἔτι διδασκαλίαν ὡς προφητείαν ἐκχεῶ*
> *καὶ καταλείψω αὐτὴν εἰς γενεὰς αἰώνων.*[51]
>
> "I will again pour out teaching like prophecy,
> and leave it to all future generations."

The wording of 8a seems to derive principally from Sir 24:30-31. This is all the more likely, since the Syrohexapla in the early seventh century still translated *διῶρυξ* ("canal, channel, brook"[52]) by ܛܦܐ (*tappā*),[53] which occurs uniquely at this point in the *Odes of Solomon*. So it is most unlikely that 𝔊 had *ἀπόρροια*, a Gnostic technical term found as a loanword in the Coptic version. This term, probably taken from Wis 7:25, will have found its way into *Ode* 6:8-18 from the mythos of the *Pistis Sophia* which surrounds the quotation.[54]

John's Gospel (Cambridge: Cambridge University Press, 1917) 66, on Origen *Comm. Rom.* 7.12 (Rom 9:1-5), where it is said of the Lord Jesus Christ (cf. 1 Cor 8:6), unus autem uterque est Deus, quia non est aliud filio divinitatis initium quam pater, sed ipsius unius paterni fontis, sicut sapientia dicit, "purissima" est "manatio" filius, "both are one God, for the deity of the Son has no source but the Father. As Wisdom says, the Son is the 'pure emanation' [Wis 7:25] of the Father, who is the source." Here Jesus Christ is truly "the *ἀπόρροια* or *manatio*." Whether this description as "an irresistible flow of water, as in the sixth *Ode of Solomon*," can be transferred to the Sophia-Christ is more doubtful.

51 Rahlfs, 2:419.

52 LEH, *s.v.* *διῶρυξ*.

53 Later the word would also be used metaphorically; see Payne Smith, 2:4476.

54 See Harnack, 32.

The particle ܓܝܪ (*gēr*), which occurs twice, does not there introduce a justification, as it does in 10, but rather serves to move forward the flow of rhetoric (like καί or δέ), while the two verbs, ܢܦܩ (Pe. *npaq*) and ܗܘܐ (*hwā*), are equivalent to Greek ἐξῆλθον and ἐγένετο (cf. Sir 24:3a, 30b, 31c-d). It is worth referring to *Ode* 30:5, where the "living" (i.e., "flowing") "spring of the Lord" (30:1-2) "flows" from "the lips of the Lord" (masculine singular active participle *nāpeq*), which corresponds to Sophia's description of herself in Sir 24:3a: ἀπὸ στόματος ὑψίστου ἐξῆλθον ("I came forth from the mouth of the Most High"). So the metaphor of the river, which originates in the brook or rivulet, may well be connected with the paradisiacal "river of joy" (cf. 11:16g [only in 𝔊], ποταμὸς χαρᾶς, and Sir 24:30b, εἰς παράδεισον) and/or the river of "rest," "which has an abundant spring" (26:12-13; cf., for the motif of searching in 26:13b, the ending of Sir 24:34b: τοῖς ἐκζητοῦσιν αὐτήν, "for all who seek her, viz., wisdom"). With regard to part 3 of *Ode* 6 (vv. 11-18) which has many cross-connections with *Ode* 11, it is also pertinent to consider whether this brimming river might be "the speaking water . . . from the [living, only in 𝔊] spring of the Lord" (11:6).

According to Emerton's detailed remarks on 8b it is most important to note that ܟܠܡܕܡ (*kol meddem*) is also "the implied object of the second and third verbs" and that the ܠ (*l-*) prefixed to ܠܗܝܟܠܐ (*l-hayklā*) is not used "to introduce the direct object" but as the preposition "to."[55] The verbs ܓܪܦ (Pe. *grap̄*, *hapax legomenon*), ܫܚܩ (Pe. *šḥaq*, *hapax legomenon*), and ܐܝܬܝ (*ʾaytī*, Aph. of ܐܬܐ [*ʾetā*]) manifest their literal meanings in the details of the representation and present no difficulty of interpretation (cf. the metaphor of the rivers in 39:1–4, 8 and that of the way in 7:13-14).[56] The problem of 8b lies in the allusion to the or a temple.[57] The simplest supposition is that, since *Ode* 6 is so strongly influenced by Sirach 24 (see Table 3), the word ܗܝܟܠܐ (Coptic ⲣ̄ⲡⲉ, both representing Greek τὸ ἱερόν or ναός),[58] which occurs only here and plays no further role, is a symbolic conflation of Sir 24:10b-11b where the Temple Mount and the city of Jerusalem are named in parallel.[59] Since the mythos takes place in some undefined and timeless past, there is no point in asking whether the Second Temple still existed in Jerusalem when this Ode was composed. The temple of this new image may not have any specific meaning, such "as the heavenly sanctuary or as the Church."[60]

The metaphor of the destructive river is now embellished with hydrological detail (9a-b), in which forms of the verbs ܟܠܐ (*klā*) and ⲁⲙⲁϩⲧⲉ (*amahte*) dominate. The negated, anomalous verb ܫܟܚ (*šk̲aḥ*) "with prosthetic Aleph"[61] is immediately followed by the Pe. *klā* in the same tense with a third masculine singular accusative suffix referring to "river" (in ℭ the object remains the same as the subject of 8, namely, ἀπόρροια). In the first half of the subject, the Syriac term "sons of men" can be replaced by the general term "men" (ℭ includes the subject in the negated third person plural of the perfect I of ϣ [*š*]). In parallel to the "restraints" (𝔖), which the Coptic describes as "fortifications and constructions,"[62] the second half of the subject speaks more generally of

55 Emerton, "Notes," 508. The word "toward" in the translation of the Coptic is intended to describe the direction "onto, to, over" (Till, 322; cf. the many possible Greek equivalents given by Crum, 757). See the detailed discussion by Worrell (p. 37), who translates 8b, "It carried away all things, and it turned toward the Temple."

56 This statement is of course true of the dwellers by the Nile or in Mesopotamia, but equally of the "inhabitants of Palestine," who are well aware "of the life-threatening, destructive power of water": "the downpours of winter rain transform dry valleys and gullies into raging torrents which carry away people, animals and buildings" (Richard Hentschke, "Wasser," *BHH* 2 [1966] 2141).

57 See Emerton, "Notes," 509–11.

58 See Payne Smith, 1:1003; Crum, 298.

59 Georg Sauer, *Jesus Sirach (Ben Sira)* (JSHRZ 3.5; Gütersloh: Mohn, 1981) 491, 564.

60 Emerton, "Notes," 511.

61 Payne Smith, *Dictionary*, 576.

62 One of many emendations of Friedrich Schultheß ("Textkritische Bemerkungen zu den syrischen Oden Salomos," *ZNW* 11 [1910] 252), might be considered here, if it were not that the stylistic form of paronomasia (see Charlesworth, "Paronomasia," 12–26) argues against the substitution of ܒܢܝܢܐ (*benyānē*, *aedificium*, *aedificatio* [Brockelmann, *Lexicon*, 78]) for ܟܠܝܢܐ (*kelyānē*). So "constructions" seems to be an addition in the Coptic, which does not derive from the Greek οἰκοδομαί. Schultheß's emendations must be considered in connection with his verdicts that the Syriac *Odes of Solomon* are

ܐܘܡܢܘܬܐ (*ʾummānwāṯā*), the *artes* or τέχναι (loanword in ℭ) of the highly skilled hydraulic engineers of antiquity.[63] Since this engineering specialty did not yet have a name, its activities had to be described in relative clauses, in 𝔖 with the participle of ܟܠܐ governing "water" in the accusative, in ℭ with the infinitive of ⲁⲙⲁϩⲧⲉ.

The reason (*gēr*) for the impotence expressed in 9a-b is given in 10, at least in 𝔖 (ℭ does not offer an explanatory conjunction). The idiomatic expression "face of the whole earth" in 𝔖 (cf. 16:16), which can be found also in 𝔊 (cf. 11:13), corresponds to "the whole earth" in ℭ. The verb ܡܠܐ (Pe. *mlā*) means literally "to fill (up)" (like πληρόω),[64] but may be translated as "to flood" in the context of this image (ℭ puns with yet another meaning of ⲁⲙⲁϩⲧⲉ). In both versions, the direct object "all things" (or "all living things") forms the *inclusio* of the detailed mythological image (8a and 10), according to which the earth—and not the sea[65] as in Hab 2:14 MT—is covered with water, and human life seems, again, to have come to an end. But the stress here, unlike in the other stories of a great flood, including the composite one of Genesis 6–8, is not on the "annihilation of humanity, the earth or the cosmos."[66]

■ **11-12** Stanza V, which marks the beginning of the third and last part of *Ode* 6, is a metaphorical description of the "living water" (18 𝔖) as the "drink" of the "Most High" (12), and is only loosely connected to the preceding parts of the Ode by the key words "know" (18; cf. 6 in part 1) and "water" (part 2). If the mythological river of stanza IV is an untamed deluge, submerging and overwhelming everything, rather than merely great and overflowing, the connection between parts 2 and 3 does not seem very logical: in fact, it demands the exercise of some poetic licence, which now sounds a conciliatory note of salvation and finds calmer waters in its detailed descriptions.

Excursus 6: "Drink," "To Drink," and "Water" in the *Odes of Solomon*, Considering also "Thirst," "River," "Spring," and "Drunkenness"

Among those few cases in which the terms and images do not bear a soteriological sense, the river of 6:8-10 may be taken as a first example. This mythological "river" (ⲓⲉⲣⲟ in ℭ, ܢܗܪܐ [*nahrā*] in 𝔖, surely ποταμός in 𝔊), whose "water" (ⲙⲟⲟⲩ in ℭ, ܡܝܐ [*mayyā*] in 𝔖, surely ὕδωρ in 𝔊) cannot be dammed, can be clearly distinguished from the "raging rivers" (39:1-4) that will finally be "obedient" (39:8c), and meanwhile the "footprints of our Lord Messiah" on their "waters" perform a saving role (39:10-12). Another contrast to the all-submerging river is found in 23:14b, where the "rivers" are "filled in" by the mythological wheel (cf. commentary on 23:11). This self-contained, and probably originally negative, mythos of the river can find a positive meaning only in the context of the whole collection of the *Odes* (see on stanza IV above).

Taken literally "sea" and "water" belong together (16:10). However, passages such as 12:2a ("like the flowing of water") and 40:2a ("as a spring gushes out its water") are metaphorical but not directly soteriological. On the edge of the soteriological are such images as 11:16g in 𝔊 ("the river of joy watered them [i.e., the roots] in paradise") and 38:17b ("[the Lord] watered it [viz., the root]"). The Aph. ܐܫܩܝ (*ʾašqī*) in *Ode* 38 probably represents the verb ποτίζω found in that part of *Ode* 11 preserved only in Greek.[67] In dualistic opposition to Gnostic salvation, the destroyer and seducer "call the many to the wedding feast (ܡܫܬܘܬܐ [*meštūṯā*]) and give them to drink the wine of their intoxication" (38:12). This drunkenness (ܪܘܝܘܬܐ [*rawwāyūṯā*]) is the "μέθη τῆς ἀγνωσίας"[68] (cf. 18:11, where "ignorance" [non-*gnōsis*] is compared to "the stink of the sea").

(1) "prose" and (2) "translations from the Greek" (Schultheß, 251–52).

63 See Payne Smith, 1:237; Kurt Galling, ed., *Biblisches Reallexikon* (HAT, Erste Reihe 1; 2nd ed.; Tübingen: Mohr Siebeck, 1977) 358–60; *MEL*, 25:49–50, *s.v.* Wasserbau.

64 See Payne Smith, 2:2117; BDAG, *s.v.* πληρόω, 1.

65 Unlike Harris and Mingana (2:235), I do not believe that Hab 2:14 and Ps 72:19 have directly influenced 6 and 10 so that "[t]he tenth verse is anticipated in the sixth." In the LXX version of Hab 2:14 (. . . ὡς ὕδωρ κατακαλύψει αὐτούς), αὐτούς seems to be due to the erroneous reading עליהם (= preposition על + 3rd masculine plural suffix) for על־ים ("of the waters"). It is, however, quite unclear which of the terms in 14a (. . . τοῦ γνῶναι τὴν δόξαν κυρίου) is the subject of κατακαλύψει. Nor is the referent of the personal pronoun αὐτούς clear.

66 Otto Biehn and Hubert Junker, "Sintflut," *LThK*² 9 (1964) 787.

67 See Payne Smith, 2:4281.

68 Herbert Preisker, "μέθη, κτλ.," *ThWNT* 4 (1942) 551; cf. *TDNT* 4:545–46.

Now follow the soteriological passages. For Gnostics, there is also a "drunkenness" that is not "irrationality (𝔊)/without *gnōsis* (𝔖)" because it is caused by "drinking" (*πίνω*, ⲥⲱ, ܫܬܐ [*šṯā*] or ܐܫܬܝ [*ʾeštī*]) the speaking and living or immortal waters of the "spring of the Lord" (ܡܒܘܥܗ ܕܡܪܝܐ [*mabbūʿeh d-māryā*]) or pleonastically of the "fountain of life of the Lord" (*πηγῆς ζωῆς κυρίου*) (11:6-7; the Syriac Pe. ܪܘܐ [*rwā*] or ܪܘܝ [*rwī*] corresponds to the Greek passive *μεθύσκομαι*, "to become drunk").[69]

This "spring of the Lord" or "spring of life" (11:6) is unlike the "abundant springs" that "let flow milk and honey for us" (4:10) and also unlike the literal "spring" of the slow flowing river, which is compared to the "rest" of the singers (26:12-13); the *πηγὴ ζωῆς* of Jewish and early Christian writings and tradition is a "common term" in "a rich transferred use."[70] One of the *Odes* is devoted exclusively to this "living spring of the Lord," and almost all the terms discussed in this excursus occur in it (30:1-7). Although "the fountain of the water of life" (cf. Rev 21:6) shows specific traits (drinking water, rest, source), it has become "quite symbolic."[71] This spring can also be linked to the already mentioned "river of joy" (11:16g in 𝔊; cf. also the "river of the water of life" in Rev 22:1-2). The "water in my right hand" (28:15) is probably drawn also from the utopian springs of theological rest and immortality of this "water of life."[72]

Two of the seven passages that mention "milk" also refer to "drinking" (see on "milk and honey" above at 4:10) and should be understood soteriologically, but they are otherwise not closely related to the material under discussion. The "drinking" of the "holy milk" is life-giving (8:16c). And even though the direct object of "to drink" in 19:1b is the "cup of milk," the metaphorical action refers to the content and not to the vessel (19:1a).

Except for 11:22b, the remaining passages occur in *Ode* 6, the subject of the current commentary. The monocolon 11:22b is part of the material preserved only in Greek and offers an exegetical problem, since the eulogy (*εὐλογημένοι*) can yield sense only by a text-critical conjecture (substitution of *δρῆσται* for ⲁⲣⲱⲥⲧⲉⲥ). If this emendation is correct, the "workers of thy waters" recall the "ministers of that drink" who are "entrusted with his water" and also called blessed (6:13). There is no doubt that the "water of the Lord," as the Coptic rightly translates it (6:13b ℭ), is the "living water" (6:18b 𝔖). It should also be clear that the "drink" given by "the Most High" and drunk by the "thirsty" to quench their "thirst" (6:11-12)[73] refers to the metaphorical water of life and only in a quite subsidiary way (by synchronicity in the context of the whole collection of *Odes*) to the water of the river of stanza IV.

Some of the key words of Sirach 24, for example, *πίνοντες* (v. 21b), *γῆν* (v. 3b), and *ὑψίστου* (vv. 2a, 3a, 23a), will have influenced the vocabulary of stanza V. "Drink" and "to drink" are meant as metaphorically as "thirst" (a *hapax legomenon*) and "thirsty ones" (cf. 30:2). This elementary human need and its proper satisfaction are raised to an existential plane and left, unlike the

69 See Payne Smith, 2:3840; BDAG, *s.v.* *μεθύσκω* ("cause to become intoxicated").

70 Wilhelm Michaelis, "*πηγή*," *ThWNT* 6 (1959) 114; cf. *TDNT* 6:113.

71 BDAG, *s.v.* *πηγή*, 1c.

72 See Bauer, 609. Leonhard Goppelt, in his account of water in the ancient Orient and the Greek-Hellenistic, Old Testament, and Jewish worlds, and in the New Testament, with its wealth of material, places the *Odes of Solomon* together with the water given to drink in the Apocalypse and the Gospel of John: "On the one side, 1QH (. . .) and even more Rev (. . .) develop what the OT says about water into the metaphor of the water of life. On the other the dualistic development of the idea is plain (even more so than in Jn) in *OdSol* 30:1 (cf. 11:6ff.), in Ign[atius] *R[om]* 7:2 and, much later, in the Mandaean writings in which water of life is a fixed metaphor for the salvation which comes from above" (Goppelt, "*ὕδωρ*," *ThWNT* 8 [1969] 326; cf. *TDNT* 8:326–27); cf. Kurt Rudolph, *Die Mandäer*, vol. 2: *Der Kult* (FRLANT 75 = N.F. 57; Göttingen: Vandenhoeck & Ruprecht, 1961) 61–66.

73 Goppelt's remarks on "*πίνω* with transferred meaning" must be considered harmonizing, when he says: "In the Gnostic *Odes of Solomon gnosis* is compared to a river, which overflows the whole earth to supply the thirsty [cf. 6:11-12], or to a paradisial spring, from which the redeemed have drunk immortality (*OdSol* 11:6-8, cf. Ps 36:9), or to a well of life, which pours forth as a word of knowledge from the lips of the Lord (*OdSol* 30). This fig. use merges into the specifically Gnostic ref. to true drinking" (Leonhard Goppelt, "*πίνω*, *κτλ.*," *ThWNT* 6 [1959] 139; cf. *TDNT* 6:139). Heinrich Schlier's position is similar, placing the *Odes* against a background of a Mandaic-Gnostic baptismal sect: "There [viz, in the *Odes Sol.*] the water that quenches thirst is the *gnosis* that is experienced" (Schlier, "Zur Mandäerfrage," *ThR* N.F. 5 [1933] 89; cf. Lattke, *Bedeutung*, 3:210–11).

similar passage in the Sermon on the Mount (Matt 5:6), without any further metaphorical explanation.

The two parallel verbs in 11b do not carry any apocalyptic or soteriological meaning,[74] but refer to the imagery of thirst, with the Syriac and Coptic versions a close match (Ethpe. ܐܫܬܪܝ [ʾeštrī] || ⲃⲱⲗ ⲉⲃⲟⲗ, both reproducing an inflection and perhaps a composite form of λύω;[75] Pe. ܕܥܟ [dʿek] || ⲱϣⲙ̄ [ōšᵉm], reproducing the passive of σβέννυμι).[76]

The common verb "to give," which, however, can bear a theological meaning in the *Odes* (see 4:3c and 4:13a-b above), is translated in the explanatory monocolon 12 (ܓܪ [gēr]) by "to offer."[77] With respect to the mythos and the return to the mythos, the *Pistis Sophia* understands the originally Greek quotation only in reference to the lack, the gift, and the reception of light (ⲟⲩⲟⲉⲓⲛ), conceived of in a Gnostic dualistic sense.[78] The text of the Ode refers to the "living water" (18), which, just because it does not exist in this world—whether as a profane or a sacramental element—must come from the "Most High," the "Lord" (13).

■ **13-17** In ܣ the composite term ܗܟܝܠ (*hākēl*) in the second place marks stanza VI as the consequence of stanza V (cf. 8:19; 39:8; 41:5);[79] Coptic lacks the conjunction or particle that would translate ἄρα or οὖν. The benediction (13) is followed by another detailed description (14-17) ending with a summarizing monocolon that does not include the Gnostic statement of salvation in 18a-b (= stanza VII).[80]

The Greek of 13a will have begun with μακάριοι, like ϭ, while ܣ expresses it with the compound of ܛܘܒܐ (*ṭūbā*) and the suffixed third plural masculine pronoun (cf. 9:8; 11:18; 12:13; 30:7). It is also likely that the *hapax legomenon* ܡܫܡܫܢܐ (*mšammšānē*) corresponds to διάκονοι (used in ϭ), although this technical term of the liturgical or cultic vocabulary can represent a number of different Greek words.[81] It has already been noted (Excursus 6 above) that the expression "ministers of that drink" (13a; cf. 12) is similar to "workers of thy waters," which is parallel to τῶν πιστῶν τῶν δούλων σου (11:22b-c; δοῦλος in the Greek of *Ode* 11 corresponds to Syriac ܥܒܕܐ [ʿabdā]).

Does it make sense to ask whether these "ministers of that drink" ever existed in a historical context? There is no hint in the *Odes of Solomon* or in any other early Christian or early Jewish writing that they stood for "the teachers, who are also missionaries"[82] or for "the preachers of the Word of God throughout the world."[83] Since 6:11-18 is a "parable about the water of life,"[84] the "ministers" and the "drink" are equally metaphorical (see on stanza V above). The "drink" in this passage, as well as in 30:2, is the "water of the Lord," a metaphor for the divine and otherworldly "element" that sustains and redeems human life,[85] and so its "ministers" are the unconstrained and active mediators of this means of salvation.[86]

The activities of these ministers are quite factually pictured (14-17), and at first glance the careful poetic structure seems to consist of bodily perceptible aspects of human existence (lips, limbs, eyes), on the one hand, and of spiritual-psychic aspects (will/joy of heart, soul, openness), on the other. This first impression is likely to

74 For the first, cf. 15:2; 17:3, 11; 18:4 [H]; 22:4, 11; 23:9; for the second, 23:20.

75 See Payne Smith, 2:4309–10; Crum, 32–33.

76 See Payne Smith, 1:931; Crum, 535; BDAG, *s.v.* σβέννυμι. See also Frankenberg, 8.

77 In ϭ, 12 does not use a causal conjunction but the *temporalis* (Till §319, "when something happened," "after something had happened"). When the quotation is repeated in the explanation (formal element Z¹) the perfect II is used, again in the third person plural, which replaces the passive (see Lattke, *Bedeutung*, 1:92). The phrase "on the dry sand" (ϭ) in place of "upon the earth" (ܣ) may reflect Egyptian conditions.

78 See Lattke, *Bedeutung*, 1:92–93, 192–99.

79 See Payne Smith, 1:1006.

80 Franzmann's argument for the connection of 13b and 18b because of "*inclusio*" convinces me the less since she herself says that "18a-b functions as a concluding summary statement. The cl[ause] introduced by ܡܛܠ ܕ in 18a appears to have little logical connection with the preceding lines" (Franzmann, 48–50, esp. 49). Verse 18, therefore, must not be translated as she does (Franzmann, 42–43). Moreover, the division of the three monocola 15-17 is unnecessary and arbitrary (Franzmann, 48).

81 See Payne Smith, 2:4225–30, esp. 4227–28.

82 Harnack, 32.

83 Theodor Zahn, "Die Oden Salomos," *NKZ* 21 (1910) 756.

84 Lattke, *Oden*, 43.

85 *MEL*⁹, 31:1646, *s.v.* "Lebenselement."

86 Potentially this can be any- and everyone. The term "entrusted" is a *hapax legomenon* in both versions:

be the correct reading. It may, however, be worth sketching the changes in structure and meaning if another point of view is taken, namely, that the "limbs" (always plural in the *Odes*) of v. 16 do not belong to an individual (cf. 8:16; 18:2[?]; 21:4[?]; 26:4[?]; 40:3) but refer to members of the group (cf. 3:2[?]; 6:2[?]; 17:15; for the question marks, consult Excursus 18).

For if the "fallen limbs" are human beings, the "setting upright" does not depict the splinting of a broken bone but a "straightening" of *lapsi*,[87]–to use an anachronistic technical term of the third century. In that case 16 and 17 would form a bicolon, parallel to 14-15, and "coming" (παρουσία) would not be "without sense"[88] but would express the "return"[89] of former members. This interpretation is tempting also because it seems to offer a rare glimpse into the inner workings of the group. However, the other interpretation is the more likely.

Except for the variants in 14b and 17, the Syriac and Coptic texts are extraordinarily close and can be used to draw clear conclusions about much of the wording of 𝔊. The verbs translated by "to revive" in 14a strictly mean "to calm" (𝔖) and "to turn" (ⲕⲧⲟ in ℭ), where the Syriac Aph. ܐܢܝܚ (*ʾanīḥ*), from the root ܢܘܚ (*nwḥ, nāḥ*) is used in an unusual manner (see Excursus 3). The participial adjective ܝܒܝܫܐ (*yabbīšā, hapax legomenon*) corresponds to the construction of the circumstantial[90] with ϣⲟⲟⲩⲉ. The basic meaning of both words is "dry" or "desiccated."[91] So this sequence of paradigmatic actions begins with the wetting of dry lips (see Excursus 16). But the connection with "water" (13; cf. 11:6) disappears completely in what follows.

In the first of the spiritual-psychic aspects, which follows chiastically, the anthropological term "will" is used atypically (see Excursus 9). The variant "joy of heart" in ℭ, in place of the Syriac ܨܒܝܢܐ (*ṣeḇyānā*), is probably a change (within the grammatical context) of the original ϑέλημα, influenced by the statement ⲁⲩⲟⲩⲣⲟⲧ ("they rejoiced") in the mythology of the *Pistis Sophia*.[92] If 𝔊 read something like ϑέλημα (κατα)σβεννύμενον[93] this would explain both the passive participle ܡܫܪܝܢ (*mšarray*) and the relative clause with the qualitative of ⲃⲱⲗ ⲉⲃⲟⲗ. In that case the two differing versions are terminologically even closer to 6:11b (see above). The Aph. of ܩܡ (*qām*), which occurs also in 16, is preceded by its direct object "will"; the different sentence structure of ℭ has no comparable form. For the subject of vv. 14-17 is in 𝔖 "the servants" from 13; in the Coptic of 14b it is "those who were drained."

Verse 15 parallels 14b with another spiritual-psychic aspect. "Soul" (ܢܦܫܐ [*nap̄šā*], ψυχή) is not here simply "self" in some sense, but means rather the living power opposed to death and dying (see Excursus 20). In another passage the notion occurs in connection with the "water from the living spring of the Lord," where this spring of rest brings "rest to the soul" (30:1-3). Monocolon 15, however, is no longer immediately concerned with a function of water, but rather with efforts on behalf of human beings with souls (7:23c) or who are "living souls" (cf. Gen 2:7 LXX: καὶ ἐγένετο ὁ ἄνθρωπος εἰς ψυχὴν ζῶσαν, "and the man became a living soul").[94] The words ܩܪܝܒܐ (*qarrīḇā*), ܢܦܩ (*npaq*), and ܐܚܕ (*ʾeḥad*), which are used in this clumsy construction, are fairly common in the *Odes of Solomon*, but occur only here in connection with "to die" or "death" (see Table 1).

Although the construction of 16 is parallel to 15, the verse is chiastically concerned with the second of the bodily aspects. The "fallen limbs" (μέλη in ℭ) should probably be considered the result not of death in battle

ܐܬܗܝܡܢ (*ʾeṯhayman*) in 𝔖, ⲧⲁⲛϩⲟⲩⲧ (*tanhut*) in ℭ; 𝔊 will have been the passive πιστεύομαι (cf. BDAG, *s.v.* πιστεύω, 3).

87 Wilhelm M. Gessel, "Lapsi, Lapsae," *LThK*³ 6 (1997) 652–53.

88 Worrell, 39.

89 BDAG, *s.v.* παρουσία, 2a.

90 Lambdin, 95–97; cf. Till §§328–34: "Der Umstandssatz."

91 See BDAG, *s.v.* ξηρός, 1; Payne Smith, 1:1543; Crum, 601.

92 See Lattke, *Bedeutung*, 1:94–95, 194–95.

93 See BDAG, *s.vv.* κατασβέννυμι and σβέννυμι, 1.

94 Rahlfs, 1:3; Brenton, 3.

(cf. 9:6) but of a crashing fall leading to broken bones and dislocated joints. In view of the Coptic (ⲧⲁϩⲟ ⲉⲣⲁⲧ⸗ [*taho erat*]), it is likely that there was only one verb in 𝔊, as Harnack correctly surmised.[95] The Syriac, repeating ܐܩܝܡܘ (*ʾaqīm*) from 14b in addition to the Aph. of ܩܡ (*qām*), depicts the bone-setting activities of the "servants" as ambulance attendants even more graphically. The Pa. ܬܪܨ (*tarreṣ*) shares the basic meaning of the root *trṣ* "to make straight,"[96] but not the special connotation found elsewhere in the *Odes* (cf. 27:3; 35:7; 42:2).

The monocolon 17 contains the third of the spiritual-psychic and of the bodily aspects. The direct objects of the common verb "to give," which is also used in ℭ and should be given no more weight here than in v. 12, are "strength" (ܚܝܠܐ [*ḥaylā*], ϭⲟⲙ [*com*]; in 𝔊 probably δύναμις or possibly ἰσχύς;[97] see Excursus 29) and "light" (ܢܘܗܪܐ [*nuhrā*], ⲟⲩⲟⲉⲓⲛ, in 𝔊 certainly φῶς; see Excursus 10). The mythos in the *Pistis Sophia* at this point shows clearly why the quotation of *Ode* 6:8-18 seemed to fit so well as the so-called solution (ⲃⲱⲗ):

> ⲁⲩϫⲓ ⲟⲛ ⲙ̄ⲡⲉⲩⲟⲩⲟⲓ̈ⲛ ⲁⲩⲱ ⲁⲩⲣ̄ⲑⲉ ⲉⲛⲉⲩⲟ ⲙ̄ⲙⲟⲥ ⲛ̄ϣⲟⲣⲡ̄. ⲁⲩϫⲓ-ⲁⲓⲥⲑⲏⲥⲓⲥ ϩⲙ̄ ⲡⲟⲩⲟⲓ̈ⲛ ⲁⲩⲱ ⲁⲩⲥⲟⲩⲛ̄ⲧⲁⲡⲟϩⲣⲟⲓⲁ ⲛ̄ⲟⲩⲟⲓ̈ⲛ ϫⲉ ⲉⲥⲏⲡ ⲉⲡϫⲓⲥⲉ.

> [T]hey have received their light again and they have become as they were at first.
> [T]hey have received *perception* (αἴσθησις) in the light, and they have known the *outpouring* (ἀπόρροια) of light, that it belongs to the height.[98]

But the metaphors of *Ode* 6 were not intended to be quite so mythological, although the key word "light" also has dualistic associations in the *Odes*. The second indirect object "eyes" (plural of ܥܝܢܐ [*ʿaynā*], as usual; ⲃⲁⲗ; in 𝔊 certainly ὀφθαλμοῖς), with the natural connection between eyes and light, presents no interpretative difficulties.[99] The first, however, presents both a serious problem in textual criticism and an interesting insight into the textual history of the *Odes of Solomon*.

It is extremely likely that the Greek original of ℭ had παρρησία (Coptic ⲡⲁⲣϩⲏⲥⲓⲁ). As written, it does not differ greatly from ⲡⲁⲣⲟⲩⲥⲓⲁ, which is regularly translated into Syriac as ܡܐܬܝܬܐ (*mēṯīṯā*), as found here.[100] If the two words παρουσία and παρρησία made equally good sense, the decision about the original reading would be extremely difficult, as the following models A–D of possible textual history show:

Model A

𝔖 ܡܐܬܝܬܐ
⇓
𝔊 παρουσία [→ παρρησία]
⇓
ℭ ⲡⲁⲣϩⲏⲥⲓⲁ

Model B

𝔊 παρουσία [→ παρρησία]
⇓ ⇓
𝔖 ܡܐܬܝܬܐ ℭ ⲡⲁⲣϩⲏⲥⲓⲁ

Model C

𝔊 παρρησία [→ παρουσία]
⇓ ⇓
ℭ ⲡⲁⲣϩⲏⲥⲓⲁ 𝔖 ܡܐܬܝܬܐ

Model D

𝔖* ܦܪܪܗܣܝܐ[101]
⇓
𝔊 παρρησία [→ παρουσία]
⇓ ⇓
ℭ ⲡⲁⲣϩⲏⲥⲓⲁ 𝔖 ܡܐܬܝܬܐ

95 Harnack, 33; cf. Frankenberg, 9 (επανωρθωσαν). On the translation of 6:16 in ℭ, see Till §236; some of the constructions in 15-17 belong to the class of improper relative clauses: "Nach einem undeterminierten Beziehungswort ersetzt ein Umstandssatz den Relativsatz" (Till §475).

96 Payne Smith, 2:4507 (*rectum fecit*).

97 See Payne Smith, 1:1258–59; Crum, 815–16.

98 Schmidt and MacDermot, *Pistis Sophia*, 135; cf. Lattke, *Bedeutung*, 1:94–95.

99 Cf. 5:5-6; 15:2-3; also Matt 6:22; Luke 11:34; Eph 1:18; 1 John 2:11. On the "parable of the eyes" in the Synoptics, which is taken from Q, see Siegfried Schulz, *Q: Die Spruchquelle der Evangelisten* (Zurich: Theologischer Verlag, 1972) 468–69.

100 See, e.g., Matt 24:3, 27; 1 Cor 15:23; 16:17; 2 Cor 7:6-7; 1 Thess 2:19; 3:13; 4:15; 5:23; 2 Thess 2:1, 8-9; Jas 5:7; 2 Pet 1:16; 3:4, 12; 1 John 2:28. Cf. Payne Smith, 1:418.

101 Or: ܦܪܗܣܝܐ, ܦܪܪܣܝܐ, ܦܐܪܪܣܝܐ, etc. (see Nöldeke §39). This model assumes that the two surviving Syriac MSS. are based not on the original Syriac

If, however, παρρησία, with the meaning of "confidence" or "fearlessness,"[102] makes better sense in the spiritual-psychic half of the tripartite construction than the Syriac reading, it is also likely that at least this Ode was originally written in Greek (Model C).

■ **18** As discussed earlier, this esoteric statement of salvation is not part of stanza VI, but a separate unit, which may be considered a "concluding summary statement"[103] because of its use of the catchwords "know" (6), "Lord" (2-3, 6, 13 [ℭ]), and "water" (9, 13).

Since 18a is an explanatory clause, dependent on 18b in 𝔖, the particle ܘ (*w-*) in 𝔖 should be translated "also." Neither the subject "everyone" of ܐܫܬܘܕܥ (*ʾeštawdaʿ*, Eshtaph. of ܝܕܥ) nor the subject "all of them" of ⲥⲟⲟⲩⲛ̄ can refer to the "servants" (13);[104] they are more likely to be the recipients in 14-17. It is, however, possible that stanza VII was originally the conclusion of stanza I (6:1-7), in which case the subject could be "all" of "us." In any case, it is wrong to import universality into this Gnostic utterance. Determining the identity of the direct object is still more difficult. The Coptic is ambivalent, since the third person suffix (-ⲟⲩ) to the *status pronominalis* ⲥⲟⲩⲱⲛ⸗ can also be interpreted as a reflexive;[105] in 𝔖 the enclitic ܐܢܘܢ (*ʾennōn*) cannot in the present context refer to "the ones who have been healed, strengthened, and so on in 14-17,"[106] but describes the "servants,"[107] and perhaps originally also those "added" (see 6 above). However it is read, 18a is "an early testimony to *gnōsis* κυρίῳ or ἐν κυρίῳ"[108] (see Excursus 7), which is quite unlike such a promise as Isa 61:9 LXX: καὶ γνωσθήσεται ἐν τοῖς ἔθνεσιν τὸ σπέρμα αὐτῶν κτλ. ("And their seed shall be known among the Gentiles," etc.).[109]

The grammatical subject changes in the Syriac of 18b.[110] If the subject of the plural of the verb "to live" (ܚܝܐ [*ḥyā*]; see Table 1) is the "servants," this statement of salvation would be a commentary on the benediction of 13. If the subject is (or includes) those "added" in v. 6, the "Gnostics" who are to be known are defined as those who were "redeemed" in this way. For the reading ⲛⲟⲩϩⲙ̄ (*nuhᵉm*) in ℭ shows that 𝔊 had a passive form of σῴζω at this point, which is idiomatically translated by the Syriac with the Pe. perfect of ܚܝܐ (see 5:3b above). This heightens the probability of a Greek original for this Ode, whose last lines might have been:

παντῶν δὲ γνόντων αὐτοὺς ἐν κυρίῳ,
σεσῳσμένοι καὶ ὕδατι ζωῆς αἰωνίου.[111]

text (𝔖*) or one of its early copies but on a Greek translation of this lost Syriac original. Such a complicated model is hardly worth considering.

102 BDAG, *s.v.* παρρησία, 3; cf. Bauer and Aland, *s.v.* παρρησία, 3: "Freimütigkeit," "Unerschrockenheit."

103 Franzmann, 49–50, although she has it continuing from 17.

104 Contra Worrell, 40.

105 See Till §§258b, 262. Schmidt and MacDermot, *Pistis Sophia* (p. 133) use "themselves."

106 Contra Franzmann, 49.

107 Harnack, 33, although he calls them "teachers."

108 Lattke, *Oden*, 108.

109 Rahlfs, 2:649; Brenton, 896. But the mention of Isaiah 61 is still pertinent, since this influential chapter (see esp. the commentary on *Ode* 36), with its message to Israel of salvation to come, shows some similarities to the detailed descriptions of *Ode* 6:14-17.

110 Harnack, 33. Diettrich's remark (p. 20) that "the constant change of subject in the Syriac can be irritating" could be applied to a number of passages in the *Odes*. I do not think that "the existing text" is "certainly corrupt," but correctly placing the elements in their context can be difficult for the translator.

111 The translation of ܡܝ̈ܐ ܚܝ̈ܐ as "water of life" (Lattke, *Oden*, 108), while verbally correct, is not quite accurate grammatically, since *ḥayyē* is the emphatic adjective of *mayyā*. On "living water," cf. 11:7 and 30:1 and parallels cited by Charlesworth (p. 33), e.g., John 4:10; 7:3; Acts 21:6; 22:1, 17; Ignatius *Rom.* 7:2.

7

Ode 7: The Lord and Father of *Gnōsis*, Epiphany and Salvation of the Son, *Gnōsis* of the Lord

(I) 1a Like the course of anger over injustice,
1b so is the course of joy over the Beloved,
1c and he brings in the fruits of it unhindered.
2a My joy is the Lord and my course is toward him;
2b this way of mine is beautiful,
3a for I have the Lord as my helper.
(II) 3b He let me know him without jealousy in his simplicity,
3c for his kindness has diminished his greatness.
(III) 4a He became like me, that I might receive him.
4b In appearance he seemed like me, that I might put him on.
5a And I did not tremble when I saw him.
5b Because he is, he had compassion on me.
6a Like my nature he became, that I might experience him,
6b and like my form, that I might not turn away from him.
(IV) 7 The Father of *gnōsis* is the word of *gnōsis*.
8a He who created Sophia (Wisdom)
8b is wiser than his works.
9a He who created me before I was,
9b knew, before I was, what I would do.
(V) 10a Therefore he had compassion on me in his great compassion,
10b and granted me to entreat of him and receive of his being.[a]
11a Because he is, he is imperishable,
11b the *plērōma* of the Aeons and their Father.
(VI) 12a He granted him to appear to those who are his,
12b that they might recognize him who made them,
12c and not suppose that they were from themselves.
(VII) 13a For toward *gnōsis* he laid out his way:
13b he made it broad and long and brought it over the whole *plērōma*.
14a And he laid upon it the tracks of his light,
14b and it [viz., the way] went from the beginning until the end.
(VIII) 15a For by him he was served,
15b and he was pleased with the Son.
16a And because of his salvation he will take possession of everything.

a 10b "Being" (ܐܝܬܘܬܐ [ʾīṯūṯā]; οὐσία in 𝔖) is a conjecture. Codex H has "sacrifice" (ܕܒܚܬܐ [*deḇḥṯā*]).

(IX) 16b And the Most High will be known in his saints,
17a to proclaim to those who have psalms for the coming of the Lord,
17b that they may go out to meet him and sing to him with joy
17c and with the cithara of many tones/voices.
(X) 18a The seers will go before him,
18b and they will appear before him.
19a And they will praise the Lord in his love,
19b because he is near and sees.
(XI) 20a And hatred will be lifted from the earth
20b and be submerged together with jealousy.
21a For non-*gnōsis* has been destroyed,
21b because the *gnōsis* of the Lord has come.
(XII) 22a Those who sing will sing the grace of the Most High Lord
22b and offer their psalms.
23a And their heart will be like the day [of the Lord?],
23b and their voices like the sublimity of the Lord.
(XIII) 23c And there shall be nothing that lives,
23d neither without *gnōsis*
23e nor without speech.
24a For he gave a mouth to his creation,
24b to open the voice of the mouth to him
24c and to praise him.
(XIV) 25a Praise/confess his power
25b and manifest his grace!
Hallelujah!

Introduction

Ode 7 is preserved in one Syriac manuscript.[1] In this Ode, which Gottfried Schille reckons among the "Hymns of epiphany"[2] (cf. *Odes* 19, 23, and 24), the tripartite structure, 1-11, 12-16a, 16b-25,[3] is as recognizable as in *Ode* 6. The multiple themes can be only partially shown in the suggested title. Certainly the theme of the Ode is not simply "the way to God"[4] or "God becoming man."[5]

1 Ms.: Codex H, 3b–5b (ꜱ). Ed./trans.: Charlesworth, 33–39; Franzmann, 51–62; Lattke, 1:95–128, and 3:XVIII–XX.
2 Gottfried Schille, *Frühchristliche Hymnen* (Berlin: Evangelische Verlagsanstalt, 1965) 114.
3 See Franzmann, 56: "There are three main sections to the Ode: 1-11, which concerns the relationship of the 'I' and the Lord; 12-16a, which deals with the Most High and the Son, and the way of the Lord; and 16b-24, which comprises detail of various groups within the community, and finally of the whole creation, engaged in praise of the Most High. The sections share a number of motifs, the most significant being that of knowledge (the root ܝܕܥ occurs ten times)." The division into microforms, which I have undertaken (Lattke, *Oden*, 42–45), confirms this analysis; see also Introduction, sec. 8.
4 Abbott, 138–236.
5 Greßmann, 442; Bauer, 584.

Indeed, it is even doubtful whether the (or an) incarnation is included in the subject matter.

Although *Ode* 7 may be a stylistic mixture and the material may have an earlier oral or written history, the excisions of Christian—or Jewish—interpolations by Harnack, Friedrich Spitta, Diettrich,[6] and others are not only not formally supported but unnecessary to the content.[7]

Except for the address in the final imperative (25),[8] the search for an envisaged audience of this Ode is also vain. A speaking "I" is to be found only in part 1, at least up to the final didactic and formulaic bicolon (11). This "I," identified as a male person only by the masculine participle in 9b, who is not identical with the writer of the Ode, distinguishes himself from the "Lord" (2a, 3a) and the creator-"Father" (7-11).

After this, things get complicated. Depending on whether the "Lord" of part 1 is or is not identical with the "Lord" of part 3, the "Father" of part 1, and the "Most High" or "Lord Most High" of part 3, there are two different interpretations possible, especially of part 2. To save repeatedly discussing both possibilities, the less likely one can be sketched briefly before the other interpretation is undertaken in full. If the "Lord" differs from the "Father" and the "Most High," who may both be described as "God," then:

1. Stanzas II and III in part 1 would refer to the relationship between the speaking "I" and the "Lord" who reveals himself, who would then "have compassion" (5b; 10a), like the "Father."
2. The "Lord" of part 1 would be identical with the "Son" of part 2, appearing, serving, and to be redeemed (12a; 15-16a); but especially
3. The poetic juxtapositions and mixing of the terms "Most High," "Lord," and "Lord Most High" in part 3 would be extremely jarring (16b-17a; 22).

In the context of the piece under consideration, this final point most clearly shows that the "Lord," "Father," "Most High," and "Lord Most High" are theologically identical and are contrasted soteriologically and mythologically with the speaking "I," who, as a devoted Gnostic, can also be the "Son." So the main reason for choosing this second interpretation is the construction of *Ode* 7, and not any possible use of the word "Lord" (ܡܪܝܐ; κύριος) as a title for God on the one hand and an emanation or person on the other, as has happened—and not only in respect of Ps 109:1 LXX—"in ref[erence] to Jesus."[9]

Such apparent terminological confusions, which also occur in other *Odes* (cf., e.g., 17:1-2 with 17:16; 29:6; 39:11), are really not surprising, since the composition and collection of the *Odes* took place in the area where early Judaism in apocalyptic and/or wisdom form, early Gnosticism in mythologically and/or philosophically soteriological form, and early Christianity in soteriologically and/or christologically theological form were becoming differentiated, and it was still possible to speak naively of the κύριος as the Highest God, Creator, and Father, and also as the Revealer and Redeemer.[10] This is not the case in *Ode* 7.

6 Harnack, 33–36; Friedrich Spitta, "Die Oden Salomos," *Monatsschrift für Gottesdienst und kirchliche Kunst* 15 (1910) 245–49, 273–78; Diettrich, 23–25.

7 Kittel, 30–32, 53–64.

8 This "invitation" leads Diettrich (p. 20) to the conclusion that this monodic "hymn" (his description of *Ode* 7) "was performed in cultic festivals;" this is only one idea among many.

9 BDAG, *s.v.* κύριος, 2bγ. See Joseph A. Fitzmyer, "κύριος, κτλ.," *EWNT* 2 (1981) 817: "The title implies that the exalted Jesus is on a par with Yahweh, yet is not identified with him—*he* is not *ʾabbāʾ*! Κύριος does not immediately mean θεός." Cf. also *EDNT* 2:330. "Jesus," of course, is not mentioned here or anywhere else in the *Odes of Solomon*.

10 This was a period before the later christological distinctions and tendencies, such as "subordinationism," "adoptianism," and "monarchianism," came into being, since they belong in the framework of the "two natures" and "Logos theology" ("Logos Christology") (see Alexander Böhlig, "Christologie," *KWCO*, 90–92).

Interpretation

■ **1-3a** The introductory metaphor[11] is truly a "splendid picture."[12] But the accent does not fall on the thrice-repeated masculine ܪܗܛܐ (*rehṭā*) in its proper and also metaphorical meaning of *cursus* or δρόμος,[13] nor on the *hapax legomena* ܚܡܬܐ (*ḥemṭā*) and ܥܘܠܘܬܐ (*ʿawwālūṯā*), but on the term "joy" in 1b and especially in 2a (cf. also 17b).

The likely equivalent for the redemptive term ܚܕܘܬܐ (*ḥaḏuṯā*), which occurs also in another introductory metaphor (15:1; cf. also 23:1; 31:3, 6; 32:1), is χαρά (as in 11:16).[14] The "motif of joy" is, in Gnosticism, closely connected with "knowledge," often "becomes the ontological token of the New Man," and displays "transcendental traits."[15] A direct influence of the emotional and erotic image of Cant 1:4, to the extent that "the identification of the Beloved leads to the identification of Canticles as the source of the 'running,'"[16] is unlikely, although the pseudo-Solomonic Song of Songs not only is an anthology of Hebrew love songs but remains a lasting source of inspiration and imagination far beyond Hellenism and late antiquity.

The final word of 1b can be parsed both as the "beloved" feminine absolute state and as the "beloved" masculine emphatic state. So Brian McNeil's question, "At 7:1, is it not more natural to translate *rḥymʾ* by 'den Geliebten' [the beloved, masculine], a reference to Christ (cf. 3:5, 7), than by 'die Geliebte' [the beloved, feminine]?,"[17] can be taken up and carried forward (on the term "Christ," see below). McNeil's suggestion, if not "more natural," is certainly correct in syntax since the *status absolutus* is not possible here. So, even grammatically, ܪܚܝܡܐ (*rḥīmā*) as *status emphaticus* must refer to the beloved as masculine.[18]

Thus, the possessive suffix (third singular feminine) of the metaphorical "fruits" of 1c can refer either to "joy," taken as a feminine noun, or, if the person moved by joy should be a woman, to the implied feminine lover or beloved. The subject of the masculine participle ܡܥܠ (*maʿʿel, hapax legomenon*, Aph. of ܥܠ [*ʿal*]) could be the "course," but the final metaphor of the comparison makes sense only if "the beloved [masculine] harvests the fruits of the joy of the beloved [feminine]"—in other words, the totality of loving companionship.[19] The negative phrase, which should perhaps read ܕܠܐ ܟܠܝܢ (*d-lā ḵelyān*) in place of ܕܠܐ ܟܠܝܢܐ (*d-lā ḵelyānā*), corresponds to the Greek adverb ἀκωλύτως (cf. Acts 28:31; etc.).[20] What hindrance there might be to love is not made clear, but the whole poetic statement, unlike 14:6-7, remains firmly grounded in human life and experience.

The statement of salvation in 2-3a now leaves this plane, but without disparaging it. The redeemed "I," while still on its way, identifies the "Lord," who is not here the "beloved," in 2a with his "joy," which is reminiscent of the theological statement of Ps 43:4, but without parallel in early Christian writings.[21] The phrase "my course" beside "my joy" picks up another key word from the comparison in 1a-b. The term "way" (2b), which is synonymous with "running," connects part 1 and part 2 (see on 7:13 below and Excursus 15). The judgment that "my way"[22] is beautiful—viz., well adapted to

11 On this form, cf. 1:1; 6:1-2; 7:1; 15:1-2a; 16:1; 28:1-2; 40:1.
12 Harnack, 33.
13 Payne Smith, 2:3835.
14 See Payne Smith, 1:1199. On the transcription of ܚܕܘܬܐ (*ḥaḏuṯā*), see Klaus Beyer, *Die aramäischen Texte vom Toten Meer samt den Inschriften aus Palästina, dem Testament Levis aus der Kairoer Genisa, der Fastenrolle und den alten talmudischen Zitaten* (2 vols.; Göttingen: Vandenhoeck & Ruprecht, 1984–2004) 2:59.
15 See Otto Michel, "Freude," *RAC* 8 (1972) 400–401; and Hans Conzelmann, "χαίρω . . . χάρις, κτλ.," *ThWNT* 9 (1973) 362; cf. *TDNT* 9:371–72.
16 Harris and Mingana, 2:246.
17 Brian McNeil, review of Lattke, *Bedeutung*, vols. 1–2 in *Ostkirchliche Studien* 29 (1980) 193.
18 Brockelmann, *Grammatik* §§89 and 191; Robinson and Brockington, 21; contra Lattke, *Bedeutung*, 1:97.
19 Lattke, *Oden*, 109.
20 Payne Smith, 1:1740; BDAG, *s.v.* ἀκωλύτως: "without hindrance."
21 In 3:5 and 3:7 the "Lord" is the "Beloved." This identification, then, surpasses the Johannine χαίρω and χαρά statements (see John 3:29; 14:28; 15:11; 16:20, 22, 24; 17:13; 1 John 1:4).
22 The strange construction in ς may be another indication of a Greek original: αὕτη ἡ ὁδός μου καλή.

its objective[23]—is justified in 3a because (ܓܝܪ [*gēr*]) the speaking "I" has the "Lord" of 2a as his "helper."[24]

Harris and Mingana were probably right to suspect that the Greek *Vorlage* of the Syriac text of 3a was *βοηθὸν γὰρ ἔχω τὸν Κύριον*.[25] The idea, which their commentary of 1920 discounted, was underpinned linguistically by Sebastian Brock in 1975:[26]

> Before Greek can be finally ruled out as the original language the following points need to be taken into consideration: in 7:3 the Syriac has *mʿaddrana ʾit li l-marya* "I have the Lord as a helper"; the construction with *lamedh* is without parallel except in (late) translation literature, where *ʾit li* is taken as a syntactic unit equivalent to ἔχω, and the Greek object, instead of becoming subject in Syriac (as normal), is mechanically introduced by *lamedh*.[27]

Verse 3a has no connection with the *παράκλητος* passages (John 14:16, 26; 15:26; 16:7; 1 John 2:1),[28] the more so as ܦܪܩܠܝܛܐ (*paraqlīṭā*) is one of many Greek loanwords found in Syriac.[29]

■ **3b-c** The Aph. ܐܘܕܥ (*ʾawdaʿ*) from the root *ydʿ*, which dominates this Ode, is found in only one other passage in the *Odes*. In that one the "perfect virgin," "Grace" personified, calls to her "elect": "my ways I shall make known to those who seek me" (33:13). The parallel is heightened by the use of the term "way" (see 2b above). Even if stanza II acts only as a "prelude to the greater detail" of stanza III, the fact that "3b introduces the theme of knowledge"[30] is important. The motif of *gnōsis* first appears here and is carried through in all three parts of the Ode (7-9, 13-14, 21, 23).

Excursus 7: "Knowledge" and "To Know" in the *Odes of Solomon*

The large number of forms derived from the root ܝܕܥ (*ydʿ*) led Kurt Rudolph to the conclusion that "the Gnostic character of the *Odes of Solomon* is certain."[31] In the same way, what Bultmann wrote about the "Gnostic usage" of (ἐπι)γινώσκω and (ἐπί)γνωσις, even before the Nag Hammadi texts or the Dead Sea Scrolls were discovered, is also valid, in the main, with respect to the *Odes of Solomon*, namely, that the specifically Gnostic "knowledge" (1) is distinct from all other kinds of knowledge;[32] (2) is "illumination given by God" and "ecstatic or mystical

23 Cf. BDAG *s.v.* καλός, 2.

24 As I concluded some time ago, "3a actually belongs to 2b as its justification" (Lattke, *Oden*, 109). In this I disagree with Franzmann (p. 53), although her translation "For I have a helper, the Lord" is correct.

25 Harris and Mingana, vol. 1, note on *Ode* 7:3a; on ܡܥܕܪܢܐ (*mʿaddrānā*), *adjutor, auxiliator, βοηθός*, etc., see Payne Smith 2:2815–16.

26 Harris and Mingana, 2:242; Sebastian Brock, review of Charlesworth in *BSOAS* 38 (1975) 143.

27 These observations, which Emerton ("Notes," 512–13) does not fully consider, are supported, independently of Brock, in a letter to me from Professor Jan Joosten (Strasbourg University) of October 1, 1996: "When I got to the Odes of Solomon . . . its linguistic form came as a shock to me. . . . The only place where I had seen anything remotely similar was in the Syrohexapla. I concluded that the Syriac text must have been translated from Greek, and I have been mystified ever since by the refusal of other Syriologists to see things the same way. . . . The syntax of 7:3a points, I believe, conclusively to a Greek *Vorlage*. . . . A meaning 'I have a helper unto the Lord' is really impossible in Syriac, for it would require ܠܘܬ ܡܪܝܐ [cf. Gal 3,24]. . . . Harris' initial idea is therefore to be retained. The syntax is that of Apoc 9:11 in the Harklean version: ܘܐܝܬ ܠܗܘܢ ܡܠܟܐ ܥܠܝܗܘܢ ܠܡܠܐܟܐ ܕܬܗܘܡܐ." My earlier translations must, therefore, be corrected (Lattke, *Bedeutung*, 1:97; *Oden*, 109), as also the note on Godfrey Rolles Driver, "Notes on Two Passages in the *Odes of Solomon*," *JTS* n.s. 25 (1974) 434–37 (Lattke, *Bedeutung*, 3:312); see also Jan Joosten, "*Odes de Salomon* 7,3a: Observations sur un hellénisme dans le texte syriaque," *ZNW* 89 (1998) 135: "The only possible translation is 'for I have as helper the Lord.'"

28 Contra Otto Betz, *Der Paraklet: Fürsprecher im häretischen Spätjudentum, im Johannes-Evangelium und in neu gefundenen gnostischen Schriften* (AGSU 2; Leiden: Brill, 1963) 216.

29 Payne Smith, 2:3299; Brockelmann, *Lexicon*, 606.

30 Franzmann, 57.

31 Kurt Rudolph, "War der Verfasser der *Oden Salomos* ein 'Qumran-Christ'? Ein Beitrag zur Diskussion um die Anfänge der Gnosis," *RevQ* 4 (1964) 525.

32 The next part of the quotation is important for the conjecture in 7:10b: "and this is in keeping with the restriction of ἀλήθεια . . . and οὐσία to the divine reality and nature" (Rudolf Bultmann, "γινώσκω, κτλ.," *ThWNT* 1 [1933] 693; cf. *TDNT* 1:694).

vision" that includes also "the way which leads to it [knowledge]" and implies "the hearing of faith"; and (3) "invests the Gnostic with the divine nature, and therefore in the first instance with immortality" in such a way that the term "can be linked and even equated with ζωή and φῶς."[33]

This survey can best be started with a listing of the occurrences in the *Odes of Solomon* of the forms derived from the root *ydʿ* in order of frequency (with numbers of occurrences in parentheses):

ܝܕܥ (*ʾiḏaʿ*)	know (32)
ܝܕܥܬܐ (*ʾiḏaʿṯā*)	knowledge, *gnōsis*, understanding (19)[34]
ܐܬܝܕܥ (*ʾeṯiḏaʿ*)	be known (5)
ܐܫܬܘܕܥ (*ʾeštawdaʿ*)	know (4 or 5)[35]
ܡܕܥܐ (*maddʿā*)	mind, understanding, *gnōsis*, knowledge (4)
ܐܘܕܥ (*ʾawdaʿ*)	make known (2)

There are a few cases in which the words are not interpreted gnostically or are of no importance for a coherent soteriological usage.[36] On the borders of use as technical terms are 3:3 ("I should not have known to love the Lord"), 18:9-10, and 38:13. This last uses "wisdoms" and "understandings/knowledges," quite unusually in the plural, as parallels, while the second passage introduces the problem of dualism, not particularly strongly expressed in the *Odes*,[37] which here takes the form of reciprocal statements (cf. 4:7):

> And nothingness thou dost not acknowledge, because neither does it acknowledge thee.
>
> And thou knowest not error, because neither does it know thee. (18:9-10)

Another step brings out the passages where parallels and synonyms illuminate the meaning of "know" and "knowledge." Among the verbs, ܝܕܥ (*ʾiḏaʿ*) defines and is defined by "to be wise"/"to be awakened" (3:11), "to put on the Name of the Most High" (39:8; see Table 2), "to hear"/"to receive" (9:6-7; cf. 8:8), "to take" (19:5), "to be at rest" (26:12). Among the nouns "*gnōsis*" corresponds to the "language" of hymnody (7:23d-e), and the "word of Truth" is closely connected with the "*gnōsis* of the Most High" (8:8).

Each occurrence of the possessive phrase "*gnōsis* of the Most High" (8:8; 11:4; 23:4 [H]) or "*gnōsis* of the Lord" (7:21; 23:4 [N]) and the term "his [viz., the Lord's/the Most High's] knowledge" expressed by a suffix (6:6; 11:4; 12:3; cf. 23:4) raises the question whether this is a case of an objective or subjective genitive, that is, whether the Syriac possessive pronouns reflect an objective or subjective use of the Greek pronoun αὐτός. The meaning of the expression "the understanding of his [viz., the Lord's] mind" with its multiplicity of possessives will need to be considered further (38:21). Expressions like "my knowledge" (8:12; 17:12), "my understanding" (17:7), and "the thought of knowledge" (15:5) in the addresses of the redeemed Redeemer are just as ambiguous.

Other uses of the "adnominal" genitive also can be difficult to interpret,[38] for example, the combinations "the Father of *gnōsis*" who is "the word of *gnōsis*" (7:7) or "the perfection [fullness] of his [viz., the Lord's] knowledge" (23:4). Interpretation is easier where the term "*gnōsis*" (positive [+]) or "non-*gnōsis*" (negative [-]) is used as an absolute (7:13 [+]; 7:21 [-]; 7:23 [+, double negative]; 11:8 [+, double negative]; 18:11 [-]; 34:5 [-]).

In addition to this absolute use of the noun ܝܕܥܬܐ (*ʾiḏaʿṯā*), which can be used synonymously (e.g., 17:7) with ܡܕܥܐ (*maddʿā*), there is also the absolute use of the transitive verb ܝܕܥ (*ʾiḏaʿ*), where the context and synonyms serve to emphasize or suppress the soteriological connotation, which can equally be positive or negative (3:11 [+]; 8:9 [-]; 18:13 [+]; 19:5 [-]; 26:12 [+]).

The transitive uses of the Pe. ܝܕܥ (*ʾiḏaʿ*) and the Eshtaph. ܐܫܬܘܕܥ (*ʾeštawdaʿ*), whose meanings are almost interchangeable, are by far the commonest.[39] When these are sorted by the direct object of "knowledge" (including the subjects of the Ethpe. ܐܬܝܕܥ [*ʾeṯiḏaʿ*]), they form two distinct groups.

In the first, "the Most High" knows the "redeemed Redeemer" (17:7) and, protologically, his "Messiah" (41:15). As the Creator he knows beforehand what his creatures will do (7:9); also "the Lord" "acknowledges his children" (41:2) as the Revealer does his own (8:14). The personified "Aeons" knew

33 Bultmann, "γινώσκω, κτλ.," *ThWNT* 1:692–96; cf. *TDNT* 1:692–96. On "Gnostic Christianity" in the early second century C.E., see Arnold Ehrhardt, "Christianity before the Apostles' Creed," *HTR* 55 (1962) 96–104.

34 Cf. esp. 11:4 (σύνεσις) and 11:18 (ἀλογιστία).

35 Cf. ⲥⲟⲟⲩⲛ̄ (*sow*^{e}*n*) in 6:18 ℭ.

36 Cf. 8:20; 12:6; 16:13; 23:10; 28:13; 38:7.

37 Rudolph, "Verfasser," 526.

38 BDF and BDR §163.

39 See Payne Smith, 1:1554–57; Payne Smith, *Dictionary*, 187–88.

their maker (12:10). And the "seal," also personified, which is itself "known" (see below), knows God's "creatures" (4:7). Only some of these statements can be described as Gnostic.

The passages in the second group, in which human beings, believers awaiting deliverance and Gnostics already redeemed, are the subject of these statements of salvation, occur more often. The objects of their knowledge are:

Creator	7:12
Most High	7:16; 9:7 (?)
Name of the Most High	39:8
Lord	12:13; see on 7:3b and 9:7 below
Mercy of the Lord	23:4; 24:14 (Way?)
Holiness of the Lord	24:14
Fountain of the Lord	30:6
Seal of the Lord	4:7
Way/ways of the Lord	3:10; 24:14 (Mercy?); cf. 33:13[40]
Revealer	8:12
Gnōsis of the Revealer	8:12
Redeemer	42:3 (N); 42:8
Origin of the Redeemer	28:16 (N)[41]
Gnostics	6:6; 6:18 (ministers of the drink?)
themselves	6:18 ℭ (?)[42]
Origin	28:16 (N) (?, see "Redeemer" above)
Ministers of the drink	6:18 (Gnostics?)
All	12:13

Ode 7:3b (see above) can also be counted, indirectly, as part of this second group, even though the grammatical subject of the statement of salvation is the "Lord." For the Aph. "let [me] know" implies that the speaking "I," who has the "Lord" as his helper in his "course" toward the "Lord" (2a-3a), has become a Gnostic.

So the speaking "I," who in part 2 will be the subject of another's discourse (12a, 15a) before the field of view in that speech widens to include a multitude in part 3, has recognized the "Lord." Whether he is a (or the) Revealer, the preeminent "son" (15), will be discussed later (see on 15b below). But it is already possible to say that the "Lord" has really appeared to him as the "Father of *gnōsis*" (7)[43] and that "without jealousy" (in 𝔊 probably ἀφϑόνως; see on 3:7 above) in or through his ܦܫܝܛܘܬܐ (*pšīṭūṯā*), which in this case corresponds to ἁπλότης, *simplicitas*.[44] These virtues can be applied theologically, because no human being is altogether without jealousy or completely single-hearted.

The anthropomorphizing phrase "let [me] know"[45] is explained in 3c (ܓܝܪ [*gēr*]) by the Lord's "kindness" (this must be χρηστότης in 𝔊; see Excursus 14), which has diminished his "greatness."[46] Grammatically, both "greatness" and "kindness" can be the subject of this theological statement of salvation. However, it makes sense as a transition to stanza III only if the prepositional ܪܒܘܬܗ (*rabbūṯeh*) draws attention to the direct object, which also shows that the term "greatness" refers to the "Most High," as it does in 36:5 and in the phrase ܪܒܘܬ ܝܐܝܘܬܐ (*rabbūṯ yāʾyūṯā*), which certainly translates the Greek μεγαλοπρέπεια.[47] But even by itself the feminine noun ܪܒܘܬܐ (*rabbūṯā*) can mean *majestas* or *magnificentia*.[48]

40 The "making known" (Aph. ܐܘܕܥ [*ʾawdaʿ*]) of the "ways" corresponds to the "knowledge" of the seekers.

41 This negative statement implies that the brothers recognize his "birth." The speaking "I" may not even be the Redeemer, but one of the redeemed, a noteworthy Gnostic.

42 Even if this statement in ℭ is intended reflexively, it still has no connection with the Greek maxim γνῶϑι σαυτόν (Bultmann, "γινώσκω, κτλ.," *ThWNT* 1:689; cf. *TDNT* 1:690).

43 This is not a case of ecstasy, nor of visual or auditory apparition. Reading more ecstatic or visionary material into the text than is actually there is unscholarly.

44 See Payne Smith, 2:3321; BDAG, *s.v.* ἁπλότης, 1; Joseph Amstutz, *ΑΠΛΟΤΗΣ: Eine begriffsgeschichtliche Studie zum jüdisch-christlichen Griechisch* (Theophaneia 19; Bonn: Hanstein, 1968) 123; see also Connolly ("Greek," 530–31), who cites 2 Cor 8:2; 9:11, 13 (ἁπλότης), and Jas 1:5 (ἁπλῶς). He declares: "The Odes were composed in Greek."

45 Literally "he made his soul known to me." The term "soul" expresses "the reflexive relation with accuracy" (Nöldeke §223).

46 For the Aph. of ܙܥܪ (*zʿar*) (*hapax legomenon*), see Payne Smith, 1:1144, *diminuit*; linguistically, cf. Sir 3:19.

47 Cf. 7:23; 15:7; 18:16; 29:3; see Jan Joosten in his previously cited letter of October 1, 1996 (n. 27 above): "Other cases could be mentioned: I think ܪܒܘܬ ܝܐܝܘܬܐ does reflect μεγαλοπρέπεια."

48 Payne Smith, 2:3787.

Since the subject of 3c is the "gentleness" or "kindness" of *God*,[49] this theological statement connects neither in wording nor in meaning with Phil 2:6-8, where the reflexive expression ἐταπείνωσεν ἑαυτόν (2:8; cf. Syriac ܘܡܟܟ ܢܦܫܗ [*w-makkek napšeh*]) refers, hymnically, to the way the Χριστὸς Ἰησοῦς (2:5) or the κύριος Ἰησοῦς Χριστός (2:11) humbles himself in the incarnation. *Ode* 7 is not about the incarnation of God but about his merciful revelation in the profound self-discovery of the speaking "I," who is preparing to apply Gen 1:26-27 to himself.

■ **4-6** The statement of salvation in 5a-b is shown to be central to stanza III[50] by the parallelism of 4a-b and 6a-b, with the mechanically recurring conjunction ܡܛܠ ܕ (*mettol d-*) + imperfect following various comparisons, which are all gnostically tinged and seem to express some kind of "consubstantiality."[51]

Harnack recognized in this "a naïve modalist (*modalistisch*) Christology . . . (differing from Phil 2)" which "portrays God as incarnate" in a Christian fashion,[52] and his influence can be felt when Kittel calls 3b-6 "indubitably Christian," saying it "obviously" refers to the incarnation;[53] when Harris and Mingana do not doubt "that the Odist is occupied in the first instance with the Incarnation";[54] when even Georg Richter much later speaks of the "incarnation of the Redeemer."[55] Luise Schottroff at least questions this interpretation by quoting 7:3-6 as an example of God "lowering himself to equality with humans" and thus one of the texts "which include the incarnation of Jesus, docetically, in a Gnostic mythos of descent and therefore are not evidence for a Gnostic mythologoumenon of incarnation."[56] So the "incarnation of Jesus" has entered the discussion, together with the term "docetic,"[57] with which Charlesworth takes issue: "The insistence that the Lord became a man shows that the Odes are not thoroughly docetic," although he finds no "polemic against Docetism" because of "the docetic overtones in other passages (viz., Odes 17:6, 28:17ff., 41:8; 42:10)."[58]

The fault in all these interpretations is that they take the "Lord" of part 1 to be the Logos of John 1:14 (ὁ λόγος σὰρξ ἐγένετο ["the *Logos* became flesh"]); the mystery of 1 Tim 3:16 (ὃς ἐφανερώθη ἐν σαρκί ["he was revealed in flesh"]); the Son of Gal 4:4 (ἐξαπέστειλεν ὁ θεὸς τὸν υἱὸν αὐτοῦ ["God sent his Son"]); or the image of Col 1:15-22 (ὅς ἐστιν εἰκὼν τοῦ θεοῦ . . . ἐν τῷ σώματι τῆς σαρκὸς αὐτοῦ διὰ τοῦ θανάτου ["he is the image of God . . . in the body of his flesh through death"]). But stanza III says nothing of all this.

The speaking "I," who will later confess his creatureliness (9) and who is equated with the manifested and to-be-redeemed Son (12a, 15b, 16a), in fact compares himself on his "course" *toward* the "Lord" (2a)[59] with this same "Lord," who has "let me know him" (3b). The vocabulary for this quadripartite comparison has been taken in part from Gen 1:26-27, and displays an early stage of naïve Gnostic use of a biblical passage, which becomes a "basic anthropological and soteriological text" in Gnosticism, where it loses all historical connection.[60] The *locus classicus* of humanity's "likeness" to God warrants closer examination:

49 See BDAG, *s.v.* χρηστότης, 2b, which lists ἀγάπη, ἔλεος, and φιλανθρωπία as parallel terms.

50 Franzmann, 58.

51 Rudolph, "Verfasser," 525–26.

52 Harnack, 34.

53 Kittel, 53–54.

54 Harris and Mingana, 2:246.

55 Georg Richter, "Die Fleischwerdung des Logos im Johannesevangelium," *NovT* 13 (1971) 104–5 = Georg Richter, *Studien zum Johannesevangelium* (ed. Josef Hainz; BU 13; Regensburg: Pustet, 1977) 167–68.

56 Luise Schottroff, *Der Glaubende und die feindliche Welt: Beobachtungen zum gnostischen Dualismus und seiner Bedeutung für Paulus und das Johannesevangelium* (WMANT 37; Neukirchen-Vluyn: Neukirchener Verlag, 1970) 223 and 281.

57 See Pierre Batiffol, "Les Odes de Salomon," *RB* 8 (1911) 176–80.

58 Charlesworth, 37.

59 This "course" may be compared to the "ascent" of 35:7:

> And I stretched out my hands in the ascent of myself (literally "soul"),
> And I directed myself toward the Most High,
> And I was moved toward him.

60 Jervell, *Imago Dei*, 169.

Genesis 1:26-27

26 And God said, "Let us make man in our image, after our likeness, and let them have dominion . . ."

ὁ ϑεός	ܐܠܗܐ	אלהים
ἄνϑρωπον	ܐܢܫܐ	אדם
κατ᾿ εἰκόνα ἡμετέραν	ܒܨܠܡܢ	בצלמנו
καὶ καϑ᾿ ὁμοίωσιν	ܐܝܟ ܕܡܘܬܐ	כדמותנו

27 So God created man in his own image, in the image of God created he him; male and female created he them.

ὁ ϑεός	ܐܠܗܐ	אלהים
τὸν ἄνϑρωπον	ܠܐܕܡ	את־האדם
κατ᾿ εἰκόνα . . .	ܒܨܠܡܗ . . .	בצלמו . . .
. . . ϑεοῦ	ܒܨܠܡ ܐܠܗܐ . . .	. . . בצלם אלהים . . .[61]

The first half of 4b clearly relates to the "likeness" of Gen 1:26 (on ܕܡܘܬܐ [*dmūṯā*] cf. 17:4; 34:4).[62] When one considers that the *hapax legomenon* ܨܘܪܬܐ (*ṣūrtā*) in the first half of 6b is both a synonym of ܕܡܘܬܐ and often used to translate εἰκών (e.g., Wis 7:26; Rom 8:29),[63] the origin of this comparison in the εἰκών/צלם passages of Gen 1:26-27 is easily seen, although Syriac also offers the term ܨܠܡܐ (*ṣalmā*).[64] After all, this is not a direct quotation but an allusion to a well-known text.

Comparisons are not equations. This is especially true in any theological discussion in which the word "god" occurs as a human attempt to make it clear that the infinite all—and finite humanity within it—is neither self-created nor able to be explained from within. The world and humanity can never attain "lordship" over themselves. What the speaking "I" is saying is a conclusion from Gen 1:26-27, not an inversion of the Judeo-Christian theologoumenon, as if he were claiming that God was made in the speaker's human image.

By placing the perfect tense at the beginning, 4a expresses the "result of a prior occurrence," and the full form ܗܘܐ (*hwā*) should not be translated as "became" but as "was" or even as "is," like γέγονε.[65] The term ܐܟܘܬ (*ʾakwāṯ*), with a personal suffix, is a construct state of an abstract noun, not recorded in use, derived from ܐܝܟ (cf. 6a-b) describing the quality of a thing or person.[66] The first of the "dependent, subordinate clauses pointing to the future,"[67] all four of which correspond to final clauses with ἵνα or ἵνα μή,[68] declares that the outcome is "receiving" or "accepting" the "Lord," who is represented by the accusative suffix. The verb ܢܣܒ (*nsab*), which is especially used to translate λαμβάνω (cf. 11:4),[69] and occurs as a parallel to "to know" (9:7), is found in the *Odes of Solomon* with the direct objects "grace" (5:3; 23:2), "*gnōsis*" (11:4), "salvation" (15:6), "life" (31:7), and "truth" (41:1). Taking into account the

61 Translation of the Hebrew from Claus Westermann, *Genesis* (2 vols.; BKAT 1.1–2; Neukirchen-Vluyn: Neukirchener Verlag, 1974–81) 1:108. See his excursus "On the History of the Interpretation of Gen 1:26–27" (1:203–14) which begins: "The statement that God made man in his own image, has, ever since the history of interpretation came into contact first with the Greek and then with the modern understanding of humanity, been discussed more than perhaps any other passage in the OT. The material about it is endless. It displays a concentration of interest in the theological discussion about mankind, in the question: What is a human being?" (1:204). From his recognition that Gen 1:26–30 "is not a statement about humanity but about an act of God" (1:214) the Old Testament scholar draws "an important theological conclusion. If this [viz., Gen 1:26-27] deals with being human as such, not something partial and not something larger than being human, then it is truly and seriously valid for all human beings. God . . . has created all of them in such a way that something can take place between the Creator and this creature. . . . Every human being, of whatever religion, and from any region where no religions are acknowledged, is made in the image of God" (1:217–18). Hebrew text from *BHS*; Syriac from *OTSy* pt. 1 fasc. 1; Greek from Rahlfs, 1:2.

62 See Payne Smith, 1:914.

63 See ibid., 2:3386.

64 See ibid., 2:3408; Koehler and Baumgartner, 3:963.

65 See Nöldeke §256.

66 Payne Smith, 1:148.

67 Nöldeke §267.

68 See Frankenberg, 9; BDF and BDR §369.

69 See Payne Smith, 2:2392.

whole context of stanza III, there is a notable parallel in 17:4, where the redeemed Redeemer says "I received the face and figure (ܕܡܘܬܐ) of a new person (πρόσωπον)."[70]

The translation of the Ethpe. of ܣܒܪ (*sbar*) by "seem" avoids giving rise to any thoughts of an epiphany in 4b. As with the intransitive use of δοκέω, the meaning is "to have the appearance of" (cf. 17:6),[71] not "to be seen" (see on 12 and 18 below). The preposition ܒ (*b*-), always used as a prefix, whose basic meaning is "in," will change in translation according to the specific term (e.g., *forma, figura, species, similitudo*; μορφή, τύπος, ὁμοίωμα, εἰκών)[72] chosen to translate ܕܡܘܬܐ (*dmūṯā*). The second final clause uses the Pe. ܠܒܫ (*lbeš*) metaphorically; like "receive" in 4a, its direct objects include "grace" (4:6; 20:7), "seal" (4:8), "holiness" (13:3), "the name of the Most High" (39:8), "incorruption" (15:8), "light" (21:3), "love" (23:3), and "joy" (23:1; for a fuller listing see Table 2, following 4:6). The speech of the perfect virgin Grace in 33:12 is not an exact parallel, but its content is very close to this passage, since the object is also a personified Power:

> And they who have put me on shall not be oppressed,
> but will gain incorruption in the new world.[73]

In order to bring out the parallelism between 4a-b and 6a-b, commentary on 5a-b is postponed (see below).

In 6a also ܗܘܐ (*hwā*) is not enclitic but corresponds to Greek ἐγένετο in the sense of "was."[74] The *hapax legomenon* ܟܝܢܐ (*kyānā*), which Syrian theologians were to use later in the debate on the dogma *de duabus in Christo naturis*, is used already here in the sense of "nature" as φύσις, bringing out most clearly the idea of consubstantiality referred to above.[75] There is a similar and contemporary use of φύσις in 2 Pet 1:4, but there it refers specifically to the "divine nature" and does not promise "a future deification, a transformation into God's proper being . . . but rather a partaking of the divine nature."[76] The word translated "experience" in the final clause actually means "learn," as in 13:2 (ܐܠܦ [*ʾilep̄*]),[77] but can be used, like μανθάνω, with a transferred meaning "to appropriate to oneself,"[78] which brings out the parallelism with "receive" (4a) and "put on" (4b) even more clearly.

ܨܘܪܬܐ (*ṣūrtā*) in 6b is also a *hapax legomenon* in the *Odes of Solomon* (see above following the quotation of Gen 1:26-27). The final clause, in this case a negative one, with the imperfect of ܗܦܟ (*hp̄ak*), goes particularly well with the synonym of ܕܡܘܬܐ (*dmūṯā*), and finds as it were a downward parallel to 8:14, where the Revealer says, "For I do not turn away my face from my own, because I know them."[79]

It is now time to turn to the central part of 4-6. Criticizing certain ideas of religion, the speaking "I," using

70 See Jervell, *Imago Dei*, 167–68, on equivalents of εἰκῶν. Since the incarnation is not a topic of stanza III, John 1:12 (ὅσοι δὲ ἔλαβον αὐτόν ["all who received him"]) cannot be adduced as a parallel (contra Harris and Mingana, 2:240). However, the Pa. ܩܒܠ (*qabbel*) used in this passage could be used as a synonym of ܢܣܒ (cf. 7:10; 8:8; 9:5; 17:14; 31:6; 41:3).

71 BDAG, *s.v.* δοκέω, 2; Payne Smith, 2:2510.

72 Payne Smith, 1:914.

73 The term "garment" (Syriac ܠܒܘܫܐ [*lbūšā*]) is also "a term synonymous with εἰκών" (Jervell, *Imago Dei*, 168).

74 See Nöldeke §299.

75 See Payne Smith, 1:1703.

76 Anton Vögtle, *Der Judasbrief / Der 2. Petrusbrief* (EKKNT 22; Solothurn/Düsseldorf: Benziger; Neukirchen-Vluyn: Neukirchener Verlag, 1994) 141.

77 Payne Smith, 1:212; 1:1599.

78 BDAG, *s.v.* μανθάνω, 3.

79 Dibelius is right to call the "soteriology" of the *Odes* "Gnostic" "not in the sense of a heresy, but of a great religious movement" (Martin Dibelius, "Ἐπίγνωσις ἀληθείας," in *Neutestamentliche Studien Georg Heinrici zu seinem 70. Geburtstag [14. März 1914]* [Leipzig: Hinrichs, 1914] 186 = *Botschaft und Geschichte: Gesammelte Aufsätze*, vol. 2: *Zum Urchristentum und zur hellenistischen Religionsgeschichte* [ed. Günther Bornkamm and Heinz Kraft; Tübingen: Mohr Siebeck, 1956] 10). He also accepts the verbs "know," "take," and "put on" as synonyms. Whether this passage can be described as "unadulterated mysticism" is more doubtful.

yet another *hapax legomenon* (ܙܘܥ, ܙܥ [*zāʿ*]), says that he did *not* "quiver or quake," did *not* "stagger,"[80] in fact did *not* have a soul-shattering (*tremendum*) experience when he saw the "Lord." This transferred and existential statement of salvation, which is in no sense the description of a vision, is answered in part 3 by the statement that the Lord "is near and sees" (19b).

The emphasis, however, is on the theological statement of 5b, where the conjunction ܡܛܠ ܕ (*meṭṭol d-*) corresponds to a justifying ὅτι. The translation of the remaining words is difficult, although a rechecking of the manuscript confirms that the pointing of ܚܰܢܢܝ[81] makes its first vowel "*a*." This leaves open two interpretations. Either this word, derived from the root *ḥn[n]* (*med. gem.*), is the adjective ܚܢܢܐ (*ḥannānā*) with a first person singular possessive suffix ("one who has compassion on me" – "my compassionator");[82] or ܚܢܢ (*ḥannan*), similar to ܩܛܠܢ (*qaṭlan*), is the Pe. perfect third singular ܚܢ (*ḥan*) with first singular accusative suffix ("he had compassion on me").[83]

If this word is interpreted as a verb, according to the second possibility, the opening words of 5b form a dependent clause, giving the reason for the main clause, "he had compassion on me."[84] This dependent clause, then, is a highly charged ontological statement, comparable to the historically influential Greek translation ἐγώ εἰμι ὁ ὤν ("I am the Being") of Exod 3:14. As in 11a or 34:4b, it is a statement of being, whether Platonically idealistic or not,[85] which surpasses the "theologically weighty parallel [Exod] 33:19."[86] Whether this mixture of theology and philosophical ontology is still acceptable after the end of the mythological era is a separate question.

If the word, however, is interpreted as a noun, 5b as a whole is the justification for the statement in 5a ("I did not tremble"). In either case the word ܗܘܝܘ (*hūyū*) is a reduplication of the personal pronoun, first as subject and then as "copula."[87] The pronoun suffixed to the "one showing compassion" corresponds to a Greek objective genitive like ἐλεήμων μου or οἰκτίρμων μου.[88]

■ **7-9** Both the introductory Gnostic definition (7), which is hardly a "*confessional* formula,"[89] and the tightly parallel tetracolon (8-9), whose subject is the relationship of the all-wise and foreknowing creator with the personified "Wisdom" and with the speaking "I" of stanzas I–V, are meant didactically. Words with the root ܝܕܥ (*ydʿ*) in 7 and 9b form the *inclusio* of stanza IV.[90]

Bauer's explanatory note on the lapidary monocolon (7),[91] which uses the enclitic personal pronoun as a copula, is far too general: "There is no knowledge without the word of knowledge, which produces it."[92] Kittel is also off target, remarking about the formulaic statement, "God gives knowledge that is of Himself as

80 See Payne Smith, 1:1105; BDAG, *s.vv.* σαλεύω and σείω.

81 See Charlesworth, *Manuscripts*, 34 line 11.

82 See Payne Smith, 1:1315.

83 Harnack (p. 34) has a note, clearly by Johannes Flemming, on the translation "he who has compassion on me," which states, incorrectly, "literally 'my compassion'" (followed by Diettrich, p. 24, and others), but then considers "perhaps it should rather be read as ܕܚܢܢܝ 'he who has had compassion on me.'"

84 Lattke, *Oden*, 110, contra Lattke, *Bedeutung*, 1:97.

85 Cf. Martin Hengel, *Judentum und Hellenismus: Studien zu ihrer Begegnung unter besonderer Berücksichtigung Palästinas bis zur Mitte des 2. Jh. v. Chr.* (WUNT 10; Tübingen: Mohr Siebeck, 1969) 295.

86 Cf. Werner H. Schmidt, *Exodus*, vol. 1: *Exodus 1-6* (BKAT 2.1; Neukirchen-Vluyn: Neukirchener Verlag, 1988) 105 and 178–79. Attention should be paid to his excursus (pp. 175–77) "On the Interpretation of Exod 3:14." Part of the text of Exod 33:19 LXX is καὶ ἐλεήσω ὃν ἂν ἐλεῶ, καὶ οἰκτιρήσω ὃν ἂν οἰκτίρω (Rahlfs, 1:145), "and I will have mercy on whom I will have mercy, and I will have pity on whom I will have pity" (Brenton, 116). The contrast between the continuation of this speech of the Lord (κύριος) to Moses in Exod 33:20, Οὐ δυνήσῃ ἰδεῖν μου τὸ πρόσωπον· οὐ γὰρ μὴ ἴδῃ ἄνθρωπος τὸ πρόσωπόν μου καὶ ζήσεται ("Thou shalt not be able to see my face; for no man shall see my face, and live"), and the present passage is worth pondering.

87 Nöldeke §§312–13.

88 Cf. BDAG, *s.vv.* ἐλεήμων and οἰκτίρμων.

89 Franzmann, 58 (emphasis added).

90 See the structural analysis of Franzmann (p. 58) and her excursus "Word" (pp. 106–8).

91 There is no good reason for dividing the single line of the manuscript into a bicolon, although it is a frequent practice (e.g., Bauer, 584; Charlesworth, 33, 35; Fanourgakis, 145; Franzmann, 51, 54; Pierre, 74).

92 Bauer, 584.

God."[93] For a start, it is worth noting similar expressions in the *Odes* themselves, for example, 8:8, "Hear the word of truth and receive the *gnōsis* of the Most High."[94] Here *gnōsis* and "word" are parallels, as are "Most High" and "truth"; in 41:9 it is the "Father of truth" rather than the "Father of *gnōsis*." In 7, the terms intermingle, so that the name "Father" (cf. 8:23; 23:22), the originator and subject of *gnōsis*,[95] is, epexegetically (cf. 1 Cor 12:8), the actual "word of *gnōsis*."[96] Whoever knows the word "Father" in existential and soteriologically theological fashion is redeemed by it and freed from the domination of earthly paternity.[97]

Here too, though in different ways from Rom 11:33 (βάθος πλούτου καὶ σοφίας καὶ γνώσεως θεοῦ, "depth of the riches and wisdom and knowledge of God") or John 1:1-14 (ἐν ἀρχῇ ἦν ὁ λόγος . . . ὁ λόγος σὰρξ ἐγένετο, "In the beginning was the *Logos* . . . the *Logos* became flesh"), the influence of wisdom literature is clear (see below). But this does not mean that "knowledge is used as an equivalent of Truth and Wisdom."[98] Charlesworth draws attention to a passage in the Qumran scrolls (1QS iii.15),[99] which, in its dualistic and predestinarian context, may be among the sources for early Gnosticism:

מאל הדעות כול הווה ונהיה
ולפני היותם הכין כול מחשבתם

From the God of Knowledge comes all that is and shall be.
Before ever they existed He established their whole design.[100]

Like the "God of Knowledge" of the Qumran Jews, the "Father" of these early Christian Gnostics is equated in 8a-9b with the Creator, viz., with no-thing and no-body in the infinite universe. The teaching on the creation, not yet attributed to an *evil* demiurge,[101] is stated in 4:15: "And Thou, O Lord, hast made all."[102]

Verse 8a depends on a self-description of "Wisdom" personified, like that in Prov 8:22a (κύριος ἔκτισέν με, "the Lord created me"), which is taken up again in 13 (see below), but the play on words with the *hapax legomenon* ܚܟܝܡܐ (*ḥakkīmā*) in 8b surely belongs to the Syriac writer of the Ode. The plural of ܥܒܕܐ (*ʿbādā*) with the possessive suffix does not translate as "deeds" (as perhaps in 12:4[f]) but as "works" in the sense of individual "creatures" (4:7) or the whole of "creation" (7:24). These last two terms are derived from the same root as the Pe. ܒܪܐ (*brā*), found only in 8a and 9a, which translates both ברא (Gen 1:1) and קנה (Prov 8:22),[103] for which the LXX uses ποιέω and κτίζω respectively.[104] The Greek wording must therefore remain uncertain (Frankenberg suggests κτίσας, which is likely).[105]

93 Kittel, 31. Abbott's long-winded exposition (pp. 162–67) is, as usual, instructive and interesting but goes far beyond what the passage actually says.

94 *Ode* 8:8 uses "the originally Persian masculine *pethghama* in place of the more usual feminine *meltha*" (Bauer, 584). See also Excursus 12.

95 Eph 1:17 has a similar genitive coupling, ὁ πατὴρ τῆς δόξης ("the Father of glory"), again denoting both the originator and the subject (cf. BDAG, *s.v.* πατήρ, 6).

96 See BDAG, *s.vv.* γνῶσις and λόγος.

97 Harris and Mingana (2:249) call a similar utterance, by the Gnostic Markos about the name of Jesus and/or Christ, "an instance of the ill-luck that the Odes had in falling into the hands of the Valentinian Gnostics."

98 Harris and Mingana, 2:244.

99 Charlesworth, 37.

100 Text from Eduard Lohse, ed., *Die Texte aus Qumran: Hebräisch und deutsch mit masoretischer Punktation, Übersetzung, Einführung und Anmerkungen* (Darmstadt: Wissenschaftliche Buchgesellschaft, 1964) 10–11; translation from Geza Vermes, *The Dead Sea Scrolls in English* (3rd ed.; London: Penguin, 1987; repr., 1990) 64. Cf. 1QH ix.26–27 [previously i.26–27]: "For thine, O God of knowledge, are all righteous deeds and the counsel of truth; but to the sons of men is the work of iniquity and deeds of deceit" (Vermes, 167–68). This parallel is not, however, as striking as 1QS iii.15.

101 Compare BDAG, *s.v.* δημιουργός, with Lampe, *s.v.* δημιουργός, A.g–i.

102 For the teaching on creation, one of the didactic themes of the *Odes of Solomon*, see also 7:24; 8:18-20b; 16:8-19. Abbott (pp. 168–78) has collected a plethora of material on the "Lord" as "Creator."

103 See Koehler and Baumgartner, 3:1039.

104 *OTSy* pt. 1 fasc. 1; pt. 2 fasc. 5; Payne Smith, 1:600.

105 Frankenberg, 9.

The speaking "I" of the first part (1-11) of the Ode now includes himself in this doctrine of creation (9a) and combines the eternal plan of the Creator (cf. 4:2b-c) with his foreknowledge (9b; cf. Charlesworth, who declares a little too emphatically that "the Odist does not express a predestinarian belief [as found in 1QS iii.13–iv.26]"[106]). What the Odist says, succinctly, if in high-flown language, using the imperfect of ܗܘܐ (*hwā*) and the participle of ܥܒܕ (*ʿḇaḏ*),[107] sounds like an abstract of Psalm 139,[108] a psalm that may also have given rise to similar utterances found in the Dead Sea Scrolls: "before creating them Thou knewest their works for ever and ever" (1QH i.7-8); "He knew their deeds before ever they were created" (CD ii.7–8).[109] This may be a case of Qumranic influence on the *Odes*.

The fact that the speaking "I" places himself on a level with preexistent "Wisdom"[110] is of more importance for the assurance of election, which the Ode ascribes to him, than his use of the verb ܥܒܕ (*ʿḇaḏ*), which, although used as a part of the language of creation in the *Odes*,[111] in this verse means only "to do" or "to make," as, for example, ἐργάζομαι or ποιέω.[112]

■ **10-11** Stanza V (10-11) marks the end of the first part, although the speaking "I" disappears as early as the end of the statement of salvation 10a-b,[113] so that the final formulaic instruction 11a-b is even more isolated. The "word-play on the root ܝܗܒ"[114] connects 5b with 10a, where the introductory prepositional phrase[115] draws the immediate consequence of 9 and, by use of the demonstrative pronoun ܗܢܐ (*hānnā*), which points to what is nearby,[116] includes the statement of salvation of 2b-6 as well as the teachings of 7-8. If the preposition ܒ (*b-*) is translated "in" or "through," the utterance about the "great compassion"[117] is reminiscent of Sir 16:12 and the formulaic expression in 1 Pet 1:3 (κατὰ τὸ πολὺ ἔλεος αὐτοῦ, "by his great mercy"), which is derived from the former. As in that pseudonymous work of the late first century C.E.,[118] the pronoun, in this passage a third masculine singular possessive suffix, refers to God as "Father," who in the Ode is also "the Lord" (ܡܪܝܐ, κύριος, see 2a-3a above), whereas in 1 Peter ὁ θεὸς καὶ πατήρ ("the God and Father") is clearly distinguished from the κύριος Ἰησοῦς Χριστός ("Lord Jesus Christ").

As in some other cases (e.g., 7:12; 10:2; 31:5), the commonly used verb ܝܗܒ (*yaḇ*) in 10b is translated "granted" (see Excursus 37), so that the dependent construction, with the conjunction ܕ (*d-*) and the two imperfect verbs "pointing towards the future,"[119] could more easily be translated by infinitives. The first imperfect clause, literally translated, says, "that I might entreat/beg of him" (on ܒܥܐ [*bʿā*], see Excursus 19). The granting of this petition, which sounds as unbounded as a dream, is delimited by the second imperfect clause, "and that I might receive of his being."[120]

The *hapax legomenon* ܕܒܚܬܐ (*deḇḥtā*), which was to be used later even of the eucharist (but cf. *Did.* 14:1-2, though the Greek there is ἡ θυσία ὑμῶν) and which corresponds to Greek θυσία,[121] is "completely

106 Charlesworth, 37.
107 See Nöldeke §§267, 277.
108 See esp. Ps 139:14-16 as part of the stanza 13-18. This psalm is "part hymn and part meditation on one of the most difficult problems in theology," which is "the divine omnipotence over space and time" (Hans-Joachim Kraus, *Psalmen* [2 vols.; BKAT 15.1–2; Neukirchen-Vluyn: Neukirchener Verlag, 1961; 3rd ed., 1966] 915, quoting Rudolf Kittel).
109 Vermes, 84, 166.
110 See Otto Plöger, *Sprüche Salomos (Proverbia)* (BKAT 17; Neukirchen-Vluyn: Neukirchener Verlag, 1984) 91–96, on "the witness of Wisdom regarding her origin" in Prov 8:22-31.
111 Cf. 4:2, 15; 7:12; 12:10; 15:7; 29:2; 36:5.
112 Payne Smith, 2:2765–66.
113 Verse 10a-b is a bicolon; subdividing b into b and c (Franzmann, 52, 54, 59) is unnecessary and hard to justify.
114 Franzmann, 59.
115 Cf. διὰ τοῦτο, BDAG, *s.v.* διά, 2b.
116 Brockelmann, *Grammatik* §84.
117 Cf. 21:1-2 where "compassion" is explained by the parallel term "salvation."
118 See Norbert Brox, *Der erste Petrusbrief* (EKKNT 21; Zurich: Benziger; Neukirchen-Vluyn: Neukirchener Verlag, 1979) 41–44.
119 Nöldeke §267.
120 The original reading was probably "being," not "sacrifice" (which is the reading of H; see next paragraph above). On the Pa. ܩܒܠ (*qabbel*) and its Greek equivalents such as δέχομαι und λαμβάνω, see Payne Smith, 2:3468.
121 Payne Smith, 1:807: etiam de eucharistia; BDAG, *s.v.* θυσία, 2.

meaningless,"[122] since there is no mention anywhere in the *Odes of Solomon* of a divine "sacrifice of the Cross,"[123] and the alternative translations "favor," "gift," "munificence," or "largesse"[124] are all uncertain. It is therefore advisable to turn to an early conjecture by Eberhard Nestle, which has important consequences for the hotly discussed question of the original language of the *Odes*.[125] For the word in 𝔊 is most likely to have been ΟΥϹΙΑ, which the Syriac translator misread as ΘΥϹΙΑ. So the Greek of 10a-b (with acknowledgment of Frankenberg)[126] was, in all probability:

διὰ τοῦτο ἠλεήσε με κατὰ τὸ πολὺ ἔλεος αὐτοῦ καὶ ἔδωκέν μοι αἰτεῖν παρ' αὐτοῦ καὶ μεταλαβεῖν τῆς οὐσίας αὐτοῦ.

The Syriac, then, should have been ܐܝܬܘܬܐ (*ʾītūtā*), though without all the philosophic-theological connotations that later accumulated around that abstract noun, derived from ܐܝܬ, which was itself originally a noun.[127] The use of *οὐσία* too will have been in a sense naïve, not connected with the debates in Platonic philosophy about "pure being and transcendence in general,"[128] and too early for the philosophic-theological discussions of the Apologists and church fathers about the being and nature of God.[129]

What the "nature"[130] of the Father is in this passage is made clear in the separate statement 11a-b, where the explanatory conjunction does not hark back to 10b. The first part of 11a, in ܡܛܠ ܕܗܘܝܘ (*mettol d-hūyū*), is an explanatory dependent clause (the Greek may have been a simple participial *ὤν*, or possibly *ὁ ὤν* [cf. Exod 3:14 LXX]), which elucidates the subsequent main clause, constructed with ܐܝܬ (*ʾīt*) and third masculine singular possessive suffix.

Although 11 is not strongly connected to 10 (or to 12), the number of terms denoting "being" in 11a reinforces the conjecture *οὐσία* in 10b. Untroubled by metaphysical, ontological, epistemological, or theological problems, the poet begins by simply stating, "He is" (cf. 16:18; 34:4-5). And, since the "Father" "is" the Creator in his divinity, he "exists,"[131] to put it uncritically, simply "imperishably" (see Excursus 28), something that can be said of no-thing and no-body in the world within the bounds of space and time. Even if the infinite universe should be eternal and therefore imperishable, *God's* imperishability transcends it. God "is" not and does not "exist" as this world is and exists.[132]

The exact interpretation of 11b depends on the meaning that the terms ܫܘܡܠܝܐ (*šumlāyā*) and ܥܠܡܐ (*ʿālmā*) bear in this passage and generally in the *Odes* (see Excursuses 22 and 35). The Gnosticizing character of this Ode makes it likely that the "Father" is not only the transcendental completion and perfection of the

122 Harnack, 34.
123 According to Bernard (p. 61), who makes this claim because he has also erroneously asserted "the fact of the incarnation" (see on 3-4 above). The case is different for NT passages such as Eph 5:2 and Heb 9:26; 10:12, where the idea of sacrifice occurs in connection with the love of Christ and the forgiveness of sin(s).
124 Harris and Mingana, 2:244.
125 A note by Nestle also deserves attention: "concerning my hypothesis of a confusion between *οὐσία* and *θυσία* in 7:12 [i.e., 7:10], it is worth comparing Mark 9:49 where the same misreading is recorded by the use of *hostia* and *substantia* in the Vetus Latina Mss" (Eberhard Nestle, review of Harnack and Diettrich in *ThLZ* 36 [1911] 587; cf. Richard Hugh Connolly, review of Kittel in *JTS* 15 [1913–14] 467).
126 Frankenberg, 9.
127 Payne Smith, 1:173; cf. Nöldeke §199.
128 Hans Joachim Krämer, *Der Ursprung der Geistmetaphysik: Untersuchungen zur Geschichte des Platonismus zwischen Platon und Plotin* (Amsterdam: Grüner, 1964; 2nd ed., 1967) 60, on Plato *Resp.* 509b (LCL 6:106–7); cf. Clemens Zintzen, ed., *Der Mittelplatonismus* (Wege der Forschung 70; Darmstadt: Wissenschaftliche Buchgesellschaft, 1981) *passim.*
129 Cf. LSJ, *s.v.* *οὐσία*; Lampe, 980–85, *s.v.* *οὐσία*; especially Origen *Cels.* 6.64 (ANF 4:602–3); Eric Osborn, *The Beginning of Christian Philosophy* (Cambridge: Cambridge University Press, 1981) 31–78; idem, *The Emergence of Christian Theology* (Cambridge: Cambridge University Press, 1993) *passim.*
130 Greßmann, 442.
131 See Nöldeke §303.
132 Grammatically it might be more correct to translate 11a-b as follows: "Because he is, he is [also] the imperishable *plērōma* of the Aeons and their father." Because of the verse form of the *Odes of Solomon*, however, it seemed better to interpret 11b in apposition to the main clause in 11a.

innumerable and limitless "worlds" (κόσμοι) but also the "fullness of the aeons beyond" (τὸ πλήρωμα τῶν αἰώνων), which sheds some light on the systematization later undertaken by the Valentinians. That he is also the "Father" of the "Aeons," that is, their creator and preserver, interprets the Gnostic term *plērōma*, as it were, in biblical fashion. It is, however, already possible to speak of the "unknown Father of the *plērōma*"[133] (but see on 16b below).[134]

■ **12** The esoteric statement of salvation in stanza VI is the beginning of the shorter part 2 (12-16a), in which the subject "he" is the same as the "Father" of part 1 (cf. the term "Son" in 15b). For "granted" as the translation of ܝܗܒ (*yab*), see the discussion of 10b. The parallelism of the beginnings of vv. 10b and 12a suggests that the indirect object of ܝܗܒ (*yab*) is identical with the speaking "I" of part 1 (cf. 2-6, 9-10). If this is so, the promise of epiphany (lit., "that he might appear"), which has remarkable parallels in other *Odes* (23:18; 41:13), also refers to this speaking "I." Even in this case, however, there is no thought of an incarnation.[135] And, though it is possible to speak of a "statement bearing a Johannine tinge" (Harnack, referring to John 1:11; 10:3, 4, 12; 13:1),[136] in fact the indirect object of the Ethpe. imperfect of ܚܙܐ (*ḥzā*)—"to those who are his"—must be related to the "Father" and not the "Son" (cf., therefore, John 17:6: σοὶ ἦσαν, "thine they were").

The parallelism of the bicolon 12b-c, which is verbally antithetical but complementary in content, uses the "word-pair ܥܒܕ—ܝܕܥ"[137] to explain the purpose of the epiphany. Those who are the "own" of the "Father" and "Lord" (cf. 26:1)[138] are to know their creator. This aim of 12b, which gives a biblical foundation to the Gnostic esoteric 12a, is undoubtedly influenced by Ps 99:3 LXX:[139]

> γνῶτε ὅτι κύριος, αὐτός ἐστιν ὁ θεός,
> αὐτὸς ἐποίησεν ἡμᾶς καὶ οὐχ ἡμεῖς,
> λαὸς αὐτοῦ καὶ πρόβατα τῆς νομῆς αὐτοῦ.

> Know that the Lord he is God;
> he made us, and not we ourselves;
> we are his people and the sheep of his pasture.

The term for "creating," which in 8a and 9a is ܒܪܐ (*brā*), is here the Pe. ܥܒܕ (*ʿbad*), a word that the Peshitta uses to translate עשׂה.[140] This word occurs regularly in the *Odes of Solomon* with the meaning "create"[141] and is also commonly used for "to do" (see 7:9a above, and elsewhere). In the use of the Eshtaph. ܐܫܬܘܕܥ (*ʾeštawdaʿ*), it can be seen how easily biblical vocabulary is used in Gnosticizing texts.

In Gnosticism, 12c especially exerted an influence, as the following quotation of *Tri. Trac.* 84,3-6 makes clear (*NHLE*, 76):

> ⲚⲈⲨⲘⲈⲨⲈ ⲀⲢⲀⲞ[Ⲩ] ϪⲈ ϨⲈⲚϢⲰⲠⲈ ⲀⲂⲀⲖ ⲘⲘⲀ[Ⲩ] ⲞⲨⲀ-
> ⲈⲈⲦⲞⲨ ⲚⲈ· ⲀⲨⲰ Ϩ[Ⲉ]ⲚⲀⲦⲀⲢⲬⲎ ⲚⲈ·

> They thought about themselves that they were beings originating from themselves alone and were without a source (-ἀρχή).[142]

133 Kurt Rudolph, *Die Gnosis: Wesen und Geschichte einer spätantiken Religion* (UTB 1577; 3rd ed.; Göttingen: Vandenhoeck & Ruprecht, 1990) 345.

134 On πατὴρ τῶν αἰώνων ("Father of the ages") in *1 Clem.* 35:3 (Ehrman, 1:96–97), see Hermann Sasse, "αἰών, αἰώνιος," *ThWNT* 1 (1933) 201; cf. *TDNT* 1:201.

135 Contra Harris and Mingana, 2:252.

136 Harnack, 35. Since "his own" in John 1:11 are treated negatively, which is not the case in the remainder of this Gospel, this reference can hardly be included. Similarly Diettrich's reference (p. 25) to John 3:27 is not relevant.

137 Franzmann, 59.

138 On the terms "his/my own," cf. also 8:14, 20; 42:20. In the immediate context of 7:12 it may be considered whether "those who are his" could be the "Aeons" of 11b, since in 12:10b they also "knew him who made them." I feel that this interpretation is too narrow. "Those who are his" refers to human beings, and potentially all of humankind since the full number of the "Gnostics" is not yet achieved.

139 Rahlfs, 2:107; Brenton, p. 758; see Harris and Mingana, 2:250; Harnack, p. 35; Diettrich, p. 25; Charlesworth, p. 38.

140 *OTSy* pt. 2 fasc. 3, on Ps 100:3; cf. Koehler and Baumgartner, 3:842–43.

141 Cf. 4:2, 15; 12:10; 15:7; 36:5.

142 Harold W. Attridge and Elaine H. Pagels, "The Tripartite Tractate. [NHC] I,5:51.1–138.27," in *Nag Hammadi Codex I (The Jung Codex)*, vol. 1: *Introductions, Texts, Translations, Indices* (ed. Harold W. Attridge; NHS 22; Leiden: Brill, 1985) 244–45.

However, there is still a long distance from *Ode* 7 to "revised traditional Valentinianism" as found in the third-century *Tractatus tripartitus* (*NHLE*, 58–60, 76). The purpose of the epiphany that the "Father" grants the being who is identical with the speaking "I" of part 1, whose revelation is not disclosed, is the theological recognition that human beings are not property, that they were made by no-thing and no-body in this world, and therefore cannot be self-originated either.[143]

■ **13-14** Even if 13a, as a sort of continuation of 8a, may be influenced by Prov 8:22 (κύριος ἔκτισέν με ἀρχὴν ὁδῶν αὐτοῦ, "The Lord created me at the beginning of his ways"), the metaphors of stanza VII already sound very much like Gnostic mythology.[144] The terms "way" and "*plērōma*" make a connection with part 1 (see 2b, 11b above). The "way" of the "Father," which is the dualistic opposite of the "way of error" (15:6), is "laid" as in 39:13 (see Excursus 15). The postpositive particle ܓܝܪ (*gēr*) does not refer causally to stanza VI but emphasizes the word "knowledge,"[145] which takes first place in ܣ, and which, with the prefix ܠ (*l*-), not only defines the "goal" of the metaphorical "way" but also its task and "outcome."[146]

There are three verbs in 13b, of which the middle one, the Aph. ܐܘܪܟ (*ʾawrek*), is a *hapax legomenon*, while the first Aph. ܐܦܬܝ (*ʾaptī*) belongs to the vocabulary of creation (16:10) and may metaphorically be used of the spreading of the "grace" of the Lord (24:13b; 24:13a also refers to the "way"). The third Aph. ܐܝܬܝ (*ʾaytī*) means literally *venire fecit*,[147] but the preposition ܥܠ (*ʿal*) presents difficulty for the translator because it "scarcely ever indicates the mere direction 'to', but often on the other hand the hostile sense 'against' [with accusative]."[148] The metaphorical ܫܘܡܠܝܐ (*šumlāyā*) is used in a concrete sense, not as an abstraction, and must be translated, as is the case with "way," by a word that will bring out the connotation of space, though without a sense of the inimical (see Excursus 35), which means that the preposition also cannot be translated "against" but must be something like "onto" or "over."[149]

Verse 14a, which is shown to be parallel with 13a by the use of ܣܡ (*sām*), speaks in an extremely mythologized fashion of the "tracks of light," which in 10:6 are laid not on a "way" but "on their hearts" (see Excursus 10). This expression is indeed "obscure"; whether it also "evidently has a special meaning"[150] is less clear. It is quite possible that Sir 50:28-29 has influenced the phraseology (cf. esp. θεὶς αὐτὰ ἐπὶ καρδίαν ["lay them to heart"] and φῶς κυρίου τὸ ἴχνος αὐτοῦ ["the light of the Lord is his path"]).[151] This does not explain the image. The "tracks," which are literally "footprints" in Greek and Syriac[152] as well as in English, can only "remain" on the water (39:10-11) as a poetic metaphor, and in the same way these signs of "the light of the Father" (cf. esp. 29:7; 39:7) are an image that people in antiquity may have interpreted by a glance at the Milky Way.[153]

143 See Lampe, 268, *s.vv.* αὐτογενής and αὐτογένητος. The use of ܢܦܫܐ (*napšā*) in 12c, as also in 3b, serves to "express the reflexive relation with accuracy" (Nöldeke §223).

144 Cf., e.g., *Gos. Truth* 37,25–38,4; *NHLE*, 49.

145 See Lattke, "Wörter," 287 = idem, *Bedeutung*, 4:135–36.

146 BDAG, *s.v.* εἰς, 4.

147 Payne Smith, 1:415.

148 Nöldeke §250; Payne Smith, 1:416. Therefore the following translations are erroneous: "to all completion" (Harnack, 35), "to all perfection" (Harris and Mingana, 2:241), "altogether to completion" (Greßmann, 443), "altogether to perfection" (Bauer, 585), "to complete perfection" (Charlesworth, 36, with misleading reference to 1QS xi.11), "to complete fulfilment" (Lattke, *Bedeutung*, 1:97), "to total perfection" (Franzmann, 54), and "to the complete *plērōma*" (Lattke, *Oden*, 111). Pierre's translation "sur toute la plénitude" ("over the whole *plērōma*") is accurate (Pierre, 75).

149 Brockelmann, *Grundriss* §§249–50.

150 Harris and Mingana, 2:245.

151 Rahlfs, 2:468; cf. Brenton, 120, in the appendix; Harris and Mingana, 2:253, whose *Expository Notes* (2:246–53) end in a wordplay: "Further illumination seems necessary." Harnack's note (p. 40 on 10:6), "The tracks are probably the rays of light," merely records his bewilderment.

152 See BDAG, *s.v.* ἴχνος, 1; Payne Smith, 2:2960.

153 The *via lactea* (Georges, 2:534) was understood mythologically, in some instances, as "the way of the gods" and in Pythagoreanism as the "way of the soul" (Jürgen Mau, "Milchstraße," *KP* 3 [1969] 1294).

On the "final summary statement" 14b, Franzmann refers to 11:4.[154] The Pa. ܗܠܟ (*hallek*), which generally means "to go" or "to walk," has as subject the "way" laid out by the "Father."[155] The expression "from the beginning until the end" (cf. 6:4 and 26:7, but esp. 11:4, ἀπ' ἀρχῆς ἕως τέλους) is in the first place an expression of completeness, as it was already in Eccl 3:11.[156] The phrase corresponding to "from the beginning to the end"[157] in the LXX is ἀπ' ἀρχῆς καὶ μέχρι τέλους, and in the Peshitta it is ܡܢ ܪܫܝܬܐ ܘܥܕܡܐ ܠܫܘܠܡܐ.[158] At the same time, and, as it were, as a condition of the completion, there is a subtext of a soteriological "statement of eternity,"[159] "God is ἀρχὴ καὶ τέλος," which makes the time aspect rather indefinite.[160]

■ **15-16a** First it is necessary to establish who or what is the subject of 15a in this mythological-soteriological statement. Since "way" (13a, 14b) is feminine in Syriac, the masculine pronoun cannot refer to it. If "by him" were to refer, causally and instrumentally, to the "Father," who is the main subject of part 2, it would be necessary to emend the passive participle of ܦܠܚ (*plaḥ*), which, taken together with ܗܘܐ (*-wā*)—as in 15b—expresses "a kind of Pluperfect,"[161] by substituting for it the passive participle of ܫܠܚ (*šlaḥ*).[162] In that case it would be possible to find similar references to sending forth, for example, Gal 4:4 and John 5:36 (cf. also John 3:16 and 1 John 4:9). Without such surgery on the text of H, and taking into account the chiastic parallelism between 15a and 15b, the third person singular masculine suffix on the preposition ܡܢ (*men*) can be interpreted as the "Son" seen as a specific being, who served the "Father," probably in spiritual fashion (cf. 20:3, "those who serve fleshly").

Although "to be sent" would fit better with the expression of epiphany in 12a, given the present state of textual criticism of the *Odes* it is not as "impossible" as Harnack thought "that the singer describes himself as the son."[163] For it is indeed the case that the phrases "by him" (15a) and "with the Son" (15b)[164] refer to the indirect object "him" in 12a and thus to the speaking "I" of part 1 (1-11). So this speaking "I," who should not be equated with either the author of the Ode or the "singer" ("Odist"), is now unmasked and identified in a fashion reminiscent of the statements in Mark 1:11 (ἐν σοὶ εὐδόκησα ["with you I am well pleased"]) and Matt 3:17 (ὁ υἱός μου ὁ ἀγαπητός, ἐν ᾧ εὐδόκησα ["my beloved Son, with whom I am well pleased"]) and also of many of the passages referring to the Son in the Gospel of John. These early Christian statements referring to the Son, together with Matt 11:27,[165] were influential in Gnosticism up to the era of Nag Hammadi, for example, *Tri. Trac.* 93,36–37: ⲉⲧⲉ ⲡⲁⲉⲓ ⲉⲛⲧⲁϥⲟⲩⲱϣⲉ· ‹ⲙ̄ⲙⲁϥ› ⲁⲩⲱ ⲁϥⲱⲕ ⲛ̄ϩⲏⲧ· ⲁⲣⲁϥ ("who is the one whom he loved and in whom he was pleased"),[166] or earlier in the same tractate (58,34–59,1):

> ⲉⲧⲉ ⲧⲁⲉⲓ ⲧⲉ ⲧⲫⲩⲥⲓⲥ ⲛ̄ⲧⲉ ⲛⲓⲡⲛ[ⲉⲩⲙ]ⲁ· ⲉⲧⲟⲩⲁⲁⲃ
> ⲛ̄ⲁⲧⲧⲉⲕⲟ ⲧⲉⲉⲓ ⲉⲧⲉⲣⲉⲡϣⲏⲣⲉ ⲙⲁⲧⲛ̄ ⲙ̄ⲙⲁϥ ⲁϫⲱⲥ ϩⲱⲥ
> ⲧⲉϥⲟⲩⲥⲓⲁ ⲧⲉ ⲛ̄ⲑⲉ ⲙ̄ⲡⲓⲱⲧ ⲉⲧⲉϥⲙⲁⲧⲛ̄ ⲙ̄ⲙⲁϥ ⲁϫⲛ̄ ⲡϣⲏⲣⲉ

> This is the nature (φύσις) of the holy imperishable spirits (πνεύματα), upon which the Son rests, since it is his essence (οὐσία), just as the Father rests upon the Son.[167]

154 Franzmann, 60.
155 Charlesworth, 38, with paleographic justification.
156 Gerhard Delling, "τέλος . . . τελειότης, κτλ.," *ThWNT* 8 (1969) 53; cf. *TDNT* 8:52.
157 Aarre Lauha, *Kohelet* (BKAT 19; Neukirchen-Vluyn: Neukirchener Verlag, 1978) 62.
158 Rahlfs, 2:244; *OTSy* pt. 2 fasc. 5, on Eccl. 3:11.
159 Delling, "τέλος," *ThWNT* 8:51; cf. *TDNT* 8:50.
160 Gerhard Delling, "ἄρχω, κτλ.," *ThWNT* 1 (1933) 478; cf. *TDNT* 1:479.
161 Nöldeke §278 B.
162 See Harris and Mingana, vol. 1, note on *Ode* 7:15a: "Perhaps we should read ܫܠܝܚ"; 2:245, "He was sent."
163 Harnack, 35.
164 See Payne Smith, 2:2313, on the passive participle of the Aph. of ܢܘܚ, ܢܚ (*nāḥ*) with the preposition ܒ (*b-*).
165 See Harris and Mingana, 2:241, on 16a.
166 Attridge and Pagels, "Tripartite Tractate," 1:262–63.
167 Ibid., 1:204–5; see also ibid., 2:244: "It should be noted that the verb (viz., ⲙⲁⲧⲛ̄, Qual. of ⲙ̄ⲧⲟⲛ) can also be translated 'be satisfied (or pleased) with.'" The Syriac of 15b also uses a word that has the basic meaning of "rest."

So this is not an intrusive "Christian interpolation"[168] but an affirmation of an early Gnosticizing Christianity. Whether this "Son" is the "Son of the Most High" par excellence, as in 41:11-16, or merely a "son" as the type of a Gnostic awaiting redemption, as in 3:7d, remains uncertain.

Nothing is said of the "Son as Savior,"[169] but the monocolon 16a, which forms the end of part 2, refers to the "son" as to be saved (*salvandus*; see Excursus 5). The future tense of the Pe. ܐܚܕ (*ʾeḥad*) does not do much to clarify the meaning of "his salvation," since this verb has a wide variety of meanings.[170] The key to understanding is rather to be found in the object "everything." The "Father" is, soteriologically and in this case also eschatologically, the "Lord of all," the "Almighty," the "All-powerful," *κύριος παντοκράτωρ*[171] (cf. 2 Cor 6:18, which also refers to "sons" and "daughters"). The Syriac phrase ܐܚܝܕ ܟܠ (*ʾaḥīd kol*), using the transitive passive participle of ܐܚܕ (*ʾeḥad*), has the meaning of "holding all things," "equivalent to omnipotent, and epithet of the true God."[172]

■ **16b-17** The third and final part of *Ode* 7 begins at stanza IX, and, although it contains new themes and utterances mainly concerned with the future (announcement, prophecy), it is closely connected to the preceding parts, especially by the use of words derived from the root ܦܪܩ (see Excursus 7), and also by the use of "Lord" as a divine title (see the introduction to the Ode above). Although Franzmann unnecessarily divides 17b into 17b-c, she correctly demonstrates that stanza IX "exhibits a kind of semantic terrace effect by the pattern of the statements of purpose—17a expresses the purpose of 16b, 17b-c expresses the double purpose of 17a."[173]

In 16b a new title of divinity, in addition to "Lord" and "Father," is introduced. *Ode* 3:6 already spoke of the "Lord Most High" (see on 22a below). Those Hellenistic listeners and readers who had been influenced by the belief in Yahweh (and Yahweh was honored with the Semitic title עליון/אל עליון) would connect *ὕψιστος* with the God of their books,[174] while those who had not been so influenced would hear it as an "attribute of Zeus."[175] In the relatively early stage of Gnosticizing utterances recorded in the *Odes of Solomon*, the doctrine of the "unknown god" is not yet strongly emphasized[176] (but cf. Acts 17:23). Instead it is announced that the "Most High" in his all-transcendent "being" (see 11a above)

168 Harnack, 35.

169 Franzmann, 60.

170 See Payne Smith, 1:114–16 (*[ap]prehendit, [ac]cepit, occupavit, tenuit, clausit, occlusit*).

171 BDAG, *s.v.* *παντοκράτωρ*.

172 Payne Smith, 1:117: "*omnitenens*, . . . pro *omnipotens*, ut Dei veri . . . epitheton; . . . pro Gr. *παντοκράτωρ* positum." Although he refers to the "redeemer" as "mediator of creation" and to "his work," Harald Hegermann's note on *Ode* 7:15-16a has some relevance: "The normally un-Gnostic idea of a general redemption is here only a background to the poetry, steeped as it is in the individualism of basically Gnostic mysticism." See Harald Hegermann, *Die Vorstellung vom Schöpfungsmittler im hellenistischen Judentum und Urchristentum* (TU 82; Berlin: Akademie-Verlag, 1961) 110–37, esp. 130, with a rather free translation.

173 Franzmann, 60. Charlesworth (p. 36) places the phrase "with joy" in 17c following Harris and Mingana's arbitrary division of the monocolon 17b (Harris and Mingana, vol. 1, note on this passage; 2:241; except for some minor textual criticisms they offer no "notes" on part 3 at all).

174 See also Luke 1:32, 35, 76; 6:35; 8:28; Acts 7:48; 16:17.

175 Georg Bertram, "*ὕψος, ὑψόω, κτλ.*," *ThWNT* 8 (1969) 613–19; cf. *TDNT* 8:614–20. The attribute, description, or appellation "Highest/Most High" is not limited to Yahweh or Zeus: it is a "basic idea" that can be applied to other names or to the bare word *θεός*. "The naming of a god as the Highest must have occurred independently in several places and have been maintained there" (Carsten Colpe and Andreas Löw, "Hypsistos [Theos]," *RAC* 16 [1994] 1038). Colpe and Löw (cols. 1054–55) distinguish the numerous examples in texts and inscriptions as follows: The Christian "Hypsistos-worship" presupposes Jewish "absorption" ("in contrasting the Semitic to the pagan testimonies to consecration and witness") and "rivalry in reciprocity" ("in contrast to the Greek"), but the separation of the Christians, "which happened for other reasons," also "led to a decrease in the description of God as the Most High, because the title was too broad to have a function in Christian theology." The numerous occurrences of the title in the *Odes of Solomon* are a sign of continuing strong Jewish influence.

176 Rudolph, *Gnosis*, 66, 70–76.

can yet be known; that is, he allows himself to be known (see 3b above). The esoteric limitation to the elect Gnostics (cf. 9:6a [used with a different term]; 23:1-3) by the use of the prepositional phrase "in" or "among" "his saints" distinguishes this soteriological becoming known from any merely natural knowledge of God.[177] It may be that the connection of the designation "saints of the Most High" with the idea of "the knowledge of the Most High" can be traced back to the "sectarians of Qumran" (cf. CD xx.8; 1QS iv.22).[178]

The preposition ܠ (*l-*) prefixed to the infinitive of the Pa. ܣܒܪ (*sabbar*) gives 17a "the sense of direction"[179] for the path that the "saints who know" are to take. As bearers of the "message of joy"[180] (cf. 12:4), they are distinguished from another subgroup of the esoteric "community,"[181] "psalmists" or "singers" (cf. 7:22; 16:1-3; 26:12). The "Lord's coming" is not the "coming of Jesus in the incarnation" (cf. Ignatius *Phld.* 9:2) or the "messianic coming of the Glorified."[182] Rather, it is the divine *parousia* of the "Lord" as the "Most High,"[183] which is pictured metaphorically and nonsacramentally as a visitation by the emperor or king in the provinces and not as the appearance of the "hidden god" at the climax of an act of worship.[184]

The phrase ܢܦܩ ܠܐܘܪܥܗ (*npaq l-ʾurʿeh*)[185] in 17b, which is reminiscent of the technical term εἰς ἀπάντησιν ("to meet")[186] in Matt 25:6 and 1 Thess 4:17, suggests the royal progress as "an ancient custom,"[187] which immediately comes under theological question. The "saints of the Most High" no longer went out with songs and music to greet the secular government. The key word "joy," which describes "to sing" eschatologically only in this passage,[188] makes a connection with the beginning of the Ode (cf. also 23:1; 31:6).

Verse 17c, in parallel with the prepositional phrase "with joy," also consists only of a prepositional phrase containing the Greek word κιθάρα,[189] where the Greek would have been κιθάρᾳ πολυφώνῳ.[190] The term ܩܠܐ (*qālā*), which became a common technical term in later Syriac liturgical history and literature,[191] can also be translated as "voice" (see on 24b below; on "sounds," see also the *hapax legomenon* ܩܝܢܢ [*qīnān*] in 14:8).

■ **18-19** Stanza X (18-19) takes the form of a further announcement or prophecy,[192] though it might even be an invitation,[193] framed extremely carefully with various parallelisms and a "terrace pattern,"[194] especially in the transition from 18a to 18b by the use of the root ܚܙܐ, to bring the whole complex of themes related to seeing and appearing to a final climax. The "I" saw the Lord (5a). The "Father," who is identical with the Lord, facilitated the epiphany/appearance of the speaking "I," who is the Son, before his "own" (12a; cf. 15b). His "own"—that is, "his saints" (16b)—are identical with the "seers" who are

177 On the "issue of a natural theology" in Rom 1:19-20, see Käsemann, *Romans*, 39–43 (German, pp. 35–39). On the "eschatological title" οἱ ἅγιοι as a "qualification of adherence to God," see Michael Lattke, "Heiligkeit III. Neues Testament," *TRE* 14 (1985) 705.

178 Lohse, *Texte*, 14–15, 104–5; Johann Maier, *Die Qumran-Essener: Die Texte vom Toten Meer* (3 vols.; UTB 1862, 1863, 1916; Munich/Basel: Reinhardt, 1995–96) 1:36, 176; Vermes, 67; cf. Bertram, "ὕψος," *ThWNT* 8:615; *TDNT* 8:617. Already Diettrich (p. 26) remarks, "but whether they [viz., the saints] still formed part of the official Jewish community, or were to be found outside it, like the Essenes and Therapeutae, cannot be determined from this Ode."

179 Nöldeke §286.

180 Diettrich, 26.

181 As Franzmann points out (p. 60).

182 Bauer and Aland, *s.v.* παρουσία, 2bα ("v[on] der messianischen Ankunft des Verklärten"); cf. BDAG, *s.v.* παρουσία, 2bα.

183 On θεϊκὴ παρουσία, see Payne Smith, 1:418.

184 BDAG, *s.v.* παρουσία, 2b, with classical references. It is quite possible that Isa 40:10 or 62:11 influenced the thought behind this passage. But "official Judaism" was not alone in "singing psalms for the coming of the Lord" (Diettrich, 26).

185 See Payne Smith, 1:396.

186 BDAG, *s.v.* ἀπάντησις.

187 Michael Lattke, "ἀπαντάω, ἀπάντησις," *EWNT* 1 (1980) 275; cf. *EDNT* 1:115.

188 See Klaus Berger, "χαρά," *EWNT* 3 (1983) 1090; cf. *EDNT* 3:455.

189 See Lattke, "Wörter," 291 = idem, *Bedeutung*, 4:139.

190 Harris and Mingana, vol. 1, note on this passage; Frankenberg, 10.

191 See Payne Smith, 2:3618–19; on Bardesanes in Ephraem, see Michael Lattke, "Sind Ephraems *Madrāšē* Hymnen?" *OrChr* 73 (1989) 39–40.

192 Lattke, *Oden*, 82.

193 See, e.g., Franzmann, 54, "Let the seers go before him."

194 Ibid., 61.

now to appear before the Lord (18a-b), who because of his *parousia* (17a) is near and sees continually (19b).

If this spiral sequence of utterances, with all the play on words, is recognized, the speculative equation of the "seers" (18a) with "prophets,"[195] or explication in the style of a targum, referring to Ps 42:2,[196] becomes unnecessary. The plural of ܚܙܝ (*ḥazzāy*) or ܚܙܝܐ (*ḥazzāyā*) can be used as a technical term for "prophets" or "sages,"[197] but here the use of the *hapax legomenon* is quite untechnical.

The choice of the verb "to go," which like the other verbs in 18b and 19a is a future imperfect, need not be explained by asserting that two very different texts (7:18 and 23:10a) contain a "word-pair ܐܙܠ-ܚܙܐ."[198] "To go" carries on the lively metaphor of "arrival" and "going forth" in stanza IX (17a-b) and is given precision by the preposition ܩܕܡ (*qḏām*) with the suffixed third masculine singular pronoun. The repetition of this preposition with suffix in 18b (after the imperfect of the Ethpe. ܐܬܚܙܝ [*ʾeṯḥzī*]) makes it clear that "will go before him" is parallel to "will appear before him" and is really no more than poetical padding in the bicolon 18a-b.

Verse 19a carries the announcement of stanza IX further, but without identifying the "seers"—the subject of the Pa. ܫܒܚ (*šabbaḥ*)—with the "singers" of the psalms in 17a-c.[199] The emphasis has passed on from singing to the cithara and falls now on the praising[200] whose object is the "Lord." The prepositional phrase "in his love" (in 𝔊 certainly ἐν τῇ ἀγάπῃ αὐτοῦ) can equally be understood adnominally or adverbially in reference to the praising.[201]

In either case, 19b expresses the condition of the possibility of praising. In 21:7 the existential nearness of the *redeemed* to his Lord is connected with praise and thanks, but in this passage it is the nearness of the *Lord* that is stressed and clarified by the active participle of ܚܙܐ (*ḥzā*), which makes a statement "without reference to a definite time."[202] Just as the "being" of the Lord God is *totally other* (5b, 11a), he "sees" already and always those whom the sight of no-thing and no-body in this world can penetrate and know.

■ **20-21** Two parallel announcements, whose imperfect futures may again be translated as imperatives[203] or optatives,[204] are justified by a statement of salvation in the perfect (21a-b), which clearly takes up the beginning of part 3 (cf. 16b). The Ettaph. ܐܬܬܪܝܡ (*ʾettrīm*), whose meaning is identical with the Ethpe., is here in 20a used with a rare negative connotation "as opposed to other actions of lifting up (exaltation) in the Odes."[205] The Syriac word for "hatred" (in 𝔊 certainly μῖσος)[206] is a *hapax legomenon*.[207] Obviously hatred will not vanish from the earth as a whole, but only from among the esoteric group of Gnostics who love each other and are hated by the world (cf. 28:12).[208]

The Ethpa. of ܛܒܥ (*ṭbaʿ*) in 20b is also a *hapax legomenon*, which predicts the disappearance of "jealousy," as it were, in the opposite direction[209] to its parallel "hatred." The noun ܛܢܢܐ (*ṭnānā*), which occurs only twice, could equally be translated "envy,"[210] "malice,"[211] or possibly even "spite."[212]

That "hatred" and "jealousy" are not purely psychological or ethical is shown by the third parallel, in the

195 E.g., Harnack, 35; Diettrich, 26.
196 See Harris and Mingana, 2:249–52.
197 Payne Smith, 1:1235–36.
198 Contra Franzmann, 61.
199 Contra Diettrich, 26; Harris and Mingana, 2:249.
200 Cf. 6:7; 14:8b; 18:1; 21:7; 26:4; 36:2c, 4; 41:1.
201 Adnominal: 8:22; 14:3, 9; 16:7; 18:1; 29:3; adverbial: 6:2; 40:4; 41:2, 6.
202 Nöldeke §269.
203 See Frankenberg, 10 (ἀρθήτω μῖσος ἐκ τῆς γῆς).
204 See Fanourgakis, 146 (ἐκλίποι μῖσος ἀπὸ τῆς γῆς).
205 Franzmann, 56; cf. 8:5; 18:1; 21:6; 41:12.
206 See Payne Smith, 2:2670.
207 On the "radical ܐ in the 3rd position" in ܣܢܐܬܐ (*seneṯā*), see Nöldeke §100.
208 On μισεῖν in John 3:20; 15:18-19; 17:14, see Lattke, *Einheit*, 45–53.
209 Payne Smith, 1:1428 (*mersus est*).
210 Harnack, 35; Diettrich, 26.
211 Bauer, *Oden*, 19.
212 Bauer, 609 on 28:11; cf. Payne Smith, 1:1489 (ζῆλος). The translation "Mißgeburt (= monster)" (Bauer, 585) has to be a misprint, perhaps due to a mix-up with 28:11a. On Tosato's imaginative suggestions (Angelo Tosato, "Gesù e gli zeloti alla luce delle *Odi di Salomone*," *BeO* 19 [1977] 145–53), see Lattke, *Bedeutung*, 3:329.

perfect, found in 21a. The objective is the soteriological annihilation (Ethpa. of ܚܒܠ [*ḥbal*]; cf. 15:9a; 31:1b; 33:9a; and Excursus 28) of the negation of *gnōsis*. The word prefaced by ܠܐ (*lā*) probably equals Greek ἀγνωσία or ἄγνοια.[213] In this passage—though not in 11:8a—it would hardly have been ἀλογιστία. And 21b would probably have had γνῶσις—unlike 11:4, which has σύνεσις. Translating the two occurrences of ܠܗ (*lāh*) by "on it" (viz., "on the earth")[214] is not merely otiose but actually wrong.[215] The genitive in the phrase "knowledge/*gnōsis* of the Lord" is not a subjective but an objective genitive in this case, perhaps with a slight connotation of provenance or inception (see on 6:6 above). "*Gnōsis*" can "come" just as much as ἡ πίστις (cf. Gal 3:23, 25), but the "γνῶσις/ἄγνοια contrast is of great importance for Gnosticism and the Hermetic literature"[216] as can be seen by an antithetical parallelism in *Corp. Herm.* 13.8:

ἦλθεν ἡμῖν γνῶσις θεοῦ·
ταύτης ἐλθούσης . . . ἐξηλάθη ἡ ἄγνοια.

Knowledge of God came to us;
when it came . . . ignorance was driven out.[217]

Knowledge of God, for a Gnostic, is also self-knowledge "because man bears within himself a spark of the divine," but in this quotation from the Hermetic texts man is "not inherently divine, but he becomes divine only through the process of regeneration."[218] In the same way, the people of the *Odes of Solomon*, in spite of their naïvely Gnosticizing language, did not consider themselves to be divine beings, but were set free to be fully human by their knowledge of the Most High as Lord.

■ **22-23b** Stanza XII, with its four announcements in parallel pairs, refers back to stanza X[219] and at the same time makes it clear that "the Lord" is truly "the Most High."[220] The clumsy participial phrase "those who sing" (= "the singers") in 22a would correspond to Greek οἱ ᾄδοντες and not οἱ ὑμνοῦντες.[221] The direct object and content of the singing (imperfect of the Pa. ܙܡܪ [*zammar*]) are God's "grace" (in 𝔊 certainly χάρις). This peculiar concept is also found in 31:3a, although there it is the justified *Lord* who "spoke grace and joy."

The word ܡܙܡܘܪܐ (*mazmōrā*), derived from the root *zmr*, which has already been used in 17a, is found also in 22b; in the plural it is translated "psalms," but these

213 Cf. BDAG, *s.vv.* ἄγνοια and ἀγνωσία, on 1 Cor 15:34; Acts 17:30; Eph 4:18; 1 Pet 1:14; 2:15.
214 See Bauer, *Oden*, 19; Bauer, 586.
215 See Brockelmann, *Grammatik* §196: "Verbs whose reference is limited to the physical or spiritual aspect of the subject are often followed by ܠ, with suffix, without change of meaning." In consequence, Charlesworth's criticism of Harris and Mingana, Bernard, Abbott, Michael MarYosip, Johannes Flemming, Jean Labourt, and Charles Bruston is as ill conceived as his statement "The verse refers to the incarnation" (Charlesworth, 38).
216 William C. Grese, *Corpus Hermeticum XIII and Early Christian Literature* (SCHNT 5; Leiden: Brill, 1979) 122.
217 Text and translation after Grese, *Corpus*, 14–15; cf. the reference to this passage in Bauer, 586. According to Irenaeus *Haer.* 1.15.2, Markos the Gnostic said: Ἀγνοίας δὲ λύσις ἡ ἐπίγνωσις αὐτοῦ ἐγίνετο, "The dissolution of ignorance was the knowledge of the Father." See Norbert Brox, *Irenäus von Lyon, Epideixis, Adversus haereses – Darlegung der apostolischen Verkündigung, Gegen die Häresien* (5 vols.; FontChr 8.1–5; Freiburg: Herder, 1993–2001) 1:244–45. Paulsen (*Studien*, 31) finds a "verbal connection" with Ignatius *Eph.* 19:3 ἄγνοια καθῃρεῖτο "ignorance was removed/destroyed"; cf. Joseph A. Fischer, *Die Apostolischen Väter* (Munich: Kösel, 1956; 9th ed., Darmstadt: Wissenschaftliche Buchgesellschaft, 1986) 158–59; Lake, 1:192–93; Ehrman, 1:238–39.
218 Grese, *Corpus*, 122.
219 See Franzmann, 61–62 (with corrections [in brackets]): "Stanza XII [not 11] returns to details concerning a group (singers) as in stanza X [not 9] (seers). The repetition of the root ܙܡܪ provides a link with stanza IX [not 8]. The use of initial 3rd pl. masc. imperf. verbs (22a-b) connects this stanza with both stanzas IX [not 8] and X [not 9]."
220 See Diettrich, 27: "This is very important, since it assures us that the whole eschatological section deals with the coming of the God of the Old Testament Covenant and not the Second Coming of Christ to judge the world."
221 Contra Frankenberg, 10.

psalms are nearer to early Jewish or "Christian songs of praise" than to the actual "OT Psalms."[222] The subject of the imperfect of the Pa. ܩܪܒ (*qarreḇ*), which is a term in the language of sacrifice (cf. 20:2, 5a; 31:4b), is the singers of 21a, who can hardly be meant for priests.

If the comparison in 23a merely refers to the brightness of day,[223] the addition in the translation would be unnecessary. It is the parallelism with 23b that suggests the "Day of the Lord" (Joel 3:4 LXX), though without the disastrous auguries of Joel 3:1-5 LXX or Acts 2:17-21. This text, which speaks of "the day of *God*, the Lord,"[224] runs, in Greek, *πρὶν ἐλθεῖν ἡμέραν κυρίου τὴν μεγάλην καὶ ἐπιφανῆ* ("before the great and glorious day of the Lord comes").[225]

In order to bring out the parallel to "heart," the *hapax legomenon* ܢܥܡܬܐ (*neʿmāṯā*) in 23b is translated as "voices" rather than "sounds" or "notes."[226] That the phrase of comparison "like the sublimity of the Lord," which is parallel to 23a, is a translation of *ὡς ἡ μεγαλοπρέπεια* is all but certain (cf. 15:7; 18:16; 29:3).[227] Since stanza XIII mentions creation, it is permissible here to allude to *1 Clem.* 60:1: *σύ, κύριε, τὴν οἰκουμένην ἔκτισας . . . θαυμαστὸς ἐν ἰσχύϊ καὶ μεγαλοπρεπείᾳ* ("thou, Lord, didst create the earth/world . . . wonderful in strength and majesty").[228]

■ **23c-24** The text of stanza XIII, which is not easy to translate, consists of one sentence brimful of negations and particles (23c-e), whose anticipatory character modally expresses a strong desire,[229] and a second, which gives a reason for the first with a teaching on creation (24a),[230] that names a double objective (24b-c) "expressing the purpose for the Lord's giving in 24a."[231]

Harris and Mingana, with a conjectural emendation (ܕܠܐ ܢܦܫܐ for ܕܢܦܫܐ), translate 23c as "And let there be nothing without life."[232] But this is unnecessary, because the composite expression ܡܕܡ ܕܢܦܫ (*meddem da-npeš*) already means anything animated,[233] which translates as "person."[234] Of course, the genitive ܕܢܦܫܐ (*d-napšā*), which is used adjectivally,[235] could be extended to mean other living creatures, but 23d makes it clear that no more is "intended here than people."[236]

If the repeated ܘܠܐ (*w-lā*) in 23d-e is translated as "neither . . . nor,"[237] the ܕܠܐ (*d-lā*) that precedes the term "*gnōsis*/knowledge" will not correspond to a mere *alpha* privative (see 21a above), but to the preposition *ἄνευ* (23d).[238] The word translated as "without speech" (= "mute") in 23e is a predicative adjective in *status absolutus* with prefixed relative particle ܕ (*d-*), which in this context would make no sense if translated as "deaf."[239]

Humans, according to the statement of creation in 24a, which refers to the Most High Lord of stanza XII, are speaking beings, endowed with life and knowledge; as such, they transcend this world and acknowledge their created existence as an underived and

222 BDAG, *s.v.* *ψαλμός*; cf. 1 Cor 14:26; Eph 5:19; Col 3:16.
223 Cf. Diettrich, 27: "[bright] like the day."
224 BDAG, *s.v.* *ἡμέρα*, 3b*β*.
225 Rahlfs, 2:522.
226 See Brockelmann, *Lexicon*, 435a; Franzmann, 62: "The parallelism of 'heart' and 'voices' is close to the association of 'heart' and 'lips' found also in 8:1; 16:2; 20:4; 21:8; 30:5; 37:2; 40:2."
227 See Frankenberg, 10; Harris and Mingana, vol. 1, note on this passage, who mention Ps 67:35 LXX. Joosten also refers to it in his letter of October 1, 1996 (n. 27 above): "I think ܪܒܘܬ ܐܝܩܘܬܐ does reflect *μεγαλοπρέπεια*."
228 Lindemann and Paulsen, 144–45; cf. Lake, 1:112–13; Ehrman, 1:142–43.
229 Nöldeke §266.
230 See Lattke, *Oden*, 88.
231 Franzmann, 62.
232 Harris and Mingana, vol. 1, note on this passage; 2:242.
233 Brockelmann, *Lexicon*, 441a: *aliquid animatum*.
234 Bauer, 586. Therefore Charlesworth (p. 36) corrected his earlier translation "anyone who breathes" (1973) to "any person" (1977).
235 Nöldeke §219 (emphatic status masculine).
236 Contra Franzmann, 56, whose translation "nothing which breathes" is in any case too free.
237 Payne Smith, *Dictionary*, 233.
238 See Payne Smith, 2:1869.
239 See Payne Smith, 1:1387 (*mutus, surdus*); BDAG, *s.v.* *κωφός*. Diettrich's criticism (p. 27) of Harris and Flemming for their translation "dumb" (and its German equivalent "stumm") is as unfounded as his own translation of 23c-e: "And there will not be any soul, whether of ignorance or of magic."

unfathomable mystery, and their immanent logic leads them to conclude from this that the mouth, with its internal or external voice,[240] which they have received from their Creator, is to be used toward him (24b) or in order to give him praise (24c), which is his alone and above all and is merited by no-thing and no-body. The word ܦܘܡܐ (*pummā*) in this verse is not so much the complex bodily organ as the ability to speak given to created humanity (see Excursus 31).[241] That is why the infinitive of the Pe. ܦܬܚ (*pṯaḥ*), with final meaning, has as direct object not the "mouth" (cf. 8:4; 16:5; 31:3; 36:7) but its "voice" (cf. 31:4; 37:1-2).

The feminine noun ܡܫܒܚܘܬܐ (*mšabbḥūṯā*), derived from the root *šbḥ*, may mean "praiseworthiness,"[242] but can also stand for the title "Excellency."[243] In that case it may correspond to the rare word ἐνδοξασμός,[244] which would be translated as "glorifying."[245] In 24c, however, the parallelism of 24b shows that the term ܠܡܫܒܚܘܬܗ (*la-mšabbāḥūṯeh*) is the Pa. infinitive ܡܫܒܚܘ (*mšabbāḥū*) with the sign of the infinitive and objective suffix.[246]

■ **25** Even without words of praise, this conclusion is a doxological imperative.[247] It is the first address to a group of believers since the imperatives of salvation in 3:11, but it does not follow "that the Odes were used in public *services*" (emphasis added), or that the passage reflects the "missionary zeal" of non-Gnostic primitive Christianity.[248]

The parallel invitations to confessing and acknowledging "making known"[249] or demonstrative and announcing "proclamation"[250] are addressed to a timeless, inclusive—despite "the use of the 2nd plural masculine"—"community"[251] of readers and listeners who will proclaim God's δύναμις (cf. 29:8a) and χάρις, so that all earthly "power"[252] and "favor"[253] are shown to be profoundly conditional.

240 Cf. 1QM xiv.6: "He . . . has opened the mouth of the dumb that they might praise [the mighty] works [of God]" (Lohse, *Texte*, 213; Vermes, 119; cf. Maier, *Qumran-Essener*, 1:147). With Paulsen, *Studien*, 31, compare Ignatius *Rom.* 7:2: *Δεῦρο πρὸς τὸν πατέρα*, "Come to the Father" (Fischer, 190–91; Ehrman, 1:278–79).

241 Diettrich (p. 27) correctly notes that ܒܪܝܬܐ (*brīṯā*) is often used to characterize "people" as "humankind."

242 Payne Smith, *Dictionary*, 304a.

243 Brockelmann, *Lexicon*, 751a (*excellentia*).

244 Payne Smith, 2:4027.

245 LSJ, *s.v.* ἐνδοξασμός.

246 Klaus Beyer, in Lattke, 3:XX n. 1. This means that the opinions expressed in Lattke, 1:127 and n. 5 on that page are incorrect.

247 Other doxological forms are listed in Lattke, *Oden*, 83; see also Introduction, sec. 8.

248 Charlesworth, 39.

249 Payne Smith, 1:1550. This is the only occasion in the *Odes* where the Aph. ܐܘܕܝ (*ʾawdī*) is not followed by a preposition (cf. 5:1; 10:5; 21:7).

250 See Payne Smith, 1:1208–9 on the Pa. ܚܘܝ (*ḥawwī*).

251 Franzmann, 62.

252 See Bauer, *Oden*, 19; Bauer, 586: "Confess his power and proclaim his goodness." The erroneous ܚܝܠܬܢܘܬܐ in Harris and Mingana, vol. 1, note on this passage (which they corrected to ܚܝܠܬܢܘܬܗ [*ḥayltānūṯeh*] in 2:246) still leads Bauer in 1964 (p. 586 n. 4), as in 1933 (*Oden*, 19 note c), to remark: "This *his* is not expressed in the available text."

253 Diettrich, 27.

8

Ode 8: Speech of the Redeemer, Revealer, and Mediator of Creation

(I) 1a Open, open your hearts to the exultation over the Lord,
1b and your love will grow from the heart to the lips,
2a to bring forth fruits to the Lord, a holy life,
2b and to speak with watchfulness in his light.
(II) 3 Rise and stand upright, [you] who were once brought low!
4a [You] who were in silence,
4b speak, now that your mouth has been opened.
5a [You] who were despised, be now lifted up,
5b (now) that your righteousness has been lifted up.
(III) 6a For the right hand of the Lord is with you,
6b and he was/became a helper for you.
7a And peace was prepared for you,
7b before ever your war happened.
(IVa) 8a Hear the word of truth
8b and receive the *gnōsis* of the Most High.
(IVb) 9a Neither your flesh will know what I say to you,
9b nor your garment what I declare to you.
(V) 10 Keep my mystery, [you] who are kept by it!
11 Keep my faith, [you] who are kept by it!
12 And know my *gnōsis*, [you] who know me in truth!
13 Love me with love, [you] who love!
(VI) 14a For I turn not my face from my own,
14b because I know them.
15a And before they yet were,
15b I perceived them.
15c And on their faces I set a seal.
16a I fashioned their members,
16b and my own breasts I prepared for them,
16c that they might drink my holy milk to live by it.
17 I was well pleased in them and I am not ashamed of them.
(VII) 18 For they are my work and the power of my thoughts.
19a Who then will stand against my work,
19b or who is he who does not obey them?
20a I willed and formed mind and heart,
20b and they are mine.

(VIII) 20c And at my own right hand I set my elect.
21a And my righteousness goes before them.
21b And they will not separate themselves from my name,
21c because it is with them.
(IX) 22a Seek and increase
22b and abide in the love of the Lord,
22c as beloved in the Beloved,
22d and as those who are kept in him who lives,
22e and as redeemed ones in him who was redeemed.
23a And you will be found imperishable
23b in all aeons/ages
23c on account of the name of your Father.
Hallelujah!

Introduction

Ode 8 is preserved in one Syriac manuscript.[1] The description of this nine- (ten-) stanza Ode[2] as a reveille,[3] like *Ode* 9, is only partially correct in both cases. In the forms used in the Ode[4] and among the theological and soteriological personae, it is first necessary to determine who the speakers are.

The speaker in stanzas IVb–VIII is a masculine "I" (see the participle in 9a etc.), but in stanzas I–IVa and in stanza IX it is not possible to say whether the speaker is "the singer" and/or "the Odist."[5] Indeed, the speaker of stanza IX may be a responding group, although there is no first person plural "we" in the passage. The same might be true of stanzas I–IVa, if this long introduction is *not* put into the mouth of the speaking "I" of stanzas IVb–VIII, as will be discussed below.

A group of persons is addressed in stanzas I–IVa, IVb–V, and IX. It should also be noted that in stanzas IVb–VIII the persons addressed in stanzas IVb–V become the topic under discussion in stanzas VI–VIII.

Returning to the problem of the speaker in stanzas I–VIII, there are (at least) two possible solutions. In the first case, the speaker of stanzas I–IVa is identical with the speaking "I" of stanzas IVb–VIII; in the second, stanzas I–IVa and stanza IX belong to the same speaker (or group of speakers), who is not identical with the speaking "I." Since the second case has dominated discussion since 1910, it will be taken up first.

The principal part[6] of *Ode* 8, in any case, is stanzas IVb–VIII. This core passage has been described as *ex ore Christi*[7] and also as a "Gnostic revelation spoken

1 Ms.: Codex H, 5b–7a (ܣ). Ed./trans.: Charlesworth, 41–44; Franzmann, 63–72; Lattke, 1:129–54 and 3:XX–XXI.

2 I have retained Franzmann's stanza numbering, although it is necessary to divide stanza IV into IVa (8a-b) and IVb (9a-b). This division results from the considerations about the speaker(s) that follow. Even with the change in speaker, there is no need to posit a "dual personality" (Harris and Mingana, 2:256).

3 Schille, 98.

4 Lattke, *Oden*, 44–47.

5 Harnack, 36; Harris and Mingana, 2:256.

6 Diettrich (p. 29), however, marks this "principal part" as beginning only in 10a, entitling it, in line with his conception, "Truth personified [in 8a] speaks through the prophet" (Diettrich, 28–29). In the title I assigned to the whole *Ode* above, this principal part is also considered.

7 Harris and Mingana, 2:257. Charlesworth accepts this description without acknowledgment and renumbers the verses (11-13 → 10b-11b; 8-21 → 8-19), continuing, "No linguistic device announces the shift in speakers, only the thoughts of the passage reflect it" (Charlesworth, 43). That is not quite correct, since the actual first-person address only commences, linguistically, at stanza IVb (9). My division follows Bauer's, but without accepting his

by God."[8] The speaking "I" does not actually claim to be "God Himself,"[9] but this identification might be deduced from the content and the context, if he should be identified with the "Lord" (1a, 2, 6, 22b) and also with the "Most High" (8b) and the "Father" (23c) in the surrounding text. But then he would also be the "Beloved" (22c) and the "Redeemed One" (22d), which led Diettrich to the logical consequence of his erroneous premise, namely, that ܐܬܦܪܩ (*ʾetpreq*) "is most probably a scribal error."[10]

If there is no reason to assume such an error, there are two possible solutions to the puzzle of the speaker. Either the "Lord" as the announcing Revealer, the redeemed Redeemer, the loving Beloved, and the selecting Mediator of creation is distinct from the "Most High" and the "Father," or the "Lord" as the "Most High" and the "Father" is distinct from the Revealer, Redeemer, and Mediator of creation, who speaks in the first person, and also from the Beloved and the Redeemed One of stanza IX.

The second possibility is valid even if the first person speaker (stanzas IVb–VIII) is identical with the speaker of the introduction (stanzas I–IVa). This, then, seems to be the most satisfactory determination of the various speakers.[11] *Ode* 8 is mainly an address of revelation with a final responsory (stanza IX), not a revelation *by* God but a revelation *of* God by a Revealer, redeemed Redeemer, and Mediator of creation, whose place in the history of religion is found in the area of intersection of early Gnosticism, early Judaism, and early Christianity.

Interpretation

■ **1-2** The speaker of stanzas I–VIII begins by calling on his hearers with a repeated imperative of ܦܬܚ (*ptaḥ*, only the Pe. and Ethpe. are used in the *Odes of Solomon*), the masculine plural of which is meant inclusively, and a metaphorical use of "hearts" (plural of ܠܒܐ [*lebbā*] + second masculine plural possessive suffix) as direct object, to "the exultation of the Lord."[12] The presupposition for this double exhortation or invitation to open the heart (in 𝔊 certainly καρδία), which is the "seat of physical, spiritual and mental life,"[13] is found in 10:1b and 10:4b, where the "Lord," also called the "Most High," "God," and "Father," opened the heart of the Redeemer (cf. Acts 16:14 and Excursus 4).

If the genitive of ܕܝܨܐ (*dyāṣā*) is objective, as in other passages (cf. 21:9b; 23:4c; 40:4a; 41:7), this hymnic motif of joyful *exultatio*[14] or ἀγαλλίασις[15] (cf., e.g., *Ps. Sol.* 5:1), which belongs theologically to no person or thing, is not pursued in this Ode past 1b and 2b.

Since 1b is not only parallel to 1a but carries the meaning forward by repeating the term "heart," the imperfect third masculine singular of the *hapax legomenon* ܣܓܝ, ܣܓܐ (*sgī*, *sgā*), which should not be corrected to ܓܣܐ (*gsā*),[16] is better translated by the future tense than by a "jussive."[17] That love (in 𝔊 certainly ἀγάπη) metaphorically comes from the heart (see Excursus 2) is unsurprising; its growth from the heart to the lips, the primary organs of speech, is, however, one of the typical, complex images of the *Odes of Solomon*, especially in its connection with the "metaphor of fruits," one of the "plant metaphors of Gnosticism"[18] (see Excursus 16).

The parallel infinitives with prefixed ܠ (*l-*) in 2a and 2b express the "purpose"[19] of the invitation (1a) and of the prediction (1b).

The two accusatives in 2a could also be understood and translated in apposition, which gives the phrase "holy life," not used in any moralizing sense, even more weight.[20] The Aph. of ܐܬܐ (*ʾetā*) is found only here

description of 9-21 as an "address of revelation *by God*" (Bauer, 586; emphasis added).

8 Greßmann, 443–44; Bauer, 586.

9 Harnack, 36.

10 Diettrich, 31.

11 Who the speaker of stanzas I–IVa is has no bearing on its content.

12 See Lattke, *Oden*, 82–83, *s.vv.* "Aufforderung" and "Einführende Aufforderung."

13 BDAG, *s.v.* καρδία, 1.

14 Payne Smith, 1:847.

15 BDAG, *s.v.* ἀγαλλίασις; cf. Frankenberg, 10.

16 Contra Hugo Greßmann, review of Labourt and Batiffol in *ZDMG* 65 (1911) 851, referring to 16:2c; 36:7b; 40:2a, 2b.

17 Franzmann, 67.

18 Gemünden, *Vegetationsmetaphorik*, 376–405, esp. 402.

19 Nöldeke §286.

20 Harris and Mingana, 2:253, followed by many interpreters. I agree with Harris and Mingana (2:255–56) in rejecting the emendations of Schultheß (p. 253) and Barth (pp. 261–62).

together with the term "fruit," in 𝔊 certainly some form of καρπός (see Excursus 11). The at-least-partially-hymnic imagery of heart–love–lips–fruits (cf. 12:2; 16:2; 21:8-9; 37:2-3; 40:2-4) is strangely interrupted and existentially expanded by the use of the unique phrase "holy life," a phrase that describes a life molded by and dedicated to God, but lived fully in the world.[21]

There is thus no longer "equivalence of bringing/producing fruits and speaking/praising."[22] It is not until 2b that the ideas of 1b return, on the new level of "holy life," expressed by the Pa. ܡܠܠ (*mallel*; cf. 10:1-2; 12:3; 29:7-9; 32:1-2; 41:14). The parallelism of stanza I can be shown as follows: 1a/2a || 1b/2b. The *hapax legomenon* ܥܝܪܘܬܐ (*ʿīrūtā*), which could also be translated as "wakefulness" (cf. the Gnostic imperative of salvation in 3:11 with the Ethpe. of ܥܘܪ, ܥܪ [*ʿār*]),[23] describes adverbially the consequences of this opening of the heart. The second adverbial phrase, using the same preposition ܒ (*b*-), describes the new habitat. "Life" (ζωή) and "light" (φῶς) belong together, in the area where the *Odes* originated,[24] as closely as "light" and "word" (see Table 1; Excursuses 10 and 12).

■ **3-5** It is amazing how the translators of the *Odes of Solomon* have passed over the "extremely unusual construction" of stanza II with its alternation of "forms addressing a person" and third person plurals in the verbs.[25] For already in a Greek version the imperatives would "clash" with the participial nominatives whose definite articles would correspond to the Syriac phrase consisting of the demonstrative pronoun ܗܢܘܢ (*hānnōn*) and the relative particle ܕ (*d*-).[26]

Stanza II is, of course, full of antitheses and parallels. Franzmann's "parallel structure," however, can only be attained by willful divisions.[27] The parallels and interminglings of imperatives of salvation (A), antithetical statements of conditions changed from the past (B), and justifying statements of salvation (C), can be shown following the manuscript by the following diagram:

(3)	A+A		⟷	B
(4a)	B			
	↑ ↓			
(4b)	A	+		C
(5a)	B		⟷	A
(5b)				C

If the meaning of the first of the imperatives, the second masculine plural of the Pe. ܩܘܡܘ, ܩܡ (*qām*),[28] here in 3 is unique in the *Odes of Solomon*, the second (*hapax legomenon* Ethpa.), derived from the same root, must be translated to show the antithesis to the third masculine plural of the Ethpa. ܐܬܡܟܟܘ (*ʾetmakkak*). There is first the firm stance and then the erect carriage, which distinguishes those who "once, in the past" (ܒܙܒܢ [*ba-zban*], another *hapax legomenon,*[29] in 𝔊 certainly ποτέ[30]) were bowed down, humbled, and degraded.[31] *Ode* 41:12 makes it clear that this antithesis of "humbled" and "exalted" refers even to the (redeemed) Redeemer (see 5a and b below).

The antithesis in 3 is carried on in 4. Verses 3-4 cannot really be called a parallel of the reveille in Eph 5:14 (in spite of the use of ܐܬܬܥܝܪ [*ʾettʿīr*]; see 2b above, and ܩܘܡ [*qūm*] in the Syriac to translate ἔγειρε ["awake"] and ἀνάστα ["arise"]).[32]

The *hapax legomenon* ܫܠܝܐ (*šelyā*) in 4a does not characterize the previous conditions positively: it was not a

21 Cf. the phrase *simul sanctus et profanus* in Michael Lattke, "Heiligkeit III. Neues Testament," *TRE* 14 (1985) 705.
22 Franzmann, 67.
23 See Payne Smith, 2:2845.
24 BDAG, *s.vv.* ζωή and φῶς.
25 See Heinz Schürmann, *Das Lukasevangelium* (2 vols.; HThKNT 3.1–2; Freiburg: Herder, 1969–94) 1:330 on Luke 6:20-21; Nöldeke §350.
26 Nöldeke §228; cf. the Greek back-translations of Frankenberg (pp. 10–11) and Fanourgakis (p. 147).
27 Franzmann, 67–68.
28 In stanza II "he" embraces "she."
29 See Payne Smith, 1:1077.
30 See BDAG, *s.v.* ποτέ.
31 Payne Smith, 2:2101; cf. BDAG, *s.v.* ταπεινόω, 2–3.
32 See Petr Pokorný, "Epheserbrief und gnostische Mysterien," *ZNW* 53 (1962) 174, 187; idem, *Der Epheserbrief und die Gnosis: Die Bedeutung des Haupt–Glieder-Gedankens in der entstehenden Kirche* (Berlin: Evangelische Verlagsanstalt, 1965) 54, 95, 119; and George W. MacRae, "Sleep and Awakening in Gnostic Texts," in Ugo Bianchi, ed., *Le origini dello gnosticismo: Colloquio di Messina, 13–18 Aprile 1966* (Leiden: Brill, 1967; repr., 1970) 504.

restful sleep or the *vita anachoretica*[33] or the "silence . . . of the Essenes."[34] It was not any sort of quiet life[35] or divine silence;[36] it was completely negative—oppression, in a sense the opposite of freedom of speech, a soteriological concept that also has social and political implications.

While the Ethpe. of ܦܬܚ (*pṯaḥ*) in 4b is a theological passive, indicating that the "mouth" descends as far as the bottom of the heart (see 1a above; cf. the parallels between "mouth" and "heart" in 10:1; 21:8; 36:7; see further Excursus 31), the imperative of the Pa. ܡܠܠ (*mallel*) makes another connection with stanza I, this time with the end in 2b.

A third antithesis in 5a describes the formerly degraded and oppressed as despised (cf. 25:5). The basic meaning of the Ethpe., identical with the Ettaph., of ܫܘܛ, ܫܛ (*šāṭ*) is best expressed by the passive of a verb such as ἀτιμάζω.[37] When those who had been dishonorably treated are exhorted to "be now lifted up" (*mekkēl* = νῦν),[38] the imperative of the Ethpe., again identical with the Ettaph. of ܪܘܡ, ܪܡ (*rām*), which is intended as a passive, not a reflexive,[39] expresses a redemptive event, the reason for which will be given in 5b.

Just because the parallel structures in stanza II are not smooth and refined (see above), there is an extra stress on 5b.[40] Since the Revealer speaks, later on, of his own "righteousness" (21a; cf. 41:12), ܙܕܝܩܘܬܐ (*zaddīqūṯā*) cannot here stand for "Jesus Christ, the Righteous One."[41] The "righteousness" of the audience, which has been "lifted up," that is "made visible" to the whole world,[42] does not mean that their *iustitia distributiva* is their own as an "attribute" or virtue, their "righteousness under the law," or the leitmotif of their whole "way of life."[43] It is the "being righteous," which is the gift of no-thing and no body in this world and exists in the paradox of divine grace and human injustice. This righteousness, handed down, as it were, in judgment, is the opposite of self-righteousness, and is both a gift and a task.

■ **6-7** While it is correct to state that stanzas II and III "are linked by the association of ܪܘܡ in 5b and ܝܡܝܢܗ in 6a (cf. 25:9)," it is quite misleading to assert that stanza III contains "statements *about* the community."[44] The statements in stanza III are in part metaphorical and in part predestinarian promises of salvation, addressed to the hearer or reader by use of the suffix ܟܘܢ (-*ḵōn*), which is intended inclusively.

According to antique superstition and theories of power, the "right," in this case the "right hand," is superior to the left in all cases and thus is not meant to be inclusive.[45] In 6a the ܝܡܝܢܐ (*yammīnā*) of the Lord expresses his unequalled "power,"[46] perhaps even at this early stage already his *bonitas*.[47]

33 Payne Smith, 2:4167.
34 Diettrich (p. 29) assumes that the *Odes* originated in that sect.
35 Cf. BDAG, *s.v.* ἡσυχία, 1.
36 See BDAG, *s.v.* σιγή, on Ignatius *Magn.* 8:2.
37 See Payne Smith, 2:4093; BAGD, *s.v.* ἀτιμάζω ("deprive someone of honor or respect").
38 See Payne Smith, 2:2104.
39 Bauer (p. 586), for instance, translates it reflexively "now raise yourselves." So do Diettrich (p. 29) and Greßmann (p. 444). Harris and Mingana (2:254) use the passive "be lifted up." Charlesworth (p. 41) and Franzmann (p. 65) do the same. I select these examples partly for their varied treatment of the manuscript divisions. Lattke, *Oden*, 114, "*wurden* nun erhöht [*were* now raised up]" is a misprint. Grammatically this translation is possible, but the sense is unlikely.
40 Why the "fourth section of the verse" should have been "omitted" from the manuscript (Diettrich, 29) is incomprehensible. In spite of her arbitrary divisions for the sake of "parallel structure," Franzmann is right that the "inclusio for the stanza" is "formed between 3a and 5b by . . . the semantically similar roots ܥܘܩ and ܪܘܡ" (Franzmann, 66–67).
41 Charlesworth, 43.
42 See Payne Smith, 2:3857; BDAG, *s.v.* ὑψόω.
43 Bauer and Aland, *s.v.* δικαιοσύνη, 2b; cf. BDAG, *s.v.* δικαιοσύνη, 3a.
44 Franzmann, 68 (emphasis added).
45 The "left" is mentioned only once in the *Odes of Solomon*. The juxtaposition of the right side and the left side in 25:7a represents completeness, wholeness (25:7b).
46 See BDAG, *s.v.* δεξιός, 1.
47 Payne Smith, 1:1605.

In synthetic parallelism, 6b draws the consequence of this promise of the presence of the Lord's right hand,[48] that the Lord—the only possible complement—is "a helper for you" (cf. 7:3; 21:2; 25:2). In 25:2 "right hand" and "helper" are soteriologically linked, and the combination in 21:2 of "helper" with the Aph. of ܪܘܡ (*rwm*) is another indication that stanzas II and III are closely connected. There is no doubting the verbal influence of Ps 118 (117 LXX), which, after emphasizing that the Lord is "good" (1-4), continues:

κύριος ἐμοὶ βοηθός,
οὐ φοβηθήσομαι τί ποιήσει μοι ἄνθρωπος.
κύριος ἐμοὶ βοηθός,
κἀγὼ ἐπόψομαι τοὺς ἐχθρούς μου (6-7).
δεξιὰ κυρίου ὕψωσέν με,
δεξιὰ κυρίου ἐποίησεν δύναμιν (16).

The Lord is my helper;
and I will not fear what man shall do to me.
The Lord is my helper;
and I shall see my desire upon mine enemies.
The right hand of the Lord has exalted me:
the right hand of the Lord has wrought powerfully.[49]

With the antithesis of war and peace, which cannot be historically verified here or in 9:6,[50] 7a specifies the "right hand of the Lord" as ܝܡܝܢܐ ܕܫܠܡܐ (*yammīnā ḏa-šlāmā*), as it will be designated also in later Syriac texts.[51] The Ethpa. ܐܬܛܝܒ (*ʾeṯṭayyaḇ*), derived from the root ܛܘܒ (*ṭwb*) meaning "to be good,"[52] which occurs only here, is a theological passive describing God as the "preparer" of peace.[53]

Charlesworth's criticism[54] of Harris and Mingana's translation of 7b ("Before ever your war happened")[55] is unfounded, because "happened" is not a simple "past tense" but an imperfect expressing potentiality, perhaps even a sort of subjunctive.[56] Even the possible but never actualized war exists, therefore, in a predestined past future out of which God's peace comes into this world of murder and manslaughter as an event of salvation.

■ **8** As discussed in the introduction to *Ode* 8, it is better to divide the tetracolon 8-9 into two bicola, 8 = stanza IVa and 9 = stanza IVb. The speaker of IVa introduces his own revelation (stanzas IVb–VIII) by the use of two parallel and inclusively intended (masculine plural) imperatives of salvation.

The exact meaning of the phrase "the word of truth," with its use of the genitive (in 𝔊 certainly [*τὸν*] *λόγον τῆς ἀληθείας*), is dependent on the mythological and kerygmatic context in each case; the passage under consideration has a strong Gnostic tinge (see Excursus 1). Similar passages in the New Testament (Col 1:5; Eph 1:13; 4:21; 2 Tim 2:15; Jas 1:8) and later Gnostic parallels in the *Pistis Sophia*,[57] the Mandaic liturgies,[58] the Manichaean *Psalm-Book*,[59] and NHC I,*4*[60] show how popular and widely used this quite unphilosophical phrase

48 On the preposition ܥܡ (*ʿam*), see Payne Smith 2:2903–4.
49 Rahlfs, 2:129–30; Brenton, 769–70.
50 See Harris and Mingana, 2:258; and Harnack, 36.
51 Payne Smith, 1:1605.
52 Payne Smith, *Dictionary*, 167.
53 See BDAG, *s.v.* *ἑτοιμάζω*, a; on *κατάπαυσις* = *τόπος* [*τῆς*] *καταπαύσεως* in *Jos. Asen.* 8:11, see Christoph Burchard, *Joseph und Aseneth* (JSHRZ 2.4; Gütersloh: Mohn, 1983) 651.
54 Charlesworth, 43.
55 Harris and Mingana, 2:254.
56 See Nöldeke §267.
57 E.g., ⲡϣⲁϫⲉ ⲛ̄ⲧⲁⲗⲏⲑⲓⲁ (*ἀλήθεια*) in chap. 98; see Schmidt, Till, and Schenke, *Schriften*, 153, line 9; cf. Schmidt and MacDermot, *Pistis Sophia*, 239.
58 מאמלא ד׳שראראׄ in no. 99 of the *Qolastā*; see Mark Lidzbarski, *Mandäische Liturgien* (Abhandlungen der königlichen Gesellschaft der Wissenschaften zu Göttingen, Philosophisch-historische Klasse, N.F. 17.1; Berlin, 1920; repr., Göttingen: Vandenhoeck & Ruprecht, 1970) 165, lines 3–4.
59 ⲡⲥⲉϫⲉ ⲙ̄ⲧⲙⲏⲉ in the *ψαλμοὶ Σαρακωτῶν*; see Charles Robert Cecil Allberry, ed., *A Manichaean Psalm-Book*, with a contribution by Hugo Ibscher (Manichaean Manuscripts in the Chester Beatty Collection 2, pt. 2; Stuttgart: Kohlhammer, 1938) 158, lines 19–21. The complete English translation of this passage according to Allberry is the following: "Christ is the word of Truth: he that hears it shall live. I tasted a sweet taste, I found nothing sweeter than the word of Truth." In this passage "the idea of Truth is as it were personified in Christ" (Siegfried Richter, *Exegetisch-literarkritische Untersuchungen von Herakleidespsalmen des koptisch-manichäischen Psalmenbuches* [Arbeiten zum spätantiken und koptischen Ägypten 5; Altenberge: Oros, 1994] 83 n. 30), which differs from *Ode* 8.

was.[61] "Truth" in 8a is neither "a Person or Hypostasis"[62] from the Wisdom tradition, nor someone who, in Johannine fashion, can call himself *ἡ ἀλήθεια,* among other descriptions (John 14:6, differing from 1:17 and 17:17), but is transcendental "reality." The imperative of the Pe. ܫܡܥ (*šmaʿ*) can be said to correspond to the call with which *Ode* 9 begins: "Open your ears, and I shall speak to you" (9:1).

Just as in 15:4-5 the hearing of "truth" corresponds to the thought of *gnōsis,* 8b illuminates the "word of truth" (cf. the conjecture at 12:1), showing it to be the content of the soteriological "knowledge of the Most High" (see Excursus 7). Between the Pa. ܩܒܠ (*qabbel*) and the other word generally used for "take," the Pe. ܢܣܒ (*nsab*), there is hardly any difference in meaning, which, despite the conventions of Syriac translation, is also broadly true of the Greek verbs *δέχομαι* and *λαμβάνω* with their various compounds.[63] The ܝܕܥܬܐ (*ʾidaʿtā*) of the Most High is not recognition of God (objective genitive), as, for example, in Rom 1:19-21; 2 Cor 10:5; Col 1:10; Eph 1:17; or 1 Pet 1:2-3,[64] but an otherworldly *gnōsis* whose originator is known to Gnostics as *their* "Most High" (genitive of source or subjective genitive; see on 12 below; cf. also already Rom 11:33).[65]

■ **9** In 9a, the third masculine singular imperfect of ܝܕܥ (*ʾidaʿ*) picks up the key word *gnōsis* (8b) of stanza IVa, while stanza IVb as a whole with its synonyms and parallelism ushers in the revelatory address, whose speaker is identified as a masculine person by the active participles (masculine singular) of the Pe. ܐܡܪ (*ʾemar*) and the Pa. ܚܘܝ (*ḥawwī*), while his audience, in spite of the four-times-repeated suffix ܟܘܢ (*-kōn*), should be understood to include both sexes.

If the verb of the main clause in 9a, which carries a future connotation, can be taken to refer also to 9b, then in each the objects of the (non-)"knowing"—that is, the revelation of the speaking "I" as unfolded in stanzas V to VIII—are introduced by the "correlative" ܡܕܡ ܕ (*meddem d-*).[66]

Parallel within the structure of stanza IVb are the anthropological-dualistic terms "flesh" (in 𝔊 probably *σάρξ* rather than *σῶμα*) and "garment." The negative meaning of ܒܣܪܐ (*besrā,* parallel to "world" in 20:3), which should not be reduced to the merely sexual, depresses the metaphorical ܠܒܘܫܐ (*lbūšā,* derived from ܠܒܫ (*lbeš*]), which is basically neutral (in 11:11 *ἔνδυμα*/ܠܒܘܫܐ is a positive parallel to "light"), so that, as the opposite of something like "soul" (*ψυχή*; cf. *Diogn.* 6.5),[67] it almost becomes the hermetic *σκῆνος*, "the body

60 ⲡⲗⲟⲅⲟⲥ ⲛ̄ⲧⲙⲏⲉ in *Treat. Res.* 43,34 and 45,3–4; see Malcolm Lee Peel, "NHC I,4: The Treatise on the Resurrection," in Attridge, *Nag Hammadi Codex I,* 1:148–49; see also Peel, "The Treatise on the Resurrection (I,4)," *NHLE,* 54.

61 See BDAG, *s.v.* ἀλήθεια, 2b; Bauer, 587.

62 Diettrich, 28.

63 Cf. in the *Odes of Solomon,* for example, 9:5b with 11:4. See Payne Smith, 2:2392–93, 3469–70; BDAG, *s.vv.* δέχομαι and λαμβάνω.

64 See BDAG, *s.vv.* γινώσκω, γνῶσις, γνωστός and ἐπίγνωσις.

65 This mixture of objective genitive and subjective genitive can be seen in *Corp. Herm.* 10:15: *οὐ γὰρ ἀγνοεῖ τὸν ἄνθρωπον ὁ θεός, ἀλλὰ καὶ πάνυ γνωρίζει καὶ θέλει γνωρίζεσθαι. τοῦτο μόνον σωτήριον ἀνθρώπῳ ἐστίν, ἡ γνῶσις τοῦ θεοῦ* ("Dieu n'ignore pas l'homme, au contraire il le connaît tout à fait bien et il veut être connu de lui. Cela seul est salutaire pour l'homme, la connaissance de Dieu" [Nock and Festugière, 1:120]).

66 Nöldeke §236.

67 The metaphorical term "garment" or "vesture" not only partakes of the negative meaning of *σάρξ* but is also involved in the dualistic contrasts with *νοῦς*, *πνεῦμα,* and *ψυχή* (see BDAG, *s.v.* *σάρξ*).

Bauer's reference to the "ignorance of the flesh" (p. 587) in the *First Book of Jeû* (chap. 4) is not quite accurate, for in this *Book of the Great κατὰ μυστήριον λόγος*—the proper "title of this treatise" (Schmidt, Till, and Schenke, *Schriften,* XXIX–XXX)—the dialogue between the apostles and Jesus runs as follows (Schmidt, Till, and Schenke, 259–60; cf. Schmidt and MacDermot, *Jeu,* 43):

<The *apostles*> answered with one voice, they said:

"Jesus, <thou living one>, O Lord, are we born of the *flesh* (κατὰ σάρκα), and <have we> known thee *according to* the *flesh* (κατὰ σάρκα)? Tell us, O Lord, *for* (γάρ) we are troubled."

The living Jesus answered and said to his *apostles*:

"I do not speak of the *flesh* (σάρξ) in which <you> dwell, *but* (ἀλλά) of the *flesh* (σάρξ) of <ignorance> and *non-understanding* (ἄγνοια) which exists in ignorance, which leads astray many from the <word> of my Father."

The background of this dialogue may be the

in which man is imprisoned [and which] keeps him from unity with God."[68]

What is so emphatically excluded by the prepositioned denials of stanza IVb is a human "pessimism" more profound than even that which is expressed in a popularly Platonic fashion by Wis 9:15:[69]

φθαρτὸν γὰρ σῶμα βαρύνει ψυχήν,
καὶ βρίθει τὸ γεῶδες σκῆνος νοῦν πολυφρόντιδα.

For a perishable body weighs down the soul,
and this earthy tent burdens the thoughtful/anxious mind.[70]

■ **10-13** In comparison with stanza II (see above), the strangeness of the construction in stanza V is lessened because the inclusively intended imperatives of salvation (masculine plural) only collide with the predicative participles (masculine plural absolute), which are also meant inclusively.[71] Verse 12 in particular forms the connection with the introduction of stanza IVa (cf. the structural analysis of Franzmann,[72] although her dissection of the four monocola into bicola is gratuitous).

There is extreme parallelism between 10 and 11, above all in the "reciprocity" expressed by the use of the Pe. ܢܛܪ (*nṭar*) and the Ethpa. ܐܬܢܛܪ (*ʾeṯnaṭṭar*), which—though not in the use of *τηρέω*—sounds almost Johannine.[73] Verse 12 is still mostly parallel to 10-11, which leaves 13 formally somewhat isolated.

The word ܐܪܙܐ (*rāzā*), early adopted from Persian, and pronounced, it seems, "with a vowel-prefix,"[74] is a *hapax legomenon* in the *Odes*, although in later Syriac literature it was to play an important role[75]—and not only as a translation of *μυστήριον*. If it is hardly defensible to insert the word "secret" into the title of the Ode,[76] it is also not proper to look for evidence of an early sacramental "*disciplina arcani*,"[77] or to proclaim "that we are here . . . totally in the realm of Wisdom literature."[78] The "secret" of the Revealer, in the context of *Ode* 8, is nothing more or less than his revelation, which has a preserving power and must, therefore, be preserved (in 𝔊 probably *τηρέω* or *φυλάσσω*).[79] It is no "secret doctrine,"[80] but a "gift of God,"[81] which the authors and readers of the *Odes of Solomon*, some of whom were certainly Gnostics, will have interpreted according to their differing traditions as the *μυστήριον τοῦ θεοῦ* (cf. 1 Cor 2:1; Col 2:2; Rev 10:7) in the beyond, or even as the historical *μυστήριον τοῦ Χριστοῦ* ("mystery of Christ" [Col 4:3]).[82]

The "faith" of the Revealer (in 𝔊 certainly [*τὴν*] *πίστιν μου*, a subjective genitive; cf. 39:13) also has powers of preservation. The imperative in 11 of the primal believer, which depicts him as *ἀρχηγὸς τῆς σωτηρίας/πίστεως* ("pioneer of salvation/faith"; cf. Heb 2:10; 12:2), is at most only indirectly a call to "faith in me."[83] Primarily this "preservation" means protected partaking in the *πίστις* of the Revealer, his trust in God, directed to no-thing and no-body in this world, which is never an "attribute" or "virtue" but only a "gift of grace."[84] The Syriac noun ܗܝܡܢܘܬܐ (*haymānūṯā*) has not yet acquired its later meaning of *religio* or *doctrina*.[85]

---

much-discussed passage 2 Cor 5:16, which Walter Schmithals (*Die Gnosis in Korinth: Eine Untersuchung zu den Korintherbriefen* [FRLANT 66 = N.F. 48; 2nd ed.; Göttingen: Vandenhoeck & Ruprecht, 1965] 292 n. 3) considers a Gnostic gloss. See also the excursus on the interpretation of 2 Cor 5:16 in Christian Wolff, *Der zweite Brief des Paulus an die Korinther* (ThHKNT 7; Berlin: Evangelische Verlagssanstalt, 1989) 123–27.

68 Grese, *Corpus*, 141; cf. *Corp. Herm.* 13:12; Nock and Festugière, 2:205; BDAG, *s.v.* *σκῆνος* on 2 Cor 5:1 and 5:4.

69 See Georgi, 436.

70 Rahlfs, 2:358; Georgi, 435–36.

71 See again Nöldeke §350.

72 Franzmann, 69.

73 See Lattke, *Einheit*, 22–24, on "lieben [to love]."

74 Nöldeke §51.

75 See Payne Smith, 2:3871–73.

76 As Abbott does (pp. 237–90), with a plethora of unsorted data.

77 As Harris and Mingana (2:257–58), correctly state countering Bernard's suggestion (Bernard, 66).

78 Diettrich, 29.

79 See BDAG, *s.vv.* *τηρέω* and *φυλάσσω*; cf. Payne Smith, 2:2353.

80 BDAG, *s.v.* *μυστήριον*.

81 Bauer, 587.

82 BDAG, *s.v.* *μυστήριον*, with more quotations, including some from magical papyri.

83 Abbott, 258. See Attridge, *Hebrews*, 88, 356–57.

84 See Bauer and Aland, *s.v.* *πίστις*, 2dγ and ζ; BDAG, *s.v.* *πίστις*, 2dγ and ζ.

85 See Payne Smith, 1:238.

In 12, the Revealer takes up key words from the introductory verses: "truth" (8a), "*gnōsis*" (8b), and "know" (9a). His own "knowledge" comes from the "Most High" (8b), which thus certifies him as the primal Gnostic. The Gnostics, who, according to their understanding, can "truly" and "really" (in 𝔊 ἐν ἀληθείᾳ or ἀληθῶς)[86] know the Revealer only in a complete antithesis to the normal and natural earthly "flesh" (9a), are called on to "know" his *gnōsis* so that they too can partake of the "*gnōsis* of the Most High."

In place of the demonstrative pronouns of 10-12 (masculine plural as above in stanza II), the correlative in 13 is constructed with the pronoun for indirect question (common plural),[87] with no detectable change in meaning.[88] Nor is there a discernible difference in meaning between the verb ܚܒ (*ḥab[b]*) used in 22 and the repeated Pe. of ܪܚܡ (*rḥem*) used here (see Excursus 2). Since the Revealer is not speaking of his own ܚܘܒܐ (*ḥubbā* [in 22c he himself is called the "beloved"]), it is correct to point to the "love" mentioned in the beginning (1b). The admonition (imperative plural + first singular accusative suffix) to love the Revealer, in this context full of "knowledge" and "knowing" (12, 14b), forms a somewhat isolated bridge to stanzas VI–VIII, in which the Revealer will speak *about* his own, and thus, indirectly, about his relationship with them.

■ **14-17** The remainder of this first person discourse does not address an audience directly. In fact, stanzas VI–VIII (i.e., 14-21) are a "report concerning the relationship of the 'I' to his chosen ones,"[89] divided and organized by various inclusions. Syntactically and semantically 14a-b and 21b-c mark either end of the whole report, made up of two promises (14a, 21b-c) and other statements of salvation. The use of ܕܝܠ (*dīl*) with the first singular possessive suffix circumscribes stanzas VI–VII—as well as stanza VII within it—and also connects them to stanza VIII (20c).

Stanza VI is marked off by 14 and 17, which "form a semantic inclusio"[90] and are chiastic in content.[91] Although stanzas IVb and V are only loosely connected by the use of the singular masculine active participle of Pe. ܝܕܥ (*ʾidaʿ*), it is 14 that begins something really new. Indeed, this is the proper beginning of the revelation, with respect to the thought and action of the Revealer as Redeemer and Mediator of the (new) creation, and also with respect to the predestined being and future existence of those whom he calls his "own" (14a, 20b), his "work" (18-19), and his "elect" (17, 20c).

The negated participle (active singular masculine) of the Aph. of ܗܦܟ (*hpak*) "denotes . . . the continuing . . . Present"[92] of the vigilance and solicitude of the Redeemer, but the following particle ܓܝܪ (*gēr*) has no justifying or explanatory meaning; its function is rather to emphasize the first word of 14a.[93] The feminine ܐܦܐ (*ʾappē*), which is never used in the singular, corresponds to the Greek neuter τὸ πρόσωπον,[94] which itself is found in Syriac as the masculine loanword ܦܪܨܘܦܐ (*parṣōpā*), which will appear immediately in this context in 15c. Here in stanza VI both words mean "features," "countenance," or "face," a *pars pro toto* for the person standing opposite, even though sometimes only metaphorically.

Excursus 8: "Countenance" and "Person" in the *Odes of Solomon*[95]

The occurrences of ܐܦܐ (thirteen times) and ܦܪܨܘܦܐ (eight times) are first shown in a diagram (see chart below) to display, by indentation, marks of repetition or parallels, and similar abbreviated notes, both the linguistic distinctions (e.g., ܡܢ ܩܕܡ [*men qdām*] = "before") and the personal relations (e.g., Redeemer, redeemed, Lord). It should be noted that

86 See BDAG, *s.vv.* ἀλήθεια and ἀληθῶς.
87 See Nöldeke §§68 and 236.
88 See the distribution in the concordance, Lattke, *Bedeutung*, 2:47, 84.
89 Franzmann, 69, "stanzas 6–9" is a misprint for "stanzas 6–8."
90 Ibid., 70.
91 *Ode* 8:14a-b is a bicolon, but 17 is a colon, with its hemistichs connected by "and." The influence of Harris and Mingana's division (vol. 1, on this passage; 2:255) of 17 into 17a-b can still be traced in modern editions and translations (see, e.g., Bauer, 587; Charlesworth, 40, 42; Beskow and Hidal, 18; Franzmann, 64–65; Pierre, 79; Azar, 102). Franzmann's thorough structural analysis (p. 70) slightly exaggerates the parallelisms in stanza VI, but her division into 14, 15-16, and 17 is correct.
92 Nöldeke §269; cf. Payne Smith, 1:1038–39.
93 See Lattke, "Wörter," 287–89 = idem, *Bedeutung*, 4:136–38.
94 Payne Smith, 1:278; BDAG, *s.v.* πρόσωπον.
95 This excursus is largely based on Lattke, "Wörter," 296–98 = idem, *Bedeutung*, 4:145–47.

the multiple related meanings of the Greek "hypostasis" *τὸ πρόσωπον* ("face, countenance, mask, role, person")[96] are to be found also in the Syriac uses of the masculine loan word ܦܪܨܘܦܐ (*p̄arṣōp̄ā*),[97] a word in which the pronunciation of the ܦ (*p̄*) in both positions is always hard.[98] Even an expression like "the surface of the whole earth" has a Syriac equivalent ܦܪܨܘܦܐ ܕܟܠܗ ܐܪܥܐ (*p̄arṣōp̄ā ḏ-ḵullāh ʾarʿā*),[99] although in most cases ܐܦܐ (*ʾappē*) is used for *πρόσωπον* rather than ܦܪܨܘܦܐ (also in the *Odes of Solomon;* see 6:10; 11:13; 16:16).[100]

ܐܦܐ	ܦܪܨܘܦܐ (*πρόσωπον*)
6:10 surface of the earth	
8:14 my ~ (Redeemer) I turn not away from my own	
	8:15 their ~ [plural] (redeemed), I sealed them
11:13 surface of the earth (*πρόσωπον* in 𝔊)	
	11:14 my ~ (Redeemer) || eyes (*πρόσωπον* in 𝔊)
13:2 your ~ (redeemed)	
13:3 your ~ (redeemed)	
15:2 my ~ (redeemed; Redeemer?)	
	15:9 ~ ܡܢ ܩܕܡ (Redeemer) || by my word
16:16 surface of the earth	
17:4 ~ and figure . . .	17:4 . . . of a new ~ [= person] I put on (redeeming Redeemed)
21:6 ~ ܩܕܡ (Lord)	
21:9 on my ~ (redeemed)	
	22:11 thy way || thy ~ [2O in ℭ]
	25:4 thy ~ [2O in ℭ] with me (God/Lord)
	31:5 his ~ [= person] was declared righteous (Son)
36:3 ~ ܡܢ ܩܕܡ (Lord)	
40:4 my ~ || spirit || soul (redeemed)	
41:6 our ~ (redeemed) in his light	
	42:13 my ~ (Redeemer)

In 11:14 the enlightened "eyes" and the bedewed "face" of the redeemed "I" are in parallel. The equivalence of ܦܪܨܘܦܐ and *πρόσωπον* is shown in the manuscripts, as is the idiomatic or traditional equation of ܐܦܐ and *πρόσωπον* in the immediate context (see on 6:10; 11:13; and 16:16).

96 Hjalmar Frisk, *Griechisches etymologisches Wörterbuch* (3 vols.; Heidelberg: Winter, 1954–72) 2:602.

97 Payne Smith, 2:3291–92; Margoliouth, *Supplement*, 278.

98 Brockelmann, *Grammatik* §30; cf. Nöldeke §25.

99 Payne Smith, 2:3291.

100 See Payne Smith, 1:278–80.

In the Greek of the "Mirror" *Ode* (13:2-3)[101] it is more than likely that πρόσωπον or πρόσωπα was the word twice translated by ܐܦܝܟܘܢ (*ʾappaykōn*). And πρόσωπον will also have been used in 21:9 (heart-mouth-lips-face); 40:4 (rejoicing and exultation); 41:6 (shining).

In *Ode* 15, it is not only difficult to identify the speaking "I" from whose countenance (ܐܦܐ) the darkness is banished (15:2). There is also the problem of translating the idiom ܡܢ ܩܕܡ ܦܪܨܘܦܝ (*men qdām parṣōp*) in 15:9a so that the parallelism with the instrumental "by my word" in 15:9b is brought out.[102] A similar construction using ܡܢ ܩܕܡ with ܐܦܐ is found in 36:3 where the exalted one says of himself that the power of the Lord's Spirit brought him forth "before the face of the Lord." In both these cases, but probably not in 21:6 (ܩܕܡ) where the exalted one "passed before" the Lord's "face," the Greek is likely to have been πρόσωπον (rather than a mere preposition).

Ode 17:4b is a special case, since both ܐܦܐ and ܦܪܨܘܦܐ occur in the one colon. In this case ܦܪܨܘܦܐ is "person," as in 31:5, which declares the justification of the Son by the Father (cf. 1 Tim 3:16 for the content). The Greek equivalent will have been πρόσωπον. It is unlikely to have been the case with ܐܦܐ here. It may have been ὄψις (cf. John 11:44 in the Peshitta). The parallel ܕܡܘܬܐ (*dmūṯā*) may have been εἶδος or μορφή.[103]

In 22:11 and 25:5 the ܦܪܨܘܦܐ in 𝔖 is equivalent to ϩⲟ (*ho*) in ℭ, a word that generally translates πρόσωπον. God's "way" and "countenance" are complementary (22:11a; in the hymn of the *Pistis Sophia* it is explained by "the light of thy countenance"). This "countenance" is in fact the presence of God's redeeming grace (25:4a). "Presence" as "regard" is also the meaning of ܦܪܨܘܦܐ in 42:13b. The descent of the Redeemer into the underworld is an acute threat to Death personified.

Ode 8:15 is the only passage where ܦܪ̈ܨܘܦܐ occurs in the plural.[104] This refers to the term "my own" in the context of stanza VI, of whom the Redeemer says, "I do not turn my face away" (8:14). For this 𝔖 has ܐܦܝ (*ʾappay*), but in both verses 𝔊 will have had πρόσωπον or πρόσωπα.

Verse 14b gives the reason for the promise of salvation in 14a. In it the "personal pronoun as object" of being known "is denoted by ܠ (*l-*)."[105] The reciprocity (see on 10-12 above) of "knowing" and "being known" in a personal sense is reminiscent of the saying of the Jesus of John 10:14 (even though the *Odes of Solomon* never mention the "Good Shepherd" or his "sheep"):

> ἐγώ εἰμι ὁ ποιμὴν ὁ καλός
> καὶ γινώσκω τὰ ἐμὰ (viz., πρόβατα)
> καὶ ⸀γινώσκουσί με τὰ ἐμά⸀ (*v.l.* γινώσκομαι ὑπὸ τῶν ἐμῶν).

> I am the good shepherd;
> I know my own [viz., sheep]
> and my own know me (*v.l.* am known of mine).

That "my own" are thought of as in some sense preexistent follows from the statement of salvation in 15a-b, where the preceding subordinate clause 15a *must retain* the particle ܕܠܐ (*d-lā*).[106] The Ethpa. of ܣܟܠ (*skal*), used only here, refers to an activity of the νοῦς. The metaphor of the predestining "perceiving," the νοεῖν or

101 See Michael Lattke, "Salomo-Ode 13 im Spiegel-Bild der Werke von Ephraem Syrus," *Mus* 102 (1989) 255–66.

102 See Payne Smith, *Dictionary*, 490: "from the presence." In 15:9a-b, the topic is the destruction of Death and his kingdom "Sheol."

103 Payne Smith, 1:914.

104 Harnack's translation of 8:13-15 is "love me with devotion, you who love, for I shall not turn my face from that which is mine. For I know them, and before they were I have recognized them and their face; I have sealed them" (p. 37). This splitting of the cola is impossible. His annotation also shows that the plural of ܦܪ̈ܨܘܦܐ was not observed: "One might also translate it: 'and their face—I sealed it,' but that seems a less good translation."

105 Nöldeke §287. The objective suffix ܗܘܢ (*-hōn*), which is used inclusively throughout stanza VI as well, makes it plain that ܕܝܠ (*dīl*) + first singular possessive suffix cannot stand for a thing that is "mine" but must apply to a number of persons who are "mine."

106 Contra Harris and Mingana, vol. 1, on this passage, where it is omitted; cf. Nöldeke §267; Charlesworth, 44.

ϑεωρεῖν,[107] appears as a precondition for the "knowing" found earlier. This speaker claims to be more than a commissioned Revealer and delegated Redeemer. Here, quite naively, is the claim, invented and defended by humankind, of *creatio ex nihilo*, which almost surpasses the early Jewish and Gnostic myths of Sophia and speculation on the Logos, as well as Christian statements about the Lord Jesus as mediator of creation (see 1 Cor 8:6; John 1:3; Col 1:16; Heb 1:2).

The cola 15c and 16a are in formally chiastic and thematically synthetic parallelism. Like the commonly paired terms "flesh and blood" (Sir 14:18; 17:31; Wis 12:5; Matt 16:17, and elsewhere in the New Testament), "members and head" (see on 17:15 below), or "heart and limbs" (18:1-2; 26:4), the pair "faces and limbs"[108] represents the complete human beings (cf. 40:3-4). By placing the plural of ܦܪܨܘܦܐ (*p̄arṣōp̄ā*; see Excursus 8 above) at the beginning, the authentically individual character of the body consisting of many members is emphasized (see Excursus 18).

The Aph. of ܬܩܢ (*tqen*) in this mythological image of the world, where the Lord already appears as *creator universi*,[109] offers no difficulties as a description of preparing and making the ܗܕܡ̈ܐ (*haddāmē*) in 16a, but the exact meaning of the Pe. ܛܒܥ (*ṭbaʿ*) in 15c, which is used transitively only here, is a very different case. Instead of using the normal Syriac noun for "seal" (ܚܬܡܐ [*ḥāṭmā*] in 4:7; 23:8–9), the author uses a verb, which can mean variously "*to imprint* a seal, *to mark, sign, seal . . . to coin*."[110] Since the Greek was most probably a form of σφραγίζω,[111] the meaning "to seal up . . . in order to keep it secret" can be excluded.[112] Tattooing also, and its connection to religious dedication,[113] or the "seal on the forehead in the cult of Mithra"[114] is unlikely. If the passage deals not only with "spiritual rebirth" but with the "primary creation,"[115] then Schenke would be right in saying that "the seal [explicitly named in 4:7 and implied here] refers to man's likeness to God, which is the original oneness of God and man."[116] This then is (Gnostic-)protological and "eschatological sealing" only in the sense that "the mark denoting ownership also carries with it the protection of the owner."[117]

The "peculiar expression" in 16b does not refer to the Father's "breasts," as in 19:3-4, so that only the theological claim of the speaking "I" brings in the idea of "God's breasts."[118] The feminine metaphor (cf. Isa 66:11)[119] describes milk as the life-giving food (16c; cf. 14:2), so it is hard to understand how this image of breasts can "pass the bound of what is acceptable to modern taste."[120]

The sequence of two final clauses, the first of which again uses ܕܝܠ (*dīl*) adjectivally (16c; cf. 16b) to stress the divine origin of the "holy milk," forms the climax of the section in 15-16. The masculine ܚܠܒܐ (*ḥalb̄ā*) is not a metaphor for "revelation as life-giving and nourishing power,"[121] nor a symbol of the Eucharist,[122] nor an expression of "longing" in "contemplation of the divine" to "eliminate the limits and divisions of gender."[123] In

107 See Payne Smith, 2:2628.
108 Which is not found in Franzmann's listing (Franzmann, 398–414).
109 Payne Smith, 2:4485.
110 See Payne Smith, *Dictionary*, 166.
111 See Payne Smith, 1:1427.
112 BDAG, *s.v.* σφραγίζω, 2.
113 Tomas Arvedson, *Das Mysterium Christi: Eine Studie zu Mt 11.25-30* (Arbeiten und Mitteilungen aus dem neutestamentlichen Seminar zu Uppsala 7; Uppsala: Wretmans, 1937) 186.
114 BDAG, *s.v.* σφραγίζω, 3, referring to Tertullian *Praescr. haer.* 40.
115 Contra Diettrich, 30.
116 Hans-Martin Schenke, *Der Gott „Mensch" in der Gnosis: Ein religionsgeschichtlicher Beitrag zur Diskussion über die paulinische Anschauung von der Kirche als Leib Christi* (Göttingen: Vandenhoeck & Ruprecht, 1962) 39.
117 BDAG, *s.v.* σφραγίζω, 3, with many references.
118 Harnack, 45; cf. Joseph Conrad Plumpe, *Mater Ecclesia: An Inquiry into the Concept of the Church as Mother in Early Christianity* (Studies in Christian Antiquity 5; Washington, D.C.: Catholic University of America Press, 1943) 33.
119 Payne Smith, 2:4391.
120 Virginia Corwin, *St. Ignatius and Christianity in Antioch* (Yale Publications in Religion 1; New Haven: Yale University Press, 1960) 79. The Pa. ܛܝܒ (*ṭayyeb̄*) comes from the same root *ṭwb* as the Ethpa. in 7a (see above); both are *hapax legomena*.
121 Otto Betz, *Offenbarung und Schriftforschung in der Qumransekte* (WUNT 6; Tübingen: Mohr Siebeck, 1960) 117; but see already Bernard, 67–68: "Word as Milk."
122 Johannes Betz, "Die Eucharistie als Gottes Milch in frühchristlicher Sicht," *ZKTh* 106 (1984) 15–18.
123 Wolfgang Speyer, "Das Weiblich-Mütterliche im

this image of "breasts" as sources of milk, it refers to the "holy" and elemental food, antithetical to everything worldly and profane.[124] In other words, the first person Revealer is not only Redeemer and (co-)Creator of "his own" but also the one who nourishes and sustains them as such. And whoever drinks this "holy milk" is enabled to live a "holy life" (see on 2a above).

The monocolon 17 returns chiastically to 14a-b (see introduction to stanza VI above), and, in the Ethpe. of ܨܒܐ (*ṣḇā*), which outdoes the expression of choice εὐδόκησα ("I am well pleased") in the christological adoption of Matt 3:17 par.,[125] it sums up the preceding reports of creation and salvation. This continuing not "being ashamed" (active masculine singular participle of ܒܗܬ [*bheṯ*]; for the syntax, cf. Rom 1:16)[126] is of course connected to the not "turning away" the face in 14a, but it also brings out an aspect that was expressed later in a long *μυστήριον*-speech of the Gnostic Redeemer (σωτήρ) "Jesus" in chap. 96 of the *Pistis Sophia*:[127]

> Because of this, I have not refrained nor (οὐδέ) been ashamed to call you "my brothers and companions," because you will become fellow-rulers/kings with me in my kingdom.

■ **18-20b** A teaching on creation, together with a heightened theological claim, is now put into the mouth of the speaking "I" (18 and 20; cf. 7:8-9; 7:24; esp. 16:8-18), interrupted by a double rhetorical question (19a-b).[128] Although 18 is a colon, not a bicolon, this beginning and the emphatic final statement of 20b form the *inclusio* of stanza VII.[129]

The particle ܓܝܪ (*gēr*), in the second place, which this time probably does supply a reason,[130] makes the connection with stanza VI. So those the Revealer, Redeemer, and (co)-Creator "has brought into being"[131] are his own, who are now an "expression" of his power.[132] It is highly likely that the gnostically limited Syriac words of creation ܥܒܕܐ (*ʿḇāḏā*) and ܚܝܠܐ (*ḥaylā*) represent the Greek nouns ἔργον and δύναμις, used in the sense of a final result.[133] The plural of the equally metaphorical ܡܚܫܒܬܐ (*maḥšaḇtā*), *cogitatio*, is more likely to stand for *(δια)λογισμοί*[134] than *νοήματα*[135] (see Excursus 9). The word ܐܝܬ (*ʾīṯ*) with third masculine plural suffix (= Greek εἰσι[ν]), meant inclusively, does not bear any particular existential emphasis.

The rhetorical question, doubled in parallel, "interrupts the report style"[136] but shows that it belongs at this point by the repetition of the key word "work" from 18 as well as by the use of the compound word ܗܟܝܠ (*hāḵēl* = ἄρα or οὖν)[137] denoting inference. As in 6:5 (cf. also 25:3) the imperfect of the Pe. ܩܘܡ, ܩܡ (*qām*), which is followed by the compound adversative preposition ܠܘܩܒܠ (*luqḇal*), bears a connotation of enmity.[138]

christlichen Gottesbild," *Kairos* N.F. 24 (1982) 155 = idem, *Frühes Christentum im antiken Strahlungsfeld: Ausgewählte Aufsätze* (Tübingen: Mohr Siebeck, 1989) 339.

124 See Payne Smith, 1:1273; BDAG, *s.v.* γάλα.

125 Harris and Mingana, vol. 1, on this passage; Payne Smith, 2:3352–53.

126 Payne Smith, 1:460.

127 Schmidt, Till, and Schenke, *Schriften*, 148, lines 10–12; cf. Schmidt and MacDermot, *Pistis Sophia*, 232.

128 Add to Lattke, *Oden*, 87.

129 Franzmann, 70. The arbitrary division of 18 into 18a and b is not original with Franzmann (pp. 60, 64) but has already appeared in, e.g., Harris and Mingana (vol. 1, on this passage; 2:255), Bauer (p. 587), and Charlesworth (pp. 40, 42). Diettrich (p. 30) and Frankenberg (p. 11) are right.

130 Lattke, "Wörter," 289 = idem, *Bedeutung*, 4:138.

131 BDGD, *s.v.* ἔργον, 3.

132 BDGD, *s.v.* δύναμις. Cf. Greßmann's excellent translation of 18: "For they are my creation and the miraculous achievement of my thoughts" (p. 445).

133 See Payne Smith, 1:1258; 2:2773; and earlier Frankenberg, 11.

134 See Payne Smith, 1:1397; BDAG, *s.vv.* διαλογισμός and λογισμός.

135 Contra Frankenberg, 11; cf. BDAG, *s.v.* νόημα.

136 Franzmann, 71.

137 See Payne Smith, 1:1006.

138 Payne Smith, 2:3471, 3523.

The interrogative ܡܢܘ (*man-ū*)[139] in 19b still shows its composite origin as ܡܢ (*man*) with the enclitic personal pronoun ܗܘ (third singular masculine), because it is followed by the negated relative particle ܕ (*d-*) introducing the participle of the Ettaph. ܐܬܛܦܝܣ (*ʾeṭṭpīs* [*πεῖσαι]), which is used for the Ethpe. Since these negated Syriac forms of this loanword can equally represent a word like ἀπειθέω or even the adjective ἀπειθής, any attempt to reconstruct the Greek of 19b would be mere guesswork.[140]

The *exact* meaning of the Greek word in its Syriac form is in any case less important than the positively oriented thought of the speaking "I," that his own can participate in the power he wields to an extent greater even than implied by Paul's question τίς καθ' ἡμῶν ("who is against us?") in Rom 8:31.[141] Even an authoritative charge like Heb 13:17, *Πείθεσθε*[142] τοῖς ἡγουμένοις καὶ ὑπείκετε ("obey your leaders and submit to them"), becomes impossible in the sociology of this religion.[143]

The nouns of 18 are transformed into verbs in 20a, where the two direct objects "mind" (in 𝔖 probably νοῦς, but see Excursus 7)[144] and "heart" (in 𝔖 certainly καρδία; see Excursus 4), which rarely occur together since they are anthropologically parallel terms of "the capability of thought,"[145] may both be governed by both verbs or each may pertain to one of them.[146] If the Pe. ܨܒܐ (*ṣbā*), the divine θέλειν,[147] corresponds to the "power" of thought in 18, the Pe. ܓܒܠ (*gbal*), which occurs only here, refers chiastically rather to the "work," and as the equivalent of πλάσσειν it brings to mind the myth of "God's creative activity in forming man" (cf. Gen 2:7).[148] According to Ps 32:15 LXX, the Lord God is particularly ὁ πλάσας . . . τὰς καρδίας αὐτῶν ("who fashioned their hearts," i.e., of the children of men [v. 13]; cf. *Barn.* 2:10),[149] so that the speaking "I," in a transferred claim for himself, could be thought to use the second verb of 20a to refer exclusively to the second object, "heart" (see above).

Verse 20b receives full stress, being verbally identical with the utterance of the redeemed Redeemer, which concludes the whole collection (42:20c). In stanza VIII, it will be seen that the "name" occurs also in the final verse (42:20a), and his own are declared "free" (42:20b), which casts more light on the double rhetorical question of 8:19a-b (see above). Whether it illuminates the problem of the redeemed Redeemer in stanza IX (8:22e) will be considered later.

■ **20c-21** The report, which began at 14, ends here (see stanza VI above). For there is an "inclusio formed by 21b-c and 14a-b."[150] In alternation, or perhaps rising sequence, of the tenses of past, continuous, and future, the Revealer and Redeemer of his elect makes another statement of salvation (20c-21a), which is immediately followed by a promise of the same in reciprocity (21b-c).

In 20c, the right hand is not a symbol of "power," contrasting with 8:6 (cf. 18:7a), but the "place of honor."[151] What is said in the New Testament, often by the use of Ps 109:1 LXX (κάθου ἐκ δεξιῶν μου . . . "sit at my right hand"), on the "enthronement of Jesus as heavenly and messianic ruler,"[152] refers here to all those elect from the

---

139 See Nöldeke §68; and also Muraoka §14.

140 On πεῖσα(ι) > ܦܝܣܐ (*pīsā*), see Payne Smith, 2:3114–19, esp. 3116; and Lattke, "Wörter," 295–96 = idem, *Bedeutung*, 4:144.

141 Cf. the relevant passages in Käsemann, *Romans*, 246-48 (German, 238–39), which show, if indirectly, how far the *Odes of Solomon* have moved beyond the bounds of dialectical theology as the word of the "Justification of the godless."

142 The Syriac translation of this imperative in Heb 13:17 is ܐܬܛܦܝܣܘ (*ʾeṭṭpīs*).

143 Erich Gräßer, *An die Hebräer* (3 vols.; EKKNT 17.1–3; Zurich: Benziger; Neukirchen-Vluyn: Neukirchener Verlag, 1990–97) 3:365, 393–94.

144 Other possible equivalents can be found in Payne Smith, 1:1560.

145 Bauer and Aland, *s.v.* καρδία, 1bβ ("des Denkvermögens"); cf. BDAG, *s.vv.* καρδία and νοῦς.

146 Although "heart" does not have quite the same connotation here as in 8:1, it may still be possible to make a connection. Only those whose "hearts" have been properly "formed" are able to "open" them to the Lord's exultation.

147 BDAG, *s.v.* θέλω, 2; Payne Smith, 2:3352.

148 BDAG, *s.v.* πλάσσω, 1b; Payne Smith, 1:640.

149 Rahlfs, 2:31; Brenton, 716.

150 Franzmann, 71. However, this is neither "the Word of the Most High" nor a "focussing on the establishment of the chosen on the right hand" (Franzmann, 71).

151 BDAG, *s.v.* δεξιός, 1b.

152 Peter von der Osten-Sacken, "δεξιός," *EWNT* 1 (1980) 686; cf. *EDNT* 1:286.

beginning (cf. 23:1-3; 33:13; also 8:17 with different terminology), who show only slight similarity to the eschatologically blessed (εὐλογημένοι) of Matt 25:33-34. The perfect of ܣܐܡ, ܣܡ (*sām*), probably representing a form of the much-used verb τίθημι (as in 25:7),[153] reports the transitive "set" or "stand" as a "past action."[154] To the ears of early Judaism as well as of early Christianity the plural of the passive participle of ܓܒܐ (*gḇā*) with its (first person singular) possessive suffix would have sounded quite familiar,[155] since both "Israelites" and "Christians" are said to be "those whom God has chosen from the generality of mankind and drawn to himself."[156]

In the same way as the speaking "I" confers theological election on himself and his own, he claims for himself in 21a the blessing promised in Isa 58:8, by the quotation of Isa 52:12,[157] in such a way that the Lord, Most High and Father (the titles of God in *Ode* 8), becomes the personified δικαιοσύνη of the speaker (cf. 9:10 and Excursus 25).[158] The comparison of the Hebrew, Greek, and Syriac texts of these verses from Deutero- and Trito-Isaiah will illustrate this interpretation:[159]

(Deutero-)Isaiah 52:12

כי־הלך	πορεύσεται γὰρ	ܡܛܠ ܕܡܪܝܐ ܐܙܠ
לפניכם	πρότερος ὑμῶν	ܩܕܡܝܟܘܢ
יהוה	κύριος	[see ܡܪܝܐ above]

(Trito-)Isaiah 58:8

והלך	καὶ προπορεύσεται	ܘܬܐܙܠ
לפניך	ἔμπροσθέν σου	ܩܕܡܝܟ
צדקך	ἡ δικαιοσύνη σου	ܙܕܝܩܘܬܟ

The feminine ܙܕܝܩܘܬܐ (*zaddīqūtā*; cf. δικαιοσύνη in 25:10 ℭ), therefore, is to be interpreted in a soteriological, not an ethical, sense. The feminine singular participle of ܐܙܠ (*ʾezal*), which it governs, is a future that includes the present.[160] The report form converts the biblical *address* (ὑμῶν and σου) into a *description*, constructed with the help of the *hapax legomenon* ܩܘܕܡܐ (*qudmā*)[161] + third plural masculine suffix, which refers to the "elect" of both sexes.

Verses 21b and 21c do not merely "have a degree of parallelism with chiasmus."[162] This final bicolon also expresses, in a concealed fashion, the idea of soteriological reciprocity found already in 10-11 above. As the Name is with them, they remain linked to the Name. But what, exactly, is the meaning of the masculine ܫܡܐ (*šmā*, in 𝔊 certainly ὄνομα) with its first person singular possessive suffix?

It would have been nice if the Revealer had come clean and revealed his name (title) or personal name. A personal name such as "Jesus" or "Jesus Christ" is not to be found in any of the *Odes of Solomon*. And whether ܡܫܝܚܐ (*mšīḥā*) is a name or merely the "designation of an office"[163] still awaits discussion (see Excursus 24). Assuming that the *Odes* are largely unified,[164] there are passages in which other titles appear, such as "Son" (cf. 23:22), the "Virgin Grace" (33:13 in the context of *Ode* 33), or "Son of God" (42:15b). But even they do not really advance matters. Since this passage is anything but "indubitably" an "utterance of God"[165] or any utterance of a canonical "Christ" (too easily proposed as an alternative by numerous authors), it is likely that, after calling on personified "Righteousness," the speaking "I" now claims the "name" which is "the hypostatized Name of God" (see Excursus 39).[166]

153 See Payne Smith, 2:2556–57; BDAG, *s.v.* τίθημι.
154 Nöldeke §255.
155 See Payne Smith, 1:636–37.
156 BDAG, *s.v.* ἐκλεκτός, 1.
157 Cf. Claus Westermann, *Das Buch Jesaja: Kapitel 40–66* (ATD 19; Göttingen: Vandenhoeck & Ruprecht, 1966; 3rd ed., 1976) 204, 264, 269; ET: *Isaiah 40–66: A Commentary* (Philadelphia: Westminster, 1969) 252, 332, 338.
158 Bauer (p. 588) also refers to Ps 85:14 (Ps 84:14 LXX), but in that passage "righteousness" goes before him, that is, the Lord.
159 Texts taken from *BHS*, 758, 766; Rahlfs, 2:638, 644; *OTSy* pt. 3 fasc. 1, pp. 96, 105.
160 See Nöldeke §270.
161 Payne Smith, 2:3495.
162 Franzmann, 71.
163 Lattke, "Messias-Stellen," 430 = idem, *Bedeutung*, 4:90.
164 As Kittel argues (pp. 64–66).
165 Contra Kittel, 65.
166 Diettrich, 31. John 17:11-12 is so complex that it can hardly shed light on this passage in the *Odes of Solomon*, but it has a textual variant that may make the use of the possessive suffix "my" less offensive. In 𝔓[66] the first scribe alters ἐν τῷ ὀνόματί σου (17:11) to ἐν τῷ ὀνόματί μου. The Name of the Father thus becomes the name of the Johannine Jesus.

If this seems too far-fetched or even blasphemous,[167] it is at least certain that in antiquity the "name" is a term of power: "In the Hellenistic linguistic usage *ὄνομα* actually becomes synonymous with *δύναμις*."[168] The grammatical structure of verbs and prepositions in 21b-c shows that "name" is conceived of not merely as an abstract magnitude or domain but as a powerful and protective hypostatization. Since the causal clause 21c, whose implied subject is "the Name," contains only the copula (in 𝔊 certainly *ἐστίν*) with the suffixed preposition ܥܡ (*ʿam*) as adverbial expression of place (metaphorically of manner), the *hapax legomenon* ܐܫܬܘܚܕ (*ʾeštawḥaḏ*), Eshtaph. of ܐܚܕ (*ʾiḥeḏ*), followed by the preposition ܡܢ (*men*) cannot be translated as a passive (e.g., "to be deserted"[169] or "robbed"[170]) but must be a reflexive, "separate themselves" (*separavit se*).[171] The imperfect then stands for the "future" and in this case without "modal colouring."[172]

At the end of his speech, it is possible to give a summary of the identity of the speaking "I." Although the Ode gives no voice to God as Most High, Father/Mother, or Lord, the exalted claim of the Revealer, Redeemer, and (co)-Creator "implies" something like a theology—not merely a "Christology."[173] If the concepts of "persons" (especially in the case of "God"), "Christ," and "consciousness" are limited, and "believers" may include Gnostics, whose Redeemer was not necessarily called "Jesus," the following characterization of the "circumstances" can be accepted: "The persons of God and Christ merge, in the consciousness of the poet, into one sublime associate of the believer."[174]

■ **22-23** Only if the speaking "I" of the preceding stanzas were to refer to himself in stanza IX in the third person (esp. in 22e) could he be thought to utter these invitations or imperatives of salvation (22) and the final promise of it (23). Since such a change is unlikely, it may be assumed that this coda[175] is the responsory to the previous revelation and is addressed to an inclusive group of "the redeemed." Whether the words are given to a single speaker or to a group depends on the use that was made of this Ode. To claim that "the Church concludes the Ode with words of holy counsel"[176] or that the "Odist" himself speaks[177] is too simplistic.

As the extended discussions of Charlesworth, Diettrich, and Franzmann demonstrate,[178] the translation of 22a presents a problem. The Syriac text is quite clear and should not be combined with 22b into a monocolon.[179] What is problematic is, first, whether the imperative of the Pe. ܒܥܐ (*bʿā*), which has neither object nor preposition, can here be translated by "seek" (its most usual meaning in the *Odes of Solomon*) or "pray" (cf. 7:10 with preposition ܡܢ [*men*]), and, second, whether the imperative of the Aph. of ܣܓܝ, ܣܓܐ (*sgī, sgā*), with

167 See the thorough discussion by Hans Bietenhard, "*ὄνομα, κτλ.*," *ThWNT* 5 (1954) 254–58, 263–66, 270–79; cf. *TDNT* 5:255–58, 264–67, 271–80.

168 Rudolf Bultmann, *The Gospel of John: A Commentary* (ed. G. R. Beasley-Murray; trans. R. W. N. Hoare and J. K. Riches; Philadelphia: Westminster, 1971) 503 n. 2, ET of *Das Evangelium des Johannes* (KEK 2. Abt.; Göttingen: Vandenhoeck & Ruprecht, 1941; repr., 1964; *Ergänzungsheft*: Neubearbeitung 1957) 385 n. 1.

169 Greßmann, 445; Bauer, 588.

170 Harnack, 37; Diettrich, 31; cf. Charlesworth, 42: "to be deprived."

171 Brockelmann, *Grammatik*, p. 173*a; cf. Payne Smith, 1:1588. It should be translated neither by "to be detached" (Harris and Mingana, 2:255) nor by "to be separated" (Franzmann, 66).

172 Nöldeke §266.

173 See Rudolf Bultmann, "Das Verhältnis der urchristlichen Christusbotschaft zum historischen Jesus," SHAW.PH 1960, p. 16 = idem, *Exegetica:* Aufsätze zur Erforschung des Neuen Testaments (ed. Erich Dinkler; Tübingen: Mohr Siebeck, 1967) 457.

174 Kittel, 66. The context of the passage is as follows: "We are faced with the same situation as in *Ode* 3. . . . Specific attributes of God are juxtaposed with clearly Christological statements." The *text* of the *Odes* knows nothing of the *doctrine* of Patripassianism; see Henri Crouzel, "Patripassianismus," *LThK*² 8 (1963) 180–81.

175 Diettrich, 31.

176 Bernard, 69.

177 Charlesworth, 42.

178 Ibid., 44; Diettrich, 31; Franzmann, 66–67.

179 Contra Harris and Mingana, vol. 1, on the passage; 2:255; Franzmann, 64, 66, 71.

the conjunction ܘ (*w*-), is meant adverbially[180] or is an independent verb form.

In consideration of Matt 7:7 || Luke 11:9 (absolute ζητεῖτε, ܒܥܘ [*bʿaw*] in ܣ), the first imperative can be accepted[181] without emendation (to ܦܪܘ [*praw*], for instance, as in Gen 1:28 and 9:1).[182] If the second imperative is taken as representing a form of πληθύνω,[183] the result, with the addition of the imperative of the Pa. ܩܘܘ (*qawwī*)[184] in 22b, is the Gnosticizing sequence "seek"[185]–"increase"[186]–"abide."

The adverbial linking of the third imperative with the (metaphorical) location "the love of the Lord" (in 𝔊 surely ἐν τῇ ἀγάπῃ τοῦ κυρίου, *genitivus subjectivus*) in 22b can probably be traced back to the tradition of John 15:9-10. That passage also demonstrates the synonymity of ܪܚܡܬܐ (*reḥmtā*) and ܚܘܒܐ (*ḥubbā*) (see Excursus 2):

(John 15:9) μείνατε ἐν τῇ ἀγάπῃ τῇ ἐμῇ — ܩܘܘ ܒܪܚܡܬܝ

(*qawwaw b-reḥmat*)

"abide in my love"

(John 15:10) μενεῖτε ἐν τῇ ἀγάπῃ μου — ܬܩܘܘܢ ܒܚܘܒܐ ܕܝܠܝ

(*tqawwūn b-ḥubbā dīl*)

"you will abide in my love"

This utterance of the Johannine Jesus, with its chain of images,[187] is simplified in *Ode* 8 to refer merely to the "Lord" as "Father" (23c).

In 22c-e, which are closely related by parallelism of both form and content, the first half-lines relate to the hearers as "beloved" (22c), those "who are kept" (22d),[188] and "redeemed ones" (22e; see Excursus 5). The second half-lines, however, refer no longer to the "Most High" and the "Father" but to the Redeemer ("Savior") as the original "Beloved" (22c), who has been living forever (22d) and therefore "was saved, not from death, but from having to die" (22e; cf. 25:17-18 and 42:10-11).[189]

In the history of religion this moves sections of the *Odes* farther from the Johannine school and toward a Gnosticism in which the mythos of the redeemed Redeemer becomes explicit.[190]

180 Interpreted in this way up to and including Lattke, *Oden*, 116. But cf., in addition to Payne Smith, *Dictionary*, 360 ("[u]sed adverbially with another verb"), Brockelmann, *Grammatik* §225: "verbs . . . are often placed side by side *without connection*" [emphasis added]. Here, however, the Aph. "increase" (Brockelmann, *Grammatik*, p. 185*a with reference to §226!) is not only placed second but also connected to the other two verbs by "and."

181 Payne Smith, 1:556; BDAG, *s.v.* ζητέω, 1b.

182 If the command to be fruitful and multiply should be behind this passage in the *Odes of Solomon*, it would in any case have a limited early-Gnostic application.

183 See Payne Smith, 2:2518; BDAG, *s.v.* πληθύνω, 1.

184 Payne Smith, 2:3509; BDAG, *s.v.* μένω.

185 I now consider "seek" preferable to "ask" (Lattke, *Oden*, 116). The implied object might be *gnōsis* or as-yet-unknown Gnostics-to-be.

186 This imperative is related less to 8:1b ("and your love will grow") than to 6:6. Again the implied object might be *gnōsis* or the number of Gnostics.

187 Lattke, *Einheit*, 24–26, 165–76.

188 On the peculiar construction of 22d, see on 4-5 above; thematically, see also 10-11.

189 Brian McNeil, "The Odes of Solomon and the Sufferings of Christ," OrChrA 205 (1978 [*Symposium Syriacum* 1976]) 33. On 22b-e in particular see *Ode* 3. Perhaps 3:7-9 should be interpreted to mean that the "Beloved" is also the "Son," which would increase the number of comparable and illuminating parallels.

190 On the redeemed Redeemer, see, e.g., *Tri. Tract.* (Valentinian, third century) 124,32–125,1: ". . . even the Son himself, who has the position of redeemer of the Totality, [needed] redemption as well" (*NHLE*, 97). On 8:22 and other passages (e.g., 41:11; 42:18) Adam refers to the "Salvator salvandus" (Alfred Adam, *Die Psalmen des Thomas und das Perlenlied als Zeugnisse vorchristlicher Gnosis* [BZNW 24; Berlin: de Gruyter, 1959] 34, cf. 44), which Schenke (p. 30) strongly refutes. But even Colpe (*Schule*, 180–81) has to admit that we here have a redeemed Redeemer.

The promise of salvation in 23 is not a monocolon,[191] nor yet a bicolon,[192] but a tricolon, clearly marked off by the letter ܗ (*h* = abbreviation of "hallelujah") and three dots in a vertical line,[193] which opens with the predicative denial ἄφθαρτος[194] emphasizing the unending existence of the redeemed (see Excursus 28),[195] underpins this with an adverbial expression denoting all places or times (see Excursus 22), and ends, non-doxologically, with the Name of the Father, who is identical with no-thing and no-body, as a powerful means to achieve this future state.[196]

Such an assurance is the *answer* to a *prayer* like that of the Johannine Jesus for those whom his transcendent Father had given, that is, entrusted, to him (cf. John 17:9 [*ὅτι σοί εἰσιν*]): *πάτερ ἅγιε, τήρησον αὐτοὺς ἐν τῷ ὀνόματί σου* ("Holy Father, keep them in thy name" [John 17:11]).[197]

191 Contra, e.g., Harris and Mingana, vol. 1, on this passage.

192 Contra, e.g., Azar, 102, 188; Charlesworth, 41–42; Franzmann, 64, 66.

193 See Charlesworth, *Manuscripts*, 39–40.

194 The masculine ܚܒܠܐ (*ḥbālā*) preceded by the negative ܕܠܐ (*d-lā*) must represent this Greek adjective with *alpha privative*. The theological passive "to be found" (Ethpe. of ܐܫܟܚ [*ʾeškaḥ*]) probably represents a form of *εὑρίσκω* (BDAG, *s.v.*). The verbs "to seek" (22a) and "to find" or "to be found" are in a very different relationship from that in Matt 7:7 or Rom 10:20 (and Isa 65:1 LXX).

195 See Payne Smith, 1:1179; BDAG, *s.v.* ἄφθαρτος.

196 See Excursus 39, and see on 21b-c above. In this case, the preposition ܠ (*l-*) after the passive verb marks the agent by which something is done or brought about (see Payne Smith, *Dictionary*, 232). This eliminates such translations as "to" (Harris and Mingana, 2:255), "au" (Pierre, 80), "pour" (Azar, 102) and "für" (Diettrich, 31).

197 On the misuse of the divine title "Holy Father" in the Roman Catholic Church [and others], see Michael Lattke, "Heiligkeit III. Neues Testament," *TRE* 14 (1985) 704.

9

Ode 9: Redemptive Address

(I) 1 Open your ears and (then) I shall speak to you.
2 Give me your soul, that I may also give you my soul.
(II) 3a The word of the Lord and (the intentions of) his will (are)
3b the holy thought which he thought about his Messiah/Anointed One.
4a For in the will of the Lord is your life,
4b and his mind/purpose is eternal life,
4c and imperishable is your *plērōma*/fullness.
(III) 5a Be rich in God the Father
5b and receive the mind of the Most High!
5c Be strong and be redeemed by his grace.
(IV) 6a For I proclaim peace to you, his holy ones,
6b so that all of those who hear should not fall in the war,
7a and those, also, who knew him may not perish,
7b and that those who will receive will not be ashamed.
(V) 8a The eternal crown is truth,
8b —blessed are those who put it on their head—
9a a stone of great price,
9b for there were wars on account of the crown.
10 And righteousness took it and gave it to you,
11a put on the crown in the true covenant of the Lord!
(VI) 11b And all those who were victorious will be written in his book,
12a for their (recording in the) book is your victory.
12b And she [viz., Victory] sees you before her
12c and wills that you are to be saved.
Hallelujah.

Introduction

This Ode is preserved in one Syriac manuscript.[1] The Ode, which consists of two parts (1-7, 8-12), is an address on redemption and can be called a "reveille"[2] only by overstressing the similarities between the openings 8:1 and 9:1.[3] To divide the song into three parts as "Introduction" (1-5), "Central Part" (6-7), and "Finale"

1 Ms.: Codex H, 7a–b (ܣ). Ed/trans.: Charlesworth, 44–49; Franzmann, 73–78; Lattke, 1:155–70 and 3:XXI–XXII.

2 Schille, 98.

3 I have chosen the title "Redemptive Address" to bring out the content of the *Ode*. To pick out the key word "*your* victory" from the end of the *Ode* in order to name the whole "The Victory of *the Lord*" (emphasis added) and to import Abrahamic traditions throughout (Abbott, 291–318) are errors.

(8-12),[4] is just as artificial as to call it a "combination of self-praise and revivalist sermon" with a reference to Matt 11:25-30.[5]

The benediction in 8b may be a later interpolation, but in the rest of the Ode the "you" who are addressed are, despite the masculine verbs and suffixes (which are intended to be inclusive) a group of redeemed, now or in the future. So it may be concluded that the masculine speaking "I" of stanzas I and IV (esp. 6a) is also the speaker in stanzas II–III and V–VI. This "I" is clearly distinguished by the content of the speech from the "Lord" (3-4, 11a-b)—from "God" the "Father" and the "Most High" (5), on the one hand, and from the "Messiah (of the Lord)" (3), on the other. Since the speaking "I" is not identical with the poet ("Odist"), the content of the Ode shows him to be the announcer of salvation and the authorized promulgator of imperatives of salvation. If this role were to be played by a woman, or if a female reader identified with the "I," only the masculine participle in 6a would need to be replaced by a feminine.

Interpretation

■ **1-2** Not too much weight should be placed on the oriental rhetoric of the invitation in stanza I, which is marked by reciprocity and close parallelism and acts as an "introductory proclamation formula."[6] Since it seems that the copyist may have carelessly omitted marks of division, 1 and 2 are perhaps actually 1a-b and 2a-b.[7]

The choice of the metaphorical plural of ܐܕܢܐ (*ʾednā*)[8] in place of "hearts" (8:1a) must be partly due to the use of the Pa. ܡܠܠ (*mallel*). The actual term "ears" in 1, as in the other passages (15:4; 16:9), refers not to the sensory organ of hearing but to "mental and spiritual understanding."[9] So this metaphorical exhortation is addressed (as in 8:1; 13:1) to the existential ability to open oneself, which is the complement of being opened by the Lord (10:1; 14:8), and it is underlined by the parallel exhortation in the following monocolon.

Idiomatically, the repeated feminine ܢܦܫܐ (*napšā*) translates as "yourselves" and "myself."[10] However, 𝔊 would not necessarily have used just the reflexive pronoun (ἑαυτούς and ἐμαυτόν). Indeed, it is probable that—whether the Greek text was the original or a translation—the word ψυχή appeared together with a personal, possessive, or reflexive pronoun.[11]

■ **3-4** Between the two direct addresses to the audience in stanzas I and III there is a lengthy statement on salvation, which is in part messianic and of which the very first word poses a number of problems. There are two terms in the *Odes of Solomon*, both of which are translated as "word": the normal feminine noun ܡܠܬܐ (*melltā*) and the "masculine loanword from Persian" ܦܬܓܡܐ (*petgāmā*).[12] Both are used to translate λόγος and ῥῆμα,[13] and they cannot simply be "allocated to hypostases of different gender."[14] "The word of the Lord" is the word of God, predating this world and not issuing from any human source; it is not identified with "divine revelation" or with the personified "Logos."[15] The choice of the rare plural of ܨܒܝܢܐ (*ṣebyānā*) not only forms an "inclusio for the Ode proper,"[16] with the use of words derived from the root *ṣbʾ* in 3a and 12c, but may also be a sign of the influence of a Davidic tradition similar to Acts 13:22, where God (ὁ θεός) is made to say: εὗρον Δαυὶδ τὸν τοῦ Ἰεσσαί, ἄνδρα κατὰ τὴν καρδίαν μου, ὃς ποιήσει πάντα τὰ θελήματά μου ("I have found in David the son of Jesse a man after my heart, who will do all my will").

"Word" and "will" are the subject of the noun clause 3a-b, and the relative clause depends on the predicate

4 Diettrich, 32.
5 Dibelius, 284.
6 David E. Aune, "The Form and Function of the Proclamations to the Seven Churches (Revelation 2–3)," *NTS* 36 (1990) 193.
7 Harris and Mingana, vol. 1, on this passage; Charlesworth, 44, 46 n. 1; Franzmann, 73–75.
8 Payne Smith, 1:39.
9 BDAG, *s.v.* οὖς, 2.
10 Emerton, 699.
11 See BDAG, *s.v.* ψυχή, 2g, with references to such New Testament passages as Matt 11:29; Mark 14:34; Luke 14:26; John 10:24; 12:27; 2 Cor 1:23; 12:15; Heb 13:17; Rev 18:14.
12 See Bauer, 584, on 7:7.
13 See Payne Smith, 2:2110–12, 3335–36.
14 Lattke, "Messias-Stellen," 434 = idem, *Bedeutung*, 4:94–96. See also Excursus 12.
15 BDAG, *s.v.* λόγος, 1aβ and 3.
16 Franzmann, 76.

"thought." The missing copula must be added in translation. There is a wordplay in the use of the common feminine noun ܡܚܫܒܬܐ (*maḥšabṯā*), with its attribute *qaddīšā* (emphatic; in 𝔊 certainly ἅγιος), and the much rarer Ethpa. of ܚܫܒ (*ḥšab*), as in 18:13 (see Excursus 9 below). The preposition ܥܠ (*ʿal*), as in many Syriac texts that indulge in wordplay on *ḥšb* derivatives, means "about" not "against."[17] The noun ܡܫܝܚܐ (*mšīḥā*) represents the Greek ὁ χριστός (see Excursus 24). If there was a Greek original—or even a parallel text—it may well have used the *nomen sacrum* $\overline{\text{ΧΟΥ}}$ in place of χριστοῦ. This would explain why the letter ܡ, with a line above it, which is a fairly rare "abbreviation," appears after the preposition at the end of that line of text, since the whole word ܡܫܝܚܗ is written out at the beginning of the immediately following line.[18]

The Syriac manuscript has a mark of division after the third word of 4a, which has been properly ignored by all editors,[19] especially since the careless copyist has made a number of other errors.[20] Verse 4a is all one sentence, and the causal particle ܓܝܪ (*gēr*), always in second place, is, as so often, superfluous.[21] The introductory preposition ܒ (*b*-), which could also have the instrumental meaning "by," picks up the key word ܨܒܝܢܐ (*ṣeḇyānā*) from 3a. The close connection thus formed between 3a and 4a is not only semantic.[22]

Verse 4b is directly parallel with 4a but is also linked semantically to 3b, especially by the use of ܬܪܥܝܬܐ (*tarʿīṯā*), which is synonymous with ܡܚܫܒܬܐ (*maḥšaḇṯā*). Since ܨܒܝܢܐ and ܡܚܫܒܬܐ belong to the "parallel word-pairs,"[23] the following excursus also considers "will."[24]

Excursus 9: "Thought," "Mind," and "Will" in the *Odes of Solomon*

The Syriac words under consideration are the nouns ܡܚܫܒܬܐ (*maḥšaḇṯā*), ܬܪܥܝܬܐ (*tarʿīṯā*), and ܨܒܝܢܐ (*ṣeḇyānā*), as well as ܪܥܝܢܐ (*reʿyānā*, not to be confused with words derived from the Semitic root I ܪܥܐ)[25] and four verbs, the Ethpa. ܐܬܚܫܒ (*ʾeṯḥaššaḇ*),[26] the Ethpa. ܐܬܪܥܝ (*ʾeṯraʿʿī*),[27] the Pe. ܨܒܐ (*ṣḇā*),[28] and the Ethpe. ܐܨܛܒܝ (*ʾeṣṭḇī*)[29] (cf. Synoptic Survey).

The words derived from the root *ṣbʾ* are relatively easy to translate, since the basic meaning of "to will" (ϑέλω, βούλομαι) and "the will" (ϑέλημα, ϑέλησις) is mostly quite clear. That the plural ܨܒܝ̈ܢܐ (*ṣeḇyānē*) was used to translate terms like νοήματα and ἐπιθυμίαι will help in finding equivalents.[30]

The proper translation of words derived from the other two roots is more complicated because the meanings of both nouns and verbs meet and intersect.

To start with some atypical and sometimes puzzling passages, "Victory" personified "wills that you are to be saved" (9:12). The virgin mother "brought forth with desire" (19:10aβ), which may be due to her masculine strength (cf. 19:10aα), or may be merely *one* of the revelatory and soteriological mythologoumena in the poem on the birth (19:10aβ-11). The "thought" in which the mythos of *Ode* 24 makes the many "perish" (24:7) only gives rise to the bewildered question, "What thought?"[31]

In contrast to the multiplicity of theological and soteriological uses of the terms under discussion, their appearance in dualistic opposition is rare. The "thinking" of the persecutors, whether mythological or historical (5:4), will become "tumors" (5:7), because they "devised a plan" in vain (5:8). The "thought of many," which came to nothing (23:19), is contrasted with the "thinking" or "thought" of the Lord (23:5; and see below). The "many" are mentioned again when the power of reason is drowned by wine (38:13).[32] A prominent redeemed person, according to his tale of salvation, receives the power to overcome the "thoughts" of many peoples (29:8). In what could be called negative predestination, the Lord annihilated the "thoughts of all those with whom the truth was not" (24:10). That ܪܥܝܢܐ (*reʿyānā*) and ܬܪܥܝܬܐ (*tarʿīṯā*) are synonyms, and not merely related as potential to performance, is shown by the "mad dogs" passage (28:13) in the first person report of a persecuted one: "Corrupt is their mind and perverted their sense" (28:14).

17 Payne Smith, 1:1393–97; 2:2886–87.
18 See Charlesworth, 46 n. 2.
19 See already Harris and Mingana, vol. 1, on this passage.
20 See Charlesworth, *Manuscripts*, 40 on 2a and 4c.
21 See Lattke, "Wörter," 289 = idem, *Bedeutung*, 138.
22 See Franzmann, 76.
23 Franzmann, 406; cf. 23:5.
24 See Kittel, 67–68.
25 See Brockelmann, *Lexicon*, 737–38; Payne Smith, 2:3946–47.
26 Payne Smith, 1:1395.
27 Ibid., 2:3944.
28 Ibid., 2:3352.
29 Ibid., 2:3352–53.
30 Ibid., 2:3354.
31 Slightly altered from Bauer, 606, "What plan?"
32 See Payne Smith, 2:3946.

Synoptic Survey*

ܐܨܛܒܝ *ʾeṣṭḇī* choose (v)	ܨܒܐ *ṣḇā* will (v)	ܨܒܝܢܐ *ṣeḇyānā* will (n)	ܐܬܚܫܒ *ʾeṯḥaššaḇ* think (v)	ܡܚܫܒܬܐ *maḥšaḇṯā* thought (n)	ܬܪܥܝܬܐ *tarʿīṯā* mind (n)	ܪܥܝܢܐ *reʿyānā* sense (n)†	ܐܬܪܥܝ *ʾeṯraʿʿī* design (v)
3:9							
							4:2
					5:7 [thinking]		
			5:8 [devise]		5:8 [plan]		
		6:14					
8:17				8:18			
	8:20						
		9:3a [desires]	9:3b	9:3b			
		9:4a			9:4b		
					9:5		
	9:12						
	10:3 [desire]						
		[11:22?]‡					
				12:4d	12:4e		
				12:7			
		14:4					
				15:5			
				16:8-9			
				16:19			
				17:5			
		18:3					
		18:8					
			18:13b	18:13b	18:14		
		19:10					
				20:2-3			
				21:5			
		23:5b		23:5a			
				23:19			
				24:7			
				24:10			
					28:14a	28:14b	
					28:19		
				29:8			
				34:1-2			
						38:13	
					38:21		
				41:10			

* The English words in the headings represent the primary meaning of each Syriac word, but occasional synonyms used in the individual Ode translations are noted in brackets for the verse in which they occur.

† In 38:13 this is hidden in the negative "senseless."

‡ The word θέλημα in the Greek manuscript is still being debated. ܣ has "remnant."

On the other side are the to-be-redeemed, the redeemed, the Redeemer, and, above all, with many names, the Being who is no-where. The discussion of the various passages will follow this ascending sequence.

The wisdom teaching of the parallelism of "simple heart," "upright thoughts," (34:1), and "enlightened thought" (34:2) is fairly commonplace. Raising the paralyzed "will" (6:14) needs a detailed description (6:14-17) and a benediction (6:13) to bring out its redemptive meaning. Those who "desire to come" to the Lord (10:3) are like those who "choose" in life and "will be living" (3:9). In Gnostic-dualistic fashion those who knew "thought and were not polluted by their thought" (18:13) because the Gnostics were "in/by the mind of the Most High" (18:14; see below).

Not many passages treat of the thought or thinking of the Redeemer, who as Revealer and Mediator "chose" his own (8:17). This choice is elucidated by the speaking "I" when he claims the elect, whose mind and heart he "willed" (8:20), as "my work" and "the strength of my thoughts" (8:18). Whether the redeemed one with his "thought of knowledge" (15:5) is also the Redeemer (cf. 15:9) will be discussed later. If such a redeemed Redeemer declares, in a mythological statement of salvation, "the thought of truth led me" (17:5), this may form the transition to the statements that refer anthropomorphically to God as the Lord, the Most High, and the Father.

This final and largest group includes 12:7, since the word, the "light and dawning of thought," is given by the Most High (cf. 12:4) to the "confessors of his thought" (12:4d) and the "preachers of his mind" (12:4e), among others. The parallelism between the synonyms ܡܚܫܒܬܐ (*maḥšabṯā*) and ܬܪܥܝܬܐ (*tarʿīṯā*) and "works" (12:4f) is found also where the "word of the Lord" and "his thought" are in parallel with "his works" and "his thought" (16:8-9; on 16:19 see below).

The predestined Gnostics are already found in the "mind of the Most High" (18:14; cf. "truth" in 18:15). The same term ܬܪܥܝܬܐ (*tarʿīṯā*) shows that the "mind (of the Most High)" is a parallel to "heart" (28:19; see on 34:1-2 below). That the "heart" is seen as the actual "place of thought"[33] (see Excursus 4) is shown clearly by two passages using ܡܚܫܒܬܐ (*maḥšabṯā*): "the thought of his heart" in 16:9, parallel to "word" and referring to the Lord, and in 41:10, referring to the "Father of truth" (cf. "his word" in 41:11).

If the Lord can be glorified in part by "the understanding of his mind" (38:21), he can also receive the "offering of his thought [= thinking of or about him]" (20:2 using a synonymous term), which is dualistically opposed to the "world" and the "flesh" (20:3). For the "thought of the Lord" and his "imperishable fellowship" mark the difference between "light" and "darkness" (21:3-5, esp. 5).

In the mythological parable of the celestial letter (23:5-22), the "thought" of the Lord is compared to the letter (23:5a) and also parallels his "will" (23:5b). Since the "will" of God the Lord is identified with his *plērōma* (18:8), the "members" of the speaking "I" are enabled to stand firm by the "will" of the Lord (18:3). The prayer that the Lord may himself be the guide to his "will" (14:4) can perhaps also be accommodated here.

All the other passages occur in stanza II of *Ode* 9. The "word of the Lord" and the rare plural of "will" are parallel (9:3a), and both are the "thought which he thought" about his Messiah (9:3b). The "will of the Lord," which is parallel to this (9:4a), is his "mind" (9:4b) or the "mind of the Most High" (9:5b), whose end and soteriological content are "eternal life" and "imperishable *plērōma*/fullness" (9:4b-c; see Table 1 and Excursus 35).[34]

The close parallelism and indeed synonymy of the terms in 3 and 4(5) serve to show that the humanly unthinkable thought of his will, which the Lord thought preordainingly about his Messiah (cf. *Ps. Sol.* 18:5, 7; Luke

33 Bauer, 610.

34 The "will and thought of God" can hardly be called a "set phrase" (contra Drijvers, "Polemik," 53–54). It may be that Theophilus of Antioch was influenced by the *Odes of Solomon* when he wrote in *Ad Autolycum* (2.22; Robert M. Grant, ed. and trans., *Theophilus of Antioch, Ad Autolycum* [OECT; Oxford: Clarendon, 1970] 62–63), discussing the Logos, about God's "wishing" and "planning": *ὁπότε δὲ ἠθέλησεν ὁ θεὸς ποιῆσαι ὅσα ἐβουλεύσατο, τοῦτον τὸν λόγον ἐγέννησεν προφορικόν, πρωτότοκον πάσης κτίσεως* ("When God wished to make what he planned to make, he generated this Logos, making him external [*sic*], as the *first-born of all creation* [Col 1:15]").

2:26), is the gift of salvation to eternal life (4a-b), both for the first hearers and for every subsequent group of those to be saved.[35]

Therefore *their* ܫܘܡܠܝܐ (*šumlāyā*) in 4c is not merely "perfection"[36] but πλήρωμα in the theological sense of "fullness" of life[37] in which the imperishable "Father" of the Aeons (cf. 7:11) "is" already the Lord and Most High (cf. 17:7; 18:5, 8; 26:7; 35:6; 36:2; 41:13).

The predicative adjective ܕܠܐ ܚܒܠܐ (*d-lā ḥḇālā*), which, taken literally, is impossible to humanity and therefore a prerogative of God (cf. 7:11; 11:12 [ἀφθαρσία]; 21:5; 22:11), serves to emphasize the transferring of the theological category *plērōma* to men, who are not, however, thereby made "God" but achieve the meaning and fulfillment of their humanity (on "imperishable," "imperishability," see also 8:23; 15:8; 17:2; 28:5; 33:12; 40:6).

■ **5** The return to direct address (cf. stanza I) takes the form of parallel imperatives of salvation. The key word ܬܪܥܝܬܐ (*tarʿīṯā*) in 5b makes the connection with stanza II (see on 4b above), while the structural parallelism of the flanking cola 5a and 5c is especially marked.[38]

The Pe. ܥܬܪ (*ʿṯar*) in 5a would certainly correspond to πλουτέω in 𝔊 (cf. 11:9).[39] Unlike Luke 12:21 (μὴ εἰς θεὸν πλουτῶν, "not rich toward God"), the preposition ܒ (*b-*) would here (and in 5c)[40] have translated ἐν, not in the sense of "[rich] in *something*,"[41] but "in" (with transferred meaning of place) or "with" (instrumental). Only here and in 10:4 is "God," identical with the "Lord" of stanza II, also called "Father" (cf. "Father" = "Most High" in 23:18; 41:13). If the edifying philosophical-theological commonplace of 5a is examined more closely,[42] it reveals a fierce polemic against the false security and glorification of worldly wealth and gain.

There are parallels in the *Odes of Solomon* to the imperative of salvation with the Pa. ܩܒܠ (*qabbel*) in 5a, in 8:8 ("receive the knowledge of the Most High"), and in 31:6 ("receive joy"). The second passage shows that the verb can be an exact synonym of ܢܣܒ (*nsaḇ*) (cf. 31:7b), especially since the "mind/purpose of the Most High" is nothing but "eternal life" (see 4b above; cf. 31:7b "immortal life"). The key words "grace" (31:7a) and "Messiah" necessitate reference to 41:3a-b as well.

The Ethpa. ܐܬܚܝܠ (*ʾeṯḥayyal*; also in 10:4 but not elsewhere in the *Odes of Solomon*), which is related to ܚܝܠܐ (*ḥaylā*; see Excursus 29), and whose imperative in 5c may be variously translated,[43] is less important than the Ethpe. of ܦܪܩ (*praq*), which forms a "word-pair"[44] with the verb of 5b and is also used as an imperative of salvation elsewhere, and which is coupled with ܛܝܒܘܬܐ (*ṭaybūṯā*, in 𝔊 certainly χάρις [cf. 33:10-11a; 34:6; Excursus 5]). "To be redeemed" and "to live" regularly occur as parallels (cf. 5:3 [with extended discussion of the Syriac translation of σωθῆναι]; 6:18 [ℭ]; 17:14; 34:6;

35 In spite of verbal similarities, the messianic statement of salvation in 3b is neither a "witness to royal messianic expectations" nor a christological "reflection" on the person of Jesus crucified (Ferdinand Hahn, "Χριστός, κτλ.," *EWNT* 3 [1983] 1151, 1165; cf. *EDNT* 3:480, 485–86). The idea of the thought thought is found more fully formed in NHC I,*5*, where not the Messiah but the Son is described as the Father's preexistent "thought" (*Tri. Trac.* 56,35–38; 125,24–27); see Attridge and Pagels, "Tripartite Tractate," 1:200–201, 318–19; *NHLE*, 63, 98).

36 Emerton, 699.

37 BDAG, *s.v.* πλήρωμα, 2–3. Actually it is possible that 𝔊 used either πλήρωσις (see Lampe, 1095) or τελειότης (BDAG, *s.v.* τελειότης) instead of πλήρωμα.

38 Cf. the structural analysis of Franzmann (p. 76): "With stanza 3 there is a return to a direct address to the community, each line commencing with a 2nd pl[ural] masc[uline] imper[ative] verb (5c doubles the pattern) which refers to some attribute of God/the Most High as source or object of the action. 5b has central position between the more strictly parallel 5a and 5c on the pattern: 2nd pl[ural] masc[uline] imper[ative] verb/s + ܒ + noun (ref. to God/the Most High). 5b and 5c are linked by the word-pair ܩܒܠ – ܦܪܩ. There is a connection with stanza 2 by the repetition of ܬܪܥܝܬܐ (4b, 5b; ref. to the Lord/Most High)."

39 Payne Smith, 2:3012.

40 One or both of these clauses might have used only an instrumental dative.

41 BDAG, *s.v.* πλουτέω, 2; cf. Bauer and Aland, *s.v.* πλουτέω, 2 ("an").

42 See BDAG, *s.v.* πατήρ.

43 "Be strong" (Harris and Mingana, 2:260; Charlesworth, 46; Emerton, 699; Franzmann, 74; German equivalent, Bauer, 588; French equivalent, Pierre, 82); "be brave" (Greßmann, 446).

44 Franzmann, 406.

38:16). Though "grace" does not recur in *Ode* 9 (but cf. 25:4 and Excursus 33), the verb "to be redeemed/saved" at the end carries a good deal of weight (see 12b below). In a transferred sense even human beings can put mercy before justice, but the only "mercy" that can redeem is the gracious power of God. So the imperatives in this passage are not calls to activity or ethical behavior but imperatives of salvation, invitations to allow oneself to be theologically enriched, empowered, and redeemed.

■ **6-7** This promise of salvation from the speaking "I" concludes the first part of *Ode* 9. Verses 6a and 1a form a sort of *inclusio,* and 6b-7 give "the purpose for the declaration of peace."[45] Harris and Mingana's statement about the dualistic terms "peace" and "war" in *Ode* 8 is true also for this passage: "There is, however, still much that is obscure in the Odist's language."[46] If the Essene Dead Sea Scrolls had already been known, they might have referred to the *War Scroll* (1QM)[47] and the Qumranic themes of "election, determination and predestination," "dualism" and "covenant," and "messianic eschatological expectations."[48] So it is not to be wondered at that Jean Carmignac, who believes that "the Odes . . . are an admirable work by a Christian formed at Qumran and transformed by the Gospel,"[49] thinks it obvious that in 8:7 and 9:6 "the author evokes the war of liberation expected at Qumran and advises his erstwhile companions that it has lost its relevance, because Christ will conquer the heart of his faithful by peace."[50] Charlesworth is more cautious, saying, "It is probable that the concept of 'war' held by the author of the Odes was influenced by Essene terminology and ideas."[51] Since Carmignac's view cannot be supported,[52] and Charlesworth also presses the point too hard that "the Odes of Solomon were influenced by Essene writings,"[53] it is better to start from the fact that in the notes that form the commentary to Charlesworth's edition there is *no* mention of a Qumranic parallel to 9:6.[54] The reference to "the apocalyptic role of the Messiah" (see 3b above) and "the notion of a final cosmic battle between good and evil . . . in the Odes"[55] should also arouse skepticism. Finally, it is necessary to take seriously the fact that parts 1-7 and 8-12 are "two basic sections,"[56] despite the repetition of the key word "war" (6b, 9b).

By using the masculine participle of ܣܒܪ (*sabbar*), the speaker of 6a appears, on the one hand, as an "evangelist" ("preacher") of the mind of the Most High (12:4e; see stanzas II–III above),[57] and, on the other, as a prophetic messenger of joy and announcer of peace (cf. εὐαγγελιζόμενος and εἰρήνη in Isa 52:7 LXX), who does not identify himself with the Χριστὸς Ἰησοῦς of Acts 10:36 or Eph 2:17. That the masculine noun ܫܠܡܐ (*šlāmā*; in 𝔊 certainly εἰρήνη) might suggest more than the merely soteriological—perhaps some christological incarnation, as, for example, in Eph 2:14 (αὐτὸς γάρ ἐστιν ἡ εἰρήνη ἡμῶν), is not even a supposition in the context of *Ode* 9. There is only one certainty, which would be accepted by Jews and non-Jews, Hellenists and Romans, philosophers and theologians—that "peace" is one of the *prima bona* (Seneca *Ep.* 66.5),[58] a gift of "messianic salvation" (John 14:27; Rom 5:1; 8:6; Col 3:15) and always a "gift of God,"[59] because the world is and

45 Ibid., 77.
46 Harris and Mingana, 2:259, on 8:7 and 9:6.
47 See Armin Lange, "Qumran (Abschnitt 1.)," *TRE* 28 (1997) 60–62.
48 See Hermann Lichtenberger, "Qumran (Abschnitte 2.–4.)," *TRE* 28 (1997) 69–71.
49 Carmignac, "Auteur," 91.
50 Ibid., 81.
51 James H. Charlesworth, "Les Odes de Salomon et les manuscrits de la mer Morte," *RB* 77 (1970) 534.
52 See Rudolph, "Verfasser," 523–24.
53 Charlesworth, "Mer Morte," 549.
54 Charlesworth, 46.
55 Aune, "Christian Prophecy," 449.
56 Franzmann, 75.
57 Payne Smith, 2:2510–11, 2515.
58 Manfred Rosenbach, ed., *L. Annaeus Seneca, Ad Lucilium epistulae morales I–LXIX – An Lucilius, Briefe über Ethik 1–69* (Darmstadt: Wissenschaftliche Buchgesellschaft, 1974) 556.
59 BDAG, *s.v.* εἰρήνη, 2b, referring to Epictetus 3.13.12: εἰρήνη ὑπὸ τοῦ θεοῦ κεκηρυγμένη διὰ τοῦ λόγου ("peace proclaimed by God through the reason [viz., philosophy]" [LCL 2.90–91]).

always will be subject to the human tendency to strike at random.[60] The adjective ܚܣܝܐ (*ḥasyā*), otherwise only in 25:10, which corresponds to Greek ὅσιος rather than ἅγιος,[61] can simply be translated as "holy" (cf. 7:16b)[62] without any reference to the "mystae of the Orphic Mysteries," or to the "Essenes."[63] The possessive suffix, which stands for the Greek αὐτοῦ, refers of course to "God," not to "peace," since God alone can grant holiness to humanity.

Verse 6b is the first of a triplet of parallel final clauses (which should be [re]-constructed in 𝔊 with ἵνα not ὅτι).[64] The direct address now gives way to statements of promises, and the audience is correspondingly enlarged to all who "hear" at any time. The object of the verb ܫܡܥ (*šmaʿ*) may be found in 8:8a ("hear the word of truth!"), both because of the bicolon 8:7 already mentioned (see above) and because of 8:8b (see below on "receive" in 7b; but see also 33:10: "listen to me [i.e., Grace personified] and you will be saved"). Line 6b somewhat overshoots the mark, after the subjunctively negated imperfect of ܢܦܠ (*npal*), by introducing the masculine ܩܪܒܐ (*qrāḇā*), which may have intruded from 8:7 or been added in contrast to "peace" and to explain "to fall." The image of the "war" (in 𝔊 certainly πόλεμος)[65] is just as literal as that of "peace" and is not limited to "psychic"[66] or "spiritual combat."[67]

While the negated imperfects "perish" (7a) and "be ashamed" (7b) are also parallel to the form of the term "fall" (6b), the parallel terms "hear" (6b), "know" (7a), and "receive" (7b) are differentiated by the aspects of present, past, and future. Not too much stress should be laid on the fact that the perfect of the Pe. ܝܕܥ (*ʾiḏaʿ*) and the future of the Pe. ܢܣܒ (*nsaḇ*) are the forms chosen.[68]

Since ἀκούω, γινώσκω, and λαμβάνω—even πιστεύω in places—occur as related terms in the Fourth Gospel,[69] it is relevant to refer to John 3:16b (ἵνα πᾶς ὁ πιστεύων εἰς αὐτὸν μὴ ἀπόληται ἀλλ᾽ ἔχῃ ζωὴν αἰώνιον, "that whoever believes in him should not perish but have eternal life"). Elsewhere in the *Odes of Solomon* ܝܕܥ (*ʾiḏaʿ*) or ܐܫܬܘܕܥ (*ʾeštawdaʿ*) and ܐܒܕ (*ʾeḇaḏ*) are only indirectly related (28:16 [N]; 33:9). But who or what is the object of "to know," represented by the third singular masculine pronominal suffix? It could as well stand for the adumbrated "war" as for the promised "peace," but in fact it is more probably meant to stand for one of the theological appellations from stanzas II–III (see Excursus 7).

In the background of 7b there may be a biblical quotation that has been influential also in other places (Isa 28:16 LXX; cf. Rom 9:33; 10:11: ὁ πιστεύων ἐπ᾽ αὐτῷ οὐ καταισχυνθήσεται, "he who believes in him will not be put to shame"). Without making any reference to "Israel's guilt and fall," the verb ܒܗܬ (*bheṯ*) expresses "eschatological putting to shame"[70] (cf. 29:1) and not merely "disconcerting" or "confusing."[71] This exclusion from "disgrace" and "shame" is not here achieved *sola fide* but is promised to those who actively "take possession" (cf. 31:7) or passively "receive" (cf. 15:6; 23:2).[72] If no putative object is introduced, the verse can be interpreted, with the absolute use of the verb ܢܣܒ (*nsaḇ*), as a soteriological utterance on human existence, which is as radical as any of the statements using πίστις/πιστεύειν.[73]

■ **8-11a** These image-filled lines are one of the most obscure and enigmatic passages in the *Odes of Solomon*. Franzmann's structural analysis sheds some light: (1) the *inclusio* between 8a and 11c is easy to see; (2) the blessing in 8b is marked as a (later?) interpolation; and (3) because of the causal particle ܓܝܪ (*gēr*), "9b seems to

60 Otto Bauernfeind, "πόλεμος, πολεμέω," *ThWNT* 6 (1959) 511; cf. *TDNT* 6:511.
61 Payne Smith, 1:1325.
62 Diettrich, 34.
63 See BDAG, *s.v.* ὅσιος, 1a.
64 Contra Frankenberg, 12.
65 Payne Smith, 2:3726.
66 Diettrich, 34.
67 Bernard, 70; Charlesworth, 46.
68 In H, 6b and 7a have marks of division, which should be ignored (see Lattke, *Bedeutung*, 1:75; Diettrich, 34). On 7a, see also Franzmann (p. 75): "The failure of H to make a punctuation break after ܢܐܒܕܘܢ indicates the copyist was unaware of the syntactic pattern of 6b-7a."
69 Lattke, *Einheit*, 28.
70 Käsemann, *Romans*, 279 (German, 266–70, esp. 269); Payne Smith, 1:460.
71 Contra Charlesworth, 46–47.
72 Because ܩܒܠ (*qabbel*) is a synonym, the following passages are also relevant: 8:8b; 9:5 (see above); 20:9; 31:6; 41:3.
73 See Payne Smith, 2:2392–93; BDAG, *s.v.* λαμβάνω; also, e.g., Schrage, *1 Korinther*, 1:337, on 1 Cor 4:7b

follow logically from 9a."[74] But whether 9a "in apposition with ܟܠܝܠܐ ܕܠܥܠܡ" refers to the subject "truth" in 8a needs further consideration.

Interpreting the meaning of the passage becomes more straightforward "when we observe the source from which the writer is working."[75] This source is Ps 20:4b LXX, where it is said in the address to the *Κύριος* (Yhwh) that *ἔθηκας ἐπὶ τὴν κεφαλὴν αὐτοῦ* [viz., *τοῦ βασιλέως*] *στέφανον ἐκ λίθου τιμίου* ("thou hast set upon his [viz., the king's] head a crown of precious stone").[76] Whether this can lead to the conclusion "that the ninth Ode of Solomon is based on the 20th Psalm of David" (a psalm that, certainly by the end of the second century C.E., was treated as a gracious promise of immortality "of the believer") may be considered less assured, in spite of the reference to 9:4.[77]

The sudden appearance of the key word ܫܪܪܐ (*šrārā*) in 8a is difficult to explain, even taking into account the "wreath of truth" of *Ode* 1 (1:2; cf. 25:10; 31:2; Excursus 1). Since the topic of stanza V as a whole is the "crown," it is preferable to consider ܟܠܝܠܐ (*klīlā*)—with the stress on "eternal" as attribute (cf. 9:4; 11:16h [*αἰώνιος*])—as the subject,[78] and not to lean too heavily on "truth" (*ἀλήθεια*), which can be interpreted dualistically as "veracity" or even as simple "reliability."[79] In that case 9a is indeed in apposition to "truth" (see below).

The benediction in 8b interrupts the connection between 8a and 9a and should be taken to be either an original interjection, addressed to a plural "you," or a general note, which made its way in from the margin. The object, formed by ܠ (*l-*) + 3rd masculine singular suffix, of the participle of the Pe. ܣܐܡ, ܣܡ (*sām*), which is meant inclusively, refers to "crown," not to "truth." Since the plural suffix on ܪ̈ܫܐ (*rēšā*) clearly envisages a number of human heads, Charlesworth's remark[80] on the "singular" of this word is unnecessary (on the image, cf. 20:8; 42:20).

The long phrase 9a may simply mean "jewel"[81] and would correspond either to Greek *λίθος τίμιος* (as in Ps 20:4 LXX)[82] or perhaps rather to Greek *λίθος πολύτιμος*[83] or *λίθος ἀτίμητος*, as in Wis 7:9.[84] The stone stands as *pars pro toto* for the whole circlet (in 𝔊 certainly *στέφανος*, as in Ps 20:4 LXX). "Jewel" and "crown" are "not two different images but one and the same, since the stone is the brilliant adornment of the crown."[85]

Although 9b logically gives the reason for 8a + 9a,[86] the mythological image remains imprecise. Since the "crown" is neither "the precious crown of the baptized"[87] nor the "*corona victoriae*" (which was later "*de martyrio usurpatur*"),[88] it is necessary to agree with Harnack that "these are not earthly wars."[89] But the image is as literal as that of 9:6, so the wars are not merely "wars of this life";[90] they are mythological battles of apocalyptic extent.[91]

(*τί δὲ ἔχεις ὃ οὐκ ἔλαβες;* ["What have you that you did not receive?"]), on Christians as "receivers of gifts from God."

74 Franzmann, 77.

75 Harris and Mingana, 2:261.

76 Rahlfs, 2:18; Brenton, 709.

77 Harris and Mingana, 2:262.

78 Contra Harris and Mingana, 2:261; Franzmann, 77.

79 See Bultmann, "*ἀλήθεια* [C.D.], *κτλ.*," *ThWNT* 1 (1933) 240 and 242; *TDNT* 1:239, 242. If ܫܪܪܐ stood for *ἀσφάλεια* rather than *ἀλήθεια* (as in *Ps. Sol.* 8:18 [= 8:20]; cf. Joseph L. Trafton, *The Syriac Version of the Psalms of Solomon: A Critical Evaluation* [with a supplement: *The Psalms of Solomon: Syriac and Greek Texts*; SBLSCS 11; Atlanta: Scholars Press, 1985] 32–33 in supplement), the meaning would be *firmitas* (Brockelmann, *Lexicon*, 802); cf. Bauer and Aland, *s.v.* *ἀσφάλεια*, 1 ("Festigkeit," "Sicherheit"); see also BDAG, *s.v.* *ἀσφαλής*, 1 ("firm").

80 Charlesworth, 47.

81 See Payne Smith, 1:916, 1626.

82 See BDAG, *s.v.* *τίμιος*, 1a.

83 See BDAG, *s.v.* *πολύτιμος*. Cf. the Syriac version of Matt 13:46, referring to the *one* pearl (*πολύτιμος μαργαρίτης*).

84 See LEH, *s.v.* *ἀτίμητος*; Georgi, 425; John Adney Emerton, *The Peshitta of the Wisdom of Solomon* (SPB 2; Leiden: Brill, 1959) 11.

85 Kittel, 68; cf. Hermann Gunkel, review of Frankenberg in *ThLZ* 38 (1913) 10.

86 See Lattke, "Wörter," 289 = idem, *Bedeutung*, 138.

87 Bernard, 70.

88 Payne Smith, 1:1732.

89 Harnack, 38.

90 Harris and Mingana, 2:263.

91 See Payne Smith, 2:3726; BDAG, *s.v.* *πόλεμος*, 1.

Not until the statement of salvation in 10 (which is not 10a-b)[92] and the imperative of salvation of 11a is there a connection made between the "crown" and the audience, which marks the benediction, 8b, even more clearly as a misplaced insertion.[93] "Righteousness" (cf. 8:21)[94] personified is God's righteousness, although not in the specifically Pauline sense.[95] The disconcerting appearance of this term has less to do with the phrase in 2 Tim 4:8 (ὁ τῆς δικαιοσύνης στέφανος, "the crown of righteousness") than with its parallelism with the term "truth" (cf. 25:10; Eph 5:9 is only verbally related). In *Corp. Herm.* 13 (204 and 206)[96] δικαιοσύνη and ἀλήθεια are also found side by side as two of the divine δυνάμεις speaking their own praise. What exactly the actions were that are adumbrated by the common verbs ܢܣܒ (*nsaḇ*) and ܝܗܒ (*yaḇ*) it is impossible to know.[97]

If the image of "putting on" the crown comes through fairly clearly, the remainder of 11a is again enigmatic. Bauer's remark that "covenant" and "book" (in stanza VI) are "common terms in the Old Testament" that "have been taken over into Christian usage"[98] is not much help in dealing with the noun ܩܝܡܐ (*qyāmā*), which occurs only here, especially since the stress is on the attributive "true" and the qualifying genitive (on "Lord," see stanza II above). Diettrich may help a little more by interpreting "covenant" as "an inner circle of Jewish believers, accepted or not accepted into the Jewish community," but also as "a more or less organised elite" of "Gnostics."[99] The translation "in the true covenant"[100] assumes that the form is emphatic masculine. Later monastic meanings that this *hapax legomenon,* derived from the root *qwm*, acquired must not be anachronistically imported here.[101]

■ **11b-12** Except for the coda 12c, which echoes the imperative of salvation in 5c, this final promise of salvation is also filled with extraordinary images, although the metaphorical "book (of life)" already had a long history (from Ps 68:29 LXX; Exod 32:32-33 via Dan 12:1; Phil 4:3; Rev 3:5; and elsewhere, to the *Gos. Truth* NHC I,*3* + XII,*2*, esp. 19,35–20,24; 21,3-5; 22,38–32,1).[102] Because of the joint usage of the roots *zkʾ* and *ktb*, which connect 11b and 12a chiastically and with a "terrace pattern,"[103] two biblical passages may have been especially influential in meaning and vocabulary:

> Ps 68:29 LXX ἐξαλειφθήτωσαν ἐκ βίβλου ζώντων καὶ μετὰ δικαίων μὴ γραφήτωσαν ("Let them be blotted out of the book of the living, and let them not be written with the righteous").[104]

> Rev 3:5 ὁ νικῶν . . . καὶ οὐ μὴ ἐξαλείψω τὸ ὄνομα αὐτοῦ ἐκ τῆς βίβλου τῆς ζωῆς ("He who conquers . . . and I will not blot out his name out of the book of life").

92 Contra Franzmann, 73–74, 77, etc.
93 Both Greßmann (p. 446) and Bauer (p. 589) enclose it in dashes, suggesting that they consider it a parenthesis.
94 In his list of "Hypostases in these *Odes,*" Diettrich (pp. XI–XII) equates "victory" (12) with "righteousness." This is hardly defensible.
95 Cf. BDAG, *s.v.* δικαιοσύνη, 2–3.
96 Grese, *Corpus*, 28, 179.
97 On the soft pronunciation of "ܬ of the 3rd sing[ular] fem[inine] in the Per[fect]" of ܢܣܒ (*nsaḇ*) and ܝܗܒ (*yaḇ*), see Nöldeke §23.G.
98 Bauer, 589.
99 Diettrich, 35.
100 See BDAG, *s.v.* διαθήκη, 2. The Syriac word cannot here mean "testament"; cf. the translation of Labourt and Batiffol (p. 12): "Put on the crown in the veritable testament of the Lord." Even the translation "in a firm alliance" (Schultheß, 254) is inappropriate, although the adjective ܫܪܝܪܐ (*šrīrā*) can be used "in the sense of firm, sure" (Bultmann, "Untersuchungen," 160 = *Exegetica*, 170).
101 Payne Smith, 2:3533. If the form were feminine absolute, the translation would be "in the true resurrection" (Payne Smith, 2:3535). The context of the *Odes of Solomon*, however, makes it possible to eliminate this meaning. Pierre's note on this point (p. 82) is too indefinite.
102 *NHLE*, 41–43.
103 Franzmann, 77–78.
104 Rahlfs, 2:72; Brenton, 738. The use of δίκαιος here may explain the appearance of "righteousness" in 10, though in a very different sense.

Because of the mention of "war(s)" (see at 6b and 9b above), the *hapax legomenon* Pe. ܙܟܐ (*zkā*)[105] and the feminine ܙܟܘܬܐ (*zākūtā*, not *zakkūtā*),[106] which is found elsewhere in Gnostic and soteriological contexts (18:7; 29:9), bear the sense of "victory" in preference to other possible meanings.[107] The masculine ܟܬܒܐ (*ktābā*) in 11b, not found elsewhere in the *Odes of Solomon*, is simply a "book" (like *βιβλίον* or *βίβλος*),[108] but in 12a, because of the Syriac sentence form,[109] it must be translated differently. The possessive suffix in 11b refers, of course, to the "Lord" of 11a.

Since there is no good reason for altering the wording of 12a,[110] a strange logical reciprocity of "victory" and "recording" becomes visible. The two actions seem to define each other, and the reason is that it is not human victory that is the cause of redemption.[111] Human beings can finally neither win nor endure forever in the written word. Even "victory" is a theological category, whose Greek expression (*ἡ νίκη ὑμῶν*[112] or *ἡ νίκη ἡ ὑμετέρα*)[113] must have sounded like a slogan against the "idea" of *Νίκη* "as a divinity."[114]

The subject of the participles expressing continuity in vv. 12b-c must be the Syriac feminine "victory." As in the case of "righteousness" in stanza V (10), this is a theological "poetic personification" but not the "concept of an angelic being."[115] There are no parallels for the peculiar use of the verbs ܚܙܐ (*ḥzā*) and ܨܒܐ (*ṣbā*), on which Harnack remarked: "This verse [i.e., 12] seems to be corrupt; it is difficult, in its present state, to make sense of it."[116] However, these metaphorical expressions belong to the imagery of the *Odes of Solomon*, and the participle in 12c shares the root of the noun ܨܒܝܢܐ (*ṣebyānā*), forming the *inclusio* of the address of redemption (see on "will" in 3a above).[117]

The subject of the Ode as a whole is "redemption," the final victory, which is humanly impossible, as the last sentence underlines by its use of the Ethpe. of ܦܪܩ (*praq*), a theological passive (cf. 9:5 and also 17:14 and 34:6, as well as Excursus 5).

105 The Ethpe. of ܟܬܒ (*ktab*) in 11b is also a *hapax legomenon*.
106 Contra Diettrich, 36.
107 Contra Diettrich, 35; cf. Charlesworth, 46–47; Payne Smith, 1:1119–21.
108 BDAG, *s.vv.* *βιβλίον* and *βίβλος*.
109 On the ending of 12a, see Nöldeke §355: "Short adverbial adjuncts to a noun are generally turned into the form of a relative clause, by means of ܕ."
110 See, e.g., Diettrich (p. 35): "the one who writes them," or even "their scribe"; Greßmann (p. 446): "your scribe."
111 Charlesworth's remark on "justification" in his notes to 12a (p. 47) is altogether off the point: "The idea that Christ's sacrifice justifies the believer (see v. 10) is paralleled by the belief that the believer also must contribute his all in the struggles for salvation."
112 Fanourgakis, 149.
113 Frankenberg, 12.
114 Walter Pötscher, "Nike (*Νίκη*)," *KP* 4 (1972) 100; see also Greßmann's translation (p. 446): "your own Nike/Victory."
115 Contra Diettrich, 36.
116 Harnack, 39.
117 See Franzmann, 76.

10

Ode 10: Mythological Address of the Redeemer and Revealer

(I) 1a The Lord directed my mouth by his word
1b and opened my heart by his light.
2a And he caused his immortal life to dwell in me
2b and granted me to speak the fruit of his peace.
(II) 3a To bring back the souls of those who desire to come to him
3b and to lead captive a good captivity for freedom,
4a I was made mighty and strengthened and took the world captive,
4b and it [viz., the captivity] became for me the glory/praise of the Most High and God, my Father.
(III) 5a And the peoples that had been scattered were gathered together
5b and I was not defiled by the sins (of the peoples).
5c Because they had praised me in the heights,
6a the tracks of light were laid on their heart.
6b And they walked in my life and were redeemed,
6c and they were my people for all eternity.
Hallelujah.

Introduction

This Ode is preserved in one Syriac manuscript.[1] In "this difficult Ode"[2] there is no reason to bisect the speaker into the "Odist" (1-3) and "Christ" (4-6).[3] Apart from the fact that the speaker does not have to be the "author (the prophet)," the terms "Messiah" and "Christ" should also be treated with circumspection.[4] Jews might consider the unitary speaking "I," who does not have a defined audience, as one anointed by the Lord, and Christians might identify him with the Jesus Christ of their still primitive Christology and proclamation of the gospel, but early Gnostics too, at the edges of these two movements, which were fanning out and occasionally

1 Ms.: Codex H, 7b–8a (ܣ). Ed./trans.: Charlesworth, 47–49; Franzmann, 79–82; Lattke, 1:171–83 and 3:XXII.

2 Harnack, 39.

3 Charlesworth, 48; Grese, *Corpus*, 178; Aune, "Christian Prophecy," 438. See already Harris and Mingana, 2:264: "In this Ode again the writer, after a short preface in which he declares himself an evangelist of the new faith, begins to speak in the Person of Christ and so continues to the end of the Ode." Kittel, also—like Greßmann (p. 446) later on—"is inclined, in *Ode* 10, to see an actual transition from the 'I' of the singer to the 'I' of Christ" (Kittel, 71). According to Bernard (p. 71), "Christ is the speaker throughout."

4 Contra Harnack, 30.

intersecting (perhaps under the influence of Hermetic thought), would have few problems in accepting him as one of their Redeemers (Liberators).

This mythological address[5] is neither a "baptismal hymn"[6] nor a "hymn of thanksgiving."[7] Diettrich's dictum, "This Ode can only be understood as an eschatological hymn of the Old Testament,"[8] is also unsatisfactory. The content of this mythos, as uttered by the Revealer, is so manifold that it cannot be reduced to the *single* theme of "leading captivity captive."[9]

Stanza I is not 1-3, but only "the first strophe (1a-2b)," which, contra Franzmann, can in part be justified by her own words: "With 3a there is a change of image to struggle, capturing and bringing back. 3a-b would be better placed with 4a because of the similarity of the motif of capture, especially since the root ܫܒܐ is repeated three times in 3b-4a."[10] Her criterion for including 3a-b "as the second strophe" of stanza I is not convincing.[11]

If the "word order" is "very free" in Syriac prose, rhetorical and poetic texts offer "unbounded possibilities."[12] Although it would be unusual, it is perfectly possible that the connected infinitive clauses of 3a-b are pre-positioned, either because they bear a heavy emphasis or to throw the stress forward onto the second part (4b) of the main clause 4a-b. This possibility would exist in Greek as well, if the Syriac were equivalent not to ὥστε,[13] but to εἰς/πρὸς τό + infinitive.[14]

Interpretation

■ **1-2** Since the Revealer, who distinguishes himself from the "Lord" (1a) the "Most High" (4a),[15] makes use of "the three most important Gnostic symbols"—"word" (1a), "light" (1b), and "life" (2a)—his place is to be found somewhere along the line linking the prologue of the Gospel of John (see John 1:1-4) with the much later "Manichaean doctrine of the primal man."[16] He does not, however, speak of his descent (his mission or incarnation) or his ascent (his exaltation or return). Later he is to be found "in the heights" (5c), so 2b (perhaps together with 4a) may refer to a mythological rather than a historical redemption, which lets him appear, in this Ode also, as the redeemed Redeemer (see Excursus 5). In any case, he is seen as preexistent in relation to the redeemed, but his revelation and power of redemption are God-given and are not from any worldly authority or power.

Of the two possible meanings of the Pa. of ܬܪܨ (*tras*), "directed" fits better in 1a than "corrected" (contrast 6:16).[17] However, this verb always has a connotation of "rectification,"[18] so the Greek equivalent might have been a form of διορθόω or κατευθύνω.[19] Its connection to ܦܘܡܐ (*pummā*) as the organ of speech is unusual, but may perhaps be explained by the occurrence of "to

5 I have, again, supplied the title. It is not unimaginable that this speech could have been put into the mouth of the Johannine Jesus and could thus have found its way into the New Testament (see Bultmann, "Bedeutung," 110, 119, esp. 135 [= idem, *Exegetica*, 65, 75, esp. 93]: "Of the *Odes of Solomon*, *Odes* 10, 31 and especially 17 and 42 describe the liberation of the captives" [slightly corrected]. Because of the largely unitary character of the *Odes of Solomon*, the speaking "I" of *Ode* 10 is also most probably masculine, although grammatical corroboration is absent. If the mythos were thought to refer to Wisdom personified, both in 𝔖 and 𝔊 the image would be feminine.

6 Contra Bernard, 71–72; Schille, 65.

7 Contra Hermann Gunkel, "Die Oden Salomos," *ZNW* 11 (1910) 311.

8 Diettrich, 36.

9 Contra Abbott, 319–43, again with a plethora of material.

10 Franzmann, 80–81.

11 This criterion is "the use of infinitives" in 3a-b (Franzmann, 81). Translators of the *Odes* have indeed treated these infinitives as dependent on 2b without always making clear what the type of dependence is.

12 Nöldeke §§324, 378.

13 As in Frankenberg, 13.

14 Cf. Heb 8:3 and to some extent also Matt 26:12; Heb 9:28; 1 Cor 11:33; 1 Thess 2:9; see also BDF and BDR §402.

15 Charlesworth, 48.

16 Hans Heinrich Schaeder, "Zur manichäischen Urmenschlehre," in Richard Reitzenstein and Hans Heinrich Schaeder, *Studien zum antiken Synkretismus aus Iran und Griechenland* (Studien der Bibliothek Warburg 7; Leipzig/Berlin: Teubner, 1926; repr., Darmstadt: Wissenschaftliche Buchgesellschaft, 1965) 268.

17 See Brockelmann, *Lexicon*, 838.

18 Harris and Mingana, 2:264; Payne Smith, 2:4508.

19 See BDAG, *s.vv.* διορθόω and κατευθύνω.

open"[20] in 1b (see below). This is the first appearance of ܡܠܬܐ (*melltā*), and it is used as an anthropomorphism for a theologically transcendent action not identifiable with any human utterance or extramundane signal.[21]

Closely paralleling 1a, as shown by the "word-pair ܡܠܬܐ - ܢܘܗܪܐ"[22] and the connection of "mouth" and "heart," which occurs several times (cf. 21:8; 36:7), the speaking "I" in 1b combines the Pe. ܦܬܚ (*ptaḥ*) with ܠܒܐ (*lebbā*) as object (cf. 8:1 and Excursus 4). This metaphorical opening is also performed by the "light" of God, which here is not τὸ φῶς τοῦ κόσμου ("the light of the world") or τὸ φῶς τῶν ἀνθρώπων ("the light of men"; cf. John 1:4, 7-9; 3:19; 8:12; 9:5; 12:46). There is a certain similarity between this ܢܘܗܪܐ (*nuhrā*) and the καθαρὸν φῶς ("pure light") of Ignatius *Rom.* 6:2, perhaps even with the νοητὸν φῶς ("intelligible light") of *Corp. Herm.* 13:200 in a context where ζωὴ καὶ φῶς appear as "divine δυνάμεις"[23] (on 6a, see Excursus 10 below).

Verse 2a is the theological climax of stanza I, in which the speaking "I," using the Aph. of ܥܡܪ (*ʿmar*), which occurs only here (but cf. 32:1), describes himself as the dwelling of "immortal life."[24] This utterance calls to mind John 1:4 (ἐν αὐτῷ ζωὴ ἦν, "in him was life") and Col 1:19 (ἐν αὐτῷ εὐδόκησεν πᾶν τὸ πλήρωμα κατοικῆσαι, "all the fulness willed to dwell in him"),[25] so that it would be possible to say that the speaking "I" of this passage has "indwelling all the powers of God in creation and re-creation."[26] The infinite world of mortal life does not contain such ܚܝܐ (*ḥayyē*), so the Revealer who has received this "divine life" is altogether removed from it. "Life" in this context is probably more than a mere "term of eschatological salvation."[27]

The common verb "to give" in 2b is translated "granted" because of the final clause (ܕ [*d-*] + imperfect of the Pa. ܡܠܠ [*mallel*]).[28] The object of "to speak" would correspond to a Greek phrase such as καρπὸς τῆς εἰρήνης ("fruit of peace") or καρπὸς εἰρηνικός ("peaceful fruit") as in Heb 12:11 (cf. Jas 3:17-18).[29] The stress, in any case, does not fall on ܦܐܪܐ (*pērā*; see Excursus 11), not, that is, on the "metaphor of fruit,"[30] which is connected as in 17:13 with the Redeemer, but on the metaphorical ܫܠܡܐ (*šlāmā*), which here too implies a literal antithesis to "war" (cf. 9:6) and thus connects to the images in stanza II, which are partly drawn from the language of warfare.

If "life" and "the peaceful fruit of righteousness" in Heb 12:9-11 are to be interpreted as "eschatological possessions,"[31] the "peace" of God, which does not exist in this world, is the protological prerequisite in this passage for the mythos of salvation.

■ **3-4** As discussed above, stanza II begins with the infinitive declarations of the aims in 4a, is united by the use of the root *šbʾ*, and finishes with the outcome of the mythological liberation, which results not in the "possession of glory in 4b"[32] but in the "glory of God."[33] Without any specific literary dependence, stanza II is full of parallels with primitive Christian traditions, which in turn are partly rooted in Jewish theologoumena.

The Aph. of ܦܢܐ (*pnā*), used only in 3a, corresponds reciprocally to the Pe. ܐܬܐ (*ʾetā*), which is modified by ܨܒܐ (*ṣbā*). Both verbs include the notion of complete

20 "Mouth" and "to open" are regularly found in association in the *Odes of Solomon*; see 7:24; 8:4; 16:5; 31:3; 36:7.

21 See 41:11, 14; also 9:3 and 32:3 among the *petgāmā* passages; and Excursus 12.

22 Franzmann, 80–81.

23 *Corp. Herm.* 13:208; cf. Grese, *Corpus*, 26–29, 179.

24 See Table 1, esp. 15:10; 28:6; 31:7; 38:3; 40:6.

25 BDAG, *s.v.* εὐδοκέω, 1.

26 Eduard Schweizer, *Der Brief an die Kolosser* (EKKNT 12; Zurich: Benziger; Neukirchen-Vluyn: Neukirchener Verlag, 1976) 67.

27 Gerhard Dautzenberg, "Leben IV. Neues Testament," *TRE* 20 (1990) 527.

28 See Charlesworth, 48: "The verb ܝܗܒ often has the meaning 'to permit', and the imperfect in a subordinate clause is often translated by the English infinitive (see Nöldeke §267)." Cf. similar constructions in 6:7; 7:10, 12, 24; 12:4; 31:1-5.

29 Formally cf. πνεῦμα ἁγιωσύνης, "intensification" of πνεῦμα ἅγιον in Rom 1:4 (BDAG, *s.v.* ἁγιωσύνη).

30 Gemünden, *Vegetationsmetaphorik*, 402.

31 Gräßer, 3:274.

32 Franzmann, 81.

33 Bauer, 590.

reversal (cf. 33:6),[34] which is reinforced by the preposition ܠܘܬ (*lwāṯ*), with a suffix referring to the "Lord" (1a) and the "Most High" (4b).[35] The plural of ܢܦܫܐ (*nap̄šā*) is not dualistically opposed to fleshly "bodies" (not even in 39:3; cf. also 6:15; 41:11, 16), but refers to living beings as a whole according to Semitic tradition, and in this case to the exercise of their wills (cf. "heart" in 6a).

The speaking "I" declares his objective in 3b, with a direct or indirect (mis-)quotation of Ps 68:19a (67:19a LXX). The parallelism with 3a is more synthetic than synonymous, since the paronomasia "taking captivity captive"[36] is a metaphor from warfare, while the *hapax legomenon* "freedom" refers to the state which can only be obtained as a gift, in which those are found who have been "freed," of whom the Redeemer can say, in the final verse of the final Ode, "and they are mine" (42:20).

Since Eph 4:8 quotes this "verse of the psalm, which originally depicted the triumphal procession of the divine ruler to his sanctuary on the heights of Mount Zion,"[37] with "an intentional alteration of the text"[38] to make it refer to "the exaltation of Christ in the highest heaven," and 4:9, assuming the idea of pre-existence, implies the victory over the "hostile forces . . . in our life"[39] following the "incarnation," this loose quotation can be added to the following conspectus.[40]

Ps 68:19a MT	עָלִיתָ לַמָּרוֹם שָׁבִיתָ שֶּׁבִי
Ps 68:19a S[41]	ܣܠܩܬ ܠܡܪܘܡܐ ܘܫܒܝܬ ܫܒܝܬܐ
Ps 67:19a LXX	ἀνέβης εἰς ὕψος, ᾐχμαλώτευσας αἰχμαλωσίαν
Eph 4:8a	ἀναβὰς εἰς ὕψος, ᾐχμαλώτευσεν αἰχμαλωσίαν
Eph 4:8a S[42]	ܣܠܩ ܠܡܪܘܡܐ ܘܫܒܐ ܫܒܝܬܐ
Ode 10:3b	ܘܠܡܫܒܐ ܫܒܝܬܐ ܛܒܬܐ ܠܚܐܪܘܬܐ [cf. ܒܡܪ̈ܘܡܐ in 5c]

Even though the key word "peacc" (εἰρήνη in Eph 4:3; cf. Col 3:15) has already turned up in 2b and the idea of ὕψος ("height") is still to come (see on 4b and especially 5c below), it is unnecessary to assume a *direct* pseudo-Pauline influence on *Ode* 10. It is, however, likely that both the "contrasting images" of Eph 4:8–10 and the poetic mythos of *Ode* 10 "can be used indirectly . . . to reconstruct a possible initial phase of Gnostic thought."[43]

The two passives, of Ethpa. ܐܬܚܝܠ (*ʾeṯḥayyal*; cf. only 9:5) and Ethpa. ܐܬܥܫܢ (*ʾeṯʿaššan*; cf. 18:2 and 32:3), as warlike images,[44] may refer only to the necessary preparation for the operation undertaken in 4a. Gnostic ears, however, might have caught a reference to the "achieved salvation,"[45] just as the term ܥܠܡܐ (*ʿālmā*) would, for them, have had a meaning closer to αἰών than to κόσμος.[46] But especially in view of 5a, the term should be interpreted as the world of humans, though without the dualism of John 16:33 (ἐγὼ νενίκηκα τὸν κόσμον, "I have overcome the world"). The Redeemer declares himself, with mythological hyperbole, victor over all humanity.

That this subjection, which means liberation, was also εἰς δόξαν θεοῦ πατρός ("to the glory/praise of

34 Payne Smith, 2:3168–69.
35 Cf. 7:2; 11:9; 15:6; 25:1; 35:7b-c; 42:17.
36 Petr Pokorný, *Der Brief des Paulus an die Epheser* (ThHKNT 10.2; Leipzig: Evangelische Verlagsanstalt, 1992) 170. The Greek wordplay in Eph 4:8 corresponds exactly to the Syriac in *Ode* 10:3b.
37 Schlier, *Epheser*, 192.
38 Rudolf Schnackenburg, *Der Brief an die Epheser* (EKKNT 10; Zurich: Benziger; Neukirchen-Vluyn: Neukirchener Verlag, 1982) 179.
39 Pokorný, *Epheser*, 170–71.
40 The words derived from root ܫܒܐ occur only in 10:3-4 in the *Odes of Solomon* (see Payne Smith, 2:4018–21). In the New Testament also and in early Christian writing, the words αἰχμαλωσία ("state of captivity, captivity, mostly in war"; or "abstr[act] for concr[ete] a captured military force, prisoners of war, captives") and αἰχμαλωτεύω ("to capture in war, capture, take captive") are rare (BDAG, *s.vv.* αἰχμαλωσία and αἰχμαλωτεύω). The "captivity" is "good" because "it leads to freedom, not to renewed slavery" (Gunkel, 311; cf. 1 Tim 1:18; 2 Tim 2:3).
41 See *OTSy* pt. 2 fasc. 3, on this passage.
42 See *NTSy*, on Eph 4:8.
43 Pokorný, *Epheser*, 172.
44 Payne Smith, 1:1261; 2:3003.
45 Gunkel, 311.
46 See Payne Smith, 2:2898–900; BDAG, *s.v.* αἰών, 2a, 3; κόσμος, 3.

God the Father"; cf. Phil 2:11) is declared by the speaking "I" in an expression referring to "voluntary captivity,"[47] which is as indefinite as the Greek phrase ἐγένετό μοι εἰς ("it became for me"; cf. 11:3a). The feminine ܬܫܒܘܚܬܐ (*tešbuḥtā*), here as elsewhere, wavers between its two meanings, "glory" (e.g., 11:17) and "praise" (e.g., 6:7).

The Redeemer and Revealer, in calling the "Lord" of 1a not only the "Most High" and "God," but also his "Father"[48] unmasks himself in this patriarchal worldview as the preeminent "Son,"[49] perhaps even as the mytho-theological "primal man" free of any earthly parentage.

■ **5-6** If ܥܡ (*ʿam*) in the last line means "my people" and not "with me,"[50] Franzmann is right when she says, "The inclusio is formed by 5a and 6c with the repetition of ܥܡܐ."[51] Much of her analysis, however, is faulty, since 5c-6a must be marked out as a separate bicolon beginning with a justification.[52] This divides stanza III into three bicola in a sequence of utterances whose eschatology seems to be removed to a mythological past.

In contrast to the negative outcome for the peoples in 1QM, the *War Scroll* of QL, xiv.5 (וּקְהַל גּוֹיִים אָסַף לְכָלָה אֵין שְׁאֵרִית),[53] 5a, with a theological passive (Ethpa. of ܟܢܫ [*knaš*]),[54] speaks of a positive assembly of the peoples, though it does not refer to πάντα τὰ ἔθνη ("all nations" [Matt 28:19; Luke 24:47]; cf. also Acts 28:28) or to τὸ πλήρωμα τῶν ἐθνῶν ("the full number of the Gentiles" [Rom 11:25]) but only to "those who desire to come to him" (3a)[55] and were "dispersed" (passive participle of Pa. ܒܕܪ [*baddar*], a word used much later "*de Nestorianis in Syria et Aegypto dispersis*").[56] Verse 5a thus reads like a variation of the prophecy in John 11:52, which has already come to pass:

ἵνα καὶ τὰ τέκνα τοῦ θεοῦ τὰ (δι)εσκορπισμένα συναγάγῃ εἰς ἕν

"to gather into one the dispersed children of God"

ܐܝܟ ܕܐܦ ܒܢ̈ܝܐ ܕܐܠܗܐ ܕܡܒܕܪܝܢ ܢܟܢܫ ܠܚܕܐ (*NTSy*).

Verse 5b is incomprehensible without some emendation. If the plural points are left on ܚܘܒܐ (*ḥawbā*), without any alteration to the text, the first person statement of the sinless Redeemer (cf. John 8:46) yields only a tortuous meaning "by sins (ὀφειλήματα or ἁμαρτίαι), which I, the Redeemer, might have committed."[57] On the other hand, removing the plural points from the manuscript text results in a reading ܚܘܒܝ, whose pronunciation *ḥob* (cf. 16:3) differs quite widely from *ḥawbay* and would have to be translated as "my love (for them),"[58] that is "for the Gentiles,"[59] which (a) "is not said"[60] and (b) does not result in a coherent meaning for the line.[61]

47 Arvedson, *Mysterium*, 198.
48 Cf. 9:5; 19:2; 23:18, 22; 41:13.
49 Cf. John 3:16, 35; 5:26; 17:1; Rom 8:3; Gal 4:4.
50 Labourt and Batiffol, 13; cf. Pierre, 85; Azar, 106.
51 Franzmann, 81.
52 Lattke, *Oden*, 121 n. 5.
53 Vermes (p. 119) translates: "He . . . has gathered in the assembly of the nations to destruction without any remnant." See Lohse, *Texte*, 213; and Maier, *Qumran-Essener*, 1:147.
54 See Payne Smith, 1:1771. There is a similar phrase in 23:17. The meaning is closer to 17:14 because of the mention of redemption. Franzmann (p. 82) notes other parallels: 17:12-16; 33:5-13; 42:14-20. Bauer's translation (p. 590) of the Ethpa. is grammatically possible but does not make good sense: ". . . and the peoples that were scattered have assembled themselves together."
55 See Bauer, 590.
56 See Payne Smith, 1:455.
57 Lattke, *Oden*, 121. The idea that the plural might refer to Christian *agapai* is rather far-fetched: "If then the plural pointing is right, and the meaning is 'loves', the Syriac will be a translation of ἐν ταῖς ἀγάπαις μου, and we are reminded at once of Jude *v.* 12" (Richard Hugh Connolly, review of Harris and Mingana in *JTS* 22 [1920–21] 83). Frankenberg's back-translation (p. 13) is erroneous: "*και ουκ εμιανθη εν ταις αμαρτιαις (αυτων).*"
58 Harris and Mingana, 2:264; Charlesworth, 48.
59 Bernard, 71; see also Labourt and Batiffol, 13.
60 Harnack, 40.
61 This is true even if 5c is taken to be the justification for 5b; see, e.g., Diettrich, 39.

This leads to Harnack's conclusion: "There may be an omission, or something else that is wrong with the text."[62] In fact, if the end of 5b is amplified to ܒܚܘܒܝ ܥܡܡܐ (*b-ḥawbay ʿammē*), the phrase using the construct state makes very good sense: "by the sins (guilt, wrongdoing) of the peoples" (cf. Dan 9:20). The omission of the plural, which has occurred just previously in 5a, is paleographically more likely than the omission of the singular term ܚܘܒܝ (*delicta populi mei*),[63] which only occurs later in 6c. This provides an explanation for the way the negation of the Ethpa. of ܛܡܐ (*ṭmā*)[64] is emphasized by putting the personal pronoun before it. The immortal Redeemer, present only in the mythos, cannot be made "common" or "profane"[65] by the sinfulness inherent in the world, which can only be absolved by forgiveness (cf. Matt 6:12, ἄφες ἡμῖν τὰ ὀφειλήματα ἡμῶν, "forgive us our debts").

Without necessarily referring to Ps 17:50 LXX (ἐξομολογήσομαί σοι ἐν ἔθνεσιν, κύριε, "I will praise you among the nations, Lord"),[66] it is likely that the Aph. form ܐܘܕܝܘ (*ʾawdīw*) in 5c carries a meaning similar to ἐξομολογέομαι ("to praise").[67] The preceding conjunction would be equivalent to the Greek causal conjunction ὅτι, which also does not necessarily follow the main clause (cf., e.g., John 20:29). The prepositional phrase "in the heights" refers not to the praise and thanks but to the object of them, expressed by ܠ (*l-*) + suffix. *Where* the assembly of the peoples took place is not mentioned. The plural of ܡܪܘܡܐ (*mrawmā*) occurs only here and corresponds to the metaphorical τὰ ὕψιστα.[68] Even in antiquity, critical ears would not have heard in this mythos the description of a place or space, but rather of a transcendence not in any sense to be identified with the skies of this world.

In the succeeding main clause, 6a, the introductory ܘ (*w-*) is to be translated "also," which can equally be used for καί. The translation of the common word ܣܘܡ, ܣܡ (*sām*),[69] even in its metaphorical connection with the preposition ܥܠ (*ʿal* = "upon") and ܠܒܐ (*lebbā*) + possessive suffix, is perfectly straightforward (see Excursus 4), but the peculiar expression "tracks of light" and its relationship to the dualism of light and darkness needs further illumination.

Excursus 10: "Light," "Tracks of Light," and "Darkness" in the *Odes of Solomon*

The masculine ܢܘܗܪܐ (*nuhrā*), which corresponds to the Greek neuter φῶς (11:19), occurs twenty times, which makes it one of the dominant terms in the imagery of the *Odes of Solomon*.[70] At least once, possibly twice, the word ܢܗܝܪܐ (*nahhīrā*, singular masculine emphatic) is used as a noun synonymous with ܢܘܗܪܐ (18:6; on 36:3 see below).[71] In its other two occurrences, it is an adjective: "light" (16:16a, modifying "day") and "clear" (34:2, modifying "thought"). The Pe. ܢܗܪ (*nhar*) and Aph. ܐܢܗܪ (*ʾanhar*) occur twice each (40:4; 41:6a; and 11:14; 41:4). *Ode* 41:4 and 41:6a each contain a statement concerning light (see below); 40:4 speaks of the shining of the soul[72] and 11:14 𝔊 of the shining of the eyes (ἔστιλβον; on the different reading of 𝔖, see that section of the commentary on *Ode* 11).

With the exception of 5:5a, where the *hapax legomenon* ܥܡܛܢܐ (*ʿamṭānā*) is found in the phrase "cloud of darkness,"[73] the Syriac word ܚܫܘܟܐ (*ḥeššōkā*)

62 Harnack, 40. Barth (p. 262), who translates the word under discussion by "faults," is less convincing in his text-critical remark that 5b "seems to be an interpolation or placed here by mistake."
63 See Payne Smith, 1:1214–15.
64 On this *hapax legomenon*, see Payne Smith, 1:1484.
65 See BDAG, *s.vv.* βεβηλόω and κοινόω, 2.
66 Rahlfs, 2:17; Brenton, 708 (corrected).
67 See BDAG, *s.v.* ἐξομολογέω, 4; Harris and Mingana, 2:265, referring to 5:1.
68 See BDAG, *s.v.* ὕψιστος, 1: "the highest heights = heaven."
69 This verb, meaning "to lay, put, set," like the verb of 5a, is a theological passive. It might also be possible to translate the Ethpe. reflexively: "the tracks of light laid themselves on their heart." Charlesworth (p. 49) is right, remarking in connection with "heart": "The translators frequently fail to represent the singular noun." But this "heart" is not the communal core of the assembly of peoples; it is the heart (see BDAG, *s.v.* καρδία) of each individual, a plurality of "hearts," as implied by the inclusively intended suffix.
70 Lattke, "Bildersprache," 106 = idem, *Bedeutung*, 4:33.
71 See Payne Smith, 2:2300.
72 As the parallels "tongue" and "limbs" (40:3), "countenance" and "spirit" demonstrate, this is not a reference to the so-called soul of light.
73 See Payne Smith, 2:2911 (masculine, *caligo, tenebrae densae*).

is used for "darkness" in each of the eight passages where it occurs. This word (singular masculine emphatic), used as a noun, corresponds in 11:19 to τὸ σκότος.[74] The Greek may have had ἡ σκοτία in some cases (cf. John 1:5; 8:12; 12:35). Even in 42:16 ζόφος would not come under consideration (cf. 2 Pet 2:4 [ܥܠܛܢܐ], but also 2 Pet 2:17 [ܚܫܘܟܐ]), and γνόφος is also unlikely (but cf. Heb 12:18). The Aph. of ܚܫܟ (*ḥšeḵ*), which occurs only twice, describes an action of the "air of fog" in 5:5b[75] and by parallelism with 5:5a is also "*de oculis*."[76]

"Light," in antiquity even more than today, was equated with "daylight" as the precondition for seeing (5:6). Those who give light to the eyes (6:17) may be said to set alight the lamp of the body (cf. Matt 6:22). And whoever surrounds a person with lamps leaves no part of that person without light (25:7). But it is the natural daylight, emanating from the sun, not its artificial substitute, that gives rise to the contrasting and dualistic imagery of light and the darkness of night (16:15-16). This opposition between light/day and darkness/night is also used mythologically, with a nod to Gen 1:1-5, so that the primal darkness is destroyed by the appearance of the Lord of the World (31:1). All the same, "darkness" is an inimical, fettering power, from which humans cannot break free by their own efforts (42:16). Even taking off the metaphorical straitjacket of "darkness" (21:3a) is possible only because the bonds had already been removed (cf. 21:2). Only when they attain the mythic-eschatological paradise can those who were planted turn away from "darkness" towards "light" (11:19).

The sun is not God. But since the sun is essential to all known life in the infinite universe, the Lord of humanity may, by a daring comparison, be depicted as a redeeming Helios, whose "rays" awaken and whose "light" drives the "darkness" away (15:2). The fact that "light" cannot finally be vanquished by "darkness" (18:6) is part of the dualistic ideology of redemption. That is why "Judaism governs the thought of the *Odes*," which are also "Gnosticizing" in their "concept of light," and the emphasis is on "light" as the "place" and "being" of the "redeemed,"[77] not on "darkness" as "place" and state of "mankind."[78]

As natural light comes, generally speaking, from above, the divine "light," which exists only as image and myth, is also located in the heights (11:11 ς; 21:3, 6; 32:1; 41:14). But into this spatial conception, in which it is possible to enter the "light of truth" like a chariot (38:1), there intrudes both a profound transcendentalism and an existential trend, which views the "light" of the Lord, the Most High, as manifesting revelation and as a means of salvation. Thus, one could speak already here and now "in his light"—or "by means of his light" (8:2). His "light" is like a garment, which can be donned (11:11; 21:3). His "light" dispels the "darkness" (15:2; cf. 41:6);[79] it is like a guide (29:7) and a device for lifting up (21:6). "Light from him who dwells within them" comes to the blessed (32:1).

Even the Redeemer's heart is opened by the "light" of the Lord (10:1b). "Light" is here parallel to "word" (10:1a); elsewhere the "word" can be said to be the source of the "light" (41:14). For the "mouth of the Lord" is the "true word" and the "entrance gate of his light" (12:3). The statement that the "word" is the "light and dawning of thought" sounds more general (12:5-7; but cf. Excursus 12). Whether the "Son of God" in 36:3 is *the Shining One*[80] or is merely called "(the) Light" will be discussed later.

It is remarkable that Conzelmann in his comprehensive article on φῶς κτλ.[81] never mentions the strange phrase "tracks of light" (7:14; 10:6). The plural of ܥܩܒܐ (*ʿeqḇā*) is found in a similarly puzzling context in 39:10-11 and must be equivalent to Greek τὰ ἴχνη.[82] In its connection with "light" in 7:14, the term retains its literal meaning of "track" (i.e., single "*footprints*" or "continuous . . . *spoor*"), which, as such, "is not imitated but followed."[83]

74 Payne Smith, 1:1402; BDAG, *s.v.* σκότος.

75 Lattke, "Wörter," 287 = idem, *Bedeutung*, 4:135.

76 Payne Smith, 1:1401.

77 Hans Conzelmann, "φῶς, κτλ.," *ThWNT* 9 (1973) 331; *TDNT* 9:340.

78 Hans Conzelmann, "σκότος, κτλ.," *ThWNT* 7 (1964) 436; *TDNT* 7:435.

79 Conzelmann interprets 41:6 altogether gnostically: "the redeemed [are] transformed into light" (see Conzelmann, "φῶς," *ThWNT* 9:332; *TDNT* 9:340.). In 22:12 ℭ, a Gnostic interpretation of the Greek original is found in the actual text, not only in the hymn of the *Pistis Sophia*.

80 Conzelmann, "φῶς," *ThWNT* 9:332; *TDNT* 9:340.

81 Conzelmann, "φῶς," *ThWNT* 9:302–49; *TDNT* 9:310–58.

82 Frankenberg, 10, 13, 33; Payne Smith, 2:2960; cf. Georg Bertram's postscript to Albrecht Stumpff, "ἴχνος," *ThWNT* 3 (1938) 409; *TDNT* 3:406 n. 20.

83 See Stumpff, "ἴχνος," *ThWNT* 3:405–7; *TDNT* 3:402–5, referring to Sir 50:29 (φῶς κυρίου τὸ ἴχνος αὐτοῦ, "the light of the Lord is their path"). Sir 50:28-29 had already been mentioned by Harris and Mingana as the "nearest Biblical passage that shows any parallelism with the [curious] expression in the Odes" (Harris and Mingana, 2:252–53).

The term *καρδία* also occurs in Sir 50:28, so even this "password"[84] in 10:6 could have been inspired by that passage in the wisdom literature. This would, however, confuse the imagery. For the metaphor of "tracks" makes sense only if it is also clear that a "track of light" was laid down by the Most High for the benefit of *other persons* to help them "find the way to life."[85]

Continuing with 6a: although the *light* connects the assembly of the peoples soteriologically with the "heights" (5c), the *tracks* of light are not intended for those on whose hearts they are placed. These "tracks of light" are metaphorically meant as pointers that will give light to future generations of persons to be redeemed.

In 6b, the mythological description goes a step further. The Pa. ܗܠܟ (*hallek̲*) describes the existential walking[86] as a past occurrence, which sounds like an attempt to trump Rom 6:4 (*οὕτως καὶ ἡμεῖς ἐν καινότητι ζωῆς περιπατήσωμεν*, "we too might walk in newness of life"), and is reminiscent of Eph 5:8 (*ὡς τέκνα φωτὸς περιπατεῖτε*, "walk as children of light") and Col 2:6 (*ἐν αὐτῷ* [viz., *Χριστῷ Ἰησοῦ*] *περιπατεῖτε*, "walk = live in him"). Since, according to 2a, the "immortal life" of the Lord dwells in the Redeemer, the adverbial phrase of situation refers here also to the divine "life." This is an even greater claim than is found in other statements and imperatives concerning "walking" (17:4c; 23:4; 33:13; 38:5). The Ethpe. of ܦܪܩ (*praq*) makes it clear that this paradoxical living/walking in the otherworldly "life" of the Redeemer is theological "redemption," which is not a consequence but a simultaneous event.

The terms "to live" and "to be redeemed" are regularly found in close proximity in the Syriac (see the commentary on 5:3 and 6:18). The material parallelism of "live/life" (cf. 3:9) and "redemption" is also found elsewhere, sometimes in reverse order (see 17:14; 26:9; 34:6; 38:16; 40:6).

Verse 6c, the "concluding statement to the actions described for the gathered people,"[87] is not simply a consequence but a final, timeless, and eternal summary of the soteriological address of revelation by the speaking "I." It is likely that the term "people," as in 31:12, is equivalent to *λαός*, which would place it on the line of development from "the people of Israel" to "the Christians."[88] The direct connection with Hos 2:23 (2:25 LXX)—"That the Gentiles should become 'my people' is from Hosea"—is not as certain as Harris and Mingana believed.[89] Only someone totally immersed in a Pauline biblical theology would claim that "the heathen have become *the* or at least *a* people of truth."[90] Without being *compelled* to speak of "the heathen" or "the people of Christ," it is still possible to agree with Gunkel: "once many peoples, now one people."[91] This idea, which can be applied to all those who are to be redeemed from the beginning to the end of time, is to be found in later, degenerate Gnostic texts, two of which may be quoted here.[92]

One of the appendixes to the Coptic *Codex Bruce* is "A Hymn to the First Mystery on the Construction of the Aeons by Jeu."[93] This "Fragment of a Gnostic Hymn" includes the following passage:

84 Gunkel, 312.

85 Bauer, 590. Harnack's note (p. 40) "the tracks are probably the rays of light" shows that he can make nothing of the phrase. Gunkel's remark (p. 312), "These tracks of light have penetrated the hearts of the heathen; they found the way by following them," is off the point. Although I quote Bauer, I cannot altogether agree with him that in "*Ode* 7,14; 39,10-13 . . . the tracks of light define a path that leads the blessed aright. In our *Ode* they are imprinted on their hearts and thus enable them to find the way into life" (p. 590).

86 See Payne Smith, 1:1014.

87 Franzmann, 82.

88 See BDAG, *s.v.* *λαός*, 4a-b.

89 Harris and Mingana, 2:265.

90 Diettrich, 39.

91 Gunkel, 312.

92 The two examples come from Majella Franzmann, "Background and Parallels of the Imagery of the Coptic, Greek and Syriac *Odes of Solomon*," unpublished manuscript resulting from an Australian Research Council research project (University of Queensland, 1990).

93 Schmidt, Till, and Schenke, *Schriften*, XXX.

ⲥⲱⲧⲉ ⲙⲙⲉⲗⲟⲥ ⲛⲓⲙ ⲛⲧⲁⲓ ⲉⲧϫⲟⲟⲣⲉ ⲉⲃⲟⲗ ϫⲓⲛ-ⲧⲕⲁⲧⲁⲃⲟⲗⲏ ⲙⲡⲕⲟⲥⲙⲟⲥ ϩⲣⲁⲓ ϩⲛ-ⲛⲁⲣⲭⲱⲛ ⲧⲏⲣⲟⲩ ⲙⲛ-ⲛⲇⲉⲕⲁⲛⲟⲥ ⲙⲛ-ⲛⲗⲓⲧⲟⲩⲣⲅⲟⲥ ⲙⲡⲙⲉϩϯⲟⲩ ⲛⲁⲓⲱⲛ ⲁⲩⲱ ⲛⲅⲥⲟⲟⲩϩⲟⲩ ⲧⲏⲣⲟⲩ ⲉⲣⲟⲩⲛ ⲛⲅϫⲓⲧⲟⲩ ⲉⲡⲟⲩⲟⲉⲓⲛ·

> Save all my members (μέλη), which have been scattered since the foundation (καταβολή) of the world (κόσμος) in all the archons (ἄρχοντες) and the decans (δεκανοί) and the ministers (λειτουργοί) of the fifth aeon (αἰών), and gather them all together and take them to the light.[94]

In the same manuscript there is the *Untitled Text.* In chap. 11—a passage that teems with terms such as "word (λόγος)," "eternal life," "light," "rest (ἀνάπαυσις)," "knowledge (γνῶσις)," "return," and "heart"—there is a rare mention of "Israel:"

ⲁⲩⲱ ⲡϣⲱⲛⲃ ⲛⲛⲉⲩⲙⲉⲗⲟⲥ ⲡⲉ ⲡⲥⲱⲟⲩϩ ⲉϩⲟⲩⲛ ⲙⲡϫⲱⲱⲣⲉ ⲉⲃⲟⲗ ⲙⲡⲓⲏⲗ

> And the uniting of their members (μέλη) was the gathering together of the dispersed of Israel.[95]

Ode 10, even if it is not yet fully Gnostic, could well have been read by Gnostics from the second century onward as *their* text. If the whole was still a little too close to Judaism or already to Christianity, even so, sections and key words could easily be incorporated into various Gnostic mythologies. Even a quotation of the whole of this mythological address would fit well into the *Pistis Sophia.*

---

94 Schmidt and MacDermot, *Jeu*, 79, lines 8–12; Schmidt, Till, and Schenke, *Schriften*, 330, lines 7–10. MacDermot's reference (p. 79 n. 1) to Hans Jonas is not relevant to this passage, because Jonas is discussing the "gathering of the self": "The way of denial of the world . . . is seen, among others, in the image of the gathering of the self out of the multiplicity of the world" (Hans Jonas, *Gnosis und spätantiker Geist,* vol. 1: *Die mythologische Gnosis. Mit einer Einleitung: Zur Geschichte und Methodologie der Forschung* [3rd ed.; Göttingen: Vandenhoeck & Ruprecht, 1964] 139).

95 Schmidt and MacDermot, *Jeu*, 247, lines 26–27; Schmidt, Till, and Schenke, *Schriften*, 350, lines 35–36. The name "Israel" is also very uncommon in the Nag Hammadi tractates. The most important passage is NHC II,*5,* where "Jesus Christ has no central function, but rather a marginal role" (*NHLE*, 171). "Thereafter he created a congregation (*ekklesia*) of angels, thousands and myriads, numberless, which resembled the congregation in the eighth heaven; and a firstborn, called Israel—which is, 'the man that sees God'; and another being, called Jesus Christ, who resembles the savior above in the eighth heaven and who sits at his right upon a revered throne, and at his left, there sits the virgin of the holy spirit, upon a throne and glorifying him" (*Orig. World* 105,20–31; *NHLE*, 176).

11

Ode 11: A Redeemed One Witnesses in Metaphorical Speech

Greek (𝔊)

(I) 1a My heart was circumcised and its flower appeared.
1b Grace grew up in it
1c and bore fruit for God.
2a The Most High circumcised me by his holy spirit
2b and laid bare toward himself my kidneys/reins
2c and filled me with his love.
3a His circumcision became my salvation.

(II) 3b I ran the way of truth in his peace,
4 from the beginning to the end I received his understanding.
5a I was set firmly on the firm rock,
5b where he also set me.

(III) 6a And the speaking water drew near to my lips
6b from the spring of life of the Lord in his lack of envy.
7 I drank—and became drunk—immortal water,
8a and my drunkenness was not irrationality.[a]

(IV) 8b But I turned away from vanities
9a to the Most High, my God,
9b and became rich by his gracious gift.
10a I left folly lying on the earth,
10b I stripped it off and cast it from me.
11a The Lord renewed me by his garment
11b and regained me by his light
12a and recalled me to life by his imperishability.

(V) 12b I became/was like (the)[b] earth that flourishes and laughs by its fruits,
13 and the Lord became/was to me like the sun over the face of the earth.
14a My eyes shone,
14b and my face was bedewed.
15 My breath was gladdened by the fragrance of the Lord's kindness.

(VI) 16a And he led me away into his paradise,
16b where is the fullness of the Lord's delight.
16c I saw beautiful and fruit-bearing trees,
16d and their crown was grown naturally.
16e Their timber [flourished][c] and their fruits laughed.
16f From immortal earth [grew] their roots,

a 8a Manuscript correction of εἰς ἀλογιστίαν to ἀλογιστία.
b 12b Manuscript correction of ἡ γῆ to γῆ.
c 16e Manuscript θάλλει to be corrected to ἔθαλλε.

16g and the river of joy watered them
16h and all around the earth of their eternal life.
(VII) 17 I worshiped the Lord because of his glory
18a and said, Lord, blessed are those planted on the earth,
18b who have a place in thy paradise
19a and grow in the growth of thy trees,
19b turned from darkness to (the)[d] light.
20a Behold, thy laborers are beautiful:
20b they bring about good transformations
21a from uselessness to goodness.
21b The bitterness of the plants is changed in thy earth.
22a And everything becomes like thy [remnant][e]
22b —blessed be the [wardens][f] of thy waters—
22c and eternal remembrances of thy faithful servants.
(VIII) 23a Generous (is) the area of thy paradise,
23b and nothing is fallow,
23c but even bears fruit.
(IX) 24a Glory to thee, God,
24b by thy paradise of eternal delight.
Hallelujah.

Syriac (S)
(I) 1a My heart was circumcised and its flower appeared,
1b and grace grew up in it,
1c and it bore fruits for the Lord.
2a For the Most High circumcised me by his holy spirit
2b and laid bare toward himself my kidneys/reins,
2c and filled me with his love.
3a And his circumcision became my salvation.
(II) 3b And I ran in his peace in the way of truth,
4 from the beginning and to the end I received his *gnōsis*/knowledge.
5a And I was firmly founded upon the rock of truth,
5b where he set me.
(III) 6a And the speaking water drew near to my lips
6b from the spring of the Lord [who is] without jealousy.
7 And I drank from the living water that dies not, and became drunk,

d 19b Manuscript correction of *τὸ φῶς* to *φῶς*.
e 22a Conjecture *λεῖμμα* for manuscript *θέλημα*.
f 22b Conjecture *δρῆσται* for manuscript ⲇⲣⲱⲥⲧⲉⲥ.

8a and my drunkenness was not without *gnōsis*/knowledge.
(IV) 8b But I abandoned vanities,
9a and returned toward the Most High, my God,
9b and became rich by his gracious gift.
10a And I left folly behind, dropped on the earth,
10b and I stripped it off and cast it from me.
11a And the Lord renewed me by his garment
11b and gained me by his light
12a and from above he gave me imperishable rest.
(V) 12b And I was like the earth that flourishes and laughs in its fruits,
13 and the Lord like the sun upon the face of the earth.
14a My eyes shone,
14b and my face received the dew.
15 And my breath rejoiced in the sweet fragrance of the Lord.
(VI) 16a And he brought me into his paradise,
16b where is the wealth of the Lord's joy.
(VII) 17 And I worshiped the Lord because of his glory
18a and said, Blessed, Lord, are they who are planted in thy earth,
18b and those who have a place in thy paradise
19a and grow in the growth of thy trees
19b and have passed from darkness to light.
20a Behold, all thy laborers are beautiful
20b who work good works
21a and turn from wickedness to thy kindness.
21b And they turned the bitterness of the trees from themselves,
21c when they were planted in your earth.
22a And everything was like thy remnant
22b and an eternal memorial of thy faithful servants.
(VIII) 23a For generous is the area in thy paradise,
23b and there is nothing in it that lies fallow,
23c but everything is filled with fruits.
(IX) 24a Glory to thee, God,
24b everlasting paradisiacal delight.
Hallelujah.

Introduction

Ode 11 survives in two manuscripts, one in Greek and one in Syriac.[1] Since this poem, in spite of the doxology (24), is not a hymn and, in spite of the themes of "spiritual circumcision" (1-3a) and "speaking waters" (6-8a), does not refer to the rite of baptism,[2] it cannot be described as a "Baptismal Hymn of Thanksgiving," similar to the "Hymns of Initiation," even though certain characteristics of the "form and language of the hymns of initiation" are found in this Ode.[3] With its abundant imagery, which really does not have "Abraham in mind,"[4] it is a metaphorical address by an "I" of indeterminate gender, a poetic tale whose audience does not come into view. Not until the "speech within the speech" (18-24)[5] does the redeemed speaker turn to the "Lord" (18a) or "God" (24), even now not to a person but to the unfathomable and forever hidden secret of the world. Throughout this Ode, described by Harris and Mingana as a "lovely psalm,"[6] the "I" is not the "Lord" (1c 𝔖, 6b, 11a, 13, 16b, 17, 18a), nor the "Most High" (2a, 9a), nor "God" (1c 𝔊, 9a, 24a).

It might have been expected that since the Greek manuscript of *Ode* 11[7] was first published in 1959, making it possible to assess the worth of an earlier back-translation,[8] the discussion on the original language of the *Odes* would have been finalized or at least moved a good step forward. This is unfortunately not the case, although Arthur Vööbus finds that "the superiority of the Syriac text" has finally been "confirmed"[9] and Luise Abramowski "can draw a valid conclusion (that the Odes were written in Syriac)."[10]

First it is necessary to emphasize that there is no *direct* connection between the Syriac codex H (ca. fourteenth century) and the Greek *P. Bodmer* XI (ca. third century).[11] Between the original manuscripts (𝔊* and 𝔖*) and the existing ones there is in each case an unknown series of copies. The seductive idea of a bilingual first publication cannot be proved:

> Thus probably not only *The Acts of Thomas* and HPrl [*The Hymn of the Pearl*], but also other important works of scripture, including Tatian's *Harmony* (*Diatessaron*, A.D. ca. 170), works of the Edessene Christian philosopher Bardaisan (born A.D. 154), and *The Odes of Solomon* (early second century A.D.?) were brought out in both Syriac and Greek.[12]

So if either 𝔊* or 𝔖* is taken to be the original version, it is still likely that among the unknown copies of each series some will have influenced the other. This is true even of possible copies in the Greek series, which may have been later than the existing manuscript. If 𝔊* was the original, then 𝔖* would have been translated

1 Mss.: *P. Bodmer* XI, 1–5 (𝔊); Codex H, 8a–9b (𝔖). Ed./trans.: Charlesworth, 49–59; Franzmann, 83–99; Lattke, 1:185–223 and 3:XXII–XXIV.

2 Contra Bernard, 73.

3 See Schille, 77, 79, 82–85.

4 Contra Abbott, 346.

5 See Lattke, *Oden*, 49.

6 Harris and Mingana, 2:269.

7 See Testuz; Lattke, *Bedeutung*, 1:1–23 and 1a:60–64 (facsimile).

8 Frankenberg, 13–14.

9 Vööbus, 289.

10 Abramowski, "Sprache," 90.

11 The experienced papyrologist Stuart R. Pickering, editor of *New Testament Textual Research Update*, suggests the following procedure for dating *P. Bodmer* XI: "I think that the fourth century provides a preferable working hypothesis, and the approach I would take is to ask to what extent, on palaeographical grounds, one can detach the hand from the fourth century" (letter of October 7, 1993).

12 Bentley Layton, *The Gnostic Scriptures: A New Translation with Annotations and Introductions* (Garden City, NY: Doubleday, 1987) 364. Layton mentions "bilingual publication" but also speaks correctly of "an early form of Syriac (the regional Aramaic dialect)" and probably accepts that "[one] version was translated from the other" (p. 364). The bilingual status of Syria, the northwestern part of the central Near East, has always been considered in the discussion of the original language of the *Odes of Solomon*, most recently by Drijvers: "Moreover, these writings were current in both a Syriac as well as a Greek version and there was a continuing tradition of translation in this bilingual area" (Han J. W. Drijvers, "Early Syriac Christianity: Some Recent Publications," *VC* 50 [1996] 173).

from a manuscript in the Greek series (including ⲋ*). In the same way, if ꞩ* was the original, ⲋ* would have been translated from the Syriac series (including ꞩ*).[13] In either case, it could be that for ꞩ "an Aramaic original was later rewritten in Middle Syriac."[14] So it may be possible to agree with Alfred Adam "that the present Syriac text is a faithful reproduction of an Aramaic original" without also accepting that the "*original* language of the Odes of Solomon" [emphasis added] was "an Aramaic which is closely related to the Syriac of Edessa."[15]

The dating of the *Odes of Solomon* to the early second century[16] and the wording of various passages argue *for* ⲋ*, but the commentary on this poem, which originated in the overlap of Judaism, early Christianity, and developing Gnosticism, must bear in mind what the Hebrew and Syriac scholar J. A. Emerton has to say at the end of his exhaustive study: "The most probable conclusion to be drawn is that the Odes of Solomon were composed in Syriac."[17]

Interpretation

■ **1-3a** Although the main topic of stanza I is "redemption" (3a) and not circumcision (of the foreskin) as such, the use of the terms *περιτέμνομαι, περιτέμνω,* and *περιτομή*,[18] or the Ethpe. ܐܬܓܙܪ (*ʾetgzar*), Pe. ܓܙܪ (*gzar*), and ܓܙܘܪܬܐ (*gzūrtā*), shapes and structures the overcharged imagery,[19] which is perhaps taken up again in stanza VII.[20] Even in 1a, the metaphor is already mixed: the circumcision of the heart, which should remove

13 In addition, even though the "original" was probably a single manuscript, the translator(s) may have had several manuscripts to use by the time they started work.

14 Klaus Beyer, letter of April 2, 1990; cf. Beyer, *ATTM*, 46, 59. Beyer's letter to me begins as follows: "You ask whether the Odes of Solomon were originally in Greek or Syriac, and I do not know. The text has ἐγένετο εἰς, but also the idiomatically Greek α-privativum." And at the end he says: "Since ἐγένετο εἰς also occurs in 8 it may have come from the LXX. That argues for a Greek original." Valuable insights can also be gained from Jan Joosten, "West Aramaic Elements in the Old Syriac and Peshitta Gospels," *JBL* 110 (1991) 271–89, and applied to the *Odes of Solomon* (e.g., p. 281 on the "Old Syriac parent text of C[uretonian] and S[inaitic]" and on later Syriac corrections "by a revisor of S" and "by a revisor of C").

15 The hypothesis "of a Hebrew original" (Carmignac, "Affinités," 96; cf. idem, "Recherches sur la langue originelle des Odes de Salomon," *RevQ* 4 [1963] 432), although refined after Grimme's early work (on Grimme, see Lattke, *Bedeutung*, 3:98–107) can be considered to have been dismissed (see already Rudolph, "Verfasser," 523–24). Carmignac's attempt "to prove that the Greek and Syriac texts of Ode xi are translations of a Hebrew poem is unconvincing" (Emerton, "Problems," 405). There is, however, value in many of Carmignac's observations on the connections between the *Odes of Solomon* and the Qumran scrolls.

16 Lattke, "Dating" = idem, *Bedeutung*, 4:113–32; idem, *Oden*, 20–35.

17 Emerton, "Problems," 406, repeated in Emerton, 687. The following note by Emerton (p. 687) on the original language of the *Odes of Solomon* is of special importance: "A technical point is perhaps worth noting in this connection. In the Odes, the third person preformative of the imperfect begins with *n*- (rather than *y*-). From the evidence of the Syriac inscriptions it seems that the change took place round about AD 200. . . . We cannot, of course, be precise in such matters, and there may well have been a time lag between the change in popular speech in some places and its appearance in inscriptions. Nevertheless, this suggests that we can scarcely date the present Syriac text of the Odes much before AD 200—though inevitably, in itself, it gives us no help in deciding whether that text is the author's original, or an edited version of the original, or a translation from Greek!"

18 BDAG, *s.vv.* περιτέμνω and περιτομή.

19 See Payne Smith, 1:699–700.

20 Franzmann, 92. Dividing 1a into a bicolon (including by Lattke, *Bedeutung*, 1:106–7) runs counter to the manuscript evidence. I shall revert to the monocolon (like Harris and Mingana, 2:265). This places the words that refer to circumcision as listed above at the beginning (1a), in the middle (2a), and near the end (3a).

the "hardness of heart" (cf. ἡ πώρωσις τῆς καρδίας [Mark 3:5; Eph 4:18], ἡ σκληροκαρδία [Mark 10:5 parr.; 16:14; cf. Rom 2:5], or τὸ σκληρὸν τῆς καρδίας [*Barn.* 9:5 in the context of *Barn.* 9]),[21] being associated with the plant imagery ("flower," "grow up," and "bear fruit") which has nothing to do with circumcision.[22] At the same time, the *hapax legomena* ܥܘܦܝܐ (*ʿup̄yā*) and ἄνθος ("flower") are not here used as "a type of that which does not last"[23] as in Isa 40:6-8, Jas 1:10-11, and 1 Pet 1:24. Although the Ethpe. of ܚܙܐ (*ḥzā*) is regularly used to translate ὤφθη, it can equally render the aorist passive of φαίνω.[24] The blossom of the heart, the soft and beautiful part of the metaphorical "seat of physical, spiritual and mental life"[25] (see Excursus 4), is exposed and thus becomes figuratively visible.

It is difficult to agree with Franzmann when she says, "There is no basic difference between the Greek and Syriac texts"[26] of 1b-c. The individual differences may not weigh heavily in textual criticism in 1b (word sequence; missing καί or δέ) or in 1c (on the alternation between κύριος ["Lord"] and θεός ["God"], cf., e.g., 5:11 and 25:1). But syntactically the Syriac text in 1b-c is quite plain (especially the verb in 1c referring to "heart"). In 𝔊, the subject of 1c is ambiguous, and the expression and construction of 1b combine to suggest a different meaning: "Since . . . καί [and] is missing and χάρις [grace] is placed at the beginning, someone with no knowledge of the Syriac would take χάρις to be the subject" of ἐκαρποφόρησεν.[27] It is difficult to decide whether the Greek image (grace bore fruit) has been moralizingly diluted or the Syriac image (the heart bore fruit) has been theologically emended (see Excursus 11 below).

The equivalence of the words in 1b accords with normal usage, although the metaphorical use of ܐܝܥܐ (*ʾiʿā*) would correspond better to ἀνατέλλω (cf. Isa 43:19; Ps 84:12 LXX). The horticultural vocabulary, however, almost forces the use of the intransitive βλαστάνω,[28] as in Matt 13:26.[29] The subject χάρις/ܛܝܒܘܬܐ (*ṭaybūṯā*), which is elsewhere likened to a garment (4:6; 20:7) or even personified (33:1, 10; see Excursus 33), is not here identified with the blossom of 1a but leads its own metaphorical life as a theological power.

The Syriac of 1c returns to the subject "heart," while 𝔊 extends the plant metaphor of 1b and allows the "grace," derived from no-thing and no-body in this world,[30] to "bear fruit,"[31] and that, theologically, for God alone (as against the ambiguity of the "Lord" in 𝔖). If the use of the Pe. ܥܒܕ (*ʿḇaḏ*) in 𝔖 should go back to 𝔖*, the expected Greek, to judge from biblical translations, would be ποιεῖν καρπόν.[32] But the synonym καρποφορεῖν, actually found in 𝔊, has been occasionally (e.g., Wis 10:7) translated by ܥܒܕ ܦܐܖ̈ܐ (*ʿḇaḏ pērē*).

If there is a verbal influence from Rom 7:4 (ἵνα καρποφορήσωμεν τῷ θεῷ, "that we may bear fruit for God"), 𝔊 has clearly understood the Pauline concept that any imperative depends on the indicative justifying faith τῇ αὐτοῦ χάριτι ("by his grace"; Rom 3:24; cf. 5:1-2). The later moralizing tendency is seen in 𝔖, but also in *Barn.* 11:11 in a *pesher*-style interpretation of baptism (ἀναβαίνομεν καρποφοροῦντες ἐν τῇ καρδίᾳ, "we come up bearing the fruit . . . in our heart").[33]

Excursus 11: "Fruit" and "Fruits" in the *Odes of Solomon*

The extensive research by Petra von Gemünden on plant imagery and metaphor[34] means that this can be a short summary dealing primarily with the question, Whose are the καρποί or ܦܐܖ̈ܐ (*pērē*) in each instance? In two cases, it must be determined who or

21 See Wengst, 160–65.
22 For the narrative in stanza I, 𝔖 uses the perfect as *tempus historicum* (Nöldeke §255), while 𝔊 employs forms of the aorist indicative.
23 BDAG, *s.v.* ἄνθος.
24 Payne Smith, 1:1234; BDAG, *s.v.* ὁράω, esp. A1d; *s.v.* φαίνω, esp. 2 and 3.
25 BDAG, *s.v.* καρδία.
26 Franzmann, 96.
27 Klaus Beyer, letter of April 2, 1990 (n. 14 above).
28 BDAG, *s.v.* βλαστάνω.
29 See Payne Smith, 1:1611; Frankenberg (p. 13) had already translated it by ἀναβλαστάνω.
30 BDAG, *s.v.* χάρις.
31 BDAG, *s.v.* καρποφορέω.
32 Payne Smith, 2:2766; BDAG, *s.v.* καρπός.
33 Wengst, 130, 172; Lake, 1:382–83. Taken together with *Barn.* 5:7 (cf. *Ode* 31:12-13) and *Barn.* 11:10 (cf. *Ode* 11:16c 𝔊), this would be another clue to the early influence (and therefore early date) of the *Odes of Solomon*.
34 Gemünden, *Vegetationsmetaphorik*, esp. 519–20, on the *Odes of Solomon*.

what "bore" the "fruits" (11:1c) or brought them up (16:2c).[35]

The images of the soil that "flourishes and laughs by its fruits" and of the trees, whose fruits "laughed" (11:16e 𝔊), are easiest to understand. They also fit with the *δένδρα ὡραῖα καὶ καρποφόρα* (11:16c 𝔊), which are transferred into a utopian paradise and can be expanded to take in the abundance of "fruits" to be found there (11:23b 𝔖) even if these "trees"/"plants" (cf. 11:19; 11:21) and "fruits" are perhaps coded references to the blessed (see on 11:18 below).[36]

Ode 7:1c is isolated because the stress is on "joy" (7:1b, 2a). In the emotional and erotic images, however, what is important is that the beloved reaps the "fruits" of the lover.[37] But since joy is a movement of the heart (cf. 6:14 ℭ; 32:1), this passage may find an indirect connection through the fact that the term "heart" occurs surprisingly often in the same context as "fruit."[38] This finding is especially important for the interpretation of 11:1c and 16:2c. Other points worth noting are that an indirect object is very rare (8:2 and 11:1, in both cases "Lord" = "God"), that there is only one adverbial description (17:13, "in[to] hearts"), and that there is only one apposition to provide any form of definition (8:2, "holy life"). So it is necessary in the fruit metaphors to seek the originators and/or owners in order to sort the passages.[39]

The "Lord" (= "God"), who is like a wreath, occupies the first place: his "fruits" are called "full and ripe" in a prayer addressed directly to him (1:5a). Also in prayer it is said, "nor wilt thou be without fruits" (4:4b). The "fruit of peace," which the living Redeemer is permitted, mythologically, to speak, also belongs to the Lord (10:2b). If it is "grace" that "bore fruit" (11:1c 𝔊), the reading belongs here (but see below). Whether this "fruit" means the "love" of 11:2c will be considered later. Since "truth" comes from the "Lord" (12:1a), the "fruits of truth," which flow from the lips of the Gnostic, must refer at least indirectly to this Lord (12:2a). In its confidence of salvation, the speaking "I" places the "rest" of the "Lord" in parallel with the "fruits" of the Lord's "love" (14:6; see on 14:7 below).

In the short first-person discourse of a redeemed one, the "Lord," the "Most High," is finally the author of the "fruits" of this person's "labor" since it is the Lord's "word" that gave them (37:3). Here again "rest" is parallel to "fruits" (37:4). The genitive phrase "of my labors" is not to be understood ethically, but in connection with the speaking "lips" of the "heart" (37:2a). In view of 11:1b-c it may be noted that the "grace of the Lord" is mentioned here also (37:4).

The "root," whose "fruits are forever" (38:17c), was planted by the "Lord" (38:17a). Therefore, the "fruits," which may stand for human beings, come predestined from the "Lord" and no other.

In only one passage does the phrase "my fruits" refer to the redeemed Redeemer, who "sowed" them "in hearts" (17:13), which leaves the impression that the seeds sprouted in the hearts and the hearts then bore "fruit."[40]

In another unique passage, the speaking "I," one who is to be redeemed, hopes to bear "fruits" (14:7b). A question to be considered later is whether these are the previously mentioned "fruits" of the "love" of the "Lord" (14:6b) or a hymnological parallel to the "odes" of "truth" (14:7a; cf. also 37:3).

It is now clear that in certain passages the "fruits," which ultimately originate from God, can be organized by the more or less abstract genitive phrase that accompanies them: "fruits of his peace" (10:2), "fruits of truth" (12:2), "fruits of thy love"

35 Of the fifteen Syriac occurrences, only one is in the singular ܦܐܪܐ (*pērā*); *καρποί* occurs three times, once as a loanword (*Ode* 1:5) and once in the purely Greek material (11:16e). The adjective *καρποφόρος* is also peculiar to 𝔊 (11:16c). The verb *καρποφορέω* is found twice, the second time without a Syriac equivalent ("everything is filled with fruits" [𝔖]). 𝔖 uses numerous verbs expressing "to bring in" (7:1, Aph. ܐܥܠ), "to bring forth" (8:2, Aph. ܐܝܬܝ), "to bear" (11:1; 14:7, ܝܠܕ), "to bring up" (16:2, ܐܣܩ), "to give" (37:3, ܝܗܒ), "to speak" (10:2, Pa. ܡܠܠ), and "to declare" (12:2, Pa. ܚܘܝ).

36 There may be similarly coded references elsewhere, e.g., 1:5; 4:4; 11:1 𝔊 (?); 14:7; 37:3 (?); 38:17.

37 As we shall see later, there are other concepts besides "joy" which help to define "fruits."

38 Cf. 4:3c; 8:1; 10:1b; 11:1; 16:2; 17:13; 37:2.

39 *Ode* 16:2c could be "his fruits," referring to the "Lord," but that is unlikely (see below).

40 It is worth quoting a note by Friedrich Hauck: "In Iranian (as in Persian and Mandaean literature) the soul is often described as a tree or a plant, which is planted by the messenger of life with a view to bringing forth fruit. Paradise is the garden, planted by God, in which the souls of the perfected are plants that bear rich and precious fruits" ("*καρπός, κτλ.*," *ThWNT* 3 [1938] 617; cf. *TDNT* 3:614). "Soul" and "heart" are anthropological parallels and even synonyms.

(14:6), "fruits of my labors" (37:3), and "fruits of the root" (38:17). The otherwise isolated passage 7:1c ("fruits of joy"; see above) and the two enigmatic ones, 11:1c and 16:2c, also belong to this group by virtue of the genitive or a possessive suffix.

Ode 16:2 may be illuminated also by 8:2, for both contain the sequence of images heart–love–lips–fruits. Syntactically, the infinitive "to bring forth (fruit)" (8:2a) depends rather on the growing of "love" (8:1b) than on the earlier "open your hearts" (8:1a). So the implied subject of 16:2c may also be "love" rather than "heart."[41] And even the direct object could refer to "love": "and brought up its/his fruits to my lips" (16:2c).

If then the metaphorical "heart" occurs regularly together with the imagery of fruit but is never involved in bringing forth or bearing the "fruit" or "fruits," the reading of 11:1c 𝔖 must be considered aberrant. Perhaps a feminine ܥܒܕܬ (*ʿeb̲dat̲*), referring to the abstract "grace," was emended to the masculine ܥܒܕ (*ʿb̲ad̲*), because of the theme "heart," at some point in the sequence of manuscripts preceding H. If the image was originally the "fruits of grace," it would have fitted well into the set of phrases with the abstract-metaphorical genitive discussed above.

The subject of 2a-c, a parallel tricolon,[42] is the "Most High," that is, "God" (9a), and not any this- or otherworldly being (see Excursus 17). There is a long history behind the metaphor of 2a. One of the major prophets already lamented threateningly, "all the house of Israel is uncircumcised in heart" (Jer 9:26). From the middle of the second century B.C.E., this prophecy was current among the groups seeking to reform Judaism: "I [i.e., the Lord] will circumcise the foreskin of their heart and the foreskin of the heart of their offspring. And I will give them a holy spirit" (*Jub.* 1:23;[43] cf. Deut 10:16; 30:6).[44] A century later the Wicked Priest is accused because "he did not circumcise the foreskin of his heart" (1QpHab xi.13).[45] The sectarian counsel to "circumcise in the Community the foreskin of evil inclinations and stiffness of neck that they may lay a foundation of truth for Israel" (1QS v.5)[46] may have been as familiar to the people of the *Odes of Solomon* as Paul's emphatic statement in Rom 2:29 that true circumcision is *περιτομὴ καρδίας ἐν πνεύματι οὐ γράμματι* ("circumcision is of the heart, in the spirit and not according to the letter"),[47] which may also have influenced the Gnostic *Gospel of Thomas*, e.g., log. 53: ⲡⲥⲃ̄ⲃⲉ ⲙ̄ⲙⲉ ϩⲙ̄ ⲡⲛ̄ⲁ ("the true circumcision in the spirit [*πνεῦμα*]").[48] The redeemed person, in witnessing that his metaphorical circumcision was the consequence of the sacred spiritual power of the Most High (cf. 3:10; etc.), acknowledges that the existential hardness of heart cannot be erased by emotional thrills or rationally moral boosting.

"Reins [kidneys]," like "heart," stands for the "inwardness" of a person.[49] The verb form *ἐγύμνωσε* is occasionally found elsewhere as equivalent to the *hapax legomenon* ܓܠܐ (*glā*).[50] So the second statement keeps the image of cutting, but adds the existential and theological acknowledgment that no human analysis or inquisition can lay bare the depths of being.

𝔊 here offers an alternative reading *ἐγύμνωσα* ("I laid bare"), which needs to be considered together with the prepositional phrase *πρὸς αὐτόν/αὑτόν*. The corresponding expression ܠܘܬܗ (*lwāt̲eh*) in 𝔖 can

41 See Gemünden, *Vegetationsmetaphorik*, 402: In "*Odes of Solomon* 7:1; 14:6-7; 16:2 the fruit imagery is directly linked to the motif of love."

42 Franzmann, 92.

43 Klaus Berger, *Das Buch der Jubiläen* (JSHRZ 2.3; Gütersloh: Mohn, 1981) 318.

44 Roger Le Déaut suggests Deut 30:6 as the origin of *Ode* 11:1-3; see "Le thème de la circoncision du coeur (Dt. xxx 6; Jér. iv 4) dans les versions anciennes (LXX et Targum) et à Qumrân," in *Congress Volume: Vienna* 1980 (*VTSup* 32; Leiden: Brill, 1981) 197–98.

45 Vermes, 289; Maier, *Qumran-Essener*, 1:164.

46 Vermes, 67; Maier, *Qumran-Essener*, 1:178.

47 See Käsemann, *Romans*, 72, 75 (German, 67, 70); Brendan Byrne, *Romans* (Sacra Pagina 6; Collegeville, Minn.: Liturgical Press, 1996) 104.

48 Kurt Aland, ed., *Synopsis Quattuor Evangeliorum* (15th ed.; Stuttgart: Deutsche Bibelgesellschaft, 1996; 4th corr. printing 2005) 532. William D. Stroker lists the Coptic text on the value of circumcision with parallels; see Stroker, *Extracanonical Sayings of Jesus* (SBL Resources for Biblical Study 18; Atlanta: Scholars Press, 1989) 33–34 (A29); cf. Käsemann, *Romans,* 75 (German, 70): "The final link in the chain is Col 2:11ff. with its understanding of baptism as the circumcision of Christ effected by the Spirit." The link between baptism and circumcision, however, is only secondary; see Everett Ferguson, "Spiritual Circumcision in Early Christianity," *SJT* 41 (1988) 490–92.

49 BDAG, *s.v.* *νεφρός*. Cf. Ps 7:10; Jer 11:20; 17:10; 20:12; Rev 2:23.

50 Payne Smith, 1:716; BDAG, *s.v.* *γυμνόω*. But

only be reflexive, so 𝔊* must also be assumed to have had the contract reflexive pronoun αὑτόν.[51] This does not help to decide the original language of the *Odes*, since πρὸς αὐτόν was rendered by ܠܘܬܗ (*lwāṯeh*), "very often" by ܠܢܦܫܗ (*l-napšeh*), or "more rarely" by ܠܩܢܘܡܗ (*la-qnōmeh*).[52] Whatever the origin of ἐγύμνωσα, it is a variant in the history of the Greek text. If the variant is accepted, αυτον (without diacritics in the manuscript) must be read as αὑτόν: "and I laid bare my innermost self to him." This transforms the theological idea of 2b into an anthropological one and dilutes its profundity.

Nor does 2c give any help in deciding the original language—the use of the preposition ܡܢ (*men*) with the verb ܡܠܐ (*mlā*) is unusual[53] (see on 12:1 below), but the use of the genitive after πληρόω is quite normal.[54] The verbs of 2c are, in a sense, opposite to those of 2b.

The image in itself is not difficult to understand, but there is a question whether the equivalent terms ἀγάπη and ܚܘܒܐ (*ḥubbā*) are meant to refer back to the terms "heart," "grace," and "fruits" in 1a-c.[55] As the power of grace itself bore fruit for "God" the "Lord" (1b-c),[56] so the "Most High" filled the inward parts laid bare toward him with his love. A person who can make this statement, rooted in the highest and most beautiful human reality, *coram Deo* of his own self, knows himself to be fundamentally affirmed and protected but also in touch with the mystery and meaning of the infinite world.[57]

With 3a, the "I" reaches the crux of stanza I. "Redemption" has *already* taken place (see Excursus 5). Thus, this final statement of salvation takes its place along a line of development that is both early Gnostic and early Christian and, taking in the teaching of Paul, leads to the paradox of realized eschatology. Comparing the differences between 𝔖 and 𝔊 with similar variations in vocabulary and word sequence in, for instance, the texts of the New Testament makes it clear that there are no wider consequences to draw. Even the fact that passages such as Gen 2:7 ("Adam became a living soul") are classed as "Hebraisms"[58] does not lead to the conclusion that the Syriac of this or other verses (10:4; 28:10; 35:2; 38:3) was translated from a Hebrew original (see already Gen 2:7 LXX, ἐγένετο ὁ ἄνθρωπος εἰς ψυχὴν ζῶσαν). And even without the influence of the Septuagint, the construction γίνεσθαι εἴς τι, as in the Greek text of this Ode, can be found in Greek in place of constructions with a double nominative.[59] The placing of ܦܘܪܩܢܐ (*purqānā*) at the end of the monocolon does not mean that 𝔖 necessarily laid extra stress on the term. The difference between 𝔖 and 𝔊 only reveals different ways of emphasizing the same soteriological concept.[60]

■ **3b-5** The "I" continues its metaphorical narration with a complete change of topic and a vocabulary strongly influenced by the psalms. The wording of 3b depends not on Wis 6:22[61] but on Ps 118:30-32 LXX

Frankenberg (p. 13) used the more common ἀνεκάλυψε.

51 See BDAG, *s.v.* ἑαυτοῦ.

52 Nöldeke §223.

53 Payne Smith, 2:2117–18.

54 BDAG, *s.v.* πληρόω, 1b.

55 Cf. 8:1; 14:6; 16:2; 18:1; 41:6; also Excursus 2.

56 In this verse it is more probable that θεός was translated as ܡܪܝܐ (*māryā*), because θεός occurs far less often, which makes it *lectio difficilior* than a translation in the reverse direction.

57 In view of the passages Deut 10:16 and 30:6, quoted in relation to 2a, which refer to the commandment to love God, and in view of Luke 11:42 ("love for God"; see Schürmann, *Lukasevangelium*, 2:314) and especially of John 5:42 (τὴν ἀγάπην τοῦ θεοῦ οὐκ ἔχετε ἐν ἑαυτοῖς, "you have not the love of God within you"), it may be asked whether the "fruit" of "grace" might not be love *directed to* the Most High, that is, whether this is a an objective genitive, although Bultmann remarks on it: "it actually makes no difference whether one takes τοῦ θεοῦ as an objective or subjective genitive or whether one believes that there is an intentional ambiguity here." See Bultmann, *Das Evangelium*, 202; ET: *John*, 269 n. 2.

58 See Nöldeke §247.

59 BDAG, *s.v.* γίνομαι, esp. 4. See on 8a below.

60 On the prepositional phrase εἰς σωτηρίαν, cf. Exod 15:2; Ps 117:14 LXX; Isa 12:2; Rom 1:16; 10:1, 10; 2 Cor 7:10; Phil 1:19; 2 Thess 2:13; 2 Tim 3:15; 1 Pet 2:2; *Barn.* 17:1; *1 Clem.* 45:1. For 11:3a (and other passages), reference should be made to Emerton, "Problems," 395–400, who thoroughly discusses "quotations of the LXX in the Greek Ode."

61 Harris and Mingana, 2:270.

with its use of the words ἔδραμον and καρδίαν (see 1a above) and the phrase ὁδὸν ἀληθείας ("way of truth").[62] The erroneous repetition of ܒܐܘܪܚܐ (*b-urḥā*) in H may be due to the different word order in 𝔊, where the accusative of ὁδός follows the aorist of τρέχω in accordance with normal usage. This "running is an emphatic form of 'walking.'"[63] "Way" occurs also as a parallel to "running" (7:2), but it is the frequent juxtaposition of "way" and "truth" that demands notice.[64] The prepositional construction ἐν εἰρήνῃ αὐτοῦ/ܒܫܠܡܗ (*ba-šlāmeh*), with its pronoun/suffix referring to the "Lord" of 2a-c, refers to the total image of running in the way of peace (cf. 35:1; 36:8).

"Beginning" and "end" in 4, describing completion, can refer temporally to the running or spatially to the way, but hardly to the direct object of λαμβάνω/ܢܣܒ (*nsaḇ*). Similar expressions are found elsewhere (6:4; 7:14; 26:7) and bear no relation to Deut 11:12.[65] The equivalent verbs (cf. 15:6; 23:2), to which the synonymous ܩܒܠ (*qabbel*) should be added,[66] do not express any active "taking" but a passive "receiving." In considering the object of these verbs the question arises whether the "knowledge (𝔖)/understanding (𝔊)" comes from and is given by the Most High or is knowledge *about* him.[67] Either is possible. What is important is that σύνεσις/ܝܕܥܬܐ (*ʾidaʿtā*) is not an achievement of human "reason" but a theological gift (see Excursus 7).[68] This meaning of σύνεσις is a synonym of soteriological γνῶσις (or ἐπίγνωσις). If these terms for "understanding" in 𝔊 and 𝔖 were already found in 𝔊* and 𝔖*, it is more likely that ܝܕܥܬܐ was used to translate σύνεσις than the reverse, because ܝܕܥܬܐ would have been preferentially translated by γνῶσις or ἐπίγνωσις rather than the less common σύνεσις.[69]

The wordplay with the root ܫܪ (*šr[r]*) in 5a 𝔖 (cf. 3b) does not prove that Syriac was the original language. Syriac translators may also have been "fond of paronomasia."[70] A. F. J. Klijn, however, remarks correctly that the adjectival phrase ἀπὸ στερεᾶς πέτρας is a lead to the correct interpretation of the Syriac "genitive of quality": "on the rock of truth" = "on a strong (firm) rock."[71] Both the passive aorist of στηρίζω[72] and the Ethpa. of ܫܪ (*šar*) have the connotation of soteriological strengthening.[73] If the use of ἀπό in place of ὑπό[74] is well within the range of possibilities, only Vööbus could maintain that there can be "no road from the Greek ΑΠΟ to Syriac ܥܠ."[75] In the present state of 𝔊 and 𝔖, there is a slight difference in meaning. 𝔖 emphasizes the metaphorical "rock,"[76] while in 𝔊 ἡ στερεὰ πέτρα—on a line of development from Isa 50:7 via *Odes Sol.* 11:5a to *Barn.* 5:15 and 6:4[77]—is not only a firm foundation but also a source of reinforcement and support.

Could there be an allusion, in connection with "water" (see stanza III below), to the "rock in the wilder-

62 The phrase ὁδὸς ἀληθείας is found also in Wis 5:6; 2 Pet 2:2; *1 Clem.* 35:5. On Wis 6:22, see the comments of Emerton, "Problems," 374–76, although he finally admits to some doubts: "were it not for the uncertainty whether there is, in fact, an echo of the passage in the Apocrypha" (p. 376).

63 Otto Bauernfeind, "τρέχω, κτλ.," *ThWNT* 8 (1969) 229; cf. *TDNT* 8:229.

64 See 17:7-8; 24:12-13; 33:8; 38:7; for the inverse, see 15:6 and 31:2; and see Excursus 1.

65 Contra Carmignac, "Affinités," 83.

66 See esp. 8:8; 9:5; 17:14; 20:9; 31:6; 41:3.

67 See Emerton, 700; see also the comment on 2c above.

68 BDAG, *s.v.* σύνεσις.

69 See Eph 3:4; Col 2:2. On the expression σύνεσιν λαμβάνειν ("receive understanding") in *Hermas, Sim.* 79 (IX.2).6, see Lake, 2:222–23; and Ehrman, 2:390–91; on σύνεσις as a Gnostic aeon, see Lampe, 1325: "as Valent[inian] aeon paired with Ἀείνους, Iren.*haer.* 1.1.2."

70 See Charlesworth, 54. Vööbus's conclusion (p. 280) that "this sort of thing can only occur if Syriac is the original language" is in this respect not correct.

71 A. F. J. Klijn, review of Testuz in *NedThT* 14 (1959–60) 447.

72 BDAG, *s.v.* στηρίζω.

73 See 36:8; 38:16; 40:5; and see Payne Smith, 2:4299. Since στηρίζω and στερεός are derived from different roots, it is not quite correct to say that "the word-play within 5a remains" (Franzmann, 96). Carmignac, "Affinités," 83, also refers to a "play on words."

74 See BDAG, *s.v.* ἀπό.

75 Vööbus, 280. Vööbus's "explanation" for the "aberration" is again that "only Syriac is the original language" (p. 280). But according to his paleographical thesis, it is equally possible that ܥܠ developed from ܠ (the sign of the *nomen agens*).

76 Cf. Pss 27:5; 40:3; 61:3 in Syriac [ܥܠ ܫܘܥܐ/ܟܐܦܐ] with Pss 26:5; 39:3; 60:3 LXX (ἐν πέτρᾳ or ἐπὶ πέτραν).

77 Wengst, 150–53.

ness" from which Moses struck water with a rod (cf. Exod 17:6; Num 20:8-11), and which Paul in 1 Cor 10:4 calls πνευματικὴ πέτρα ("spiritual rock")[78] and identifies allegorically with ὁ Χριστός? But, just as the "way of truth" in 3b cannot be likened to the Johannine Jesus,[79] so any specifically Christian interpretation of the rock symbolism or of the Ode as a whole must be carefully avoided.[80]

A Christian reader will probably connect 5b with Eph 2:6 ([ὁ θεός] . . . συνήγειρεν καὶ συνεκάθισεν ἐν τοῖς ἐπουρανίοις ἐν Χριστῷ Ἰησοῦ, "God . . . raised us up with him, and made us sit with him in the heavenly places in Christ Jesus"), but the narrative perfect of συγκαθίζω[81] as well as the perfect of the Aph. of ܬܩܢ (*tqen*) preceded by the unemphasized pronoun[82] serve to underline the idea of making firm in 5a. Greek translators of ܣ* would be unlikely to have hit on the unusual compound συγκαθίζω as a transitive equivalent of ܐܬܩܢ (*ʾatqen*).[83] On the other hand, in a Syriac translation from 𝔊*, the prefix σύν would bite the dust. It is, however, very possible that συγκαθίζω, with its connotation of fellowship, represents a Christian strain in the Greek tradition of the *Odes*, which may have been occasioned by a christological interpretation of πέτρα (see, e.g., Justin *Dial.* 113.6, λίθος καὶ πέτρα . . . ὁ Χριστός, "Christ . . . a Stone and a Rock,"[84] where the next paragraph refers to "circumcision of the heart" [καρδίας περιτομὴν περιετμήθησαν; see stanza I above]). What the imagery of stanza II may have meant originally is probably unrecoverable today.

■ **6-8a** Stanza III, with its new themes, forms a unit of two bicola.[85] The images of "water" and "spring" are only loosely connected to the preceding images of "way" and "rock" (see stanza II above). The connection is probably due to external nature rather than any literary model.[86] In 𝔊, the verb λαλέω (6a) and the noun ἀλογιστία (8a), with related meaning, form a sort of *inclusio* to stanza III.

A "stream of water" may "produce sounds."[87] This poetic image of "speaking water" in 6a, then, refers to the nature of flowing water and not to any deeper meaning extending to the soteriological (cf. 6:18; 30:1).[88] Although ἐγγίζω and ܩܪܒ (*qreb*) are both *hapax legomena*, there is a similar image of "approaching in space"[89] by the use of the Ethpa. in 19:1 ("a cup of milk was offered to me"). In 30:5, a living spring "flowed" from the "lips of the Lord," but in this verse the redeeming water "drew near to" the "lips" of the speaking "I".[90]

78 BDAG, *s.v.* πέτρα.

79 Contra Charlesworth, 54, who refers to John 14:6.

80 See Diettrich, 40, who interprets *Ode* 11 as a "Jewish song." On the symbolism of the rock in the Syriac church, see Robert Murray, *Symbols of Church and Kingdom: A Study in Early Syriac Tradition* (London/New York: Cambridge University Press, 1975) 205–38; on 11:5 but also on 22:12 and 31:11, see idem, "The Rock and the House on the Rock: A chapter in the ecclesiological symbolism of Aphraates and Ephrem," *OrChrP* 30 (1964) 352–54 (in Appendix I: "Firm Rock").

81 BDF and BDR §343.

82 "Unaccented ܗܘ before a third masculine singular perfect is idiomatically Syriac" (Klaus Beyer, letter of April 2, 1990; see n. 14 above).

83 Payne Smith, 2:4485–86.

84 Goodspeed, 230; Marcovich, *Dialogus*, 265; ANF 1:255.

85 H marks no division in 6. The separation of 6 into 6a-b is necessary, but 7 ought not to be segmented into 7a and b (contra Franzmann, 83, 85, 93). ܣ again—as in stanza I—uses the perfect as *tempus historicum* (Nöldeke §255) for the narration in stanza III while 𝔊 again has indicative forms of the aorist.

86 Even with the terms μεθυσθήσονται and πηγὴ ζωῆς in Ps 35:9-10 LXX, it is incorrect to say: "Here we have clearly the key to the Odist's expressions; here is the fountain of the Lord of which the believer drinks plenteously, and here is the divine intoxication" (Harris and Mingana, 2:269). See already the criticism of Hans Lewy, *Sobria ebrietas: Untersuchungen zur Geschichte der antiken Mystik* (BZNW 9; Gießen: Töpelmann, 1929) 85.

87 BDAG, *s.v.* λαλέω; cf. φωνὴ ὑδάτων in BDAG, *s.v.* ὕδωρ, 1.

88 The discovery of the Greek text has shown that the back-translations of Frankenberg (p. 13) and Lewy (*Sobria*, 84) (ὕδατα λογικά) were over-determined.

89 BDAG, *s.v.* ἐγγίζω.

90 See Excursus 16. There may be a connection between τὸ ὕδωρ τὸ λαλοῦν (6a) and ὕδωρ δὲ ζῶν καὶ λαλοῦν (Ignatius *Rom.* 7:2; Fischer, 190; Ehrman, 278–79 ["living water, which is also speaking"]), although the contexts are very different. If the late date for Ignatius's epistles (Reinhard M. Hübner, "Thesen zur Echtheit und Datierung der sieben Briefe des Ignatius von Antiochien," *ZAC* 1 [1997] 66–67) and the early date for the *Odes of Solomon* (Lattke, "Dating" = idem, *Bedeutung*, 4:113–32; idem, *Oden*, 20–53; see also Introduction, sec. 4) were both correct, there could be only

In 6b the Syriac and Greek texts differ slightly. The phrase πηγὴ ζωῆς ("spring of life") in 𝔊 originates in biblical tradition[91] and is not merely a "symbol of doctrine."[92] In 𝔖, unlike 30:1, ܚܝ̈ܐ (*ḥayyē*) does not occur, although it appears with emphasis in 7 (see below). Perhaps it was misplaced at some point in the sequence of copying. So the genitive of ܡܪܝܐ (*māryā*) refers immediately to the "spring," while the genitive of κύριος ("Lord") can refer equally well to the "living spring" and to "life" itself. What is important, in both cases, is that the metaphors of "water," "spring," and "life" allude to what can be procured, in this world, not even by means of sacraments.[93] Even if the "water" should stand for "*gnosis* that can be experienced,"[94] it is still a gift and cannot be alienated. The final predicate (ܕܠܐ ܚܣܡ [*d-lā ḥsām*], masculine *status absolutus*) must refer to the "Lord," as is made plain by the slightly different Greek construction.[95] Even so, ἀφθονία stresses "abundance"[96] and demands more than a psychological interpretation.[97]

Since the discovery of the Greek text of *Ode* 11,[98] it is clear that many of Hans Lewy's opinions[99] cannot be supported. This is especially true for 7-8a, even if he is *conceptually* correct in saying that "the author here describes the μέθη τῆς γνώσεως," which "on the basis of Gnosticism" reveals "a striking parallelism to Philo's θεία καὶ νηφάλιος μέθη."[100] *Linguistically,* the "drunkenness caused by this divine water" is, however, not described as "a μέθη τῆς γνώσεως" nor placed "diametrically opposite to the μέθη τῆς ἀγνωσίας."[101] Finally, 7 and 8a would provide persuasive arguments for Greek rather than Syriac as the "original language" of the *Odes*.[102]

Accepting the appearance of ܚܝ̈ܐ (*ḥayyē*) as a variant within the Syriac tradition (see above), the preposition ܡܢ (*men*), which is placed after the fairly common Pe. ܐܫܬܝ (*ʾeštī*)[103] and the Pe. ܪܘܐ/ܪܘܝ (*rwā/rwī*),[104] found only here, is more important than might be thought at first. Because in 𝔊 there is no ἀπό or ἐκ that would be its equivalent and the first verb, πίνω,[105] is separated by the passive of μεθύσκω[106] from the accusative of ὕδωρ which it governs, the question arises whether a Syriac original, *with* the preposition, would not have been more literally translated into Greek. If the translation was in the other direction, the insertion of ܡܢ is idiomatically necessary (see Excursus 6). The expression ὕδωρ

one explanation forthcoming: "This lovely psalm was known . . . also to Ignatius" (Harris and Mingana, 2:269). On Ignatius *Rom.* 7:2, see William R. Schoedel, *Ignatius of Antioch: A Commentary on the Letters of Ignatius of Antioch* (Hermeneia; Philadelphia: Fortress, 1985) 185.

91 See Ps 35:10 LXX; Jer 2:13; 17:13; cf. John 4:14; Rev 21:6; *Barn.* 11:2.

92 Siegbert Uhlig, *Das äthiopische Henochbuch* (JSHRZ 5.6; Gütersloh: Mohn, 1984) 720, on *1 Enoch* 96:6.

93 See Hans-Josef Klauck, *Herrenmahl und hellenistischer Kult: Eine religionsgeschichtliche Untersuchung zum ersten Korintherbrief* (NTAbh N.F. 15; Münster: Aschendorff, 1982) 213–14, with a reference to a Gnostic "water eucharist."

94 Heinrich Schlier, "Zur Mandäerfrage," *ThR* N.F. 5 (1933) 89.

95 See the commentary on 3:6. Note that 𝔊 does not use the adverb ἀφθόνως (see Frankenberg, 13, and Lewy, *Sobria*, 84) but the prepositional phrase ἐν ἀφθονίᾳ αὐτοῦ.

96 BDAG, *s.v.* ἀφθονία.

97 See Charlesworth, 52: "generously."

98 Testuz.

99 Lewy, *Sobria*, 82–89.

100 Ibid., 86.

101 Ibid., 85.

102 Contra Lewy, *Sobria*, 83, who, however, declares that the determination of the original language is "irrelevant" for his purposes "since there is full agreement that the author belonged to both languages and cultures and had internalized the vocabulary and ideas of the Gnostics who wrote in Greek."

103 Payne Smith, 2:4349; cf. 8:16; 19:1; 30:7; 38:12.

104 Payne Smith, 2:3840.

105 Bauer and Aland, *s.v.* πίνω; there is no reference to this passage in BDAG, *s.v.* πίνω.

106 See Bauer and Aland, *s.v.* μεθύσκω, which erroneously cites *Ode* 11:6 *s.v.* μεθύω. A remark by Franzmann (p. 97) on 7 𝔊 shows that her division of 7 𝔖 into 7a-b is arbitrary: "7 would require *ΑΠΟ ΥΔΑΤΟΣ ΤΟΥ ΑΘΑΝΑΤΟΥ* to maintain the parallelism of 6b and 7b in Syriac."

τὸ ἀθάνατον ("immortal water"), amplified in ܣ by ܚܝܐ (*ḥayyē*),[107] introduced probably from 6b, has the same meaning as ὕδωρ ζῶν, derived from biblical tradition (cf. Zech 14:8; John 4:10-11; 7:38), an expression whose influence extends further (Ignatius *Rom.* 7:2).[108] This metaphor of the "immortal water" that does not exist in real life forms part of the "immortality" that can only be asserted of God (see Table 1).

In opposition to the "intoxication of ignorance"[109] in 38:12-13, the speaking "I" in 8a explains the *ebrietas*[110] attained through the theological "water of life," within the widespread group of images of "drunkenness"[111] as *gnōsis* (see Excursus 7). The extremely rare term ἀλογιστία, not found even in Philo,[112] which would later be used as the opposite of ἀλήθεια (Tatian *Or.* 17.1),[113] is a striking image of the unreason of μέθη,[114] and its very rarity suggests that it was in the original text. A translation into Greek of ܕܠܐ ܝܕܥܬܐ (*d-lā ʾidaʿtā*) would more probably have used ἄγνοια or ἀγνωσία.[115]

■ **8b-12a** Continuing to use verb forms in the historic perfect in ܣ and the aorist in 𝔊, the speaking "I" again changes the topic of its narration and the imagery becomes somewhat more abstract. Verses 8b-9a and 10a-12a could almost be two strophes, with the second longer one a variation on the shorter.[116] Despite the minimal variation in content between 𝔊 and ܣ, linguistically there are some hotly contested differences in stanza IV that argue against a Syriac original.

The introductory "adversative particle" of 8b highlights the double negative in 8a, which expresses a positive, but at the same time indicates "that the preceding is to be regarded as settled," thus forming "the transition to something new."[117] This new thing consists, in the first place, in turning completely away from the μάταια (more likely than μάταιοι).[118] 𝔊 expresses the extent of this turning and rejection in 9a with only one composite verb ἐκτρέπω[119] and the subsequent preposition ἐπί, while ܣ uses two verbs, the Pe. ܫܒܩ (*šḇaq*), as in 10a (cf. 15:6; 33:1, 7), and the Ethpe. of ܦܢܐ/ܦܢܝ (*pnā/pnī*; cf. 33:6).[120] If these differences existed already in 𝔊* and ܣ*, a Greek original becomes more probable, since the Greek language offers a translator two or more suitable verbs.[121] The use of ܠܘܬ (*lwāṯ*) to translate ἐπί is unproblematic,[122] as are the two theological terms ὕψιστος/ܡܪܝܡܐ (*mrayymā*) and θεός/ܐܠܗܐ (*ʾallāhā*), attesting to the categorical rejection and conversion, the

107 The Syriac noun "life" and the plural adjective "living" have the same spelling.

108 BDAG, *s.v.* ὕδωρ, esp. 2; cf. Walter Bauer and Henning Paulsen, *Die Briefe des Ignatius von Antiochia und der Brief des Polykarp von Smyrna* (HNT 18: Die Apostolischen Väter 2; 2nd ed.; Tübingen: Mohr Siebeck, 1985) 77; Lewy, *Sobria*, 85, 91.

109 Lewy, *Sobria*, 85.

110 Payne Smith, 2:3841.

111 Jonas, *Gnosis*, 115–18.

112 See Günter Mayer, *Index Philoneus* (Berlin/New York: de Gruyter, 1974).

113 Goodspeed, 284.

114 BDAG, *s.v.* μέθη.

115 Payne Smith, 1:1560; Frankenberg, 13; Lewy, *Sobria*, 73–74, 85, 89. The Greek text οὐκ ἐγένετο εἰς ἀλογιστίαν was corrected, whether to match the Syriac or another Greek version, to οὐκ ἐγένετο ἀλογιστία ("was not irrationality"); on ἐγένετο = ἦν, see BDAG, *s.v.* γίνομαι. On the construction ἐγένετο εἰς, see the commentary on 3a above.

116 Franzmann, 93–94, with analytical detail. I do not agree with the running on of 8b into 9a in 𝔊, which results in one over-length line (see Franzmann, 86, 88, 97). Frankenberg's back-translation into Greek of stanza IV (pp. 13–14) differs more than usual from the Greek codex.

117 BDAG, *s.v.* ἀλλά, esp. 3; cf. Nöldeke §155; Payne Smith, 1:192: ܐܠܐ = ܐܢ + ܠܐ.

118 BDAG, *s.v.* μάταιος ([*Ode*] 11:9, not 16:9). As a masculine, ματαίων can refer to μάταιοι, that is, θεοί ("idols") or to adversaries ("vain ones"). As a neuter, it refers to μάταια ("what is worthless, empty"), which is similar in meaning to κενά (see Payne Smith, 2:2747 on the emphatic feminine plural ܣܪܝܩܬܐ [*srīqāṯā*]).

119 BDAG, *s.v.* ἐκτρέπω, 1.

120 Payne Smith, 2:3167.

121 See ibid., 2:4037–38.

122 Ibid., 2:1920.

first of which already occurred in 2a while the second now appears in apposition to it (cf. also the doxology in 24a).[123]

The imperative of salvation of 9:5, where being rich "in God the Father" is parallel to being redeemed "by his grace," is similar to this statement of salvation, 9b, where the making rich, which has already taken place, is connected to God's χάρισμα (on ܡܘܗܒܬܐ [*mawhabtā*], see 15:7; 35:6). The expression πλουτέω ἔν τινι means "to be plentifully supplied with something,"[124] so the wealth of the redeemed one is the divine "gift of grace."[125] But ἐν as well as ܒ (*b-*) can be translated as the instrumental preposition "with."[126] It is also worth alluding to the striking Judeo-Christian definition of χάρισμα τοῦ θεοῦ ("gift of God") as ζωὴ αἰώνιος ("eternal life") in Rom 6:23, with a forward glance to 12a.

The second strophe of stanza IV begins with a parallel bicolon. The rare adverb χαμαί in 10a is another pointer to a Greek original. The prepositional phrase ἐπὶ τὴν γῆν would have been expected as the translation of ܥܠ ܐܪܥܐ (*ʿal ʾarʿā*), although there is no stress here on the term "earth/land" (see 12b-13, 16f, 16h, 18, 21 below). For the rest, 𝔊 and 𝔖 correspond practically word for word, which allows a wordplay on the root ܫܕܐ (*šdʾ*) in 𝔖. However, such a paronomasia is not yet proof of a Syriac original. Therefore, it is not possible to say: "The play is lost in the Greek."[127] While ἀφίημι and ܫܒܩ (*šbaq*) are often used as equivalents[128] (but see on 8b above), it is here less likely that the *hapax legomenon* ܫܛܝܘܬܐ (*šāṭyūṯā*) was translated by ἀφροσύνη than the reverse.[129] In 𝔖 there is now a wider range of connotations[130] than in 𝔊, where ἀφροσύνη is the negative of φρόνησις and thus more limited in meaning.[131]

The images of 10b show that "folly" can be treated as a garment, which can be stripped off.[132] Because of the negative character of folly, the second verb ῥίπτω has not only the parallel meaning of "throw off" (cf. Acts 22:23) but adds a certain harshness (on ܫܕܐ [*šḏā*], see 21:2).[133] This also casts a clearer light on the rather neutral verb κεῖμαι[134] in 10a, which 𝔖 correctly interprets by its use of the participle of ܫܕܐ (*šḏā*).

The actions of the "I," especially in 8b-9a and 10a-b, are matched like the coin to the die by three parallel actions of the "Lord" (11a-12a), which should not be mistaken for any actual renewal, reclothing, or illuminating. They are purely images of existential/theological redemption.

In 11a, as a comparison with 8:9 and 25:8 makes clear, the terms ἔνδυμα and ܠܒܘܫܐ (*lḇūšā*) are in fact neutral. At this point, they refer to the invisible "garment of light,"[135] without any mythological elaboration.[136] It may be that 𝔊, by adding ἐν, is trying to say that the "Lord's" ἐγκαινίζειν[137] (on 36:5 see below) did not take place *by [means of]* but *in* the garment, which is not received from anyone in this world.

If 11b 𝔖 were the original, the verb ܩܢܐ (*qnā*) would hardly have been translated by ἀνακτάομαι;[138] κτάομαι would have been a more obvious choice.[139] The fact that ἀνακτάομαι can have the transitive meanings "refresh," "revive," "restore," and even "win a person over"[140] suggests to Klijn "that the Syriac translator may have chosen the wrong sense of the Greek word,"[141] and even

123 The number of occurrences of "Lord" in *Ode* 11 (cf. κύριος/ܡܪܝܐ [*māryā*] in 6, 11, 13, 15, 16, 17, and 18), however, far outweighs the frequency of the titles "God" and "Most High." In 1c ܡܪܝܐ (*māryā*) translates θεός (see above on 1c).
124 BDAG, *s.v.* πλουτέω, esp. 2.
125 BDAG, *s.v.* χάρισμα.
126 Lattke, *Oden*, 127.
127 Emerton, "Problems," 380.
128 Payne Smith, 2:4037–38.
129 See ibid., 2:3126 (ܦܟܝܗܘܬܐ [*pakkīhūṯā*]); 2:4131.
130 E.g., μωρία, cf. 1 Cor 3:19; *Diogn.* 3:3; ἄνοια, cf. 2 Tim 3:9; ἀλογία, see Lampe, 78 (not in BDAG).
131 See Bertram, "φρήν, κτλ.," *ThWNT* 9 (1973) 224, on Philo; cf. *TDNT* 9:228–29.
132 BDAG, *s.v.* ἀποδύομαι, does not mention *Ode* 11:10. On ܫܠܚ (*šlaḥ*), see also 15:8; 21:3.
133 Cf. BAGD, *s.v.* ῥίπτω, 1.
134 See BDAG, *s.v.* κεῖμαι.
135 Bauer, 591.
136 See Wilhelm Bousset, *Hauptprobleme der Gnosis* (Göttingen: Vandenhoeck & Ruprecht, 1907; repr., 1973) 303, esp. on *Asc. Isa.* 9:1-2, 9-13.
137 BDAG, *s.v.* ἐγκαινίζω; see also Payne Smith, 1:1206 on the Pa. ܚܕܬ (*ḥaddeṯ*).
138 BDAG, *s.v.* ἀνακτάομαι.
139 BDAG, *s.v.* κτάομαι; Payne Smith, 2:3651–52.
140 LSJ, *s.v.* ἀνακτάομαι.
141 Klijn, "Review of Testuz," 448.

Emerton finds it "a good argument prima facie for the priority of the Greek"[142] (on the Syriac, see 23:3; 41:9). The metaphorical action of the "Lord" is brought about by the power of his "light" (see Excursus 10), which in biblical texts is already compared to a divine "garment" (cf. *ἀναβαλλόμενος φῶς ὡς ἱμάτιον* in Ps 103:2a LXX).

The prefix of the verb *ἀναζῳοποιέω* (12a),[143] a Gnosticizing reinforcement–and therefore restriction–of *ζῳοποιέω* (cf. Rom 4:17; 1 Cor 15:22; John 5:21),[144] does not by any means lead to the conclusion "that there is no path to the Syriac version from this *ἀνεζωοποίησεν*."[145] In fact, the opposite is true. It also brings into question Luise Abramowski's confident judgment, "a Greek origin for the Odes . . . can no longer be convincingly upheld."[146] With Sebastian Brock, Emerton, and Klijn,[147] and against Abramowski and Vööbus,[148] it will be shown that it is possible to make out the path from Greek to Syriac.

If 𝔊* already had *ἀνεζῳοποίησέν με,* the prefix would have been translated into Syriac by ܡܢ ܠܥܠ (*men l-ʿel*).[149] This prepositional phrase would have been used with ܐܚܝܢ (*ʾaḥyan* = Aph. of ܚܝܐ [*ḥyā*] + first singular objective suffix): "he made me alive." Because of the confusability of the "letters *ḥet, yod, nun,*"[150] this term could have been misread in the course of the Syriac textual tradition as ܐܢܝܚܢ (*ʾanīḥan* [found in H]): "he gave me rest" (see Excursus 3).

As in 6b the instrumentally intended phrase *τῇ ἀφθαρσίᾳ αὐτοῦ* in 12a was translated by ܕܠܐ ܚܒܠ (*d-lā ḥbāl*). This Syriac phrase presents some difficulties. It may refer predicatively to the Aph. of ܢܘܚ, ܢܚ (*nāḥ*) or attributively to the implied term "rest." Originally, it was closely connected with the idea of making alive, a thought that can be thought only of God (cf. 7:11; 15:8). There is no connotation of a "life free from corruption . . . in the sense of an ascetic ideal."[151]

■ **12b-15** The redeemed "I" continues its tale with a new set of images, still using the historic perfect in 𝔖 or the aorist in 𝔊, beginning with "a double simile (12b-13)"[152] and linking the two by the repetition of *γῆ*/ܐܪܥܐ (*ʾarʿā*). As in 8, there has been a correction in the Greek manuscript in 12b (deletion of the definite article *ἡ*), which emphasizes the nonspecific character of "earth" or "land."[153] The image of 12b is of a tract of land ready for harvest. What the "fruits" are is not specified. The participles of the two verbs are formally equivalent and should be understood metaphorically, as in 16e.[154] The occidental Valentinian Ptolomaeus (second half of the second century C.E.) used a similar metaphor at the end of his *Letter to Flora*:

> . . . *ἐάν γε ὡς καλὴ γῆ καὶ ἀγαθὴ γονίμων σπερμάτων τυχοῦσα τὸν δι᾽ αὐτῶν καρπὸν ἀναδείξῃς*.[155]
>
> . . . when, like a beautiful and good piece of land sown with fertile seed, you have brought forth its fruits.[156]

If 𝔊* of 13 already had *μοι ἐγένετο* (cf. 3a), it is possible that either the corresponding phrase ܗܘܐ ܠܝ (*hwā lī*) was missing in 𝔖* or that it was omitted at some point

142 Emerton, "Problems," 381.
143 Cf. Lampe, 102: "restore to life."
144 See BDAG, *s.v.* *ζῳοποιέω*.
145 Vööbus, 282.
146 Abramowski, "Sprache," 83.
147 Sebastian Brock, "Review of Charlesworth," in *BSOAS* 38 (1975) 143; Emerton, "Problems," 381–82; idem, "Notes," 513; Klijn, "Review of Testuz," 448.
148 Abramowski, "Sprache," 82–83; Vööbus, 281–83.
149 See Payne Smith, 2:2880: mainly used for *ἄνωθεν* and other prepositions, but also for the *ἀνα-* of *ἀναγεννηθείς* in "Clem. Rom. Rec. 142. 28."
150 Abramowski, "Sprache," 83.
151 Contra Vööbus, 282. See Excursus 28.
152 Franzmann, 94.
153 The term "earth" does not yet show the technical meaning it assumes in 16f, 16h, 18, and 21. The forms of *γίνομαι* can equally well be translated "became" or "was."
154 On *θάλλω*/ܫܘܚ (*šwaḥ*), see the commentary on 16e below and see also BDAG, *s.v.* *θάλλω*; Payne Smith, 2:4091; on *γελάω*/ܪܘܙ (*rwaz*), see BDAG, *s.v.* *γελάω*; Payne Smith, 2:3845–46. From a purely lexical standpoint, it also seems likelier here that Syriac is translated from Greek.
155 Epiphanius, *Haer.* 33.7.10; Völker, *Quellen*, 93.
156 Hans Leisegang, *Die Gnosis* (KTA 32; Leipzig: Kröner, 1924) 308.

in the Syriac transmission of the text.[157] The effect of the comparison in 13 𝔖 is more impersonal than in 13 𝔊, which is reminiscent of 15:2 (see Excursus 10). The metaphorical "face of the earth" stands for the "surface of the earth" (as in 6:10 and 16:16).[158] The "Lord" has been mentioned before (1, 6, 11) and will occur again in stanzas VI–VII. If the term stands for "God" (9, 24) or the "Most High" (2, 9), this comparison of the completely transcendent with the "sun," so necessary to the life of all beings, is profoundly and negatively distinct theologically from any deification of the stellar object such as appears indirectly in a prayer from the *Greek Magical Papyri*:

> *ἀνέθαλεν ἡ γῆ σοῦ ἐπιλάμψαντος καὶ ἐκαρποφόρησεν τὰ φυτὰ σοῦ γελάσαντος.*[159]
>
> The earth flourished when you [viz., Helios] shone forth, and the plants became fruitful when you laughed.[160]

The parallel bicolon 14, accepting Willem Baars's conjecture,[161] gives further evidence for a Greek original of the *Odes of Solomon*.[162] The parallelism of "eyes" and "face," which in 𝔊 are subjects of their respective verbs, makes it probable that 𝔖*, as a translation from 𝔊*, used the Aph. of ܙܗܪ (*zhar*): ܐܙܗܪܘ ܥܝܢ̈ܝ = "my eyes shone."[163] Except for the word order, this is an exact translation of 𝔊.[164] The word ܐܙܗܪܘ, whose final vowel is mute (*ʾazhar*), was then misread as and corrected to ܐܢܗܪ (*ʾanhar*). This caused an ambiguity in 𝔖, because ܐܢܗܪ (*ʾanhar*) can be either third masculine singular or third feminine plural of the perfect Aph. of ܢܗܪ (*nhar*). Taken as masculine, this would make the "Lord" the subject of the first verb in 𝔖, destroying the parallelism. The *hapax legomenon* *δροσίζω*[165] (cf. Ignatius *Magn.*14) has no Syriac equivalent, so the passive had to be constructed by use of the active Pa. ܩܒܠ (*qabbel*) followed by ܛܠܠܐ (*ṭallā*) as the object (and retaining the Greek loanword *πρόσωπον* as subject)[166] (see Excursus 8).

The monocolon 15—like 13, it should not be divided into a bicolon[167]—has the *hapax legomenon* *ἀναπνοή*/ܢܫܡܬܐ (*nšamtā*), which as a third term parallel to "eyes" and "face" describes the organ of breath consisting of nose and mouth together.[168] The term *εὐωδία*/ܪܝܚܐ (*rēḥā*), which, except for the emendation suggested in 35:3, is also a *hapax legomenon*,[169] is found here with an underlying suggestion of something pleasant, which is intensified by the genitive of *χρηστότης*[170] and the adjective ܒܣܝܡܐ (*bassīmā*), respectively. Referring to the "Lord," the expression is, of course, anthropomorphic. Whether it is also a metaphor for the "revelation of God on earth"[171] depends on answering the question whether the redeemed "I" is still on earth or already metaphorically at the gates of paradise (see stanza VI below).

Since wordplay by itself cannot decide for or against either language as the original, and since the expression ܪܝܚܐ ܒܣܝܡܐ (*rēḥā bassīmā*) would more normally have been translated by *ὀσμὴ εὐωδίας*,[172] Vööbus's pleading for a Syriac original[173] collapses. On the other hand, if 𝔊 is reasonably close to the original (𝔊*), neither the adjectival interpretation of *εὐωδία χρηστότητος*

157 See the summary of variant readings in Lattke, *Bedeutung*, 1:46–51.

158 On the use of *πρόσωπον* and ܐܦ̈ܐ (*ʾappē*), see Lattke, "Wörter," 296–98 = idem, *Bedeutung*, 4:145–47.

159 *PGM* 4.1611–14.

160 Hans Dieter Betz, ed., *The Greek Magical Papyri in Translation, Including the Demotic Spells* (2nd ed.; Chicago/London: University of Chicago Press, 1986) 68. What sort of comparison Bardaisan drew between the divine father and the sun, which caused Ephrem to attack him, is unknown (see Harris and Mingana, 2:270).

161 Willem Baars, "A Note on Ode of Solomon xi 14," *VT* 12 (1962) 196.

162 Contra Charlesworth, 55; and Lattke, *Bedeutung*, 3:260.

163 See Payne Smith, 1:1090.

164 See BDAG, *s.v.* *στίλβω*.

165 See BDAG, *s.v.* *δροσίζω*.

166 See Payne Smith, 1:1471.

167 Contra Harris and Mingana, 2:267; Charlesworth, 50, 52.

168 LSJ, *s.v.* *ἀναπνοή*; Payne Smith, 2:2476–77.

169 See BDAG, *s.v.* *εὐωδία*; Payne Smith, 2:3854.

170 See BDAG, *s.v.* *χρηστότης*.

171 Suggested by Ernst Lohmeyer, *Vom göttlichen Wohlgeruch* (SHAW.PH 1919, 9. Abh.; Heidelberg: Winter, 1919) 32, discussing 2 Cor 2:14-16; Eph 5:2; Phil 4:18; Ignatius *Eph.* 17:1; Ignatius *Magn.* 10:2; cf. Rom 2:4; 11:22; Eph 2:7; Titus 3:4.

172 See Payne Smith, 1:551; 2:3854.

173 Vööbus, 283–84.

("fragrance of gentleness" = "gentle fragrance") nor the paronomasiac translation of εὐφραίνομαι (passive)[174] by the Ethpa. of ܒܣܡ (*bsem*)[175] (see Excursus 14) could be considered unusual. This stanza too offers little "in favour of a Syriac original."[176]

■ **16** Whether there were ever lines matching 16c-h in ܣ* or in any recension of the Syriac cannot (yet) be determined.[177] If this "description of paradise," perhaps in connection with an equally imaginary "tour of heaven" for the speaking "I,"[178] was not contained in 𝔊*, it must have been added at some point in the tradition of the Greek text. It now forms part of stanza VI[179] and makes a charming addition to the early representations of paradise, all of them more or less based on the "story of paradise Gen 2:4b–3:24,"[180] with their various forms and functions, their multiple locations, and their aim of "adding a cosmological and eschatological aspect" to the "protological sense" of Genesis 2–3.[181]

The term παράδεισος/ܦܪܕܝܣܐ (*pardaysā*), borrowed from the Persian, occurs only in 20:7 and in *Ode* 11 (vv. 16, 18, 23, 24).[182] Following the usage of the LXX, the meaning of παράδεισος is already firmly established in early Judaism and primitive Christianity as a "place of the blessed" above the earth.[183] After the "gradual rising" of the preliminary stanzas IV and V, 16a-b is "an introduction to the entire section dealing with the Lord's Paradise," and the first bicolon of stanza VI "forms an inclusio"[184] with 24b of stanza IX. The Syriac form of ܐܘܒܠ (*ʾawbel*, Aph. of ܝܒܠ [*ybl*])[185] with accusative suffix, in 16a, does not correspond to μετήγαγέ με,[186] and probably not to ἐπήγαγέν με either,[187] but most likely to ἀπήγαγέν με (emending the manuscript ⲠⲎⲄⲀⲄⲈⲚ ⲘⲈ), although not with any "legal meaning." [188]

Unlike its occurrence in 41:10, the metaphorical masculine term πλοῦτος/ܥܘܬܪܐ (*ʿutrā*),[189] which is of great importance in Mandaean writings,[190] is here more closely defined by a genitive phrase. The word ܒܘܣܡܐ (*bussāmā*),[191] derived from the root *bsm*, connects back to stanza V (15 ܣ), while the phrase ἡ τρυφή certainly comes from the LXX, where the expression παράδεισος τῆς τρυφῆς is found (Gen 3:23-24; Ezek 31:9; Joel 2:3; see also *Diogn.* 12:1).[192]

It will be noticed that the material preserved only in 𝔊, 16c-h, has a number of verbs in the imperfect, which

174 See BDAG, *s.v.* εὐφραίνω.

175 See Payne Smith, 1:549.

176 Contra Emerton, "Problems," 382.

177 I cannot share Charlesworth's conviction: "It appears that they are authentic and the copyist of H omitted them because of *parablepsis*, an error which he commits with astonishing frequency" (Charlesworth, 56–57).

178 Gemünden, *Vegetationsmetaphorik*, 384.

179 Unlike Franzmann (pp. 97–98), I do not treat the purely Greek material as "Stanza 7" or divide 16e into a bicolon.

180 Fritz Stolz, "Paradies I. Religionsgeschichtlich. II. Biblisch," *TRE* 25 (1995) 708.

181 Simone Rosenkranz, "Paradies III. Jüdisch," *TRE* 25 (1995) 711. Cf. *Jub.* 3:9, 12, 15-35; 4 Ezra 3:6; 4:7-8; 6:2-3; 7:36, 123; 8:52; *1 Enoch* 24:3–25:7; 32:3-6; *2 Enoch* 8:1-8; 1QH xvi (prev. viii).4-20. To these should be added the beginning of the *Apocalypse of Peter,* a text that was already noted by Richard Hugh Connolly, "The Odes of Solomon: Jewish or Christian?" *JTS* 13 (1911–12) 302–3. Part of it is preserved in Greek in the fragmentary "Parchment codex of Akhmim" (text and German translation in Albrecht Dieterich, *Nekyia: Beiträge zur Erklärung der neuentdeckten Petrusapokalypse* [3rd ed.; Darmstadt: Wissenschaftliche Buchgesellschaft, 1969 = 2nd ed.; Leipzig/Berlin: Teubner, 1913] 2–9). The "depiction of the place of the blessed" is far shorter than the gruesome description of the "place of the damned" (1).

182 See Lattke, "Wörter," 295 = idem, *Bedeutung,* 4:143–44.

183 Cf. *Ps. Sol.* 14:3; Luke 23:43; 2 Cor 12:4; Rev 2:7; *Diogn.* 12:1; and see Payne Smith, 2:3239; BDAG, *s.v.* παράδεισος.

184 Franzmann, 94, 97; see also Adolf Büchler, "A Study of Ode XI," *Abstract of Proceedings for the Year 1911-1912, Society of Historical Theology* (Oxford, 1912) 20–21, 24–25.

185 See Payne Smith, 1:1539.

186 Contra Frankenberg, 14.

187 Found in all editions since Testuz, 64; see BDAG, *s.v.* ἐπάγω.

188 See BDAG, *s.v.* ἀπάγω.

189 Payne Smith, 2:3012; BDAG, *s.v.* πλοῦτος.

190 E. S. Drower and R. Macuch, *A Mandaic Dictionary* (Oxford: Clarendon, 1963) 347.

191 Payne Smith, 1:550.

192 In Ezek 28:13 the sequence is reversed (ἐν τῇ τρυφῇ τοῦ παραδείσου τοῦ θεοῦ); Joachim Jeremias translates τρυφή by "Üppigkeit [profusion]";

is suitable to the "description"[193] of paradise, and also, on the whole, goes against the idea of a translation from Syriac.[194] Franzmann's division of this description of paradise into two strophes marked by *inclusio*,[195] 16c-e (καρποφόρα/καρποί) and 16f-h (ἀθανάτου γῆς/γῆς ζωῆς αἰωνίας), is justified. The image completely ignores localization and concentrates on the "trees," which had already taken up a dominant role—as ξύλα—in Gen 2:8-17 and 3:1-24. The interest in this passage, however, is not limited to those two biblical ξύλα but extends to the δένδρα[196] in general. Looking forward to stanza VII, it must be asked whether these "trees" may be metaphors for the persons who, in that stanza, are blessed for being "planted." In that case, though, the details should not be taken allegorically.

The aorist of θεάομαι[197] is not used to mean a supernatural vision, since the "I" is already mythologically in paradise. This change in location does involve being "caught up" (cf. 2 Cor 12:2-4),[198] but the seeing is done in the normal way. The expression δένδρα ὡραῖα ("beautiful trees") is found also in *Barn.* 11:10, a "prophetic saying of uncertain origin,"[199] but not in Gen 2:9 or Ezek 47:7, 12, passages that surely influenced this newly coined phrase.[200]

The word στέφανος in 16d, unlike 20:7, refers to the crown of the tree, that is, the upper part of a tree including the leaves and living branches. This "wreath" corresponds, in the bilingual and metaphorical thought of the author(s), to the more flexible Syriac term ܟܠܝܠܐ (*klīlā*).[201] Such a polysemous use of στέφανος calls into question the apodeictic judgment of Adam that this "is impossible in Greek."[202] For "it is difficult to see why it should be regarded as impossible for a writer in Greek to think of such a figure of speech."[203] The description of this "crown," with use of the imperfect tense, depicts it as "self-grown, natural"[204] and thus emphasizes the beauty of its growth.

The manuscript ⲑⲁⲗⲗⲉⲓ in 16e must be another of the "errata" that "were not corrected."[205] In conformity with ἐγέλων, the imperfect of γελάω, it should be read as ἔθαλλε. Both verbs are found already in 12b and are meant metaphorically in both cases. In order to bring out this metaphorical character of θάλλω, it is better translated as "burst out"[206] rather than "flourish, grow up."[207] The plural τὰ ξύλα cannot here be restricted to "trees"[208] but must mean collectively all the "living" wood of stems and branches.[209] Reasoning from γελάω to an underlying Syriac *Grundschrift* with ܓܚܟ (*g̱ḥaḵ*),[210] in view of the use of θάλλω/ܫܘܚ (*šwaḥ*) and γελάω/ܪܘܙ (*rwaz*) in 12b, is at least "open to question": "If the earth can laugh, or rejoice, in its fruits, why should not the fruits themselves be said to laugh?"[211]

see Jeremias, "παράδεισος," *ThWNT* 5 (1954) 763 n. 6; *TDNT* 5:766 n. 6, which does not translate "Üppigkeit."

193 BDR §327 ("*Schilderung*"); BDF §327 ("to portray").

194 The comments of Joachim Begrich ("Der Text der Psalmen Salomos," *ZNW* 38 [1939] 139) on the use of the imperfect in the *Psalms of Solomon* are worth noting in this connection. Unfortunately a comparable Syriac text is not available here.

195 Franzmann, 98.

196 See BDAG, *s.v.* δένδρον.

197 See BDAG, *s.v.* θεάομαι.

198 See Hans Windisch, *Der zweite Korinterbrief* (repr. of 1924 edition, ed. Georg Strecker; KEK; Göttingen: Vandenhoeck & Ruprecht, 1970) 369–80, on 2 Cor 12:2-4.

199 BDAG, *s.v.* ὡραῖος.

200 Wengst, 173 ("Neubildung"). If Barnabas found the expression δένδρα ὡραῖα in the paradisology of *Ode* 11, this raises the question whether his reference to "another prophet" (ἕτερος προφήτης [*Barn.* 11:9]) refers to the author of the Greek *Ode(s) of Solomon*.

201 Payne Smith, 1:1732–33; see also BDAG, *s.v.* στέφανος.

202 Alfred Adam, "Die ursprüngliche Sprache der Salomo-Oden," *ZNW* 52 (1961) 150.

203 Emerton, "Problems," 400.

204 Lampe, 273, *s.v.* αὐτοφυής, 1.

205 Lattke, *Bedeutung*, 1:14. I cannot agree with Charlesworth (57 n. 32): "The present tense is probably an error by the Greek translator."

206 *MEL*, 32:2527, *s.v.* strotzen; cf. Friedrich Kluge, *Etymologisches Wörterbuch der deutschen Sprache* (22nd ed.; ed. Elmar Seebold; Berlin/New York: de Gruyter, 1989) 709.

207 BDAG, *s.v.* θάλλω.

208 BDAG, *s.v.* ξύλον.

209 Johannes Schneider, "ξύλον," *ThWNT* 5 (1954) 37; cf. *TDNT* 5:37.

210 Charlesworth, 57, correcting "noun" (1973) to "verb" (1977).

211 Emerton, "Notes," 514; cf. Franzmann, 90.

Verse 16f needs a verb.[212] The term γῆ, by the addition of ἀθάνατος, which can really only refer to "God,"[213] acquires a completely new meaning compared to 11:10 and 11:12-13, a meaning that will remain in 11:18 and 11:21 (cf. also 15:10). Even if the roots of the trees in this utopian paradise are visible on the surface[214] (cf. 38:17), they originate in the indescribable depths of this special land.[215]

There must have been a reason why the definite article was added before ποταμός in the Papyrus, turning it into a specific river, known perhaps to the scribe and his readers as a river of joy (16g). Whether this was a reference to the "river of the water of life" in the heavenly Jerusalem (Rev 22:1-2)[216] or to the earlier one of Ezek 47:6-7; 47:12, is difficult to decide, since there are no known parallels to ποταμός χαρᾶς.[217] The transitive verb ποτίζω in its usual sense of "to water/irrigate"[218] continues the description, also in the imperfect tense; its direct object αὐτάς refers to the "roots" of 16f.

Although 16h "is very peculiar,"[219] the form κύκλῳ, which has fossilized into an "(improper) preposition of place," followed by the genitive,[220] serves to describe further the irrigating action of the river. The genitive phrase ζωῆς αἰωνίας αὐτῶν refers back rather to the δένδρα of 16c than the ξύλα and καρποί of 16e. These "trees," like those in *Ps. Sol.* 14:3, receive the theological attribute of "eternal life."[221] It is not only the soil of this paradise that shares the divine immortality (16f); so do the δένδρα that grow from this γῆ and are rooted in it. In stanza VII the images of vegetation take on meanings beyond mere flora (and fauna), so these "trees" of stanza VI should probably also be understood parabolically.

■ **17-22** After the general introduction (stanza VI), stanzas VII–IX take the form of a lengthy "speech within the speech."[222] This speech of the "I" transported to paradise is also largely metaphorical, and it is addressed to the "Lord" (17-18a) as "God" (24a). After an introduction of its own (17), the speech begins with a benediction (18-19), before carrying on the descriptions of the paradise (18-23) that had been begun in the Greek *Sondergut* of 16c-h, and finishes with a doxology (24). Despite the general unanimity of 𝔖 and 𝔊, there are some significant differences, which pose difficulties for the commentator (see on 21-22 below).

With the perfect of ܣܓܶܕ (*sḡeḏ*; cf. 39:13), the aorist of προσκυνέω, the "I" in 17 relates its prayerful obeisance, which can, metaphorically, be paid only to the "Lord," because this stooped posture, worshiping genuflection, and devout prostration may not be performed before any merely human being.[223] The use of the improper preposition ἕνεκα reveals the divine "doxa" as the cause of the "worshiping."[224] Δόξα, like ܬܫܒܘܚܬܐ (*tešbuḥtā*), at this point means "glory" in the sense of "radiance" from beyond, *magnificentia*;[225] in the final doxology the stress will be placed on praising (see on 24 below).

The "I," which up to now has been merely narrating,

212 See Emerton, 701: "came up."
213 See BDAG, *s.v.* ἀθάνατος.
214 BDAG, *s.v.* ῥίζα.
215 BDAG, *s.v.* γῆ, esp. 6b.
216 See BDAG, *s.v.* ποταμός.
217 See BDAG, *s.v.* χαρά; Lampe, 1123. Pierre displays more certainty: "An allusion to the river of life, which encircles Jerusalem, the city of God (see Ps 46[45]:5; Gen 2:10; Rev 22:2)." See Pierre, "Odes de Salomon," 697.
218 BDAG, *s.v.* ποτίζω.
219 Carmignac, "Affinités," 91. Adam ("Sprache," 150), indeed, refers to a failed Greek "construction" and believes it "an unsuccessful attempt at translating a Syriac text" that may have originally read: "And all around was the country of their life in eternity." I disagree.
220 BDAG, *s.v.* κύκλῳ.
221 *Ps. Sol.* 14:3a-b: *ὅσιοι κυρίου ζήσονται ἐν αὐτῷ εἰς τὸν αἰῶνα· ὁ παράδεισος τοῦ κυρίου, τὰ ξύλα τῆς ζωῆς, ὅσιοι αὐτοῦ* (Rahlfs, 2:483), "The faithful of the Lord will live eternally by this (law), the park of the Lord, the trees of life (are) his faithful" (Holm-Nielsen, 91).
222 Lattke, *Oden*, 49, 87. Cf. 33:6-13; 38:10b-14; 42:15c-18, which show similar forms.
223 See Payne Smith, 2:2522; BDAG, *s.v.* προσκυνέω; see also Heinrich Greeven, "προσκυνέω, προσκυνητής," *ThWNT* 6 (1959) 759–67; *TDNT* 6:758–66.
224 Here also, ἕνεκα is rather *propter* than *causa* (BDF and BDR §216). The choice of ἕνεκα + genitive in preference to διά + accusative, as an equivalent of ܡܛܠ (*meṭṭol*), can be equally that of a translator or of the original author. I prefer the latter (see BDAG, *s.v.* ἕνεκα; Payne Smith, 2:2076–77).
225 BDAG, *s.v.* δόξα; Payne Smith, 2:4027.

now quotes itself (aorist εἶπα, perfect of ܐܡܪ [ʾemar])[226] as addressing the "Lord" in the second person,[227] but not speaking directly to those "planted" (cf. 38:16; 38:19-21) whom it calls blessed. The image of these πεφυτευμένοι (perfect participle passive of φυτεύω),[228] ܢܨܝܒܝܢ (nṣīḇīn) is of "trees" (19a, 21b 𝔖; see 16c 𝔊 above) or "plants" (21b 𝔊).[229] But by this time it is clear that the flora of the benediction (18-19) are also meant metaphorically for and identified with the "laborers" (20-21) and the "servants" (22b 𝔖, 22c 𝔊).[230] The γῆ/ܐܪܥܐ (ʾarʿā) of the "Lord" is the "immortal earth" of the mythological paradise (see on 16f, 16h in stanza VI above). To divide 18a into a bicolon[231] is to overlook the Syriac construction ܛܘܒܐ (ṭūḇā) + suffix followed by ܠ (l-) + pronoun + ܕ (d-).[232]

In 18b, 𝔊 uses apposition to express what 𝔖 says by the use of preceding ܘ (w-).[233] The correspondence of ἔχω and ܐܝܬ (ʾīṯ) + ܠ (l-) is quite regular, but the demonstrative pronoun ܗܢܘܢ (hānnōn, masculine plural)[234] has to depend on ܠ (l-).[235] The terms τόπος/ܐܬܪܐ (ʾaṯrā)[236] do not carry any specialized meaning, but the key word "paradise," picked up from 16a, does (see above and cf. also 23a). An influence of John 14:2-3 (ἑτοιμάσαι/σω τόπον ὑμῖν) on these passages is perhaps less likely than the influence that *Ode* 11 seems to have exerted on the Valentinians, for example, in *Gos. Truth* 36,35-39 ("He [viz., the perfect Father] is good. He knows his plantings, because it is he who planted them in his Paradise. Now his Paradise is his place of rest").[237]

Colossians 2:19 (πᾶν τὸ σῶμα . . . αὔξει τὴν αὔξησιν τοῦ θεοῦ, "the whole body . . . grows with a growth that is from God") may perhaps be found in the background of 19a 𝔊 (καὶ αὐξανόμενοι ἐν τῇ αὐξήσει τῶν δένδρων σου, "and grow in the growth of thy trees"), although the Syriac of this passage in *Ode* 11 makes use of forms of ܐܝܥܐ (ʾiʿā) rather than words derived from the root ܪܒ (rb[b]). The passive of αὐξάνω means "to grow" and is also used of "plants."[238] The participles of the verbs are as close in meaning as the nouns αὔξησις and ܡܘܥܝܬܐ (mawʿīṯā). However, 𝔖 shows a clearer connection with the plant kingdom.[239] The readers of 𝔊 have already come across the "trees" (see 16c above, δένδρα ὡραῖα). For readers of 𝔖, the plural of ܐܝܠܢܐ (ʾīlānā) is something new, and their knowledge of the biblical stories may have led them to think first of Gen 2:9, with the "tree of life" (ܐܝܠܢܐ ܕܚܝܐ [ʾīlānā ḏ-ḥayyē]) and the "tree of knowledge" (ܐܝܠܢܐ ܕܝܕܥܬܐ [ʾīlānā ḏ-iḏaʿtā]).[240] In view of 21b 𝔖, they will have soon realized that the subject is more generally a "divine plantation."[241]

Both versions use verbs in 19b, which later formed part of the language of conversion. Both the aorist passive participle of μεταβάλλω[242] and the Pa. perfect of ܫܢܐ (šnā)[243] place the turning from "darkness" to "light" in the past, and 𝔊 also stresses the passive nature of this

226 BDAG, *s.v.* εἶπον; Payne Smith, 1:243–44.
227 See Franzmann, 95.
228 BDAG, *s.v.* φυτεύω.
229 Payne Smith, 2:2435–36.
230 All the masculine forms of verbs and nouns in stanza VII are to be taken as including the feminine.
231 As do Bauer (p. 591), Charlesworth (pp. 51, 53), and Franzmann (pp. 84–85). Diettrich (p. 43), despite an unorthodox interpretation, is among those who treat it correctly.
232 The change from ἐπὶ τῆς γῆς (18a) to ἐν τῇ γῇ (21b) may not be unintentional, even though both phrases can be translated by "on the earth" (BDAG, *s.v.* ἐπί). This distinction, while the Syriac remains unchanged, also rather suggests a Greek original.
233 It is noticeable that throughout stanza VII καί occurs far less often than its Syriac equivalent (17, 18b, 19b, 21a, 21b).
234 Nöldeke §67.
235 Cf. Charlesworth, 57 n. 36: "The Greek leaves out the pronoun but it may be contained in the article." This note, however, refers not to "Thy" but to "who" (p. 53).
236 See BDAG, *s.v.* τόπος; Payne Smith, 1:425–26.
237 *NHLE*, 48.
238 BDAG, *s.v.* αὐξάνω.
239 Payne Smith, 1:1611–12. The translator(s) may be responsible for this clarification.
240 Suggested by Diettrich, 44; cf. Payne Smith, 1:154; *OTSy* pt. 1 fasc. 1, on this passage.
241 See Bauer's reference (p. 591) to Reitzenstein, *Das iranische Erlösungsmysterium,* 138–46. With due caution concerning dates of origin, I accept Reitzenstein's conclusion (p. 146): "That Mandaean and Manichaean poetry must be included in any explanation of the *Odes of Solomon* seems to me to be clearly shown in this case also." Reference should also be made to Arnold-Döben's research on metaphor (Victoria Arnold-Döben, *Die Bildersprache des Manichäismus* [AMRG 3; Cologne: Brill, 1978]

profound transformation. It is quite clear that more is meant in this passage than the natural preference of plants for light, and there are many other examples of the duality of light and darkness to be found[244] (cf. 15:2; 21:3; Excursus 10). As in 8a and 12b, the article preceding $\varphi\tilde{\omega}\varsigma$ in 19b 𝔊 was marked for deletion in the manuscript, perhaps to align it with σκότος which has no article.[245]

Since 20 and 21 belong together, 20a-b is not "an insertion into the parallel bicola" 19a-b and 21a-b;[246] the "laborers" introduced in 20a by the demonstrative particle ἰδού/ܗܐ (*hā*), which aims at "arousing the attention of hearers and readers," must be the metaphorical plants in human guise.[247] In keeping with the closeness of the tree imagery, the adjectival plurals of καλός/ܫܦܝܪ (*šappīr*) are not translated as "excellent"[248] or "fine"[249] but as "beautiful," synonymically with ὡραῖος (see 12c above).[250] This predicative adjective refers to the participle of ἐργάζομαι,[251] used as a noun, which may originally have been translated by ܦܠܚܝܟ (*pālḥayk*)[252] and only later equated with ܦܥܠܝܟ (*pāʿlayk*). It is this noun, derived from ܦܥܠ (*pʿal*), that is most commonly used to translate ἐργάτης (*operarius*).[253]

By reversing some of Luise Abramowski's arguments,[254] it can be shown how in 20b-21a the way leads from original Greek to Syriac. The plural of μεταβολή,[255] a term for conversion related to μεταβάλλω (19b), is first translated by the plural of ܥܒܪܐ (*ʿeḇrā* or *ʿḇārā*, *transitus*).[256] When this ܥܒܪܐ was reinterpreted as ܥܒܕܐ,[257] perhaps influenced by other words from the root *ʿbd* in 20b and 22b (see below), the participle of ܗܦܟ (*hp̄aḵ*), also an important word in the language of conversion,[258] had to be added in 21a. This turning around was taken further theologically, by adding ܕܝܠܟ (*dīl* + suffix). So 𝔊 preserves the original metaphorical sense of the passage: not *God*'s "kindness" but the "sweetness" of the *trees*, and "good" not referring moralizingly to human *works* but referring to radical *conversion*. The laboring "trees" bring about, analogously to "the natural processes of growth,"[259] good transformations of rooted "evil" to paradisiacal "goodness."[260] In the end, the subject, as in Matt 7:17-20, is not δένδρα but πίστοι δοῦλοι (see 22b-c below).

Compared to the Syriac 21b-c, the Greek 21b is *lectio brevior*, and briefly declares the transmutation (μεταλλάσσομαι, probably passive rather than middle).[261] The "bitterness of the plants" concerns not merely the unpalatability or poisonous nature of their "roots" and "fruits" but also the "water" drawn into them and stored as sap.[262] If the manuscript reading is indeed ἐν τῇ γῇ σου ("in thy earth") and not ἐν πηγῇ σου ("by thy spring"),[263] the transmutation takes place in the soil of paradise (see 16f-h above). Drawing the metaphorical water, which is essential to life, from the "river of joy" (16g), these

7-44; eadem, "Die Symbolik des Baumes im Manichäismus," *Symbolon: Jahrbuch für Symbolforschung* N.F. 5 [1980] 9–29; eadem, *Die Bildersprache der Gnosis* [AMRG 13; Cologne: Brill, 1986] 135–52).

242 BDAG, *s.v.* μεταβάλλω; Lampe, 848–49.

243 Payne Smith, 2:4234–35.

244 See Charlesworth, 57 n. 38.

245 BDAG, *s.v.* σκότος.

246 Contra Franzmann, 95, 98.

247 See BDAG, *s.v.* ἰδού; Payne Smith, 1:959.

248 Bauer, 592 ("trefflich").

249 See BDAG, *s.v.* καλός.

250 See Payne Smith, 2:4275–76.

251 BDAG, *s.v.* ἐργάζομαι.

252 Payne Smith, 2:3147–48.

253 Ibid., 2:3202.

254 Abramowski, "Sprache," 80–81.

255 Lampe, 849–50.

256 Payne Smith, 2:2787–88.

257 Ibid., 2:2773–74.

258 Ibid., 1:1035–36.

259 BDAG, *s.v.* ποιέω, esp. 2g.

260 BDAG, *s.vv.* πονηρία and χρηστότης; see also Payne Smith, 1:441, 551. There seems no good reason why ἀγαθάς cannot refer to μεταβολάς (contra Adam, "Sprache," 150 ["must refer to persons"]). Cf. Emerton, "Problems," 383, in opposition: "Nor is there any need to follow them [viz., Adam, "Sprache"; Vööbus] in maintaining that *ΑΓΑΘΑΣ* should not be applied to *ΜΕΤΑΒΟΛΑΣ*, but only to people." In the same breath he sets to rights the use of ποιέω: "there is evidence for a tendency in popular Hellenistic usage to replace the middle by the active voice."

261 See BDAG, *s.v.* μεταλλάσσω.

262 See BDAG, *s.v.* πικρός.

263 Franzmann, 91; contra Lattke, *Bedeutung*, 1:23, 112; and William R. Schoedel, "Some Readings in the Greek Ode of Solomon (Ode XI)," *JTS* n.s. 33 (1982) 180.

"plants"/"trees," springing up in darkness and marked by foulness, are redeemed and partake theologically of its gladness and sweetness (21a) and may—though perhaps by a misplaced marginal note—be praised as mysterious agents of the water of the Lord (see on 22b 𝔊 below).

If this interpretation is correct, the Syriac 21b-c must be considered another example of moralizing. The theological present passive of *μεταλλάσσω* is translated by the Aph. perfect of ܗܦܟ (*hp̄ak*), which refers back to 21a[264] and is reinforced by the reflexive use of the preposition ܡܢܗܘܢ (*men* + personal suffix). The general term *φυτά*[265] is replaced by the more specific plural of ܐܝܠܢܐ (*ʾīlānā*) from 19a. But the idea of "plant" is found in 21c, where the Ethpe. of ܢܨܒ (*nṣab*) makes a connection with 18a and is placed at the end in a relative clause with ܡܐ ܕ (*mā d-*).[266] The masculine ܡܪܪܐ (*mrārā*), derived from ܡܪ (*mar*), and generally used in the plural,[267] corresponds to the adjective *πικρός* used as a noun, *τὸ πικρόν* ("bitterness"). This deprives the literal translation of *ἐν τῇ γῇ*, ܒܐܪܥܐ (*b-arʿā*), referring back to 18a, of its instrumental meaning.[268]

Neither 𝔊 nor 𝔖 mentions the "tree of bitterness," *arbor amaritudinis* (*Act. Pet.* 8),[269] or the "bitter tree," *τὸ δένδρον τὸ πικρόν* (*Act. Thom.* 44).[270] Therefore, Daniel Plooij's earlier studies are not much help in explaining the "at first sight somewhat peculiar expression" in 11:20.[271] But the phrase "bitterness of the trees" (𝔖) or "bitterness of the plants" (𝔊) may have influenced the later wording of "bitter tree."[272]

Discussion of 22b 𝔊 will be postponed, since it is probably a marginal note that is more applicable to 20-21 than 22 (see at end of stanza VI below); the remaining bicolon 22, with the exception of the much-discussed word "remnant," is practically identical in 𝔖 and 𝔊. It cannot, however, be characterized as an "insertion into the bicolon formed by 21c [21b 𝔊] and 23a";[273] it is rather the final conclusion from what has been previously described in this address.[274]

The use of *ὡς* in 22a may seem to be a "Semitism,"[275] but this does not militate against a Greek original.[276] The subject *τὰ πάντα*, to which ܟܠܡܕܡ (*kol meddem*) corresponds exactly, does not refer to the cosmic "All" but to everything that has been named so far. If *θέλημα*, as found in the manuscript, represents the original wording, the translation would be: "And everything was as your will (i.e., according to your desire)"[277] (for the

264 Payne Smith, 1:1038–39.
265 BDAG, *s.v.* *φυτόν*.
266 See Payne Smith, 2:1979, 2436.
267 See ibid., 2:2199, 2203.
268 Only if the imagery is to be allegorically understood is it necessary to search for a morally personal signification of "bitterness." Diettrich (p. 44) already tried to interpret "bitterness" as "wedlock." Vööbus (pp. 286–87) goes further: "The sequence of ideas in the text of our *Ode* is quite clear—the decision against the libido and for abstinence on the part of the Blessed could not be more clearly expressed." Both refer to the *Gospel of the Egyptians*. Vööbus (p. 287) dismisses the metaphorical text of 𝔊 as a "misunderstanding": "from the point of view of the mental world of ascetic Christianity it should, strictly speaking, be called nonsense." Emerton ("Problems," 384), on the other hand, referring to 42:12 and 28:15 (cf. also 31:12), correctly makes the point that "bitterness does not always stand for lust in the Odes."
269 *AAAp*, 1:55, line 29; cf. *NTApoc* 2:295.
270 *AAAp*, 2.2:161, lines 16–17; cf. *NTApoc* 2:358.
271 Daniel Plooij, "De Boom der Bitterheid," *Theologisch tijdschrift* 46 (1911–12) 294.
272 Plooij ("Boom," 300), thinks it "clear that the 'bitter tree' is nothing but the tree of knowledge in Eden, so named because it is the cause of sin and death among mankind." See Gilles Quispel, *Makarius, das Thomasevangelium und das Lied von der Perle* (NovTSup 15; Leiden: Brill, 1967) 29.
273 Franzmann, 96, 98.
274 Franzmann (pp. 84–85, 87, 89) places 23a at the end of stanza VII (𝔖)/VIII (𝔊). Her reasons are not convincing. On the contrary, she herself, in her analysis of 23b-c 𝔖, mentions the "link between the bicolon and the previous stanza" (p. 96). I prefer to place 23a at the beginning of stanza VIII and will defend the placing at that point.
275 BDAG, *s.v.* *ὡς*.
276 I cannot agree with Emerton ("Problems," 387), that "the use of *ΩΣ* tells strongly in favour of the view that the Greek Ode is a translation of the Syriac."
277 BDAG, *s.vv.* *θέλημα* and *πᾶς*.

wording, see Mark 4:11; for the meaning, Matt 6:10). It would then be possible to agree with Marc Philonenko that "the meaning is excellent and the formulation has many Qumranic parallels (cf. 1QH i.8; i.20; x.9; 1QS xi.18)."[278] However, 𝔖—next to the perfect ܗܘܐ (*hwā*)—has nothing equivalent to "will," but instead the term ܫܪܟܢܐ (*šarkānā*), a word that is regularly used to translate λεῖμμα, κατάλειμμα, and ὑπόλειμμα[279] (cf. Rom 9:27; 11:5), which makes it necessary to consider an emendation.

The Syriac emendations ܐܫܟܪܐ (*ʾaškārā*),[280] ܫܘܟܢܐ (*šūḵānā*),[281] and ܨܒܝܢܐ (*ṣeḇyānā*)[282] tend to make the situation more difficult, while the conjectural Greek λεῖμμα is a simple solution. It was not an original θέλημα that was misheard or misread as λεῖμμα.[283] It is θέλημα which is the corruption of λεῖμμα. Supposing that 𝔊* had λεῖμμα, it is still possible that it was a translation from 𝔖*, and θέλημα was later substituted for λεῖμμα. If 𝔊* was the original and 𝔖* a translation, then the Syriac version preserves the text of 𝔖* whereas the Greek version does not preserve that of 𝔊*. Even if this is the case, Philonenko's conclusion, "the Syriac text of this Ode is a translation from the Greek," still stands.[284]

It is now possible to examine the statement in 22a, which, with the use of "remnant" (cf. Hebrew שארית), takes up "an Old Testament motif" that "had already exerted a wide influence in Judaism as well as being of great significance in early Jewish Christian circles."[285] This vague term does not refer to the "quantity of the faithful"[286] so much as to the fact that there is a group of the elect and faithful. The idea of election here is not concerned with eschatological historicity or the relation between the Children of Israel and all other peoples, but is limited to the paradisiacal realm beyond where the redeemed whom the Lord has "planted" (18a) metaphorically live, grow, and thrive. Theologically, the beings who become the "remnant" face the "Lord," which means that Harnack's dictum, "as they partake of God's being, this appears in them and they become, as it were, parts of God,"[287] cannot be upheld.

Verse 22a is followed immediately by 22c 𝔊 or 22b 𝔖. The singular ܕܘܟܪܢܐ (*duḵrānā*), which translates μνεῖαι, may have originally been plural ܕܘܟܪܢ̈ܐ (*duḵrānē*), losing its plural points as being dependent on ܗܘܐ (*hwā*).[288] With the attribution of eternity, the "remembrance(s)," constructed with an objective genitive, acquire directly an enduring soteriological and theological meaning, which also reflects indirectly on the "remnant" and which is not to be found in the human sphere, where memories are shorter (cf. 16h 𝔊).[289] These δοῦλοι/ܥܒܕ̈ܐ (*ʿaḇdē*), who will from now on be loyal and faithful, are the dwellers in paradise, who have been described as

278 Marc Philonenko, "Conjecture sur un verset de la onzième Ode de Salomon," *ZNW* 53 (1962) 264.

279 Payne Smith, 2:4332–33.

280 Emerton, "Problems," 390–91.

281 Abramowski, "Sprache," 82.

282 Schoedel, "Readings," 176. See already Carmignac, "Affinités," 94, although he appends three question marks. Later on, Carmignac seems to have given up this idea (Carmignac, "Auteur," 429–31). Vööbus (p. 289), too, thinks in terms of a Syriac word for "will" in the original.

283 As Klijn did earlier ("Review of Testuz," 448), Philonenko ("Conjecture," 264) considers ΛΕΙΜΜΑ "a corruption of ΘΕΛΗΜΑ," saying, "the text which the Syriac translator had before him was doubtless as follows: ΚΑΙ ΓΕΙΝΕΤΕ ΤΑ ΠΑΝΤΑ ΩϹ ΤΟ ΛΕΙΜΜΑ ϹΟΥ." Schoedel ("Readings," 176), too, would like to keep θέλημα.

284 So it is "unnecessary to emend the text (viz. of 𝔖)" (Charlesworth, 59). But that does not mean that it is "unlikely" that the Syriac text—not Codex H but 𝔖*—was a translation "from Greek" (Charlesworth, 58). I do agree, however, that "it is improbable that a Hebrew original lies behind the Syriac text" (Charlesworth, 59). According to Emerton ("Problems," 386–87), "it could be suggested that *ΤΟ ΛΕΙΜΜΑ* was the original Greek reading and that it was a translation of the Syriac."

285 Käsemann, *Romans,* 275–76 (German, 266) on Rom 9:27; see Volkmar Martinus Herntrich and Gottlob Schrenk, "λεῖμμα, κτλ.," *ThWNT* 4 (1942) 198–221; *TDNT* 4:194–214. See also Charlesworth, 59: "The biblical source of inspiration may be the vision that a remnant of Israel will be saved, a pervasive characteristic of Jewish thought since Isaiah and Jeremiah (viz. Is 10:19-23)."

286 Käsemann, *Romans,* 300 (German, 290), on Rom 11:5.

287 Harnack, 41.

288 See BDAG, *s.v.* μνεία; Payne Smith, 1:898.

289 Cf. *Paraph. Shem* 46,2-3, 12, 22 (*NHLE*, 360: "immortal memorial") and also *1 Clem.* 45:8: καὶ

"trees" and "plants" but also as "laborers" and who are now "slaves" of the Lord because they are no longer subject to anyone.[290]

Note on 22b preserved only in 𝔊. It is not impossible "that this line is authentic because it makes sense within the context of the Greek."[291] But the structure of 22 becomes "more complex by the further insertion of the eulogy 22b . . . into the bicolon formed by 22a and 22c."[292] So it is advisable to treat 22b 𝔊 as another section peculiar to 𝔊 and, unlike the previous passage 16c-h (see above), as a marginal note that found a place between 22a and 22c by a copyist's error. It also offers a text-critical puzzle.[293]

Given that ⲇⲣⲱⲥⲧⲉⲥ in the manuscript needs emendation, the suggestions of *δρῶντες*, as a participle of *δράω*[294]—or even *ἐρῶντες*[295]—are not as convincing, because of the following genitive, as *δράσται*[296] or *δρῆσται*.[297]

The masculine *δρήστης* (Attic *δράστης*), meaning "worker" or "slave,"[298] is a less common synonym for *διάκονος* and *δοῦλος*, or even *ἐργαζόμενος* (20a). This eulogy[299], then, is reminiscent of the benediction in 6:13a, where ℭ uses the loanwords *μακάριοι* and *διάκονοι*. In the imagery of stanzas VI and VII, the "workers" or "slaves" of the waters of the Lord are also the *φυτά* (21b 𝔊), which both depend on the *ὕδατα* (on the plural of *ὕδωρ*, cf. Rev 7:17)[300] and serve and preserve them. Hence, the choice of "wardens" to translate the emended ⲇⲣⲏⲥⲧⲁⲓ.[301]

■ **23** Without 23a, it would have been all but impossible to make sense of stanza VIII, particularly the Syriac version. That is why the division in this case follows Emerton rather than Franzmann.[302] So stanza VIII is a tricolon, like stanza I, and 23b and 23c are seen to be in synonymous parallelism.[303] Contrary to Charlesworth's notion that 23b 𝔊 "looks like a literal translation of the Syriac,"[304] it is exactly in 23c that a decisive argument for a Greek original can be found.

Verse 23a takes up terms from 18b, laying stress on "paradise" (see on 16a above) not on *τόπος*/ܐܬܪܐ (*ʾaṯrā*). It is not concerned, therefore, with a *specific* place or with a "place of special meaning," but quite generally with a "place to stay,"[305] so the difference between the Syriac construction (with preposition ܒ [*b*-]) and the Greek (with genitive) is trivial. The addition of ܓܝܪ (*gēr*) followed by ܘ (*w*-) in 23b is not meant causally,[306] and thus it does not form a connection back from 23a to stanza VII (22b-c). The adjectives *πολύς*/ܣܓܝ (*saggī*), used predicatively, are placed emphatically at the beginning, qualifying the singular "place" or "space."[307]

In contrast to the formulaic brevity of 23b in 𝔊, the Syriac expressly makes the connection to *παράδεισος* by the use of ܒܗ (preposition ܒ [*b*-] + third masculine singular suffix). For the remainder, the translation of

ἔγγραφοι ἐγένοντο ἀπὸ τοῦ θεοῦ ἐν τῷ μνημοσύνῳ αὐτοῦ [*αὐτῶν*] *εἰς τοὺς αἰῶνας τῶν αἰώνων* ("and [they] were enrolled/inscribed by God in his [or: their own] memorial for ever and ever" [Lake, 1:86–87; cf. Ehrman, 1:116–17; Fischer, 82]).

290 BDAG, *s.v.* *δοῦλος*; Payne Smith, 2:2772–73. The adjective *πιστός* (BDAG, *s.v.* *πιστός*) corresponds to the Syriac term ܡܗܝܡܢܐ (*mhaymnā*) derived from ܗܝܡܢ (*haymen*), which may equally be an active or a passive participle (Payne Smith, 1:232–33).

291 Charlesworth, 58.

292 Franzmann, 98–99.

293 Emerton ("Problems," 388–89) sees three possibilities for "the additional line": that it was (1) "original," (2) "a gloss," or (3) "added by a translator from Syriac into Greek." He is inclined to accept it as part of the original *Ode*: "It is possible that the line once existed in Syriac and that it was lost by *homoioteleuton*" (p. 389).

294 Carmignac, "Affinités," 94; Franzmann, 87, 91; Lattke, *Oden*, 132.

295 Schoedel, "Readings," 177–78.

296 Testuz, 66.

297 Charlesworth, 51.

298 LSJ, *s.v.* *δρήστης*.

299 On the acclamation *εὐλογημένος*, see BDAG, *s.v.* *εὐλογέω*.

300 BDAG, *s.v.* *ὕδωρ*.

301 I believe that 22b 𝔊 must be interpreted within the imagery of its context. I would therefore question Emerton's reference ("Problems," 389) to 11:6-7: "The waters referred to are presumably those of verses 6 ff., possibly the waters of baptism."

302 Emerton, "Problems," 389; Franzmann, 98–99.

303 Franzmann (p. 96) correctly refers to 4:4: "23b-c is a formula used also in 4:4 with ref. to the Lord." She also brings out the parallelism of 23b and 23c.

304 Charlesworth, 59.

305 BDAG, *s.v.* *τόπος*, esp. 1e.

306 See Lattke, "Wörter," 289 = idem, *Bedeutung*, 4:138.

307 BDAG, *s.v.* *πολύς*; Payne Smith, 2:2518–19.

ἀργέω by a following passive participle, derived from the root *bṭl*, used predicatively, is idiomatically correct Syriac.[308] The Greek verb, used to describe the delay in rebuilding the temple (1 Esdr 2:26),[309] means here "be fruitless, ineffectual."[310] Since it is negated, the emphasis, of course, is not on the barrenness but on the fruitfulness announced, with a higher step in comparison, in 23c.[311]

Assuming that καὶ καρποφορεῖ in 23c is the correct reading and that it was found already in 𝔊*,[312] and assuming also that the subject ܟܠܡܕܡ (*kol meddem*), as in 22a, represents the text of 𝔖*, the Greek can claim unquestionable superiority over the Syriac. The adverb καί preceded by ἀλλά raises the comparison a step higher,[313] which means it could not be translated by ܐܦ (*ʾāp̄*). Paraphrasing it with "all" as the opposite of οὐδέν is both logical and also gives the same sense. If the cases had been reversed, the Syriac phrase would have been translated by πάντα. So it is incorrect to say, with Carmignac, "the Greek omits 'all.'"[314] Indeed, the missing πάντα is a strong argument for the priority of 𝔊. It is not vitiated by the slight difference between καρποφορεῖ[315] and the idiomatically Syriac expression with the passive participle of ܡܠܐ (*mlā*).[316]

■ **24** None of the other closing doxologies (16:20; 17:16; 18:16; 20:10) presents such difficulties as this one at the end of the bilingual *Ode* 11. As can be seen from Emerton's detailed study,[317] Vööbus oversimplifies in his theory "of the superiority of the Syriac text," claiming that 𝔖 is "clear and comprehensible" while commenting on 𝔊 only: "By such stammering acclaim he [i.e., 'the Greek'] reveals that he has not quite understood the original doxology."[318] Carmignac goes deeper, maintaining that "paradise" is misplaced in 𝔖 and emending it ("in the Paradise of eternal delights"), and then concludes: "The two endings are equally plausible, although the error in the Syriac prompts one to give preference to the Greek."[319] Emerton points to the LXX as the source for 24b[320] but cannot decide "whether the Greek is original."[321]

There is no difficulty in 24a, where δόξα corresponds to the *hapax legomenon* ܫܘܒܚܐ (*šubḥā*), with the meaning of "praise," "glory," even "honor,"[322] unlike 17:16, where δόξα/ܬܫܒܘܚܬܐ (*tešbuḥtā*) means "glory" in the sense of "splendor." The personifying address puts θεός in the dative into apposition with the personal pronoun.[323] If ܐܠܗܐ (*ʾallāhā*) is a vocative, the apposition is somewhat loose.[324] "God" is the same as the one who has previously been addressed as "Lord" and has also been called the "Most High" (9a). And the "I" at the end of its speech within a speech (see on 18a above) can utter such θεολογία[325] just because no-body can rightfully receive "glory" in an act of worship.

308 Payne Smith, 1:511; cf. Sebastian Brock, review of Charlesworth in *BSOAS* 38 (1975) 142: "useless," "unprofitable."

309 BDAG, *s.v.* ἀργέω.

310 Lampe, 223.

311 If Ephraem in his "*Madrāšā De Paradiso* 7,21" quoted the Syriac text of 23b ("certain quotation" according to Harris and Mingana, 2:18; cf. Murray, *Symbols*, 25, 255), 𝔖* would have been available in the fourth century (see Lattke, "Ode 13," 256 = idem, *Bedeutung*, 4:76). Such evidence of reception is not directly helpful in historical criticism.

312 See Lattke, *Bedeutung*, 1:10.

313 See BDAG, *s.vv.* ἀλλά, 1 and 4; καί, 2; BDF and BDR §448, 1 and 6.

314 Carmignac, "Affinités," 94.

315 Cf. the aorist of καρποφορέω in 1c, καρποφόρα in 16c. Here in 23c the form καρποφορεῖ is made parallel to ἀργεῖ (23b).

316 This expression (cf. Payne Smith, 2:2118–19) is also made to fit the parallelism of 23b and 23c in 𝔖.

317 Emerton, "Problems," 391–92, 396.

318 Vööbus, 289–90.

319 Carmignac, "Affinités," 95.

320 See Gen 2:23-24; Joel 2:3; Ezek 31:9; cf. Ezek 28:13; 31:16, 18; 4 Esdr 7:36.

321 Emerton, "Problems," 396. 4 Esdr 7:36 shows that the Greek text is preferable to the Syriac. A reference to *Ps. Sol.* 14:3-4, and Trafton's remark on it, "On the identification of the holy ones with the trees in paradise, cf. OdesSol 11.16-23," should also be added (Trafton, 133). The term ܡܫܪܪܐ (*mšarrā*) in *Ps. Sol.* 14:4 (Trafton's 14:3) is not a "misspelling" of ܡܫܪܫܐ (*mšaršā*) as Holm-Nielsen (91) believes.

322 BDAG, *s.v.* δόξα; see also Payne Smith, 2:4026; Lattke, *Hymnus*, 479, 487.

323 There is no special significance to the definite article preceding "God" since θεός occurs "somet[imes] with, somet[imes] without the art[icle]" (BDAG, *s.v.* θεός, 3).

324 Nöldeke §§212–13.

325 See Lampe, 627.

Emerton's statement that 24b 𝔊 "does not make sense" does not make sense.[326] The dative of παρά-δεισος is clearly instrumental, so the only question is whether σου refers to the word that precedes it (viz., παραδείσῳ) or the one that follows (viz., τρυφῆς). It could equally well be read as "by the paradise of your everlasting delight." The difference between the two possibilities is minimal; the mythological idea, that a paradisiacal utopia can be an instrument for glorifying God (cf. already 16a-b), is stupendous.

Verse 24b 𝔖 can also be translated two ways. The masculine ܒܘܣܡܐ (*bussāmā*),[327] corresponding to τρυφή,[328] has to be in apposition with "God" and not parallel to the first word of 24a.[329] However, since the ܒ (*b*-), which follows the relative particle ܕ (*d*-), is not only "the proper preposition to indicate locality and time" but also "to express instrumentality,"[330] 24b 𝔖 could also be translated instrumentally as "delight, which is by the everlasting paradise" or "everlasting delight, which is by the paradise" (cf. esp. 38:19-21). It is, however, more probable that "delight" is qualified by the temporal expression ܕܠܥܠܡ (*da-l-ʿālam*) as "everlasting delight" and placed in paradise by the locating preposition ܒ (*b*-): "everlasting delight, that is in paradise" = "everlasting paradisiacal delight."[331] Whether God is described as delight *in* or *by* paradise is less important, however, than the fact that the doxology expressed in 24a acquires a reciprocal character: "God" becomes the "delight" of those who honor him (cf., e.g., 7:2-3; 11:15; 15:1).

Finally, it is again necessary to ask which of the two versions of 24b is more likely to reflect the original.[332] The texts in 𝔖 and 𝔊 may be considered equal linguistically, but the Greek, being the theological *lectio difficilior*, can perhaps therefore claim priority. So Emerton's conclusion, "the doxology thus does not help us to decide which is the original language," may be questioned.[333]

326 Emerton, "Problems," 391. Adam ("Sprache," 151) comes to a similar conclusion: "The final doxology, as found in the Greek text (V. 24), does not make sense."

327 Payne Smith, 1:550–51.

328 BDAG, *s.v.* τρυφή, 3: "joy, delight."

329 Emerton, "Problems," 391; contra Adam, "Sprache," 151.

330 Nöldeke §248.

331 Klaus Beyer in Lattke, 3:XXIV n. 1.

332 See Klijn, "Review of Testuz," 448.

333 Emerton, "Problems," 392. As previously mentioned (see before stanza I above), Emerton ends his detailed study by saying (p. 406): "The most probable conclusion to be drawn is that the Odes of Solomon were composed in Syriac." But it may not be unimportant to quote Brock's statement: "Finally it must be remembered that the Odes are transmitted both in Syriac and in the Graeco-Latin world in conjunction with the Psalms of Solomon, where the Syriac is definitely a translation from the Greek; moreover, where the Greek vocabulary of Ode 11 overlaps with that of the Psalms of Solomon, the Syriac will be found to use the same word in both Odes and Psalms in all cases but one." See Sebastian Brock, review of Charlesworth, in *BSOAS* 38 (1975) 143.

12

Ode 12: The Truth, the Word, and the Aeons

(I) **1a** The word[a] of truth filled me,
1b in order that I might speak it.
2a And like the flowing of water,
2b truth flowed from my mouth,
2c and my lips declared its fruits.
3a And it increased in me its *gnōsis*,
3b because the true word is the mouth of the Lord
3c and the gate of his light.

(II) **4a** And the Most High gave it [viz., the word] to his Aeons,
4b the interpreters of his beauty,
4c and the narrators of his glory,
4d and the confessors of his thought,
4e and the preachers of his mind,
4f and the teachers of his works.

(III) **5a** For the swiftness of the word is indescribable,
5b and like its narration, so are its swiftness and sharpness,
5c and its course is limitless.
6a And it never falls, but abides,
6b and known[b] is neither its descent nor its way.
7a For as its work, so is its expectation,
7b for it is the light and dawning of thought.

(IV) **8a** And the Aeons spoke to one another by it (viz., the word)
8b and they acquired speech, those who were silent.
9a And from it was friendship and harmony,
9b and they spoke, one to another, that which they had [viz., the word].
10a And they were goaded by the word
10b and knew him who had made them, because they were in harmony.
11a Because the mouth of the Most High spoke to them,
11b also, by it/him his [the Most High's] explanation ran.

(V) **12a** For the dwelling-place of the word is man,
12b and its truth is love.

(VI) **13a** Blessed are they who by it have understood everything,
13b and have known the Lord in his truth.
Hallelujah.

a 1a Read singular ܦܬܓܡܐ (*petḡāmā*) instead of the plural.

b 6b Read Passive ܝܕܝܥ instead of Active ܝܕܥ.

Introduction

Ode 12 is preserved in one Syriac manuscript.[1] Although the personified "word" is one of the dominant topics of this difficult poem,[2] the complex mixture of mythological imagery cannot simply be called "hymn on the Word, the Logos."[3] Since stanzas I and VI frame this composition, which is mainly founded on Wisdom 7 and Sirach 24,[4] the key word "truth" must also receive its due weight (1a, 13b).[5] The stanzas between are concerned with the "Aeons" (II and IV) and the "word" (III and V). The Gnostic speaking "I" disappears at the end of the introductory metaphorical address (stanza I), and even the final benediction (stanza VI) does not bring it back. As in many of the other *Odes* the audience is not specified.

Interpretation

■ **1-3** If the Persian loanword ܦܬܓܡܐ (*peṯgāmā*), "word," were to keep the plural points of the manuscript, 1a would be left without a subject. Although Harris and Mingana keep the plural ܦܬܓܡ̈ܐ (*peṯgāmē*) in their edition and translation,[6] they consider Newbold's emendation ("Read without points")[7] "grammatically more correct."[8] Without the plural points, it is easier to reconstruct a possible Greek original: Ἐπλήρωσέν με ὁ λόγος τῆς ἀληθείας (cf. 11:2c). In place of ὁ λόγος 𝔊 could equally have had τὸ ῥῆμα, because this personification is not "the Logos."[9] The genitive phrase ὁ λόγος τῆς ἀληθείας would have been ambiguous, unlike New Testament occurrences of the term (Eph 1:13; Col 1:5; 2 Tim 2:15; Jas 1:18), a nuance that has disappeared in the Syriac. The possible Greek original should probably have been translated, "The word filled me *with* truth."[10] In view of 3b, the Syriac translation "word *of* truth" is acceptable. The divine "word of truth" would then be the "true word," which is not attainable by any human being (3b; see Excursus 1). Verse 2b however, even in 𝔖, allows the original meaning of 1a 𝔊 to show through (see Excursus 12 at 8b below).

The conjunction ܡܛܠ ܕ (*meṭṭol d-*) at the beginning of 1b corresponds to Greek ἵνα (+ subjunctive). On the other hand, it is not possible to decide whether the Pa. ܡܠܠ (*mallel*) represents λαλέω (cf. linguistically Eph 4:25; John 8:40) or λέγω (cf. in substance John 8:45-46; 16:7). Although the masculine suffix on ܠ (*l-*) can equally refer to the "word,"[11] and although the combination of λαλέω (rather than λέγω) with λόγος or ῥῆμα as direct object is very common,[12] 2b suggests that it may refer rather to "truth," which is the object of this inspired Gnostic speaking (cf. 18:15).[13]

1 Ms.: Codex H, 9b–10b (𝔖). Ed./trans.: Charlesworth, 59–63; Franzmann, 100–108; Lattke, 1:225–46 and 3:XXIV.

2 See Harris and Mingana, 2:275: "It is not an easy Ode to translate nor to understand."

3 Contra Wilhelm Bousset, *Kyrios Christos: Geschichte des Christusglaubens von den Anfängen des Christentums bis Irenaeus* (2nd ed.; Göttingen: Vandenhoeck & Ruprecht, 1921; repr. of 5th ed., 1965) 305. Similarly Newbold ("Bardaisan," 186) considers it an "Ode to the Word," and Harris and Mingana (2:275) "a Hymn concerning the Divine Logos, or the Divine Wisdom which becomes the Logos." Quasten, too, is thinking of the Logos of John 1 when he heads it "Ode 12 sings of the Logos"; see Johannes Quasten, *Patrology*, vol. 1: *The Beginnings of Patristic Literature* (Utrecht/Antwerp: Spectrum, 1950; repr., 1966) 164. *Ode* 12 is not a "eulogy" (Harnack, 42) nor one of the "reveilles" (Schille, 99). Diettrich, who considers *Ode* 12 "a liturgical hymn," provides a *Formgeschichte* that is as fanciful as his theory that stanza IV "is a prophetically themed retrospective on the activity of the Logos . . . in the origin of the Essene sect" (Diettrich, 46).

4 See J. Rendel Harris, *The Origin of the Prologue to St John's Gospel* (Cambridge: Cambridge University Press, 1917) 54; Harris and Mingana, 2:273–76.

5 At 6:8a, Table 3 draws attention to the pervasive influence of Sirach 24.

6 Harris and Mingana, vol. 1, on this passage; 2:272.

7 Newbold, "Bardaisan," 185.

8 Harris and Mingana, 2:273. They explain it thus: "The copyist was possibly puzzled, as every other Syrian Christian would be, with the fact that λόγος was expressed by the inadequate vocable ܦܬܓܡܐ, and put the plural dots over it, signifying that it meant 'words' *in concreto*." Franzmann (p. 102) also thinks the plural "a copyist's error."

9 BDAG, *s.v.* λόγος.

10 See BDAG, *s.v.* πληρόω; on ܡܠܐ (*mlā*), see Payne Smith, 2:2117–18.

Verse 2a-b cannot be separated from 2c (cf. 40:2). This brings Franzmann's analysis into question.[14] As in similar comparisons,[15] the "truth," which has filled the "I" (1a 𝔊) and flows out of or from its "mouth," is compared to "running water."[16] The idea of water is not emphasized in *Ode* 12 (see Excursus 6). The term "mouth," however, is used also in 3b and 11a, although in a different context (see below and cf. 10:1).

Verse 2c is parallel to 2b. The "lips" stand for the speaking mouth (cf. 21:8; Excursus 16). What the lips of the mouth "declared" (in the sense of "reveal" or "announce"; see commentary on 7:25)[17] are probably not the "fruits" of truth,[18] but those of the mouth (in 𝔊 probably καρποὺς αὐτοῦ).[19] In both cases. the transferred sense is of *spoken* "gain"[20] and not of moral "fruits" (unlike καρπὸς ἀληθείας, "fruit of truth," in *Hermas, Sim.* 96 [IX.19].2).[21]

As "word" is the subject of 1a, it is also the subject of 3a, contained in the Aph. of ܣܓܝ (*sgī*) / ܣܓܐ (*sgā*).[22] 𝔊 would have had ἐπλήθυνε.[23] The masculine suffix of ܝܕܥܬܐ (*ʾidaʿtā*) is indeterminate because the subject in the text of the Syriac manuscript is not the "word" but the "Lord" (3a; cf. "he" in 1a [H]) as the "Most High" (4a, etc.). Even in 𝔖 as emended, there are two possibilities for the referent. Either the personified Word increased the "*gnōsis*" of the "truth" (αὐτῆς in 𝔊) or of the "Word" itself (αὐτοῦ in 𝔊). In either case it deals with objects of *gnōsis* (see Excursus 7).

If 3b-c are the justification of 3a, their subject is the "true word"[24] to which two parallel predicates are annexed. The very free word order of the Syriac[25] is quite compatible with a possible Greek original "with nominal predicate,"[26] ὅτι στόμα τοῦ κυρίου ὁ λόγος ἐστιν (ὁ ἀληθινός/ἀληθής)[27] | καὶ θύρα τοῦ φωτός αὐτοῦ. This justification is more of a didactic saying[28] than "a concluding confessional statement."[29]

Metaphorically, "mouth" in 3b stands "by metonymy for that which the mouth utters" (see Excursus 31).[30] The theologically predicative "mouth of the Lord" deliberately removes the personified "Word" from earthly reality or human possession. If Sir 24:3 (ἀπὸ στόματος ὑψίστου ἐξῆλθον, "I came forth from the mouth of the Most High") already influenced the language of 3b—and not only 11a—this audacious equation of "word" and "mouth of the Lord" surely trumps even the self-praise of the Hellenistic-Judaic "Sophia."[31]

---

11 Franzmann, 104. Charlesworth (p. 61) translated it, "That I may proclaim Him." His explanation—"'Him' refers either to God the Father or to His Son"—is found only in the original printing of 1973 (p. 62).
12 See BDAG, *s.v.* λαλέω.
13 Bauer, 592, among many others.
14 Franzmann (p. 104) divides them 2a-b, 2c-3a.
15 See Introduction, sec. 8.
16 On possible Greek models for the words ܪܕܐ (*rdā*) and ܪܕܝܐ (*redyā*) from the one root, see Payne Smith, 2:3818, 3821.
17 On the Pa. ܚܘܝ (*ḥawwī*), see Payne Smith, 1:1208–9.
18 Bauer, 592.
19 Thus a reference to *Gos. Phil.* 84,10-13 ("Ignorance is a slave. Knowledge is freedom. If we know the truth, we shall find the fruits of the truth within us" [*NHLE*, 159]) is of limited relevance.
20 See BDAG, *s.v.* καρπός.
21 Ehrman, 2:436–37; cf. Norbert Brox, *Der Hirt des Hermas* (KAV 7; Göttingen: Vandenhoeck & Ruprecht, 1991) 436, 445. See also Excursus 11.
22 Grammatically, it can also be translated as "and she [i.e., Truth] increased in me her/his *gnōsis*." Because of the reasons given in 3b-c, the translation suggested above is preferable.
23 See Payne Smith, 2:2518; Frankenberg, 14 ("επληθυνε εν εμοι την γνωσιν αυτου").
24 Contra Franzmann, 104.
25 Nöldeke §324.
26 See BDF and BDR §472.
27 The adjective ܫܪܝܪܐ (*šarrīrā*) may even be a Syriac addition, making a connection with 1a.
28 See Introduction, sec. 8.
29 Franzmann, 104.
30 BDAG, *s.v.* στόμα. Pierre (p. 92) says much the same: "Assimilation de l'organe (ici: la bouche) à sa fonction, sa puissance actualisée (le verbe)."
31 There is also a certain parallelism with Ignatius *Rom.* 8:2 (τὸ ἀψευδὲς στόμα, ἐν ᾧ ὁ πατὴρ ἀληθῶς ἐλάλησεν, "He is the mouth which cannot lie, by which the Father has spoken truely"; cf. Lake, 1:236–37, with Ehrman, 1:280–81). "Ignatius uses the term στόμα . . . to emphasize the revelatory activity of the Son" (Bauer and Paulsen, 77–78). *Ode* 12, however, never mentions the "Son."

Verse 3c is hardly likely to have been inspired by Ps 118:105 LXX or Prov 6:26,[32] for the stress is not on "light" as the "element and sphere of the divine"[33] (cf. esp. 1 John 1:7b; Excursus 10), but on the term "gate" used uniquely here in parallel to "mouth."[34] Thus, a transferred theological function is ascribed to "word" without characterizing this otherworldly "word" as the "light."[35]

■ **4** Following on from the parallel statements about the true word (3b-c) is a mythological "poem,"[36] which, after the introductory monocolon 4a, displays five parallel appositions to "Aeons." The first word of each line, 4b-f, is a so-called *nomen agentis*,[37] which in 𝔊 would probably have been a nominalized participle or a noun.[38] Whether the five parallel constructions with the genitive were equivalent to the Greek genitive (e.g., τῆς δόξης αὐτοῦ) or accusative constructions (e.g., τὴν δόξαν αὐτοῦ) is as uncertain as the exact Greek words that correspond to most of the words in stanza II.[39] The insertion of ܕܝܠ (*dīl-*) in 4b makes it quite clear that the nouns in the genitive refer not to the "word" but to the "Most High."[40]

The "Most High" in 4a (cf. 11a) is identical with the "Lord" in this Ode (3b, 13b). He is called κύριος τῶν κυρίων καὶ θεὸς τῶν θεῶν καὶ βασιλεὺς τῶν αἰώνων (Greek *Enoch* 9:4)[41] according to Jewish tradition, but is also regarded as being above and beyond all hierarchies of the boundless cosmos. This negative theo-logic needs to be kept in mind in trying to understand correctly the downward gradations of the human attempts at description of the Most High, beginning with his being (4b-c), then his thought (4d-e), and finally his works (4f). The masculine accusative suffix on ܝܗܒܗ refers to the "word" of stanza I (and of stanzas III–V). The verb *yab* itself, corresponding to ἔδωκεν (cf., e.g., 4:3c), functions mythologically similarly to its use in John 3:16, where, however, it expresses the sending of the Son of God into the sphere of human history.[42] This compass, considered as the total of all the "eras of history," "generations,"[43] or "worlds,"[44] is not here under consideration. The plural of ܥܠܡܐ (*ʿālmā*) or αἰών stands for a personification of the supramundane *plērōma* (= "totality of aeons";[45] see Excursuses 22 and 35). Harnack, referring also to 7:11, remarks on Flemming's translation "worlds":

> Probably the original had "aeons;" and then we must recognize that we have here a Judaism with "Gnostic" lineaments; but this "Gnostic" trait had penetrated even into Pharisaic doctrines from where Paul picked it up. The Aeons are the mediators and heralds of God. The shift in meaning from Ps 19:1-2 to this text is hardly noticeable.[46]

32 Contra Diettrich, 47.
33 BDAG, *s.v.* φῶς; see also Payne Smith, 2:2301.
34 On ܬܪܥܐ (*tarʿā*), see Payne Smith, 2:4505; on θύρα, see BDAG, *s.v.*
35 So this verse must be distinguished from such passages as John 1:4, 5, 7-9; 3:19a; 8:12a; 9:5; 12:35-36; 12:46. *Ode* 12 may also have influenced the Valentinian *Gospel of Truth*; see, e.g., 26,28–27,7: "Truth appeared; all its emanations knew it. They greeted the Father in truth with a perfect power that joins them with the Father. For, as for everyone who loves the truth—because the truth is the mouth of the Father; his tongue is the Holy Spirit—he who is joined to the truth is joined to the Father's mouth by his tongue, whenever he is to receive the Holy Spirit, since this is the manifestation of the Father and his revelation to his aeons" (*NHLE*, 44). At the same time Newbold's remark ("Bardaisan," 187) on 4a is justified: "These [worlds] are not Valentinian aeons." Perhaps "not" should be changed to "not yet."
36 See Introduction, sec. 8.
37 Nöldeke §130.
38 As Frankenberg already recognized (p. 15), although he put them all in apposition to "word." Cf. the criticism of Harris and Mingana, 2:273–74: "Frankenberg unnecessarily suggests to read . . . singular with reference to λόγος."
39 The latter is a common problem, found also in lists and catalogues in the New Testament and Philo.
40 See Nöldeke §225.
41 See Uhlig, *Henochbuch*, 524.
42 See Lattke, *Einheit*, 64–85.
43 See Charlesworth, 61.
44 See Harris and Mingana, 2:272. "Hardly = worlds, but Aeons as beings" (Bauer, 592, referring to "Excerpta ex Theod. 7,1: 'Since the Father was unacknowledged he wished for acknowledgment from the Aeons.' Common in Manichaean writings"). See also the last note on stanza I above.
45 Lampe, 56.
46 Harnack, 42. Diettrich (p. 47) repeats this statement but omits the last sentence.

Although the word given to the Aeons reverberates five times, it still requires a great deal of imagination to see a reference "to the five Books of the Law, or the five senses."[47] More important is the perception that this poetical list of synonyms and aspects does not arise from any strong desire to make conceptual distinctions. Especially the synonyms of the appositional—and approving—characterizations of the personified Aeons make it difficult to find plausible Greek equivalents and therefore do the same to attempts at translation into modern languages. Because of the strict parallelism of 4b-f, it will be best to begin by considering the five *hapax legomena*[48] that form the first word of each line and after that to discuss the various aspects of the Most High.

The meaning of the plural ܡܬܪ̈ܓܡܢܐ (*mtargmānē*), derived from ܬܪܓܡ (*targem*), one of the "quadriliterals," in 4b is reasonably clear.[49] 𝔊 will have had a term derived from the root ἑρμην-.[50] There is no necessary connotation of "translate" or "interpret," since ἑρμηνεύω, for example, can mean simply "proclaim, discourse on."[51]

To comprehend the *hapax legomenon* ܡܬܢܝܢܐ (*mtannyānā*) in 4c, it is necessary to consider 5a-b (see below) and also to include the basic meaning of the Pa. of ܬܢܐ (*tnā*).[52] This suggests that the translations of this unusual word by *enuntians*,[53] "annunciator,"[54] or "repeater"[55] are less suitable than "narrator."[56] The Greek equivalent can only be conjectured.

There is no reason at all, in 4d, to ignore the meaning of the *hapax legomenon* ܡܘܕܝܢܐ (*mawdyānā* = *confessor*),[57] derived from the Aph. ܐܘܕܝ (*ʾawdī*), in order to translate it as "annunciator"[58] or "preacher."[59] In this case, it is likely that 𝔊 used some form of *(ἐξ)ομολογέω*. If, however, it governed the dative, the meaning would change to "to praise."[60]

That the *hapax legomenon* in 4e, ܡܣܒܪܢܐ (*msabbrānā*), was already a technical term equivalent to *evangelista* is most unlikely. What is certain is that it has to be related to the Pa. of ܣܒܪ (*sbar*), and so a form of εὐαγγελίζομαι is to be expected in 𝔊[61] (on the Pa., cf. 7:17; 9:6; 13:2). Varying translations attempt to reflect this expectation, for example, "heralds,"[62] "preachers,"[63] "messengers,"[64] or "evangelists."[65]

The *hapax legomenon* in 4f, ܡܢܟܦܢܐ (*mnakkpānā*), is especially hard to translate. The major dictionaries are unsatisfactory.[66] Here, too, it is necessary to attend to the meaning of the Pa. of ܢܟܦ (*nkep̄/nkap̄*).[67] If 𝔊 used one of the participles of σωφρονίζω, the Aeons appear in the final line of this mini-poem as those who, by the Word, "bring" the works (i.e., the "creatures")[68] of the Most High "to their senses" and "advise" them to be sensible.[69] So they are less "purifiers,"[70] "hallowers,"[71] or "devotees"[72] than "instructors,"[73] "educators,"[74] or quite simply "teachers."[75]

47 Contra Pierre, 92.
48 The fact that all five lines begin with a *hapax legomenon* is not enough to prove that this short poem was originally independent. If *Ode* 12 also had a Greek original and stanza II had, at least sometimes, used participles, the Greek text—and even more 𝔊*—might have employed few or no *hapax legomena*.
49 Cf. Nöldeke §130: "interpreter;" Payne Smith, 2:4497: *interpres*.
50 LSJ, *s.v.* ἑρμην-; Lampe, 549; cf. also compounds with δι- or μεθ-.
51 BDAG, *s.v.* ἑρμηνεύω, 1.
52 Payne Smith, 2:4465: *narravit*.
53 Brockelmann, *Lexicon*, 829.
54 Bauer, 592 ("Verkünder").
55 Harris and Mingana, 2:272.
56 Harnack, 42, and Diettrich, 47 ("Erzähler"); Charlesworth, 61, and Franzmann, 101 ("narrator").
57 Payne Smith, 1:1551; Harris and Mingana, 2:272; et al.
58 Harnack, 42, and Diettrich, 47 ("Verkünder").
59 Bauer, 592.
60 BDAG, *s.v.* [ἐξ]ομολογέω.
61 Payne Smith, 2:2510–11, 2515.
62 Harris and Mingana, 2:272; Harnack, 42 ("Herolde").
63 Charlesworth, 61; Diettrich, 47 ("Prediger").
64 Franzmann, 101; Bauer, 592 ("Boten").
65 Labourt and Batiffol, 15 ("Evangélistes"); Pierre, 92 ("évangélisateurs").
66 Payne Smith, 2:2378 (*castigator*); Brockelmann, *Lexicon*, 430 (*sanctificans [sive observans]*).
67 See Payne Smith, 2:2376–77.
68 Ungnad and Staerk, 15; Bauer, 592.
69 BDAG, *s.v.* σωφρονίζω.
70 Franzmann, 101.
71 Lattke, *Bedeutung*, 1:115 ("Heiliger").
72 Lattke, *Oden*, 136 ("Verehrer").
73 Harris and Mingana, 2:272.
74 Bauer, 592 ("Erzieher").
75 Charlesworth, 61. Diettrich (p. 47) remarks on his translation ("and those who maintain the chastity

Working again from 4b to 4f there will be a shorter discussion of the aspects of the "Most High" of 4a (see above). In general, it may be said that his "beauty" and "glory" correspond to his "thought" and "mind" and that his "works" arise from his "mind." The "Aeons" themselves, who are in some sense also his "works" (see below), play their role, made possible by his "word," because they have the "mouth of the Lord" and the "gate of his light" (3b-c) and can use words to describe the "Most High" (4b-e) and instruct the works of his creation also in words (4f; see on stanza IV below).[76]

The term ܝܐܝܘܬܐ (*yāʾyūṯā*) in 4b, derived from the root ܝܐܝ, which is no longer in use,[77] does not mean μεγαλοπρέπεια, as it does, for example, in 7:23,[78] but simple "beauty," not including any sense of "majesty."[79] Since it is a parallel term to δόξα (4c), 𝔊 cannot have used δόξα in this line.[80]

The term ܬܫܒܘܚܬܐ (*tešbuḥtā*) is often used hymnically, but in 4c it is certainly equivalent to δόξα in the sense of "glory"[81] (see Excursus 21), not of "praise,"[82] "honor"[83] or ἔπαινος.[84]

The terms ܡܚܫܒܬܐ (*maḥšaḇṯā*) and ܬܪܥܝܬܐ (*tarʿīṯā*) in 4d-e are synonymous and could be translated in several ways (see Excursus 9). To vary Descartes, it is not true that the "Most High" *is*, because people *think* him. Rather humans have thought of and named a Most High as their Lord who does not exist in himself or think on his own. And the secret of his creative thought, which serves to explain the secrets of humanity and the cosmos, forms part of the concept of his being.

Since the cosmos—as well as the chaos—of the eternal and unbounded universe, including humanity on earth and all possible living beings, is not lord over itself and does not even form a hierarchy with a Most High at the apex, this congeries can be described both as a singular, his "work" (8:18-19; 16:6), and as a plural, his "works," as in 4f (cf. esp. 16:9). Even Sophia herself is included among them (7:8), so the Aeons, as personified "higher" beings, are also within the ambit of this term, derived from ܥܒܕ (*ʿḇaḏ*).[85] Whether the Greek equivalent of the plural of ܥܒܕܐ (*ʿḇāḏā*) was ἔργα[86] or rather ποιήματα (cf. Rom 1:20)[87] or κτίσματα,[88] must be left undecided.

■ **5-7** Even if the manuscript text of 5 and 6b is "in disorder,"[89] it is no more "unintelligible"[90] than a number of other passages in the *Odes of Solomon*. Harris and Mingana assume that 5b "is certainly corrupt" and hypothesize "that a dittographical error from the copyists has crept into the text of the second line,"[91] which is unconvincing. All that is necessary are their relatively slight text-critical emendations in 5b (suffixes third masculine singular for third feminine singular) and 6b (passive participle for active), which Franzmann also accepts.[92] Thus emended, the text is still difficult and needs help from 3b-c in the interpretation. The topic of stanza III is the "true word" of stanza I. Franzmann's deduction from her analysis, "The structure of the strophes is chiastic," shows clearly that 6a occupies a central position.[93] The structure of stanza III can be shown by a diagram:

of his works [servants?]") as follows: "The worlds or aeons as representatives of an active chastity, as against the general idea of pairing in the universe (cf. Gen 1:12, 21, 24, 27; Sir 33:15; 42:24), is possible in Palestine only among the Essenes and a small group of rabbis. Outside Palestine there are also the Therapeutae." This theory must be considered very far-fetched.

76 I cannot agree with Newbold ("Bardaisan," 188) that "worlds" (his translation in 4a) probably means "planets," so I do not see any link to ancient astrology, such as can be detected in the works of, for example, Bardesanes.

77 Cf. יאה in Koehler and Baumgartner, 364; יאא in Drower and Macuch, 183.

78 Contra Frankenberg, 15.

79 Contra Lattke, *Oden*, 136.

80 See Payne Smith, 1:1534, suggesting other possibilities.

81 BDAG, *s.v.* δόξα; Payne Smith, 2:4027–28.

82 Harris and Mingana, 2:272; Bernard, 75.

83 Diettrich, 47 ("Lob").

84 Frankenberg, 15; Tsakonas, 75.

85 See Payne Smith, 2:2773–74.

86 BDAG, *s.v.* ἔργον.

87 BDAG, *s.v.* ποίημα.

88 BDAG, *s.v.* κτίσμα.

89 Bauer, 593.

90 Newbold, "Bardaisan," 185.

91 Harris and Mingana, 2:274.

92 Franzmann, 103.

93 Ibid., 105. Whether 6a is treated as a monocolon, following the manuscript, or divided into a bicolon

5a-b					A
	5c			B	
		6a	C		
	6b			B'	
7a-b					A'

The well-known problems in 5a-b disappear if the wordplay with ܬܘܢܝܐ (*tunnāyā*) is transposed into Greek and the genitive, expressed by a suffix in 𝔖 (and surely by αὐτοῦ in 𝔊), is read as a *subjective* genitive. In the first place, it is said that the "swiftness of the word" is ἀδιήγητος[94] or even ἀνεκδιήγητος.[95] The ܓܝܪ (*gēr*) in second place—and followed by ܘ (*w-*) in 5b—does not have any causal force.[96] The feminine suffix of ܐܝܬ (*ʾīṯ*) (Greek merely ἐστίν) refers to the feminine ܩܠܝܠܘܬܐ (*qallīlūṯā*), which occurs only in 5a and 5b, and which in 𝔊 would most probably have been τὸ τάχος.[97]

The parallel term ܚܪܝܦܘܬܐ (*ḥarrīpūṯā*) occurs only in 5b; it is commonly used for fast and sudden movement (cf. 39:4)[98] and may have corresponded to ὀξύτης[99]—provided that it was not an addition peculiar to 𝔖. It brings in the idea of "speed" and "sharpness" as comparisons to help in picturing the "narration" that the "word" itself has initiated.[100] What constituted *this* ܬܘܢܝܐ (*tunnāyā*; in 𝔊 probably διήγησις)[101] is not mentioned, quite logically in view of 5a. "Narration," after all, is a basic function of the word. On the other hand, this "word" is just about as difficult to delineate as the "Lord" or the "Most High" himself.

So the complementary statements of 5c and 6b belong to the *via negationis*, which as "a necessary part of the theology of any age" characterizes "negative theology."[102] The *hapax legomenon* ܣܘܝܟܐ (*suyyāḵā*) in 5c, derived from ܣܘܟ, ܣܟ (*sāḵ*) and negated by ܕܠܐ (*d-lā*), most probably corresponded to the predicative adjective ἀπέραντος,[103] which in antiquity was used to express the limitlessness of space and time,[104] and also of God.[105] The subject of this negative statement—constructed with ܐܝܬ (*ʾīṯ*) + third feminine singular possessive suffix = ἐστίν—is the feminine ܗܠܟܬܐ (*hlaḵṯā*), which can mean the ability to walk (or move?),[106] but in this context probably stands for δρόμος. In place of Pierre's interpretation of it as "a term which likens the running of the Word to the gift of the Law and the obedience to the commandments" (referring to Ps 19:4-5),[107] it may be seen as a polemical term emphasizing the limited "*courses* of the stars."[108]

Verse 6a, "the central focus of the stanza,"[109] interrupts the connection between 5c and 6b. Considering all the words of motion that precede and follow it, it is impossible to translate the participle of ܩܘܡ, ܩܡ (*qām*) used with infinitive absolute[110] by a simple "stand," meaning to stop or stand still,[111] while the reference to the "polar word-pair ܢܦܠ - ܩܘܡ" with "the contrasting

(as Franzmann, 100–101, 105, does) makes no difference.

94 BDAG, *s.v.* ἀδιήγητος ("indescribable").

95 BDAG, *s.v.* ἀνεκδιήγητος; see also Harris and Mingana, 2:274. Barth's reference (p. 263) to Ps 19:4 and his translation ("without an audible sound") cannot be supported.

96 See Lattke, "Wörter," 289 = idem, *Bedeutung*, 4:138.

97 See Payne Smith, 2:3618; BDAG, *s.v.* τάχος; Frankenberg, 15.

98 Payne Smith, 1:1381.

99 Frankenberg, 15; see also Tsakonas, 75; Fanourgakis, 151.

100 This fact is occluded when Franzmann (p. 105) speaks of *all* the nouns in 5b and 7a as "attribute[s] of the Word." The influence of Wis 7:24a cannot be overlooked (πάσης γὰρ κινήσεως κινητικώτερον σοφία, "For wisdom is more mobile than any motion"). Cf. also Heb 4:12-13, speaking of ὁ λόγος τοῦ θεοῦ ("the word of God").

101 See Payne Smith, 2:4466; BDAG, *s.v.* διήγησις.

102 See Herbert Vorgrimler, "Negative Theologie," *LThK*² 7 (1962) 864–65.

103 Payne Smith, 2:2551; BDAG, *s.v.* ἀπέραντος.

104 LSJ, *s.v.* ἀπέραντος.

105 Lampe, 182.

106 Brockelmann, *Lexicon*, 176–77 ("*facultas eundi*").

107 Pierre, 92–93.

108 See BDAG, *s.v.* δρόμος.

109 Franzmann, 105.

110 The infinitive absolute "serves to give more emphasis to the verb, by contrasting the action with some other one or by giving expression to its intensity" (Nöldeke §295; cf. 28:4).

111 Contra Bauer, 593; Charlesworth, 61; Lattke, *Oden*, 137.

action of standing over against falling" is not very helpful.[112] This polysemous verb, with a basic meaning of "arose",[113] must be interpreted here as having one of its multiple transferred meanings that express transcendental being, continuance, and abiding, as, for example, *διαμένω*[114] or simple *μένω* in opposition to *(ἐκ)πίπτω*[115] (cf. 1 Cor 13:8, 13).[116]

The positive second half of 6a emphasizes, by contrast (*ἀλλά* in 𝔊), the dominating negative statement of the first half. In order to come to some understanding of this central mythologoumenon, constructed of the active participle[117] of ܢܦܠ (*npal*) with an adverbial ܠܐ ܡܬܘܡ (*lā mtōm* = *οὐδέποτε*, *nunquam*) and "without reference to a definite time,"[118] it can be compared to the affirmation of salvation in Rom 9:6a, *οὐχ οἷον δὲ ἐκπέπτωκεν ὁ λόγος τοῦ Θεοῦ* ("It is not as though God's word has failed").[119]

The active participle of ܐܝܕܥ (*ʾidaʿ*) as it stands in the manuscript of 6b makes no sense, but only a minimal text-critical emendation is required to change ܝܕܥ (*yādaʿ*) into the passive ܐܝܕܝܥ (*ʾidīʿ*).[120] This would suggest, in parallelism with 5c, that the Greek, whether original or a translation, would have used a predicative adjective such as *ἄγνωστος*,[121] which refers equally to the *hapax legomenon* ܡܚܬܬܐ (*maḥḥtā*) and the more common term ܐܘܪܚܐ (*ʾurḥā*, without topical parallels in the *Odes of Solomon*). It is noteworthy that the term used for "descent" is not the technical term ܡܚܬܬܐ (*maḥḥattā*), incarnation, but another noun, ܡܚܬܬܐ,[122] also derived from the Pa. of ܢܚܬ (*nḥet*). It is impossible to tell whether the Greek word was *κάθοδος* or *κατάβασις*. Both of these words later became technical terms for the christological *descensus*.[123] In the antique mythos of *Ode* 12 the "descent" starts down from the "Most High" (4a), that is, from the transcendental heights,[124] arrives among the Aeons of stanzas II and IV, and probably continues as the "way" to reach humankind (see on 12a below).

Verse 7a-b, which is to some extent parallel to 5a-b, not only justifies 6b but, by use of the term ܥܒܕܐ (*ʿbādā*), encompasses everything spoken by the "word." Verse 7b at the same time justifies 7a and also forms the connection to stanza IV. The term *ἔργον*, which would have been used in the Greek of 7a, is not here in opposition to *λόγος* and does not refer to any particular "accomplishment."[125] It is also unlikely that there was any influence from John 17:4. The stress in this typical comparison in 7a[126] is not, after all, on "work" but on the *hapax legomenon* ܣܘܟܝܐ (*sukkaya*), derived from the Pa. of ܣܟܐ (*skā*). For the Greek equivalent *προσδοκία* ("expectation"),[127] it is necessary to decide whether the *αὐτοῦ*, which undoubtedly followed it, is a subjective or objective genitive. For the use of this strange term is only understandable if it is used to mean that the advent of the personified word—or perhaps just its "work"—is expected.[128]

With only slight justification, 7b implies that the "expectation" of 7a is already fulfilled. The last word of stanza III (ܐܝܬ + third masculine singular possessive suffix, in 𝔊 certainly *ἐστίν*) could be taken to refer to "expectation," but the statement should rather be understood as an additional—and positive—characterization of the "word." Its first part is reminiscent of 41:14, though

112 Contra Franzmann, 105, cf. p. 404 with references to 6:16 and 18:2-3.
113 See Payne Smith, 2:3522–26 ("*surrexit*").
114 Frankenberg, 15.
115 See BDAG, *s.vv.* *μένω* and *πίπτω*.
116 Forms or compounds of *ἵστημι* are less likely (BDAG, *s.v.* *ἵστημι*).
117 The misprint *nāpāl* for *nāpel* in Harris and Mingana (in vol. 1 on this passage) is still to be found in Charlesworth, 60.
118 Nöldeke §269.
119 Käsemann, *Romans*, 260 (German, 250); Payne Smith, 2:2412; BDAG, *s.v.* *ἐκπίπτω*.
120 Harris and Mingana, vol. 1, on this passage; 2:272. Charlesworth's note (p. 63 n. 10) on this emendation cannot be passed over in silence. It is true that H has ܝܕܥ (with a dot over the first letter). However, this does not mark it as "imperfect 3ms" but as a *qāṭel*-form (see Nöldeke §6) like ܢܦܠ in 6a. Thus, the assertion that "the dot over the *Nūn* is the sign the copyist used to distinguish an initial *Nūn* . . . from an initial *Yūdh*. . . . Hence we have a modal imperfect" is erroneous.
121 See Frankenberg, 15; Franzmann, 103; BDAG, *s.v.* *ἄγνωστος*.
122 Payne Smith, 2:2346.
123 See Lampe, 690, 705.
124 Cf. 10:5; 21:1; 22:1; 23:5; 36:1-2.
125 Payne Smith, 2:2773–74; BDAG, *s.v.* *ἔργον*.
126 See Introduction, sec. 8.
127 See BDAG, *s.v.* *προσδοκία*; Payne Smith, 2:2624.
128 I do not agree with Franzmann (p. 105) that "[t]he combination of the elements of expectation and the light/dawning of thought in relation to the

with less of a Johannine tinge (cf. John 1:4-5 and 1:9). In the context of *Ode* 12 this statement surpasses 3c in that "word" is no longer merely the *gate* of divine light but is itself named as this "light"[129] (see Excursus 10).

Like the "light," the genitive phrase that follows is not concerned with mental activity. The *hapax legomenon* ܕܢܚܐ (*denḥā*), derived from ܕܢܚ (*dnaḥ*) and probably equivalent to Greek ἀνατολή ("dawn[ing]"),[130] is not here intended as an astronomical or geographical term, nor does it carry any messianic connotation (cf. Luke 1:78); instead its transferred meaning is governed by the feminine ܡܚܫܒܬܐ (*maḥšabṯā*), derived from the root *ḥšb*. As this word is not a reference to the "clear thought" of 34:2, nor yet, in the first place, to an anthropologically Gnostic idea (cf. 15:4-5; 18:14), it becomes necessary to refer back to the human description of the Most High (see on 4d above) and also to find other theological and soteriological parallels.[131] Which of the many possible equivalents (e.g., [δια]λογισμός, σύνεσις, [δια]νόημα)[132] may have been found in 𝔊 is unknown.

■ **8-11** There is no cause to disturb the structure of these four bicola by dividing 10b into 10b-c.[133] When Franzmann additionally divides 8b into 8b-c, her analysis of stanza IV becomes quite obscure.[134] Connecting back to stanza II, the mythological narration tells what happened to the "Aeons" and what they did. At the same time, the personified "word" directly and indirectly forms part of the topic because of the link to 7b. Verses 8-9 may have been influenced by Ps 18:3-4 LXX, but the Gnosticizing aeonology has departed markedly from the biblical imagery, although it has not yet achieved a "Gnostic Aeon-genealogy."[135]

That the Aeons were considered speaking beings could be deduced already from the aeonology of stanza II. What is new in 8a is the idea that the "Aeons," which here are neither eras nor generations, spoke *to each other* (Pa. ܡܠܠ [*mallel*], as in 9b; cf. also 11a) by the word that was given to them (4a; here just ܒ [*b-*] + third masculine singular suffix). The phrase ܚܕ ܠܚܕ (*ḥaḏ l-ḥaḏ*), and the similar phrase ܚܕ ܠܘܬ ܚܕ (*ḥaḏ lwāṯ ḥaḏ*) in 9b, correspond to a Greek phrase including ἀλλήλων,[136] for example, ἐν ἀλλήλοις and/or εἰς ἀλλήλους[137] or even πρὸς ἀλλήλους.

Harnack already found the "sense" of 8b "obscure" but still proposed an intuitive solution: "the Aeons, which had no speech of their own, acquired language by the gift of the word."[138] Harris and Mingana accepted this for their translation ("And those that were silent acquired speech") as "[the] only meaning the Syriac sentence can have,"[139] based on Connolly's convincing proposition "that the Syriac of *v.* 8ᵇ is merely an attempt at translating literally καὶ τὰ ἄφωνα ἔμφωνα ἐγένετο"[140] (cf. Isa 53:7 and Acts 8:32). The hypothesis can be refined further by observing the grammatical gender of αἰών and adjusting the word order to a more idiomatic Greek, which produces καὶ ἔμφωνοι ἐγένοντο οἱ ἄφωνοι as a possible Greek original. This results in the collapse of Franzmann's justification for her idiosyncratic translation: "The sense of this line is that the aeons came into being by the Word, a concept supported by 10b."[141] Neither the reference to 10b nor the incidental mention of 16:19a sheds much light, linguistically or topically, on 8b in the context of its bicolon. Even in a form-critical analysis, 8b cannot be classified as "a formula"/"formular saying."[142]

The circumlocutory paraphrase of οἱ ἄφωνοι (by demonstrative pronoun + participial adjective + enclitic form of ܗܘܐ [*hwā*]) is nothing unusual.[143] Taken by itself, the first part of 8a is quite ambiguous and could indeed mean the same as 16:19a. There would be several

Word in 7a-b suggests some link with the Lord as the sun (cf. esp. in 15:1 where the aspect of expectation also occurs)."

129 See Payne Smith, 2:2301–2 on ܢܘܗܪܐ (*nuhrā*); BDAG, *s.v.* φῶς.

130 Payne Smith, 1:927; BDAG, *s.v.* ἀνατολή, 3.

131 Cf. 16:8-9, 19; 17:5; 21:5; 41:10; see also Excursus 9.

132 See Payne Smith, 1:1397.

133 As do Harris and Mingana, vol. 1, on this passage, 2:273; Bauer, 593; Charlesworth, 60–61.

134 Franzmann, 100, 102, 105–6. Two misprints mar the Syriac text: for ܒܕ ܠܘܬ ܒܕ read ܚܕ ܠܘܬ ܚܕ (Franzmann, 100).

135 See Harnack, 42.

136 BDAG, *s.v.* ἀλλήλων.

137 Payne Smith, 1:1194.

138 Harnack, 42.

139 Harris and Mingana, 2:275, cf. 2:272.

140 Connolly, "Greek," 534.

141 Franzmann, 102–3.

142 Ibid., 105, 107.

143 On the plural of ܫܬܝܩ (*šattīq*), see Payne Smith, *Dictionary*, 601; Payne Smith, 2:4357.

possible interpretations of the third plural masculine perfect of ܗܘܐ (*hwā*) as well as of the preposition ܒ (*b*-), for example, "they were in/by the word" or "they became by the word." But, as previously remarked, those translations make no sense. So it is necessary to follow Connolly, who, making an analogy with Luke 24:5 (ἐμφόβων δὲ γενομένων αὐτῶν – ܘܗܘܝ ܒܕܚܠܬܐ [*wa-hway b-deḥltā*], Peshitta), postulated a literal interim translation of ܒܡܠܬܐ: "with- (*or* in-) speech."[144] The meaning of 8b is thus closer to the statement in 8:4, "you who were in silence, speak, for your mouth has been opened." In addition, it is notable that, in all of *Ode* 12, only here is the feminine ܡܠܬܐ (*melltā*) used. The translator(s) did so to show that this "word" is neither synonymous nor identical with the personified "word" of the remainder of *Ode* 12. The excursus that follows will demonstrate that the statement of 8a is unique in its formulation.

Excursus 12: "Word" and Words of Speaking in the *Odes of Solomon*

In the Syriac text of the *Odes of Solomon* there are two terms (ܡܠܬܐ [=M] and ܦܬܓܡܐ [=P]; see below) that are translated by "word," and they are used indiscriminately to translate λόγος and ῥῆμα.[145] These Greek terms, in their turn, are "full synonyms" in the LXX "to reproduce the idea of דָּבָר" and are "much influenced" by the Hebrew word.[146] It can be assumed that especially λόγος in 𝔊 had "dianoetic force" in the *Odes of Solomon* as well (and they thus share at least *one* important characteristic of the Greek λόγος tradition) and also carries the "dynamic" connotation of דָּבָר and דְּבַר־יְהוָה.[147] Along the evolutionary lines, which originate in the Hebrew writings and continue in the Greek writings of the Bible, the "most important attribute of דָּבָר, and of λόγος and ῥῆμα as translations, is truth" (with special reference to Ps 119:160).[148]

Since the term "word" is found neither in *Ode* 1 nor in *Ode* 11, the two Syriac words can only be considered in isolation, without being able to determine which was the Greek equivalent. The masculine ܦܬܓܡܐ (*petḡāmā*) occurs thirteen times, and, with the emendation of 12:1a, is always in the singular; it dominates *Ode* 12. Setting aside the unusual passage 12:8b (see above), the feminine ܡܠܬܐ (*melltā*) occurs eleven times, is also generally used in the singular, and is found noticeably often "within a phrase introduced by ܒ" (cf. 10:1; 15:9; 16:19; 29:9; 29:10; 39:9).[149]

But even in the *Odes of Solomon,* the two Syriac words may be synonyms; compare, for example, 9:3 and 16:8 ("word of the Lord"); 42:14 and 15:9 ("my [i.e., the redeemed Redeemer's] word"); 8:8, etc., and 41:11 (in connection with "truth").[150] Even when "word" is in parallel with the divine "thought"/"thinking," M is not used exclusively (16:8, 19; 41:11); P occurs as well (9:3). The same is true of the close connection with "light" (M in 10:1; 41:14; P in 12:3; 32:2).

When comparing the statements about the "word"—and about "to speak"—in the *Odes of Solomon* with the "usage of λέγω, λόγος, ῥῆμα, λαλέω in

144 Connolly, "Greek," 534.

145 Payne Smith, 2:2110–11, 3335–36.

146 Otto Procksch, "λέγω, κτλ. C. 'Wort Gottes' im AT," *ThWNT* 4 (1942) 91; *TDNT* 4:92.

147 Procksch, "λέγω," *ThWNT* 4:90–91; *TDNT* 4:92.

148 Procksch, "λέγω," *ThWNT* 4:92; *TDNT* 4:93. The "much misunderstood Ps 119," which is "a treasure-trove of the varieties and nuances of the term דָּבָר" receives individual treatment from Procksch ("λέγω," *ThWNT* 4:99–100; *TDNT* 4:100). The limits of the influence it had on the *Odes of Solomon* become clear, for example, in the recognition that "תּוֹרָה as alternative to דָּבָר (v 1. 18. 34. 44. 51. 61. 72. 97. 126. 136. 163)" is quite insignificant (p. 100). If a statement like Ps 119:160a influenced the prologue of *Ode* 12, the plural found in Ps 118:160 LXX (ἀρχὴ τῶν λόγων σου ἀλήθεια) may help to explain the plural points on ܦܬܓܡܐ (see on 12:1a above).

149 Franzmann, 106. There are two criticisms to make of Franzmann's "Excursus: 'Word' in the Odes" (pp. 106–8). In the first place, she has not noticed the exceptional position of ܒܡܠܬܐ (*b-melltā*) in 12:8b. Second, she refers to the feminine ܡܠܬܐ in 41:11 and 41:14 not as "it" but as "he," "him." It is doubtful whether this can be done in the context of 41:11-16a. Even if 𝔊 had λόγος (and not ῥῆμα), the Syriac could have used a masculine construction in 41:14 to make it clear that ܡܠܬܐ was used as a masculine, as can be seen in John 1:1, 14 and Rev 19:13 (see Payne Smith, 2:2110). If the term in 41:11a had been a masculine (= ὁ Λόγος, "the Logos"), it would have to be distinguished from the "word" in 41:14.

150 In the passages quoted as comparisons, the word ܦܬܓܡܐ (hereinafter P) is found in the first, and the word ܡܠܬܐ (hereinafter M) in the second.

ancient Greek,"[151] with the concept of "Logos in Ancient Greece and Hellenism,"[152] or even with the use of "word" and "to speak" in the New Testament,[153] it is immediately evident that the contemporary breadth of meaning has been severely limited in the poetical forms of the *Odes of Solomon*. In each case, it will be necessary to examine possible influences and cross-connections within the area defined by the Hellenistic doctrines of the Logos, early Gnostic mythologies, and early Jewish or Christian theologies together with the "testimony to the λόγος in the prologue to John's Gospel."[154] So what follows will be only a summary overview, noting also passages where terms of speaking bear some relation to statements about the "word."

The most common word of speaking is the Pa. ܡܠܠ (*mallel*). If 6:1b is included (strings "speak"), it occurs twenty-one times, four of them in *Ode* 12. The association with "spirit" (6:2a; 16:5a) and "breath" (18:15a), which signify a kind of inspiration, is also quite striking. The term ܡܠܠ (*mallel*) in Syriac is generally used to translate λαλέω.[155] On the other hand, ܐܡܪ (*ʾemar*) is only used five times. Like λέγω/εἶπον/εἶπα, it is used to introduce direct speech (11:18; 33:5; 38:10; 42:15). Even in 8:9a it refers back to the imperative in 8:8.[156] In three passages it appears with other words of speaking: ܚܘܝ (*ḥawwī*) in 8:9b ("declare"); ܐܟܪܙ (*ʾakrez*) and ܩܥܐ (*qʿā*) in 33:5b ("preaching"; "crying out"); and ܩܥܐ by itself in 42:15b ("cry out"; cf. also ܣܒܪ [*sabbar*, "proclaim"] in 7:17; 9:6; ["declare"] in 13:2; ܓܥܐ [*gʿā*, "cry to"] in 26:4a).

The "Father of *gnōsis*" is characterized as the "word (P) of *gnōsis*" in 7:7. The parallel imperatives of salvation in 8:8a-b ("Hear the word [P] of truth | and receive the *gnōsis* of the Most High") are the basis for the subsequent dualistically used words of speaking in 8:9a-b (see above). The "word (P) of truth" in 12:1a ≤ corresponds to the "true word" in 12:3b, which is called the "mouth of the Lord"—and therefore probably also the "mouth of the Most High" (12:11a)—and the "gate of his light" (12:3b-c). The personification of the speedy and sharp "word (P)" in *Ode* 12, which reaches an apex in 12:12 ("the dwelling-place of the word is man"), on the one hand "seems . . . to let through in glimpses . . . a memory of a pre-Christian mythos of the 'Word.'"[157] On the other hand, especially in 12:11a, it is clear that "word" still bears the sense of "the spoken word"[158] and results in the speech both of the speaking "I" and of the "Aeons" (12:1b, 8a, 9b). "His word (M)" in 41:11a probably refers to the "Father of truth" (41:9a). Whether M in 41:11a is identical with M in 41:14 and what relationship it may have to John 1:1-14 still await elucidation.[159] The "word (P)" at the center of *Ode* 32 comes from personified "Truth" (2) and is parallel to "joy" (1a) and "light" (1b). The personified "word (P)" of the Lord/Most High comes to the speaking "I" (37:3a) bearing gifts of eschatological "fruits" of labor (3b) and "rest" (4).

In 9:3, the "word (P) of the Lord" and his "desires" are protologically equated with his holy "thought" about the Messiah. In 16:8, the "word (M) of the Lord" is again parallel to his "thought." It could equally be said that his "word" and his ܡܚܫܒܬܐ (*maḥšabtā*, "thought, thinking") are complementary, like the manifest and invisible realms they probe. Although "word" may retain some dianoetic connotations, the dynamic sense is dominant. This dynamism expresses itself when the "Lord" directs the mouth of the speaking "I" by his "word (M)" (10:1a); when the "power of his word (M)" is specifically mentioned (16:7); when the heavenly hosts are subjected to his "word (M)" (16:14; cf. ῥῆμα in Sir 16:28); when

151 Albert Debrunner, "λέγω, κτλ. A. Die Vokabeln λέγω, λόγος, ῥῆμα, λαλέω im Griechentum," *ThWNT* 4 (1942) 71–76, esp. 73–74; *TDNT* 4:71–77, esp. 73–74.

152 Hermann M. Kleinknecht, "λέγω, κτλ. B. Der Logos in Griechentum und Hellenismus," *ThWNT* 4 (1942) 76–89; *TDNT* 4:77–91.

153 See Gerhard Kittel, "λέγω, κτλ. D. 'Wort' und 'Reden' im NT," *ThWNT* 4 (1942) 100–147; *TDNT* 4:100–143; BDAG, *s.vv.* εἶπον, λαλέω, λέγω, λόγος, ῥῆμα.

154 Kittel, "λέγω," *ThWNT* 4:134–40; *TDNT* 4:127–36, has now been completely superseded by Michael Theobald, *Die Fleischwerdung des Logos: Studien zum Verhältnis des Johannesprologs zum Corpus des Evangeliums und zu 1 Joh* (NTAbh N.F. 20; Münster: Aschendorff, 1988); see Michael Lattke, review of Theobald, *Fleischwerdung*, in *Colloquium* 25/1 (1993) 39–40.

155 Payne Smith, 2:2109; see also 2:2115 on 11:6, where ܡܠܠܐ (*mallālā*) corresponds to a participle of λαλέω.

156 See Payne Smith, 1:243–44.

157 Schnackenburg, *Johannesevangelium*, 1:266, quoted after Theobald, *Fleischwerdung*, 482.

158 Bultmann, *Johannes, Ergänzungsheft,* 14 n. 1; ET *John,* 14 n. 3.

159 See Lattke, "Messias-Stellen," 443–44 = idem, *Bedeutung*, 4:104–6.

the "Aeons"/"Worlds" are made/endure by his "word (M)" (16:19); when metaphorical wars are fought and enemies defeated by his "word (M)" (29:9-10); and when mythological rivers are bridged by his "word (M)" (39:9a). In certain passages the dianoetic aspect is transferred to the parallel term "thought" (16:8; see above) or the "thought of his heart" (16:19; cf. 41:10b in the transition to 41:11a).

The shared term "in need" may provide a connection between 18:4 and 24:9. In the first passage, God's "word (P)" is parallel to his "perfection" (18:5). What sort of "password" the "word (P)" in the second part of the mythos of *Ode* 24 may have been must be further examined. At any rate, its connection to 24:10-12 shows that it is closely related to "truth."

In most cases, "word" is recognizable as a soteriological power, the word of God, which acts creatively and liberatingly as no cosmic power or existential maxim can. As the "word (P) of *gnōsis*" *is* the "Father of *gnōsis*," so it would be possible in a number of contexts to substitute "God" or "Lord" or "Most High" for the "*Word* of the Lord/the Most High." For the content of his "word (M/P)" is nowhere articulated. The same is true of the "word (M)" of the redeemed Redeemer—or redeeming Redeemed One—in 15:9b ("Sheol has been destroyed by my word"). Even in 42:14c it is not clear of what the redeemed Redeemer's "word (P)" that will not fail consists. Since so many of the *Odes of Solomon* are put into the mouth of the Redeemer, his word assumes a poetic character in his words.

The preposition ܡܢ (*men*) in 9a shows the origin of the two synonyms, not by reference to a spiritual source but as the gift of relationship among the "Aeons." In this hendiadys,[160] the stress is not on the *hapax legomenon* ܪܚܡܘܬܐ (*rāḥmūṯā*, in 𝔊 surely φιλία; see Excursus 2),[161] but on the term of harmony ܫܘܝܘܬܐ (*šawyūṯā*), which is derived from the root ܫܘܐ (*šwā*; in 𝔊 perhaps ὁμαλότης but more probably ἰσότης),[162] as is evident from its repetition in 10b. If the term had been ἰσότης in 𝔊, the focus would not have been on the later principle that "παντὶ ἀνθρώπῳ . . . ἰσότης ἐστὶ κατὰ τὴν φύσιν ['For every human being there is equality by nature'] Bas[il], *ep.* 262.1,"[163] nor on the christological and theological content of the word. Since φιλία, in a transferred sense, can also be equivalent to "harmony,"[164] both words emphasize the "concord" of the "Aeons."[165] The Pythagorean harmony of the spheres and the "common ownership of the Essenes"[166] are both foreign to this passage.

Verse 9b is a slightly altered repetition of 8a. In 8a the "Aeons" spoke to each other *by* the word; in 9b they speak the word *itself.* It was given to them by the "Most High" (4a). The idiomatic Syriac construction (*meddem . . . lhōn*) seems to be a translation of ἅ/ἅτινα ἔσχοσαν.[167]

As Harris and Mingana themselves admit, their text-critical suggestion ("ܘܐܙܕܪܪܘ for ܘܐܙܕܩܬܘ")[168] for the beginning of 10a is "a daring emendation in view of the fact that in the previous lines mention is made of the 'sharpness' of the word."[169] The Ethpe. of ܙܩܛ (*zqaṭ*), inserted in the margin of manuscript H, is used metaphorically for "incited, stimulated,"[170] and is certainly a translation of a passive form of κεντρόω.[171] The "sharpness" of 5b reappears here as the prick of a goad.[172] Unlike in 9a, ܡܢ (*men*) here, following the "passive," "denotes, generally, the starting point of the action, *i.e.* the *agent.*"[173]

Closely connected to 10a and also harking back to 9a, the monocolon 10b combines a Gnosticizing saying about "knowing" (see Excursus 7) with a biblical saying on creation (cf. 4:15; 7:12; 16:19). The personified "Aeons" knew their creator, the "Most High" (11a). So even these beings, who are believed to inhabit the higher realms, are not masters of themselves. The

160 The synonyms are so closely connected that the translation of the verb ܗܘܐ (*hwā*) can remain in the singular.
161 See Payne Smith, 2:3883.
162 See Payne Smith, 2:4082–83; BDAG, *s.v.* ἰσότης, 1.
163 Lampe, 677.
164 Ibid., 1478.
165 Bauer, 593. Harnack (p. 43) is of the opinion that "it is probable that the subject changes in 8b and the reference is to the human beings to whom the word came; consequently the subject of 9b-11 is also humanity." But humans are first mentioned in 12a. The homogeneity of 8-11 makes it unlikely that humanity forms part of the subject matter of this second "aeonology."
166 Diettrich, 49.
167 Frankenberg's retroversion (p. 15) ("α εγενετο αυτοις") is hardly correct.
168 Harris and Mingana, vol. 1, on this passage.
169 Harris and Mingana, 2:275.
170 Payne Smith, 1:1151 ("*incitatus, stimulatus est*").
171 See Lampe, 744.
172 See BDAG, *s.v.* κέντρον.
173 Nöldeke §249 D.

second half, with the composite particle ܟܕ (*ba-d*) emphasizes, in this case, not so much the cause[174] as the simultaneity ("while," "meantime"),[175] which in 𝔊 would be indicated by a participle (γενόμενοι ἐν τῇ ἰσότητι). While the "Aeons" received their "harmony" from the "word," their activity and response carry them past "speaking" to "knowing."

As in some other passages in the *Odes of Solomon*, 11a precedes and gives the reason for the main clause 11b, which has not been clearly shown in any translation. For this reason the ܘ (*ʾu-*), which is equivalent to καί, has to be translated by "also"—not by "and." The Greek of 11a might even have used a genitive absolute construction (perhaps λαλοῦντος τοῦ στόματος ὑψίστου αὐτοῖς). The "speaking" of the "Aeons" is finally due to the mythological fact that the "mouth of the Most High" (cf. στόματος ὑψίστου in Sir 24:3)[176] has spoken to them at and since their creation.

Since the "Most High" in *Ode* 12 (4a, 11a) is identical with the "Lord" (3b, 13b), the phrase "the mouth of the Most High" means the "true" personified "word," which is the "mouth of the Lord" (3b). Therefore it is almost unnecessary to ask whether the third masculine singular suffix on ܒ (*b-*) + ܐܝܕܐ (*ʾidā*, "hand") in 11b refers to the "mouth" or the "Most High." Even so, both possibilities should be discussed.

Taking ܪܗܛ (*rheṭ*) here—like τρέχω—to mean "run" in the sense of "proceed quickly"[177] (cf. 2 Thess 3:1 [ἵνα ὁ λόγος τοῦ κυρίου τρέχῃ]), the first possible translation would be: "By it [i.e., the mouth] his [i.e., the Most High's] exposition ran." In this case the suffix of the *hapax legomenon* ܡܦܫܩܢܘܬܐ (*mp̄aššqānūṯā*), derived from the Pa. of ܦܫܩ (*pšaq*), would correspond to Greek αὐτοῦ as an objective genitive. By the "mouth" or the "word," then, the "Most High"/"Lord" would be interpreted and the "Aeons" would do the interpreting.

In the other possible translation, αὐτοῦ would be taken as a subjective genitive: "By him [i.e., the Most High] its [i.e., the mouth's] exposition ran." So the divine "mouth" or the true "word" would be the authority performing the exegesis.[178] Who or what was being explicated may perhaps be gathered from stanza II (4b-f), where, however, it is the "Aeons" that are the "interpreters," etc.

Whichever way this difficult colon (the core of bicolon 11) was intended, it is reminiscent of John 1:18 (μονογενὴς θεός/υἱός . . . ἐξηγήσατο, "the only God/Son . . . has made him known"), where "God," the invisible power, is "the object, which must follow ἐξηγήσατο."[179] The direction in which this interpretation "ran" becomes clearer from the following verses, although 12a cannot be used as a basis for 11b.[180]

■ **12** It is very tempting to interpret this parallel bicolon, with the unique image in 12a and the new terms "man" and "love," in a poetic didactic fashion, constructing an anthropological, philosophic connection between language and humanity, on the one hand, and reality and Eros, on the other. But however didactic these statements in their simple construction with the copula (ἐστίν in 𝔊) may be, they must be read and understood in the limiting and Gnosticizing context of the mythology of *Ode* 12.[181]

174 Payne Smith, 1:449.

175 Nöldeke §§155, 360 A.

176 "The Peshitta of Sirach has ܕܐܠܗܐ, where again we see the Odist to be independent of the Peshitta. The whole of Ode XII is a Wisdom composition, showing striking parallels with the *Praises of Wisdom* in Sirach xxiv" (Harris and Mingana, 2:276).

177 BDAG, *s.v.* τρέχω; Payne Smith, 2:3833–34 (*progressus est*).

178 See Payne Smith, 2:3328 (*expositio, explicatio*); BDAG, *s.vv.* ἐξήγησις and ἑρμηνεία.

179 Walter Bauer, *Das Johannesevangelium* (HNT 6; Tübingen: Mohr Siebeck, 1933) 30. C. H. Dodd (*The Interpretation of the Fourth Gospel* [Cambridge: Cambridge University Press, 1953; 1st pb. ed., 1968] 272) quotes 12:11-12, with other passages, to demonstrate that "the idea of Christ as Word—the spoken word of God though conceived in some sort hypostatically—is to be found in writings emanating from a circle whose thought certainly resembles that of the Fourth Gospel in some respects."

180 Contra Diettrich, 49.

181 Only certain parts of the *Odes of Solomon* can be called didactic. This means that Drijvers's opinion that "[t]he *Odes of Solomon* are deeply considered, didactic poems" and "moulded by an anti-Marcionite, philosophical habit of thought" is far too broad, and definitely questionable on the subject of Marcionism (Drijvers, "Salomoschriften," 732).

The particle ܓܝܪ (*gēr*, in 𝔊 γάρ or δέ) in 12a, followed by ܘ (*w*-) in 12b, has no "causal force" but at most expresses continuation and connection,[182] so stanza V cannot be thought to give a reason for the last line of stanza IV (see above). The connection to 11b consists in the fact that 12a can be considered the terminus of the expository run, but at the same time stanza V returns to the starting point of the whole Ode.[183] The speaking "I" includes himself in the comprehensive term "man," although this meaning is not intended to be "universalized."[184] For the idiomatic ܒܪ ܐܢܫܐ (*bar nāšā*)—literally "son of man"—is here neither the title ὁ υἱὸς τοῦ ἀνθρώπου (36:3 may be different)[185] nor a "substitute for 'I.'"[186]

The third singular masculine suffix in 12b stands for ܦܬܓܡܐ (*petḡāmā*), the personified "word (of the Most High)," which has informed the Ode from 1a onward. This "word," like God himself, exists as a power in the words of humans. Since it is inalienable, it can sojourn, even among Gnostics, only as a nomad. Although the use of the *hapax legomenon* ܡܫܟܢܐ (*maškṇā*), "dwelling place," derived from ܫܟܢ (*šḵen*) and in 𝔊 certainly σκηνή,[187] may have been influenced by John 1:14 (ἐσκήνωσεν ἐν ἡμῖν, "dwelt among us"), the "word" does not become human σάρξ ("flesh") but takes up temporary "residence" in the persons of Gnostics.[188]

The parallelism of 12a-b is purely formal, since 12b reverts from the human plane (12a) to the mythological, otherworldly one. Just as ܫܪܪܐ (*šrārā*) expresses the continuing "truth" and "reality" of the divine "word" (see on 1a above),[189] ܚܘܒܐ (*ḥubbā*) is the "love of the Most High," which cannot be identified with any human inclination or attachment (see 18:1 and Excursus 2). The Greek word will have been ἀγάπη.[190]

■ **13** In the final and inclusively intended benediction (cf. 30:7), the compound ܛܘܒܐ (*ṭūḇā*) with third plural masculine possessive suffix refers to both of the relative clauses following the dative ܠܐܝܠܝܢ (*l-ayllēn*), which are in a synthetic parallelism. Whether the synonymous verbs appeared in 𝔊 as participles (μακάριοι οἱ . . .) or as finite forms with the relative pronoun οἵ(τινες) cannot be determined. Nor is it possible to decide whether the Eshtaph. of ܝܕܥ (*ʾiḏaʿ*) in 13a corresponds to the verb ἐπιγινώσκω[191] or whether the Pe. of the same verb in 13b represents the commoner γινώσκω.[192] Since a direct influence of 1 Cor 2:6-14 or the relevant Johannine passages (see John 8:32; 14:7, 17; 17:3, 25) cannot be ascertained, it remains to note the connection between stanzas VI and I (see on stanza V above; also Excursuses 1 and 7).

As in 11b, the phrase ܒܝܕ ܗܢܐ (*b-yaḏ hānnā*, literally, "by the hand of this" = "by this") has a meaning similar to διὰ τούτου,[193] while the masculine demonstrative pronoun can only refer to "word."[194] The generalizing phrase ܟܠ ܡܕܡ (*kol meddem*), equivalent to πάντα rather than πᾶν (cf. Matt 11:27), does not, of course, mean the universe.[195] In the context of *Ode* 12 it means, in the first place, all of the preceding (cf. formally Mark 4:11). But because this verse concerns soteriological knowledge, it is permissible to include the fullness of salvation (cf. 23:19; 34:5).

182 See BDAG, *s.v.* γάρ; Lattke, "Wörter," 289 = idem, *Bedeutung*, 4:138.
183 See Franzmann's analysis (p. 106).
184 Contra Diettrich, 49.
185 Examples of idiomatically correct translations are "Mensch" [human being] (Harnack, 43; Diettrich, 49; Bauer, *Oden*, 29); "man" (Harris and Mingana, 2:273; Charlesworth, 61; Franzmann, 102); "l'homme" [man] (Azar, 112). Emerton (p. 703) varies between "a man," "man," and "the Son of man." Pierre (p. 94) alone keeps the complete phrase "fils d'homme" [son of man].
186 See Ferdinand Hahn, "υἱός," *EWNT* 3 (1983) 927–35; *EDNT* 3:387–90.
187 See Payne Smith, 2:4156; cf. Lattke, 1:244 ("Zeltwohnung").
188 BDAG, *s.v.* σκηνή.
189 BDAG, *s.v.* ἀλήθεια.
190 On 12:12b, see Lattke, *Einheit*, 58: "In this context it is unlikely that 'love' was limited to a psychological or ethical meaning. It is impossible to claim a parallelism with the idiosyncratic use of 'love' in John's Gospel, but there are similarities."
191 See Payne Smith, 1:1557; BDAG, *s.v.* ἐπιγινώσκω.
192 See Payne Smith, 1:1554–55; BDAG, *s.v.* γινώσκω.
193 Frankenberg, 15.
194 Bauer, *Oden*, 29. Grammatically it could also refer to "truth," but 13b makes this implausible. Charlesworth's translation, "by means of Him" (pp. 62–63), interprets "Him" as referring to "the personal 'Word', the 'Lord.'" That would make "Him" in 13a identical with the "Lord" in 13b, which is scarcely possible.
195 BDAG, *s.v.* πᾶς, 1dβ.

The term "truth" (see on 12b above), which has up to now been connected to the personified "word," comes out in 13b with a new profundity as the abstract sphere in which the "Lord" can be thought of as the "Most High" (cf. 17:5-7) and known by Gnostics. For the "Most High" is the "Father of truth" (41:9). This "truth," which does not exist in the cosmos, is not here an instrument (ܒ [*b*-] = "by") of *gnōsis*, but belongs with God himself among extramundane objects of knowledge. Anyone who knows the "Lord" (cf. 7:3, 12, 16; 9:7) is "blessed"[196] and already eschatologically "saved."[197]

196 BDAG, *s.v.* μακάριος.

197 Bauer, 593.

13

Ode 13: Admonitory Parable of the Mirror

1a Behold, our mirror is the Lord.
1b Open the eyes and look at them in/by him,
2a and learn how your face is!
2b And declare hymns to his spirit!
3a And wipe [the dirt, hatred?][a] from your faces,
3b and love his holiness and put it on!
4 Then you will be always unblemished with him.
Hallelujah!

a 3a The word ܨܝܬܐ (*ṣayyāttā*) in H does not make sense; see Excursus 13 below.

Introduction

Ode 13 is preserved in one Syriac manuscript.[1] This Ode, in spite of its brevity, is full of problems. The question whether "Lord" in 1a (+ 1b, 2b, 3b, 4) means the Judeo-Christian *Κύριος*/יהוה or the Christian and Gnostic-Christian *Κύριος Χριστός* depends entirely on the decision whether the image of the "mirror" is or is not an allusion to Wis 7:26 and thus represents a part of Sophia-Christology.[2] Verse 1b contains another strong argument for a Greek original (see below). And the *crux interpretum* in 3a has not yet been solved and is probably insoluble without the discovery of further manuscript evidence.[3]

A "reveille" it is not.[4] The admonitions of 1b-3b are not exhortations but examples of "imperatives of salvation,"[5] and they are framed by the image of an undefined group of speaker and audience at the beginning (1a) and by the final promise of salvation (4) addressed again to an inclusive group. The closing Hallelujah is abbreviated, uniquely in H, "for lack of space."[6]

According to Franzmann's analysis[7] (ABC D C'B'A'), 2b (= D) receives the greatest emphasis "by its position at the centre of the two reflexively congruent sections" 1b + 2a and 3b + 3a.

Interpretation

■ **1-4** Whether the Greek of 1a used *ἐστίν* can be left undecided. The simile, introduced by the demonstrative particle[8] and effected by the use of the copula, contains two important postulates: (1) that "the mirror in its material and psychological aspects cannot be eliminated from human life;"[9] and (2) that the group uttering the metaphor declares that it acknowledges no other earthly or cosmic Lord, and thus that no mirrors, whether naturally occurring, or cunningly crafted and designed

1 Ms.: Codex H, 10b (ܣ). Ed./trans.: Charlesworth, 63–65; Franzmann, 109–10; Lattke, 1:247–55 and 3:XXV.

2 See Harald Hegermann, "*σοφία*," *EWNT* 3 (1983) 623–24; *EDNT* 3:261; François Bovon, *New Testament Traditions and Apocryphal Narratives* (PTMS 36; Allison Park, Pa.: Pickwick, 1995) 127–31; on *1 Clem.* 36:2, see Horacio E. Lona, *Der erste Clemensbrief* (KAV 2; Göttingen: Vandenhoeck & Ruprecht, 1998) 391–97.

3 See the detailed studies by Majella Franzmann, "'Wipe the harlotry from your faces': A Brief Note on Ode of Solomon 13,3," *ZNW* 77 (1986) 282–83, and Lattke, "Ode 13" = idem, *Bedeutung*, 4:75–87.

4 Contra Schille, 97.

5 See Introduction, sec. 8.

6 Lattke, *Bedeutung*, 1:59; see Charlesworth, *Manuscripts*, 47.

7 Franzmann, 110.

8 Payne Smith, 1:959; BDAG, *s.v.* *ἰδού*.

9 Hildegard Urner-Astholz, "Spiegel und Spiegelbild," in Erich Dinkler, ed., *Zeit und Geschichte: Dankesgabe an Rudolf Bultmann zum 80. Geburtstag* (Tübingen: Mohr Siebeck, 1964) 668.

by humans, can have any magical or other powers over them.

The "mirror"-image of Wis 7:25-26 is relevant for those, like Harris and Mingana,[10] who take the "Lord" to be the kerygmatically exalted Christ, because in this passage it says of σοφία ("Wisdom"):[11]

25ἀτμὶς γάρ ἐστιν τῆς τοῦ θεοῦ δυνάμεως
καὶ ἀπόρροια τῆς τοῦ παντοκράτορος δόξης εἰλικρινής·
διὰ τοῦτο οὐδὲν μεμιαμμένον εἰς αὐτὴν παρεμπίπτει.
26ἀπαύγασμα γάρ ἐστιν φωτὸς ἀιδίου
καὶ ἔσοπτρον ἀκηλίδωτον τῆς τοῦ θεοῦ ἐνεργείας
καὶ εἰκὼν τῆς ἀγαθότητος αὐτοῦ.

25For she is a breath of the power of God,
and a pure emanation of the glory of the Almighty;
therefore nothing defiled gains entrance into her.
26For she is a reflection of eternal light,
a spotless mirror of the working of God,
and an image of his goodness.

The influence of this passage on New Testament[12] and other early Christian writings (e.g., *2 Clem.* 36:2; *Teach. Silv.* 112,36–113,7) is beyond doubt.[13] But even though it is likely that the people of the *Odes of Solomon* were familiar with the Wisdom Literature and its development, *Ode* 13 is not concerned with the mirroring of God but with God the "Lord" as the "mirror" for theological self-understanding (1b-2a),[14] and the consequent summons to purification (3a) and metaphorical change of raiment (3b).[15]

So one should rather assume that the (pseudo-) Platonic dialogue *Alcibiades* I (ἢ περὶ φύσεως ἀνθρώπου), which was "highly esteemed in Antiquity and for centuries . . . used as an introduction to Platonic

10 Harris and Mingana, 2:276–78.

11 Rahlfs, 2:355; Georgi, 428.

12 See, e.g., 2 Cor 3:18; 4:4, 6; Col 1:5; Heb 1:3. On 1 Cor 13:12, see Weiß, *Korintherbrief*, 319–20; Johannes Behm, "Das Bildwort vom Spiegel 1. Korinther 13,12," in Wilhelm Koepp, ed., *Reinhold-Seeberg-Festschrift*, vol. 1: *Zur Theorie des Christentums* (Leipzig: Deichert, Scholl, 1929) 315–42; Gerhard Kittel, "αἴνιγμα (ἔσοπτρον)," *ThWNT* 1 (1933) 177–79; *TDNT* 1:178–80; Ceslas Spicq, *Notes de lexicographie néo-testamentaire* (3 vols.; OBO 22.1–3; Fribourg: Editions universitaires; Göttingen: Vandenhoeck & Ruprecht, 1978–82) 1:292–95, esp. 294.

13 The "Egyptian alchemist Zosimus," who "in the twelfth part of his book περὶ ἀρετῆς πρὸς θεοσέβειαν, according to ancient tradition" described "the mirror as the representation of the divine spirit," received "his strongest stimulus from Wis 7:36" (Urner-Astholz, "Spiegel," 656). If *Ode* 13 is at all related to "the religious ideas of Zosimus" (Urner-Astholz, "Spiegel," 657, following Richard Reitzenstein, *Historia Monachorum und Historia Lausiaca: Eine Studie zur Geschichte des Mönchtums und der frühchristlichen Begriffe Gnostiker und Pneumatiker* [FRLANT 24; Göttingen: Vandenhoeck & Ruprecht, 1916] 244, 262; cf. Lattke, *Bedeutung*, 3:167), it would still be fallacious to interpret the earlier Ode in the light of later speculative ideas. See also Dibelius's criticism of Reitzenstein: "More likely is that Zosimus, writing in the 3rd/4th century CE, took a popular idea, about forgetting the image in the mirror, which no longer seemed to make sense to him and limited it to an enchanted mirror" (Martin Dibelius, *Der Brief des Jakobus* [KEK 15; ed. Heinrich Greeven; 11th ed.; Göttingen: Vandenhoeck & Ruprecht, 1964] 147–48). Norbert Hugedé thoroughly confutes Reitzenstein's theory (see Hugedé, *La métaphore du miroir dans les Epîtres de saint Paul aux Corinthiens* [Bibliothèque théologique; Neuchâtel/Paris: Delachaux et Niestlé, 1957] 66–68). See also Carsten Colpe, "Die Christologie der Oden Salomos im Zusammenhang von Gnosis und Synkretismus," ed. Michael Lattke, in Julia Männchen, ed., with Torsten Reiprich, *Mein Haus wird ein Bethaus für alle Völker genannt werden (Jes 56,7): Judentum seit der Zeit des Zweiten Tempels in Geschichte, Literatur und Kult: Festschrift für Thomas Willi zum 65. Geburtstag* (Neukirchen-Vluyn: Neukirchener Verlag, 2007) 48–49.

14 Simone Pétrement, too, regards the "Lord" of *Ode* 13 as "Savior" and remarks: "One must also note that for these Gnostics there is a knowledge of the self (or more precisely of the origin of the self), but there is not, properly speaking, a *search* for the self. The knowledge was given without search, by the revelation of the Savior" (Pétrement, *A Separate God: The Christian Origins of Gnosticism* [trans. Carol Harrison; London: Darton, Longman & Todd, 1991] 138).

15 It follows that the later verse from *Act. John* 95 ("I am a mirror to you who know me") is only a formal

philosophy,"[16] prompted the choice of the "mirror"-image.[17] In explaining the Delphic saying "*Γνῶθι σαυτόν*,"[18] the eye that sees itself is compared to a mirror.[19] The point is made that "the face (*τὸ πρόσωπον*) of a person who looks into another's eye is shown in the optic (*ἐν τῇ ὄψει*) confronting him, as in a mirror (*ὥσπερ ἐν κατόπτρῳ*)."[20] In a later addendum to discussions on the "soul" (*ψυχή*) that knows itself, and "wisdom" (*σοφία*) as "the virtue of the soul" (*ἡ ψυχῆς ἀρετή*), Socrates sums up:[21]

> *Ἆρ᾽ οὖν ὅτι ὥσπερ κάτοπτρά ἐστι σαφέστερα τοῦ ἐν τῷ ὀφθαλμῷ ἐνόπτρου καὶ καθαρώτερα καὶ λαμπρότερα, οὕτω καὶ ὁ θεὸς τοῦ ἐν τῇ ἡμετέρᾳ ψυχῇ βελτίστου καθαρώτερόν τε καὶ λαμπρότερον τυγχάνει ὄν;*
>
> *Εἰς τὸν θεὸν ἄρα βλέποντες ἐκείνῳ καλλίστῳ ἐνόπτρῳ χρῴμεθ᾽ ἂν καὶ τῶν ἀνθρωπίνων εἰς τὴν ψυχῆς ἀρετήν, καὶ οὕτως ἂν μάλιστα ὁρῷμεν καὶ γιγνώσκοιμεν ἡμᾶς αὐτούς.*
>
> As mirrors are truer and clearer and brighter than the mirror within the eye, so also God is by his nature a clearer and brighter mirror than the most excellent part of our own soul?
>
> And therefore by looking at God we shall use the finest mirror of the human soul and its virtue; and by such means we shall best see and come to know ourselves.

Ode 13 uses the key words and similes of this popular dialogue, without in any way taking on its *philosophical* content of self-knowledge and doctrines of the soul. What the Greek word was that corresponds to the *hapax legomenon* ܡܚܙܝܬܐ (*maḥzīṯā*), derived from ܚܙܐ (*ḥzā*), is difficult to determine and not of crucial importance.[22] In any case, the *Κύριος* (see 1:1 and *passim* in nearly all the *Odes*), originating in Jewish tradition, has moved into the place of the divine (*τὸ θεῖον*) and the philosophical god (*θεός*).[23]

The imperative of ܦܬܚ (*pṯaḥ*; cf. 9:1) in 1b is logically followed by the imperative of ܚܙܐ (*ḥzā*; cf. 15:3; 16:9). If the plural of ܥܝܢܐ (*ʿaynā*) were "a homonym like the German 'das Gesicht' or the Greek *αἱ ὄψεις* [meaning both 'eyesight' and 'face']."[24] one would not, in view of the *Alcibiades I* 132b–133c, have to suspect a mistranslation. But here the "eyes"[25] are not compared to a mirror, so Frankenberg's text-critical remark—"13:1 the ܐܝܟ of the Syriac refers to the eyes, the translator

parallel, since this hymn is spoken by the Gnostic Christ (see Lattke, *Oden*, 139 n. 1; Charlesworth, 64; *NTApo*⁵ 2 [1989] 167; *NTApoc* 2:183; Willy Stölten, "Gnostische Parallelen zu den Oden Salomos," *ZNW* 13 [1912] 40). Already Diettrich (p. 50) was very critical of the use of Wis 7:26: "the reference to Wis 7:26 is quite misleading since there Wisdom is the mirror of the Lord." Thus "Eikon (*εἰκών*) and mirror are" not "synonyms" in the Ode (contra Jervell, *Imago Dei*, 185), unlike Wis 7:26. And *Ode* 13 makes no mention of a "seal" (contra Schenke, 39; but see on 4:7-8 above).

16 Heinz Hofmann, ed., *Platon, Ion, Hippias II, Protagoras, Laches, Charmides, Euthyphron, Lysis, Hippias I, Alkibiades I* (Darmstadt: Wissenschaftliche Buchgesellschaft, 1977) 528–29.

17 Two passages in Gregory Thaumaturges' *Panegyricum in Originem* (third century) are also influenced by this dialogue, where he speaks of "self-reflection as in a mirror" (119 and 142); see Peter Guyot, trans., and introduction by Richard Klein, *Gregor der Wundertäter, Oratio prosphonetica ac panegyrica in Origenem–Dankrede an Origenes*, with appendix: *Origenis epistula ad Gregorium Thaumaturgum* (FontChr 24; Freiburg: Herder, 1996) 170–71 and 180–81.

18 *Alcibiades I*, 124b, 129a (LCL 8.172–73, 194–95); Hofmann, 592, 612.

19 *Alcibiades I*, 132d-e (LCL 8.208–9); Hofmann, 624–25.

20 *Alcibiades I*, 133a (LCL 8.210–11); Hofmann, 626–27.

21 *Alcibiades I*, 133c; Hofmann, 628–29. These two paragraphs are found only in quotations by Eusebius and Stobaeus and are omitted in the Loeb edition.

22 Payne Smith, 1:1237; BDAG, *s.v.* *ἔσοπτρον*.

23 Even if *Ode* 13 has "nothing specifically Christian" to say (Harnack, 43; similarly Diettrich, 50), it can undergo a Christian reading, like many of the Psalms. Already in antiquity it would have been read christologically as well as merely theologically.

24 Bauer, 593; see also Payne Smith, 2:2867.

25 𝔊 would probably have had the accusative plural of *ὀφθαλμός*, used in the sense of "mental and spiritual understanding" (BDAG, *s.v.* *ὀφθαλμός*).

has misunderstood the Greek αὐτους"[26]—is probably correct. Preuschen goes so far as to call the enclitic object ܐܢܢ (ʾennēn) "nonsense" and comments: "The Syriac translator read βλεπετεαυτους and understood it as βλέπετε αὐτούς. So he translated it as ܚܙܘ ܐܢܢ (*ḥzaw-ennēn*)."[27] For him "this proves conclusively that the Syriac is translated from Greek."[28] The preposition ܒ (*b*-) with masculine suffix cannot refer to the Syriac feminine "mirror," so it refers to the masculine "Lord." However, if 𝔊 had ἐν αὐτῷ, that could have referred equally to ὁ κύριος as to a neuter like ἔσοπτρον or κάτοπτρον.[29] Since the "mirror" is equated with the "Lord," the question to which of them it refers may be considered less important than the fact that the preposition here bears the full weight of its locative and instrumental meaning.[30]

The use of ܐܦ̈ܐ (ʾ*appē*) in the parallel lines 2a and 3a supports the supposition that the Greek of 1b had the reflexive pronoun αὑτούς rather than αὐτούς. The collective plural ܐܦ̈ܐ, which probably corresponded to the terms πρόσωπον/πρόσωπα, is parallel to this pronoun.[31] The "face" represents the "self" of the hearers. The verb ܝܠܦ (ʾ*ilep̄*), which occurs only here and in 7:6,[32] stands for an existential μανθάνειν, very close to knowing. In fact 2a is almost a variation on Γνῶθι σαυτόν!

This self-recognition in and by the "Lord" is not an end in itself and not the ending. On the contrary, the central monocolon 2b immediately interrupts the nascent "self-reflection"[33] and soteriologically demands "hymns" celebrating, praising, and addressed to the spiritual power of the Lord (cf. 6:7). The plural of ܬܫܒܘܚܬܐ (*tešbuḥtā*) may represent ὕμνοι or αἰνέσεις, but it could also refer to Jewish Psalms or Odes.[34] The stress is on the praise and glory, which cannot be rendered to any being or power of this world, so it should be no surprise that the indirect object of the Pa. of ܣܒܪ (*sb̲ar*)—which would in 𝔊 be ἀπαγγέλλω, εὐαγγελίζομαι or κηρύσσω[35]—is the ܪܘܚܐ (*rūḥā*) of the Lord.[36]

The meaning of the Pa. of ܫܘܐ (*šwā*) in 3a can only be "wipe off."[37] It is equally clear that the members of the imagined audience are being called upon to remove something that is on their faces or can be read in their faces. And this "something" is in opposition to "holiness" (3b) and "being unblemished" (4). But what is this "something," the term for which can be clearly read ܨܝܬܐ, with the pointing of *ṣayyāttā* = *venatrix*,[38] which makes no sense at all?

Excursus 13: The *crux interpretum* in *Ode* 13:3a

Harris and Mingana consider the manuscript ܨܝܬܐ "meaningless" and emend it to ܨܝܬܐ (*ṣāyīṯā*), which they translate as "filth," calling it "almost certain," although "phonetically it is more correct to read ܨܐܝܬܐ."[39] Kittel[40] and Bauer[41] both print ܨܝܬܐ, without any further explanation. A variant of this

Semitic would have had "*your* eyes." Therefore, a Greek original is likely (see Klaus Beyer in Lattke, 3:XXV n. 1).

26 Frankenberg, 38.

27 Erwin Preuschen, "Ein Übersetzungsfehler in den Oden Salomos," *ZNW* 16 (1915) 234.

28 Ibid., 234–35; he then (p. 235) draws another consequence: "The idea that Bardasanes might have been the author now has no foundation." On this theory of Frankenberg and Preuschen, see Harris and Mingana, 2:277: "The point deserves a careful consideration."

29 See LSJ, *s.v.* κάτοπτρον.

30 See Nöldeke §248.

31 See Excursus 8 and Payne Smith, 1:278; BDAG, *s.v.* πρόσωπον. "Face," of course, is singular only for each member "of the 2nd pl. group which is addressed" (Franzmann, 109).

32 BDAG, *s.v.* μανθάνω; see also Payne Smith, 1:212–13.

33 Urner-Astholz, "Spiegel," 649.

34 See Payne Smith, 2:4027–28.

35 See Payne Smith, 2:2510–11; BDAG, *s.vv.* ἀπαγγέλλω, εὐαγγελίζομαι, κηρύσσω.

36 On the Spirit of God, see BDAG, *s.v.* πνεῦμα, esp. 5; Payne Smith, 2:3850–53, esp. 3852.

37 See Payne Smith, 2:4080; BDAG, *s.v.* ἐκμάσσω.

38 Brockelmann, *Lexicon*, 627a. The misprint ܨܝܬܐ in Charlesworth (1973, p. 64) was corrected in the revised reprint (1977, p. 64). The reference to Brockelmann, *Lexicon*, 626, "hunting" or "booty" (Charlesworth, 64) is off the mark. Emerton's remark (p. 704) on ܨܝܬܐ "The Syriac word here is otherwise unknown" is very odd.

39 Harris and Mingana, vol. 1, on this passage; 2:276–77; see also Payne Smith, *Dictionary*, 471, feminine emphatic of ܨܐܐ.

40 Kittel, 168.

41 Bauer, *Oden*, 28.

well-accepted emendation is ܨܐܬܐ.[42] These more or less well attested words, derived from the root ܨܐܝ (Pa. also ܨܐܐ), can be used both directly and in a transferred sense to mean "dirt" and "impurity"[43] and thus would include most of the meanings of *ἡ ῥυπαρία, τὸ ῥυπαρόν,* or *ὁ ῥύπος*.[44]

Charlesworth, quoting *Act. John* 28–29,[45] suggests a different and also paleographically acceptable emendation: "It is possible that ܨܝܪܬܐ (i.e., *ṣīrtā*), the pass. part. of ܨܪ (i.e. *ṣār*), was the original form in the manuscript. This restauration would present the following meaning: 'And wipe the paint from your face'. In favour of this translation is the minor emendation required."[46] This suggestion, which Pierre seems to accept,[47] faces the same problem as the adjective ܨܐܝܬܐ (ܨܝܬܐ), where, as Charlesworth remarks, "a noun is needed."[48] But even if ܨܝܪܬܐ is to be translated as "painting,"[49] meaning "makeup," this conjecture, just because of the connection made with *Act. John* 28–29, makes no sense because it bears a negative connotation.[50] Charlesworth's concluding remark, "Of course a 'painted face' has pejorative connotations in the Old Testament (e.g., see Ezek 23:40, 2 Kgs 9:30, and Jer 4:30),"[51] cannot alter this opinion.

Since the Syriac letters ܨ and ܣ, and ܙ and ܣ, or ܙ and ܨ are interchangeable, it is not necessary to limit the search for a paleographically acceptable emendation of the Syriac to the suggestions that have already been made. So Franzmann's suggestion "that originally ܨܝܬܐ read as ܙܢܝܘܬܐ (i.e. *zānyūtā*) . . . , being a conscious or unconscious allusion to Hos 2,4"[52] certainly deserves consideration. This word is equivalent to *πορνεία* in the LXX.[53] The image would have to refer to the Hebrew text, since in the Greek translation it is the Lord (*κύριος*) who threatens, among other things, *καὶ ἐξαρῶ τὴν πορνείαν αὐτῆς ἐκ προσώπου μου* ("and I will remove her fornication out of *my* presence" [Hos 2:4 LXX]).[54] The reason for the change from the Hebrew text may have been that the female "emblems," described by the abstract plurals זנונים and נאפופים, which "were affixed to the face or the bosom and could be removed,"[55] had long ago disappeared, so that the words were not understood. Therefore, even without considering the problems of converting ܙܢܝܘܬܐ via ܨܢܝܘܬܐ to ܨܝܬܐ, "the ܢ becoming ܝ and ܘ becoming ܪ, or the ܢ dropping out and ܘ becoming ܝ,"[56] this emendation is rather unlikely. But the final note contains a valuable contribution to this problem: "My thanks to Prof. Sebastian Brock for his suggestion that ܨܚܢܘܬܐ could give the same sense in Ode 13,3, although without verbal correspondence with Hos 2,4."[57]

It is possible that Ephraem knew *Ode* 13.[58] Although it would be anachronistic to interpret the "Mirror"-*Ode* by its influence on the six so-called "Hymns (ܡܕܖ̈ܫܐ)" and four "Sermons (ܡܐܡܖ̈ܐ)," which were written some two centuries later, it may be that the "stereotypical moral vocabulary of the mirror image" in Ephraem has preserved the desired original word from 3a.[59] So it is perhaps permissible to end this excursus by quoting the last paragraphs from my essay:[60]

> The simplest restoration of the current text would be a retransformation of ܨܝܬܐ (*ṣayyāttā*) into ܨܐܬܐ (*ṣāṭā*) or ܨܐܘܬܐ (*ṣāūṭā*, as in Text no. 10 from Ephraem = Sermones II, Sermo 1, 1639–44). The latter word ("dirt," "uncleanness," Greek commonly *ῥύπος*) has a number of spellings, e.g. ܨܐܝܘܬܐ (*ṣāyūṭā*) and even ܨܝܘܬܐ.[61] That it caused difficulties and confusion can be seen from the reading ܨܐܘܝܘܬܐ in MS Y of Ephraem.

42 Proposed by Grimme, on this passage; see Payne Smith, *Dictionary*, 472; Nöldeke §78.
43 Payne Smith, 2:3349–51.
44 See BDAG, *s.vv. ῥυπαρία, ῥυπαρός, ῥύπος*; Spicq, 2:784–85.
45 Cf. *NTApo*^{5} 2 (1989), 160; *NTApoc* 2:176.
46 Charlesworth, 64.
47 Pierre, 96; idem, "Odes de Salomon," 700.
48 Charlesworth, 64.
49 "Passive participles are employed both as substantives and adjectives" (Nöldeke §284).
50 See Lampe, 593, on the verb *ζωγραφέω*.
51 Charlesworth, 65; these three passages refer only to eye shadow and mascara.
52 Franzmann, "Note," 282.
53 LEH and BDAG, *s.v. πορνεία*.
54 Rahlfs, 2:491; Brenton, 1071 (my emphasis).
55 Hans Walter Wolff, *Dodekapropheton 1: Hosea* (BKAT 14.1; 2nd ed.; Neukirchen-Vluyn: Neukirchener Verlag, 1965) 40.
56 Franzmann, "Note," 283.
57 Franzmann, "Note," 283; on *ṣaḥnūṯā*, see Payne Smith, 2:3394 (*impuritas, ἀσέλγεια*).
58 See Harris and Mingana, 2:18–20, 277.
59 See Lattke, "Ode 13," 258, 263–64 = idem, *Bedeutung*, 4:78, 84–85, both with synoptic summary.
60 Lattke, "Ode 13," 265–66 = *Bedeutung*, 4:86–87.
61 See Payne Smith, 2:3350–51.

So it is not far from this possible reading to the *crux*, just a spelling mistake (misread or misheard) from ܨܐܝܘܬܐ or ܨܝܘܬܐ to the similar outlines of ܨܝܬܐ, which the *Serta*-script of Codex H clearly and nonsensically perpetuated as *ṣayyāttā*.

Ephraem's stereotypical semantic field offers a different solution, based in literary history and tradition, starting from the well-attested confusion between *Ṣāḏē* and *Semkaṯ*.[62] The emendation in my edition ܣܢܐܬܐ (*seneṯā*, "hatred"; cf. *Ode* 7:20) is not used in any of the 10 Ephraem passages cited. The root ܣܢܐ, however, and especially the partial synonym ܣܢܝܘܬܐ (*sanyūṯā*) with the double meaning of *odium* ("hatred") and *deformitas* ("ugliness"), clearly belongs to the morality of the mirror image in Ephraem and might probably have belonged to it as early as *Ode* 13. In that case, the misspelling (mishearing) in the Syriac manuscript tradition could have been the "missing link," which gave rise to the "nonsense reading" ܨܢܐܬܐ or ܨܢܝܘܬܐ, with some sort of pointing, which was finally miscorrected to the ܨܝܬܐ of the existing manuscript. It is, after all, likely that Ephraem, who appears to quote *Ode* 11:23a, would have known the *Odes* and among them *Ode* 13 also. It is even more likely that the mirror image was already present in pre-Ephraem Syriac metaphor and literature. Ephraem, as usual, gave a personal slant to his poetical expression of it.[63] So it is possible that Ephraem found "dirt" in the Mirror-*Ode* and that he added his favourite "hatred/ugliness" to the imagery.

As 3a draws the conclusion from 2a, 3b carries on from 1b, for self-reflection is followed by the turn toward the "Lord." The *hapax legomenon* ܩܕܝܫܘܬܐ (*qaddīšūṯā*), which must have been ἁγιότης in 𝔊,[64] referring to God's "holiness as the supernatural creator,"[65] is not confined by the contrast with 3a but rather is prompted by the key word "spirit" in 2b.[66] If μῖσος was originally in the Greek of 3a,[67] the peculiar use of ܪܚܡ (*rḥem*) would be easier to explain (see Excursus 2). Whether 𝔊 used a form of ἀγαπάω or of φιλέω cannot be decided.[68]

Since it is possible, metaphorically, to "put on" "grace" (4:6; 20:7; 33:12), "imperishability" (15:8), "light" (21:3), "joy" (23:1), "love" (23:3), and the "name of the Most High" (39:8), "putting on" the "holiness" of the "Lord" makes an addition to the distinctive imagery of the *Odes of Solomon*, but it also forms a connection to St. Paul and the deutero-Pauline epistles (see esp. 1 Cor 15:53-55; Col 3:10; Eph 4:24). In this transferred sense, the verb ܠܒܫ (*lḇeš*) is an exact translation of the middle voice of ἐνδύω and means "acceptance."[69] The feminine objective suffix refers to "holiness."

In the concluding promise of salvation (4), using the imperfect of ܗܘܐ (*hwā*) and the composite expression of continuance ܒܟܠܙܒܢ (*b-ḵol zḇan*),[70] which points forward to 14:1, the phrase ܕܠܐ ܡܘܡܐ (*d-lā mūmā*), which can refer to both body and soul, must not be narrowly moralized.[71] The Greek correspondence or *Vorlage* was probably ἄμωμος rather than ἀμίαντος.[72] Unlike 39:6, this term of perfection, excluding any error or shortcoming, is a consequence of the use of the key word "holiness." But, since 4 depends structurally on 1a, the "mirror" image may also have exerted an indirect influence. The prepositional phrase with ܠܘܬ (*lwāṯ*) and third masculine singular suffix, reminiscent of John 1:1-2 and referring

62 Payne Smith, 2:2489, 3349, etc.

63 See Lattke, *Bedeutung*, 3:233, on Edmund Beck, "Das Bild vom Spiegel bei Ephräm," *OrChrP* 19 (1953) 5–24, who distinguishes five different groups in Ephraem's uses of the mirror image.

64 See Payne Smith, 2:3501; on Heb 12:10, see Gräßer, 3:272.

65 Michael Lattke, "Heiligkeit III. Neues Testament," *TRE* 14 (1985) 704.

66 On "holy spirit," see 6:7; 11:2; 14:8; 23:22; see also 31:5 ("holy Father") and 32:3 ("holy power of the Most High").

67 See Payne Smith, 2:2570.

68 See BDAG, *s.vv.* ἀγαπάω, φιλέω; Payne Smith, 2:3879–80.

69 BDAG, *s.v.* ἐνδύω; Payne Smith, 2:1887 (rather incomplete); see Michael Lattke, "Die Bedeutung der apokryphen *Salomo-Oden* für die neutestamentliche Wissenschaft," in Peter Slater and Donald Wiebe, eds., *Traditions in Contact and Change: Selected Proceedings of the XIVth Congress of the International Association for the History of Religions (Winnipeg, Man., August 15–20, 1980)* (Studies in Religion 3; Waterloo, Ont.: Wilfrid Laurier University Press, 1983) 297–80 = idem, *Bedeutung*, 4:62.

70 Payne Smith, 1:1078, *s.v.* ܙܒܢܐ (*zaḇnā*); BDAG, *s.v.* ἀεί.

71 Payne Smith, 2:2037.

72 BDAG, *s.vv.* ἀμίαντος, ἄμωμος.

to the "Lord," also forms a connection to 14:1 and corresponds to Greek πρὸς αὐτόν ("with him").[73] Even in the mythological age of the *Odes of Solomon* this was not necessarily an indication of place. What it promises is an existential "closeness" to the "Lord," such as is not found even in human love and solidarity.[74]

73 Frankenberg, 15.

74 As a postscript, it may be noted that Abbott's suggestion that *Ode* 13 derives from Exod 38:8 is indeed "extremely fanciful" (Abbott, 401). His excursus "Ephrem's Use of the Language of the Odes" is of some use (Abbott, 413–16).

14

Ode 14: Childlike Trust in the Lord

(I) 1a As the eyes of a son upon his father,
1b so my eyes, Lord, are always toward thee.
2 Because with thee are my sources of milk and my delight.
(II) 3a Turn not thy mercy from me, Lord,
3b and take not thy kindness from me.
4a Stretch out to me, my Lord, thy right hand continually,
4b and be my guide until the end, to/according to thy will!
5a I shall be beautiful before thee because of thy glory,
5b and because of thy name I will be saved from the Evil One.
(III) 6a And both thy rest, Lord, will abide with me
6b and also the fruits of thy love.
7a Teach me the odes of thy truth,
7b that I may bear fruits by/in thee.
8a And open the cithara of thy holy spirit to me,
8b that I may praise thee with all the tones, Lord.
(IV) 9a And according to the multitude of thy mercies
9b so thou wilt grant me.
(V) 9c And hasten to grant our petitions,
10 and thou art able for all our needs.
Hallelujah.

Introduction

Ode 14 is preserved in one Syriac manuscript.[1] In his *editio princeps*—and also in the revised edition—Harris says this on *Ode* 14: "In this Psalm the canonical Psalter is somewhat more closely imitated than is generally the case with our collection. . . . But the Psalm is by no means a cento from the canonical Psalter, even though it does not contain anything that could, at the first reading, be definitely labelled as Christian."[2] At first sight this description appears correct, but the survey of the literary forms[3] reads, in part, like poetic variations on themes of the Lord's Prayer (Matt 6:9-13; Luke 11:2-4; *Did.* 8:2), which, taken in its Jewish context, does presuppose many biblical traditions.[4] The fact that the eschatological petitions of the Lord's Prayer for forgiveness of debts/trespasses and preservation from temptation (e.g., by Satan) do *not* have direct correspondences in *Ode* 14 is just as revealing as the agreement on the topics of "Father" (1a), "Lord" (*passim*; cf. βασιλεία, δύναμις), "will" (4b), "glory" (5a; cf. δόξα), "name"

1 Ms.: Codex H, 10b–11b (ܣ). Ed./trans.: Charlesworth, 65–66; Franzmann, 111–15; Lattke, 1:257–68 and 3:XXV.
2 Harris, 110.
3 Lattke, *Oden*, 51.
4 See, e.g., Joachim Gnilka, "Vaterunser. I. Biblisch," *LThK*[2] 10 (1965) 625–26. Rudolf Abramowski, who had great difficulty in classifying this *Ode* (pp. 51–52), already remarks on the relationship between the *Ode* and the Lord's Prayer (p. 46): "The form of this lovely prayer, with its invocation, petitions and explanatory ending corresponds closely to the Lord's Prayer." That this *Ode* "is spoken throughout *ex ore catechumini*" (Bernard,

(5b), "evil/the Evil One" (5b), and "needs" (10; cf. ἐπι-ούσιος in Matt 6:11; χρεία in Matt 6:8).[5]

The "I" of indeterminate gender in stanzas I–IV, who stands before the "Lord" as "thou" in all its forms, is not to be identified with either the persona of the author/poet or with anyone of importance officiating in the liturgy. The "we" of stanza V is equally indeterminate and cannot be identified with any specific group of persons. Poetically, stanza V may be considered "a communal response,"[6] but that does not make it "an addition to the self-contained Ode in 1-9b."[7] Anyone using this homogenous poem as a prayer will be reminded, as with the plurals of the Lord's Prayer, that even in the secrecy of their chamber, *coram Deo*, no one is alone; all who are necessitous are interconnected.[8]

Interpretation

■ **1-2** If the stylistic device of comparison is "a means to make easier the visualization and comprehension of some common content of the connected regions,"[9] the *tertium comparationis* is in no sense the power of sight or a belief in authority. The common content of 1a-b is trust, almost a primal trust. As a similar comparison in 40:1 makes clear, the imagery in the *Odes of Solomon* is not confined to the masculine gender, a point also made by the intrusion of the term "breasts" in 2.[10]

While the sense of primal existential trust connects the comparison to the Lord's Prayer (see above), the *words* clearly derive from Ps 122:2 LXX: ὡς ὀφθαλμοὶ δούλων/παιδίσκης εἰς . . . οὕτως οἱ ὀφθαλμοὶ ἡμῶν πρὸς κύριον τὸν θεὸν ἡμῶν ("as the eyes of servants/a maid-servant to . . . so our eyes are directed to the Lord our God").[11] This wording also explains the change from ܥܠ (*ʿal*) in 1a to ܠܘܬ (*lwāṯ*) + second masculine singular suffix in 1b. But it is in no sense a "raising" of the eyes to "heaven" as God's "dwelling."[12]

The justification and expansion of the comparison in 2 shows that stanza I is a tricolon, as is the case with other comparisons (7:1; 15:1-2a; 40:1). Bauer, quite

77) is just as fanciful as Diettrich's supposition (p. 50) "that the song, despite its first-person formulation, was sung in divine service," stanzas I–IV "by a cantor"—"possibly two singers dividing it between them"—and stanza V "as a final chorus by the congregation."

5 Édouard Massaux compares *Ode* 14:5b explicitly only with Matt 6:13; see Massaux, *The Influence of the Gospel of Saint Matthew on Christian Literature before Saint Irenaeus,* book 2: *The Later Christian Writings* (ed., with introduction and addenda, Arthur J. Bellinzoni; trans. Norman J. Belval and Suzanne Hecht; New Gospel Studies 5.2; Leuven: Peeters; Macon, Ga.: Mercer University Press, 1992) 63–64. This is surprising, since he refers to the address *Πάτερ ἡμῶν* in Matt 6:9. The superficiality of the comparison with the *Ode* can be seen from his statement that "Odes Sol. 14 consists of a prayer of the Son to his Father" (Massaux, *Influence*, 64). This criticism does not detract from the value of the material Massaux has collected.

6 Franzmann, 115.

7 Ibid., 114.

8 This problematizes Kittel's statement (p. 12) that the *theme* of *Ode* 14 is "I and God."

9 Gero von Wilpert, *Sachwörterbuch der Literatur* (KTA 231; 5th ed.; Stuttgart: Kröner, 1969) 820; see Lattke, "Bildersprache," 101–2 = idem, *Bedeutung*, 4:26–28; Lattke, *Oden*, 88 (see also Introduction, sec. 8).

10 On the androgynous or bisexual nature of God, see *Corp. Herm.* 1:9 and *Asclepius* 20–21 (Carsten Colpe and Jens Holzhausen, eds., *Das Corpus Hermeticum Deutsch* [Stuttgart-Bad Cannstatt: Frommann-Holzboog, 1997] 13, 279–82; cf. also 614). A quotation from the so-called *Poimandres* will be sufficient illustration: "The spirit, god, which is androgynous and is life and light, bore, by the word, another spirit, the demiurge" (*Corp. Herm.* 1:9; Colpe and Holzhausen, 13). A text like this shows that the imagery of the *Odes of Solomon* would have posed little difficulty to people of the second century.

11 Rahlfs, 2:142; Brenton, 776.

12 Contra Franz Joseph Dölger, *Sol Salutis: Gebet und Gesang im christlichen Altertum. Mit besonderer Rücksicht auf die Ostung in Gebet und Liturgie* (Liturgiegeschichtliche Forschungen 4–5; 2nd ed.; Münster: Aschendorff, 1925) 315–16. The ideas of 1-2 show a relationship with *Ode* 13. If this was not planned from the first, it may still have given the impetus for the placing of *Odes* 14–16, which also begin with an introductory comparison.

correctly, reproduces the plural of the masculine ܬܕܐ (*tdā*) with first singular possessive suffix by "breasts for me."[13] This peculiar image (cf. 8:16; 19:3-4) is not of the "site" of the "loving dedication" of the speaker,[14] but of "God's breasts."[15] The translation by "sources of milk" is meant to reflect both the basic meaning of a source of food as also the metaphor of fullness and fertility, which cannot be expressed by "consolations."[16] 𝔊 probably had *μαστοί μου*.[17]

The plural copula ܐܢܘܢ (*ʾennōn*) refers to the second subject as well, the singular *hapax legomenon* ܦܘܢܩܐ (*punnāqā*), which follows, and which should not be translated as a plural.[18] As an abstract term parallel to "breasts," its meaning here, "in a good sense," is the "delight"[19] or "enjoyment"[20] derived from the sources of milk, but without a paradisiacal flavor.[21]

■ **3-5** The parallelisms of these three bicola[22] serve to consolidate the logical progression of negative petition, positive petition, and final confidence in salvation. Contrary to the impression that Diettrich gives by quotations from the "canonical Psalter,"[23] stanza II also uses themes from the Lord's Prayer (see above), especially in 4-5.

The negative petitions of 3a-b allow the speaker to express something quite positive. For the negated imperfects of ܐܣܛܝ (*ʾasṭī*, Aph. of ܣܛܐ, *hapax legomenon*)[24] and ܢܣܒ (*nsab*; cf. 4:13),[25] which are "the direct contrary of the Imperative,"[26] allow one to draw the conclusion that the "Lord" can be believed to have "mercy" and "kindness."[27] This conclusion follows especially from the use, twice, of the preposition ܡܢ (*men*) with first singular possessive suffix. Although the plural ܪܚܡܐ (*raḥmē*) is synonymous with ܚܘܒܐ (*ḥubbā*) in 6b, it is closer to *misericordia* than to *amor* in this passage (see Excursus 2).[28] The equivalent in 𝔊 would then have been ἔλεος.[29] The exact translation of this term is not perhaps as important as the recognition that it transcends theologically even a mother's love and that it is elucidated by the parallel term ܒܣܝܡܘܬܐ (*bassīmūtā*), probably corresponding to the Greek χρηστότης.[30]

Those who know themselves to be in God's "mercy" (ἔλεος) and "kindness" are *finally* independent of kindness "whether public or private,"[31] however pleasant and important such manifestations and experiences may be.

Excursus 14: "Kindness" and "Delight" in the *Odes of Solomon*

For words derived from the root *bsm*, there is, in the first place, Joseph Ziegler's acute observation: "The Greek parallel could be χρηστός, χρηστότης. This seems to have been the model in the *Odes* as well, if a Greek original is accepted."[32] When *Ode* 11 𝔊 was published in 1959,[33] Ziegler's remarks on ܒܘܣܡܐ (*bussāmā*) in 11:16b and 11:24b were confuted.[34] It is now confirmed that the masculine word indeed

13 Bauer, 594; his note "probably only a simile like 1 Thess 2:7" is superfluous.
14 Suggested by Diettrich, 51.
15 Harnack, 44.
16 See Harris and Mingana, 2:278; and Charlesworth's criticism (p. 66).
17 See Payne Smith, 2:4391; BDAG, *s.v.* μαστός; Frankenberg, 16.
18 See Harris and Mingana, 2:278: "delights"; Frankenberg, 16 (αἱ τρυφαί).
19 BDAG, *s.v.* τρυφή.
20 Ungnad and Staerk, 16.
21 See Payne Smith, 2:3179–80.
22 See Franzmann, 113–14.
23 Diettrich, 50–51 nn. 4–9.
24 Payne Smith, 2:2594–95.
25 Ibid., 2:2392–93.
26 Nöldeke §266.
27 The corresponding Greek verbs were probably in the first place a transitive ἀφίστημι (BDAG, *s.v.* ἀφίστημι, "withdraw") and in the second αἴρω (BDAG, *s.v.* αἴρω) rather than ἀφαιρέω or (even less likely) λαμβάνω (BDAG, *s.vv.* ἀφαιρέω, λαμβάνω).
28 See Payne Smith, 2:3882.
29 See Konrad Weiß, "χρηστός, κτλ.," *ThWNT* 9 (1973) 474 lines 40–47; *TDNT* 9:485–86.
30 Frankenberg, 16; Franzmann, 407, referring to Col 3:12.
31 Weiß, "χρηστός," *ThWNT* 9:478; *TDNT* 9:488–89.
32 Joseph Ziegler, *Dulcedo Dei: Ein Beitrag zur Theologie der griechischen und lateinischen Bibel* (AtAbh 13.2; Münster: Aschendorff, 1937) 99.
33 Testuz 1959.
34 Ziegler (*Dulcedo*, 99 n. 80) considered it "uncertain" whether 𝔊 had used τρυφή. He therefore translated "the final word of praise" in *Ode* 11 with "sweetness of Paradise" (p. 100).

corresponds to τρυφή, which is therefore included in this excursus as "delight" (cf. the exegesis on the two passages). The Ethpa. of ܒܣܡ (*bsem*), which occurs three times, is not a translation of χρηστεύομαι,[35] but quite certainly represents the passive εὐφραίνομαι.[36] So words from the root *bsm* also express joy.[37] Thus, Ziegler's statement must be modified—only the two occurrences of the adjective ܒܣܝܡܐ (*bassīmā*) and the nine occurrences of the feminine ܒܣܝܡܘܬܐ (*bassīmūṯā*), in their various constructions, correspond to Greek χρηστός or χρηστότης, with a considerable loss in the breadth of meaning of the Greek.[38] The connotations of practical usefulness and moral purpose are totally missing in the *Odes of Solomon*.

The two Greek terms and their Syriac equivalents can be outlined only against the background of their use, on the one hand, in describing God's "sovereign 'clemency,' 'mildness' or 'magnanimity'" and, on the other, "in hymns of praise to God."[39] Their translation by "kind" and "kindness" can variously be made clearer by substituting "good," "friendly," "good to taste" (e.g., 30:4a, of the springwater), "goodness," "friendliness," "magnanimity."[40]

The terms considered here are sometimes more closely defined by the words used as antonyms. The statement that "his kindness has diminished his greatness" (7:3c) gives the reason for recognizing the "Lord." Human "wickedness" (πονηρία) is contrasted with God's "kindness" (11:21a).[41]

In certain passages, the term "kindness" is given an instrumental character by the use of verbal and prepositional constructions. The "breath" of a redeemed one is "gladdened by the fragrance of the Lord's kindness" (11:15 𝔖).[42] In 17:7 there is a question as to whether the "Most High" glorified the redeemed Redeemer "by his benevolence" (H) or is himself glorified by it (N). The "I" in 25:12a "was justified by his [viz., the Lord's] kindness" (Greek loanword χρηστός in ℭ). "Kindness" is a term used for the most part theologically in the *Odes of Solomon*, and even the mythological "Son of God" can be appealed to for his "kindness" (42:16a).

In the complex and difficult image 19:1b ("I drank it [i.e., the milk] in the sweetness of the Lord's kindness"), ܚܠܝܘܬܐ (*ḥalyūṯā*) stands for "sweetness in the literal sense of taste, while the second term combines this sensory meaning with a transferred sense—both sweetness and kindness."[43] In the little poem of birth, 19:10-11, the statement that the "mother," *inter alia*, "guarded with kindness" (11b) is also hard to interpret.

In 20:9b, the "kindness" of the "Lord" is parallel to his "grace"—and perhaps also to his "glory" (20:9a; cf. "grace and joy," 31:3a). The key word "glory," after all, also turns up in *Ode* 14 (see on 14:5a below) in close proximity to the parallelism of "kindness" and "mercy" (14:3a-b).

The pair of negative petitions in 3 is followed by a pair of positive petitions in 4a-b, which, in synthetic parallelism, transfer the ideas of "trust" and "power"[44] to the "Lord," signifying a radical refusal to follow a leader or render total obedience to any will in this world.

The *hapax legomenon* ܐܘܫܛ (*ʾawšeṭ*, Aph. of the root *yšṭ*, which is not found as a Pe.) commonly has the object "hand"; it corresponds to ἐκτείνω.[45] This Greek verb is less commonly found than δίδωμι[46] with δεξιά as its object. As in 8:6, ܝܡܝܢܐ (*yammīnā*) refers metaphorically to the right *hand* of the "Lord," which may have caused

35 See Weiß, "χρηστός," *ThWNT* 9:481; *TDNT* 9:491–92.
36 Payne Smith, 1:549; BDAG, *s.v.* εὐφραίνω.
37 Though the Syriac equivalent of τρυφή can be translated by "joy" (see on *Ode* 11 above), it must be distinguished from ܚܕܘܬܐ (*ḥaḏuṯā*) and χαρά (see Excursus 32).
38 See Weiß, "χρηστός," *ThWNT* 9:472–80; *TDNT* 9:483–91.
39 Weiß, "χρηστός," *ThWNT* 9:473, 479; *TDNT* 9:484, 491.
40 Weiß, "χρηστός," *ThWNT* 9:472–75, 478–79; *TDNT* 9:483–86, 489–90.
41 On πονηρός as antonym of χρηστός, see Weiß, "χρηστός," *ThWNT* 9:472; *TDNT* 9:483.
42 𝔖 here substitutes the adjective ܒܣܝܡܐ (*bassīmā*) for the noun. For ܐܬܒܣܡ (*ʾeṯbassam*)/εὐφραίνομαι cf. also 20:8a ("be joyful" in Paradise) and 28:2a ("my heart is delighted").
43 Ziegler, *Dulcedo*, 103.
44 BDAG, *s.v.* δεξιός.
45 Payne Smith, 1:1636; BDAG, *s.v.* ἐκτείνω, "stretch out."
46 BDAG, *s.v.* δίδωμι, esp. 16.

complaints of discrimination from the left-handed even in antiquity.[47]

Their parallelism endows both the expression in 4a ܒܟܠܙܒܢ (*b-kol zḇan*), repeated from 1b, and also the phrase in 4b (*ʿdammā l-ḥarṯā*), equivalent to εἰς τέλος, with a temporal meaning, indeed a meaning surpassing all categories of time: "to the end," "for ever and ever," "altogether."[48] The similarly imperative petition that the Lord will be "guide" (𝔊 would more probably have used γίνου than ἴσθι) uses the *hapax legomenon* ܡܕܒܪܢܐ (*mdabbrānā*), derived from ܕܒܪ (*dḇar*; Pa. *dabbar*), which in this case is the equivalent of ἡγούμενος,[49] not of καθηγητής.[50] Despite a superficial likeness, there is no reference to Ps 48:15 (47:15 LXX).[51] When it is remembered that the "present participle (ὁ) ἡγούμενος" was used "of men in any leading position,"[52] the attack on political, military, and religious leaders becomes clear.

Although the preposition ܥܠ (*ʿal*) "scarcely ever indicates the mere direction 'to',"[53] the final phrase of 4b does not absolutely have to correspond to κατὰ τὸ θέλημά σου.[54] This interpretation would obviously come very close to the petition in the Lord's Prayer, Matt 6:10: γενηθήτω τὸ θέλημά σου ("thy will be done")—ܢܗܘܐ ܨܒܝܢܟ (*nehwē ṣeḇyānāḵ*). But ܨܒܝܢܐ (*ṣeḇyānā*) may also be a soteriological and theological description of the goal (cf. 9:4; 18:8; Excursus 9) to which the "I," in poetic freedom, asks to be guided. In any case, this is not any legalistic or moralistic limitation of the will of God, which cannot ever be completely grasped and is not to be identified with any "act of will."[55]

In accordance with their chiastic construction, 5a and 5b reciprocally interpret each other. The imperfects of these parallel statements of confidence in salvation could also be translated as optatives rather than future tenses, and the same can be said of vv. 6a and 9b.[56] The first problem is to find the correct interpretation in 5a of the *hapax legomenon* ܫܦܪ (*šp̄ar*) with the preposition ܩܕܡ (*qḏām*) and second masculine singular suffix. Finding the Greek equivalent is also difficult.[57] The proper shade of meaning depends also on deciding whether ܬܫܒܘܚܬܐ (*tešbuḥtā*) here means "glorification" as in praise (cf. 6:7; 16:20; 18:16; 31:3, which would be Greek διὰ τῆς δόξης σου with an objective genitive)[58] or "glory" (with a subjective genitive σου in 𝔊; see Excursus 21). In the first case, it would be pleasing/acceptable *coram Deo;*[59] in the second, it would be a beauty based on the δόξα.[60] In either case, the speaker is looking forward to salvation. The key word "glory" may have its source in the "final doxology" of early date at the end of Matt 6:13.[61]

Even if the verbal influence of the Psalms, some of which evince fervent trust (cf. Ps 30:4 LXX[62] and also especially Ps 142:10-11 LXX,[63] which uses the terms θέλημα ["will"], ὁδηγήσει ["shall guide"], ἕνεκα τοῦ ὀνόματός σου, κύριε ["Lord, for thy name's sake"], and the rare transitive ζήσεις με ["thou shalt quicken me"]), cannot be excluded, 5b is an assemblage of themes from the Lord's Prayer. It is not concerned with "calling on the name of the Lord"[64] nor yet with "God hallowing himself."[65] The term ܫܡܐ (*šmā*)/ὄνομα (certainly its Greek equivalent) denotes the Name of God, taken over from Judaism, which "appears almost as a representa-

47 See Payne Smith, 1:1605.
48 BDAG, *s.v.* τέλος, esp. 2aα; see also Payne Smith, 1:129–30.
49 Payne Smith, 1:817; BDAG, *s.v.* ἡγέομαι, esp. 1.
50 Contra Frankenberg, 16.
51 Contra Harris and Mingana, 2:279. Heb 2:10 and 12:2, calling Jesus ἀρχηγός, are not parallels to *Ode* 14:4, where it is God the Lord, not "the Redeemer, who receives the title of leader" (contra Käsemann, *Wandering People*, 131; *Gottesvolk*, 81).
52 BDAG, *s.v.* ἡγέομαι, esp. 1.
53 Nöldeke §250.
54 Apart from Frankenberg, 16, see, e.g., Harris and Mingana, 2:278; Bauer, 594.
55 See BDAG, *s.v.* θέλημα; Payne Smith, 2:3354.
56 See Nöldeke §266; Emerton, 704.
57 See Payne Smith, 2:4272–73.
58 On the "word-pair" with "name," see Franzmann, 408.
59 See BDAG, *s.vv.* ἀρέσκω, esp. 2, or εὐαρεστέω, esp. 1, εὐάρεστος.
60 See BDAG, *s.v.* καλός; but also esp. LEH and Lampe, both *s.v.* ὡραιόομαι.
61 See Joachim Gnilka, "Vaterunser. I. Biblisch," *LThK*² 10 (1965) 626.
62 Harris and Mingana, 2:279.
63 Rahlfs, 2:157; Brenton, 783–84.
64 Lattke, *Oden*, 140.
65 Gnilka, "Vaterunser," 625, on Matt 6:9.

tion of the Godhead"[66] (see Excursus 39). As the "Lord" of the world and of humankind *is in* his "Name," the suppliant "I" hopes for salvation *by* that Name.[67]

When it is realized that the text of the Lord's Prayer is never quoted, although some of its themes and terms are treated to poetic variations, the substitution in 5b of the favorite soteriological verb ܐܬܦܪܩ (*ʾeṯpreq*, Ethpe. from ܦܪܩ [*praq*]; see Excursus 5), which would here certainly represent a passive of Greek σῴζω,[68] for the Pa. ܦܨܝ (*paṣṣī*), which translates ῥύομαι in Matt 6:13, can well be passed over. The masculine ܒܝܫܐ (*bīšā*) is "commonly used in Syriac literature to render 'the Evil One,'"[69] but its employment does not lead to any clear conclusions on the connotation of πονηρός, which will have been the most likely term used in 𝔊.[70] As in Matt 6:13, it is impossible to decide whether it means "the evil one," that is, "the devil," or "evil" in the abstract,[71] perhaps even in a "universalizing" sense.[72] Whether as a personified being or as a cosmic principle, ὁ πονηρός/ ܒܝܫܐ or τὸ πονηρόν is a dualistically negative and inimical power from which the "I" wishes to escape and will be able to.

■ **6-8** There is a point to be added to Franzmann's description of the structure of these three bicola.[73] Stanzas II and III are mirror images, in that an expression of trust in salvation (6a-b; cf. 5a-b) is now followed by two petitions (7-8; cf. 3-4).[74] If the author(s) and their mouthpiece seem for the moment to have lost sight of the Lord's Prayer (but see on stanza V below), the central terms and images of the *Odes of Solomon* are here gathered together.

The parallel lines 6a-b both begin with ܘ (*ʾu-*), corresponding to Greek καί . . . καί. Both subjects govern the imperfect of Pa. ܩܘܝ (*qawwī*), which is singular under the influence of "rest"; this verb probably does not represent a simple future—or even an optative (see on 5a above)—of μένω.[75] Far more likely is the use of a composite like παραμένω or προσμένω with a dative of the personal pronoun.[76] The feminine ܢܝܚܘܬܐ (*nīḥūṯā*) is not equivalent to Greek φιλανθρωπία[77] or to the term of "virtue" πραότης/πραΰτης.[78] As usual, the Syriac term is a synonym of ܢܝܚܬܐ (*nyāḥtā*; cf. 35:1) and ܢܝܚܐ (*nyāḥā*) and means also "quietness"[79] (see Excursus 3, and esp. the commentary on *Ode* 26:3b, 10a, 12a-b). In a personal invocation, the "I" expresses its complete trust that the eschatological (perhaps with an early Gnostic tinge) ἀνά-/κατάπαυσις of the "Lord" will remain with him or her, where one can attain true "rest" and abide in it.[80] One who is in God's "rest" does not need a day or place of repose.

In parallel to the "rest" of the "Lord" are the "fruits" of his "love" (see Excursuses 2 and 11). There is no reason "to delete" 6b,[81] or to doubt that the Greek expression was οἱ καρποὶ τῆς ἀγάπης σου,[82] but Petra von Gemün-

66 BDAG, *s.v.* ὄνομα; see also Payne Smith, 2:4199–4200.
67 See 8:21, 23; 15:8; 25:11 (𝔖); 39:8; 42:20. On *Hermas, Vis.* 23 (IV.2).4, see Brox, *Hirt*, 173.
68 Payne Smith, 2:3294; BDAG, *s.v.* σῴζω, esp. 2b.
69 Harris and Mingana, 2:279.
70 It is not the context but the grammar that decides "that 'evil' is personified" in 𝔖 (Charlesworth, 66). Diettrich (p. 51) also interprets the Syriac word as "diabolus" and refers to 33:4 and also to "the depiction of Satan as chief of the evil spirits and essence of wickedness" in *Jub.* 10:5-11; 23:29.
71 BDAG, *s.v.* πονηρός.
72 Suggested by Carsten Colpe and Wilhelm Schmidt-Biggemann, eds., *Das Böse: Eine historische Phänomenologie des Unerklärlichen* (Suhrkamp Taschenbuch Wissenschaft 1078; Frankfurt a.M.: Suhrkamp, 1993) 43–44.
73 Franzmann, 114.
74 Franzmann (p. 114) establishes the following points of structure: "6a and 6b are parallel with ellipsis"; "7a-b and 8a-b are alternately parallel." Also she says of 6a-b: "The bicolon is given emphasis by its position in the centre of the main body of the address to the Lord (3-9b)."
75 Payne Smith, 2:3509–10; BDAG, *s.v.* μένω.
76 See BDAG, *s.vv.* παραμένω, προσμένω.
77 Contra Frankenberg, 16.
78 See BDAG, *s.v.* πραότης/πραΰτης; Friedrich Hauck and Siegfried Schulz, "πραΰς, πραΰτης," *ThWNT* 6 (1959) 645–51; *TDNT* 6:645–51. This term of "virtue" seems to be the influence under which translators use words like "gentleness" to represent the Syriac; see, e.g., Ungnad and Staerk, 16; Bauer, 594 ("Milde"); Harris and Mingana, 2:278; Charlesworth, 66. If the terms πραότης/ πραΰτης were used in 𝔊, reference should be made to *Diogn.* 7:4.
79 Payne Smith, *Dictionary*, 338.
80 See BDAG, *s.vv.* ἀνάπαυσις, κατάπαυσις.
81 Contra Diettrich, 51.
82 Frankenberg, 16.

den has not interpreted the "fruit metaphor" of this passage.[83] The simplest explanation would make the "fruits" quite generally "results" or "gain."[84] However, it could also be an early Gnostic metaphor for other redeemed ones who join the "I" to make a "we" (see on stanza V below).[85] As the "love" of the "Lord" brings forth these "fruits," which stand metaphorically for persons, the "I" also will be instrumental in the future in bearing such "fruit" (see on 7b below). If this image seems to some to lack evidence and to show too much boldness, they will have to content themselves with the finding that the "content" of the "fruit metaphor" in 6b is not "tangible,"[86] and the one in 7b can only be taken as a parallel of 8b.

The petition of 7a uses Pa. ܐܠܦ (*ʾallep̄*), which in John 8:28 translates διδάσκω.[87] Among the passages in the *Odes of Solomon* that deal with the divine ܫܪܪܐ (*šrārā*; see Excursus 1), 7a is unique in combining it with the plural of the hymnic ܙܡܝܪܬܐ (*zmīrtā*), a term found in the title of the individual *Odes*,[88] in 26:2 as a parallel to "hymn" (26:1); this term can, generally speaking, be equated with "psalm" or "song." Similar genitive phrases are "odes of the Lord" (26:8) and "odes of his rest" (26:3; cf. 36:2, again in close proximity to a mention of "rest" [36:1], and 40:3).[89] This, of course, raises the question whether the "odes of thy truth" refer to particular sections of the *Odes of Solomon*. But it is more likely that these "ode" passages caused the whole collection to be called the "*Odes* of Solomon," as well as providing the word as a title for each individual Ode (note especially the title of *Ode* 11).

The objective of 7b has already been outlined (see 6b above). In a sense, stanza III is like an optical illusion. Concentrating on 6-7 brings out one set of meanings for the plural of ܦܐܪܐ (*pērā*), while looking at 7-8 changes them to another. The parallel structure of 7-8 seems to make 8b the explanation of 7b. So the intended καρποφερεῖν (cf. 11:1) or καρποὺς φερεῖν/ποιεῖν of the speaking "I" would be nothing but the singing of praises as a result of the teaching of 7a (cf. esp. 16:2). Even if 7b and 8b are not strictly parallel (see on 8a below), and despite all ambiguities and difficulties in understanding the entwined images, one thing is clear: the "fruits" do not represent virtues or good works.[90]

A remark by Bauer points the way to interpreting 8a: "8a may be an abridgment of 'open my mouth' (7:24) so that it becomes the instrument of thy holy spirit (6:1-2)."[91] It follows that the Greek loanword κιθάρα, unlike its use in 26:3, has the metaphorical meaning of "mouth" (cf. 7:24; 12:2; 16:5; 36:7). Verse 8a, then, is not a mere parallel of 7a,[92] but brings in a new theme in logical sequence. The petition for teaching is followed by a petition for its use: "open my mouth, the cithara of thy holy spirit" (cf. 3:10 for the "spirit of the Lord" as teacher; on the "holy spirit" or "spirit of holiness," cf. also 6:7; 11:2; 19:2, 4; 23:22).

The concluding statement of the goal in 8b is more or less parallel to 7b (see above). It is uncertain which Greek verb corresponded to the subjunctive imperfect of the Pa. ܫܒܚ (*šabbaḥ*). It must have been a hymnic term like αἰνέω, δοξάζω, or ὑμνέω.[93] Furthermore, the *hapax legomenon* ܩܝܢܢ (*qīnān*, absolute state feminine plural of ܩܝܢܐ [*qīnā*]; cf. ὁ φθόγγος in 1 Cor 14:7)[94] carries a

83 Gemünden, *Vegetationsmetaphorik*, 402, referring to *Odes* 7:1 and 16:2.

84 BDAG, *s.v.* καρπός, esp. 2.

85 See Victoria Arnold-Döben, *Die Bildersprache der Gnosis* (AMRG 13; Cologne: Brill, 1986) 148.

86 Gemünden, *Vegetationsmetaphorik*, 401.

87 Payne Smith, 1:213; BDAG, *s.v.* διδάσκω. The reference to John 8:28 is important because the Jesus of the Fourth Gospel is there speaking of the teaching of the heavenly Father.

88 See Payne Smith, 1:1136–37; BDAG, *s.v.* ᾠδή.

89 See Franzmann, "Man of Rest," 411: "By comparison, the concepts of truth and rest permeate the Odes and are strongly linked."

90 See BDAG, *s.v.* καρπός.

91 Bauer, 594. Diettrich's translation (p. 52), "open to me the zither of thy spirit," is grammatically defensible, but the sense is unlikely.

92 See Lattke, "Wörter," 291 = idem, *Bedeutung*, 4:139.

93 Payne Smith, 2:4023–24; BDAG, *s.vv.* αἰνέω, δοξάζω, ὑμνέω.

94 Payne Smith, 2:3603–4; see also BDAG, *s.v.* φθόγγος. The misprint ܩܬܢ in Charlesworth 1973 (p. 65) was corrected to ܩܝܢܢ in the 1977 reprint (p. 65). Even if the terms κιθάρα and φθόγγος originate with Paul, this passage in the *Odes* does not have any implication of speaking with tongues or prophecy.

sense of hymnody and music making in addition to the prayerful glorification.[95]

■ **9a-b** This expression of confidence in salvation, which concludes the "I" section by taking up the comparative particles from 1a-b,[96] is incomprehensible without reference to a Greek original, even though 9a uses only the Syriac vocabulary of the Psalms (cf. Ps 25:7; 51:3).[97] Whether 9a had ὡς or καθώς cannot be decided, but 9b must have had οὕτως (cf. 29:2; 36:5) because the Syriac construction (cf. 15:7; 29:3) could easily have dispensed with ܗܟܢܐ (*hākannā*). This excludes at least part of Frankenberg's back-translation καὶ κατὰ τὸ μέγεθος τοῦ ἐλέου σου δώσεις μοι.[98] The noun here, derived from ܣܓܐ (*sgā*), as in 16:7, will have corresponded to τὸ πλῆθος (cf. Ps 50:3 LXX; *1 Clem.* 18:2).[99] But probably the most important word in 9a was identical with the equivalent of ܪܚܡܐ (*raḥmē*) in 3a (see on ἔλεος above).

It is only in 9b that the speaker first expresses actual confidence. Here also the imperfect future ܢܬܠ (*nettel*) could be translated as an optative (see on 5 above). 𝔊 would have used a form of the common verb (ἀπο)δίδωμι[100] or one of a less common verb, such as χαρίζομαι.[101] The application of it to God the Lord can have been a soteriological variation on the use of ἀποδώσει and δός in Matt 6:6 and 6:11, the more so since the infinitive of ܢܬܠ (*nettel*) occurs also in 9c. The content of this confiding statement remains quite undefined and thus outdoes any human need for love and even the unconcealed expectation of a child or baby.

■ **9c-10** "The singular speaker makes way for a plurality."[102] This fact does not give a license to consider stanza V "an addition to the self-contained Ode in 1-9b,"[103] especially since this response, combining petition (9c) and trust in salvation (10), is, by repetition of ܢܬܠ (*nettel*) and address to the identical "Lord," firmly attached to stanzas II–IV, and now as a communal "we" brings the previous variations on text and context of the Lord's Prayer to an almost doxological conclusion. It might even be considered superfluous to cite the similarly doxological passage Phil 4:19-20,[104] since the terms χρεία, αἰτέω, and δύναμις in Matt 6:8 and 6:13 are quite sufficient for interpretation. A reconstruction of the possible Greek original is placed at the end of this commentary.

Since the Saph. of ܪܗܒ (*rheb*), which occurs only in 9c, is often used adverbially,[105] 𝔊 is likely to have had ταχέως.[106] Instead of the infinitive of ܢܬܠ (see on 9b above) that follows this imperative, 𝔊 will have used an imperative of δίδωμι. The plural ܫܐܠܬܐ (*šelāṯā*)[107] is again a *hapax legomenon* and refers to the content of the prayers. The Greek phrase τὰ αἰτήματα ἡμῶν, which is likely to have been the grammatical object of the insistent imperative, is also concerned with "that which is prayed for."[108]

In the bicolon 9c-10, 10 is more a justification of 9c than a parallel, although the nouns with plural suffixes at the ends of the lines form "a semantic link."[109] The central part of the address—ܡܨܐ ܟܠܗܝܢ (*mṣē kullhēn*)—evokes *omnipotens*, which is equivalent to the "Hellenistic divine title" παντοδύναμος.[110] Taken as a whole, however, the language of the verse raises the cosmic component of this all-powerfulness to an existential

95 See Lattke, *Hymnus*, 251–53 = idem, *Bedeutung*, 4:107–10.
96 Franzmann, 114: "inclusio."
97 *OTSy*, pt. 2 fasc. 3, pp. 25 and 56.
98 Frankenberg, 16.
99 See BDAG, *s.v.* πλῆθος; Payne Smith, 2:2520–21 on ܣܘܓܐ (*sogā*).
100 BDAG, *s.vv.* ἀποδίδωμι, δίδωμι.
101 See Payne Smith, 2:2480–81; BDAG, *s.v.* χαρίζομαι.
102 Bauer, 594.
103 Franzmann, 114.
104 Contra Harris and Mingana, 2:280; Lattke, *Oden*, 141.
105 See Payne Smith, *Dictionary*, 531.
106 BDAG, *s.v.* ταχέως; Payne Smith, 2:3828.
107 See Payne Smith, 2:4008.
108 BDAG, *s.v.* αἴτημα; cf. ܫܐܠܬܟܘܢ in Matt 6:8 in the Peshitta.
109 Franzmann, 115.
110 See Payne Smith, 2:2190; Georgi, 428, on Wis 7:23.

level and attaches it to the plural of ܚܫܚܬܐ (*ḥšaḥṯā*). This *hapax legomenon,* which includes all the "necessaries of life,"[111] reproduces the plural of χρεία (Matt 6:8)[112] and includes "the bread that we need."[113] The passive participle of ܡܨܐ (*mṣā*), which is also used only here, is the normal equivalent of δυνάμενος.[114] So the Greek original of the Syriac text was constructed with a following accusative, and in this case the verb to be supplied is not ποιεῖν but πληροῦν.[115] The original Greek of this passage can then be restored with some assurance:

καὶ δὸς ταχέως τὰ αἰτήματα ἡμῶν,
καὶ σὺ εἶ πάσας δυνάμενος χρείας ἡμῶν.

111 Payne Smith, *Dictionary*, 162.
112 Payne Smith, 1:1400–1401; BDAG, *s.v.* χρεία.
113 Joachim Gnilka, "Vaterunser. I. Biblisch," *LThK*² 10 (1965) 626, on ἐπιούσιος in Matt 6:11.
114 Payne Smith, 2:2190–91.
115 See BDAG, *s.v.* δύναμαι.

15

Ode 15: Address of the Redeemed One and Redeemer: The Lord as the Sun

(I) 1a As Helios is joy to those who seek his day,
1b so my joy is the Lord,
2a because he is *my* Helios.
2b And his rays awakened me,
2c and his light dispelled all darkness from my face.
(II) 3a I obtained eyes through him
3b and saw his holy day.
4a I had ears
4b and heard his truth.

5a I had the thought of *gnōsis*
5b and was delighted by him.
(III) 6a I forsook the way of error and went to him
6b and received salvation from him without envy.
7a And according to his gracious gift he gave to me,
7b and according to his magnificence he made me.
8a I put on imperishability by his name
8b and took off perishability by his grace.
9a Death was annihilated before my face
9b and the realm of the dead [Sheol] destroyed by my word.
(IV) 10a And he rose on the land of the Lord—immortal life.
10b And it [viz., life] was known by his believers
10c and given without stint to those who trust in him.
Hallelujah.

Introduction

Ode 15 is preserved in one Syriac manuscript.[1] The word "Redeemer" in the title assigned to this "Ode of the Sun" depends on a single suffix in 9b. If "my word" were to be emended to "his word,"[2] *Ode* 15 would have only one redeemed speaker of indeterminate gender, for whom "death and hell" are already "finished with."[3] The manuscript text of 9b, however, is *lectio difficilior*, so Rudolf Abramowski's "enigmatic second 'I,'" who is "a prominent member of the community of the Odes,"[4] should be accepted as the speaker, one who is not merely *redeemed* but in some more or less mythological fashion can *act to redeem* others. Facing the "I" is the "Lord," described in metaphorical and soteriological-theological fashion (*passim*). It is not made clear who the

1 Ms.: Codex H, 11b–12a (ܣ). Ed./trans.: Charlesworth, 66–69; Franzmann, 116–20; Lattke, 2:1–16 and 3:XXV–XXVI.

2 Harris, 111; Harnack, 45; Kittel, 45. Frankenberg (p. 17) also puts a question mark after *μου*. Although Harris and Mingana (2:281–82) do not discuss this problem, Harris's original note is relevant (p. 111): "There is one passage which is either obscure, incorrect or extravagant where the writer says that 'Sheol has been abolished by my word.' Unless there has been a transition of personality, this seems extravagant, and invites the correction 'has been abolished at His word.' In any case, I think the Psalm is a Christian one."

3 Bauer, 594.

4 Abramowski, 58.

speaker of stanza IV is. Thematically, however, at least 10b-c concerns a number of people and so form a sort of *inclusio* with 1a.[5] More difficult to imagine and somewhat hypothetical is the proposition that only in the two over-length lines, 1a and 10c, "a singer would treat these in an antiphon mode, differentiating them by rhythm/melody from the remainder of the Ode to emphasise the introduction and conclusion."[6]

Gottfried Schille[7] reckons *Ode* 15 among his "hymns of initiation," but the fact that "garment of immortality" is a "common description of baptism"[8] in early Christian writings is not sufficient reason to call this Ode a "baptismal hymn." *Ode* 15 is indeed a "song of the sun" and as such can be read as a *theological* polemic against the "sun worship of antiquity," but that does not make it an "Easter hymn," and it does not mention *Christ* as the "true sun" whose "beams wondrously illuminate" the newly baptized;[9] in fact, it compares *God* the Lord to the "sun." It is equally inexplicable how *Ode* 15 can be likened to one of the *carmina Christo quasi deo* ("hymns to Christ as to a god") of which the younger Pliny writes.[10]

Interpretation

■ **1-2** Following Wolfgang Fauth into the "theology of the sun" of antiquity and the "heliolatry" of the "pre-syncretic phase"[11] makes it possible to understand the full extent of the polemic contained in the first comparison (1-2a) and the statement of salvation that follows (2b-c). Helios is stripped of his eminence when the "I" declares the Creator and Redeemer to be the eschatological and transcendent "object of joy."[12] The speaker endorses the importance of the sun to life, by declaring the "Lord," who is not to be equated with any individual star nor with the total cosmos and/or chaos of the universe, to be *his* metaphorical Helios. This is the dialectical content of the first strophe of stanza I, which is "constructed on a (circular) terrace pattern."[13]

In 𝔊 the construction of the introductory comparison in 1a-b will have used ὡς . . . οὕτως.[14] And the noun ܚܕܘܬܐ (*ḥaḏuṯā*), which can be of either gender, probably corresponded to the equally metonymic use of the noun ἡ χαρά.[15] Even in the bilingual area to which the Syriac version of the *Odes of Solomon* belongs, the great importance of ἥλιος, equivalent to ܫܡܫܐ (*šemšā*), was well understood.[16] The simile of "sun" and "joy," accomplished by use of the copula, assumes that people in general are not afraid of light but appreciate the "day" from sunrise to sunset. The verb form of ܒܥܐ (*bʿā*) is a continuing participle, and the verb can be used transitively to mean "need" or "request";[17] in this context its meaning is nearer to "seek" or "desire" in the sense of "wish for."[18] The third masculine singular possessive suffix to ܝܘܡܐ (*yawmā*) refers to the "sun"[19] and thus describes

5 Franzmann, 120.

6 Ibid. Although Diettrich's division of *Ode* 15 into an "introductory part" (1-2) and a "main section" of two strophes (3-6, 7-10) is quite acceptable (p. 52), I prefer Franzmann's more detailed and reasoned analysis (pp. 118–20).

7 Schille, 76.

8 Franz Joseph Dölger, *Sol Salutis: Gebet und Gesang im christlichen Altertum. Mit besonderer Rücksicht auf die Ostung in Gebet und Liturgie* (Liturgiegeschichtliche Forschungen 4.5; 2nd ed.; Münster: Aschendorff, 1925) 369–70; see also Bernard, 79.

9 Basilius Steidle, "'Die Oden Salomons,'" *Benediktinische Monatsschrift zur Pflege religiösen und geistigen Lebens* 24 (1948) 242 (see also p. 241: "Der Herr meine Sonne. 15. Ode Salomons").

10 Contra Charlesworth, 68, speaking of "psalm[s]"; on *carmen* in Pliny, see Lattke, *Hymnus*, 86–88.

11 Wolfgang Fauth, *Helios megistos: Zur synkretistischen Theologie der Spätantike* (Religions in the Graeco-Roman World 125; Leiden: Brill, 1995) xvii–xxxiii.

12 See BDAG, *s.v.* χαρά. Charlesworth (p. 68) is wrong to doubt that ܚܕܘܬܐ (*ḥaḏuṯā*) translates as "Freude [joy]," saying, "the noun means 'gladness', 'mirth', and 'joy'."

13 Franzmann, 118.

14 Cf. 6:1-2; 7:1-2; 14:1; 16:1; 28:1; 40:1-2; BDAG, *s.v.* ὡς.

15 Payne Smith, 1:1199–200; BDAG, *s.v.* χαρά. See Excursus 32.

16 See BDAG, *s.v.* ἥλιος; Payne Smith, 2:4223–24.

17 Payne Smith, 1:556–57.

18 See BDAG, *s.v.* ζητέω, and Klijn, 303.

19 Johannes Baptist Bauer, Review of Lattke 1979, 1979a, 1980, *Kairos* N.F. 23 (1981) 121–22.

the "day"–ἡμέρα[20] in 𝔊—as in a sense the product and possession of the heavenly body that dispenses light and warmth (cf. 16:15-16).

The key word "day" is not transferred to the "Lord" until 3a; in 1b the speaking "I" is content with the vivifying "joy" as the term of comparison. The place of "Helios" is taken theologically by the "Kyrios," the totally transcendent creator and governor of all the cosmic powers, including the sun.

Verse 2a justifies 1b, returning, with ܗܘܝܘ (*hūyū*, pronoun + copula),[21] to the origin of the simile (the "sun") but surpassing such a simple comparison as the one in 11:13 ("the Lord *like* the sun"). The "Lord" is not merely, as it were, the object of "joy": he is the metaphorical "sun," which ousts the ancient sun god from his sacred position.[22]

Without allegorizing, the speaking "I," in the second strophe of stanza I, emphasizes the two most important functions of the sun on earth and among humankind in two parallel terms—in 𝔊 certainly ἀκτῖνες ("rays"; cf. Wis 2:4) and φῶς ("light")—and transfers them dualistically to the awakening and enlightening power of the Lord, which has been active from times past. Syntactically, the masculine suffixes of ܙܠܝܩܘܗܝ (*zallīqē*, *hapax legomenon*)[23] and ܢܘܗܪܐ (*nuhrā*), corresponding to Greek αὐτοῦ, can refer to the "sun" or to the "Lord," which makes no difference in a real comparison (see also on 10a below).

The Aph. of ܩܘܡ, ܩܡ (*qām*), which probably reproduces ἀνίστημι rather than ἐγείρω, in 2b is not used in a parallel sense elsewhere in the *Odes of Solomon*,[24] but, since it presupposes a preceding sleep, it is reminiscent of Eph 5:14 (in the context of 5:6-14, with the contrast of σκότος ["darkness"]–φῶς ["light"]), though it says nothing of "*baptism* as illumination by the sun" [emphasis added]; it is quite unnecessary to make a connection between any and every existential awakening and illumination and Christian baptism, much less the "baptismal experience."[25]

There is no reason to suppose that ܐܦܐ (*ʾappē*) in 2c should *not* correspond to τὸ πρόσωπον.[26] The speaking "I" uses "face" to signify the whole "person" (see Excursus 8).[27] The power of the divine "light" was existentially so great that *all* shackling, crippling, and benighting "darkness" (in 𝔊 σκοτία or σκότος) was "dispelled" (on the dualism of light and darkness, see Excursus 10).[28] In this statement of salvation, the speaker appears as a poetic persona, freed internally and externally from the *mixtum compositum* of light and dark. In stanzas II and III, further consequences of this soteriological self-perception are explored in detail.

■ **3-5** The speaking "I" transfers the classical description of Helios as "seeing all and hearing all . . . and therefore knowing all,"[29] in three parallel bicola, not to the Lord but, in part, to himself. The "Lord," as the "sun," is certainly present in this threefold perfect-tense statement of salvation. Both the instrumental phrases with ܒ (*b-*) + suffix, which frame the stanza in 3a and 5b, and the suffixes in 3b and 4b refer to the Lord/Helios. *Ode* 15:3-4 may, like 16:9, be under the influence of Prov 20:12 LXX,[30] a saying couched in the vocabulary of Wisdom literature:

20 BDAG, *s.v.* ἡμέρα.

21 See Nöldeke §312 C.

22 For Diettrich (pp. 53–54), *Ode* 15 is "from a–z a Jewish song" that even radiates "an Essene-Therapeutic atmosphere." This idea leads him to make the following misleading assertion (among others): "God as the sun of his faithful already occurs in Psalm 84:12" (p. 54). But Ps 85:12 (84:12 LXX) says only: "righteousness looks down from heaven" (δικαιοσύνη ἐκ τοῦ οὐρανοῦ διέκυψεν).

23 Payne Smith, 1:1131; see also BDAG, *s.v.* ἀκτίς.

24 See BDAG, *s.v.* ἀνίστημι; Payne Smith, 2:3527–28.

25 Hugo Rahner, *Griechische Mythen in christlicher Deutung: Gesammelte Aufsätze* (Zurich: Rhein-Verlag, 1945; 3rd ed., 1966) 118.

26 Contra Frankenberg, 16: ἔμπροσθέν μου λύει.

27 BDAG, *s.v.* πρόσωπον; see also Payne Smith, 1:278–79.

28 On ܫܪܐ (*šrā*), see Payne Smith, 2:4305–9; BDAG, *s.v.* λύω.

29 Wolfgang Fauth, *Helios megistos: Zur synkretistischen Theologie der Spätantike* (Religions in the Graeco-Roman World 125; Leiden: Brill, 1995) xix.

30 Diettrich, 54.

οὖς ἀκούει καὶ ὀφθαλμὸς ὁρᾷ·
κυρίου ἔργα καὶ ἀμφότερα.

The ear hears, and the eye sees:
even both of them are the Lord's work.[31]

The phraseology of 3a, which differs from 4a and 5a, can best be explained by assuming a Greek original, where *ἐκτησάμην* was used with *ἐν αὐτῷ* or *δι᾽ αὐτοῦ*.[32] The ܒ (*b*-) + third masculine singular suffix make it clear that not only the acquisition of "eyes" for "spiritual perception,"[33] but also the other faculties mentioned later are gifts and not the results of individual prowess.

Verse 3b picks up the key word ܝܘܡܐ (*yawmā*) from 1a and, by adding the otherworldly adjective ܩܕܝܫܐ (*qaddīšā*), removes it from the grasp of Helios. The verb form of ܚܙܐ (*ḥzā*), ܚܙܝܬ (*ḥzēt*), could correspond to various Greek words (e.g., *ἔβλεψα*, *εἶδον,* or *ἑώρακα*),[34] but the phrase *τὴν ἁγίαν αὐτοῦ ἡμέραν*, or something very like it, is likely to have formed the object.[35] This "day," spiritually perceived, "is obviously not the day of the Messiah," unlike 41:4.[36] In fact, no particular day is specified.[37] It is a natural phenomenon that is transferred to the "Lord," an act that relativizes or even negates its original meaning.

The "ears," also limited to "spiritual understanding,"[38] which form the subject of the idiomatic verb construction[39] with ܗܘܐ (*hwā*) + ܠ (*l*-) + first singular suffix,[40] also come from the "Lord" (see on 3a above). What the speaker "heard," that is, understood or grasped,[41] was the Lord's "truth" in the sense of "divine reality,"[42] which exists only in the word (cf. 8:8). Therefore ܫܪܪܐ (*šrārā*)[43] or *ἀλήθεια*,[44] unlike Rom 1:25, does not in 4b mean the "true God" (see Excursus 1).

Excursus 9 postponed consideration of 5a: "Whether the redeemed one with his 'thought of knowledge' (15:5) is also the Redeemer (cf. 15:9) will be discussed later." The commentary on 9b will return to this question. Two points need to be decided here: first, whether ܝܕܥܬܐ (*ʾidaʿtā*) corresponds to the technical term *γνῶσις* (see Excursus 7),[45] and, second, whether the grammatical form of "*gnōsis*" or "knowledge" is a subjective or objective genitive.

1. Even without Harris and Mingana's suggested emendation of ܐܬܦܢܩܬ (*ʾetpannqet*) to ܐܬܦܪܩܬ (*ʾetparqet*) in 5b (see below),[46] the juxtaposition with "salvation" (6c) gives the term *γνῶσις*/ܝܕܥܬܐ a Gnosticizing tinge.

2. In the genitive phrase, that is not simply a parallel expression, as, for example, *γνῶσις καὶ σύνεσις* ("knowledge and understanding") in Prov 2:6 LXX,[47]

31 Rahlfs, 2:217; Brenton, 807. See Plöger, 234–35 on this saying: "That this is merely a remark about God the creator who fashioned eyes and ears, which are so important in human life, is very unlikely. Ps 94:9 couples a similar statement with the warning that Jahwe, who has made the organs of sight and hearing, can himself hear all and see all." So statements about Helios have also already been made about Yahweh.

32 On the Pe. ܩܢܐ (*qnā*), which can also mean "to own," see Payne Smith, 2:3651–52; on *κτάομαι*, see BDAG, *s.v.*

33 See Payne Smith, 2:2867, *s.v.* ܥܝܢܐ (*ʿaynā*); BDAG, *s.v.* *ὀφθαλμός*, 2.

34 See BDAG, *s.vv.* *βλέπω*, *εἶδον*, *ὁράω*; Payne Smith, 1:1233–34.

35 Frankenberg, 16.

36 Diettrich, 54.

37 Therefore, it is not even "the day" of Diettrich's hypothesis "on which the singer, in an act of initiation, 'received the idea of knowledge'" (Diettrich, 54).

38 See Payne Smith, 1:39–40 *s.v.* ܐܕܢܐ (*ʾednā*); BDAG, *s.v.* *οὖς*, 2.

39 This verb construction does not correspond to *ἐγένετό μοι* (contra Frankenberg, 16) but to a form of *ἔχω* (e.g., *ἔσχον*); see also Klaus Beyer in Lattke, 3:XXVI nn. 1 and 2.

40 See Payne Smith, 1:983–84; BDAG, *s.v.* *ἔχω*, 1bα, "of parts of the body" as object.

41 Payne Smith, 2:4214 *s.v.* ܫܡܥ (*šmaʿ*); BDAG, *s.v.* *ἀκούω*.

42 Rudolf Bultmann, "*γινώσκω, κτλ.*," *ThWNT* 1 (1933) 693; *TDNT* 1:694.

43 Payne Smith, 2:4303–4.

44 See BDAG, *s.v.* *ἀλήθεια*.

45 See Payne Smith, 1:1559–60; BDAG, *s.v.* *γνῶσις*.

46 Charlesworth (p. 68) is not quite right when he says: "Harris-Mingana proposed in 1916 to emend the text to 'and I was saved', but correctly ignored the emendation in 1920." In a text-critical note on their translation "delighted," Harris and Mingana say: "In view of the next verse where mention is made of salvation we have suggested the probable ܐܬܦܪܩܬ 'and I was saved'" (2:281).

47 Brenton, 789; cf. Diettrich, 54.

but sounds more like "thought of Truth" (in 17:5) or even φωτισμὸς τῆς γνώσεως (2 Cor 4:6),[48] the feminine ܡܚܫܒܬܐ (*maḥšab̲tā*)[49] is qualified by the following feminine ܝܕܥܬܐ (*ʾid̲aʿt̲ā*).[50] Even in 𝔊, γνῶσις was not the content or object of "thought" but a soteriological power, a gift from God, to guide the thought (on the coming of the "*gnōsis* of the Lord," cf. 7:21).[51]

It is possible that in 5b the Ethpa. from the root *pnq* appeared already in 𝔖* (a *hapax legomenon* like the noun in 14:2).[52] But even in a transferred sense this verb does not fit as easily into the soteriological and mythological context of *Ode* 15 as the paleographically very similar form of the Ethpe. of ܦܪܩ (*pᵉraq*; cf. 17:4 and 38:16).[53] If 𝔖* had ܐܬܦܪܩܬ (*ʾetparqet̲*), then 𝔊 or rather 𝔊* would probably have used a form of σῴζω.[54] The idiomatic expression "by him"—lit., "by his hand"—corresponded to δι᾽ αὐτοῦ,[55] and the relative pronoun, there also, referred to the "Lord" and not to "*gnōsis*."

■ **6-9** This stanza, composed of four more or less parallel strophes, is not a "report about the 'I' and how the Lord acted on his behalf,"[56] but a mythological address by the speaking "I." The dualistic statements of salvation in 6 and 8 are in the first person; in those of 7, the Lord is shown as having acted in the past, while the parallel mythologoumena of 9 are in the theological passive. The redeemed "I," at the generalizing apex of stanza III, metamorphoses into a mediator of victory over death and Hades, who, in the light of similar passages in other *Odes*, should be described as the redeeming Redeemed One.

Following the division of 6 in H, with 6b extending from ܘܐܙܠܬ (*w-ezlet̲*) to ܚܣܡܐ (*ḥsāmā*), gives this colon an almost ridiculous length. An earlier editorial division of 6b into 6b-c[57] can be avoided by lengthening 6a instead. This gives 6a two complementary verbs of motion, the first of which may have been in a participial construction in 𝔊 (e.g., τὴν ὁδὸν τῆς πλάνης ἀφεὶς ἦλθον πρὸς αὐτόν).

Excursus 15: "Way" and Some Terms of Motion in the *Odes of Solomon*

Given the importance of ἡ ὁδός in Greek literature, in the LXX, in the works of Philo, in the New Testament, and in the Apostolic Fathers,[58] it is no surprise that the feminines ὁδός (11:3) and ܐܘܪܚܐ (*ʾurḥā*, twenty occurrences) have a role in the dualistic-mythological images of the *Odes of Solomon*.[59] Since statements containing "way" are often juxtaposed with terms of motion, and there is indeed a good deal of poetical movement in the *Odes* (esp. in *Odes* 7, 17, 23, 33, 38, and 39), this excursus will include derivatives of the roots ܐܙܠ, ܗܠܟ, ܢܚܬ, ܥܒܪ, ܪܗܛ, and ܪܗܛ, but not ones from ܐܬܐ, ܢܦܩ, or ܩܪܒ.[60]

As a beginning, it can be stated that there seems to be no sign of an ethical doctrine of the two ways.[61] In the *Odes of Solomon*, "way" is not used "in the most comprehensive sense" for a "tendency" or "doctrine,"[62] nor is it a term for the *religio Christiana*.[63]

48 See BDAG, *s.v.* φωτισμός, b.
49 See Payne Smith, 1:1397. Frankenberg (p. 16) chose νόημα for his retroversion. But there are a number of other possibilities (e.g., διανόημα, διάνοια, and σύνεσις). In any case, "thought" is parallel to "eyes" and "ears" in 3a and 4a.
50 Payne Smith, 1:1559–60.
51 BDAG, *s.v.* γνῶσις.
52 See Payne Smith, 2:3179.
53 Payne Smith, 2:3294. A plausible cause for the change from manuscript ܐܬܦܪܩܬ to ܐܬܦܨܝܬ may be that the speaker only refers to his "salvation" in 6c. The copyist (or translator) wanted to be more logical than the poet.
54 See BDAG, *s.v.* σῴζω.
55 Frankenberg, 16; see also Payne Smith, 1:1547–48.
56 Contra Franzmann, 119, whose meticulous structural analysis contains many valuable insights.
57 Lattke, *Bedeutung*, 1:118–19; Franzmann, 116–17.
58 Wilhelm Michaelis, "ὁδός, κτλ.," *ThWNT* 5 (1954) 42–118; *TDNT* 5:42–114.
59 See BDAG, *s.v.* ὁδός; Payne Smith, 1:375.
60 On the roots discussed here, see Lattke, 3:356 ("gehen," etc.), 3:360 ("irregehen," etc.), 3:358 ("herabsteigen," etc.), 3:359 ("hinübergehen," etc.) and 3:361 ("laufen," etc.). On the roots excluded from the discussion, see Lattke, 3:360 ("kommen," etc.), 3:349 ("ausgehen," etc.), and 3:363 ("nahen," etc.).
61 See BDAG, *s.v.* ὁδός, 3; Michaelis, "ὁδός," *ThWNT* 5:43–46, 57–58, 71–75, 98–100; *TDNT* 5:43–46, 57–60, 70–75, 93–96; Ferdinand R. Prostmeier, *Der Barnabasbrief* (KAV 8; Göttingen: Vandenhoeck & Ruprecht, 1999) 529–61.
62 BDAG, *s.v.* ὁδός, 3c.
63 Payne Smith, 1:375.

The four occasions where the plural "ways" is used have no special significance (compare 3:10 [plural] with 24:13 [singular]; 33:7 [plural] with 15:6 [singular]; 33:8 [plural] with 11:3 [singular]; 33:13 [plural] with 17:8 [singular]).

Biblical tradition, which speaks of "the way or ways of God or the Lord,"[64] exerts some influence but does not dominate.[65] So, for instance, in 3:10 the Spirit teaches mankind to know the "ways" of God. But even here the context is already very Gnosticized.

Moving on from this passage through the occurrences of "way" in the *Odes of Solomon*, which are difficult to categorize, the first stop is at *Ode* 7, where the introductory comparison uses ܪܗܛܐ (*rehṭā*, "course") as a synonym for "way" (7:1-2). This "way," set toward knowledge (*gnōsis*) and perfection (*plērōma*) and leading from the beginning to the end, receives "tracks of his light" (7:13-14 in part 2).[66] In the third part the seers "go" before the Lord (7:18).[67]

In *Ode* 11, which is preserved in two languages, the traditional phrase "way of truth" is interpreted by the word *gnōsis* (cf. σύνεσις in 𝔊) without the later conception of *gnōsis* "as the way."[68] According to 12:6, the personified "word of truth" (cf. emendation to 12:1a) does not know "its descent (ܡܚܛܐ [*maḥṭā*]) nor its way."

Leaving 15:6 aside till the end of this excursus, the next stop is *Ode* 17, where verbs of motion become numerous. To "walk" in the "figure of a new person" is more or less identical with being redeemed (17:4). And to "follow" the "thought of truth" is the opposite of to "go astray" (17:5; cf. also 18:10, 14). The redeemed Redeemer, to whom the Most High gave "the way of his steps" (17:8a), "went toward all my shut in ones to free them" (17:11).

In the dualistic mythos of *Ode* 22, "way" (ϩⲓⲏ [*hyē*] in ℭ) may be part of the traditional eschatology. The "way" is leveled for the believers (22:7). However, this way is not from the first identical with the incorruptible "way" of 22:11.

At the end of the first part of *Ode* 23, the Gnostic imperative of salvation, "walk in the knowledge of the Lord (or the Most High)!" (23:4a), prefaces a lengthy promise of salvation. In the second part "those who saw" the mysterious heavenly letter "went after" it (23:10). The even more enigmatic "wheel" (= "chariot"?) "crossed over . . . many forests and made a wide way" (23:15).[69]

In *Ode* 24, "the Lord revealed his way and spread widely his grace" (24:13). The final bicolon moves this perhaps biblically influenced mythos into a more Gnostic light (24:14).

Whether "error," another of the terms of movement, at the beginning of *Ode* 31 is a personification of the dualistic "darkness" and/or identical with "immobility" (ἀνοδία in 𝔊?) will be considered later (cf. 31:1-2).

The first part of *Ode* 33 begins with a fusillade of verbs of motion: "But Grace again ran/ran back and abandoned Corruption, and she descended into him" (33:1). In the second part, the perfect Virgin calls upon the sons and daughters of men to turn back, to come, and to abandon the "ways of this destruction" (33:6-7). As a result, she promises to enter into them and make them wise in or on the "ways of truth" (33:8). She calls on her elect to walk in her ways (33:13a) with the promise, "my ways I shall make known to them who seek me" (33:13b). It should be noted, incidentally, that three of the four occurrences of "way" in the plural are found in this second part of *Ode* 33.

The didactic statement of 34:1-2, in which the dangerous "way" is parallel to "barrier" and "whirlwind," falls outside the pattern. None of these ills can affect those who have a simple heart, upright thoughts, or clear thought.

In *Ode* 38, the "way" occurs only once: "Truth went on the right way" (38:7). But this ode teems with other words of motion. "Truth" personified—it is said—"led me . . . and caused me to pass over gulfs" (38:1-2); "went with me . . . and did not allow me to err" (38:4; cf. 38:15). The redeemed "I" is protected against all dangers because it "walked" with Truth

64 Michaelis, "ὁδός," *ThWNT* 5:51; *TDNT* 5:51.

65 "The way of God" is "normally in the Old Testament God's commandment, sometimes also his action. . . . Ways of God as spatially localised areas in heaven or the underworld, described in detail in Akkadian or Egyptian texts, are not found in the Old Testament. There is also no trace of the deification of a way in the Old Testament" (Markus Zehnder, "Zentrale Aspekte der Semantik der hebräischen Weg-Lexeme," in Andreas Wagner, ed., *Studien zur hebräischen Grammatik* [OBO 156; Freiburg: Universitätsverlag; Göttingen: Vandenhoeck & Ruprecht, 1997] 160; see also the illustration on p. 170).

66 In 10:6, the "tracks of light" are set on the hearts of the assembled peoples. Thereafter, it is said of the redeemed "and they walked in my life" (6b).

67 This and similar statements must be distinguished from 8:21 ("and my righteousness goes before them") and 20:9 ("and his glory will go before thee"), which derive from Isa 58:8.

68 See Michaelis, "ὁδός," *ThWNT* 5:47; *TDNT* 5:47.

69 And continuing "the 'scroll' descended to the feet" and "unto the feet ran the wheel" (23:16a-b).

and therefore did not "err" (38:5). The use of the verb ܛܥܐ (*ṭʿā*) in 38:4-5 goes with the frequent use of "error" in 38:6-10 (see on *Ode* 31 above and on *Ode* 15 below).

Ode 39 also is full of movement. The verb ܥܒܪ (*ʿbar*) is used to "cross over" metaphorical rivers (39:5, 7-9, 13; cf. "steps" and "fords" in 39:2). If the "sign" appears first as the "Lord" and then as the "way" (39:7), this can be compared to John 14:5-6. The final, indirectly doxological statement of salvation begins: "A way has been established for those who cross after him [i.e., the Lord Messiah] and for those who follow in the path of his faith" (39:13).

The extraordinarily difficult passage 41:11-16a begins with a statement of salvation that belongs to this group: "And his word is with us in all our way" (41:11a). Whether this "way" is more than simply "manner of life" needs to be elucidated.[70] A similar question mark hangs over "the way of the upright/righteous one" in 42:2b, with its expansion of the phrase from *Ode* 27.

It is now time to return to the explication of *Ode* 15. The term "error," which has already been encountered in a number of contexts, occurs in 15:6 in the genitive qualifying "way." Anyone unaware of the dualistic personification of ܛܥܝܘܬܐ (*ṭāʿyūṯā*; cf. 18:10, 14; 31:2; 38:6, 8, 10) would be likely to take it as a deviation, a mistake that needs to be corrected (cf. Jas 5:20, ἐκ πλάνης ὁδοῦ).[71]

Verse 6a can hardly be influenced by Ps 95:10.[72] If "error" were to be considered a personification (see last paragraph of Excursus 15 above), as in various other passages, it would be a subjective genitive: the speaking "I" "forsook" the way[73] taken by the πλάνη[74]—probably opposed by an equally personified ἀλήθεια. If ܛܥܝܘܬܐ (*ṭāʿyūṯā*) means no more than *error* or even *ignorantia*,[75] then "error" would qualify the "way" of life. This would make it a statement of conversion related to Justin's declaration of a later date that "some are . . . quitting the path of error" (τινάς . . . ἀπολείποντας τὴν ὁδὸν τῆς πλάνης [Justin *Dial.* 39.2]).[76] Whatever the exact meaning of "error" here, the speaking "I," with his oppositional verbs, expresses a radical change. One who metaphorically and theologically goes to the Lord existentially leaves everyone and everything behind.[77]

This profound reversal in 6a corresponds to the simultaneous attainment of σωτηρία (certainly the Greek term in 𝔊; see Excursus 5).[78] That this occurs in 6b "in connection w[ith] Jesus Christ as Savior"[79] is not evident. The verb ܢܣܒ (*nsab*), like its equivalent λαμβάνω, can mean "to take,"[80] but here—especially with the preposition ܡܢ (*men*), with a third masculine singular suffix, which represents ἀπό/παρά/ὑπό τινος—it stands for "receive," "get," or "obtain." The phrase ܕܠܐ ܚܣܡܐ (*d-lā ḥsāmā*) is so grammatically stereotyped that it is impossible to determine whether it is used attributively or predicatively.[81] On the assumption that it refers neither to the verb nor to the "redemption," but to the "Lord" "as a characteristic of God,"[82] it is likely that the Greek original was ἐν ἀφθονίᾳ αὐτοῦ (cf. 11:6) and not the adverb ἀφθόνως (see commentary on 3:6).[83]

Neither 7a nor 7b belongs among the usual metaphorical comparisons. This means that the particle of comparison ܐܝܟ (*ʾak*) is better translated by "according to" (cf. 29:2a, 3a-b; 36:5b; 42:16a) than by "as."[84] The particle ܐܝܟ (*ʾak*), used without "so," is simply a translation of κατά.[85] Whether the paronomasia with the derivatives of the root ܝܗܒ[86] reflects a similar play on δόμα and ἔδωκεν[87] or perhaps even on χάρισμα und ἐχαρισάμην[88] is not easy to decide. In view of 11:9 χάρισμα

70 See Michaelis, "ὁδός," *ThWNT* 5:43; *TDNT* 5:43.

71 See Dibelius, *Jakobus*, 306, on Jas 5:20.

72 Contra Diettrich, 54.

73 See Payne Smith, 2:4037 *s.v.* ܫܒܩ (*šbaq*); BDAG, *s.vv.* ἀπολείπω, ἀφίημι.

74 See BDAG, *s.v.* πλάνη.

75 Payne Smith, 1:1494.

76 Goodspeed, 135; Miroslav Marcovich, *Iustini Martyris Dialogus cum Tryphone* (PTS 47; Berlin/New York: de Gruyter, 1997) 134; ANF, 1:214.

77 The preposition ܠܘܬ (*lwāt*) with third masculine singular suffix, following the perfect of ܐܙܠ (*ʾezal*), refers to the Lord as the sun.

78 See Payne Smith, 2:3295; BDAG, *s.v.* σωτηρία.

79 BDAG, *s.v.* σωτηρία, 2.

80 Payne Smith, 2:2392–93; BDAG, *s.v.* λαμβάνω.

81 See Robinson and Brockington, 24.

82 Drijvers, "Polemik," 47.

83 Van Unnik, "De ἀφθονία van God," 10.

84 Contra Lattke, *Oden*, 143.

85 Payne Smith, 1:146–47; BDAG, *s.v.* κατά.

86 Payne Smith, 1:1564–68.

87 See BDAG, *s.vv.* δόμα, δίδωμι. In this case there could have been an influence from Ps 67:19 LXX via Eph 4:8. The influence of these passages can also be traced in 10:3-4.

88 See BDAG, *s.vv.* χάρισμα, χαρίζομαι.

is probably the one to argue for as the "free gift of redemption" (cf. 35:6; Rom 5:15-16; 6:23),[89] which leaves ἔδωκεν as the normal equivalent of ܝܗܒ (*yab*).

It is easier to determine that ܪܒܘܬ ܝܐܝܘܬܐ (*rabbūt yā'yūtā*) in 7b "does reflect μεγαλοπρέπεια or the like" (cf. 7:23b)[90] and that the perfect of ܥܒܕ (*ʿbad*) with accusative suffix stands for an aorist form of ποιέω.[91] The usage of the Greek verb for "God's creative activity"[92] includes redemption as a new creation. So the Greek of 7 may have run as follows:[93]

καὶ κατὰ τὸ χάρισμα/δόμα αὐτοῦ ἔδωκέν μοι,
καὶ κατὰ τὴν μεγαλοπρέπειαν αὐτοῦ ἐποίησέν με.

The next two bicola derive from 1 Cor 15:53-55[94] with some influence from 1 Cor 15:42.[95] As can be seen from the passage *Treat. Res.* 48,38–49,4,[96] this Pauline utterance also inspired Gnostics of later periods. The terms "put on" (ἐνδύομαι), "incorruption" (ἀφθαρσία; cf. ἀθανασία), "corruption" (φθορά; cf. τὸ φθαρτόν) and "death" (θάνατος) come from 1 Corinthians 15, but the general context of the ἀνάστασις τῶν νέκρων (1 Cor 15:42) is altogether wanting. The speaking "I" at first speaks only of itself and complements the ideas it takes up by two terms of power (see Excursuses 33 and 39), which also figure among the objects that can be metaphorically "donned" (cf. 4:6; 20:7; 39:8; Table 2).

The perfect of ܠܒܫ (*lbeš*) in 8a must correspond to a form of the verb ἐνδύομαι (cf. Eph 4:24 and Col 3:10, which deal with "putting on" the new person),[97] and so the antithetical perfect of ܫܠܚ (*šlaḥ*) in 8b would represent a form of ἀπεκδύομαι (cf. Col 3:9, referring to the old person), or of ἀποδύομαι (cf. 11:10 𝔊) or ἐκδύομαι (cf. 2 Cor 5:4).[98]

The negation of ܚܒܠܐ (*ḥbālā*) in 8a corresponds to ἀφθαρσία "as a quality of the future life."[99] As in 11:12, this is the inalienable incorruptibility of the Lord, which is not to be found in this world (cf. 33:12). When the "I" buttresses this eschatologically paradoxical statement of salvation by the parallel statement 8b, the declaration put into his mouth is that he has put the human "state of being perishable" totally behind him.[100]

So far the basic ideas have been Pauline (although somewhat altered by being displaced into the past), and the two terms of power, "name" and "grace," used instrumentally, continue on the line of Pauline theologizing. The possibility of a change from "corruption" to "incorruption" is not innate, nor is this change the result of "apocalyptic destiny" expressed by δεῖ:[101] it can occur only through the power of God. The difference between ܒܝܕ (*b-yad*, literally "by the hand") in 8a and the simple ܒ (*b-*) in 8b is slight.[102] Perhaps the variation reflects a Greek original that had δι᾽ὀνόματος αὐτοῦ in the first case and merely χάριτι αὐτοῦ in the second.[103] It is more important to note that redemption occurs in other passages as well by God's "name" or "grace" (cf. 8:23; 14:5 and 9:5; 25:4; 29:5).[104]

Another word derived from the root *ḥbl* in 9a connects this final bicolon to 8a-b. What is annihilated is not what is "mortal"[105] but the power of θάνατος itself, which is inimical to all that lives. This staggering statement is quite remote from Pauline thought, since people continue to die (cf. 1 Cor 15:26 and 54, quoted from

89 BDAG, *s.v.* χάρισμα.
90 Letter from Jan Joosten, October 1, 1996.
91 Payne Smith, 2:2765–66.
92 BDAG, *s.v.* ποιέω.
93 Cf. Frankenberg, 17.
94 Bauer, 595.
95 See Hans Conzelmann, *Der erste Brief an die Korinther* (KEK 5; 2nd ed.; Göttingen: Vandenhoeck & Ruprecht, 1981) 359–60; ET *1 Corinthians: Commentary on the First Epistle to the Corinthians* (trans. James W. Leitch; ed. George W. Macrae, S.J.; Hermeneia; Philadelphia: Fortress Press, 1975) 282–83.
96 Peel, *Rheginos*, 34, 93–94; idem, "The Treatise on the Resurrection (I,*4*)," *NHLE*, 56.
97 Payne Smith, 2:1887–88; BDAG, *s.v.* ἐνδύω.
98 Payne Smith, 2:4171–72; BDAG, *s.vv.* ἀπεκδύομαι, ἀποδύομαι, ἐκδύω.
99 BDAG, *s.v.* ἀφθαρσία; cf. Payne Smith, 1:1179.
100 BDAG, *s.v.* φθορά, 5 ("destruction"). See Excursus 28.
101 Conzelmann, *Korinther*, 359; *1 Corinthians*, 291–92, on 1 Cor 15:53.
102 See Payne Smith, 1:431–32, 1547–48.
103 Frankenberg, 17.
104 On ܫܡܐ (*šmā*), see Payne Smith, 2:4199–200; BDAG, *s.v.* ὄνομα; on ܛܝܒܘܬܐ (*taybūtā*), cf. Brockelmann, *Lexicon*, 270; Payne Smith, *Dictionary*, 171–72; BDAG, *s.v.* χάρις.
105 As suggested, e.g., by Diettrich, 55.

Isa 25:8), and closer to the so-called *realized eschatology* found in some Johannine and deutero-Pauline works. The speaking "I" is now found in God's imperishable realm, which does not exist here and now. Therefore "death" is already annihilated before the *speaker's* face, that is, before him personally. This is the zenith of statements using the Ethpa. of ܚܒܠ (*ḥbal*; cf. 7:21 [ignorance/non-*gnōsis* destroyed]; 31:1 [darkness destroyed]). If the verb from 1 Cor 15:26 was reserved for 9b (see below), the verb in 9a 𝔊 is more likely to have been a form of *(κατα)φθείρω* than of *ἀφανίζω*.[106] The preposition ܩܕܡ (*qdām*), amplified by a preceding ܡܢ (*men*), "without perceptible modification of the meaning," simply means "before."[107] Making the loanword *πρόσωπον* the "object" and not the "active subject" of 9a is possible only if "*his* word" in 9b is taken as the original reading and the phrase "*my* word," found in the manuscript, is explained away as "one of the many inconsequential scribal variants."[108] Such emendations and interpretations are the product of dogmatically induced wishful thinking. Just *because* the text in 9b raises such problems, the expression arising from *πρὸ προσώπου μου* must be understood grammatically as *subjective*.[109] The "I" plays a redeemed and redeeming part in the destruction, described in the theological passive, that results in eternal life (see on 10a below).

At least since Wis 16:13, the parallel "death" and "Hades," the mythical "place of the dead" (cf. the variant reading in 1 Cor 15:55),[110] has formed part of the imagery current in the ancient world. The bicolon in question is:[111]

σὺ [viz., *κύριε*] *γὰρ ζωῆς καὶ θανάτου ἐξουσίαν ἔχεις*
καὶ κατάγεις εἰς πύλας ᾅδου καὶ ἀνάγεις.

For you have power over life and death;
you lead mortals down to the gates of Hades and back again.[112]

Verse 9b may imply a *descensus ad inferos* (cf. 29:4; 42:11). But there is no discernible connection with baptism.[113] And neither the "kingdom of the dead" nor "death" is in any sense personified. If the Ethpa. of ܒܛܠ (*bṭel*), synonymous with the verb in 9a, translates a passive form of *καταργέω*,[114] that is further evidence of the influence of Pauline usage (cf. 1 Cor 15:26, *ἔσχατος ἐχθρὸς καταργεῖται ὁ θάνατος*). But even in this case, Hades would be *already* "annihilated"—and that primarily by the power of God, as shown by the use of the theological passive. But now ܒܡܠܬܝ (*b-mellaṯ*, with silent first singular suffix),[115] which, like its possible Greek equivalents *(ἐν) τῷ λόγῳ/ῥήματί μου*, can be taken instrumentally, causatively, or associatively,[116] introduces a new demythologizing element. For the theological destruction, although objectively a result, occurred kerygmatically simultaneously with or by the word of the redeemed Redeemer (cf. 17:8-11).[117] What word the "word" is, is not said. Perhaps the speaker includes all the previous statements of salvation of his first-person discourse in this final word of stanza III by which or among which the mythos of Hades was irrevocably brought to nought.

106 See Payne Smith, 1:1176–77; BDAG, *s.vv.* *ἀφανίζω*, *καταφθείρω*, *φθείρω*.
107 Nöldeke §156.
108 Suggested by Kittel, 75.
109 BDAG, *s.v.* *πρόσωπον*.
110 BDAG, *s.v.* *ᾅδης*.
111 Rahlfs, 2:370; Georgi, 459.
112 In Syriac writings, *ᾅδης* is generally represented by the Hebrew loanword שְׁאוֹל (Payne Smith, 2:4009–10). Wis 16:13 is no exception (see Emerton, *Wisdom*, 30).
113 Contra W. K. Lowther Clarke, "The First Epistle of St Peter and the Odes of Solomon," *JTS* 15 (1913–14) 51.
114 Payne Smith, 1:510; BDAG, *s.v.* *καταργέω*.
115 See Nöldeke §50.
116 See Payne Smith, 1:429–32; BDF and BDR §§195–98, §219.
117 Among those who do *not* emend the manuscript text are Bauer, 595: "by my word"; Emerton, 705: "at my word"; Pierre, 703: "in my word." Charlesworth's note on his translation ("by my word"), "The noun is ܡܠܬܐ, but ܦܬܓܡܐ would have been more appropriate" (pp. 68–69), does not address the problem posed by 9b (see Excursus 12).

■ **10** This final tricolon is an esoteric statement of salvation, no longer couched in the first person, but also not in the form of a response. The suffixes in 10b and 10c make it "impossible" that stanza IV concerns the "resurrection" and even less likely that it deals with the "ascension of life personified, i.e. Christ."[118]

If the subject of ܣܠܩ (*sleq*) in 10a[119] is "the Lord as sun, indicating a return to the imagery of stanza I, thus providing a semantic as well as syntactic inclusio (1a, 10c) for the Ode,"[120] then "the concept 'life' has been clearly set out by the previous statements" in 8-9.[121] The "land" or "country of the Lord" is not "Palestine," the literal "Holy Land,"[122] but, as in 11:16, 18, and 21, the γῆ of the utopian paradise (cf. also 11:13, where the "Lord" is compared to the "sun"). The introduction of this new image mixes the metaphor of the sun that awakens (2b), which rises anew every day, with that of plant life. This is the reason for choosing the perfect of ܣܠܩ (*sleq*), which represents not Greek ἀνέτειλεν[123] but a form of ἀναβαίνω.[124] The clichéd expression ܚܝܐ ܕܠܐ ܡܘܬܐ (*ḥayyē d-lā mawtā*), which is commonly but incorrectly taken to be the direct subject, and for which the corresponding Greek will have been *(ἡ)* ζωὴ ἀθάνατος, withdraws the divine "life" from this worldly disposition, and it should probably be taken as the result of the rising.[125] If "immortal life" were taken to be in apposition, the image would be parallel to *Diogn.* 9:6 (God as ζωή among other attributes) and perhaps also to 1 John 5:20 (οὗτός ἐστιν ὁ ἀληθινὸς θεὸς καὶ ζωὴ αἰώνιος). But the two following statements suggest rather "the life radiating to believers" from the Lord as sun.[126] The term "life" (literally "life without death") in this context corresponds to the eschatological ζωὴ αἰώνιος.[127]

The verbs at the beginning of 10b and 10c must refer to the plural ܚܝܐ (*ḥayyē*) in 10a. The life of salvation is not here an immediate consequence of soteriological perception. Rather, it is itself "known" (in 𝔊 certainly ἐγνώσθη; see Excursus 7).[128] Following the perfect of the Ethpe. of ܝܕܥ (*ʾidaʿ*), "ܠ *very often denotes the agent*, the logical Subject."[129] This logical subject of the completed knowledge in 10b, whether active or passive, is the ܡܗܝܡܢܐ (*mhaymnē*, plural participle of the Paiel of ܐܡܢ [*ʾeman*]).[130] Because of its parallelism with 10c the whole expression, whose application is limited to Gnostics, would have corresponded to τοῖς πιστοῖς αὐτοῦ in 𝔊 (see on 4:3 above; πιστός as loanword in 22:7 ℭ),[131] probably with the sense of τοῖς εἰς αὐτὸν πιστεύουσι.[132]

The parallel perfect of the Ethpe. of ܝܗܒ (*yab*) in 10c is indeed the "return of a verb form" from 7a, but only an "apparently intentional *inclusio*" (cf. rather 6:12 and 22:10).[133] The *hapax legomenon* ܕܠܐ ܚܘܣܪܢܐ (*d-lā ḥusrānā*), derived from ܚܣܪ (*ḥsar*), must be taken adverbially.[134] It expresses the opposite of lack, "damage," or "loss."[135]

118 Kittel (p. 76) validly opposing Grimme, 133.
119 Verse 10a returns to the introductory comparison, where the "Lord" was linked with "Helios." In consequence, a text-critical emendation of the singular ܣܠܩ to the plural, agreeing with the plural form of "life," seems superfluous (contra Schultheß, 254, and Klaus Beyer in Lattke, 3:XXVI n. 3).
120 Franzmann, 120.
121 Kittel, 76.
122 Contra Diettrich, 55.
123 Contra Frankenberg, 17; see Payne Smith, 2:2646–47; BDAG, *s.v.* ἀνατέλλω.
124 BDAG, *s.v.* ἀναβαίνω. The verb ܣܠܩ (*sleq*) is occasionally used for daybreak (equivalent to ὄρθρος, cf., e.g., Gen 19:15 and Tob 8:18), but in this case ἀνατέλλω would have corresponded to ܕܢܚ (*dnaḥ*; see Payne Smith, 1:926).
125 Cf. 10:2; 28:6; 31:7; 38:3; 40:6. A few samples of free translation of the Syriac: Harris and Mingana, 2:281: "And there hath gone up deathless life in the Lord's land"; Bauer, 595: "And there grew up in the Lord's land life without death"; Pierre, 101: "It rose up in the Lord's land, immortal life." A Greek text using the singular ἡ ζωή would admit of such translations.
126 BDAG, *s.v.* ζωή; cf. Payne Smith, 1:1254.
127 BDAG, *s.v.* ζωή, 2bα.
128 BDAG, *s.v.* γινώσκω.
129 Nöldeke §247.
130 Payne Smith, 1:232–33.
131 See BDAG, *s.v.* πιστός.
132 Frankenberg, 17.
133 In part contra Diettrich, 55.
134 See Payne Smith, 1:1340, ἀζημίως.
135 See BDAG, *s.v.* ζημία, and LSJ, *s.v.* ἀζήμιος.

It is certainly not the equivalent of περισσῶς.[136] The indirect object, dependent on the theological passive (ܠ [*l*-] "marking the dative"),[137] in spite of the use of ܟܠܗܘܢ (*kullhōn*), does not expand the circle of recipients to universality. On the contrary, the relative clause, beginning with the correlative ܐܝܠܝܢ (*ʾayllēn*),[138] serves to narrow it esoterically. Only those who, believing in the Lord, are ones who "trust in him" (cf. 23:2; 33:13) have been—and are—partakers of this "life." This statement, with its use of the participle ܬܟܝܠܐ (*tḵīlā*), derived from the Ethpe. ܐܬܬܟܠ,[139] bears a resemblance to the close connection between πιστεύω and ζωή in the Gospel of John.[140] A retroversion of stanza IV into the original Greek shows this resemblance still more clearly:

καὶ ἀνέβη[141] ἐν τῇ γῇ κυρίου—ἡ ζωὴ ἀθάνατος,
καὶ ἐγνώσθη [ἡ ζωὴ] ὑπὸ τοῖς πιστοῖς αὐτοῦ
καὶ ἐδόθη ἀζημίως πᾶσιν ἐπ᾽ αὐτῷ πεποιθόσιν.[142]

136 Contra Frankenberg, 17.
137 Nöldeke §247.
138 Ibid., §236.
139 See Payne Smith, 2:4433.
140 See BDAG, *s.v.* ζωή.
141 The Syriac translators and/or scribes clearly took no offense at the statement in 10a, which they interpreted as follows: "And he [viz., Helios as Lord] rose on the land of the Lord."
142 The second perfect of πείθω has present meaning (see BDF and BDR §341). With the dative of a person it comes near to "believe in" (BDAG, *s.v.* πείθω). The Syriac equivalent regularly uses ܥܠ (*ʿal*) "de fiducia in Deo" (Payne Smith, 2:4433).

16

Ode 16: Hymnic Self-Portrait and Doctrine of Creation

(I) 1a As the work of the ploughman is the ploughshare,
1b and the work of the helmsman, the steering of the ship,
1c so my work, also, is the psalm of the Lord in his hymns.
2a My craft and my service are in his hymns,
2b because his love has nourished my heart,
2c and unto my lips brought up his/its fruits.
3a For my love is the Lord,
3b therefore I will sing to him.
4a For I am strengthened in his hymns,
4b and I have faith by/in him.
(II) 5a I will open my mouth and his spirit will speak through me
5b [of] the glory of the Lord and his beauty,
6 the work of his hands and the labor of his fingers,
7 the multitude of his mercy and the power of his word.
(III) 8a For the word of the Lord searches what is invisible,
8b and his thought [searches] what is manifest.[a]
9a For the eye sees his works,
9b and the ear hears his thought.
(IV) 10 He spread out the land and placed the waters in the sea,
11 he stretched out the heaven and fixed the stars,
12a and set in order the creation and established it,
12b and he rested from his works.
(V) 13a And the created things run in their courses
13b and work their works
13c and do not know how to stop and stand still.
14 And the powers are subject to his word.
(VI) 15a The treasury of light is the sun,
15b and the treasury of darkness is the night.
16a For the sun makes the day that it is bright,
16b but the night brings darkness over the face of the earth.
17a And their reception [is] one from the other:
17b they complete the beauty of God.
(VII) 18a And there is nothing that is beyond the Lord,
18b because he was, before everything came to be.
19a And the aeons were by his word
19b and by the thought of his heart.

a 8b For the alternative translation "and investigates his thought," see commentary on 8b.

(VIII) 20 Glory and honor to his name!
Hallelujah.

Introduction

Ode 16 is preserved in one Syriac manuscript.[1] Franzmann's division and analysis do not contradict the perception that *Ode* 16 comprises two parts: "In [vv] 1-7 the speaker in the first person singular discusses his work of singing of the Lord in His praises or hymns."[2] Whether the first section was ever independent or not, now it serves "as an introduction to a longer didactic poem extending from [v] 8 to [v] 20 in which the 'I' of the speaker disappears completely."[3] *Ode* 16, as a whole, is therefore not a "hymn."[4] Diettrich's reconstruction of the "strophic architecture," which he calls "masterly," makes use of alternating groups, which others find it difficult to identify.[5] On the other hand, his detection of a somewhat Old Testament "joy in nature" and the conclusion that the "content" of the whole of the Ode seems to be "uncontaminated by specifically Christian ideas,"[6] are valid, which is why the Ode does not seem to contain any specific "anti-Jewish polemics" either.[7]

Interpretation

■ **1-4** Early in the second century C.E., Arrian puts into the mouth of his teacher, the Stoic Epictetus, the declaration: *νῦν δὲ λογικός εἰμι· ὑμνεῖν με δεῖ τὸν θεόν. τοῦτό μου τὸ ἔργον ἐστίν,* "But as it is, I am a rational being, therefore I must be singing hymns of praise to God. This is my task" (1.16.20-21 [LCL 1:112–13]).[8] It is not only the little hymn on the creator-god and the mention of practical activities like ἀρνοῦν in its context (1.16.16-17) that make it resemble *Ode* 16, but especially the use of the terms δεῖ and ἔργον. The triple use of the noun ܥܒܕܐ (*ʿḇāḏā*) is the point of comparison in this introductory simile (cf. 15:1).[9] In this conventional "list of callings" (cf. 1 Cor 9:7; 2 Tim 2:4-6),[10] which is probably not influenced by Sirach 38 and does not have any reference "to the responsibility of guiding and directing a group in its liturgical gatherings,"[11] it is hard, at first sight, to find a connection. "Work" here does not mean anything "creative" (unlike 16:6 [singular] or 16:9 [plural]; cf. 8:18-19; 12:4); it is simply a general description of human activity.[12]

The abbreviated description of 1a needs no further explanation, since the agrarian *hapax legomena* ܐܟܪܐ (*ʾakkārā*)[13] and ܩܢܩܢܐ (*qēqnā*)[14] would have brought to mind familiar associations even among city-dwellers in antiquity, but 1b, a nominative clause without even a copula, presents some problems. For instance, it is not at all clear what sort of "ship" or "boat" it is.[15] Nor is it known what part the "helmsman" played in the chain of command,[16] for the very rare term ܓܪܪܐ (*grārā*) means "pulling,"[17] and is not in any sense the "Peal act[ive]

1 Ms.: Codex H, 12a–13a (ܣ). Ed./trans.: Charlesworth, 69–73; Franzmann, 121–29; Lattke, 2:17–39 and 3:XXVI–XXVII.

2 Gerald R. Blaszczak, *A Formcritical Study of Selected Odes of Solomon* (HSM 36; Atlanta: Scholars Press, 1985) 29.

3 Ibid., 29. This is one of the four Odes (16, 31, 33, and 36) that Blaszczak subjected to form-critical analysis and which therefore have a running commentary (Blaszczak, 29–41, esp. 30: "commentary"; cf. Michael Lattke, review of Blaszczak in *ThLZ* 112 [1987] 183–85 = idem, *Bedeutung*, 4:175–77). The value of this detailed commentary is enhanced by the exhaustive annotations referring to earlier writings on the *Odes* (Blaszczak, 115–20).

4 Contra Eissfeldt §93 n. 2; Grese, *Corpus*, 175, 179.

5 Diettrich, 57–59.

6 Ibid., 56.

7 Harnack, 46, contra Harris, 112–13; see on 13c below.

8 See Kroll, *Hymnodik*, 70; and Lattke, *Hymnus*, 40.

9 Lattke, *Oden*, 282: "like . . . as." Blaszczak (p. 30) remarks sadly: "The exact point of the simile is unclear."

10 Gemünden, *Vegetationsmetaphorik*, 324.

11 Contra Blaszczak, 30.

12 See Payne Smith, 2:2773; BDAG, *s.v.* ἔργον, 2.

13 Payne Smith, 1:190; cf. BDAG, *s.v.* γεωργός.

14 Payne Smith, 2:3611; cf. BDAG, *s.v.* ἄροτρον.

15 Payne Smith, 1:216; BDAG, *s.v.* πλοῖον (the reference to *Ode Sol.* 11:9 should be deleted). How Charlesworth (p. 72) knows that the ship is a galley remains obscure.

16 On the Greek loanword κυβερνήτης, see Payne

part[iciple] of ܓܪ."[18] The transitive "pulling" of ships is often mentioned in classical times,[19] but this is hardly the task of the helmsman. If, however, one considers that the Syriac term, emended early and unconvincingly to ܫܪ̈ܐ,[20] corresponds to the noun ἡ σύρσις[21] (which is related to σύρω and used for the "*drawing* of a plough by oxen") and that the Aph. of ܓܪ (*gar*[*r*]) can also mean "he led" and the masculine noun ܓܪܘܪܐ (*gārūrā*) means "someone who leads,"[22] this insight helps the images of 1a-b to cohere, in that both describe an activity of pulling and guiding. As the farmer guides the plough through the soil, the helmsman pilots the ship through water.[23]

With 1c the agrarian and nautical images melt into thin air. From here to the end of the first part (stanzas I–II) the dominant terms and ideas are those that give rise to the partial title "Hymnic Self-Portrait." The "work" of the speaking "I," who must not be simply identified with (one of) the author(s) of the *Odes of Solomon*, is now and in the future to sing hymns to God. Both the genitive following ܡܙܡܘܪܐ (*mazmōrā*; cf. 7:17, 22)[24] and the third masculine singular suffix of ܬܫܒܘܚܬܐ (*tešbuḥtā*; cf. 13:2; 40:2 [N]; 41:4)[25] are objective (see Excursus 21). "Psalms" and "hymns" are not here terms denoting the word of God, even though biblical texts are included in their meaning.

Verse 2a is not a repetition of 1c but a hendiadys elucidating "work," which, accepting the adverbial expression of place, emphasizes the hymnic character of the speaker's activity. The word ܐܘܡܢܘܬܐ (*ʾummānūṯā*) corresponds to ἡ τέχνη (cf. 6:9 ℭ).[26] Finding an exact Greek equivalent to ܦܘܠܚܢܐ (*pulḥānā*) is much more difficult (see on 6 below).[27]

The "state" expressed by the copula ܐܢܝܢ (*ʾennēn*)[28] is supported in the first place by 2b, but also by 2c. The *hapax legomenon* ܬܪܣܝ (*tarsī*) is often used for τρέφω.[29] Transferring the tender image of nourishing "love" to the Lord and the "heart" as the center of personal life, the speaking "I" in his hymnic function declares his utter independence of any material nourishment (see Excursuses 2 and 4).[30]

Although the subject of the participle of ܓܣܐ (*gsā*) with following ܗܘܐ (*-wā*), expressing "continuation or repetition in past time," in 2c,[31] could be "love"[32]—or even the "Lord"—the equivalence of this verb form to ἐρεύγεται suggests rather that the "heart" of the speaking "I" continually brought up its "fruits" through its mouth (cf. 40:2b).[33] The suffix of the plural of ܦܐܪܐ (*pērā*) can again refer to the "Lord," the "heart," or "love." Bauer[34] ("her [love's] fruits") and Diettrich[35] ("its [the heart's] fruits"; cf. Ps 44:2 LXX: Ἐξηρεύξατο ἡ καρδία μου λόγον ἀγαθόν, "My heart has uttered a good matter")[36] specify whose "fruits" they are, while Baarda[37] and Blaszczak[38] are less definite. The verdict

Smith, 2:3512; BDAG, *s.v.*; Lattke, "Wörter," 292 = idem, *Bedeutung*, 4:141.

17 Payne Smith, 1:768 (*tractio*); Ungnad and Staerk, 17 ("das ziehen [*sic*] [= hauling]").

18 Contra Charlesworth, 72.

19 See LSJ, *s.v.* ἕλκω.

20 Schultheß, 254; see also Payne Smith, 2:2814.

21 LSJ, *s.v.* σύρσις.

22 Payne Smith, 1:767–68: ܓܪ = *duxit;* ܓܪܘܪܐ = *qui ducit*.

23 Harris and Mingana (2:284), referring to Ephrem, go so far as to say: "The verb ܓܪ is very frequently used to express 'steering' of a ship." Countering Schultheß, they say: "Further, ܫܪ̈ܐ is generally used in the plural and refers to tools whose function is to strengthen the construction of a ship." The translation of ܫܪ̈ܐ by "jackstaff [to attach a flag to a ship's mast]" (Diettrich, 57) lacks relevance to the task of the helmsman.

24 Payne Smith, 1:1137; cf. BDAG, *s.v.* ψαλμός.

25 Payne Smith, 2:4027–28; BDAG, *s.v.* ὕμνος.

26 Payne Smith, 1:237; BDAG, *s.v.* τέχνη.

27 See the numerous equivalents in Payne Smith, 2:3150.

28 Nöldeke §315.

29 Payne Smith, 2:4501; BDAG, *s.v.* τρέφω.

30 On ܚܘܒܐ (*ḥubbā*), see Payne Smith, 1:1171; BDAG, *s.v.* ἀγάπη; on ܠܒܐ (*lebbā*), see Payne Smith, 2:1877; BDAG, *s.v.* καρδία.

31 Nöldeke §277.

32 Suggested, e.g., by Bauer, 596 ("sie [= she, i.e., love]").

33 Payne Smith, 1:757; BDAG, *s.v.* ἐρεύγομαι.

34 Bauer, 596.

35 Diettrich, 57.

36 Rahlfs, 2:46; Brenton, 724.

37 Tjitze Baarda, "'Het uitbreiden van mijn handen is Zijn teken': Enkele notities bij de gebedshouding in de Oden van Salomo," in *Loven en geloven: Opstellen . . . aangeboden aan Nic. H. Ridderbos* (Amsterdam: Ton Bolland, 1975) 249.

38 Blaszczak, 31.

depends partly on the decision whether the image of fruits "here probably refers to the hymns or praises"[39] but partly also on the connection in the *Odes* between the terms "love," "heart," "fruits" and the always plural term ܣܦܘܬܐ (*sep̄wāṯā*).[40]

Excursus 16: "Lips" in the *Odes of Solomon*

The plural of ܣܦܬܐ (*sep̄ṯā*) occurs twelve times in the *Odes of Solomon*, but never in the sense of riverbanks or the seashore.[41] The term "lips," whether in a literal or a transferred sense, generally refers to the organ of speech and is thus parallel to "tongue" (40:2c-3a)[42] or to "mouth" (12:2; 21:8; cf. 16:5 and Excursus 31). The positive connection with "heart," which also forms a parallel (20:4; 30:5), is notable, since "heart" and "lips" are so often contrasted elsewhere (e.g., Isa 29:13 LXX in Mark 7:6 and Matt 15:8).[43] But, although "fruits" are juxtaposed with "lips" (12:2; 16:2) and "hymns" are also important in the context (16:2; 40:2; cf. 21:9), the phrase "fruit of the lips" is not found in the *Odes of Solomon*.[44]

The function of the human "lips" in speech is subordinated in only two cases, once to their experience of dryness and once to their employment in drinking. Lips can be "parched" (6:14). And the redeeming water of the spring of the Lord (see on 30:5 below) "drew near to" the "lips" of the speaking "I" (11:6).

Notable among the remaining passages is the transference of "lips" of the mouth to the "lips" of the heart (37:2, parallel to "voice"). The reason for this grotesque image is to be found in the close connection between "lips" and "heart" already mentioned (see Excursus 4). Equally notable is the transference of human "lips" to the "lips of the Lord," which are the source of the living spring of the Lord (30:5a).[45] Who is meant by the term "Lord" in this passage will have to be elucidated. It must also be decided whether the expression "the blessing of his lips," which, together with other of his actions, serves to glorify the Lord alone, refers to God or to another "Kyrios" (38:19-20). It should be kept in mind, moreover, that the so-called Son of God, the redeemed "Redeemer," spoke in Hades "with living lips" (cf. 42:14, 15, 18).

The expression "from the heart to the lips" (8:1), referring to the increase in love, is also in the background of the formulations in 16:2 and 21:8. Therefore "heart"—rather than "love"—is the subject of 16:2c (cf. also 36:7). Whatever the translation of 21:8-9, two points are firmly established: the parallelism of "mouth" and "lips" (cf. 12:2) and the movement from the inside to the outside (i.e., from the heart via the mouth and lips to the countenance). Depending on the translator's decision, it may either be "the exultation over the Lord together with his praise" (21:9b) or the "heart" of the speaking "I" that sprang forth upon his "lips" (21:8).

The equivocal statement of 16:2c must be taken together with 12:2 and 40:2. The last-mentioned passage also uses the participle of ܓܣܐ (*gsā*). The speaking "I" compares its "heart," which brings forth hymns of the Lord, to a bubbling spring (40:2a-b; cf. again 36:7). And in parallel the "lips" utter the hymn (40:2c). The "I" of *Ode* 12 similarly compares the flow of truth from its "mouth" with a stream of water (12:2a-b). The "lips," the outermost part of the "mouth," "declare its fruits" (12:2c); whether the suffix of ܦܐܪܐ (*pērē*) refers to "truth" or "mouth" is of no particular moment, since the truth flows from the mouth.

Near the end of Excursus 11, in light of 8:2 and 11:1c ܣ, it was proposed that the subject of 16:2c

39 Ibid., 31.

40 Payne Smith, 2:2694–95; BDAG, *s.v.* χεῖλος.

41 Payne Smith, 2:2694; BDAG, *s.v.* χεῖλος, 2.

42 Amazingly "speaking with tongues" never occurs in the *Odes of Solomon*; see BDAG, *s.v.* γλῶσσα, 3, with references.

43 See LSJ, 1982, "ἀπὸ χειλέων, opp. ἀπὸ καρδίας." An exception is *Ps. Sol.* 15:3 (Rahlfs, 2:484; *OTP*, 2:664; cf. Holm-Nielsen, 92–93), which does not make a contrast between "heart" and "lips" either. The text of the tricolon is:

> ψαλμὸν καινὸν μετὰ ᾠδῆς ἐν εὐφροσύνῃ καρδίας,
> καρπὸν χειλέων ἐν ὀργάνῳ ἡρμοσμένῳ γλώσσης,
> ἀπαρχὴν χειλέων ἀπὸ καρδίας ὁσίας καὶ δικαίας.

> A new psalm with song with a happy heart,
> the fruit of the lips with the tuned instrument of the tongue,
> the first fruits of the lips from a devout and righteous heart.

44 Cf. Hos 14:3 in Heb 13:15 (καρπὸς χειλέων, parallel to θυσία αἰνέσεως); Prov 18:20 (καρποὶ χειλέων, parallel to καρποὶ στόματος); 1QH i.28; *Ps. Sol.* 15:3 (see previous note).

45 The parallel to this is the soteriological transference of the term "heart" from the individual to the Lord in 30:5b.

might be "love" and not the "heart," and that the suffix of the direct object should be referred to "love." Revisiting the first part of this statement, we can reword the translation of 16:2c as, "And up to my lips it [viz., the heart] brought forth its [viz., love's] fruits." The hymnic context of 16:1-7, in contrast to 14:6b, suggests that the "fruits" of the love of the Lord are the glorification of God, which the "heart" may bring forth, but which are actually the results of that nurturing love (16:2b).

Having dealt with the problem in 2c (see the end of the excursus above), the next passage is the tetracolon 3-4. Franzmann has established that "the two bicola have an inverted pattern of A B B A."[46] The connection of the key words with those in 1-2 has been brought out by Blaszczak.[47]

As in other passages where the particle ܓܝܪ (*gēr*) is followed by "a subordinating conjunction" (3b) or even only an introductory ܘ (*ʾu-* [4b]), the clauses 3a and 4a that it introduces are not strictly causal.[48] In fact, 3a is connected reciprocally to 2b, as the nurturing love of the Lord is answered by the "love" of the speaker for the Lord. For the confession, constructed by use of the copula (cf. formally 15:1, "my joy is the Lord"), says nothing more than 5:1b ⲋ ("I love thee [viz., the Lord]").

This reciprocal love is, according to 3b, "the motive and the ground for his praises."[49] Frankenberg in his retroversion (διὰ τοῦτο αὐτὸν ὑμνῶ)[50] misses the connection of ܐܙܡܪ (Pe. *ʾezmar* or Pa. *ʾezzammar*)[51] with the key word "psalm" in 1c and the fact that ܠ (*l-*) + third singular masculine suffix is not here a "sign of the accusative" but a "sign of the dative."[52] So the Greek of 3b would probably have been διὰ τοῦτο ψαλῶ αὐτῷ (cf. Eph 5:19; Col 3:16).[53] There is no reason to construe the imperfect of ܙܡܪ (*zmar* or *zammar*) as anything but a future.[54]

Verse 4a (like 3a) is connected to 2b. The love of the Lord has nourished the heart of the speaking "I" (2b) and its whole being is "strengthened." The masculine passive participle of the Pa. ܚܝܠ (*ḥayyel*) as the perfect expresses the completion of the action.[55] Whether 𝔊 used a form of (ἐν)δυναμόω or of (ἐπι)στηρίζω is hard to decide (see Excursus 29).[56] The repetition of the adverbial term of place (see 1c-2a above on ܒܬܫܒܚܬܗ [*b-tešbḥāteh*]), as well as the relationship of 4a, as consequence, to 2b, as cause, makes an instrumental translation, "by his praises," unlikely.[57] The suffix of the plural of ܬܫܒܘܚܬܐ (*tešbuḥtā*) should again be taken objectively, corresponding to an objective genitive in 𝔊 (ἐν τοῖς ὕμνοις αὐτοῦ).

It is difficult to decide whether the ܒ (*b-*) + third masculine singular suffix in 4b specifies, in a transferred and perfervid sense, the "place" where the "I" has its existential foundation[58] or refers to the theological "tools"[59] that shape the confiding faith. The answer probably depends, even more than usual, on the personal theology of the hearers or readers.[60] Since the second part of the Ode brings the creator God face to face with the creation, the translation "by him" is likely to be preferable to "in him" or even "to him."[61]

■ **5-7** The speaking "I," whose vocabulary is strongly influenced by the Bible, continues its hymnic self-por-

46 Franzmann, 126.
47 Blaszczak, 31.
48 See Lattke, "Wörter," 289 = idem, *Bedeutung*, 4:137–38.
49 Blaszczak, 31.
50 Frankenberg, 17.
51 See Lattke, 3:XXVI n. 4.
52 Payne Smith, *Dictionary*, 232.
53 See Payne Smith, 1:1136; BDAG, *s.v.* ψάλλω.
54 See, e.g., Bauer, 596: "therefore I must sing to him."
55 Nöldeke §278.
56 Payne Smith, 1:1260; BDAG, *s.vv.* δυναμόω, ἐνδυναμόω, 1; ἐπιστηρίζω, στηρίζω, 2.
57 Blaszczak, 27; Charlesworth, 71. Contrast, e.g., Bauer, 594 ("*among* his praises"), Franzmann, 122: ("*in* his praises"), Pierre, 103 ("*in* his praises" [emphases added]).
58 On ܗܝܡܢܘܬܐ (*haymānūtā*), see Payne Smith, 1:238; BDAG, *s.v.* πίστις, esp. 2: πίστιν ἐν τ[οῖς] θεοῖς ἔχειν. "Faith" here still means "steadfastness" and not "the Christian faith, religion, doctrine, creed" (Payne Smith, *Dictionary*, 103).
59 Nöldeke §248.
60 See the many meanings of ἐν in BDAG, *s.v.*
61 Contra Ungnad and Staerk, 17; Harnack, 45; Diettrich, 57; Greßmann, 451; Bauer, 596. "To him" would be a possible translation only if the Greek had been καὶ πιστεύω εἰς αὐτόν. But this would have been translated into Syriac using a construction with ܗܝܡܢ (*haymen*) + ܒ (*b-*); see Payne Smith, 1:232. The complete line of 4b ⲋ could correspond

trait, with the formal section (5a) giving way to description of the content (5b-7). Because of the "internal parallelism" of 5a (verbs), on the one hand, and 5b-7 (nouns as object), on the other, it is necessary to revise previous editorial divisions into 5a-c, 6a-b, and 7a-b[62] and, with Franzmann, to accept the line divisions of the manuscript.[63]

A further examination of H has shown that v. 5a offers the only form of the Pa. of ܦܬܚ (*ptaḥ*).[64] The verb is also found elsewhere in connection with ܦܘܡܐ (*pummā*) (7:24; 31:3; see Excursus 31),[65] a combination that may depend on Ps 77:2 LXX (ἀνοίξω . . . τὸ στόμα μου, "I will open my mouth").[66] The imperfect of ܡܠܠ (*mallel*), parallel to the first verb and making an *inclusio* with the last word of stanza II, marks an important change of direction. It is not the speaking "I" that will speak ecstatically in or by the spirit of God (cf. 1 Cor 14:2):[67] it is the power of the spirit of God (cf. 3:10) that will make use of the opened mouth—and limited human speech—to "proclaim" what follows.[68] In view of 6:2 and 18:15, this human concept could be described as "inspiration."[69] This ܪܘܚܐ (*rūḥā*) is not envisioned as an "*independent . . . personality*."[70] Like the personified "word of the Lord" (see 8a below) and his "wisdom,"[71] his "spirit" is also a theological force, differing from all immanent powers of the illimitable universe. Even if this articulate force is not transformed into a "vehicle for the self-revelation of the divine" by its presence in the speaking "I,"[72] it is still true that the hymnic human utterances about God are traced back to what humans call the spiritual power of God. Grese puts it quite simply: "God is the source of the hymn."[73]

What the spirit intends to say through the "I" is shown in the remainder of stanza II by the three pairs of parallel accusatives, which, like most pleonastic lists, are only meant as examples. All six of these objects refer to the "Lord," explicitly mentioned in v. 5b. The object ܬܫܒܘܚܬܐ (*tešbuḥtā*), as in 12:4c, means δόξα in the sense of "glory" (cf. 11:17 and Excursus 21).[74] And the parallel ܝܐܝܘܬܐ (*yāʾyūtā*), as in 12:4b, simply means "beauty."[75] The terms are probably intended reciprocally to explain each other.

The separate sections of 6 are not meant as parallels to the two parts of 5;[76] it is the whole, internally parallel colon that describes the way in which God's δόξα becomes, as it were, visible (cf. Rom 1:19-23). It is obvious that the interchangeable terms of creation are based on biblical models.[77] Both ܐܝܕܐ (*ʾidā* = χείρ) and ܨܒܥܐ (*ṣebʿā* = δάκτυλος) are anthropomorphically used for God's creative—and also perhaps for his historically active—power.[78] Since ܦܘܠܚܢܐ (*pulḥānā*) is here parallel to ܥܒܕܐ (*ʿbādā*), the noun, derived from ܦܠܚ (*plaḥ*), should be translated by "work," not "service"[79] as in 2a, or "plantation."[80] Both terms describe God's

only to καὶ πίστιν ἔχω (ἐν) αὐτῷ / διὰ αὐτοῦ in 𝔊 (cf., e.g., Rom 11:36). The English translation of Harris and Mingana (2:236), "in Him," found also in a number of later works, is ambiguous and thus escapes criticism.

62 Lattke, *Bedeutung*, 1:75, 1:120–21.

63 Franzmann, 126.

64 This means that a correction must be made to the concordances in Lattke, *Bedeutung*, 2:159; and *Oden*, 274; cf. Charlesworth, *Manuscripts*, 50; Payne Smith, 2:3338; BDAG, *s.v.* ἀνοίγω, esp. 5b.

65 See Payne Smith, 2:3063–64; BDAG, *s.v.* στόμα.

66 Rahlfs, 2:82; Brenton, 744.

67 See BDAG, *s.v.* πνεῦμα, esp. 6e.

68 BDAG, *s.v.* λαλέω. See Acts 2:11: . . . λαλούντων αὐτῶν ταῖς ἡμετέραις γλώσσαις τὰ μεγαλεῖα τοῦ ϑεοῦ ("telling in our own tongues the mighty works of God"). If ܡܠܠ is to be translated by "speak," the direct objects of the transitive verb in Syriac must be annexed to the English verb by "about/of." On the translation of ܪܘܚܐ as "power of the spirit," see 3:10.

69 See BDAG, *s.v.* πνεῦμα on *Asc. Isa.* 1:7: τὸ πν[εῦμα] τὸ λαλοῦν ἐν ἐμοί ("the Spirit that speaks in me").

70 BDAG, *s.v.* πνεῦμα, esp. 8.

71 See Johannes Marböck, "Heiliger Geist I. Biblisch-theologisch: 1. Altes Testament u. Judentum," *LThK*³ 4 (1995) 1305.

72 Richard Schaeffler, "Geist II. Begriffsgeschichte," *LThK*³ 4 (1995) 374.

73 Grese, *Corpus*, 179.

74 Payne Smith, 2:4027–28; BDAG, *s.v.* δόξα.

75 Payne Smith, 1:1534.

76 Contra Blaszczak, 32.

77 E.g., Ps 8:4 (ἔργα τῶν δακτύλων σου); 8:7 (ἔργα τῶν χειρῶν σου); 18:2 LXX (ποίησις χειρῶν); 101:26 LXX; cf. Isa 66:2; Acts 7:50; Heb 1:10.

78 See Payne Smith, 1:1546; BDAG, *s.v.* χείρ, esp. 2b, and Eduard Lohse, "χείρ, κτλ.," *ThWNT* 9 (1973) 416; *TDNT* 9:427; Payne Smith, 2:3357; BDAG, *s.v.* δάκτυλος.

79 Contra Lattke, *Oden*, 145.

80 See Klijn, 303, contra Lattke, *Bedeutung*, 1:121.

creative action and historical power (cf. 8:18-19 and see 8a and 12b below; contrast 13b; see Excursus 27). To determine the Greek term that paralleled *ἔργον* is even more difficult than in 2a.[81] It will most likely have been one that emphasized the activity rather than its outcome.

The first part of the phrase introduced by an "object marker" in 7 is quite likely to be based on Ps 51:1 (cf. Ps 50:3 LXX: *τὸ πλῆθος τῶν οἰκτιρμῶν σου*, "the multitude of thy compassion").[82] This means that, as in 14:9, ܪ̈ܚܡܐ (*raḥmē*) is not translated by "love"[83] but by "mercy," "compassion" (see Excursus 2).[84] It signifies "the whole of salvation history as God's self-revelation."[85] The parallel second section of 7, therefore, also carries more weight than merely calling attention to "the creative power of the word as agent in creation."[86] The word in question, ܥܘܫܢܐ (*ʿušnā*), derived from ܥܫܢ (*ʿšen*), has a qualitative meaning of strength, corresponding perhaps to *δύναμις* or *ἰσχύς*,[87] and this emphasizes the already dynamic character of "word" (on ܡܠܬܐ [*melltā*] and its possible equivalents *λόγος* and *ῥῆμα*, see Excursus 12). The Word-made-flesh of John 1:1-14 is not under consideration. The mighty "word" of the Lord is inalienable. It must not be too hastily identified with any written or printed text, since it can be known and recognized only by its illumination of the mystery of the world and the story of humanity.

At this point the hymnic self-portrait is cut short, but its final term, as well as some of the references to the creation in 5b-7, form a bridge to the second part of *Ode* 16 (stanzas III–VII).

■ **8-9** The second part of *Ode* 16, a didactic poem on aspects of the creation,[88] comprises stanzas III to VII and is framed by the theological terms "word" (8a, 19a) and "thought" (8b, 19b). This doctrine of creation is not a "hymn" and does not confine itself "*completely* within the bounds of the OT" [emphasis added].[89]

The tradition underlying stanza III is fairly clearly that of 1 Cor 2:9-10, with the Greek of Prov 20:12 (*οὖς ἀκούει καὶ ὀφθαλμὸς ὁρᾷ· κυρίου ἔργα καὶ ἀμφότερα*, "The ear hears, and the eye sees: even both of them are the Lord's work") and Prov 20:27 (*φῶς κυρίου πνοὴ ἀνθρώπων, ὃς ἐρευνᾷ ταμίεια κοιλίας*, "The spirit of man is a light of the Lord, who searches the inmost parts of the belly").[90] But if 8a does not say that the Spirit searches all things (*τὸ γὰρ πνεῦμα πάντα ἐραυνᾷ* [1 Cor 2:10]; cf. Rom 8:27), if it is "the word of the Lord" that performs this continuing function,[91] this leads to a reference to Heb 4:12 (*ὁ λόγος τοῦ θεοῦ* [ܡܠܬܗ ܕܐܠܗܐ] . . . *κριτικὸς ἐνθυμήσεων* [ܡܒܨܝܢܘܬܐ] *καὶ ἐννοιῶν καρδίας*, "the word of God . . . discerning the thoughts and intentions of the heart"). For there also the *λόγος τοῦ θεοῦ* is not the "*revelation of God* through Jesus" but God's examining and judging "power."[92] According to 1 Cor 2:10, "the penetration to the depths of God . . . is reserved for the Spirit alone":[93] the transference of this humanly conceived examining to the powerful "word of the Lord" is evidence that the Pauline *πάντα* has here been limited to "the invisible." If the negative particle ܠܐ (*lā*), which was inserted into H as a correction in this passage, belonged, like the participle ܒܨܝܐ (*bāṣyā*) that was also added above the line, to the text being copied, the phrase containing the passive participle of ܐܬܚܙܝ (*ʾeṯḥzī*) must correspond to the neuter *τὰ ἀόρατα*, "the invisible world" (cf. Col 1:16).[94] Even "things invisible" (cf. 30:6) form part of God's "works" (see on 9a below).

Without the Greek text of 8b, the alternative interpretations of this line must be considered equal. Either ܘܕܓܠܐ is parsed as *ʾu-dāḡlā* (active feminine participle

81 See Payne Smith, 2:3150.
82 See Blaszczak, 33; *OTSy*, pt. 2 fasc. 3, p. 56: ܣܘܓܐܐ ܕܪ̈ܚܡܝܟ; Rahlfs, 2:53; Brenton, 727–28.
83 Contra Lattke, *Oden*, 145.
84 BDAG, *s.v.* *οἰκτιρμός*; Payne Smith, 2:3882.
85 See Käsemann, *Romans*, 326 (German, 314), on Rom 12:1.
86 Blaszczak, 33.
87 Payne Smith, 2:3004; BDAG, *s.vv.* *δύναμις*, esp. 1; *ἰσχύς*.
88 See Blaszczak, 29.
89 Contra Bauer, 597.
90 Rahlfs, 2:217; Brenton, 807.
91 Nöldeke §269; on the feminine active participle of the *hapax legomenon* ܒܨܐ (*bṣā*), see Payne Smith, 1:568; *OTSy*, pt. 2 fasc. 5, on Prov 20:27; BDAG, *s.v.* *ἐραυνάω*.
92 See Gräßer, 1:236, 240.
93 Schrage, *1. Korinther*, 1:257.
94 Payne Smith, 1:1234; BDAG, *s.v.* *ἀόρατος*.

of the Pe. ܕܓܠ [*dḡal*])[95] or as *ʾu-ḏa-ḡlē* (passive masculine participle of the Pe. ܓܠܐ [*glā*]).[96] The first reading provides a transitive parallel to the participle of ܒܨܐ (*bṣā*) in 8a, makes the "word of the Lord" the implied subject, and casts "thought" as the direct object. The other reading of the unpointed text gives rise to a chiasmus, where "his thought" is parallel to "word of the Lord" and the form ܓܠܐ (*glē*) shows similarities to the participle ܡܬܚܙܐ (*meṯḥzē*) in 8a. Both possibilities make good sense, so it is unnecessary to follow Barth's suggestion: "For the meaningless ܘܕܓܠܐ read ܘܓܠܐ '(the word of God) reveals his thoughts' . . . the only meaning that fits with the continuation."[97] All the same, this early textual criticism adumbrated the controversy between Brock and Charlesworth.

Harris and Mingana and Charlesworth[98] take the feminine noun ܡܚܫܒܬܐ (*maḥšaḇṯā*), derived from ܚܫܒ (*ḥšaḇ*), to be the object of ܕܓܠܐ (*dāḡlā*), which brings out the Pauline model. The "thought" of the Lord could then correspond to the "depths of God" (*τὰ βάϑη τοῦ ϑεοῦ*) of the "apocalyptic wisdom tradition," that is, "God's unfathomability and immeasurability."[99] In the context of the *Odes of Solomon,* this idea is supported by 12:4 and 16:9 ("thought" as object parallel to "works"; see Excursus 9).

Brock,[100] on the other hand, takes "that which is revealed" to be another object of ܒܨܝܐ (*bāṣyā*, 8a) and "his Thought" to be the subject of 8b, in which case the "invisible" and the "manifest" are chiastically complementary[101] as the *πάντα* of 1 Cor 2:10. This reading is supported also by other passages in the *Odes of Solomon* where "word" and "thought" are parallel or juxtaposed (esp. 9:3; cf. 12:7; 16:9; 41:10-11; see Excursus 12). Charlesworth[102] may consider the Syriac scholar Brock a critic "unfamiliar with the scholarly debates," but Blaszczak's verdict, which is endorsed by Franzmann,[103] that "Brock's interpretation, is, on the whole, more convincing than that of Charlesworth, given the parallelism, and the good sense it makes of the difficult Syriac of the verse,"[104] must be taken seriously.

The parallel bicolon 9a-b is connected to 8a by the participle of ܚܙܐ (*ḥzā*), expressing duration, and it exhibits a partial chiasmus (A B C || B' A' C');[105] Blaszczak refers it to the partly apocryphal tradition of 1 Cor 2:9 and *Gos. Thom.* log. 17.[106] The parallelism of "eye(s)" and "ear(s)" has already been noted in 15:3-4 (see the commentary on that passage). According to the "Jahwe proverb" (Prov 20:12), "eye" and "ear" are *κυρίου ἔργα*[107] and the human eye in 9a sees "the works of God in creation" (in Blaszczak's happy translation).[108] The plural of ܥܒܕܐ (*ʿḇāḏā*) means the same as the singular (see 6 above), which would have agreed better with the parallel "thought" in 9b.

"Hearing," like "seeing," is not limited to "sense perception"[109] but includes "understanding" (cf. 8:8; 15:4).[110] The human ear does not, in some mysterious way, hear the "thought" of God expressed in imagined words (see 8b above) but understands "the thought or design of God made manifest in the created world."[111] The repetition of ܡܚܫܒܬܗ (*maḥšaḇṯeh*) in 9b rather supports Brock's interpretation of 8b. It could, after all, be thought strange to have both the "word of the Lord"

---

95 Payne Smith, 1:821; Brockelmann, *Lexicon*, 141: *examinavit*; cf. Frankenberg, 17: *στοχάζεται*. Cf. Harris and Mingana (2:284): "The verb ܕܓܠ is not duly catalogued in the *Thesaurus*, and this has given rise to many inadmissible theories about this sentence." Kittel (p. 77), who calls 8b "corrupt," suggests an "emendation" that is grammatically impossible.

96 Payne Smith, 1:717: *manifestus*.

97 Barth, 263.

98 Harris and Mingana, 2:283; Charlesworth, 69, 71; idem, "Haplography and Philology: A Study of *Ode of Solomon* 16:8," *NTS* 25 (1978–79) 221–27.

99 Schrage, *1. Korinther*, 1:257.

100 Sebastian Brock, review of Charlesworth [1973] in *JBL* 93 (1974) 624.

101 See BDAG, *s.v.* *φανερόω*; Eph 5:13 [14]: *τὸ φανερούμενον*.

102 James H. Charlesworth, "Haplography and Philology: A Study of *Ode of Solomon* 16:8," *NTS* 25 (1978–79) 221.

103 Franzmann, 124.

104 Blaszczak, 34; see on 9b below.

105 Franzmann, 127.

106 Blaszczak, 34–35.

107 See Plöger, 234.

108 Blaszczak, 35.

109 See BDAG, *s.v.* *εἶδον*.

110 See Payne Smith, 2:4214: *mente percepit*; BDAG, *s.v.* *ἀκούω*.

111 Blaszczak, 35, referring to Rom 1:20.

and the human ear directed toward the "thought" of the Lord to examine and understand it.

■ **10-12** As Grese has declared, "ECL [= early Christian literature] taught that the God it worshipped was the creator of the world."[112] This doctrine is inherited from Jewish writings, including the Old Testament. What is important is not so much any poetico-mythological embroidery but the general acceptance of an omnipotent "creator of the world."[113]

In order to understand the details of *Ode* 16, it will be necessary to refer to a number of Old Testament texts and also to observe omissions. God's *ποιεῖν* (Gen 1:1, 16; Exod 20:11; Ps 145:6 LXX) is not mentioned, nor his *καλεῖν* (Gen 1:10). The "seventh day," sanctified by God (Gen 2:2-3; Exod 20:11; see on 12b below), is altogether missing. The creation of humanity as male and female in God's image (Gen 1:27) is not made explicit. The sequence "earth/land," "sea," "heaven," and "stars" can be found more or less complete, sometimes merely summarized and attended by various verbs, for example, in Gen 2:1 (*ὁ οὐρανὸς καὶ ἡ γῆ καὶ πᾶς ὁ κόσμος αὐτῶν*); Exod 20:11 and Ps 145:6 LXX (*οὐρανός, γῆ, θάλασσα*); Isa 44:24 (*οὐρανός, γῆ*; cf. Gen 1:1 and Zech 12:1); and Ps 135:5-9 LXX (*οὐρανοί, γῆ, ὕδατα, ἥλιος, ἄστρα*).[114]

Another text, nearly contemporary with the *Odes of Solomon*, that also bears the imprint of these and related texts, is *1 Clem.* 33:2-7, although this includes among its representative *ἔργα ἀγαθά* ("good works") of the *δημιουργὸς καὶ δεσπότης τῶν ἁπάντων* ("Creator and Master of all things") the production of animals and the creation of humans as well as the fixing and ordering of the firmament and the separation of land and sea.[115] One important conclusion from this comparison of two early Christian texts, both "under the influence of antiquated forms,"[116] is that the activities, reported in widely varying terms, are not meant to be descriptions of technical projects or scientific explanations.

Franzmann has demonstrated that 10-12a is a tricolon "with internal parallelism" and "word-pairs."[117] So 10-11 should be left as single cola, as in H, not divided into two bicola, as has often been done following Harris and Mingana.[118] The third masculine singular personal pronoun, which is placed first for "emphasis"[119] and which must represent Greek *αὐτός*,[120] cannot refer to the "word" of 7-8,[121] but must refer to the divine Lord, the powerful creator.[122] This pronoun is the subject of the seven[123] verbs that follow it, which use the perfect as a "tense of *narration*" and also, in 10-12a, as looking back on "the *completed result*."[124]

That this didactic poem begins with the spreading out of the land, not mentioned elsewhere, is not due to any apologetic impulse.[125] Since an act of creation is not here in question, Gunkel's statement that "this psalm can be considered as a conscious rejection of the doctrine that the world is evil and not of God"[126] is rather beside the point. Although ܐܪܥܐ (*ʾarʿā*), in opposition to "heaven" in 11, could mean "earth"—already long known to be a sphere, though still considered the center of the universe until the time of Copernicus—in 10 it is used for the "land," which rises above the "surface of the water" of this world.[127] The Aph. of ܦܫܛ/ܦܫܛ

112 Grese, *Corpus*, 175–76. Cf. *Corp. Herm.* 13:17, where God is called *τῆς κτίσεως κύριος, κτίσας τὰ πάντα,* and *πασῆς φύσεως κτίστης* ("Lord of creation," "who created all things," "creator of all nature"); Grese, *Corpus*, 24–25, lines 176, 181, and 26–27, line 193; see also Colpe and Holzhausen, 184–85.

113 Jacob Jervell, *Die Apostelgeschichte* (KEK 3; Göttingen: Vandenhoeck & Ruprecht, 1998) 185. On Acts 4:24 (cf. also 14:15), Jervell comments (p. 185): "In early Judaism, God is not only the one who brought Israel out of the land of Egypt but also the creator."

114 The "moon" clearly had no significance (see Ps 135:9 LXX), not even in stanza VI, which has the "sun" as its topic. On these and further Old Testament parallels, see Greßmann, 452.

115 See Ehrman, 1:92–95; Lona, 351–61.

116 Gunkel and Begrich, *Einleitung*, 6.

117 Franzmann, 127.

118 Harris and Mingana, 2:283; contra Lattke, *Bedeutung*, 1:75, 120–21.

119 Nöldeke §312 B.

120 See Frankenberg, 17.

121 Contra Charlesworth, 72, who even discovers similarities to the Prologue to John's Gospel.

122 See Kittel, 77 ("Schöpfermacht").

123 Perhaps the fact that there are seven verbs conceals an allusion to the seven days of creation in Gen 1:1-24.

124 Nöldeke §§255–56.

125 Contra Blaszczak, 35.

126 Gunkel, 327.

127 Payne Smith, 1:397; BDAG, *s.v.* *γῆ*, esp. 4.

(*pṯā/pṯī*), which is used in 7:13 about the way of *gnōsis*, corresponds to the Greek verb πλατύνω.[128] This image of the broadening of the land clearly implies an image of the "water" (ܡ̈ܝܐ [*mayyā*]) being pushed aside and confined in the "sea." It makes no difference which particular image of the "ocean" the author had in mind. Any seas and large lakes, already described as θάλασσα, were included as opposites to the continents.[129] In the context of 10-11, "sea" together with γῆ and οὐρανός also "denote[s] the whole universe"[130] (cf., e.g., Acts 4:24). The use of the *hapax legomenon* ܐܘܬܒ (*ʾawteḇ*, Aph. of ܝܬܒ [*ʾiteḇ*])[131] makes it unlikely that the masculine ܝܡܐ (*yammā*) was meant to include the great rivers, such as the Nile or the Euphrates (cf. Isa 27:1; Jer 51:36; Ezek 32:2).

The Pe. ܡܬܚ (*mṯaḥ*) can be used literally to mean pitching a tent (cf. 42:9) or in a transferred sense, as here in 11, for spreading out the canopy of heaven.[132] This image is found already in Isa 44:24 (ἐξέτεινα τὸν οὐρανόν), Ps 103:2 LXX, and Zech 12:1 (ἐκτείνων οὐρανόν) but not in early Christian writings except for *Hermas, Vis.* 3 (I.3).4 (πήξας τὸν οὐρανόν, quoting Isa 42:5).[133] The verb and the whole of the second half of 11 make it clear that the "heaven" is the "firmament" that overarches the earth and is visible as bearer of the "fixed stars" but is not the "abode" of the creator or of God himself.[134] Whether the *hapax legomenon* ܟܘܟ̈ܒܐ (*kawkḇē*)[135] corresponds to τοὺς ἀστέρας (cf. Gen 1:16) or to τὰ ἄστρα (cf. Ps 135:9 LXX, which includes the moon, not mentioned in this Ode) cannot be decided. What is important is that the "stars," as parts that arise and perish in the infinite and eternal all, are neither "living beings endowed with reason" nor "gods."[136] Their innumerability (cf. Gen 22:17) is not treated as important, nor is their usefulness to humankind.[137]

But what is meant by the Aph. of ܬܩܢ (*tqen*), hardly distinguishable from its Pa. ܬܩܢ (*taqqen*), which is repeated in 12a? The sense of the verb covers a number of Greek equivalents from "to create" via "to fix" to "to put in order."[138] The idea is probably not based on Gen 1:17 (יתן, ܝܗܒ, ἔθετο). As no other *Vorlage* (model) has been identified, the exact meaning can only be conjectured. Considering 13, it is probably intended to emphasize the creatureliness of the stars.

Verse 12a, where ܐܬܩܢ (*ʾaṯqen*) recurs, is just as enigmatic. The object here is the whole of creation, unless, as in 7:24, ܒܪܝܬܐ (*brīṯā*) is limited to the "world of men" or perhaps to all living "creatures."[139] This, then, would concern the formation and setting up of humankind, since they must in the last instance refer their origin and upright stance to God the Lord as the mystery of creation or consider themselves a product of blind evolution and a helpless toy of cosmic forces. The Aph. of ܩܘܡ, ܩܡ (*qām*) probably does not imply any eschatological awakening.[140]

Verse 12b[141] undoubtedly depends on Gen 2:2 (on "his works," see 9a above):

וישבת . . . מכל־מלאכתו

ܘܐܬܬܢܝܚ . . . ܡܢ ܟܠܗܘܢ ܥܒ̈ܕܘܗܝ

καὶ κατέπαυσεν . . . ἀπὸ πάντων τῶν ἔργων αὐτοῦ.[142]

128 Payne Smith, 2:3334; BDAG, *s.v.* πλατύνω: "to make broad, enlarge."
129 See Payne Smith, 1:1600.
130 BDAG, *s.v.* θάλασσα.
131 Payne Smith, 1:1644; cf. BDAG, *s.v.* καθίζω, esp. 1.
132 Payne Smith, 2:2247.
133 Ehrman, 2:180–81; see BDAG, *s.vv.* ἐκτείνω, πήγνυμι.
134 On the *hapax legomenon* ܫܡ̈ܝܐ (*šmayyā*), see Payne Smith, 2:4208; BDAG, *s.v.* οὐρανός.
135 Payne Smith, 1:1694.
136 BDAG, *s.v.* ἀστήρ. In biblical and other early Christian creation stories, God is the meta-eternal and meta-infinite creative power invoked to explain the secrets of the elements and powers of the universe, which human thought cannot quite fathom.
137 BDAG, *s.v.* ἄστρον.
138 See Payne Smith, 2:4484–86.
139 Payne Smith, 1:601; BDAG, *s.vv.* κτίσις, κτίσμα.
140 See Payne Smith, 2:3527–28.
141 The enclitic ܗܘ (*-w*) emphasizes the preceding verb (see Nöldeke §221).
142 See *BHS*, p. 3; *OTSy*, pt. 1 fasc. 1, on this passage; Rahlfs, 1:3.
143 Payne Smith, 2:2311–12.

Unlike any of the other passages (see Excursus 3), the Ethpe. of ܢܘܚ, ܢܚ (*nāḥ*)[143] here refers to the Creator himself, though without mentioning the Sabbath. Whether "the omission of the reference to the seventh day" is really "an unmistakable case of anti-Judaic polemic"[144] will be discussed at 13c.[145]

■ **13-14** The plural of ܒܪܝܬܐ (*brītā*) in 13a does not stand for κτίσις, as in Rom 1:25 or *Ode* 8:22, but either for κτίσεις[146] or—more likely—for κτίσματα as individual "component parts of creation."[147] This term connects stanza V to stanza IV (see 12a above), but in the transition to stanza VI it now refers to the constellations[148] and their "works" (as distinct from 12b). The paronomasias in 13a (root ܪܗܛ) and 13b (root ܥܒܕ) are not a conclusive indication of a Syriac original,[149] since they would also be possible in 𝔊 (e.g., using δρόμος and δραμεῖν [cf. Ps 18:6 LXX, where, however, the text has ὁδόν, not δρόμον] and ἔργον and ἐργάζομαι). Whether the reference is especially to the "paths of the sun and moon" (Dio Chrysostom in his Borysthenian address [36.42], well known in the second century)[150] or more generally to all the ἄστρων δρόμοι (Marcus Aurelius 7.47),[151] it is impossible to say. The breadth of the parallel (or perhaps explanatory) term "powers" in 14 suggests the latter. What is most noticeable about the visible stars, besides their light, is the regularity of their paths across the sky,[152] and in a poetic sense there is no difference between the fixed stars and the planets known to antiquity on this score. The third feminine plural suffix, as well as the feminine plural active participle of the Pe. ܪܗܛ (*rheṭ*), expressing duration, refers to the "creatures," the subject of 13a-c.

Except for the shared subject, the structure of 13b is identical to that of 13a.[153] In spite of this parallelism, 13b is more than a mere interpretation of 13a.[154] In fact, the wordplay with ܥܒܕܐ (*ʿbāḏā*) and ܥܒܕ (*ʿebaḏ*; cf. linguistically 11:20), which points back to the use of "work" in 1a-c rather than to the idea of creation in 6, 9a, and 12b, brings a new aspect that will be elucidated by example in 16a (again employing the Pe. ܥܒܕ).[155] Since in antiquity it was believed that the "changes in the weather" were caused by the "rising and setting of specific stars or constellations,"[156] these occurrences could be considered their "works." But this understanding should be limited to the beneficent aspects of giving light, direction, and warmth.[157]

Franzmann notes that the two infinitives, depending on the negated participle of the Pe. ܝܕܥ (*ʾidaʿ*) in 13c, refer to the activities mentioned earlier in the verse.[158] The infinitive of the Pe. ܩܘܡ, ܩܡ (*qām*) is the opposite of "run" (13a), and the infinitive of the Pe. ܒܛܠ (*bṭel*) is opposed to "work" (13b).[159] The negation of "stop" and "stand still," together with a reference to "Justin's *Dialogue with Trypho* c. 22," elicited the following from

144 Harris and Mingana, 2:288; Harnack (p. 46) disagrees.

145 On the source and meaning of the "discussion of God's resting," see Westermann, *Genesis*, 1:230–44.

146 Frankenberg, 18.

147 BDAG, *s.v.* κτίσμα; Payne Smith, 1:601.

148 Bauernfeind doubts "the use of δρόμος in relation to the stars in a lit[eral] one" (Otto Bauernfeind, "τρέχω, κτλ.," *ThWNT* 8 [1969] 233 n. 2; *TDNT* 8:233 n. 2).

149 See Charlesworth, "Paronomasia," 14.

150 Winfried Elliger, *Dion Chrysostomos, Sämtliche Reden* (BAWGR; Zurich/Stuttgart: Artemis, 1967) XL–XLIII, 521.

151 Willy Theiler, ed. and trans., *Kaiser Marc Aurel, Wege zu sich selbst* (BAWGR; 2nd ed.; Zurich/Munich: Artemis, 1974) 164.

152 On the plural of ܪܗܛܐ (*reḥtā*), see Payne Smith, 2:3835.

153 Franzmann, 127.

154 Contra Blaszczak (pp. 36–37), who takes "created things" far too broadly and fails to observe references to "heavenly luminaries" earlier than 14.

155 See Payne Smith, 2:2765–74.

156 See Emilie Boer, "Sternbilder, Sternglaube, Sternschnuppen," *KP* 5 (1975) 365.

157 In spite of verbal similarities, 12:5-7 is not parallel to 16:13. Compared to the belief in the stars and the astrology/astronomy of classical times, the poetic statements in 11 and 13 are very restrained; see Franz Boll, Carl Bezold, and Wilhelm Gundel, *Sternglaube und Sterndeutung: Die Geschichte und das Wesen der Astrologie* (Mit einem bibliographischen Anhang von Hans Georg Gundel; 7th ed.; Darmstadt: Wissenschaftliche Buchgesellschaft, 1977) 44–58.

158 Franzmann, 128.

159 Franzmann's reference to Matt 20:6 (p. 124) is not as helpful as Charlesworth's to *1 Enoch* 2:1 (p. 72); cf. Greßmann, 452.

Harris: "On examining the Ode more closely we detect an unmistakable case of anti-Judaic polemic. . . . It is clear, then, that the 16th Ode means to say that the Sabbath is not kept by the Heavenly bodies."[160] Harnack immediately countered this in a note on 13c: "He [i.e., Harris] makes a comparison with Justin, Dial. 22, which, in an anti-Jewish polemic, says that τὰ στοιχεῖα οὐκ ἀργεῖ οὐδὲ σαββατίζει. But the phrase 'οὐ σαββατίζει' does not occur in the text under consideration, so this is not a case of anti-Jewish polemic."[161] Friedrich Spitta added that any "polemic against the Sabbath" is already "excluded" by 12b.[162] And H. M. Slee, only a little later, drew on two passages in Philo (*Cher.* 87–88 and *Migr. Abr.* 91–92) to establish that "[i]t appears . . . that a thoughtful Jew could reflect on the unceasing activity of the heavenly bodies, and yet keep the Seventh Day; and this . . . seems to make it doubtful whether any anti-Judaic polemic is to be detected in this Ode."[163] Finally, in the transition to 14, one may quote Blaszczak: "The Odist, however, is interested not in the question of sabbath rest but in God's sovereignty as Creator; expressed by the fact that while God rests, creation continues doing the work assigned to it."[164]

The connection of 14 with the preceding tricolon is not as problematic as Franzmann makes it,[165] when Sir 16:27-28 is taken into consideration. This passage does not mention *powers*, but speaks of the incessant "works" (ἔργα) of the created *works* (also ἔργα) of the Lord: καὶ ἕως αἰῶνος οὐκ ἀπειθήσουσιν τοῦ ῥήματος αὐτοῦ, "and they never disobey his word."[166] In *Ode* 16, the plural of ܚܝܠܘܬܐ (*ḥaylūṯā*) is not a parallel term to "archangel" (4:8),[167] but is equivalent to δυνάμεις as a more general designation for "supernatural beings"[168] including the "created things" = "stars" (see Excursus 19). There is no poetic intention behind the illusory connection with 13b by the use of the masculine plural passive participle of the Eshtaph. of ܥܒܕ (*ʿḇaḏ*). If the *hapax legomenon* in 𝔖 represents a form of ὑποτάσσεσθαι,[169] there is still the question whether the passive means "to be subjected" or "to subject oneself, obey."[170] Only the second meaning would be possible if 𝔊 had used the passive of πείθω or the active of ὑπακούω.[171] The term ܡܠܬܐ (*melltā*) with third masculine singular possessive suffix at the end of stanza V refers to the "word of the Lord" (see 7-8 above, 19 below, and Excursus 12). This calls into question the potency of the heavenly "powers" and subjects their activity to the word of the creator.

■ **15-17** The easily intelligible terms in stanza VI can be divided into two opposed groups: "light," "sun," bright "day" versus "darkness" and "night." These are terms drawn from the daily and nightly experience of sighted persons (see Excursus 10). The artistic structure of the two bicola 15 and 16, each of which consists of an antithetical parallelism, is not content to arrange them schematically but alternates direct and indirect antitheses. Direct opposites are "light" and "darkness" (15a-b), "night" and "day" (15b-16a); but "sun" and "night" (15a-b, 16a-b) and "day" and "darkness" (16a-b) are indirect opposites, which, as a comparison with a disturbing line in the dialogue between Orestes and Iphigenia from Euripides' *Iphigenia in Taurus* (νύξ—φῶς)[172] shows, is not unusual. The omission of the word "moon" depends on the poetic introduction of ܣܝܡܬܐ (*sīmṯā*).[173] This word, which occurs only here, corresponds to the metaphorical use of the noun ὁ θησαυρός and is to be translated as "treasury" not "treasure."[174] Since it is possible that

160 Harris, 112–13.
161 Harnack, 46.
162 Friedrich Spitta, "Zum Verständnis der Oden Salomos," *ZNW* 11 (1910) 275.
163 H. M. Slee, "A Note on the Sixteenth *Ode of Solomon*," *JTS* 15 (1913–14) 454.
164 Blaszczak, 36.
165 Franzmann, 128; see also Greßmann, 452; and esp. Charlesworth, 72.
166 Rahlfs, 2:404; Sauer, *Sirach*, 546.
167 See Payne Smith, 1:1261.
168 BDAG, *s.v.* δύναμις, esp. 5.
169 See Payne Smith, 2:2772; BDAG, *s.v.* ὑποτάσσω.
170 E.g., Harnack, 46: "and his hosts obey his word."
171 BDAG, *s.vv.* πείθω, 3b, ὑπακούω, 1.
172 *Iphigenia in Tauris*, line 1026; see Gustav Adolf Seek, ed., Ernst Buschor et al., trans., *Euripides, Sämtliche Tragödien und Fragmente* (OG/Ger.; 6 vols.; Darmstadt: Wissenschaftliche Buchgesellschaft, 1972–81) 4:74, 508.
173 See Emerton's remark on 15a: "The poet wishes to speak of the storehouses, or treasuries, of light and darkness; and, while the sun can obviously be described as the storehouse of light, the moon cannot be regarded as the storehouse of darkness because it shines and is a source of light" ("Notes," 516).
174 Johannes Bapt. Bauer, review of Lattke, *Bedeutung*, vols. 1, 1a, and 2, in *Kairos* N.F. 23 (1981) 121; Payne Smith, 2:2563; BDAG, *s.v.* θησαυρός, 1.

this unusual word—and perhaps more—originated in contemporary imagery, it is worth quoting a passage from *1 Enoch* 41 in a slightly abbreviated form:

> 5. And I saw the storerooms of the sun and the moon, from what place they come out and to which place they return, and their glorious return. . . . 6. From the first is the sun. . . . 7. After that is found the . . . path of the moon. . . . And the two will gaze directly into the glory of the Lord of the Spirits. They give thanks, they praise, and do not economize (on energy), for their very essence generates new power. 8. Surely the many changes of the sun have (both) a blessing and a curse, and the course of the moon's path is light to the righteous (on the one hand) and darkness to the sinners (on the other), in the name of the Lord of the Spirits, who created the distinction between light and darkness. . . .[175]

In 15a, ܢܘܗܪܐ (*nuhrā*) refers only to the light of the sun, thus deviating from the accepted dualistic-soteriological use of the term "light." [176] And unlike in 15:2, the term "sun" does not refer to the "Lord."[177] The term ܚܫܘܟܐ (*ḥeššōḵā*) in 15b and 16b may correspond either to ἡ σκοτία or to τὸ σκότος,[178] but ܠܠܝܐ (*lēlyā*) certainly corresponds to ἡ νύξ.[179]

As in 15:1, v. 16a now juxtaposes "day" and "sun." Emerton detects a problem in treating "sun" as the subject of the Pe. ܥܒܕ (*ʿḇaḏ*), which is pointed as a perfect, and at first thinks of God's "single act of creation in the past."[180] His suggestion is "to ignore the diacritical point, and to vocalize the first verb as a participle"[181] in parallel to the verb of 16b, and this acquires added weight because a reexamination of the facsimile of MS. H reveals yet another point below the letter ܒ, which now only looks like a tiny ring.[182] In any case, this changes the reading from *ʿḇaḏ* to *ʿāḇeḏ*.[183] Regardless, the "sun" is the subject of 16a, and its continuous "making" is one of the "works" of 13b.[184] The particle ܠ (*l-*) preceding ܝܘܡܐ (*yawmā*), then, must be "the sign of the direct object."[185] In a final clause, the adjective ܢܗܝܪ (*nahhīr*), probably corresponding to Greek φωτεινός,[186] modifies "the natural day, the period bet[ween] the rising and setting of the sun."[187]

As a poetic variation, 16b uses "night" as the subject with the participle of the Aph. of ܐܬܐ (*ʾeṯā*), which may represent a form of ἄγω or φέρω.[188] The direct object is "darkness," and thus the terms have changed sides when compared to 16a. 𝔊 will also have used πρόσωπον τῆς γῆς for the "surface of the earth,"[189] and probably ἐπί[190] (cf. 11:13) for the preposition of place.

According to Emerton, "[v]erse 17 is difficult to translate."[191] If the monocolon of the manuscript is divided into a bicolon, there is no verb for 17a. Even so, 17a functions as an easily comprehensible "nominal clause."[192] Since there is no need to insert an instrumental ܒ (*b-*) between the ܘ (*u-*) and ܩܘܒܠܐ (*qubbālā*) with its suffix,[193] Emerton's translation, "And their reception (is) by one from the other," makes good sense.[194] This sense becomes even clearer if the conjectural Greek wording was similar to καὶ ἡ ἀποδοχὴ αὐτῶν παρὰ ἀλλήλων.[195] This reciprocal "reception"[196] is enacted between "day" and "night" and/or between "sun (light)" and "darkness."

175 Cf. Gen 1:14; *OTP* 1:32–33; Uhlig, *Henochbuch*, 583, whose translation differs.
176 Payne Smith, 2:2301; BDAG, *s.v.* φῶς.
177 On ܫܡܫܐ (*šemšā*) and ἥλιος, see Payne Smith, 2:4223; BDAG, *s.v.* ἥλιος.
178 Payne Smith, 1:1402; BDAG, *s.vv.* σκοτία, σκότος.
179 Payne Smith, 2:1950; BDAG, *s.v.* νύξ.
180 Emerton, "Notes," 516.
181 Ibid., 517.
182 See Charlesworth, *Manuscripts*, 51.
183 See Nöldeke §10.
184 Similarly Blaszczak, 37.
185 Emerton, "Notes," 517; cf. Payne Smith, 1:1576.
186 Payne Smith, 2:2299; BDAG, *s.v.* φωτεινός.
187 BDAG, *s.v.* ἡμέρα.
188 Payne Smith, 1:417; BDAG, *s.vv.* ἄγω, φέρω.
189 See Lattke, "Wörter," 297 = idem, *Bedeutung*, 4:145; BDAG, *s.v.* πρόσωπον; Payne Smith, 1:278–80.
190 Payne Smith, 2:2886, *s.v.* ܥܠ (*ʿal*).
191 Emerton, "Notes," 517.
192 Ibid., 519.
193 Contra Harris and Mingana, 2:285.
194 In opposition to Charlesworth's translation (p. 71), Emerton states: "Against his rendering stands the difficulty of justifying either 'by' or 'portion'" ("Notes," 518).
195 See Payne Smith, 2:3474; LSJ, *s.v.* ἀποδοχή; Spicq, 1:132.
196 See LSJ, *s.v.* ἀποδοχή; Hermann Menge and Otto Güthling, *Enzyklopädisches Wörterbuch der griechischen und deutschen Sprache,* vol. 1: *Griechisch-*

The participle ܡܡܠܠܝܢ (*mmallēn*) in 17b, which corresponds to a form of *(ἀνα)πληρόω*,[197] may be taken for a mistake in the text as copied and corrected to ܡܡܠܠܝܢ (*mmallīn*) and translated as "They speak the beauty of God,"[198] which, in view of Ps 18:2 LXX (*Οἱ οὐρανοὶ διηγοῦνται δόξαν θεοῦ*, "The heavens declare the glory of God"),[199] would make good sense. But Charlesworth is right: "The emendation is not necessary."[200] For Emerton, who takes "the sun and the night of verses 15-16" as subjects in these verses, "it is not clear how they can be said to complete the beauty of God."[201] But a poet who undertakes to ascribe the human term ܝܐܝܘܬܐ (*yāʾyūṯā*) to God (5b; cf. 12:4) may also exercise the license, by use of the *hapax legomenon* ܡܠܠܝ (*mallī*), to let parts and phenomena of creation "bring to full expression" the "beauty" of God, which is otherwise indescribable (cf. Col 1:25).[202]

■ **18-19** Anyone reading or hearing 18a-b, the zenith of the doctrine of creation extending from 8 to 19, would be reminded of the vocabulary of Deutero-Isaiah in the use of the compound and metaphorical preposition ܠܒܪ ܡܢ (*l-ḇar men*). For *πάρεξ ἐμοῦ* (Isa 43:11; cf. Hos 13:4) or *πλὴν ἐμοῦ* (Isa 44:6, 8; 45:5-6, 21) in the LXX is always reproduced by ܠܒܪ ܡܢ (*l-ḇar men*) in the Syriac translations of the Bible.[203] This connection with the biblical passages can be made the more easily, because in one text there is also mention of "sun," "light," and "darkness." Since these terms have just occurred in stanza VI, it is pertinent to quote part of Isa 45:5-7:

> 5. . . . *ἐγὼ κύριος ὁ θεός, καὶ οὐκ ἔστιν ἔτι πλὴν ἐμοῦ θεός, . . .*
> 6. *ἵνα γνῶσιν οἱ ἀπὸ ἀνατολῶν ἡλίου . . . ὅτι οὐκ ἔστιν πλὴν ἐμοῦ· . . .*
> 7. *ἐγὼ ὁ κατασκευάσας φῶς καὶ ποιήσας σκότος, . . .*

> . . . I am the Lord God, and there is no other God beside me; . . .
> That they that come from the east . . . know that there is no God but me . . .
> I am he that prepared light, and formed darkness. . . .[204]

But such comparisons with "passages which assert that 'except for' Jahwe there is no true God" and "that there is no savior besides him"[205] do not explicate this *hapax legomenon* in the context of 18a-b. For 18a is based on 18b (cf. 7:9, 11) and plays a dialectical game with "nothing" (18a) and "everything" (18b).[206] Since the statement is not identical to 34:5a-b ("for everything is above, and below there is nothing"), one might refer to Wisdom and primitive Christian traditions here, for example, Prov 8:22-23 or Col 1:15, which may even have had some verbal influence (cf. also *Hermas*, *Sim.* 89 [IX.12].2). But they do not further the search for the meaning, because the "Lord" of *Ode* 16 is the creator God, whose habitation cannot be localized.

It is possible to advance a step by transforming the negative statement 18a into a positive, which fits into a Stoic tradition that can be traced from 1 Cor 8:6 to Rom 11:36 and on to Marcus Aurelius 4.23.[207] What is important are the formulaic expressions that refer to *θεός*, *ἐξ αὐτοῦ . . . τὰ πάντα* ("from him [viz., God]

Deutsch (17th ed.; Berlin-Schöneberg: Langenscheidt, 1962) *s.v.* *ἀποδοχή* ("Wiederempfangen").

197 Payne Smith, 2:2121; BDAG, *s.vv.* *ἀναπληρόω*, *πληρόω*.

198 Harris and Mingana, 2:284; similarly Emerton, "Notes," 517, 519; Blaszczak, 28, 38; cf. Payne Smith, 2:2109.

199 Rahlfs, 2:17; Brenton, 708.

200 Charlesworth, 73. Instead of Charlesworth's (p. 73) *1 Enoch* 69:20, I would prefer to quote 69:25 as a parallel: "All these believe and give thanks in the presence of the Lord of the Spirits; they glorify with all their might, and please him in all this thanksgiving; they shall thank, glorify, exalt the Lord of the Spirits forever and ever!" (*OTP* 1:49; cf. Uhlig, *Henochbuch*, 629 [his v. 24], whose translation differs somewhat).

201 Emerton, "Notes," 517.

202 I cannot subscribe to Franzmann's verdict (pp. 128–29) that "[t]here is a subtle antithesis between ܘܟܠܗܘܢ . . . and ܡܡܠܠܝܢ" and that it is clear "that merismus is intended by the logic of the movement from opposition to completion."

203 *OTSy*, pt. 3 fasc. 1 and fasc. 4, on these passages.

204 Rahlfs, 2:628; Brenton, 881.

205 Karl Elliger, *Deuterojesaja*, vol. 1: *Jesaja 40,1–45,7* (BKAT 11.1; Neukirchen-Vluyn: Neukirchener Verlag, 1978) 325.

206 Franzmann, 129.

207 See Norden, *Theos*, 240–50, 348–54. "Marcus transfers the formula from God to *Φύσις* who, in Stoic doctrine, is co-essential with him, and therefore uses *ἐν σοί* in the second clause" (ibid., 242).

. . . are all things" [Rom 11:36]); ἐξ οὗ τὰ πάντα ("from whom are all things" [1 Cor 8:6]); and ἐκ σοῦ πάντα, ἐν σοὶ πάντα ("from you [viz., *Physis*] is everything, in you is everything" [Marcus Aurelius 4.23]).[208] This may be called "panentheism," for, although the word was coined only in the nineteenth century for this "doctrine of God encompassing all," it and its ancient roots[209] "unlike pantheism, preserve . . . the dependence of the world on God and his transcendence."[210] Even more cogent is a reference to the *creatio ex nihilo*,[211] which in the final analysis deals with "God's deity,"[212] an idea that must be theologically supported, even if the universe is eternal and infinite.

How should the preposition ܠܒܪ ܡܢ (*l-ḇar men*) in 18a, with the prefixed relative particle ܕ (*d-*), be translated? It corresponds more closely to πάρεκ/παρέκ[213] than to πλήν, and, even in metaphorical use, it preserves its basic sense of place, so "beyond" is preferable to "except" or "besides."[214] Since 18a presupposes the transcendence of the "Lord," its teaching that nothing—not even an archetype or ψυχή—is transcendent, all is immanent, is quite abstract in comparison with later mythological statements.[215]

Verse 18b gives the basis for 18a. The causal ܡܛܠ ܕ (*meṭṭol d-*)[216] is followed by the pre-positioned "personal pronoun of the 3rd person" giving "greater prominence to" the "Lord" of 18a.[217] The following word is first opposed to ܠܝܬ (*layt*) by the use of ܐܝܬ (*ʾīṯ*) with a suffix "strengthened by an enclitic ܗܘܐ (*-wā*)."[218] This compound may remind one of ἦν or *erat* in John 1:1,[219] but it goes transcendentally beyond the beginning, which is the topic in John and also in Gen 1:1. In order to express God's transcendence, its absolutely other and unknown being must be removed, by an imperfect of ܗܘܐ (*hwā*), dependent on ܡܢ ܩܕܡ ܕ (*men qḏām d-*), into the primordial nothingness.[220] Only thus can He be and remain "Lord of all."[221] Since this "Lord" is not one of the classical "gods," 18b can even accept the famous saying of Heraclitus: κόσμον τόνδε, τὸν αὐτὸν ἁπάντων, οὔτε τις θεῶν οὔτε ἀνθρώπων ἐποίησεν, ἀλλ' ἦν ἀεὶ καὶ ἔστιν καὶ ἔσται, "This world-order [the same of all] did none of gods or men make, but it always was and is and shall be" (B 30).[222]

The second bicolon of stanza VII could be simply explicated by referring to a number of the excursuses (4; 9; 12; 22). The first question that arises is whether the plural of ܥܠܡܐ (*ʿālmā*) corresponds to αἰῶνες or to κόσμος. Bauer avoids the Gnostic term "aeons" (cf. 7:11) and uses the neutral term "worlds," since "the conclusion is far removed from dualism and pessimism."[223] However, the plural of αἰών, in a spatial and temporal sense, can also mean "eras of the world" or the "world" as a whole,[224] so it is unnecessary to think of personified beings in this context. Thus, it is quite probable that 𝔊 used οἱ αἰῶνες[225] in a spatial sense, not a temporal one.[226] Of course, 19a reminds one of John 1:10 (καὶ ὁ

208 Willy Theiler, ed. and trans., *Kaiser Marc Aurel, Wege zu sich selbst* (BAWGR; 2nd ed.; Zurich/Munich: Artemis, 1974) 82.

209 See John Macquarrie, "Panentheismus," *TRE* 25 (1995) 612.

210 Ulrich Dierse and Winfried Schröder, "Panentheismus," *HWP* 7 (1989) 48, who do not mention Stoicism at all.

211 Schrage, *1. Korinther*, 2:242.

212 Käsemann, 310 (ET, 320).

213 See Frankenberg, 18.

214 Payne Smith, 1:576; LSJ, *s.v.* πάρεκ.

215 E.g., the *Untitled Text*, chap. 22: "And nothing exists outside of him. . . . There is no place (τόπος) outside of him" (Schmidt and MacDermot, *Jeu*, 276; Schmidt, Till, and Schenke, *Schriften*, 367, lines 9–13).

216 See Nöldeke §360.

217 Ibid., §227.

218 Ibid., §301.

219 See Charlesworth, 73.

220 See Nöldeke §267.

221 Ibid., §217.

222 *FVS* 1:157–58; see G. S. Kirk et al., *The Presocratic Philosophers: A Critical History with a Selection of Texts* (2nd ed.; Cambridge: Cambridge University Press, 1983; repr., 1990) 197–98; Bruno Snell, ed., *Heraklit, Fragmente* (OG/Ger.; 6th ed.; Munich: Heimeran, 1976) 14–15. Parallels from Qumran, already noted by Carmignac ("Auteur," 83) and Charlesworth (p. 73), are listed by Blaszczak (p. 39).

223 Bauer, 597; cf. Charlesworth, 72.

224 BDAG, *s.v.* αἰών; cf. Payne Smith, 2:2898–900.

225 Contra Diettrich, 59.

226 Blaszczak (p. 40) agrees.

κόσμος δι᾽ αὐτοῦ ἐγένετο – ܘܟܠܗ ܒܐܝܕܗ ܗܘܐ) and thus of the personified Logos (cf. Heb 1:2).[227] But the Lord's ܡܠܬܐ (*melltā*) is not "Christ as the Word,"[228] any more than it is in 12:10; it is God's creative word, referred to in 7, 8, and 13, as his power.

In 19b, the parallel to "word" is the phrase "the thought of his heart." The combination of ܡܚܫܒܬܐ (*maḥšabtā*) and ܠܒܐ (*lebbā*) is something of a tautology, but it emphasizes that the "heart" is the "site of thought" (cf. 41:10-11).[229] "Word" and "thought" are also the two sides of the "Greek term *λόγος*."[230]

■ **20** There are three doxologies in the *Odes of Solomon* that are in the third person and addressed to God's "name" (cf. 18:6; 20:10 [= 16:20]; Excursus 39). The two hymnic terms correspond, without doubt, to Greek *δόξα* und *τιμή*[231] (see Excursus 21). The terms originate in the vocabulary of the Psalms, for example, the call to praise in Ps 95:7b LXX (*ἐνέγκατε τῷ κυρίῳ δόξαν καὶ τιμήν*, "bring to the Lord glory and honor"),[232] where the "indirect speech," as in the Ode, "contains in itself the act of praise."[233] This allows no conclusion as to any "cult" for the *Sitz im Leben* of the Ode (cf. Ps 28:1 LXX).[234]

If this two-part doxology was mediated by New Testament texts, it will not have been through anthropological passages such as Heb 2:7 (cf. Ps 8:6 LXX) or christological ones such as Heb 2:9 or 2 Pet 1:17. Tripartite forms like Rom 2:7, 10 and 1 Pet 1:7 do not come under consideration either, even if the terms used, *δόξα* and *τιμή*, in addition to meaning "praise and heavenly recognition,"[235] primarily express "the essential being of God" (cf. Rev 4:9).[236] The texts that come closest to the concluding formula of *Ode* 16 are the doxology in 1 Tim 1:17, framed under "the influence of the Greek-speaking Jewish diaspora,"[237] and the ending of the so-called heavenly liturgy, Rev 4:11.[238] As evidence for a connection to these two passages, there is the fact that in the first the *βασιλεὺς τῶν αἰώνων* ("king of ages") is mentioned (see on 19a above) and the second addresses the "Lord" and "God" in the vocabulary of creation (*σὺ ἔκτισας τὰ πάντα*, "thou didst create all things"), which is reminiscent of stanza VIII.

227 See Gräßer, 1:59–60.
228 Contra Dodd, *Interpretation*, 272.
229 Bauer, 610.
230 Dodd, *Interpretation*, 273.
231 Payne Smith, 1:1624; 2:4027; BDAG, *s.vv.* *δόξα*, *τιμή*, 2.
232 Rahlfs, 2:105; Brenton, 756.
233 Andreas Wagner, "Der Lobaufruf im israelitischen Hymnus als indirekter Sprechakt," in idem, ed., *Studien zur hebräischen Grammatik* (OBO 156; Fribourg: Academic Press; Göttingen: Vandenhoeck & Ruprecht, 1997) 152–54.
234 Ibid., 143, 154. Blaszczak's enumeration of possible cults is purely speculative, as he himself says: "On the basis of the evidence culled from the *Ode* alone, we cannot ascertain the *Sitz im Leben*" (Blaszczak, 40).
235 Käsemann, 55 (ET, 59).
236 Karl Hermann Schelkle, *Die Petrusbriefe. Der Judasbrief* (HThKNT 13.2; 2nd ed.; Freiburg/Basel/Vienna: Herder, 1964) 36.
237 See Lorenz Oberlinner, *Die Pastoralbriefe* (3 vols.; HThKNT 11.2, 1–3; Freiburg: Herder, 1994–96) 1:47.
238 Heinrich Kraft, *Die Offenbarung des Johannes* (HNT 16a; Tübingen: Mohr Siebeck, 1974) 100–102.

17

Ode 17: Mythological Address of the Redeemed Redeemer with a Christological Doxology

(I) 1a I was crowned by my God,
1b and he is my living crown/wreath.
2a And I was justified by my Lord,
2b and my salvation is imperishable.

(II) 3a I was released from vanities and am not a man condemned
3b <***>[a]
4a My bonds were severed by her/it (= <***>?);
4b I received the face and figure of a new person.

(III) 4c And I walked in it and was saved.
5a And the thought of Truth led me
5b and I followed it and did not go astray.
6a And all who saw me were amazed,
6b and I seemed to them like a stranger.
7a And he who knew made me great,
7b the Most High [b]in his complete *plērōma*.
7c And he glorified me[c] by his benevolence
7d and lifted up my *gnōsis* [knowledge] to the height of Truth.
8a And thence he gave me the way of his steps.

(IV) 8b And I opened the gates that were shut,
9a and broke the bars of iron.
9b My own iron glowed
9c and melted before me.
10a And nothing seemed shut to me,
10b because I was the opening[d] of everything.
11a And I went toward all my shut-in ones[e] to set them free,
11b lest I leave any who is bound or who binds.

(V) 12a And I gave my *gnōsis* [knowledge] without jealousy
12b and my consolation through my love.
13a And I sowed my fruits in hearts
13b and transformed them by/in me.
14a And they received my blessing and lived,
14b and were gathered to me and were saved,
15 because they were my members and I their head.

(VI) 16 Glory to thee, our Head, Lord Messiah.
Hallelujah.

a 3b See commentary on 3-4b.
b 7b The text preserved in N begins here with ܒܟܠܗ.
c 7c ܘܫܒܚܢܝ H; ܘܫܒܚܢ N.
d 10b ܡܛܠ ܕܦܬܚܐ H; ܡܛܠ ܕܦܬܚܐ ܓܒܪ̈ N.
e 11a ܐܣܝܪ̈ܝ H; ܐܣܝܪ̈ܐ N; ܐܣܘܪ̈ܝ *v.l.* of another codex in H.

Introduction

Ode 17 is preserved completely in one Syriac manuscript and partly in another.[1] "This Ode is as difficult as the 10th, which is closely related to it."[2] The interpretation is made more difficult because from 7b onward there are two Syriac manuscripts of the *Odes of Solomon*.[3] But even the necessary textual criticism does not provide the main difficulty, which is that the "I" of stanzas I–III, who is to be distinguished from the author or performer of the Ode, speaks of his salvation by "God" the "Lord" and the "Most High," while the speaking "I" of stanzas IV–V describes himself as the "head" and speaks of his own already accomplished liberation and salvation of his "members" (15). There is no indication of a change of grammatical subject, so it is necessary to refer to the final collective doxology, strongly marked by Jewish expectations of the Messiah, to the whole of the highly mythologized first-person address, and to interpret *Ode* 17 as a unity.

To maintain that "[Jesus] Christ speaks" only from 6a[4] on is as arbitrary as declaring *Ode* 17 to be "full of the thought of the Redemption of the Baptized."[5] Equally, the division of connected sections into a "supreme moment of baptism" (1-4) and "hymns of initiation" (5 onward) is justified by neither content nor form.[6] So to begin with, "it is not advisable to cut the Ode in two and assume that an interpolator foolishly mistook the prophetic singer of the first part for the Messiah."[7] The content of the Ode can then be given in précis as "the redeemed one . . . becomes the Redeemer."[8]

Richard Reitzenstein's idea of the "redeemed Redeemer," in the sense of the Manichean mythos, is not completely applicable to *Ode* 17.[9] But this text—like 8:22—shows many similarities with the diversified "Gnostic idea of the Redeemer, which closely connects the Redeemer with the redeemed."[10] Adolfo Omodeo goes even further, saying that *Ode* 17, ending "con un motivo ecclesiastico," is a "documento interessante della religiosità gnostica."[11]

Since there is no mention of a descent by the first-person Redeemer or of ܫܝܘܠ (*šyōl* [שְׁאוֹל]; cf. 15:9; 29:4;

1 Mss.: Codex H, 13a–14a; Codex N, 149ʳ (s). Ed./trans.: Charlesworth, 73–77; Franzmann, 130–38; Lattke, 2:41–66 and 3:XXVII–XXVIII.

2 Harnack, 46.

3 See Lattke, *Bedeutung*, 1:32–77.

4 Charlesworth, 75; Grese, *Corpus*, 178.

5 Bernard, 82.

6 Contra Schille, 78, 86.

7 Gunkel, 306, contra Harnack, 82, 95, 107. Kittel (p. 86), although he comes to the "conclusion" that "an 'I', different from the first, speaks in the second part of the Ode," considers "Harnack's assumption of a quite dim-witted interpolator . . . inadequate, since even such a one must have had a reason for connecting the two parts." Kittel's own solution (p. 86: "the poet generalizes his individual experience of salvation") is quite as problematic as the "conclusion" of Diettrich in 1911, which he calls "wrong" (Kittel, 78). I am not convinced by Diettrich's attempted change of grammatical subject, either. He refers to Wisdom personified in Proverbs 8 and Sirach 24 and says: "The other speaker is not the revealed Christ but Truth personified" (Diettrich, 60). This makes it necessary for him to delete "head" and "anointed one" in the doxology as "Christian interpolations" (Diettrich, 63).

8 Gunkel, 307. In agreement with Gunkel (p. 307), *Ode* 17 can be described as "Song of the Triumph of the Christ." Although Rudolf Abramowski (p. 57) remarks on 8:22, "Even the true-born son is redeemed," he considers that the speaker of *Ode* 17 is "the liberated human being" (p. 60), "a leading member of the community glimpsed in the Odes" (p. 58). But note what Abramowski (p. 57) says on the "two Christs" in discussing 41:15a: "Finally there will be no distinction between the actual and the adopted son." For the "basic purpose" of the *Odes of Solomon* is "the Christ likeness of the Christ believers" (p. 68).

9 Richard Reitzenstein, *Das mandäische Buch des Herrn der Größe und die Evangelienüberlieferung* (SHAW.PH 1919, 12. Abh.; Heidelberg: Winter, 1919) 31–32; idem, *Das iranische Erlösungsmysterium*, 83–92, esp. 86–88. Wolf-Peter Funk (*Die zweite Apokalypse des Jakobus aus Nag-Hammadi-Codex V* [TU 119; Berlin: Akademie-Verlag, 1976] 147) also questions the applicability of the "redeemed Redeemer" to "the speaker in *Odes of Solomon* 17." At the same time he shows that this undivided speaker, like the James of the *Second Apocalypse of James*, is "the type of the subsidiary redeemer, who unites the function of redeemer with the need for redemption in his own person."

10 Rudolph, *Gnosis*, 142.

11 Adolfo Omodeo, "Le Odi di Salomone," *ParPass* 1 (1946) 106–7.

42:11)/Hades (cf. Homer *Iliad* 5.646 [πύλας Ἀίδαο];[12] *Odyssey* 10.490–11.640),[13] it will become necessary to examine whether in stanza IV "the *descensus ad inferos* is under consideration."[14]

Interpretation

■ **1-2** Because of the parallel construction of 1-2, it is better not to follow H but to treat 1 also as a bicolon.[15] That means that the fill word ܕܝܢ (*dēn*), derived from the Biblical Aramaic אדין, which "has acquired its current usage and placing after the first word, following the example of the Greek δέ,"[16] not only has no "syntactic or other function, apart from the poetic,"[17] but has no function in 𝔖, except perhaps as *inclusio* for stanza I. Certainly the particle, which corresponds more to δέ (or καί) than to γάρ, does not "couple" *Ode* 17 to *Ode* 16.[18] In the parallel construction of stanza I, the verbs and the nouns used instrumentally in 1a and 2a interpret each other, as do the grammatical subjects in 1b and 2b, the first singular suffixes of which refer them to the "I," and which are connected to their predicates by a copula.

In both 1a and 2a the preposition ܒ (*b*-) must be translated as "through" or "by," not "in."[19] Although the *hapax legomenon* ܐܬܟܠܠ (*ʾetkallal*), corresponding to the theological passive of στεφανόω, which is quite commonly used later in martyrologies (but cf. *Mart. Pol.* 17:1),[20] imports a term of the vocabulary of "championship" into the metaphorical statement of salvation,[21] it does not imply a personal victory. For this honor to the victor was not given διὰ τὴν εὐσέβειαν, as recorded in an inscription on Delos about the author of a hymn to Sarapis (*IG* 11, fasc. 4, no. 1299, line 9),[22] but without any pious precondition and without any statues visibly erected in a temple (*IG*, line 10: εἰκόνι χαλκεῖ . . . ἐν τῷ ναῷ). And "God" is not here, or anywhere in the *Odes of Solomon*, in competition with Hellenistic gods and goddesses, like the "imperially established" god Sarapis,[23] but as "Lord" (2a) and "Most High" (7b) He transcends all the world.

For 1b the only comparisons are 5:12 and possibly *Ode* 1, if the "Lord," who is also likened to a "wreath" in that Ode, is actually "God" and not the "Kyrios Christos" (see the analysis of 1:1 and 9:8). In any case, this "wreath," which "God" bestows, is not "the baptismal crown,"[24] and not "the living one,"[25] but the "crown of life,"[26] the "salvation at the end of the world."[27] What is unique about this eschatological image is its application to the speaking "I," who will be revealed later as the Redeemer and "Messiah." That he is Jesus is only an assumption, but the most likely one.

Unlike the "hymn to Christ" in 1 Tim 3:16, *Ode* 17:2a is not a "step-up"[28] but simply a parallel statement to

12 Helmut van Thiel, *Homeri Ilias* (Bibliotheca Weidmanniana II; Hildesheim/Zurich/New York: Olms, 1996) 97.

13 Helmut van Thiel, *Homeri Odyssea* (Bibliotheca Weidmanniana I; Hildesheim/Zurich/New York: Olms, 1991) 141–61.

14 Harnack, 47, who decides that it is "not necessary." There are extensive notes by August Vogl—their editor, Brian McNeil, goes so far as to call them a commentary on *Ode* 17 as well as *Odes* 22, 24, and 42 (Vogl, "Oden Salomos 17, 22, 24, 42: Übersetzung und Kommentar," ed. Brian McNeil, *OrChr* 62 [1978] 60–63). In his "editor's notes" McNeil says: "This study forms part of the projected dissertation, 'Christus und Scheol', a study of the treatment in earliest Syriac literature of the descent of Christ to Hades, which was left unfinished at P. Vogl's untimely death in 1972" (p. 75).

15 Already in Harris and Mingana, 2:289; Franzmann, 132, with reasons; Vogl (p. 60) differs.

16 Brockelmann, *Grundriss*, 2:482; cf. idem, *Grammatik*, 44.

17 Contra Lattke, "Wörter," p. 290 = idem, *Bedeutung*, 4:138.

18 Contra Zahn, 692.

19 Franzmann, 131; contra Vogl, 61, who ignores the simile in 5:12.

20 Payne Smith, 1:1731; on *Mart. Pol.* 17:1, see Gerd Buschmann, *Das Martyrium des Polykarp* (KAV 6; Göttingen: Vandenhoeck & Ruprecht, 1998) 328.

21 See BDAG, *s.v.* στεφανόω.

22 Petrus Roussel, ed., *Inscriptiones Deli* (*IG* 11.4; Berlin: Reimer, 1914) 131.

23 Hans Wolfgang Helck, "Sarapis," *KP* 4 (1972) 1549.

24 Contra Bernard, 82.

25 As Vogl (p. 61) thinks.

26 Bauer, 597.

27 Dibelius, *Jakobus*, 119, on Jas 1:12; for other citations, see Payne Smith, 1:1732; BDAG, *s.v.* στέφανος.

28 See Jürgen Roloff, *Der erste Brief an Timotheus*

1a. The connection between the theological passive ἐδικαιώθη—a "use of the word that is quite contrary to St. Paul's usage"[29]—and the Ethpa. of ܙܕܩ (*zdaq*) is the "aspect of winning."[30] But this passage is not concerned with "the exaltation of Jesus"[31] or the "resurrection" in the sense of a final "*confirmation* of his appearance in the realm of the flesh," which will take place "in the realm of the spirit."[32]

As 2b shows, the justification brought about a "salvation" (in 𝔊 certainly σωτηρία; cf. 11:3 and Excursus 5) that cannot be shaken.[33] That it is "imperishable," like eternal life,[34] means that it—and thus the speaking "I"—can partake of the being of God, which does not exist in the infinite universe of beginnings and endings (see Excursus 28). This could lead one, even without recourse to the vocabulary of the mystery religions,[35] to speak of a "deification" as a total "change of being."[36] But the redeemed speaker, who does not allude to any preexistence or incarnation in his case, still distinguishes himself (see on 4b below: πρόσωπον) from "God" the "Lord," the "Most High" (1a, 2a, 7b).

■ **3-4b** Since the somewhat negative statements of salvation in stanza II again merge into "a positive conclusion" (4b), followed immediately by 4c, it would be possible to part company with Franzmann[37] and move 4b to the beginning of stanza III. However, her divisions, apart from her emendation of H, where "3 stands as one line,"[38] are more convincing than earlier attempts.[39] But the easy transition from stanza II to stanza III is less important than the neglected question about the clearly legible instrumental expression ܒܐܝܕܝܗ (*b-iḏēh*) in 4a: "Lit[erally] 'by her hands,' but what is the antecedent of that feminine singular suffix?"[40] The unfounded emendation to "his hands" or "his hand" of Harnack and Diettrich[41] is as unsatisfactory as Harris and Mingana's far-fetched explanation for the emendation.[42] It makes better sense to assume that a line is missing between 3a and 4a in which there was a feminine noun—as subject or object—perhaps ܛܝܒܘܬܐ (*ṭaybūṯā*),[43] ܐܝܕܥܬܐ (*ʾiḏaʿṯā*, cf. 11:4) or ܡܘܗܒܬܐ (*mawhabṯā*; cf. the contexts of 11:9; 15:7; 35:6), or else a causal conjunction and perhaps the term ܢܣܒܬ (*nesbeṯ*), as at the end of 4b.[44]

In 3a, the speaking "I," by the use of the Ethpe. of ܫܪܐ (*šrā*), connects his own experience, expressed in the theological passive, with his activity in the liberation of others (see 11a below).[45] In conjunction with the

(EKKNT 15; Zurich: Benziger; Neukirchen-Vluyn: Neukirchener Verlag, 1988) 203; Lorenz Oberlinner, *Die Pastoralbriefe* (3 vols.; HThKNT 11.2, 1–3; Freiburg: Herder, 1994–96) 1:166.

29 Martin Dibelius, *Die Pastoralbriefe* (HNT 13; 4th ed., ed. Hans Conzelmann; Tübingen: Mohr Siebeck, 1966) 50.

30 Roloff, 205, although he objects to Werner Stenger's exaggeration (*Der Christushymnus 1 Tim 3,16: Eine strukturanalytische Untersuchung* [Regensburger Studien zur Theologie 6; Frankfurt/M.: P. Lang; Bern: H. Lang, 1977] 38)); cf. Payne Smith, 1:1084; BDAG, *s.v.* δικαιόω. "To be justified" = "to be victorious" (Bultmann, "Bedeutung," 128 = idem, *Exegetica*, 85; but see Excursus 25); see also Felix Christ, *Jesus Sophia: Die Sophia-Christologie bei den Synoptikern* (AThANT 57; Zurich: Zwingli, 1970) 71 n. 243.

31 Dibelius, *Pastoralbriefe*, 50; similarly Oberlinner, *Pastoralbriefe*, 1:166. Stenger (*Christushymnus*, 155) takes the statement of justification in 2a, in view of 7b, to be "a Gnostic 'demythologizing' and explicatory reception of the biblical idea of exaltation."

32 Roloff, 205–6.

33 See Payne Smith, 2:3295; BDAG, *s.v.* σωτηρία.

34 Payne Smith, 1:1179; BAGD, *s.v.* ἄφθαρτος.

35 Richard Reitzenstein, *Die hellenistischen Mysterienreligionen nach ihren Grundgedanken und Wirkungen* (repr. of 3rd ed. 1927 [Teubner]; Darmstadt: Wissenschaftliche Buchgesellschaft, 1966) 252–65.

36 See Roloff, 205; BDAG, *s.v.* δικαιόω.

37 Franzmann, 134.

38 Ibid., 132.

39 E.g., Harris and Mingana, 2:289; Charlesworth, 75.

40 Lattke, *Oden*, 147.

41 Harnack, 46; Diettrich, 61.

42 Harris and Mingana, 2:291: "The writer seems to have thought that he was emancipated 'by the thought of Truth' (fem.) which follows in the next verse, and so added the feminine suffix."

43 See Grimme, 41.

44 This presumed lacuna of 3b is shown by <* * *> in the text (cf. textual criticism of 23:4b). Since the papyrus of *Ode* 11 has an insertion in the manuscript (see Lattke, *Bedeutung*, 1a:62 on 11:16) a similar omission in copying or even translating is quite conceivable.

45 "The preposition ܠ with reflexive personal pronoun often stands alongside of a verb, without essentially modifying its meaning (*Dativus ethicus*)" (Nöldeke §224).

preposition ܡܢ (*men*), the verb corresponds to a form of ἀπολύω.[46] As in 11:8b, the feminine emphatic plural of ܣܪܝܩܐ (*srīqā*) is more likely to correspond to μάταια than to μάταιοι.[47] The meaning is not the "nothingness" of opponents or idols but the futility and decay of this world and age (cf. Rom 8:18-21). The liberation from it is simultaneously—not as a consequence—the lifting of damnation (cf., besides Rom 8:1, Mark 16:16). The participle of ܚܐܒ, ܚܒ (*ḥāḇ*), together with ܐܝܬ (*ʾīṯ*) + first singular suffix, cannot be the translation of the adjective ἔνοχος used with a genitive[48] but, according to the construction used, represents either κατάκριτος or ἀκατάκριτος.[49] The basic forensic meaning of these terms has been expanded into general and mythological use.

Without further speculation on the actuality and wording of any missing second colon 3b (see <* * *> above), it is time to turn to 4a, where the mythological imagery continues in parallel with 3a. Although the two *hapax legomena* ܚܢܩܐ (*ḥnāqē*, plural of ܚܢܩܐ [*ḥnāqā*]) and ܐܬܦܣܩ (*ʾeṯpassaq*) may be verbally reminiscent of Ps 2:3a (Διαρρήξωμεν τοὺς δεσμοὺς αὐτῶν ["Let us break through their bonds"]; cf. ܢܦܣܩ ܚܢܩܝܗܘܢ [*npasseq ḥnāqayhōn*]),[50] there is here no allusion to the "bonds" of the "rule of Yahweh and his anointed."[51] For the "bonds" or "fetters" in this text (as in 22:4) are a negative image of subjection and mundanity, which of course includes "external powers."[52] What power—described by a feminine term—representing "God" the "Lord" mythologically broke the bonds cannot be determined. On the whole, one may echo Vogl's resigned conclusion: "A workable, reasoned explanation of this difficult passage cannot be found."[53]

Verse 4b is the first climax of *Ode* 17; indeed Greßmann, using Dibelius's work somewhat freely, calls it the "key to understanding this Ode."[54] But the speaker is not an "initiate"[55] who becomes "godlike."[56] First, it is clear that the "I" does not use the Greek loanword ܦܪܨܘܦܐ (*parṣōpā* = πρόσωπον) as meaning his "face" but as his "person" in the classical sense of his rhetorical and social "role" (see 31:5 and for the sense again 1 Tim 3:16).[57] Second, there is the question what the Greek equivalent of ܐܦܐ (*ʾappē*) was. "Perhaps ὄψις is the best candidate (cf. John 11:44 in the Peshitta). Then ܕܡܘܬܐ could represent εἶδος or μορφή."[58] The emphasis is on the *newness* of the person/role, which may be compared to 11:11 ("The Lord renewed me by his garment") and 33:12b ("incorruption in the new world"; cf. also 36:5). The Pe. ܢܣܒ (*nsaḇ*)—like its equivalent (ἀνα)λαμβάνω—can be used more actively as "to take" or more passively as "to receive."[59] The two senses are here united. The speaking "I" received the appearance and shape of a new *persona* and took on a new role, which is further described in stanza III in relation to "truth" and the

46 Payne Smith, 2:4309; BDAG, *s.v.* ἀπολύω; Frankenberg, 18: ἀπολέλυμαι.

47 Payne Smith, 2:2747; BDAG, *s.v.* μάταιος.

48 Contra Frankenberg, 18.

49 See Payne Smith, 1:1214; BDAG, *s.vv.* κατάκριτος, ἀκατάκριτος; Nöldeke §303. This verse should be compared to 31:8, where the justified Lord (31:5) says: "They condemned me . . . who had not been condemned."

50 Rahlfs, 2:1; Brenton, 699; *OTSy*, pt. 2 fasc. 3, on this passage.

51 Kraus, *Psalmen*, 11, 16, 22; see also Payne Smith, 1:1324, 2:3195; BDAG, *s.vv.* δεσμός and διαρρήγνυμι, διαρήσσω.

52 Kraus, *Psalmen*, 16.

53 Vogl, 61.

54 Greßmann, 452.

55 Contra Martin Dibelius, "Ἐπίγνωσις ἀληθείας," in *Neutestamentliche Studien Georg Heinrici zu seinem 70. Geburtstag (14. März 1914)* (Leipzig: Hinrichs, 1914), quoted from idem, *Urchristentum*, 74.

56 Contra Greßmann, 452.

57 See BDAG, and Frisk, *s.v.* πρόσωπον. "Person" in the sense of "personality" or "individuality" is a later "creation of the Christian tradition, although the abstract use of the word in the vocabulary of rhetoric and law will have prepared the ground for it" (Manfred Fuhrmann, "Person I. Von der Antike bis zum Mittelalter," *HWP* 7 [1989] 269). The "Christian dogma," in which the idea of person is very important (ibid., 274–80), must not be covertly inserted into the *Odes of Solomon*.

58 Lattke, "Wörter," 298 = idem, *Bedeutung*, 4:146–47; see also Payne Smith, 1:278–80, 914; BDAG, *s.v.* μορφή (Mark 16:12; Phil 2:6-7). It must be remembered that in Gen 1:26 ὁμοίωσις and ܕܡܘܬܐ (*dmūṯā*) are equivalent (cf. 7:4 and BDAG, *s.v.* ὁμοίωμα, 3 [Rom 8:3; Phil 2:7]). Frankenberg's retroversion (p. 18) of ܐܦܐ (*ʾappē*) to εἶδος cannot be supported.

59 Payne Smith, 2:2392; BDAG, *s.vv.* ἀναλαμβάνω,

"Most High" and the experience of being a stranger, which appears in its full weight in stanzas IV–V.[60]

■ **4c-8a** As already noted at the beginning of stanza II, stanza III flows on from II, with 4c connecting to 4b by the use of ܒܗ (*b-* + third masculine singular suffix), which refers to "person." There is a similarly easy connection from stanza III to IV in 8a-b. Since both "truth" in 5a and 7d and the words derived from the root ܗܠܟ in 4c and 8a form the *inclusio* of stanza III, the commentary should follow Franzmann's analysis, including her division into the shorter strophes 4c-5b, 6a-b, and 7a-8a.[61] Vogl's artificially constructed bicola only serve to divide connected statements of salvation as well as self-descriptions of the speaking "I."[62]

The "being saved" of 4c is not a consequence of "walking" in the new role but synonymous with it.[63] The "I" had, after all, already witnessed to its own eternal "salvation" in 2b. The Pa. ܗܠܟ (*hallek*) in this verse probably corresponds to the soteriological use of περιπατέω,[64] and the Ethpe. of ܦܪܩ (*praq*) certainly represents a passive form of σῴζω.[65]

The third feminine singular suffix in 5b refers to ܡܚܫܒܬܐ (*maḥšabṯā*) in 5a; the emphasis is not on "thinking" or "thought"[66] but on the personified ܫܪܪܐ (*šrārā*; cf. *Ode* 38 and Excursus 1). In 𝔊 the genitive of ἀλήθεια ("truth") will have been understood as a subjective one.[67] The Pe. ܕܒܪ (*dbar*), perhaps inspired by Wis 9:11 (ὁδηγήσει με, "she will guide me"), which occurs again in *Ode* 38:1, also belongs to the extended imagery of ways and walking.[68] Because of the connection with the key word *gnōsis* (see on 7d below), there is a similarity with a singular saying in *Corp. Herm.* 10.21: ὁ νοῦς . . . ὁδηγεῖ αὐτὴν ἐπὶ τὸ τῆς γνώσεως φῶς ("the *Nous* . . . guides her [viz., the soul] to the light of *gnōsis*").[69]

Further terms of motion in 5b argue for the continuity of 4c-5b. The speaking "I," in following the "thought" of "truth" personified, did not go astray.[70] The combination of ܐܙܠ (*ʾezal*) and ܒܬܪ (*bāṯar*) + third feminine singular suffix corresponds to a form of the verb ἀκολουθέω,[71] though not in the sense of follower-disciple. The negated Pe. ܛܥܐ (*ṭʿā*) is not so much a denial of error or deception as an affirmation of the mythological guidance.[72] Frankenberg's retroversion of 5b (καὶ ἀκολουθήσας αὐτῇ οὐ πεπλάνημαι) can be accepted.[73]

Harnack already made a connection between the singular bicolon 6 and the "person" statement in 4b.[74]

λαμβάνω. In any case, the expression λαμβάνειν πρόσωπον, which goes back to the Old Testament, is not in question here (cf. Luke 20:21; Gal 2:6; BDAG, *s.v.* πρόσωπον, 1b).

60 The term "person" is not to be found among the words describing the objects of the metaphorically used verbs "to put on, to don, to dress oneself" (see Table 2). So one must question whether "the idea of raiment" is really to be found in the "background" and whether the subject is actually the "putting on or wearing the likeness of the heavenly Redeemer" (see Egon Brandenburger, *Adam und Christus: Exegetisch-religionsgeschichtliche Untersuchung zu Röm. 5,12-21 [1. Kor. 15]* [WMANT 7; Neukirchen-Vluyn: Neukirchener Verlag, 1962] 147–48). Brandenburger (p. 150) combines 17:4 with 17:14-15 and declares: "*Ode Sol.* 17 shows how, in Christian Gnosticism, the extra-Christian Adam-Anthropos-theory, already merged with the concept of the enormous, all-encompassing Anthropos (primeval man), consisting of head and members, that belonged originally to a purely cosmological theory, was taken up and used in reference to Christ the Redeemer."

61 Franzmann, 134.

62 Vogl, 60.

63 Cf. 8:22 on the redeemed Redeemer; and 10:6 on the close connection of these verbs.

64 Payne Smith, 1:1014; BDAG, *s.v.* περιπατέω. Cf. Rom 6:4 for the expression; also the imperatives of salvation in 23:4 and 33:13.

65 See Excursuses 5 and 15; also Payne Smith, 2:3294; BDAG, *s.v.* σῴζω.

66 See Excursus 9; also Payne Smith, 1:1397.

67 Payne Smith, 2:4304; BDAG, *s.v.* ἀλήθεια.

68 Payne Smith, 1:811. "The ܬ of the 3rd sing[ular] fem[inine] in the perf[ect] (at least according to the usual pronunciation) remains always soft" (Nöldeke §23.G).

69 Colpe and Holzhausen, 99, 111; BDAG, *s.v.* γνῶσις.

70 Cf. 15:6; 38:4-5; Wis 5:6; but Jas 5:19 is not a parallel.

71 Payne Smith, 1:107, 626; BDAG, *s.v.* ἀκολουθέω.

72 Payne Smith, 1:1492; BDAG, *s.v.* πλανάω.

73 Frankenberg, 18.

74 Harnack, 46, with references to 28:14 and 41:8; cf. also 28:8 and Franzmann, 135.

This new guise/role is a good reason for the amazement at the stranger, although he is not a completely "new man."[75] The only thing that can be said about the astonished spectators in this mythological-soteriological context is that they did not recognize the redeemed speaker. The common word ܚܙܐ (*ḥzā*), used in this nonspecific way in 6a, will refer primarily to non-Gnostics, although "members" who are yet to be redeemed may be included (see on 15 below).[76] This passage, unlike 28:8 and 41:8, uses the *hapax legomenon* ܬܡܗ (*tmah*),[77] which can represent a number of Greek verbs. No particular emphasis seems to be laid on the marvelous.[78]

The statement in 6b with the unique occurrence of the Greek loanword ξένος[79] is quite unconnected to any possible Docetism in the *Odes of Solomon*, which Charlesworth seems to suspect;[80] it is a common motif in Hellenism, as can be seen from Luke 24:16: *οἱ δὲ ὀφθαλμοὶ αὐτῶν ἐκρατοῦντο τοῦ μὴ ἐπιγνῶναι αὐτόν* ("But their eyes were kept from recognizing him").[81] The Ethpe. of ܣܒܪ (*sḇar*) does not imply any sort of epiphany (cf. already 7:4b). Instead of Frankenberg's free retroversion (*καὶ ὡς ξένον με ἐνόμισαν*),[82] it may be preferable to use δοκέω (with dative of the person) and suggest the following for a Greek equivalent: *καὶ ὡς ξένος ἔδοξα αὐτοῖς*.[83]

Several authors have remarked that something is wrong with the beginning of the last strophe of stanza III. Labourt and Batiffol say that "it is impossible that one suffix suffices for two verbs."[84] Instead of "inserting ܠ after ܗܘܐ ܝܕܥ" they prefer to assume "the omission of several words." Harris and Mingana accept this suggestion,[85] while Charlesworth translates "He who knew,"[86] and Vogl takes the expression ܘܗܘ ܕܝܕܥ ܗܘ to be "simply a statement about God" and translates it, "the one who knows."[87] This also solves the next problem, which could have complicated things further. For if the last word of line 7a in the manuscript were ܘܪܒܝܢ, it would have to be emended, and the emendation is less likely to be Harris and Mingana's ܘܪܒܝܢܝ ("and brought me up")[88] than Charlesworth's ܘܐܘܪܒܢ (assuming "haplography").[89] Vogl makes any emendation unnecessary, since according to his reading the last word is ܐܘܪܒܢ.[90] The term ܪܒܝܢ (*rabbyan*) is the Pa. of ܪܒܝ (*rabbī*) + first singular accusative suffix,[91] while ܐܘܪܒܢ (*ʾawrḇan*) is the Aph. of ܪܒ (*ʾireḇ*) with suffix.[92] The participle of ܝܕܥ (*ʾidaʿ*), therefore, is not modified by the suffix ܗܘܐ (*-wā*),[93] but is used as a predicative adjective with enclitic ܗܘ (*-ū*).[94] The only problem lies in the absolute use of ܝܕܥ or γινώσκω,[95] which does not fit into the general pattern of its use in the *Odes of Solomon* (but cf. 26:12 and Excursus 7, especially on the subjective genitive).

If Vogl's reading is correct, 7b is in apposition to the subject of 7a, which must be construed as a relative clause. This makes an end of translations that insert "is."[96] It is true that "7a and 7b form the inclusio for the major section of the strophe (7a-d) by the repetition of

75 Contra Harnack, 46.

76 On the possible verbs of seeing, see Payne Smith, 1:1233.

77 Payne Smith, 2:4455.

78 But cf. BDAG, *s.v.* θαῦμα κτλ.

79 See Lattke, "Wörter," 294 = idem, *Bedeutung*, 142–43; Franzmann, "Strangers," 29–31.

80 Charlesworth, 76; cf. the comprehensive discussion in Labourt and Batiffol, 94–98.

81 See Wolfgang Wiefel, *Das Evangelium nach Lukas* (ThHKNT 3; Berlin: Evangelische Verlagsanstalt, 1987 [©1988]) 409; Rudolf Bultmann, *Die Geschichte der synoptischen Tradition* (2nd ed., 1931; Afterword by Gerd Theissen; FRLANT 29 = N.F. 12; 10th ed.; Göttingen: Vandenhoeck & Ruprecht, 1995) 310. In Mark 16:12 it is even said that the Risen One ἐφανηρώθη ἐν ἑτέρᾳ μορφῇ ("appeared in another form"; see on 4b above). *Ode* 17, however, shows no trace of the "motif of recognition" (Wiefel, 408–9).

82 Frankenberg, 18.

83 Payne Smith, 2:2510; BDAG, *s.v.* δοκέω.

84 Labourt and Batiffol, 18.

85 Harris and Mingana, vol. 1, on this passage; 2:291.

86 Charlesworth, 75.

87 Vogl, 60, 62.

88 Harris and Mingana, 2:291.

89 Charlesworth, 74, 76.

90 A recent rechecking of H has shown that the reading ܗܘ ܐܘܪܒܢ gives a more likely division of the letter sequence ܗܘܐܘܪܒܢ than ܗܘܐ ܘܪܒܢ; see Charlesworth, *Manuscripts*, 53 line 2.

91 Payne Smith, 2:3171; BDAG, *s.v.* ἐκτρέφω.

92 Payne Smith, 1:1628; BDAG, *s.v.* μεγαλύνω.

93 Cf. Nöldeke §277.

94 Ibid. §269.

95 Payne Smith, 1:1554; BDAG, *s.v.* γινώσκω.

96 E.g., Bauer, *Oden*, 37; Bauer, 597: "and he, who has knowledge, and allowed me to grow, *is* the Most High in his perfection." According to Bauer's own reading, he should have translated "who *had* knowledge" (see Nöldeke §277). My own earlier

the root ܫܠܡ,"[97] but 7b-d are also dominated by words derived from the root ܪܘܡ, most importantly the divine title ὕψιστος = ܡܪܝܡܐ (*mrayymā*). What the meaning of ܫܘܡܠܝܐ (*šumlāyā*)/πλήρωμα is in this passage will become clearer following this excursus (see also Excursus 35).

Excursus 17: "To Exalt" and "To Be Exalted," "Most High," and "Height" in the *Odes of Solomon*

If the passages in the *Odes of Solomon* containing these terms, together with other related passages containing such terms as "descent" (12:6), "descended" (42:12), and "ascent" (35:7), "above"[98] and "below" (34:4-5), "causes me to descend" (22:1) and "to ascend" (22:1), "caused me to ascend" (29:4),[99] were marked on a graph, as suggested by Franzmann in "The World-View of the Odist," which she sees as "a universe radically divided into two regions: light and darkness,"[100] the spatial distribution would appear quite clearly. But even the terms "above" and "below," taken together with John 8:23, open the door to the great classical philosophical debates on earth, heaven, and cosmos.[101] Since "heaven" occurs only once among the statements of creation (16:11),[102] it is not possible to declare generally for the *Odes of Solomon* that "to imagine the deity in heaven and to equate heavenly and divine is a presupposition for primitive Christianity as much as for Judaism and Hellenism."[103] There is also the question whether "paradise" is to be placed in the spheres above (11:16-24; 20:7)[104] or the realm of the dead, thought to be subterranean (see 15:9; 29:4; 42:11). A unitary "worldview" can no more be found in the *Odes of Solomon* than in Greco-Roman literature,[105] the Old Testament,[106] the New Testament,[107] or the systems of Gnosticism,[108] not to mention all the varied pseudepigrapha of early Judaism and primitive Christianity. This note of caution refers to all the mythological elements in the soteriology of the *Odes of Solomon*.[109] In addition, for some of the terms under discussion, it will be necessary to consider to what extent they were intended to carry a mythologically spatial meaning, whether they would already have been interpreted existentially in antiquity, and how profoundly the theology in each case would have influenced the production and use of these soteriological poems. The majority of the words under consideration are derived from the root ܪܘܡ, ܪܡ (*rām*), so they will first be listed in dictionary order, with the number of times each is used and suggestions as to possible Greek equivalents.

- Ethpe. ܐܬܬܪܝܡ (*ʾettrīm* [8]), usually like a passive of ὑψόω, sometimes as a passive of (ἐπ)αἴρω.[110]
- Palp. ܪܡܪܡ (*ramrem* [2]), like (ἀν)υψόω;[111] synonym of Aph. ܐܪܝܡ (see below).
- Masculine emphatic passive participle ܡܪܝܡܐ (*mrayymā* [28]), like ὁ ὕψιστος; in 3:6 and 23:18 it may be an attributive adjective;[112] next to ܡܪܝܐ (*māryā*, "Lord") it is the most common name/title for "God" (ܐܠܗܐ [*ʾallāhā*] occurs only fifteen times).

translations must also be amended (Lattke, *Bedeutung*, 1:123; idem, *Oden*, 147).

97 Franzmann, 135.

98 The reading of 11:12a 𝔖 ("from above he gave me rest") is probably secondary to the one in 𝔊 ("he recalled me to life").

99 *Ode* 29:4 speaks of the "mouth of death" in parallel to the "deeps of Sheol" (cf. 15:9 and 42:11).

100 Franzmann, "Study," 384–86 ("The World-View of the Odist").

101 See Friedrich Büchsel, "ἄνω, κτλ.," *ThWNT* 1 (1933) 377; *TDNT* 1:377; idem, "κάτω, κτλ.," *ThWNT* 3 (1938) 642; *TDNT* 3:640; Hermann Sasse, "αἰών, αἰώνιος," *ThWNT* 1 (1933) 203–5; *TDNT* 1:203–5; idem, "γῆ, ἐπίγειος," *ThWNT* 1 (1933) 677; *TDNT* 1:678–79; idem, "κοσμέω, κόσμος, κτλ.," *ThWNT* 3 (1938) 869–87; *TDNT* 3:869–88; Helmut Traub, "οὐρανός, κτλ. A, C–E," *ThWNT* 5 (1954) 497–501; *TDNT* 5:497–501.

102 Gerhard von Rad, "οὐρανός, κτλ. B," *ThWNT* 5 (1954) 503; *TDNT* 5:504.

103 Büchsel, "ἄνω," *ThWNT* 1:376; *TDNT* 1:376–77.

104 See the "Diagram of the Ophites" in Rudolph, *Gnosis*, 78–79.

105 See Frederick C. Grant, "Weltbild I D. Griechisch-römische Welt," *RGG*^{3} 6 (1962) 1613–15, but also idem, *Hellenistic Religions: The Age of Syncretism* (Library of Liberal Arts; Indianapolis: Bobbs-Merrill, 1953, repr., 1977) 178–96: "Sallustius concerning the gods and the universe."

106 See Hans Wilhelm Hertzberg, "Weltbild II. Im AT," *RGG*^{3} 6 (1962) 1615–18.

107 See Erich Dinkler, "Weltbild III. Im NT," *RGG*^{3} 6 (1962) 1618–21.

108 Rudolph, *Gnosis*, 76–98.

109 On the New Testament, see Rudolf Bultmann, "Mythos und Mythologie IV. Im NT," *RGG*^{3} 4 (1960) 1278–82.

110 Payne Smith, 2:3858; BDAG, *s.vv.* αἴρω, ἐπαίρω, ὑψόω.

111 Payne Smith, 2:3858; BDAG, *s.v.* ὑψόω; *LEH*, *s.vv.* ἀνυψόω, ὑψόω.

112 Payne Smith, 2:3858; BDAG, *s.v.* ὕψιστος.

- Aph. ܐܪܝܡ (ʾarīm [9]), not only like ὑψόω, also like (ἐπ)αίρω;[113] synonym of Palp. ܪܡܪܡ (see above).
- Masculine noun ܪܘܡܐ (*rawmā* [2 in H, 3 in N]), either like ὑψηλός used as a noun (τὰ ὑψηλά) or like ὕψος/ὕψωμα;[114] synonym of ܡܪܘܡܐ (see below).
- Masculine singular adjective ܪܡܐ (*rāmā* [1]), probably like ὑψηλός (cf. commentary on 33:3).[115]
- Adjective used as noun ܡܪܘܡܐ (*mrawmā* [6 in H, 5 in N]), usually like ὕψος, in 10:5 like ἐν ὑψηλοῖς;[116] synonym of ܪܘܡܐ (see above).

The atypical occurrences, in which there is neither mythological exaltation nor existential raising up, may be taken first. Waves "rise up" (39:11); hatred is to be "lifted" from the earth (7:20); wisdom is lacking among those who "were arrogant" (24:11). "Lifting" the "arms" "on high" (21:1) is no more than "stretching out" or "extending" the hands (cf. 27:1; 35:7; 37:1a; 42:1). *Ode* 21:1—as well as 35:7 and 37:1a—is in an Ode that contains several occurrences of raising up (see below). The same may be said of 25:8 s ("you removed from me my garments of skin"; see on 25:9 below). The "lifting up" of the voice gains in meaning by being directed to the "Most High" (31:4; 37:1b). The passage where the *hapax legomenon* ܪܡܐ (*rāmā*) is combined with ܪܫܐ (*rēšā*) to mean "peak" has already been mentioned (33:3). The image is probably of a "high" mountain in this world, rather than the mythological "heights," which will be discussed next.

That the terms ܪܘܡܐ (*rawmā*) and ܡܪܘܡܐ (*mrawmā*) are synonyms is shown by 36:1b-2a in H. The "height" of the Lord is described by the parallel terms "*plērōma*/perfection" and "glory" (36:2b; cf. 17:7b). That is why the "heights" not only complement the points of the compass (26:5-6) by adding the vertical dimension, but also signify the transcendence of the "Lord," the "Most High" (26:7 and context). This is where the praising in the "heights" takes place (10:5c; cf. 29:11). The "height" in 21:1a probably describes only the direction of the lifted arms (see above), but the "height of truth" in 17:7d abstractly presents a Gnostic goal. Without the help of mythological dualism it is hardly possible to understand the descent from "the height" and the ascent from the "deeps" (22:1; cf. 34:4-5). How the will that descended from "on high" (23:5) is connected with the heavenly letter will have to be considered in the commentary on *Ode* 23.

Certain occurrences of "height" are expressly connected with the active verbs "exalt" and "raise up," whose subject is the "Most High" (17:7d, with "understanding" as object) or the "spirit of the Lord" (36:1). "My helper" who "lifted me up" (21:2) also refers to this Lord. The dualism of light and darkness (21:3; see on 21:6 below) should not limit the metaphorical content of this verb to movement in space. On the other hand, theological "exaltation" is more than an enthusiastic lifting of the emotions. This is relevant to 25:9a, which depends on Ps 117:16 LXX (δεξιὰ κυρίου ὕψωσέν με), and to 29:3a-b, where the two Syriac verbs are used as parallels. Whether these verbs describe a lifting up that rescues from the mythological place of Hades, as envisaged in 29:4, will be discussed later (meanwhile cf. Ps 30:3 and Wis 16:13). Since theologically both "doxa" and "height" can be attributed to the Lord (cf., e.g., Luke 2:14, δόξα ἐν ὑψίστοις θεῷ), the hymnic parallel of "praise" and "exalt" offers no conceptual difficulties (26:4b).[117]

The use of ܐܪܝܡ (*ʾarīm*) and ܪܡܪܡ (*ramrem*) in an active sense corresponds to the use of ܐܬܬܪܝܡ (*ʾettrīm*) as a theological passive. It is noticeable that "to be exalted" is twice used as the opposite of a negative term. In the first case, the despised are exhorted: "now be lifted up" (8:5a; on the sense of the same verb together with "righteousness" as subject in 8:5b, see the commentary on *Ode* 8). In the second case also, the key word "righteousness" appears, referring this time to the Savior as "the man who was humbled and was exalted" (41:12).[118] Whether the phrase that follows it, ܒܙܕܝܩܘܬܐ ܕܝܠܗ (*b-zaddīqūṯā ḏīleh*), should be understood instrumentally[119] will be discussed in the exegesis. Just as ambiguous is the term ܒܢܘܗܪܐ (*b-nuhrā*), which follows the first person statement in 21:6 ("I was lifted up"). The question is whether "light" is the "means of exaltation" (see Excursus 10) or is meant in some spatial sense in this verse. Finally, there is 18:1a, where the Gnostic "I" says: "My heart was lifted up by the love of the Most High and overflowed." The

113 Payne Smith, 2:3858–59; BDAG, *s.vv.* αἴρω, ἐπαίρω, ὑψόω.

114 Payne Smith, 2:3860; BDAG, *s.v.* ὕψος.

115 Payne Smith, 2:3861; BDAG, *s.v.* ὑψηλός.

116 Payne Smith, 2:3864; BDAG, *s.vv.* ὑψηλός, ὕψος.

117 See Georg Bertram, "ὕψος, ὑψόω, κτλ.," *ThWNT* 8 (1969) 605; *TDNT* 8:608.

118 See Bertram, "ὕψος," *ThWNT* 8:606, on Phil 2:8-9; *TDNT* 8:608.

119 See Lattke, *Oden*, 210.

parallelism of ܐܬܬܪܝܡ (ʾettrīm) and ܐܬܝܬܪ (ʾetyattar) suggests that the meaning is existential, not spatial.

The frequency of the use of ܡܪܝܡܐ (*mrayymā*), corresponding to ὁ ὕψιστος ("the Most High"), as a "title of God" in the *Odes of Solomon*, as compared to early Christian writings—and also to the Qumran texts—is quite striking.[120] For Hellenistic people and Greek-speaking Jews, this "name of God" was very familiar. The original image of spatial or celestial heights was no longer dominant by the time the *Odes of Solomon* were composed. This is true also of the *Odes* themselves, where this "title" is an expression of profound monotheism with no implication of any hierarchy of gods. For this reason it may have seemed to non-Jewish Greek and other inhabitants of the Roman Empire that their pantheons were being besieged by this "Hypsistos."[121]

Before discussing the individual passages, a simplified table can show how often the four theological terms "Most High," "God," "Lord," and "Father" define each other in their immediate context in the *Odes of Solomon*.

Most High	God	Lord*	Father†
2	2	2	2
3	3	3	3
1	–	1	1
4	4	–	–
14	–	14	–
3	–	–	3
1	–	–	–
–	6	6	–
–	1	–	1
–	–	3	3
–	–	–	2

* Only 29 occurrences are relevant. "Lord" actually occurs much more often; cf. Lattke, *Oden*, 268–69. Given how often they are used "Lord" and "Most High" are found together 20 times.

† Only 12 of the 14 occurrences need to be noticed; 14:1 and 31:13 do not fit the parameters.

It is significant that "Most High" is very seldom found in a context of mythologically conceived spatial elevation or any other-worldly place (35:7; perhaps also 17:7 and 41:13 according to the sense of *plērōma*). Even the "rest with the Most High" need not be understood in a metaphorically transferred sense as describing a place (26:10). It is possible to raise one's voice to the Most High (31:4; 37:1), just as one may glorify him (29:11; cf. 10:4) or simply address him confidingly (5:2). The abandonment of vanities corresponds to a turning toward the Most High (11:9), who is known by his saints (7:16).

Actions of the Most High are very rarely expressed in human terms. Metaphorically, the Most High circumcises by his holy spirit (11:2) or breathes his breath into the Gnostics (18:15).

If 3:6b and 23:4b (H) are accepted as statements concerning the ἀφθονία of the Most High (cf. 11:6b), they fit into the pattern of the many genitive constructions, including the drink "*from* the Most High" (6:12), his "word" given to the Aeons (12:4), and the "son of truth *from* the Father, the Most High" (23:18; see on 41:13 below). Without finally deciding what sort of genitive it is in each case, it is possible to list the terms thus qualified: "grace" (7:22), "love" (18:1), "*gnōsis*" (8:8; 23:4), "mind" (9:5; 18:14), "mouth" (12:11), "spirit" (28:19), "holy power" (32:3; cf. Luke 1:35), "greatness" (36:5), "name" (39:8), and "son of the Most High" (41:12; cf. Luke 1:32). This son, who has already been mentioned (41:12, "humbled and exalted"), is also said to have appeared "in the *plērōma* of his father" (41:13). This neatly returns us to the apposition in 17:7b.[122]

As in several other cases, the meaning of the masculine ܫܘܡܠܝܐ (*šumlāyā*), derived from the Shaph. ܫܡܠܝ (*šamlī*), here wavers between τελειότης[123] and πλήρωμα.[124] Because of the Gnostic tinge this word has in the *Odes of Solomon*, "*plērōma*" can be left untranslated, even if it was not yet a technical term, but became one perhaps partly under the influence of the *Odes*.[125] The

120 Cf. Bertram, "ὕψος," *ThWNT* 8:613–19; *TDNT* 8:614–20; Carsten Colpe and Andreas Löw, "Hypsistos (Theos)," *RAC* 16 (1994) 1051–52, although the *Odes of Solomon*, unfortunately, are not mentioned there.

121 Colpe and Löw, "Hypsistos (Theos)," *RAC* 16 (1994) 1039–51.

122 In the commentary on *Ode* 36, Blaszczak's eight-part "survey" of the "motif of ascent to the heavens" will be more fully considered (Blaszczak, 15–25). But reference to it must be made here together with mention of Schnackenburg's excursus entitled "Exaltation and Glorification of Jesus" (Schnackenburg, *Johannesenvangelium*, 2:498–512). It is astounding how few cross-connections there are on this subject between the Fourth Gospel and the *Odes of Solomon*.

123 BDAG, *s.v.* τελειότης; cf. Greßmann, 453 and Bauer, 597 ("perfection").

124 Payne Smith, 2:2128; BDAG, *s.v.* πλήρωμα.

125 See Rudolph, *Gnosis*, 450, *s.v.* "Pleroma," esp. 76.

preposition of place ܒ (*b-*) and the appositional "ܠܗ . . . with a pronominal suffix of its own"[126] that precedes ܫܘܡܠܝܗ (*šumlāyeh*) declare this "complete perfection" to be the mythological domain of the Most High, a place that exists only in words. Philosophically the *plērōma* is "complete t[ranscendence],"[127] distinct even from Augustine's "region of unending abundance" (*Conf.* 11.10.24).[128]

Vogl prefers the N reading ܘܫܒܝܚ (*wa-šb̲īḥ*, "and the glorified one"),[129] but Franzmann has shown that "[t]he context of 7-8a demands the H reading."[130] The Pa. ܫܒܚ (*šabbaḥ*), with first singular objective suffix, here in 7c means not "to praise" but "to make glorious."[131] As a ruler in antiquity, by his "clemency, mildness and magnanimity," would honor an individual,[132] so the prepositional phrase with ܒܒܣܝܡܘܬܐ (*bassīmūṯā*) appears to equip the Most High with the noble human quality of χρηστότης (see Excursus 14). However, it is more probably intended instrumentally, qualifying the making glorious of the redeemed Redeemer *by* the Most High.[133]

With "added emphasis by the repetition of the root ܪܘܡ,"[134] the speaking "I" reaches the summit, in the fullest sense of the word, of his own redemption in 7d (see Excursus 17 above). The object ܡܕܥܐ (*maddʿā*), with first singular possessive suffix, which is far removed from the "heretical *Gnosis*,"[135] has no object of its own and thus appears to be an absolute value (cf. 8:12; 17:12). Gnostics understood this *intellectus*-term, derived from ܝܕܥ (*ʾid̲aʿ*),[136] in their own way and related it to 7a ("he who knows"). By this metaphorical raising up to the "height of truth" (see Excursus 1), the "understanding" of the redeemed one partakes of the "*gnōsis*" of the Lord and Most High in the *plērōma*.[137]

The prepositional phrase with the adverb of place ܬܡܢ (*tammān*; cf. its other occurrence in 22:6), which corresponds as a whole to the adverb ἐκεῖθεν,[138] and the redundant expression with ܐܘܪܚܐ (*ʾurḥā*)[139] and the plural of ܗܠܟܬܐ (*hlak̲t̲ā* or *hellak̲t̲ā*)[140] anchor the final monocolon 8a firmly in stanza III,[141] but also mark the transition to stanza IV. That the Psalms stood sponsor to both terms of motion is clear (cf. Ps 36:23 LXX, etc.; Excursus 15). The destination of the journey is not yet announced (but see on 11a below). There is no good reason to emend the third masculine singular possessive suffix, which can be clearly read in both H and N, and to read ܕܗܠܟܬܝ, as Gunkel does.[142] That this manuscript suffix refers back to "truth"[143] in 7d is less than compelling, especially as Diettrich demands a "translation of the Greek αὐτῆς"—that is, of a feminine pronoun—as the starting point.[144] It would be preferable to find a reference from the Syriac suffix to "*gnōsis*" in 7d, which would then be to some extent personified. But the best interpretation of the metaphorical "way of his steps" is as a gift from the "Most High." This gift—

126 Nöldeke §218.

127 Jens Halfwassen, "Transzendenz; Transzendieren," *HWP* 10 (1998) 1444.

128 Joseph Bernhart, *Augustinus, Confessiones – Bekenntnisse* (Lat.-Ger.; Munich: Kösel, 1955; 4th ed., 1980) 464 (*regio ubertatis indeficientis*).

129 Vogl, 62.

130 Franzmann, 133.

131 Payne Smith, 2:4023–24; BDAG, *s.v.* δοξάζω.

132 See Konrad Weiß, "χρηστός, κτλ.," *ThWNT* 9 (1973) 473; *TDNT* 9:484.

133 Cf. John 8:54; 12:28; 13:31; 17:1, 4.

134 Franzmann, 135.

135 Bauer and Aland, *s.v.* γνῶσις, 3; cf. BDAG, *s.v.* γνῶσις, 3.

136 See Payne Smith, 1:1560, with a remark on the Nestorian vowelization of ܡܕܥܝ in 1 Cor 14:14 (ὁ δὲ νοῦς μου).

137 Cf. 7:7, 13; 23:4; and Excursus 7.

138 Payne Smith, 2:4459; BDAG, *s.v.* ἐκεῖθεν. Gunkel (p. 306) assumes that this term does not mean "thence" but "then" because that is possible "in later Greek."

139 Payne Smith, 1:375; BDAG, *s.v.* ὁδός.

140 Brockelmann, *Lexicon*, 176; Payne Smith, 1:1015; BDAG, *s.vv.* διάβημα, πορεία.

141 Franzmann, 135.

142 Gunkel, 306. This would make the (first singular) genitive ܕܗܠܟܬܝ (*d-halk̲āt̲*) refer directly to the steps of the speaking "I." It does not make a great difference, since the complete expression "the way of my steps" would still be the direct object of the common verb ܝܗܒ, which gets its theological coloring only from its subject "the Most High" (cf. Payne Smith, 1:1564–65; BDAG, *s.v.* δίδωμι).

143 This connection is necessary for Diettrich (p. 60), who considers 8a "the key to understanding the *Ode*" and contends that from here on "another person" is the speaker, namely, "truth personified." I cannot agree with his reasoning.

144 Diettrich, 62.

or license[145]—is also a task with which stanzas IV–V are concerned.[146]

■ **8b-11** With 8a as preparation, 8b inaugurates a new stanza, of which the first three bicola are framed by words derived from the root ܦܬܚ (8b and 10b), while the final bicolon (11) "concludes the key motif of imprisonment" by repeating the root ܐܣܪ as well as "the double play on ܐܣܪ."[147] All the mythological statements of salvation, filled with images of activity, depict the performance of the steps of redemption by the Most High (8a). This "second part" of *Ode* 17 "shows how he (viz., the Redeemed One) becomes the Redeemer."[148] Gunkel's inference, which has been influential, that these "steps," or perhaps "hidden paths," lead the Redeemer "to the Underworld," where he is himself "again fettered" in "Hades," has, however, been contradicted and doubted from the first.[149]

Certainly the terminology of stanza IV evokes a prison. Whether this metaphorical prison is Hades or the "prison" of this "world"[150] will be taken up at the end of these commentaries (see Excursus 42). For the exegesis of this stanza, it is of minor importance whether the statements of *Ode* 17 do or do not refer to Hades and its gates.[151] Since neither the pairing "death"/"realm of the dead" (cf. 15:9; 29:4; 42:11) nor the "dead" nor "souls" are mentioned,[152] readers contemporary with the *Odes* would have thought in the first place of the technical term ܒܝܬ ܐܣܝܪܐ (*bēṯ ʾasīrē*), which is often used to translate φυλακή (cf. Acts 5:19; 12:10; 16:26–27),[153] but also for δεσμωτήριον (cf. Acts 5:23).[154] More important

145 See Bauer, 597.

146 Erik Peterson (*Studien*, 280) rightly stresses the key word γνῶσις, but goes too far by making a connection between 7d-8a and the "teaching of the two ways."

147 Franzmann, 135–36.

148 Gunkel, 307.

149 Ibid.; of the contrary opinion are, e.g., Harnack, 47; Labourt and Batiffol, 73; Harris, 114. Those who follow Gunkel in finding in *Ode* 17 a descent into hell, a journey to Hades, or a *descensus ad inferos*—or at least think it possible—include, in chronological order, Karl Gschwind, *Die Niederfahrt Christi in die Unterwelt: Ein Beitrag zur Exegese des Neuen Testamentes und zur Geschichte des Taufsymbols* (NTAbh 2.3–5; Münster: Aschendorff, 1911) 228–34, esp. 232 ("if this is really meant for a descensus"); Daniel Plooij, "Der Descensus ad inferos in Aphrahat und den Oden Salomos," *ZNW* 14 (1913) 227–28; Martin Dibelius, *Die Isisweihe bei Apuleius und verwandte Initiations-Riten* (SHAW. PH 1917, 4. Abh.; Heidelberg: Winter, 1917; quoted from idem, *Urchristentum*, 30–79) 74; Reitzenstein, *Das mandäische Buch*, 30–32 ("descent into hell = ascent to heaven"); cf. idem, *Das iranische Erlösungsmysterium*, 87; Carl Schmidt and Isaak Wajnberg, *Gespräche Jesu mit seinen Jüngern nach der Auferstehung: Ein katholisch-apostolisches Sendschreiben des 2. Jahrhunderts* (Leipzig, 1919; repr., Hildesheim: Olms, 1967) 564–65; Kroll, *Hymnodik*, 77; cf. idem, *Gott und die Hölle: Der Mythos vom Descensuskampfe* (Studien der Bibliothek Warburg 20; Leipzig/Berlin, 1932; repr., Darmstadt: Wissenschaftliche Buchgesellschaft, 1963) 36; Greßmann, 452; Otto Weinreich, *Gebet und Wunder: Zwei Abhandlungen zur Religions- und Literaturgeschichte* (originally in *Genethliakon* [Tübinger Beiträge zur Altertumswissenschaft 5; Stuttgart: Kohlhammer, 1929], 169–464; repr., Darmstadt: Wissenschaftliche Buchgesellschaft, 1968) 281; Johannes Quasten, "Der gute Hirte in frühchristlicher Totenliturgie und Grabeskunst," in *Miscellanea G. Mercati*, vol. 1: *Bibbia – Letteratura cristiana antica* (Studi e testi 121; Vatican City: Biblioteca Apostolica Vaticana, 1946) 398; Werner Bieder, *Die Vorstellung von der Höllenfahrt Jesu Christi: Beitrag zur Entstehungsgeschichte der Vorstellung vom sog. Descensus ad inferos* (AThANT 19; Zurich: Zwingli, 1949) 174–76; Bauer, 597; Murray, "Rock," 357; John Dominic Crossan, *The Cross That Spoke: The Origins of the Passion Narrative* (San Francisco: Harper & Row, 1988) 365; Sebastian P. Brock, "The Gates/Bars of Sheol Revisited," in William L. Petersen, Johan S. Vos and Henk J. de Jonge, eds., *Sayings of Jesus: Canonical and Non-Canonical. Essays in Honour of Tjitze Baarda* (NovTSup 89; Leiden: Brill, 1997) 12.

150 Rudolph, *Gnosis*, 142.

151 Cf., e.g., Homer *Il.* 5.646; *Od.* 11.571 and 14.156; Matt 16:18; and see BDAG, *s.v.* ᾅδης.

152 See Harris, 114: "liberation of souls."

153 BDAG, *s.v.* φυλακή, 3: "prison."

154 BDAG, *s.v.* δεσμωτήριον: "prison, jail"; Payne Smith, 1:320–22.

than any specific correspondence is the recognition "that the language is taken from the 107th Psalm."[155] Following Brock, then, the verse Ps 106:16 LXX (Ps 107:16 Peshitta) as well as the related verse Isa 45:2 may be quoted here, before the exegesis proper, to set it in perspective as an ancient—and even a modern—reader would see it.

Psalm 106:16 LXX[156]	Psalm 107:16 Pesh.[157]
συνέτριψεν πύλας χαλκᾶς	ܬܒܪ ܬܪܥܐ ܕܢܚܫܐ
καὶ μοχλοὺς σιδηροῦς συνέκλασεν	ܘܡܘܟܠܐ ܕܦܪܙܠܐ ܓܕܡ

Isaiah 45:2 LXX[158]	Isaiah 45:2 Pesh.[159]
θύρας χαλκᾶς συντρίψω	ܬܪܥܐ ܕܢܚܫܐ ܐܬܒܪ
καὶ μοχλοὺς σιδηροῦς συγκλάσω	ܘܡܘܟܠܐ ܕܦܪܙܠܐ ܐܓܕܡ

Brock is right to call 8b-9a "a combination" "which links up with Isa 45:1-2 more closely than with Ps 106 (107)."[160] The first two words of 8b seem to be influenced by the context of the passage from Isaiah.[161] For that reason, the term ܬܪܥܐ (*tarʿā*), derived from ܬܪܥ (*traʿ*), which is also found in the singular in 42:17, is more likely to stand for *θύρα*[162] than for *πύλη*,[163] although the latter term is more commonly used as the Greek equivalent.[164] Like the verb ܦܬܚ (*pṯaḥ*),[165] the intransitive passive participle ܐܚܝܕܐ (*ʾaḥīḏā*), from ܐܚܕ (*ʾeḥad*), is an established term in the language dealing with prisons and prisoners.[166] The plural of ܗܘܐ (*hwā*) makes it clear that the "gates" or "doors" have been barred in a long-ago mythic past.[167]

Verse 9a, parallel to 8b, describes how the breach was achieved. All the words used are represented in the second lines of the Old Testament texts quoted above, and only the *hapax legomenon* ܓܕܡ (Pa. *gaddem*)[168] shows a difference of form; the Greek will have been *συνέκλασα*. In place of "break"[169] one might translate *συγκλάω* by "smash" or "shatter."[170] As in the texts quoted, the genitive of ܦܪܙܠܐ (*parzlā*), qualifying the plural of the Greek loanword ܡܘܟܠܐ (*mukḻā*),[171] would translate the Greek adjective *σιδηροῦς*.[172]

The play on words immediately following in 9b, by the repetition of the term ܦܪܙܠܐ (*parzlā*), which now

155 Harris and Mingana, 2:293; cf. Murray, "Rock," 356–57.

156 Rahlfs 2:119–120.

157 *OTSy*, pt. 2 fasc. 3, p. 130. Brock (p. 12) translates: "he has shattered the gates of bronze, and the bars of iron he has broken."

158 Rahlfs, 2:627.

159 *OTSy*, pt. 3 fasc 1, p. 82. Brock (p. 12) translates: "the gates of bronze shall I shatter, and the bars of iron shall I break."

160 Brock, 12. These two passages have also influenced other early Christian writings (cf. *Barn.* 11:4; *Act. Thom.* 10), Nag Hammadi and Manichean texts (see Brock, 12–14; Franzmann, 136; Paul-Hubert Poirier, "La *Prôtennoia Trimorphe* [NH XIII,1] et le vocabulaire du *Descensus ad inferos*," *Mus* 96 [1983] 197–200; S. Richter, *Untersuchungen*, 262–64), and other Syriac writings (see Brock, 15–23).

161 Cf. Isa 45:1: *Οὕτως λέγει κύριος ὁ θεὸς τῷ χριστῷ μου . . . ἀνοίξω ἔμπροσθεν αὐτοῦ θύρας* ("Thus saith the Lord God to my anointed . . . I will open doors before him")—ܗܟܢܐ ܐܡܪ ܡܪܝܐ ܠܡܫܝܚܗ . . . ܐܦܬܚ ܩܕܡܘܗܝ ܬܪܥܐ (Rahlfs, 2:627; Brenton, 880; *OTSy*, pt. 3 fasc. 1, p. 82). One might even speculate that the term "Messiah" at the end of *Ode* 17 comes from this Isaian passage, where it is used of the Persian king Cyrus (see Karl Elliger, *Deuterojesaja*, vol. 1: *Jesaja 40,1–45,7* [BKAT 11.1; Neukirchen-Vluyn: Neukirchener Verlag, 1978] 491).

162 BDAGD, *s.v.* *θύρα*. This is not a reference to the door that was opened in heaven; cf. Rev 4:1 (*θύρα ἠνεῳγμένη ἐν τῷ οὐρανῷ* ["in heaven an open door"]—ܬܪܥܐ ܦܬܝܚܐ [*tarʿā pṯīḥā*]).

163 BDAG, *s.v.* *πύλη*.

164 In addition to Ps 106:16 LXX, cf. Ps 9:14b LXX: (*κύριος*) *ὁ ὑψῶν με ἐκ τῶν πυλῶν τοῦ θανάτου*, "thou that liftest me up from the gates of death"); Rahlfs, 2:7; Brenton, 702; see also Payne Smith, 2:4505.

165 Payne Smith, 2:3337; BDAG, *s.v.* *ἀνοίγω*.

166 Payne Smith, 1:116–17; BDAG, *s.v.* *κλείω*.

167 See Nöldeke §278.B.

168 Payne Smith, 1:657.

169 BDAG, *s.v.* *μοχλός*.

170 BDAG, *s.v.* *συγκλάω*.

171 Lattke, "Wörter," 293–94 = idem, *Bedeutung*, 4:141–42.

172 Payne Smith, 2:3253; BDAG, *s.v.* *σιδηροῦς*. That the wording of 9a is so similar to that of the Syriac of Isa 45:2 is not an argument for a Syriac original (see Brock, 12 n. 21).

means "iron implement,"[173] can be reproduced in Greek by using the related term σίδηρος. The image is not of "fetters" shackling the Redeemer[174] but of his "sword,"[175] or some other iron implement,[176] that became heated in breaking the iron bars and thus "glowed."[177] This mythological statement is, of course, hyperbole, when compared to "iron glowing in the furnace,"[178] and is immediately surpassed by 9c.

Again in 9c, the liberator does not say "his fetters melted like wax."[179] The preposition ܩܕܡ (*qdām*) + first singular suffix that follows would make no sense in such an image.[180] The Ethpa. of ܦܫܪ (*pšar*), which probably corresponds to an intransitive passive form of τήκω,[181] instead describes in compelling imagery exactly what the consequences of the glowing are. Once the gates are opened and the bars are broken, the redeemed Redeemer has no more need of his weapon. He could, in any case, easily have performed a miracle to open the doors.[182]

The bicolon 10a-b declares more than merely a miracle, especially in the reason given in 10b, which is reminiscent of John 10:9 (ἐγώ εἰμι ἡ θύρα, "I am the door").[183] One might indeed ask why there was all the warlike effort in 8b-9c if the speaking "I," as he claims by the *hapax legomenon* ܦܬܚܐ (*ptāḥā*), is himself the "opening of everything."[184] The "solving of riddles" (λύσεις αἰνιγμάτων), as in Wis 8:8c, is not in question here.[185] The insertion of the particle ܓܝܪ (*gēr*) in N is "redundant after ܡܛܠ ܕ."[186] The subject of the explanatory clause is the emphasized pronoun "I."[187] The phrase ܟܠܡܕܡ (*kol meddem*), which, used as a noun, transmits a sense of universality,[188] refers to every existential prison and forms a verbal antithesis to the negated ܡܕܡ (*meddem*) in 10a.[189] Without seriously changing the meaning the ܠܐ (*lā*) could alternatively be thought to negate the Ethpe. of ܚܙܐ (*ḥzā*), which, taken together with ܠܝ (*lī*), would correspond to the Greek ἐφάνη μοι.[190] The particle ܟܕ (*kad*), occurring before the participle of ܐܚܕ (*ʾeḥad*; see above), can be left untranslated since it only "denotes present action or state."[191]

Stanza IV concludes with the statement of salvation in 11. This bicolon provides an interesting insight into the textual history of the Syriac *Odes of Solomon*. The limiting reading in H is nearer to the original than the generalizing variant ܐܚܝܕܐ (*ʾaḥīdē*) by which N expands liberation to "all who are shut in," perhaps influenced by 10b. Whether this generalization originated with the copyist of N or was found already in an earlier codex can no longer be determined. But when H was written, the person who dictated it, or the scribe himself, had at least two manuscripts to work from.[192] Both might have been earlier than N. In one of them, the reading was ܐܣܝܪܝ (*ʾasīray* = "my fettered ones"), which was possibly meant to harmonize the wording of 11a and 11b.

To a certain extent the participle[193] of ܐܙܠ (*ʾezal*), which is transposed into a mythic past by the enclitic ܗܘܝܬ (*-wēt*), takes up in 11a the theme of 8a (see Excursus 15).[194] The preposition ܥܠ (*ʿal*) gives the verb an adversarial sound,[195] but the corresponding Greek prepositions ἐπί or πρός would be neutral or at least

173 Payne Smith, 2:3253 (*instrumentum ferreum*).
174 Contra Zahn, 692, and Gunkel, 307, who refer to Pss 105:18 and 107:10.
175 BDAG, *s.v.* σίδηρος.
176 See LSJ, *s.v.* σίδηρος.
177 On the *hapax legomenon* ܪܬܚ (*rtaḥ*), see Payne Smith, 2:3994; BDAG, *s.v.* ζέω.
178 Albrecht Oepke, "ζέω, κτλ.," *ThWNT* 2 (1935) 878; *TDNT* 2:876.
179 Contra Gunkel, 307.
180 Payne Smith, 2:3492.
181 BDAG, *s.v.* τήκω; Payne Smith, 2:3329.
182 See Weinreich, *Wunder*, 200–452, esp. 411–52 ("Materialien").
183 See Ernst Olof Percy, *Untersuchungen über den Ursprung der johanneischen Theologie: Zugleich ein Beitrag zur Frage nach der Entstehung des Gnostizismus* (Lund: Håkan Ohlssons, 1939) 285.
184 Payne Smith, 2:3339; Lampe, *s.vv.* ἄνοιγμα, ἄνοιξις (Frankenberg, 19).
185 Contra Diettrich, 62; cf. Georgi, 431.
186 Vogl, 63.
187 See Nöldeke §301, on the use of suffixed ܐܝܬ (*ʾīt*) together with the first singular of ܗܘܐ (*hwā*).
188 See Nöldeke §§217–19.
189 Payne Smith, *Dictionary*, 253: "nothing at all."
190 Frankenberg, 19; Payne Smith, 1:1234; BDAG, *s.v.* φαίνω, φαίνομαι.
191 Payne Smith, *Dictionary*, 204.
192 See Charlesworth, 76 n. 15.
193 Harris and Mingana (vol. 1, on this passage) pointed this form as a Pe. third singular masculine perfect, which is still to be found in Charlesworth (p. 74).
194 See Nöldeke §299.
195 Payne Smith, 1:107; Payne Smith, *Dictionary*, 9.

ambiguous.[196] The plural passive participle of ܐܚܕ (ʾeḥaḏ; see on 8b and 10a above), used as a noun, is preceded by appositional "ܠܟܠ . . . with a pronominal suffix of its own."[197] In H this apposition, connecting 11a to 10b, is limited, by the first singular possessive suffix of ܐܚܝܕܐ (ʾaḥīḏē), to "all *my* shut-in ones" or "prisoners."[198] Bauer's translation, "And I went to all my people, who were locked up," hits the nail on the head.[199] The infinitive of ܫܪܐ (šrā; cf. 22:4), followed by the direct object, defines the purpose of this forcible entry or going toward.[200] The exact translation of the verb ("rescue," "set free," "let out") is not as important as the fact that the Redeemer, by this transitive term, alludes to his own liberation (cf. the Ethpe. in 3a).

Verse 11b shows an insignificant variant reading.[201] As the "tense of dependent, subordinate clauses pointing to the future," the imperfect of ܫܒܩ (šḇaq), which could represent a variety of Greek verbs,[202] together with the negative conjunction "lest,"[203] gives assurance that this liberation was carried through. The direct object of the verb is equivalent to τινά.[204] As in 10a, the ܟܕ (kaḏ) preceding the passive participle of ܐܣܪ (ʾesar)[205] is to be left untranslated (see above). The awkward construction with the relative particle ܕ (d-) preceding the active participle of the same verb[206] suggests that the ending of this concluding verse of stanza IV in 𝔊 might have been: . . . τινὰ δέσμιον/δεδεμένον καὶ δεσμεύοντα/δέοντα.[207] An allusion to the Jewish scribes and Pharisees (Matt 23:4) is as unlikely as one to Peter's power of the keys (Matt 16:19) or to Paul's persecution of Christians (Acts 22:4). Gunkel interprets this difficult verse as "No demon any longer had power to bind, none of the dead remained imprisoned."[208] Countering this imaginative interpretation, Diettrich comes nearer to the point, especially in view of the use the key word *gnōsis* in 12a, when he refers only to those "fettered and fettering in ignorance."[209] The prison in question is not Hades (whether hell or the underworld), nor some place of habitation in "the heavenly regions,"[210] nor even the "world" as such,[211] but "non-*gnōsis*" recorded as already destroyed in 7:21.

■ **12-15** Although there is no change of speaker in stanza V, the grammatical subject changes from "I" (12-13) to "they" (14-15), marking off two separate strophes.[212] With the repetition of the verb "to give" (see 8a above) and the connection back to "knowledge" (7d),

196 BDAG, *s.vv.* ἐπί, πρός.
197 Nöldeke §218.
198 Greßmann, 453.
199 Bauer, 598.
200 Payne Smith, 2:4305–6; BDAG, *s.vv.* ἀπολύω, λύω.
201 "Or" (N) against "and" (H) preceding the last word; see Charlesworth, 76–77: "ܐܘ . . . stands alone on the left margin and cannot be a prefixed Waw."
202 Cf. Ps 15:10 LXX; also Payne Smith, 2:4037–39; BDAG, *s.vv.* ἀπολείπω, ἀφίημι, ἐγκαταλείπω.
203 Payne Smith, *Dictionary*, 233.
204 Payne Smith, 1:283.
205 See Payne Smith, 1:320–22; BDAG, *s.v.* δέσμιος.
206 Literally ". . . and who [is] binding" = ". . . and who binds."
207 BDAG, *s.vv.* δεσμεύω, δέω.
208 Gunkel, 308; Bauer (p. 598) agrees.
209 Diettrich (p. 62) refers to 10:3 in saying "there is no idea of . . . a *descensus ad inferos*." I do not agree that "Truth personified is speaking here." Harris and Mingana conclude from a single passage in Ignatius *Phld.* 8:1 (*πιστεύω τῇ χάριτι Ἰησοῦ Χριστοῦ, ὃς λύσει ἀφ᾽ ὑμῶν πάντα δεσμόν,* "I have faith in the grace of Jesus Christ, and he shall loose every bond from you" [Lindemann and Paulsen, 222–23]; Lake, 1:246–47; cf. Ehrman, 1:290–91, whose translation differs from Lake's) that "Ignatius knew the Odes closely" (Harris and Mingana, 2:45). The commentators on Ignatius's letters do not think it necessary to refer to *Ode* 17:11 (see Bauer and Paulsen, 85; Schoedel, *Ignatius*, 206). The correct reference is Isa 58:6 (λῦε πάντα σύνδεσμον ἀδικίας, "loose every burden of iniquity"; Rahlfs, 2:644; Brenton, 893). The influence of Isaiah is not confined to the New Testament but can be seen also in Ignatius and the *Odes of Solomon*.
210 See Schlier, *Epheser*, 16, in chap. 1 ("Himmelfahrt des Erlösers" [Ascent to Heaven of the Redeemer]).
211 Rudolph, *Gnosis*, 142.
212 Franzmann, 136. It must be noted that the speaking "I" of *Ode* 17 returns as subject at the end of 15. It may be poetic accident that the terms "head" (15-16) and "crown/wreath" (1b) form a sort of *inclusio* for the whole *Ode*.

though with a change of expression, stanza IV, in retrospect, seems almost like an excursus.

In 12a, the speaking "I" uses the commoner *intellectus*-term ܝܕܥܬܐ (*ʾidaʿtā*), derived, like the one in 7d, from the root ܝܕܥ, which does not form a "word-pair"[213] with ܚܘܒܐ (*ḥubbā*) here or in 8:12-13. There was no generally accepted term for the soteriological *gnōsis*[214] at the time the *Odes* were composed. This is true especially for 𝔊 (cf. 11:4; Excursus 7). So it becomes very difficult to decide whether 𝔊 used γνῶσις, ἐπίγνωσις, or σύνεσις, and whether the terms used in 7d and 12a were also different in 𝔊.[215] Because of the parallelism of 12a and 12b, the first singular possessive suffix (in 𝔊 μου or ἐμήν) clearly refers to the Redeemer's own recognition of being redeemed, which he passed on to those he himself liberated (see Excursus 37). It is also clear that the cliché ܕܠܐ ܚܣܡ (*d-lā ḥsām*), a masculine in the absolute state, cannot be the predicate of ܝܕܥܬܐ (cf. 15:6), but as an adverb, like the Greek ἀφθόνως, refers to the first person singular of the Pa. of ܝܗܒ (*yab*).[216] This lack of "jealousy" is in no sense a psychological state; it stresses the generosity and abundance of the giving.[217]

The next statement of salvation, in 12b, is also dependent on the verb in 12a, so that by *parallelismus membrorum* the ungrudgingness and the ἀγάπη, also not to be taken psychologically, reciprocally interpret each other.[218] What meaning should one assign to the *hapax legomenon* ܒܥܘܬܐ (*bāʿūtā*), derived from ܒܥܐ (*bʿā*) and parallel to *gnōsis*, of which Harris and Mingana say, "The sense is very doubtful"?[219] The feminine noun cannot, here, be a translation of δέησις.[220] It makes good sense, however, when seen as the translation of παράκλησις, which Harris and Mingana confirm, referring to the "Lewis text" of Luke 2:25.[221] This makes it unnecessary to accept the convoluted translation "resurrection."[222] The suggestion, which was first mooted by Charles Cutler Torrey, does not improve the sense of the bicolon 12a-b, as Charlesworth would have it.[223] On the contrary, the "consolation" of the speaking "I," who will be acclaimed later as "Messiah" (see on 16 below), and his gift of *gnōsis*—not yet a technical term—are the two sides of one soteriological coin.

In 13a it looks almost as if the direct object of the metaphorical Pe. ܙܪܥ (*zraʿ*)—used only here—has anticipated the results of the harvest. But καρπός can also be used "for the seed of the fruit," at least from the LXX onwards.[224] The Greek equivalent of the verb was certainly σπείρω followed by εἰς or ἐν.[225] What is meant by the plural of ܦܐܪܐ (*pērā* [+ first singular possessive suffix]) is hard to guess, since the usage is peculiar to this

213 Contra Franzmann, 69, 136, 402.

214 Ernst Olof Percy, *Untersuchungen über den Ursprung der johanneischen Theologie: Zugleich ein Beitrag zur Frage nach der Entstehung des Gnostizismus* (Lund: Håkan Ohlssons, 1939) 292.

215 Payne Smith, 1:1559–60; BDAG, *s.vv.* γνῶσις, ἐπίγνωσις, σύνεσις.

216 Van Unnik, "De ἀφθονία van God," 10; cf. Drijvers, "Polemik," 45 ("adverbial nuance"); Payne Smith, 1:1333.

217 See LSJ, *s.v.* ἀφθον-.

218 Cf. 42:7, 9; Excursus 2 and Lattke, *Einheit*, 58; Payne Smith, 1:1171; BDAG, *s.v.* ἀγάπη; Frankenberg, 19.

219 Harris and Mingana, 2:291.

220 Payne Smith, 1:557; BDAG, *s.v.* δέησις. Gunkel (p. 308) goes so far as to say: "Christ *preached* . . . in the underworld and entreated so powerfully for them" (referring to 1 Pet 4:6). The use of "entreaty" at this point carries on from Gunkel to Greßmann (p. 453) and Bauer (p. 598), and down to Vogl (p. 61).

221 Harris and Mingana, 2:292: "consolation"; cf. BDAG, *s.v.* παράκλησις. Klijn (p. 303) admits the possibility of this somewhat unusual meaning, but prefers "interrogation" "although it does not fit the context quite well." That "'in my love' refers to both members of parallelism" (Harris and Mingana, 2:291–92) is not really likely.

222 Contra Charlesworth, *Reflections*, 138–46. I do not believe that this translation needs to be seriously considered in spite of McNeil's reference to an unpublished "typescript of a French translation of the Odes by Fr Pierre Yousif" (Brian McNeil, review of Lattke, *Bedeutung*, vol. 3 in *JSS* 33 [1988] 286). And the fact that the terms "transformation" and "transition (μεταβολή) into newness" occur in NHC 1,*4* in the context of a discussion of "resurrection (ἀνάστασις)" (*Treat. Res.* 48,4; 48,35–38; Peel, *Rheginos*, 33–34, 92) is also no reason to advocate "resurrection" as the translation here.

223 Charlesworth, *Reflections*, 145–46, with additional wide-ranging hypotheses on the origin of the *Odes of Solomon* in West Syria/North Palestine.

224 Dibelius, *Jakobus*, 258, on Jas 3:18; cf. Prov 11:30a.

225 Payne Smith, 1:1158; BDAG, *s.v.* σπείρω.

passage (see Excursus 11).[226] Even Petra von Gemünden can only say "*Odes of Solomon* 17:13, where the Redeemer sows his fruits (!) in the hearts of the faithful, is thought-provoking."[227] Perhaps the metaphorical term refers to the "yield" of the "works" of the redeemed Redeemer,[228] or perhaps only to the "*gnōsis*" (12a), "consolation" (12b), and "blessing" (14a).[229] It is remarkable that the plural of ܠܒܐ (*lebbā*) has no suffix. Even so, the "heart" as the sensible center of life belongs to those redeemed who will be called "members" (see Excursus 4).[230] One might even say that the term "hearts" signifies the redeemed persons. Given its intellectual sense, the term fits well with "knowledge" in 12a.

The direct object of the Shaph. of ܚܠܦ (*ḥlap̄*), which is used only here in 13b in a positive sense, may refer to "hearts."[231] But it is also possible that the enclitic personal pronoun ܐܢܘܢ (*ʾennōn*) already refers to the subject of 14a. The detailed discussions of ܒܝ (*bī*), which led Harris and Mingana to suggest radical emendations,[232] are based on false premises. The preposition with first singular pronominal suffix corresponds to a phrase like ἐν ἐμοί, which describes the "closeness" of the Redeemer and his people.[233] If the instrumental translation "by me"[234] is rejected in favor of the locative "in me," in a transferred sense, the partly chiastic parallelism of 13a and 13b comes out even more clearly.[235] This would bring a reminiscence of the formulaic ἐν κυρίῳ and/or ἐν Χριστῷ of the New Testament.[236]

The "giving" of 12a corresponds to the "receiving" of 14a (see Excursus 41). With so many possible equivalents it is hard to determine what the Greek was for the Pa. ܩܒܠ (*qabbel*).[237] The texts, however, offer a combination of εὐλογία ("blessing"; Heb 6:7, with genitive) or ζωή ("life"; *2 Clem.* 14:5, with accusative) and the verb μεταλαμβάνω.[238] In connection with the term ܒܘܪܟܬܐ (*burkṯā*), derived from ܒܪܟ (*brek̠*), which occurs again in 38:20 in the context of vegetation imagery, attention may be drawn to the Pauline expression in Rom 15:29, εὐλογία Χριστοῦ ("blessing of Christ"), later expanded to εὐλογία τοῦ εὐαγγελίου τοῦ Χριστοῦ ("blessing of the gospel of Christ").[239] The second verb of 14b does not follow from the first but expresses a simultaneous experience of redemption. The eschatological Pe. ܚܝܐ (*ḥyā*), which, because of its parallelism with the second verb of 14a, must represent ζάω,[240] in a statement more radical than even John 5:25, moves the accomplished deed back into the mythological past.

Having referred to John 11:52 in connection with 10:5a (cf. 22:2), the reference can be complemented by Eph 4:16 where the Ethpa. of ܟܢܫ (*knaš*) is the revised translation of συμβιβαζόμενος.[241] However, it is more probable that 𝔖 used a theological passive of συνάγω, though not with reference to πάντα τὰ ἔθνη as in Matt 25:32, but limited to the redeemed.[242] The preposition ܠܘܬ (*lwāṯ*) with first singular suffix is not equivalent to εἰς or ܠ (*l-*) as in John 11:52; here it represents παρά (with dative) or πρός (with accusative) and again serves to describe the close "connection" between the Redeemer and the redeemed.[243] In parallel with "live," the Ethpe. of ܦܪܩ (*praq*) stresses once again the achieved salvation, which ultimately unites the "members" and the "head" (15).[244]

226 Payne Smith, 2:3227.
227 Gemünden, *Vegetationsmetaphorik*, 402.
228 See BDAG, *s.v.* καρπός.
229 The idea that the terms "to sow," "fruits," and "blessing" were chosen because of Ps 106:37-38a LXX can, I think, be dismissed (contra Harris and Mingana, 2:294).
230 Payne Smith, 2:1877; BDAG, *s.v.* καρδία.
231 Franzmann, 136. See also Payne Smith, 1:1286; 𝔖 may have used a form of μεταστρέφω or μετασχηματίζω; see BDAG on these words.
232 Harris and Mingana, 2:292.
233 See BDAG, *s.v.* ἐν, 4, with references to comparable passages in the NT.
234 As in Bauer, 598; Lattke, *Oden*, 149.
235 See Franzmann, 136.
236 See Joseph A. Fitzmyer, "κύριος, κτλ.," *EWNT* 2 (1981) 817–18 ("union of the Christian with Christ"); *EDNT* 2:330; Ferdinand Hahn, "Χριστός, κτλ.," *EWNT* 3 (1983) 1156–60; *EDNT* 3:482–84.
237 Payne Smith, 2:3468.
238 BDAG, *s.v.* μεταλαμβάνω.
239 NA[27], p. 438; BDAG, *s.v.* εὐλογία, 3bα; Payne Smith, 1:614.
240 See Table 1; also Payne Smith, 1:1251; BDAG, *s.v.* ζάω.
241 Payne Smith, 1:1771.
242 BDAG, *s.v.* συνάγω.
243 Payne Smith, 2:1918; BDAG, *s.vv.* παρά, πρός.
244 See also on 4c above; and Excursus 5. See also Payne Smith, 2:3294; BDAG, *s.v.* σῴζω, passive.

The reason for this act of redemption is given by the monocolon 15, which is more than "a summary line to the preceding bicolon."[245] A "change of subject" by itself is no reason why 15 "must be divided into two sections."[246] Neither is there anything about "members of the head of truth personified."[247] Although it uses the plural of ܗܕܡܐ (*haddāmā*), which is certainly equivalent to τὰ μέλη, and metaphorically describes the aggregate of the redeemed,[248] 15 lies on the line of development of the Pauline and deutero-Pauline statements on the "body" (σῶμα) or "body of Christ and its members," on the one hand,[249] and the "body"—sometimes = ἐκκλησία—and its "head" (κεφαλή), on the other.[250] The "members" and the "head"[251] that surmounts them come together as a soteriological unity in the image of an enlarged human body, which is not the same as the macrocosmic "body" and only throws a very unclear light on the "mythos of the primal man as Redeemer" as developed in Gnosticism .[252]

■ **16** In this closing doxology (cf. also 11:24; 18:16; 20:10), the "we" of the redeemed—and in liturgical use the Christian congregation[253]—responds to the speaking "I," who, in addition to his role as Redeemer and "head" of the "members," is now accorded the same title κύριος/ܡܪܝܐ (*māryā*) as his original "God" and "Lord" (1a, 2a).[254] It is easy to assume that the whole phrase in apposition to ܠܟ (*l-* + second singular suffix) is an "acclamation" (cf. Rom 10:9; 1 Cor 12:3).[255] Considering, however, that the word ܪܫܐ (*rēšā*), "head," with first plural possessive suffix, refers back to the end of stanza V, it may be that the original acclamation had only two parts, which were Κύριος Χριστός (cf. Rom 16:18; Col 3:24). Such an acclamation becomes possible only if ܡܫܝܚܐ (*mšīḥā*) has become an accepted sobriquet[256] of Ἰησοῦς/ܝܫܘܥ (*Yeššūʿ*). But the name "Jesus" does not occur in the *Odes of Solomon* and should not be imported unnecessarily into the "Messiah" passages either.[257]

245 Franzmann, 136.
246 Contra Diettrich, 63.
247 Diettrich, 63, with an unconvincing reference to the term "people" in 10:6.
248 Payne Smith, 1:974–75; BDAG, *s.v.* μέλη; Johannes Horst, "μέλος," *ThWNT* 4 (1942) 561; *TDNT* 4:557.
249 Cf. Rom 12:5; 1 Cor 6:15 (σώματα = μέλη Χριστοῦ); 12:27; Eph 4:25; 5:30; also Ignatius *Eph.* 4:2 (μέλη . . . τοῦ υἱοῦ αὐτοῦ).
250 Cf. Eph 1:22-23; 4:15; 5:23; Col 2:9-10 (κεφαλὴ πάσης ἀρχῆς); 1:18; and cf. Ignatius *Trall.* 11:2, for the only juxtaposition of κεφαλή and μέλη. Mußner calls 17:15-16 Gnostic "soma hypothesis," which "must be a secondary construction on the basis of Colossians and Ephesians"; see Franz Mußner, *Christus, das All und die Kirche: Studien zur Theologie des Epheserbriefes* (Trierer theologische Studien 5; Trier: Paulinus, 1955; 2nd ed., 1968) 162. See also Petr Pokorný, *Der Epheserbrief und die Gnosis: Die Bedeutung des Haupt-Glieder-Gedankens in der entstehenden Kirche* (Berlin: Evangelische Verlagsanstalt, 1965), 51, 66, 114, and Klauck, *Herrenmahl*, 343.
251 On ܪܫܐ (*rēšā*) and κεφαλή, see Payne Smith, 2:3899–900; BDAG, *s.v.* κεφαλή; Michael Lattke, "κεφαλή," *EWNT* 2 (1981) 706; *EDNT* 2:286.
252 See Excursuses 18 and 23 and Heinrich Schlier, "κεφαλή, ἀνακεφαλαιόομαι," *ThWNT* 3 (1938) 675–77; *TDNT* 3:675–78. Two decades later Schlier adds, on 17:14-16, "The (new) man is formed in the unity of the members that gather around and about him, and of the (redeeming) head" ("Corpus," *RAC* 3 [1957] 450). This still shows traces of the influence of Käsemann, who mentions the "primal man" at various points in the context of *Ode* 17; see Ernst Käsemann, *Leib und Leib Christi: Eine Untersuchung zur paulinischen Begrifflichkeit* (BHTh 9; Tübingen: Mohr Siebeck, 1933) 141, etc. Actually Käsemann should have laid more weight on 17:15, as Karl Martin Fischer confirms: "It is possible that Colossians/Ephesians exerts some influence. In any case the text does not say that the members had already been parts of the body and that the redemption was a *restitutio in integrum;* they only became members by their redemption. So the text is just a poetic variation on the biblical imagery, depicting the unconditional relationship of the Redeemer and redeemed. The mythos of the fall of primal man cannot be read into this passage" (Karl Martin Fischer, *Tendenz und Absicht des Epheserbriefes* [FRLANT 111; Göttingen: Vandenhoeck & Ruprecht, 1973] 61). Whether this gives sufficient weight to the causal conjunction of 15 may be left undecided.
253 "The first person plural pronoun again suggests that these *Odes* were used in primitive Christian services" (Charlesworth, 77).
254 See BDAG, *s.v.* κύριος; Payne Smith, 2:2204–5.
255 See Ernst Käsemann, "Formeln II. Liturgische Formeln im NT," *RGG*[3] 2 (1958) 994.
256 See Gerhard Schneider, "Ἰησοῦς," *EWNT* 2 (1981) 446 ("Beiname"); *EDNT* 2:182 ("a name").

In three of these seven passages there is no doubt that the title "Messiah" = "Anointed" (9:3; 29:6; 41:3). The most difficult passage (41:15a) probably also belongs here.[258] In the other three cases, it is not immediately obvious whether *Χριστός*/ܡܫܝܚܐ is already a name or still a messianic title (*χριστός* or *μεσσίας*; cf., e.g., Matt 1:16; John 1:41; 4:25) used in apposition to "Lord" (17:16; 24:1a N; 39:11b).[259] So in this case it is quite possible that both "Lord" and "Messiah"/"Anointed One"[260] are in apposition to "our head," which would then have to be marked off by a comma (so Greßmann and Bauer, who, however, choose "Christ" for their translations and thus achieve ambiguity).[261]

In retrospect to the Pauline and deutero-Pauline epistles and in respect of Christian usage, it must be admitted that the hearers and readers would be likely to understand the term "Messiah" to mean "(Jesus) Christ" (but see Excursus 24).

257 This doxology/acclamation could have found a place among the Pauline and deutero-Pauline congregations. But in the relevant epistles the combination *κύριος Ἰησοῦς* occurs regularly and the three-part phrase *κύριος Ἰησοῦς Χριστός* (and similarly in various permutations; see Gerhard Schneider, "*Ἰησοῦς*," *EWNT* 2 [1981] 444–47; *EDNT* 2:182; Joseph A. Fitzmyer, "*κύριος, κτλ.*," *EWNT* 2 [1981] 818; *EDNT* 2:330; Ferdinand Hahn, "*Χριστός, κτλ.*," *EWNT* 3 [1983] 1157–60; *EDNT* 3:479–81) is still commoner. The reason why the name "Jesus" is avoided may perhaps be found in the area of what is called "Docetism" in the Christology of the *Odes of Solomon* (Labourt and Batiffol, 94–98).

258 See Lattke, "Messias-Stellen," 442–45 = idem, *Bedeutung*, 104–6.

259 Payne Smith, 2:2241; BDAG, *s.v. κύριος*.

260 Harnack's translation (p. 47), with a note that 11-15 are "certainly messianic." Diettrich's omission (p. 63) of "our head" and "the anointed" is arbitrary.

261 Greßmann, 453; Bauer, 598.

18

Ode 18: The *Plērōma* and the Gnostics

(I) 1a My heart was lifted up by the love of the Most High and overflowed,
1b that I might glorify him through my name.
2a My members were strengthened,
2b that they might not fall from his power.
3a Infirmities fled[a] far from my body,
3b and they stood fast[b] for the Lord by/according to his will,
3c because his kingdom is firm/true.
(II) 4a Lord, do not, because of those who are in need,
4b turn away[c] thy word from me.
5a Nor, because of their works,
5b withhold thy *plērōma* from me.
6a The light shall not be vanquished by darkness,
6b nor shall truth flee from falsehood.
7a Thy right hand shall establish our salvation unto victory,
7b and thou wilt collect from every place
7c and protect every one[d] who is held fast by evil.
8a Thou, my God, falsehood and death are not in thy mouth,
8b but the *plērōma* is thy will.
(III) 9a And vanity thou knowest not,
9b because neither does it know/acknowledge thee.
10a And thou knowest not error,
10b because[e] neither does it know/acknowledge thee.
(IV) 11a And non-*gnōsis* appeared like spray
11b and like the stink of the sea.
12a And the vain ones thought about it that it is great,
12b and they came[f] to resemble it and became futile.
(V) 13a And they understood, those who understand,
13b and thought and were not polluted by their thoughts,
14a because they were by/in the mind of the Most High.
14b And they laughed at those who were walking[g] in error,
15a but they also spoke the truth
15b from the breath that the Most High breathed into them.
(VI) 16 Glory and majesty to his name.
Hallelujah.

a 3a ܐܬܪܚܩܘ N; ܐܪܚܩܘ H.
b 3b ܘܩܡܘ N; ܘܩܡ H.
c 4b ܬܫܕܐ N; ܬܫܪܐ H.
d 7c ܠܟܠ ܡܢ erroneous in H and N; see commentary below.
e 10b ܡܛܠ N; ܡܛܠ ܐܠܐ H.
f 12b ܘܐܬܘ N; ܐܬܘ H.
g 14b ܕܡܗܠܟܝܢ N; ܗܘܘ ܕܡܗܠܟܝܢ H.

Introduction

Ode 18 is preserved in two Syriac manuscripts.[1] A decade after the *editio princeps* of 1909, Harris and Mingana still note, sadly, "This is a very difficult Ode to interpret: we have not succeeded in finding any Scripture coincidences that could be depended upon,"[2] although they refer to John 1:5 (on 6a) and Ps 119:43 (on 4). In consequence, they do not accept Diettrich's simplistic injunction: "Since this Ode is unencumbered by any specifically Christian ideas it should be interpreted conventionally as a Jewish work."[3] Rudolf Abramowski, as so often, comes closest to the facts when, after quoting 18:11-14a, he says, very circumspectly, "From this passage, as well as all the contextual thought forms, and the destiny of the Redeemer, it is clear that we are dealing with a specific form of Gnosticism."[4]

Diettrich thinks that 1-10 was "sung antiphonally by the prophet and the congregation" and at the end of the "prophecy" (11-16) concludes "with an eschatological image."[5] A different extreme of form criticism is represented by Schille, who declares 1-3 to depict the "supreme moment of baptism."[6] Finally, Pierre rather contradicts her own observations, maintaining that *Ode* 18 "is laid out like a liturgy in two parts (v.1-8 and 9-16)."[7] In contrast to these divisions, there is Franzmann's reasoned analysis, which distinguishes the two sections, 1-8 and 9-15, and determines that a "personal song" is followed by "a teaching song."[8] That only one person is speaking both in 6-7 and in the whole of the second part—the "I" who stands before the "Most High" (1a, 14-15), the "Lord" (3b, 4a), and "God" (8a)—cannot be doubted. Even the beginning of the didactic part (9-10) is addressed to the second person singular, as was the end of the first part (8a-b). However, when Abramowski lists *Ode* 18 among the *Odes of Solomon* "in which it is impossible to determine which of the two sons is speaking,"[9] it is necessary to remark that, from a grammatical point of view and before any detailed commentary is undertaken, the speaking "I"—who is not identical with the poet or with any person performing the poem—might equally well be a "daughter." Whether this possibility remains open will have to wait for further exegesis (see on 2a below).

Interpretation

■ **1-3** The statements of salvation in the three, more or less parallel bicola 1, 2, and 3a-b, whose dependent imperfect verbs in 1b and 2b point, in the mythological past of the action, "toward the future,"[10] are completed by a causal statement (3c). The conclusion of stanza I—like the conclusion of the first part as a whole (8)—is less "a concluding confessional statement"[11] than a didactic one serving to connect the two parts of *Ode* 18 more closely in a formal sense. The strongest connection is made by the use of the term ܡܪܝܡܐ (*mrayymā*), corresponding to the Greek title of God, (ὁ) ὕψιστος ("[the] Most High"; see Excursus 17), in 1a and 15b, thus encompassing the whole Ode.

The passive Ethpe. of ܪܘܡ, ܪܡ (*rām*) in 1a can include a spatial component in its meaning,[12] but here it refers

1 Mss.: Codex H, 14a–15a; Codex N, 149ʳ (ܣ). Ed./trans.: Charlesworth, 77–81; Franzmann, 139–45; Lattke, 2:67–89 and 3:XXVIII–XXIX.
2 Harris and Mingana, 2:297.
3 Diettrich, 63.
4 Abramowski, 62. Bauer's title for this Ode (p. 598), "The Victory of *Gnosis* over its Opponents," is close to the one I have chosen. Frankenberg (p. 49) mentions a "sort of Gnosticism (or mysticism)" whose "characteristic" is "that it sets the soul in place of the congregation and attempts to experience the historical salvation by Christ in a psychological fashion." With quotations from the homilies of Makarios (fourth century), he reaches the conclusion that "the spiritual emotion, which this poem projects, is as clear as possible" (pp. 50–51), with which not many will agree.
5 Diettrich, 64–66.
6 Schille, 87. See the commentary on 17:1-4.
7 Pierre, 109.
8 Franzmann, 142.
9 Abramowski, 59.
10 Nöldeke §267.
11 Franzmann, 143.
12 Payne Smith, 2:3858.

to the existential elevation or raising up of the $\kappa\alpha\rho\delta\acute{\iota}\alpha$ or ܠܒ (*leb̲*) (see Excursus 4), which is the center of the life of the speaker. The ἀγάπη or ܚܘܒܐ (*ḥubbā*), which is used instrumentally—or even in a transferred sense as a place—and to emphasize unity, is not "love" for the "Most High" but the power of his own love that can be found only in the speech and imagery of human beings (see Excursus 2).[13] Perhaps the second verb in 1a should be moved to the beginning of 1b, as Frankenberg does: καὶ ἐπερίσσευσεν. . . .[14] Since the *hapax legomenon* ܐܬܝܬܪ (Ethpa. *ʾetyattar*),[15] derived from ܝܬܪ (*ʾiṯar*), corresponds to περισσεύω rather than to αὐξάνω/αὔξω,[16] it may be translated by "overflow"[17] or "abound,"[18] but not by "increase,"[19] much less by "improve."[20]

If the construction of the imperfect of the Pa. ܫܒܚ (*šabbaḥ*) with the prefixed conjunction ܕ (*d-*) and third singular masculine objective suffix corresponded to a subjunctive form of δοξάζω, the Syriac verb would share in the ambiguity of its Greek equivalent with its meaning wavering between "to praise" and "to glorify."[21] But 𝔊 could have used another verb for this construction of praising (e.g., αἰνέω or ὑμνέω) in place of ἵνα αὐτὸν δοξάσω (or δοξάζω).[22] More important than this is the question whether the expression ܫܡܝ (*šem* with first person possessive suffix), which is well attested, should be emended, with Schultheß, to ܫܡܗ ("in his name").[23] The recognition "that ܒ means not only 'by means of' but also 'with,' 'according to'"[24] does not give much help toward a solution. The suggested emendation does not, in fact, make any better sense, even if "the meaning of *name* is strictly adhered to,"[25] so it is necessary to find an explanation for the text as it stands. In the first place, one can make reference to 42:20a ("I set my name upon their head"), but this also does not lead any further. Bauer's remark that "name," "like ὄνομα," can stand for the "person" (see Excursus 39)[26] is not much more helpful. Whether the speaker of *Ode* 18 is more than just some redeemed, pleading, and teaching person, who, by the power of naming himself, intends to glorify and praise the Most High, can only be decided by examining the meaning of two terms that appear in the lines immediately following, namely, "members" (2a) and "body" (3a).

Excursus 18: "Members" and "Body" in the *Odes of Solomon*

For a start, the term ܗܕܡܐ (*haddāmā*), which occurs only in the plural, corresponds in all nine cases to the plural of τὸ μέλος.[27] Although the masculine ܦܓܪܐ (*pağrā*) might, in the very passage where ℭ uses the loanword σῶμα (22:9), be considered the equivalent of σάρξ, this term, occurring both in the singular and the plural, in fact always corresponds to σῶμα (cf. also 18:3 and 39:3),[28] a word of great significance throughout Greek antiquity. Both of these anthropological terms are typically used in both a literal and a transferred sense, as is also the case in the *Odes of Solomon*.

The decision about which meaning to assign is made easier, since the context in each case offers human and generally corporeal parallel terms. In 22:9, there can be no question that "bodies" means every part of the living person that is not the skeleton. The new "bodies" of this mythological-theological awakening were stretched over the "dead

13 See Payne Smith, 1:1171; BDAG, *s.v.* ἀγάπη.
14 Frankenberg, 19.
15 Payne Smith, 1:1649.
16 See BDAG, *s.v.* περισσεύω.
17 Lattke, *Bedeutung*, 1:125; cf. Greßmann, 453: "fließt über [overflows]."
18 Diettrich, 64; Bauer, 598.
19 Contra Lattke, *Oden*, 150.
20 Harnack, 48. Diettrich (p. 64) imports the idea of inspiration when he says: "The heart of the inspired one is so filled with the spirit that it bubbles over like a spring (cf. 16:3)."
21 Payne Smith, 2:4023–24; BDAG, *s.v.* δοξάζω. Cf. 7:19; 21:7; 26:4; 36:2, 4.
22 Frankenberg, 19.
23 Schultheß, 254. Diettrich (p. 64) declares the "emendation by Harris [*sic*]" to be "unnecessary" and does not consider whether the terms "members" and "body" refer to the "community."
24 Payne Smith, *Dictionary*, 186; Charlesworth, 79.
25 Bauer, 598.
26 Bauer, 598; cf. BDAG, *s.v.* ὄνομα, esp. the passages with ἐν ὀνόματι Ἰησοῦ Χριστοῦ and ἐν ὀνόματί μου.
27 Payne Smith, 1:974–75; BDAG, *s.v.* μέλος; Johannes Horst "μέλος," *ThWNT* 4 (1942) 559–61; *TDNT* 4:555–57.
28 See Payne Smith, 2:3033; BDAG, *s.v.* σῶμα; Eduard Schweizer, "σῶμα," *EWNT* 3 (1983) 772–79; *EDNT* 3:322–25.

bones" like tents (cf. 25:8, "garments of skin").[29] In 39:3 "bodies" is parallel to "souls." This is meant as an expression not of Platonic dualism but of the existential "unity" of the individual.[30] The "limbs" that were set upright in 6:16 are probably also envisaged literally, as shown by the parallels "lips" (14) and "souls" (15). When the Redeemer says, in 8:16a, that he assembled the "members" of his people (14a), the parallel term "faces" (15c) again emphasizes the completeness of the persons. This will hold also for 40:3b N ("my limbs are fat/lush in his odes"), where "tongue" (3a) and "face" (4a), "spirit" (4b) and "soul" (4c) are parallel terms. "Heart" is another term from the human anatomy that can be used to represent the totality of the person. Its hymnic use in 26:4a means that "members" in 26:4b cannot be (mis)-interpreted metaphorically. Accordingly, it might be reasoned that "members" in 18:2a is parallel with "heart" in 1a and is intended to distinguish the periphery from the center. Against this, however, is the use of "body" in the immediate context (see on 18:3a-b below).

Except for one doubtful passage (see the commentary on 6:2a), all the other occurrences of the plural ܗܕܡ̈ܐ (*haddāmē*), corresponding to Greek μέλη, are used in a metaphorical sense. Although the beginning of *Ode* 3 is missing, the parallel structure of 3:2 strongly suggests that the term "members" describes those belonging to the "Lord" (3:3). Some light is cast on this idea by the somewhat anomalous statement of salvation, "I had members of myself" (21:4a), uttered by the Redeemer.[31] This speaker has nothing to say about his own role as Redeemer, but 17:15 makes it clear that the redeemed "members," together with the Redeemer, who describes himself as their "head," form a complete unity modeled on the ideal human body.

This leaves one last passage in which "members" occurs and also "body" (18:2-3). The usage of *Ode* 17 cannot, of course, be immediately transferred to the meaning of the Ode following, but the verbs in 18:2b and 3b as well as "the only occurrence of the 1st pl. in this Ode"[32] (see on 7a below) strongly suggest that "members" and "body" are synonymous metaphors. If that is so, the speaking "I" of *Ode* 18 must be identified with the "head" in 17:15-16, or even with the great "anthropos" of later Gnosticism.

This excursus has shown that the speaking "I" of *Ode* 18 must be connected with this "body" made up of Gnostic "members."[33] In the beginnings of the Christian tradition, he will have been recognized as "Christ"[34] and therefore as "son" and "Lord."[35] The subject of the Ethpa. ܐܬܥܫܢ (*ʾetʿaššan*) in 2a, however, is theologically the "Most High" (1a), who, on the Jewish line of development, is the "Lord" par excellence (3b) and can be addressed as such (4a). What the Redeemer himself experienced mythologically (cf. 10:4) is here declared soteriologically of his "members."[36] It is impossible to say what the theological passive may have been in 𝔊.

The opening words, ܐܟ ܕܠܐ (*ʾak d-lā*), of the final clause (2b) mean "that not," "lest."[37] 𝔊 may have actually used ὥστε μή followed by the infinitive of πίπτω.[38] Unlike 6:16, where the fallen "members" are probably not meant metaphorically, the imperfect of the Pe. ܢܦܠ (*npal*), followed by the preposition ܡܢ (*men*), is quite likely to have been used here in a transferred sense.[39] The same would be true of πίπτω, which would have had ἀπό or ἐκ followed by the genitive of δύναμις.[40] If

29 This metaphor is particularly striking in Syriac because ܦܓܪܐ (*pagrā*) can also translate σκῆνος (2 Cor 5:1) and σκήνωμα (2 Pet 1:13).

30 See Eduard Schweizer, "σῶμα," *EWNT* 3 (1983) 772; *EDNT* 3:322.

31 See Bauer, 601.

32 Franzmann, 143.

33 The *Odes of Solomon* never describe this "body" as ܥܕܬܐ (*ʿettā*) or ἐκκλησία (see Payne Smith, 2:2802). This means that one should not import Pauline ideas to interpret σῶμα as the Christian "community" (see Peter Stuhlmacher, *Biblische Theologie des Neuen Testaments*, vol. 2: *Von der Paulusschule bis zur Johannesoffenbarung. Der Kanon und seine Auslegung* [Göttingen: Vandenhoeck & Ruprecht, 1999] 10, on Col 1:18a).

34 Cf. Col 1:18; 2:19; Ignatius *Trall.* 11:2; and see BDAG, *s.v.* κεφαλή, 1b.

35 Abramowski, 53.

36 See Payne Smith, 2:3003–4.

37 Nöldeke §364.B.

38 Frankenberg, 19; BDAG, *s.vv.* μή, πίπτω.

39 Payne Smith, 2:2413: *defecit, descivit, deseruit.* There is little justification for the translation "that they might not fall *before* his power" (Harnack, 48 [emphasis added]).

40 BDAG, *s.v.* πίπτω; on ܚܝܠܐ (*ḥaylā*), see Payne Smith, 1:1258; BDAG, *s.v.* δύναμις. Because of the occurrence of the same verb as in 2a and of the phrase "power of the Most High," reference should be made from this passage to 32:3.

the "members" are thought to be in mythological high places, the verb "to fall" acquires a spatial meaning in addition to its primary existential one.

The plural of ܟܘܪܗܢܐ (*kurhānā*) in 3a is meant metaphorically—unlike its use in 25:9—as part of the image evoked by "body" and "members." Whether 𝔊 used the plural of ἀσθένεια, μαλακία, or νόσος[41] is less important than the possible reason for the differing derivatives of the root ܪܚܩ,[42] both of which are *hapax legomena.* The reflexive Ethpa. ܐܬܪܚܩ (*ʾeṯraḥḥaq*) of N as well as the intransitive Aph. ܐܪܚܩ (*ʾarḥeq*) of H are possible translations of the aorist ἀπέστην,[43] which often duplicates the prefix of ἀφίστημι with the preposition ἀπό.[44] These variants in 𝔖 are a further indication of a possible Greek original of the *Odes.*[45] The "infirmities"—or simply "weaknesses"—that fled from the metaphorical "body" are parallel to the existential strengthening recorded in the statement of salvation in 2a.

In 3b there is another variant, where N should again be preferred as the *lectio difficilior.*[46] If ܩܡ (*qām*) is more than a variant due to mishearing when the text was read aloud, it still does not necessarily follow that "the context appears to demand the sing[ular] reading from H, with ܦܓܪܝ as the (understood) subj[ect]."[47] For the plural ܗܕܡܝ̈ (*haddāmay*), which the speaking "I" uses to describe the various parts of his "body," also belongs to the context of 2-3b. The translation of the verb ܩܘܡ, ܩܡ (*qām*) by "stand up,"[48] or even more by "arise,"[49] does not make much sense in this context. This Pe. perfect, which corresponds to the intransitive aorist of ἵστημι, has the figurative meaning "to stand fast"[50] and thus forms a counter to πεσεῖν in 2b (cf. Rom 11:20).[51] The middle phrase of 3b corresponds to a "dative of advantage" (τῷ κυρίῳ, similar to Rom 14:4),[52] but the noun ܨܒܝܢܐ (*ṣeḇyānā*), with prefix ܒ (*b-*) and third singular masculine possessive suffix, refers rather to the theological means than to the metaphorical place of standing and points the way to an interpretation of 8b (see Excursus 9).[53]

The didactically causal 3c, whose subject ܡܠܟܘܬܐ (*malkūtā*, "kingdom," in 𝔊 certainly βασιλεία) is not among the dominant images of the *Odes of Solomon* (cf. only 22:12; 23:12), refers in the first place to 3b.[54] The monocolon also serves as the conclusion to stanza I, because "true" in the Semitic sense of "firm" and "reliable"[55] is also included in what Franzmann calls the "semantic context in 2-3."[56] Indeed the predicate ܫܪܝܪܐ (*šarrīrā*) could easily be a translation of βεβαία (cf. Rom 4:16 and 2 Cor 1:7).[57] It is more likely, however, to represent ἀληθής or ἀληθινή,[58] since these two adjectives can also express transcendent reality and dependability. Where the "Lord," the "Most High," rules and cares for his kingdom, merely human sovereignty no longer has existential meaning. Put positively, the theological reign shows itself in freedom from weakness (2a) and sickness (3a) and is a parallel term to δύναμις (2b).[59]

■ **4-8** If stanza II were divided into the independent sections 4-5, 6, and 7-8, the "structure" that Franzmann has demonstrated, with 6a-b in a "central position," 7 connected to 6 by the "repetition of the root ܪܒܐ" and the relationship of 8a-b with 5b (ܫܘܡܠܝܐ) and 6b (ܕܝܠܘܬܐ), would be completely obscured.[60] The connection between "word" (4b) and "mouth" (8a) may be added to

41 Payne Smith, 1:1812; BDAG, *s.vv.* ἀσθένεια, μαλακία, νόσος.
42 Payne Smith, 2:3888.
43 BDAG, *s.v.* ἀφίστημι.
44 See Frankenberg, 19: ἀπέστη . . . ἀπὸ τοῦ σώματός μου.
45 It is more than possible that at least some copyists of the Syriac text had one or more Greek texts available for comparison purposes.
46 The subject in N is "members"; in H, "body."
47 Contra Franzmann, 141.
48 Bauer, 598.
49 Greßmann, 454.
50 BDAG, *s.v.* ἵστημι; cf. Payne Smith, 2:3524.
51 The contrast is only between the verbs as such. The negation in 2b converts the two statements into a positive parallel.
52 BDF and BDR §188 (*dativus commodi*).
53 See Payne Smith, 2:3354; BDAG, *s.v.* θέλημα, 2b.
54 See Frankenberg, 19; Franzmann, 143: "clear word-play intended between ܫܪܝܪܐ and ܩܘܡ."
55 Bultmann, "Untersuchungen," 160 = idem, *Exegetica*, 170.
56 Franzmann, 141.
57 BDAG, *s.v.* βέβαιος; Payne Smith, 2:4303.
58 BDAG, *s.v.* ἀληθής or ἀληθινός (ἀληθινή).
59 Cf. the additions at the end of the Lord's Prayer in Matt 6:13, where βασιλεία and δύναμις are also parallel terms. The importance of the Lord's Prayer in the *Odes of Solomon* has already been shown in the commentary on *Ode* 14.
60 Franzmann, 143–44.

the final group. A Greek original can be perceived more clearly in stanza II than in some other passages, even if not all concepts—and particularly not all terms—can be reduced to one Greek equivalent.

The structure of the first two bicola[61] is masterful. Verses 4a-b and 5a-b are parallel, but 4a and 5b, on the one hand, and 4b and 5a, on the other, show antithesis, thus creating a chiasmus. So "need" is opposed to "perfection" and "word" and "works" are contrasted, as so often.[62]

Following stanza I, 4a changes to the form of a petition. The statements of 4-7 convey a profound trust in salvation, so that the numerous imperfects must be translated variously by future indicatives, optatives, jussives, and prohibitives.[63] As a start, the negations in 4a and 5a give rise to quite emphatic prohibitives. The first composite word, ܕܠܡܐ (*da-l-mā*), following the key word "Lord," a form of address repeated from 3b, means "that not/lest"[64] and corresponds to the negative particle μή or μήποτε.[65] The second composite word, ܐܦܠܐ (*ʾāp̄ lā*), at the beginning of 5a is a translation of μηδέ or μήτε.[66] The imperfects governed by the particles are both found in the second line (4b and 5b), which perhaps contributed to the confusion about line division in the manuscripts.

The convoluted phrase consisting of a preposition, a correlative, and the plural of the verbal adjective ܚܣܝܪܐ (*ḥassīrā*)[67] translates διὰ τοὺς ὑστεροῦντας[68] or ὑστερουμένους,[69] which depends on the Pauline discussion of the "body" consisting of many "members" (cf. 1 Cor 12:12-31, esp. v. 24). In contrast to 24:9, these are not "bad."[70] Nor is there a "consciousness of sin."[71] "Those who are in need" (literally, "those who [are] needing/lacking") are the weaker "members" of the "body," who have not yet attained the high status of the speaking "I" (see on 1a above, especially the disquisition on περισσεύω).

Because 4b may refer to Ps 118:43a LXX (μὴ περιέλῃς ἐκ τοῦ στόματός μου λόγον ἀληθείας, "take not the word of truth utterly out of my mouth")[72] and/or Ps 50:13a LXX (μὴ ἀπορρίψῃς με ἀπὸ τοῦ προσώπου σου, "Cast me not away from thy presence"),[73] the imperfect of ܫܕܐ (*šḏā*) in N is to be preferred to that of ܫܪܐ (*šrā*) in H.[74] The easily misspelled word in N is also the *lectio difficilior.* If the verb, whose basic meaning is "throw (away)," represents not ῥίπτω (as in 11:10) but ἀπορρίπτω, it can perfectly well be translated by "banish."[75] Although it is often impossible to decide whether ܦܬܓܡܐ (*petgāmā*) represents λόγος or ῥῆμα (see Excursus 12), in this case the influence of the vocabulary of the Psalms would suggest a preference for λόγος.[76] However, even ῥῆμα is the powerful "word" of God, which can be uttered by no human voice (see on 8a below). It is certainly not "the word of the inspired one, who has just spoken and will speak again in prophetic words at the end of the *Ode.*"[77] This interpretation is at once excluded because "word" is parallel to the term *plērōma* in 5b.[78]

The plural of ܥܒܕܐ (*ʿbāḏā*) in 5a is the first term that stands in antithesis to the "word" of 4b and at the same time elucidates the need of the "members" (4a). This expression, which corresponds to τὰ ἔργα αὐτῶν ("their works") as a description for inadequate

61 Diettrich (p. 65), by circular reasoning, treats 4 and 5 as monocola. Franzmann (p. 141) correctly shows that 4 should be divided.
62 BDAG, *s.v.* ἔργον.
63 Nöldeke §266.
64 Ibid. §373.
65 Payne Smith, 2:1983; BDAG, *s.vv.* μή, μήποτε.
66 Payne Smith, 1:327; BDAG, *s.vv.* μηδέ, μήτε.
67 See Nöldeke §§118, 236.A.
68 Frankenberg, 19.
69 See Payne Smith, 1:1340–41; BDAG, *s.v.* ὑστερέω.
70 Contra Harnack, 48.
71 Contra Diettrich, 65.
72 Rahlfs, 2:133; Brenton, 770. Although the terms "mouth" and "truth" do not occur in 4b, they are found later in this passage (see on 6b and 8a below).
73 Rahlfs, 2:53; Brenton, 728.
74 See Harris and Mingana, 2:298: " ܬܫܕܐ . . . should be right"; Payne Smith, 2:4062.
75 BDAG, *s.v.* ἀπορρίπτω.
76 Used by Frankenberg, 19; his retroversion, ἀφαίρει, does justice neither to H nor to N.
77 Diettrich, 65.
78 Diettrich (p. 65) also involves himself in a contradiction, taking the "perfection" of 5b as the "total perfection of God's kingdom," "that is expressed in the end of time, which the prophecy will reveal."

"performance,"[79] hardly resonates with the Pauline ἔργα νόμου ("works of law"),[80] but—especially in view of the dualism of 6a-b—shows a certain connection to τὰ ἔργα τοῦ σκότους ("the works of darkness") in Rom 13:12.[81]

These "works," which are to be understood as "an expression of existential commitment, not just moral conduct,"[82] prompt the speaking "I," in his second prohibitive petition, to pray that they will not obstruct the acceptance of him, together with his members, into that "invisible and encompassing transcendental sphere."[83] On the line of development of Col 2:9 (πλήρωμα τῆς θεότητος, cf. Col 1:19) and Eph 3:19 (πλήρωμα τοῦ θεοῦ), πλήρωμα/ܫܘܡܠܝܐ (*šumlāyā*) is not yet a "Gnostic technical term,"[84] but it is more than mere "perfection,"[85] or "completeness."[86] It is, in Gnosticizing fashion, the monistic "fullness" of the "unknown God,"[87] which does not allow a final dualism. The imperative of the Pe. ܟܠܐ (*klā*), generally accompanied by ܡܢ (*men*), probably translates a form of ἀπέχω.[88] The "I" uses this verb to ask to partake in God's "fullness," which will thus be extended eschatologically to the metaphorical "body" and its "members."

The central bicolon, 6, in which the speaking "I," in full confidence of salvation, utters two more prohibitives, interrupts the direct address. The formulation of these negated imperatives, which, although it is within the dualistic tradition, allows no scope, theologically or soteriologically, to the negative powers of "darkness" and "falsehood," cannot be *directly* derived from 1QS iii.13–iv.26,[89] or from *Jos. Asen.* 8:10,[90] or from New Testament passages like Rom 13:12 or John 1:5.[91] This means that, in spite of the similarity between *Ode* 18 and 1QS iii.19, it is incorrect to conclude that the author(s) "knew the most important document of the community which contains their Qumran rules and guidelines for living."[92]

The terms ܢܘܗܪܐ (*nuhrā*) and ܫܪܪܐ (*šrārā*) are found

79 BDAG, *s.v.* ἔργον; cf. Payne Smith, 2:2773.
80 BDAG, *s.v.* ἔργον, 1cβ.
81 See Käsemann, *Romans*, 360 (German, 350). Käsemann refers here to 1QM xv.9: "for they are a congregation of wickedness and all their works are darkness" (Maier, *Qumran-Essener*, 1:149; Vermes, 121). St. Paul and the people of the *Odes* may indeed have been influenced by the vocabulary of Qumran, but they have distanced themselves theologically, each in his or her own direction.
82 Käsemann, *Romans,* 363 (German, 350).
83 See Heinrich Schlier, "Pleroma," *LThK*² 8 (1963) 560, where, however, *Ode* 18 is not considered.
84 BDAG, *s.v.* πλήρωμα; Payne Smith, 2:2128.
85 Contra Greßmann, 454; Bauer, 598. Since Harris and Mingana (2:295), this important term has been translated as "perfection" (e.g., Charlesworth, 79; Franzmann, 140). Frankenberg (p. 19) uses τελειότης in 5b but τελείωσις in 8b. Varying the Greek in this fashion seems a mistake to me.
86 Contra Harnack, 48; Diettrich, 65.
87 Rudolph, *Gnosis*, 76, etc.
88 Payne Smith, 1:1738; LSJ, *s.v.* ἀπέχω: "keep off or away."
89 See Maier, *Qumran-Essener*, 1:173–74; Vermes, 64–65; Charlesworth, 80.
90 See Christoph Burchard, *Joseph und Aseneth* (JSHRZ 2.4; Gütersloh: Mohn, 1983) 650–51. The passage in Joseph's prayer to the Lord, God and Most High, runs as follows in Burchard's preliminary edition and translation: καὶ καλέσας ἀπὸ τοῦ σκότους εἰς τὸ φῶς / καὶ ἀπὸ τῆς πλάνης εἰς τὴν ἀλήθειαν / καὶ ἀπὸ τοῦ θανάτου εἰς τὴν ζωήν ("and [who] called from darkness to light / and from error to truth / and from death to life"); see Christoph Burchard, "Ein vorläufiger Text von Joseph und Aseneth," *Dielheimer Blätter zum Alten Testament* 14 (Oktober 1979) 12.
91 If καταλαμβάνειν in John 1:5 is correctly translated as "overcome," this verse (καὶ τὸ φῶς ἐν τῇ σκοτίᾳ φαίνει, καὶ ἡ σκοτία αὐτὸ οὐ κατέλαβεν, "And the light shines in the darkness, and the darkness has not overcome it") would come closest to the passage under consideration. In that case *Ode* 18:6 as well as 1 John 2:8 (ἡ σκοτία παράγεται κτλ.) would be witnesses to "the early interpretation and influence of this verse" (Theobald, *Fleischwerdung*, 215).
92 Charlesworth, *Reflections*, 14. Charlesworth is of the opinion that *Ode* 18:6 "contains a thought virtually identical to that encountered in 1QS 3.19. In both collections light (ܢܘܗܪܐ = אור) is contrasted to darkness (ܚܫܘܟܐ = חושך [N.B. medial consonant in final position]) and falsehood (ܕܓܠܘܬܐ) or perversity (העול) is antithetical to truth (ܫܪܪܐ = האמת)" (ibid., 15; correction made to a misprinted ܓܠܘܬܐ).

repeatedly in close connection in the *Odes of Solomon*.[93] So in 6a—differing, perhaps, from 36:3—the nominalized adjective ܢܗܝܪܐ (*nahhīrā*) should, with Charlesworth,[94] be equated with τὸ φῶς and not, with Frankenberg,[95] to ὁ φωστήρ. The Gnosticizing and metaphorically understood opposing power ܚܫܘܟܐ (*ḥeššōḵā*), equivalent to Greek ἡ σκοτία or τὸ σκότος,[96] cannot and will not be ultimately victorious (cf. 15:2). What is less important is whether the Ethpe. of ܙܟܐ (*zḵā*), found only here, is a translation of a passive form of ἡττάομαι[97] or of νικάομαι.[98]

Verse 6b also uses warlike vocabulary: the prohibitive imperfect of the Pe. ܥܪܩ (*ʿraq*) must correspond to a construction with φεύγω + ἀπό.[99] The dualism of "truth" and "falsehood," also a Gnosticizing trait, is closely related to the contrast between "truth" and "error" by the use of this verb (38:6). This opposition occurs also in *Ode* 18 (see on 14b and 15a below). The term ܫܪܪܐ (*šrārā*; the Greek must have been ἀλήθεια) is commonly used and important in the *Odes of Solomon* (see Excursus 1), but the feminine ܕܓܠܘܬܐ (*daggālūṯā*), derived from the root ܕܓܠ (in 𝔊 probably τὸ ψεῦδος rather than τὸ ψεῦσμα), occurs exactly three times, twice in *Ode* 18 alone.[100]

At 7a the speaking "I" resumes its direct address, which continues to the end of stanza II. Following the prohibitive statements, there are three verbs in the imperfect without negation, which can be translated without modal inflection. Since the introductory phrase using the term ܙܟܘܬܐ (*zāḵūṯā*), corresponding to εἰς νῖκος ("unto victory"), connects with the verb of 6a,[101] the term of "power," ܝܡܝܢܐ (*yammīnā* = ἡ δεξιά [i.e., χείρ]) with second masculine singular possessive suffix, must be the subject.[102] This puts σωτηρία/ܦܘܪܩܢܐ (*purqānā*), the object of the common verb ܣܐܡ, ܣܡ (*sām, in* 𝔊 more probably τίθημι [+εἴς τι] than the transitive παρίστημι),[103] distinguished by the first person *plural* suffix, squarely into the center of the declaration of trust in future salvation (see Excursus 5).[104] The topic is the "salvation" of the "members" together with the speaking "I," who is the "head" of this metaphorical body (cf. 7:16a; 17:2). This certainty of victory comes into sharper focus in contrast with the classical "custom of speaking of the emperor's νίκη as the power that grants him the victory,"[105] but there may also be some influences from Pauline sayings such as 1 Cor 15:54 from Isa 25:8 LXX: κατεπόθη ὁ θάνατος εἰς νῖκος ("Death is swallowed up in victory"); 1 Thess 5:9: ἔθετο ἡμᾶς ὁ θεός . . . εἰς περιποίησιν σωτηρίας ("God has destined us . . . to obtain salvation").[106]

In spite of the fact that there are two verbs in 7b and 7c, the two lines are so intertwined that the relative clause with preceding ܟܠ (*kol*), which forms the direct object of the imperfect of the Pa. ܢܛܪ (*naṭṭar*), with

93 Cf. 12:1-3; 15:2-4; 25:7-10; 32:1-2; 38:1; 41:14-16; cf. in 31:1-2 the terms "darkness" and "truth of the Lord"; see also Excursus 10.

94 Charlesworth, *Reflections*, 15.

95 Frankenberg, 19; see also Payne Smith, 2:2300; BDAG, *s.vv.* φῶς, φωστήρ.

96 BDAG, *s.vv.* σκοτία, σκότος; Payne Smith, 1:1402.

97 Frankenberg, 19. In that case 𝔊 would probably have used τῷ σκότει or τῇ σκοτίᾳ rather than ὑπὸ τοῦ σκότου ("a masc[uline] word since Homer"; see BDAG, *s.v.* σκότος).

98 See Payne Smith, 1:1120; BDAG, *s.vv.* ἡττάομαι, νικάομαι.

99 Frankenberg, 19: μηδὲ φυγέτω, although he then continues ὑπὸ τοῦ ψεύδους.

100 See on 8a below, and cf. 3:10. See also Payne Smith, 1:822; BDAG, *s.v.* ψεῦδος. In the New Testament, the term ܟܕܒܘܬܐ (*kaddābūṯā*) is used in preference to ܕܓܠܘܬܐ (*daggālūṯā*) to translate τὸ ψεῦδος (Payne Smith, 1:1679). But this is not true of 1 John 2:21 (πᾶν ψεῦδος ἐκ τῆς ἀληθείας οὐκ ἔστιν).

101 Payne Smith, 1:1120–21; BDAG, *s.v.* νῖκος; see Bultmann, "Bedeutung," 129 = idem, *Exegetica*, 86.

102 Cf. 8:6; 14:4; 19:5 ("*plērōma* of the right hand"); 25:2 ("right hand of salvation"); 25:9. See Payne Smith, 1:1605; BDAG, *s.v.* δεξιός.

103 Contra Frankenberg, 19; cf. Payne Smith, 2:2556–57; BDAG, *s.v.* τίθημι.

104 On the translation of ܣܡ (*sām*)/τίθημι by "establish," see Brockelmann, *Grammatik*, 186*; BDAG, *s.v.* τίθημι.

105 BDAG, *s.v.* νίκη.

106 If these passages did indeed exert an influence, this would strengthen the case for a Greek original of the *Odes of Solomon*, since the Syriac New Testament (*NTSy*, 100, 137) translates εἰς νῖκος as ܒܙܟܘܬܐ (*b-zāḵūṯā*) but σωτηρία as ܚܝܐ (*ḥayyē*); correct ܟܙܟܘܬܐ to ܒܙܟܘܬܐ in Lattke 2:78 n. 2.

future meaning, in 7c, is also the direct object of the imperfect of the Pa. ܩܒܠ (*qabbel*) in 7b.[107] Both Syriac verbs, which form a logical sequence, and their possible Greek equivalents demand an object in the accusative, in this case πάντα κτλ. (see Excursus 4).[108] The prepositional phrase in 7b refers only to the first verb and is the equivalent of the adverb παντόθεν,[109] so that the preposition ܡܢ (*men*) bears no particular emphasis, which falls instead on the ingathering of the dispersed. Why this first section of the statement should be "a polemic against the nationalism of the Pharisees"[110] is incomprehensible. The full meaning becomes clear in 7c, not so much in the verb "protect" as in the emphatic feminine plural of the nominalized adjective ܒܝܫܐ (*bīšā*) and the intransitive masculine singular passive participle of ܐܚܕ (*ʾeḥad*), which has already occurred in the prison vocabulary of 17:8b-11.[111] The preposition ܒ (*b-*), which follows the relative particle, should be taken instrumentally (like ἐν in Rom 7:6), although it can also have a spatial meaning in a transferred sense.[112] It could be translated as "all who are enmeshed in evils"[113] or perhaps "bad luck"[114] or "misfortunes."[115] But these translations both lay too much weight on "personal conduct"[116] and are too weak. The "evils" are not only an individual's "wickedness" and "works" (5a), but—as in Rom 1:29—are existential, even ontological "characteristics" of this darkened world in which the Gnostic "members" also must still live.[117] It makes little difference whether ܒܝܫܬܐ (*bīšāṯā*) translates αἱ κακίαι[118] or τὰ πονηρά.[119] One may, however, agree with Frankenberg that ܐܚܝܕ (*ʾaḥīḏ*) corresponds to the participle of the passive κατέχομαι,[120] which can be used to express being bound or confined by the "law" (cf. Rom 7:6) or by "disease."[121]

In describing the form of 8 as a "concluding confessional statement concerning God,"[122] it is important not to overlook the didactic nature of the parallel bicolon, which leads on into stanza III (see on 3c above). The introductory second masculine singular personal pronoun ܐܢܬ (*ʾat*) is also typically found elsewhere at the end of a complete Ode or part of one (4:15; 14:10; 42:18); the theological (ontological) problems can be greatly simplified by returning to two passages, which have been previously discussed and contain numerous parallel terms,[123] before attempting to interpret the current one.

107 This does not mean that 7b-c should be run on as one overlong line (contra Frankenberg, 19). Since the imperfects in 7b-c can also be read as third feminine singular perfects, they may equally be thought to refer to the "right [hand]" of 7a (so Charlesworth, 80). I cannot follow Charlesworth's subtleties in the further interpretation of ܡܢ ܠܟܠ (H + N). Harris and Mingana (2:297) invert the manuscript order to ܠܟܠ ܡܢ and translate the resulting phrase as "whomsoever" (2:295; cf. Payne Smith, *Dictionary*, 215).

108 See Payne Smith, 2:3468; BDAG, *s.vv.* δέχομαι, λαμβάνω (and, in some cases, composites of these verbs); Payne Smith, 2:2355; BDAG, *s.vv.* διαφυλάσσω (e.g., Luke 4:10 from Ps 90:11 LXX), τηρέω (e.g., 1 Thess 5:23), φρουρέω (e.g., Phil 4:7), φυλάσσω (esp. 2 Thess 3:3, κύριος . . . φυλάξει ἀπὸ τοῦ πονηροῦ, "the Lord . . . will guard you from evil").

109 Payne Smith, 1:426; BDAG, *s.v.* παντόθεν ("everywhere").

110 Diettrich, 65, perhaps thinking of John 11:52.

111 See Payne Smith, 1:116–17. This participle is not one of the verbal adjectives that double the middle radical; see Nöldeke §118.

112 "Eus. Theoph. i. 35. 5" has an expression in a similar form: . . . ܒܚܫܘܟܐ ܕܒܝܫܬܐ ܐܚܝܕܝܢ ܗܘܘ, *tenebris pravitatum tenebantur* (Payne Smith, 1:117).

113 Bauer, 598.

114 Greßmann, 454.

115 Emerton, 708.

116 *MEL*, 32:2781, *s.v.* verstricken.

117 See Michael Lattke, "κακία," *EWNT* 2 (1981) 584–85; *EDNT* 2:237. It may be useful to draw attention to the following Gnosticizing saying in *Corp. Herm.* 6.4: ὁ γὰρ κόσμος πλήρωμά ἐστι τῆς κακίας ("for the cosmos is the fullness of evil"); cf. Colpe and Holzhausen, 69.

118 BDAG, *s.v.* κακία.

119 BDAG, *s.v.* πονηρός, 2c; cf. Payne Smith, 1:440.

120 Frankenberg, 19.

121 BDAG, *s.v.* κατέχω, 1d.

122 Franzmann, 143.

123 These are parallels not only to 8a (cf. esp. 12:3) and 8b (cf. esp. 9:4) but to the whole of stanza II and also other passages in *Ode* 18.

12:3 And it[124] increased in me its *gnōsis*,[125]
because the true word is the mouth of the Lord
and the gate of his light.

9:4 For in the will of the Lord is your life,
and his mind/purpose is eternal life,
and imperishable is your *plērōma*/fullness.

A modern who considers "God" a useful "auxiliary construction for the understanding of the world,"[126] drawing on negative theology, might interrogate this ancient text as follows: If God does not simply exist, how is it possible to proclaim the nonexistence of "falsehood" and "death" in his "mouth" (= in his "word") or to assert that his "will" can have an intention? In answering these and similar questions, which must occasionally be put quite bluntly, it is not sufficient to retreat from the sphere of knowledge and research to a sphere of belief and religion. Rather, it is necessary to accept that even in antiquity the users of the terms of "being" such as εἰμί[127] and ܐܝܬ[128] in positive and negative contexts were well aware of the "analogous uses of the words in our language," which always "imply a tale"—or a teaching—"spoken in μεταφέρειν."[129]

The emphatic address in 8a is directed to "God" (in 𝔊 θεός μου or a similar expression), who is identical with the "Most High" (1a, 14a, 15b) and the "Lord" (3b, 4a; see the table in Excursus 17). The term "falsehood" harks back to the dualism implicit in 6b (see also *Hermas, Man.* 28 [III].1: οὐδὲν παρ' αὐτῷ ψεῦδος, "there is no lie in him").[130] Although this is, strictly speaking, the only term that can be used with the anthropomorphism ἐν τῷ στόματί σου (cf. 12:3; 26:10), both non-"falsehood" (= "truth") and non-"death" (= eternal, immortal "life"),[131] used in this absolute way, are "properties of God."[132] Just as there is a connection between ܦܘܡܐ (*pummā*), "mouth," and God's "word" (4b), the rare words "breath" and "breathed" (15b) will refer back to this organ of speech imagined for the Most High (see Excursus 31).[133]

Introduced by the adversative particle ܐܠܐ (*ʾellā*; in 𝔊 presumably ἀλλά) and with the subject "the will" postponed to the end, the predicate noun *plērōma* occupies the center of the didactic 8b. This determining address, prepared for by 3b and 5b, shows the Gnostic-theological term "fulness" in its most eschatological light. God's transcendental being is, of course, not theo-ontologically a process of "becoming,"[134] but soteriologically it is not yet completed.[135]

■ **9-10** Verse 9 marks the beginning of the second, didactic part, which is firmly attached to the first by being a personal address (in stanza III only). The words now put into the mouth of the speaking "I" of this Ode may be a "fragment" traditional with the people of the

124 The subject of 3a is the "word of truth" (12:1a).
125 Either the knowledge/*gnōsis* of "truth" or of the "word."
126 Winfried Schulze, "Der Fragebogen," *Forschung & Lehre* 6 (Bonn: Deutscher Hochschulverband, 1999) 616.
127 BDAG, *s.v.* εἰμί.
128 Nöldeke §§199, 301–8.
129 Eberhard Jüngel, "Thesen zum Verhältnis von Existenz, Wesen und Eigenschaften Gottes," *ZThK* 96 (1999) 405. Not everything that Jüngel says in his "proposition" on a "theology rooted in the gospel," given his presupposition of a "vocabulary of the Christian faith," can be applied to the *Odes of Solomon,* since they originated in an area influenced by early Judaism, Christianity, and Gnosticism.
130 Lindemann and Paulsen, 378–80; Ehrman, 2:240–41.
131 Cf. 10:2; 15:10; 28:6; 31:7; 38:3; 40:6.
132 Brox, *Hirt,* 199. Rev 14:5, in a blended quotation of Ps 31:2 LXX, Isa 53:9, and Zeph 3:13, says of the ἄμωμοι that ἐν τῷ στόματι αὐτῶν οὐχ εὑρέθη ψεῦδος. Wilhelm Bousset finds it "unclear" why "their truthfulness is emphasized" (see Bousset, *Die Offenbarung Johannis* [Göttingen: Vandenhoeck & Ruprecht, 1906; repr., 1966] 382), but Heinrich Kraft points out that "the blamelessness is God's doing" (Kraft, *Die Offenbarung des Johannes* [HNT 16a; Tübingen: Mohr Siebeck, 1974], 190; cf. p. 186, where the word "nicht" [= not] must be inserted into the translation of Rev 14:5).
133 See Payne Smith, 2:3063–64; BDAG, *s.v.* στόμα.
134 On this formulation, see Eberhard Jüngel, *Gottes Sein ist im Werden: Verantwortliche Rede vom Sein Gottes bei Karl Barth. Eine Paraphrase* (2nd ed.; Tübingen: Mohr Siebeck, 1967) III and throughout.
135 Nor is Jüngel concerned with a "developing God." "God's being is not the same as God's becoming, but God's being is ontologically placed" (Jüngel, *Gottes Sein ist im Werden,* III). The statement in the foreword to his first edition (1966, p. III), "But

Odes of Solomon, but is surely no poetic "patchwork,"[136] consisting, as it does, of two "completely parallel sentences."[137] The scarlet thread that winds through the reciprocity of these two bicola is the active singular participle, feminine or masculine, of the Pe. ܝܕܥ (*ʾidaʿ*). This emphasizes the "continuing as well as the momentary present" of the statements.[138] 𝔊 would have played with forms of γινώσκω and/or οἶδα in a similar way,[139] which suggests the following retroversion, with acknowledgments to Frankenberg,[140] suggesting alternative verbs in progressive "kinds of action (*Aktionsarten*) in the present stem":[141]

9 καὶ τὴν ματειότητα σὺ οὐ γινώσκεις/οἶσθα
ὅτι οὐδὲ αὐτή σε γινώσκει/οἶδε

10 καὶ οὐ γινώσκεις/οἶσθα σὺ πλάνη
ὅτι (ἀλλ')[142] οὐδὲ αὐτή σε γινώσκει/οἶδε

This reconstruction of a possible Greek original, whose word order—especially in the use of the accented σύ and the enclitic σε—cannot be certainly determined, has been placed before the exegesis proper to show that the two personified and parallel terms, ܣܪܝܩܘܬܐ (*srīqūṯā*) in 9a and ܛܥܝܘܬܐ (*ṭāʿyūṯā*) in 10a, are most probably equivalent to ἡ ματαιότης and ἡ πλάνη.[143]

Although the key word ܣܪܝܩܘܬܐ (*srīqūṯā*),[144] which may have come from Rom 8:20, is a *hapax legomenon,* its meaning is elucidated by other forms of ܣܪܝܩܐ (*srīqā*; cf. 5:9; 11:8b; 17:3; 18:12a) as well as by the other *hapax legomenon* derived from the root ܣܪܩ, the Ethpa. ܐܣܬܪܩ (*ʾestarraq* [18:12b]; see below). To import the long philosophical discussion on "nothing," which extends from Parmenides and Plotinus to Heidegger and Sartre, into 9a,[145] and to confront the negations of 9a and 10a with the theological dogma of "God's omniscience"[146] would be an overinterpretation of stanza III. "Nothingness" here is related to the power of "death" (8a), the personified "vanity" and "impermanence" of all that is and who are unredeemed,[147] but without reference to the terms κτίσις and ἐλπίς of Rom 8:18-25. Just as in English it is possible to say that one does not acknowledge him/her—that is, one has nothing (left) in common with this person (cf. already Mark 14:71; 2 Cor 5:16)—it is said of the God, who is being addressed, that he neither knows nor acknowledges[148] "nothingness."

The reason for this non-"relationship"[149] is given, reciprocally, in 9b (cf. Gal 4:8-9; 1 Thess 4:5). For Paul, humankind, γνόντες τὸν θεὸν οὐχ ὡς θεὸν ἐδόξασαν ἢ ηὐχαρίστησαν, ἀλλ' ἐματαιώθησαν ἐν τοῖς διαλογισμοῖς αὐτῶν ("although they knew God they did not honor him as God or give thanks to him, but they became futile in their thinking" [Rom 1:21]), but here the ματαιότης is from the outset judged incapable of "knowing" God and thus "acknowledging" him as God. Therefore this inimical power, like the πλάνη ("error"), is described as "evil" (7c) and "ignorance" (non-*gnōsis*; see on 11a below).

All that has been said about reciprocal nonacknowledgment in 9a-b can be transferred to 10a-b, but the textual criticism of the readings in 10b needs careful attention. Verse 10b in N begins ܡܛܠ ܕܐܦ (*meṭṭol d-āp̄*

the God whose being is becoming may experience *death* as a human," is not easily applicable to the *Odes of Solomon*.

136 Agreeing and disagreeing with Diettrich, 64.

137 Kittel, 88.

138 Nöldeke §269.

139 BDAG, *s.vv.* γινώσκω, οἶδα; Payne Smith, 1:1554–55.

140 Frankenberg, 19–20.

141 BDF and BDR §318.

142 This putative variant in 𝔊 will be discussed later. Diettrich (p. 65) translated the Syriac particle ܐܠܐ as "but," placing it at the end of 10a and anachronistically used "false teaching" to translate ܛܥܝܘܬܐ (*ṭāʿyūṯā*).

143 BDAG, *s.vv.* ματαιότης, πλάνη; Schenke, *Herkunft*, 26.

144 Payne Smith, 2:2750.

145 See Theo Kobusch, "Nichts, Nichtseiendes," *HWP* 6 (1984) 805–11, 834–36.

146 See Raphael Schulte, "Allwissenheit Gottes," *LThK*[3] 1 (1993) 421.

147 See BDAG, *s.v.* ματαιότης.

148 See BDAG, *s.v.* γινώσκω, 1b, 7.

149 See BDAG, *s.v.* οἶδα, 2.

lā),[150] but in H it begins ܐܠܐ ܡܛܠ ܕܐܦܠܐ (*ʾellā meṭṭol d-āp̄ lā*),[151] which means that there must have been Greek texts, of which some at least had ὅτι ἀλλ' οὐδέ, although others may have had only ὅτι οὐδέ.[152] The phrase ἀλλ' οὐδέ meaning "but not even" is translated into Syriac in the New Testament and elsewhere by three different expressions: ܘܐܦܠܐ (Acts 19:2), ܐܠܐ ܐܦܠܐ (Luke 23:15; 1 Cor 3:2; 4:3) and ܐܦ . . . ܠܐ (Gal 2:3).[153] This weakens the case for a speculative original ܐܠܗܝ (= "my God").[154] Charlesworth has some reason to call ܐܠܐ "an error in H." But this is true only for the word order; his argument that "the form for God in the *Odes* is ܐܠܗܐ" is incorrect.[155] Franzmann's reason for preferring N is weak, since she herself points out that the parallelism of 9b and 10b is upset by the "addition of ܗܝ for emphasis."[156] So it is not because ܐܠܐ is not found in N, but following accepted conventions of translation that the advice of Harris and Mingana "not to take any notice of it in the translation" can be followed.[157] But this seemingly minor variant is very important when the original language of the *Odes of Solomon* comes under discussion.

Although the feminine ܛܥܝܘܬܐ (*ṭāʿyūṯā*), derived from the root ܛܥܐ, has been used to translate ἀγνόημα (Gen 43:12) and even ἄγνοια (Acts 17:30),[158] in 10a and elsewhere in the *Odes of Solomon,*[159] it corresponds to ἡ πλάνη. The second personified power is not simply "erring" (*errare humanum est*), not committing a philosophical "error," but—as the opposite of ἀλήθεια and thus parallel to "falsehood" (6b)—the fundamental "delusion" and "error," which is itself astray and misleads humankind.[160] Perhaps this πλάνη, this lack of (re)cognition of God, which receives "emphasis" in 10b by the use of the enclitic third feminine singular pronoun,[161] influenced the "fall of the Aeons"[162] as described in the *Gospel of Truth* (= NHC 1,*3*).

■ **11-12** This new section, which is loosely connected to stanza III "by the repetition of the roots ܥܒܪ (11a) and ܣܪܩ (12a, 12b)"[163] and by the later reuse of the term "error" (14b), contains Gnostic-dualistic teaching with a polemical edge that affects both the negative view of the past in stanza IV and its positive companion piece stanza V. The speaker no longer uses a direct address and does not explicitly include himself as he "contrasts . . . the final fate of ignorance and its followers . . . with the final fate of *gnōsis* and its followers."[164]

The subject of the vivid images of 11a-b is "ἄγνοια or ἀγνωσία, the opposite of γνῶσις" (cf. 7:21; 28:13; and see Excursus 7).[165] The Ethpe. of ܚܙܐ (*ḥzā*), twice coupled with the particle of comparison ܐܝܟ (*ʾak̠* = ὡς or ὡσεί [cf. Luke 24:11]), translates φαίνομαι (as in 11:1),[166] but there is no sense of an epiphany here, and the meaning is close to "look like."[167] Because the images are close and parallel, the feminine ܥܘܪܐ (*ʿūrā*), from the root ܥܘܪ, cannot in 11a be translated as "chaff" or "dust,"[168] as in 29:10,[169] but must also refer to the "sea," as a translation of ἡ ἄχνη.[170] Thus, it is "anything that comes off the surface"[171] and should be translated as "spray"[172] rather than "foam."[173]

150 Lattke, *Bedeutung*, 2:197. N does have a mark of division between 10a and 10b (contra Lattke, *Bedeutung*, 1:75).
151 Charlesworth, *Manuscripts*, 55.
152 BDAG, *s.v.* οὐδέ.
153 See *NTSy* on these passages. Generally οὐδέ is translated as ܐܦܠܐ, sometimes as ܘܠܐ, and rarely as ܠܐ on its own.
154 Contra Richard Hugh Connolly, review of Bernard in *JTS* 14 (1912–13) 312.
155 Charlesworth, 80; cf. the occurrences of ܐܠܗܝ, ending in silent *Yūdh*, in 4:1; 11:9; 17:1; 18:8; 25:1; 40:1.
156 Franzmann, 142, 144.
157 Harris and Mingana, 2:297.
158 Payne Smith, 1:1494.
159 Cf. 15:6; 18:14; 31:2; 38:6, 8, 10; and see Excursus 38.
160 BDAG, *s.v.* πλάνη; Lampe, 1089.
161 Nöldeke §312.B.
162 Carsten Colpe, "Gnosis II (Gnostizismus)," *RAC* 11 (1981) 572.
163 Franzmann, 144.
164 Diettrich, 66.
165 Bauer, 599.
166 See Payne Smith, 1:1234.
167 BDAG, *s.v.* φαίνω, 2.
168 Nor as "straw."
169 BDAG, *s.v.* χνοῦς. On ὁ χνοῦς, cf. Ps 1:4 in *Barn.* 11:7.
170 See Payne Smith, 2:2841; cf. Wis 5:14, and the note, including some textual criticism, by Georgi, 417–18.
171 LSJ, *s.v.* ἄχνη.
172 See LSJ.RevSup, *s.v.* ἄχνη.
173 See already Greßmann, 454.

Parallel to this "spray," which spatters face and eyes, is the *hapax legomenon* ܣܪܝܘܬܐ (*saryūṯā*) in 11b. This feminine, derived from ܣܪܐ (*srā*) or ܣܪܝ (*srī*), does not here mean "mist,"[174] nor "foam," as Charlesworth translates it[175] in preference to Harris and Mingana's "scum."[176] Even Franzmann's translation, "filth,"[177] is not as close as "stink," "foulness," or "filthiness."[178] The key to understanding the term in this passage is that, with or without ܪܝܚܐ (*rēḥā*), it corresponds to δυσωδία,[179] meaning "stench."[180] The alternative term σαπρία, on which Greßmann bases his translation "decay,"[181] cannot form part of a *maritime* image describing a fogging of the sight and stimulation of the sense of smell. This metaphor of the foul-smelling "sea,"[182] which, unlike 16:10, could also be a large "lake,"[183] was so widespread that it is not really possible to be sure that it was rooted in personal "experience" and to use it as "evidence of a Palestinian provenance for the Odes."[184] The metaphor may be elucidated, without reference to disturbing natural phenomena, by a warning from one who possessed the γνῶσις ϑεοῦ—actually equated with Ἰησοῦς Χριστός[185]—in full measure against the "stench of the teaching of the ruler of this age," δυσωδία τῆς διδασκαλίας τοῦ ἄρχοντος τοῦ αἰῶνος τούτου (Ignatius *Eph.* 17:1).[186]

The two third feminine singular suffixes and the enclitic personal pronoun ܗܝ (*-y*) in the second bicolon refer to "non-*gnōsis*" used absolutely and already in the process of becoming a technical term, which is sharply differentiated from merely human ignorance and lack of knowledge, while the subject of all three verbs in 12a-b is the plural of the masculine passive participle of ܣܪܩ (*sraq*),[187] which can be considered a personification, and is the antecedent of the third masculine plural pronoun ܗܢܘܢ (*hennōn*). The wordplay in 𝔊 would have used οἱ μάταιοι.[188] If the Valentinians, not much later, hung such a polemical label on *their* opponents, it would explain the branding of the "followers of Valentinian" and other "heretics" by the orthodox as μάταιοι.[189] What is important is that this is a polemical term that may even date back to St. Paul, as in the amended quotation from Ps 93:11 LXX in 1 Cor 3:20: κύριος γινώσκει τοὺς διαλογισμοὺς τῶν σοφῶν [for ἀνθρώπων] ὅτι εἰσὶν μάταιοι ("The Lord knows that the thoughts of the wise are futile").

As in other passages the Pe. ܣܒܪ (*sḇar*) in 12a is closely connected with the verb in 11a (cf. 7:12a, 12c; 28:9a–b).[190] This could represent a form of νομίζω,[191] but a form of δοκέω is more likely, which suggests a retroversion as follows: καὶ ἔδοξαν οἱ μάταιοι αὐτὴν εἶναι μεγάλην.[192] The delusion of these "vain" opponents consisted, therefore, in believing their non-existent *gnōsis* to be "great," that is "powerful" and "important."[193]

174 Contra Bauer, 599.
175 Charlesworth, 79.
176 Harris and Mingana, 2:296.
177 Franzmann, 141.
178 Payne Smith, *Dictionary*, 391.
179 Payne Smith, 2:2724; Frankenberg (p. 20) already uses it, although in 11a he has χνοῦς.
180 Lattke, *Bedeutung*, 1:127; BDAG, *s.v.* δυσωδία.
181 Greßmann, 454; see also Friedrich Rehkopf, *Septuaginta-Vokabular* (Göttingen: Vandenhoeck & Ruprecht, 1989) 257: "Fäulnis."
182 Payne Smith, 1:1600.
183 BDAG, *s.v.* ϑάλασσα. The translation "swamp" is quite arbitrary, since the "bad smell" can certainly arise from the "sea" (see Harnack, 48). Both the "Sea of Galilee" and the "Dead Sea" were called ϑάλασσα in antiquity.
184 Charlesworth, 81.
185 "The equation of Christ and knowledge intensifies the measure of heresy, in Ignatius' mind, since it demonstrates their ἄγνοια towards both donor and gift" (Bauer and Paulsen, 41).
186 Bauer and Paulsen, 41; Fischer, 154–57; Ehrman, 1:236–37.
187 Payne Smith, 2:2747.
188 See 9a above, "nothingness"; 12a below, the last verb of stanza IV. See also BDAG, *s.v.* μάταιος.
189 Cf. Irenaeus *Haer.* 3.11.9; 5.1.2; and see Brox, *Irenäus,* 3:116–17; 5:28–29.
190 The Ethpe. of ܣܒܪ (*sḇar*) is also closely associated with the Ethpe. ܐܬܚܙܝ (*ʾeṯḥzī*); cf. 7:4; 17:6; 34:5.
191 Payne Smith, 2:2509–10; BDAG, *s.v.* νομίζω; see Frankenberg, 20: ἐνόμιζον.
192 See BDAG, *s.v.* δοκέω, 1c, translated with following "acc[usative] and inf[initive] w[ith] subj[ect] not identical;" on the construction with ܠ = *de* (Payne Smith, 2:2510), cf., e.g., 2 Cor 11:16.
193 Bauer, 599; BDAG, *s.v.* μέγας, 4b; Payne Smith, 2:3783–84.

The lack of the introductory particle ܘ (*w*-) in H might be interpreted as putting even more emphasis on 12b, but it is probably only the copyist's carelessness.[194] In 12b—and therefore in stanza IV as a whole—the stress is not on the normally important term ܕܡܘܬܐ (*dmūṯā*) but on the final verb.[195] The complete preceding phrase[196] "simply means, 'they resembled it' in Syriac"[197] and may be only an idiomatic translation of καὶ (αὐτοὶ) ὡμοιώθησαν αὐτῇ.[198] The use of the redundant common word ܐܬܐ (*ʾeṯā*) transformed the ambivalent καί into ܘ (*w*-), on the one hand, and ܐܦ (*ʾāp̄*), on the other.[199] The Ethpa. ܐܣܬܪܩ (*ʾestarraq*), which is connected to the words in 9a and 12a derived from the same root ܣܪܩ, occurs only here and very probably translates ἐματαιώθησαν (cf. Rom 1:21).[200] It is a powerful word, which—in the theological passive—passes the final judgment appropriate to the nature of the "empty ones."

■ **13-15** This Gnostic-dualistic teaching, placed in antithesis to stanza IV, can be called esoteric on a number of levels. This conclusion would be reinforced if the sometimes difficult construction of stanza V were to conceal historical memories among the mythologoumena. Since it has become progressively more likely that *Ode* 18 was originally composed in Greek and is strongly influenced by Pauline thought, some parts of stanza V can be elucidated. Other literary influences may also be present. First it must be noted that stanza V consists of two tricola, and the last line of each emphasizes the "Most High," which also acts as the *inclusio* for the whole Ode.

The correlative ܐܝܠܝܢ ܕ (*ʾayllēn d*-) in 13a followed by the active masculine plural participle of ܝܕܥ (*ʾidaʿ*) probably stands for Greek οἱ γνόντες or possibly οἱ γινώσκοντες.[201] Those "who understand" are not simply "the wise";[202] they are the "possessors of knowledge."[203] At this time γνωστικός was not yet used as a technical term.[204] If it may be assumed that 𝔊 also indulged in wordplay, 13a could have begun καὶ ἔγνωσαν.[205] The absolute use of both these forms leads to the conclusion that *gnōsis*—with or without the existence of γνῶσις as a technical term—was a positive in opposition to "non-*gnōsis*" (cf. 11a; see Excursus 7).[206]

Verse 13b also shows paronomasia, based, most probably, on a play with (δια)λογίζομαι and διαλογισμός. The prepositional phrase, consisting of ܒ (*b*-) and the plural of the feminine ܡܚܫܒܬܐ (*maḥšabṯā*) (which could easily—without the negative tinge—have come from Rom 1:21) is not to be interpreted instrumentally,[207] and is in contrast to the negative statement in 24:10.[208] Although many Greek words can be used as equivalents to ܚܫܒ (*ḥšab*; cf. 5:8 and 9:3),[209] διελογίσαντο or simple ἐλογίσαντο is more likely as the original word here than διενοήθησαν.[210] At any rate, even in 𝔖, the two terms used in this wordplay do not present much difficulty in comprehension (see Excursus 9), but the Ethpa. ܐܬܛܢܦ (*ʾeṭṭannap̄*), which occurs only here, is not so easily understood.[211] There are only two Greek verbs that correspond to it, namely, μιαίνω or μολύνω,[212] and both also correspond to Pa. and Ethpa. forms derived

194 Made more probable by the fact that ܣܪܝܩܐ (*srīqā*) in 12a does not have its plural pointing (see Lattke, *Bedeutung*, 1:70 n. 2; Franzmann, 142).

195 Instead of referring to *Odes of Solomon* 7:4; 17:4; 18:12; 34:4, Jervell (*Imago Dei*, 167) quite generally—and probably mistakenly—lists "OdSal 34,14; 18,4; 7,4."

196 Literally, "in its form, likeness." The possessive pronoun refers to non-*gnōsis*, not to the "vain ones."

197 Harris and Mingana, 2:297.

198 See BDAG, *s.v.* ὁμοιόω; Bauer, 599: "and they became like it."

199 It is possible that the variant reading in H may be explained by this ambivalent meaning of καί (= "and/also").

200 BDAG, s.v. ματαιόω; Payne Smith, 2:2749; Frankenberg, 20.

201 See Nöldeke §236; Payne Smith, 1:1555; BDAG, *s.v.* γινώσκω.

202 Suggested by Harris and Mingana, 2:296; Charlesworth, 79.

203 Bauer, 599.

204 See Lampe, 320.

205 Frankenberg, 20.

206 Harris and Mingana (vol. 1, on this passage; 2:296) and Charlesworth (p. 79), by emending H without explanation (there is no line break marked in N) and moving the first verb of 13b to the end of 13a, soften the harshness of the absolute use of "know."

207 Contra Charlesworth, 79.

208 Payne Smith, 1:1397; BDAG, *s.vv.* διαλογίζομαι, διαλογισμός.

209 Payne Smith, 1:1395.

210 See Frankenberg, 20.

211 Payne Smith, 1:1490.

212 BDAG, *s.vv.* μιαίνω, μολύνω.

from the roots ܛܢܦ and ܣܘܦ.[213] So all that can be said is that this must be interpreted as a transferred meaning, although it does not refer to ritual uncleanness or to moral blemishes. It is rather the radical negation of any connection with "nothingness" (9a; cf. 12b), "error" (10a; 14b), and "falsehood," the opposite of "truth" (6b; 15a).

If Franzmann is right in detecting a vocabulary of creation connecting 14a with 15b,[214] the causal clause 14a may have been influenced by Rom 1:18-25, with its emphasis on the creator. What is said there about *all* created humanity is here narrowed to focus on the Gnostics. For it is only they who "were" by/in the "mind" or "thought" of the "Most High," which means, on the one hand, they "came into being"[215] and, on the other, they existed (in 𝔊 ἐγένοντο).[216] The interchangeability of ܬܪܥܝܬܐ (*tarʿītā*) and ܡܚܫܒܬܐ (*maḥšabtā*) is shown by the statement in 16:19 at the end of a more general teaching on creation ("And the aeons were by his word / and by the thought of his heart").[217]

The apparently innocent ܓܚܟܘ (*gḥek*), "they laughed,"[218] in 14b reveals its sharp point only when looking back at the polemics of stanza IV. But the underlying verb καταγελάω (+ genitive of those ridiculed) is, in its own right, a strong statement of "superiority."[219] In this way, the Gnostics laid claim to God's "superiority" and his personified "wisdom."[220] The involved correlative construction with the masculine plural active participle of the Pa. ܗܠܟ (*hallek*), "walking," which is used negatively only here and which H pedantically removes into the past by the use of ܗܘܘ (*hwaw*), conceals the more elegant genitive of a participle of περιπατέω.[221] The use of this verb, which will have occurred with ἐν πλάνῃ, is not confined to Johannine dualism (cf. ἐν τῇ σκοτίᾳ in John 8:12; 12:35; 1 John 2:11); its metaphorical meaning is characteristic especially of the writings of the Pauline circle.[222] Though the key word ܛܥܝܘܬܐ (*ṭāʿyūtā*) may, because of the likely context, have been taken from Rom 1:27, it is not used for "idolatry" or "deification of created beings"[223] but belongs to a wider vocabulary of a "dualism, which speaks, in texts of diverse origin, with a unitary terminology that is however applied in a graduated fashion."[224] Here πλάνη is not as definitely personified as it often is (see on 10 above), and that is due, partly, to the contrast that follows immediately.[225]

The term "truth" in 15a also appears less strongly personified than elsewhere (see Excursus 1). As in 31:2, ἀλήθεια/ܫܪܪܐ (*šrārā*) is contrasted with "error," but this "truth," as direct object of the Pa. ܡܠܠ (*mallel*), almost becomes a "revelation" (cf. 12:1; Excursus 12).[226] The third masculine personal plural pronoun ܗܢܘܢ (*hennōn*), emphatically placed at the beginning and preceded by redundant ܘ (*u*-), is given even greater

213 Payne Smith, 1:1454, 2:2541.
214 Franzmann, 142.
215 Ibid.
216 Frankenberg, 20.
217 If Franzmann's interpretation of 14a should be incorrect, ܗܘܘ (*hwaw*) would be neutral. The prepositional phrase would then not be understood instrumentally, but in a transferred sense as describing the place of the power in the mind of the "Most High." And there is another consideration. If stanza V is not two tricola but three bicola, 14a would be the justification preceding 14b and the "thought of the Most High" would be the antithesis of "error," which would be unusual when compared to other passages (cf. 9:3-5; 12:4; 28:19; 38:21).
218 A subscript point in both manuscripts shows this verb to be a Pe. (contra Lattke, *Bedeutung*, 2:63; idem, *Oden*, 271; idem, 2:86; and Charlesworth, 78, where it is shown as a Pa.). Both the Pe. and the Pa. are used with the preposition ܥܠ (*ʿal*). The Pe. corresponds more often to καταγελάω than to γελάω (Payne Smith, 1:703; BDAG, *s.vv.* γελάω, καταγελάω).
219 Karl Heinrich Rengstorf, "γελάω, καταγελάω, γέλως," *ThWNT* 1 (1933) 657–58; *TDNT* 1:660.
220 Cf. ἐκγελάω in Pss 2:4; 36:13; 58:9 LXX; ἐπιγελάω in Prov 1:26; and see Rengstorf, "γελάω," *ThWNT* 1:659; *TDNT* 1:661.
221 Payne Smith, 1:1014; BDAG, *s.v.* περιπατέω.
222 Cf., e.g., Rom 8:4; 2 Cor 10:2 (with κατὰ σάρκα); Eph 4:17 (with καθώς); Col 3:7; Eph 2:2 (with ἐν).
223 Herbert Braun, "πλανάω, κτλ.," *ThWNT* 6 (1959) 244; *TDNT* 6:243.
224 Braun, "πλανάω," *ThWNT* 6:241; *TDNT* 6:240.
225 Charlesworth (p. 81) remarks on 14b: "The meaning of this line seems contrary to the Christian kerygma. Could it be influenced by the Qumranic injunction to hate 'the sons of darkness'?"
226 See Bultmann, "Untersuchungen," 159–61 = idem, *Exegetica*, 170–72.

prominence by the particle ܕܝܢ (*dēn*).[227] But whether 𝔊 had καὶ αὐτοί[228] or αὐτοὶ δέ to "underline" the "contrast" between 14bβ and 15a[229] cannot be determined with certainty. Even καὶ αὐτοὶ δέ would not be an unthinkable construction.[230]

Verse 15b, containing a wordplay and two *hapax legomena,* is certainly an allusion to Gen 2:7, which also has the Pe. ܢܦܚ (*npaḥ*), representing ἐνεφύσησεν ("breathed") in the LXX.[231] The deviation from Gen 2:7 in the use of the uncommon ܢܦܚܐ (*npāḥā*)—in place of ܢܫܡܬܐ (*nšamtā*), corresponding to ἡ πνοή—can be traced to 𝔊, where the wordplay will have demanded τὸ φύσημα.[232] On a higher level, however, the inspired, "truth"-speaking Gnostics are distinguished from the common people, who became living beings by God's πνοὴ ζωῆς ("breath of life"; Gen 2:7: לְנֶפֶשׁ חַיָּה—εἰς ψυχὴν ζῶσαν—ܠܢܦܫܐ ܚܝܐ). By this even the "Most High," though he retains his Jewish and Christian titles "Lord" (3b, 4a) and "God" (8a), is removed out of the reality of his creation, an idea that does not occur in other Odes (cf. the teaching on creation in 4:15; 7:24; 16:8-9).

■ **16** The final doxology, perhaps a respond, which differs completely in terminology from 11:24 𝔖 but is connected to the other doxologies by the term ܬܫܒܘܚܬܐ (*tešbuḥtā* = δόξα in 11:24 𝔊; cf. 16:20; 17:16; 20:10) and the mention of God's "name" (16:20; 20:10), forms the last link in the chain of argument for a Greek original of this Ode. As has been shown for 7:23 and 15:7 (and cf. 29:3), the construction with ܪܒܘܬܐ (*rabbūṯā*) and ܝܐܝܘܬܐ (*yāʾyūṯā*) is a translation of μεγαλοπρέπεια.[233] This term originates in the Septuagint,[234] and though it does not occur in the New Testament, it is found in *1 Clem.* 60:1.[235]

Because of the parallelism between the two terms of eminence, the first word of 16 is not here "laud" or "glorification," but describes the "glory" that belongs only to the one "Most High."[236] This means that Franzmann's statement, "16 forms the inclusio for the Ode with 1b,"[237] is not quite correct. The word ܫܡܐ (*šmā* = ὄνομα), prefixed with the "sign of the dative,"[238] stands here—unlike in 1b—for the "most holy name of God," which represents "the being that bears it" and does not exist in a this-worldly manner.[239] Perhaps it would be better to say that human language has attached this "name" to the "Most High." In 𝔊 the final doxology of *Ode* 18 would have been:[240]

δόξα καὶ μεγαλοπρέπεια τῷ ὀνόματι αὐτοῦ.

227 See Lattke, "Wörter," 290 = idem, *Bedeutung*, 4:138.
228 Frankenberg, 20.
229 BDAG, *s.v.* δέ.
230 BDAG, *s.v.* δέ.
231 Rahlfs, 1:3; *OTSy*, pt. 1 fasc. 1, p. 3; Payne Smith, 2:2408; BDAG, *s.v.* ἐμφυσάω.
232 LSJ, *s.v.* φύσημα; Payne Smith, 2:2409. There is no reason to omit the noun as Frankenberg (p. 20) does in his retroversion καὶ αὐτοὶ ἐλάλησαν ἀλήθειαν ἀφ᾿ οὗ ἐνεφύσησεν ἐν αὐτοῖς ὁ ὕψιστος. The preposition ἐν, on the other hand, is unnecessary.
233 Payne Smith, 1:1534, 2:3787; BDAG, *s.v.* μεγαλοπρέπεια.
234 See LEH, *s.v.* μεγαλοπρέπεια: "majesty." Cf. Pss 8:2; 20:6 (δόξαν καὶ μεγαλοπρέπειαν); 28:4; 67:35; 70:8; 95:6; 110:3; 144:5, 12 LXX.
235 In the New Testament, cf. 2 Pet 1:17: ὑπὸ τῆς μεγαλοπρεποῦς δόξης ("by the Majestic Glory").
236 Payne Smith, 2:4027–28; BDAG, *s.v.* δόξα.
237 Franzmann, 145, with reference to the terminology of Ps 144:1-2 and Ps 144:21 LXX.
238 Payne Smith, *Dictionary*, 232.
239 BDAG, *s.v.* ὄνομα, esp. 4; Payne Smith, 2:4199.
240 See Frankenberg, 20.

19

Ode 19: The Milk of the Father and the Mother of the Son

(I) 1a A cup of milk was offered to me,
1b and I drank it in the sweetness of the Lord's kindness.
2a The Son is the cup,
2b and he who was milked, the Father,
2c and [the one] who[a] milked him, the Spirit of holiness.
(II) 3a Because his breasts were full
3b and it was not desirable that his milk should be poured out/discharged for no reason/uselessly,
4a the Spirit of holiness opened his [viz., the Father's][b] bosom
4b and mixed the milk of the two breasts of the Father.
5a And she/it gave the mixture to the world, while they did not know,
5b and those who receive [it] are in the *plērōma* of the right [hand].
(III) 6a The womb of the Virgin caught [it],
6b and she conceived and gave birth.
7a And the Virgin became a mother in great compassion[c]
7bα and she was in labor and bore a son.
(IV) 7bβ And she felt no pains/grief,
8 because it was not useless/for no reason.
9a And she did not require a midwife,
9b|10aα because he [viz., God] kept her alive | like a man.
(V) 10aβ She brought forth by/in the will [of God]
10b and brought forth by/in [his] manifestation
10c and acquired by/in [his] great power
11a and loved by/in [his] salvation
11b and guarded by/in [his] kindness
11c and made known by/in [his] greatness.
Hallelujah.

a 2c ܘܡܚܠܒܬܗ N; ܡܚܠܒܬܗ H.
b 4a ܥܘܒܗ H and N (see commentary).
c 6a-7a Latin (𝔏); cf. ANF, 7:110 and 239: Solomon in his 19th Ode said this / according to Solomon it was written thus:
6a The womb of the Virgin was weakened,
6b and she received young and she was made pregnant.
7a And the Virgin became a mother in great compassion.

Introduction

Ode 19 is preserved in two Syriac manuscripts; some verses are quoted by Lactantius in his *Divinae institutiones* and its "Epitome."[1] The *editio princeps* finally put it beyond doubt that the Latin quotation in Lactantius in the early fourth century indeed forms part of *Ode* 19.[2] This does not mean that there was ever a complete Latin version.[3] Even though it is all but certain "that Lactan-

1 Mss.: H, 15a–b; N, 149r (𝔖). Latin quotation of 19:6-7a: Lactantius *Inst.* 4.12.3 + Epit. 39.2 (𝔏). Ed./trans.: Charlesworth, 81–84; Franzmann, 146–52; Lattke, 2:91–112 and 3:XXIX–XXX.

2 See Harris and Mingana, 2:7–11, on the *Testimonia adversus Iudaeos* in Latin that were employed and compiled much earlier; Lattke, *Bedeutung*, 3:5–6.

3 Harris and Mingana (2:9) say that it is "almost

tius did not know a Greek version of the Odes," this does not necessarily lead from the Latin testimonium to a "translator" "whose command of Syriac was incomplete."[4] In fact, the possibility of a Greek *Vorlage* must be kept in mind not only for 𝔖 but also (*sit venia verbo*) for ℭ.

Ode 19, which Schille counts among the "hymns of epiphany,"[5] consists of a metaphorical address that is bizarre even for the *Odes of Solomon* (1-5)[6] and a nativity hymn (6-11). The mythos ends with a small poem (10-11) that is formally reminiscent of the "Aeon"-poem in 12:4 and the "Christ hymn" in 1 Tim 3:16.[7] The original connection between these parts is a matter for the exegesis.

If the ideas of "Trinity" and "trinitarian" are applied to stanzas I–II, this anticipation of later Christian doctrine concerning God, which was in any case formally "modelled on the middle Platonic triad of ἕν—νοῦς—πνεῦμα,"[8] is as questionable as assertions of a "triune God"[9] in reference to tripartite formulations in the New Testament (Matt 28:19; cf. 2 Cor 13:13; Eph 4:4-6). The assignment of stanzas III–V to early Christian Mariology seems less problematic, although the name "Mary" does not occur. It remains to be seen whether the second part of *Ode* 19 is more Mariological—by emphasis on a virgin birth perhaps—than its christological and soteriological application by Lactantius.[10] The "Son" of the "Father" is mentioned near the beginning (immediately after the introduction of the speaking "I," an inclusive concept, who vanishes completely with the beginning of 2a), which poses a logical problem, since the birth of the—or a—son is not mentioned until 7a. If the first part is in some sense a prelude in heaven,[11] then the introduction 1a-b, which is palpably realistic and personalized in spite of its metaphorical content, does not fit easily. Perhaps it is necessary, because of this problem and because the term "Lord" occurs only in 1b, to deviate from Franzmann's division and treat the bicolon 1a-b as a stanza in its own right. Since Franzmann, however, marks off 1, 2, and 3 as separate strophes of stanza I,[12] the extra division may be avoided.

It is preferable, however, not to follow Franzmann, but to treat 3a-b as the beginning of stanza II, not the end of stanza I.[13] This will become clear in the commentary.

Interpretation

■ **1-2** If Clement of Alexandria, "the first Christian scholar,"[14] had known *Ode* 19, his sometimes extravagant discourses on the life-giving "milk, that flows from tender loving breasts" (*Paed.* 1.35.3),[15] on the "Logos, which is metaphorically called milk" (1.36.1),[16] on the close "connection" between "breasts" and "birth mother" (1.39.3),[17] on the transformation of "blood" into "milk" (1.39.4; cf. 1.45.1),[18] on the quadernity "Father"—

certain, as a result of recent investigations, that the *Testimony Book* in its earliest form antedates the New Testament, and is of Apostolic origin." From this it follows that "the force is taken out of attempts to find parallels to the *Odes of Solomon* elsewhere in Lactantius" (Harris and Mingana, 2:11). But cf. Emerton, 685 n. 2; Darrell D. Hannah, "The *Ascension of Isaiah* and Docetic Christology," *VC* 53 (1999) 185.

4 Alfred Adam, *Sprache und Dogma: Untersuchungen zu Grundproblemen der Kirchengeschichte* (ed. Gerhard Ruhbach; Gütersloh: Mohn, 1969) 131.

5 Schille, 116.

6 See Lattke, "Bildersprache," 104 = idem, *Bedeutung,* 4:31.

7 Oberlinner, *Pastoralbriefe,* 1:162–69.

8 Jörg Ulrich, *Phoebadius, Contra Arianos—Streitschrift gegen die Arianer* (FontChr 38; Freiburg: Herder, 1999) 11.

9 Ibid., 7.

10 See Lattke, *Bedeutung,* 3:6.

11 See Han J. W. Drijvers, "The 19th Ode of Solomon: Its Interpretation and Place in Syrian Christianity," *JTS* n.s. 31 (1980) 345, who even, alluding to Goethe's play *Faust,* calls it a "Prologue in Heaven."

12 Franzmann, 149.

13 Contra Lattke, 3:93–97.

14 Berthold Altaner and Alfred Stuiber, *Patrologie: Leben, Schriften und Lehre der Kirchenväter* (7th ed.; Freiburg/Basel/Vienna: Herder, 1966) 191.

15 Stählin, 1:235. For the Greek text of *Paed.* 1.35–52, see Otto Stählin, ed., *Clemens Alexandrinus,* vol. 1: *Protrepticus und Paedagogus* (3rd ed. by Ursula Treu; GCS; Berlin: Akademie-Verlag, 1972) 111–21.

16 Stählin, 1:236.

17 Ibid., 1:240.

18 Ibid., 1:240, 244, etc.

"Logos"—"Holy Spirit"—"Virgin Mother . . . Church" (1.42.1),[19] and on the "milk of the Father" and his "pacifying breasts" (1.43.3-4)[20] would have been enriched by a number of images, which he would hardly, despite his polemics against "Gnostics" (52:2),[21] have considered "grotesque" or "tasteless," much less "horrible."[22] Whether the same goes for Irenaeus may be seen from the following quotation:

> And therefore he [i.e., *dominus noster*/ὁ Κύριος ἡμῶν] who was the perfect bread of the Father offered himself to us as milk [*lac*/γάλα] to children, which is the meaning of his appearance as a man, so that we, being nourished by the breast of his body and accustomed by this milk to eat and to drink the word of God, are enabled to hold within us the bread of immortality, which is the spirit of the Father. (*Haer.* 4.38.1)[23]

In view of the eucharistic texts that use the term "cup," it is tempting to "consider a connection with a rite of some kind."[24] The term ܟܣܐ (*kāsā*) occurs again only in 2a and corresponds to τὸ ποτήριον.[25] The genitive of ܚܠܒܐ (*ḥalḇā*), which immediately follows, would then point to a "milk sacrament," but already Harnack rebutted this.[26] Harris and Mingana also distance themselves from the idea "that the author was patronizing a milk-sacrament, like that of certain early heretics."[27] Since none of the other "milk"-passages shows ritual or sacramental traits (cf. 4:10; 8:16; 35:5; 40:1), 1a is also "no more than an image,"[28] which will be illuminated by the near allegorical equation of the "son" and the "cup" in 2a.[29] The Ethpa. of ܩܪܒ (*qreḇ*), "was offered," also forms part of the picture (cf. 11:6, where 𝔊 has ἐγγίζω). It has no sacrificial meaning and corresponds more closely to the passive of προσφέρω[30] than to any form of προσάγω.[31]

Since both "cup" and "milk" are masculine in Syriac and neuter in Greek, the third masculine singular objective suffix, corresponding to αὐτό, of the Pe. of ܐܫܬܐ (*šṯā*)[32] in 1b can refer equally to the "vessel" and to its "contents," especially since they are often identified.[33] This is as important as the statement that "the cup stands, by metonymy, for what it contains."[34] Although the "cup"—and thus the "milk"—is identified with the "son" (2a), the "milk" actually comes from the "Father" (2b, 3a-b, 4b).[35] Allegorically, therefore, the "son" is

19 Ibid., 1:242.
20 Ibid., 1:243. In another passage Clement says: "That is why seeking is called μαστεύειν, because the loving breast of the Father gives milk to the babes who are seeking the word" (*Paed* 1.46.1; Stählin, 1:245). The New Testament passages on "milk" (1 Cor 3:2 and 1 Pet 2:2) also play their proper parts in Clement's work. On Clement's expositions, see Johannes Betz, "Die Eucharistie als Gottes Milch in frühchristlicher Sicht," *ZKTh* 106 (1984) 10–16. Schenke (*Herkunft*, 29) considers the beginning of *Ode* 19 "a very good parallel" to *Gos. Truth* 24,9-11.
21 Stählin, 1:250.
22 For these adjectives, see Bauer, 599; Zahn, 770; Spitta, 266.
23 Brox, *Irenäus*, 4:334–35; see also Frederick Cornwallis Conybeare, "Note on the Odes of Solomon," *ZNW* 14 (1913) 96.
24 Klauck, *Herrenmahl*, 213.
25 Cf. Matt 26:27; Mark 14:23; Luke 22:17, 20; 1 Cor 11:25; and see Payne Smith, 1:1776; BDAG, *s.v.* ποτήριον.
26 Harnack, 49.
27 Harris and Mingana, 2:310.
28 Harnack, 49.
29 The equation of the "milk of God" with "knowledge of God (truth)" by Diettrich (p. 68) is even more aberrant than Bernard's idea (p. 86) "that the Milk of the Father is the Word, which is the spiritual food of the baptized Christian." On the connection between "word" and "son," however, see 41:11-14.
30 BDAG, *s.v.* προσφέρω.
31 BDAG, *s.v.* προσάγω; cf. Payne Smith, 2:3723.
32 Formed "*cum prothesi literae* ܐ" (Payne Smith, 2:4349).
33 BDAG, *s.v.* πίνω.
34 BDAG, *s.v.* ποτήριον.
35 It will become clear that being offered and drinking (1a-b) is one instance of the more general actions described in 5a-b.

derived from the "Father." Many of the authors and recipients of New Testament writings would agree.[36] The long prepositional phrase, overflowing with genitives, in which 𝔊 would surely have used γλυκύτης (cf. Wis 16:21; *1 Clem.* 14:3)[37] and χρηστότης (with the exception of 42:16 used only of God),[38] could be unraveled with reference to 28:15 so that "the sweetness (of Christ)" is shown to be "a manifestation of the kindness (of God)."[39] What must be kept clearly in mind, though, is that "Christ" or "Messiah" is *expressly* not mentioned. The "sweetness"[40] in this soteriological image of drinking milk refers, in any case, to this nourishment, which, on the one hand, originates from the androgynous Father[41] and, on the other, represents the Son.

What follows is no longer told in the first person and can hardly be called an "elaboration of verse 1: how man can appropriate God's kindness."[42] The highly mythological tricolon 2a-c, where Drijvers, like many preceding commentators since Harris,[43] finds "a Trinitarian context,"[44] nowhere says that "God's kindness, His milk, is given to the world by His Son, the cup."[45] Nor is it correct to speak of "an intra-trinitarian milking."[46] In the first place, the "cup" that is drunk, with genitive of "milk" understood, is identified by use of the copula (ܐܝܬܘܗܝ + third masculine singular possessive suffix)[47] as the "son." 𝔊, also, would have used υἱός ἐστιν as a nominal predicate to begin the line. It is as clear here as in 23:22 that this is the "authentic son of God."[48]

Many male, and some female, commentators, such as Virginia Corwin,[49] find the extreme image in 2b, which is produced by the wordplay with the Ethpe. of ܚܠܒ (*ḥlab*)—and the Pe. of the same verb in 2c—even more disturbing than the image of "breasts" in 8:16 and 19:3-4. The Greek had no equivalent to this wordplay, but a solitary instance like this cannot support "a form of early Syriac" as the "original language of the *Odes*."[50] The only possible verb in 𝔊 would be ἀμαλγέω,[51] which

36 See Ferdinand Hahn, "υἱός," *EWNT* 3 (1983) 920–24; *EDNT* 3:383–87. This text does not share the cosmological undertones of, e.g., *Corp. Herm.* 10:14 (Colpe and Holzhausen, 107).

37 See BDAG, *s.v.* γλυκύτης; Payne Smith, 1:1281. On the reference to *Wisdom,* see Lona, 220: "γλυκύτης, whose basic meaning is sweetness, is used figuratively for the tenderness of God, as in Wis 16:21."

38 BDAG, *s.v.* χρηστότης; Payne Smith, 1:551.

39 Suggested by Drijvers, "Ode 19," 341, translating ܒ (*b-*) as "with" not "in."

40 Human breast milk has a sugar content almost twice that of most mammalian milk types that are used as human food (see *MEL,* 16:230–31, 671; L. A. Moritz, "Milch," *KP* 3 [1969] 1293). On "sweetness in the sense of something that can be tasted," see Ziegler, *Dulcedo,* 103.

41 Wolfgang Speyer, *Frühes Christentum im antiken Strahlungsfeld: Ausgewählte Aufsätze* (Tübingen: Mohr Siebeck, 1989) 339, on *Ode* 8:16.

42 Drijvers, "Ode 19," 341.

43 Harris, 117: "tritheism." As far as I can see, Harnack avoids trinitarian concepts in both *Ode* 19 and *Ode* 23 (Harnack, 49, 55, 108). On the trinitarian interpretation of E. E. Fabbri ("El símbolo de la leche en las Odas de Salomón," *Ciencia y fe* 17 [1961] 277), see Lattke, *Bedeutung,* 3:257. Bruce Chilton ("God as 'Father' in the Targumim, in Non-Canonical Literatures of Early Judaism and Primitive Christianity, and in Matthew," in James H. Charlesworth and Craig A. Evans, eds., *The Pseudepigrapha and Early Biblical Interpretation* [JSPSup 14; Studies in Scripture in Early Judaism and Christianity 2; Sheffield: Sheffield Academic Press, 1993] 164) speaks only of "incipient trinitarianism."

44 Drijvers, "Ode 19," 341.

45 Ibid.

46 Contra Lattke, "Bildersprache," 105 = idem, *Bedeutung,* 4:32.

47 See Nöldeke §303.

48 Abramowski, 53, who, however, also finds "trinitarian passages" and distinguishes the "milk" from the "cup."

49 Virginia Corwin, *St. Ignatius and Christianity in Antioch* (Yale Publications in Religion 1; New Haven: Yale University Press, 1960) 79.

50 See Charlesworth, "Paronomasia," 12; idem, *Reflections,* 147. He omits these "milk" and "milking" passages from his list headed "Repetition" (*Reflections,* 148–53).

51 As Frankenberg already recognized (p. 20).

does not occur anywhere in early Christian writings and only twice in the LXX (Job 10:10; Prov 30:33). It is used mainly together with γάλα "of animals milked."[52] For the theological interpretation of ܐܒܐ (*ʾabā*, Greek πατήρ, also a predicate), one may refer to other passages in the *Odes of Solomon*.[53]

If in 2c the Greek equivalent of the predicate ܪܘܚܐ (*rūḥā*), "Spirit," was the neuter πνεῦμα (whether with an attributive ἅγιον or the genitive of ἁγιωσύνη as in Rom 1:4),[54] it would be more accurate to replace "She who milked Him"[55] with an impersonal construction. Such a translation (also subversive) would make it clear that the holy pneuma of God is not meant as a person, a point that even Tertullian might now concede, although he became "the pioneer of the Trinitarian formula 'tres personae–una substantia' (three persons–one substance/nature)."[56] The "spirit" is more a power, the living "spiritual power" of God, which cannot be intellectually circumscribed (cf. 3:10; 28:7). Even if the historical Jesus was a (Davidic) person who, according to Rom 1:3-4, became the "Lord" and "Son of God" of the primitive gospel ἐν δυνάμει κατὰ πνεῦμα ἁγιωσύνης ἐξ ἀναστάσεως νεκρῶν ("in power according to the Spirit of holiness by his resurrection from the dead"), this kerygmatic origin has been long forgotten and the "Son" removed protologically into the transcendence of God.[57] Just as they are beyond time and space, where there is no place, so "father" and "son," despite their anthropomorphic designations, are not persons.

■ **3-5** In spite of the poetical reasons that Franzmann[58] adduces for the division between the bicola 3a-b and 4a-b, it is better to interpret the statements of 3a-b as the reason for 4a-b (or even 4a-5a).[59] While the image of 3a (except for the androgynous aspect) is easy to follow, a convincing translation of 3b is fraught with difficulties. The plural of ܬܕܐ (*tdā*), because of "both" in 4b, must refer to οἱ μαστοί.[60] But this is not a male chest (cf. Rev 1:13, literally, "nipples"); the image bestows a "mother's breast"[61] on the "Father." The *hapax legomenon* ܐܬܡܠܝ (*ʾetmlī*, Ethpe. of ܡܠܐ [*mlā*]), "were full," may even be part of a play on words on *plērōma* (see on 5b below), which would suggest that 𝔊 used a form of πληρόω (perhaps πεπληρωμένοι),[62] rather than ἐπλήσθησαν.[63]

Verse 3b is the continuation of 3a.[64] The outcome to be avoided is expressed by the imperfect of the Ethpe. of ܫܕܐ (*šdā*). Since it refers to the "milk" of the full "breasts," its meaning is clear, and the probable Greek equivalent will have been a form of βάλλω–or perhaps of ἀποβάλλω or ἐκβάλλω.[65] The proper translation of the masculine singular participle of the Ethpe. ܐܬܒܥܝ (*ʾetbʿī*), which occurs only here, and the adverb ܣܦܝܩܐܝܬ (*spīqāʾīt*), whose recurrence in 8 serves to connect the two parts of *Ode* 19, is much more difficult. The *hapax legomenon* ܡܬܒܥܐ (*metbʿē*), negated by ܠܐ (*lā*), is hardly likely to be connected to χρεία or δεῖ/ἔδει in this passage (see Excursus 19).[66] Logically it must refer to the spilling of the milk, which is "undesirable."[67] If 𝔖 used the adverb ܣܪܝܩܐܝܬ (*srīqāʾīt*) instead of ܣܦܝܩܐܝܬ (*spīqāʾīt*),[68] it would be easier to translate.[69] But there is no sign, here or in 8, of a scribal error, so the meaning of the adverb remains undecided among *vacue, temere,*

52 LSJ, *s.v.* γάλα; Payne Smith, 1:1273.

53 Cf., e.g., 7:7, 11; 9:5; 10:4; 23:18, 22; 31:5; 41:9, 13).

54 BDAG, *s.v.* ἁγιωσύνη; Payne Smith, 2:3501–2, *s.v.* ܩܘܕܫܐ (*qudšā*).

55 Drijvers, "Ode 19," 339; Franzmann, 147.

56 Manfred Fuhrmann, "Person I. Von der Antike bis zum Mittelalter," *HWP* 7 (1989) 276; see also Eric Osborn, *Tertullian, First Theologian of the West* (Cambridge: Cambridge University Press, 1997) 116–43: "Trinity and christology."

57 At this point it is necessary to remember that the name "Jesus" does not occur in the *Odes of Solomon*. But if *Ode* 19 arose in a primitive Gnostic milieu, as, for example, Heinrich Schlier ("γάλα," *ThWNT* 1 [1933] 645: *TDNT* 1:647) suggests, one should probably assume a certain amount of Christian influence.

58 Franzmann, 150.

59 See Bauer, 599; contra Lattke, 3:96.

60 Payne Smith, 2:4391.

61 BDAG, *s.v.* μαστός.

62 BDAG, *s.v.* πληρόω.

63 Frankenberg, 20; cf. BDAG, *s.v.* πίμπλημι.

64 If 3a explained only 3b, then ܘ (*ʾu-*), equivalent to καί (BDAG, *s.v.*), in 3b must be translated by "also."

65 Payne Smith, 2:4064; BDAG, *s.vv.* ἀποβάλλω, βάλλω, ἐκβάλλω.

66 Payne Smith, 1:557; BDAG, *s.vv.* δεῖ, ἔδει, χρεία.

67 Bauer, 599; see also Harris and Mingana, 2:298 ("not desirable"); Drijvers, "Ode 19," 339.

68 Drijvers ("Ode 19," 341) leaves a false impression, printing ܣܦܝܩܐܝܬ ܠܐ and translating it literally as "not empty."

sine justa causa, and *inaniter.*[70] So the various translations, "to no purpose,"[71] "pointlessly,"[72] "ineffectually,"[73] "uselessly,"[74] "without purpose,"[75] "without cause,"[76] can all be justified, and it is wrong to say dogmatically: "the giving of the milk is according to God's purpose—that is the only correct interpretation of ܠܐ ܣܪܝܩܐܝܬ."[77] The "giving" of the "milk" is not mentioned until later (see on 5a below).

Even if 3a-4a and 4b-5b were treated as tricola, there would still be a logical connection between 4a and 4b. But, even without following Franzmann's analysis (see on 3a above), the second bicolon of stanza II is even more close-knit, so that 4b is a consequence of 4a, or perhaps the two occurred simultaneously in the mythological past. That 4a-5a describes "actions by the Spirit of holiness" personified[78] is clear from the feminine endings of the verbs ܦܬܚܬ, ܡܙܓܬ and ܝܗܒܬ (all are third feminine singular Pe. perfect, like the verb ܚܠܒܬ in 2c, which also refers to the holy spirit).

The point over the third singular suffix of ܥܘܒܐ (*ʿubbā*)—and not ܟܪܣܐ (*karsā*) = *uterus* as in 19:6a and 28:2b—is clearly visible in both manuscripts, and presents the greatest problem for the interpretation of 4a. The simplest solution would be to omit this point, anticipating the feminine ܪܘܚܐ (*rūḥā*), perhaps reasoning as did Harris and Mingana: "Both MSS. read . . . ܥܘܒܗ̇ under the influence of the preceding and following feminine verbs."[79] If this theory was true of s*—with or without an ambiguous Greek original *τὸν κόλπον αὐτοῦ* ("his bosom")—then the Syriac women and men who originally read or heard it will have understood and imagined it as something completely female. Whether they would have accepted Drijvers's interpretation, which far outruns the point that has been reached in the text, is a very different question:

The idea expressed in this verse is that the Holy Spirit functions as the womb of the Father in which His grace in the shape of the milk from His two breasts is received—she "opened her womb"—and thereupon brought forth and given to the world. The milk from the two breasts of the Father is, so to speak, his "sperma", "used for self-fertilization", to let His grace be born! In other and perhaps more dogmatically defined terms: the Logos being with and in God is brought forth by the Holy Spirit and as *λόγος προφορικός* given to the world.[80]

That Drijvers takes ܥܘܒܐ (*ʿubbā*) to be the equivalent of *ὁ κόλπος* is clear from his further exposition (see on 5 below; cf. John 1:18). But by translating *κόλπος*/ܥܘܒܐ not as "bosom" or "breast" but as the much less usual "lap/womb,"[81] his phrase "as the womb of the Father" thrusts aside the actual wording of the text ("[she] opened her womb"). The text also has nothing to say of "[having] received" and "brought forth." The equation of "milk" and "sperma," despite the rhetorical restriction, is hard to follow and clashes violently with the images of "breasts" and "drinking." It would be possible to identify the "milk" with the Logos of John 1:18, except that *Ode* 19 speaks only of the "Son."[82] And "self-fertilization" could only be performed by the "spirit" who opens her own "womb" (cf. Exod 13:2, quoted in Luke 2:23, where the term *διανοίγω*/ܦܬܚ is used but not *κόλπος*/ܥܘܒܐ).[83] In the context of stanza II, this makes as little sense as the alternative idea that she "opened" her "bosom."[84]

The emendation of ܥܘܒܗ̇ (*ʿubbāh*) to ܥܘܒܗ (*ʿubbeh*) is, however, a very minor change to the manuscript text, and it can be justified by appeal to the probable Greek original. In the same way as other "parts of the

69 See Payne Smith, 2:2750.
70 Payne Smith, 2:2705; cf. Brockelmann, *Lexicon*, 492.
71 Harris and Mingana, 2:298.
72 Bauer, 599 ("zwecklos").
73 Charlesworth, 82.
74 Lattke, *Bedeutung*, 1:129 ("unnütz"); cf. Greßmann, 455.
75 Drijvers, "Ode 19," 339.
76 Franzmann, 147; Lattke, *Oden*, 153 ("grundlos").
77 Drijvers, "Ode 19," 341.
78 Franzmann, 150.
79 Harris and Mingana, 2:299.
80 Drijvers, "Ode 19," 341.
81 BDAG, *s.v.* *κόλπος*; Payne Smith, 2:2823.
82 Conversely, John 1:18 speaks only of the "Logos," since the variant reading *υἱός* in 1:18 is a late emendation for *θεός*; see Theobald, *Fleischwerdung*, 197, etc.
83 BDAG, *s.v.* *διανοίγω*.
84 See Diettrich, 69; Harnack, 49.

body"—or anything "whose interior is thereby made accessible"[85]—can be opened (cf. 4:10; 10:1), the holy pneuma, named in 2c, "opens" his, that is, the Father's, "breast" or "bosom" (τὸν κόλπον αὐτοῦ in 𝔊). In the context of stanzas I–II, this opening is all but synonymous with "milking" (2c).

The terms in 4b have all occurred previously except for the *hapax legomena* ܡܙܓ (*mzag̱*) and ܬܪܝܢ (*trēn,* δύο).[86] It is perhaps not unimportant that the Pe. ܚܠܛ (*ḥlaṭ*), which would go better with ܚܘܠܛܢܐ (*ḥulṭānā*), is *not* used here (cf. 5a), since in Syriac writings it is also used "of the union of divine and human nature in Christ."[87] The Pe. ܡܙܓ (*mzag̱*) is another indication of "a Greek origin," apart from speculation on the derivation of "mingle" and "mixing-jug" from Prov 9:2, 5 LXX.[88] For 𝔊 would have used a form of *(συγ)κεράννυμι*,[89] which makes a nice wordplay with κρᾶσις (5a). A polemic against "wine," or the mixture of wine and water common from ancient times, is not, despite 38:12, to be found here, since the passage concerns "milk" as an *image,* not as a drink. Since a "bosom" generally harbors two "breasts" (cf. δύο μαστοί σου in Cant 4:5), the number "two" does not contribute any particular "emphasis."[90] This also invalidates speculations about "two different constituents."[91]

The definition of κρᾶσις—and consequently also of the *hapax legomenon* ܚܘܠܛܢܐ (*ḥulṭānā*) in 5a[92]—as "an εἶδος μίξεως in which the constituents are liquids"[93] dates back to antiquity. It would be anachronistic to load later christological theories onto this image of "mixture."[94] The "mixture" in question is the "milk" expressed from the Father's pair of maternal "breasts" into the "cup," which is the "son." This is given by the spirit to the "world" of individual beings (cf. τὸν υἱόν ... ἔδωκεν in John 3:16).[95] The ambiguous noun ܥܠܡܐ (*ʿālmā*) here probably stands for κόσμος, as in John 1:10 and 3:16, and not for αἰών (see Excursus 22). The "Aeons" are not under discussion here, unlike in 7:11 or 16:19.[96] The plural of the active participle of ܝܕܥ (*ʾidaʿ*) refers to those who did *not* know, and is therefore—like the term κόσμος/ܥܠܡܐ—related to John 1:10 (ὁ κόσμος αὐτὸν οὐκ ἔγνω, "the world knew him not"), as Drijvers rightly points out.[97] The common verb "to give" bridges the gap between mythological transcendence and the human world in its multiplicity.[98]

Verse 5b, untroubled by the logical contradiction of not-knowing and accepting (see Excursus 7), narrows the general statement in 5a in a manner reminiscent of John 1:12 (ὅσοι δὲ ἔλαβον αὐτόν, "But to all who received him"). The probable Greek verb λαμβάνω, however, is not represented by the Pa. ܩܒܠ (*qabbel*), as in the Syriac New Testament[99] (cf. in the *Odes of Solomon* 8:8; 9:5; 20:9; 31:6; 41:3), but by the Pe. ܢܣܒ (*nsaḇ*; cf. in the *Odes of Solomon* 5:3 𝔖; 11:4; 15:6; 23:2; 30:2; 31:7).[100] This verb, like "to know" previously, has no direct object, but there can be no doubt that the "mixture" given in 5a is meant.[101] It does not say that the soteriological nourishment, implied by the enclitic, and inclusively meant, third masculine plural personal pronoun, gives a place in the "*plērōma* of the right hand." Only the predestined are exempted from the world's general lack of knowledge and are found in the "fullness" of

85 BDAG, *s.v.* ἀνοίγω.
86 Payne Smith, 2:4468.
87 Payne Smith, 1:1277: *De unione divinae et humanae in Christo naturae.*
88 Harris and Mingana, 2:309–12, esp. 310. Prov 9:1-6 does seem to have influenced the image of the "mixing-jug (κρατήρ)" in *Corp. Herm.* 4:4-6; see Colpe and Holzhausen, 43–53, esp. 43 and 49–50.
89 BDAG, *s.vv.* κεράννυμι, συγκεράννυμι; cf. Payne Smith, 2:2059.
90 Contra Diettrich, 69.
91 Drijvers, "Ode 19," 342.
92 Payne Smith, 1:1279.
93 LSJ, *s.v.* κρᾶσις.
94 See Lampe, *s.v.* κρᾶσις, 4.
95 See Lattke, *Einheit*, 64–85.
96 Contra Schlier, "γάλα," *ThWNT* 1:645; *TDNT* 1:647. There is no good reason to emend the text to read ܥܠܡ̈ܐ, since κόσμος/ܥܠܡܐ conveys a plural sense (cf. Harris and Mingana, 2:299–300).
97 Drijvers, "Ode 19," 342. Since the particle ܟܕ (*kad̲*) "esp[ecially] before a participle or adjective, denotes present action or state" (Payne Smith, *Dictionary*, 204) the literal translation "while they do not know" (Lattke, *Oden*, 154) should be "while they did not know" (see Bauer, 599: "without anyone knowing"; Drijvers, "Ode 19," 340: "without their knowing").
98 Cf. 4:3, 9, 13; 7:24; 12:4; 17:12; 37:4.
99 *NTSy*, on this passage.
100 Payne Smith, 2:2393.
101 See Harris and Mingana (2:299), who insert "it."

the power of God as symbolized by his right hand (cf. 18:7; 25:2; see Excursus 35). These are able and allowed to receive the gift and to form an esoteric group that includes the singular "I" of 1a-b. This, then, is the compass, both thematic and structural, of the first part of *Ode* 19.

■ **6-7bα** Stanza III marks the beginning of the second part of *Ode* 19, which is connected to the first part by four terms: (1) the Pe. ܢܣܒ (*nsab*)[102] in 5b and 6b; (2) "son" in 2a and 7b; (3) the unusual adverb ܣܦܝܩܐܝܬ (*spīqāʾīt*) in 3b and 8; (4) "kindness" in 1b and 11b. This can certainly be called a "loose connection."[103] That this connection consists of the "acknowledgment of God" leading to a general "filiation to God"[104] may be considered doubtful. In the case of 𝔖, Drijvers may be right when he declares that "from verse 6 the world functions as a scene of action to which the mixture ... is given."[105] He identifies the "virgin" and "mother" with "Mary,"[106] following the example not only of later Syrians but also of Lactantius in the early fourth century[107] and the testimonia he probably used, which may have dated back to the first half of the second century.[108] It follows that the "son" of Parts 1 and 2 must be treated theologically and christologically as the same *persona*, although in Part 2 he plays only a minor role.[109]

If the Latin quotation of 6-7a is subjected to serious textual criticism, it is necessary to conclude that there is something wrong with the Syriac text as transmitted. For there are two things "required" to solve the puzzle of *infirmatus* (6a 𝔏), and also of *grauata* (6b 𝔏): "it must give an intelligible meaning to the verse, and it must account both for the present form of the Syriac text and for the 'infirmatus est' of Lactantius."[110]

Peter Cameron relates the history of the research on this passage and then proposes a new solution for the first word of 6a,[111] but another solution, also taking into account the *crux* in 6b, is more satisfying. 𝔊 would surely have used ἐξελύθη.[112] This aorist passive of ἐκλύω was correctly translated by *infirmatus est*, since *infirmo* is regularly used in the context of *corpus*.[113] The equally possible translation *defectus est* would not have suited in this case (cf. Mark 9:3; Matt 15:32). In the same way ἐξελύθη became ܥܦܬ (*ʿāpat*) in 𝔖, again the only correct translation.[114] This at some point became ܓܦܬ (*gāpat*), as

102 It is remarkable that the Pa. ܩܒܠ (*qabbel*), used in translating John 1:11-12 and Luke 1:31, occurs in neither of these verses.

103 Harnack, 50. Kittel (p. 90) even speaks of a "close connection" and stresses its "Christianity," pointing to "many New Testament resonances in this particular poem."

104 Diettrich, 70.

105 Drijvers, "Ode 19," 345.

106 Ibid., 346.

107 Although Syriac is probably not the original language, that text will be used for the commentary. The Latin quotation by Lactantius, however, plays a decisive part in the attempt to reconstruct the original and thus is worth quoting here (see Lattke, *Bedeutung*, 1:128):
Solomon in ode undeuicesima ita dicit / apud Solomonem ita scriptum est:

> [6a] infirmatus est uterus uirginis
> [6b] et accepit fetum, et grauata est
> [7a] et facta est in multa miseratione mater uirgo.

The English translation can be found in the notes on the translation of the *Ode*.

108 Cf. Harris and Mingana, 2:7–12.

109 The influence that *Ode* 19 exerted should also ensure its acceptance in collections of early texts referring to Mary; see Walter Delius and Hans-Udo Rosenbaum, *Texte zur Geschichte der Marienverehrung und Marienverkündigung in der Alten Kirche* (KIT 178; 2nd ed.; Berlin/New York: de Gruyter, 1973) 12–13.

110 See Peter Cameron ("The Crux in Ode of Solomon 19:6: A New Solution," *JTS* n.s. 42 [1991] 594), who does not touch on the problem in 6b.

111 According to Cameron, original ܥܦܬ (*ʿp̄āt*) = "blossomed/flourished/bloomed," root ܥܦܐ, became ܥܦܬ (*ʿāpat*) = "infirmatus est," root ܥܘܦ, which was corrupted to ܓܦܬ (*gāpat*) = "caught," root ܓܘܦ (Cameron, "Crux," 590, 594–95).

112 See already Frankenberg, 40; BDAG, *s.v.* ἐκλύω: "become weary *or* slack." But cf. Nestle's criticism of the "equation ἐκλύεσθαι = infirmari" (Eberhard Nestle, review of Frankenberg in *Theologisches Literaturblatt* 32 [1911] 534). Connolly's appealing suggestion (*infirmatus est* = ἠκράτησεν, "simple corruption" of ἐκράτησεν in 𝔊) is hardly feasible, because κρατέω normally corresponds to ܐܚܕ (Connolly, "Odes," 308).

113 Georges, 1:242.

114 See already William Emery Barnes, "The Text of the Odes of Solomon," *JTS* 11 (1909–10) 574; Barth, 263–64; Payne Smith, 2:2835.

found in H and N.[115] That may not have been a simple scribal error (according to Cameron, "the same confusion" as in *Ode* 38:3),[116] but an intentional attempt to connect the two parts of the Ode more closely.[117] The physical tiredness of pregnancy is changed into a process in which the womb or the developing "maternal body" becomes a trap to capture the "mixture" of the "milk" of the "father," which represents the "son."[118] The transcendent "son" of the "father" is thus transformed by mythological pregnancy and birth into the "son" of the "mother" (7b).

In spite of the *later* Christian equation of the ܒܬܘܠܬܐ (*btūltā*) with Mary—and the "son" with Jesus Christ—at the time of composition of the *Odes* it can be said for certain only that the influential prophecy of Isa 7:14 LXX is behind the text of this verse:

> ... *δώσει κύριος αὐτὸς ὑμῖν σημεῖον· ἰδοὺ ἡ παρθένος ἐν γαστρὶ ἕξει* [*v.l.* *λήψεται*] *καὶ τέξεται υἱόν, καὶ καλέσεις τὸ ὄνομα αὐτοῦ Εμμανουηλ.*
>
> . . . the Lord himself shall give you a sign; behold, a virgin shall conceive in the womb, and shall bring forth a son, and thou shalt call his name Emmanuel.[119]

This allusion could, of course, have been drawn from one of the many passages that also make use of Isa 7:14 (cf. Matt 1:23; Luke 1:31; Rev 12:1-5). If 𝔊 used the equivocal word *παρθένος*,[120] it could be allegorical, perhaps as "truth personified."[121] Kittel calls this exegesis "adventurism" on Diettrich's part,[122] for there is nothing in this birth mythos to suggest it. Certainly it concerns a young woman, who may have been accepted as a "virgin."[123] There is no question of a "cult,"[124] and as little of the "conception by the Virgin" in any dogmatic sense.[125] The silence regarding any male participant or any sexual intercourse only intensifies the spotlight cast on the *mythi persona*.

The construction in 6b with the Pe. ܢܣܒ (*nsab*) and the *hapax legomenon* ܒܛܢܐ (*baṭnā* = *conceptio*)[126] must have corresponded to a form of *συλλαμβάνω*.[127] As already noted, there is no direct route from ܝܠܕܬ (*yeldat*)[128] to the passive participle of *gravo*.[129] In a review of the two bicola 6a-b and 7a-bα in 𝔖, it is noticeable that the mention of birth in 6b is premature and out of place. Its proper place is in 7b (see below). The following reconstruction of the textual history of these verses attempts to solve this discrepancy. The Greek text did not use *ἐγέννησε(ν)* or *ἔτεκε(ν)* but *ἐβαρήθη*.[130] This form of *βαρέω*, referring to the pregnant woman, was

115 See Payne Smith, 1:687; Brockelmann, *Lexicon*, 110.

116 Cameron, "Crux," 595.

117 That the transitive verb is left without a direct object is of minor importance, since the verb ܢܣܒ (*nsab*) in 5b is also used without one.

118 See Payne Smith, 1:1834–35; BDAG, *s.vv.* *γαστήρ*, *κοιλία*.

119 Rahlfs, 2:575; Brenton, 842; cf. *OTSy*, pt. 3 fasc. 1, p. 12: . . . ܒܬܘܠܬܐ ܒܛܢܐ ܘܝܠܕܐ ܒܪܐ . . . .

120 Payne Smith, 1:624; BDAG, *s.v.* *παρθένος* ("virgin," "girl").

121 Diettrich, 70, with references to 33:5 and 38:10.

122 Kittel, 90.

123 The difficulty in 4a might be made easier if the "virgin" were an embodiment of the "spirit of holiness." In the *Gospel of the Hebrews* frg 5 (Erich Klostermann, *Apocrypha II: Evangelien* [KlT 8; Bonn: Marcus & Weber, 1904] 4) or frg 3 (Philipp Vielhauer and Georg Strecker, "Judenchristliche Evangelien," *NTApo* [5th ed., 1987], 1:146; "Jewish-Christian Gospels," *NTApoc*, 1:177), there is "the extraordinary notion that the Holy Spirit (רוחא דקדשא [feminine gender]) was the mother of Christ" (BDAG, *s.v.* *μήτηρ*). I refrain from comment.

124 See Fidelis Buck, "Are the 'Ascension of Isaiah' and the 'Odes of Solomon' Witnesses to an Early Cult of Mary?" in C. Balić, O.F.M., ed., *De primordiis cultus mariani 4* (Acta Congressus Mariologici-Mariani in Lusitania anno 1967 celebrati; Rome: Pontificia Academia Mariana, 1970) 399; and Lattke, *Bedeutung*, 3:289–90, on this article.

125 See Quasten, 163–64.

126 Payne Smith, 1:514.

127 BDAG, *s.v.* *συλλαμβάνω*: "*conceive* in the sexual sense." The translation of *συνέλαβεν* by *accepit fetum* is idiomatically correct and need raise no question (see Georges, 1:60–64, esp. 61, and 1:2743: "fruit of the womb").

128 Payne Smith, 1:1593 *s.v.* ܝܠܕ (*ʾiled*); BDAG, *s.v.* *τίκτω*.

129 Georges, 1:2975–76.

130 LSJ, *s.v.* *βαρέω*: *οἷον βεβαρημένος* = "as though pregnant."

translated by *grauata est*.[131] In S* the corresponding word was ܝܩܪܬ (*yeqrat*),[132] which was changed—perhaps under the influence of 7bα—to ܐܝܠܕܬ, or perhaps was intentionally corrected (see on the painlessness in 7bβ below). At any rate, the two aspects of pregnancy, *infirmatus est* and *grauata est*, are complementary, a point that has escaped researchers to date.

Franzmann has shown that the division in the manuscripts[133] should be changed and that 7b should be subdivided into 7bα and 7bβ.[134] This brings out the parallelism of 7a-bα. The Latin translation of 7a raises no text-critical problems. The story itself is clear. A "virgin" became a "mother."[135] That is the explicit and implicit plot of quite a number of stories, and it has a long history, that began, according to the Bible, with Gen 4:1 and still continues. The story here, however, is not a variation on "how the virgin came by a child."[136] The difficulties arise in understanding the prepositional phrase with the plural noun ܪ̈ܚܡܐ (*raḥmē*) and the attributive adjective ܣ̈ܓܝܐܐ (*saggīyē*). The phrase must be taken adverbially, as C does. And, considering stanza V and also Luke 1:58 (ἐμεγάλυνεν κύριος τὸ ἔλεος αὐτοῦ, "the Lord had shown great mercy"), the emphasis is not on the great "love" or "sympathy" of the woman, but rather on the "mercy" of God (see Excursus 2).[137]

Verse 7bα is also comprehensible, except for the identity of the "son," which depends on the intended unity of the Ode[138] and/or the influence it exerted, of which the only surviving evidence is the quotation by Lactantius. It is a description of the last throes of becoming a mother. The *hapax legomenon* ܚܒܠ (*ḥabbel*, Pa. of *ḥbal*, corresponding to ὠδίνω)[139] is followed by the Pe. ܝܠܕ (*ʾiled*), already discussed (see on 6b above), which now appears in its right place. At the end of the "birth-pangs" (cf. Rev 12:2) comes the delivery. Whether a—or the—child was thus brought into the *world*, again depends on how historically this mythos is taken.[140]

If one both accepts and corrects Frankenberg's retroversion,[141] it may be possible to attempt a reconstruction of the original Greek of stanza III as follows, with the deciding words from C in parentheses:

ἐξελύθη (*infirmatus est*) ἡ γαστήρ/κοιλία τῆς
　　παρθένου
　καὶ συνέλαβε καὶ ἐβαρήθη (*grauata est*)
καὶ ἐγένετο μήτηρ ἡ παρθένος ἐν πολλῷ ἐλέει
　καὶ ὠδίνησε καὶ ἔτεκε(ν) (τὸν) υἱόν.

■ **7bβ-10aα** Despite H and N, 7bβ does not belong to the end of stanza III (see above) nor 10aα to the beginning of stanza V.[142] Verses 10aα and 9b together form the last line of this section (stanza IV), which consists of two bicola, linguistically and mythologically among the most difficult passages of the *Odes of Solomon*.[143] It is necessary to observe every nuance in attempting to fathom the original meaning of the words and ideas before later Mariological concepts obscured them. Unlike the Christian "interpolation" in *Asc. Isa.* 11:2-22, *Ode* 19 does not emphasize the miracle of parthenogenesis. In the *Ascension of Isaiah,* Joseph cared for his affianced Mary "as a holy virgin, although she was with child," and one of the responses to the unexpected two-month child,

131 See BDAG, *s.v.* βαρέω, and cf. Vulgate Matt 26:43; Luke 9:32; 2 Cor 1:8; 5:4; 1 Tim 5:16.
132 Payne Smith, 1:1623, *s.v.* ܝܩܪ (*ʾiqar*).
133 See Lattke, *Bedeutung*, 1:128–29.
134 Franzmann, 150–51.
135 Payne Smith, 1:221–22; BDAG, *s.v.* μήτηρ.
136 See *MEL*, 31:1392.
137 Payne Smith, 2:3882; BDAG, *s.v.* ἔλεος (probably not τὰ σπλάγχνα); Georges, 2:943; contra Lattke, *Oden*, 154.
138 See Kittel, 18–20, 88–92.
139 See Payne Smith, 1:1175–76; BDAG, *s.v.* ὠδίνω.
140 The reference to Revelation 12 is especially apt, since the provenance of that mythos of the "woman" and the "birth of the child" is still unknown (see Bousset, *Offenbarung*, 335–58). Taking into account Isa 7:14 and 66:6-8, Kraft comes to the conclusion that "the birth of the boy was understood as the birth of the Messiah" (Kraft, *Offenbarung*, 164–65, on Rev 12:2).
141 Frankenberg, 20.
142 Franzmann, 149.
143 This renders unnecessary the conjectures of James Lagrand ("How was the Virgin Mary 'Like a Man' [ܐܝܟ ܓܒܪܐ]? A Note on Mt. i 18b and Related Syriac Christian Texts," *NovT* 22 [1980] 104), who adds ܐܝܟ ܓܒܪܐ to 10a ("She brought forth, as a man, of the will"): "This reading has the virtue, at least, of avoiding the misunderstanding that Mary herself was the object of a male's desire in her role in the divine plan. She was given grace to transcend normal sexuality in bringing new life to mankind and so become the only human parent, father-mother, of the Son of God." The same is

(viz., Jesus) seems to originate in a parallel tradition (v. 14: "many said 'she has not given birth: the midwife has not gone up [to her], and we have heard no cries of pain'").[144] Since the "son" has already been born in 7bα, stanza IV starts with the details about the mother and the birth (7bβ-9a) and ends with the mythological-theological explanation why a midwife was not needed (9b|10aα). This takes up the great compassion of 7a and leads on to the six prepositional clauses in 10aβ-11c, which all refer to the God, who is the mystery that is not identified with any thing or anyone in this world, and the marvel of every birth.

Although she was "in labor" (7bα), the mother-to-be was not affected by pain. She did not feel it, and the birth caused her no distress. This psychosomatic double meaning can result from the construction of the *hapax legomenon* ܟܐܒ "*cum* ܠ *pers.*"[145] in the same way as by the use of the passive of ὀδυνάω.[146] If 𝔊 used καὶ οὐ ὠδυνήθη the paronomasia with ὠδίνησε in the previous verse would be both audible and visible.

The feminine form of ܗܘܐ (*hwā*) at the end of 8 is the verb of the causal clause explaining the first negative statement of stanza IV, while the enclitic ܗܘܐ, as in Syriac texts in general, is "combined with" a qualitative adverb,[147] in this case ܫܦܝܩܐܝܬ (*spīqāʾīṯ*).[148] Determining the translation of this adverb is as difficult here as in 3b (see above). The history of the theological use of οἰκονομία,[149] which "becomes important in later patristic writings," begins with God's "plan of salvation" in Eph 1:10 and 3:9,[150] so it may be possible to accept Drijvers's reference to "God's *oeconomia* or providence,"[151] without following him as to the "date" ("about A.D. 200") or "Syriac as the original language of the Odes."[152]

Parallel to 7bβ, 9a also begins by negating the multivocal verb ܒܥܐ (*bʿā*), whose exact shade of meaning in this context must be carefully determined. Since 3b has a *hapax legomenon* derived from this root, it forms another connection between the two parts of the Ode, at least in 𝔖.

Excursus 19: "Request" and "Seek" in the *Odes of Solomon*

Although almost all of the twelve occurrences of the Pe. ܒܥܐ (*bʿā*) can be translated as "to seek" or "to petition,"[153] the multiplicity of its meanings is just about as great as that of the Greek verbs ἀνα-, ἐκ-, ἐπιζητέω and ζητέω without a prefix, to which may be added at least some of the meanings of παρακαλέω.[154] Some of the meanings established by Bauer (and the other scholars who worked on his dictionary) for the Greek verbs cited may be listed here: "look, search;"[155] "seek out, search for";[156] "search for, seek after";[157] "strive for, aim at, desire to obtain, wish for";[158] "summon to one's aid, call upon for help; . . . request, implore, appeal to, entreat."[159]

true of Pieter W. van der Horst's remark on 10a: "One can only speculate about the possibility that the author . . . had a theory on female seed in mind" ("Sarah's Seminal Emission: Hebrews 11:11 in the Light of Ancient Embryology," in David L. Balch et al., eds., *Greeks, Romans, and Christians: Essays in Honor of Abraham J. Malherbe* [Minneapolis: Fortress Press, 1990] 302 n. 72).

144 See Detlef G. Müller, "Die Himmelfahrt des Jesaja," *NTApo* (5th ed., 1989) 2:549–50, 560–61; "The Ascension of Isaiah," *NTApoc* 2:605, 618.

145 Payne Smith, 1:1657. The point above the word in H shows that it is to be read as the active participle *kāʾeḇ*, while N uses a point below the word to show that it is the third masculine singular perfect of the Pe. ܟܐܒ (*keḇ*).

146 BDAG, *s.v.* ὀδυνάω; LSJ, *s.v.* ὀδυνάω; LEH, *s.v.* ὀδυνάω.

147 Nöldeke §308, where one of the examples has ܛܒܐܝܬ.

148 "In 19:7bβ-8 ܗܘܐ (*hwā*) + adverb is unusual. One would expect an adjective. So the translation should be: 'But she was not in pain, because *it* did not happen without a reason' (cf. Nöldeke §254.C), unless a participle has been omitted" (Klaus Beyer in Lattke, 3:XXIX n. 2).

149 See Lampe, 940–43.

150 Jürgen Goetzmann, "οἰκονομία," *CBB* 1:643.

151 Drijvers, "Ode 19," 341, 346.

152 Ibid., 351.

153 "To need," which I have used in earlier translations (Lattke, *Bedeutung*, 1:129; idem, *Oden*, 155), is probably incorrect.

154 Payne Smith, 1:556; BDAG, *s.vv.* ἀναζητέω, ἐκζητέω, ἐπιζητέω, ζητέω, παρακαλέω. One might consider the closeness of meaning of "to ask for" and "to request." In the New Testament, the manuscripts are often undecided between forms of ζητέω and, for example, ἐκζητέω.

155 BDAG, *s.v.* ἀναζητέω.

156 BDAG, *s.v.* ἐκζητέω.

157 BDAG, *s.v.* ἐπιζητέω.

158 BDAG, *s.v.* ζητέω.

159 BDAG, *s.v.* παρακαλέω, esp. 1c, 2.

The shade of meaning of the Syriac also depends partly on the grammatical context: whether it is used absolutely (8:22), enclosed between the conjunction ܕ (*d-*) and the preposition ܡܢ (*men*, 7:10); precedes an infinitive (20:6; 28:18); or has a direct object (19:9 and 28:17; with ܠ [*l-*] 24:5, 33:13, 38:14e; as a suffix, 26:13 and 42:5). As in Greek, it can be explicitly opposed to "finding" (28:17).[160]

There are two *hapax legomena* derived from the root ܒܥܐ, whose meaning, in the context of the *Odes of Solomon*, is in dispute. In 17:12b the feminine ܒܥܘܬܐ (*bāʿūṯā*) makes no sense if taken as the equivalent of δέησις, but it does as the equivalent of παράκλησις as in Luke 6:24 and 2 Cor 8:4.[161] The redeemed Redeemer gave his "consolation" in parallel to *gnōsis* (see commentary on that passage). The negated participle of the Ethpe. in 19:3b serves rather to describe something as undesirable than to exclude a necessity (see above).

The verb ܒܥܐ is translated once only by "entreat" (7:10b). My earlier translation of 8:22a[162] ("Bittet viel [ask much]") has been revised, for linguistic reasons, to "seek and increase." In the other passages, the basic meaning "to seek" also makes good sense.

The verb is subordinated when used with an infinitive. In the ethical passage 20:6b, the stress is on the exhortation not to "deceive" one's "neighbor." And in the "Report by the Persecuted and Preexistent One,"[163] the verb, qualified by the adverb "vainly," describes the unsuccessful attempt of his opponents to "destroy the memory" of him (28:18b).

In this latter passage, the verb "to seek" has gained in emphasis because it is closely connected to the statement that the opponents "sought" the "death" of the speaking "I" (28:17a)—without success. So it is not only the syntax but the poetic or mythological context that determines the shade of meaning of the multivocal verb. Sometimes it may be necessary to consider an opposite that is merely implied. So the "seeking" of the day of sun (15:1a) has as its background the thought that some might avoid and fear the light. And those who do *not* seek the "thinking heart" (38:14e), clearly, for whatever reason, lack application and desire to do so.

The didactic statement of comparison on "a river which has an increasingly abundant spring and flows for the help of those who seek it" (26:13; both nouns, "river" and "spring," are masculine in Syriac) is difficult. Less problematic are the two cases where the speaking "I" describes itself as the object sought. In the first case, it is the "Virgin" (no relation to *Ode* 19) called "Grace" and "Judge" (33:13b). In the second, it is the redeemed Redeemer, sought by those who hoped in him, in contrast to his persecutors (42:5b).

The final pair of examples is connected by the verb "to give birth." In the statement "they sought the Lord like those who are about to give birth" (24:5b), it is not clear who the implied subject represented by "they" is or what is the precise shade of meaning of "sought."[164] Assuming that the meaning is positive, the statement comes near the negated statement of 19:9a, since these persons who are giving birth are also "seeking" the "Lord" and not a midwife.

It is certain that in 9a 𝔊, the word corresponding to the *hapax legomenon* ܚܝܬܐ (*ḥayyṯā*),[165] derived from ܚܝܐ (*ḥyā*), was the feminine μαῖα, a relatively rare word, whether in the Bible or early Christian texts,[166] but the Greek verb meaning "seek, request" can only be guessed at (see Excursus 19 above). What happens here is not a search, thus distinguishing this passage from *Protev. Jac.* 18:1 (ἐξῆλθεν ζητῆσαι μαῖαν Ἑβραίαν).[167] In fact, she did not "ask for," "desire," or "require" a "midwife."[168]

160 See BDAG, *s.v.* εὑρίσκω.

161 See Payne Smith, 1:557; BDAG, *s.v.* παράκλησις.

162 Lattke, *Bedeutung*, 1:103; idem, *Oden*, 152.

163 Lattke, *Oden*, 67.

164 On this verse, Bauer (p. 605 n. 4) remarks "this is in many respects an enigmatic *Ode*."

165 This word "*eam indicat qui in vitam inducit*" (Payne Smith, 1:1256). In Syriac there is an overtone of resurrection that is not relevant here.

166 Payne Smith, 1:1254; Brockelmann, *Lexicon*, 228–29; BDAG, *s.v.* μαῖα.

167 Albert Fuchs, *Konkordanz zum Protoevangelium des Jakobus* (Studien zum Neuen Testament und seiner Umwelt, Serie B, 3; Linz: Selbstverlag of SNTU, 1978) 109; see also Oscar Cullmann, "Kindheitsevangelien," *NTApo* (5th ed., 1987) 1:345; "Infancy Gospels," *NTApoc*, 1:433, which should have mentioned Exod 1:15-22. The statement in Exod 1:19, Οὐχ ὡς γυναῖκες Αἰγύπτου αἱ Εβραῖαι, τίκτουσιν γὰρ πρὶν ἢ εἰσελθεῖν πρὸς αὐτὰς τὰς μαίας (Rahlfs, 1:87; "The Hebrew women are not as the women of Egypt, for they are delivered before the midwives go in to them" [Brenton, 70]), may also be relevant to *Ode* 19:9.

168 See Bauer, 600.

As 8 gives the reason for 7bβ, 9b + 10aα[169] give the reason for the negative statement of 9a. If the subject of the Aph. of ܚܝܐ (*ḥyā*)[170] were the "son," born in 7bα, it would be possible to refer to the only other occurrence of ܓܒܪܐ (*gaḇrā*) in 41:12. But this assumption is even less plausible than referring the whole comparative phrase to the third singular objective suffix of the verb.[171] Without necessarily agreeing on "the image of the husband," Franzmann's conclusion, "Thus ܐܝܟ ܓܒܪܐ refers to the Father rather than to the Virgin,"[172] should be accepted. So the subject of this causal clause is "God" as the "Lord" (cf. 2b). Emending ܓܒܪܐ to ܓܢܒܪܐ (*gabbārā*, *heros*, γίγας or simply ἀνήρ)[173] and referring to Neh 1:5 or Ps 18:6 LXX[174] makes the interpretation no easier. The Greek may be partially reconstructed, omitting the verb, as ὅτι (αὐτός) . . . αὐτὴν ὡς ἀνήρ.[175] When the meaning of the verb has become clearer, it will be possible to consider ἀνήρ/ܓܒܪܐ further.

The Aph. ܐܚܝ (*ʾaḥḥī*), which is used for the actions of the Redeemer in 41:11a and 41:16a, can stand for a number of Greek verbs: διατρέφω,[176] ζάω,[177] ζῳογονέω,[178] ζῳοποιέω,[179] ἰάομαι,[180] but above all σῴζω.[181] Drijvers's reference to God as σωτήρ/ܡܚܝܢܐ (*maḥḥyānā*)[182] in Luke 1:47 is quite acceptable,[183] but not his contention that 19:9b alludes to Ps 22:10-11.[184] Even if "the aphel of ܚܝܐ" can be translated by the verb "to deliver,"[185] it cannot be used in the technical sense of "God's delivering action" as obstetrician. This pun is possible in English, but there is no evidence for a similar wordplay in either Syriac or Greek literature. If the putative "Greek original" had used μαιόομαι/μαιεύομαι to make a paronomasia with μαῖα—or even μαίομαι—in 9,[186] this verb, whatever its form, would have been translated not by ܐܚܝ but by the Aph. ܐܘܠܕ (*ʾawleḏ*) (cf. Exod 1:16).[187] So it is better to leave the various meanings of "deliver" to one side and consider, among the possible translations of the Greek verbs listed above, such terms as "let live,"[188] "give life," "preserve." If there was any influence from the context of Exod 1:15-22, 𝔊 might have used a form of ζῳογονέω. It is more probable, however, that 𝔊 had ἐζωοποίησεν[189] or ἔσωσεν. In this combination, the comparison of God to "a man" lays "special emphasis on manliness"[190] in the sense of strength and decisiveness, rather than on the subsidiary meanings of "husband" or "bridegroom."[191]

■ **10aβ-11** Even after Drijvers's "closely reasoned interpretation of the 19th Ode of Solomon in which a well-

169 Beyer (in Lattke, 3:XXX n. 1) translates: "because he [*viz.*, God] assisted at the birth like a man (a male midwife)."
170 This term and the word "midwife" are a "most noteworthy example of repetition" (Charlesworth, "Paronomasia," 16; idem, *Reflections*, 152), but they are not a conclusive argument for "Syriac (or Aramaic)" as the original language, since the wordplay on ὠδυνήθη and ὠδίνησε, as outlined here, is possible only in Greek.
171 The implausibility is even greater, since the comparative phrase ܐܝܟ ܕܓܒܪܐ, linguistically similar to 38:1a, would be expected in place of ܐܝܟ ܓܒܪܐ (*ʾaḵ gaḇrā*). The Greek, in this case, would have been ὡς ἄνδρα.
172 Franzmann, 149.
173 Payne Smith, 1:646.
174 Suggested by William Emory Barnes, "The Text of the Odes of Solomon," *JTS* 11 (1909–10) 574.
175 Frankenberg, 20; αὐτός may be omitted.
176 Cf. Ps 32:19 LXX; and see LEH, *s.v.* διατρέφω.
177 Cf. Ps 40:3 and 118:50 LXX; and see LEH, *s.v.* ζάω: "to quicken, to give life."
178 Cf. Exod 1:17-18; 1 Tim 6:13; and see BDAG, *s.v.* ζῳογονέω.
179 Cf. Rom 4:17; 8:11; John 5:21, etc.; also συζωοποιέω in Col 2:13 and Eph 2:5; and see BDAG, *s.v.* ζῳοποιέω.
180 Cf. Ps 29:3 LXX; Eccl 3:3; and see BDAG, *s.v.* ἰάομαι.
181 BDAG, *s.v.* σῴζω: "save, keep from harm, preserve, rescue;" Payne Smith, 1:1252.
182 The doubling of the first radical is based on the fact that ܡܚܝܢܐ is derived from the Aph. (Drijvers, "Ode 19," 347; see Brockelmann, *Grammatik*, 142–43).
183 Drijvers, "Ode 19," 347; cf. Payne Smith, 1:1257.
184 Drijvers, "Ode 19," 347; cf. already Harris and Mingana, 2:299, 305, 307.
185 Drijvers, "Ode 19," 340, 347.
186 See Harris and Mingana, 2:301.
187 See LSJ, *s.v.* μαιόομαι; LEH, *s.v.* μαιόομαι; Payne Smith, 1:1594: *obstetricavit, obstetricis munere functus est.*
188 Bauer (*Oden*, 41): "meaning that God, in this case, performed the duties of a midwife."
189 Frankenberg, 20.
190 BDAG, *s.v.* ἀνήρ.
191 BDAG, *s.v.* ἀνήρ; Payne Smith, 1:644–45.

defined Trinitarian theology regarding the incarnation is expounded in a hymnical but very reflected wording,"[192] what Harris and Mingana had to say of 10b-11c is still true: "The concluding sentences of the Ode are almost unintelligible, and without adequate motive."[193] In fact, this poem on the birth, which is connected to the previous sections of the Ode by the terms "kindness" (1b) and "brought forth" (7bα), could be considered a "sub-ode,"[194] particularly as it is reminiscent of the hymn in 1 Tim 3:16.[195] Both of these six-line works show the following "characteristics of the formulaic style of solemn utterances:"[196]

> The statements refer to a common subject, and are maximally concise, of equal length, placing the words in exactly equivalent positions, using the same construction wherever possible and following each other asyndetically.

This form criticism (*Formgeschichte*) gives an initial reason why the adjective ܣܓܝܐܐ (*saggīyā*) in 10c must be seen as an "addition."[197] But in attempting to explain both this disturbance of the equality of length and the peculiar repetition of the verb in 10aβ and 10b, it is necessary to go a step further. The simple explanation is that ܣ is a translation from 𝔊. For there is only one Syriac verb to translate the two Greek verbs τίκτω and γεννάω (cf. Luke 1:57; John 16:21). And in 10c there was a composite noun with the prefix πολυ-.[198]

The certainty of these two conclusions, unfortunately, does not lead to an equal ease in retroversion. Except for the terms "give birth" (see above), "will" (θέλημα), "salvation" (σωτηρία), and "kindness" (χρηστότης; see on 1b above), the verbs and nouns of stanza V have such a breadth of meaning that each can represent several Greek words. These choices are somewhat narrowed because the verbs reflect in a logical sequence "the chronological order of events in a birth process."[199] However, the nouns, which refer to God[200]—and not to the mother[201]—show no clear ordering and, as in so many set forms and catalogues, are more or less interchangeable. Even if it were possible to find the exact equivalent for the sextuple preposition ܒ (*b*-)[202] (dative with or without ἐν, κατά with accusative, etc.), which has already appeared in 7a, it would still be possible to translate it as "in" instead of "by."[203] The linguistic and systematic exactitude that Drijvers desires is here unattainable.[204]

The fact that none of the five transitive verbs has an object is a consequence of the poetic form. Even though τίκτω, for instance, can be used absolutely (as in John 16:21 or Gal 4:27), in 10b-11c, the direct object "him," referring to the son, is understood.[205] The verbs, all in the third feminine singular perfect, whose subject is the "mother" (7a), will be considered first.

In ܣ the Pe. ܐܠܕ (*ʾileḏ*) refers back to 6b and 7bα.[206] As has already been discussed, the most likely equivalent in 10aβ will have been ἔτεκεν in its literal sense.[207] Since γεννάω also means "to bear (of women),"[208] 10b 𝔊 may have used ἐγέννησεν as a poetic variant, which might be represented in English by "to bring forth." The issue follows the labor.

192 Drijvers, "Ode 19," 348–50, esp. 350.
193 Harris and Mingana, 2:306.
194 Franzmann, 151.
195 Bauer (p. 600), who here also speaks of a "closing hymn."
196 Kroll, *Hymnodik*, 79.
197 Franzmann, 151.
198 Cf. Payne Smith, 2:2519, on ܣܓܝܐܐ (*saggīyā*): "Usurpatur etiam ad Gr. composita reddenda."
199 Drijvers, "Ode 19," 350.
200 According to Harris and Mingana (2:302, 306), only "will" refers, without doubt, to God; the other nouns "seem to refer to the Virgin."
201 See, e.g., Bauer, 600; Charlesworth, 82–83.
202 On the lack of any objects for the verbs, see the commentary.
203 See, e.g., Bauer, 600.
204 Drijvers, "Ode 19," 350. Hubert Grimme ("Die 19. Ode Salomos," *ThGl* 3 [1911] 17) transforms the prepositional phrases of 10aβ-11c into direct objects, employing the specious argument that the Syriac ܒ (*b*-) "must have originated in a confusion of the Hebrew את = *nota accusativi* with את = 'with.'" See Wilhelm Gesenius, *Hebräisches und aramäisches Handwörterbuch über das Alte Testament* (ed. Frants Buhl; 17th ed., Berlin: Springer, 1915; repr., 1962) 76–77. In this way, the "abstract nouns" become personifications of the son of God made flesh.
205 Harris and Mingana, 2:299.
206 Payne Smith, 1:1593.
207 BDAG, *s.v.* τίκτω.
208 BDAG, *s.v.* γεννάω.

The Pe. ܩܢܐ (*qnā*) in 10c moves a step further. With the sense of "acquire" and "possess," it probably stands for κτάομαι.[209] Although ἔχω can also refer to children,[210] in that case ἔσχεν would normally be translated by ܗܘܐ + ܠ.[211]

Verse 11a uses the Aph. ܐܚܒ (*ʾaḥḥeḇ*), which is a synonym for ܪܚܡ (*rḥem*; cf. 40:1b, speaking of a woman who loves her children), a verb used to translate both ἀγαπάω and φιλέω (see Excursus 2).[212] Generally speaking, once a child is there, it is loved. Even fathers can understand that.

This close connection and affection give rise to care and protection. The meaning of the Pa. of ܢܛܪ (*nṭar*) in 11b is clear, even if it is not possible to choose between the various Greek equivalents διαφυλάσσω, συντηρέω, τηρέω, φρουρέω, or φυλάσσω.[213]

The Pa. ܚܘܝ (*ḥawwī*) in 11c is the final step in these actions by the mother,[214] and so the translation "reveal" is somewhat misleading.[215] It is possible that the mother "announced" the event.[216] But it is preferable to stay with the basic meaning of "to show" or "exhibit."[217] This final clause simply means, "she shows it [viz., the child] to the others."[218] There is no allusion to the presentation of Jesus in the Temple (Luke 2:22).

Any logical connection between the prepositional phrases and the verbs they qualify is not apparent. The six nouns that are to be considered next, like "mercy" in 7a, refer to God, and their complete interchangeability can be easily demonstrated.

Any attempt to refer "will" in 10aβ to the woman giving birth falls to the ground when ܐܝܟ ܓܒܪܐ (*ʾaḵ gaḇrā*) is removed (see on 9b|10aα above). It is possible to refer to Rom 2:18 for the absolute use of θέλημα/ܨܒܝܢܐ (*ṣeḇyānā*) as "Will of God,"[219] although there the Syriac text actually has the explanatory ܨܒܝܢܗ (*ṣeḇyāneh*; see Excursus 9).[220] But there are even stronger connections to Eph 1:9-11 (οἰκονομία in context; see on 8 above) and especially to John 1:13.[221] Christian readers could thus connect the efficacy of God's will with the ineffectiveness of θέλημα σαρκός ("will of the flesh") and ἀνδρός ("[will] of man"] in the formation of the τέκνα θεοῦ ("children of God"; cf. John 1:12-13).

The *hapax legomenon* ܬܚܘܝܬܐ (*taḥwīṯā*) in 10b, which comes from the same root as the Pa. ܚܘܝ (11c), is difficult to translate. It is used for ἀνάδειξις (Sir 43:6; Luke 1:80), ἀπόδειξις (1 Cor 2:4), ἔνδειγμα (2 Thess 1:5), ἔνδειξις (Rom 3:26; 2 Cor 8:24; Phil 1:28), ὑπόδειγμα (2 Pet 2:6), and ὑποτύπωσις (1 Tim 1:16). It is notable that of all these terms only the last, a compound of τύπος, is listed in *Theologisches Begriffslexikon zum Neuen Testament* (see CBB), and there is no collective theological term for their various meanings.[222] An allusion to the manifestation of John the Baptist to the people of Israel is no more likely than a reference to other omens or prototypes. The most likely equivalent in 𝔊 would be ἀπόδειξις[223] or ἔνδειξις, so that the demonstrative term "proof" would be a suitable translation.[224]

The compound noun for the Greek of 10c can only be the rare term πολυκρατία ("*multa potestas*").[225] The *hapax legomenon* ܐܘܚܕܢܐ (*ʾuḥdānā*), derived from ܐܚܕ (*ʾeḥaḏ*), is most commonly used for the often doxological Greek term of power and sovereignty τὸ κράτος.[226]

209 Payne Smith, 2:3651–52; BDAG, *s.v.* κτάομαι; see Frankenberg, 20: ἐκτήσατο.
210 BDAG, *s.v.* ἔχω.
211 Payne Smith, *Dictionary*, 101.
212 Payne Smith, 1:1169; BDAG, *s.vv.* ἀγαπάω, φιλέω.
213 This last used by Frankenberg, 20; cf. Payne Smith, 2:2355; BDAG, *s.vv.* διαφυλάσσω, συντηρέω, τηρέω, φρουρέω, φυλάσσω.
214 See Payne Smith, 1:1208–9.
215 Contra Lattke, *Bedeutung*, 1:129; idem, *Oden*, 155.
216 BDAG, *s.v.* ἀναγγέλλω, or more likely ἀπαγγέλλω, as in Frankenberg, 20: ἀπήγγειλεν.
217 See Harris and Mingana, 2:299; and, e.g., BDAG, *s.vv.* δείκνυμι, ἐπιδείκνυμι.
218 Drijvers, "Ode 19," 350; instead of "it" Drijvers should have used "him" referring to the son of v. 7ba.
219 Harris and Mingana, 2:308.
220 *NTSy*, 67; see Payne Smith, 2:3354; BDAG, *s.v.* θέλημα.
221 Mentioned already by Harris and Mingana, 2:306; Drijvers, "Ode 19," 349.
222 See Payne Smith, 1:1211–12; BDAG, *s.vv.* ἀνάδειξις, ἀπόδειξις, ἔνδειξις, ὑπόδειγμα, ὑποτύπωσις.
223 Frankenberg, 20.
224 Cf. Rom 3:26 and 1 Cor 2:4, and on these Käsemann, *Romans*, 99–101 (German, pp. 93–95); and Schrage, *1 Korinther*, 1:233.
225 *ThGL*, 7:1392.
226 Payne Smith, 1:120; BDAG, *s.v* κράτος.

However, the Greek text of the Ode, for the reasons already given, did not use ἐν πολλῷ κράτει[227] but ἐν πολυκρατίᾳ.[228]

The emendations that Harris and Mingana proposed for the central soteriological term ܦܘܪܩܢܐ (*purqānā*) can be left to one side,[229] since σωτηρία makes the best sense of 11a (see Excursus 5). Neither this prepositional phrase, nor the ones in the two following lines, shows any "double tendency" or says anything of "the situation in which he [viz., her son] has been delivered from her";[230] they deal only with "God's redemption."[231]

The commentary on 1b may suffice to demonstrate that ܒܣܝܡܘܬܐ (*bassīmūṯā*), "kindness," in 11b translates ἡ χρηστότης,[232] but in 11c ܪܒܘܬܐ (*rabbūṯā*) could represent ἡ μεγαλειότης, ἡ μεγαλωσύνη, or τὸ μέγεθος.[233] As in 36:5, the "greatness" is that of God as the "Most High" (cf. Luke 9:43; Eph 1:19; Heb 1:3), which was a provocation to others besides the Hellenistic devotees of Artemis (Acts 19:27-28).[234] In all the other occurrences, the construct state of the Syriac term is paired with ܝܐܝܘܬܐ (*yā'yūṯā*) as a translation of μεγαλοπρέπεια (7:23; 15:7; 18:16; 29:3). The terms "kindness" and "greatness" are also found as a theological pairing in 7:3, where they may be said to confront one another.[235]

The mention of John the Baptist above (see Luke 1:5-25, 57-80) is a reminder that his disciples too could have appropriated the second part of *Ode* 19 to celebrate the birth of their Master (cf. Matt 11:11; Luke 9:7; Acts 19:3). Especially stanza V, the small poem on birth, could be applied to all such heroic mothers as Elizabeth and Mary. Whatever the original *Sitz im Leben* of the poem was, its place in the present *text* ensures its position and exposition as part of the early history of Mariology.[236] It should, however, be observed that later readers cannot approach *Ode* 19 as innocently as people of the early second century did when "orthodoxy and heterodoxy"[237] were still a simmering *mixtum compositum.* So this is an occasion to exclaim with Bauer: "What diversity was accommodated in primitive Christianity!"[238]

227 Contra Frankenberg, 20.

228 Cf. LSJ, *s.v.* πολυκρατής: "very mighty."

229 Harris and Mingana, 2:303.

230 Contra Drijvers, "Ode 19," 350.

231 Ibid.

232 Frankenberg, 20: ἐν χρηστότητι.

233 Payne Smith, 2:3787; BDAG, *s.vv.* μεγαλειότης, μεγαλωσύνη, μέγεθος.

234 Rick Strelan, *Paul, Artemis, and the Jews in Ephesus* (BZNW 80; Berlin/New York: de Gruyter, 1996) 143.

235 See the commentary on that *Ode*.

236 José Maria Bover ("La Mariología en las Odas de Salomon," *EstEcl* 10 [1931] 349) even speaks of "the brilliant Mariology of *Ode* 19." His Greek retroversion takes due note of the poetic character of stanza V, although his choice of words is not always felicitous (p. 350). His "theological interpretation" runs far ahead of the text (pp. 353–58). The "anti-Docetism," which according to Drijvers ("Polemik," 51) "is clearly seen in verses 6-11 of *Ode* 19," eludes me.

237 Walter Bauer, *Orthodoxy and heresy in earliest Christianity* (translated by a team from the Philadelphia Seminar on Christian Origins; ed. Robert A. Kraft and Gerhard Krodel; Philadelphia: Fortress, 1971); ET of *Rechtgläubigkeit und Ketzerei im ältesten Christentum* (ed. Georg Strecker; BHTh 10; 2nd ed.; Tübingen: Mohr Siebeck, 1964).

238 Ibid., 237 (English), 239 (German). A piece of "Gnostic-Christian editing" of the "principal book of the Naasenes, which Hippolytus quotes" shows that Gnostic congregations could read *Ode* 19 in a very different manner (see Richard Reitzenstein, *Poimandres: Studien zur griechisch-ägyptischen und frühchristlichen Literatur* [Leipzig, 1904; repr., Darmstadt: Wissenschaftliche Buchgesellschaft, 1966] 81–82). But Reitzenstein specifically avoids the "conclusion that a *Jewish* congregation used to celebrate the mysteries of the Μήτηρ μεγάλη" (p. 82; quotation from Hippolytus, p. 96 n. 6). The passage from Hippolytus *Ref.* 5.8.45 (Paul Wendland, ed., *Hippolytus Werke*, vol. 3: *Refutatio omnium haeresium* [GCS 26; Leipzig: Hinrichs, 1916; repr., Hildesheim/New York: Olms, 1977] 97), is as follows: αὕτη γάρ ἐστιν ἡ παρθένος ἡ ἐν γαστρὶ ἔχουσα καὶ συλλαμβάνουσα καὶ τίκτουσα υἱόν [cf. Isa 7:14], οὐ ψυχικόν, οὐ σωματικόν, ἀλλὰ μακάριον αἰῶνα αἰώνων (cf. already the reference in Stölten, 43–44)—"For this is the virgin who carries in her womb and conceives and brings forth a son, not animal, not corporeal, but blessed for evermore" (ANF 5:560).

The article by Edward Engelbrecht, "God's Milk: An Orthodox Confession of the Eucharist," *JECS* 7 (1999) 509–26, who maintains (p. 510) "that the Odist used milk as an analogy for the nurturing presence of Christ in the baptismal eucharist" appeared after this manuscript was complete. His most important contribution is the statement

(p. 524) that "[t]he image of God's milk, even God nursing, was not foreign to early orthodoxy as these many examples show. In view of the broad acceptance of this imagery by orthodox writers, ascription of such language to Gnosticism seems unwarranted. Inspired by ancient physiology and applied to the eucharist, the milk analogy provided useful rhetoric in defense of orthodox doctrine." Otherwise, Engelbrecht's article does not materially affect the exegesis of *Ode* 19:1-6.

Darrell D. Hannah's article ("The *Ascension of Isaiah* and Docetic Christology," *VC* 53 [1999] 165–96), in which he quotes *Ode* 19:6-11 in Emerton's translation (Emerton, 709–10), also appeared after the completion of this manuscript; he concludes that "[i]t would seem then that we may add the *Odes of Solomon* to the *Protevangelium of James* and Clement of Alexandria as second or third century witnesses to a miraculous, but not docetic, understanding of the birth of Jesus. I would suggest that the *Ascension of Isaiah* also stood within this tradition" (p. 185).

20

Ode 20: From Righteousness to Glory

(I) 1a I am a priest of the Lord,
1b and to him I serve as a priest,
2 and to him I offer the sacrifice of his thought.
3a For neither like the world
3b nor like the flesh is his thought,
3c nor like those who serve in a fleshly way.
4a The sacrifice of the Lord is righteousness
4b and purity of heart and lips.
(II) 5a Sacrifice thy kidneys[a] without blemish,
5b and let not thy bowels oppress [another's] bowels,
5c and let not thy "soul" oppress [another] "soul."
6a Do not possess a stranger among thy blood kin,
6b nor seek to defraud thy neighbor,
6c nor deprive him of the covering of his nakedness.
(III) 7a But put on the grace of the Lord without envy,
7b and come into his paradise,
7c and make thyself a wreath from his tree,
8a and set [it] on thy head and rejoice,
8b and lean on his mildness/rest.
(IV) 9a And his glory will go before thee,
9b and thou shalt receive of his kindness and of his grace,
9c and truly thou wilt be fat in the glory of his holiness.
(V) 10 Glory and honor to his name! Hallelujah.

a 5a Codex N has ܟܘ̈ܠܝܬܝ (*kulyāṯ*), "my kidneys."

Introduction

Ode 20 is preserved in two Syriac manuscripts.[1] The stanzaic divisions on which this commentary is based follow the analysis of Franzmann, with one exception. The remarkable instruction, 5a, which includes a negation, does not sit easily as the culmination of stanza I after the parallel bicolon 4a-b. As the beginning of stanza II, its sacrificial terminology connects backwards to stanza I, and it also initiates a series of addresses to an undefined second person singular, that is, to anyone in the target audience who reads or hears the Ode, which continues to the end of stanza IV. Verse 5a-c are additionally connected by the metaphorical use of three terms that each express the psychosomatic unity of the human being. Stanza II, beginning with the invitation in 5a, followed by a sequence of five prohibitions, is the only example of ethical paraenesis in the *Odes of Solomon*.

The introductory "self-description"[2] as "priest of the Lord" cannot be used to draw conclusions about the

1 Mss.: Codex H, 15b–16a; Codex N, 149ʳ (ܣ). Ed./trans.: Charlesworth, 84–87; Franzmann, 153–58; Lattke, 2:113–29 and 3:XXX.

2 Lattke, *Oden*, 57; see Introduction, sec. 8.

person of the author or his office in the community. Instead, the priesthood is bestowed on the masculine "I" of this Ode, who never speaks of himself again after 1-2, to give his teaching (3-4), paraenesis (5-6), invitation to salvation (7-8) and promise of salvation (9) an authority that was widely accepted in antiquity. That the "Lord" (1-4, 7-10) is the Judeo-Christian God and not the Kyrios Christos needs no further proof, even if *Ode* 20 were to have been *used* in marginally Gnostic circles. That it *originated* among the less than orthodox cannot be deduced from the text of this Ode.

Interpretation

■ **1-4** The speaking "I" introduces himself in 1a-b with two *hapax legomena.* This "priest" is not a Stoic σοφός who has "achieved understanding" of "sacrifices, founding of temples, purifications"—περὶ θυσιῶν, ἱδρύσεων, καθαρμῶν (Diogenes Laertius 7.119),[3] nor one who performs the services in the Jewish temple, as, for example, Zechariah (Luke 1:5-23, esp. vv. 5 [ἱερεύς] and 8 [ἱερατεύειν]), but stands on the line from Exod 19:6 to 1 Pet 2:5, 9 (ἱεράτευμα) or from Isa 61:6 to Rev 1:6; 5:10; 20:6 (ἱερεῖς) as one chosen "in metaphor and symbol" and set apart as the representative of the "people of God."[4] The Greek of 1a-b is easy to reconstruct (ἱερεὺς κυρίου εἰμὶ καὶ αὐτῷ ἱερατεύω):[5] in 𝔖, the verbal ܐܝܬ (*ʾīṯ*) with first singular possessive suffix stands for εἰμί,[6] and the enclitic ܗܘ (*-ū*) gives prominence to the personal pronoun attached to ܠ,[7] while the participle of the Pa. ܟܗܢ (*kahhen*) with enclitic ܐܢܐ (*-nā*) expresses "the continuing as well as the momentary Present."[8]

The monocolon 2 is again characterized by paronomasia (words derived from the root ܩܪܒ in this case), but its retroversion into Greek is more problematic. The verb and both nouns have a number of possible equivalents. Clearly the Pa. of ܩܪܒ (*qreḇ*) is a term of sacrifice,[9] but it could represent θύω[10] (cf. θῦσον τῷ θεῷ θυσίαν αἰνέσεως, "offer to God the sacrifice of praise," in Ps 49:14 LXX, although 𝔖 there uses ܕܒܚ)[11] or the technical term προσφέρω,[12] which is often used with θυσία. The term ܩܘܪܒܢܐ (*qurbānā*), which appears only here and in 4a, might—like ܕܒܚܬܐ (*deḇḥṯā*) in 7:10—stand for θυσία.[13] It is, however, much more likely that 𝔊 used προσφορά in a transferred sense.[14] The terms προσφέρω and προσφορά would also lend themselves to paronomasia,

3 H. S. Long, ed., *Diogenis Laertii vitae philosophorum* (2 vols.; Oxford: Clarendon, 1964, 1966) 347; Otto Apelt, trans., and Klaus Reich, ed., *Diogenes Laertius, Leben und Meinungen berühmter Philosophen* (2 vols.; Philosophische Bibliothek 53–54; 2nd ed.; Hamburg: Meiner, 1967) 2:62–63.

4 Norbert Brox, *Der erste Petrusbrief* (EKKNT 21; Zurich: Benziger; Neukirchen-Vluyn: Neukirchener Verlag, 1979) 99, 105. Hugo Greßmann ("Die Oden Salomos," *Deutsche Literaturzeitung* 32 [1911] 1355) objects to Diettrich's attempt "to find the singer among the Essenes." His own argument that 20:1 presupposes "the universal priesthood" overlooks the esoteric nature of the statement. Even Rudolf Abramowski's statement that "the mysterious second 'I' in the Odes is without doubt an outstanding member of the community and its minister that can be glimpsed in the Odes" probably goes too far (Abramowski, 58).

5 Frankenberg, 21; cf. Payne Smith, 1:1683; BDAG, *s.v.* ἱερεύς.

6 Nöldeke §§199, 303.

7 Ibid. §221.

8 Ibid. §269. In 𝔊, 1 may have been a monocolon. The structure of stanza I in 𝔊 would then have been bicolon (1-2) / tricolon (3) / bicolon (4).

9 Payne Smith, 2:3722: *obtulit sacrificia.*

10 BDAG, *s.v.* θύω.

11 Rahlfs, 2:52; Brenton, 727; cf. *OTSy*, pt. 2 fasc. 3, p. 56.

12 BDAG, *s.v.* προσφέρω.

13 Payne Smith, 2:3725–26; BDAG, *s.v.* θυσία; cf. Johannes Behm, "θύω, κτλ.," *ThWNT* 3 (1938) 189; *TDNT* 3:190.

14 BDAG, *s.v.* προσφορά.

a point missed by Frankenberg when he used προσάγω and δῶρον.[15] The precise *meaning* of the feminine noun ܡܚܫܒܬܐ (*maḥšabṯā*) cannot be determined (see Excursus 9), but the *use* of the term is of great importance, since the objective genitive of its form ("his thought" = thinking of or about him)[16] bursts all religious and intellectual bounds. Like λογικὴ λατρεία ("spiritual worship") in Rom 12:1, this no longer concerns sacramental acts or liturgical celebrations.

This "thinking" of the Lord in an objective—and also transcendental—sense is skillfully made the single and central subject (in 3b) of the negative teaching in 3a-c.[17] The particle ܓܝܪ (*gēr*) does not serve any "real, causal function."[18] Even though the terms "world," "flesh," and "fleshly" are not overtly contrasted with positive terms, their full meaning can be grasped only in opposition to "not-world," "spirit," and "spiritual." Thinking God in this radical fashion leaves behind all categories of being in the cosmos (see Excursus 22).[19]

The anthropological term σάρξ/ܒܣܪܐ (*besrā*) in 3b anchors the universality of the *theologia negativa* historically (cf. 8:9). The term "flesh" must not be limited to the physical "substance" of human beings, and even less can it be reduced to their sexuality. What is denied here is the possibility of "finite humanity" to think of God as God.[20] Where right thinking of God—it might be called radical theology—manages to flash like lightning and becomes available for metaphorical sacrifice, it is, as it were, God's holy πνεῦμα itself at work. The influence here is more Pauline than Johannine.

The adverb ܒܣܪܢܐܝܬ (*besrānā'īṯ*), "fleshly," in 3c, which corresponds to σαρκικῶς or σαρκίνως,[21] repeats the idea of 3b. The unspoken contrast with πνευματικῶς ("spiritually") is more intensely Pauline[22] than Ignatius *Eph.* 10:3 (cf. also 8:2). Whether the demonstrative pronoun ܗܢܘܢ (*hānnōn*, masculine plural) points polemically at known "others"[23] cannot be determined. But the term of ministry ܦܠܚ (*plaḥ*, Pe. masculine plural active participle) leads to a positive continuation of the teaching.[24]

The "information on true sacrifice"[25] in 4a-b "is given in strict accord with the prophets and psalmists."[26] A few examples will suffice to demonstrate the origins of this anti-ritualistic stance (on Hos 6:6, cf. also Matt 9:13; 12:7):

Hos 6:6 LXX

διότι ἔλεος θέλω καὶ οὐ θυσίαν καὶ ἐπίγνωσιν θεοῦ ἢ ὁλοκαυτώματα.

For I desire mercy and not sacrifice, and the knowledge of God rather than whole burnt-offerings.[27]

Ps 50:18-19 LXX

ὅτι εἰ ἠθέλησας θυσίαν, ἔδωκα ἄν·
ὁλοκαυτώματα οὐκ εὐδοκήσεις.
θυσία τῷ θεῷ πνεῦμα συντετριμμένον,
καρδίαν συντετριμμένην καὶ τεταπεινωμένην ὁ θεὸς οὐκ ἐξουθενώσει.

15 Frankenberg, 21.
16 If the term "his thought" is taken as a subjective genitive, the sacrificial statement of 2 loses its meaning.
17 On ܠܐ (*lā*) with enclitic ܗܘܬ (*hwāṯ*) "having nothing of the force of a verb," see Nöldeke §§299, 328.B. The subject of the three comparisons is feminine and therefore cannot be "sacrifice" (contra Lattke, *Oden*, 156), but must be "his thought." This skillful construction is one of the reasons for Gunkel's verdict: "Aesthetically the quality of the Odes of Solomon can be very high" (Hermann Gunkel, "Salomo-Oden," *RGG*[1] 5 [1913] 230).
18 Lattke, "Wörter," 289 = idem, *Bedeutung*, 4:138.
19 See Payne Smith, 2:2899; BDAG, *s.v.* κόσμος.
20 See Payne Smith, 1:553–54; BDAG, *s.v.* σάρξ.
21 BDAG, *s.v.* σαρκικῶς; Lampe, 1223; Payne Smith, 1:554.
22 See BDAG, *s.v.* σαρκικός.
23 Nöldeke §67.
24 On ܦܠܚ, see Payne Smith, 2:3147–49, with numerous possible Greek equivalents.
25 Abramowski, 52.
26 Hermann Gunkel, *Reden und Aufsätze* (Göttingen: Vandenhoeck & Ruprecht, 1913) 180.
27 Rahlfs, 2:495; Brenton, 1074 [slightly corr.].

For if thou desiredst sacrifice, I would have given it:
thou wilt not take pleasure in whole burnt-offerings.
Sacrifice to God is a broken spirit:
a broken and humbled heart God will not despise.[28]

Prov 21:3 LXX

ποιεῖν δίκαια καὶ ἀληθεύειν ἀρεστὰ παρὰ θεῷ μᾶλλον ἢ θυσιῶν αἷμα.

To do justly and to speak truth are more pleasing to God than the blood of sacrifices.[29]

The genitive "of the Lord" (in 𝔊 certainly [τοῦ] κυρίου) is, of course, not a subjective one. The κύριος/ܡܪܝܐ (*māryā*) is the transcendental destination of the metaphorical "sacrifice" and thus its negating qualification. The self-canceling idea of "sacrifice" endures only because of tradition and the religious and sacramental environment. What matters, however, are the existential correspondences with the thought of God. What is needed is not mere devotion but the δικαιοσύνη/ܙܕܝܩܘܬܐ (*zaddīqūtā*), "righteousness," and καθαριότης/ܕܟܝܘܬܐ (*dakyūtā*), "purity," of the human thinking "heart" and the conversing and speaking "lips," which are appropriate to the "Lord" (see Excursuses 4 and 16). The combination of these two exemplary terms of human integrity—made attainable by God—arises from a tradition found, for example, in Ps 17:21, 25 LXX; and 2 Kgdms 22:25 (. . . κατὰ τὴν δικαιοσύνην μου καὶ κατὰ τὴν καθαριότητα τῶν χειρῶν μου . . . , "according to my righteousness, and according to the purity of my hands").[30] The first term does not describe either self-righteousness or an attribute resulting from the observance of a code of law (see Excursus 25).[31] And the *hapax legomenon* in 4b is no longer connected to any idea of ritual purity (cf. Mark 7:1-23).[32] Both terms cover a far wider area than the six subsequent imperatives, and their existential theological authenticity must be continually actualized.

Before turning to 5-6, it will be useful to list some other texts that are likely to have exerted an influence on *Ode* 20.[33] Isaiah 61 has not yet been sufficiently considered. Whether Sir 33:31 is among the influences may seem doubtful because of the negativity of its context in Sir 33:24-32 (but see on 6a below).

Table 4: Influence of Exodus 22:25-27 and Isaiah 58 on *Ode* 20

Exodus 22	Terms, Statements, Ideas	*Ode* 20
24	ἀργύριον	6b
25	τὸ ἱμάτιον τοῦ πλησίον	6b-c
26	περιβόλαιον, τὸ ἱμάτιον ἀσχημοσύνης αὐτοῦ	6c
26	ἐλεήμων γάρ εἰμι	7a
Isaiah 58		*Ode* 20
2	δικαιοσύνη	4
3	ὑποχειρίους . . . ὑπονύσσετε (oppression)	5b-c
6-7	prisoners, the hungry, poor, naked	4-6
8	δικαιοσύνη σου, καὶ ἡ δόξα τοῦ θεοῦ	4 and 9a, 9c (cf. 8:21)
10	ἄρτον ἐκ ψυχῆς σου, ψυχὴν τεταπεινωμένην	5c-6a
11	καὶ τὰ ὀστᾶ σου πιανθήσεται	9c

28 Rahlfs, 2:53; Brenton, 728.
29 Rahlfs, 2:217; Brenton, 807.
30 Rahlfs, 1:15, 2:615; Brenton, 435, 707.
31 See Payne Smith, 1:1085; BDAG, *s.v.* δικαιοσύνη.
32 See Payne Smith, 1:895; LEH, *s.v.* καθαριότης.
33 Cf. Connolly, "Greek," 531–34; Harris and Mingana, 2:315–17.

Table 5: Influence of Isaiah 61 on *Ode* 20

Isaiah 61	Terms, Statements, Ideas*	*Ode* 20
3	δικαιοσύνη/ܙܕܝܩܘܬܐ, φύτευμα . . . εἰς δόξαν	4 and 9
5	ἀλλογενεῖς/ܢܘܟܪܝܐ	6
6	ὑμεῖς δὲ ἱερεῖς κυρίου κληθήσεσθε	1
7	εὐφροσύνη/ܚܕܘܬܐ	8a
8	κύριος ὁ ἀγαπῶν δικαιοσύνην/ܕܝܢܐ	4
	καὶ μισῶν ἁρπάγματα ἐξ ἀδικίας	5-6
10	ἀγαλλιάσθω ἡ ψυχή μου ἐπὶ τῷ κυρίῳ	8a
	ἐνέδυσεν γάρ με (ܐܠܒܫܢܝ) ἱμάτιον σωτηρίου καὶ χιτῶνα εὐφροσύνης	7-8
11	δικαιοσύνη/ܙܕܝܩܘܬܐ, ἀγαλλίαμα/ܬܫܒܘܚܬܐ	4 and 9

* The references to Syriac terms are taken from *OTSy*, pt. 3 fasc. 1, pp. 110–11. On the influence of Isa 61 on Matt 5:3 and the Sermon on the Mount in general, cf. Michael Lattke, "Glückselig durch den Geist (Matthäus 5,3)," in C. Mayer et al., eds., *Nach den Anfängen fragen: Gerhard Dautzenberg zum 60. Geburtstag am 30. Januar 1994* (Gießener Schriften zur Theologie und Religionspädagogik des Fachbereichs Evangelische Theologie und Katholische Theologie und deren Didaktik der Justus-Liebig-Universität 8; Gießen: Selbstverlag, 1994) 363–82.

■ **5-6** "Such moral exhortations . . . are not to be found elsewhere in the *Odes*."[34] Except for the second part of 6a, the metaphorical imperative in 5a and the remaining five prohibitives offer no difficulties to comprehension when considered in the light of Exod 22:25-27 and Isaiah 58 and 61. Conversely, determining the Greek text is very hard.

The main reason for disregarding Franzmann's analysis, according to which "5a functions as the concluding exhortation/invitation of the first stanza,"[35] is the hortatory address to the second person singular that continues to the end of *Ode* 20. Also beginning stanza II with ܘ (ʾ*u*-) in 5b would be clumsier than it is in 9a. Another reason for moving the imperative, which is connected to the vocabulary of sacrifice in stanza I, into the first strophe of stanza II (5a-c) is the metaphorical use of three anthropological terms. An idiomatic translation of these "aspects" derived from the Semitic "biblical body symbolism"[36] is not easy, even if it is almost certain that the Greek terms were οἱ νεφροί,[37] τὰ σπλάγχνα, and ἡ ψυχή (see below). The reading ܟܘܠܝܬܝ ("my kidneys") in N does not make sense and counts among the few scribal errors of this manuscript.[38] For the Pa. ܩܪܒ (*qarreb*), reference can be made to 2, but the strange negation of ܡܘܡܐ (*mūmā*) deserves careful consideration (see also 13:4 and 39:6). The complete Syriac phrase ܕܠܐ ܡܘܡܐ cannot really be either the attribute or the predicate of "kidneys." But such a form with ܕܠܐ (*d-lā* = *sine*)[39] has become so worn down with use that two Greek equivalents are possible. Either the accusative plural of ἄμωμος referred attributively to "kidneys,"[40] or the adverb ἀμώμως qualified the verb. In either

34 Harnack, 51.
35 Franzmann, 156.
36 Schroer and Staubli, *Körpersymbolik*, 24–26, throughout.
37 BDAG, *s.v.* νέφρος; cf. Payne Smith, 1:1740, plural of ܟܘܠܝܬܐ (*kūlīṯā*).
38 See Lattke, *Bedeutung*, 1:38–39.
39 Payne Smith, 2:1869.
40 Suggested by Frankenberg, 21.

case, the word, drawn from the vocabulary of sacrifice, refers to a moral "stance."[41] Actually there is little difference between a blameless offering of the existentially innermost and the offering of a blameless inwardness. This demand forms the positive and quasi-theological[42] foundation of the following paradigmatic and negated imperfectives.

Klijn is right to criticize the translation of ܪܚܡܐ (*raḥmē*) in 5b as "flesh," pointing out that the term means "intestines."[43] Since this term corresponds to τὰ σπλάγχνα and stands for the "bowels" as "the seat of the emotions,"[44] "heart" would be a possible English translation.[45] But to avoid confusion, since the term "heart" is used to translate καρδία/ܠܒܐ (*lebbā*) and has an intellectual component (see Excursus 4), the word "bowels" may be used as denoting the "innermost" parts though without narrowing the sense of the whole line to a "protest against assault in the religious sphere."[46] Whether the Pe. ܐܠܨ (*ʾelaṣ*), which occurs only twice, corresponds to θλίβω[47] or—but less probably—to παρενοχλέω,[48] the parallel prohibitions of 5b and 5c refer neither to proselytizing nor to religious "persecutions,"[49] but to everyday vexations.

The translation of ܢܦܫܐ (*napšā*)[50] already presents difficulties in 5c before its recurrence in 6a. To begin with, there can be no doubt that the Greek of 5c used ψυχή, and the line, omitting the verb noted before, may be reconstructed as καὶ ἡ ψυχή σου μή . . . ψυχήν.[51] The meaning of "soul" in the passage will be made clearer by the following excursus.

Excursus 20: "Soul" in the *Odes of Solomon*

Occurring as it does twenty-three times, the term ܢܦܫܐ (*napšā*) would seem to be one of the more important ones in the *Odes of Solomon*.[52] The plural of ψυχή is used once as a loanword (6:15 ℭ), which suggests that this polysemous term in the history of philosophy and religion,[53] as well as biblically Jewish and early Christian anthropology,[54] must have played a similar role in 𝔊.[55] This expectation is, however, less than certain, since 𝔖, in particular, belongs to the Semitic tradition in which the "reflexive relationship is paraphrased" with "soul."[56] In certain cases, it is not clear whether that idiom is being used. So the first task will be to sort out the passages where 𝔊 used not ψυχή but a reflexive pronoun.

In reference both to the "Lord" (7:3b) and to his creatures (7:12c), "soul" is used "to express the reflexive relationship with accuracy."[57] The much-debated phrase "blood of thy soul" (20:6a) cannot have corresponded to any form of αἷμα τῆς ψυχῆς σου in 𝔊 (see below). The statement of the redeemed one in 21:4a ("And I had members of/with myself") could have been constructed with "soul" only in Syriac. As H makes clear by adding ܡܢ (*men*), 32:2 N speaks of "truth, who is/was itself" (H "from itself"). The first person statements in 35:7 imply that "ascent of my soul" reflexively refers to the whole

41 BDAG, *s.v.* ἄμωμος; Payne Smith, 2:2037.
42 The indirect object of the verb in 5a must be the "Lord" of stanza I. All that was said about "sacrifice" and "sacrifice of the Lord" in that stanza also pertains in this one.
43 Klijn, 303, contra Lattke, *Bedeutung*, 1:131.
44 BDAG, *s.v.* σπλάγχνον; Payne Smith, 2:3882.
45 Lattke, *Oden*, 156. In this passage and within the given sentence structure, translations such as "mercy" or "love" do not make sense (see Excursus 2).
46 Diettrich, 77.
47 BDAG, *s.v.* θλίβω; Payne Smith, 1:217–18.
48 Used by Frankenberg, 21; see BDAG, *s.v.* παρενοχλέω; LEH, *s.v.* παρενοχλέω.
49 BDAG, *s.v.* θλίβω.
50 This could be translated as "life" or "self." The commentary and Excursus 20 consider the problems posed in translating terms such as "kidneys (reins)" and "soul."
51 See Frankenberg (p. 21), who uses ἀδικείτω, the same verb as he uses in 5b.
52 See Payne Smith, 2:2430–32.
53 Albert Dihle, "ψυχή, κτλ. A. C. E.1–3," *ThWNT* 9 (1973) 604–14, 630–33, 657–59; *TDNT* 9:608–17, 632–35, 656–58; Friedo Ricken, "Seele I," *HWP* 9 (1995) 1–8; Horst Seidl, "Seele V. Kirchen- und philosophiegeschichtlich," *TRE* 30 (1999) 749–51.
54 Gerhard Dautzenberg, "Seele IV. Neues Testament," *TRE* 30 (1999) 744–48; Edmond Jacob, "ψυχή, κτλ. B," *ThWNT* 9 (1973) 614–29; *TDNT* 9:617–31; Karin Schöpflin, "Seele II. Altes Testament," *TRE* 30 (1999) 737–40; Eduard Schweizer, "ψυχή, κτλ. D," *ThWNT* 9 (1973) 635–57; *TDNT* 9:637–56.
55 BDAG, *s.v.* ψυχή.
56 Eduard Lohse, "ψυχή, κτλ. C.II," *ThWNT* 9 (1973) 634; *TDNT* 9:635–37; Günter Stemberger, "Seele III. Judentum," *TRE* 30 (1999) 740.
57 Nöldeke §223.

of the redeemed being and not some "ascension of the soul" by itself to heaven.[58] In *Ode* 38, there is no hint that the joy of the speaking "I" is confined to his "soul" and does not extend to the whole of his "self" (38:15c). But this case may already belong rather to the blurred boundary.

The place of the loving "I" is taken by the synonymous "my soul" (3:5a-b). In this case, 𝔊 will have had ἡ ψυχή μου in accordance with biblical usage.[59] Similarly "us" is parallel to the accusative "our souls" (41:11a-b), which in 𝔊 was τὰς ψυχὰς ἡμῶν. These two passages demonstrate that "soul" was not considered a dicho- or trichotomous part of a human being,[60] but still "describes the total human being, not something that a person possesses, but what he is."[61] But because—even without a "doctrine of the immortality of the soul"—"ψυχή came to be favoured as the term for a survival that is not ended by death" (cf. Matt 10:28),[62] the soteriological teaching of 41:16a also refers to human beings in their entirety, "that he [i.e., the Redeemer, Son, and Messiah] might give life to souls forever by the truth of his name." How esoterically this is intended will be discussed in its proper place.

Three more passages where the plural of ψυχή/ܢܦܫܐ (*napšā*) occurs can be elucidated by what has been said above. That the "souls of those who desire to come to him" (10:3) refers to integral, purposeful living beings is clear from the syntax.[63] The "bodies" and "souls" (39:3) threatened by the "power of the Lord" are not "in opposition"; they describe the "whole person" from different aspects.[64] Even though it could be suggested that "souls that were near to expiring" (6:15 𝔖) might be understood to be parts separated from the body, the parallelism of the mental-spiritual aspects in 6:13-17 must be considered. This leads to the interpretation of "soul" as the "life-force that resists death and dying."[65] Because of this use of the term "soul" for one facet,[66] it can be used as a parallel to "face" and "spirit" (40:4a-c).[67] Each of these facets describes the human being "as . . . a *person*."[68] The compound expression in 7:23c, ܡܕܡ ܕܢܦܫܐ (*meddem d-napšā*), also means "person," since no animal has been endowed with *gnōsis* and speech.[69]

There are some borderline cases where it is difficult to determine whether ܢܦܫܐ and/or ψυχή merely describes a reflexive relationship or bears greater weight. One passage has already been mentioned (see on 38:15c). In 9:2, where "your soul" is a reciprocal parallel to "you," 𝔊 would have had τὴν ψυχὴν ὑμῶν or τὴν ψυχὴν τὴν ὑμετέραν. The phrase "my soul," however, was not necessarily τὴν ψυχήν μου or τὴν ἐμὴν ψυχήν but could have been a simple ἐμαυτόν. Since "your soul" is parallel to "your ears" (9:1), the two cola are complementary challenges to the circumference and the center.[70]

Ode 26:9a-b may have used ἑαυτόν twice in place of ܢܦܫܗ (*napšeh* = "his soul") (see the text-critical discussion on that passage). But if ψυχή/ܢܦܫܐ, at least in 26:9b, means "life,"[71] then the use of ζωή/ܚܝܐ (*ḥayyē*) is a semantic play on words that tests the boundaries of translation and even "the boundaries of the study of religion."[72]

With the occurrence of the term "life," which plays a key role in discussions of ψυχή,[73] it is time to examine the last three passages. The question whether there may be some soul/body dualism

58 Contra Bauer, 615.
59 Schweizer, "ψυχή," *ThWNT* 9:638–40; *TDNT* 9:639–42.
60 See Albert Dihle, "ψυχή," *ThWNT* 9:657–59; *TDNT* 9:656–58; Karl-Wolfgang Tröger, "ψυχή, κτλ. E.4," *ThWNT* 9 (1973) 659–61; *TDNT* 9:658–60.
61 Jacob, "ψυχή," *ThWNT* 9:616; *TDNT* 9:620.
62 Schweizer, "ψυχή," *ThWNT* 9:645, 656; *TDNT* 9:645–46, 654.
63 Cf. Dihle, "ψυχή," *ThWNT* 9:613; *TDNT* 9:616; Jacob, "ψυχή," *ThWNT* 9:618; *TDNT* 9:621–22.
64 Schweizer, "ψυχή," *ThWNT* 9:638, 645; *TDNT* 9:639–40, 645–46.
65 See commentary on that passage; cf. Dihle, "ψυχή," *ThWNT* 9:613; *TDNT* 9:616: the "quintessence of human life."
66 Cf. Schroer and Staubli, *Körpersymbolik*, 61–73.
67 Cf. Jacob, "ψυχή," *ThWNT* 9:626; *TDNT* 9:628–29; Karin Schöpflin, "Seele II. Altes Testament," *TRE* 30 (1999) 739, on the relationship of *rû^{a}ḥ* and *näfäš*.
68 Schweizer, "ψυχή," *ThWNT* 9:655; *TDNT* 9:654–55.
69 Bauer, 586.
70 See Schroer and Staubli, *Körpersymbolik*, 138, on "ear" and "heart" as "the outer and inner aspects of the process of understanding."
71 See Gerhard Dautzenberg, "Seele IV. Neues Testament," *TRE* 30 (1999) 745–46, and elsewhere on "the composition of Mark 8:35ff. par."
72 Hans-Peter Hasenfratz, "Seele I. Religionsgeschichte," *TRE* 30 (1999) 733.
73 Cf. Alexander Sand, "ψυχή," *EWNT* 3 (1983) 1199-1202; *EDNT* 3:501-03.

arising from "popular philosophical doctrine of the soul"[74] is pertinent, especially to the first two. When it is said of the "spring of the Lord" that it "gives rest to the soul" (30:3), it is necessary, as always, to look at the context. This shows that it is the "physical life" of the "thirsty" who are being summoned that is in question (30:2).[75] The final blessing also asserts that "they rested" (30:7) in wholeness. In the case of the imperative of salvation in 31:7, one may consider whether the best translation is "gain yourselves"[76] or whether "your souls" expresses some essence of those who are to be redeemed. If "soul" is replaced by "life," the parallel imperative of salvation 31:7b ("take unto you immortal life") reopens the questions noted previously (see on 26:9 above).

So how is the repeated ψυχή/ܢܦܫܐ in 20:5c to be translated? Is the inner aspect, which is emphasized in the context, to be glossed over and the repetition reduced to "let not another's life be subjected to ill-treatment?"[77] Or is the sense limited to the "essence of the person" in question?[78] The succeeding tricolon is concerned with relationships among actual, embodied human beings, so the meaning could encompass real "life" and perhaps even the total "person," both of the one addressed and of every other human being.[79]

Harris and Mingana in their translation show their perplexity about 6a by an ellipsis: "Thou shalt not acquire a stranger . . . ."[80] The literal translation of ܒܕܡܐ ܕܢܦܫܟ (*ba-d̲mā d̲-napšāk̲*) as "by the blood of thy soul"—as they remark—"has no meaning."[81] Diettrich correctly interprets the first half of 6a as "an unconditional prohibition of obtaining slaves."[82] The radicalism of the prohibition could even be compared to similar reports about the "Essenes" (see Josephus *Ant.* 18.1.5)[83] and the "Therapeutae," who relied on "nature" (φύσις) (Philo *Vit. cont.* 70).[84] But Diettrich's division of ܒܕܡܐ into ܒܕ (*bad̲* = "for [he]") and ܡܐ (*mā* = "the same, that") is grammatically incorrect.[85] Even my emendation of the text, suggested earlier, to ܒܕܕܡܐ ܕܢܦܫܟ ("since he [is] of thy blood")[86] fails because a "stranger" is, of course, not one who is "related by blood."[87] The interpretation of ܕܡܐ as the active participle of *dmā* ("to be like")[88] is just as unconvincing, since the prefix ܒ (*b-*) would then be a conjunction.[89]

Already Connolly said that the Pe. ܩܢܐ (*qnā*) does not here mean "to acquire" but "to possess."[90] That is, it represents a form of ἔχω negated by μή.[91] In his review of Harris and Mingana's edition (1916, 1920), Connolly goes even further: "The obscure expression in Ode xx 6 . . . is surely derived from Ecclesiasticus xxxiii 31."[92] Raimund Köbert takes up this suggestion and, by comparing the Hebrew fragment (אל תקנא בדמי נפש)[93] with the Greek text (ὅτι ἐν αἵματι ἐκτήσω αὐτόν) and the Peshitta (*wlâ tetkattaš nûkrāyâ badmâ dĕnap̄šāk* [*sic*]) together with a conjecture of an unrecorded Pe. ܩܢܐ,[94] achieves the following translation: "Stranger, do not

74 Cf. Karl-Wolfgang Tröger, "ψυχή, κτλ. E.4," *ThWNT* 9 (1973) 657; *TDNT* 9:656.
75 Cf. Schweizer, "ψυχή," *ThWNT* 9:638, etc.; *TDNT* 9:639–40, etc.
76 Berger and Nord, 963.
77 Berger and Nord, 954.
78 Dihle, "ψυχή," *ThWNT* 9:613; *TDNT* 9:616.
79 Jacob, "ψυχή," *ThWNT* 9:616; *TDNT* 9:620; cf. Schweizer, "ψυχή," *ThWNT* 9:648; *TDNT* 9:648–49, with reference to Rom 2:9 and 13:1 "in traditional Jewish contexts."
80 Harris and Mingana, 2:312.
81 Ibid., 2:315. Bauer (p. 601) actually does translate this "strange, perhaps impossible, phrase" as "by the blood of thy soul." It is pertinent to remark, already here, that ܒ (*b-*) is used in a locative sense, perhaps more commonly than in an instrumental one.
82 Diettrich, 77. Gunkel (*Aufsätze,* 181) calls this prohibition a "feat in cultural history" and points out that "the early Christian Church never attained it."
83 Alfred Adam and Christoph Burchard, *Antike Berichte über die Essener* (KIT 182; 2nd ed.; Berlin: de Gruyter, 1972) 37.
84 Ibid., 19.
85 Harris and Mingana (2:313–14) object to this division and translation ("for he is the same as you are"); cf. Nöldeke §§258, 348, 363.
86 Lattke, *Bedeutung*, 1:131; on ܒܕܕܡܐ (*baddmā*), see Payne Smith, *Dictionary*, 35; Nöldeke §§26.B, 155.C.
87 See Lattke, *Oden*, 156.
88 Charlesworth, 86.
89 See, however, Brockelmann, *Grammatik*, §§163–66; idem, *Grundriss*, 2:363–77 (§§237–41).
90 Connolly, "Greek," 532.
91 Payne Smith, 2:3651–52; BDAG, *s.vv.* ἔχω, μή. The perfect of κτάομαι, meaning "to possess," may also be considered (BDAG, *s.v.* κτάομαι). On the omission of the preposition ܒ (*b-*), see Edwin A. Abbott and Richard Hugh Connolly, "The Original Language of the Odes of Solomon," *JTS* 15 (1913–14) 46–47.

envy your own blood kin."[95] Apart from the fact that an "influence of the Hebrew Sirach" is unlikely and that Köbert does not consider the preposition ܒ (*b-*) either, it is actually quite uncertain that Sir 33:31 had any impact. That difficult passage is quite pragmatic in the context of an "exhortation to strive for personal independence and also to treat slaves strictly but considerately."[96] The focus of 6a, however, is that there should be no stranger kept as a slave within the family.

So by (1) interpreting the negated imperfect of ܩܢܐ as forbidding all slave owning; (2) taking the term ܢܘܟܪܝܐ (*nukrāyā*) as the equivalent of ἀλλότριος and the opposite of kin (cf. Matt 17:25-26 with the terms ἀλλότριοι and υἱοί);[97] (3) reading the preposition ܒ (*b-*) not in an instrumental but in a locative sense; (4) construing αἷμα/ܕܡܐ (*dmā*), which should not be emended, as "*genus*" or "kin";[98] and finally (5) resolving the genitive construction with ܢܦܫܐ (*napšā*) and a personal suffix as a normal "expression of reflexive relationship" (see Excursus 20 above),[99] the translation of 6a 𝔖 can be illuminated by the probable Greek text, *Μή* (+ a form of ἔχω or κέκτημαι)[100] ἀλλότριον ἐν τῷ ἰδίῳ αἵματί σου (in a purely linguistic sense, cf. John 5:34).[101]

The last two prohibitions are totally clear, even if they are meant to be limited to "members of the same ethnic group" (cf. Matt 5:43, etc.)[102] or only to immediate neighbors. The nominalized adjective ܩܪܝܒܐ (*qarrībā*), derived from ܩܪܒ (*qreḇ*), which occurs only here in the sense of ὁ πλησίον,[103] is traceable to Exod 22:25 (see Table 4 above), but it has no connection with "sacrifice" as a noun (2, 4a) or verb (2, 5a), although it shares their root. The imperfect of the Pe. ܒܥܐ (*bʿā*) pillories even the attempt to deceive (see Excursus 19), but the emphasis is on the infinitive of ܢܟܠ (*nkel*), which corresponds rather to πτερνίζειν than to κατεσθίειν.[104] The use of πτέρνα[105] in 6b 𝔊 would have brought up ideas of "underhanded" plots against goods and chattels as well as against faith and trust.[106]

In 6c, where the objective suffix refers to the "neighbor" of 6b, there is another echo of Exod 22:26. The Aph. ܐܚܣܪ (*ʾaḥsar*) is a *hapax legomenon* expressing the causation of a lack.[107] The word ܬܟܣܝܬܐ (*taksīṯā*) is a term for the simplest clothing.[108] This basic covering is necessary even in the warmer climes, since, especially in Judeo-Christian tradition (from Gen 3:7 to Rev 16:15), the nakedness of the "private parts" is both subjectively and objectively embarrassing.[109]

92 Richard Hugh Connolly, review of Harris and Mingana in *JTS* 22 (1920–21) 83; see also idem, "The Odes and Psalms of Solomon: An Amends," *JTS* 22 (1920–21) 160.

93 Köbert fills out the fragmentary stich as follows:]אל תקנא ב[דמי] נפש ("Ode Salomons 20,6 und Sir 33,31," *Bib* 58 [1977] 529). Köbert refers to Charlesworth (p. 86 n. 4) instead of to Connolly.

94 See Payne Smith, 2:3656–57.

95 Köbert, "Ode Salomons 20,6 und Sir 33, 31," 530. Franzmann, without accepting "Köbert's suggestion of treating ܢܘܟܪܝܐ as a vocative," concludes that "then ܢܘܟܪܝܐ may be a *terminus technicus* in the *Odes* for a member of the believing community addressed here" (Franzmann, "Strangers," 31; see also idem, 155).

96 Victor Ryssel, "Die Sprüche Jesus', des Sohnes Sirachs," *APAT* 1 (1900; repr., 1962) 398–400.

97 Payne Smith, 2:2380; BDAG, *s.v.* ἀλλότριος.

98 Payne Smith, 1:910; BDAG, *s.v.* αἷμα.

99 Nöldeke §223.

100 For the various possible constructions "in a prohibitive sense in independent clauses, to express a negative wish or a warning," see BDAG, s.v. μή, c.

101 BDAG, *s.v.* ἴδιος; BDF and BDR §286. The reading τιμῇ for αἵματι (Frankenberg, 21) stems from an emendation "ܝܩܪܐ for ܕܡܐ" (ibid., 40; cf. Harris and Mingana, 2:313–14). Connolly ("Greek," 532) reconstructs the emended text as follows: οὐχ ἕξει (or the like) ἀλλότριον τὸ ἴδιον αἷμα–"thou shalt not regard as an alien thine own (flesh and) blood."

102 BDAG, *s.v.* πλησίον.

103 See Payne Smith, 2:3727.

104 Contra Frankenberg, 21; cf. Payne Smith, 2:2371; Otto Klein, *Syrisch-griechisches Wörterbuch zu den vier kanonischen Evangelien nebst einleitenden Untersuchungen* (BZAW 28; Gießen: Töpelmann, 1916) 114; LEH, *s.v.* πτερνίζειν.

105 See LSJ, *s.v.* πτέρνα.

106 See BDAG, *s.v.* πτέρνα.

107 Payne Smith, 1:1340.

108 Payne Smith, 1:1782; *OTSy*, pt. 1 fasc. 1, p. 169; see also BDAG, *s.v.* ἔνδυμα.

109 On the *hapax legomenon* ܦܘܪܣܝܐ (*pursāyā*), see Payne Smith, 2:3277; BDAG, *s.v.* ἀσχημοσύνη; LEH, *s.v.* ἀσχημοσύνη.

■ **7-8** If stanza II leaves "the impression of a foreign body within the Odes,"[110] stanza III is filled with terms and images that occur also elsewhere and have largely been discussed previously. There is, however, no reason to excise 5 and 6—much less 4[111]—because the "technically excellent link"[112] between stanzas II and III is made "by the semantic connection between the covering of nakedness in 6c and ܠܒܫ in 7a."[113] Counting the verbs shows that there are six imperatives of/invitations to salvation in the five (or four [H]) cola that follow each other logically; they differ from a similar series of invitations in 30:1-3 by not having a causal clause but instead continuing into the prophecies of salvation in stanza IV.

The particle ܕܝܢ (*dēn*), which follows the introductory imperative ܠܒܫ (*lbeš*) in 7a, has no syntactic function, and the later imperatives (7b-8b) and promises (9a-c) succeed each other connected by a more or less meaningless ܘ (*ʾu-*).[114] As in 4:6, the feminine ܛܝܒܘܬܐ (*ṭaybūṯā*; χάρις in 𝔊) is the object of the metaphorical verb (see Table 2). This "grace" is qualified by the "Lord" of 1a and 4a. The ambiguous phrase ܕܠܐ ܚܣܡܐ (*dlā ḥsāmā*) could refer adverbially to the salvific action of "putting on,"[115] or as predicate could describe "grace" as a garment,[116] but in this passage it is the attribute of the "Lord," with whom "there is no jealousy" (3:6b; in addition to the exegesis of this verse, see the remarks on 7:3; 11:6; and 23:4). In 𝔊, 7a would have run as follows: *ἔνδυσαι δὲ τὴν χάριν τοῦ κυρίου τοῦ ἀφθόνου* (or *κυρίου ἐν ἀφθονίᾳ αὐτοῦ* as in 11:6).

The imperative of ܐܬܐ (*ʾeṯā*), "come," in 7b is an example of the soteriological use of that common word (cf. 10:3; 30:2; 33:6). Together with the following preposition ܠ (*l-*), it corresponds to *ἔρχου εἰς* or *ἔλθε εἰς*.[117] The use of the loanword *παράδεισος* does not allude to Isa 58:11 Peshitta, in spite of the occurrence of ܦܪܕܝܣܐ (*p̄ardaysā*) in that verse.[118] Thus, there is no basis for the controversy between Harris and Mingana, who argue for "a Syriac original for this Ode,"[119] and Connolly, who thinks that "this Ode was composed in Greek."[120] For even if Isa 58:11 LXX had *παράδεισος* and not *κῆπος*,[121] the verse would still not be about the "paradise" of the Lord as a *locus beatorum* (see the commentary on 11:16-24).[122] Charlesworth's reference to *Apoc. Mos.* 20:1 really concerns only 7a;[123] however, there is a parallel to this entry into paradise in *T. Abr.* A XI.[124] But no literary connection has been established between the *Odes of Solomon* and the *Apocalypse of Moses* or the *Testament of Abraham*.

Not only the mythological term "paradise" but also the associated "tree" (7c; elsewhere in the plural: 11:16, 19, 21) finally derives from the primary text of all later Jewish, Christian, and Gnostic traditions about paradise.[125] As the third masculine singular possessive suffix in 7b refers to the "Lord" of 7a existing in the divine power of the human word, so in 7c it refers to the metaphorical place in 7b. This eschatological invitation transports the person addressed—presumably together with those who hear or read this text—into the primal garden, fails to differentiate between the trees of knowledge and of life, and with the word "wreath" adds a new feature to the ancient picture. The *στέφανος*/ܟܠܝܠܐ (*klīlā*) is neither the "Lord" (1:1; 5:12) nor the "wreath

110 Kittel, 93.
111 Grimme, 124: a "three-part intrusion."
112 Kittel, 93.
113 Franzmann, 157.
114 Lattke, "Wörter," 290 = idem, *Bedeutung*, 4:138. Some of these particles could be left untranslated, since they are merely equivalent to a comma.
115 Frankenberg, 21: *ἔνδυσαι . . . ἀφθόνως*; see Charlesworth, 86: "generously"; also Payne Smith, 1:1333.
116 Bauer, 601: "generously given," in which case the Greek would have been something like *τὴν χάριν . . . τὴν ἄφθονον*.
117 Payne Smith, 1:414; BDAG, *s.v.* *ἔρχομαι*, 1a*β*.
118 *OTSy*, pt. 3 fasc. 1, p. 105.
119 Harris and Mingana, 2:316.
120 Connolly, "Greek," 534.
121 See Rahlfs, 2:644.
122 Payne Smith, 2:3239. Charlesworth (p. 86 n. 5) notes that "Harris-Mingana misread H." Their text-critical apparatus still states, erroneously, "H ܠܦܪܕܝܣܐ" (Harris and Mingana, vol. 1, on this passage). Gunkel (*Aufsätze*, 181) replaces the integral "thou" with "the soul," stating that "clothed in the garment of divine grace, the soul enters Paradise."
123 Charlesworth, 86; see Otto Merk and Martin Meiser, *Das Leben Adams und Evas* (JSHRZ 2.5; Gütersloh: Mohn, 1998) 830; they also discuss the readings *χάρις* and *δικαιοσύνη*.
124 BDAG, *s.v.* *ἔρχομαι*, 1a*β*: *εἰς τὸν παράδεισον*; Enno Janssen, *Testament Abrahams* (JSHRZ 3.2; Gütersloh: Mohn, 1975) 229.
125 Greßmann (p. 456) even imports a plural: "and

of truth" (see discussion of 1:2-4), nor yet "truth" as in 9:8-11a.[126] The image is of joyous and unrestrained merrymaking, an activity of which the "flower-children"[127] of the twentieth century are only the latest discoverers.

The first imperative of 8a is the logical sequel of 7c. Although there is no objective suffix, it is clearly the "wreath" of 7c that is to be put on the head (cf. 9:8, 11a). This missing object in 𝔖 could be most easily explained if 𝔊 had a participle of τίθημι.[128] This would be an important indication of a Greek *Vorlage*. That the term κεφαλή/ܪܫܐ (*rēšā*), which occurs often in the *Odes of Solomon*, should be found in connection with "wreath" or "crown" is hardly surprising (cf. 1:1, 4; 5:12; 9:8; see also Excursus 23). If the imperative of the Ethpa. of ܒܣܡ (*bsem*) represents εὐφραίνου in 𝔊 (cf. 11:15; 28:2; see also Excursus 14), then "paradise" included the classical "pleasures of the table" (cf. Luke 12:19).[129]

It is strange that Judith Hoch Wray does not mention 20:8b in her summary, "Rest in Other Early Christian Literature," or anywhere else.[130] Perhaps it was omitted because 8b does not fit comfortably into the assessment that the *Odes of Solomon* "present inner-peace and tranquility as a result of trusting in Christ."[131] The first question is, again, Who or what is the antecedent of the possessive suffix of ܢܝܚܘܬܐ (*nīḥūtā*)? It might, like the "tree" of 7c, refer to "paradise," expressing a paradisal "rest."[132] But here also it most probably stands for "the rest of God, the Lord and Most High" (see Excursus 3). The transition to stanza IV enhances this probability. It also closes the circle of stanza III. Beginning with the metaphorical invitation to put on the "grace of the Lord" (7a), it ends with a similarly transferred imperative of salvation to support oneself or lean on the "rest" of the same Lord (cf. Ps 70:6a LXX).[133]

■ **9** Three promises of salvation, in which the imperfect verbs show no "modal colouring,"[134] "result from the acceptance of the invitations" in stanza III.[135] Dominating, and also forming an *inclusio*, is the term ܬܫܒܘܚܬܐ (*tešbuḥtā*), whose "concordant translation," as demanded by Klijn,[136] would not be easy even if, in 9a and 9c as well as in the final doxology, it always represented the equally polysemous term δόξα (see Excursus 21). But even a comparison of the equivalents in Isa 58:8 (כְּבוֹד יְהוָה, δόξα τοῦ θεοῦ, ܐܝܩܪܗ ܕܡܪܝܐ) with those in Isa 61:11 (תְּהִלָּה, ἀγαλλίαμα, ܬܫܒܘܚܬܐ),[137] shows that things are not so simple.

make yourself a wreath from his trees." Cf. Gen 2:9, 17; 3:3, 6, 22, 24.

126 Contra Diettrich, 78. These interpretations fall short of the mark because the "wreath" is the direct object of the reflexive imperative of ܥܒܕ (*ʿbad*). This common verb here represents ποιέω/ποιέομαι, a sense that does not occur elsewhere in the *Odes of Solomon* (Payne Smith, 2:2765–66; BDAG, *s.v.* ποιέω).

127 See *MEL*, 31:1257, *s.v.* Hippie.

128 Payne Smith, 2:2556–57; BDAG, *s.v.* τίθημι; see Frankenberg, 21: θέμενος.

129 See Payne Smith, 1:549; BDAG, *s.v.* εὐφραίνω, 2.

130 Judith Hoch Wray, *Rest as a Theological Metaphor in the Epistle to the Hebrews and the Gospel of Truth: Early Christian Homiletics of Rest* (SBLDS 166; Atlanta: Scholars Press, 1998) 25–32.

131 Ibid., 32. This description fits better with lines 43,35-37 of NHC 1,*4* and recalls Peel's statement: "Such 'rest' seems to denote both the cessation of anxiety about death and the afterlife and a present anticipation of the fully-resurrected state" (Peel, *Rheginos*, 143). The text of the passage cited is: ". . . Rest, which we have received through our Saviour (σωτήρ), our Lord Christ (χρηστός)" (Peel, *Rheginos*, 29). In this important treatise on resurrection, whose "author is a Christian Gnostic whose thought displays the influence of Middle Platonism as filtered through a late and somewhat vaguely articulated Valentinian Gnosticism" (Malcolm L. Peel, "The Treatise on the Resurrection [I,*4*]," *NHLE*, 53), there is no mention of a place of paradise. For this reason it has not been listed in Franzmann's collection (Franzmann, "Background").

132 The term "rest" in this verse may be a translation of πραΰτης (Payne Smith, 2:2316; BDAG, *s.v.* πραΰτης; Greßmann, 456: "kindness;" Bauer, 601: "mildness") but φιλανθρωπία (Frankenberg, 21) is impossible.

133 On the Ethpa. of ܣܡܟ (*smaḵ*), a *hapax legomenon*, see Payne Smith, 2:2660: *innisus est*.

134 Nöldeke §266.

135 Franzmann, 158: "The repetition of ܛܝܒܘܬܐ (7a, 9b) and the root ܒܣܡ (8b, 9b) links this stanza with stanza 3."

136 Klijn, 303.

137 *BHS*, 766, 771; Rahlfs, 2:644, 2:649; *OTSy*, pt. 3 fasc. 1, pp. 105, 111.

A further uncertainty is found in 9a. The question is, What or who is the referent of the third masculine singular possessive suffix that corresponds to the genitive αὐτοῦ? If there is an echo here of Isa 58:8 LXX (in 𝔊 perhaps προπορεύσεται ἔμπροσθέν σου ἡ δόξα αὐτοῦ), then a subjective genitive, as in 11:17 and 36:2, would refer to God's otherworldly "glory," suitably paralleled by the "gentleness" and "grace" of 9b. If, however, it is an objective genitive, his "honor" would be meant as "praise," which would fit better with the doxology. Finding a unique solution to this question is made more difficult because readers and listeners might differentially make associations with the visual "brightness" or the aural impression of angelic hymnody. How interchangeable the verbs ܐܙܠ (*ʾezal*) and ܗܠܟ (*hallek*) are is shown by comparing 9a with the Syriac translation of Isa 58:8.[138] The use of the Pa. ܗܠܟ (in place of the Pe. ܐܙܠ) weakens the repeated statement of Harris and Mingana "that the Odist has been imitating the Syriac text of Isaiah."[139]

The term χάρις/ܛܝܒܘܬܐ (*ṭaybūṯā*), "grace," is taken up in 9b with poetic freedom (see 7a above).[140] The Pa. ܩܒܠ (*qabbel*), as in most cases, means "to receive" and thus accords with the passive sense of ܢܣܒ (*nsab*; cf. 5:3; 11:4 [ἔλαβον]; 23:2).[141] The term χρηστότης/ܒܣܝܡܘܬܐ (*bassīmūṯā*), "kindness," can be used parallel to "mercy" and "rest" (14:3; 25:12), but in this case the term derived from ܒܣܡ is juxtaposed with "grace" (see Excursus 14). A passage like 17:7c may be taken as strengthening the case for translation of ܬܫܒܘܚܬܐ (*tešbuḥtā*) in 9a and 9c by "glory."

The same question as in 9a about ܬܫܒܘܚܬܐ arises in 9c. Is the topic God's own "brightness"[142] or the "praise" of his holiness?[143] There is also the question whether the preposition ܒ (*b*-) is used locatively or instrumentally. If it is instrumental, and the other term is used hymnically, the promise contained in the verb would be diminished from a comprehensive show of grace to a collaboration in the felicity of paradise. But if the radical conception of God requires the idea of a pure gift, then the Lord's ܚܣܝܘܬܐ (*ḥasyūṯā*) cannot carry any taint of human or hierarchical ὁσιότης.[144] The term ܫܪܪܐ (*šrārā*) cannot here bear the full weight of its meaning (see Excursus 1); it corresponds, in connection with the preposition ܒ (*b*-), to the Greek phrase ἐν ἀληθείᾳ or to the adverb ἀληθῶς[145] and serves only to reinforce the Pe. ܕܗܢ (*dhan*), whose basic meaning is "to grow fat" (cf. 40:3). Since it is more than likely that Isa 58:11 LXX influenced 9c,[146] this use of the imperfect of ܕܗܢ anticipates the translation of πιανθήσεται by ܬܬܕܗܢ in the Hexapla.[147] Instead of assuming an influence by ܕܘܗܢܐ (*dūhānā*),[148] one should ask whether the Syriac text of the *Odes of Solomon* might not have influenced the "Syro-Hexaplaris" of the early seventh century.[149]

■ **10** Instead of referring to the identical doxology at 16:20, the exegesis of that passage will in large part be repeated here.[150]

There are three doxologies in the *Odes of Solomon* that are in the third person and are addressed to God's "name" (cf. 16:20 [= 20:10]; 18:6; see Excursus 39). The two hymnic terms correspond, without doubt, to Greek

138 *OTSy*, pt. 3 fasc. 1, p. 105: ܘܬܐܙܠ. Isa 58:8 is also quoted, in part, in 8:21a. My earlier note on 20:9a (Lattke, *Oden*, 116, 157) should be revised, because it is not a "continuation" of this quotation, instead substituting δόξα for δικαιοσύνη.

139 Harris and Mingana, 2:316.

140 If N does substitute ܛܒܘܬܗ for ܛܝܒܘܬܗ (Harris and Mingana, vol. 1, on this passage, repeated by Charlesworth, 85, 87, but cf. his remark on 25:4 [idem, 102 n. 5], which is true of this passage also), the copyist probably noticed that "grace" had already been put on in 7a.

141 BDAG, *s.v.* λαμβάνω.

142 Lattke, *Bedeutung*, 1:131.

143 See Charlesworth, 86.

144 See Payne Smith, 1:1327–28; Brockelmann, *Lexicon*, 245; BDAG, *s.v.* ὁσιότης.

145 BDAG, *s.vv.* ἀλήθεια, ἀληθῶς; cf. Bultmann, "Untersuchungen," 160 = idem, *Exegetica*, 170 n. 1). Berger and Nord (p. 954) simply omit the phrase in their translation. Instead of "glorious holiness" it would be more accurate to say "holy glory."

146 Connolly, "Greek," 534.

147 See Payne Smith, 1:826–27; LEH, *s.v.* πιαίνω.

148 So Harris and Mingana, 2:316, referring to Isa 58:11a Peshitta; see Payne Smith, *Dictionary*, 85: "fat, fatness, rich food."

149 See Wolfgang Hage, "Bibelübersetzungen," *KWCO*, 78; Sebastian P. Brock, "Bibelübersetzungen I. Die alten Übersetzungen des Alten und Neuen Testaments," *TRE* 6 (1980) 185–87.

150 "10 functions as the concluding doxology for the Ode (cf. 16:20; 18:16). It is connected with the

δόξα and *τιμή* (see Excursus 21).[151] The terms originate in the vocabulary of the Psalms, for example, the call to praise in Ps 95:7 LXX (*ἐνέγκατε τῷ κυρίῳ δόξαν καὶ τιμήν*, "bring to the Lord glory and honor"),[152] where the "indirect speech," as in the Ode, "contains in itself the act of praise."[153] This allows no conclusion as to any "cult" for the *Sitz im Leben* of the Ode (cf. Ps 28:1 LXX).[154]

If this two-part doxology was mediated by New Testament texts, it will not have been through anthropological passages such as Heb 2:7 (cf. Ps 8:6 LXX) or christological ones such as Heb 2:9 or 2 Pet 1:17. Tripartite forms such as Rom 2:7, 10 and 1 Pet 1:7 do not come under consideration either, even if the terms used, *δόξα* and *τιμή*, in addition to meaning "praise and heavenly recognition,"[155] primarily express "the essential being of God" (cf. Rev 4:9).[156] The texts that come closest to the concluding formula of *Ode* 20 are the doxology in 1 Tim 1:17, framed under "the influence of the Greek-speaking Jewish diaspora,"[157] and the ending of the so-called heavenly liturgy, Rev 4:11.[158] But the connection with these two passages is not as clear as it is in *Ode* 16. For the only link between 20:10 and the rest of the Ode is the repetition of ܬܫܒܘܚܬܐ (*tešbuḥtā*), in a distinctly hymnic sense, unlike its use in 9a and 9c.

preceding stanza by the repetition of ܬܫܒܘܚܬܐ" (Franzmann, 158).

151 Payne Smith, 1:1624, 2:4027; BDAG, *s.vv.* δόξα, τιμή.

152 Rahlfs, 2:105; Brenton, 756.

153 Wagner, "Lobaufruf," 152–54.

154 Ibid., 143, 154. Blaszczak's enumeration of possible cults is purely speculative, as he himself says (on 16:20): "On the basis of the evidence culled from the *Ode* alone, we cannot ascertain the *Sitz im Leben*" (Blaszczak, 40).

155 Käsemann, *Romans*, 59 (German, 55).

156 Karl Hermann Schelkle, *Die Petrusbriefe. Der Judasbrief* (HThKNT 13.2; 2nd ed.; Freiburg/Basel/Vienna: Herder, 1964) 36.

157 See Oberlinner, *Pastoralbriefe*, 1:47.

158 See Kraft, *Offenbarung*, 100–102.

21

Ode 21: Address by the Exalted, Redeemed, and Glorifying One

(I) 1a **I raised my arms on high**
1b **to the compassion of the Lord,**
2a **because he cast my bonds away from me.**
2b **And my helper lifted me up**
2c **to his compassion and his salvation.**
(II) 3a **And I put off darkness,**
3b **and I put on light.**
4a **And I had members of/with myself,**
4b **in/among which/whom there was no[a] pain**
4c **nor affliction nor suffering.**
5a **And supremely helpful to me was**
5b **the thought of the Lord**
5c **and his imperishable fellowship.**
(III) 6a **And I was lifted up by/in the light**
6b **and passed before his face.**
7a **And I was near him,**
7b **while I praised**
7c **and gave thanks to him.**
(IV) 8a **My heart overflowed**
8b **and found itself in my mouth**
8c **and dawned upon my lips.**
9a **And upon my face increased**
9b **the exultation over the Lord together with[b] his praise.**
Hallelujah.

a 4b H omits ܠܐ.
b 9b ܒܬܫܒܘܚܬܗ N; ܘܬܫܒܘܚܬܗ H.

Introduction

Ode 21 is preserved in two Syriac manuscripts.[1] It is possible to determine that the "I" of this "intensely personal Ode"[2] is to be considered male by noting two masculine participles (7b-c). This will also have been true of 𝔖.[3] Whether it is possible to go further and identify the redeemed and glorifying one with "the risen Christ,"[4] or indeed with any other redeemer, depends essentially on the meaning of the term "members" in 4a-c.[5]

Only if the details of later baptismal rites are read into this Ode ("outstretching of the hands *after* baptism"; "release from the bonds of sin"; "clothing the neophytes in white robes") and at the same time 4a-c is interpreted as a statement about the connection between body and soul as well as about "the . . . beneficial influence of baptism upon the health of the body"[6] is it possible to consider *Ode* 21 a "baptismal hymn."[7] Although "setting free" is mentioned, this Ode is still hardly a "hymn of thanks"[8] or a "prayer of thanks."[9] This first person speech is, in fact, a series of statements of salvation (2-7a) introduced by a self-descriptive image

1 Mss.: Codex H, 16a–b; Codex N, 49ʳ–149ᵛ (𝔰). Ed./trans.: Charlesworth, 87–88; Franzmann, 159–63; Lattke, 2:131–46 and 3:XXX–XXXI.
2 Franzmann, 163.
3 See Frankenberg, 21; Payne Smith, *Dictionary*, 204, *s.v.* ܟܕ.
4 Connolly, "Odes," 302.
5 Abramowski (p. 59) counts *Ode* 21 among the "*Odes* where it is impossible to see which of the two sons is the speaker." Reizenstein (*Das iranische Erlösungsmysterium*, 89) places it beside the "Mandaic Hymns of the Soul." Kroll (*Hymnodik,* 76) compares it to "the solemn announcement of the mystae during the rites of Isis in Apuleius."
6 Bernard, 90–91.
7 Schille, 63.
8 Suggested by Bultmann, "Bedeutung," 135 = idem, *Exegetica*, 93.
9 Suggested by Diettrich, 78.

of the upraised arms (1) and followed by more hymnodic self-descriptions (7b-9). The κύριος/ܡܪܝܐ (*māryā* [1b, 5b, 9b], "Lord")—who is not directly addressed—is the merciful God who alone is worthy of praise, and not the Kyrios Christos or any terrestrial being, and he is located, even without the use of the title "Most High," in the mythological but also existential "heights" (1a-b, 2b-c, 6a).[10]

Harnack was right in his finding that "there is nothing Christian about this *Ode*."[11] Diettrich agrees, but draws the extraordinary conclusion that *Ode* 21 is "therefore connected to the Old Testament," "perhaps ... the Therapeutae."[12] For it is impossible to ignore the fact that this Ode contains "a certain insight into Gnostic spirituality."[13] Like Kurt Rudolph, Eduard Lohse quotes *Ode* 21, avoiding one-sidedness in his remarks that the speaking "I" "combines Old Testament turns of phrase with Gnostic ideas, that the redeemed one puts on a body of light, which the darkness cannot overpower, and that it is borne upward into the perpetual fellowship of the world of light."[14] Whether "the 30th Psalm should be the key to the 21st Ode"[15] will have to be examined as carefully as the assertion "that the Odist was working from the Syriac or Aramaic Psalter."[16]

Interpretation

■ **1-2** Since *Ode* 21 is not a prayer addressed to God (see above), it may be doubted that the raising of the arms is meant to portray the "image of a person praying with arms stretched wide and hands raised."[17] This passage does not actually mention raising the hands or stretching out the arms (but cf. 27:1; 35:7; 37:1; 42:1). So the following functional translation, "I raised my arms in prayer, to thank God for his mercy,"[18] is misleading. Although the plural of ܕܪܥܐ (*drāʿā*), "arms," is occasionally used for χεῖρες κτλ. ("hands," e.g., Luke 4:11, quoting Ps 90:12 LXX),[19] here it corresponds to the accusative plural of βραχίων.[20] The Aph. of ܪܘܡ, ܪܡ (*rām*), which functions as a past tense, must have been settled on because of the use of the mythic-theological term ܡܪܘܡܐ (*mrawmā*), which makes possible, though only in 𝔖, the paronomasia with Aph. ܐܪܝܡ (*ʾarīm*) in 1a and 2b (cf. 36:1-2 and see Excursus 17). In 𝔊, the word for "height" would have been τὰ ὑψηλά or τὸ ὕψος.[21] But the two forms of ܐܪܝܡ cannot have corresponded to forms from one verb in Greek. The verb ὑψόω could have been used in 2b (see below). In 1a, however, it could only have been αἴρω or ἐπαίρω.[22] But that is not what wrecks Harris and Mingana's assertion that "we find the very assonance that the Odist has imitated"[23] only in the Syriac translation of Ps 30:2a. The fact that contradicts it is the quite different direction of the two statements. The speaker of Ps 30 (29 LXX)—like the one of *Ode* 26:4—is concerned to "exalt" the *Lord* (ὑψώσω σε), but the "I" of this Ode raises his *arms*. One may agree with Harris and Mingana that certain concepts in the last part of Psalm 30 influenced the terminology of *Ode* 21. But none of the examples taken from Ps 30:11-13 shows that "the Odist . . . was working . . . on the Syriac Psalter" or that the "dependence of the Ode on the

---

10 In Charlesworth's translation (pp. 87–88), it is not clear who is meant by the "Lord." Berger and Nord's translation (pp. 954–55) is somewhat free, but they correctly use "God" for ܡܪܝܐ (*māryā*) in two instances. This does not, however, decide whether "the speaker" of this *Ode* is "Jesus Christ himself" (Berger and Nord, 933).

11 Harnack, 52.

12 Diettrich, 79.

13 Rudolph, *Gnosis*, 239.

14 Eduard Lohse, *Umwelt des Neuen Testaments* (GNT 1; Göttingen: Vandenhoeck & Ruprecht, 1971; 3rd ed., 1976; 4th ed., 1978) 204.

15 Harris and Mingana, 2:321.

16 Ibid., 2:323. Occasionally the editorial divisions differ from those of H and/or N for reasons of versification (Lattke, *Bedeutung*, 1:75). Although N has a singular in two places (1a, 8c), it is clear, even without plural pointing, that the meaning is plural (Lattke, *Bedeutung*, 1:46). These are not properly speaking variant readings.

17 This *orans* gesture is "a common attitude of prayer in antiquity, the depiction of which is not specifically Christian" (Gudrun Bühl, "Orans, Orante, Oranten," *LThK*^{3} 7 [1998] 1083).

18 Berger and Nord, 954.

19 Rahlfs, 2:100; *OTSy*, pt. 2 fasc. 3, p. 109.

20 Payne Smith, 1:953; BDAG, *s.v.* βραχίων.

21 BDAG, *s.vv.* ὑψηλός, ὕψος.

22 See Payne Smith, 2:3858–59. Both words are admittedly used with the object "hands" to describe the position of prayer (BDAG, *s.vv.* αἴρω, ἐπαίρω).

23 Harris and Mingana, 2:322.

Psalm can be seen in its texture throughout."[24] In fact, a closer examination shows that, in addition to the general influence of the language of the Psalms (see below, esp. on 2a), it is Psalm 117 LXX that has most strongly influenced *Ode* 21, particularly in the first part, rather than Psalm 30 (Psalm 29 LXX).[25]

Table 6: Influence of Psalm 117 LXX on *Ode* 21

Ps 117 LXX	Terms, Statements, Ideas*	*Ode* 21
1-4	*τὸ ἔλεος αὐτοῦ*/ܪܚܡܘܗܝ	1b and 2c
6a, 7a	*κύριος ἐμοὶ βοηθός*/ܡܪܝܐ ܡܥܕܪܢܝ	2b
14a	*ὕμνησίς μου*/ܫܘܒܚܝ	(7b)
14b	*ἐγένετό μοι εἰς σωτηρίαν*/ܦܘܪܩܢܐ	2c
16a	*δεξιὰ κυρίου ὕψωσέν με*/ܐܪܝܡܬܢܝ	2b
19b	*ἐξομολογήσομαι τῷ κυρίῳ*/ܐܘܕܐ ܠܡܪܝܐ	(7c)
21a	*ἐξομολογήσομαί σοι*/ܐܘܕܐ ܠܟ	(7c)
21b	*ἐγένου μοι εἰς σωτηρίαν*/ܦܘܪܩܢܐ	2c
24b	*ἀγαλλιασώμεθα*/ܢܕܘܨ	9b
28a, 28c	*ἐξομολογήσομαί σοι*/ܐܘܕܐ ܠܟ/ܐܫܒܚܟ	(7c)
28d	*ἐγένου μοι εἰς σωτηρίαν*	2c
29a	*ἐξομολογεῖσθε τῷ κυρίῳ*/ܐܘܕܐ	(7c)
29b	*τὸ ἔλεος αὐτοῦ*/ܛܝܒܘܬܐ	1b and 2c

* Cf. Rahlfs, 2:129–31. The Syriac terms are taken from *OTSy*, pt. 2 fasc. 3, pp. 140–42. Verses in brackets are not as markedly influenced. A comparison of the Syriac translation of Ps 118 with the terms used in the Syriac of *Ode* 21 shows that the translation of the Psalm is not likely to have influenced the Ode directly much less predominantly.

The prepositional phrase at the beginning of 1b is not merely "in parallel to ܠܪܘܡܐ" in 1a,[26] but stands in apposition to it, interpreting the spatial term in existentially soteriological fashion. The term *τὸ ἔλεος*/ܚܢܢܐ (*ḥnānā*), used in Judaism and early Christianity and clearly taken from the vocabulary of the Psalms, would have been comprehensible also to persons who knew of and prayed for the mercy of the Greco-Roman gods.[27] "Compassion" here receives its particular nuance from the genitive of *κύριος*/ܡܪܝܐ (*māryā* = "God"). This "Lord," however, *is* not—not in the heights nor in the deeps, not as a picture nor as a statue, not as a person nor as a concept. Since this Ode has nothing to say of creation, it is altogether focused on the power of salvation of this peerless Lord.

According to Franzmann, "2a has the central position between the parallel bicola."[28] What the apocryphal Paul, later in the second century, will say in general of "God"[29] is uttered here by the speaking "I" as the precondition that will allow him to raise his arms. The

24 Ibid.

25 It should be remembered that vv. 22-23 and 25-26 of Psalm 117 LXX reverberated strongly in early Christian writings (see Michael Lattke, "κεφαλή," *EWNT* 2 [1981] 703; *EDNT* 2:285).

26 Franzmann, 161.

27 See Payne Smith, 1:1315; BDAG, *s.v.* ἔλεος.

28 Franzmann, 161.

29 Carl Schmidt and Wilhelm Schubart, eds., *ΠΡΑΞΕΙΣ ΠΑΥΛΟΥ – Acta Pauli: Nach dem Papyrus der Hamburger Staats- und Universitäts-Bibliothek* (Veröffentlichungen aus der Hamburger Staats- und Universitäts-Bibliothek, Neue Folge der Veröffentlichungen aus der Hamburger Stadt-

plural of ܐܣܘܪ̈ܐ (ʾ*asūrā*) means not only the "chains of darkness" (42:16): it images a complete existential lack of freedom (cf. 25:1). The removal of the fetters is liberation *from* the world.[30] It is very tempting to accept Diettrich's suggestion that the Pe. ܫܕܐ (*šḏā*) in the manuscripts is a scribal error and should be read as ܫܪܐ (*šrā*).[31] One could point to the two readings of 18:4, and especially to the text of Ps 116:16b (115:7c LXX), which runs διέρρηξας τοὺς δεσμούς μου ("thou hast burst my bonds asunder").[32] But ἀπο(ρ)ρίπτω/ρίπτω/ܫܕܐ makes sense also, especially in connection with 11:10 and 18:4, and "fetters" can be considered a peculiarly irksome form of "clothing,"[33] so the reading in H and N should be accepted as the *lectio difficilior*.[34]

There is a certain parallelism between 1a-b and the statement of salvation made by the speaking "I" in 2b-c, but now it comprehends his whole existence, and the subject of it is the Lord who is his "helper." There can be no doubt that the term ܡܥܕܪܢܐ (*mʿaddrānā*) corresponds to the nominalized adjective βοηθός (cf. 7:3; 8:6; 25:2).[35] Because there are significant departures from the Syriac text of Psalm 118 (see Table 6 above),[36] there are grounds to assume that not only βοηθός but also ὕψωσέν με, (εἰς) τὸ ἔλεος αὐτοῦ and εἰς σωτηρίαν (αὐτοῦ) came into the Greek original of the Ode from Ps 117 LXX and were later translated into Syriac, not always using the same words as the translator(s) of the Syriac Bible. From this it follows that the Aph. of ܪܘܡ, ܪܡ (*rām*) in v. 2c probably does not correspond to ἀναλαμβάνω (cf. Ezek 3:14). The use of ὑψόω, however, might have an undertone of a "euphemism" for dying—in Johannine congregations, even for death on the cross[37]—which, however, is not applicable in this context.

Repeating the beginning of 1b, 2c expresses the most comprehensive idea of redemption (see Excursus 5). That is really all that needs to be said. Like "mercy," σωτηρία/ܦܘܪܩܢܐ (*purqānā*) is qualified by the third masculine singular suffix—in 𝔊 by the personal pronoun—and thus distinguished from the "salvation" available, for instance, in the cult of Attis or the rites of Isis.[38] The pious understood this familiar term and yet were unsettled in their piety.

■ **3-5** On the heights of the Lord, the speaking "I" must take off the "darkness" of the world and put on the divine "light" (cf. 11:1; see Table 2; Excursus 10). These dualistic metaphors are far from a monotheistic statement of creation like Isa 45:7 (ἐγὼ ὁ κατασκευάσας φῶς καὶ ποιήσας σκότος), but are comparable to some passages in the New Testament[39] and their formal simplicity conceals no hint of any rite of anointing.[40]

The tricolon 4a-c is decisive in determining whether the exalted and redeemed "I" is just any—or even an outstanding—representative of the group that composed and used this Ode (or collection of Odes). Even if the

bibliothek 2; Glückstadt/Hamburg: Augustin, 1936) 30: ἐκ δεσμῶν ἐρύσατο τὸν κόσμον ὅλον.

30 See Payne Smith, 1:323; BDAG, *s.v.* δεσμός.

31 Diettrich, 79.

32 Rahlfs, 2:129; Brenton, 769; cf. *OTSy*, pt. 2 fasc. 3, p. 140 (ܫܪܝܬ ܡܢܝ ܐܣܘܪ̈ܝ); Payne Smith, 2:4307. A verbal allusion to this Psalm is the more likely, since Ps 116:16b (115:7c LXX) also seems to have influenced *Ode* 29:11. However, one could refer equally to Ps 106:14b LXX (τοὺς δεσμοὺς αὐτῶν διέρρηξεν), both because the key words σκότος and θάνατος appear in close context (106:14a), and also because Ps 106:16 LXX (together with Isa 45:2) influenced *Ode* 17:9. The Syriac text of Ps 107:14b differs considerably from that of this *Ode* (*OTSy*, pt. 2 fasc. 3, p. 130: ܘܢ̈ܬܩܝܗܘܢ ܦܣܩ; cf. also Luke 8:29 and BDAG, *s.vv.* δια[ρ]ρήγνυμι, διαρήσσω).

33 BDAG, *s.v.* ῥίπτω, ῥιπτέω, 1.

34 See Payne Smith, 2:4063: *abjecit*.

35 Payne Smith, 2:2815–16; BDAG, *s.v.* βοηθός.

36 The use of the terms ܚܢܢܐ (*ḥnānā*) and ܦܘܪܩܢܐ (*purqānā*) in 2c are evidence for a Greek original that was influenced by Ps 117 LXX. These two important terms do not appear in Psalm 30 and are not used in the Syriac translation of Psalm 118.

37 BDAG, *s.vv.* ἀναλαμβάνω, ὑψόω.

38 BDAG, *s.v.* σωτηρία.

39 See Hans Dieter Betz, "2 Cor 6:14–7:1: An Anti-Pauline Fragment?" *JBL* 92 (1973) 91. Cf. John 8:12; 12:46; 2 Cor 6:14; Eph 5:8.

40 Contra Jarl E. Fossum, *The Image of the Invisible God: Essays on the Influence of Jewish Mysticism on Early Christology* (NTOA 30; Fribourg: Academic Press; Göttingen: Vandenhoeck & Ruprecht, 1995) 84, 98. Fossum's statements are made in connection with the metamorphosis of Enoch into an angel, "the transformation ritual consisting of unction and vesting with 'clothes of glory.'" On the image of "garments," see Alois Kehl, "Gewand (der Seele)," *RAC* 10 (1978) 990 ("more probably" Gnostic); Philipp Vielhauer, *Oikodome: Aufsätze*

"limbs" denote the individual "immortal body,"[41] it would not be impossible to rebut Harris and Mingana's doubtful question that "the present Ode can hardly be *ex ore Christi?*"[42] (comparing it to "the 36th Ode"). The reference to *Ode* 36 could equally have been to *Ode* 17, at the end of which the redeemed Redeemer describes himself as the "head" of his "members" and is immediately praised as "our head, the Lord Messiah" (17:15-16; see the discussion of 18:2-3).

First, it must be stated that the term ܢܦܫܐ (*napšā*) with first singular possessive suffix in this passage expresses "the reflexive relation"[43] and has nothing to do with any body/soul dualism (see Excursus 20), so it does not represent ψυχή in 𝔊 and should not be translated by "soul."[44]

Second, the equally idiomatic construction of ܗܘܐ with ܠ (*hwā* + *l*-) means "was his" or "he had."[45] Emerton[46] repeats Harris and Mingana's imprecise translation ("my soul acquired members"),[47] and even Charlesworth does not fully correct it ("I myself acquired members").[48] If the expression ܗܘܘ ܠܝ ܗܕܡܐ (*hwāw lī haddāmē*), "I had members," corresponded to the Greek γέγονε ἐμοὶ μέλη,[49] then "members" would be the subject of 4a in both 𝔖 and 𝔊. Much more probably 𝔊 had a form of ἔχω with μέλη as the direct object, while the duplication of the reflexive relationship that is unavoidable in Syriac (ܠܝ [*lī*] and ܠܘܬ ܢܦܫܝ [*lwāṯ napš*]) was simply not present in 𝔊: καὶ ἔσχον μέλη (. . .).[50] Whether παρά or πρός was used near the end of the line is as unimportant as the form taken by "me" or "myself" (ἐμοί, ἐμέ, ἐμαυτῷ, ἐμαυτόν).

So far the conclusions and corrections still allow the interpretation of the "limbs" as the personal σῶμα πνευματικόν (1 Cor 15:44)—that only God can give—and it is possible to imagine the statement of salvation coming from the mouth of the/an exalted Christ. At the same time, it is necessary to raise the question whether the exalted one—Christian head or Gnostic primal man—is not speaking of the "members" added to him and redeemed with him (cf. Rom 12:4-5; 1 Cor 12:12, 27; see Excursus 18). The only argument *against* this assumption is the fact that the speaking "I" speaks only of himself in all other parts of this Ode. If one acknowledges the influence of Romans 8 on the three *hapax legomena* in 4b-c, that makes room for the idea that the imagery of "members" originates in Pauline theology, making it unnecessary to assume a "background of Hellenistic (Adam-anthropos-)mysticism with a Gnostic cast."[51]

The search for a model for the list of three strongly negated terms[52] leads not to the Psalms (unlike stanza I, see above) or to other Jewish texts (such as Wis 8:16 or Josephus *Bell.* 2.151)[53] but to Rom 8:18-35, with 8:18 the most certain point of attachment. It is only as a whole that the dependence of these terms on Romans 8 becomes probable, since the first two Syriac words can each represent a large number of Greek words.[54] The equivalent Pauline statements can be distributed among the *hapax legomena* as follows.

- ὀδύνη/ܟܐܒܐ (*kēḇā*): πᾶσα ἡ κτίσις συστενάζει καὶ συνωδίνει (*v.l.* ὀδύνει) ἄχρι τοῦ νῦν ("the

zum Neuen Testament [vol. 2] (ed. Günter Klein; ThBü 65; Munich: Kaiser, 1979) 46 ("process of salvation").

41 Harnack, 52; Diettrich, 79.

42 Harris and Mingana, 2:322.

43 See Nöldeke §223.

44 Contra Harris and Mingana, 2:320; also Greßmann, 456; Bauer, 601, among others. Correct translations by Franzmann (p. 160: "with me"), Pierre (p. 120: "près moi-même"), among others.

45 Payne Smith, 1:984 (*fuit ei, habuit*).

46 Emerton, 711.

47 Harris and Mingana, 2:320.

48 Charlesworth, 88.

49 BDAG, *s.v.* γίνομαι, 4bγ (γέγονε ἐμοί: "someth[ing] has come to me = I have something").

50 BDAG, *s.v.* ἔχω.

51 Contra Egon Brandenburger, *Adam und Christus: Exegetisch-religionsgeschichtliche Untersuchung zu Röm. 5,12-21 (1. Kor. 15)* (WMANT 7; Neukirchen-Vluyn: Neukirchener Verlag, 1962) 148; see also Peel, *Rheginos*, 88.

52 The omission of ܠܐ (*lā*) in 4b H is "an undoubted scribal error" (Diettrich, 79). The word ܟܕ (*kaḏ*) is not separately translated, since it merely "denotes present action or state" (Payne Smith, *Dictionary*, 204; Nöldeke §155.C).

53 Diettrich, 79, refers to Josephus; cf. Alfred Adam and Christoph Burchard, *Antike Berichte über die Essener* (KlT 182; 2nd ed.; Berlin: de Gruyter, 1972) 27.

54 See Payne Smith, 1:220, 1391, 1658.

whole creation has been groaning in travail together until now" [Rom 8:22])

- ϑλῖψις/ܐܘܠܨܢܐ (*ʾulṣānā*): *τίς ἡμᾶς χωρίσει ἀπὸ τῆς ἀγάπης τοῦ Χριστοῦ* (*v.l.* *ϑεοῦ*); *ϑλῖψις* . . . ; ("Who shall separate us from the love of Christ [God]? Shall tribulation . . . ? [Rom 8:35])
- παϑήματα/ܚܫܐ (*ḥaššē*): *οὐκ ἄξια τὰ παϑήματα τοῦ νῦν καιροῦ πρὸς τὴν μέλλουσαν δόξαν ἀποκαλυφϑῆναι εἰς ἡμᾶς* ("the sufferings of this present time are not worth comparing with the glory that is to be revealed to us" [Rom 8:18])

The main difference between that important chapter of Paul's letter, which also influenced other passages of the *Odes of Solomon* (e.g., 18:9 and 28:4), and the statement of salvation in this Ode is that the attributes of world and time are already removed. To this extent it may be considered a case of *realized eschatology*,[55] such as can also be found in the deutero-Pauline writings in the New Testament (see esp. Colossians and Ephesians).[56]

In the tricolon 5a-c, the speaking "I" returns to his personal salvation, adding two slightly ambiguous genitive constructions to a predicative adjective that makes the connection back to the key word "helper" in stanza I (2b) and is qualified by an adverb of comparison. The feminine form of ܡܥܕܪܢܐ (*mʿaddrānā*), which occurs only here, must correspond to the (unnominalized) adjective *βοηϑός* ("helpful"),[57] while the *hapax legomenon* ܝܬܝܪܐܝܬ (*yattīrāʾīṯ*), derived from the root ܝܬܪ, is more likely to represent *περισσῶς* than *μᾶλλον* or *μάλιστα*.[58] The construction ܗܘܬ ܠܝ (*hwāṯ lī*) does not have the same meaning as ܗܘܘ ܠܝ (*hwaw lī*) in verse 4a (cf. also 17:15 and 25:6) or in 10:4 (cf. 11:3; 28:10; 38:3). The nearest would be 38:5a, although that has no predicate. Verse 5a 𝔊 probably used *ἐγένετό μοι* as a substitute for a form of *εἰμί*.[59]

In the double subject of 5b-c, the second is modified by the originally predicative expression ܕܠܐ ܚܒܠܐ (*dlā ḥḇālā* = *ἐν ἀφϑαρσίᾳ* or *ἄφϑαρτος*, "imperishable";[60] see Excursus 28), which in this passage has been worn down to an attribute. The form that the first part took in 𝔊 cannot be accurately determined (see Excursus 9). More important is the question what sort of genitive is involved in the *κοινωνία αὐτοῦ* and the "thought of the Lord." Referring back to 9:3b, one must conclude that ܡܚܫܒܬܐ (*maḥšaḇṯā*) is used anthropomorphically to denote God's own soteriological[61] "thinking." That the speaking "I" imagines that his own thought of God can bring about salvation is unlikely (cf. 20:2). Thus, ܫܘܬܦܘܬܐ (*šawtāp̄ūṯā*), also, is more likely to mean God's "fellowship" with the redeemed one(s) than some "sharing" in the "Lord" attained by personal desire and striving.[62]

■ **6-7** The statement of salvation, 6a, in the theological passive, is in some sense a repetition of 2b and begins a gradual shift into a hymnic self-portrait (7b-9). The Ettaph. = Ethpe. of ܪܘܡ, ܪܡ (*rām*) is used in a similar statement in 41:12, but here there is no humbling to complement the exaltation and no definite identification of the speaker with the preexistent Savior (41:11-16a). Diettrich justifies his translation ("I was lifted up into the light")[63] by some far-fetched references to Old Testament passages (Ps 36:9; Job 33:28; Mic 7:9).[64] The speaker, who, according to 3b, is already clothed in

55 See Robert P. Carroll, "Eschatology," in Richard J. Coggins and James L. Houlden, eds., *A Dictionary of Biblical Interpretation* (London: SCM; Philadelphia: Trinity Press International, 1990) 202.

56 See Andreas Lindemann, "Eschatologie III: Neues Testament," *RGG*[4] 2 (1999) 1557.

57 See Payne Smith, 2:2816; BDAG, *s.v.* *βοηϑός*.

58 Frankenberg, 21; see also Payne Smith, 1:1651; BDAG, *s.vv.* *μάλιστα*, *μᾶλλον*, *περισσῶς*.

59 Bauer and Aland, *s.v.* *γίνομαι*, II; BDAG, *s.v.* *γίνομαι*.

60 Payne Smith, 1:1779; BDAG, *s.v.* *ἄφϑαρτος*.

61 Anyone with *Ode* 9 in ear or eye would be likely to take the "thought" of God *messianically* and to accept the speaking "I" as Messiah.

62 Payne Smith, 2:4355; BDAG, *s.v.* *κοινωνία*. An ecclesial or sacramental *participatio* is not intended here, even though ܫܘܬܦܘܬܐ (*šawtāp̄ūṯā*) was later used for this (Payne Smith, 2:4355). This limitation is applicable also to the statement in the prayer in 4:9a: "thou gavest us thy fellowship."

63 Diettrich, 80.

64 Greßmann (p. 456) and Bauer (p. 602) offer similar translations. But in that case the particle should be ܠ (*l-*), not ܒ (*b-*). Greßmann's explanation that it deals with "his [viz., the Lord's] light" is factually correct.

divine "light," is either—instrumentally—exalted by that very agency (Greek ὑψώθην)[65] or he is—in the spatial imagination of classical mythology—brought closer to the Lord in this sphere that is the opposite of darkness (cf. 7a).[66]

Even in the second edition of Harris's publication of the *Odes*, 6b still has ܥܒܕܬ (*ʿebdet*, "I served") for ܥܒܪܬ (*ʿebret*).[67] However, both manuscripts witness to the perfect of the Pe. ܥܒܪ (*ʿbar*), the Greek equivalent of which cannot be certainly determined, because of the wide uses and connotations of this verb.[68] There may be a parallel to Heb 4:14 ([ἔχομεν] ἀρχιερέα μέγαν διεληλυθότα τοὺς οὐρανούς, Ἰησοῦν τὸν υἱὸν τοῦ θεοῦ, "we have a great high priest who has passed through the heavens, Jesus, the Son of God"). The meaning of the verb becomes more sharply defined by the prepositional phrase ܩܕܡ (*qdām*) + ܐ̈ܦܐ (*ʾappē*) + third masculine singular possessive suffix, which clearly stands for πρὸ προσώπου αὐτοῦ ("before his face"; see Excursus 8).[69] The image is more one of walking past rather than crossing over or traversing (unlike 23:15 and 39:5, 7-9, 13).

Tricolon 7 shows even more parallels with Ode 36 (esp. 2c-4 and 6b). In Ode 36, the exalted one is himself called ܢܗܝܪܐ (*nahhīrā*), while in this Ode the divine "light" appears variously as a garment, a medium, and a space. But the speaking "I" of each Ode emphasizes his closeness to the "Lord" (21:7a; 36:6b). It is likely, in view of 5c, that 7a was influenced by Wis 6:19,[70] which says: ἀφθαρσία δὲ ἐγγὺς εἶναι ποιεῖ θεοῦ ("And immortality brings one near to God").[71] Despite the two expressions ܕܠܐ ܚܒܠܐ (*dlā ḥbālā*) and ܡܩܪܒܝܢ (*mqarrbīn*), there is no need to suppose a direct influence from the Peshitta.[72] How dualistic and esoteric 7a is can be seen by comparison with *1 Clem.* 27:3 (πάντα ἐγγὺς αὐτῷ ἐστίν, "all things are near to him"),[73] where "trust in God is based in the theology of creation"[74] in a far more general fashion (and cf. *1 Clem.* 27:6, πάντα ἐνώπιον αὐτοῦ εἰσίν, "Everything is before him").[75]

As in 4b, the simultaneous actions of the speaking "I" during his closeness to God are prefaced by ܟܕ.[76] The Greek of 7b-c will also have used participles. The Aph. ܐܘܕܝ (*ʾawdī*) + ܠ (*l-*), which normally corresponds to εὐχαριστέω or the middle voice of ἐξομολογέω, does not mean "to confess"[77] but to "give thanks" or "praise,"[78] so the parallel verbs of 7b-c are very close. For the Pa. ܫܒܚ (*šabbaḥ*) also regularly shows hymnic characteristics, even as translation for δοξάζω.[79] The excursus that follows will deal primarily with the various nuances of ܫܒܚ and ܬܫܒܘܚܬܐ (on *tešbuḥtā*, see 9b below).

Excursus 21: "Acclaim," "Honor," "Glory," and "Praise" in the *Odes of Solomon*

For various reasons, some prefatory remarks are necessary. First, it must be kept in mind that restriction of meaning of the Greek δόξα under the influence of

65 See BDAG, *s.v.* ὑψόω; Payne Smith, 2:3857; see also Excursus 10: "a device for lifting up."

66 Such progress is illustrated by a passage in the *Corp. Herm.* 1:26: "And then, liberated by the powers of the celestial harmony, he [the inner being] comes into the eighth order . . . and sings praises to the Father with those who (really) are. And all there rejoice at his coming. . . . And then they go up to the Father in an orderly procession . . ." (Colpe and Holzhausen, 19–20). About the "goal" of Gnostics "to become gods" (Colpe and Holzhausen, 20), *Ode* 21 has nothing to say. On the ancient idea that God is ἐν τῷ φωτί, or even himself φῶς, see 1 John 1:5, 7.

67 Harris, on this passage, p. 119. This error had already been noticed by Schultheß (p. 254; cf. Diettrich, 80). That older translations are based on this misreading is not surprising (see, e.g., Ungnad and Staerk, 22: "schaffte [made]"; Frankenberg, 21: ἐποίησα). But it is strange that Emerton (p. 711) still uses "worked" in translating H.

68 See Payne Smith, 2:2783–84; Klein, *Wörterbuch*, 76–77.

69 Payne Smith, 1:278, 2:3492–93; BDAG, *s.vv.* πρό, 7; πρόσωπον.

70 Suggested already by Harris and Mingana, 2:322.

71 Rahlfs, 2:353; Georgi, 422.

72 *OTSy*, pt. 2 fasc. 5, on this passage; Payne Smith, 2:3722–32, 3727; BDAD, *s.v.* ἐγγύς.

73 Lake, 1:54–55; Ehrman, 1:84–85.

74 Lona, 315; Lindemann and Paulsen, 110.

75 Ehrman, 1:84–85; cf. Lake (1:54–55), whose translation differs.

76 Payne Smith, 1:1676.

77 Contra Lattke, *Oden*, 158 n. 4.

78 Payne Smith, 1:1550; BDAG, *s.vv.* εὐχαριστέω, ἐξομολογέω.

79 Payne Smith, 2:4023–24; BDAG, *s.v.* δοξάζω.

כָּבוֹד had already been completed before the *Odes of Solomon* were composed.[80] Educated Greek-speakers without a knowledge of the Septuagint would have found this usage of δόξα and δοξάζω rather limited, since the further meanings of the Syriac ܫܒܚ (*šabbaḥ*), ܫܘܒܚܐ (*šubḥā*), ܡܫܒܚܢܐ (*mšabbḥānā*) and ܬܫܒܘܚܬܐ (*tešbuḥtā*) used "e sensu Graecae vocis δόξα" are also absent.[81] Second, the breadth of meaning of the terms ܐܘܕܝ (ʾ*awdī*), ܬܘܕܝܬܐ (*tawdītā*), and the derivates from root ܫܒܚ already mentioned make it difficult to determine the Greek equivalent in a number of cases, and thus an accurate translation becomes very difficult or nearly impossible.[82] Third, while this excursus will include terms from the roots ܣܓܕ (cf. προσκυνέω in 11:17) and ܪܘܙ (i.e., "rejoicing" and "rejoice") as well as the terms τιμή/ܐܝܩܪܐ (ʾ*iqārā*) and τιμάω/ܝܩܪ (*yaqqar*), words derived from the root ܙܡܪ—although meanings such as ὕμνος intersect the senses being considered—will be saved until later (see Excursus 26).

First come the few cases where the terms under consideration do not refer only to God the Lord and Most High. The Redeemer may be the object of the Aph. ܐܘܕܝ (ʾ*awdī*), "because they had praised me in the heights" (10:5c). Similarly, the redeemed Redeemer is the object of the Pa. ܫܒܚ (*šabbaḥ*) in 17:7c H (see below on the reading of N). However, the subject of "glorified" is, there also, the Most High, who lifts up the redeemed to partake of his own being. When the redeemed one in *Ode* 29 says that the Lord made him "according to his glory" (2a), the topic again is the δόξα of God, which is parallel to his μεγαλοπρέπεια (3b: "majesty"; cf. 7:23; 15:7; 18:16). Only the doxology of 17:16 allots the ܬܫܒܘܚܬܐ (*tešbuḥtā*), which is the prerogative of God alone, to "our head," the "Lord Messiah." In consequence of 17:7c H, it could be maintained that *this* Lord shares in the divine δόξα (*praises to God*), just as he bears the divine title "Lord."[83] It is not likely that the doxological term was restricted to a purely hymnic sense in this passage.[84]

In addition to this messianic doxology at the end of *Ode* 17, there are four final theological doxologies, two of which are identical. In 11:24a, δόξα corresponds to the *hapax legomenon* ܫܘܒܚܐ (*šubḥā*), which is not always the case, as in Eph 1:14 where δόξα—not τιμή—is translated by ܐܝܩܪܐ (ʾ*iqārā*).[85] The Greek of 16:20 and 20:10 can be reconstructed with confidence: δόξα/ܬܫܒܘܚܬܐ καὶ τιμή/ܐܝܩܪܐ τῷ ὀνόματι αὐτοῦ.[86] The name of God receives, in addition to the praise and acclaim flowing from his glory, the special "honor" that is its due.[87] The doxology 18:16 shows a variation from the regular pairing of δόξα and τιμή, and is also easily reconstructed: δόξα/ܬܫܒܘܚܬܐ καὶ μεγαλοπρέπεια/ܪܒܘܬܐ ܠܫܡܗ τῷ ὀνόματι αὐτοῦ (cf. Ps 20:6 LXX).[88] Not all the terms derived from the root ܝܕܐ, which is not used in the Pe., are used in doxologies and praise. But even though the Aph. ܐܘܕܝ (ʾ*awdī*) in 7:25—parallel to the Pa. ܚܘܝ (*ḥawwī*)—means to "confess" and may be opposed to the political and religious ὁμολογεῖν Καίσαρα,[89] the ending of *Ode* 7 forms a kind of doxological imperative, especially since the infinitive of the Pa. ܫܒܚ (*šabbaḥ*), which speaks of "praising" the Lord, has only just occurred (7:24c).

The remaining occurrences of ܐܘܕܝ show the same breadth of meaning as εὐχαριστέω and/or ἐξομολογέομαι (5:1a [ⲟⲩⲱⲛϩ ⲉⲃⲟⲗ]; 10:5c [see above]; 21:7c [see below]). It must always be remembered that the verbs ὁμολογέω and ἐξομολογέομαι, "in the sense 'to praise,' 'to thank,' 'to confess,' 'to extol' (הוֹדָה) are true lexical Hebraisms which have made themselves at home in the usage of the Jewish world to which the LXX belongs."[90] The *hapax legomenon*

80 See Gerhard Kittel, "δοκέω, κτλ.," *ThWNT* 2 (1935) 235–40, 245–51; *TDNT* 2:232–37, 242–48; Gerhard von Rad, "δοκέω, κτλ. C. כָּבוֹד im AT," *ThWNT* 2 (1935) 241–45; *TDNT* 2:238–42.

81 See Payne Smith, 2:4024: *cogito, censeo*; 2:4026: *opinio*; 2:4027: *qui cogitat*; 2:4028: *opinio, dogma*. The misleading equivalent κυριότης for ܬܫܒܘܚܬܐ has slipped into Syriac lexicography from the context of 2 Pet 2:10 and Jude 8 (Payne Smith, 2:4027; on δόξαι, see BDAG, *s.v.* δόξα).

82 See Payne Smith, 1:1550–53, 2:4023–28.

83 See BDAG, *s.v.* δόξα, 3.

84 See Lattke, *Hymnus*, 253.

85 Payne Smith, 2:4026.

86 See Payne Smith, 1:1624–25; BDAG, *s.v.* τιμή.

87 It follows that the object of the Pa. ܝܩܪ (*yaqqar*), which occurs only once and corresponds to the verb τιμάω (Payne Smith, 1:1623; BDAG, *s.v.* τιμάω), is quite probably the "name of the Lord" (41:5; the "Lord" is also a possible object). Another passage, where the Pe. ܣܓܕ (*sged*) is used, runs "revere his name" (39:13b). The phrase ܝܩܝܪܬ ܕܡܝܐ (*yaqqīraṯ dmayyā*), referring to a "stone" in 9:9a, is only distantly related to this excursus.

88 See Lattke, *Oden*, 152.

89 See Otto Michel, "ὁμολογέω, κτλ.," *ThWNT* 5 (1954) 205; *TDNT* 5:205.

90 Michel, "ὁμολογέω," *ThWNT* 5:204; *TDNT* 5:204–5.

ܡܘܕܝܢܐ (*mawdyānē*) still clearly connotes proclaiming and witnessing (12:4d, the "Aeons" as "confessors of his thought"),[91] but the *hapax legomenon* ܬܘܕܝܬܐ (*tawdīṯā*) in 26:6, found between ܬܫܒܘܚܬܐ (*tešbuḥtā* [26:5]) and ܫܘܡܠܝܐ (*šumlāyā* [26:7]), is not so easily placed on the ladder of possible meanings.[92]

The Ethpa. ܐܫܬܒܚ (*ʾeštabbaḥ*) occurs only once (38:19a, "the one Lord was glorified"), but the Pa. ܫܒܚ (*šabbaḥ*) occurs ten times each in H and N. The manuscripts disagree twice. In 17:7c H, the redeemed Redeemer says that the Most High "glorified" him (see above). N uses the *hapax legomenon* ܫܒܝܚܐ (*šḇīḥā*) instead, referring directly to the Most High as ἔνδοξος[93] and thus also showing the influence of "the Biblical δόξα vocabulary."[94] In 36:4a, the reading in H is the *hapax legomenon* ܡܫܒܚܢܐ (*mšabbḥānē*), a *nomen agentis* formed from the active participle ܡܫܒܚ (*mšabbaḥ*).[95] In translation it is all but impossible to differentiate this from the participle itself,[96] used in N; both come out as "while I was glorious among the glorious." These then are the two main translations: "glorify" and "laud"/"praise," and it is easier to distinguish them in some cases than others. The objects of praise are the holy spirit of the Lord (6:7b) and, more especially, the Lord himself.[97] Where there is no direct object (36:2c and perhaps 36:4a [see above]), the context allows one to conclude that this praising takes place in the heights of the Lord (see on 36:2 below). Objects of glorification, on the other hand, are the redeemed Redeemer (17:7c H; see above) and the Most High (18:1b), who thus receives his own δόξα (see also on 18:16 above).

Of the thirty-seven passages in which ܬܫܒܘܚܬܐ (*tešbuḥtā*) occurs, the doxologies have already been discussed (16:20; 17:16; 18:16; 20:10).[98] A certain conclusion on the connotation of this doxological and hymnic term can be drawn in the cases where it occurs in the plural ܬܫܒܚܬܐ (*tešbḥāṯā*).[99] The consistent translation of this plural by the term "hymns," while not arbitrary, does not impose any conclusion as to the Greek wording of any given passage (13:2b, "declare hymns to his spirit"; 16:1c, "his hymns"; 16:2a, "his hymns"; 16:4a, "his hymns"; 40:2b, "my heart gushes out praises of the Lord" [N; on H, see below]; 41:4b, "who gave of his praises").[100] In some other cases, the context permits a translation of the singular by "hymn," or some similar musical term (6:7a, "praise for his name"; 26:1a, "I poured out a hymn to the Lord"; 31:3b, "he spoke a new hymn to his name"; 40:2b H, "praise" [on N, see above]; 40:2c, "my lips bring forth a hymn to him"; 41:16b, "a new hymn for the Lord").

Before turning to the four borderline cases (10:4b; 21:9b; 26:5b; 29:11a), which form the bridge to the doxological sense of "glory," it is time to deal with the five occurrences of "exult," some of which are connected to the passages with "praise" already considered. The verb "to exult," in both its appearances (40:4; 41:7), is found in the immediate vicinity of ἀγαλλίασις/ܕܝܨܐ (*dyāṣā*). All these passages speak of the "exultation over the Lord" (expressly 8:1a; 21:9b; 41:7; implied in 23:4c and 40:4a), which always translates an objective genitive.[101] This means that in 21:9b ܬܫܒܘܚܬܐ should also be translated by "praise"[102] and not by "glory." And that brings up the borderline cases mentioned above.

How completely the meanings of "praise" (ὕμνος, κτλ.) and "glory" (δόξα, "as the word to translate Hebrew *kāḇôḏ* in the LXX")[103]—via the sense "honor"[104]—are intertwined can be shown by example. An act of salvation could equally well have occurred to the "glory" of the Lord as to his "praise" (10:4b). The parallelism of 26:6b ("confession") suggests the use of "hymn" in 26:5b ("*his* is the hymn"),

91 See Payne Smith, 1:1551; Lampe, *s.v.* ὁμολογητής.

92 Payne Smith, 1:1552: תּוֹדָה, εὐχαριστία, εὐλογία, ὁμολογία. Other terms derived from the root ܝܕܐ, such as ܫܘܕܝܐ (*šūḏāyā*) in 31:13a ("promises") and ܐܫܬܘܕܝ (*ʾeštawdī*) in 4:11 ("promised") and 31:13b ("promised"), are not used in senses relevant to this excursus. On ܫܘܡܠܝܐ (*šumlāyā*), see Excursus 35.

93 Payne Smith, 2:4025.

94 Kittel, "δοκέω," *ThWNT* 2:257; *TDNT* 2:254.

95 Nöldeke §130; Payne Smith, 2:4027.

96 Payne Smith, 2:4024.

97 See 7:19a; 14:8b; 21:7b; 26:4b; 41:1a.

98 Cf. 11:24 using the synonym ܫܘܒܚܐ (*šuḇḥā*).

99 See Payne Smith, 2:4028: ᾄσματα, ὕμνοι, ᾠδαί, κτλ. Note that Philo of Alexandria, for instance, always calls the Davidic Psalms ὕμνοι (Lattke, *Hymnus*, 129).

100 It is always possible that different Greek manuscripts of the *Odes of Solomon* had variant readings.

101 See commentary on 8:1.

102 Bauer, 602: "*Preis*"; Charlesworth, 88.

103 Harald Hegermann, "δόξα," *EWNT* 1 (1980) 834; *EDNT* 1:345.

104 On "honor," see Moshe Weinfeld, "כָּבוֹד *kāḇôḏ*," *ThWAT* 4 (1984) 26; *TDOT* 7:25–26.

since "to give *kābôd* is often tantamount to a confession,"[105] but the parallel with *plērōma* points toward a connotation of "glory" (see on 36:2b below). And in 29:11a, unlike 6:7, the verb "to give" creates ambiguity in the meaning of its object ܬܫܒܘܚܬܐ, "I gave δόξα/כָּבוֹד to the Most High."[106]

In the remaining passages, ܬܫܒܘܚܬܐ means "glory," occasionally with leanings toward "honor" or "renown." The Lord is "worshiped" in paradise because of his δόξα (11:17). The "Aeons" to whom the Most High has given the word are not only the interpreters of his "beauty" (12:4a-b) but in a parallel also the narrators of his δόξα (12:4c). This "glory" influences the future beauty of one of the first-person speakers (14:5a).[107] The parallelism with "beauty" in 16:5b directs attention to the "glory of the Lord" (i.e., the content of the hymn) rather than to the performance. *Ode* 20:9a is under the influence of Isa 58:8, so that there, as also in 20:9c ("glory of his holiness"), the reference is to the weighty and brilliant δόξα τοῦ ϑεοῦ.[108] In the case of 29:2a, it has already been noted at the beginning of this excursus that the "glory" of the Lord is parallel to "his majesty" (29:3b). One of the clearest testimonies to the meaning of "glory" for ܬܫܒܘܚܬܐ is found in 36:2b in the context of the utterance of the exalted one, closely related to *Ode* 21: "The Spirit of the Lord rested upon me, / and she lifted me up to the height / and set me on my feet in the height of the Lord / before his *plērōma*/fullness and his glory" (36:1-2).

After this excursus only the final hymnic self-description remains to be discussed, and its formal problems have already been fully treated by Franzmann.[109]

■ **8-9** Whatever the original divisions within 8-9,[110] these image-filled and poetical lines deserve more than just "some explanation."[111] For, despite the occurrence of ἐξερεύγομαι/ܐܒܥ, καρδία/ܠܒܐ, and χείλη/ܣܦܘ̈ܬܐ in the first lines of Psalm 45 (44 LXX), it is not certain "that the Odist was imitating the 45th Psalm" nor "clear that the Odist was working from the Syriac or Aramaic Psalter."[112] At variance with their own translation, in which they clearly made "my heart" the object of the Aph. of ܢܒܥ (*nbaʿ*) and the "Lord" is understood as the subject of the verb ("He made my heart overflow"), Harris and Mingana insert the phrase "a good word" into their exegesis (cf. λόγον ἀγαθόν in Ps 44:2 LXX; ܡ̈ܠܐ ܛ̈ܒܬܐ in Ps 45:2 Peshitta)[113] as the object of ܐܒܥ and then find in that "the clue to the meaning of the Odist's words."[114] This correctly makes ܠܒ (*leb*) the subject of 8a, but, contrary to the usage of the verbs ἐξερεύγομαι[115] and ἐρεύγομαι,[116] omits any explicit object.[117] When the verb, whose causative sense should not be overemphasized,[118] is used absolutely, its equivalents are less likely to be ἀναγγέλλω (Ps 18:2 LXX) or (ἐξ)ερεύγομαι[119] than ἐκβλύζω (as in Prov 3:10)[120] or πηγάζω.[121] Thus, Franzmann correctly translates it: "My heart overflowed."[122] The speaking "I" compares his "heart" to a spring that gushes and bubbles up (cf. 40:2, where the verb ܓܣܐ [*gsā*] occurs twice; see Excursus 4).

Is "heart" also the subject of the passive verb in 8b (Ethpe of ܐܫܟܚ [*ʾeškaḥ*]; in 𝔊 certainly εὑρέϑη ἐν τῷ στόματί μου)?[123] This same question arises also for the verb

105 Moshe Weinfeld, "כָּבוֹד *kābôd*," *ThWAT* 4 (1984) 27; *TDOT* 7:26.

106 Kittel, "δοκέω," *ThWNT* 2:248, with reference to Isa 42:12; *TDNT* 2:244.

107 See commentary on 14:5a-b.

108 On Isa 58 cf. Moshe Weinfeld, "כָּבוֹד *kābôd*," *ThWAT* 4 (1984) 37; *TDOT* 7:35.

109 Franzmann, 161–62.

110 See Lattke, *Bedeutung*, 1:75.

111 Harris and Mingana, 2:323.

112 Ibid.

113 Rahlfs, 2:46; *OTSy*, pt. 2 fasc. 3, p. 49.

114 Harris and Mingana, 2:323. These statements could be quite seductive in the attempt to identify the speaking "I" of *Ode* 21, since "[t]he opening of the 45th Psalm, as is well known, is one of the proof passages for the doctrine of the Logos" (Harris and Mingana, 2:323). I can make nothing of their following proposition: "The Odist, working from a Syriac original, indulges his fondness for paronomasia by contrasting the verb which is used in the Psalm (ܢܒܥ = *eructavit*) with a similar verb (ܒܥܐ = *quaesivit*); the word-play cannot be reproduced in any other language." Does this imply that 8a should have the Aph. of ܒܥܐ?

115 LEH, *s.v.* ἐξερεύγομαι.

116 BDAG, *s.v.* ἐρεύγομαι.

117 *Ode* 26:1 is different: "I poured out a hymn to the Lord / because I am *his*."

118 Contra Bauer, 602; Lattke, *Oden*, 159, 175.

119 Contra Frankenberg, 22: ἠρεύξατο.

120 See LSJ, *s.v.* ἐκβλύζω.

121 LSJ, *s.v.* πηγάζω; Payne Smith, 2:2271.

122 Franzmann, 160; see already Harnack, 52; and Diettrich, 80.

123 See Payne Smith, 2:4149–50; BDAG, *s.v.* εὑρίσκω.

in 8c. The noun ܕܝܨܐ (*dyāṣā* [9b]), which is also masculine, is the subject of the verb in 9a, and it might also be the subject of 8c (thus, "There arose . . . and increased . . . the exultation . . ."). Indeed, the "exultation over the Lord" could even, grammatically, be the subject of 8b, although that would leave 8a quite disconnected.[124] However, it is impossible to ignore the relationship between "mouth" and "lips," on the one hand (cf. 12:2), and "heart" and "lips," on the other (cf. 16:2; 37:2; 40:2), so 8a-c and 9a-b should be considered the two halves of stanza IV. This division also brings into focus the parallelism of "heart" and "face" as terms describing the oneness of an individual (cf. 41:6). The spiritual center of the person is considered the source, so to speak, of the words that fill the "mouth" and set the "lips" in motion. In stanza IV, this flow of words must be related to the "exultation" of 9b.

In 8c, the "heart," "in a very smudged image," appears not like the "sun" or some star but as a power that bursts out of the "lips" of the speaking "I" from the depths of his personality (see Excursus 16).[125]

The two terms "mouth" (8b) and "lips" (8c) name important parts of the human "face" (πρόσωπον in 𝔊), which in the final bicolon,[126] with repeated use of the preposition ܥܠ (*ʿal*), represents the speaking "I" as a whole, as one who is "affected by anything pleasant," here by the exultation and praise (see Excursus 8).[127] The Pe. ܐܪܒ (*ʾireḇ*) most probably corresponds to the passive form ἐμεγαλύνθη,[128] which can be variously translated.[129]

The excursus for this Ode dealt extensively with the terms "exultation" and "praise." The variant reading in H (ܘ [*ʾu-*] for ܒ [*b-*]) makes it quite clear that ܬܫܒܘܚܬܐ in 9b cannot be translated "glory," much less "splendor."[130] In both manuscripts the use of the hymnic terms is pleonastic or even hendyadic, since "ἀγαλλιᾶσθαι and its derivative ἀγαλλίασις (or ἀγαλλίαμα)" means here, as well as in the LXX and the New Testament, "*jubilant and thankful exultation*."[131] Those who join in this not purely religious "exultation over the Lord"[132] are eschatologically liberated from any ritual and mandated cheering of this world.

124 As Franzmann (pp. 160, 163) does.

125 BDAG, *s.v.* ἀνατέλλω, 2; on ܕܘܨ, see Payne Smith, 1:926.

126 N seems to have a mark of division after ܐܦܝ (see Lattke, *Bedeutung*, 1:75, 2:198), while H treats 9 as a monocolon (see Charlesworth, *Manuscripts*, 59) and has been published and translated thus (Harris and Mingana, vol. 1 on this passage [2:320 differs]; Bauer, 602; Charlesworth, 87–88). Frankenberg (p. 22), who did not know N, still reaches the correct conclusion and makes a division accordingly:

> καὶ ἐμεγαλύνθη ἐπὶ τοῦ προσώπου μου
> ἀγαλλίασις τοῦ κυρίου καὶ δόξα αὐτοῦ.

127 Nöldeke §250.

128 Payne Smith, 1:1628; Frankenberg, 22.

129 BDAG, *s.v.* μεγαλύνω, 1: increase, grow.

130 Contra Diettrich, 80. Instead of "exultation" Diettrich uses the fine translation "joyful welcome" and admits that the last word of 9b might be "only a liturgical indication that the 'song of praise' of the congregation (the doxology) is to be inserted here" (Diettrich, 80 n. 7).

131 Rudolf Bultmann, "ἀγαλλιάομαι, ἀγαλλίασις," *ThWNT* 1 (1933) 19; *TDNT* 1:20.

132 Bauer, *Oden*, 45 ("Jubel über den Herrn").

22

Ode 22: Dualistic Mythos with Traditional Eschatology

Syriac (ܣ)

(I) 1 [Thou] who leadest me down from the height and up from the deeps,
2 and [thou] who gatherest those that are in the middle and joinest them[a] to me.
3 [Thou] who scatteredst my enemies and my adversaries.
4 [Thou] who gavest me power over bonds, that I might loose them.
5a [Thou] who didst overthrow, by my hands, the seven-headed dragon.
5b And thou didst set me over its root[b] that I might destroy its seed.
(II) 6a Thou wert there and helped me,
6b and in every place thy name surrounded[c] me.
7a Thy right [hand] destroyed the poison of evil[d],
7b and thy hand leveled the way for those who believe in thee.
(III) 8a And thou didst choose them from the graves
8b and didst separate them from the dead.
9a Thou didst take dead bones
9b and stretch bodies over them.
10a And they were motionless,
10b and thou gavest [them] energy[e] for life.
(IV) 11a Imperishable were thy way and thy countenance;
11b thou hast brought thy world to destruction/corruption,
11c that everything might be dissolved and renewed
12a and thy rock might be the foundation of everything.
12b And upon it thou hast built thy kingdom,
12c and it became[f] the dwelling place of the saints.
Hallelujah.

Coptic (ℭ)

(I) 1 He who brought me down from the high places which are above, and has brought me up from the places in the depth below.
2 He who there has taken those that are in the midst and has taught them about them.
3 He who has scattered my enemies and my adversaries (ἀντίδικοι).
4 He who has given me authority

a 2 H omits ܠܗܘܢ.
b 5b ܥܩܪܗ N; ܥܩܪ̈ܘܗܝ H.
c 6b ܟܪܟܢܝ N (cf. ℭ); ܟܪܟܢܝ H.
d 7a ܠܡܪܬܗ ܕܒܝܫܘܬܐ N; ܠܡܪܬܗ ܒܝܫܘܬܐ H.
e 10b ܡܥܒܕܢܘܬܐ N; ܡܥܒܕ̈ܢܘܬܐ H.
f 12c ܗܘܬ N; ܗܘܝܬ H.

(ἐξουσία) over bonds, to release them.
5a He who has smitten (πατάσσω) the serpent with seven heads by my hands.
5b He has set me up over its root, so that I might wipe out its seed (σπέρμα).
(II) 6a And thou wast with me, helping me;
6b in all places thy name surrounded me.
7a Thy right [hand] has destroyed the poison of the slanderer;
7b thy hand has smoothed the way for thy faithful ones (πιστοί).
(III) 8a Thou hast redeemed them from the graves (τάφοι)
8b and hast removed them from the midst of the dead.
9a Thou hast taken dead bones
9b [and] thou hast clothed them with a body (σῶμα).
10a And to those that do not move
10b thou hast given energy (ἐνέργεια) of life.
(IV) 11a Thy way has become indestructibility, and thy countenance;
11b thou hast brought thy aeon (αἰών) to destruction,
11c that all should be dissolved and made new,
12a and that thy light should be a foundation for them all.
12b Thou hast built thy wealth upon them,
12c and they have become a holy dwelling place.

Introduction

Ode 22 is preserved in three manuscripts, two Syriac and one Coptic.[1] Schille counts *Ode* 22 among the "hymns of the Cross triumphant" in the train of Eph 2:14-18 and Col 2:9-15, but still describes it as "purely a hymn of the Savior."[2] However, neither his remarks on the change from the narrative in the first person by a speaking "I" of undetermined gender (1-5 or 1-6) to the "address" directed to one whose acts occur in the mythic past (6-12 or 7-12)[3] nor his reference to "hymn no 7 in the *Psalms of Thomas*, which is closest in style to this *Ode*"[4] make it clear who this "Savior" may be.[5] For this "song

1 Mss.: Codex H, 16b–17a; Codex N, 149ʳ (ܣ); Codex A, 74ʳa–b (ϲ). Ed./trans.: Charlesworth, 88–91 (ϲ only referred to in footnotes); Franzmann, 164–72; Lattke, 2:147–68 and 3:XXXI–XXXII.

2 Schille, 43.

3 This character, first indirectly described and then addressed, is represented in stanza I by the repeated "He." But see Klaus Beyer in Lattke, 3:XXXI n. 2.

4 Schille, 43 n. 87.

5 "ThPs 7 is a hymn of praise to the Living Spirit" (Peter Nagel, *Die Thomaspsalmen des koptisch-manichäischen Psalmenbuches* [Quellen: Ausgewählte Texte aus der Geschichte der christlichen Kirche,

of triumph" is extraordinary,[6] not so much in its mixture of dualistic mythology with elements of Jewish and Christian eschatology, as in the inclusion of the speaking "I"—as a character that is carried up from below and down from above and supported from the heights, and performs both redeeming and destructive acts—in the acts of leadership and redemption of the mighty "He" in the "heights" (stanza I), who is identical with the "Thou" addressed in stanzas II–IV as helper, giver of life, renewer, and builder. This being is God, that is, no-one and no-thing anywhere in the universe from its "heights" to its "deeps." Since neither the term "God" nor the terms "Lord," "Most High," or "Father" occur in this Ode, it will be necessary to "pay careful attention to the periphrases which the Odist employs to describe the Divine Nature and the Divine Action."[7] These "Targumisms" are, on the one hand, the use of the pronouns "He" and "Thou" in stanzas I and III, and, on the other, especially the terms "name" (6b), "right hand" (7a), "hand" (7b), "way" (11a), and "countenance" (11, see below),[8] which avoid the name of God and can therefore not really be considered anthropomorphizing.

From Harris and Mingana[9] to Charlesworth,[10] the generally accepted heading referring to the speaking "I" has been "Christ speaks."[11] A Christian congregation using this Ode would agree. If the Ode was originally "a Jewish product"[12] or had been at all disseminated in Jewish circles, the speaker might have been considered to be the (or a) Jewish Messiah. Although Harnack, too, is only prepared "to consider pre-existence," he also notes: "But whether it is the Messiah who speaks is questionable; in any case it cannot be Jesus Christ."[13] The first conclusion, then, is that the "I" of 1-6 considers itself a secondary redeemer (4-5), portraying itself as one whom the proper Redeemer leads and supports. Its personal redemption is mentioned, if at all, only in 1 ("who leads me up . . . from the deeps"), and so the identification of "Christ Himself" as "speaker of this Ode" is intimately connected to the claim that this verse refers to "Christ ascending from Hades."[14] This claim has been very influential,[15] quite ignoring Harnack's skepticism on a *descensus ad inferos*: "That seems to me quite unlikely, in

N.F. 1; Berlin: Evangelische Verlagsanstalt, 1980] 93). "The possibility of an exchange of function between saviors and the allocation of the function to a single savior show that the Manichaean mythos had not yet attained its final didactic form" (ibid., 95). *Ode* 22 belongs to a still earlier phase.

6 Gunkel, 309, in agreement with Harnack. "The Gnostic character of this song of triumph . . . cannot be doubted" (Harnack, *Pistis Sophia*, 44). Harnack has nothing to say about "Christ's descent into hell" in his remarks on this *Ode*, which are now partially superseded (contra Gunkel, 309). The less exact description of *Ode* 22 as a "song of thanksgiving" (e.g., Gunkel, 309; Colpe, "Überlieferung," 77–78) can also be traced back to Harnack and his observation on 6-7: "In this lovely expression of gratitude the Savior-Aeon celebrates his victory" (Harnack, *Pistis Sophia*, 45; see Excursus 22).

7 Harris and Mingana, 2:331.

8 Whether "rock" or "foundation of everything" (12a) is also a surrogate for God (Harris and Mingana, 2:331) will be discussed later.

9 Harris and Mingana, 2:325.

10 Charlesworth, 89.

11 See also Gunkel, 309, and many others.

12 Harnack, 52, referring to Harris, 1909. Harnack has a question mark at the end of this quotation from Harris, which I have not been able to verify.

13 Harnack, 52, reversing his earlier opinion (idem, *Pistis Sophia*, 44: "I" = "Christ").

14 Harris and Mingana, 2:327. "The opening sentence suggests Him that descended and ascended again; and the account of dead men taken from their graves and clothed again with flesh can hardly be anything else than the emancipation of the souls that are imprisoned in Hades. The Odist has no knowledge of a general resurrection . . . and he has a strong doctrine of the Descent into Hades (see Ode xlii, for example)."

Günther Bornkamm (*Mythos und Legende in den apokryphen Thomas-Akten: Beiträge zur Geschichte der Gnosis und zur Vorgeschichte des Manichäismus* [FRLANT 49 = N.F. 31; Göttingen: Vandenhoeck & Ruprecht, 1933] 31) represents the opposite extreme when he remarks on *Ode* 22: "so the believer . . . can take up the role of Christ, performing the same works as he does."

15 As was done for 17:8b, a selection of those who see in *Ode* 22 a descent into hell or a *descensus ad inferos* may be listed in chronological order: Gunkel, 309; Gschwind, *Niederfahrt*, 228–29; Connolly, "Odes," 300–302; Clarke, 51; Kittel, 95; Reitzenstein, *Das mandäische Buch*, 30–32 ("descent into hell" = "ascent to heaven"); cf. idem, *Das iranische Erlösungsmysterium*, 84–86; idem, "Weltuntergangsvorstellungen: Eine Studie zur vergleichenden

spite of a few verses which could be interpreted in this way."[16] We shall see.

Interpretation

■ **1-5** Although *Ode* 22 does not display any express forms of praise and can therefore hardly be called a "hymn," the following remarks by Josef Kroll on the style of "the third-person mythos" of stanza I, which—probably already in the "primary Greek text"—includes the "I," and shifts to direct speech are very important: "first come long asyndetic participial or relative predications, which always begin with the article[17] or a relative pronoun[18] followed by short lines in the form of main clauses with anaphoric 'Thou' . . . ."[19] The change from third person to second person[20] is not at all unusual (see 5b below). The demonstrative pronoun ܗܘ (*hāw*), placed emphatically at the beginning of the line, is transformed, in all five cases, to a "correlative" by the following "relative conjunction" ܕ (*d-*), though the "other term" is not made explicit, since ܗܘ has a "tendency to weaken its demonstrative signification."[21]

Even if the first monocolon falls under the influence of Rom 10:6-7 (εἰς τὸν οὐρανόν ["into heaven"] || εἰς τὴν ἄβυσσον ["into the abyss"] or Χριστὸν καταγαγεῖν ["to bring Christ down"] || Χ. ἐκ νεκρῶν ἀναγαγεῖν ["to bring Christ up from the dead"]; cf. Heb 13:20), Diettrich could still be right in saying that the speaker is "in the spirit" and "positions himself at the end of time."[22] But then there is the question whether this proposition, which is intended to counter the identification of the speaker with "Christ," can be harmonized with the first part of 1 without needing to assume the preexistence of "human souls." The Aph. participle of ܢܚܬ (*nḥeṯ*), used only once, corresponds to the Greek κατάγων,[23] beginning the wordplay with the three composite ἄγω verbs (κατάγων and ἀνάγων in 1, συνάγων in 2). "Lead down" is connected to the "heights" of the Lord (cf. 17:7; 21:1; 36:1-2; see Excursus 17), so *1 Clem.* 4:12 is not a direct parallel (κατήγαγεν εἰς ᾅδου, "brought down into Hades").[24] Because the Aph. of ܣܠܩ (*sleq*) is used elsewhere (29:4, 6) about a redeemed one who is distinguished from the "Lord's Messiah/Anointed," the leading up in the second half of 1 may be imagined as being "*from the (realm of the) dead* represented as subterranean."[25] The ܥܘܡܩܗ ܕܫܝܘܠ (*ʿumqēh da-šyōl*) are not under consideration here, only the lowest "deeps," as contrasted with the "height,"[26] but these could be held to be the κατώτατα τῆς γῆς, which might be considered "Hades" (Ps 62:10 LXX; cf. Ps 85:13 LXX).[27] On the one hand, it would have been possible for the speaker, who is being led upward, to have been rescued from the *lower world* but not to be thought of as a Messiah. On the other, however, it is unlikely that the statement about being led downward and the later ones about playing the part of mediator and being given power to save and to destroy (4-5) do not describe some preexistent Redeemer. So in the context of stanza I, there is no mention of the descent of the Crucified into "hell" (*descensus ad inferos*), but of one who was brought up (again) after being led down to the lowest regions

Religionsgeschichte," *Kyrkohistorisk årsskrift* 24 (1924; Uppsala/Stockholm, 1925) 140–41, 151; Schmidt and Wajnberg, *Gespräche*, 565–67; Greßmann, 457; Schlier, *Christus*, 14; Kroll, *Hölle*, 36; Quasten, "Hirte," 398; Bieder, *Höllenfahrt*, 177; Bauer, 602; Vogl, 63–66; Poirier, "Descensus," 198; John Dominic Crossan, *The Cross That Spoke: The Origins of the Passion Narrative* (San Francisco: Harper & Row, 1988) 366.

Pierre (pp. 122–24) does not consider whether *Ode* 22 deals with Christ's descent into hell.

16 Harnack, 54.

17 "I assume, judging by Greßmann's translation, that the original Greek text of the hymn began: ὁ κατάγων με ἐκ τῶν ἄνω, ὁ ἀνάγων με ἐκ τῶν κάτω. That would be a typically un-Hellenistic style" (Kroll, *Hymnodik*, 72).

18 "According to the translation of Ungnad and Staerk . . . one would have to assume an anaphoric οὗτός ἐστιν ὅς, which is also a well known figure in a hymn in oriental style . . . Greßmann's translation is the more plausible" (Kroll, *Hymnodik*, 72 n. 1, with a concluding reference to Frankenberg).

19 Kroll, *Hymnodik*, 72.

20 Ibid., 73.

21 See Nöldeke §§67, 228, 235–36.

22 Diettrich, 82.

23 Frankenberg, 22; Kroll, *Hymnodik*, 72.

24 Lake, 1:16–17; Ehrman, 1:42–43; Lindemann and Paulsen, 84; cf. BDAG, *s.v.* κατάγω; Payne Smith, 2:2344–45.

25 BDAG, *s.v.* ἀνάγω; Payne Smith, 2:2648–49.

26 BDAG, *s.v.* κατώτερος; Payne Smith, 2:4425–26.

27 In 2 Pet 2:4 the aorist active participle ταρταρώσας (a correction is needed in Payne Smith, 2:4424) is not translated by a Syriac verb. Instead,

among which Hades and/or Tartarus may be found (see Excursus 42).[28]

To express the closeness of 1 and 2, the Syriac text begins with ܘ (ʾu-). However, both stylistic considerations and the Coptic text make it unlikely that the Greek of 2 began with *καί*. The difference between the Syriac and Coptic of the second half of this monocolon is more important.[29] The long-standing suggestion that the participle of the Pe. ܪܕܐ (*rdā*), corresponding to ⲧⲥⲁⲃⲟ, should be read for ܪܡܐ (*rāmē*)[30] is supported by two other considerations. First, the object ܠܗܝܢ (*lhēn*) is missing from H. And, second, when the quotation is taken up again in the *Pistis Sophia,* the word is not ⲁϥⲧⲥⲁⲃⲟⲟϊ ("he taught *them*") but ⲁϥⲧⲥⲁⲃⲟϊ ("he taught *me*").[31] This eliminates the need for Carmignac's reference to "the root YRH" in Hebrew, with the meanings "to throw" and "to teach," since ܪܕܐ, unlike ܐܘܪܝ and ܐܠܦ, does display "a visual likeness" to ܪܡܐ,[32] and this makes it possible to reconstruct the route to the Coptic and to the Syriac manuscripts as follows.

The wording of the Greek original was either *καὶ παιδεύων με περὶ αὐτῶν* or *καὶ περὶ αὐτῶν παιδεύων με*. This wording is put beyond doubt by the variant ⲁⲩⲱ ⲁϥⲧⲥⲁⲃⲟϊ ⲉⲣⲟⲟⲩ in the quotation of the Coptic translation. The reading of the translation proper, ⲁϥⲧⲥⲁⲃⲟⲟⲩ, is due not to a version of the "paraphrases" but to the "improvisation" of the translation and its "freedom" in quotation.[33] The original Syriac translation would then have been either ܘܪܕܐ ܠܟܠܗܝܢ ܠܝ or ܘܪܕܐ ܠܝ ܠܟܠܗܝܢ. When ܘܪܕܐ was miscopied as ܘܪܡܐ (as found in H and N), ܠܟܠܗܝܢ no longer made any sense. In consequence, the H line of development simply omitted the prepositional phrase, while the N line amended it to ܠܗܝܢ (*lhēn*). Thus, the two Syriac readings regained a certain amount of meaning.[34]

Both in the Greek and Coptic texts, and in the Syriac, the activity of the second verb must also concern the object of the first. 𝔊 used *συνάγω*, the third of the composite -*ἄγω* verbs.[35] The Syriac Pa. ܟܢܫ (*kanneš*) is a *hapax legomenon*[36] but has a certain parallelism to the soteriological use of the related Ethpa. (cf. 10:5; 17:14; 23:17). But what is the meaning of the feminine plural of ܡܨܥܝܐ (*meṣʿāyā*)? "Does it mean earth lying in the middle between heaven and the underworld?" asks Harnack.[37] He answers himself with scholarly resignation: "I cannot understand the verse."[38] If the equivalent of the plural ܡܨܥܝܬܐ (*meṣʿāyātā*) was *τὰ ἐν τῷ μέσῳ* in 𝔊,[39] which would agree with the Coptic, then one might imagine a whole cosmic "public"[40] about which the "I" was instructed. If the hearers knew only the Syriac version, they would be reminded of astronomical aeons or spheres, but might equally limit their ideas to the inhabitants of Earth,[41] who were "assigned" to the speaking "I" (see Excursus 18).[42] The subject of this

the same expression is used as an indirect equivalent, as is found in *Ode* 22:1 for the "deeps" (*NTSy*, 168; on "Tartarus," see BDAG, *s.v.* *ταρταρόω*), a point that is noted neither in *NTGr* IV.1.2, p. 225, nor in *NTGr* IV.2.2, p. B 85).

28 BDAG, *s.v.* *ταρταρόω*; LSJ, *s.v.* *τάρταρος*. The hymnus in the *Pistis Sophia*, whose first solution (ⲃⲱⲗ) is the quotation of *Ode* 22, supplies the logical connections missing in the *Ode* (see Lattke, *Bedeutung*, 1:134–35, 216, 222–25).

29 Crum (p. 622) remarks on ϥι ⲛ̄ⲙⲁⲩ, "but Od Solom 22_{2} ܡܟܢܫ." This variant may be due to the hymn of Pistis Sophia (see Lattke, *Bedeutung*, 1:134–35).

30 See Diettrich, 82; Payne Smith, 2:3819.

31 See Lattke, *Bedeutung*, 1:134–35; and Crum, 434. The text-critical notes in Charlesworth (p. 89) fuse these two words into ⲁϥⲧⲥⲁⲃⲟⲟϊ. Reference could be made to Acts 7:22, where *ἐπαιδεύϑη* is translated by ܐܬܪܕܝ (*ʾetrdī*).

32 Jean Carmignac, "Recherches sur la langue originelle des Odes de Salomon," *RevQ* 4 (1963) 432; cf. Koehler and Baumgartner, 416–17.

33 See Kragerud, *Pistis Sophia,* 83–90, as well as Lattke, *Bedeutung,* 1:224.

34 On the *hapax legomenon* ܪܡܐ (*rmā*), see Payne Smith, 2:3922–23: *[con-, in-]jecit, immisit.* Charlesworth has another explanation for the omission in H: "the cause seems to be *parablepsis* facilitated by the initial *Lāmadh* in ܠܗܝܢ and in ܠܝ" (see Charlesworth, 91 n. 3).

35 See BDAG, *s.v.* *συνάγω*.

36 See Payne Smith, 1:1770–71.

37 Harnack, 53.

38 Ibid. For the Gnostics of the *Pistis Sophia* there was no problem: "The expression *Middle Place* or a similar one is often found in the *Pistis Sophia* (pp. 121.21; 121.31; 121.33; 127.6; 128.5; etc.); also among the Valentinians (Irenaeus *Haer.* 1.7.1; 2.30.2)" (Bauer, 602).

39 Cf. Frankenberg, 22: *τὰ μέσα*.

40 BDAG, *s.v.* *μέσος*, 1b.

41 See Payne Smith, 2:2193–94.

42 Bauer, 602.

verse is not simply a "middling *understanding*" of the "celestial world,"[43] but deals with persons or personified powers found below the "heights" of the Lord and above the lowest "deeps."

Beginning with 3, all actions were played out in the mythological past. In 𝔊 the synonymous accusatives ἐχθρούς and ἀντιδίκους would have been the objects of the not certainly determinable verb equivalent to the Pa. ܒܕܪ (*baddar*).[44] "Scatter" in 3 is the opposite of "gather" in 2 (cf. again 10:5). As will be shown in 29:5, the redeemed one, who is distinguished from the Messiah, himself humbled his "foes."[45] The *hapax legomenon* ܒܥܠܕܝܢܐ (*bʿeldīnā*), corresponding to ἀντίδικος in 𝔊 and 𝔆, is a judicial term,[46] but it is used in a more general sense here and, together with its synonym, forms a hendiadys. Because both are in the plural, neither of the dualistic terms can refer to the "devil." The form that the enmity of these opponents took is not explained. "Enemies" and "adversaries" cannot, in any case, be demythologized as "spiritual powers like sin or ignorance."[47]

Again in the fourth monocolon there is no doubt that 𝔊 had ἐξουσία where 𝔖 uses ܫܘܠܛܢܐ (*šulṭānā*).[48] This term, with its connotation of the perfect "power" of Jesus, is normally found as a loanword in Sahidic but is often translated by ⲉⲣϣⲓϣⲓ in Bohairic.[49] Since the "power" was granted to the speaker, it is in the last analysis the "power of God" that is meant.[50] The genitive plural of δεσμός/ܐܣܘܪܐ (*ʾasūrā*) specifies over what the "power" has dominion.[51] It is not the "fetters" of the "I" that are in question (but cf., e.g., 21:2) but those of the πιστοί (7b 𝔆) or the "saints" (12c 𝔖) who will be introduced later. Someone who already knew the whole collection of the *Odes* would also be reminded of the "chains of darkness" (42:16b).[52] The construction with ܐܝܟ ܕ (*ʾak̲ d-*) + imperfect of ܫܪܐ (*šrā*) + object ܐܢܘܢ (*ʾennōn*) is based on a Greek construction containing the following elements: ὡς as a "final particle" + subjunctive or infinitive of λύω + object αὐτούς.[53] The statement of 4 challenges the miracle-working claims of Isis,[54] but Christian readers could also read it as a parallel to a positive and comprehensive assurance from Ignatius of Antioch (*Phld.* 8:1): *πιστεύω τῇ χάριτι Ἰησοῦ Χριστοῦ, ὃς λύσει ἀφ᾽ ὑμῶν πάντα δεσμόν* ("I believe in the gracious gift that comes from Jesus Christ, who will loose every bond from you").[55] A direct influence from Isa 58:6 (λῦε πάντα σύνδεσμον ἀδικίας, "loose every burden of iniquity"; cf. Acts 8:23 and *Barn.* 3:3, 5) is unlikely, although this prophetic passage certainly affected the *Odes of Solomon* (cf., e.g., 8:21 and 20:5, 9).

Verse 5a becomes even more mythological. First it needs to be understood that the "serpent-like hybrid" bears a negative "connotation" and is not—unlike the East Asian variety—a "kindly celestial." "Many-headedness" often emphasizes "the danger of the malignant dragon."[56] "Myths of combat with dragons ... are found in all of western Asia from India to Egypt and Greece." Remembering that even before Rev 12:3-10 and 20:2 an "angel"—and especially *Μιχαὴλ ὁ ἀρχάγγελος ... τῷ διαβόλῳ διακρινόμενος* ("the archangel Michael, contending with the devil" [Jude 9])—had played the "part of the one who slays the dragon," one

43 Contra Diettrich, 82.
44 Payne Smith, 1:454; see also Crum, 782; BDAG, *s.vv.* διασκορπίζω, σκορπίζω.
45 See Payne Smith, 1:562, *s.v.* ܒܥܠܕܒܒܐ [*bʿeldb̲āb̲ā*]; BDAG, *s.v.* ἐχθρός.
46 Payne Smith, 1:562; BDAG, *s.v.* ἀντίδικος, 1–2: "opponent" "in a lawsuit."
47 Contra Diettrich, 82.
48 Payne Smith, 2:4179.
49 See, e.g., Crum, 59.
50 BDAG, *s.v.* ἐξουσία, 3.
51 Cf. 17:11 on the related verb. See Payne Smith, 1:323; BDAG, *s.v.* δεσμός.
52 Diettrich's explanatory addition "bonds [of the body]" (p. 83) is both arbitrary and restrictive.
53 See Nöldeke §§63, 364.B; Payne Smith, 2:4305–9; BDAG, *s.v.* λύω. Contra Frankenberg, 22: . . . τοῦ λύειν τοὺς δεσμούς.
54 BDAG, *s.v.* λύω, 2: ἐγὼ τοὺς ἐν δεσμοῖς λύω.
55 Fischer, 200; Ehrman, 1:291.
56 The first part of this paragraph is based on Christoph Uehlinger, "Drache I. Religionsgeschichtlich," *RGG*⁴ 2 (1999) 966.

might cast Michael as the speaker of *Ode* 22. Attractive as such an alternative to a political Messiah may be (cf. ἐξουσία τοῦ χριστοῦ αὐτοῦ, "authority of his Christ," in Rev 12:10; and see on 12b below), the use of the *hapax legomenon* δράκων/ὄφις/ϩⲟϥ/ܬܢܝܢܐ (*tannīnā*), "dragon," as "a figurative term for the devil"[57] is far more certain. A search for its mythological abode finds no trace of it in any subterranean hell.[58] The battle is more likely to take place in heaven (cf. ἐν τῷ οὐρανῷ in Rev 12:7). The picture becomes clear enough[59] if one draws on the drama and imagery of Rev 12:3 and 12:9: [(3)]δράκων . . . ἔχων κεφαλὰς ἑπτά . . . [(9)]ἐβλήθη ὁ δράκων . . . ὁ ὄφις . . . Διάβολος . . . Σατανᾶς, ὁ πλάνων τὴν οἰκουμένην ὅλην, ἐβλήθη εἰς τὴν γῆν ("dragon, with seven heads" . . . "the dragon was thrown out . . . the serpent . . . Devil . . . Satan, the deceiver of the whole world–he was thrown down to the earth"). But, unlike in Rev 12:9, where the "dragon" or the "serpent" is only "cast out into the earth" as a "preliminary to the establishment of the kingdom of God in heaven (and later also on earth)"[60] (but see on 12b below), here it is "overthrown" altogether–indeed in ℭ it is put to death.[61] Since πατάσσω is not consistently employed as a loanword in translations into Coptic,[62] 5a ℭ does not guarantee that 𝔊 used πατάξας.[63] Other Greek terms, such as καθαιρέω, κατασκάπτω, καταστρέφω, or πορθέω[64] must be considered as the possible original of the Pa. ܨܚܦ (*saḥḥep̄*), which occurs only here, and for which ℭ substituted πατάσσω as seeming even more forceful.[65] The idiomatic expression ܒܐܝܕܝ (*b-iḏay*) in this case probably did not correspond to simple δι᾽ ἐμοῦ,[66] but, as in ℭ (ϩⲛ̄ ⲛⲁϭⲓϫ [*hᵉn na-cič*]), to the fuller phrase διὰ [τῶν] χερσίν μου.[67]

The change in 5b 𝔖 to direct address marks the beginning of the transition from stanza I to stanzas II–IV and is not necessarily a sign of "corrupted text,"[68] even though the Coptic text speaks *for* "a probable emendation ܐܘܩܡܬܢܝ."[69] While the common word ܩܘܡ, ܩܡ (*qām*) raises no difficulties,[70] the plural ܥܩܪܘܗܝ (*ʿeqqāraw*) in H makes it clear that Harnack[71] was by no means the first to think the "image" of the "root" "peculiar." Does "this peculiar image . . . refer to the origins from which the dragon may reform itself?"[72] Or is the image "illuminated by a reference to the Greek *Acts of John* (chap. 98) where the Gnostic writer of the *Acts* refers to Σατανᾶς καὶ ἡ κατωτικὴ ῥίζα, which root he identifies with the nature of created things?"[73] Neither suggestion meets the case. A more apposite reference would be to *Act. John* 114: τὰ τέκνα . . . καὶ ὅλη ἡ ῥίζα αὐτοῦ ("his children . . . and all his root").[74] From this, one may conclude that ῥίζα/ܥܩܪܐ (*ʿeqqārā*) here probably means "clan"[75] and is closely connected to the term σπέρμα/ܙܪܥܐ (*zarʿā*), which means "descendants" as in 31:13b.[76] This juxtaposition of terms can be traced

57 BDAG, *s.v.* δράκων; see Crum, 740–41; Payne Smith, 2:4463.
58 See Harnack, 53.
59 Kittel, 95.
60 See Rudolf Hoppe, "Die Johannesoffenbarung: Das Ringen um das rechte Verständnis eines schwierigen Bibeltextes," in Herbert W. Wurster and Richard Loibl, eds., *Apokalypse: Zwischen Himmel und Hölle* (Passau: Archiv des Bistums & Oberhausmuseum; Regensburg: Pustet, 2000) 149–54, esp. 150, 154.
61 See BDAG, *s.v.* πατάσσω; LEH, *s.v.* πατάσσω.
62 See Crum, 921.
63 Frankenberg, 22.
64 See Payne Smith, 2:2591–92; BDAG, *s.vv.* καθαιρέω, κατασκάπτω, καταστρέφω, πορθέω.
65 See, e.g., Crum, 311. Possibly this came about under the influence of the hymnus in the *Pistis Sophia* (Lattke, *Bedeutung*, 1:136–37). One may refer to Rom 16:20 for the sense (ὁ δὲ θεὸς τῆς εἰρήνης συντρίψει τὸν σατανᾶν, "the God of peace will soon crush Satan"), but Harris and Mingana's explanation (2:330) is linguistically unsatisfactory.
66 Contra Diettrich, 83; Frankenberg, 22.
67 As in Mark 6:2; Acts 5:12; 14:3; 19:11; on the seven heads, see Excursus 23. See BDAG, *s.v.* χείρ; Charlesworth, 90: "by my hands."
68 Franzmann, 169.
69 Harris and Mingana, 2:326. They call the reading of H and N "not very grammatical" but then note, oddly, about their emendation: "On the other hand, note that the Coptic text is *against* the emendation" [emphasis added].
70 See Payne Smith, 2:3522–25.
71 Harnack, 53.
72 Diettrich, 83, agreeing with Harnack.
73 Harris and Mingana, 2:329.
74 *AAAp*, 2.1:214; Knut Schäferdiek, "Johannesakten," *NTApo* (5th ed., 1989) 2:190; "The Acts of John," *NTApoc*, 2:204.
75 Bauer and Aland, *s.v.* ῥίζα, 1b ("Geschlecht"); cf. BDAG, *s.v.* ῥίζα, 1b; cf. Payne Smith, 2:2970.
76 BDAG, *s.v.* σπέρμα, 2a; Payne Smith, 1:1159.

back as far as Pindar.[77] Any influence from Gen 3:15 or "an interpretation of the third chapter of Genesis" is unlikely.[78] The mythological dragon-serpent of *Ode* 22 bears no relation to the snake in the garden of Genesis 3. Since the "dragon"—Satan or the devil—has already been overthrown or killed (5a), the command to destroy in the final clause was also carried out in the mythological past (on the Aph. of ܐܒܕ [ʾebad], cf. 6:3; 24:10; 33:2). So here—in contrast to the New Testament—there is no longer any power hostile to God, nor any τέκνα τοῦ διαβόλου ("children of the devil"; cf. 1 John 3:10).

■ **6-7** All the statements of good and ill fortune in stanzas II–IV are in the form of a direct address, but the speaking "I" expressly includes itself only in the parallel bicolon 6a-b. This change from third to second person began in ܣ with 5b, underlining the connection between stanzas I and II.[79] The first pair of statements, although they seem quite general, in fact refer, because of the adverbial expressions ἐκεῖ/ܬܡܢ (*tammān*) in 6a and πανταχοῦ/ܒܟܠ ܐܬܪ (*b-kol ʾatar*) in 6b, directly to the mythological circumstances of 1-5.[80] The variant in 6a ℭ, replacing the location "there" by the existential "with me,"[81] does not authorize the emendation ܥܡܢ for ܬܡܢ.[82] However, it may be concluded from the use of † ⲚⲦⲟⲟⲧ≈, corresponding to the *hapax legomenon* ܥܕܪ (Pa. *ʿaddar*), that 𝔊 used the verb βοηθέω.[83] The Syriac objective suffix quite regularly corresponds to the Greek dative μοι (cf. Matt 15:25; Mark 9:22; Acts 16:9; 2 Cor 6:2). It will be shown below that the connection between 6 and 7 is closer than may appear at first sight (and cf. already 8:6 and 25:2).

Charlesworth turns the facts upside down when he remarks on 6b: "The variant reading between C [= *Pistis Sophia*] and H reveals the originality of the Syriac, precisely because it is easy to confuse a *Bēth* with a *Kāph*."[84] Diettrich had already stated that ܒܪܝܟ (*brīḵ*) in H is "clearly a copyist's mistake" for ܟܪܝܟ (*krīḵ*) in ܣ*.[85] But this mistake speaks for a Greek original, which must have had κύκλῳ μου.[86] This improper preposition was correctly translated into Syriac and Coptic. N preserves the passive participle of ܟܪܟ (*kraḵ*),[87] but on the line leading to H—or even by the scribe of H—it was mistaken for ܒܪܝܟ, and this was accepted, at first, by translators (e.g., Harnack: "and everywhere your name is blessed by me"; Ungnad and Staerk: ". . . hallowed").[88] This line of reasoning is supported by the remarks on ܟܪܝܐ/ܟܪܘܢܐ in 2 (see above). The Gnostic interpretation of the hymn in the *Pistis Sophia* is interesting in its entirety, but what is especially noteworthy is the way in which the "hypostatization of the Name of God"[89] is replaced by the dominant term "light" (see on 12a below; also Excursus 39).[90]

The antithetical parallelism of 7a-b is brought out even more clearly by the synonymity of the two terms of power, ܝܡܝܢܐ (*yammīnā*) and ܐܝܕܐ (*ʾidā*).[91] The use of the term referring to the right hand of God in 7a makes "some connection between 6 and 7,"[92] since the "right [hand]" is also found elsewhere in connection with the equally theological term "helper" (cf. esp. 8:6 and 25:2). The *Vorlage* of ⲦⲀⲔⲟ and ܚܒܠ (Pa. *ḥabbel*) is likely to have been φθείρω or some compound of it (see Excursus 28).[93] As in 1 Cor 3:17, only God—that is, no political

77 See LSJ, *s.v.* ῥίζα: ῥίζα σπέρματος.
78 Contra Harris and Mingana, 2:330.
79 Emerton (p. 712) inserts "*It is thou*" at the beginning of 6 and remarks: "The syntactical relationship of this verse to verses 1-5 is difficult."
80 See BDAG, *s.vv.* ἐκεῖ, πανταχοῦ; Payne Smith, 1:426, 2:4459.
81 See Crum, 169, *s.v.* ⲙⲛ̄-.
82 Contra Frankenberg, 40. His emendation runs counter to his own retroversion into Greek (p. 22: ἐκεῖ). The Coptic variant may derive from the hymn in the *Pistis Sophia*, which incidentally also uses the singular "place" (see Lattke, *Bedeutung*, 1:137). This is a good example of the reciprocal influence of quotation and hymn.
83 Payne Smith, 2:2813–14; Crum, 426; BDAG, *s.v.* βοηθέω.
84 Charlesworth, 91.
85 Diettrich, 83; see also Frankenberg, 40; Harris and Mingana, vol. 1, on this passage.
86 BDAG, *s.v.* κύκλῳ, 1.
87 Payne Smith, 1:1823: "active, *circumdans*."
88 Harnack, 53; Ungnad and Staerk, 23.
89 Diettrich, 83.
90 Bultmann quotes *Ode* 22:6 and notes: "That the 'name' provided help rests on the concept of the magic name, which the Redeemer brings down from the heights" (see Bultmann, "Bedeutung," 108 = idem, *Exegetica*, 64), which hardly seems germane. To his reference to 42:20 another to 8:21 may be added.
91 See Payne Smith, 1:1605; BDAG, *s.v.* δεξιός.
92 Franzmann, 170.

power or religious institution—has the right to "destroy" and "cause to perish" any κακία (πονηρία).[94] Slightly altering Schrage, one could say: "Whom" or what the speaker "has in view" among the possible objects of this cutting verb "is uncertain."[95] The variants in the manuscripts already bear witness to this uncertainty. While they agree on the term "poison" (𝔊 could have been ἰός, πικρία, or χολή),[96] N uses the emphatic feminine singular of the adjective ܒܝܫܐ (*bīšā*) as a noun, which can be equivalent to ܒܝܫܬܐ (*bēštā*) and is used to translate κακία or πονηρία, while H keeps it as an adjective.[97] If, as Zahn supposes and Diettrich too thinks "very likely,"[98] 𝔊 had used τοῦ πονηροῦ, 𝔖 would not have had ܒܝܫܬܐ (*bīštā*) but ܒܝܫܐ (*bīšā*).[99] So in H "his evil poison"[100] or "his wicked venom" can only refer to the "dragon" (5), which is the devil.[101] In N, on the other hand, the connection to the mythology of stanza I is looser, since the "poison of evil" stakes out a far larger dualistic position. In ℭ also, the "poison of the slanderer"[102] does not refer to a particular opponent of God, but to any person who speaks ill.[103] The Coptic version may have been indebted to Rom 3:13-14, which in its turn was influenced by Ps 10:7 and 139:4 LXX with their key words "mouth," "tongue," and "lips."

Unlike in Isa 40:3,[104] it is the "hand" of the Most High himself that prepared the "way" (7b). Whether the *hapax legomenon* ܐܫܘܝ (Aph. *ʾašwī*) corresponded to a form of εὐθύνω or εὐθεῖαν ποιέω (cf. Isa 40:3)[105] or of ὁμαλίζω (cf. Isa 45:2)[106] is more difficult to decide than that the *Vorlage* of ܐܘܪܚܐ (*ʾurḥā*) was ἡ ὁδός (see Excursus 15).[107] In spite of traditional eschatology, this last term develops its own dualistic-Gnostic existence in the *Odes of Solomon* (cf. 24:13; 39:13) and will recur in *Ode* 22 in this sense (see on 11a below). The connection between stanzas I and II seems somewhat remote in the use of χείρ/ܐܝܕܐ (see on 5a above; also Excursus 27)[108] and in the imagery of preparing the way, which has less to do with the "being led" of stanza I than with the "foundation" of the redeemed laid by the hand of the Lord (38:16b; see on 12a below). Here too the way of salvation was smoothed only for the Gnostic πιστοί (ℭ). But 𝔊 probably used τοῖς εἴς σε πιστεύουσιν (see Excursus 34)[109] rather than simply τοῖς πιστοῖς σου.[110]

■ **8-10** Although Diettrich emphasizes the "join" between stanza III and 7b and correctly recognizes that this is only a "raising of the faithful" by their God, he considers 8-10 an "intrusion in our collection" and "an intolerable interruption" of what he calls the "responses" to 1-6, and decides "for reasons of both content and form 8-10 should be struck out as a later interpolation."[111] Kittel dismisses this as "merely the fanciful aestheticism of a modern critic."[112] The only reason for considering these three bicola an insertion would be the link between 11a and 7b in the repetition of the term "way." But this is not a strong enough reason, since the inclusively meant object ܐܢܘܢ (*ʾennōn*, enclitic third masculine plural personal pronoun) in 8a-b refers to the "faithful" of 7b.

Before the exegesis proper, it is necessary to discuss the problem of the verb forms in stanza III. On this, Franzmann remarks as follows:

93 See Crum, 405; Payne Smith, 1:1175–76; BDAG, *s.v.* φθείρω, and also διαφθείρω and καταφθείρω.
94 Schrage, *1 Korinther*, 1:306.
95 Ibid., 1:305.
96 Payne Smith, 2:2203–4; Crum, 196; BDAG, *s.vv.* ἰός, πικρία, χολή.
97 Payne Smith, 1:440; BDAG, *s.vv.* κακία, πονηρία.
98 Zahn, 698; Diettrich, 83.
99 See BDAG, *s.v.* πονηρός, 1b (as subst.). Diettrich's reference to *Ode* 14:6 is the more irrelevant, since he himself notes about that verse: "Evil (malum) is always *bîštâ* in the Peshitta of the Psalter" (see Diettrich, 51 n. 11).
100 Harnack, 53.
101 Harris and Mingana, 2:328.
102 Harnack, 53.
103 See Crum, 731, 755.
104 Cf. Mark 1:3; Matt 3:3; Luke 3:4; John 1:23.
105 BDAG, *s.v.* adj. εὐθύς, 1.
106 See BDAG, *s.v.* ὁμαλίζω; Frankenberg, 22: ὡμάλισεν.
107 Payne Smith, 1:375; BDAG, *s.v.* ὁδός.
108 See BDAG, *s.v.* χείρ; Payne Smith, 1:1546–47.
109 Frankenberg, 22; cf. BDAG, *s.v.* εἴς.
110 See BDAG, *s.v.* πιστός.
111 Diettrich, 81.
112 Kittel, 94.

8a, 8b, 9a, 9b, 10b: The Coptic gives the verbs in the 2nd masc. sing. In the margin of his personal copy of his 1911 edition, Harris changed the translation of the verbs from 2nd masc. sing. to 3rd fem. sing. (subject ܐܢܬܝ). The changes found their way into Harris and Mingana vol. 2 and subsequently into Charlesworth 1977 and Emerton [1984]. Charlesworth indicates for 8a (91, n. 11) that the unpointed Syriac text could be interpreted either as 2nd masc. sing. or as 3rd fem. sing. This is only true if the verb is Pael rather than Peal. One must question how Charlesworth has arrived at the Pael for 8a rather than the Peal which he had used for the remaining verbs of 8b, 9a, 9b and 10b. The choice of the Pael would appear to have been made for the convenience of supplying the possibility of a 3rd fem. sing. subj.[113]

Even though the pointing of H and N may not be the final arbiters for the critical edition, the points that are found over and under the verbs of 8-9 and 10b strongly suggest that they are Pe. forms. In 9b, the ambiguous pointing of ܘܩܪܡܬ in H,[114] which does not suit the reading of *ʾu-qermaṯ*,[115] needs to be emended to read the Pe. *wa-qramt* instead of the Pa. *ʾu-qarremt*. This slight move of the *Pṯāḥā*-points from the ܩ to the ܘ can be justified because the Pa., in spite of overlapping meanings, is found far less often than the Pe. of ܩܪܡ,[116] and the pointing of N also indicates a Pe. rather than a Pa.[117] So the verb forms make it difficult to speak of "Coptic variants," which removes the support from Charlesworth's verdict: "These pronominal variants suggest that the Coptic ultimately goes back to a Syriac *Grundschrift*."[118]

Whether stanza III deals with the "raising of the dead from *Sheol*" [emphasis added] is far less clear than "the influence of Ezekiel, ch. xxxvii."[119] As in, for example, Matt 27:52 or John 5:28, 8-10 form part of a rich tradition following the two-part vision of Ezek 37:1-14, although they do not depict the "raising of Israel from the dead."[120] For "Israel" is not mentioned, either in reference to πᾶς οἶκος ("whole house") or in reference to γῆ/ܐܪܥܐ (*ʾarʿā*, "land") or λαός ("people"; cf. Ezek 37:11-14).[121] Other important terms that do not occur are "spirit/wind" (Ezek 37:1, 5-6, 8-10, 14), "dry" (Ezek 37:2, 4, 11), "sinews" (Ezek 37:6), and "skin" (Ezek 37:6, 8). In place of the dominant terms "to live," "to make/become alive" (Ezek 37:5-6, 9-10, 14) the noun "life," found only in the LXX, ζωή/ⲱⲛϩ/ܚ̈ܝܐ (*ḥayyē*), is used (*Ode* 22:10b; cf. Ezek 37:5); and for σάρκες (plural) or ܒܣܪܐ (singular) there is the synonym σώματα/ܦܓܖ̈ܐ (*pagrē*, "bodies") in 𝔖 and σῶμα ("body") in ℭ (*Ode* 22:9b; cf. Ezek 37:6, 8). The term τάφοι/ܩܒܖ̈ܐ (*qaḇrē*, "graves") in *Ode* 22:8a comes from Ezek 37:12-13, ⲕⲱⲱⲥ/ܡܝ̈ܬܐ (*mīṯē*, "the dead") in 8b from Ezek 37:9 LXX (νεκροί),[122] and ⲕⲁⲥ/ܓܖ̈ܡܐ (*garmē*, "bones") in 9a from Ezek 37:1, 3-4, 7, 11 (ὀστᾶ in the LXX regularly corresponds to ܓܖ̈ܡܐ). The verb form ܩܪܡܬ (*qramt*, "stretch") in 9b corresponds to the form of ἐκτείνω used in Ezek 37:6 (ἐκτενῶ), which raises the question whether it is really "not the right word to use."[123]

Even if the verbs of 8a-b do not occur in the model, this statement of salvation is greatly influenced by Ezek

113 Franzmann, 168.
114 Charlesworth, *Manuscripts*, 60, line 9.
115 As in Harris and Mingana, vol. 1, on this passage; Charlesworth, 89.
116 See Payne Smith, 2:3747.
117 See Lattke, *Bedeutung*, 2:198, line 7.
118 Charlesworth, 91. This verdict is related to a stemma that Charlesworth himself calls only a working hypothesis (idem, 14).
119 Harris and Mingana, 2:328. In what follows Harris and Mingana's careful conclusion must always be kept in mind: "On the whole, we suspect Syriac origin for the Ode, but the case is not nearly so strong nor so convincing as some which we had from the Psalms" (2:329). It should also be remembered that a Greek original could have been translated with the help of a Syriac version of the Bible.
120 Walther Zimmerli, *Ezechiel* (2 vols.; BKAT 13.1–2; Neukirchen-Vluyn: Neukirchener Verlag, 1969) 885–902.
121 See Rahlfs, 2:838; Brenton, 1029; *OTSy*, pt. 3 fasc. 3, pp. 82–83.
122 The "slain" of Ezek 37:9 are ܩ̈ܛܝܠܐ in the Syriac translation and not ܡܝ̈ܬܐ, which suggests that the LXX was used.
123 Harris and Mingana, 2:328.

37:9 and 37:12-13 LXX: [(9)]. . . ἐμφύσησον εἰς τοὺς νεκροὺς τούτους ("breathe upon these dead") . . . [(12)]. . . ἐγὼ ἀνοίγω ὑμῶν τὰ μνήματα καὶ ἀνάξω ὑμᾶς ἐκ τῶν μνημάτων ὑμῶν ("I will open your tombs, and will bring you up out of your tombs") . . . [(13)]καὶ γνώσεσθε ὅτι ἐγώ εἰμι κύριος ἐν τῷ ἀνοῖξαί με τοὺς τάφους ὑμῶν τοῦ ἀναγαγεῖν με ἐκ τῶν τάφων τὸν λαόν μου ("And ye shall know that I am the Lord, when I have opened your graves, that I may bring up my people from their graves").[124] Since the loanword τάφοι occurs in ℭ, it is likely that 𝔊 had ἐκ τῶν τάφων and not ἐκ τῶν μνημάτων.[125] Only God can "choose" (𝔖) or "redeem" (ℭ) from the "graves" or "tombs." Although the reading ⲥⲱⲧⲉ ⲉⲃⲟⲗ makes sense, it may be a scribal error in the *Pistis Sophia*: "Od Solom 22 $_8$ ܓܒܝܬ reading ? ⲥⲟⲧⲡⲟⲩ."[126] This would be another indication that the *Vorlage* of the Pe. ܓܒܐ (*gḇā*) was a form of ἐκλέγομαι ("choose").[127]

Parallel to 8a, 8b admits that the chosen ones (cf. 8:20; 23:2-3; 33:13) were separated from the rest of the "dead" (cf. Matt 25:32).[128] Although this could refer to "all those who are in the underworld" (cf. 42:14),[129] the image in fact confines itself to earthly graveyards and does not venture into the deeps of Hades. The emphasis is rather on the idea that a part of mankind is not counted among the elect and must rely on the mercy of a re-creator who may be more all-embracing.

Even the "elect" became nothing but "bones" in death (cf. the phrase ὄστεα νεκρῶν in Matt 23:27). The plural emphatic passive participle ܡܝ̈ܬܐ (*mīṯē*) in 9a is influenced by the nominalized adjective νεκροί in Ezek 37:9 LXX, just as the same form ܡܝ̈ܬܐ is used in the same sense in 8b.[130] Since the Syriac of Ezek 37:1-14 does not use ܡܝ̈ܬܐ, it follows that there can be "preference for one version over the other,"[131] specifically for 𝔊 used in conjunction with a Greek text of Ezekiel. The "taking" of the dead ὀστᾶ/ܓܪ̈ܡܐ (*garmē*, "bones")[132] shows some similarities to God's creative act in Gen 2:21 (ἔλαβεν/ܢܣܒ [*nsaḇ*], "he took").

Since σάρξ/ܒܣܪܐ (*besrā*, "flesh") has a negative connotation for the people of the *Odes of Solomon* (cf. 8:9; 20:3), the term σάρκες (Ezek 37:6, 8) will have been replaced by the more neutral σώματα/ܦܓܪ̈ܐ (*pağrē*, "bodies"), as the use of the loanword σῶμα in ℭ proves.[133] The verb ἐκτείνω/ܩܪܡ (*qram*), which in Ezek 37:6 refers only to the "skin," is extended to refer to the whole "body," stretched also like a σκῆνος ("tent"; cf. 2 Cor 5:1) over the skeleton.[134] The image, then, offers no basis for the statement, "It was not the right word to use, but he [i.e., the Odist] took it from his context, i.e. from the Hebrew or the Syriac. We take it that he was using a Syriac text of Ezekiel."[135]

On the third bicolon (10a-b), which is most likely meant as an antithetical parallelism, even Harris and Mingana have to acknowledge: "the sentence has a Greek look, for ܡܥܒܕܢܘܬܐ stands for ἐνέργεια, and the word is actually preserved in the Coptic."[136] The word ܡܥܕܪܢܘܬܐ (*mʿaḏrānūṯā*) in 10b H is an error, although it does make a certain sense ("help" in place of "energy"). Whether the participle of ܙܘܥ, ܙܥ (*zāʿ*) actually derives from σεισμός/ܙܘܥܐ (*zawʿā*) in Ezek 37:7 is less important than determining the exact meaning of 10a. For the negated masculine plural participle of

124 Rahlfs, 2:838; Brenton, 1029.

125 See BDAG, *s.vv.* μνῆμα, τάφος; Payne Smith, 2:3482. The term τάφος corresponds to Syriac ܩܒܪܐ (*qaḇrā*), while the sense of μνημεῖον is usually reproduced by ܒܝܬ ܩܒܘܪܐ (*bēṯ qḇūrā*) (Payne Smith, 2:3482). But ܩܒܪܐ is occasionally also used for μνημεῖον (e.g., John 5:28; 11:31; 12:17; 19:42; 20:11).

126 Crum, 362.

127 BDAG, *s.v.* ἐκλέγομαι, 1; Payne Smith, 1:636–37; Crum, 365.

128 Unlike in 3:4a, there is no doubt that ܦܪܫ (*praš*) here translates ἀφορίζω (BDAG, *s.v.* ἀφορίζω; Payne Smith, 2:3299–301).

129 BDAG, *s.v.* νεκρός, on 1 Pet 4:6.

130 See Payne Smith, 2:2055–56.

131 Harris and Mingana, 2:329.

132 BDAG, *s.v.* ὀστέον; Payne Smith, 1:782.

133 See Payne Smith, 2:3033.

134 See BDAG, *s.vv.* ἐκτείνω, σκῆνος; Payne Smith, 2:3746–47. It is clear that ℭ pictured σῶμα more like a garment in which the dead bones were clothed.

135 Harris and Mingana, 2:328.

136 Ibid., 2:328.

the Ethpe. ܐܬܬܙܝܥܘ (ʾettzīʿ) could mean ἀμετακίνητοι ("immovable")[137] as in 1 Cor 15:58 or μὴ πτυρόμενοι (not "intimidated")[138] as in Phil 1:28. In the latter case, the motionlessness would already be a positive result of God's creative power, and the parallelism would be synthetic, not antithetic.[139] However, it is more likely that the original expression was μὴ κινούμενοι or ἀσάλευτοι (cf. Acts 27:41, but not Heb 12:28).[140] With antithetical parallelism, the dramatic contrast is heightened when the skeletons, even though covered by bodies, still remain inanimate.

Verse 10b is the climax of stanza III with its theological use of the common verb "to give,"[141] whose direct object, ἐνέργεια/ܡܥܒܕܢܘܬܐ (maʿbdānūtā), as a *hapax legomenon,* emphasizes the activity of the "supernatural" God.[142] The implied indirect object ܐܢܘܢ (ʾennōn), from 8a-b, has to be added. The preposition ܠ (l-) prefixed to the term ζωή/ܚܝܐ (ḥayyē), taken from Ezek 37:5 LXX, gives the "Object,"[143] which is the opposite of being dead, but only receives its full meaning of eternal and immortal "life" in the context of all the *Odes* taken together (see Table 1).[144]

■ **11-12** The key word "way" connects back to the end of stanza II (see on 7b above), but the complex subject matter of stanza IV presupposes the eschatological content of stanza III. There are difficulties posed by the manifest differences between ℭ and 𝔖 in 12a-b (see below), and also by the placing of the final word of 11a and its connection to the purport of 11b. If the Greek loanword πρόσωπον were to be detached from the end of 11a—as in H and N—and even, perhaps, allowed to become a colon in its own right, as 11b "with (ܗܘܐ) ܗܘܬ ܚܒܠܐ ܠܐ understood,"[145] the verse structure would be disrupted. If ܘܦܪܨܘܦܟ (ʾu-parṣōpāk) were placed at the beginning of 11b—as in the manuscripts—it would have to be translated by something like "you brought your person/self (cf. 31:5) into your world, into destruction."[146] Even if—speaking theologically rather than christologically—the term "countenance" is chosen instead of "person/self," the construction with twofold use of ܠ (l-) would still mean much the same, so that already Diettrich had to "emend" ܐܝܬܝܬ to ܐܝܬܝ ("and thy countenance 'has' brought thy world to destruction").[147] Since this at least takes into account the accusative of αἰών in ℭ, one could, instead of making such an assault upon the text, imagine that in 𝔊* the phrase καὶ τὸ πρόσωπόν σου was a gloss on 11a (either between the lines or in the margin) and slipped from there into different places in the text of the Syriac and Coptic translations. The main idea of 11a, in any case, is that the "way" prepared by God's "hand" for the "faithful" (πιστοί in 7b ℭ) was ἄφθαρτος or even ἡ ἀφθαρσία (see Excursuses 8, 15, and 28).[148]

If ܠܚܒܠܐ (la-ḥbālā = εἰς φθοράν) is not to be emended to ܠܠܐ ܚܒܠܐ (l-lā ḥbālā = εἰς ἀφθαρσίαν), it is still possible to mitigate the harshness of the negative statement in 11b by expanding the translation of 11b-c as follows: "You *only* brought your world to destruction, in order that everything might be dissolved and *then* renewed" [emphasis added].[149] The first question that must be asked is whether the term ܥܠܡܐ (ʿālmā), with its second masculine singular suffix, stands for κόσμος or αἰών. Both Greek words occur as loanwords in the *Pistis Sophia*, so does the use of αἰών (ℭ) here mean that that term was also used in 𝔊?

Excursus 22: "Aeon" and "World" in the *Odes of Solomon*

It was only because of "this use of κόσμος in Hellenistic Judaism" that the Aramaic term עָלְמָא, like the Hebrew עוֹלָם, "began to take on what had hitherto

137 BDAG, *s.v.* ἀμετακίνητος.
138 BDAG, *s.v.* πτύρω.
139 See Eissfeldt §6.1.
140 BDAG, *s.vv.* ἀσάλευτος, κινέω (opposite of "living"); Payne Smith, 1:1106.
141 Cf. 4:3, 9, 13; 7:24; 9:2; 15:7; 17:8; 22:4; 29:2; 31:5.
142 BDAG, *s.v.* ἐνέργεια; Payne Smith, 2:2776–77.
143 See Nöldeke §247.
144 BDAG, *s.v.* ζωή; Payne Smith, 1:1254.
145 Franzmann, 170.
146 Schultheß, 254. Schultheß has "the world," not "your world." See also Emerton's note (p. 712): "According to the punctuation of the Mss 'thy person' goes with the next line to give 'And thou didst bring thy person into the world, even into corruption.'" But Emerton also moves the phrase back to 11a. Frankenberg (p. 22) in his retroversion converts ܠܥܠܡܟ into the dative τῷ κόσμῳ σου and ܠܚܒܠܐ into the prepositional phrase of purpose εἰς ἀναίρεσιν.
147 Diettrich, 83.
148 BDAG, *s.vv.* ἀφθαρσία, ἄφθαρτος; see Crum, 405; Payne Smith, 1:1179.
149 Berger and Nord, 956.

been an alien spatial significance."[150] In the LXX the originally temporal term is usually represented by αἰών and αἰώνιος,[151] but never by κόσμος.[152] The masculine Syriac noun ܥܠܡܐ (*ʿālmā*), also, is still strongly attached to עוֹלָם/αἰών,[153] as can be seen most clearly in the phrases ܠܥܠܡ (*l-ʿālam* = εἰς τὸν αἰῶνα), ܕܠܥܠܡ (*da-l-ʿālam* = αἰώνιος), and ܡܢ ܥܠܡ (*men ʿālam* = ἐκ τοῦ αἰῶνος).[154] But at the same time ܥܠܡܐ can also be found as a translation for κόσμος in the full extent of its later senses from "universe" and the "wide world" to "humankind."[155]

This ambiguity or polysemy is mirrored in the use of the singular (seventeen or eighteen times) and plural (nine or ten times) of ܥܠܡܐ in the *Odes of Solomon*. ℭ uses the loanword αἰών once (22:11), but elsewhere one finds the normal Coptic word for eternity ⲉⲛⲉϩ (6:18; 25:12).[156] The adjective αἰώνιος, found in the material preserved only in Greek (11:16h, together with ζωή), has its normal meaning "eternal" in the other two passages (11:22, 24).[157]

In all five cases where 𝔖 has ܕܠܥܠܡ, its correspondence to the Greek adjective αἰώνιος can be assumed or even observed (6:18 [living water]; 9:4 [life]; 9:8 [crown]; 11:22 [memorial/remembrance]; 11:24 [paradise/delight of paradise]).

In the formulaic use of "eternity/eternities," the commonest is a combination of singular and plural (10:6 [my people]; 23:24 [divine reign]; 25:12 [rest]; 32:3 [unshakable]). The singular ܠܥܠܡ (38:17 H; 41:16 [give life]) and the plural ܠܥܠܡܝܢ (38:17 N [fruits]) by itself have the same meaning as ܠܥܠܡ ܥܠܡܝܢ (*l-ʿālam ʿālmīn*). The plural is used with the assumption "that there are a number of αἰῶνες, that is, *ages and periods of time* whose endless sequence constitutes eternity."[158]

At this point the question arises whether the plural ܥܠܡ̈ܐ (*ʿālmē*) used with the preposition ܒ (*b-*) and ܟܠܗܘܢ (*kullhōn*) refers to eternal "periods of time" or infinite "spheres of the cosmos" (8:23 ["imperishable . . . on account of the name of your Father"]).[159] On the borderline of the idea of "Aeons" as "persons," there is the statement about the "*plērōma* of the Aeons" and their "Father" (7:11) "in which it would be impossible to substitute αἰώνιος for τῶν αἰώνων."[160] The "Aeons" appear fully personified as recipients of the word (12:4) by which they spoke to each other (12:8). This matches the statement that the "Aeons" came into existence by the word of the Lord (16:19). As in Ignatius *Eph.* 19:2, these are more likely to be "personified αἰῶνες"[161] than a "plurality of κόσμοι" or the "Platonic duplication of the κόσμος."[162]

In the remaining six cases, the singular ܥܠܡܐ is used. When a "new aeon" is mentioned (33:12), one may conclude that there is an idea of an old, current, and perishing "aeon."[163] As a parallel to "flesh," in another passage, ܥܠܡܐ is not αἰών but κόσμος (20:3).[164] Behind the expression "before the foundation of the world" (41:15), there is a concept of "preexistence" and also a *spatial* idea of the "creation . . . of the κόσμος" (cf. parallel passages).[165] Deceivers of the "world" (38:11) are reminiscent of

150 Hermann Sasse, "κοσμέω, κόσμος, κτλ.," *ThWNT* 3 (1938) 881; *TDNT* 3:882.

151 Hermann Sasse, "αἰών, αἰώνιος," *ThWNT* 1 (1933) 199; *TDNT* 1:199; Horst Dietrich Preuß, "עוֹלָם *ʿôlām*, עָלַם *ʿālam*," *ThWAT* 5 (1986) 1147; *TDOT* 10:533.

152 See Horst Balz, "κόσμος," *EWNT* 2 (1981) 767; *EDNT* 2:310.

153 Payne Smith, 2:2898.

154 Payne Smith, 2:2899; BDAG, *s.v.* αἰών; Traugott Holtz, "αἰών," *EWNT* 1 (1980) 106–8; *EDNT* 1:45; Horst Balz, "αἰώνιος," *EWNT* 1 (1980) 112; *EDNT* 1:46–47.

155 Payne Smith, 2:2899–900; BDAG, *s.v.* κόσμος.

156 See Crum, 57.

157 See Sasse, "αἰών," *ThWNT* 1:208; *TDNT* 1:208; Balz, "αἰώνιος," *EWNT* 1 (1980) 111; *EDNT* 1:46.

158 See Sasse, "αἰών," *ThWNT* 1:199; *TDNT* 1:199, on this "linguistic usage in Hellenistic Judaism."

159 See Sasse, "αἰών," *ThWNT* 1:201; *TDNT* 1:201.

160 Ibid.

161 Sasse, "αἰών," *ThWNT* 1:208; *TDNT* 1:207.

162 Sasse, "κοσμέω," *ThWNT* 3:873, 878; *TDNT* 3:873, 879.

163 Some considerations on the usage and terminology are that "Paul uses the phrase κόσμος οὗτος along with αἰὼν οὗτος . . . and in the same sense" (Sasse, "κοσμέω," *ThWNT* 3:884–85; *TDNT* 3:885; cf. 1 Cor 2:6; 3:19; 5:10; 7:31; Eph 2:2). After discussing Johannine usage, Sasse (p. 885) continues: "although κόσμος takes the place of αἰών to describe what Jewish apocalypticism called עוֹלָם הַזֶּה, New Testament writers avoid the term κόσμος in descriptions of the 'future world.'" On the Jewish-apocalyptic and Christian dogma of the two aeons, see Sasse, "αἰών," *ThWNT* 1:204–7; *TDNT* 1:204–07; Richard Löwe, *Kosmos und Aion: Ein Beitrag zur heilsgeschichtlichen Dialektik des urchristlichen Weltverständnisses* (NTF, 3. Reihe, 5. Heft; Gütersloh: Mohn, 1935; repr., Münster: Stenderhoff, 1983) 39–48.

164 See Alexander Sand, "σάρξ," *EWNT* 3 (1983) 550–52; *EDNT* 3:231–32.

165 Sasse, "κοσμέω," *ThWNT* 3:884; *TDNT* 3:885.

κοσμοπλάνης in *Did.* 16:4.[166] This refers to the world of humanity, as does the statement about the capture of the ܥܠܡܐ/κόσμος (10:4). The cosmos of humankind, which does not understand, is also the target of 19:5, but ܥܠܡܐ in 22:11 𝔖 is not so limited. This finally brings back the question posed immediately before this excursus: Did the Greek text of this verse use αἰών?

If 11b 𝔊 used the term αἰών, which seems likely given the quotation in the *Pistis Sophia*, then 𝔖 took it to mean κόσμος in the sense of God's own creation (cf., e.g., John 1:10). The Gnostics of the *Pistis Sophia* were aware of the saying συντέλεια τοῦ αἰῶνος ("close of the age") from Matt 13:39 (e.g., chap. 86;[167] cf. Matt 13:40, 49; 24:3; 28:20), but they pulled the teeth of this negative statement by transforming God's "world" into the personified "thirteenth Aeon," which is not only the earlier habitation of the Pistis Sophia, but is, with her, identical with the "power" of the First Mystery (chaps. 70–71).[168] This also explains the difference between ℭ and 𝔖. The ruling God of the Syriac text—based on the vocabulary of 𝔊 (ἄγω, αἰών σου, εἰς φθοράν)—consigns, in eschatological terms, his own world, which had become autonomous and self-regulated, to "destruction/corruption" and "dissolution,"[169] while in ℭ the aeon-power, discussed above, is led upward "above the chaos (χάος) and above the destruction" (according to the second solution in chap. 71).[170]

The intention expressed in 11c differs in the Syriac and Coptic versions; whereas 𝔖 has ܟܠܡܕܡ (*kol meddem*), referring to ܥܠܡܟ (*ʿālmāḵ*) and corresponding to πάντα,[171] ℭ uses ⲧⲏⲣ⸗ with third plural suffix;[172] in addition, the two verbs describing actions passively endured by "everything" or "them all" are directed at differing objects, the dissolution of the chaotic "matter (ὕλαι)" as against the renewal of "all my powers" in "the" or "thy light" (chaps. 70–71).[173] The verbs agree: both the Ethpe. of ܫܪܐ (*šrā*) and ⲃⲱⲗ ⲉⲃⲟⲗ correspond to the passive of λύω,[174] and the *hapax legomenon* ܐܬܚܕܬ (*ʾeṯḥaddaṯ*) and ⲣ-ⲃⲣⲣⲉ to the passive of ἀνακαινόω or ἀνακαινίζω.[175] This soteriological renewal, which has already taken place, is now described in more detail.

Whether the subject "your rock," so abruptly introduced in 12a 𝔖, represents λίθος or πέτρα in 𝔊 is hard to decide. Both terms can be ascribed to "Christ" as in 1 Pet 2:4-8; 1 Cor 3:11.[176] This "rock" does not refer to the Peter of Matt 16:18, even though, in the image of the "process of salvation," the reference to building may have been influenced by that passage.[177] The predicate noun ܫܬܐܣܬܐ (*šeṯesṯā*)/ⲥⲛⲧⲉ certainly corresponds to θεμέλιος[178] and may also refer to "Christ," as does 1 Cor 3:11.[179] At any rate, ܟܐܦܐ (*kēp̄ā*) is more than just a "foundation for the building of a house" (cf. Matt 7:24-25 and Luke 6:48).[180] It is possible that ℭ originally had ⲡⲉⲕⲱⲛⲉ instead of ⲡⲉⲕⲟⲩⲟⲉⲓⲛ.[181] But the reinterpreta-

166 BDAG, *s.v.* κοσμοπλάνης: "deceiver of the world"; *Did.* 16:4: ὡς υἱὸς θεοῦ ("as a son of God"; cf. Ehrman, 1:442–43; Lindemann and Paulsen, 20).
167 Schmidt, Till, and Schenke, *Schriften*, 123, line 9; 126, lines 31–32; Schmidt and MacDermot, *Pistis Sophia*, 191 and 196.
168 Schmidt, Till, and Schenke, *Schriften*, 100, line 22; 101, line 25; 103, lines 21–24; Schmidt and MacDermot, *Pistis Sophia*, 156–58, 161. See also Schmidt, Till, and Schenke, *Schriften*, 399 *s.v.* "Äon, der dreizehnte [Aeon, the thirteenth]," and 414 *s.v.* "Mysterium, das erste [Mystery, the first]."
169 Payne Smith, 1:415–16, 1179; BDAG, *s.vv.* ἄγω, φθορά; Klein, *Wörterbuch*, 32.
170 Schmidt, Till, and Schenke, *Schriften*, 103, line 24; Schmidt and MacDermot, *Pistis Sophia*, 161; see also Crum, 405.
171 Payne Smith, 1:1737.
172 See Till §194.
173 Schmidt, Till, and Schenke, *Schriften*, 100, lines 24–25; 103, lines 25–26; Schmidt and MacDermot, *Pistis Sophia*, 156 and 161.
174 Omitted in Payne Smith, 2:4309–10; see BDAG, *s.v.* λύω, esp. 3 on 2 Pet 3:10-12 ("final conflagration"); Crum, 32–33.
175 Payne Smith, 1:1207; BDAG, *s.vv.* ἀνακαινίζω, ἀνακαινόω; Crum, 43.
176 BDAG, *s.vv.* λίθος, πέτρα; Payne Smith, 1:1663.
177 Vielhauer, *Oikodome*, 46. See Murray's cautious assessment ("Rock," 352): "But possibly vv. 11-12 are addressed to Christ. In any case there seems to be a clear allusion to the foundation of the Church."
178 Payne Smith, 2:4348; Crum, 345.
179 BDAG, *s.v.* θεμέλιος.
180 BDAG, *s.v.* πέτρα.
181 Crum, 524; Franzmann, 172: "your stone."

tion of 11c (see above), as well as the hymn of the Pistis Sophia and the second solution of this hymn, suggest that the phrase "your rock/stone," which is difficult to interpret, was replaced by "your light."[182] The term πάντα/ܟܠ ܡܕܡ (*kol meddem*) connects 12a to 11c, and there is "a kind of terrace pattern" in both 12 𝔖 and 12 ℭ, which may help to find the feminine referent of ܥܠܗ̇ (*ʿlēh*): "12b refers to ܟܐܦܟ in 12a, and 12c refers to ܡܠܟܘܬܟ in 12b."[183]

According to 12b 𝔊 and 𝔖, God has built his βασιλεία/ܡܠܟܘܬܐ (*malkūṯā*) on his own metaphorical bedrock.[184] Unlike 18:3 and 23:12, in this passage the term "basileia," which plays a more subordinate role here than in Jewish writings and the Synoptic Gospels,[185] and which in ℭ might originally have been ⲙⲛ̄ⲧⲣ̄ⲣⲟ, rather than the ⲙⲛ̄ⲧⲣⲙ̄ⲙⲁⲟ of Codex A,[186] stands for an extended and habitable "kingdom" and not for the "kingship" of God, which guarantees the freedom of its inhabitants.

In 12c the reading of N, for reasons of both form and content, is to be preferred to the direct address ("thou was/becamest") in H,[187] since the N variant refers to the metaphorical "kingdom" of the previous step of the terrace. Although the *hapax legomenon* ܡܥܡܪܐ (*maʿmrā*), derived from ܥܡܪ (*ʿmar*), is found in conjunction with ܒܝܬ (*bēṯ*) also in Ps 71:3,[188] there is no connection between this Psalm and *Ode* 22. A better comparison is Eph 2:22, where the church is called a κατοικητήριον τοῦ θεοῦ ("dwelling place of God"),[189] and mention is made of συμπολῖται τῶν ἁγίων καὶ οἰκεῖοι τοῦ θεοῦ ("fellow citizens with the saints and members of the household of God") in the same context (Eph 2:19).[190] The genitive of ἅγιοι/ܩܕܝܫܐ (*qaddīšē*, "saints")—differing perhaps from the Qualitative[191] ⲟⲩⲁⲁⲃ in ℭ—makes no connection with God's "holy place" (4:1) but serves as a link to the beginning of the next Ode.

182 See Lattke, *Bedeutung*, 1:211, 224.

183 Franzmann, 170. The differences between 𝔖 and ℭ can best be described as follows: "In the Syriac, the stone is the foundation of everything, the kingdom is built on the stone, and the kingdom is the habitation of the holy. In the Coptic, the light is the foundation of everything, the wealth is built, not upon the light, but upon everything, and everything becomes a holy dwelling" (Franzmann, 172).

184 Payne Smith, 1:542, 2:2143; BDAG, *s.vv.* βασιλεία, οἰκοδομέω.

185 Gustaf Dalman's chapter "Die Gottesherrschaft" is still of fundamental importance; see Dalman, *Die Worte Jesu mit Berücksichtigung des nachkanonischen jüdischen Schrifttums und der aramäischen Sprache*, vol. 1: *Einleitung und wichtige Begriffe. Mit Anhang: A. Das Vaterunser; B. Nachträge und Berichtigungen* (2nd ed.; Leipzig: Hinrichs, 1930) 75–119.

186 Franzmann, 168, 172; Crum, 296, 299.

187 Contra Diettrich, 84.

188 *OTSy*, pt. 2 fasc. 3, p. 78.

189 See *NTSy*, on this passage: ܡܥܡܪܐ ܕܐܠܗܐ.

190 See Payne Smith, 2:2922; BDAG, *s.v.* κατοικητήριον. It is surprising that in the chapter "Der Leib Christi als himmlischer Bau [The Body of Christ as a Celestial Building]," Schlier (*Christus*, 46–60) does not mention *Ode* 22:12, even to exclude it. This omission has also had an effect on dictionary references (see, e.g., Otto Michel, "οἶκος, κτλ.," *ThWNT* 5 (1954) 139, 145–47 [on οἰκοδομέω], 158 [on κατοικητήριον]; *TDNT* 5:137, 143–44, 155–56). Even Schlier's commentary on Ephesians passes over this passage in silence (see Schlier, *Epheser*, 140–45).

191 Lambdin, 86–88.

23

Ode 23: Mythological and Metaphorical Account of the Heavenly Letter (with Didactic Introduction and Invitation)

(I) 1a Joy belongs[a] to the saints,
1b and who will put it on
1c except they alone?
2a Grace belongs to the elect,
2b and who will receive it
2c except those who trust in it from the beginning?
3a Love belongs to the elect,
3b and who will put it on
3c except those who gained it from the beginning?
(II) 4a Walk in the *gnōsis* of the Lord[b]:
4b then you will know the grace of the Lord without envy[c],
4c both[d] for the exultation over him and for the perfection of his *gnōsis*.
(III) 5a And his thought was like a/the letter,
5b and his will flew down from the height.
6a And it was sent like an arrow from the bow
6b that is shot with force.
(IV) 7a And many hands rushed at the letter,
7b to snatch and take and read it;
8a but it escaped from their fingers.
(V) 8b And they were afraid of it and of the seal upon it,
9a because it was not possible for them to break its[e] seal,
9b for the power that was on the seal was mightier than they.
(VI) 10a Then those who saw the letter followed it,
10b that they might perceive where it would settle
10c and who would read it
10d and who[f] would hear it.
(VII) 11a But a/the wheel received it,
11b and it [the letter] came upon it.
12a And with it was a sign
12b of kingship and of governance.
13a And everything that disturbed the wheel[g]
13b it mowed down and cut to pieces[h].
14a And it heaped up a multitude of those who stood[i] in its way,
14b and covered up rivers
15a and passed through and uprooted many forests[j]
15b and made a wide way.
16a The "scroll" descended to the feet,
16b because to the feet[k] ran the wheel
16c and that which had come upon it.
(VIII) 17a The letter was also[l] a decree.

a 1a H omits ܗܝ.
b 4a ܡܪܝܐ N; ܡܪܝܬܐ H.
c 4b H omits ܕܡܪܝܐ ܠܛܝܒܘܬܗ ܘܬܕܥܘܢ.
d 4c H omits ܘ.
e 9a ܚܬܡܗ̇ N; ܚܬܡܗ H.
f 10d ܘܫܡܥ N; ܘܕܫܡܥ H.
g 13a H omits ܠܗ̇ before ܠܓܝܓܠܐ.
h 13b H omits second ܗܘܬ.
i 14a ܕܣܘܩܒ̈ܠܐ N; ܕܣܘܩܒ̈ܠܝܐ H.
j 15a ܥܒ̈ܐ H; ܥܒ̈ܝܐ N.
k 16b ܠܪ̈ܓܠܐ N; ܠܪܓܠܐ H.
l 17a ܘܦܘܩܕܢܐ N; ܕܦܘܩܕܢܐ H.

17b And[m] because all places were gathered together,
18a at its[n] head appeared a head that manifested itself,
18b that is the Son of Truth from the Most High Father.
19a And he inherited everything and took possession.
(IX) 19b Then the thought of the many ceased[o].
20a And all the apostates were bold and [yet] fled,
20b and the persecutors were extinguished and blotted out[p].
(X) 21a But the letter became a great tablet
21b that was entirely covered with writing by the finger of God.
22a And the name of the Father was upon it
22b and of the Son and of the Holy[q] Spirit,
22c to reign as king for ever and ever. Hallelujah.

m 17b H omits ܘ.
n 18a ܒܪܝܫܗ̇ N; ܒܪܝܫܗ H.
o 19b ܘܒܛܠܬ N; ܘܐܬܒܛܠܬ H.
p 20b ܘܐܬܛܫܝܘ N; ܘܐܬܛܫܘ H.
q 22b ܪܘܚܐ ܩܕܝܫܐ N; ܪܘܚܐ ܕܩܘܕܫܐ H.

Introduction

Ode 23 is preserved in two Syriac manuscripts.[1] "This Ode is the most difficult of all the hymns in the collection. It contains an account of a mysterious letter, shot from heaven like an arrow from a bow, sealed with a terrible seal, written with the finger of God, and inscribed with the name of the Trinity. No one, so far, has succeeded in breaking this seal; it is too strong for the critics."[2] The final sentence of this introduction, written after a decade of intensive research on the *Odes*,[3] not only criticizes such confident assertions as Spitta's, "the sense of this *Ode* will soon be deciphered"[4] (countering Harnack's claim that the "description" in stanza VII "is incomprehensible"),[5] but also takes the edge off their own final assessment that everything but stanza VII "appears to be cleared up."[6]

This commentary on the mythological and metaphorical narration (5-21) with its Gnostic and Wisdom introduction (1-4) and unmistakably Christian ending (22) will have to navigate between the two extremes of Greßmann's attempts at solution from the history of religion[7] and Drijvers's soteriological-theological reading.[8]

Interpretation

■ **1-3** The main part, beginning at 5, is preceded by a didactic introduction of three rhetorical questions. This "didactic poem" with the one "great denominator *ṭaibuta* [*sic*] χάρις"[9] may be addressed only to the

1 Mss.: Codex H, 17a–18b; Codex N, 149v (ܣ). Ed./trans.: Charlesworth, 92–96; Franzmann, 173–82; Lattke, 2:169–92 and 3:XXXII–XXXIII.
2 Harris and Mingana, 2:336.
3 See Lattke, *Bedeutung*, 3:31–178.
4 Spitta, 297.
5 Harnack, 55.
6 Harris and Mingana, 2:340.
7 Hugo Greßmann, "Die Oden Salomos," *Internationale Wochenschrift für Wissenschaft, Kunst und Technik* 5 (1911) 14–18; idem, "Ode Salomos 23," SPAW.PH (1923) 618–24.
8 Han J. W. Drijvers, "Kerygma und Logos in den Oden Salomos dargestellt am Beispiel der 23. Ode," in Adolf M. Ritter, ed., *Kerygma und Logos: Beiträge zu den geistesgeschichtlichen Beziehungen zwischen Antike und Christentum. Festschrift für Carl Andresen zum 70. Geburtstag* (Göttingen: Vandenhoeck & Ruprecht, 1979) 156–70; cf. Lattke, *Bedeutung*, 3:337.
9 Abramowski, 50.

audience glimpsed in the transition of 4a-c (see stanza II below). But these esoterica, linked to the end of Ode 22—like the "quite impersonal description of the letter, the wheel, the head"[10]—have a more general significance (cf. *Ode* 32) and can be thematically integrated with most of the remaining of the *Odes*—unlike the subsequent narration. These rhetorical questions, however, are hardly comparable in function to John 1:1-18 in the history of salvation as a "prologue"[11] to the principal section notable for its mythological content and "fanciful imagery."[12]

In Wis 3:1-9 there is a "poem of Wisdom,"[13] which ends as follows:[14]

οἱ πεποιθότες ἐπ᾽ αὐτῷ συνήσουσιν ἀλήθειαν,
καὶ οἱ πιστοὶ ἐν ἀγάπῃ προσμενοῦσιν αὐτῷ·
ὅτι χάρις καὶ ἔλεος τοῖς ἐκλεκτοῖς αὐτοῦ.

Those who trust in him will understand truth,
and the faithful will abide with him in love,
because grace and mercy are upon his elect ones.

This accumulation of related key words, *πέποιθα*, *ἀγάπη*, *χάρις*, and *ἐκλεκτός*, but also *συνίημι* (see on 4b below), leads Harris and Mingana to the correct conclusion: "So far we might classify the Ode as one of the Wisdom Odes, and as half-Gnostic" (cf. Wis 4:15).[15] Considering the discrepancy between the Greek text and Syriac translation of Wis 3:9 and 4:15,[16] it is possible, at least in the case of *Ode* 23:1-4, to take the further step of agreeing with Greßmann that "the interpretation must rest on the original Greek."[17]

All three parallel teachings (1a, 2a, and 3a) reflect the use of *εἶναί τινος* in the sense of "belong."[18] The central term *χάρις*/ܛܝܒܘܬܐ (*taybūṯā* [2a]), which refers to God's redeeming and exclusively justifying "act of grace,"[19] allows the conclusion that *χαρά*/ܚܕܘܬܐ (*ḥaḏuṯā* [1a]) also describes the soteriological "state of joy,"[20] and that *ἀγάπη*/ܚܘܒܐ (*ḥubbā* [3a]) is God's own "love," not a pious love of God, much less the various kinds of love among human beings (see Excursus 2).[21]

Because 4 is a direct address, it is not possible to limit the nominalized plural of *ἅγιος*/ܩܕܝܫܐ (*qaddīšā*; cf. 7:16; 22:12 ܣ)[22] or the similar form of *ἐκλεκτός*/ܓܒܝܐ (*gaḇyā*; cf. 4:8; 8:20; 33:13)[23] to "angels." Both terms, which appear conjoined in the "commendatory postscript" of *Mart. Pol.* 22:1 (*ἐπὶ σωτηρίᾳ τῇ τῶν ἁγίων ἐκλεκτῶν*, "for the salvation of the Holy Elect"),[24] refer primarily to an esoteric Gnosticizing group of human beings. The masculine plurals in 1a, 2a, and 3a should, of course, be understood inclusively.

The central lines of the three strictly parallel tricola also interpret each other. The conjunction *καί*/ܘ (*ʾu-*) and interrogative pronoun *τίς*/ܡܢܘ (*man-ū*) are followed in two cases by the imperfect with future sense of *ἐνδύομαι*/ܠܒܫ (*lḇeš*) in a metaphorical sense (1b; 3b; see Table 2).[25] Since the central verb *λαμβάνω*/ܢܣܒ (*nsaḇ*) in 2b fluctuates between active and passive meanings ("take" or "receive"),[26] this note on the verb of the preceding and following verses is relevant: "The mid[dle] sense is not always clearly right; the pass[ive] is somet[imes] better."[27] The object suffixes in ܣ, of course, take their gender from their referents "joy" (feminine), "grace" (feminine), and "love" (masculine), but all three correspond to the accusative of *αὐτή*.[28]

Although the final lines 1c, 2c, and 3c all begin with the particles *εἰ μή*/ܐܠܐ ܐܢ (*ʾellā ʾen*),[29] the remainder of 1c abandons parallelism, replacing the demonstrative pronoun ܗܢܘܢ (*hānnōn*, third masculine plural) and the relative conjunction ܕ (*d-*) with the personal pronoun

10 Kittel, 20.
11 Drijvers, "Ode 23," 156–57.
12 Greßmann, "Ode 23," 619.
13 Georgi, 410.
14 See Rahlfs, 2:348.
15 Harris and Mingana, 2:337. Neither the introduction nor the main section qualifies *Ode* 23 as an "Epiphany hymn" (contra Schille, 116).
16 Emerton, *Wisdom*, 4, 6.
17 Greßmann, "Ode 23," 616.
18 BDF and BDR §162 (7).
19 Cf. 5:3; 9:5; 25:9; 29:5; 34:6; 37:4; and see Excursus 33; also Brockelmann, *Lexicon*, 270; BDAG, *s.v.* *χάρις*, 4.
20 Cf. 7:2; 15:1; 31:3, 6-7; 32:1; and see Excursus 32; also BDAG, *s.v.* *χαρά*; Payne Smith, 1:1199.
21 BDAG, *s.v.* *ἀγάπη*; Payne Smith, 1:1171.
22 BDAG, *s.v.* *ἅγιος*; Payne Smith, 2:3500.
23 BDAG, *s.v.* *ἐκλεκτός*; Payne Smith, 1:637 (plural masculine emphatic passive participle).
24 Lake, 2:340–41; see also Buschmann, 373.
25 See BDAG, *s.v.* *ἐνδύω*; Payne Smith, 2:1887.
26 See BDAG, *s.v.* *λαμβάνω*; Payne Smith, 2:2392.
27 BDAG, *s.v.* *ἐνδύω*, 2b.

ܗܢܘܢ (*hennōn*), which refers to the "holy ones" of 1a and by the use of ܒܠܚܘܕ (*ba-lḥōḏ*), an "adv[erb] formed from ܒ, ܠ and r[oo]t ܚܕ"[30] (𝔊 must have been αὐτοὶ μόνοι), dualistically excludes all other persons. This forms the link to the "elect ones," who are defined as those who "trust" in grace (2c; cf. 15:10; 33:13; in 𝔊 probably πεποιθότες ἐπ' αὐτῇ)[31] and as those who "gained" love and to whom, therefore, it "belongs" (3c; cf. 33:12; John 5:42; 1 John 4:16).[32] The prepositional phrase ܡܢ ܒܪܫܝܬ (*men b-rēšīt*), which in 𝔊 would have been ἀπ' ἀρχῆς rather than ἐξ ἀρχῆς (cf. 4:14; 41:9; 2 Thess 2:13 *v.l.*; and see Excursus 23 below),[33] expresses the fact that "joy, grace, and love are *predestined gifts*."[34]

■ **4** In this tricolon, whose "inclusio . . . is formed by the repetition of ܝܕܥܬܗ in 4a and 4c,"[35] as in stanza I, the key word "grace" occupies a central position (see 2a above). N should be considered the primary text for the following reason. H omits the major part of 4b, as Charlesworth explains: "The cause is *parablepsis* facilitated by the *homoeoteleuton* of the repeated ܕܡܪܝܐ."[36] However, the omission must have occurred at an earlier stage of the transmission, since 4a in H does not have ܡܪܝܐ (*māryā*) but ܡܪܝܡܐ (*mrayymā* = "Most High").[37] So it was already theologically established in the source document of H that the "Lord" of stanza II is the "Most High" (see 18b below) and not his "son" (see 22b below). The ܘ (*ʾu-*) that H omits at the beginning of 4c (= 4b[H], since the stanza is only a bicolon in H) is merely a stylistic difference.

There is no reason to believe that the Greek text of the imperative of salvation in 4a should have begun with πορεύεσθε.[38] The Pa. ܗܠܟ (*hallek*), "walk," can be assumed to represent a form of περιπατέω (cf. 10:6; 17:4; 33:13; 38:5).[39] The appended prepositional phrase emphasizes the figurative sense of the verb as the "walk of life" (cf., from a stylistic point of view, Col 2:6: ἐν αὐτῷ περιπατεῖτε, "live in him").[40] The "*gnōsis* of the Lord" here, as in Rom 11:33 (βάθος . . . γνώσεως θεοῦ, "depth of . . . knowledge of God"), is "knowledge as possessed by God."[41]

It is only in the promise of salvation of 4b (N) that the hearers are first said to "know" (cf. 8:12). The object of "know" is not the "Lord" himself, but his "grace" (cf., but only linguistically, 2 Cor 8:9: γινώσκετε γὰρ τὴν χάριν τοῦ κυρίου ἡμῶν Ἰησοῦ [Χριστοῦ]). Although Wis 3:9 had some influence (see above on stanza I), the imperfect of ܝܕܥ (*ʾidaʿ*) represents a form of γινώσκω, not of συνίημι.[42] This is the more likely since the "praise" of the "knowledge of God" in Rom 11:33 corresponds to the question in 11:34, τίς γὰρ ἔγνω νοῦν κυρίου; ("For who has known the mind of the Lord?").[43] And it is to this "Lord," not to his "grace,"[44] that the clichéd expression ܕܠܐ ܚܣܡܐ (*d-lā ḥsāmā*)[45] refers, which

28 Frankenberg, 22; Greßmann, "Ode 23," 617.
29 BDAG, *s.v.* εἰ, 6iα; Payne Smith, 1:192, 249.
30 Payne Smith, *Dictionary*, 46.
31 Payne Smith, 2:4433; BDAG, *s.v.* πείθω.
32 Payne Smith, 2:3651; BDAG, *s.vv.* ἔχω (aor[ist] 2: ἔσχον), κτάομαι (perf[ect] κέκτημαι = pres[ent] "possess"). Greßmann ("Ode 23," 617) prefers the aorist and offers this retroversion: εἰ μὴ οἱ ἐκτήσαντο αὐτὴν ἀπ' ἀρχῆς. Ignatius *Eph.* 14:2 is not a parallel in content, since it deals with human love as the opposite of hatred (οὐδὲ ἀγάπην κεκτημένος μισεῖ [Fischer, 153–55, with references to 1 John 3:6 and 5:18]; cf. Ehrman, 1:232–35).
33 Payne Smith, 2:3908; BDAG, *s.v.* ἀρχή .
34 Bernard, 98. Although Gal 5:22 mentions ἀγάπη and χαρά among others as καρπὸς τοῦ πνεύματος, the passage probably did not influence *Ode* 23 (contra Bernard, 98, who also mentions "the baptized" here).
35 Franzmann, 178.
36 Charlesworth, 95.
37 Greßmann bases his retroversion on H (ἐν τῇ γνώσει τοῦ ὑψίστου), which would be appropriate for 8:8. His text-critical note is unfortunately erroneous (see Greßmann, "Ode 23," 617).
38 Contra Frankenberg, 23; Greßmann, "Ode 23," 617.
39 Payne Smith, 1:1014.
40 BDAG, *s.v.* περιπατέω, 2.
41 Payne Smith, 1:1559; BDAG, *s.v.* γνῶσις, 1; cf. 6:6; 7:7, 21; 8:8, 12; 12:3; 17:7; and see Excursus 7.
42 BDAG, *s.v.* γινώσκω; Payne Smith, 1:1554–55; Greßmann "Ode 23," 617: γνώσεσθε.
43 Käsemann, 307; ET, 318.
44 Contra Greßmann, "Ode 23," 617; Klijn, 304.
45 Emerton, 713: "who is without envy."

need not be equated with the adverb ἀφθόνως (cf. the discussion and reconstruction of 20:7a).[46]

The repeated ܘ + ܠ in 4c (ʾu-la- and wa-l- in N; on H see above) represents καὶ εἰς . . . καὶ εἰς.[47] In the case of the first goal, it is difficult to decide whether the masculine ܕܝܨܐ (dyāṣā), derived from ܕܘܨ, ܕܨ (dāṣ), is a translation of ἀγαλλίαμα, ἀγαλλίασις or εὐφροσύνη.[48] What seems more important is that the possessive suffix of ܕܝܨܐ corresponds to the objective genitive αὐτοῦ (cf. 8:1; 21:9; 40:4; 41:7). The same is true of the possessive suffix of ܝܕܥܬܐ (ʾidaʿtā) at the end of stanza II, so that, by the inclusion of 4b, it alludes to the "knowledge" that is directed toward God the Lord and Most High and cannot be bounded by any epistemology. Such *gnōsis* in its "fullness" is the soteriological complement of God's *plērōma* (17:7; see Excursus 35).[49] Whether there is a reference "to the Incarnation"[50] will have to be discovered now in the exegesis of the main part of the Ode.

■ **5-6** Although it is hardly possible to find a connection between stanzas I–II and stanzas III–X, the two possessive suffixes in 5a and b refer, in the existing form of *Ode* 23, to the "Lord" (N) or "Most High" (H) of 4, who is identical with the "Most High Father" and "Father" (see 18b and 22a below). To get a feeling for the meaning it held for its original readers and hearers, it is necessary to skim through the whole section and discover that the strange "letter" (5a), which is sealed up from the many (8b), is a "tablet" written by the "finger of God" (21) for the Gnostics, that contains the Christian titles the "Father," the "Son," and the "Spirit" (22a-b). So this mythological writing belongs to a widespread species of "heavenly letters," which was no novelty in religious history for the generality of persons in ancient times, nor yet a theological book with seven seals for the elect.

In stanza III, the "letter"[51] from heaven is introduced in a comparison (5a), but the other metaphors and comparisons refer to ܨܒܝܢܐ (ṣebyānā, "will" [5b]). Since it is impossible to ascertain the exact meanings of the parallel terms ܡܚܫܒܬܐ (maḥšabtā) and ܨܒܝܢܐ (ṣebyānā) (see Excursus 9),[52] it should not surprise that Frankenberg translates them by βουλή/προαίρεσις[53] while Greßmann uses ἐπίνοια/βουλή,[54] which comes nearer to the basic meanings of the roots ܚܫܒ and ܨܒܐ (both retroversions agree on ἐγένετο ὡς).[55]

46 Contra Frankenberg, 23. Emerton's suggested alternative translation (p. 713) is not quite grammatically correct, since ܕܠܐ ܚܣܡܐ is attributive (emphatic masculine, its status agreeing with ܡܪܝܐ), as in the Greek phrase χάρις τοῦ κυρίου τοῦ ἀφθόνου. Drijvers's interpretation is strained: "The second line of verse 4 is anti-Marcionite in its emphasis that the Lord knows no envy; this leads back to Paradise and the beginning of the history of salvation" (see Drijvers, "Ode 23," 157).

47 BDAG, *s.v.* καί, 1f.

48 Payne Smith, 1:847; BDAG, *s.vv.* ἀγαλλίασις, εὐφροσύνη; LEH, *s.vv.* ἀγαλλίαμα, ἀγαλλίασις, εὐφροσύνη. "Esth. viii. 16" is the first reference following ܕܝܨܐ in Payne Smith (1:847), which raises a suspicion that Abbott's unsustainable hypothesis (p. 420) that *Ode* 23 is "an allusion to that deliverance of Israel which is mentioned in the book of Esther and which gave rise to one of the most popular festivals of the Jews, Purim" is not due only to the key word "letter."

49 BDAG, *s.v.* πλήρωμα, 2; Payne Smith, 2:2128.

50 Suggested by Drijvers, "Ode 23," 157.

51 Harnack (p. 54) is not correct in saying: "It is not clear that he [viz., the singer] intends something specific by the letter." The specificities of the letter are elucidated step by step in the subsequent stanzas. On the placing of *Ode* 23 in the species of "heavenly letters," see Rudolf Stübe, *Der Himmelsbrief: Ein Beitrag zur allgemeinen Religionsgeschichte* (Tübingen: Mohr Siebeck, 1918) 33–37; Adolf Deissmann, *Light from the Ancient East: The New Testament Illustrated by Recently Discovered Texts of the Graeco-Roman World* (trans. Lionel R. M. Strachan; New York/London: Harper, 1927) 245 n. 2, ET of *Licht vom Osten: Das Neue Testament und die neuentdeckten Texte der hellenistisch-römischen Welt* (4th ed.; Tübingen: Mohr Siebeck, 1923) 208 n. 2; Walther Koehler, "Himmelsbrief," *RGG*² 3 (1928) 1901–2; Alfred Bertholet, *Die Macht der Schrift in Glauben und Aberglauben* (Abhandlungen der Deutschen Akademie der Wissenschaften zu Berlin, Philologisch-historische Klasse, Jahrgang 1948, Nr. 1; Berlin: Akademie-Verlag, 1949) 9–13; Johannes Schneider, "Brief," *RAC* 2 (1954) 566 (= "revelation of God"), 576. On the different classes of "heavenly letters," see also Georg Graf, "Der vom Himmel gefallene Brief," *Zeitschrift für Semitistik und verwandte Gebiete* 6 (1928) 10–23. If the "letter" is imagined as a scroll (see 8b and 16a below), the metaphor of the "arrow" is easier to understand.

52 Payne Smith, 1:1397, 2:3354.

53 Frankenberg, 23.

54 Greßmann, "Ode 23," 617.

God's "will" is the subject of 5b ꜱ, but poetic logic suggests a glance further back to 5a at the "thought" like a/the "letter." And stanzas IV–VI will continue with the subject of this semi-personified heavenly letter. Looking forward to the new images of 6, it is preferable to consider the Pe. ܢܚܬ (*nḥeṯ*) as describing a "flying down" rather than a "descending." Whether 𝔊 used *κατέβη*[56] or *κατῆλθεν* (cf. Jas 3:15)[57] is impossible to decide.[58] The term "height" (in 𝔊 either *τὸ ὕψος* or *τὰ ὕψιστα*) stands for heaven in a transcendent and theological sense (see Excursus 17).[59] But for the ancients, the distinction between that and the starry skies was even less sharp than it is for moderns, so that the two terms of battle, *βέλος*/ܓܐܪܐ (*gērā*) and *τόξον*/ܩܫܬܐ (*qeštā*), "arrow" and "bow," would have likely evoked the constellation *Τοξότης/Sagittarius* or even an actual "deity."[60] The *hapax legomenon* ܐܫܬܕܪ (Ethpa. *ʾeštaddar*), "was sent," really goes better with the feminine Syriac word "letter" as subject than with the masculine ܨܒܝܢܐ (*ṣeḇyānā*).[61] If 𝔊 had used a finite form of *ἀποστέλλω* or *πέμπω*, it would have been ambiguous, although the second of the possible verbs is regularly used in connection with "a document, a letter."[62] So the "letter" intrudes into the already mixed metaphor.

The Ethpe. of ܫܕܐ (*šḏā*), "shot," in 6b unambiguously refers to the "arrow," and will have corresponded to Greek *βεβλημένον*.[63] This is reinforced by the idiomatic use of ܩܛܝܪܐ (*qṭīrā*, passive participle of ܩܛܪ [*qṭar*]) with the instrumental preposition ܒ (*b*-), which is more likely to have translated *μετὰ βίας* ("with force") than the adverb *βιαίως* ("forceful").[64] None of these images agrees with Drijvers's hypothesis that "Christ represents the thought and will of God"[65] and "that the incarnate Logos who carries out God's plan from beginning to end, is compared to the heavenly letter, indeed in some sense is that letter."[66] After all, the name of the "Logos"/"Son" is written *on* the letter (see 22b below).

■ **7-8a** Though 7-10 are closely connected, they can be divided by content and form into three sections (7-8a, 8b-9, and 10). The first section can be characterized as follows: "The central focus of the tricolon is the violent intention expressed by the series of three Peal infinitives in 7b. 7a and 8a are closely connected semantically, the action in 8a following easily from 7a."[67]

The Greek original of stanza IV is easy to make out, especially as the objective suffix occurs only once in 7b (third feminine singular = *αὐτήν* in 𝔊), and it will make the interpretation of this dramatic scene easier if a reconstruction, based on the retroversions of Frankenberg and Greßmann, is inserted here:

> *καὶ ὥρμησαν ἐπὶ τὴν ἐπιστολὴν χεῖρες πολλαί*
> *τοῦ ἁρπάσαι καὶ λαβεῖν καὶ ἀναγνῶναι αὐτήν·*
> *καὶ ἔφυγεν ἀπὸ τῶν δακτύλων αὐτῶν.*[68]

Stanza IV is enclosed by the parallel terms of power *χείρ*/ܐܝܕܐ (*ʾiḏā* [7a]) and *δάκτυλος*/ܨܒܥܐ (*ṣeḇʿā* [8a]), "hand" and "finger," both of which mythologically stand for "hostile power,"[69] though without "anti-Jewish

55 See BDAG, *s.v.* *γίνομαι*.
56 Greßmann, "Ode 23," 617.
57 Frankenberg, 23.
58 Payne Smith, 2:2343; BDAG, *s.vv.* *καταβαίνω*, *κατέρχομαι*.
59 Payne Smith, 2:3860, 3864; BDAG, *s.vv.* *ὕψιστος*, *ὕψος*.
60 See Payne Smith, 1:767, 2:3772; Friedrich Hauck, "*βέλος*," *ThWNT* 1 (1933) 607; *TDNT* 1:608–9; Emilie Boer, "Sternbilder, Sternglaube, Sternschnuppen," *KP* 5 (1975), 361.
61 Perhaps the word "arrow," which is masculine in Syriac and occurs in the immediately following comparison, influenced the form of the verb.
62 BDAG, *s.vv.* *ἀποστέλλω*, *πέμπω*; cf. the Pa. ܫܕܪ (*šaddar*) in Payne Smith, 2:4069.
63 Greßmann, "Ode 23," 617; cf. Payne Smith, 2:4064.
64 Contra Frankenberg, 23; cf. Payne Smith, 2:3589.
65 Drijvers, "Ode 23," 159.
66 Ibid., 160–61.
67 Franzmann, 179.
68 On the "*final* (or *consecutive*)" use of the infinitive with *τοῦ*, see BDF and BDR §400 (5). Frankenberg does not explain why he substituted *δακτυλίων*, (signet-) "rings," for "fingers" in his text-critical appendix (pp. 37–44) or in his discussion of *Ode* 23 (pp. 89–91). In other respects, his translation and reconstruction of 8a is to be preferred to Greßmann's (*ἐξέφυγεν δὲ τοὺς δακτύλους αὐτῶν*), although Syriac often uses ܘ (*ʾu- or w-*) for the particle *δέ*, which better brings out the contrast between 7a and 8a (see Greßmann, "Ode 23," 617; also BDAG, *s.v.* *δέ*).
69 BDAG, *s.vv.* *δάκτυλος*, *χείρ*; Payne Smith, 1:1546–47, 2:3357.

prejudice."[70] Terms of multitude are numerous in this Ode (see 14a, 15a, 19b below). There are also mythological connections to *Ode* 38, which mentions both the "many" led astray and the "hands of the Deceivers" (38:12a, 15b). The adjective "many"[71] has here a clear "negative connotation,"[72] but only in the sense of a thronging and dangerous mob, not as an opposite to "Christian coteries . . . , which consider themselves an (intellectual) elite superior to the Jews, who could not defeat the Christ."[73]

The contrasting verbs of 7a and 8a form part of the *inclusio* of stanza IV and contribute to the sense of personification. The thing that has come down from on high begins to behave independently, is assaulted,[74] but "escapes" triumphantly.[75] The "fingers" of the hostile "hands" are finally powerless before the "finger of God" (see 23:21b below).

What these antagonistic powers unsuccessfully intended is explained in the central colon 7b. They wanted to "snatch" or even "steal" the letter.[76] Therefore the infinitive of λαμβάνω/ܢܣܒ (*nsab*) in this case can only mean active taking possession (see Excursus 41).[77] The verb ἀναγινώσκω/ܩܪܐ (*qrā*), which occurs again in 23:10, has "to call out" as its primary meaning in Syriac,[78] so the aim of the assault was to "read" aloud or "recite"[79] the letter and thus appropriate it.

■ **8b-9** The internal logic that Greßmann reconstructed in the "first part (v. 5-10)"[80] has provoked a rejoinder from Franzmann: "This stanza appears to interrupt the flow of the report from stanza 4 to stanza 6, by providing a commentary on the attitude towards the letter of those against it and a statement about the power of its seal."[81] This observation on the form of the stanza is the more pertinent since the fear evoked by the "letter" and its "seal" (8b) is so unlike the attacking frenzy of the previous image (7a-b).

"Who 'they' are is not revealed by the impersonal use of the 3rd person plural."[82] Clearly, there has been a scene change. Center stage is the thrice-repeated σφραγίς/ܚܬܡܐ (*ḥāṯmā*, "seal").[83] Although the translators avoided the Syriac term ܛܒܥܐ (*ṭabʿā*),[84] the question raised by Rev 5:1-3 is equally relevant here, in a slightly amended form: "how should one" "picture to oneself" the document and its "seal"?[85] It is clear that the "letter" that aroused fear[86] was "sealed" to "keep secret" its contents.[87] This reinforces the notion, influenced by Ezek 2:9 (κεφαλὶς βιβλίου, "roll, volume of a book"), that the letter is a scroll (see 16a below).[88]

The fear is explained in 9a by a statement that is reminiscent of Rev 5:3 (οὐδεὶς ἐδύνατο . . . ἀνοῖξαι τὸ βιβλίον, "no one . . . was able to open the scroll"). Linguistically, it is based on a construction with ἐξῆν

70 Drijvers, "Ode 23," 162.
71 Payne Smith, 2:2518.
72 Drijvers, "Ode 23," 162, referring to 25:5.
73 Ibid.
74 The Pe. ܪܗܛ (*rheṭ*) corresponds to τρέχω everywhere else (even in 16b; cf. Payne Smith, 2:3833–34), but here, combined with the preposition ܥܠ (*ʿal*), it represents the Greek expression ὁρμάω ἐπί τινα (BDAG, *s.v.* ὁρμάω: "rush at, fall upon someone").
75 BDAG, *s.v.* φεύγω. The Pe. ܥܪܩ (*ʿraq*) in 20a has a different connotation; see Payne Smith, 2:2997 and BDAG, *s.v.* ἐκφεύγω.
76 See BDAG, *s.vv.* ἁρπάζω and διαρπάζω as possible originals of ܚܛܦ (*ḥṭap̄*, Payne Smith, 1:1447–48).
77 BDAG, *s.v.* λαμβάνω; Payne Smith, 2:2392.
78 Payne Smith, 2:3712–14, 3717.
79 BDAG, *s.v.* ἀναγινώσκω.
80 Greßmann, "Ode 23," 619.
81 Franzmann, 179.
82 Lattke, *Oden*, 165. I now withdraw my assertion that there are "direct or indirect connections" between *Ode* 23 and the "so-called 'Hymn of the Pearl.'" But cf. Johan Ferreira, *The Hymn of the Pearl: The Syriac and Greek Texts with Introduction, Translations, and Notes* (Early Christian Studies 3; Sydney: St Pauls Publications, 2002) 48–49, 74 nn. 77 and 78.
83 BDAG, *s.v.* σφραγίς; Payne Smith, 1:1410.
84 See Payne Smith, 1:1429.
85 Bousset, *Offenbarung*, 255.
86 See Payne Smith, 1:862, *s.v.* ܕܚܠ (*dḥel*): "cum ܡܢ pers., vel rei;" BDAG, *s.v.* φοβέω transitive (+ τί).
87 See BDAG, *s.vv.* κατασφραγίζω and σφραγίζω. This fear in 8b has as little connection with the "fear of the Jews and their rulers of the Christ" (Drijvers, "Ode 23," 162) as with theological "reverence" (see BDAG, *s.v.* φοβέω, 2).
Drijvers correctly emphasizes that the "seal" of *Ode* 23 is neither the "seal of baptism" nor a "talisman against the wicked archons" (see Drijvers, "Ode 23," 162 n. 31, with references).
88 On ancient letter rolls, see Peter L. Schmidt, "Epistolographie," *KP* 2 (1967) 324; on ancient seals, see Frederick Norman Pryce and Donald Emrys Strong, "Seals," *OCD*[2] (1970) 968–69. It should be

+ dative of the person + present/aorist infinitive.[89] If the Greek expression had been οὐκ ἴσχυον,[90] it would have been represented by the negated Pe. perfect ܐܫܟܚ (ʾeškaḥ). The combination of the adjectival passive participle of ܫܠܛ (šlaṭ) with an enclitic ܗܘܐ (-wā) makes it clear that the unsuccessful attempt occurred in the "past."[91] That the infinitive of the Pe. ܫܪܐ (šrā) corresponds to an infinitive of λύω[92] is corroborated by Rev 5:2 (λῦσαι τὰς σφραγῖδας αὐτοῦ, "to break its seals"; cf. also the textual variants in Rev 5:5). It is interesting that H, by the use of the third masculine singular possessive suffix, ascribes the "seal" not to the letter scroll (as N does) but directly to the Lord or the Most High, whom the seal represents, as his "mark of ownership"[93] or "sign of possession."[94]

This Lord and Most High is also the referent of the term δύναμις/ܚܝܠܐ (ḥaylā, "power") in 9b (cf. 32:3; 39:1; and see Excursus 29).[95] The clumsy Syriac structure is probably due to a repetition of the article in 𝔊 (perhaps ἡ δύναμις ἡ ἐπὶ τῆς σφραγῖδος), and ܓܝܪ (gēr) is thus actually a causal particle corresponding to γάρ,[96] not to ἐπεί.[97] Unlike the numerous seals surviving from antiquity that bear symbols of rulers or deities, this mythological "seal"—and thus the whole heavenly letter—bears the "power of God,"[98] which, in its mysterious superiority,[99] is similar to no-thing and no-body.

■ **10** The mythological narrative now turns to a third group, who are as indeterminate as the assailants of stanza IV and the fearful ones of stanza V. Despite the "Johannine theology, which recognises a direct connection between hearing, following and understanding," stanza VI is not an allusion to John 1:37-39 and does not lay any "emphasis on seeing."[100] With the "word-pair ܐܙܠ – ܚܙܐ",[101] 10a paints a lively picture in which the "letter" almost becomes a person to be "followed" (cf. linguistically, 17:5).[102] There is, however, no trace of discipleship. The use of the Pe. ܚܙܐ (ḥzā) has no parallel in the *Odes of Solomon*, and the many Greek equivalents available make it nearly impossible to reconstruct.[103] At any rate, the retroversion οἳ εἶδον αὐτήν deserves a large question mark.[104]

The goal of the pursuers is shown by the conjunction ܕ (d-) with the imperfect of ܝܕܥ (ʾidaʿ).[105] The verb, which refers to three future circumstances, might well be translated as "learn."[106] Verse 10a is one of the "few cases in which the words are not interpreted Gnostically or are of no importance for a coherent soteriological usage" (Excursus 7). Since the Pe. ܫܪܐ (šrā) has just been used in 9a, "it is perhaps not too fanciful to assume that in the use of the verb ܫܪܐ = to settle (intransitive), the overtones of the transitive meaning 'to break' (e.g. a seal) or 'to open' (e.g. a letter) might resonate with it."[107] However, passages such as Rev 12:12 and 13:6 suggest that the Greek *Vorlage* of this intransitive verb was

---

noted that the Greek βιβλίον can be translated by ܐܓܪܬܐ, as in Matt 19:7 (Payne Smith, 1:33).

89 As Greßmann, "Ode 23," 617, rightly has it: οὐκ ἐξῆν αὐτοῖς λῦσαι . . . ; see BDAG, *s.v.* ἔξεστιν, 1b; Klein, *Wörterbuch*, 100.

90 Frankenberg, 23.

91 Brockelmann, *Grammatik*, §214; see Payne Smith, 2:4177, 4180–81.

92 Payne Smith, 2:4305–6, 4307; BDAG, *s.v.* λύω.

93 Peter Welten, "Siegel und Stempel," in Galling, 299–307, esp. 299.

94 Drijvers, "Ode 23," 162.

95 Payne Smith, 1:1258; BDAG, *s.v.* δύναμις.

96 Greßmann, "Ode 23," 617; cf. Lattke, "Wörter," 289–90 = idem, *Bedeutung*, 4:138.

97 Contra Frankenberg, 23.

98 BDAG, *s.v.* δύναμις.

99 The Syriac phrase ܡܝܬܪ ܡܢ (*myattar men*) does not correspond to μείζων (BDAG, *s.v.*) but to the comparative κρείττων/κρείσσων (Payne Smith, 1:1653), which means "more prominent, higher in rank, preferable" (BDAG, *s.v.* κρείττων) and also "stronger, more powerful, mightier," "surpassing" (Adolf Kaegi, *Benselers griechisch-deutsches Schulwörterbuch* [12th ed.; Leipzig/Berlin: Teubner, 1904] 513, with numerous similar senses).

100 Contra Drijvers, "Ode 23," 163.

101 Franzmann, 180.

102 Payne Smith, 1:107, *s.v.* ܐܙܠ (*ʾezal*) + ܒܬܪ (*bāṯar*); Nöldeke §156; BDAG, *s.v.* ἀκολουθέω + dative.

103 Payne Smith, 1:1233.

104 See Frankenberg, 23; Greßmann, "Ode 23," 617.

105 See Payne Smith, 1:1554–55.

106 BDAG, *s.v.* γινώσκω; Drijvers, "Ode 23," 155. On the three participles in 10b-d, see Nöldeke §272: "in a considerable number of instances the Part[iciple] stands for a future action, instead of the Imp[er]f[ect], even in dependent clauses."

107 Drijvers, "Ode 23," 163.

σκηνόω,[108] not a paronomastic *καταλύω*[109] or the middle voice of *καταπαύω*.[110]

The final bicolon 10c-d, which, following the manuscripts, is properly "divided into two parts,"[111] also depends on the verb *γινώσκω*/ܝܕܥ (*ʾidaʿ*) and makes the heavenly letter an object to be read aloud (see on 7b above) and therefore heard. The expected paronomasia of 𝔊 with *γινώσκω* (10b) and *ἀναγινώσκω* (10c) was not reproduced in 𝔖. Like ܚܙܐ (*ḥzā*) in 10a, the Pe. ܫܡܥ (*šmaʿ*) in 10d has no parallel in the *Odes of Solomon*, although the verb, corresponding to *ἀκούω*, occurs a number of times.[112]

■ **11-16** In spite of some "correspondence" between the Hindu "wheel of sovereignty"—and the Buddhist "wheel of teaching"—and the "wheel" of stanza VII, which is also "seen almost as an autonomous being,"[113] "the wheel refers to the chariot of God, the Merkabah, as described in detail in Ezekiel 1, the site of God's glory."[114] If one asks the right question, "Is there anything in Scripture about which the writer appears to be thinking?,"[115] it is impossible to overlook the heterogeneous description of that prophet's vision, and thus one will avoid being carried away by the implausible speculation that the term *τροχός*/ܓܝܓܠܐ (*gīglā*) describes "here, as elsewhere, the heavenly sphere or rather the study of the heavenly sphere, i.e. the Chaldaean lore."[116]

The reason why the "wheel" in 11a stands for the whole "chariot"[117] is not to be found in the "combination of the Merkabah and the Cross . . . by Ephraem Syrus" and the "connection" he makes "to the Ark of the Covenant (Ex[od] 37:6-9),"[118] but in Ezekiel's avoidance of the term "chariot" (see Ezek 1:15-21; 3:13; 10:2-7).[119] If "the vocabulary was in process of development" at that time,[120] at least the term "chariot" or "royal chariot" had been "expressly" introduced by Ezek 43:3 LXX (*ἡ ὅρασις τοῦ ἅρματος*, "the vision of the chariot")[121] well before Ephraem. Whether this chariot wheel[122] belongs to a four-wheeled vehicle is as difficult to determine as

108 BDAG, *s.v.* *σκηνόω*; should be added to Payne Smith, 2:4306 or 4308.

109 Suggested by Greßmann, "Ode 23," 617.

110 Frankenberg, 23.

111 Contra Diettrich, 87.

112 See BDAG, *s.v.* *ἀκούω*; Payne Smith, 2:4214. If the image were not of reading or reciting (10c), the personified "letter" might itself have been taken to be a speaking and therefore audible being.

113 Greßmann, "Ode 23," 623; see also Kittel, 96–98; Bauer, 604.

114 Drijvers, "Ode 23," 165; see also Hermann Gunkel, *Das Märchen im Alten Testament* (Religionsgeschichtliche Volksbücher für die deutsche christliche Gegenwart, II. Reihe, 23.–26. Heft; Tübingen: Mohr Siebeck, 1921) 59–62; Charlesworth, 96.

115 Abbott, 417; see also 426–30.

116 Contra Diettrich, 87. Starting from the fact that the constellation *Ursa major*, called ܐܕܠܐ (*ʾādlā*) in Syriac (Payne Smith, 1:37), is also known as ܓܝܓܠܐ ܪܒܬܐ (*gīglā rabbtā*) (Payne Smith, 1:713), I have tried to find a matching reference to a "great wheel," perhaps *ὁ τροχὸς ὁ μέγας*, for the constellation *Plaustrum magnum* or *Currus magnus* (see LSJ, *s.vv.* *ἅμαξα* and *Ἄρκτος*), in ancient Greek writings. This would have made it possible to interpret *Ode* 23 astronomically, although the processes it describes do not match the behavior of the fixed stars. Chris Montgomery was a great help in this research, which unfortunately had a negative result. However, Syriac usage shows that "wheel" can be used for "wain." The phrase *τροχὸς τῆς γενέσεως* (Jas 3:6; BDAG, *s.v.* *τροχός*) has no more connection with this passage than the *τροχὸς ἁμάξης* of Isa 28:27. In a discussion of Daniel C. Snell ("The Wheel in Proverbs xx 26," *VT* 39 [1989] 503–7, esp. 504–5), Franzmann has shown that "a study of Ode of Solomon xxiii both indicates that it may have closer links to Prov. xx 26 than the Hittite texts cited by Snell and sup[p]orts the interpretation of the image in an agricultural sense" (see Majella Franzmann, "The Wheel in Proverbs xx 26 and Ode of Solomon xxiii 11-16," *VT* 41 [1991] 121).

117 Lattke, *Oden*, 166: "synecdoche"; see also Drijvers, "Ode 23," 166: "pars pro toto."

118 Drijvers, "Ode 23," 165.

119 Zimmerli, *Ezechiel*, 64–68.

120 Ibid., 66.

121 Ibid., 1071.

122 On the expression "chariot wheels," cf., e.g., 3 Kgdms 7:19 (*καὶ τὸ ἔργον τῶν τροχῶν ἔργον τροχῶν ἅρματος*, "And the work of the wheels was as the work of chariot wheels"; Rahlfs 1:643; Brenton, 453). The interpretation of the wheel as the "wheel of fortune" is far-fetched (Preserved Smith, "The Disciples of John and the Odes of Solomon," *The Monist: A Quarterly Magazine Devoted to the Philosophy of Science* 25 [1915] 180; cf. Lattke, *Bedeutung*, 3:164–65).

the exact nuance of the Pa. ܩܒܠ (*qabbel*). However, 11b suggests that the wheel is more likely to have passively received or accepted the letter, represented by the third feminine singular objective suffix, than to have actively laid hold of it and seized it (see Excursus 41).[123]

In 11b, it becomes manifest that "[t]he limits of the stanza are clearly delineated by the exclusive use of the key word ܓܠܓܠܐ and by the inclusio formed between 11a-b and 16b-c by the occurrence of ܓܠܓܠܐ in 11a and 16b and by ܐܬܝܐ ܗܘܬ/ܐܬܐ ܗܘܐ ܥܠܝܗ in 11b and 16c."[124] The construction Pe. ܐܬܐ (*ʾeṯā*), "came," with preposition ܥܠ (*ʿal*) corresponds to ἔρχομαι + ἐπί[125] and leaves the impression of a mythological invasion, "distinctly referred to the past" by the use of the participle ܐܬܝܐ (*ʾāṯyā*) and enclitic ܗܘܬ (*-wāṯ*).[126]

Verse 12 is only a monocolon in H, but that is at least doubtful for N. The term σημεῖον/ܐܬܐ (*ʾāṯā*, "sign") in 12a, quite unlike 27:2 and 42:1, does not refer to "the Cross as a symbol of power" (cf. 29:7-8 and 39:7).[127] The first question is whether the third feminine singular possessive suffix of the preposition ܥܡ (*ʿam*) refers to the "letter" or the "wheel." In the light of 22c, it would have to refer to the first term.[128] That would make the "sign" something like a "seal" on the "letter" (cf. Rom 4:11). On the other hand, one might say that the "letter" itself, with its inscription (21-22), is the "sign." In that case, the suffix refers to the "wheel." So in either case—directly *as* the letter or indirectly *on* the letter—the "sign" is attached to the "wheel."

In 12b the "sign" is modified by the genitives of ܡܠܟܘܬܐ (*malkūṯā*) and ܡܕܒܪܢܘܬܐ (*mḏabbrānūṯā*). The first term corresponds to βασιλεία and cannot be restricted to "Christ's kingdom" (cf. 18:3 and 22:12).[129] The still rarer second term may correspond to ἡγεμονία as an equivalent parallel to βασιλεία.[130] But κυβέρνησις is also possible,[131] so the following categorical assertion by Drijvers may only be valid for 36:8: "The Greek οἰκονομία is identical to the Syriac ܡܕܒܪܢܘܬܐ (*mḏabbrānūṯā*) and means divine providence."[132]

That 13-15 describes "conflicts"[133] is much clearer than the amount of the violence and destruction described.[134] For the exact nuances of the plethora of *hapax legomena* ܐܙܝܥ (*ʾazīʿ*, Aph. of *zāʿ*), ܚܨܕ (*ḥṣaḏ*), ܦܣܩ (Pa. *passeq*), ܚܡܠ (*ḥmal*), ܬܡܪ (*ṭmar*), and ܥܩܪ (*ʿqar*) can no longer be determined.[135] Some of the verbs seem connected to harvest (cf. Rev 14:15-16).[136] But the main impression is that the "wheel" was caused to tremble (13a); it chopped up everything (13b), heaped up all that was disturbing and "opposed" in a great pile (14a),[137] and used it to fill up whole rivers (14b). How un-"sophisticated"[138] and incomprehensible all this was can be seen by the reading "peoples" in 15a (N) in place of the *hapax legomenon* "forests" (H), a variant perhaps derived from Ezek 3:6, based on an interpretation of

123 See Payne Smith, 2:3468.

124 Franzmann, 180.

125 See Payne Smith, 1:414; BDAG, *s.v.* ἔρχομαι.

126 See Nöldeke §277. There is no parallel to the verbs ܐܬܐ and ܩܒܠ (with its synonym ܢܣܒ) in the *Odes of Solomon*.

127 Contra Drijvers, "Ode 23," 163; see Payne Smith, 1:412–13; BDAG, *s.v.* σημεῖον; Lattke, "Bildersprache," 100–101 = idem, *Bedeutung*, 4:24–26. "The stanza has strong semantic links to 39:7-9 (the sign from the Lord, the disturbing/dangerous action of passing over rivers) with some common vocabulary— ܐܬܐ, ܥܒܪ, ܢܗܪ̈ܘܬܐ, ܐܘܪܚܐ" (Franzmann, 180).

128 Zahn, 766.

129 Contra Drijvers, "Ode 23," 164.

130 Frankenberg, 23; Greßmann, "Ode 23," 617; cf. Payne Smith, 1:817–18; BDAG, *s.v.* ἡγεμονία: "chief command."

131 BDAG, *s.v.* κυβέρνησις: "administration."

132 Drijvers, "Ode 23," 164.

133 Harris and Mingana, 2:340.

134 Drijvers contradicts himself rejecting Daniélou's (see Jean Daniélou, *Théologie du judéo-christianisme* [Tournai: Desclée, 1958] 306–7) "equation of the cross and the wheel" and yet theorizing that behind the description of 13-15 there is "the symbolism of the cross as an axe or a ploughshare" (see Drijvers, "Ode 23," 165, 167).

135 See Payne Smith, 1:1106–7, 1351, 2:3195, 1:1303–4, 1486, 2:2968–69, listed in sequence as above.

136 See Majella Franzmann, "The Wheel in Proverbs xx 26 and Ode of Solomon xxiii 11–16," *VT* 41 (1991) 122; BDAG, *s.vv.* θερίζω, συνάγω.

137 See Payne Smith, 2:2520–21, 3476; BDAG, *s.vv.* ἐναντίος, πλῆθος.

138 Contra Drijvers, "Ode 23," 171.

ܥܩܪ (*ʿqar*) as "extirpate" instead of "uproot,"[139] though it does not fit as well with the ruthless image of track breaking (15b). It does not seem that "way" has any salvific connotation here, unlike other passages.[140] If ὁδός/ܐܘܪܚܐ (*ʾurḥā*) carries a positive sense, then the Pe. ܥܒܕ (*ʿbad*) would have the more neutral meaning "to lay,"[141] which would summarize and lead on to the more peaceful image of 16a-c, though the motion is still rolling forward. Since 18a has a play on the word κεφαλή/ܪܫܐ,[142] it is possible that in 16a also the term ܪܫܐ (*rēšā*) does not mean "head"—as the opposite of "feet"—but translates κεφαλίς and is derived from the LXX.[143]

Excursus 23: "Head," "Beginning," and "Head and Feet" in the *Odes of Solomon*

The two Syriac terms ܪܫܐ (*rēšā*, seventeen times in the singular, three times in the plural) and ܪܫܝܬܐ (*rēšītā*, in the phrase ܡܢ ܪܫܝܬܐ only in 11:4, elsewhere seven times in the synonymous phrase ܡܢ ܒܪܫܝܬ [*men b-rēšīṯ*]) may occasionally be interchangeable in translating ἀρχή = "beginning" (cf. 26:7),[144] but in the *Odes of Solomon* they are generally distinguished, in that the second expression is typically used like ἐξ/ἀπ᾿ ἀρχῆς in prepositional constructions,[145] while the first has a wider field of use and meaning.[146] In most cases it is clear that κεφαλή corresponds to ܪܫܐ and also to ⲁⲡⲉ.[147]

Except in 24:8a ("acted destructively . . . from the beginning") the passages where ἀρχή/ܪܫܝܬܐ occurs are theological and/or soteriological in nature with a strong emphasis on eschatological predestination and elements of dualism. "From the beginning" everything was set in order before God (4:14). "From the beginning and until the end," it is true that everything is of the Lord (6:4). The way that leads toward *gnōsis* goes "from the beginning until the end" (7:14). The redeemed one received the *gnōsis* of the Lord/the Most High "from the beginning until the end" (11:4). Trust in grace as well as possession of love "from the beginning" identifies the elect (23:2-3). The Father of Truth gained the redeemed Redeemer "from the beginning" (41:9).

The transition to passages using ܪܫܐ is to be found in 26:7, which also mentions the "extremity" of the heights (cf. 6:4; 7:14; 11:4). So the question is whether 𝔊 had ἀρχή or ἄκρον in place of ܪܫܐ (cf. Matt 24:31).[148] It seems to be a mixed metaphor, perhaps attempting to picture a three-dimensional infinity. It has a certain affinity to 33:3, which mentions the "summit of a peak" and the "end[s] of the earth."

Among the three witnesses to the plural of ܪܫܐ, 31:13 does not fit the pattern, since it occurs in the compound expression ܪܫܝ ܐܒܗܬܐ (*rēšay ʾabāhātā*), meaning "forefathers" or "ancestors" (cf. Rom 4:1).[149] In a sort of malediction dating back to Ps 7:17, the plural stands for the whole body of each of the persecutors (5:7 𝔖), as ℭ quite correctly interprets it.[150] The seven heads of the dragon-serpent in 22:5 are, of course, reminiscent of the "visions in Revelation" (cf. Rev 12:3; 13:1; 17:3).[151]

The use of a plural possessive suffix creates an impression of multiple heads in some other passages. In addition to the idiomatic phrase "head downwards" (39:1), this occurs in the statement of the redeemed Redeemer: "I set my name upon their head" (42:20; see Excursus 39). The blessing of those who set "on their head" the crown that is equated with truth (9:8; cf. 9:11a) already belongs to the next set of occurrences.

That "wreath" or "crown" belongs with "head" is clear even if κεφαλή/ܪܫܐ is not expressly

139 Payne Smith, *Dictionary*, 425.

140 Cf. 7:13; 22:7; 39:7b, 13a.

141 See Payne Smith, 2:2765–66.

142 Frankenberg (p. 91) refers only here to κεφαλὶς βιβλίου (cf. Ps 39:8 LXX; Rahlfs, 2:41).

143 See BDAG, *s.v.* κεφαλίς: "roll." In the Syriac translation of Ps 40:8 and Heb 10:7 ܪܫܐ is used (*OTSy*, pt. 2 fasc. 3, p. 43), while in the Syriac translation of Ezek 2:9 and 3:2-3 the term is ܟܪܟܐ (*kerkā*) (*OTSy*, pt. 3 fasc. 3, p. 4; Payne Smith, 1:1827, where the note to "Aq. Ps. xxxix. 8" should be observed: εἴλημα = ܟܪܟܐ).

144 Payne Smith, 2:3900, 3908.

145 Cf. 4:14; 6:4; 7:14; 11:4; 23:2, 3; 24:8; 41:9. In 6:4 and 7:14, 𝔊 will have used a complementary εἰς τέλος as in 11:4 𝔊. The term ܪܫܝܬܐ does not occur as an equivalent of ἀπαρχή.

146 See Payne Smith, 2:3899–900: κεφαλή, ἄκρον/ἄκρα, ἀρχή/ἄρχων, κεφαλίς. The entry "*caput, capitulum*, pars libri s. tractatus, κεφαλίς, Hex. Ez. ii. 9, iii. 1 sqq." (Payne Smith, 2:3900) is partly misleading, because in this passage κεφαλίς means "roll, volume (of a book)" (LEH, s.v. κεφαλίς).

147 See Crum, 13, on 1:1 and 1:4.

148 BDAG, *s.v.* ἄκρον: "from one end."

149 See Payne Smith, 1:5, 2:3900; BDAG, *s.v.* προπάτωρ.

150 Heinrich Schlier, "κεφαλή, ἀνακεφαλαιόομαι," *ThWNT* 3 (1938) 673; *TDNT* 3:674; Michael Lattke, "κεφαλή," *EWNT* 2 (1981) 705; *EDNT* 2:285.

151 Lattke, "κεφαλή," *EWNT* 2:707; *EDNT* 2:286.

mentioned (cf. 17:1). In all the other passages with "crown/wreath," there are also references to "head." The whole collection of *Odes* begins with the simile: "The Lord is on my head like a wreath" (1:1 ℭ; cf. 1:4 also with the Coptic term ⲁⲡⲉ). This simile has its parallel in 5:12 𝔖. The invitation to enter paradise is paired with the imperative of salvation to put a wreath from the divine tree on the "head" (20:7-8). The term "mildness/rest" (20:8) connects this with 35:1, where a "cloud of peace" is placed on/over the "head" of the redeemed one.

Within the range of images of "rest" (28:3; see Excursus 3), there is also the concept of 28:4b ("my head is with him"), although the connection may well be rather with the redeeming "blessing" (28:4a) that descends on the "head" as representing the whole person.

The image of the "Head, the Lord Messiah" and his "members" (17:15-16) is clearly influenced by the New Testament (cf. Eph 4:15; and see Excursus 18).[152] What looks like a play on ܪܫܐ in 23:18a 𝔖 may have been more clearly differentiated in 𝔊 by the use of the two terms ἀρχή (for the "beginning" = "head" of the letter) and κεφαλή (for the "Head which manifested itself"). Whether this "Head" should be equated with the "Son of Truth" (23:18b) will be discussed in what follows. In 24:1 N, on the other hand, there is a true wordplay with κεφαλή/ܪܫܐ in that the "Lord Messiah," on whose "head" the dove settled, is described as the "Head" of this symbolic bird steeped in tradition.

The term ܪܓܠܐ (*reglā*) occurs five times and always, except in the phrase ܡܢ ܪܓܠ (*men rgel*) in 39:9 ("on foot") and in a variant reading of H (see on 23:16b below), in the plural.[153] Where it is said of death personified that its "head" and "feet" became slack (42:13), the emphasis is on the whole even more than on the "opposition of above and below."[154] In the first person address of the exalted one, prophetic influence is detectable: "She [*viz.*, the spirit of the Lord] stood me up on my feet in the height of the Lord" (36:2; cf. Ezek 2:2; 3:24). That "foot" or "feet" in 23:16b bears "the more general sense of the *lower* end"[155] is shown clearly by the emphasized "descent from above" that precedes it (see above on 5a-b).[156] Since the chariot "wheel" and the "letter" perform this downward movement together and the "Head" only manifests itself later (see on 18 below), ܪܫܐ in 23:16a 𝔖 must mean that which came upon the "wheel" (23:16c), that is, the "letter" visualized as a κεφαλίς. Only this interpretation, which is also another pointer to a Greek original,[157] can make sense of the syntax of 16b-c in relation to 16a.

The Pe. ܢܚܬ (*nḥet*) in 16a picks up the mythological image of the descent from on high (see on 5b above). Since it does not concern "the descent of the head to the feet," but describes the going down of the "(letter)-scroll" (in 𝔊 κεφαλίς, derived from Ezek 2:9 and 3:2-3) to the metaphorical lowest point, it cannot be "an allegory of the humiliation, i.e. the Crucifixion."[158]

The explanatory character of 16b-c, including the repetition of ܪܓܠܐ (*reglā*) following a slightly changed preposition (in 𝔊 probably ἕως [16b] succeeding εἰς/πρός [16a]),[159] reinforces the theory that ܪܫܐ is not "head" as opposed to "feet" but stands for the thing that came on the "wheel," a term that also originates in the prophetic vocabulary (16c; see above on ܐܬܐ [*ʾeṯā*] in 11b).[160]

152 Michael Lattke, "κεφαλή," *EWNT* 2 (1981) 707; *EDNT* 2:286.

153 See Payne Smith, 2:3810–11; BDAG, *s.v.* πούς.

154 Michael Lattke, "κεφαλή," *EWNT* 2 (1981) 706; *EDNT*, 2:285.

155 Konrad Weiß, "πούς," *ThWNT* 6 (1959) 624; *TDNT* 6:624.

156 Jonathan Z. Smith, "Geburt in verkehrter oder richtiger Lage?" in Wayne A. Meeks, ed., *Zur Soziologie des Urchristentums: Ausgewählte Beiträge zum frühchristlichen Gemeinschaftsleben in seiner gesellschaftlichen Umwelt* (ThBü 62; Munich: Kaiser, 1979) 304.

157 Contra John Healey, "*Odes of Solomon*," in Ken Parry et al., eds., *The Blackwell Dictionary of Eastern Christianity* (Oxford: Blackwell, 1999) 351.

158 Contra Drijvers, "Ode 23," 168. The excursus that immediately precedes this paragraph has demonstrated that Drijvers's claim (p. 168), "head (ܪܫܐ [*rēšā*]) always stands for the Messiah in the *Odes of Solomon*," is mistaken.

159 See Payne Smith, 2:1919, 2799.

160 N has the third masculine singular perfect Pe. while H uses the active participle of ܐܬܐ. In the construction with the enclitic ܗܘܐ (*-wā*), there is less difference than Muraoka tries to make out (Muraoka §§85 and 86; for preference, see Nöldeke §§263 and 277). Drijvers's translation of ܥܠ (*ʿal*) with third singular suffix as "on him" instead of "on it" leaves a false impression (see Drijvers, "Ode 23," 155). Diettrich (p. 88) is quite mistaken in interpreting ܐܬܐ as *ʾāṯā* and translating it as "a certain mark on it." Our translation is identical with Harris and Mingana's translation (2:334).

Even if 𝔊 had used ἔδραμε(ν)—and not ἔτρεχε(ν)—in 16b,[161] the use of ܪܗܛ (*rheṭ*) obliterated the connection, both in derivation and sense, between τρέχω and τροχός.[162] Instead, the impression left by 𝔖 is that the action of the "wheel" is the counterpart of the violence of the hands that rushed at the heavenly letter (see above, 7a; see also 16:13, on the course of the stars).

■ **17-19a** Both Frankenberg[163] and Greßmann[164] let the poem run on from 16c to 17a so that their retroversion ἐπιστολὴ ἦν διαταγῆς, corresponding to the reading of H, is unproblematical. The transition from stanza VII to stanza VIII is, indeed, smooth, since the "letter" of 17a is identical with the ἐπ' αὐτοῦ ἐρχόμενον of 16c.[165] All the same, 17a is also a new beginning and the first step in the unrolling of the document (see 21a below for the complete unrolling). The reading of N, ܐܘܦܘܩܕܢܐ (*ʾu-puqdānā*), presupposes an adverbial καί ("also, likewise")[166] in 𝔊. Whether ܗܘܬ (*hwāt*) is a translation of ἦν or ἐγένετο is unimportant. The heavenly letter reveals itself not as "one of recommendation"[167] nor as "one of command"[168] but directly as διαταγή or ἐπιταγή.[169]

In the H tradition, 17b provides the rationale for 17a, but the N reading, beginning with "and," must be a prepositioned justification for 18a, where καί/ܘ (*w-*) again means "also."[170] The plural of ܐܬܪܐ (*ʾaṯrā*) will here stand for all χῶραι rather than all τόποι, not, therefore, unlike 4:2, for all "the multiplicity of creation."[171] In addition to the parallel sense in 18:7 ("from every place"), there are, on the one hand, 10:5 and 17:14, where the Ethpa. of ܟܢܫ (*knaš*) is also used in contexts of salvation and allusion to the head,[172] and, on the other, 22:2 and 42:14, referring to soteriological assembling. 𝔊 will probably not have used συνῆλθον[173] but rather συνήχθησαν.[174] This assembling or coming together was a directive from the letter, not the reason for it, and may have had something to do with the "will" of the "Lord" (see 5b above).

Verse 18a "is the central focus of the stanza."[175] Here, at last, there is reference to the "Head," which "manifested itself" (in 𝔊 ἐφάνη; cf. 7:12 and 41:13).[176] The wordplay on ܪܫܐ can be heard only in Syriac, because 𝔊 will have had ἀρχή for the beginning of the letter (N) or the decree (H)[177] and κεφαλή, not ἄρχων,[178] for the "Head" that reveals itself (see Excursus 23 above). The Ethpe. of ܓܠܐ (*glā*) can also be taken as a passive and corresponds to a form of ἀποκαλύπτομαι or φανεροῦμαι.[179]

The problem at the beginning of 18b 𝔖 (ܘܒܪܐ [*wa-ḇrā*]) can be solved by assuming that 𝔊 used an explicative καί to make an apposition to "Head."[180] The genitive expression "Son of Truth" can certainly mean "the true Son of the Most High Father."[181] More important is the fact that "truth" is an "attribute of the height" (cf. 17:7d and see Excursuses 1 and 17). So the

161 BDAG, *s.v.* τρέχω.
162 See Payne Smith, 2:3833; LSJ, *s.v.* τροχός.
163 Frankenberg, 23.
164 Greßmann, "Ode 23," 618.
165 Ibid.
166 BDAG, *s.v.* καί, 2.
167 Harris and Mingana, 2:334, referring to 2 Cor 3:1.
168 Charlesworth, 95; similarly Franzmann, 176; cf. already Greßmann, "Ode 23," 620: "Befehlsbrief." These authors follow Harris and Mingana in prefering the H reading ܕܦܘܩܕܢܐ (*d-puqdānā*).
169 Payne Smith, 2:3215; BDAG, *s.vv.* διαταγή: "ordinance" (cf. Rom 13:2; Acts 7:53), ἐπιταγή: "direction;" "order;" "injunction" (cf. Rom 16:26). I cannot accept Drijvers's interpretation: "Verse 17 says that the letter contained a commandment that all countries should assemble and alludes to passages such as John 11:52; 12:32; Acts 1:8; 2:39; Eph 2:14-16; Phil 2:10, which, in various ways, deal with the unifying power of the proclaimed word of God" (see Drijvers, "Ode 23," 168).
170 Contra Klijn, 304.
171 See Payne Smith, 1:425; BDAG, *s.v.* χώρα; Greßmann, "Ode 23," 618 (χῶραι); Frankenberg, 23 (τόποι).
172 Payne Smith, 1:1771.
173 Contra Greßmann, "Ode 23," 618.
174 Frankenberg, 23; see also Payne Smith, *Dictionary*, 15; BDAG, *s.v.* συνάγω.
175 Franzmann, 181.
176 BDAG, *s.v.* φαίνω, 2.
177 Drijvers, "Ode 23," 169: "head of a letter"; cf. BDAG, *s.v.* ἀρχή, 1a: "the beginning . . . in a book." Reverting to 16a, Greßmann supposed there also that ἡ ἀρχή was the model for ܪܫܐ and interpreted this term, as in 18a, as "dominion": "the dominion descended to the feet."
178 Contra Greßmann, "Ode 23," 618, 620: "Ruler."
179 Payne Smith, 1:717–18; BDAG, *s.vv.* ἀποκαλύπτω, φανερόω, 1aβ "esp. of Christ."
180 BDAG, *s.v.* καί, 1c; Franzmann, 182.
181 Drijvers, "Ode 23," 156; cf. Bultmann, "Untersuchungen," 160 = idem, *Exegetica*, 170: "The genuine Son of the Father."

"Son of Truth" must be identical with the "Son of the Most High" (41:13) and closely connected to the "Father of Truth" (41:9). Just as "Father" and "Son" also occur together elsewhere (19:2; 23:22), there are parallels for the juxtaposition of ܐܒܐ (ʾaḇā) and ܡܪܝܡܐ (9:5; 10:4; 31:4-5; 41:13; ὕψιστος/*mrayymā* should be taken attributively as in 3:6). It is pure speculation "to assume, that verse 18 . . . shows apologetic and anti-heretical tendencies in its emphatic identification of the true Son . . . with the Crucified."[182]

Even more fanciful is Drijvers's suggestion that the monocolon 19a, which may even belong to stanza IX, and its object πάντα/ܟܠܡܕܡ (*kol meddem*) could be "connected to an anti-Jewish prejudice."[183] At best one may play with the idea that "everything" glances back at the complete assembly of mythological "places" or "lands" (see 17b above). The Pe. ܝܪܬ (*ʾireṯ*) expresses a soteriological aspect, as in 31:12, which surpasses such theological promises as Matt 5:15 or 25:34, but in an exclusive fashion.[184] Here the Pe. ܢܣܒ (*nsaḇ*) is a synonym of the previous verb, and the object "everything" expands its meaning further than in 2a, so that it forms an affirmative counterpart of the negative purpose of the pursuers in 7b (see Excursus 41).

■ **19b-20** The transition from stanza VIII to IX is also smooth,[185] but stanza IX still refers rather to stanza IV, and its key word "thought" makes it antithetical to 5a in stanza III. The accumulation of the particles ܘ (ʾ*u*- and *w*-) and ܕܝܢ (*dēn*) argues for a Greek original, which also explains the variant readings in 19b. If 𝔊 had κατηργήθη but not ἐματαιώθη,[186] the reading in N, third feminine singular Pe. perfect of ܒܛܠ (*bṭel*), is an exact rendering of the passive of καταργέω,[187] while the use of the Ethpa. ܐܬܒܛܠܬ (*ʾeṯbaṭṭlaṯ*) in H, though not wrong in itself, seems pedantic.[188] The *Vorlage* of ܘ . . . ܕܝܢ is probably καὶ . . . δέ.[189] The "thought of the many" is the opposite of the "thought" of the Lord and thus of the heavenly letter (see 5a above). The "many" refers in the first place to the "many hands" of 7a (cf. 25:5; 38:12). In addition, however, these "many," whom Drijvers incorrectly equates with "the Jews,"[190] are described as "renegades"[191] and "persecutors" (20a-b).

The *hapax legomenon* ܡܣܛܝܢܐ (*masṭyānē*) in 20a, derived from ܣܛܐ (*sṭā*) or the Aph. ܐܣܛܝ (ʾ*asṭī*), describes persons whose activity can be characterized by ἀστοχέω and/or ἀφίστημι.[192] Thus, this rare term could be rendered by "tempter."[193] A better translation, however, would be "apostates."[194] There is as little reason for the "emendation of ܐܡܪܚܘ to ܐܣܬܪܚܘ" as for the assumption that "the original reading was ܐܡܪܕܘ" or "may have been ܐܡܪܕܘ."[195] For even after the flight, which does not seem consistent with "boldness,"[196] there will be another mention of persecution and annihilation (see 20b below). So the Aph. of ܡܪܚ (*mraḥ*) makes

182 Contra Drijvers, "Ode 23," 169.
183 Drijvers, "Ode 23," 169.
184 See Payne Smith, 1:1634; BDAG, *s.v.* κληρονομέω.
185 Franzmann, 182: "connecting link."
186 Contra Frankenberg, 23; Greßmann, "Ode 23," 618.
187 BDAG, *s.v.* καταργέω: "cease, pass away;" Payne Smith, 1:509.
188 See Payne Smith, 1:510.
189 BDAG, *s.v.* δέ, 5b: "and also."
190 Drijvers, "Ode 23," 169.
191 This is Bauer's translation (p. 605), following Greßmann (p. 459), who, in his theory of sovereignty, even spoke earlier of "renegade revolutionaries" (Greßmann, "Ode 23," 620).
192 BDAG, *svv.* ἀστοχέω: "deviate," ἀφίστημι, 1: "cause to revolt," 2a: "fall away."
193 Drijvers, "Ode 23," 156; see also John A. Emerton and Robert P. Gordon, "A Problem in the Odes of Solomon xxiii. 20," *JTS* n.s. 32 (1981) 444: "all who led astray." I do not understand how Drijvers could translate 20a as "all the tempters fled headlong" ("Ode 23," 156). It is quite unlikely that Charlesworth's translation (p. 95: "Then all the seducers became headstrong and fled") could have influenced him.
194 Payne Smith, 2:2595; BDAG, *s.v.* ἀποστάτης; Lampe, *s.v.* ἀποστάτης. Whether this implies that the many persecutors had defected from the people of the *Odes* must be left in the realm of speculation.
195 Emerton and Gordon, 445–46; see also Barth, 264 ("All the errant ones perished") on the suggested "emendation."
196 Emerton and Gordon, 444.

good sense as a translation of τολμάω,[197] and the καί/ܘ (*wa-*) before ἔφυγον/ܥܪܩ (*ʿraq*) takes on the meaning "and yet" (cf. 18:6 as contrast; 38:6 as parallel).[198] As the heavenly letter fled from the fingers of the many hands (8a), so those who had originally been audacious were finally "put to flight."

Presumption is thus a characteristic of the "persecutors" (in 𝔊 οἱ διώκοντες),[199] as was shown already in stanza III (see on 7a-b above). Even if the active participle of ܪܕܦ (*rdap̄*) in 20b should refer not only to the mythological pursuit of the letter but also to a historical persecution "in a religious sense,"[200] there are no grounds for claiming, here or in 42:5, that "the persecutors are meant for the Jews."[201] They are also only very indirectly "persecutors of the Son."[202] Two graphic verbs picture the annihilation of the "persecutors." The Pe. ܕܥܟ (*dʿek*) corresponds to the passive of σβέννυμι, which means not merely "to become limp,"[203] but "to be extinguished, go out."[204] The reading ܐܬܥܝܝܛܘ (*ʾeṯʿayyaṭ*) in H—for ܐܬܥܛܝܘ (*ʾeṯʿṭīw*) in N—is simply a spelling mistake, and its sense is "clearly inferior."[205] That does not mean that the *Vorlage* of the Ethpe. of ܥܛܐ (*ʿṭā*) was ἠφανίσθησαν, as Greßmann has it,[206] since a passive form of ἐξαλείφω or even of ἐξολεθρεύω is also possible.[207] The meaning, at least, is clear. The opponents have lost the match.

■ **21-22** The letter scroll, which was defined as a "decree" in 17a and partly unrolled, is now opened and flattened out, taking on the form of a tablet. Although stanza X is "certainly Christian," these verses are not an "appendix," and the letter should not "be thought analogous to the Tables of the Law."[208] For Greßmann, who also refers to the "Mosaic Tables," the "secret of the letter is completely" elucidated.[209] This statement is exaggerated, as are references to the "Nova Lex" or the "Trinity."[210]

As in 19b, the particles ܘ . . . ܕܝܢ (*wa-* . . . *dēn*) in 21a translate καὶ . . . δέ (see above). Unlike in 17a, however, ܗܘܬ (*hwāṯ*) here corresponds to ἐγένετο and not to ἦν. But just as Greßmann is correct on these two linguistic points, he is quite misleading in his translation of the Greek loanword ܦܢܩܝܬܐ (*p̄enqīṯā*), which occurs only here, by πλάξ,[211] since no contrast is intended to the stone πλάκες/ܠܘܚܐ (*lūḥē*) of Exod 31:18.[212] Since neither ܟܬܒܐ (*kṯāḇā*), as in 9:11, nor ܟܪܟܐ (*kerkā*) is the term chosen,[213] the thing is not a "codex"[214] or "a large volume"[215] but a πίναξ μέγας.[216] So the "letter scroll" (ἐπιστολή = κεφαλίς [16a]) has become a poster, a placard to inform and remind the public.[217]

The "finger of God" opposes the fingers of the hostile hands in stanza IV (see on 7-8a above), but in 21a it does not represent "God's power."[218] Not until the

197 Payne Smith, 2:2222; BDAG, *s.v.* τολμάω: "to dare," "have courage," "presume."
198 BDAG, *s.vv.* καί, φεύγω; Payne Smith, 2:2997.
199 Greßmann, "Ode 23," 618.
200 Otto Knoch, "διώκω," *EWNT* 1 (1980) 818; *EDNT* 1:338–39.
201 Drijvers, "Ode 23," 169.
202 Greßmann, "Ode 23," 620. See Payne Smith, 2:3824; BDAG, *s.vv.* διώκω, ἐκδιώκω.
203 Drijvers, "Ode 23," 156, 169, clearly depending on Bauer, 605.
204 BDAG, *s.v.* σβέννυμι; Payne Smith, 1:931; cf. Greßmann, "Ode 23," 618: ἐσβέσθησαν.
205 Emerton and Gordon, 444; cf. Lattke, *Oden*, 167: "erzürnt [angered]."
206 Greßmann, "Ode 23," 618; on this passive, see BDAG, *s.v.* ἀφανίζω: "perish," "disappear"; Emerton and Gordon, 444: "were blotted out."
207 BDAG, *s.vv.* ἐξαλείφω, ἐξολεθρεύω; Payne Smith, 2:2857.
208 Harnack, 55.
209 Greßmann, "Ode 23," 620.
210 Drijvers, "Ode 23," 169; see already Abramowski (p. 53), who remarks on "the two Trinitarian passages" 19:2 and 23:22.
211 Greßmann, "Ode 23," 618, clearly dependent on Frankenberg, 23.
212 See BDAG, *s.v.* πλάξ; Payne Smith, 2:1906; Rahlfs, 1:141; *OTSy*, pt. 1 fasc. 1, p. 193.
213 See Payne Smith, 1:1827.
214 Zahn, 765.
215 Charlesworth, 95.
216 LSJ, *s.v.* πίναξ. The size of the "tablet" is expressly emphasized, so the diminutives πινακίδιον, πινάκιον or πινακίς will hardly come under consideration. On the loanword itself, see Lattke, "Wörter," 296 = idem, *Bedeutung*, 4:144.
217 See Kaegi, 716: "Erinnerungstafel"; LSJ, *s.v.* πίναξ, 6: "public notice-board." If one wishes to picture this mythological metamorphosis, one might imagine the flattened scroll, made of some suitable material, pasted to a flat board, or it might perhaps have resembled a thin plate once it had been unrolled.
218 BDAG, *s.v.* δάκτυλος; Payne Smith, 2:3357.

instrumental phrase τῷ δακτύλῳ τοῦ θεοῦ[219] is reached is there any suggestion of "the Tables of the Law" of Exod 31:18 and Deut 9:10.[220] The passive participle of ܟܬܒ (*ktab*),[221] however, is derived from the context of Ezek 2:9-10 (see on 16a above) as well as from Exod 31:18. The adverb ܡܫܡܠܝܐܝܬ (*mšamlyāʾīt*) at the end of 21b, derived from the Shaph. passive participle ܡܫܡܠܝ (*mšamlay*),[222] which must have been τελείως in 𝔊,[223] refers to ὅς γέγραπται or simply γεγραμμένος—"covered w[ith] writing."[224] The image of a *large* tablet would imply many γεγραμμένα (Ezek 2:10). What follows, clearly, are only the most important ones.

A "triadic formula" like 22a-b (cf. Matt 6:13 [doxology]; *Did.* 7:1; 2 Cor 13:13)[225] is still, in the history of dogma, a long way short of "trinitarian belief"[226] and even predates the tradition of the so-called *Gospel of Truth* (NHC I,*3* and XII,*2*); Robert M. Grant, comparing the two,[227] makes the following connection: "What the Odes have in common with the Gospel of Truth is a speculative Jewish Christianity which comes close to Gnosticism but is not fully Gnostic."[228] The ὄνομα/ܫܡܐ (*šmā*) of the divine "Father" is mentioned elsewhere (8:23; see Excursus 39). "Father," "Son," and "Spirit of holiness" also occur together in a less formulaic expression (19:2). The attributive adjective ܩܕܝܫܐ (*qaddīšā*) in N is replaced, again, by the genitive of ܩܘܕܫܐ (*qudšā*) in H. The difference in meaning between the two expressions is no greater than between πνεῦμα ἅγιον and πνεῦμα ἁγιωσύνης (Rom 1:4).[229]

The infinitive of the Aph. ܐܡܠܟ (*ʾamlek*) in 22c, "to reign," which in 𝔊 would have been βασιλεῦσαι rather than βασιλεύειν,[230] refers to all three names in 22a-b; it casts a light backward to the "sign" of the βασιλεία in 12a-b and, together with the phrase expressing eternity, εἰς τοὺς αἰῶνας τῶν αἰώνων, brings to mind Rev 11:15 (cf. also *Mart. Pol.* 20–22; and see Excursus 22).[231]

219 Greßmann, "Ode 23," 618.

220 Heinrich Schlier, "δάκτυλος," *ThWNT* 2 (1935) 21; *TDNT* 2:20–21. Exod 31:18 is quoted in *Barn.* 4:7 and 14:2. Prostmeier (p. 466 n. 9) has shown "that for Christians the meaning of the biblical image 'the finger of God' presented problems."

221 The gender of this participle is determined by the feminine gender of ܠܘܚܝܬܐ. If 𝔊 also used a participle, its gender would equally have been determined by the gender of the term used to denote the tablet.

222 Payne Smith, 2:2123, 2129.

223 Greßmann, "Ode 23," 618; BDAG, *s.v.* τελείως: "fully, perfectly, completely, altogether."

224 BDAG, *s.v.* γράφω, 2b.

225 Alexander Sand, *Das Evangelium nach Matthäus* (Leipzig: St. Benno, 1989 = RNT; Regensburg: Pustet, 1986) 596, on Matt 28:19.

226 Charlesworth, 96. A reading of the pertinent chapter on the apologetics of the late second century shows that Drijvers's contention about 22a-c, "But with this trinitarian formula we approach the early Antiochene theology of the Trinity, as represented by Theophilus *Ad Autolycum* II, 10, which also connects with the prologue to the Gospel of John" (Drijvers, "Ode 23," 170), cannot be upheld; see Robert M. Grant, ed. and trans., *Theophilus of Antioch, Ad Autolycum* (OECT; Oxford: Clarendon, 1970) 38–41.

227 Robert M. Grant, "Notes on Gnosis," *VC* 11 (1957) 145–51; see also Lattke, *Bedeutung*, 3:243.

228 Robert M. Grant, *Gnosticism and Early Christianity* (2nd ed.; New York: Columbia University Press, 1966) 134. Schenke (*Herkunft*, 26–29), on the other hand, sees the *Odes of Solomon* as the "only Gnostic texts" that contain the "key ideas" of this "homily by an unnamed Gnostic," and he draws the "conclusion" that "the so called *Evangelium Veritatis* was produced by a Gnostic group to which the author of the *Odes of Solomon* also belonged."

229 See BDAG, *s.v.* ἁγιωσύνη.

230 Greßmann, "Ode 23," 618; Payne Smith, 2:2140; BDAG, *s.v.* βασιλεύω.

231 On this passage in the *Martyrdom of Polycarp*, see Buschmann, 354–75, with numerous doxological parallels.

24

Ode 24: Dove and Messiah, Disaster and Floods, Depraved Ones and Gnostics

(I) 1a The dove flew onto the head of our Lord[a] Messiah,
1b because he was her Head.
2a And she cooed on/over him,
2b and her voice was heard.
(II) 3a And the inhabitants were afraid,
3b and the sojourners were disturbed.
4a The birds[b] gave up their wing [beat],
4b and all creeping things[c] died[d] in their hole.
(III) 5a And the primal deeps were opened and covered.
5b And they sought the Lord like those who are about to give birth,
6a and/but he was not given to them for food[e],
6b because he was not their own.
(IV) 7a But the primal deeps were submerged in the submersion of the Lord
7b and perished in that thought in which they had been from before.
8a For they were destructive from the beginning,
8b and the end/completion/goal of their destruction was life.
(V) 9a And all[f] that was lacking perished through/was destroyed by them,
9b because they[g] could not give the [pass]word, that they might abide.
(VI) 10a And the Lord destroyed the thoughts
10b of all those with whom the truth was not.
11a For they lacked wisdom,
11b those who were arrogant in their heart.
12a And they were rejected,
12b because the truth was not with them.
(VII) 13a For the Lord showed his way
13b and spread out his grace.
14a And those who knew/understood it
14b know/understand his holiness. Hallelujah.

a 1a H omits ܪܫܗ ܕܡܪܢ ("head of our Lord").
b 4a ܦܪܚܬܐ H; ܦܪܚܬ N.
c 4b ܪܚܫܐ N; ܪ̈ܚܫܐ H.
d 4b ܡܝܬ N; ܡܝܬܘ H (+ correction in N).
e 6a ܠܡܐܟܘܠܬܐ N; ܡܐܟܘܠܬܐ H.
f 9a ܟܠ N; ܕܟܠ H (scribal error).
g 9b H omits ܠܗܘܢ (see commentary).

Introduction

Ode 24 is preserved in two Syriac manuscripts.[1] To give an idea of the manifold themes in this apocalyptic and mythic poem, with an unnamed speaker,[2] addressed to an unknown audience, some of the salient terms were selected for the heading. Schille lists *Ode* 24 again among the "Epiphany hymns,"[3] which describes neither the form nor the content of this partly dualistic mythos, the apparent unity of which must be explicated. This poetic unity does not entail complete coherence of the three or four sections[4] of this mysterious and hard-to-fathom Ode, but it does link the individual parts and leads to the conclusion that even in stanzas VI–VII the subject is the *Κύριος Χριστός*.[5]

Whether and to what extent this "didactic poem," which Rudolf Abramowski connects with the beginning of *Ode* 31,[6] alludes to the reports of Christ's baptism, on the one hand, and—whether linked with this or not—to early traditions of his descent into the underworld (hell, Hades), on the other, will have to be continually examined in the exegesis to follow. Although Drijvers's projected study of *Ode* 24 never appeared, his proposition, "I do not think that *Ode* 24 has anything to do with the baptism of Jesus; it refers rather to 'apocalyptic' occurrences derived from a Christian exegesis of Noah's Flood," must be taken into consideration.[7]

Interpretation

■ **1-2** Although later sections of this Ode may have been influenced by the biblical story of the Flood, this "dove" in 1-2 cannot have come from Gen 8:8-12. Noah may be a "model of righteousness" and thus a "pattern for a faith that provides the strength to survive,"[8] but neither in early Judaism nor in Christian tradition is he considered to be a pattern of the Messiah/Christ.[9] Since ܝܘܢܐ (*yawnā*), whose wings are compared in 28:1 to the "wings of the Spirit,"[10] is not here a "symbol of peace," "sacrificial animal,"[11] or "symbol of the soul,"[12] the

1 Mss.: Codex H, 18b–19b; Codex N, 149ᵛ (ܣ). Ed./trans.: Charlesworth, 97–100; Franzmann, 183–88; Lattke, 2:193–214 and 3:XXXIII–XXXIV.

2 Except for the reading in N ("the head of *our* Lord"), there is no indication in this Ode of a speaking "I" or "we."

3 Schille, 119.

4 Previously I believed that this Ode consisted of "three unequal parts": 1-4; 5-12; 13-14 (Lattke, *Oden*, 169). However, I am now uncertain whether stanza II (3-4) should belong to I or to III or form an independent unit.

5 Without the context, one might assume that the "Lord" of stanzas VI–VII, perhaps also of stanzas III–IV, is God. That may be why the tradition behind H eliminated the christological reference to the "head of our *Lord*" (1a).

6 Abramowski, 52.

7 Drijvers, "Ode 23," 168; see already Spitta, 279–82; Zahn, 767–70; Paul Kleinert, "Zur religionsgeschichtlichen Stellung der Oden Salomos," *ThStK* 84 (1911) 597; J. Rendel Harris, "Two Flood-Hymns of the Early Church," *Exp*, 8th Ser., 2 (1911) 410–17, continuation of idem, "The Thirty-Eighth Ode of Solomon," *Exp*, 8th Ser., 2 (1911) 28–37. Vogl (pp. 66–69, 75) clearly considers *Ode* 24 merely a "Sheol" *Ode*, but Heinz Kruse offers an actual commentary, from which much can be learned even if one disagrees with his thesis; see Kruse, "Die 24. Ode Salomos," *OrChr* 74 (1990) 25–43.

8 Gräßer, 3:117 and 119, on Heb 11:7.

9 Even Harris, for whom "the Dove must be Noah's dove," can extricate himself only by declaring, "unless the Messiah is Noah, some change must have been made in the text" (see J. Rendel Harris, "Two Flood-Hymns of the Early Church," *Exp*, 8th Ser., 2 [1911] 416).

10 Payne Smith, 1:1580.

11 There is no reason to assume that it is a "turtle dove" (*τρυγών*) "as a sacrificial animal of poor people" (BDAG, *s.v.* *τρυγών*; cf. Luke 2:24). Anyone for whom the "dove" was connected to the "worship of Aphrodite" (Will Richter, "Taube," *KP* 5 [1975] 535) would now have to connect this Near Eastern sacred bird with a new cult. Greßmann's and Reitzenstein's theories will be discussed further on (see below on Hugo Greßmann, "Die Sage von der Taufe Jesu und die vorderasiatische Taubengöttin," *ARW* 20 [1920–21] 1–40, 323–59; and Reitzenstein, "Weltuntergangsvorstellungen").

12 See Benedikt Schwank, "Taube. I. Biblisch," *LThK*³ 9 (2000) 1277; Hans-Walter Stork, "Taube. II. Ikonographisch," *LThK*³ 9 (2000) 1278; Buschmann, 314.

origins of this "dove" must be sought in the Synoptics,[13] whence the preposition ἐπί/ܥܠ (*ʿal* [1a, 2a]) and the key word φωνή/ܩܠܐ (*qālā* [2b]) would also have come. But this has not yet said anything about the meaning of the bird.

Christian readers will think of the "baptism of Jesus" and take the "dove" for the symbolic "embodiment of the Spirit,"[14] but the "being baptized" is of only "marginal concern."[15] Kruse disputes any connection with "Spirit" or "baptism,"[16] and calls "the dove the mystical body of Christ, the Church"[17]—an extravagant interpretation, which Kleinert had already rejected,[18] but which Leone Tondelli also entertained.[19] Even after eliminating such theories, based on 17:14-16, there still remains Stephen Gero's statement: "there is absolutely no reason to assume that the dove is to be identified with, or is meant as a symbol for, the Spirit."[20] Gero also holds to "the baptismal setting" and comes to the conclusion that this is a tradition in which "a dove, not yet identified with the Holy Spirit, flew down upon Jesus and revealed his (royal or Messianic?) dignity to the whole world."[21] He sees this tradition as an opposite of the "version of the baptism of Jesus with the Holy Spirit without dove" in the *Gospel of the Hebrews*.[22] What Gero calls a "revelatory function" and an "election motif"[23] is hardly to be found in *Ode* 24. As will be shown later, "this is the ancient motif of the dove as servant and messenger."[24]

Even if the "dove" and other terms in stanza I originated in baptismal traditions, no stress is laid on baptism or on the Spirit.[25] Only the typical actions of the symbolic bird and the relation between the "dove" and the "Messiah" are shown. Where the dove's flight began is not explained. All that is said is that the dove, known from previous tradition, "flew" according to H "onto the Messiah," but according to N "onto the head of our Lord Messiah."[26] That the longer reading in N is also the *lectio difficilior* can be justified, on the one hand,

13 See Matt 3:16-17; Mark 1:10-11; Luke 3:22; cf. John 1:32; BDAG, *s.v.* περιστερά.

14 Zahn, 767.

15 Herbert Braun, "Entscheidende Motive in den Berichten über die Taufe Jesu von Markus bis Justin," *ZThK* 50 (1953) 39 = idem, *Gesammelte Studien zum Neuen Testament und seiner Umwelt* (2nd ed.; Tübingen: Mohr Siebeck, 1967) 168.

16 Kruse, "Die 24. Ode," 30.

17 Ibid., 28.

18 Kleinert, "Stellung," 597.

19 Leone Tondelli, *Le Odi di Salomone: Cantici cristiani degli inizi del II secolo. Versione dal siriaco, introduzione e note* (Preface by Angelo Mercati; Rome: Ferrari, 1914) 219.

20 Stephen Gero, "The Spirit as a Dove at the Baptism of Jesus," *NovT* 18 (1976) 18.

21 Gero, "Spirit," 19.

22 Kruse ("Die 24. Ode," 28) is only in partial agreement. Referring to Gero, Brock also remarks: "The scene of this very obscure poem is certainly Christ's Baptism, but it is not clear whether the dove is used as a symbol of the Holy Spirit" (see Sebastian P. Brock, *The Holy Spirit in the Syrian Baptismal Tradition* [Syrian Churches Series 9; Poona: Anita Printers, 1979] 15).

23 Gero, "Spirit," 19.

24 Kleinert, "Stellung," 597.

25 According to Omodeo (p. 116), "we have here an expansion of the story of the baptism of Jesus." The emphasis is on "Christian redemption" and the sealing up of "the abyss" (see on 5a below). In syllogistic and very dogmatically trinitarian fashion, E. E. Fabbri links his solution of the riddle of *Ode* 24 to the baptism of Jesus in the Jordan (see Fabbri, "El enigma de la 24ª Oda de Salomón," *Ciencia y fe* 16 [1960] 383, 388–98). Angelo Tosato, too, insists that especially 24:1, 2, 5, 7 refer to "the baptism of Jesus" and that the dove in 24:1-2 "has become a symbol . . . of the Spirit" (see Tosato, "Il battesimo di Gesù e le *Odi di Salomone*," *BeO* 18 [1976] 262–65, esp. 264–65).

26 Unlike the Gospel tradition, which has καταβαίνω/ܢܚܬ (*nḥeṯ*), the verb here is (ἐπι)πέτομαι/ܦܪܚ (*praḥ*); see Payne Smith, 2:3254; LSJ, *s.v.* πέτομαι; BDAG, *s.vv.* ἐπιπέτομαι, πέτομαι. This variant may have influenced Justin in the following passages: *Καὶ τότε, ἐλθόντος τοῦ Ἰησοῦ ἐπὶ τὸν Ἰορδάνην ποταμόν, . . . , ὡς περιστερὰν τὸ ἅγιον πνεῦμα ἐπιπτῆναι ἐπ᾽ αὐτὸν ἔγραψαν οἱ ἀπόστολοι αὐτοῦ τούτου τοῦ Χριστοῦ ἡμῶν* ("And then, when Jesus had gone to the river Jordan, . . . the Holy Ghost lighted on Him like a dove, [as] the apostles of this very Christ of ours wrote" [Justin *Dial.* 88.3; Marcovich, *Dialogus*, 223; Goodspeed, 202; ANF 1:243]); *τὸ πνεῦμα οὖν τὸ ἅγιον . . . ἐν εἴδει περιστερᾶς ἐπέπτη αὐτῷ* ("The Holy Ghost . . . lighted on Him in the form of a dove" [*Dial.* 88.8; Marcovich, *Dialogus*, 224; Goodspeed, 203; ANF 1:244]). So it is not necessary to seek refuge in "an old pre-canonical gospel tradition" (Kruse, "Die 24. Ode," 27). The verb by itself does not

by "a remarkable parallel in Efrem,"[27] and, on the other, by the theologically disturbing identity of the "Messiah" with the "Lord" of the remainder of the Ode (stanzas III–IV, esp. stanzas VI–VII). Perhaps people were later offended that the "head" of Christ, of which there is no mention in the baptismal tradition, should have been described as a perch for a bird. Even in the twentieth century, Grimme dismissed the N reading as "senseless."[28] What the wordplay may have been in 𝔊, similar to that on Syriac ܪܫܐ (*rēšā*), is uncertain, since only 1a N establishes *κεφαλή* as the Greek equivalent of this polysemous term (see Excursus 23). The term ⲭⲣⲓⲥⲧⲟⲥ/ܡܫܝܚܐ (*mšīḥā*), on the other hand, is quite certain and cannot be construed as a spelling mistake for ⲛⲟⲥⲥⲓⲁ.[29] But is it a name or a title?

Excursus 24: "Messiah" and "Anoint" in the *Odes of Solomon*

The name "Jesus" (ܝܫܘܥ [*Yeššūʿ*], *Ἰησοῦς*) does not appear anywhere in the *Odes of Solomon*, and the emphatic passive participle of the Pe. ܡܫܚ (*mšaḥ*), ܡܫܝܚܐ (*mšīḥā*) = "the anointed one," is found only seven times (9:3; 17:16; 24:1; 29:6; 39:11; 41:3, 15). There is also a single occurrence of the verb "to anoint" in the third masculine singular perfect with first singular objective suffix (36:6). 𝔊 could have used the "Hellenized transliteration" *Μεσσίας* (cf. John 1:41; 4:25).[30] But it is more likely to have had *Χριστός* in the "Messiah"-passages. The question is where and in what circumstances should the highly mythologized title *Χριστός*/ܡܫܝܚܐ, with various possible parallels such as "Head," "Lord," or "Son," be considered a proper noun and thus a sort of second cognomen[31] that alludes to the name of the "Christian" Jesus.[32]

Without repeating the work of previous researchers on "the Christ of the *Odes of Solomon*,"[33] on "Christ as Lifegiver,"[34] or on all "the Messiah-Passages of the *Odes of Solomon*,"[35] this excursus will content itself with a logical summary of the main statements and a discussion of problems in their immediate context. In connection with "the Messiah," it will at once be noticed that "[s]ome passages are deeply Jewish, others apparently gnostic [*sic*], and yet others patently influenced by Christian ideas and teachings."[36]

Even linguistically, 41:15a is the most difficult of the "Messiah" passages: "The Christ/Messiah [= subject] in truth is (only) one [= predicate noun]."[37] But the context "is clearly the most Christian interpretation of the Messiah in the *Odes*."[38] The next bicolon, 41:15b-16a, emphasizes, on the one hand, the pre-

enforce a "motif of selection by the bird," as Braun would have it (see Herbert Braun, "Entscheidende Motive in den Berichten über die Taufe Jesu von Markus bis Justin," *ZThK* 50 [1953] 40 = idem, *Gesammelte Studien zum Neuen Testament und seiner Umwelt* [2nd ed.; Tübingen: Mohr Siebeck, 1967] 169).

27 Kruse, "Die 24. Ode," 26–27.

28 Hubert Grimme, "Zur Handschrift N der Oden Salomos," *OLZ* 15 (1912) 494.

29 Contra Spitta, 281; see also Gero, "Spirit," 28: "totally arbitrary."

30 BDAG, *s.v.* *Μεσσίας*.

31 A "cognomen" is, "in ancient Rome, a third name, originally only applied to patricians, which served to distinguish members of the same *gens* (e.g. Gaius Julius *Caesar*)" (MEL, 31:1509).

32 See BDAG, *s.v.* *Χριστός*. Paul already "often also joins to the title the name Jesus and/or Christ" (Joseph A. Fitzmyer, "*κύριος, κτλ.*," *EWNT* 2 [1981] 818; *EDNT* 2:330). In most of the passages quoted, *κύριος* is found together with *Ἰησοῦς* or with *Ἰησοῦς Χριστός*/*Χριστὸς Ἰησοῦς*. As David Edward Aune puts it, "Paul assumes but does not argue that Jesus is the Messiah" (see Aune, "Apocalypticism 1–3 & 5," *DNTB* [2000] 55). It is true for the New Testament as a whole but "especially the Pauline epistles that 'Christ' becomes a quasi name, not just a title" (Craig A. Evans, "Messianism," *DNTB* [2000] 704).

33 Abramowski, 52–62.

34 E. E. Fabbri, "El tema del Cristo vivificante en las Odas de Salomón," *Ciencia y fe* 14 (1958) 485–91, 496–97.

35 Lattke, "Messias-Stellen," 435–45 = idem, *Bedeutung*, 4:94–106.

36 James H. Charlesworth, "Odes of Solomon," *DNTB* (2000) 750. By placing the origin of the *Odes* "before A.D. 125," he can state: "Thus the *Odes* seem to have been composed when Judaism, gnostic ideas . . . and Christian affirmation were mixing easily." This agrees with my own dating (Introduction, sec. 4) and my concept of "an age . . . when Judaism, Gnosticism and Christianity intersected and partly overlapped each other like three non-concentric circles" (Lattke, *Oden*, 18).

37 Lattke, *Oden*, 210; see also idem, "Messias-Stellen," 442–45 = idem, *Bedeutung*, 4:103–6.

38 Charlesworth, "Odes," 751.

existence of the "Messiah" (= humbled and exalted "Redeemer," "son of the Most High" [41:11-13]) and, on the other, his task of giving life "by the truth of his name," so ὄνομα/ܫܡܐ (*šmā*) could here also refer either to "(Jesus) Christ" as a "personal name" or to "Messiah" as a "title."[39]

In any case, the word occurs earlier in the *Ode* as an appellation and a soteriological term: "life we receive by *his* Messiah/Anointed One" (41:3b). This subordinates the "Messiah" exclusively to the "Lord" and "Most High," "God" and "Father" in whose "will" and "thought" is rooted the salvific "eternal life," which does not exist in this world: "the holy thought which he thought about *his* Messiah" (9:3b; cf. 9:4a-b). Although the royal aspect of the Jewish title "Messiah" is not stressed, the expression "his Messiah" or "the Messiah of the Lord" (as used in 29:6a) is reminiscent of *Ps. Sol.* 18:5.[40] But just as *Ps. Sol.* 17:32 and 18:7 mention the χριστὸς κύριος,[41] in the *Odes of Solomon* the "Messiah *of* the Lord" is immediately (29:6b) himself described as κύριος/ܡܪܝܐ (*māryā*). In the doxology 17:16, which Jews, Christians, and Gnostics "could have recited,"[42] the terms "Lord" and "Messiah" are used in apposition to the address "our Head" (cf. Eph 4:15 and Excursus 23). Particularly in this Gnosticizing *Ode*, it is difficult to identify the "Lord Messiah" with the "Lord Jesus," even though Christian users would have done so.

Whether the "footprints of our Lord Messiah" (39:11b), which are like wood on the water (39:10), are "an allusion to the account of Jesus walking on the water"[43] must be elucidated in the context of the whole symbolic address.

If there is any connection between the name or title and the first person statement of an exalted one that "he [viz., God] anointed me" (36:6a)[44] and "I became/was one of those near/related to him" (36:6b), the statement may refer to the "'human being's' [Jesus' (?)] sonship of God brought about by the spirit" (cf. 36:3b-c, on "human being" as a "son of God").[45]

Particularly for 24:1, the question arises whether "Messiah" in the two Syriac manuscripts is used as a name or a title. If it were a name, as in Col 3:17 and 3:24, the translations would have to be: "The dove flew onto the head of our Lord [Jesus] Christ" (N) and ". . . to/down to [Jesus] Christ" (H). But the general usage of the *Odes of Solomon*, which sedulously avoids the name "Jesus," suggests rather that the term was originally intended as a title of the Redeemer and that only later and in exclusively Christian usage was the title "Messiah" equated with the name of the exalted "(Jesus) Christ."[46] In this passage, it is also the "Messiah" of the Lord God, but this "Anointed One" is placed "on a par with Jahwe" by the term κύριος/ܡܪܝܐ (*māryā*) "yet not identified with him."[47]

The causal conjunction ܡܛܠ ܕ (*meṭṭol d-*) in 1b, which corresponds to ὅτι,[48] produces a unique linkage.[49] If ܗܘܐ (*hwā*) + ܠ (*l-*) stands for Greek ἦν—or perhaps ἐγένετο (cf. linguistically, Acts 1:16)—followed by a dative,[50] the translation will be "because he [viz., the Messiah] was Head for her."[51] On the other hand, if the Syriac phrase corresponds to a form of ἔχω, with the implied object αὐτόν,[52] then the translation becomes "because she had him [viz., the Messiah] as her Head."[53] Assuming that ܪܫܐ (*rēšā*) here also corresponds to κεφαλή, and not to ἄρχων,[54] the Greek text will not

39 BDAG, *s.vv.* ὄνομα, 1a and 3.

40 Charlesworth, "Odes," 750.

41 Lattke, "Psalms," 856.

42 Charlesworth, "Odes," 750.

43 Ibid., 751.

44 In connection with "*Jesus*, the Christ," cf. Luke 4:18; Acts 10:38; Heb 1:9 (BDAG, *s.v.* χρίω).

45 Lattke, "Messias-Stellen," 440 = idem, *Bedeutung*, 4:101–2.

46 A discussion of the most recent research into the title *Christos* can be found in Ferdinand Hahn, *Christologische Hoheitstitel: Ihre Geschichte im frühen Christentum* (UTB 1873; 5th ed.; Göttingen: Vandenhoeck & Ruprecht, 1995) 466–72. For this excursus, his conclusion (p. 467) that "it is clear, that even where Χριστός was used as a name it carries connotations of a title" is significant.

47 Joseph A. Fitzmyer, "κύριος, κτλ.," *EWNT* 2 (1981) 817; *EDNT* 2:330.

48 See Payne Smith, 2:2077; BDAG, *s.v.* ὅτι, 4a-b: "because," "since," "for."

49 Franzmann's translation "the head was hers" inverts the meaning (see Franzmann, 184; see also Kruse's criticism ["Die 24. Ode," 28 n. 10]). Construing 1b correctly is achieved by reference not to John 4:18 (contra Franzmann, 185) but rather to Matt 14:4 and especially to Acts 13:5 (Payne Smith, 2:4225).

50 BDAG, *s.vv.* εἰμί, γίνομαι.

51 Payne Smith, 1:984: *fuit ei.*

52 Payne Smith, 1:984: *habuit.*

53 BDAG, *s.v.* ἔχω.

54 Hugo Greßmann, "Die Sage von der Taufe Jesu und die vorderasiatische Taubengöttin," *ARW* 20 (1920–21) 27: "Fürst [ruler]."

have been merely ὅτι κεφαλὴ ἐγένετο[55] but something like ὅτι εἶχεν/ἔσχεν αὐτὸν κεφαλήν. The possibility that ἄρχοντα might after all have been used and not κεφαλήν,[56] must remain open[57] in spite of McNeil's[58] criticism.

What this causal connection may be hinges on the symbolism of the "dove," to which it is necessary to return, even though it may never be possible to explain it satisfactorily. Those who connect it to τὸ πνεῦμα/ ܪܘܚܐ (*rūḥā*) would have to accept a certain "subordination of the Spirit to the Messiah."[59] Those, however, who did not close off the symbolism by identifying the "dove" with the "Spirit"[60] could only conclude from 1b that the "dove" that flew onto the "Messiah" was playing a secondary role. There is a second-century witness to this very idea: ἡ περιστερὰ δὲ σῶμα ὤφθη, ἣν οἱ μὲν τὸ ἅγιον πνεῦμά φασιν, οἱ δὲ ἀπὸ Βασιλείδου τὸν διάκονον ("The dove, which appeared in bodily form, is called the Holy Spirit by some, but by the followers of Basilides, the servant" [Clement of Alexandria *Exc. ex Theod.* 16]).[61] Although Basilides was "perh[aps] also an author of *Odes*,"[62] his school is in no sense "the exact circle of Gnostics in which the *Odes of Solomon* originated."[63] What is possible is that the Basilidians read their interpretation of the "dove" of baptism into *Ode* 24, for they "claimed secret apostolic traditions and exotic revelations from apocryphal prophets."[64]

Summarizing—and excluding interpretations of the "dove" as "bridal bird,"[65] "bird of death," "sacrifice," "symbol of simplicity," symbol of "authentic divine sonship," or "bird of peace"[66]—it is possible to say, with all due circumspection, that the ancients would have imagined a "bird of the gods" or "divine bird," which is here seen as a servant "bird of the Messiah."[67] Jewish readers would, even without mention of the temple, recognize that "the dove could mediate the *Bath Qōl*," and "in the early church" for the Christian users of the *Odes of Solomon* "[t]he dove as a sign of the Holy Spirit is the centre and p[oin]t of all statements."[68]

The Pe. ܙܡܪ (*zmar*) in 2a describes another typical behavior of the "dove." Like ᾄδω, this Syriac verb can be used for "all kinds of vocal sounds."[69] Since neither περιστερά/ܝܘܢܐ (*yawnā*) nor any other variety of dove or pigeon is classified as a songbird, it should be called "cooing" (according to Greeven, although even he follows convention in quoting 24:2a: "It sang above him").[70] Kruse, also, who can hear the "dove/church" allegorically singing or chanting psalms above the Lord Christ, admits that "the dove is known as an imperfect singer."[71] According to Greßmann, the dove "sings" "about him."[72] By this interpretation of the prepositional phrase ("about him," not "above him"), Greßmann can determine *what* the legendary dove utters, and he declares this to be the "essential idea" of *Ode* 24: "She proclaims

55 As in Frankenberg, 24.

56 BDAG, *s.vv.* ἄρχων, 1b; κεφαλή, 2.

57 Lattke, 2:195; cf. already idem, *Bedeutung*, 1:147.

58 Brian McNeil, review of Lattke, *Bedeutung*, vols. 1–2 in *Ostkirchliche Studien* 29 (1980) 193.

59 Lattke, *Oden*, 169; a previous reference to Origen, *De princ.*, book 1 introduction 4, is mistaken and should be removed (contra Lattke, *Oden*, 169 n. 3). Cf. Murray's remark (*Symbols*, 314) on "passages close to the theme of Christ's baptism" and especially on *Ode* 24:1-2: "Here the 'Dove' appears to be subordinated to Christ, but in other passages the Spirit appears as his mother, for example in *Ode* 36,3."

60 Greßmann, "Taufe," 29; Gero, "Spirit," 19.

61 Greßmann, "Taufe," 29. Friedrich Sühling links this statement, on the one hand, to a later remark by Tatian ("pneuma" = "logos" = "servant of the God who has suffered") and, on the other, to *Ode* 24: "If Christ is the ruler of the dove, then the dove must be subject to him, she is the servant of Christ" (see Sühling, *Die Taube als religiöses Symbol im christlichen Altertum* [RQSup 24; Freiburg im Breisgau: Herder, 1930] 74). In connection with classical presuppositions, another remark by Sühling (p. 75) is of some importance: "It is interesting to note that in antiquity the doves that carried the food of the gods to Zeus were called διάκονοι."

62 Winrich A. Löhr, "Basilides," *LThK*³ 2 (1994) 59.

63 Contra Greßmann, "Taufe," 29.

64 Löhr, "Basilides," *LThK*³ 2 (1994) 59.

65 Kruse, "Die 24. Ode," 30.

66 Heinrich Greeven, "περιστερά, τρυγών," *ThWNT* 6 (1959) 65–71; *TDNT* 6:65–72.

67 Greeven, "περιστερά," *ThWNT* 6:64, 70; *TDNT* 6:64, 70.

68 Greeven, "περιστερά," *ThWNT* 6:68, 70; *TDNT* 6:69, 70.

69 LSJ, *s.v.* ἀείδω; cf. BDAG, *s.v.* ᾄδω; Payne Smith, 1:1136.

70 Greeven, "περιστερά," *ThWNT* 6:66–67; *TDNT* 6:67–68.

71 Kruse, "Die 24. Ode," 32.

72 Greßmann, "Taufe," 28; also Vogl, 66.

the inauguration of the reign of the Christ."[73] But there is no support for such speculative assertions in stanza I or in any later sections of the text.[74] If the preposition ܥܠ (*ʿal*), which has occurred already in 1a, derives from Matt 3:16 (cf. also Luke 3:22 and John 1:32; Mark 1:10 originally had εἰς), the prepositional phrase in 𝔊 was ἐπ' αὐτῷ.[75]

The consequence of the cooing of the dove is, in 2b, that her "sound" or "call" was heard.[76] At first sight this construction with the Ethpe. of ܫܡܥ (*šmaʿ*) seems as vague as ἠκούσθη.[77] However, within the mythological context one must assume that the "voice" of the "dove" that originated in the "baptismal miracle"[78] was felt to be uncanny by humans (see 3a-b below) and other forms of life (see 4a-b below). This agrees with Kruse: "The voice of the dove is heard around the world."[79]

■ **3-4** The manuscripts have no mark of division between 3a and 3b.[80] The reason why this first part of stanza II has generally been treated as a bicolon, at least since Harris and Mingana,[81] lies in the double synthetic parallelism (3a-b || 4a-b; 3a || 3b; 4a || 4b). And in the apocalyptic statement of disaster of stanza II, this stylistic device makes it possible to answer Kruse, who, having allegorically divided the "inhabitants" as the "Jews" from the "sojourners" as the "heathen" and cannot, therefore, "perceive both groups negatively," asks: "But why is it necessary to distinguish two groups?"[82] The two groups, in each case, delineate "all mankind"[83] and "every creeping thing" and "every winged creature" (Gen 7:14). So in 4a neither the reading of N (ܦܪܚܬ [*perḥat*] = "she [viz., the dove] flew") nor the equation of the reading of H (ܦܪܚܬܐ [*pāraḥtā*]) with the "dove" of stanza I accords with the form and sense of the line.[84]

The two *hapax legomena,* ܬܘܬܒܐ (*tawtābē*) and ܥܡܘܪܐ (*ʿāmōrē*) in 3b and 3a, are complementary parallel terms,[85] and, in addition, the Pe. ܕܚܠ (*dḥel*) in 3a and the Ethpe. of ܙܘܥ, ܙܥ (*zāʿ*) in 3b can also be interchanged.[86] The verb of 3a probably corresponds to ἐφοβοῦντο,[87] but the *Vorlage* of the verb of 3b is not so clear. In addition to ἐσαλεύθησαν,[88] it would be possible to use a passive form of πτύρω, πτοέω, σείω, or ταράσσω.[89] What is certain is that the two verbs have negative connotations as in 23:8b; 25:11a (ܕܚܠ); and 39:5 (ܐܬܬܙܥ ܠܐ, where it is negated as a positive indication of the believers). The "inhabitants" in 3a are the settled "residents" of town and countryside.[90] The Greek term would

73 Greßmann, "Taufe," 28.

74 See Reitzenstein's criticism of Greßmann ("Taufe"): "But I can no more accept his derivation of it from a folk-tale or the notion of an election as king than his analysis of the Gospel records of the baptism of Christ" (see Reitzenstein, "Weltuntergangsvorstellungen," 167). How tenuous Greßmann's associations are can be shown by a remark in his summary: "If *Ištar* was indeed the goddess of the doves there could have been a story how she sent a dove onto the head of the chosen and thus singled him out from the rest of mankind" (see Greßmann, "Taufe," 359).

75 Frankenberg, 24; see also Bauer, 605: "above him."

76 Payne Smith, 2:3618–19; BDAG, *s.v.* φωνή, which can be translated neutrally as "voice."

77 Payne Smith, 2:4215; BDAG, *s.v.* ἀκούω.

78 On the "baptismal miracle" within the "Mythos," see Dibelius, 270–74, esp. 273: "The 24th *Ode of Solomon* provides the necessary cosmic background to this mythical event; the dove sings above the Anointed One and the world trembles in fear and terror of death."

79 Kruse, "Die 24. Ode," 33.

80 Lattke, *Bedeutung*, 1:146.

81 Harris and Mingana, 2:341.

82 Kruse, "Die 24. Ode," 34.

83 Gunkel, *Aufsätze*, 171.

84 Harnack (p. 56) has at least noticed the parallelism between 4a and 4b, remarking about Flemming's almost correct translation: "The dove here represents the spirit of life; when she lets her wings grow lax death appears." On the basis of a free and inaccurate rendering by Harris and Mingana (2:341: "The birds took to flight"), Charlesworth's version (p. 98) is even looser: "The bird began to fly." His annotation overlooks the *parallelismus membrorum* but adds some fanciful embroidery to the text: "The reference in this line is to 'the dove' in v. 1. The meaning seems to be that while she had fluttered over the Lord's head, she now has begun to fly" (see Charlesworth, 99 n. 4).

85 Payne Smith, 1:1647, 2:2920.

86 Payne Smith, 1:862–63, 1106; cf. the complex construction of 1 Pet 3:6 in *NTSy*.

87 BDAG, *s.v.* φοβέω, though not in sense (2): "to have respect."

88 Frankenberg, 24; BDAG, *s.v.* σαλεύω.

89 BDAG, *s.vv.* πτοέω, πτύρω, σείω, ταράσσω.

90 Lattke, *Oden*, 169.

hardly have been ἔνοικοι,[91] but either οἱ κατοικοῦντες or οἰκήτορες.[92] As a complement–not an antithesis or a synonym–the "aliens" of 3b are "sojourners" who will in 𝔊 have been described by the nominalized adjective οἱ πάροικοι (cf. Acts 7:6).[93] So these are not "the residents."[94]

Because of the *parallelismus membrorum* (see above), 4a has to be interpreted by 4b. That means that line 4a, which is difficult to translate, must relate the death of all "birds."[95] Since the story of the Flood begins to exert its influence in this bicolon, it is easy to discover the Greek originals of the two subjects in 4 (cf. Gen 6:7; 7:8, 14, 23).[96] The collective noun ܦܪܚܬܐ (*pāraḥṯā*) in 4a H translates τὰ πετεινά,[97] including all sorts of birds[98] and fowl,[99] in fact all flying creatures. Verse 4a as a whole has been very variously translated. The many meanings of the Pe. ܫܒܩ (*šḇaq*) can be reduced here to two, ἀφίημι and καταλείπω, both in the sense of "give up" or "abandon."[100] An English translator can say: "The birds dropped their wings,"[101] but the German translation, "Die Vögel senkten ihre Flügel [the birds lowered their wings]",[102] is less accurate. Instead of amplifying the verb's basic meaning, "to leave," by adding another meaning such as "to hang"[103] or "to fall,"[104] it is preferable to consider the direct object πτέρυγας/ܓܦܝܗ̈ (*geppē*), with its third feminine singular possessive suffix, as describing an actual thing, which also expresses "wing beat" as its proper action.[105]

Paralleling 4a, 4b concerns the "death" of all ἑρπετά/ܪܚܫܐ (*raḥšā*).[106] This second collective noun includes more than merely "worms,"[107] comprising rather all "creeping things."[108] That makes the translation of the *hapax legomenon* ܚܘܠܢܐ (*ḥullānā*)–the Greek equivalent of which was τρώγλη, not ὀπή,[109] much less σκέπη (as in Cant 2:14a)–as "crack" far too narrow.[110] The idea is of the "cave" or "hole"[111] where all "creeping things" can take shelter. But this shelter now becomes an apocalyptic death trap. Since 4a-b deals with actual *creatures* of the air and earth, they should not be allegorically equated with "evil spirits," as Kruse does.[112]

■ **5-6** So far things seemed innocent (stanza I) or at least, in spite of the incipient cataclysm, reasonably clear (stanza II), but from stanza III onward "the confusion is such" that Harnack "can only say that this is a description of the early stages of the [Last] Judgment that even extends to the realm of the dead, but that no further

91 Contra Frankenberg, 24.
92 BDAG, *s.vv.* κατοικέω, οἰκήτωρ.
93 BDAG, *s.v.* πάροικος; cf. the translations by Diettrich (p. 90) and Gunkel (*Aufsätze*, 169).
94 Contra Harnack, 56.
95 This is Schultheß's translation (p. 255) of the collective noun. "The drooping of a bird's wings presages its death" (Spitta, 280). Once in Sydney I observed how quite a large bird became trapped between two of the boulders that are laid out around the Opera House. After a few attempts, it seemed that the creature gave up trying to free itself since its wings had no power to help it. Only the small head was still visible but did not move. None of the white tourists knew what to do in this predicament, but an Aboriginal man arrived and extricated it with a quick jerk. Almost immediately the wings came back to life and the bird that had so recently appeared dead flew up and away.
96 Rahlfs, 1:8–10; *OTSy*, pt. 1 fasc. 1, pp. 10–13.
97 Payne Smith, 2:3255; Brockelmann, *Lexicon*, 594; BDAG, *s.v.* πετεινόν.
98 Kleinert, "Stellung," 597; Diettrich, 90; Lattke, *Oden*, 169, and others.
99 Zahn, 768; Kruse, "Die 24. Ode," 34.
100 Payne Smith, 2:4037–39; Brockelmann, *Lexicon*, 753; BDAG, *s.v.* ἀφίημι, καταλείπω.
101 Newbold, "Bardaisan," 196.
102 Vogl, 66, clearly depending on Greßmann, "Taufe," 27.
103 E.g., Hugo Duensing, "Zur vierundzwanzigsten der Oden Salomos," *ZNW* 12 (1911) 87; Bauer, 605.
104 Zahn, 768: "Let fall" = "lose."
105 BDAG, *s.v.* πτέρυξ; *MEL*, 30:870: "Flügelschlag"; Payne Smith, 1:763–64.
106 The plural ܪ̈ܚܫܐ (*raḥšē*) in H has the same sense as the singular (Payne Smith, 2:3892). That the singular in N has a plural sense is shown by the plural ending that was added to the verb ܡܝܬ (*mīṯ*). In both manuscripts the possessive suffixes, which refer to the collective noun, are in the singular.
107 Contra Lattke, *Oden*, 169, and numerous predecessors.
108 BDAG, *s.v.* ἑρπετόν; LSJ, *s.v.* ἑρπετόν: "creeping thing, reptile, esp. snake."
109 Frankenberg, 24.
110 Contra Lattke, *Oden*, 169.
111 See LSJ, *s.v.* τρώγλη; Payne Smith, 1:1270.
112 Kruse, "Die 24. Ode," 34.

explanation is possible."[113] He does, however, dispute the linking of the "baptism" to the *descensus ad inferos*, observing: "the Messiah does not, in this Ode, descend to the underworld and does not execute judgment here."[114] The second part of this statement results from the fact that he was not yet aware of the second Syriac manuscript in which 1a mentions the "Lord Messiah." Whether the realm of the dead is under discussion remains to be decided. At any rate, even decades after Harnack, and in spite of numerous contributions, some of which Kittel has winnowed through in a quest for unanimity,[115] it is still true that "[t]he detailed exegesis of the whole poem is an extraordinarily difficult task."[116]

Although there is no attempt at a new "depiction of Noah's Flood,"[117] 5a does contain an "allusion to the Flood."[118] The terms of this mythical monocolon[119] are derived from Gen 7:11 and 8:2 LXX, that is, from the beginning and the end of the mythos.

> Gen 7:11: . . . *τῃ ἡμέρᾳ ταύτῃ ἐρράγησαν πᾶσαι αἱ πηγαὶ τῆς ἀβύσσου, καὶ οἱ καταρράκται τοῦ οὐρανοῦ ἠνεῴχθησαν,*
>
> . . . on this day *all the fountains of the abyss* were broken up, and the flood-gates of heaven *were opened.*
>
> Gen 8:2: *καὶ ἐπεκαλύφθησαν αἱ πηγαὶ τῆς ἀβύσσου καὶ οἱ καταρράκται τοῦ οὐρανοῦ . . .*
>
> And *the fountains of the deep were closed up*, and the flood-gates of heaven, . . .[120]

In connection with the plural of *ἄβυσσος*/ܬܗܘܡܐ (*thōmā*),[121] which is not found in the original story, there is no need to look for additional sources (e.g., Exod 15:5, 8 or Ps 32:7; 134:6 LXX). It is the plural *αἱ πηγαί*, which gave rise to the plural *ἄβυσσοι*/ܬܗܘ̈ܡܐ (*thōmē*), which is linked to both the verbs *ἀνοίγω* and *ἐπικαλύπτω*, derived from the LXX.[122] So the image is of a great "original flood," not of the bottomless pit as such or of the "realm of the dead" as the prison of (disobedient) spirits.[123] If the intended image had been of "Hades," whether as "the whole realm of the dead" or only the abode "for ungodly souls,"[124] one would have expected S to use the term ܫܝܘܠ (*šyōl*), which occurs

113 Harnack, 56–57.

114 Ibid., 57.

115 Kittel, 100–104.

116 Gero, "Spirit," 18.

117 Contra Kleinert, "Stellung," 597.

118 Contra Bieder, *Höllenfahrt*, 173. Kleinert ("Stellung," 597) believes that in 3-6 there has been a "transposition of lines," which does not make the exegesis easier. Bieder (*Höllenfahrt*, 174) argues for a *descensus* without "a preaching in Hades."

119 Franzmann (p. 187) in her analysis maintains that 5-6 are two bicola, and thus she speaks of a "personification of the deep abysses." However, there is no *parallelismus membrorum*, so it is simpler to divide stanza III into one introductory monocolon and one narrative tricolon.

120 Rahlfs, 1:10; Brenton, 8–9 (emphasis added). In the Peshitta, both Gen 7:11 and 8:2 use ܬܗܘܡܐ (*thōmā*) to translate תהום/*ἄβυσσος* (*OTSy*, pt. 1 fasc. 1, pp. 12–13). Although *ἠνεῴχθησαν* is translated by ܐܬܦܬܚܘ (*ʾetpṯaḥ*, as in *Ode* 24), the translation of *ἐπεκαλύφθησαν* differs (ܐܣܬܟܪܘ [*ʾestkar*]). The second verb in 5a is found in Gen 7:19-20 as the translation of *ἐπεκάλυψεν*, but this linguistic finding mainly shows the direct influence of the LXX on this *Ode*. Newbold's reflections ("Bardaisan," 199) on "abysses" do not contribute much to the understanding of the text.

121 BDAG, *s.v.* *ἄβυσσος*; Payne Smith, 2:4394 (as he points out, the word ܬܗܘܡܐ [*thōmā*] derives ultimately from the Assyrian name *tiāmatu*); cf. Johannes Renger, "*Tiāmat*," *DNP* 12/1 (2002) 527–28.

122 BDAG, *s.vv.* *ἀνοίγω*, *ἐπικαλύπτω*; cf. Payne Smith, 2:3338, on the Ethpe. of ܦܬܚ (*pṯaḥ*) and 1:1780–81, on the Ethpa. of ܟܣܐ (*ksā*). The logic of the opening and closing of the primal deeps obviates the need for a text-critical emendation of ܘ (*w-*) for ܕ (*d-*) between the two verbs (contra Harnack, 56). Diettrich (p. 90) accepts this "textual emendation" and even claims that it is "necessary" for "stichic symmetry."

123 Joachim Jeremias, "*ἄβυσσος*," *ThWNT* 1 (1933) 9; *TDNT* 1:9–10. Thus, the common translation of ܬܗܘ̈ܡܐ as "Abgründe [abysses]" is not the best (see, e.g., Harnack, 56; Spitta, 280; Zahn, 768; Diettrich, 90; Duensing, "Oden," 87; Greßmann, "Taufe," 28; Bieder, *Höllenfahrt*, 173). Bauer's translation (p. 605) is possible in consideration of Amos 9:3 (*τὰ βάθη*/ܬܗܘ̈ܡܐ), but in this case "deeps" is not as good as "primal deeps."

124 Joachim Jeremias, "*ᾅδης*," *ThWNT* 1 (1933) 147; *TDNT* 1:147.

three times as a parallel to "death" in the *Odes* (15:9; 29:4; 42:11).[125]

"The subject" of 5b "cannot be the abysses."[126] This statement is correct, even if "primal deeps" replaces "abysses." The identification of the subject of 5b with that of 5a has produced some amazing metaphors (e.g., Duensing: "cries of the abysses," accepting an unnecessary emendation of ܩܥܝܢ [*qāʿēn*] for ܒܥܝܢ [*bāʿēn*] from Zahn and Diettrich; Greßmann: "the abysses . . . open and close their jaws spasmodically . . . and snap at the Lord"; Bieder: "a number of abyssoi that open and close their mouths like fish").[127] The metaphor in 5b is difficult even if the third person plural of the original Greek verb[128] is taken impersonally and an implied subject like "persons" is added.[129] The direct object of the verb, whose action takes place in the mythological past, might, in H, be *God* the "Lord," who, after all, even in the Old Testament lets almost all living creatures perish (Gen 6:7, 13, 17; 7:21-23). In N, however, the expanded version of 1a makes it clear that the people "sought" the *Messiah* but not ὡς τὰς τίκτουσας.[130] It is *humanity* that is compared to "those who are about to give birth,"[131] whose birth-pangs are often used as a "metaphor for the distress" of a "crisis situation" (cf. as a sort of compendium 1QH xi [= previously iii].7-18).[132]

Women in labor have always prayed for *relief* by the birth, but these people in their affliction sought the "Lord" (Messiah) in a transferred sense as "nourishment" or "food," as can be deduced from 6a.[133] Even in H, the *hapax legomenon* ܡܐܟܘܠܬܐ (*mēkultā*), derived from ܐܟܠ (*ʾekal*), can only be construed as a double nominative (instead of the construction in N with εἰς/ܠ [*l-*]), so Zahn's translation "no food *was* given them" is impossible.[134] The indirect object αὐτοῖς/ܠܗܘܢ (*lhōn*) does not refer to the image of "those who give birth" but to the "seekers" of 5b, gendered masculine, but, as in 𝔊, intended inclusively, who were *not* given the "Lord"

125 Although Kruse ("Die 24. Ode," 34–35) also uses "abysses" in his translation, referring to *Ode* 31:1 and Gen 1:2, he carefully distinguishes between ܬܗܘܡܐ and the "realm of the dead" (Hebrew/Syriac "Sheol") and concludes: "There is no link to the concept of a descensus."

126 Spitta, 280. Spitta also points to the correct biblical passages (Gen 6:21; 7:11, 19; 8:2). However, he then continues rationalistically: "So in v. 3 [=5] the section that is so important for understanding the whole has been omitted, namely, that the earth was covered with water to the height of the mountains, and probably that, parallel to the story of Noah's flood, all cattle perished and not even human beings were saved. Since v. 4 [=6] says that they did not receive food, it may have been remarked in the preceding section that they had fled up the barren mountains and tried to save themselves by clinging to floating tree trunks."

127 Duensing, "Oden," 86; Zahn, 768; Diettrich, 90; Greßmann, "Taufe," 28; Bieder, *Höllenfahrt*, 174.

128 On the possible originals, see Excursus 19. In 𝔖, the action "is distinctly referred to the past" by the use of ܗܘܘ (*hwaw*), placed at the beginning and thus not enclitic (Nöldeke §277; cf. Payne Smith, 1:556), together with the active participle of the Pe. ܒܥܐ (*bʿā*).

129 "For 'one' it is much more customary to employ the third plur[al] (without subject). . . . *Οἱ ἄνθρωποι* may also appear as subject" (BDF and BDR §130 [2]). Examples of such uses of ζητέω without subject, limited to the New Testament, are Mark 12:12; John 7:30; 10:39; Rom 11:3 (quotation of 3 Kgdms 19:10, 14 LXX). The statement of 5b refers to human beings, not to the animals of 4a-b.

130 Contra Frankenberg, 24. For a contorted attempt to explain the accusative, see Frankenberg's commentary (p. 51): "The abyss attempts to swallow God's Anointed One as it has swallowed so many before him."

131 Diettrich, 90.

132 Maier, *Qumran-Essener*, 1:67–70, esp. 68; Vermes, 171–72; Carmignac, "Auteur," 83; Lohse, *Texte*, 120–21; Charlesworth, 100. The construction in 𝔖, where the verb "to seek" has a masculine ending but the demonstrative pronoun ܗܢܝܢ (*hānnēn*) and the participle of ܐܝܠܕ (*ʾiled*) are feminine (Payne Smith, 1:1593; Brockelmann, *Lexicon*, 301), may be another indication that there was an original Greek construction using the feminine participle of γεννάω or τίκτω (BDAG, *s.v.* γεννάω, τίκτω; cf. John 16:21 on the synonymity of the verbs). The use of the verb ζητέω (or a similar one) without an expressed subject makes its third person plural ending ambiguous.

133 If the subject of "to seek" is not "abysses" or "animals" then "animal feed" is no longer a possible translation (contra Gunkel, *Aufsätze*, 170; Greßmann, "Taufe," 27–28; Bauer, 605). At the same time, an "allusion to the eucharistic tradition is quite unlikely" (Lattke, *Oden*, 170).

134 Zahn, 768. This translation leads Zahn to more

as (their) "food."[135] That *βρῶμα* and *βρῶσις*[136] are used metaphorically can be seen from passages like John 4:34 or 4:32 (and cf. John 6:27, 55), so that there is no need to refer to Gen 1:30 (*εἰς βρῶσιν*) or Gen 6:21 (*ἀπὸ πάντων τῶν βρωμάτων*), much less to Ps 73:14 LXX.[137]

The extreme negation in 6b explains why their search was unsuccessful.[138] Thus, a dualism is introduced into the mythology that completely cuts off the rejected ones from the "Lord," as will become even clearer further on.

■ **7-8** The allusion to the tale(s) of the "Lord's" baptism in 7a is just as vague as that in 1a. Even if the act of baptism is not particularly emphasized in the narrative, the translation of ܛܘܒܥܐ (*ṭubbāʿā*) by "seal"[139] must not distract attention from the fact that "the immersion of the Lord"—or "the submersion of the Lord"[140]—"refers to the Baptism . . . of the Messiah."[141]

The repetition of the subject of 5a alludes, in the first place, to the waters of Genesis 6–8. The "primal deeps," which had been stopped up at that time, now, as it were, disappear eschatologically; as the image of God's anger over his human creation, they finally "sink" at—or because of—the redeeming act of the baptism of the Lord accepted as Messiah and adopted Son of God.[142] The construction with ܘ (*wa-*) and ܕܝܢ (*dēn*) argues that 𝔖 is a "slavish translation."[143]

Who or what is the subject of 7b? If one keeps open all possibilities in connection with the "grotesque concoction,"[144] it might have been that in parallel to 5b—and under the influence of Gen 6:5, 11-13, 17, and 8:21[145]—the topic has shifted to the corrupt "humanity" of that time. But since *φθείρω* (Gen 6:11) and *καταφθείρω* (Gen 6:12, 13, 17; 9:11) can be used both for the works of the inhabitants of earth and for the divine annihilation by the Flood (see on the root ܚܒܠ in 8a-b below), the implicit subject of the verb form ܐܒܕܘ (*ʾeḇad*, third plural masculine perfect of Pe. ܐܒܕ [*ʾeḇad*]), in the synthetic *parallelismus membrorum* with 7a, is most likely to be ܬܗܘ̈ܡܐ (*thōmē*).[146] This assumption accords

flights of interpolation in 6b: "because there was not (the food, which is) theirs." Since for Zahn (p. 769) the "Flood is a symbolic prologue to the Last Judgment," he refers to the following passages in the New Testament: Matt 24:37-39 (*τρώγοντες*/ܐܟܠܝܢ ["eating"]); 1 Pet 3:20-21 (*ἀντίτυπον . . . σῴζει βάπτισμα . . . δι᾽ ἀναστάσεως Ἰησοῦ Χριστοῦ*, "Baptism, which corresponds to this, . . . saves . . . through the resurrection of Jesus Christ"); 2 Pet 2:5-7. The author of the *Ode*, "despite the link to the baptism of Jesus, focuses his attention on the end of the world." So Zahn interprets the "abysses" by the use of the term *ἄβυσσος* in Revelation (cf. Rev 9:1-2; 20:1-3, 10). Even though this can hardly be correct, the following remarks by Zahn are relevant: "The author is no copyist, but, in his own fashion, a poet who uses the ideas he has learned from the Old Testament and the Christian writings he has encountered, to construct new images." The results may occasionally be some very mixed metaphors.

135 Among the many occurrences of the verb "to give," either as the Pe. ܝܗܒ (*yaḇ*) or as the Ethpe. ܐܬܝܗܒ (*ʾeṯīheḇ*), the following may be selected for contrast: "Give me your soul, that I may also give you my soul" (9:2); "and [life was] given without stint to those who trust in him" (15:10c).

136 BDAG, *s.vv.* *βρῶμα*, *βρῶσις*; Payne Smith, 1:181.

137 Contra Reitzenstein, "Weltuntergangsvorstellungen," 167, who, in any case, equates the "baptism story" with the "descent into hell."

138 See Nöldeke §328.B; Harris and Mingana, vol. 1, on this passage: "Intensive negative."

139 E.g., by Harnack, 57; Zahn, 768; Newbold, "Bardaisan," 197; Gunkel, *Aufsätze*, 170–71; Greßmann, "Taufe," 27–28; Reitzenstein, "Weltuntergangsvorstellungen," 167. Kruse ("Die 24. Ode," 25) translates the term as "ruin" and distinguishes it from the "baptism of Jesus *by water*" (p. 36). Vogl (pp. 67–68), however, properly mentions "submersion" and emphasizes the "play on words." The free translation by Berger and Nord (p. 758), "The Lord let the flood flow into the deeps," is unacceptable.

140 Harris and Mingana, 2:341.

141 Burkitt, 384; see also E. E. Fabbri, "El enigma de la 24ª Oda de Salomón," *Ciencia y fe* 16 (1960) 385; Emerton, 715; Brockelmann, *Lexicon*, 267.

142 See Payne Smith, 1:1427; BDAG, *s.v.* *δύ[ν]ω*; LSJ, *s.vv.* *δύω*, *καταδύω*.

143 Zahn, 768. If this remark by Zahn is justified, his emendations and retroversion of the verb as *ἐσφράγισαν* are indefensible.

144 Gunkel, *Aufsätze*, 172.

145 Spitta, 279.

146 Franzmann, 187, with reasons.

with the *opinio communis*, but in the construing of the second part of 7b this majority of translators[147] confronts a small number who do *not* feel the need to insert a correlative demonstrative pronoun.[148] If this short relative clause, with its unconstrained word order and the rare, but not impossible, use of ܕ (*d-*) without a correlative, refers to the subject of the verb, then, considering the prepositional phrase with ܒ (*b-*), the feminine demonstrative pronoun ܗܝ (*hāy*), and the ambiguous term ܡܚܫܒܬܐ (*maḥšabtā*), which Spitta even dismisses as "meaningless,"[149] we face the question: "What is the plan?"[150]—"What thought, idea, notion or proposal?" (see Excursus 9).[151]

These difficulties can be partially resolved by consulting the translations of Harris and Mingana and of Charlesworth[152] and also making use of Frankenberg's retroversion into Greek.[153] If the subject of 7b is identical with that of 5a and 7a, the Greek text may have run approximately as follows: καὶ ἀπώλοντο [viz., οἱ ἄβυσσοι] ἐν τῷ/τῇ . . .[154] ᾧ/ᾗ ποτὲ ἦσαν/εἶχον, "and they perished in/because of that thought/plan in which they had once been" (7b). In that case, ܡܚܫܒܬܐ (*maḥšabtā*) does not refer in any sense to God's "plan of salvation" but to the "intention"[155] or "purpose"[156] of the annihilating and now annihilated "primal deeps" (see Excursus 28).

The Pa. ܚܒܠ (*ḥabbel*), which derives from a different root from that of ܚܒܠ (*ḥbal*) and cannot, therefore, be translated as "travail,"[157] in 8a takes up the key word (κατα)φθείρω of the Flood metaphor to define the somewhat vague term ܡܚܫܒܬܐ (see 7b above).[158] Always in the past, though not in any otherworldly preexistence, the "primal deeps" have wielded destructive power, so that it is incorrect to say: "For they became corrupt."[159] The point at issue is what the Flood, in the service of God, has achieved "from the beginning" (see Excursus 23).[160]

The term ܚܘܒܠܐ (*ḥubbālā*) in 8b is also derived from the root ܚܒܠ (*ḥabbel*), so neither can it be translated as "travail" (see above). As *nomen actionis,* it means "*destructio*."[161] The *hapax legomenon* ܫܘܠܡܐ (*šullāmā*), as the opposite of "beginning" in 8a, denotes both the "end" (τὸ τέλος) and the "fulfillment" (ἡ τελείωσις). Although there may also be a hint of συντέλεια,[162] the soteriological term ܚܝ̈ܐ (*ḥayyē*)[163] and the construction, parallel to 7b, with ܐܝܬܘܗܝ ܗܘܐ (*ʾītaw-wā*) describe

147 Among them Ungnad and Staerk, 26; Diettrich, 91; Gunkel, *Aufsätze,* 170; Greßmann, 459; Vogl, 67; Emerton, 715; Lattke, *Oden,* 170; Pierre, 133; Azar, 136. Franzmann (p. 187), who insists on the division of 7b into 7b-c in spite of the witness of the manuscripts (see also Lattke, *Bedeutung,* 1:76, 146–47), explains this majority opinion as follows: "7c comprises a rel[ative] cl[ause] referring to the 3rd pl. masc. subj. of 7b (ܬܗܘ̈ܡܐ understood)."

148 See Nöldeke §236. Apart from Frankenberg (p. 24) and Charlesworth (pp. 97–98), see especially Harris and Mingana (2:341): "And they perished in the thought which they had existed in from the beginning." The remark "This is the only meaning the Syriac sentence can have" refers to this line as well as to 7a (Harris and Mingana, 2:343). This conclusion has not yet been taken seriously enough.

149 Spitta, 282.

150 Bauer, 606.

151 Diettrich's interpretation of 7b (p. 91), "as is shown by the next verse, the subject is the fallen angels," is wide of the mark.

152 Harris and Mingana, 2:341; Charlesworth, 98.

153 Frankenberg, 24; see Nöldeke §§303, 347.

154 Frankenberg prefers ποτέ to τὸ πρότερον (cf. Payne Smith, 2:3495; BDAG, *s.vv.* ποτέ, πρότερος), while I would more cautiously not try to determine the precise original of ܡܚܫܒܬܐ (Frankenberg, 24: βουλῇ).

155 BDAG, *s.v.* βουλή.

156 BDAG, *s.v.* νόημα, and other terms, such as [δια-]λογισμός, ἐνθύμησις, or ἐπίνοια, which could also be considered as the Greek original.

157 Contra Harris and Mingana, 2:341; Charlesworth, 98; cf. Brockelmann, *Lexicon,* 211; Payne Smith, 1:1175–76 is less clear.

158 𝔊 may very well have used δέ rather than καί in 8b. Translating the preposition ܒ (*b-*) as "in" in 7a-b is at best an approximation of its meaning.

159 Contra Emerton (p. 715), who also offers "travailed" as an alternative.

160 See BDAG, *s.v.* ἀρχή. Diettrich (p. 91) translates: "For they had sinned in the beginning." Linguistically, this is a possible translation, but it ends on the wrong track when associated with the "fallen angels."

161 Payne Smith, 1:1180.

162 BDAG, *s.v.* συντέλεια. Cf. Matt 13:39, 40, 49; 24:3; 28:20; Heb 9:26.

163 Why "life is thought of as a personification (hypostasis)" in this passage (Diettrich, 91) is incomprehensible. Kruse ("Die 24. Ode," 37) does

the "goal" that is, in mythological guise, now attained by those who are not among the condemned (see Table 1).[164]

■ **9** According to Kruse, "24:9 is enigmatic."[165] So it is not surprising that some translators are not content with as literal a translation as possible,[166] but give their intuition free rein.[167] But even an idiomatic translation of this bicolon[168] is fraught with linguistic difficulties, partly because of the "obvious" "change of scene."[169] In stanza V the Flood mythos leaves only a dying echo in 9a.[170] All else is preparation for stanza VI.

In spite of the repetition of the Pe. ܐܒܕ (*ʾeḇaḏ*), the subject of 9a is not identical with that of 7b, unless, indeed, the earlier passage already spoke of "human beings." Here, at least, "all that was lacking"—even without the insertion of "wisdom"[171]—refers to "human opponents."[172] This is made clear by 9b, not by the plural suffix of the preposition ܡܢ (*men*), which refers back to the "primal deeps" of stanzas III–IV. The phrase ܡܢܗܘܢ (*mennhōn*), because of its unusual placing, must be taken as a translation of ὑπὸ αὐτῶν,[173] although it is possible that the Greek original had ὑπὸ αὐτούς, which was misinterpreted by the Syriac translator.[174] This results in two possible translations: "perished through them . . ." and "was destroyed by them . . ." (1 Cor 10:9-10 offers a linguistic comparison).

My earlier alternative translation of 9b (= 9b-c),[175] which had already been suggested by Newbold ("Because it was not possible to give them the Word"),[176] cannot be sustained in the face of the idiomatic use of ܐܝܬ (*ʾīṯ*) + ܠ (*l-*).[177] If the "lack" in 9a should refer not to "truth" (10b) or "wisdom" (11a) but to the unattainable "word" in 9b,[178] then 9b would give only a negative reason for this lack. But probably 9b needs to be taken more radically, as the reason why that which had a lack perished or was destroyed. Whether the Greek original of this statement, set in the mythological past, was made with ἔχω + infinitive[179] or with γίνομαι + dative of the person + infinitive[180] is not very important. It is more important that the imperfect of the Pa. ܩܘܝ (*qawwī*), which corresponds to a subjunctive or infinitive of the verb μένω, represents the opposite (which has *here* been ruled out) of a verb of destruction and condemnation (9a; cf. 8:22 and the use of μένω in, e.g., John 8:31; 12:46; 15:4-6, 9-10). The condemned, indeed, lack the "word on which everything depends"[181] that would enable them to "abide," namely, the "password" when challenged.[182] A Christian-Gnostic parallel is found

consider the paradox of "destruction" and "life" and remarks on the "ambiguity of the images," but, like Drijvers ("Polemik"), he erroneously involves the heretic Marcion.

164 See Payne Smith, 2:4188; BDAG, *s.v.* τέλος, 3, referring to Rom 6:21-22.

165 Kruse, "Die 24. Ode," 37.

166 E.g., Ungnad and Staerk, 26.

167 E.g., Gunkel, *Aufsätze*, 170.

168 I now accept the manuscript evidence that 9 is a narrative bicolon whose clotted Syriac derives from a more elegant Greek construction (contra Lattke, *Oden*, 170; and idem, *Bedeutung*, 1:146–47). Franzmann in her edition (p. 183) follows Lattke, *Bedeutung*, 1:146, but in her translation she limits 9c to the final dependent clause "that they might abide" (Franzmann, 184).

169 Kruse, "Die 24. Ode," 37.

170 Cf. Gen 6:7, 13, 17; 7:4, 21-23.

171 Diettrich, 91, referring to 11a; but cf. also 18:4.

172 Kruse, "Die 24. Ode," 38. The variant ܕܟܠ (*d-kol*) in H is a scribal error (Lattke, *Bedeutung*, 1:64–67).

173 Contra Frankenberg, 24 (καὶ ἀπώλετο αὐτῶν πᾶν τὸ ὑστεροῦν); cf. Payne Smith, 2:2157, 2159; BDAG, *s.v.* ὑπό, A.a.; on ἀπόλλυμαι cf. BDAG, *s.v.* ἀπόλλυμι, 1b.

174 BAGD, *s.v.* ὑπό, B. The preposition ܡܢ (*men*) could also represent an original ἀπό (BDAG, *s.v.*) or even διά (BDAG, *s.v.*). An instrumental use of the dative does not come under consideration.

175 Lattke, *Oden*, 170.

176 Newbold, "Bardaisan," 197.

177 Payne Smith, *Dictionary*, 14; Nöldeke §307. The omission of ܠܗܘܢ (*lhōn*) by H is among those that "make it hard to suppress a certain mistrust of H" (Lattke, *Bedeutung*, 1:67).

178 Kruse, "Die 24. Ode," 37, with various speculations on the "truths of faith."

179 BDAG, *s.v.* ἔχω.

180 BDAG, *s.v.* γίνομαι.

181 Kruse, "Die 24. Ode," 37.

182 Bauer, 606; cf. *Asc. Isa.* 10:24-31; C. Detlef G. Müller, "Die Himmelfahrt des Jesaja," *NTApo* (5th ed., 1989) 2:560, "The Ascension of Isaiah," *NTApoc* 2:617–18. Vogl's translation (p. 67) is: "since it . . . was impossible to give a reason that they might remain." He misreads Bauer's translation, "Losungswort [password]," as "Lösungswort [word of solution]" and thus shows from two aspects that he has grasped the special character of this "word" as little as Harris and Mingana (2:341), who translate: "For it was not permitted to them

in *Testimony of Truth* (NHC IX,*3*): "They do not have the word which gives [life]" (34,24-26).[183] Since ܦܬܓܡܐ (*petḡāmā*) is the direct object of the infinitive of ܢܬܠ (*nettel*), the term could be a translation of ἀπόκρισις (cf. John 1:22 and 19:9 as purely linguistic parallels).[184] It is also possible that ܝܗܒ ܦܬܓܡܐ (*yab̲ petḡāmā*) is a translation of ἀποκρίνομαι (cf. John 18:22)[185] or even of λόγον ἀποδίδωμι = "give account."[186] But considering "a marked syntactic similarity between 9b and 12b"[187] and its close connection with "truth," this retroversion may be too formal, and λόγος or ῥῆμα would be a more likely original (see Excursus 12), the soteriological meaning of which can be found in the *Odes of Solomon* themselves (cf. 7:7; 8:8; and esp. the whole of *Ode* 12).[188]

■ **10-12** "The inclusio for the stanza is formed by the repetition of ܫܪܪܐ ܠܘܬܗܘܢ (ܗܘܐ) ܠܝܬ in 10b and 12b."[189] This by itself is reason enough not to treat 12b as a gloss.[190] The myth of Noah's Flood belongs to an earlier part of the Ode and should not be imported into these dualistic sentences of doom. While in H stanzas VI and VII can be referred to *God*'s judgment, on the one hand, and to *God*'s mercy and holiness, on the other (see on 1a and 5b above), in N—and probably also in the Greek original—both the negative and positive theologoumena are attributed to the Messiah "Lord," the *Κύριος Χριστός* (see the discussion on "Lord" in *Ode* 1), which can be supported by reference to other passages in the *Odes of Solomon* (e.g., 17:16; 29:6; 31:1-5; 39:11; and perhaps also 27:1 and its doublet in 42:1).[191]

By the parallelism with 12a, it becomes clear that in 10a the annihilation expressed by the Aph. of ܐܒܕ is not limited to the "thoughts," that more is intended than cleansing (Pe. *ʾeb̲ad̲* in 7a and 9a; Aph. *ʾawbed̲* also in 6:3a; see Excursus 28). For the rare plural of ܡܚܫܒܬܐ (*maḥšab̲tā*), reference can be made to the equally negative statement in 29:8 and the Gnostically positive antithesis in 18:13 (see the summary in Excursus 9). The full negativity of this close association of the (probably more existential than intellectual) term ܡܚܫܒܬܐ, which has already been used for the destructive plans of the "primal deeps" (7b), and the central dualistic term ܫܪܪܐ (*šrārā*, 10b, 12b) can be appreciated only by contrast with the personal statement of the redeemed Redeemer: "The thought of truth led me" (17:5a; see Excursus 1). The missing enclitic ܗܘܐ (*-wā*) in the idiomatic construction with ܠܝܬ (*layt*) + ܠܘܬ (*lwāt̲*), which corresponds to ἔχω and was probably negated, can, in all likelihood, be traced back to the use of a participle in 𝔊 (πάντων τῶν ἀλήθειαν μὴ ἐχόντων).[192]

In N, 11a-b appears as a monocolon, while H inserts a completely erroneous mark of division partway through 11b so that the second part of 11b seems to be part of 12a.[193] This poetic confusion has been finally untangled by Harris and Mingana.[194] The central bicolon refers to both the adjacent bicola, 10 and 12, offering two reasons for the destruction and rejection. The following observation reveals even more: "The synonymous descriptions in 11a and 11b (lack of wisdom, haughtiness of heart) are also ironically antithetical: being needy/lacking over against being haughty."[195] The perfect of the Pe. ܚܣܪ (*ḥsar*) is used only in 11a; it resonates weakly with the verbal adjective ܚܣܝܪ (*ḥassīr*) in 9a,[196] and may

to make a defence for themselves that they might remain."

183 Søren Giversen and Birger A. Pearson, "The Testimony of Truth (IX,*3*)," *NHLE*, 451; reference from Franzmann, "Background."

184 Frankenberg, 24; see BDAG, *s.v.* ἀπόκρισις.

185 BDAG, *s.v.* ἀποκρίνομαι.

186 BDAG, ἀποδίδωμι, 2c; Payne Smith, 1:1566.

187 Franzmann, 187. She also draws attention to the parallel in v. 10 (p. 187, where "10a" is a misprint for "10b").

188 Diettrich's reference (p. 91 n. 7) to the "word (of truth)" is justified. His references to "Ode 22,12. 35,4 f." seem to be misprints for *Ode* 12:12 and *Ode* 38:4–5.

189 Franzmann, 188.

190 Contra Grimme, 103; cf. Lattke, *Bedeutung*, 3:101.

191 Unfortunately, apart from one obscure statement, Abramowski (p. 69) contributed nothing to this problem in *Ode* 24.

192 Frankenberg, 24, though he adds an unnecessary παρ' αὐτοῖς; see Payne Smith, 2:1918. In my earlier, and different, translation of 10b and 12b (Lattke, *Oden*, 171) I assumed that 𝔖 was based on a construction with ἦν/ἐγένετο + preposition παρά/πρός + personal pronoun. It is also possible that the Greek construction of 10b differed from that of 12b.

193 Lattke, *Bedeutung*, 1:76–77.

194 Harris and Mingana, vol. 1, on this passage; 2:342.

195 Franzmann, 188.

196 See Nöldeke §118; Payne Smith, 1:1339.

be under the influence of Pauline language (e.g., Rom 3:23).[197] The term ܚܟܡܬܐ (*ḥekmtā*), parallel to "truth," probably represents σοφία,[198] but neither as personified "Wisdom" (cf. 7:8) nor as the "pragmatic wisdom such as the Qoheleth wished to convey to its readers."[199] The idea of Χριστός as θεοῦ σοφία is also not in question here (cf. 1 Cor 1:24). The stress is more on the connection between σοφία and γνῶσις (1 Cor 12:8; see 14a-b below).[200] Within the setting of 11a-b, "wisdom" consists, above all, in not being "presumptuous."[201] It is also possible, however, that the participle of the Ethpe. of ܪܘܡ, ܪܡ (*rām*), used in this way only here, could be a translation of a form of ὑψόω.[202] The term καρδία/ܠܒܐ (*lebbā*) means the "center of personal life" (see Excursus 4). If in this passage it was meant as the "organ of thought," the idea would connect less to "wisdom" than to the "thoughts" of 10a.

The verb ܐܘܒܕ (*ʾawbeḏ*) in 10a is matched in harshness by the Ethpe. of ܣܠܐ (*slā*) in the strangely abbreviated but therefore more inexorable verdict 12a, which only H clumsily attempts to lengthen (see above). As a predestining sentence of doom, based on the cause given in 12b, it carries not merely disparagement and contemptuous dismissal[203] but also eschatological rejection.[204] This rejection was not visited on the redeemed Redeemer (cf. 42:10) nor on those to whom the Redeemer "gives life" and whom he "does not reject" (41:11b, with use of the negated Aph. ܐܣܠܝ [*ʾaslī*]). And this positive face of the Gnostic-dualistic mythos now appears.

■ **13-14** Although stanza VII is in some sense a "coda," the two bicola can hardly "explain why the judgment (v. 2-8 [= 3-12]) can fall so heavily on the 'ignorant.'"[205] In fact, within a profound dualism, after the prevailing negatives[206] the positive side of the medal is now exhibited. So the conjunction ὅτι/ܡܛܠ ܕ (*meṭṭol d-*) in 13a is not, as in 12b, meant causally,[207] nor is it "unusual";[208] it expresses a "loose subordination" that should be translated by "for."[209] Since the "Lord" of stanza VII is identical to the one of stanza VI (see above), John 14:6 cannot be cited to explain the "way" of the Κύριος Χριστός.[210] Among the *Odes of Solomon*, the most important comparison is the promise of the perfect virgin Grace: "my ways I will make known" (33:13). An equally Gnostic juxtaposition of "way" and the Aph. ܐܦܬܝ (*ʾap̄tī*), as in 13b, is to be found in 7:13a-b, but in that passage it is *God*'s "way" to the "*plērōma*." However, taking into account 7:25b (where "grace" is the direct object of the Pa. ܚܘܝ [*ḥawwī*]), a comparison with 7:13 demonstrates the breadth of the imagery in the *Odes of Solomon*. Perhaps it was the key word "truth" in 12b that led to the use of "way" as the object of the first verb (cf. also 11:3b and 33:8c in contrast to 15:6a and 31:7a), which represents either δείκνυμι or φανερόω (see Excursus 15).[211]

197 BDAG, *s.v.* ὑστερέω.
198 Payne Smith, 1:1267–68; BDAG, *s.v.* σοφία.
199 Thomas Krüger, *Kohelet (Prediger)* (BKAT 19 [Sonderband]; Neukirchen-Vluyn: Neukirchener Verlag, 2000) 18; cf. 44–47.
200 Diettrich (p. 91) points out, correctly, that "the thought cannot be confined in national boundaries."
201 BDAG, *s.v.* ἐπαίρω, 3 (passive): "W[ith] the dat[ive] to denote the basis for the presumption."
202 Payne Smith, 2:3857; BDAG, *s.v.* ὑψόω; Frankenberg, 24: οἱ κατὰ τὰς καρδίας ὑψούμενοι.
203 As for Frankenberg, 24; BDAG, *s.v.* ἐξουθενέω.
204 Payne Smith, 2:2637; BDAG, *s.v.* ἀποδοκιμάζω.
205 Contra Diettrich, 89.
206 Franzmann (p. 188) correctly observes the "generally negative flavour of the Ode," but does not point emphatically enough to the themes of destruction and rejection.
207 Contra Emerton, 715.
208 Contra Franzmann, 188.
209 BDAG, *s.v.* ὅτι, 4b; Payne Smith, 2:2077; Bauer, 606; Harris and Mingana, 2:342; Charlesworth, 99. "Subordination with ὅτι and διότι is often very loose so that it must be translated 'for'" (BDF and BDR §456 [1]). Cf. the following passages: Matt 7:13-14; 11:29-30; John 1:16-17; 1 Cor 1:25; 4:9; 2 Cor 4:6; 7:8, 14. In *NTSyr* ܡܛܠ ܕ is used in John 1:17 and 1 Cor 1:25.
210 Even so, it is worth referring to Bultmann's collection of parallels under the heading "He has shown/prepared the way for his own" (Bultmann, "Bedeutung," 133–34 = idem, *Exegetica*, 90–92). Kruse ("Die 24. Ode," 38) correctly identifies the "Lord" with "Christ," but then refers to the "way" in 11:3b, which is hardly relevant, and connects this with the "circumcision," interpreted as "baptism," of 11:1a, 3a and also with the self-revelation of the Johannine Jesus in John 14:6.
211 Payne Smith, 1:1208–9; BDAG, *s.v.* φανερόω.

"Way" (13a) would be more suitable than "grace" as the object of the Aph. of ܦܬܐ (*ptā*) or ܦܬܝ (*ptī*) in 13b.[212] The Greek original will have had *τὴν χάριν* parallel to *τὴν ὁδόν* and a form of *πλατύνω*[213] where 𝔖 has ܐܦܬܝ (*ʾaptī*). Even though the same verb is used, there is no allusion to the end of the story of Noah in Gen 9:27.[214]

The wordplay with the Eshtaph. perfect (14a) and the active participle (14b) of ܝܕܥ (*ʾidaʿ*) can certainly represent a similar Greek play on (*ἐπι*)*γινώσκω* and *οἶδα*. But nothing more can be deduced because of the large number of possible equivalents.[215] As has been shown in Excursus 7, it is difficult to determine whether the feminine objective suffix refers to "way" or to "grace."[216] It cannot, however, represent *αὐτόν*.[217] The "Lord" of these Gnostics, assured of salvation, not only participates actively in the exercise of God's grace (13b) but also partakes of *ὁσιότης*/ܚܣܝܘܬܐ (*ḥasyūtā*, "holiness") of the Lord God (cf. 20:9c, where the "kindness" and "grace" of 9b are parallel to the "glory of his holiness"). Although in Jewish and early Christian tradition the almighty Lord God and "King of all peoples" is *μόνος ὅσιος* (Rev 15:4; 16:5), the *Κύριος Χριστός*, described as the "son" and the "high priest," can also, at least in primitive Christianity, be called *ὅσιος* (Heb 7:26), with a reference to Ps 15:10 LXX (Acts 2:27; 13:35).[218] So it is not altogether surprising that the "Lord Messiah" of *Ode* 24 (N) should be characterized by the *theological* term "holiness."[219]

212 See on 7:13 above; also Excursus 33. The translation "and lavishly dispensed his grace" (Kruse, "Die 24. Ode," 26) is too free. Even if John 1:17 is accepted as a parallel, it is necessary to contradict the reference to "the anti-Marcionite *aphthonia*" (ibid., 38).

213 Frankenberg, 24.

214 Payne Smith, 2:3334; BDAG, *s.v.* *πλατύνω*.

215 Payne Smith, 1:1554–57; BDAG, *s.vv.* *γινώσκω*, *ἐπιγινώσκω*, *οἶδα*.

216 "The Syriac has a feminine pronoun that may refer either to 'way' or to 'goodness'" (Bauer, 606). The second term is translated here by "grace" (Charlesworth, 99; Pierre, 134: "Grâce").

217 Contra Frankenberg, 24; Bauer, 606, although his n. 2 is accurate. Diettrich (p. 92) translates the suffix as a feminine pronoun to refer to "grace," but Charlesworth (p. 100)—following Ungnad and Staerk (p. 26)—valiantly declares: "The pronoun refers to 'way.'"

218 BDAG, *s.v.* *ὅσιος*; Payne Smith, 1:1327–28; Brockelmann, *Lexicon*, 245.

219 Michael Lattke, "Heiligkeit III. Neues Testament," *TRE* 14 (1985) 705.

25

Ode 25: A Redeemed One Speaks of Being Saved

Syriac (𝔖)

(I) 1a I was rescued from my bonds
1b and fled to thee, my God,
2a because thou wast the right [hand] of salvation
2b and *my* helper.

(II) 3a Thou hast restrained those who arise against me,
3b and they were no more seen[a],
4a for thy face was with me,
4b which saved[b] me by thy grace.

(III) 5a But I was despised and rejected in the eyes of many,
5b and I was/became like lead in their eyes.
6 And I had strength from thee and help.

(IV) 7a Thou didst set a lamp for me on my right [side] and on my left,
7b that[c] there might not be anything without light about me.

(V) 8a And I was covered with the covering of thy spirit,
8b and thou didst remove from me my garments of skin.
9a For thy right [hand] exalted me,
9b and thou didst cause infirmity to pass from me.

(VI) 10a And I was strong/mighty in thy truth[d],
10b and holy by thy righteousness.
11a And all my adversaries feared me,
11b and I became the Lord's by the name of the Lord,
12a and I was justified by his kindness,
12b and his rest is for all eternity.
Hallelujah.

Coptic (ℭ)[e]

(I) 1a I was rescued from my bonds;
1b I fled to thee, Lord,
2a for thou hast been a right [hand] for me, saving me
2b and helping me.

(II) 3a Thou hast hindered those who arise against me,
3b and they have not appeared,
4a for thy face was with me,
4b saving me by thy grace.

(III) 5a I was despised before many, and they rejected me;
5b I became like lead before them.
6 I received a power from thee, helping me.

(IV) 7a For thou hast placed lamps on my right [side] and my left,
7b that no side of me might be without light.

a 3b ܐܬܚܙܝܘ N; ܐܚܙܝܘܗܝ H.
b 4b ܦܪܩ H; ܦܪܩܐ N.
c 7b ܕܠܐ N; ܘܠܐ H.
d 10a ܒܫܪܪܟ N; ܒܫܪܪܐ H.
e (ℭ) On variants in ℭ, see commentary.

(V) 8a Thou coveredst me with the covering of thy mercy,
8b and I rose above the garments of skin.
9a It was thy right [hand] that exalted me,
9b and thou hast taken away sickness from me.
(VI) 10a I became strengthened by thy truth,
10b [and] pure by thy righteousness.
11 Those who rose against me became far from me,

12a and I was justified by thy kindness,
12b for thy rest is for all eternity.

Introduction

Ode 25 is preserved in two Syriac manuscripts and in the Coptic *Pistis Sophia*.[1] There is great relief in Harris and Mingana's declaration: "This Ode is of a much more intelligible structure than those which immediately precede."[2] However, this does not mean that "it poses no exegetical problems."[3] On the contrary, even the identity of the redeemed "I" is hard to ascertain, since *Ode* 25 belongs to those "*Odes* where it is impossible to determine which of the two sons is speaking."[4] If it emerges that the address to "God" (1b 𝔖) or the "Lord" (1b ℭ; 11b 𝔖) is to be understood as being, at least in part, "*ex ore Christi*,"[5] then, although there is no mention in this Ode of acts of salvation by the redeemed and justified one, it would be necessary to contradict Spitta's statement that "the 25th and 26th *Odes* contain no Christian ideas."[6] Jewish influence is evident, but this Ode, which the *Pistis Sophia* interprets Gnostically, especially in relation to the term "light," belongs "clearly among those that can be described as Gnostic in their own right."[7] *Ode* 25 is no more a "baptismal hymn,"[8] even, according to Bernard, "placed in the mouth of the neophyte,"[9] than an "unalloyed prayer of thanksgiving"[10] or "hymn of thanksgiving."[11] It is a personal testimony of salvation, which, at the end of the Syriac text, merges into a theological statement of eternity in the "rest" of the totally other-worldly "Lord."

1 Mss.: Codex H, 19b–20a; Codex N, 149^v–150^r (𝔖); Codex A, 70^{v}b–71^{r}b (ℭ). Ed./trans.: Charlesworth, pp. 100–103; Franzmann, 189–98; Lattke, 2:215–33 and 3:XXXIV–XXXV.
2 Harris and Mingana, 2:347.
3 Diettrich, 92.
4 Abramowski, 59.
5 Harris and Mingana, 2:347.
6 Spitta, 282.
7 Lattke, *Bedeutung*, 1:222.
8 Schille, 63.
9 Bernard, 107.
10 Abramowski, 52.
11 Colpe, "Überlieferung," 77. This latter classification has an extended history. Already Gunkel in his two articles in *RGG* (see Hermann Gunkel, "Salomo-Oden," *RGG*^{1} 5 [1913] 228; idem, "Salomo-Oden," *RGG*^{2} 5 [1931] 88), mentions "hymn of thanksgiving" in connection with *Ode* 25, and this clearly influenced Bultmann ("Bedeutung," 135 = *Exegetica*, 93). The influence of Gunkel and Begrich (*Einleitung*, 6, 265, 292) can also be traced in the cases of Günter Morawe, "Vergleich des Aufbaus der Danklieder und hymnischen Bekenntnislieder (1 QH) von Qumran mit dem Aufbau der Psalmen im Alten Testament und im Spätjudentum," *RevQ* 4 (1963) 347, 355, and Eissfeldt, §93 n. 2, who preceded Colpe, "Überlieferung," 77, in describing the *Ode* as a "song of thanksgiving." Cf. Buschmann, 226–90, esp. 230, 266, on *Mart. Pol.* 14.

Interpretation

■ **1-2** The "I" of indeterminable gender begins the "description of salvation"[12] with a synthetic *parallelismus membrorum* (1a-b), which exhibits both chiasm and antitheses.[13] Although the verb "to flee" in the second half of the bicolon might suggest the active voice for translating the Ethpe. of ܦܠܛ (*plaṭ*),[14] used only in 1a, the general tenor of the Ode, and especially the sense of 2a-b, argues rather for the passive.[15] So ⲛⲟⲩϩⲙ̄ ⲉⲃⲟⲗ (*nuhᵉm ebol*) is not to be understood reflexively either,[16] but as a translation of the passive of ἐξαιρέω.[17] Since the "I" of the Ode is not merely the "soul,"[18] the metaphorical ⲙⲣ̄ⲣⲉ/ܐܣܘܪܐ (ʾ*asūrē*), "bonds," does not describe the body, σάρξ or σῶμα, but stands for the dark "imprisonment" in the world (cf. esp. 21:2 and 42:16).[19]

The existential flight to "God"[20] also states a mythological destination, as will be seen (see 9a [exaltation], 12b [rest] below). Connolly on 1b refers to Ps 142:9b LXX and infers that it is "a translation of πρὸς σὲ κατέφυγον."[21] Of course, ἔφυγον, rather than κατέφυγον, could also have been the original of ⲡⲱⲧ/ܥܪܩ (*ʿraq*).[22] With a glance back at John 20:28, where Thomas addresses the miraculously present Jesus as ὁ κύριός μου καὶ ὁ θεός μου ("My Lord and my God!"), the θεός/ܐܠܗܐ (ʾ*allāhā*) here could be interpreted as the risen Κύριος Χριστός (see on 11b ܣ below). In the context of *Ode* 25 and of the *Odes of Solomon* as a whole, it is more probable that the address is directed to the Most High, who does not exist and is therefore able to liberate completely and be the ultimate refuge.[23] So it is possible to read the whole Ode as being spoken by the supreme Christian Son of God.

The Coptic version of 2a-b, which differs widely from the Syriac and is marked by the erroneous repetition of ⲉⲕⲛⲟⲩϩⲙ̄ ⲙ̄ⲙⲟⲓ̈ ⲁⲩⲱ, can be simply explained by reference to the hymn of the *Pistis Sophia*.[24] As in a number of other passages (8:6; 14:4; 18:7; 22:7), ܝܡܝܢܐ (*yammīnā*) refers to God's right hand as the symbol of his power, here soteriologically qualified by the genitive of σωτηρία/ܦܘܪܩܢܐ (*purqānā*), "salvation." Both the redeeming "right hand" and the term "helper" used with the unidiomatic ܕܝܠ (*dīl* = μου), which "emphasises the owner,"[25] are under the literary influence of Ps 117:6-7 LXX (κύριος ἐμοὶ βοηθός, "the Lord is my helper") and Ps 117:16 LXX (δεξιὰ κυρίου, "the right

12 Reitzenstein, *Das iranische Erlösungsmysterium*, 91.
13 Franzmann, 193. On the differences in the division of 1a-b and 2a-b in Mss. H and N, see Lattke, *Bedeutung*, 1:76.
14 Payne Smith, 2:3153; Bauer, 606: "Entronnen bin ich [I escaped]"; Franzmann, 190: "I escaped."
15 Harris and Mingana, 2:346; Charlesworth, 101: "I was rescued."
16 Crum, 244; on the passive sense of the I. infinitive, see Till §255.
17 BDAG, *s.v.* ἐξαιρέω, 2.
18 Contra Frankenberg, 52–53.
19 BDAG, *s.v.* δεσμός; Crum, 182; Payne Smith, 1:323. In the hymn of the *Pistis Sophia*, the "bonds" are matter-of-factly interpreted as "bonds of darkness" (Lattke, *Bedeutung*, 1:148–49).
20 The reading κύριος/ⲭⲟⲉⲓⲥ (*čoïs*) of ϲ depends on the mythological context in which *Ode* 25 appears in the *Pistis Sophia* (Lattke, *Bedeutung*, 1:202–5). Cf. the discussion of this divine title in the commentary on *Ode* 1.
21 Connolly, "Greek," 536. His deduction is important since Psalm 142 LXX has left more traces on the *Ode* than Psalm 132 (131 LXX), quoted by Harris and Mingana (2:349–51). Ps 142:10a LXX, after all, has σὺ εἶ ὁ θεός μου (Rahlfs, 2:157). For other references, see below on 4a (face); 10a (truth); 10b (righteousness); 11b ܣ (name).
22 BDAG, *s.vv.* φεύγω, καταφεύγω; Crum, 274; Payne Smith, 2:2997.
23 Vincent Brümmer does not touch on liberation and refuge in his remark that "God does not exist as a palpable object but as the highest being, in relation to which the believer claims to act and by such actions to attain the good life" (see Brümmer, "Gott IV. Religionsphilosophisch," *RGG*⁴ [2000] 1112, at the end of sec. 3: "Transzendenz und Wirklichkeit Gottes"). On the systematic and theological question "Does God exist?," see also Christoph Schwöbel, "Gott V. Dogmatisch. 1–2," *RGG*⁴ (2000) 1125–26.
24 Lattke, *Bedeutung*, 1:148–49. My earlier marking of the dittography needs to be corrected (cf. Franzmann, 191).
25 Connolly, "Greek," 537; Nöldeke §225.

hand of the Lord"). So 2a-b 𝔊 can be reconstructed somewhat as follows: *καὶ ἦσθα/ἐγένου ἡ δεξιὰ (μου) σωτηρίας καὶ βοηθός μου* (see Excursus 5).[26]

■ **3-4** An accumulation of Greek loanwords is not proof of a Greek original. But, taken with the syntax of 4b and the constructions of the verbs in 3a-b, the occurrence of *κωλύω* (3a ℭ), *πρόσωπον* (4a 𝔖), and *χάρις* (4b ℭ) does point strongly in that direction. The statement of salvation in 3a, addressed to God or the Lord, also mentions "adversaries,"[27] who will recur (11a; cf., for content not vocabulary, Ps 142:3, 9, 12 LXX). The Pe. ܟܠܐ (*klā*) clearly derives from *κωλύω*,[28] while the two constructions describing the adversaries represent either *ἀνθίστημι* or *ἀντιτάσσω*[29] and correspond to the accusative of a participle with dative of the person.[30]

The Ethpe. of ܚܙܐ (*ḥzā*) can be used to translate *ὤφθησαν*,[31] but the Coptic ⲟⲩⲱⲛϩ̄ ⲉⲃⲟⲗ suggests rather that the Greek of 3a was *καὶ οὐκέτι ἐφανερώθησαν*.[32] The omission of the adverb in ℭ can most probably be explained by the Gnostic interpretation in the hymn of the *Pistis Sophia* ("and they could not come near me").[33] The reading of H in 𝔖 (ܠܐ ܐܚܙܝܘܗܝ [*lā ʾeḥzēw*] = "I shall not see him") was described as "meaningless" already by Diettrich.[34]

The causal conjunctions, in both ℭ and 𝔖, at the beginning of 4a correspond to *ὅτι* and explain both the "action of God" in 3a[35] and the absence of the adversaries in 3b. The "presence of God's redeeming grace" has taken their previous, mythological, place (cf. Ps 142:7c LXX).[36] The Coptic ϩⲟ (*ho*), like the Syriac ܦܪܨܘܦܐ (*parṣōpā*), is masculine.[37] The underlying neuter *πρόσωπον* does not here mean "person"[38] but "face" or "countenance" as the bearer of God's presence, though not in connection with a ritual.[39]

Verse 4b is not a simple "rel[ative] cl[ause]"[40] in either ℭ or 𝔖. But since ܗܘ ܕ (*hāw d-*) etc. "are gradually approximating to the meaning of the definite article, for which in fact they are directly used by certain translators from the Greek,"[41] the clumsy beginning of 4b 𝔖 corresponds to a participle[42] with article, which gives the complete apposition to *πρόσωπον* the *appearance* of a relative clause (*τὸ σώσαν με [ἐν τῇ] χάριτί σου*).[43] The juxtaposition of *χάρις*/ܛܝܒܘܬܐ (*ṭaybūṯā*) and *σῴζω*/ܦܪܩ (*praq*) may derive from Eph 2:5, 8 (*χάριτί ἐστε σωσῳσμένοι*, "by grace you have been saved"); in any case, it serves as a connection between stanzas I and II.

■ **5-6** Deviating from Franzmann's verse division—she follows the manuscripts in the abscission of the last word of 6, and in addition she links 6a-b ℭ with 7a-b ℭ[44]—stanza III, in both languages, will be treated as a tricolon.[45] The monocolon 6, which should not be divided on the pattern of 2a-b into an even less acceptable bicolon (see above), forms the conclusion of the first part of *Ode* 25.[46]

26 See BDAG, *s.vv.* *βοηθός, δεξιός, σωτηρία*; Payne Smith, 1:1605, 2:2815, 3295. A comparison with the Syriac translation of Ps 118:6-7 and 118:16 (Peshitta) reinforces the impression that the model of 2a-b was found in Psalm 117 LXX; cf. *OTSy*, pt. 2 fasc. 3, p. 141: ܝܡܝܢܗ ܕܡܪܝܐ (Ps 118:16); ܡܪܝܐ ܡܥܕܪܢܝ (Ps 118:6-7).

27 Franzmann, 194.

28 BDAG, *s.v.* *κωλύω*; Payne Smith, 1:1738–39.

29 BDAG, *s.vv.* *ἀνθίστημι, ἀντιτάσσω*: "set oneself against"; cf. Payne Smith, 2:3522–23; Crum, 394.

30 See, e.g., Frankenberg, 24: *ἐκώλυσας τούς μοι ἀνθισταμένους*.

31 BDAG, *s.v.* *ὁράω*.

32 BDAG, *s.v.* *φανερόω*; Payne Smith, 1:1234; Crum, 486.

33 Lattke, *Bedeutung*, 1:146.

34 Diettrich, 92.

35 Franzmann, 194.

36 Lattke, "Wörter," 298 = Lattke, *Bedeutung*, 4:147.

37 See Crum, 646; Payne Smith, 2:3291.

38 Contra Bauer, 606.

39 BDAG, *s.v.* *πρόσωπον*; see also Gräßer, 2:191–92, on Heb 9:24.

40 Contra Franzmann, 194; cf. Lambdin, 95–97: "The Circumstantial."

41 Nöldeke §228.

42 H uses the Pe. perfect of ܦܪܩ (*praq*) instead of the Pe. participle ܦܪܩܐ (*pārqā*). Perhaps N's use of the participle was determined by the Greek original.

43 See BDAG, *s.v.* *ὁ, ἡ, τό*, 2cβ. I cannot understand how Frankenberg (p. 24) could translate it by *ὁ τῇ χάριτι σώσας με*. Harris and Mingana (vol. 1, on this passage) claim a reading of ܒܛܝܒܘܬܟ in 4b N, on which Charlesworth (p. 105 n. 5) correctly remarks: "*Yūdh* was written, but its ink coalesced with that of the *Bēth*."

44 Franzmann, 194, 196.

45 Cf. Lattke, *Bedeutung*, 1:76–77.

46 Franzmann, 194.

Anyone who is aware of the statements about the Son of Man in the Synoptics (cf., e.g., Mark 8:31; 9:12; Luke 9:22; 17:25) would attribute the first person utterance of 5a, with its two passive verbs, to the risen Lord. Harris and Mingana should have pointed to these passages in support of their impression that certain verses of *Ode* 25 "have an appearance of being *ex ore Christi*."[47] In spite of the differences between the Peshitta and the Philoxenian text of Mark 9:12,[48] it is possible to say that the Greek *Vorlage* of the Ethpe. of ܫܐܛ, ܫܛ (*šāṭ*) was ἐξουδενήθην/ἐξουθενήθην/-ώθην ("treat with contempt"),[49] and that of the synonymous ܣܠܐ (*slā*) was ἀπεδοκιμάσθην ("reject, declare useless").[50] The idiomatic prepositional phrase employing the term "eyes," which may not have occurred in 𝔊,[51] might mean simply *coram* or ἐναντίον,[52] but the plural of ܣܓܝ (*saggī*) is reminiscent of the "many" of 23:19b, denoting a larger group than the adversaries of 3a and 11a.[53] The immediate mythological enemies, whom Franzmann equates with the "many,"[54] have already vanished (3b) and exist only in the fear they feel (11a).

Harris and Mingana consider that the comparison drawn in the judgment of the "many" between the despised and rejected "I" and the heavy element[55] μόλιβος/μόλυβδος/ⲧⲁϩⲧ̄/ܐܒܪܐ (*ʾabārā*) in 5b is "not a very happy image."[56] They suggest emending ܐܒܪܐ to ܐܒܝܕܐ (*ʾabīdā* = "a lost, damned [man]"), as in 28:9.[57] Diettrich, however, had already pointed to the concept of "*inferiority*" connected with "lead" (cf. Jer 6:29; Ezek 22:18).[58] So the *hapax legomenon,* modified by ὡς/ܐܝܟ (*ʾak*), does not refer to the weight of the lead, but to the fact that, in spite of its usefulness, it is a "valueless . . . metal."[59] Lines 5a and 5b are thus "semantically equivalent."[60]

Except for the final word, which, following H—and perhaps N also—has been unpoetically isolated as 6b by some commentators,[61] the Greek text of 6 cannot be recovered. The beginning could have been a form of ἔχω with accusative, or a construction such as ἐγένετό μοι.[62] A variety of prepositional phrases with genitive σου could be represented by ܡܢ ܠܘܬܟ (*men lwāṭāk*) and ⲉⲃⲟⲗ ϩⲓⲧⲟⲟⲧⲕ̄ (*ebol hitook-ᵉk*).[63] The masculine ܥܘܫܢܐ (*ʿušnā*), "strength," derived from the root ܥܫܢ, is used to translate δύναμις,[64] but also ἰσχύς and even κράτος.[65] The same goes for ϭⲟⲙ.[66] More important than determining the Greek equivalents is the fact that the Ethpe. of ܥܫܢ (*ʿšen*) is also put into the mouth of the redeemed

47 Harris and Mingana, 2:347. It should be noted, however, that Harris and Mingana remark only a little further on (p. 348): "It is not, however, easy to see how to refer this Ode generally to the mouth of Christ."

48 See Klein, *Wörterbuch*, 74: Ethpe of ܣܠܐ; 99: Ettaph. = Ethpe. of ܫܐܛ, ܫܛ.

49 Payne Smith, 2:4093; BDAG, *s.v.* ἐξουδενέω.

50 Payne Smith, 2:2637; BDAG, *s.v.* ἀποδοκιμάζω. This latter verb not only shares a root with the word ܣܘܠܢܐ (*sulānā*) in 28:11, but is also the verb applied to the non-Gnostics (24:12). There is also a similar, more complex, utterance by the redeemed Redeemer in 42:10: "I was not rejected, though I was reckoned to be so" (Harris and Mingana, 2:347).

51 If 𝔊 did use ὀφθαλμός, it could have been in a variety of constructions, e.g., ἀπέναντι τῶν ὀφθαλμῶν τῶν πολλῶν (BDAG, *s.v.* ἀπέναντι, 1bβ: "before" the many; cf. Rom 3:18) or ἐν τοῖς ὀφθαλμοῖς τῶν πολλῶν (BDAG, *s.v.* ὀφθαλμός, 2), where the latter construction can also be translated as "in" or "before" and can include a "verdict." But perhaps ℭ suggests that ὀφθαλμός was not used, in which case the text might have been ἔναντι/ἐναντίον τῶν πολλῶν (BDAG, *s.v.* ἔναντι, 2: "before," or metaphorically "in the eyes; in the judgment").

52 Payne Smith, 2:2868; BDAG, *s.v.* ἐναντίον.

53 See Payne Smith, 2:2518; BDAG, *s.v.* πολύς, 2aβℵ: [οἱ] πολλοί.

54 Franzmann, 194.

55 In the hymn of the *Pistis Sophia* (Lattke, *Bedeutung*, 1:150), the "lead" is interpreted as "heavy matter (ὕλη)," so that the comparison is limited to weight.

56 Harris and Mingana, 2:347.

57 Ibid.

58 Diettrich, 93.

59 Hugo Blümner, "Blei," PW 3, 1 (= 5. Halbband, 1897) 561; Bauer, 606; BDAG, *s.v.* μόλιβος; Crum, 462; Payne Smith, 1:19.

60 Franzmann, 194.

61 E.g., Harris and Mingana, vol. 1, on this passage; 2:346; Charlesworth, 101; Franzmann, 189–90 (see above).

62 Frankenberg, 25; see also Crum, 578–79.

63 Payne Smith, 2:1919; Crum, 429.

64 Payne Smith, 2:3004; BDAG, *s.v.* δύναμις.

65 BDAG, *s.vv.* ἰσχύς, κράτος.

66 Crum, 815–16.

Redeemer: "I became strong and powerful" (10:4). The final word, ܥܘܕܪܢܐ (*ʿudrānā*), parallel to "strength," is the Greek noun *βοήθεια*,[67] which is also connected to "divine help" in other contexts in ancient writings.[68] That ℭ—as it does for "helper" in 2b—uses a circumstantial clause[69] may be due to the influence of the soteriological interpretation in the hymn of the *Pistis Sophia.*[70]

■ **7** Considering the preceding and succeeding statements of salvation, the following remark by Franzmann is somewhat exaggerated and in any case, according to her analysis, can refer only to 𝔖: "By its position, 7 is a central focus of the Ode, describing a watershed action by God which moves the 'I' out of the situation of oppression."[71] It is more correct to say that the "lamps" of 7a and the "light" of 7b form "a loose kind of inclusio,"[72] which actually argues against her different arrangement for ℭ. Even here it is still possible that the speaker is not just any redeemed person but is the so-called "Son of God" (36:3). The image of "light," which fascinated the Gnostics of the *Pistis Sophia,* belongs to the process of redemption and is not to be compared to the *ὅπλα τῆς δικαιοσύνης τῶν δεξιῶν καὶ ἀριστερῶν* ("weapons of righteousness for the right hand and for the left") of 2 Cor 6:7.[73]

The *hapax legomenon* ܫܪܓܐ (*šrāḡā*, "lamp") in 7a, which stands, like ϩⲏⲃⲥ̄ (*hēbᵉs*),[74] for *λύχνος*,[75] is virtually duplicated in 𝔖 by the construction with ܡܢ (*men*) . . . ܘܡܢ (*ʾu-men*) and also in ℭ (where the translation of *ἐκ δεξιῶν μου* and *ἐξ ἀριστερῶν μου* is even clumsier than in 𝔖). Since this term is the direct object of the Pe. ܣܘܡ, ܣܡ (*sām*),[76] the object envisaged is an ancient "source of light" in a quite literal sense, and with or without a stand.[77] Unlike in 2a and 9a, the term "right" here refers not to the right hand but to the right side (as 7b ℭ makes explicit), which is complemented by the left side, and thus cannot be meant as the "place of honor," unlike in 8:20c.[78] In this passage "right" and "left" are both terms of place, not surrogates for "good" and "evil."[79]

The entirety of the person, expressed by "right + left," is more strongly emphasized in 7b 𝔖 than in ℭ, where "the final . . . ϫⲉⲕⲁⲥ"[80] in fact supports the reading ܕܠܐ (*dlā* = *ἵνα μή*). Since the sense of the future tense statement in H ("and there will not be anything without light about me")[81] hardly differs from N, the variant ܘܠܐ (*ʾu-lā*) in H may not be a misspelling of ܕܠܐ. Neither of them is actually "better Syriac."[82] Since the expressions ܕܠܐ ܢܘܗܪܐ (*d-lā nuhrā*) and ⲁⲧⲟⲩⲟⲉⲓⲛ represent *ἀφώτιστον*,[83] such translations as "unenlightened" and even more "unbaptized" are not under consideration.[84] There is merely a denial that it is dark (cf. such "light"/"darkness" passages as, e.g., 15:2; 21:3; 42:16).[85]

In trying to trace the inspiration for the images of stanza IV, one finds not only Ps 131:17b LXX (*ἡτοίμασα λύχνον τῷ χριστῷ μου*, "I have prepared a lamp

67 Payne Smith, 2:2815.
68 BDAG, *s.v.* *βοήθεια*.
69 Till §§328–34; Lambdin §23.1.
70 Lattke, *Bedeutung*, 1:150–51: "power . . . by saving me." The Coptic text in Franzmann (p. 191) has the misprint ⲁⲥϯ for ⲉⲥϯ. I agree with her emphasis on the close connection between 6 and 2b (p. 197). On the other hand, to base "a loose pattern of A B A' for the first three stanzas" on the repetition of the root ܥܕܪ (p. 194) seems to me exaggerated. The pattern is rather that the emphasis in stanzas I–III is on the statements of salvation, although each stanza begins on a negative note (1a, 3a, 5a).
71 Franzmann, 194.
72 Ibid., 195.
73 Contra Diettrich, 93; see the discussion of that passage in Margaret E. Thrall, *A Critical and Exegetical Commentary on the Second Epistle to the Corinthians*, vol. 1: *Introduction and Commentary on II Corinthians I–VII* (ICC; Edinburgh: T&T Clark, 1994) 461–63.
74 Crum, 658.
75 Payne Smith, 2:4325–26; BDAG, *s.v.* *λύχνος*.
76 The Syriac verb, like ⲕⲱ in ℭ, corresponds to the common verb *τίθημι* (BDAG, *s.v.* active, middle), rather than to *ἵστημι* (BDAG, *s.v.*). Neither here nor in 8:20c is there any reason to look for a compound term (contra Frankenberg, 25).
77 Helga Weippert, "Lampe," in Galling, 200.
78 See BDAG, *s.vv.* *ἀριστερός*, *δεξιός*.
79 Contra Diettrich, 93.
80 Till §362.
81 Lattke, *Oden*, 173.
82 Contra Charlesworth, 102 n. 7.
83 Frankenberg, 25.
84 Lampe, 279; contra Bernard, 107.
85 LSJ, *s.v.* *ἀφώτιστος*.

for mine anointed")[86] but also the accounts of the transfiguration in the Synoptic Gospels (Mark 9:2-10; Matt 17:1-9; Luke 9:28-36), in which the christological titles *ὁ υἱός μου ὁ ἀγαπητός* ("my beloved Son")[87] and *ὁ υἱὸς τοῦ ἀνθρώπου* ("the Son of man")[88] occur. The importance of these passages, in this context, lies in the description of the metamorphosis of Jesus shaped by the resurrection kerygma, a description that may also have inspired stanza V:[89]

Matthew 17:2	Mark 9:2-3	Luke 9:29
καὶ μετεμορφώθη ἔμπροσθεν αὐτῶν, καὶ ἔλαμψεν τὸ πρόσωπον αὐτοῦ ὡς ὁ ἥλιος, τὰ δὲ ἱμάτια αὐτοῦ ἐγένετο λευκὰ ὡς τὸ φῶς.	*καὶ μετεμορφώθη ἔμπροσθεν αὐτῶν, καὶ τὰ ἱμάτια αὐτοῦ ἐγένετο στίλβοντα λευκὰ λίαν, οἷα γναφεὺς ἐπὶ τῆς γῆς οὐ δύναται οὕτως λευκᾶναι.*	*καὶ ἐγένετο ἐν τῷ προσεύχεσθαι αὐτὸν τὸ εἶδος τοῦ προσώπου αὐτοῦ ἕτερον καὶ ὁ ἱματισμὸς αὐτοῦ λευκὸς ἐξαστράπτων.*
And he was transfigured before them, and his face shone like the sun, and his garments became white as light.	and he was transfigured before them, (3) and his garments became glistening, intensely white, as no fuller on earth could bleach them.	And as he was praying, the appearance of his countenance was altered, and his raiment became dazzling white.

The two "lamps" of 7a could stand for *Μωϋσῆς καὶ Ἠλίας* (Mark 9:4; Matt 17:3; Luke 9:30), since they are described as *ὀφθέντες ἐν δόξῃ* ("appearing in glory") in Luke 9:31. The emphatic negation of a lack of light/darkness in 7b may be a variation on the two comparisons in Matt 17:2 (especially *ἔλαμψεν* and *φῶς*). Perhaps the attention to clothing (*ἱμάτια* [Matthew/Mark] or *ἱματισμός* [Luke]) explains the choice of imagery in stanza V.

■ **8-9** Even if ܠܒܘܫܐ (*lḇūšā*), which is only seldom used to translate *χιτών*,[90] represents, as it mostly does, the Synoptic key word *ἱμάτιον* (Mark 9:3) and its possible influence on the imagery of stanza V (see on stanza IV above), the speaking "I" now fixes on the protological *Urzeit* of biblical humankind and connects the eschatological *Endzeit* of the Spirit with the vocabulary of the Psalms and soteriology in general. Although the Greek of this passage can only be approximated, it is one where the fact of a Greek original is seen particularly clearly. Also 8a is important as a pointer to an early date for the *Odes of Solomon*.[91]

The loanword *σκεπάζω* in ℭ is evidence that the Ethpa. of ܟܣܐ (*ksā*), "I was covered," in 8a translates *ἐσκεπάσθην*.[92] If ϩⲁ(ⲉ)ⲓⲃⲉⲥ is not a mistake for ϩⲃⲟⲟⲥ or ϩⲃⲥⲱ,[93] then this term, which is usually used for "shade,"[94] and the feminine ܬܟܣܝܬܐ (*taḵsīṯā*), later used "de baptismo," both represent *σκέπη* and not *ἱμάτιον*, *περιβόλαιον*, or *σκέπασμα*.[95] This word, *σκέπη*, means "protection" and "shade" but is not limited to trees (cf., e.g., Hos 14:8 LXX).[96] Its primary meaning is "blanket" or "covering,"[97] and the Greek text also paired it with the verb in a play on words.[98] This fine image of the protection and clothing by God's covering Spirit bears similarities to the "wings of the Spirit" (28:1); in

86 Rahlfs, 2:147; Brenton, 778; cf. Harris and Mingana, 2:349–51.

87 Thus Mark 9:7; Matt 17:5. Luke 9:35 seems to have changed *ἀγαπητός* to *ἐκλελεγμένος* (on this reading and other variants, see Kurt Aland, ed., *Synopsis of the Four Gospels* [8th ed.; Stuttgart: German Bible Society, 1987] 153).

88 Thus Mark 9:9; Matt 17:9. Luke 9:36 or 9:37 omits the term "son of man" (see Aland, *Synopsis*, 154). Reference has already been made to a number of "son of man" passages in the Synoptics in the second paragraph of the commentary on stanza III.

89 Harris and Mingana (2:349–50) find it suggestive "for the transference of ideas" that vv. 9a, 16a, and 18a of Ps 132 (131 LXX) also make "reference to clothing." I am not as convinced as Harris and Mingana of the relevance of this aspect of the Syriac translation of Psalm 132 and the Targum. Their remarks on "right" and "left" are indeed "speculations" (Harris and Mingana, 2:351).

90 See Klein, *Wörterbuch*, 63.

91 See Introduction, sec. 4.

92 Payne Smith, 1:1780–81; BDAG, *s.v.* *σκεπάζω*; on the "missing passive" in Coptic, see Till §326.

93 See Crum, 659–60.

94 Westendorf, 564; still found in Lattke, *Oden*, 174.

95 Crum, 657; Payne Smith, 1:1782.

96 BDAG, *s.v.* *σκέπη*. *Ode* 25:8a 𝔖 could also be translated as "I was sheltered/protected by the shelter/protection of thy spirit."

97 Kaegi, 809.

98 What Charlesworth (p. 102 n. 9) has to say about the use of the Aph. of ܪܘܡ in 8b and 9a goes for a Greek-speaking author as well: "the Odist was

ℭ, because of a misreading or misspelling of ⲡⲉⲕⲡ̅ⲛ̅ⲁ (= *nomen sacrum* abbreviation of ⲡⲉⲕⲡⲛⲉⲩⲙⲁ) as ⲡⲉⲕⲛⲁ, it was so altered that it can be described as ruined.[99]

In H, the point *under* the middle letter signifies the vowel *Ḥḇāṣā*, so it is the *Quššāyā* point *above* the ending of ܐܪܝܡܬ in N that makes it clear that in 8b the verb should be read as *ʾarīmt*, the Aph. second masculine singular perfect of ܪܘܡ, ܪܡ (*rām*), which fits better into the context of stanza V than the first person *ʾarīmeṯ*.[100] As, in the beginning, the Lord God clothed Adam and Eve in "garments of skins" (Gen 3:21), he equally mythologically, at the end of time, takes away the "garments of skin" from the speaking "I":[101] "The situation of Gen 3:21 is reversed."[102] The translation of χιτῶνες δερμάτινοι by ܠܒܘܫܝ ܕܡܫܟܐ (*lḇūšay d-meškā*) suggests an early date both for the Greek original and for the Syriac translation (the latter because of the inconsistency with the Peshitta ܟܘܬܝܢܝܬܐ ܕܡܫܟܐ [*kuṯīnyāṯā ḏ-meškā*]).[103] The sense of this passage is also seen to be early, since the Genesis quotation was connected in later Gnosticism with the covering of souls by "bodies," whereas this image of befurred animal hides makes no contrast yet between the "physical body" and the "robe of light."[104] Even Harnack's Hellenistic interpretation goes beyond the actual text: "The 'clothes of skin' are the body, which has been replaced by a new spiritual body."[105] To begin with, one should note what Claus Westermann says of the protective "action of the creator for his creature" in Gen 3:21: "Clothes are a necessity of life for human beings to survive in the world in which they must now

a master of paronomasia." Harris and Mingana (2:348) had already remarked on the "Semitic play on words in verses 8, 9." That is quite admissible, since translators may also indulge in wordplay.

99 See Harnack, 58; Franzmann, 192. The variant "mercy" in ℭ cannot derive from the context, because the hymn of the *Pistis Sophia* at this point is far removed from the quotation from the *Odes of Solomon* (Lattke, *Bedeutung*, 1:150–51). Charlesworth's idea (p. 102) that "[t]he confusion could also have originated within the Syriac text (e.g., ܪܚܡܝ is similar to ܪܘܡܝ)" is far-fetched.

100 Contra Harris and Mingana, vol. 1, on this passage; Quispel, *Makarius*, 55; Charlesworth, 101–2; Franzmann, 190. The variant text of ℭ is derived from the hymn of the *Pistis Sophia:* "I have become raised over all my materials (ὕλη) because of thy light" (Schmidt and MacDermot, *Pistis Sophia*, 150; Lattke, *Bedeutung*, 1:150–51).

101 Cf. Schultheß's translation "thou hast taken away" (Schultheß, 255). He also accepts a "Greek *Vorlage*" and criticizes the reading of H. The Syriac verb cannot here be a translation of ὑψόω (unlike in 9a), but must represent a verb like αἴρω or ἀφαιρέω (BDAG, *s.vv.* αἴρω, ἀφαιρέω; Payne Smith, 2:3858–59).

102 Bauer, 607.

103 See *OTSy*, pt. 1 fasc. 1, p. 6. The term χιτών is translated into Syriac by ܠܒܘܫܐ in only a very few cases. Later on ܠܒܘܫܐ is more often used for ἱμάτιον. On the Coptic translation, see Crum, 582, 597.

104 Wayne A. Meeks, "The Image of the Androgyne: Some Uses of a Symbol in Earliest Christianity," *HR* 13 (1973) 183–89, esp. 187; see also Alois Kehl, "Gewand (der Seele)," *RAC* 10 (1978) 951. In addition to the important articles by Meeks and Kehl, mention must be made of the ones by Grese and Quispel. It is questionable whether *Ode* 28:5 deals with a σῶμα πνευματικόν (Grese, *Corpus*, 92, referring to Pauline passages such as 1 Cor 15:35-54 and 2 Cor 5:1-4) or with "the putting off of the old man and the putting on of the new" as in Eph 4:22-24; Col 3:9-10; *Odes Sol.* 11:10-11; 15:8 (Grese, *Corpus*, 93). Quispel (*Makarius*, 55, 123), who misprints *Ode* 25:8 as "24,8," may be right on the dualism of "body" and "soul" in the *Hymn of the Pearl*: "To return to Paradise the soul must take off the δερμάτινος χιτών." He is correct in saying: "It is not certain that the *Odes of Solomon* were written in Syriac in Edessa. They might also have been composed in Greek in the Hellenistic areas to the west. But they were translated into Syriac very early and are characteristic of Syriac Christianity." But whether *Ode* 25:8 in particular, in addition to its slight allusion to "paradise," shows "how to interpret this passage in the Hymn of the Pearl," is as questionable as the comparison with a Gnostic statement in the *Gospel of Truth* (see Charlesworth, 102–3 n. 10).

105 Harnack, 58, with reference to "the Jewish philosophical exegesis of Gen 3:21 (Philo)."

subsist."[106] The speaking "I" is eschatologically relieved of this requirement of life, since the redemption by light demands a different covering (7a-8a), which must not be confused with the white "garments" of Mandaean "rituals" or "early Christian baptismal liturgies."[107]

The statement of 9a, which harks back to 2a, depends on Ps 117:16a LXX (δεξιὰ κυρίου ὕψωσέν με, "The right hand of the Lord has exalted me").[108] The play on words with the Aph. of ܪܘܡ, ܪܡ (*rām*), which Harris and Mingana bring out,[109] did not occur in 𝔊. What the speaker means by the verb in 9a is elucidated by the adjacent verses of the Psalm, 117:15b and 16b LXX: Δεξιὰ κυρίου ἐποίησεν δύναμιν ("the right hand of the Lord has wrought mightily/powerfully").[110] Even if there should be an allusion to Acts 2:33 (τῇ δεξιᾷ οὖν τοῦ θεοῦ ὑψωθείς, "Being therefore exalted at the right hand of God"), what happens here is an "enhancement" in "power" and "strength,"[111] not any sort of rapture (see Excursus 17).

Unfortunately, the pointing of ܐܥܒܪܬ in the manuscripts does not admit of a decision whether this Aph. perfect of ܥܒܪ (*ʿbar*) in 9b is a second masculine or a third feminine singular (in H there is a point above the letter ܒ, but in N it is under and between the two letters ܒܪ).[112] What is more important is that 9b is parallel to 9a and therefore both expands and elucidates that statement of raising up. There are so many possible equivalents both for the Aph. ܐܥܒܪ (*ʾaʿbar*) and the Coptic verb ϥι (*fi*) that suggesting a verb for the Greek original could only be guesswork.[113] The case of the noun ϣωνε/ܟܘܪܗܢܐ (*kurhānā*) is different: the only likely Greek equivalents are ἀσθένεια (1 Cor 15:43; 2 Cor 13:4), μαλακία, or νόσος,[114] with a slight possibility of ἀρρωστία (cf. 18:3).[115] The raising up that bestows strength and power corresponds to the liberation from sickness and weakness—a truly paradisal state.

■ **10-12**[116] Franzmann's reasons for segregating 12b (as "Stanza 7") are as unconvincing as her description of the monocolon as a "concluding confessional statement."[117] The interpretation of stanza VI is made more difficult by the fact that 11b 𝔖 does not have a Coptic equivalent (signified by a line space in the translation). Since the bicolon 12a-b in ℭ carries on the direct address to God, and since the hymn in the *Pistis Sophia* does not refer to a narrative statement of salvation similar to 11b 𝔖, this line must have been lost already in the Coptic translation of *Ode* 25 from which the writer copied. So the "carelessness" noted by Harnack[118] is more likely to have occurred during the translation from Greek to Coptic than in the manuscript tradition of ℭ. Perhaps, though, it was not carelessness but the deliberate omission of a difficult passage in 𝔊. It is also possible that 11b is the result of a purely Syriac amplification that necessitated the change in 12 𝔖 from direct address to narrative.[119] In any case, the line, which Harris and Mingana consider at length[120] and which is important to the identification of the speaking "I," must be treated fully as an integral part of the Syriac text.

Many of the key words of stanza VI can be found in Psalm 132 (131 LXX), which Harris and Mingana adduced for 7-8 because of the metaphor of clothing (vv. 9, 16, 18) and the term λύχνος (v. 17):[121] the terms

106 Claus Westermann, *Genesis* (2 vols.; BKAT 1.1–2; Neukirchen-Vluyn: Neukirchener Verlag, 1974, 1981) 1:366–67.
107 Meeks, "Image of the Androgyne," 187–88, who, following Bernard, considers *Ode* 25 "a baptismal hymn."
108 Rahlfs, 2:130; Brenton, 770. The fact that the Peshitta of Ps 118:16 reproduces the Septuagint text and therefore resembles this passage (*OTSy*, pt. 2 fasc. 3, p. 141: ܝܡܝܢܗ ܕܡܪܝܐ ܐܪܝܡܬܢܝ) cannot, after all the previous evidence, be used to argue for a Syriac original.
109 Harris and Mingana, 2:348; Charlesworth (p. 102) is similar.
110 Rahlfs, 2:130; Brenton, 770.
111 BDAG, *s.vv.* δύναμις, ὑψόω, 2.
112 Franzmann, 193.
113 Payne Smith, 2:2785–86; Crum, 620–22.
114 BDAG, *s.vv.* ἀσθένεια, μαλακία, νόσος.
115 Frankenberg, 25; Payne Smith, 1:1812; Crum, 571.
116 Line 11b is not found in ℭ, and there is no equivalent for it in the hymn of the *Pistis Sophia*.
117 Franzmann, 196–98.
118 Harnack, 58.
119 Franzmann (p. 193, on 12a-b) drew my attention to the confusion of "thy" and "his" in my preliminary translation, Lattke, *Bedeutung*, 1:153, for which I thank her.
120 Harris and Mingana, 2:143–47.
121 Ibid., 2:349–51.

"truth" (v. 11), "righteousness" (v. 9), "enemies" (v. 18), "rest" (vv. 8, 14), and "forevermore/ever" (vv. 12, 14). But after the discovery of the influence of Psalm 142 LXX (see on 1b and 4a above), there are a number of additional words and phrases that may have been used as models:[122] ἐν τῇ ἀληθείᾳ σου || ἐν τῇ δικαιοσύνῃ σου ("in thy truth" || "in thy righteousness") in Ps 142:1c-d LXX, δικαιωθήσεται ("shall be justified") in Ps 142:2b LXX, ἐχθρός/ἐχθροί ("enemy/enemies") in Ps 142:3a, 9a, 12a LXX, and ἕνεκα τοῦ ὀνόματός σου, κύριε ("Lord, for thy name's sake") in Ps 142:11a LXX. Linguistically, these words and phrases are even more striking and less dependent on conjecture than the similarities found in Psalm 132 (131 LXX).

The *parallelismus membrorum* in 10a-b, influenced by Ps 142:1 LXX, casts doubt on the reading ܒܫܪܪܐ (*ba-šrārā*) of H. Since "truth" is an "attribute of the height" (see Excursus 1; cf. 17:7d) and can therefore be "equivalent" to "light,"[123] it would be possible to see the words "truth" and "rest" as the *inclusio* of stanza VI, which would retrospectively increase the mythological coloring of "exalt" in 9a. But ἀλήθεια/ܫܪܪܐ (*šrārā*) in 10a is probably a "means of the salvation" of God (see Excursus 1), while the *hapax legomenon* ܚܝܠܬܢܐ (*ḥayltānā*) would carry, for later Syriac ears, an echo of the "name of Yahweh,"[124] but in the earlier Greek–Syriac bilingual days would allow the meanings of the adjectives δυνατός and ἰσχυρός to shine through.[125] The former adjective, which can be used of God and of powerful persons, might have been suggested by the noun δύναμις (Ps 117:15-16 LXX; see on 9a above).

The juxtaposition of the adjectives κραταιός and ἀμάχητος in 10a-b may seem arbitrary,[126] but the following suggestion for the adjectives in 10b 𝔖 must be given some weight: "in place of ܘܚܣܝܐ (*ʾu-ḥasyā*), which is nugatory in this context, read ܘܚܣܝܢܐ (*ʾu-ḥassīnā*)."[127] Even Harris and Mingana call this suggestion, which would again stand for ἰσχυρός or δυνατός, "possible."[128] Unfortunately, the Coptic qualitative ⲧⲃ̄ⲃⲏⲩ contradicts this theory.[129] The only term that would be translated by both ܚܣܝܐ and ⲧⲃ̄ⲃⲏⲩ is ὅσιος ("holy"), a term that applies not only to pious human beings, but in paradoxical exclusivity can be used of "God" (Rev 15:4 [μόνος ὅσιος]; 16:5 [ὁ ὅσιος])[130] and by theological transference—possibly even here (see on 11b below)—also of the heavenly "Christ" (Acts 2:27; 13:35 [ὁ ὅσιός σου, quoting Ps 15:10 LXX]; Heb 7:26).[131] This prepositional clause is parallel to 10a and is also meant instrumentally; the Greek text will have used the word δικαιοσύνη (cf. ℭ). What does God's "righteousness" mean here?

Excursus 25: "Righteousness" and "Justification" in the *Odes of Solomon*

Although the terms derived from the root *zdq* that will be discussed here are relatively rare and narrow in meaning in the *Odes of Solomon* as compared to the common occurrence and breadth of use of the biblical δικαιοσύνη and δικαιόω,[132] one would have thought that, following the controversy between Käsemann and Bultmann,[133] the matter would have been discussed or at least mentioned in the festschrift for Käsemann that bears the title *Rechtfertigung* (= Justification). Otto Betz points out that "the experience of contested exegeses" has shown "the close connections of *truth* and *righteousness* . . . in Qumran,"[134] but apparently he sees no need to adduce *Ode* 25:10.

The Pa. ܙܕܩ (*zaddeq*) occurs only once (29:5b), corresponding to δικαιόω, but the Ethpa. ܐܙܕܕܩ (*ʾezdaddaq*) is found three times in important passages where it corresponds to the passive of δικαιόω.[135] Commonest, with seven different instances, is the noun δικαιοσύνη/ܙܕܝܩܘܬܐ (*zaddīqūtā*), which is never opposed as *righteousness*

122 Rahlfs, 2:156–57; Brenton, 783–84.
123 Bultmann, "Untersuchungen," 161 = idem, *Exegetica*, 171.
124 Gesenius, *s.v.* צְבָאוֹת; Payne Smith, 1:1261–62.
125 BDAG, *s.vv.* δυνατός, ἰσχυρός.
126 Frankenberg, 25.
127 Ibid., 41; Payne Smith, 1:1337.
128 Harris and Mingana, 2:347.
129 Crum, 399.
130 See BDAG, *s.v.* ὅσιος, 2a-b.
131 See BDAG, *s.v.* ὅσιος, 1b; Payne Smith, 1:1325.
132 Bo Johnson, "צָדַק *ṣādaq*," *ThWAT* 6 (1989) 922–23; *TDOT* 12:262–63; Gottlob Schrenk, "δίκη, δίκαιος, κτλ.," *ThWNT* 2 (1935) 194–223; *TDNT* 2:192–219.
133 Ernst Käsemann, "Gottesgerechtigkeit bei Paulus," *ZThK* 58 (1961) 367–78; Rudolf Bultmann, "Δικαιοσύνη θεοῦ," *JBL* 83 (1964) 12–16.
134 Otto Betz, "Rechtfertigung in Qumran," in Johannes Friedrich et al., eds., *Rechtfertigung: Festschrift für Ernst Käsemann zum 70. Geburtstag* (Tübingen: Mohr Siebeck; Göttingen: Vandenhoeck & Ruprecht, 1976) 23; cf. 18 n. 5.
135 Payne Smith, 1:1083–84; BDAG, *s.v.* δικαιόω.

based on faith to *righteousness based on the law*.[136] The adjective "righteous" is not used at all.[137]

The redeemed speaker of *Ode* 29, who is justified by the "grace" of the Lord, is clearly distinguished from the "Lord's Messiah" (29:5), in whom the "I" believes and who may also be considered "Lord" (29:6). So this individual passage using the Pa. *zaddeq* cannot immediately be brought together with the three Ethpa. passages under the heading "Ascent," referring to the delegated Revealer.[138] On the other hand, "justify" in 29:5, and in at least two other passages using the passive, means "lead to victory" (cf. 1 Tim 3:16).[139] It is only in 31:5 that the "person" of the "Lord" is found, justified by his holy Father, whom it may be possible to equate, in his character of Redeemer, with the speaking "I" of the redeemed Redeemer in *Ode* 17: "And I was justified by my Lord, and my salvation is imperishable" (17:2). The confusing use of the title, or name, "Lord" will be discussed later (see on 11b ܣ below). Since the "adversaries" are mentioned in 25:11a, the justification of 25:12a could be interpreted as a "victory," especially if 25:10b indicates "entry into the sphere of righteousness."[140] The correctness of this interpretation depends largely on the answer to the question who is actually being "justified" here (see below).

In three passages, δικαιοσύνη/ܙܕܝܩܘܬܐ (*zaddīqūṯā*) refers to the Redeemer and Revealer. The "I" of 8:21a describes the Most High Lord "as the personified δικαιοσύνη of the speaker," applying Isa 58:8 soteriologically,[141] which raises the question whether the statement about the exalted one's "own righteousness" (41:12) should be understood similarly. The exalted one of *Ode* 36 says of himself: "My heart gushed forth a flood of righteousness" (36:7b).

The next two passages belong together, since they both deal with human righteousness. But "righteousness" must be taken theologically: both in 8:5a and in 20:4a, it "exists in the paradox of divine grace and human injustice," on the one hand,[142] and, on the other, as one of the possible "existential correspondences with the thought of God."[143]

"Righteousness" personified, in 9:10, is "God's righteousness, although not in the specifically Pauline sense."[144] *Ode* 25:10b is, however, the only passage where there is a problem in deciding the exact connotation in 𝔊 of the genitive σου, referring to "God" (1 ܣ) or the "Lord" (1 ℭ). Its original meaning in Ps 142:1 LXX need not be taken into account. Whether the parallel prepositional expressions with "truth" and "righteousness" are meant instrumentally or metaphorically of place (i.e., of sphere), this genitive, like the Pauline phrase δικαιοσύνη θεοῦ, may be intended subjectively, expressing "God's saving activity" or God's "power of salvation."[145] However, it may also be a "*gen[itivus] auctoris*," which identifies the "gift"[146] "that God . . . gives,"[147] which would entail certain consequences for the interpretation of the previously mentioned "justification" in 25:12a. Perhaps it is necessary, as with Rom 3:21–26, to "be aware of the double meaning of δικ[αιοσύνη] θεοῦ,"[148] and that even—surpassing Paul's declaration of faith—in the case of the redeemed Redeemer (cf. 17:2 and 41:12).

The central place that Franzmann awards to 11a ܣ,[149] and which her own analysis denies to 11 ℭ,[150] cannot be defended on the grounds of form or of meaning (see at the beginning of stanza VI above). In both versions, the speaker refers back to the adversaries of 3a. But since, according to 3b, these inimical powers have already disappeared, it is only their fear that can be detected

136 Payne Smith, 1:1085; BDAG, *s.v.* δικαιοσύνη. The connection with "grace" and "to believe" (29:5-6) is relevant only to the Pa. ܙܕܩ (*zaddeq*), not to the noun ܙܕܝܩܘܬܐ (*zaddīqūṯā*).

137 Contra Arvedson, *Mysterium*, 40. Therefore in Käsemann's comment on Heb 5:13, "The λόγος δικαιοσύνης is the teaching regarding the state of the baptized as δίκαιος, a role that it assumed in Christian Gnosticism," his reference to *Ode* 25:10-12 and *Ode* 29:5 is misleading (see Käsemann, *Wandering People*, 188–89; *Gottesvolk*, 120).

138 Contra Bultmann, "Bedeutung," 128 = idem, *Exegetica*, 85; Christ, *Sophia*, 71; Stenger, *Christushymnus*, 155–57.

139 Bauer, 610; Bultmann, "Bedeutung," 128 = idem, *Exegetica*, 85: "to be justified" as "to be victorious."

140 Christ, *Sophia*, 71.

141 See commentary on 8:21a.

142 See commentary on 8:5b.

143 See commentary on 20:4a.

144 See commentary on 9:10; on the juxtaposition of δικαιοσύνη and ἀλήθεια, cf. *Corp. Herm.* 13:8, Colpe and Holzhausen, 180.

145 Käsemann, "Gottesgerechtigkeit," 370, 378; see also BDAG, *s.v.* δικαιοσύνη, 3a: "characteristic."

146 BDAG, *s.v.* δικαιοσύνη, 2.

147 Bultmann, "Δικαιοσύνη θεοῦ," 12 = idem, *Exegetica*, 470.

148 Bultmann, "Δικαιοσύνη θεοῦ," 13 = idem, *Exegetica*, 470.

149 Franzmann, 195.

150 Ibid., 197.

from afar.[151] It is very likely that 𝔊 had ἐφοβήθησαν ἀπ᾽ ἐμοῦ.[152] Whether the generalizing "all my adversaries," only found in 𝔖, has a historical basis or is purely mythological cannot be determined (see on 3 and 5 above). Nothing in the remainder of *Ode* 25 elucidates this problem.

With line 11b, which is peculiar to 𝔖, comes a return to the problems noted at the beginning of stanza VI. If this monocolon existed in a Greek form, it would have contained the term *κύριος* twice and *ὄνομα* once: . . . *τοῦ κυρίου (ἐν) (τῷ) ὀνόματι κυρίου*. This predicative statement of salvation by "belonging,"[153] whether the construction contained ἐγενόμην or not, can only mean "I became a Christian by the name of Christ,"[154] if the speaker is not identified as ὁ *Χριστός*. In that case, the title *κύριος* would refer to Christ.[155] But if the speaker is the ***Κύριος Χριστός*** himself, the repeated term *κύριος* must refer to "God"/"the Lord" of 1b, who is also present everywhere in the context of stanza VI. And a third possibility is that the speaker is neither the ***Κύριος Χριστός*** nor another redeemer, in which case he would be speaking of two separate *κύριοι*, as in 29:6, namely, the Christ and the Lord his God (in that order, hardly vice versa). In the later history of the *Odes of Solomon,* it is necessary to consider all three—perhaps even more—possibilities, since the original meaning and intention are hidden in the darkness surrounding the *Odes*' composition and dissemination.

Even without the use of the loan word *χρηστός* in the abstract Coptic term ⲙⲛ̄ⲧⲭⲣⲏⲥⲧⲟⲥ, it would be clear that ܒܣܝܡܘܬܐ (*bassīmūṯā*) in 12a corresponds to the Greek feminine *χρηστότης* (see Excursus 14). Since "gentleness" and "grace" are parallel terms (20:9), the following statement of salvation by a redeemed speaker —not identified with the Messiah—is a striking parallel: "And I humbled my enemies / and he (viz. the Most High Lord) justified me by his grace" (29:5a-b; see Excursus 25 above).[156] In spite of the general unity of the *Odes of Solomon*, however, it is necessary to keep open the possibility that here in *Ode* 25 the speaker may yet be the "Anointed One/Messiah of the Lord" (29:6) and his "justification" may be more an acknowledgment (as "righteous")[157] than a "victory."[158]

The idea of victory, which may lie behind 12a, must not be allowed to distort the image of "rest" in 12b and lead to the interpretation of this soteriological[159] term merely as quiet after the storm. But this is "the eternal rest of God,"[160] which may Gnostically be transformed into "abiding with him [viz., God]."[161] That it is "available for the believer" is not stated.[162] Arvedson calls *Ode*

151 That the opponents in ℭ "became far" (11) is due to the extremely mythological hymn of the *Pistis Sophia:* "And the emanations of the Authades (*Αὐθάδης*) . . . have gone far from me" (Lattke, *Bedeutung*, 1:152–53; cf. 224 on the liberties taken in quoting).

152 Frankenberg, 25; BDAG, *s.v.* *φοβέω*; Payne Smith, 1:862.

153 On the construction at the beginning, see BDF and BDR §162 (7).

154 Harris and Mingana, 2:143.

155 Since there is no "equivalent Greek sentence" in which ***Χριστοῦ*** could take the place of ***Κυρίου***, there also cannot be in 12a an "employment of the favourite paronomasia between *χρηστός* and *χριστός*" (Harris and Mingana, 2:143). Nor is 11b 𝔖 "a reference to Isaiah xliv. 5" (ibid., 2:349).

156 Berger and Nord (p. 959) clearly take this as a licence for their functional translation "By his *grace* he acknowledges me as righteous" [emphasis added]. Their remark on the "2nd person" in ℭ is correct, but fails to notice that, without 11b, there is no reason to make the change to the 3rd person that occurs in 𝔖.

157 Berger and Nord, 959.

158 Bultmann, "Bedeutung," 128 = idem, *Exegetica*, 85.

159 It is instructive to look at the Gnostic interpretation of this word that plays such an important part in Gnosticism: "For thou dost save, at all times!" (Lattke, *Bedeutung*, 1:152–53). In terms of the interaction between the hymn of the *Pistis Sophia* and the quotation from the *Odes of Solomon,* it is worth noting that the causal particle ϫⲉ also occurs in 12b ℭ.

160 See commentary on 3:5.

161 Berger and Nord, 959. This "rest" may have been inspired by Psalm 131 LXX, to which Harris and Mingana refer: *ἀνάστηθι, κύριε, εἰς τὴν ἀνάπαυσίν σου* ("Arise, o Lord, into thy rest") in Ps 131:8a LXX, and: *Αὕτη ἡ κατάπαυσίς μου εἰς αἰῶνα αἰῶνος* ("This is my rest for ever") in Ps 131:14a LXX (Rahlfs, 2:147; Brenton, 778).

162 Contra Wray, *Rest*, 26. Her summary (p. 32) is imprecise: "Rest" is "present inner-peace and tranquillity as a result of trusting in Christ (*Odes of Solomon*)." As shown in Excursus 3, the *Odes of Solomon* themselves contain a number of Wray's (p. 32) "variety of meanings."

25 “classical” in relation to the “Gnostic theology of rest,”[163] which he defines as follows: “The transcendent, perfect, non-material world, compared to the material world, is changeless and therefore described as the place of rest.”[164] However, and especially in this Ode, “the connection with the idea of rest derived from the OT and Wisdom literature” is clearer than the “influences of Platonic and neo-Pythagorean philosophy” that Arvedson emphasizes.[165]

163 Arvedson, *Mysterium*, 204.

164 Ibid., 205.

165 Ibid. For the sake of completeness, there is another interpretation of 12 𝔖 to be considered, which does not come into question for the Coptic version. The terms “kindness” (12a) and “rest” (12b) with their 3rd masculine singular suffixes, whose equivalents in 𝔊 were modified by the genitive *σου*, could, in the light of the terms *ἀναπαύω* (“give rest”), *ἀνάπαυσις* (“rest”), and *χρηστός* (“easy”) in Matt 11:28-30, be considered to refer to the “Son” and Revealer of the “Father,” addressed as *κύριε τοῦ οὐρανοῦ καὶ τῆς γῆς* (“Lord of heaven and earth”; cf. Matt 11:25-27). One who reads or hears the text under this interpretation *must* identify the “Lord,” mentioned twice in 11b 𝔖, with the *Κύριος (Ἰησοῦς) Χριστός*, “Lord (Jesus) Christ,” which means that he cannot be identical with the “I” of *Ode* 25.

26

Ode 26: Ode on the Odes of the Lord

(I) 1a I let a hymn to the Lord well forth,
1b because I am *his*.
2a And I will recite *his* holy ode,
2b because my heart is with him.
3a For his cithara is in my hands,
3b and the odes of his rest shall not cease!
4a I will cry to him with all my heart;
4b I will praise and exalt him with all my limbs.
(II) 5 For from the east to the west *his* is the hymn,
6 and from the south to the north *his* is the confession/thanksgiving,
7 and from the beginning of the heights to their end *his* is the *plērōma*.
(III) 8a Who can write the odes of the Lord,
8b or who can read them [aloud]?
9a Or who can instruct his self/soul for life
9b so that his self/soul may be redeemed?
10a Or who can rest with/upon the Most High
10b that he may speak from his mouth?
11a Who can interpret the ode[a] of the Lord
11b so that he who interprets will be liberated
11c and [that] he[b] who is interpreted will remain?
(IV) 12a For it is enough to know and to be at rest.
12b For the singers stand up in rest
13a like a river that has an abundant spring
13b and flows for the help of those who seek it.
Hallelujah.

a 11a ܬܕܡܪ̈ܬܗ H and N; originally probably ܙܡܝܪܬܗ (see commentary).

b 11c ܡܛܠ ܠܒܪ ܕܗܘ̇ N; ܡܛܠ ܠܒܪ ܗܘ̇ H (see commentary).

Introduction

Ode 26 is preserved in two Syriac manuscripts.[1] Of this Ode, which may even incorporate a little "ode within the ode" at 5-7[2] and provides "an understanding of the role of the odist,"[3] it can be explicitly said that it contains "no Christian idea,"[4] and even the "Gnostic content" is

1 Mss.: Codex H, 20a–21a; Codex N 150[r] (ܣ). Ed./trans.: Charlesworth, 103–6; Franzmann, 199–203; Lattke, 2:235–47 and 3:XXXV.

2 Franzmann, "Man of Rest," 418.

3 Franzmann, "Study," 397.

4 Spitta, 282. Greßmann, on the other hand, boldly declares that "content and spirit are specifically Christian, since only a Christian can hymn the ineffable mystery of salvation" (see Hugo Greßmann, "Die Oden Salomos," *Die Christliche Welt: Evangelisches Gemeindeblatt für Gebildete aller Stände* 25 [1911] 635).

"only weakly discernible."[5] These conclusions, however, offer no justification for the statement that "this *Ode* is filled from beginning to end with the spirit of the Old Testament."[6] That this Ode, which combines "intentional monotony and an elevated vocabulary"[7] and gives "expression" to "joyful enthusiasm,"[8] is in its whole "structure an Old Testament *hymn*"[9] is, in view of other formal components, a very questionable assertion.[10]

Whether the *Odes of Solomon* were ever—either by their author or by later users referring to 26:3b and 8a—called "Odes of Rest in the Lord"[11] cannot be ascertained.[12] Franzmann's connection between "the importance for the Odes of the concept of rest and, in particular, its importance for the role of the odist," on the one side, and the description of Solomon as ἀνὴρ ἀναπαύσεως ("man of rest") in 1 Chr 22:9,[13] on the other, is less forced: "Thus . . . the idea of rest is so important for the work that the odist, or final redactor of the Odes (if there was more than one author), or a later copyist may well have considered 'Solomon' to be a fitting pseudonym for the work."[14]

Interpretation

■ **1-4** Only if the first verb of 4b, which Frankenberg omits,[15] was a form of ὑμνέω in 𝔊 can Franzmann's statements—"1a and 13a form the inclusio for the Ode by the repetition of the root ܢܒܥ. The repetition indicates that the image of 13 is implicit in 1a (cf. also e.g. 40:2). The inclusio for the stanza is formed by the repetition of the root ܫܒܚ in 1a and 4b"[16]—be considered valid at least for the Greek text of stanza I. They are true for the Ode as a whole only in 𝔖, a point suggested by the translation of the Aph. of ܢܒܥ (*nba*ʿ) by "let . . . well forth."[17] The *Vorlage* for "the Odist's own prelude"[18] is Ps 44:2 LXX (Ἐξηρεύξατο ἡ καρδία μου λόγον ἀγαθόν, λέγω ἐγὼ τὰ ἔργα μου . . . , "My heart has uttered a good matter: I declare my works . . .")[19] and also especially Ps 118:171-72 LXX (ἐξερεύξαιντο τὰ χείλη μου ὕμνον, . . . φθέγξαιτο ἡ γλῶσσά μου τὸ λόγιόν σου, "Let my lips utter a hymn, . . . Let my tongue utter thine oracle").[20] The Greek of 1a, then, used both ἐξερεύγομαι and ὕμνος,[21] and in 2a-b the equivalent of the Pa. ܡܠܠ (*mallel*) was φθέγγομαι, also taken from Ps 118:171 LXX, while only καρδία μου came from Ps 44:2 LXX. This renders superfluous Harris and Mingana's vague reference to the Peshitta and Targum.[22] For "recite" in 2a one could substitute "proclaim," which would bring out the parallelism with 4a even more clearly (see Excursus 12).[23] The "Lord" in 1a (cf. 8a, 11a) is the Most High κύριος (cf. 10a), for whom a "hymn" was poured out in the past and for whom, with repeated and emphasized ܕܝܠܗ (*dīleh*) in 2a, a "holy ode" will resound in an indeterminate future.[24] The parallel causal clauses starting

5 Greßmann, "Oden," 635.
6 Diettrich, 94.
7 Abramowski, 52.
8 Kroll, *Hymnodik*, 70.
9 Greßmann, "Oden," 635.
10 See Lattke, *Oden*, 62–65.
11 H. J. E. Westerman Holstijn, *Oden van Salomo: Zangen van rust in den Heere. Een bundel lyriek uit de tweede eeuw uit het Grieksch vertaald en metrisch bewerkt* (Zutphen: Ruys, [1942]) 7.
12 See Charlesworth, 105.
13 Rahlfs, 1:797; Brenton, 557.
14 Franzmann, "Man of Rest," 419–20.
15 Frankenberg, 25.
16 Franzmann, 201.
17 See Payne Smith, 2:2271. Harris and Mingana (2:353) emphasize: "There is . . . no need to change the tense of the opening verse." This shows that Diettrich's reading *ʾab̲ʿet̲* and its "derivation" from ܒܥܬ (*bʿet̲*) are not merely superfluous but far-fetched (see Diettrich, 94; Payne Smith, 1:567).
18 Harris and Mingana, 2:355–56.
19 Rahlfs, 2:46; Brenton, 724.
20 Rahlfs, 2:140; Brenton, 775. Comparing the text with the Peshitta (*OTSy*, pt. 2 fasc. 3, pp. 49, 150), a Greek *Vorlage* seems more likely, because it is only in the LXX that ἐξερεύγομαι and ὕμνος occur together as they do in 1a.
21 On the expressive verb, see LSJ, *s.v.* ἐρεύγομαι: "vomit forth."
22 Harris and Mingana, 2:356.
23 BDAG, *s.v.* φθέγγομαι.
24 The term ܕܝܠܗ in 1b as well as 2a corresponds to the genitive αὐτοῦ. In the first case, it expresses "relationship" (BDF and BDR §162), while in the second it is in some sense an "objective genitive" (BDF and BDR §163). H marks the personal pronoun ܐܢܐ (*ʾenā*) in 1b with a subscript point as an enclitic (contra Harris and Mingana, vol. 1, on this passage; Charlesworth, 103).

with ܡܛܠ ܕ (*meṭṭol d-* = ὅτι [1b, 2b])[25] are hardly distinguishable by their content, since "I" and "heart" both express the unity of the person (see Excursus 4).

Excursus 26: "Ode," "Psalm," and "To Sing" in the *Odes of Solomon*

Except for the uncertainty in 26:12b (ܡܙܡܪܢܐ [*mzammrānē*] = οἱ ψάλλοντες [?]), there is no room to doubt that the terms derived from the root *zmr* are equivalent to the Greek words tabulated (with number of occurrences):[26]

ᾄδω	ܙܡܪ (*zmar* [2])
ψάλλω	ܙܡܪ (*zammar* [4])
ᾠδή	ܙܡܝܪܬܐ (*zmīrtā* [6])
ψαλμός	ܡܙܡܘܪܐ (*mazmōrā* [3])

This excursus is more closely connected to others (e.g., Excursuses 12, 16, 21, and 31) than most. The term ܩܠܐ (*qālā*) will be discussed in the last-mentioned excursus (but see below on 7:17c [tone] and 24:2b [voice]), while this excursus includes, almost by default—in addition to "tongue" (40:3)—a number of other musicological *hapax legomena*, namely, the plural forms ܢܥܡܬܐ (*neʿmāṯā* [7:23b]),[27] ܥܢܝܢܐ (*ʿenyānē* [40:3]),[28] and ܩܝܢܬܐ (*qīnāṯā* [14:8b]),[29] whose Greek equivalents are not as plain as the "psalms," "hymns," and Spirit-filled "odes/songs" of Col 3:16 and Eph 5:19.[30]

The first aggregation of such terms occurs in *Ode* 7, where 7:17 speaks of "those who have psalms for the coming of the Lord, / that they may . . . sing to Him with joy / and with the cithara of many tones." And a little further on, "Those who sing[31] will sing the grace of the Most High Lord / and offer their psalms" (7:22).

The hymnic self-portrait of *Ode* 16 conspicuously omits the term "ode," which has a bearing on the statements about the purpose and attitude of the "I" of *Ode* 26: "my work is the psalm of the Lord in his hymns" (16:1c). The self-description, "For my love is the Lord, / therefore I will sing to him" (16:3), also refers to "hymns" (16:1c, 2a, 4a). And the persons who are exhorted to praise the Lord make a similar statement: "Let us sing in his love" (41:2b; cf. 41:1a and 4b).

The passages where "ode" rather than "psalm" occurs also have a hymnic context. Indirectly this is true of 26:11a, if the assumption that originally it read the "odes of the Lord" and not the "wonders of the Lord" is correct (see the commentary on this passage below). In *Ode* 36 the identity of the speaker partly determines the meaning of the glorifying he performs "by the composition of his [viz., the Most High's] odes."[32] The term "composition" may also play a part in the connection between *Odes* 36 and 26. In H, 40:2c-3 makes a parallel between "lips" and "tongue" that seems to reflect the one between "hymn" and the "odes." The more extended version of 40:3a-b in N, which is not as closely connected to the "hymns" of 2b-c, can be translated, "And my tongue is sweet in his anthems / and my limbs are fat/lush in his odes."[33]

The terms "rest" and "cithara" (with all its tones) stamp the hymnic context of the confiding plea, addressed to the Lord who is like a father: "Teach me the odes of thy truth" (14:7a). It may be possible to find a connection between this singular passage and *Ode* 26, which does not employ the term "truth," by observing that "the concepts of truth and rest permeate the Odes and are strongly linked."[34] So the "odes of truth" (14:7a) are related to the "odes of rest" (26:3b; "cithara" occurs in 3a; note also the "singers" standing in "rest" in 12b), and they are, in fact, the "odes of the Lord" (26:8a). The singular of "ode" (26:2a) is primarily to be understood as the parallel of the singular of "hymn" (26:1a), not as a description of stanza II (= 26:5-7) or of *Ode* 26 as a whole.

As in the phrase "holy life," which occurs only in 8:2, the adjective ἁγία/ܩܕܝܫܬܐ (*qaddīštā*) in 2a qualifies the

25 This parallelism means that 1, in spite of the manuscripts, is also a bicolon.

26 BDAG, *s.vv.* ᾄδω, ψάλλω, ψαλμός, ᾠδή; Payne Smith, 1:1136–37. The exclusive use of "ode," "psalm," and "to sing" in the translation of these terms is merely conventional. "Song" would serve just as well. And the Pe. *zmar* could be distinguished from the Pa. *zammar* by using "chant" for the latter in allusion to the Greek ψάλλω (see Lattke, *Hymnus*, 2 n. 5, and 251–53: "Oden Salomos"). In 24:2a, *zmar* is translated by "coo," characterizing the vocalization of the dove.

27 Payne Smith, 2:2405–6.

28 Ibid., 2:2929–30.

29 Ibid., 2:3603.

30 See BDAG, *s.v.* πνευματικός, 2aβ.

31 This is the only occurrence of the Pa. participle ܡܙܡܪ (*mzammar*), used in the masculine *status absolutus* (Payne Smith, 1:1136: *canens*).

32 Lattke, *Oden*, 195; Abramowski, 57–58.

33 See Lattke, *Oden*, 206.

34 Franzmann, "Man of Rest," 411; see the commentary on this *Ode*.

"ode" to and on the Lord as something brought about by and "dedicated to God"[35]—even, perhaps, as something "*inspired*," but without limiting this "personal song of a Gnostic" to the religious sphere of "worship" and the "church."[36]

In the immediately preceding excursus, it was noted that the Greek loanword κιθάρα in 3a is one of the links connecting 14:6-8 with *Ode* 26.[37] The adjective "holy" would be almost better suited to this metaphorical stringed instrument, which is not the "holy Spirit,"[38] than to the "ode" intended to be performed with instrumental accompaniment (2a; on the prepositional phrase with ܐܝܕܐ [ʾ*idā*], see Excursus 27).

The imperfect of ܫܠܝ (*šlī*), which can also be translated by a future tense, cannot in 3b mean "remain calm," unlike 31:10a ("I . . . was silent and remained calm"). Rather, it means "to cease," and the negation emphasizes its eschatological continuance. 𝔊 is likely to have had a wordplay with παύομαι and ἀνά-/κατάπαυσις.[39] Even though a subjective genitive may be excluded, the phrase "odes of his rest," which Wray does not explicate,[40] remains ambiguous. Like "truth" (14:7a), the Lord's "rest," which cannot be found in the life of this world, may be the object that the "odes" long for. However, the divine "rest" may also be seen as a transcendental "place" (see on 10a and 12b below), and thus the genitive may reveal the *original* source and habitation of these poems (see Excursus 3).

The *parallelismus membrorum* and the repetition of ܟܠ (*kol*) in 4a-b underline the strong emphasis on the completeness of the individual that is already evident in the use of the two anthropological terms "heart" and "limbs" (see Excursuses 4 and 18). The *hapax legomenon* ܓܥܐ (*gʿā*) in 4a, like βοάω, expresses "a solemn proclamation."[41] The repetition of πρός/ܠܘܬ (*lwāt*) from 2b defines the direction, which, according to classical ideas, is upwards.[42]

The hymnic synonyms in 4b form both the conclusion and the *inclusio* of stanza I (see 1a above, "hymn"). The Pa. ܫܒܚ (*šabbaḥ*) can mean to "glorify" or to "laud" (Excursus 21). If 𝔊 did not use δοξάζω but ὑμνέω in a wordplay with ὕμνος (1a), the translation as "praise" would be even more suitable, matching other passages (see 7:19; 17:8; 21:7; 41:1). The Palp. ܪܡܪܡ (*ramrem*), as a synonym of *šabbaḥ*, is also used hymnically, but corresponds more to ὑψόω or ἀνυψόω than to μεγαλύνω (see Excursus 17).[43]

■ **5-7** This stanza abandons the first person and forms, in a tricolon, a self-contained and poetically free hymnic confession, which Franzmann calls an "ode-within-the-ode" (formally, cf. 12:4 and 19:10-11).[44] The three artistically varied constructions, with ܕܝܠ (*dīl*) + possessive suffix + enclitic personal pronoun, corresponded in 𝔊 to αὐτοῦ, with more or less emphasis and with or without ἐστίν in a word order that may have mirrored 𝔖. These genitives, referring to the "Lord" and "Most High," must be examined for their specific meanings.[45]

The building blocks of this poem, which may be quoted from a preexisting work, are taken not only from Ps 107 (106 LXX), as Harris and Mingana point out,[46] but also from Ps 112:3-5 LXX, and there may even be some Synoptic influence (Luke 13:29).[47] For the use of

35 BDAG, *s.v.* ἅγιος, 1a.
36 Heinrich Schlier, "ᾄδω, ᾠδή," *ThWNT* 1 (1933) 163–64; *TDNT* 1:164–65.
37 See Lattke, "Wörter," 291 = idem, *Bedeutung*, 4:139–40.
38 Contra Diettrich, 95.
39 BDAG, *s.vv.* παύομαι, ἀνάπαυσις, κατάπαυσις; Payne Smith, 2:4163–64.
40 Wray, *Rest*, 26, 32.
41 BDAG, *s.v.* βοάω, 1c; Payne Smith, 1:759.
42 Whether a distinction was made in 𝔊 between πρὸς αὐτῷ (2b) and πρὸς αὐτόν (4b) (Frankenberg, 25) can no longer be determined (cf., e.g., John 1:1-2).
43 Contra Frankenberg, 25; see Payne Smith, 2:3858: *magnificavit*.
44 Franzmann, "Study," 397.
45 In spite of Franzmann's stated reason (p. 201) and reversing the division in my earlier edition (Lattke, *Bedeutung*, 154–55), I am keeping the division shown in both manuscripts, which may be evidence for less-emphasized constructions in 𝔊.
46 Harris and Mingana, 2:354.
47 On Matt 24:27 and 24:31, see Pierre, 139.

the preposition of place ܥܕܡܐ (*ʿdammā*) + ܠ (*l-*), which can represent ἕως (as in Matt 24:27: ἀπὸ ἀνατολῶν . . . ἕως δυσμῶν, "from the east . . . as far as the west") as well as μέχρι (Ps 112:3a LXX: ἀπὸ ἀνατολῶν ἡλίου μέχρι δυσμῶν, "From the rising of the sun to his setting"),[48] betrays diverse influences on 5 and 6. Further, the cardinal points in 6 are reversed, as can be seen from the passages where the four are sequentially listed.

Ps 106:3b LXX	ἀπὸ ἀνατολῶν καὶ δυσμῶν καὶ βορρᾶ καὶ θαλάσσης. "from the east, and west, and north, and sea [south]."[49]
Luke 13:29	ἀπὸ ἀνατολῶν καὶ δυσμῶν καὶ ἀπὸ βορρᾶ καὶ νότου.[50] "from east and west, from north and south."

If ܬܫܒܘܚܬܐ (*tešbuḥtā*) in 5 is taken to be the parallel of ܫܘܡܠܝܐ (*šumlāyā*) in 7, the Greek equivalent must have been δόξα (cf. Ps 112:4b LXX: ἐπὶ τοὺς οὐρανοὺς ἡ δόξα αὐτοῦ, "his glory is above the heavens"). Then δόξα αὐτοῦ would be interpreted as a subjective genitive and would be translated as "his glory" (see Excursus 21). But the cardinal points, also called the four "winds" (Mark 13:27; Matt 24:31), show that 5-6 are in a synthetic *parallelismus membrorum* in which *tešbuḥtā* and the *hapax legomenon* ܬܘܕܝܬܐ (*tawdītā*) complement each other and may be meant as synonyms. So the Greek of 5-6 can only have used an objective genitive in each case; but even so it remains impossible to decide whether 5 had δόξα[51] or ὕμνος, and whether 6—influenced by Ps 106:1 LXX (Ἐξομολογεῖσθε τῷ κυρίῳ, "Give thanks to the Lord")[52]—used the rare term ἐξομολόγησις[53] or one of the commoner ones such as εὐχαριστία[54] or ὁμολογία.[55] Frankenberg even suggests ἔπαινος,[56] which may be a reference to Ps 112:1-3 LXX (αἰνεῖτε occurs three times). In this case the ambiguities of the Syriac text must remain unresolved.

The meaning of the image of the "heights" in 7, perhaps inspired by Ps 112:5 LXX (τίς ὡς κύριος ὁ θεὸς ἡμῶν ὁ ἐν ὑψηλοῖς κατοικῶν, "Who is as the Lord our God who dwells in the high places?"),[57] will have to be explored.[58] If the intention is to extend the cardinal points into the third dimension, it would reach from the ἀρχή to the equally transcendent τέλος of the "heights" of the "Most High," defining the mythological space of his "*plērōma*" (see Excursus 35). However, if, as in Matt 24:31, it is an ἄκρον of the celestial "heights" that is visualized and the distance to the (far) τέλος (see Excursus 23), the Lord's ܫܘܡܠܝܐ (*šumlāyā*) might be the same as his "perfection."[59]

■ **8-11** The five rhetorical questions of stanza III (8a, 8b, 9a, 10a, 11a), all constructed with active participles,

48 Rahlfs, 2:126; Brenton, 768 [*sic*].
49 Rahlfs, 2:119; Brenton, 764.
50 The minor variants in Luke make no difference here (cf. NA[27] on this passage). The reading θαλάσσης in the LXX (Rahlfs, 2:119), as well as ܝܡܐ (*yammā*; *OTSy*, pt. 2 fasc. 3, p. 129; corrected to ܬܝܡܢܐ in MS. 10t2) in the Syriac, is due to a misspelling in the Hebrew text (cf. the emendation proposed in *BHS*, 1190). Instead of ומִיָּם "it should read וּמִיָּמִין" (Kraus, *Psalmen*, 735), that is, "from the south" (ibid., 734). If this line in the *Ode*, with its reversed sequence of "north" and "south," does not derive from Luke 13:29, *Ode* 26:6 may be an early attempt at emendation of the biblical text. For the *hapax legomena* of the cardinal points, see, in the sequence found in 5-6, Payne Smith, 1:928, 2:2985, 1:1606, 772; BDAG, *s.vv.* ἀνατολή, δυσμή, νότος, βορρᾶς.
51 Frankenberg, 25.
52 Rahlfs, 2:119; Brenton, 764.
53 Harris and Mingana, 2:354: "thanksgiving," but cf. BDAG, *s.v.* ἐξομολόγησις: "praise of God."
54 Payne Smith, 1:1552; BDAG, *s.v.* εὐχαριστία, 2: "thanksgiving."
55 Franzmann, 200; BDAG, *s.v.* ὁμολογία, 2: "confession."
56 Frankenberg, 25; BDAG, *s.v.* ἔπαινος, 1: "praise."
57 Rahlfs, 2:126; Brenton, 768.
58 Diettrich (p. 95) says: "i.e. from the topmost heights to the lowest deeps." This explanation is as far off the mark as Berger and Nord's free translation (p. 959) "and from the highest peak to the deepest valley."
59 Diettrich, 95: "Vollendung"; cf. Berger and Nord, 959: "Vollkommenheit"; Harris and Mingana, 2:352, and Charlesworth, 104: "perfection." Unlike the corresponding terms in 5-6, ܫܘܡܠܝܐ (*šumlāyā*) in 7 is written with a suffix: ܫܘܡܠܝܗ (*šumlāyeh*). The difference is probably not critical, since ܕܝܠ (*dīl*), here ܕܝܠܗ (*dīleh*), can be used with "a suffix attached to the governing member" (Nöldeke §225).

do not expect direct answers, but the question of 11a, whose construction differs from the others, is followed by a double statement of objectives (11b-c), which are also relevant to 8-10. Neither optatives[60] nor imperatives are suitable for the translation of these "questions."[61] That there was a Greek original is extremely likely, but neither the syntax nor the vocabulary is as easy to reconstruct as Frankenberg believes.[62]

The "odes" to and about the "Lord" in the first two questions refer back to the "odes of his rest" (see 3b above; cf. 10a and Excursus 26). The verbs of 8a and 8b complement each other, meaning "to compose" and "to read (aloud)."[63] It is more, therefore, than merely writing down and reciting.

Verse 9a-b is directed "against the idea of redeeming oneself."[64] The Syriac paronomasia on ܢܦܫܐ (*napšā*) would not have occurred in 𝔊. The terms would have been ζωή (9a) and ψυχή (9b), meaning "life," unless 9a had σωτηρία as the *Vorlage* of ܚ̈ܝܐ (*ḥayyē*),[65] in which case there might have been a wordplay with the passive of σῴζω in 9b. It is tempting to point to Col 3:16 (νουθετοῦντες ἑαυτούς, "admonish one another") for the reflexive use of ܪܕܐ (*rḏā*), but this Pe., which appears in 13b in the sense of "to flow," does not here mean "admonish"[66] but something like παιδαγωγέω[67] or, more likely, παιδεύω.[68] But these classical ideas of education and culture are turned reflexively and by use of the preposition εἰς/πρός/ܠ (*l*-) toward a connotation of "life" in salvation—or even to "salvation" itself (see Table 1).

Verse 9b names the first of three, or perhaps four, objectives, in a construction using a conjunction and an imperfect. The Ethpe. of ܦܪܩ (*praq*), whose grammatical subject is ψυχή/ܢܦܫܐ (*nafšā*),[69] corresponds to a theological passive of σῴζω,[70] which means that it opposes any possibility of "self-redemption" (see above; also Excursus 5). This criticism is probably not under the influence of Mark 8:35 or Luke 9:24.

The "Most High" of 10a is the same as the "Lord" of *Ode* 26 (see Excursus 17). Whether the Ethpe of ܢܘܚ, ܢܚ (*nāḥ*), here and in 12a, corresponds to ἀναπαύομαι as the "goal of gnosticism [*sic*]"[71] or to ἐπαναπαύομαι[72] ("rely on"; contrast Rom 2:17 [νόμῳ])[73] or even to καταπαύομαι[74] cannot be decided and is less important than the remainder of the image, which includes both the "odes of his rest" (3b) and the "singers" who "stand in rest" (12b). The verb "to rest" is combined with the preposition ܥܠ (*ʿal* = ἐπί or πρός) in other passages as well (30:2b [+ "living spring of the Lord"]; 36:1a [+ "me"]; cf. also 28:3a; 35:6b). Someone at rest with the Most High needs no other rest, but does not enter into a personal relationship with him. For the God who does not exist is personal only insofar as the miraculous human personality confesses and understands itself as God's (redeemed) creation that does not exist of itself and cannot be delivered by any-body.

The second objective, in 10b, repeats the Pa. ܡܠܠ (*mallel*) from 2a and declares that the "sacred texts"[75] on the "Lord" and his "rest" come, in the final analysis, out of the metaphorical "mouth of the Lord" and can claim to be in some sort inspired and prophetic utterances.[76] So the *Odes to* and *about* the Lord (objective genitive) are

60 Contra Harris and Mingana, 2:355.
61 Contra Berger and Nord, 959.
62 Frankenberg, 25–26.
63 Payne Smith, 1:1850, 2:3712–14; see also BDAG, *s.vv.* ἀναγινώσκω and γράφω.
64 Harnack, 59; Diettrich, 95.
65 Payne Smith, 1:1254.
66 BDAG, *s.v.* νουθετέω.
67 Frankenberg, 25.
68 Payne Smith, 2:3819; BDAG, *s.v.* παιδεύω; LSJ, *s.v.* παιδεύω.
69 Contra Lattke, *Bedeutung*, 1:155, and idem, *Oden*, 175.
70 See Payne Smith, 2:3294; BDAG, *s.v.* σῴζω.
71 BDAG, *s.v.* ἀναπαύω, 3b.
72 BDAG, *s.v.* ἐπαναπαύομαι, 2.
73 Frankenberg (pp. 25–26) is somewhat cavalier in his distinction between ἀναπαυόμενος (10a) and ἐπαναπαύεσθαι (12a). However, his use of the preposition ἐπί in 10a evens it out to some extent.
74 BDAG, *s.v.* καταπαύομαι, 3; cf. Payne Smith, 2:2311–12.
75 Berger and Nord, 959.
76 See Aune, "Christian Prophecy," 447.

still, paradoxically, his *own* songs (subjective genitive) whose human authors and performers are, in a sense, only speaking tubes.[77]

The final rhetorical question in 11a refers neither to translation as a craft nor to the composition of edifying targumim. The term ܬܪܓܡ (*targem*)—and the Ethpa. in 11c from the same root—corresponds to the composite διερμηνεύω or to the simple ἑρμηνεύω, both of which mean "to explain," "to interpret,"[78] while the participle ܡܫܟܚ (*meškaḥ*) idiomatically represents δύναται + infinitive. Both Syriac manuscripts have the plural of ܬܕܡܘܪܬܐ (*tedmurtā*), that is, ܬܕܡܪ̈ܬܐ (*tedmrātā*),[79] as the object of the imperfect of ܬܪܓܡ, which is dependent on ܡܫܟܚ + ܕ (*d-*). Harris and Mingana consider that the origin of this *hapax legomenon* lies in θαυμάσια in Ps 106:8, 15, 21, 24, 31 LXX.[80] But the term "wonders" makes an awkward object for the verb "to interpret."[81] And it is also doubtful that "the Odist is imitating" the "refrain" of Psalm 107 (106 LXX).[82] That doubt is only increased by the observation that in H the word is almost certainly an emendation of an original ܙܡܝܪܬܗ (*zmīrteh*).[83] Unless this was a mistake, under the influence of 2a and 8a ("odes" and "odes of the Lord"), there must have been a manuscript original with the reading ܙܡܝܪܬܗ in the singular, as well as at least one with the reading of N. How early or late these lost Syriac manuscripts may have been cannot be determined. But "ode of the Lord" (probably found in 𝔊 also) fits much better into *Ode* 26 than the somewhat gratuitous phrase "wonders of the Lord."

The reciprocally complementary bicolon 11b-c begins to yield its meaning as a statement of outcome and to widen the field of the two previous final clauses 9b and 10b, by the use of the two verbs ܐܫܬܪܝ (*ʾeštrī*, Ethpe. of ܫܪܐ [*šrā*]) and the Pa. ܩܘܝ (*qawwī*).[84] The latter verb refers to the "Lord," the "Most High," as the topic of the "ode" (cf. Ps 9:8 and 101:13 LXX), but in the case of the first there is a question whether it is to be understood as "to perish"[85] or should rather be taken to mean "be liberated."[86] The text of the Greek version must remain pure speculation.[87]

■ **12-13** Not only the simile in 13, but even the first word of 12a is difficult to interpret. For that active masculine participle of ܣܦܩ (*sfaq*) might still refer to the unnamed exegete of 11a-b and have the meaning of ἱκανός (as,

77 Harnack (p. 59) draws attention to 10a-b, saying, "this thought gives the key to the attitude of the singer in a number of the *Odes*."

78 BDAG, *s.v.* διερμηνεύω, 2, and ἑρμηνεύω, 1; Payne Smith, 2:4495–96.

79 See Payne Smith, 1:922.

80 Harris and Mingana, 2:354.

81 Johannes Behm, "ἑρμηνεύω, ἑρμηνεία, κτλ.," *ThWNT* 2 (1935) 659; *TDNT* 2:661–62.

82 Harris and Mingana, 2:355.

83 I noted this in my edition after a personal examination of H (Lattke, *Bedeutung*, 1:154). The result was confirmed and refined by another close examination of ܬܕܡܪ̈ܬܗ (Charlesworth, *Manuscripts*, 67 line 13). The first letter, ܬ, differs from its normal shape because it overwrites the letter ܙ. The second letter, ܕ, had to be squeezed in. The fourth letter (ܪ̈ with a point below it) looks as though two joined letters (ܝܪ)—with a point below the first of them as in 66, lines 13 and 15, 67, line 8—had been amalgamated into one rather oddly shaped letter (ܪ̈). Not merely the shape of the letter, but the placing of the second point, indicating the plural, looks very different from that in the words listed, to which it was compared.

84 Payne Smith, 2:3509; see also BDAG, *s.v.* μένω, 1aβ. On the reading of H, see the following remark of Harris and Mingana (2:353): "If ܡܛܠ meaning 'because' is separated by a particle from the noun, verb, or pronoun, the letter ܕ can be omitted." However, it is questionable whether ܡܛܠ ܕ in 11b has a causal meaning, translated by "because" or "for" (see, e.g., Bauer, 608; Lattke, *Oden*, 176). It seems to me that so far it has been overlooked that (1) the insertion of the particle ܓܝܪ (*gēr*) between ܡܛܠ (*meṭṭol*) and ܕ (*d-*) differentiates this passage from all other occurrences of ܡܛܠ ܕ (see Lattke, *Bedeutung*, 2:130–31), and (2) that ܡܛܠ ܕ and imperfect corresponds to ἵνα (Payne Smith, 2:2077). My feeling that ܡܛܠ ܓܝܪ ܕ is a translation of ἵνα γάρ is supported by the fact that this phrase can be found from Homer (*Iliad* 10.127; Helmut van Thiel, *Homeri Ilias* [Bibliotheca Weidmanniana II; Hildesheim/Zurich/New York: Olms, 1996] 180) onward and becomes common about the beginning of the Christian era. I am indebted to Jeffrey Gibson and Rick Strelan for this information.

85 Bauer, 609; Franzmann, 200: "be dissolved." The only argument *for* this interpretation of 11b would be the contrast with "remain" in 11c.

86 See Payne Smith, 2:4309–10.

87 Frankenberg (p. 26) suggests a passive of λύω.

e.g., in 2 Cor 3:5 with a following infinitive).[88] More probably, however, it introduces the teaching of stanza IV as the equivalent of an impersonal ἀρκεῖ.[89] If that is so, this modest word, which was also used by philosophers, expresses "particularly clearly the profoundest character of the underlying view of life,"[90] in this case by the absolute use of the infinitives of two verbs that convey the Gnostic "relationship between knowledge and rest," as the coordination of the nouns γνῶσις and ἀνάπαυσις does in Clement of Alexandria (*Paed.* 1.29.3).[91]

Verse 12b, using a *hapax legomenon* derived from the root *zmr*, which may stand for the Greek οἱ ψάλλοντες[92] (see Excursus 26), introduces a multitude of "singers" too large to fit into any liturgical setting.[93] Whether the participle of the common verb ܩܐܡ, ܩܡ (*qām*) is meant to convey finding the soteriological "place to stand," which plays a role in both the "Qumranic and New Testament writings" in different ways,[94] is doubtful, in view of the occurrence of the undeniable *terminus technicus* "rest." Neither here nor in 14:6 can ܢܝܚܘܬܐ (*nīḥūṯā*) mean ἡ πραΰτης.[95] In fact the feminine, used as a synonym of κατάπαυσις/ܢܝܚܬܐ (*nyāḥtā*; cf. the variants in 35:1a), connects with the "odes of his rest" in 3b, where ܢܝܚܐ (*nyāḥā*) is the equivalent of ἀνάπαυσις.[96] This varied rendering in ꜱ may suggest that the Syriac translators were not as Gnostically alert to the technical differences between ἀνάπαυσις and κατάπαυσις as the Coptic translators of the *Pistis Sophia*. Commentators who, quoting Wis 3:3 and 4:7, think of "rest in the life beyond,"[97] are equally lacking in Gnostic understanding. For Gnostics, "rest" is not a "possession" but a transcendent place "in this life" (*contra* Diettrich, who even tries to construe the "singer[s]" as "God's rest" and interprets the Ethpe. of ܫܪܐ [*šrā*] in 11b as "die").[98]

Franzmann has already discussed the "simile" of 13a-b and excluded some possibilities. She seems to consider the singers to be the subject of the compari-

---

The rest of his retroversion of these two lines is as imaginative as the translations and interpolations of Harnack (p. 59), Diettrich (p. 95), or Bernard (p. 109). Log. 1 of the so-called *Gospel of Thomas*, "Whoever finds the meaning (ἑρμηνεία) of these words will not taste death" (Kurt Aland, ed., *Synopsis Quattuor Evangeliorum* [15th ed.; Stuttgart: Deutsche Bibelgesellschaft, 1996; 4th corr. printing 2005] 519), can be adduced as a parallel to the use of "to interpret." This parallel is among those collected by Franzmann ("Background") although she refers to the English translation of NHC II,*2* (32,11-14 = *NHLE*, 126). That Sir 47:17 is the source of the key word of *Ode* 26 is hardly likely. In that verse it is said of Solomon: ἐν ᾠδαῖς καὶ παροιμίαις καὶ παραβολαῖς καὶ ἐν ἑρμηνείαις ἀπεθαύμασάν σε χῶραι ("The countries marveled at thee for thy songs, and proverbs, and parables, and interpretations") (Rahlfs, 2:462; Brenton, 117, in Appendix; cf. *APAT* 1:461 and *APOT* 1:498.

88 See BDAG, *s.v.* ἱκανός, 2: "fit, appropriate," with a "connotation *worthy*."

89 Payne Smith, 2:2703–4; BDAG, *s.v.* ἀρκέω, 1; LSJ, *s.v.* ἀρκέω; cf. Harnack, 59: ἀρκεῖ γὰρ γιγνώσκειν καὶ ἀναπαύειν.

90 Gerhard Kittel, "ἀρκέω, κτλ.," *ThWNT* 1 (1933) 465; *TDNT* 1:465.

91 Bauer, 608; see also Harnack, 59–60; Diettrich, 95; Harris and Mingana, 2:354. The passages to which Bauer (p. 608) refers are worth noting, because both in frg. 4b of the *Gospel of the Hebrews* and in log. 2 of *P.Oxy.* 654 (= log. 2 of the *Gospel of Thomas*) the verb "to seek" (see 13b below) plays a leading role beside the term "rest." On the verbs "to rest" and "to know," which betray "a Gnostic understanding" (Helmut Koester, *Introduction to the New Testament*, vol. 2: *History and Literature of Early Christianity* [2nd ed.; New York/Berlin: de Gruyter, 2000] 223), see Excursuses 3 and 7.

92 Frankenberg, 26.

93 Franzmann, 203.

94 Walter Grundmann, "Stehen und Fallen im qumrânischen und neutestamentlichen Schrifttum," Hans Bardtke, ed., *Qumran-Probleme: Vorträge des Leipziger Symposions über Qumran-Probleme vom 9. bis 14. Oktober 1961* (SSA 42; Berlin: Akademie-Verlag, 1963) 146, 153, 161.

95 BDAG, *s.v.* πραΰτης; Payne Smith, 2:2316 (the usage reference "liber ܩܡ ܒܢܝܚܘܬܐ [*qām b-nīḥūṯā*] *in pace stetit*, absolutus est, finem laboris accepit," is not relevant here).

96 It is a question worth pursuing whether *Dial. Sav.* 120,1-8, that is, the beginning of NHC III,*5*, has influenced the formulation of 12a-b (see Stephen Emmel, ed., *Nag Hammadi Codex III,5: The Dialogue of the Savior* [NHS 26; Leiden: Brill, 1984] 40–41).

97 Diettrich, 95; see also Georgi, 410, 414.

98 Diettrich, 95.

son, saying, "it is this experience of rest which enables them to flow to the help of others."[99] However, the comparative particle ὡς/ܐܝܟ (ʾak̲) only connects the "river"—with its "abundant spring" (cf. 4:10; 11:6; 30:1-2; 40:1-2)[100]—and its steady flow[101]—with the "rest."[102] This determination of the exact terms of comparison is necessary because the referent of the ambiguous masculine suffix at the end of 13b cannot be the masculine ܡܒܘܥܐ (*mabbūʿā*, in 𝔊 πηγή)[103] or ܥܘܕܪܢܐ (*ʿud̲rānā*, in 𝔊 βοήθεια), but is the (also masculine) term ܢܗܪܐ (*nahrā*, in 𝔊 ποταμός). In the simile, the desired "stream" or "river" is the theological "rest," which is the actual goal of the soteriological "seeking" (see Excursus 19). This somewhat lightens the obscurity of the ornate imagery. A reconstruction of the Greek of 13a-b may be attempted, making critical use of Frankenberg's retroversion[104] and continuing from ἐν ἀναπαύσει (12b)[105] as follows:

ὡς/ὥσπερ/ὡσεὶ ποταμῷ τῷ ἔχοντι πλουσίαν
  πηγήν
καὶ ῥέοντι εἰς βοήθειαν τῶν αὐτὸν (ἐκ)ζητούντων.

---

99 Franzmann, 203.
100 The idiomatic construction with ܐܝܬ (*ʾīt̲*) + ܠ (*l-*) translates a form of ἔχω (Payne Smith, 1:172; Nöldeke §307). This is not the "river of joy" in paradise (11:16g). And the remark of Harris and Mingana (2:353), "The Ode here returns to its keynote ܐܫܕ ('I poured out'), with the reference to the 'abundant fountain' (ܡܒܘܥܐ)," is only relevant to 𝔖. Matters were different for 𝔊 (see 1a above).
101 "The river's flow is at rest, because it is steady and does not suddenly flood or dry up" (Harnack, 60). The Pe. ܪܕܐ (*rd̲ā*), also found in 9a, here means "to flow" (Payne Smith, 2:3818; cf. BDAG, *s.v.* ῥέω). There is no visible connection with the ποταμοί . . . ὕδατος ζῶντος ("rivers of living water") of John 7:38.
102 Harris and Mingana, 2:355. Their reference to the "work, preserved only in Syriac, *On the Theophany*, i.e., the incarnation of God" (Berthold Altaner and Alfred Stuiber, *Patrologie: Leben, Schriften und Lehre der Kirchenväter* [7th ed.; Freiburg/Basel/Vienna: Herder, 1966] 221) is of interest in its historical effect rather than as an aid in interpreting the *Odes*. It might be enlightening to discover whether the *Odes of Solomon* had any influence on this work by Eusebius that is so often cited by Payne Smith.
103 *Barn.* 1:3, where the text ἀπὸ τοῦ πλουσίου τῆς πηγῆς κυρίου ("from the abundance of the Lord's fountain") is corrupt (Ehrman, 2:12–13; Lindemann and Paulsen, 26; see also Prostmeier, 136–37), is another passage that may play an important part in dating the *Odes of Solomon* in the first quarter of the second century (cf. Introduction, sec. 4).
104 Frankenberg, 26.
105 Harnack, 60.

27

Ode 27: The Crucifixion Interpreted as Ascent into Heaven

1 I stretched out my hands and hallowed my Lord,
2 because the spreading out of my hands is his sign[a],
3 and my stretching [up] is the wood, which is upright/correct.
Hallelujah.

a 27:2 ܐܬܗ ܗܝ H; ܐܬܬܗܝ N.

Ode 42 Stanza I

1a I stretched out my hands and drew near to my Lord,
1b because the spreading out of my hands is his sign,
2a and my stretching [up] is the straight wood,
2b that was hung upon the way of the upright one.

Introduction

Ode 27 is preserved in two Syriac manuscripts.[1] There is only one thing certain about it. This shortest of the surviving *Odes of Solomon* has in 42:1-2 "the only doublet to be found in the collection."[2] All else is moot, and will yield its meaning only when the gestures of the imagery, as well as the two terms ܐܬܐ (*ʾāṯā*) and ܩܝܣܐ (*qaysā*), can be elucidated, preferably by finding Greek equivalents and applicable biblical quotations. Tracing its later influence, if any, is more important for dating the *Odes of Solomon* than for interpreting the original meaning of the symbols.[3]

The two most important questions, to begin with, are: (1) is the "Lord" of 27:1 and 42:1a the Most High God or the Kyrios Christos? (2) Is the speaker, who is the same in both texts, *any* "praying person,"[4] or is he, whether praying or not, the redeemed Redeemer who is named the "Son of God" in *Ode* 42 (esp. 42:15-18)? The answer to these questions will decide whose and what the "sign" is and who is referred to by the term ܬܪܝܨܐ (*trīṣā*) in 42:2b. Expanding Franzmann's short excursus,[5] the excursus for this Ode precedes the commentary.

Excursus 27: "Hand," "Right Hand," "Arm," and "Finger" in the *Odes of Solomon*

Because of the parallelism of ϭⲓϫ (*cič*)/ܐܝܕܐ (*ʾiḏā*) and ⲟⲩⲛⲁⲙ/ܝܡܝܢܐ (*yammīnā*) in 22:7, the term "the right hand," which occurs nine times, will be included in this excursus.[6] Paralleling the plural of "hands," the plural "fingers" is found twice (16:6;

1 Mss.: Codex H, 21a; Codex N, 150ʳ (ܣ). Ed./trans.: Charlesworth, 106–7; Franzmann, 204–6; Lattke, 2:249–56 and 3:XXXV.

2 Harnack, 60. Since *Ode* 27 is almost identical to stanza I of *Ode 42*, that stanza, which is one line longer, will be included, in preliminary fashion, in this exegesis. The text, with the verse numbering of *Ode* 42, is printed below *Ode* 27.

3 See Introduction, sec. 4.

4 "The one who prays images the Cross" (Berger and Nord, 960). This remark is used to justify their free translation of 27:3, "When I stand erect I am the upright (*Pfahl*) of the Cross." And their translation of 42:2b is even freer: "It [viz., the Cross] was carried up the way (of suffering) of the righteous" (Berger and Nord, 970). Unfortunately, the images are not so plain.

5 Franzmann, 205, comparing 27:1-3; 35:7; 37:1; 42:1-2.

6 Crum, 483, 839; Payne Smith, 1:1546, 1605. In 8:20c, the phrase "to my right" refers to the right side, not the right hand. The term "the left" occurs only once (25:7). Here, too, the phrase "on my right and left" refers to both sides of the person.

23:8a).[7] In place of the only singular ܨܒܥܐ (*ṣeḇʿā*), 23:21b, speaking of the "finger of God" writing, could just as easily have used the term "hand."[8] The term ܕܪܥܐ (*drāʿā*), also occurring three times, is brought in because the "arm of the bridegroom" includes his hand (42:8a), and the "lifting up" of the "arms" "on high" to the "compassion of the Lord" (21:1) shows strong similarity to the images of 35:7 and 37:1 and can thus be related to 27:1-3 and 42:1-2.[9]

The identity of the speaking "I" of *Ode* 21 has already been discussed and left unresolved (see introduction to and exegesis of *Ode* 21:1-2), and the question of the identity of the redeemed speaker will arise again for *Odes* 35 and 37. Since it is not inescapably necessary "to admit" that the "I" of 42:1-2 is not the same as the "I" of the rest of the Ode, the second question in the introduction to *Ode* 27, concerning the identity of the "I" of this Ode, remains, so far, unanswered.

In the twenty-two occurrences of "hand/s," it is first necessary to select out all the cases where the singular ܐܝܕܐ (*ʾiḏā*) or plural ܐܝܕܐ̈ (*ʾiḏē*), with a suffix and preceding preposition ܒ (*b-*), is used idiomatically for "by," which is sometimes made even clearer by parallelism with that preposition (singular in 12:11b, 13a; 15:5, 8a [parallel with ܒ]; 18:1b [parallel with ܒ]; 31:7a; plural in 17:4a; 31:4b; 33:11a). The phrase "by the hand" in 38:16b probably also simply means "by." *Ode* 22:5a is borderline, since the mythological annihilation of the seven-headed monster would have been accomplished by "hands."

Before discussing the main "hand/s" passages, there is room for a short note on the subject of the (power of the) "right hand," which has irked left-handers in all eras. Except in 28:15a ("water in my right hand") and the two passages 8:20c and 25:7 (see above), δεξιά/ܝܡܝܢܐ (*yammīnā*) refers anthropomorphically to God's right "hand" as the saving "power"[10] that is *with* the persons addressed (8:6a), can be stretched out (14:4a), leads to victory (18:7a), characterizes the *plērōma* (19:5b), but is also qualified by "salvation" (25:2a), has the power to lift up (25:9a), is instrumental in planting eschatologically (38:20b) but can also destroy dualistically (22:7a).

In the last passage mentioned, the "hand" of God that prepares the way of the believers occurs as a parallel term to his "right hand." The "work of his hands" and the "labor of his fingers" were already hymned in the context of his creation (16:6). There are no other direct references to the "hand/s" of God, but the "hands" of the singer of the *Odes* hold the cithara of the Lord (26:3a), and conversely the many "hands" and "fingers" of the pursuers snatch at the heavenly letter (23:7-8a), and the "hands of the Deceivers" are unsuccessful (38:15a).

The remaining passages are closely connected, a connection underpinned by the use of the roots *pšṭ* and *trṣ*. The imagery is clearest at the end of *Ode* 35, where the speaking "I" makes three parallel statements. He stretched out his hands in the "ascent" (35:7a); he directed himself toward the Most High (35:7b); and he was saved toward him (35:7c). There is no mention of prayer. Thus, the gesture of the hands cannot immediately be interpreted as an early position for praying. The parallelism of 35:7a and 35:7b suggests a lifting up of the hands.[11] This is related to the beginning of *Ode* 21: "I lifted up my arms on high / to the compassion of the Lord" (21:1a-b). There too one sees a connection with "salvation" (21:2c); praise and rejoicing come later (21:7–9). So it is more than questionable whether, as Berger and Nord imagine, the redeemed speaker lifted up his arms "to pray."[12]

Ode 37:1a displays the shortest form of the statement under discussion: "I stretched out my hands toward the Lord" (N; H reads "toward my Lord"). The expression ܐܪܝܡܬ (*ʾarīmeṯ*), paralleling ܦܫܛܬ (*pešṭeṯ*), refers, unlike 21:1a, to the "voice" lifted up toward the Most High (37:1b) as the utterance of the heart (37:2a), but there is no evidence that this conversation with the "Most High" is a formal liturgical prayer, or a "hymn."[13] And whose the "hands"

7 On *Ode* 16:6, see the discussion of δάκτυλος θεοῦ in Luke 11:20 "and its *Umwelt*" by Pieter Willem van der Horst, "'The Finger of God:' Miscellaneous Notes on Luke 11:20 and Its *Umwelt*," in William L. Petersen, Johan S. Vos, and Henk J. de Jonge, eds., *Sayings of Jesus: Canonical and Non-Canonical. Essays in Honour of Tjitze Baarda* (NovTSup 89; Leiden: Brill, 1997) 89–103.

8 See BDAG, *s.vv.* δάκτυλος, χείρ.

9 Like the other terms, "arm" can also be a "symbol of God's power" (BDAG, *s.v.* βραχίων). In Syriac writings, "arms" may sometimes stand for Greek "hands" (see Payne Smith, 1:953, on Matt 4:6 and Luke 4:11 [from Ps 91:12 or 90:12 LXX]). In 38:3b, H has "arms of immortal life" in place of N's "step of immortal life."

10 BDAG, *s.v.* δεξιός, 1b.

11 See Berger and Nord's metaphrastic translation (p. 965): "I raised my hands."

12 Berger and Nord, 954.

13 As Berger and Nord (p. 966) suppose ("Lied"). Correct ܐܪܝܡܬܐ to ܐܪܝܡܬ in Lattke, 2:251.

and "voice" may be must await the explication of that short Ode.

There is no mention of "praise" or "prayer" in *Ode* 27 or in its doublet *Ode* 42:1-2 and the general context of that stanza.[14] So it is doubtful whether this "stretching out" of the hands is meant as a gesture of prayer. In order to understand it as such,[15] it is necessary to accept as a fact that this "stretching out" is described as the image of the upright or extended "wood" (27:3; cf. 42:2a) and that the wood is a symbol of the hands extended upward. Further, this extension (root *pšṭ*), whether expressed as a verb or a noun, is distinguished from the "stretching" or "spreading" out of those same "hands" defined as a "sign" of the Lord (27:2; 42:1b), "hands" that, in *Ode* 42, belong *prima facie* to the redeemed Redeemer. This means that in *Ode* 27 also, the speaker may be this Redeemer, who differentiates in his utterance between two gestures, the "stretching" upward (of the "hands" and thus of the whole body) and the "spreading" out to both sides (of the arms and the palms of the hands), which people in antiquity would have recognized from images of their gods.[16]

What follows is an attempt, differing even from McNeil, to interpret both 27:1-3 and 42:1-2 as spoken *ex ore Christi*.[17] Since the "Savior" (42:18b) is not praying in a rite of baptism or in a liturgical sacramental context,[18] but speaking symbolically of the cross,[19] the rhetorical gestures of the hands and the whole body language are a "simulation of the cross."[20] But by this "the idea of the crucifixion is deflected."[21] There is no emphasis, at any rate, on "death on the cross" as the cruel ending of a historical conflict, much less on any theological idea of atonement.[22] There is very little "interpretation *about* the cross."[23] The cross is rather construed ahistorically by two intersecting motions that are quite similar to the ancient "gesture of prayer,"[24] but without emphasis on prayer of any sort.[25]

Instead of a "polemic against the habitual way of praying,"[26] this may be an early polemic against the emphasis on the cross, which survived into the later concept of the "cross of light" and the "polemics against

14 Contra Berger and Nord, 960, 970.

15 See Schroer and Staubli, *Körpersymbolik*, 177.

16 See, e.g., ibid., 199. A particularly beautiful example for the extended arms of a deity is a 90-cm statuette of the Egyptian "tutelary goddess Selket." "She stands erect with her feet together. Her arms are spread to embrace and protect right out to the tips of her fingers" (Jürgen Settgast, ed., *Tutanchamun* [Mainz: Philipp von Zabern, 1980] 56, with illustrations).

17 McNeil ("Source," 343) uses 27; 35:7 (+ 39:10b); and 42:1-2 to construct a poetical *Vorlage* that is used also in *Act. Pet.* 38. He recognizes the following distinctions: "As these three passages stand in the *Odes*, 27:1-3 is written *ex ore odistae*; 35:7 may be either *ex ore odistae* or *ex ore Christi*; and 42:1 f. is probably *ex ore Christi*, like the rest of this *Ode*."

18 Contra Daniel Plooij, "The Attitude of the Outspread Hands ('Orante') in Early Christian Literature and Art," *ExpT* 23 (1911–12) 202; Martin Dibelius, *Die Isisweihe bei Apuleius und verwandte Initiations-Riten* (SHAW.PH 1917, 4. Abh.; Heidelberg: C. Winter, 1917), quoted from idem, *Urchristentum*, 73–74.

19 Klijn, 304.

20 Rudolph, *Gnosis*, 239.

21 Abramowski, 64; on its later development, see Heinrich Schlier, *Religionsgeschichtliche Untersuchungen zu den Ignatiusbriefen* (BZNW 8; Gießen: Töpelmann, 1929) 102–10: "Das πάθος Christi und die Kirche."

22 Georg Richter, "Die Fleischwerdung des Logos im Johannesevangelium," *NovT* 13 (1971) 104 = idem, *Studien*, 167.

23 Spitta, 262, on Harnack, 60.

24 Spitta, 260.

25 Harris and Mingana's remark (2:357) is thus somewhat misleading: "There can be no doubt that this Psalm [viz., *Ode* 27] is based upon the early Christian attitude in prayer, which was cruciform, and upon the habit of the early Christians of finding the Cross everywhere in the outward world." Spitta's interpretation (pp. 259–67), which, in opposition to Harnack's Christian interpretation, eliminates the cross completely and regards *Ode* 27 as "purely Jewish," will be discussed later. Harnack's query (p. 60) about a possible "symbolism of the cross in Judaism" has been answered in a number of Dinkler's publications (see, e.g., Erich Dinkler, "Jesu Wort vom Kreuztragen," in *Neutestamentliche Studien für Rudolf Bultmann zu seinem siebzigsten Geburtstag am 20. August 1954* [ed. Walther Eltester; BZNW 21; Berlin: Töpelmann, 1954] 125; idem, "Die Taufterminologie in 2 Kor. i 21 f," in *Neotestamentica et Patristica: Eine Freundesgabe, Herrn Professor Dr. Oscar Cullmann zu seinem 60. Geburtstag überreicht* [NovTSup 6; Leiden: Brill, 1962] 187; idem, *Signum crucis: Aufsätze zum Neuen Testament und zur Christlichen Archäologie* [Tübingen: Mohr Siebeck, 1967] 15–21, 51–52, 113; idem, "Kreuz. I-II C 2," *LCI* 2 [1970] 563–70). An enquiry to Prof. Erich Dinkler elicited the following: "On

the use of a physical cross in praying."[27] Bearing in mind that, according to iconography, the symbol of the cross was, even in pre-Christian and non-Christian contexts, a "mysterious, magically powerful, life-giving sign,"[28] that this *orans* position was an expression of the "expectation of resurrection,"[29] and that Christ sometimes "ascends in such a posture,"[30] it may not be too daring to suggest that the "Son of God" and "Savior" (42:15b, 18b) is interpreting the experience of the cross as his "ascent into heaven" (cf. 35:7a: "ascent").[31] So it is not a mystical "hastening to Christ" that is in question but his own mythological "approach"[32] to the "Lord" (27:1; 37:1a; 42:1a) and "Most High" (35:7b; 37:1b).[33]

Interpretation

Both in the concise version (27) and in the altered and extended form (42:1-2), the self-describing speaker is "Christ himself, with no likelihood of a change of speaker."[34] Both *Odes*, therefore, are "Christian."[35] Even if *Ode* 42 is under the influence of Psalm 88 (87 LXX), as Harris and Mingana convincingly suggest,[36] the first half of 27:1 is more probably quoted from Isa 65:2 (ἐξεπέτασα τὰς χεῖράς μου, "I have held out my hands," also quoted in Rom 10:21).[37] That words are attributed to the "Son of God" (42:15) and "Savior" (42:18) that were originally put into the mouth of God the "Lord" is not so surprising, considering the ambiguous use of the title "Lord" in the *Odes of Solomon* (see, e.g., 17:16; 29:6; 39:11). Of the multiple meanings of the Pe. ܦܫܛ (*pšaṭ*), its use in 27:1 and 42:1a can only correspond to ἐκπετάννυμι in the sense of "extend,"[38] not to ἐκτείνω[39] or to πλατύνω.[40] This upward gesture is amplified in two different ways. In 27:1, the *hapax legomenon* ܩܕܫ (*qaddeš*) immediately reminds the hearer of the first petition of the Lord's Prayer (Matt 6:9; Luke 11:2)[41] and the biblical tradition that lies behind it. With-

---

the one hand, there is of course a Jewish cross as an eschatological seal deriving ultimately from Ezek 9:4-6; . . . On the other hand, I consider the passage in *Ode* 27 a Christian interpolation" (personal communication, July 6, 1974).

26 Peterson, *Studien*, 22.

27 Ibid., 24–25; Erich Dinkler, "Kreuz. I–II C 2," *LCI* 2 (1970) 564–65; Wilhelm Bousset, "Platons Weltseele und das Kreuz Christi," *ZNW* 14 (1913) 284.

28 Wilhelm Bousset, *Kyrios Christos: A History of the Belief in Christ from the Beginnings of Christianity to Irenaeus* (Nashville/New York: Abingdon, 1970) 307, ET of *Kyrios Christos,* 238.

29 Gerhard Seib, "Orans, Orante," *LCI* 3 (1971) 353; cf. Oskar Holl, "Handgebärden," *LCI* 2 (1970) 215.

30 Alfred A. Schmid, "Himmelfahrt Christi," *LCI* 2 (1970) 268.

31 Stock's remark on the art history of the "Ascension of Jesus Christ" refers to more recent works, but deserves consideration also for Christianity of the early period: "The extended arms in the frontally viewed upward movement may be considered a gesture of benediction (Luke 24:50)" (see Alex Stock, "Himmelfahrt/Himmelfahrt Jesu Christi: V. Kunstgeschichtlich," *RGG*⁴ 3 [2000] 1750).

32 Franz J. Dölger, "Beiträge zur Geschichte des Kreuzzeichens V," *JAC* 5 (1962) 9–10.

33 As far as I can see, Bertram never mentions the *Odes of Solomon* in his study on the ascension of Christ from the cross (see Georg Bertram, "Die Himmelfahrt Jesu vom Kreuz aus und der Glaube an seine Auferstehung," in Karl Ludwig Schmidt, ed., *Festgabe für Adolf Deissmann zum 60. Geburtstag 7. Nov. 1926* [Tübingen: Mohr Siebeck, 1927] 208 etc.). "Summarising," he says (pp. 215–16), "among the ideas of the earliest congregation concerning the entry of Jesus into the glory of heaven, there was, besides the waking from the dead or resurrection and ascension from the grave or after a shorter or longer stay, also, among certain traditions, an important place for the concept of the ascension of Jesus directly from the cross" (see esp. Phil 2:5-11; 1 Tim 3:16; 1 Pet 3:18-19).

34 Vogl, 71.

35 Staerk, 301.

36 Harris and Mingana, 2:407.

37 Isa 65:2 is also quoted in *Barn.* 12:4. The *Odes of Solomon* may have formed a link in the section "On the Cross (12:1-11)" (see Prostmeier, 432–47).

38 See Bauer and Aland, *s.v.* ἐκπετάννυμι: "ausstrecken"; BDAG, *s.v.* ἐκπετάννυμι: "an imploring gesture (cp. JosAs 12:1)." The term διαπετάννυμι, as in Ps 87:10 LXX, would not have served as well here (cf. LEH, *s.v.* διαπετάννυμι: "to open and spread out").

39 However, this verb is used elsewhere for the extending of the hands of "one who is crucified" (BDAG, *s.v.* ἐκτείνω, 1; see Bauer and Aland, *s.v.* ἐκτείνω, 1: "Ausbreiten d[er] Hände der Gekreuzigten"; cf. John 21:18; *Barn.* 12:2).

40 Contra Frankenberg, 26.

41 Berger and Nord (p. 960), by adding "with my

out addressing the Lord, the speaker "hallows" him; that is, he treats and regards him "as holy."[42] Perhaps influenced by Ps 87:10 LXX (πρὸς σέ, "to thee"), and certainly in parallel to *Ode* 35:7b-c, the speaker in 42:1a uses the preposition of place ܠܘܬ (*lwāṯ*) and the Ethpa. of ܩܪܒ (*qreḇ*), which corresponds to the intransitive use of προσάγω.[43] This strongly supports the interpretation of the "cross-event"[44] as an ascension.

Except for the nonsensical misspelling of ܐܬܗ ܗܝ (*ʾaṯeh-ī*) as ܐܬܬܗܝ (*ʾettahhī*)[45] in 27:2 N, the wording of this only weakly causal clause is identical in the two versions.[46] The masculine ܡܬܚܐ (*mṯāḥā*), derived from the root *mtḥ* and found only in 27:2 and 42:1b, is more than a synonym of ܦܫܝܛܘܬܐ (see 27:3; 42:2a below); as the equivalent of ἔκτασις,[47] it images the spreading out sideways of the hands and arms along the horizontal beam of the cross.[48] This, then, is not a gesture symbolizing an approach or a rising up[49] but God's "sign" as a "sign of salvation,"[50] or perhaps his "token."[51] Like all the other passages in which the term "sign," ܐܬܐ (*ʾāṯā*), occurs (23:12; 29:7; 39:7),[52] this verse is not concerned with a "miracle." Since the enclitic third feminine singular personal pronoun, replacing the copula, emphasizes the noun predicate,[53] Harris and Mingana's suggested emendation ("correction to ܐܬܗ ܗܘ")[54] is as pointless as Vogl's defense of it.[55]

In 27:3 and 42:2a, the stretching out of the "hands" (27:1; 42:1a) becomes the stretching "upward"[56] of the whole body of the speaker, which both interprets and transforms the meaning of the upright post, here called ξύλον, of the cross.[57] The noun ܦܫܝܛܘܬܐ (*pšīṭūṯā*), derived from the root *pšṭ*, does not, here, stand for ἁπλότης, as in 7:3, much less for "liberality."[58] Neither should the wordplay in ܫ tempt one to accept ἐκπέτασις as the Greek equivalent or original (cf. *Did.* 16:6).[59] Considering the expanded paronomasia of 42:2a and the use of ܬܪܝܨܐ (*trīṣā*) in the short relative clause qualifying ξύλον/ܩܝܣܐ (*qaysā*) in 27:3, instead of τὸ ἀνάκυπτον,[60]

words," "express . . . the verbal performance (glorification)," which is not stressed here.

42 BDAG, *s.v.* ἁγιάζω, 3. Grammatically it is already very difficult to construe "my hands" as the direct object of the second verb of 27:1 (contra Harris and Mingana, 2:356), but the translation "I sanctified [my hands] to the Lord" (Diettrich, 97, and others) makes even less sense (preferable are, e.g., Bauer [p. 608] and Charlesworth [p. 106]: "I . . . hallowed my Lord"). Note the contrast with Luke 24:50 (ἐπάρας τὰς χεῖρας αὐτοῦ εὐλόγησεν αὐτούς).

43 Payne Smith, 2:3723; BDAG, *s.v.* προσάγω, 2.

44 Sasagu Arai, *Die Christologie des Evangelium Veritatis: Eine religionsgeschichtliche Untersuchung* (Leiden: Brill, 1964) 94.

45 Payne Smith, 2:4393: passive "*impeditus, retardatus est.*"

46 See BDAG, *s.v.* ὅτι, 4a–b.

47 Frankenberg, 26.

48 Harnack, 60; Payne Smith, 2:2248; Lampe, 439.

49 Contra Spitta, 260.

50 Erich Dinkler, "Kreuz. I–II C 2," *LCI* 2 (1970) 563.

51 BDAG, *s.v.* σημεῖον, 1. This "sign" has hardly any connection with the much discussed σημεῖον τοῦ υἱοῦ τοῦ ἀνθρώπου ("sign of the Son of man") of Matt 24:30, since there is no mention of a "cosmic cross appearing in the sky" (Ulrich Luz, *Das Evangelium nach Matthäus* [4 vols.; EKKNT 1.1–4; Zurich/Düsseldorf: Benziger; Neukirchen-Vluyn: Neukirchener Verlag, 1985–2002] 3:434; but cf. *Did.* 16:6 and *Barn.* 12:4). A more cogent reference would be to Ἰησοῦν Χριστὸν καὶ τοῦτον ἐσταυρωμένον ("Jesus Christ and him crucified") as proof of the δύναμις θεοῦ ("power of God" [1 Cor 2:2, 5]; cf. also 1:17-18; Gal 3:1; Phil 2:8-9). It could be interpreted as a sign of power. Some of my earlier remarks on the term "sign" will have to be revised (Lattke, "Bildersprache," 100–101 = idem, *Bedeutung*, 4:24–26).

52 See Payne Smith, 1:412.

53 See Brockelmann, *Grammatik*, § 218.

54 Harris and Mingana, 2:357.

55 Vogl, 72. The point above the letter ܬ in the manuscripts is intended "to signify the fuller, stronger pronunciation" (Nöldeke §6; see also Brockelmann, *Grammatik* §5); it is not a sign of "*Qushshāyā*" (contra Charlesworth, 146).

56 Kittel, 141.

57 On ܩܝܣܐ (*qaysā*), see Payne Smith, 2:3606; BDAG, *s.v.* ξύλον, 2c. Spitta's attempt (p. 261) to compare the "extending of the hands" to the "growth of a tree, that raises its branches to the sky," must be considered a failure.

58 Contra Lattke, *Oden*, 212; see Payne Smith, 2:3321.

59 BDAG, *s.v.* ἐκπέτασις: "spreading out, opening."

60 Frankenberg, 26 and 41.

the ideal suggestion would be ὀρθότης.[61] Thus, the stretching upward suggesting the ascension is equated with the cross, and the predicative adjective ὀρθός/ ܬܪܝܨ (*trīṣ*, *status absolutus*) carries the double meaning of "upright" and "correct."[62]

The displacement of ܬܪܝܨܐ (*trīṣā*) to the end of 42:2b and the attributive use of ܦܫܝܛܐ (*pšīṭā*) in 42:2a in place of the adjective of 27:3 lead one to suppose that ὄρθιος was originally used with a similar double meaning.[63] This straight and upright cross is characterized, in the relative clause 42:2b, as hanging, if properly understood as a symbol, "upon the way," meaning the "way of life,"[64] of the metaphorically "upright one" (ܬܪܝܨܐ personified from ܬܪܝܨ [*trīṣ*] of 27:3). Whether this ὁδός/ܐܘܪܚܐ (*ʾurḥā*) derives from Isa 65:2 LXX (ὁδῷ ἀληθινῇ ["in a true way"])[65] is hard to say. The simplest explanation for the strange use of the Ethpe. of ܬܠܐ (*tlā*), which is found only here, is that a passive form of κρεμάννυμι or perhaps an intransitive of κρέμαμαι has been torn from its connection with ξύλον in the context of crucifixion (cf. Luke 23:39; Acts 5:30; 10:39; Gal 3:13)[66] and used in an original fashion referring to this reinterpreted "wood" (= "cross"). So the nominalized and inclusively used adjective ܬܪܝܨܐ (*trīṣā*) does not mean "Christ" as "the Upright One,"[67] but any and all upright and just persons (see above)[68] who are not among the "persecutors" of the speaking "I" (42:5, 7a). This eliminates the necessity of any emendations of ostensible "corruptions" in the text, including Kittel's.[69]

---

61 LSJ, *s.v.* ὀρθότης: "upright posture, erectness"; see Lampe, 972, with later citations "of faith and doctrine."

62 Payne Smith, 2:4510; BDAG, *s.v.* ὀρθός, 1a and 2. In support of this contention, attention may be drawn to the Ethpa. ܐܬܬܪܨ (*ʾettarraṣ*), which occurs as a *hapax legomenon* in the significant parallel: "I stretched out my hands in the ascent of myself / and I erected myself towards the Most High" (35:7).

63 Payne Smith, 2:3319; LSJ, *s.v.* ὄρθιος: "upright," "straight." The adjective ܦܫܝܛܐ cannot here mean "simple" as it does in 34:1b ("heart"), where ܬܪܝܨܐ is used as a parallel in 34:1d ("upright thoughts").

64 BDAG, *s.v.* ὁδός, 3b.

65 Rahlfs, 2:652 (see critical apparatus!); Brenton (p. 899) differs.

66 Payne Smith, 2:4442; BDAG, *s.v.* κρεμάννυμι: "hang."

67 Contra Kittel, 140; Emerton, 730.

68 See also BDAG, *s.v.* δίκαιος, 1.

69 Kittel, 140. Connolly's remarks, in which he draws on *Ode* 39, which also uses the terms "sign," "way," and "wood" (39:7, 10) to help his interpretation deserve special attention. His desperate attempt to remove the "cross" and to make the "wood" into a "wooden road-post" must also be judged "a violent one" (Connolly, "Odes," 304–5).

Schenke (*Herkunft*, 28) sees 41:15a as a "polemic against other schools of Gnosticism" and summarizes the Christology of the *Odes of Solomon* as follows: "The Logos, Christ, the Son and the Redeemer are one and the same. This Christ is crucified and endures physical death. But Death has no power over him, so he rises from the dead." In his annotated translation (p. 37) of the so-called *Evangelium Veritatis,* there is, quite correctly, no mention of *Odes Sol.* 27:3 and 42:1-2 at *Gos. Truth* 20,25-27 ("He was nailed to a tree; he [viz., Jesus] published the edict of the Father on the cross"). The "re-interpretation of earlier terms" (Michael Lattke, "Zwanzig nicht so rätselhafte Limericks zum Johannesevangelium mit einem unmissverständlichen Nachtrag," in Stefan Schreiber and Alois Stimpfle, eds., *Johannes aenigmaticus: Studien zum Johannesevangelium für Herbert Leroy* [BU 29; Regensburg: Pustet, 2000] 226) occurs in different ways both in the *Gospel of Truth* and in the *Odes of Solomon*. But why "wood" should be a "symbol of salvation" only in the *Gospel of Truth*–and not also in the *Odes of Solomon*–is a mystery (contra Sasagu Arai, *Die Christologie des Evangelium Veritatis: Eine religionsgeschichtliche Untersuchung* [Leiden: Brill, 1964] 95).

28

Ode 28: The Spirit of Life and "My Redemption"

(I) **1a** **Like the wings of doves over their nestlings**
1b **and the beaks of their nestlings toward their beaks,**
1c **so also are the wings of the Spirit over my heart.**
2a **My heart is delighted and leaps for joy,**
2b **like the babe that leaps in its mother's womb.**

(II) **3a** **I had faith, therefore also[a] I was at rest,**
3b **for he is faithful, in whom I had faith.**

(III) **4a** **He richly blessed me,**
4b **and my head is with him.**
4c **And the blade [war] shall not separate me from him**
4d **nor the sword.**
5a **For I prepared myself[b], before destruction came,**
5b[A] **and was established by his wings, imperishably.**
[or]
5b[B] **and was laid in his bosom, imperishably.**

(IV) **6** **And immortal Life embraced[c] and kissed me,**
7a **and from it is the Spirit within me.**
7b **And it cannot die,**
7c **because it is life[d].**

(V) **8a** **They were amazed, those who saw me,**
8b **because I was persecuted.**
9a **And they thought I had been swallowed up,**
9b **because I seemed to them like one of the lost.**

(VI) **10a** **But my oppression**
10b **was/became salvation for me.**

(VII) **11a** **And I was [the target of] their contempt,**
11b **because there was no jealousy in me.**
12a **Because I did good to everybody,**
12b **I was hated.**

(VIII) **13a** **And they surrounded me like mad dogs,**
13b **ones that in ignorance attack their masters.**
14a **For their mind is corrupt**
14b **and their sense perverted.**

(IX) **15a** **But I, I held water in my right [hand]**
15b **and forgot[e] its/their bitterness by my sweetness.**

(X) **16a** **And I did not perish,**
16b **because I was not their brother,**
16c **and neither did they know my origin[f].**

a 3a H omits ܐܦ.
b 5a ܐܬܛܝܒܬ N; ܛܝܒܬ H.
c 6 ܘܓܦܦܢܝ N; ܘܓܦܦܢ H.
d 7c Adjective "alive" in H.
e 15b ܛܥܝܬ N; ܛܥܝܢܬ H.
f 16c ܠܝܠܕܘܬܝ ܐܫܬܘܕܥܘ N; ܐܒܘܬܗܘܢ ܠܝܠܕܘܬܝ H.

17a And they sought my death, but did not find [it],
17b because I was older than their memory,
17c and in vain they cast lots[g] over me.
18a And those who were after me[h]
18b sought vainly to destroy the memory of the one who was before them.
(XI) 19a For the mind of the Most High is unprejudiced,
19b and his heart is better than/superior to all wisdom.
Hallelujah.

g 17c ܢܦܣܝܢ N and another MS. in H; ܠܦܣܝܢ H.
h 18a ܒܬܪܝ H; ܒܬܪ N.

Introduction

Ode 28 is preserved in two Syriac manuscripts.[1] If the first person statement of 17a leads to the conclusion that "this cannot be the Christ,"[2] then these partly didactic and partly self-descriptive utterances of the believing (3a), blessed (4a), imperishable (5b), but also persecuted (8b), hated (12b), and surrounded (13a) speaker are put into the mouth of an undoubtedly masculine redeemed one (10b, 16b ["brother"]), in whom the Spirit of life personified resides (7a). That this redeemed one is himself a Redeemer[3] is not stated in *Ode* 28. It would be necessary to draw on 42:10 as a parallel to permit the question: "Did the Savior die?"[4] It is the statements of the redeemed Redeemer in 42:10-11 that convinced Kittel that 28:17a must also be considered "a saying of the Risen One," but without "hinting at Docetism."[5]

The division of *Ode* 28 into two "sub-odes," 1-7 and 8-19,[6] goes back a long way and depends on the distinction between "two separate speakers/subjects."[7] On the basis of Harnack's superseded theory of a Christian reworking of Jewish material,[8] but at the same time criticizing it, Spitta declares it "proved that all of the section 8-18 is Christian and only 1-7 belongs to the Jewish original."[9] Even Kittel, who witnesses to the unity of the *Odes of Solomon*, thinks that "in this *Ode* there seems to be an abrupt change of speaker."[10] This claim of an

1 Mss.: Codex H, 21a–22a; Codex N, 150ʳ (ܣ). Ed./trans.: Charlesworth, 107–11; Franzmann, 207–16; Lattke, 2:257–81 and 3:XXXVI–XXXVII.
2 Harnack, 61.
3 Bauer, 608.
4 McNeil, "Sufferings," 31.
5 Kittel, 108; on 41:15, see McNeil, 174; idem, "Le Christ en vérité est Un," *Irénikon* 51.2 (1978) 199, 201.
6 See, e.g., Franzmann, 211; Lattke, *Oden*, 178.
7 Diettrich's assumption (p. 99) that "truth personified" can be the "speaking subject" of 8-19 is no more convincing than the "stichic changes" that were achieved only by editorial deletions.
8 Harnack, 74–97. So he describes the allegedly Jewish "I" of *Ode* 28 as a "mystic, who observes how his self, by the revelation and recognition of God and a truly loving relationship with him, is redeemed, finds sanctuary and is raised into eternity" (Harnack, 86). Later, however, Harnack argues for the literary "unity" of the *Odes of Solomon* (see Adolf Harnack, review of Harris and Mingana in *ThLZ* 46 [1921] 7; cf. Lattke, *Bedeutung*, 3:181).
9 Spitta, 284. The verses quoted as 8-18 correspond to 8-19 in the numbering used since Harris and Mingana (vol. 1, on this passage; 2:357–59; cf. Lattke, *Bedeutung*, 3:44–45). Charlesworth (pp. 107–8) revised the numbering from 4c onward (4c-d = 5; 5 = 6; . . . 19 = 20). Berger and Nord (pp. 960–61) accept this unmotivated re-numbering, which causes unnecessary difficulties in communication. Charlesworth has made some changes to his English translation (cf. Charlesworth 1973, 109–10, with idem 1977, 109–10).
10 Kittel, 110. He is even inclined to see "the first part [1-7] as an introduction to the second [8-19]." Similarly Bernard (p. 111) declares at 8: "At this point there is a transition of personality, and the remaining verses are spoken *ex ore Christi*." Charlesworth (p. 109) follows Harris and Mingana (2:358) by dividing the two parts with the note in brackets, "Christ speaks."

abrupt change in the middle of the "account of redemption,"[11] which cannot really be subsumed by form into the class of "hymns of initiation,"[12] can only arouse general distrust in textual divisions[13] and distinctions between one speaking "I" and another.

Literary allusions to the passion narratives of the Gospels and Johannine Christology cannot be excluded,[14] and an attempt must be made, even in the first part, so-called, to find, in addition to the "Old Testament passages which are in the mind of the Odist,"[15] New Testament and other, perhaps even early Christian-Gnostic passages that permit a unitary explanation. Not until every "possibility of interpreting him as the Christ" has been excluded can one "take 1-7 as utterances of a human singer,"[16] while any naïve identification of the fictive "I" with the actual author of the Ode is precluded in any case. As the term "Spirit" encloses 1-7, the term "heart" in 1c-2a and 19b encloses the whole Ode. Negative themes are not confined to 8-18 but can already be seen in 4c-d and 5a (see Excursus 28 below). Conversely, positive statements are also found outside 1-7 in 10b, 15, 16a, 17a, 18b, and 19.

Interpretation

■ **1-2** Emerton[17] brackets 1b for good reason, because the imagery appears so profuse. The only comparison in 1a and c is the protection and warmth of the "wings."[18] The plural of ܝܘܢܐ (*yawnā*), "doves," bears no emphasis. Thus, there is no relation to the meaning of the "dove" of 24:1-2 (see the commentary on that passage). As will be seen, stanza I bears the imprint of the Lukan childhood narrative, to which Heinz Schürmann gave the title "Prelude: The Origin of Jesus in God."[19] So there is no idea of baptism, whether of Jesus or of Christians.[20] In the search for the origin of the similes in 1a-b, it is rather the mention of "two young pigeons" in Luke 2:24 (*δύο νοσσοὺς περιστερῶν*) that may serve as an explanation for the term ܦܪܘܓܐ (*parrūgā*),[21] which occurs only in 1a and 1b. In the unbridled imagery of 1b, the plural of ܦܘܡܐ (*pummā*) is not just "mouths"[22] but specifically "beaks."[23]

The term *πνεῦμα*/ܪܘܚܐ (*rūḥā*), "Spirit," in 1c may also have been taken from Luke 1:35. Differing from Luke, the speaking "I," who may be considered *υἱὸς θεοῦ* ("Son of God" [Luke 1:35]; cf. *Ode* 36:3c; 42:15b) and perhaps even a messianic *υἱὸς ὑψίστου* ("Son of the Most High" [Luke 1:32]; see 19a below),[24] claims for himself the fictive promise of the Lukan angel; the term "heart" here, as in 2a, stands for the whole of the person (see Excursus 4).

In the bicolon 2a-b, the Lukan influence can be seen clearly as well as the Greek *Vorlage* of ܣ. The participle of the Ethpa. of ܒܣܡ (*bsem*) is not found in the Peshitta

11 Reitzenstein, *Das iranische Erlösungsmysterium*, 91.
12 Schille, 77.
13 An exception, of course, is the division into eleven stanzas by Franzmann's textual analysis. Some other examples of division may be mentioned. Greßmann originally only heard "Christ" speaking in this "*psalm of thanksgiving*," with occasional Gnostic and Docetic overtones (see Greßmann, "Oden," 675–76); he later distinguishes between the "singer" of 1-2 and "Christ" in 3-19 (see Greßmann, 461). Bauer (p. 608) makes a division between 4 and 5, because from 5 onward "the Redeemer and the redeemed coalesce." Pierre draws a line between 10 and 11: "En effet, le premier mouvement (v. 1-10) présente une situation irénique et édénique, tandis que le second (v. 11-19) engage un procès mortel" (see Pierre, 143; with similar arguments, see idem, "Odes de Salomon," 722).
14 See Quasten, 165, on 8-19.
15 Harris and Mingana, 2:360.
16 Kittel, 107–8.
17 Emerton, 718.
18 Payne Smith, 1:763–64; BDAG, *s.v.* *πτέρυξ*.
19 Schürmann, *Lukasevangelium*, 1:18. His reference to "PsSal 28,3" clearly refers to *Ode* 28:2 as numbered by Harris and Mingana and should be corrected. I do not believe that the "wings" are taken from Matt 23:37 || Luke 13:34, as Connolly suggests, but he is on the right track when he says: "Ode 28 contains two very suspicious coincidences with St Luke's Gospel" (see Connolly, "Odes," 306).
20 Contra Bernard, 111; Tosato, "Battesimo," 266.
21 Payne Smith, 2:3233; BDAG, *s.v.* *νοσσός*.
22 As in Harris and Mingana, 2:357, and many more.
23 Payne Smith, 2:3063–64; Bauer, 608 ("Schnäbel" [beaks]); cf. Lampe, 1262, *s.v.* *στόμα*.
24 Schürmann, *Lukasevangelium*, 1:47–56.

of Ps 16:9,[25] so it must derive from Ps 15:9a LXX: ηὐφράνθη ἡ καρδία μου ("my heart rejoiced").[26] Perhaps the first participle of ܕܘܨ, ܕܨ (*dāṣ*) in 2a represents ἀγαλλιᾶται (cf. ἠγαλλιάσατο ["exulted"] in Ps 15:9b LXX; ܕܨ [*dāṣ*] in Ps 16:9b Peshitta).[27] But it is more likely that the combination of Luke and the Psalm verse led to the use of σκιρτᾷ, even here.[28]

The basis of 2b is undoubtedly Luke 1:41, 44 (ἐσκίρτησεν ἐν ἀγαλλιάσει τὸ βρέφος ἐν τῇ κοιλίᾳ αὐτῆς/μου, "the babe in her/my womb leaped for joy"). But this statement about the "movements" of the babe "in the womb" of the mother-to-be Elizabeth is torn out of its context and a revised wording is put into the mouth of the speaking "I" "as an expression of joy."[29] This is not an attempt to outdo John the Baptist, but rather a hidden allusion to the relationship of the son, symbolized by his "heart" (see above), to his mother, who, like Jesus, is never named in the *Odes of Solomon* (but cf. "virgin" in 19:6-7 where the term ܟܪܣܐ [*karsā*] also occurs). The reason for this strange silence may perhaps be found in 36:3a.[30]

Finally, it has to be noted that stanza I does not "speak of inspiration by the Spirit,"[31] but that the messianic "I" is describing the life-giving and protective power of the Holy Spirit before and during his birth. Neither the doves and their nestlings nor the fetus within the womb is important as a fact of natural history.[32] These details, taken from literary stock or personal experience, are meant to focus attention on the central image of 1c and the first half of 2a.

■ **3** There is nothing against putting this concentrated and partly didactic statement of salvation into the mouth of Christ, who now, as one regenerate and exalted kerygmatically by God, speaks of his own relationship to God.[33] The main reason *for* this interpretation is found less in the contested genitive of the phrase πίστις (Ἰησοῦ) Χριστοῦ in the Pauline epistles[34] than in the early Christian description of Jesus as ὁ τῆς πίστεως ἀρχηγὸς καὶ τελειωτής ("the pioneer and perfecter of faith") in Heb 12:2, especially since the general connection between "rest" and "belief" is made also in Hebrews (4:3).[35]

Although God, or in this Ode the "Most High" of 19a, is the object of πιστεύω/ܗܝܡܢ (*haymen*) in 3b, the unconditional statement of faith in 3a is still impressive.[36] Corresponding to the transcendental belief in

25 *OTSy*, pt. 2 fasc. 3,13: ܚܕܝ (*ḥdī*).

26 Rahlfs, 2:12; Brenton, 705; Payne Smith, 1:549; BDAG, *s.v.* εὐφραίνω, 2.

27 Payne Smith, 1:846; BDAG, *s.v.* ἀγαλλιάω.

28 Frankenberg, 26.

29 BDAG, *s.v.* σκιρτάω.

30 See Murray, *Symbols*, 314.

31 Contra Kittel, 105.

32 On the *hapax legomenon* βρέφος/ܥܘܠܐ (*ʿūlā*), see BDAG, *s.v.* βρέφος, 1; Payne Smith, 2:2832–33.

33 I cannot agree with Kittel (p. 107), who finds it "extremely difficult" to accept this twofold affirmation of faith "as an utterance of Christ." On the contrary, Jesus should be found among the "scriptural examples of faith" (Lampe, 1086, *s.v.* πίστις, N).

34 Cf. Rom 3:22, 26; Gal 2:16; 3:22; Phil 3:9; also Gal 2:20 and Eph 3:12. "The πίστις Χριστοῦ in Paul is taken as a subj[ective] gen[itive]" by several authors (BDAG, *s.v.* πίστις, 2bβ, with references to earlier material), but cf. Gerhard Barth, "πίστις, πιστεύω," *EWNT* 3 (1983) 221; *EDNT* 3:95, who argues for an objective genitive.

35 On Heb 4:3, see Gräßer, 1:207–11; BDAG, *s.v.* πιστεύω, 2b. The connection between πιστεύω, πίστις, and ἐπαναπαύομαι in *Corp. Herm.* 9:10 is of a very different kind: "And when he has considered it all and is satisfied that it agrees with what the word imparted, *he is convinced and finds rest in his assured conviction*" (Colpe and Holzhausen, 90 [emphasis added]).

Looking back to *Ode* 27 and my suggested heading "The Crucifixion Interpreted as Ascent into Heaven," it may be worth partially quoting Heb 12:2: ἀφορῶντες εἰς τὸν τῆς πίστεως ἀρχηγὸν καὶ τελειωτὴν Ἰησοῦν, . . . ὑπέμεινεν (τὸν) σταυρόν . . . ἐν δεξιᾷ τε τοῦ θρόνου τοῦ θεοῦ κεκάθικεν ("looking to Jesus the pioneer and perfecter of our faith, who . . . endured the cross . . . and has taken his seat at the right hand of the throne of God"); see Gräßer, 3:236–44, for the exegesis and history of interpretation of this passage.

36 BDAG, *s.v.* πιστεύω, 2b; Payne Smith, 1:232. Frankenberg (p. 26) chose the proper Greek verb, but not the form that would correspond to the perfect of the loanword ܗܝܡܢ, which was probably ἐπίστευσα, but could also have been ἐπίστευον or πεπίστευκα (on the description "loanword," see Brockelmann, *Grammatik* §180.D).

God is the existential intensity of trust, which believes absolutely and eschatologically in no-thing and no-body. If 𝔊 had διὰ τοῦτο καί or διὸ καί between the two verbs,[37] the omission of the post-positioned καί/ܐܦ (ʾāp̄) in H is simply an attempt to clarify some possibly ambiguous syntax.[38] The use of the Ethpe. of ܢܘܚ, ܢܚ (nāḥ) is important because it connects to another first person statement (35:6b), where even Kittel admits "the possibility" that it is an utterance of Christ.[39] Whether the Greek equivalent was a form of ἐπαναπαύομαι[40] is not certain, since a form of ἀναπαύομαι could also have been used.[41]

The description of God as πιστός ("faithful") has deep roots in Judaism (e.g., Ps 144:13 LXX; *Ps. Sol.* 14:1; 17:10) and is found often in early Christian writings.[42] This adjective is translated in 3b by the passive participle ܡܗܝܡܢ (*mhayman*), alluding in a set form to the powerful name "of God as the One in whom we can have full confidence."[43] Profound belief in[44] God and speaking of God (theo-logy) define themselves reciprocally: "The power of faith is practically identified with the power of God."[45]

■ **4-5** In a miscellany of allusions to biblical and early Christian texts, the speaking "I" continues his tale of salvation, in which the subject of 4a refers back to the object of the formula in the preceding verse (see on stanza II above). Kittel's reasons for depriving the "Christ" of the utterances in stanza III are insufficient,[46] even though not all the texts employed originate in christological contexts. After all, Jesus, who was proclaimed the messianic εὐλογημένος,[47] was described as εὐλογημένος ("blessed") even before he was born (Luke 1:42), so one can imagine the Christ of *Ode* 28 applying the blessing of Abraham from Gen 22:17 and Heb 6:14 (εὐλογῶν εὐλογήσω σε, "Surely I will bless you"),[48] and the logical connection drawn between πιστεύω (πίστις) and εὐλογέομαι in Gal 3:9 (ὥστε οἱ ἐκ πίστεως εὐλογοῦνται σὺν τῷ πιστῷ Ἀβραάμ, "So then, those who are men of faith are blessed with Abraham who had faith"), to himself.[49] In 𝔊 the simple ηὐλόγησέ με[50] would have been expanded by a preceding participle of εὐλογέω.[51]

Verse 4b, which is not in any sense a "mystical concept,"[52] belongs both to the imagery of "rest" (3a) and to the whole pictorial idea of the ancients that blessing descends from above—onto the head by metonymy for the

37 BDAG, *s.v.* διό; Payne Smith, 2:2077.

38 Connolly even considers the construction "I believed, therefore" an imitation of Ps 115:1 LXX or 2 Cor 4:13 (ἐπίστευσα, διὸ [καὶ] ἐλάλησα) and a proof that "the author has only too successfully disguised his scriptural allusions" (see Connolly, "Greek," 535).

39 Kittel (p. 107) also refers to 36:1a (see commentary on that passage).

40 BDAG, *s.v.* ἐπαναπαύομαι; Frankenberg, 26: ἐπανεπα[υσάμ]ην.

41 Payne Smith, 2:2311; BDAG, *s.v.* ἀναπαύομαι.

42 See 1 Cor 1:9; 10:13; 2 Cor 1:18; 1 Thess 5:24; Heb 10:23; 11:11; 1 Pet 4:19; 1 John 1:9; Ignatius *Trall.* 13:3.

43 BDAG, *s.v.* πιστός, 1aβ; Payne Smith, 1:233. Therefore, in this case, the Kyrios Christos is not intended, although it might otherwise have been considered (cf. 2 Thess 3:3; 2 Tim 2:13).

44 The Syriac preposition ܒ (*b*-) with the third masculine singular suffix corresponds to εἰς or ἐν (Payne Smith, 1:232; BDAG, *s.v.* πιστεύω, 2aβ and 2aε).

45 Gerhard Ebeling, "Jesus und Glaube," *ZThK* 55 (1958) 96 = idem, *Wort und Glaube* (3rd ed.; Tübingen: Mohr Siebeck, 1967) 239. Elsewhere in this important article, Ebeling says: "Faith is power, indeed it is participation in God's omnipotence" (*ZThK* 55 [1958] 105 = *Wort und Glaube*, 248). Since "rest" is a term of salvation, the following is also relevant to *Ode* 28:3a: "Faith, finally, is always faith in salvation and so it is salvation itself" (*ZThK*, 109; *Wort und Glaube,* 252). Ebeling also says, "it should be impossible, considering how Jesus speaks of faith, to exclude him from the faith" (*ZThK,* 98; *Wort und Glaube,* 240).

46 Kittel, 107.

47 See Ps 117:26 LXX in Mark 11:9 par; Matt 23:39; Luke 13:35.

48 The *infinitus absolutus* in 𝔖 "serves to give more emphasis to the verb, by contrasting the action with some other one, or by giving expression to its intensity" (Nöldeke §295; see also 12:6a).

49 Just as a footnote, it may be remarked that the key word πιστός, which describes the Most High God in 3b, occurs also in Gal 3:9.

50 Frankenberg, 26.

51 BDAG, *s.v.* εὐλογέω; Payne Smith, 1:611–12.

52 Contra Kittel, 107.

whole person (see Excursus 23). This pleasing picture of physical closeness, which corresponds so well to one of the possible translations of 5b (see below), does not need to be distorted by emendations to its simple expression.[53]

The bicolon 4c-d, constructed with "synonymous parallelism," is clearly an allusion to and an application of Rom 8:35 (*τίς ἡμᾶς χωρίσει ἀπὸ τῆς ἀγάπης τοῦ Χριστοῦ; θλῖψις . . . ἢ μάχαιρα;* "Who shall separate us from the love of Christ? Shall tribulation . . . or sword?"), although this expression of "fervent relationship with God" is not connected to any "spiritual symbolism of love and marriage."[54] Comparison with Rom 8:35 in the Peshitta demonstrates that the Syriac of *Ode* 28—whether original or translated from the Greek—dates back to a time when χωρίζω could still correspond to ܦܠܓ (*plag̱, pleg̱*) and μάχαιρα could be translated by ܚܪܒܐ (*ḥarbā*) or the Persian loanword σαμψήρα with the possible connotation of an actual "execution" among the list of adverse circumstances in Rom 8:35.[55]

Although the reading ܥܬܕܬ in 5a H can make sense in translation (as the Pa. *ʿattdet*),[56] the reading ܐܬܥܬܕܬ (*ʾetʿattdet*) in N is to be preferred.[57] Since the middle voice of κατασκευάζω and παρασκευάζω can be synonymous,[58] Frankenberg's choice of παρεσκεύασμαι is on the right track.[59] All the same, the middle aorist παρεσκευσάμην must be considered as well as the perfect as a possible *Vorlage*.[60] Because of the warlike terms in 4c-d, on the one side, and the word "destruction" in the dependent clause of 5a, on the other, the verb acquires military undertones (cf. 1 Cor 14:8). Before turning to 5b, there is time to discuss the word ܐܒܕܢܐ (*ʾabdānā*) and related terms.

Excursus 28: "Ruin," "Destruction," and "Imperishability" in the *Odes of Solomon*

Under these three key words, a survey can be taken of the terms in the *Odes of Solomon* derived from the roots ܐܒܕ and ܚܒܠ.[61] The more or less numerous Greek equivalents will occasionally be mentioned here, but the likelihood of their use can only be determined in the actual context of each term. On the whole, however, it is possible to say that the Pe. ܐܒܕ (*ʾeb̲ad̲*) and the Aph. ܐܘܒܕ (*ʾawbed̲*)—in spite of sometimes being used as synonyms of the Ethpa. ܐܬܚܒܠ (*ʾet̲ḥabbal* [33:9]) or the Pa. ܚܒܠ (*ḥabbel* [22:5; 22:7; 33:2])—correspond to forms of ἀπόλλυμι, while the masculine ܐܒܕܢܐ (*ʾab̲dānā*) is mostly used to represent ἀπώλεια and ὄλεθρος.[62] The words

53 As undertaken by, e.g., Greßmann (p. 462) and Bauer (p. 609) in their translations.

54 Walter Baumgartner, "Das trennende Schwert in Oden Salomos 28,4," in idem, ed., *Festschrift Alfred Bertholet zum achtzigsten Geburtstag* (Tübingen: Mohr Siebeck, 1950) 274–75, 281 = idem, *Ausgewählte Aufsätze zum Alten Testament und seiner Umwelt* (Leiden: Brill, 1959) 50–52, 57.

55 Cf. Wilhelm Michaelis, "μάχαιρα," *ThWNT* 4 (1942) 531; *TDNT* 4:526; Käsemann, *Romans*, 249 (German, p. 240). The term ܦܠܓ in this context does not sit well as a translation of μερίζω (Frankenberg, p. 26; cf. Payne Smith, 2:3134; BDAG, *s.v.* μερίζω); it goes much better with χωρίζω (BDAG, *s.v.*; cf. Brockelmann, *Lexicon*, 569: "separavit"). This verb, found in Rom 8:35, was later generally translated by ܦܪܫ (*praš*).

The term ܣܝܦܐ (*saypā*), used in the Peshitta in Rom 8:35, is often found as a translation of μάχαιρα. But the two Syriac words for weaponry used in *Ode* 28 can also translate μάχαιρα (cf. Lattke, "Wörter," 298–99 = idem, *Bedeutung*, 147). I suspect that in this case the loanword σαμψήρα, which is not found in the LXX or the New Testament, corresponds to μάχαιρα, and ܚܪܒܐ (*ḥarbā*) is used metaphorically perhaps for πόλεμος (BDAG, *s.v.* πόλεμος; cf. Payne Smith, 1364–65, with additional terms). That would have mitigated the tautology in 𝔖. But perhaps 4c was additionally influenced by Ps 21:21a LXX (ῥῦσαι ἀπὸ ῥομφαίας τὴν ψυχήν μου).

56 Diettrich, 100: "Vorbereitung habe ich getroffen [I made preparation]."

57 Harris and Mingana, vol. 1, on this passage; 2:358: "I was ready."

58 LSJ, *s.v.* κατασκευάζω, 3.

59 Frankenberg, 26.

60 BDAG and LSJ, *s.v.* παρασκευάζω; Payne Smith, 2:3009.

61 Payne Smith, 1:8; 1:1175–77, 1179–80.

62 Neither Payne Smith (1:8) nor Margoliouth, *Supplement* (1), refers to ὄλεθρος (see *NTSy* on 1 Cor 5:5; 1 Thess 5:3; 2 Thess 1:9). The frequency of the three terms from the root ܐܒܕ in the *Odes of Solomon* is: the Pe. nine times, the Aph. five times, and ܐܒܕܢܐ (*ʾab̲dānā*) three times.

derived from the root *ḥbl* occur more frequently and correspond in the main with the large family of words related to φθείρω (e.g. δια-, καταφθείρω, φθορά, δια-, καταφθορά, ἀφθαρσία, ἄφθαρτος) but also sometimes to ἀφανίζω and ἀφανισμός as well as ὀλεθρεύω and ὄλεθρος. Apart from the two *hapax legomena* ܡܚܒܠܢܐ (*mḥabblānā*, *nomen agentis* in 38:9a: "corruptor")[63] and ܚܘܒܠܐ (*ḥubbālā*, *nomen actionis* in 24:8b: "destruction"), the forms most generally found are ܚܒܠܐ (*ḥbālā*), used both positively and negatively,[64] and forms of the Pa. *ḥabbel* (eight or nine times) and the Ethpa. *ʾetḥabbal* (eight or seven times; see the variants in 38:9b).

The terms discussed here are especially plentiful in four of the *Odes*. In *Odes* 24 and 28, the terms from the root ܐܒܕ are in the majority (with two forms from the root ܚܒܠ in each), and *Ode* 38 uses only words from the root ܚܒܠ (see also Excursus 38). In *Ode* 33 the use of the two roots is all but equal (four against five times). *Odes* 1, 3–4, 10, 12–14, 16, 18–20, 23, 25–27, 29–30, 34–37, and 41 do not use any of these terms, which does not mean that all of them show only the redemptive aspect of the dualism.[65]

In the dualism of the Odes, ܚܒܠܐ (*ḥbālā*) and (ܕ)ܠܐ ܚܒܠܐ ([*d*-]*lā ḥbālā*) are explicitly opposed (15:8). "Perishability" and "imperishability" are thus the objects of the metaphorically used verbs "to doff" and "to don" (see Table 2). The statement that God's way and face were "imperishable" while the Creator brought his own world to "destruction" (22:11 𝔖) is also dualistic. The partakers of this "imperishability" of God and his *plērōma* (7:11) are the elect (8:23; 9:4; 11:12; 21:5; 33:12; 40:6) and first among them the redeemed Redeemer (17:2). Whether ܕܠܐ ܚܒܠܐ in 28:5b is to be taken adverbially (ἀφθάρτως, ἐν ἀφθαρσίᾳ) or corresponds to a construction with genitive will be decided later. Just as Grace personified abandoned "Corruption" (33:1), so the ones whom she addresses are called to "leave the ways of this destruction" (33:7). The Syriac phrase "corruptor of corruption" (38:9a) is probably intended superlatively as the "Archcorruptor."[66]

Where the *gnōsis* of the Lord has come, non-*gnōsis* is "destroyed" (7:21, Ethpa. of ܚܒܠ). The "destruction" of death (15:9a)[67] and darkness (31:1b) belongs to the same dualistic tradition. The redeemed, on the contrary, are not "corrupted" and do not "perish" (33:9a). In 39:10a and 12, where the Messiah's footprints on the water are not "wiped away" or "destroyed," the use may be considered anomalous.[68]

God's right hand can be the subject of the Pa. ܚܒܠ (*ḥabbel*) when it destroys the poison of evil (22:7 𝔖; ℭ differs). In general, however, the subjects are the negative adversarial powers, such as the mythological primal deeps (24:8a) or the metaphorically raging rivers (39:3), and the enigmatic bridegroom (38:9a) who, together with his bride, according to N (38:9b), "corrupts" the world (38:11; cf. 38:14c). The passive participle ܡܚܒܠܐ (*mḥabblā*) describes the "corrupt" spirit of the persecutors (28:14a).[69]

Closest to the Pa. ܚܒܠ (*ḥabbel*) is the Aph. ܐܘܒܕ (*ʾawbed*), which also brings on the words derived from the root ܐܒܕ and involves a short look back over passages already discussed. In 22:5b, there is mention of "destroying" the seed of the dragon-serpent (see on 22:7a above). The "destroying" with "destruction" (33:2a) is parallel to the "corruption" of its whole contrivance (see on 33:2b above). In two cases, the Lord is the subject of "to destroy." He "destroys" what is alien (6:3a) and the thoughts of those who have not the truth (24:10). The futility of the hostile attempts at "destruction" (28:18b) complements the statement of the speaking "I" that he did not "perish" (28:16a).

This final verb form is the Pe. ܐܒܕ (*ʾebad*). What is visible will perish (5:14a) like those who were before (24:7b), as indeed all that is lacking has already "perished" (24:9a; see on 24:10a above). Error "perished/was lost" from the Lord (31:2a). On the other hand, the Gnostics and those who are wise will not "perish" (9:7a; 33:9b; on 33:9a, see above). Although the speaking "I" seemed like one of the "lost" (28:9b), he "did not perish" (28:16a).

---

63 This term is not found in Brockelmann, *Lexicon*, 211. It can be used both as an adjective and as a noun (see Payne Smith, *Dictionary*, 263).

64 The negation by preceding ܠܐ (*lā*) or ܕܠܐ (*d-lā*), corresponding to an *alpha privativum,* transforms ܚܒܠܐ into a term of salvation such as "imperishability," "incorruptibility," "imperishable," or "indestructible." Because of the ambiguity in 28:5b, *lā ḥbālā* occurs either four or five times and *d-lā ḥbālā* either nine or eight times.

65 Cf., e.g., 18:12; 23:13-15, 19b-20; 25:3, 5, 11; 29:5, 8-10; 34:5; 35:3. See Table 1, and also 9:4; 15:8-10; 17:1-2; 24:8; 28:5-7, 16-18; 38:8-16; 40:6; 42:10-11.

66 See Bauer, 618; Lattke, *Oden*, 200.

67 "Sheol" in 15:9b is parallel to "death" and is the object of the Ethpa. of ܒܛܠ (*bṭel*), which is also used in 23:19b H.

68 In 39:12, the Ethpe. ܐܬܥܛܝ (*ʾetʿṭī*) is another synonym for the Ethpa. ܐܬܚܒܠ (*ʾetḥabbal*).

69 The passive participle of ܫܚܠܦ (*šaḥlep̄*) is the parallel in 28:14b ("perverted"). The masculine subject of 33:2a-b will be discussed in its place.

This background makes the connotation of ܐܒܕܢܐ (*ʾabdānā*) somewhat clearer, although the subject of 33:2a is still hard to determine: "And he [who(?)] destroyed with destruction before him" (see on 33:2a-b above). But there must be a connection between this statement and the promise of the Virgin Grace that follows: "I bring you forth from destruction" (33:8b). As the opposite of "imperishable" or "imperishability" (see on 28:5b below), "destruction" appears in 28:5a signifying more than merely the consequences of battle and sword (see on 28:4c-d above). Whether corresponding to ἀπώλεια[70] or to ὄλεθρος,[71] this "destruction" is eschatological "ruin" and "death" (see on stanza IV below).

There are two possible translations of 5b, both of which must be considered.[72] The *hapax legomenon* ܟܢܦܐ (*kenp̄ā*) in 5b is not the term used for "wings" in other passages (cf. ܓܦ̈ܐ [*geppē*] in 24:4; 28:1a; 28:1c). Even if the plural ܟܢ̈ܦܐ (*kenp̄ē*) + third masculine singular suffix, as in Ps 36:8b (35:8b LXX: ἐν σκέπῃ τῶν πτερύγων σου, "in the shelter of thy wings"), refers to the "cherub wings" of Yahweh,[73] those "wings" are not in any sense "wings of the Spirit" (see 1c above). This leads to the supposition that 𝔊 had neither σκέπη nor πτέρυξ (translation A).[74] An alternative suggestion for the Greek word is κόλπος (translation B), which makes ܟܢ̈ܦܐ (*kenp̄ē*) synonymous with ܥܘܒܐ (*ʿubbā*; cf. linguistically and partly also in content Luke 16:23; John 1:18; 13:23), and it makes better sense of the Ethpe. of the common verb "to lay, put, place."[75]

The trite Syriac phrase ܕܠܐ ܚܒܠܐ (*d-lā ḥḇālā*) presents problems in both possible translations, since it can be taken adverbially, and thus as corresponding to the adverb ἀφθάρτως or to the prepositional phrase ἐν ἀφθαρσίᾳ (cf. 11:12; 1 Cor 15:42; Eph 6:24). Even in the singular it could be used to translate the plural adjective ἄφθαρτοι (cf., e.g., 1 Cor 15:52).[76] But since the phrase ܠܐ ܚܒܠܐ (*lā ḥḇālā*), corresponding to the Greek term ἀφθαρσία, represents a masculine and occurs elsewhere as well (15:8a; 33:12b), it is also possible that ܟܢ̈ܦܘܗܝ ܕܠܐ ܚܒܠܐ (*kenp̄aw d-lā ḥḇālā*) is an idiomatic Syriac construction with genitive and should be translated "wings of imperishability" or "bosom of imperishability."[77]

■ **6-7** Before Burkitt published manuscript N,[78] 6 began with the word ܢܦܩܘܢ (*nap̄qūn* [H]), an easy spelling mistake to make,[79] which has no possible connection with the second verb. Instead of saying "read ܐܫܩܝܢܝ ('gave me to drink') for ܢܫܩܢܝ"[80] the Semitic scholar Friedrich Schultheß, who argued for a Greek original and some of whose emendations were proved correct by N,[81] should have substituted ܥܦܩܢܝ (*ʿap̄qūn*) for ܢܦܩܘܢ. The parallelism of the two erotic, rather than mystical, *hapax legomena* ܥܦܩ (*ʿp̄aq*) and ܢܫܩ (*nšaq*) supports the reading of N, but does not make it possible to reconstruct the original text by a back-translation.[82]

The speaking "I" of stanza IV connects back to the key word ܠܐ ܚܒܠܐ(ܕ) in 5b ("imperishable" or "imperishability"; see above) and affirms his close relationship to "Life" personified and its spiritual power, which is itself immortal life. Outdoing John 5:26a (ὁ πατὴρ ἔχει ζωὴν ἐν ἑαυτῷ, "the Father has life in himself"), God,

70 BDAG, *s.v.* ἀπώλεια, 2.
71 BDAG, *s.v.* ὄλεθρος.
72 Harris and Mingana (2:358) interpret the ambiguous phrase ܕܠܐ ܚܒܠܐ (*d-lā ḥḇālā*) as an attribute ("immortal" or "incorruptible"). If the construction with ܕ (*d-*) is actually a genitive (see Bauer, 609), the two possibilities for translating 5b would be: (A) "and I was established by the wings of imperishability," or (B) "and I was laid in the bosom of imperishability."
73 See Kraus, *Psalmen*, 283.
74 Payne Smith, 1:1767.
75 See Payne Smith, 2:2560–61, with numerous Greek equivalents that are irrelevant here.
76 Contra Franzmann, 210.
77 See above. That ܠܐ ܚܒܠܐ (*lā ḥḇālā*) is used as equivalent to ἀφθαρσία suggests an early date for the translation. In the Peshitta, ἀφθαρσία is translated by ܠܐ ܡܬܚܒܠܢܘܬܐ (*lā meṯḥabblānūṯā*) (Rom 2:7; 1 Cor 15:50, 53, 54; 2 Tim 1:10; see Payne Smith, 1:1181).
78 Burkitt, 372–85.
79 Payne Smith, 2:2419; see also Frankenberg, 26: ἐξῆλθε.
80 Schultheß, 255, followed by Frankenberg, 26: ἐπότισε.
81 See Lattke, *Bedeutung*, 3:71–72.
82 On the first verb, see Payne Smith, 2:2948: περιλαμβάνω (LSJ, *s.v.*) or ἐναγκαλίζομαι (Lampe, *s.v.*), and on the second, see Payne Smith, 2:2478: καταφιλέω or φιλέω (BDAG, *s.vv.*).

the "Most High" (see 19a below), is now introduced *as* "immortal life"[83] and thus is described as the power of life itself.[84] The charming image of "being embraced and kissed" is not an example of the Gnostic "sacrament of the bridal chamber,"[85] although the kiss may be interpreted "in its original meaning as transferring powers and spiritual gifts."[86]

Why 7 should be "an undoubted gloss" is as hard to understand as why the antecedent of the third masculine plural suffix in 7a is "bosom" (5b) rather than "life" (6).[87] Continuing with John 5:26b (τῷ υἱῷ ἔδωκεν ζωὴν ἔχειν ἐν ἑαυτῷ, "so he has granted the Son to have life in himself"), the speaking "I" of *Ode* 28 first declares that τὸ πνεῦμα/ܪܘܚܐ (*rūḥā*) is in him and that this "Spirit"—feminine only in the Semitic languages—comes from God, or, in later dogmatic usage, "proceeds from the Father."[88] But since the *pneuma* itself is also "life" (7c N) or "alive" (H), the whole of 7 lies on a trajectory shared by the Fourth Gospel (see John 1:4; 4:24; 6:63).[89] The term "Spirit" connects back to 1c. This may justify regarding 1-7 as a self-contained part of *Ode* 28. But it will not do to expand the link between stanzas I and IV into an "associated motif of new life (the foetus in 2b and the implied 'conception' [?] of the Spirit [7a] from the actions of embracing and kissing [6])."[90]

The negated participle of ܐܫܟܚ (*ʾeškaḥ*) in 7b must refer to the feminine ܪܘܚܐ (*rūḥā*)[91] and, with following ܠ (*l-*) + infinitive of ܡܘܬ, ܡܝܬ (*māt*), corresponds to the Greek expression οὐ δύναται ἀποθανεῖν ("it cannot die").[92] In a transferred sense, the divine spiritual power cannot lose "the ultimate, eternal life,"[93] because as the *holy* spirit it stands with the Most High above all the spheres of the cosmos.[94]

■ **8-9** Stanza V is the beginning of the "second part of the Ode."[95] Franzmann even calls it "Sub-ode 2."[96] But the speaking "I," who talks of the persecution, oppression, hatred, and murderous intentions he suffered from his enemies, is identical with the one who has already

83 The subject of 6 can also be translated as "deathless life" (Harris and Mingana, 2:358) or "life without death" (Bauer, 609; Lattke, *Oden*, 179). But the Greek *Vorlage* was most probably ἀθάνατος ζωή (Frankenberg, 26; on Wis 1:15; cf. Emerton, *Wisdom*, 2), so the negated form is most properly translated as "immortal" (BDAG, *s.v.* ἀθάνατος). Bauer (p. 609 n. 7) points out that "the (great) life" occurs "often in Mandaean writings as a description of God." The theological wisdom that "human beings are not immortal" (see Sauer, *Sirach*, 144) was known far beyond Sir 17:30 (οὐκ ἀθάνατος υἱὸς ἀνθρώπου [Rahlfs, 2:406]) and forms the necessary negative complement to the imagery of this passage.

84 Cf. 10:2a; 15:10a; 31:7b; 38:3b; 40:6a in Table 1.

85 Contra Gustav Stählin, "φιλέω, κτλ.," *ThWNT* 9 (1973) 144; *TDNT* 9:145.

86 Karl-Martin Hofmann, *Philema hagion* (BFCThM 38; Gütersloh: "Der Rufer" Evangelischer Verlag, 1938) 87. Robert McQueen Grant finds in 6-7 an allusion to *Gos. Phil.* 59,4-6 and 63,35-36 (NHC II, *3)* (see Grant, "The Mystery of Marriage in the *Gospel of Philip*," *VC* 15 [1961] 139), but neither Schenke nor Franzmann mentions *Ode* 28 (see Hans-Martin Schenke, *Das Philippus-Evangelium (Nag-Hammadi-Codex II,3)* [TU 143; Berlin: Akademie-Verlag, 1997] 29, 37, 264, 335; Majella Franzmann, "The Concept of Rebirth as the Christ and the Initiatory Rituals of the Bridal Chamber in the *Gospel of Philip*," *Antichthon* 30 [1996] 43–47).

87 Contra Diettrich, 100.

88 Bernd Jochen Hilberath, "Heiliger Geist II. Theologie- u[nd] Dogmengeschichtlich," *LThK*[3] 4 (1995) 1309.

89 On 2 Cor 3:17a, however, see the excursus entitled "ὁ δὲ κύριος τὸ πνεῦμά ἐστιν" by Margaret E. Thrall, *A Critical and Exegetical Commentary on the Second Epistle to the Corinthians*, vol. 1: *Introduction and Commentary on II Corinthians I–VII* (ICC; Edinburgh: T&T Clark, 1994) 278–82.

90 Contra Franzmann (p. 213), who finally also doubts this conclusion based on ܒܝ (*bī*) in 7a.

91 Bauer, 609.

92 Frankenberg, 26; Payne Smith, 2:2055–56, 4147–48; BDAG, *s.vv.* ἀποθνῄσκω, δύναμαι.

93 BDAG, *s.v.* ἀποθνῄσκω, 1bα.

94 See 7a; also cf. 11:2a; 13:2b; 14:8a; 19:2c, 4a; 23:22b; 36:1a.

95 So called by Kittel, 108.

96 Franzmann, 213. Logically that would mean dividing the *Ode* into three parts, since the teaching of stanza XI cannot be integrated with the so-called second part.

achieved rest and been embraced by life in 1-7. Therefore, "Christ speaks" does not begin here[97] but continues from the previous part. There are reminiscences of the stories of the "passion" of Jesus Christ,[98] but on the whole the statements of salvation laid down in stanzas I–IV dominate the autobiographical fragments of stanzas V–X, and they are enriched by a mythological consciousness of preexistence (see on 16c-18 below) as well as being contrasted with the illusions and lack of awareness of the onlookers and adversaries, but they cannot be located in world history.

Even if there is a hidden allusion in 8b to John 5:16 (ἐδίωκον οἱ Ἰουδαῖοι τὸν Ἰησοῦν, "the Jews persecuted Jesus"), rather than to the wider *κόσμος* canvas of John 15:20 (ἐμὲ ἐδίωξαν, "they persecuted me"), there is no reference to "the Jews" or to the vivid description of the healing on the Sabbath. So the indeterminate "those" of 8a refers generally to the astonished onlookers in this world.[99] Bauer's reference to Isa 52:13-15 suggests that 𝔊 may have used a form of θαυμάζω.[100] Although 17:6a uses the synonymous ܬܡܗ (*tmah*), the Greek equivalents of which largely overlap with those of the Ethpa. of ܕܡܪ (*dmar*), used here and in 41:8a, the three passages are closely related.[101] An awareness of the general unity of the *Odes of Solomon* leads one to the conclusion that the same redeemed Redeemer is speaking in all three of the *Odes*, 17, 28, and 41, although his redemptive acts are not particularly described in *Ode* 28 (but see on 12a below).

The relationship of the Ethpe. of ܪܕܦ (*rdap̄*), which occurs only in 8b and corresponds to a passive of διώκω, with the "persecutors" of 42:5a (on the form ܪܕܘܦܝ [*rādōp̄ay*], cf. 5:4a) supports the connection that has just been established with *Ode* 42, which is another mythological address by the redeemed Redeemer.[102]

The Pe. ܣܒܪ (*sḇar*) in 9a, whose subject is just as undefined as that of 8a, makes, only in 𝔖, a further connection with 17:6a-b (but see on 9b below). The Ethpe. ܐܣܬܒܪ (*ʾestḇar*) in 17:6b, unlike the form in this verse, could not correspond to a form of λογίζομαι, νομίζω, or οἴομαι/οἶμαι.[103] Although the *hapax legomenon* ܐܬܒܠܥ (*ʾeṯblaʿ*, Ethpe. of ܒܠܥ [*blaʿ*]), "was swallowed up," must correspond to a passive form of καταπίνω,[104] it is not intended as an allusion to Isa 25:8 (as quoted by Paul in 1 Cor 15:54) or to 2 Cor 5:4. The following ܠ (*l-*) with first singular suffix is, in the case of this passive verb, not a "sign of the agent."[105] This fairly common Syriac construction could have found entrance here if 𝔊, after a verb of supposing or thinking, had the accusative ἐμέ and the infinitive καταποθῆναι.

The Ethpe. of ܚܙܐ (*ḥzā*) in 9b is synonymous with the form used in 17:6b. The phrase ἔδοξα αὐτοῖς was suggested there as the equivalent; here it can only be ἐφάνην.[106] The verb φαίνομαι/ܐܬܚܙܝ (*ʾeṯḥzī*) with dative constructed with an intransitive form of δοκέω + dative of the person (see the commentary on that verse).

97 See Harris and Mingana, 2:358; Charlesworth, 109.

98 Quasten, 165.

99 Payne Smith, 1:921.

100 Bauer, 609; BDAG, *s.v.* θαυμάζω.

101 Franzmann (p. 213) does not mention 17:6a but remarks that "8a is strikingly similar to 41:8a, both in vocabulary and construction." The parallel passages may be translated as follows:

> 17:6 And all who saw me were amazed,
> and I seemed to them like a stranger
> (ξένος).
>
> 41:8 They will be amazed, all those who see me,
> because I am of another race (γένος).

102 See Payne Smith, 2:3825; BDAG, *s.v.* διώκω.

103 Payne Smith, 2:2509–10; BDAG, *s.vv.* λογίζομαι, νομίζω, οἴομαι/οἶμαι. Frankenberg translated 17:6b quite freely (p. 18: καὶ ὡς ξένον με ἐνόμισαν), but in this passage chose the less used verb οἶμαι or οἴεσθαι (ibid., 26: ᾤοντο). I believe that ἐνόμισαν was used *here* and that 17:6b 𝔊 was

104 Payne Smith, 1:538; BDAG and LEH, *s.v.* καταπίνω; see Frankenberg, 26: κατεπόθην.

105 Payne Smith, *Dictionary*, 232. The statement that "the preposition ܠ with reflexive personal pronoun often stands alongside of a verb, without essentially modifying its meaning (*dativus ethicus*)" (Nöldeke §224) is relevant here as well as for 7:21.

106 Frankenberg's retroversion of 9b is again too free (see p. 26: ὅτι ἐνόμισάν με ὥς τινα τῶν ἀπολωλότων). Moreover, ὡς ἕνα would have been expected instead of ὥς τινα (cf. as linguistic comparisons Mark 6:15 and Luke 15:19).

of the person and a following ὡς/ ܐܟ (ʾak̲) means, in this context, "look as if."[107] The passive participle ܐܒܝܕܐ (ʾab̲īd̲ē) signals the appearance, for the well informed, of the ἀπολλύμενοι ("those who are perishing") of Paul, who are the opposite of the σῳζόμενοι ("who are being saved"; see 1 Cor 1:18; 2 Cor 2:15; 4:3; Excursus 28).[108] The speaking "I" of this Ode obviously does not belong among "those who are lost"—who are spoken of later in 2 Thess 2:10 in a similarly undefined manner[109]—although, for him, in the general context of the *Odes of Solomon*, ὁ λόγος τοῦ σταυροῦ ("the word of the cross") would probably have been μωρία ("folly") rather than δύναμις θεοῦ ("power of God" [1 Cor 1:18]). That the Christ of *Ode* 28 is not only among "those who are to be saved" but has already been mythologically "saved"[110] is expressed in a paradox in the next bicolon.[111]

■ **10** The use of ܕܝܠ (*dīl*) is, again, "unidiomatic,"[112] and, taken with the construction ܘ (*w*-) . . . ܕܝܢ (*dēn*), it suggests a Greek original for this paradoxical statement of salvation, which "is reminiscent of the similar paradox" of 24:8b.[113] There is no reason to think "that in this passage, as well as that, there is some confusion in the text."[114]

The declaration of stanza X is more like a pithy summary of all the negative and positive points of *Ode* 28 than merely "a positive commentary/confessional statement in the midst of the descriptions of persecutions,"[115] and it reads like an answer to the prayer of Ps 118:134a LXX: λύτρωσαί με ἀπὸ συκοφαντίας ἀνθρώπων ("Deliver me from the false accusation of men").[116] If this theory is accepted, the original Greek of the verse may be tentatively reconstructed: καὶ ἡ συκοφαντία δὲ ἡ ἐμὴ λύτρωσίς μοι ἐγένετο (or καὶ ἡ συκοφαντία δὲ ἡ ἐμὴ ἐγένετό μοι λύτρωσις).[117]

Naturally, "my oppression" refers to the perfidy and adversity that the speaking "I" has *suffered*.[118] The *hapax legomenon* συκοφαντία/ܛܠܘܡܝܐ (*ṭlumyā*)[119] is in opposition to the commoner term ܦܘܪܩܢܐ (*purqānā*), which here probably represents not σωτηρία but λύτρωσις (see Excursus 5).[120] That the two Greek terms could be used as synonyms can be seen from Luke 1:68-69 (ἐποίησεν λύτρωσιν, κέρας σωτηρίας, "he redeemed," "horn of salvation").

■ **11-12** Unless one of the "swords" of 4c-d originated in Ps 21:21a LXX (see on 4c-d above), the influence of this psalm, which is "quoted a number of times in the passion story [of Jesus Christ]" and "was interpreted by the early church"—although "mistakenly"—as one of the numerous "prophecies of the Messiah,"[121] begins to show itself here. For the *hapax legomenon* ܣܘܠܢܐ (*sulānā*) in 11a is undoubtedly founded on the rare term ἐξουδένημα in Ps 21:7b LXX.[122] In this way, the speaking "I" conveys that in the eyes of the onlookers and persecutors (see 8 above) he has become an "object

107 BDAG, *s.v.* φαίνω, 2; Payne Smith, 1:1234.
108 BDAG, *s.v.* ἀπόλλυμι.
109 Wolfgang Trilling, *Der zweite Brief an die Thessalonicher* (EKKNT 14; Zurich: Benziger; Neukirchen-Vluyn: Neukirchener Verlag, 1980) 109.
110 BDAG, *s.v.* σῴζω, 2b.
111 Both the Syriac manuscripts treat 8a-b and 9a-b as monocola, but 10a-b and 11a-b are monocola only in N, while H treats them as bicola (see Lattke, *Bedeutung*, 76).
112 Connolly, "Greek," 537.
113 Harnack, 61. Diettrich (p. 101) disputes this relationship and merely has the speaking "I" saying: "I was oppressed but now I am saved." But in connection with "oppression," he does refer to Ps 119:134.
114 Harnack, 61.
115 Franzmann, 213.
116 Rahlfs, 2:138; Brenton, 774; cf. *OTSy*, pt. 2 fasc. 3, p. 148.
117 Because of καί . . . δέ (BDAG, *s.v.* δέ, 5b: "and also," "but also"), μου would hardly have been used here by itself (Connolly, "Greek," 537). Linguistic comparisons can be made with New Testament passages: John 3:29; 7:6, 8; 8:17; 1 Cor 16:21; Col 4:18; 1 John 1:3.
118 See BDAG, *s.v.* συκοφαντέω.
119 LEH, *s.v.* συκοφαντία; Payne Smith, 1:1478. The Ethpe. of ܛܠܡ (*ṭlam*) occurs twice. In both cases, it is emphasized that the redeemed are *not* oppressed (4:6; 33:12).
120 Payne Smith, 2:3295; BDAG, *s.v.* λύτρωσις.
121 Kraus, *Psalmen*, 184.
122 Payne Smith, 2:2638; Alfred Rahlfs, *Psalmi cum Odis* (VTG 10; 3rd ed.; Göttingen: Vandenhoeck & Ruprecht, 1979) 109, with the variants ἐξουθένημα, ἐξουδένωμα, ἐξουθένωμα. On the transcription of ܣܘܠܢܐ (*sulānā*), see Nöldeke §128.A.b; Beyer, *ATTM*, 1:104 and 106 n. 1.

of contempt."[123] Translations of the word as *fimus*,[124] "refuse,"[125] "condemnation,"[126] "dung,"[127] or "scum"[128] are misleading because the redeemed Redeemer is, after all, *not* rejected (cf. 42:10a using the Ethpe. ܐܣܬܠܝ [*ʾestlī*]) but only the target of contempt and hatred (see on 12b below). The redeemed one of *Ode* 25 also says of himself only that he was "despised and rejected *in the eyes of many*" (25:5a ܣ).[129]

The strange rationalization for this negative attitude of contempt by the first positive personal account in 11b does not contain any "historical clue" for some negated "zealotry."[130] The despised one does not say he was no ζηλωτής, but declares himself free of ζῆλος/ܛܢܢܐ (*ṭnānā*) "in a bad sense."[131] But there is no allusion to the ζῆλος θεοῦ, whether in the objective (as in Rom 10:2 ["zeal for God"]) or in the subjective sense (as in 2 Cor 11:2 ["divine jealousy"]).[132] In the context of stanza VII, this widespread human fault, closely related to hatred (7:20a),[133] is used to describe the opposite of the good (28:12a).

Reference to the description in the *Epistle to Diognetus* of the Christians and those who "hate" them, which is patterned after Paul, will throw some light from the late second century on the self-description in 12a-b, whose causal introduction must not be narrowed down to a merely ethical statement.[134] A short quotation from *Diogn.* 5:16-17 will suffice: ἀγαθοποιοῦντες ὡς κακοὶ κολάζονται· . . . καὶ τὴν αἰτίαν τῆς ἔχθρας εἰπεῖν οἱ μισοῦντες οὐκ ἔχουσιν ("When they do good they are buffeted as evil-doers, . . . and those who hate them cannot state the cause of their enmity").[135] But the *hapax legomenon* ܐܣܬܢܝ (*ʾestnī*, Ethpe. of ܣܢܐ [*snā*]), which corresponds to a passive of μισέω,[136] is more closely related to utterances, based partly on Ps 34:19 LXX and Ps 68:5 LXX, of the Johannine Jesus (see John 15:18 and 15:23-25: ἐμὲ πρῶτον ὑμῶν μεμίσηκεν . . . ὁ ἐμὲ μισῶν καὶ τὸν πατέρα μου μισεῖ . . . μεμισήκασιν καὶ ἐμέ . . . ἐμίσησάν με δωρεάν, "it has hated me before it hated you," "He who hates me hated my Father also . . . hated both me . . . They hated me without a cause").[137] Since ethics plays such a small part in the *Odes of Solomon* (cf. only 20:5-6), there may, in 12a, be an obscure allusion to the redeeming function of the speaking "I."[138] And the participle ܥܒܕ (*ʿābed*), associated with the enclitic form ܗܘܝܬ (*-wēt*), can extend to take in the mythological past (see on 16c below).[139]

■ **13-14** The word "dog" is used "in invective (as early as Homer),"[140] but its use in 13a depends on Ps 21:17a LXX (ὅτι ἐκύκλωσάν με κύνες πολλοί, "For many dogs have compassed me").[141] The change from κύνες πολλοί to κύνες λυσσῶντες as the *Vorlage* of ܟܠܒܐ ܦܩܪܐ (*kalbē paqrē*) makes another "verbal connection" with the

123 LEH and LSJRevSup, *s.v.* ἐξουδένημα; BDAG, *s.v.* ἐξουθένημα.
124 Brockelmann, *Lexicon*, 475.
125 "Auswurf" (Greßmann, 462; Bauer, 609).
126 "Verwerfung" (Harnack, 61; Diettrich, 101).
127 "Mist" (Lattke, *Bedeutung*, 1:159).
128 "Abschaum" (Lattke, *Oden*, 179).
129 The construction with ܘ (*ʾu-*) . . . ܕܝܢ (*dēn*) suggests, as in 10a, that 𝔊 used καί . . . δέ, which might yield the following: καὶ ἐγενόμην δὲ ἐξουδένημα αὐτῶν (Frankenberg, p. 26, omits all the particles). However, it is hardly possible to reconstruct the exact word sequence.
130 Harnack, 61; Diettrich, 101; Kittel, 108. Tosato, "Zeloti," has already been considered at 7:20b.
131 BDAG, *s.v.* ζῆλος, 2: "jealousy, envy."
132 See Payne Smith, 1:1489.
133 I assume that Frankenberg's retroversion of ܛܢܢܐ as μῖσος is simply a mistake, which could have perhaps crept in from 7:20a (see Frankenberg, 26: ὅτι μῖσος οὐκ ἦν ἐν ἐμοί).
134 Both Syriac manuscripts make 12a-b a bicolon, leading me to suspect that some of the Greek original may have been omitted, which would account for the shortness of 12b.
135 Lake, 2:360–61; see also Ehrman, 2:140–41; Wengst, 320–21.
136 Payne Smith, 2:2669; BDAG, *s.v.* μισέω.
137 Schultheß (p. 255) suggests replacing ܐܣܬܢܝܬ (*ʾestnīt*) by ܐܣܬܠܝܬ (*ʾestlīt*): "I was rejected." There is no reason for this modification of a well-attested text. On John 15:20, see on 8b above.
138 On ܛܒܬܐ (*ṭābtā*) + ܥܒܕ (*ʿbad*), see Payne Smith, 1:1437–38, 2:2765–66; BDAG, *s.vv.* ἀγαθοποιέω or ἀγαθός (ἀγαθόν + ἐργάζομαι or ποιέω).
139 "The part[iciple], properly expressing only a condition, is distinctly referred to the past by subjoining ܗܘܐ, or, though not so frequently, by placing that word before it. Thus there arises a form expressing duration or repetition in past time; ܥܒܕ ܗܘܐ is nearly = *faciebat*" (Nöldeke §277).
140 BDAG, *s.v.* κύων, 3; cf. LSJ, *s.v.* κύων, with references.
141 Rahlfs, 2:20; Brenton, 710; cf. Ps 21:21b LXX,

letters of Ignatius of Antioch (Ignatius *Eph.* 7:1).[142] Anyone thinking only—or also—of John 10:24 (ἐκύκλωσαν οὖν αὐτὸν οἱ Ἰουδαῖοι, "the Jews gathered round him") might even generalize it to "the Jews" as the opponents. In either case, the Pe. ܚܕܪ (*ḥdar*), which occurs only here, translates ἐκύκλωσαν and expresses "hostile intent."[143] The "dogs" of Phil 3:2 or Rev 22:15 or one of the "dogs" of Marcion (cf. Hippolytus *Elench.* 7.30.1)[144] do not come into consideration.

Verse 13b expands the image, referring to a specific and undesirable behavior of rabid dogs.[145] The plural of ܡܪܝܐ (*māryā*) is unique in the *Odes of Solomon* and is probably meant inclusively, and the use of the Pe. ܐܙܠ (*ʾezal*) is also unusual.[146] The description also includes the "ignorance" characteristic of "unreasoning animals."[147] The compound expression ܠܐ ܝܕܥܬܐ (*lā ʾidaʿtā*) immediately brings in an association with the opposite of *gnōsis* (cf. 7:21, 23; 11:8a [S]; 18:11a; 34:5c.).

Verse 14a-b with its synonymous *parallelismus membrorum* leaves the metaphor behind. The speaking "I" puts forward a very negative opinion of the psychic and existential constitution of those who hate and persecute him. Because of the overlap between admissible translations, it is not possible to reduce the related terms ܬܪܥܝܬܐ (*tarʿītā*) and ܪܥܝܢܐ (*reʿyānā*) to a one-to-one equivalence with the Greek words φρόνησις and διάνοια (see Excursus 9).[148] The passive participle of the Pa. ܚܒܠ (*ḥabbel*) in 14a, however, can be referred back to a passive form of διαφθείρω or καταφθείρω (Excursus 28).[149] Since the passive participle of ܫܚܠܦ (*šaḥlep̄*) in 14b is used in a very negative sense, it can hardly correspond to διάφορος,[150] so Frankenberg may be right to think of a form of ἀλλοιόω as *Vorlage*.[151] The participle ἠλλοιωμένος could serve as aptly as an indicative could.[152] In any case, the opponents designated by the pejorative epithet "dogs" are not among those whom the redeemed Redeemer soteriologically "transformed" (17:13b).

■ **15** If stanza IX is a self-contained "parallel bicolon,"[153] then the third masculine plural suffix in 15b must refer primarily to the "water" in 15a. So, contrasted to "sweet water," the topic here would be "water that is not potable."[154] This interpretation excludes clarifications like "water of perception,"[155] "Waters of Baptism,"[156] or "water of life,"[157] but may lead to the verdict "that he [viz., the speaking 'I'] holds the bitter water in his right hand is a most mysterious statement."[158]

where the singular ῥομφαία is parallel to κύων (21:21a; see on 4c-d above).

142 Paulsen, *Studien*, 31, on *Ode* 7:21. "The Syriac of the *Ode* (*klbʾ pqrʾ*) represents the exact equivalent of the Greek involved" (Schoedel, *Ignatius*, 59); a reference to Payne Smith, 2:3224, should be appended to Payne Smith, 1:1742. Fischer (p. 147) translates the adversarial κύνες λυσσῶντες as "hydrophobic dogs"; Lindemann and Paulsen (p. 183) call them "mad dogs," while Ehrman (1:227) uses "raving."

143 Payne Smith, 1:1203; BDAG, *s.v.* κυκλόω, 1a.

144 Paul Wendland, ed., *Hippolytus Werke*, vol. 3: *Refutatio omnium haeresium* (GCS 26; Leipzig: Hinrichs, 1916; repr., Hildesheim/New York: Olms, 1977) 215; Konrad Preysing, trans., *Des heiligen Hippolytus von Rom Widerlegung aller Häresien (Philosophumena)* (BKV 40; Munich/Kempten: Kösel & Pustet, 1922) 217.

145 Dogs that attack their own mistress or master are totally uncontrollable. Nowadays they are put down or at least sent to the pound.

146 See Payne Smith, *Dictionary*, 9: "with ܥܠ [*ʿal*] to march against, assault, invade."

147 Harnack, 61; BDAG, *s.v.* ἄλογος, 1.

148 Contra Frankenberg, 27; see Payne Smith, 2:3946–49.

149 Payne Smith, 1:1176; BDAG, *s.vv.* διαφθείρω, καταφθείρω.

150 Payne Smith, 1:1287; LSJ, *s.v.* διάφορος.

151 Frankenberg, 27: ἠλλοίωται.

152 LSJ, *s.v.* ἀλλοιόω.

153 Franzmann, 214, with which I agree.

154 BDAG, *s.v.* πικρός, 1. This parallelism is also evident in the first singular suffixes of 15a and 15b. Harris and Mingana's (2:359) translation "their bitterness," referring to the persecutors, is accepted by many later writers, including Franzmann (209). This suggests a completely different interpretation (see below).

155 Diettrich, 101: "Wasser der Erkenntnis."

156 Bernard, 112.

157 Bauer, 609; Berger and Nord, 961: "Wasser des Lebens."

158 Harnack, 61. Pierre (p. 146) interprets the "water" as the "Word of God" and speculates on "a double meaning." Frankenberg (p. 42 [corr.]) emends "ܡܪܝܐ for the meaningless ܡܝ̈ܐ and ܒܝܡܝܢܟ for ܒܝܡܝܢܝ." This assault on the manuscript text enables him to propose a hypothetical and very different reconstruction: ἐγὼ δὲ κύριε ἀντειχόμην τῆς δεξιᾶς σου (p. 27). It is quite unlikely that ἀντέχομαι was translated as any form of ܐܚܕ (*ʾeḥad*).

Spitta's opinion that "here is an echo of Gethsemane" (cf. Matt 26:39 parr.) and that "the basic idea clearly is τὸ πικρὸν τοῦ θανάτου ποτήριον"[159] is valid only insofar as it is possible to posit a more or less direct connection with the passion narratives and with the image of a ποτήριον.[160] Since Psalm 22 (21 LXX) has been shown to have been used in the composition of *Ode* 28, the keyword ὕδωρ/ܡܝܐ (*mayyā*), "water," may have come from Ps 21:15a LXX (in the total context of Ps 21:15-16 or even 15-19 LXX)[161] and become conflated with the "right hand" mentioned in Matt 27:29 (κάλαμον ἐν τῇ δεξιᾷ αὐτοῦ, "a reed in his right hand").[162] That *Ode* 28 concerns itself also, subtly and ahistorically, with the narratives of the crucifixion will become clear in stanza X.

In transitive use, the passive participle of the Pe. ܐܚܕ (*ʾeḥad*) means to "have" or to "hold" and, like its probable Greek equivalents ἔχω and κρατέω, is commonly juxtaposed with "hand(s)."[163]

Without hypothesizing, as Harris and Mingana do, the "insertion of a conjectural clause,"[164] the contrast of ܡܪܝܪܘܬܐ (*marrīrūtā*) and ܚܠܝܘܬܐ (*ḥalyūtā*), "bitterness" and "sweetness," in 15b poses no great difficulties.[165] The parallelism of the verbs in 15a-b and "the semantic similarity with 31:12"[166] could be used to support the reading of H (ܛܥܢܬ [*ṭeʿneṯ*]).[167] On the other hand, ܛܥܢܬ may be a mistake for ܛܥܝܬ (*ṭʿēṯ*), and therefore the original Syriac, like N, stemmed from a form of ἐπιλανθάνομαι.[168] It is impossible to be sure which is right. Rather than the rare, and perhaps less applicable, word πικρότης,[169] 𝔊 would have used πικρία to modify "water" (cf. linguistically Eph 4:31),[170] opposing it to the γλυκύτης, normally reserved for God, claimed by the speaking "I."[171]

The previously mentioned alternative interpretation must now be considered; it may even have been possible in 𝔊 if 15a had had τὰ ὕδατα (cf. Rev 7:17) in place of τὸ ὕδωρ. For then the pronoun αὐτῶν in 15b, corresponding to the suffix ܗܘܢ (*-hōn*), could refer equally well to the "water" and to the mad dogs of pursuers and haters. That "bitterness" in the latter sense could be understood as "their bitterness" is shown by a strange passage in the "oldest section" of the *Acts of Philip*.[172] There, in chap. 141 (35), the contrast between the γλυκύτης of Jesus and the adversarial πικρανθέντες[173] is combined with an allusion to the "gall"[174] of Matt 27:34: καὶ αὐτός

159 Spitta, 283.

160 BDAG, *s.v.* ποτήριον, a. The text Spitta quotes is repeated three times in the A revision of the *Testament of Abraham*. This "bitter drink of death" is, of course, Death personified (*T. Abr.* I and XVI; see Enno Janssen, *Testament Abrahams* [JSHRZ 3.2; Gütersloh: Mohn, 1975] 206 and 244).

161 Rahlfs, 2:20.

162 The key word κάλαμος, "reed," makes a connection to the mocking in Matt 27:48, where there is a visible influence from Ps 68:22b LXX (cf. John 19:28-30).

163 BDAG, *s.vv.* ἔχω, κρατέω; Payne Smith, 1:117–18.

164 Harris and Mingana, 2:361: "that I might put out their flame."

165 Payne Smith, 1:1281, 2:2202. Aphraates also traditionally expresses this contrast when he says: "Sweetness overcomes bitterness" (see Harris and Mingana, 2:359).

166 Franzmann, 211. The emphasis falls on "semantic," since the verb of 31:12a ("And I endured their bitterness/cruelty in humility") is not identical with that of 28:15b. In fact, 31:12a uses the *hapax legomenon* ܣܒܠ (*sḇal*).

167 Payne Smith, 1:1498; BDAG, *s.v.* βαστάζω = "take up," "carry, bear," but also "carry away, remove."

168 Payne Smith, 1:1492; BDAG, *s.v.* ἐπιλανθάνομαι, 1: "forget."

169 LSJ and LSJRevSup, *s.v.* πικρότης.

170 BDAG, *s.v.* πικρία.

171 BDAG, *s.v.* γλυκύτης; see Frankenberg, 27. The epithet was applied also to Aphrodite. In later Christian writings, the γλυκύτης was transferred from Θεός to Χριστός (Lampe, 316). On the "philosophical overtones" of "sweetness" as a term of theological relationship in Wis 16:21a, see Georgi, 460, and the passage to which he refers in Ziegler, *Dulcedo*, 12–14.

Frankenberg's alleged "understanding of the text of the *Odes of Solomon*" (p. 3) can be seen in his explanation of 28:15 (p. 56): "The spirit in the human being must endure much from the unprovoked frenzy of its persecutors; it suffers their demonic hatred patiently without retaliation (v. [15]); the unmerited injustice serves to purify it so that it is mature and worthy at last to enter into its inheritance."

172 Aurelio de Santos Otero, "Jüngere Apostelakten," *NTApo* (5th ed., 1989) 2:425; "Later Acts of the Apostles," *NTApoc* 2:469.

173 See BDAG, *s.v.* πικραίνω, 2: "embitter."

174 See BDAG, *s.v.* χολή, 1.

ἐστιν ὁ ἔχων τὴν γλυκύτητα, καὶ ἐνέπτυσαν αὐτὸν ποτίσαντες αὐτὸν χολήν, ἵνα ποιήσῃ τοὺς πικρανθέντας τῆς γλυκύτητος αὐτοῦ γεύσασθαι ("He it is who has sweetness, and they spat upon him, giving him gall to drink, in order that he might make those who were embittered to taste of his sweetness").[175] This means that the exact significance of the "water" again becomes an open question, unless one accepts Harris and Mingana's learned and desperate explanation: "the dogs were mad and would run away at the sight of water. *Hydrophoria*, if we may say so, was the natural cure for *hydrophobia*."[176]

■ **16-18** The speaking "I" now makes a connection back to ܐܒܕܢܐ (*ʾabdānā*) in 5a, interpreted as eschatological ruin and death (see the end of Excursus 28), with clear allusions to the Johannine Revealer and some reinterpretation of the passion narratives. Since it can be confidently assumed that 𝔊 used ἀπόλλυμι (middle voice in 16a; active in 18b) and ζητέω (with accusative in 17a; with infinitive in 18b), what is true for 𝔖—(1) "16a and 18b form the inclusio for the stanza proper by the repetition of the root ܐܒܕ,"[177] and (2) "17a and 18b form the inclusio for the second strophe by the repetition of ܒܥܐ"[178]—will also have held good for 𝔊.

Greßmann[179] and others use the term "Docetism" in reference to stanza X. The applicability of this modern term is somewhat questionable, since the speaking "I" did not die or suffer death even "in seeming (τὸ δοκεῖν [Ignatius *Trall.* 10; *Smyrn.* 2; 4:2])."[180] So it is necessary to be careful and merely say that the language of 28:16-18—and also of 42:10—is "undeniably open to a docetic interpretation."[181]

The explanation of 16a offered in 16b, which shows some parallelism with 17b and is therefore made into an independent colon in N (and see Franzmann on the "parallelism between 16b and 16c"),[182] demands, as in the case of 8a-b, a reference to 17:6 and 41:8. The *hapax legomenon* ܐܚܐ (*ʾaḥā*) may derive from Ps 21:23a LXX (τοῖς ἀδελφοῖς μου, "to my brethren"), but the speaking "I" does not here use it to separate himself from the "religious community of the Israelites."[183] On the contrary, the negation of this masculine and, in contrast to the suffix ܗܘܢ (*-hōn* = αὐτῶν), noninclusive term "brother" brings out the profound alienness of the persecuted and hated one who did not perish.

This nonrelation is further explained in 16c by the fact that the persecutors did not know his "origin" (on the Eshtaph. of ܝܕܥ [*ʾidaʿ*], see Excursus 7).[184] This distinguished them from the true Gnostics (8:12; 42:3, 8). The *hapax legomenon* ܐܝܠܝܕܘܬܐ (*ʾilīdūtā*), corresponding to Greek ἡ γένεσις, should not be narrowly interpreted as "birth," as H shows, in what might be called an ontological variant ("my origin was not like theirs").[185]

175 *AAAp*, 2.2:77 lines 4–6; Bernard, 112, for whom "it is more probable that the Odist is still thinking of the incidents of the Passion."
176 Harris and Mingana, 2:361.
177 Franzmann, 214.
178 Ibid., 215.
179 Greßmann, 676.
180 See Theresia Hainthaler, "Doketismus," *LThK*³ 3 (1995) 301. Schenke (*Herkunft*, 28) considers that the "Christ" of the *Odes of Solomon* does "die" the "death of this world." He bases this opinion on 42:10-11 and calls the Gnostic Christology of the *Odes of Solomon* and the *Gospel of Truth* "non-Docetic Christology" (ibid., 27). This question will be further discussed in connection with *Ode* 42.
181 Brian McNeil, "The Provenance of the Odes of Solomon: A Study in Jewish and Christian Symbolism" (Ph.D. diss., Cambridge, 1977–78) 146–47; see also idem, "Le Christ," 199; idem, "Sufferings," 31–33. On "the naive Docetism" of John, see Ernst Käsemann, *The Testament of Jesus according to John 17* (Philadelphia: Fortress Press, 1968) 66, ET of *Jesu letzter Wille nach Johannes 17* (3rd ed.; Tübingen: Mohr Siebeck, 1971) 62.
182 Franzmann, 211.
183 See Kraus, *Psalmen*, 182; Payne Smith, 1:110–11; BDAG, *s.v.* ἀδελφός.
184 "This negative statement implies that the brothers recognize his 'birth'" (Excursus 7, n. 43). The remainder of the note has now been further illuminated. Cf. also John 7:28; 8:57-58.
185 See Payne Smith, 1:1596; BDAG, *s.v.* γένεσις. Charlesworth (p. 110) prefers H and remarks: "In this verse in H we find one of the strongest docetic passages in the Odes."

An acquaintance with John 7:34 (ζητήσετέ με καὶ οὐχ εὑρήσετέ [με], "you will seek me and you will not find me") will remove any problems in understanding the mention of "death" in 17a (cf. also Matt 26:4; Luke 22:2; John 5:18; 7:1). Where this passage differs from the tradition is in the impotence[186] of the unnamed adversaries (who may be, e.g., the ἀρχιερεῖς ["chief priests"], πρεσβύτεροι ["elders"], γραμματεῖς ["scribes"], οἱ Ἰουδαῖοι ["the Jews"] of the Gospels).

The reason for the "immortality" of the "Messiah," which pervades the whole Ode, as given in 17b, parallel to 16b-c, is another break from the tradition, namely, that "he existed in a time beyond the reach of memory [since time immemorial]."[187] This is not "personified wisdom" "speaking,"[188] but Jewish and Hellenistic teaching on חכמה/σοφία (e.g., Prov 8:22-31; Wis 7:22–8:1)[189] may have influenced the speaker's self-description "of his preexistence."[190]

There is no doubt that 17c is adapted from Ps 21:19b LXX (καὶ ἐπὶ τὸν ἱματισμόν μου ἔβαλον κλῆρον, "and cast lots upon my raiment")[191] and also alludes to the canonical passion narratives (Matt 27:35; Mark 15:24; Luke 23:34; John 19:23).[192] On the one hand, the imagined scene at the foot of the cross is personalized by replacing the ἱμάτια/ἱματισμός by the actual speaking "I," so that the conduct toward him becomes senseless as well as useless.[193] On the other hand, in contrast to the Gospels, there is no mention of crucifixion at all.[194]

Although 18a-b cannot be called "a manifest imitation of the thought of John 1:30," Spitta's references to the linguistic building blocks ὀπίσω and ἔμπροσθέν are valid (and cf. John 1:15).[195] Accepting the original reading of H, ܒܬܪܝ (*bāṯar*, with first person singular suffix),[196] together with the mark of division, again differing from N, after ܡܓܢ (*maggān*), a parallelism emerges between 17c and 18a: "and they threatened me in vain" || "and those who were after me vainly."[197] But according to the line division in N, 18b is parallel to 17c. Unlike the *hapax legomenon* ܣܪܝܩܐܝܬ (*srīqāʾīṯ*) in 17c,[198] where there are a number of possible equivalents (e.g., εἰκῇ, κενῶς, εἰς κενόν, ματαίως), in 18b the *Vorlage* of ܡܓܢ (*maggān*) can only be the adverb δωρεάν, which is not, in this case, influenced by Gal 2:21.[199] The term ܕܘܟܪܢܐ (*duḵrānā*), repeated from 17b, is now used by

186 Frankenberg (p. 27) was right to consider ἐδύναντο as an alternative to εὗρον (Payne Smith, 2:4147–48). On the verb "to seek," see Excursus 19.

187 Spitta, 283; on ܕܘܟܪܢܐ (*duḵrānā*), see Payne Smith, 1:898; BDAG, *s.v.* μνεία, 1. *Ode* 11:22 suggests that the *Vorlage* was μνεία. But μνήμη is also possible (Frankenberg, 27; BDAG, *s.v.* μνήμη, 1). Charlesworth's variant reading ܕܟܪܢܗܘܢ (p. 108) cannot be confirmed in N. This renders his note that "Harris-Mingana failed to note N's variant, 'their garment' [*sic*]," void (Charlesworth, 110).

188 Contra Diettrich, 102.

189 See Georgi, 427–29.

190 Kittel, 109; on ܩܫܝܫܐ (*qaššīšā*), see Payne Smith, 2:3766–67; BDAG, *s.v.* πρεσβύτερος. According to Harnack (p. 61), "there is no idea of Christ," and therefore he tones down "preexistence" to "predestination."

191 Rahlfs, 2:20; Brenton, 710.

192 No particular importance attaches to the variation between κλῆρον and κλήρους (BDAG, *s.v.* κλῆρος). Noteworthy is that ἔβαλον κλῆρον is translated by the participle of the Pe. ܢܦܣ (*npas*; Payne Smith, 2:2416), that is, that ܦܣܐ (*pessā*) is not yet used (see Payne Smith, 2:3183; *OTSy*, pt. 2 fasc. 3, p. 22, and *NTSy* on the passages named above). This is another sign that the original language of the *Odes of Solomon* was Greek.

193 The reading of N, which attests this deed, is supported by a note in the margin of H. The text of H reads *gāzmīn* (see Payne Smith, 1:698: *irruit in, impetum fecit in*), the participle of the Pe. ܓܙܡ (*gzam*), in place of ܢܦܣܝܢ (*nāp̄sīn*).

194 See BDAG, *s.v.* σταυρόω.

195 Spitta, 283; the reference to John 1:15 is from Gillis Peterson Wetter, *"Der Sohn Gottes": Eine Untersuchung über den Charakter und die Tendenz des Johannes-Evangeliums. Zugleich ein Beitrag zur Kenntnis der Heilandsgestalten der Antike* (FRLANT 26 = N.F. 9; Göttingen: Vandenhoeck & Ruprecht, 1916) 24. Whether from the viewpoint of form or of substance, it is quite arbitrary to "strike out" 18a-b as a "later interpolation" (contra Diettrich, 102).

196 The lack of a suffix in N is probably due to a mishearing because the suffix is silent; it would make sense only if construed as an adverb (but on ܡܢ ܒܬܪ [*men bāṯar*], see Payne Smith, 1:627; Brockelmann, *Lexicon*, 56; Payne Smith, *Dictionary*, 57).

197 See Lattke, *Bedeutung*, 1:76–77; idem, *Oden*, 180.

198 Payne Smith, 2:2750.

199 Payne Smith, 2:2005; BDAG, *s.v.* δωρεάν, 3: "in vain, to no purpose."

the speaking "I" of himself in the third person,[200] again representing himself as being preexistent (cf. in 41:9a the Ethpe. of ܕܟܪ [*dkar*]: "for the Father of Truth remembered me"). The strongly emphasized lack of success of the intended destruction echoes the statements of 16a and 17a and is underlined by the repetition of the root ܐܒܕ (in the Aph. ܐܘܒܕ) and the Pe. ܒܥܐ (see above): ܒܥܘ ܠܡܘܒܕܘ (*bʿaw l-mawbādū*).

■ **19** The speaker now abandons the first person and, in a didactic and confessional[201] *parallelismus membrorum*, whose introductory conjunction ܡܛܠ ܕ (*meṭṭol d-*) carries no more weight than a loosely subordinating ὅτι,[202] describes the transcendent one who is superior even to him (on the "Most High," see Excursus 17). The anthropomorphic terms ܬܪܥܝܬܐ (*tarʿīṯā*) and ܠܒܐ (*lebbā*) are in profound contrast to the "corrupted mind" of the persecutors (14a), who are likened to dogs, but they also serve as the *inclusio* of the whole Ode (1c-2a).[203]

Understanding and translating the negated participle of the Ethpa. ܐܬܩܕܡ (*ʾeṯqaddam*)[204] presents great difficulty. It could mean χωρὶς προκρίματος ("without favor") as in 1 Tim 5:21, emphasizing God's lack of prejudice in contrast to human "partisanship."[205] Because προκαταλαμβάνω is used so often in the LXX, Frankenberg chose οὐ προκαταλαμβάνεται[206] for his retroversion of ܡܬܩܕܡܐ (*meṯqaddmā*). That may be what Ungnad and Staerk were thinking of when they translated it by "not to be overtaken."[207] The most likely Greek original, however, is a passive form of προλαμβάνω, although not in the sense of Wis 17:16c[208] or Gal 6:1,[209] but either in the sense "to be overtaken"[210] or "to be preoccupied."[211] So the difficult expression could be translated as "not to be overtaken" or as "unprejudiced."[212] That ܬܪܥܝܬܐ (*tarʿīṯā*), which cannot easily be specified precisely because of the number of possible equivalents, is shown, by its parallelism with "heart," to be a synonym of the (dia)noetic term ܡܚܫܒܬܐ (*maḥšaḇṯā*) can be seen from passages like 16:19b and 41:10b (cf. 12:4d-e and see Excursus 9). "Eternal life" (9:4b, 5b), in which the Gnostics (18:14a; 38:21b), and especially the speaking "I" of *Ode* 28 (see 6-7 above), partake, is found only in this "spirit" or "thought" of the Most High.

The ancient theory of the heart "as the site of thinking"[213] is applied to the Most High in 19b (cf. again 16:19; 41:10; and see Excursus 4). The expression ܡܝܬܪ (*myattar*), derived from ܐܝܬܪ (*ʾiṯar*) and followed by the preposition ܡܢ (*men*), corresponds to κρείττων rather than to βελτίων and means not merely "better" but "more prominent, higher in rank, preferable."[214] That the absolute form ܚܟܡܐ (*ḥeḵmā*) is used, not at all

200 The use of the third person instead of the first in 18a has only syntactic reasons and is not particularly "remarkable" (contra Spitta, 283).
201 According to Franzmann (p. 215), "19a is a concluding confessional statement with a loose chiastic pattern by the placement of the key words ܬܪܥܝܬܗ and ܠܒܗ and their respective qualifiers."
202 BDAG, *s.v.* ὅτι, 4b.
203 Franzmann, 211.
204 This *hapax legomenon* is derived from the root *qdm* (Lattke, *Bedeutung*, 2:161; Payne Smith, 2:3490) and is found only twice in the *NTSy* (Gal 6:1; 1 Tim 5:21; cf. George Anton Kiraz, *A Computer-Generated Concordance to the Syriac New Testament according to the British and Foreign Bible Society's Edition* [6 vols.; Leiden: Brill, 1993] 2476).
205 BDAG, *s.vv.* πρόκριμα, πρόσκλισις.
206 Frankenberg, 27; LEH, *s.v.* προκαταλαμβάνω.
207 Ungnad and Staerk, 30.
208 Georgi, 463: "überrascht" = "surprised."
209 Heinrich Schlier, *Der Brief an die Galater* (KEK 7; 4th ed.; Göttingen: Vandenhoeck & Ruprecht, 1965) 268; Hans Dieter Betz, *Galatians: A Commentary on Paul's Letter to the Churches in Galatia* (Hermeneia; Philadelphia: Fortress Press, 1979; 2nd printing, 1984) 291: "detected."
210 LEH, *s.v.* προλαμβάνω; see on προκαταλαμβάνω above.
211 Lampe, 1155: "esp. with evil things."
212 See already Lattke, *Oden*, 181; contra idem, *Bedeutung*, 1:159: "uncomprehended." Harnack (p. 62) and Greßmann (p. 462) offer "nicht zuvorkommen [= not forestall]." Charlesworth (p. 111) considers "anticipate" and "overtake" but prefers "cannot be prepossessed" (p. 110). Franzmann (p. 210) opts for "not to be anticipated." Bauer's "nicht zu überflügeln [= not to be outflanked]" makes, in German, an intentional or unintentional connection with the wings at the beginning of the *Ode* (see Bauer, 610). Berger and Nord's translation (p. 961), "for God's mind cannot be outwitted," is much too free.
213 Bauer, 610.
214 BDAG, *s.v.* κρείττων; see Payne Smith, 1:1653.

"senselessly," to mean "wisdom"[215] is a consequence of its juxtaposition with ܟܠ (*kol*) in the construct state.[216] In addition, the ܟܠ makes clear that this σοφία/ܚܟܡܬܐ, in a reminiscence of Paul's judgment on the "wisdom of this world," cannot be identical even with the personified "Sophia" of 7:8a, much less with the speaking "subject," whom Diettrich constantly invokes.[217] Slightly emending Frankenberg's retroversion[218] results in the following reconstruction of the last line of this Ode: καὶ ἡ καρδία αὐτοῦ κρείττων πάσης σοφίας.

215 Contra Diettrich, 102.

216 Nöldeke §202.D, 218; see Payne Smith, *Dictionary*, 141–42: "more defined and restricted sense."

217 Diettrich, 99, etc.; see also BDAG, *s.v.* σοφία, 1a; Payne Smith, 1:1267.

218 Frankenberg, 27.

29

Ode 29: Address of a Redeemed Believer in Christ (in Part as a Narrative)

(I) 1a The Lord is my hope;
1b I shall not be ashamed in him.
(II) 2a For according to his glory he made me,
2b and according to his grace[a] he also gave to me,
3a and according to his mercy he raised me up,
3b and according to his majesty he exalted me.
(III) 4a And he caused me to ascend from the deeps of Sheol,
4b and from the mouth of Death he drew me.
5a And I humbled my enemies,
5b and he [viz., the Most High Lord] justified me by his grace.
6a For I believed in the Messiah/Anointed One of the Lord,
6b and it seemed to me/I saw that he is the Lord.
(IV) 7a And he showed me[b] his sign
7b and led me by his light
8a and gave me the rod of his power,
8b that I might subdue the thoughts of the peoples;
8c and to humble the tyranny of the mighty,
9a to make war by his word,
9b and to take the victory by his power.
(V) 10a And the Lord cast down my enemy[c] by his word,
10b and he [viz., the enemy] became like chaff that the wind carries away.
(VI) 11a And I gave praise to the Most High,
11b because he made great his servant
11c and the son of his handmaid. Hallelujah.

a 2b ܠܛܝܒܘܬܗ N; ܠܛܒܘܬܗ H.
b 7a ܠܝ N; ܠܗ H.
c 10a ܠܒܥܠܕܒܒܝ N; ܠܒܥܠܕܒ̈ܒܝ H (probably plural; see Codex H, 22b line 16).

Introduction

Ode 29 is preserved in two Syriac manuscripts.[1] This difficult unitary Ode, which could be simplified only by the omission of 6a-7a,[2] is no more a mere "song of thanksgiving" than *Ode* 25[3] and, like *Ode* 28, does not belong to the species "hymn of initiation."[4] To some extent one could agree with Pierre that the narrative line from *Ode* 28 carries on to *Ode* 29.[5] But it is impossible to make a really close connection between these two

1 Mss.: Codex H, 22a–23a; Codex N, 150^r (ܣ). Ed./trans.: Charlesworth, 111–13; Franzmann, 217–21; Lattke, 3:1–19.

2 Harnack, 62; Diettrich, 102; but cf. Kittel, 110: "not correct."

3 Gunkel, *Aufsätze*, 183; Greßmann, 463; Günter Morawe, "Vergleich des Aufbaus der Danklieder und hymnischen Bekenntnislieder (1 QH) von Qumran mit dem Aufbau der Psalmen im Alten Testament und im Spätjudentum," *RevQ* 4 (1963) 347; Bauer, 610; Buschmann, 230, 266.

4 Schille, 77. Although neither manuscript marks a caesura at 1, 5, and 7, which underlines the narrative character of the *Ode*, I will adhere to the divisions into 1a-b, 5a-b, and 7a-b, accepted since Harris and Mingana (vol. 1, on these passages; 2:362–63; cf. Charlesworth, 111; Franzmann, 217; Azar, 146, 228), for ease in communication. N,

Odes, because the ill-defined speaker is contrasted also with the "Lord's Christ."[6] Even in 8-10 any idea "that Christ is the speaker" can be excluded.[7] Spitta considers the "subject" of 7-9 to be "Christ" rather than "God"[8] and therefore claims: "The description . . . can only fit an apostle of Christ, and in fact delineates St Paul." He goes so far as to call *Ode* 29 an "Ode of St Paul,"[9] a thesis Kittel rejects for its "inherent improbability."[10] Equally validly, one could take the speaker of *Ode* 29 to be the "handmaid" of 11c and of feminine gender, because of the allusion to the Magnificat, and call it an "Ode of the Virgin Mary" (cf. Luke 1:47-55). What is most likely is that the speaker described himself at the end as the "servant" (11b) and "son of his handmaid" (11c). But this verdict, that there is a masculine speaker, depends vitally on the assumption that the twinned object of the verb in 11b-c—emphatically indicated by ܠ (*l*-) and the third singular masculine suffix—does not rather refer back to the "Lord's Anointed/Messiah" in 6a. If it should be the latter, the speaker of undetermined gender remains completely hidden in the shadows of the history of dogma and religion.

The "I" does not directly address the "Lord" (1-10) who can be identified with the "Most High" (11a). Instead, the speaking "I" makes soteriological statements, in the third person, on the activities, most of which relate to it itself, of the "Lord" and "Most High," and in the first person tells of its own deeds, resulting from the divine actions for good or ill. With the many "echoes of Old Testament Psalms"[11] this Ode is "more like a cento from the Psalms than an interpretation of a single Psalm."[12]

Interpretation

■ **1** In *Ode* 5:2, 10a and 41:1c the use of ἐλπίς/ܣܒܪܐ (*sabrā*) is influenced by Ps 145:5b LXX, but the beginning of this Ode is a free expression of the connection between "hope" and not being "ashamed" or "humiliated" (cf. Pss 24:20b; 30:2a LXX; Phil 1:20).[13] Because of the key word κύριος/ܡܪܝܐ (*māryā*), it is the latter Psalm that is the likely model: Ἐπὶ σοί, κύριε, ἤλπισα, μὴ καταισχυνθείην εἰς τὸν αἰῶνα ("Lord, I have hoped in thee; let me never be ashamed").[14] Harris and Mingana's reference to the "closeness of the agreement with the Peshiṭta"[15] should not lead one to overlook the fact that the idiomatic construction of ܒܗܬ (*bhet*) with the preposition ܒ (*b*-)[16] can be based on the middle or passive voice of ἐπαισχύνω with the accusative of the person.[17] If the Greek of 1b had been οὐ καταισχυνθήσομαι ἐν αὐτῷ,[18] it would be necessary to refer to Phil 1:20 (ἐν οὐδενὶ αἰσχυνθήσομαι/ܒܡܕܡ ܠܐ ܐܒܗܬ [*b-meddem lā ʾebhat*]),[19] where it is immediately preceded by ἐλπίς, "hope," while the term αἰσχυνθήσομαι itself,

only, makes a division between 11b and 11c, but not in the fashion in which Franzmann has placed and analyzed it (see Franzmann, 217–18, 221).

5 Pierre, "Odes de Salomon," 724 n. 29: "Le cadre narratif de l'ode 29 se situe dans la ligne de l'ode 28."

6 See Abramowski, 53 and 57, on 6a-b.

7 Harris and Mingana, 2:365. Their reason for that idea is the assumption that the "word" in 9a and 10a is the "Logos." Kittel (p. 112) has discussed Buhl's theory that Christ and humanity coalesce in the "I" of *Ode* 29 (see Frants Buhl, "Salomos Oder," *Teologisk tidsskrift for den danske folkekirke*, 3. Række, 2 [1911] 114; cf. Lattke, *Bedeutung*, 3:87–88). I cannot see why there should be any thought of a change of speaker.

8 Spitta, 284.

9 Ibid., 285.

10 Kittel, 112.

11 Bauer, 610.

12 Harris and Mingana, 2:364.

13 See BDAG, *s.vv.* αἰσχύνω, καταισχύνω.

14 Rahlfs, 2:28; Brenton, 714.

15 Harris and Mingana, 2:364. In the *Pšīttā* (Nöldeke §26), Ps 31:2a reads as follows: ܒܟ ܡܪܝܐ ܣܒܪܬ ܠܐ ܐܒܗܬ ܠܥܠܡ (*OTSy*, pt. 2 fasc. 3, p. 30). The preposition ܒ (*b*-) with second masculine singular suffix refers to the "Lord" but is governed by the verb "to hope."

16 The third singular masculine suffix of this preposition in 𝔖 can refer to either the "Lord" or "hope." In 𝔊 the corresponding form of αὐτός referred unmistakably to the "Lord."

17 Payne Smith, 1:460; BDAG, *s.v.* ἐπαισχύνω; on the lack of distinction between αἰσχύνω, ἐπαισχύνω, and καταισχύνω, see Rudolf Bultmann, "αἰσχύνω, κτλ.," *ThWNT* 1 (1933) 188; *TDNT* 1:189.

18 Frankenberg, 27.

19 See *NTSy* on this passage.

in addition to "being ashamed," suggests "the sense of *being disillusioned*."[20]

■ **2-3** On the whole, what has been said about 15:7a-b can be repeated here. In spite of the insertion of the ܗܟܢܐ ܐܦ (*hākannā ʾāp̄*), which can only correspond to οὕτω,[21] in 2b, to interrupt the repetitions of this quadripartite *parallelismus membrorum*, the statements of salvation in stanza II are not among "the usual metaphorical comparisons" of the *Odes of Solomon*.[22] The parallelism with 15:7 is the more striking, since 15:9 also deals with the annihilation of "death" and the destruction of his "realm" (see below on 4a-b). The relationship of the four nouns may suggest a chiastic structure for 2a, 2b, 3a, 3b: ABB'A'.[23] This observation is reinforced by the juxtaposition of "glory" and "majesty" in the doxology of 18:16.

Unlike the indirect doxology of 11a, in 2a δόξα/ܬܫܒܘܚܬܐ (*tešbuḥtā*) should be translated as "glory" (see Excursus 21). Diettrich's reference to Ps 8:5-6 and Wis 7:2 are as wrongheaded as his suggestion that the verb ποιέω/ܥܒܕ (*ʿbad*) refers to "the shaping in the womb and not to the birth of the *new* man."[24] The common verb "to make" can, of course, be used, like ܒܪܐ (*brā*; cf. 7:8-9) as a term of creation (cf. 7:12b; 12:10b), but here, as in 15:7b and 36:5a, it is used of eschatological re-creation and renewal (cf. 36:5b). This is confirmed by the soteriological third-person statements that follow and continue, perhaps even past the end of 3b.

In 2b the speaking "I" refers the statement of salvation to itself, not by the use of the objective suffix but by the dative preposition ܠ (*l*-) + first singular suffix, a further deviation from strict parallelism, which in 𝔊 would have been an intrusive ἔδωκέν/δέδωκέν μοι. Although the reading ܛܒܘܬܐ (*ṭābūṯā*) of H makes sense (cf. 20:9; 41:5),[25] the reading in N is to be preferred, in view of the parallelism with χάρισμα/ܡܘܗܒܬܐ (*mawhabtā*) in 15:7a and the use of χάρις/ܛܝܒܘܬܐ (*ṭaybūṯā*) in 15:8b (cf. 21:2a, with its reference to χάρις καὶ ἔλεος in Wis 3:9c and 4:15a).[26] God did not bestow "grace" itself on the speaking "I," which differs from the statements in the Pauline and deutero-Pauline epistles.[27] Since the metaphorical object that is "given" in 8a has not yet been mentioned (see below), and it is not acceptable simply to import the eschatological "rest" of 37:4, the use of the common verb ܝܗܒ (*yab*) in this general fashion serves to emphasize the extent of God's grace (cf. 2 Thess 1:12), especially God's claimed "gracious deed," even more than the "beneficent disposition," that the speaking "I" claims for itself (see Excursus 33).[28] And in 5b this "grace" will be demonstrated in action.

A glance at 14:9a-b shows that ܝܗܒ (*yab*) could also have been used in 3a. Instead the Aph. of ܪܘܡ, ܪܡ (*rām*) serves soteriologically to define God's ἔλεος/ܪܚܡܐ (*raḥmā*) more closely (cf. 21:2b-c; 25:9; 36:1b; and see Excursus 17). And in return, the verb[29] of course characterizes God's "mercy" (cf. 14:3a; 16:7; and see Excursus 2).

The use of the Palp. of ܪܘܡ, ܪܡ (*rām*) in 3b should not obscure the basic parallelism of 2a and 3b.[30] That in 𝔖 the verbs of 3a and b share a root does not argue for a Syriac original. Indeed, a poetic contrast between two Greek verbs would more strongly suggest a Greek

20 Bultmann, "αἰσχύνω," *ThWNT* 1:190; *TDNT* 1:190.
21 Frankenberg, 27.
22 See commentary on 15:7a. Frankenberg (p. 27) uses the preposition κατά not only in 2a and 3a-b but also in 2b. There is a variation in the construction of 36:5a-b similar to that in 29:2a-b.
23 Jouko Martikainen, *Gerechtigkeit und Güte Gottes: Studien zur Theologie von Ephraem dem Syrer und Philoxenos von Mabbug* (Göttinger Orientforschungen, I. Reihe: Syriaca 20; Wiesbaden: Harrassowitz, 1981) 33.
24 Diettrich, 104. He seems to contradict himself when, in reference to 15:7, he points to "the same eschatological ideas" in 29:2 (ibid., 55 n. 2).
25 Payne Smith, 1:1439; BDAG, *s.v.* ἀγαθωσύνη.
26 Although Martikainen (p. 33) reads ܛܒܘܬܐ, he translates the term as "goodness," not "grace," in line with the subject of his book.
27 Cf. Rom 1:5; 12:3, 6; 15:15; 1 Cor 1:4; 3:10; 2 Cor 8:1; Gal 1:15; Eph 3:2, 7-8; 2 Tim 1:9.
28 See BDAG, *s.v.* χάρις, 2a, 3b.
29 It can be taken for granted that 𝔊 also used different verbs here and in 3b. Frankenberg (p. 27) suggests ὑψόω in 3a and a form of αἴρω in 3b. The reverse is more likely, but composites of either or both of these Greek verbs cannot be ruled out (Payne Smith, 2:3858).
30 Martikainen (p. 33) remarks correctly on 29:2-3: "The first and fourth lines correspond, as do the second and third." In the structure of the Ode as a whole, it follows that "2a and 3b form the inclusio for the stanza" (Franzmann, 219).

original. That the compound expression ܪܒܘܬ ܝܐܝܘܬܐ (*rabbūṯ yāʾyūṯā*), "majesty," is a translation of μεγαλοπρέπεια has already been demonstrated for three earlier occurrences (7:23b; 15:7b; 18:16; cf. also 36:5a). But this example by itself cannot prove the existence of a Greek original, since in bilingual Syria this expression of the Psalmist, as well as other noun and verb equivalences such as are found in stanza II, must have become set expressions quite early.

■ **4-6** Verse 6b, in spite of Franzmann's analysis, belongs to the end of stanza III,[31] not to the beginning of stanza IV.[32] This deepens the impression that that intractable key word, the "Lord," is the *inclusio* of 1-6 and concludes the first half of *Ode* 29.

Verse 4a-b chiastically[33] forms a synonymous *parallelismus membrorum*, deriving its mythological imagery from the Psalms,[34] which spread from there into the Wisdom literature.[35] While "Death" and "Hades" have theologically been finally overcome for the redeemed and Redeemer of *Ode* 15 (15:9; but cf. again 42:11 and Excursus 42), in this passage the "realm of the dead" and "death" are still active as uncanny and savage "alien powers."[36] That will continue until ὁ θάνατος as ἔσχατος ἐχθρὸς καταργεῖται (1 Cor 15:26: "The last enemy to be destroyed is death").[37] The speaking "I," who is neither the Κύριος Ἰησοῦς (Heb 13:20) nor Χριστός (Rom 10:7; cf. 10:9), is not describing a "rescue from deadly danger"[38] or "recovery from mortal illness":[39] it is expanding on the soteriological details of the re-creation and exaltation described in stanza II. Since the actual topic is the re-awakening by the Lord Most High who alone[40] has "power of life and death" (Wis 16:13),[41] the "I" places itself as close as possible to the redeemed Redeemer.[42] There is no trace of a *descensus ad inferos*.[43] The Aph. of ܣܠܩ (*sleq*) is used in 4a, as in 22:1, for the mythological leading upward, a verb whose root is also found in the noun "ascent" (cf. 35:7a). 𝔊 most probably used a form of ἀνάγω.[44] Whether the plural of ܥܘܡܩܐ (*ʿumqā*) represents a singular βάθος[45] is questionable and, in view of Ps 85:13 LXX (καὶ ἐρρύσω τὴν ψυχήν μου ἐξ ᾅδου κατωτάτου, "and thou hast delivered my soul from the lowest hell"), even unlikely.[46] The plural "deeps," which is not found in this Psalm either, is most easily explained by assuming that 𝔊 used the superlative κατώτατα, which is plural in form (cf. the analogous τὰ κατώτατα τῆς γῆς in Ps 62:10 and 138:15 LXX).[47]

The anthropomorphizing term ܦܘܡܐ (*pummā*), which corresponds to στόμα,[48] is used only here in 4b in the sense of "maw" or "gullet" (see Excursus 31). "Death" thus appears as "an apocalyptic monster,"[49] unless the image should be referred to τὸ στόμα τῆς γῆς ("the mouth of the earth") of Num 16:30 and Rev 12:16a (cf.

31 Charlesworth, 112.
32 Franzmann, 217–19.
33 Ibid., 219–20.
34 Cf. in the LXX Pss 15:10; 17:6; 29:4; 85:13; 114:3, 8; 115:6.
35 Cf. Wis 16:13; but also Hos 13:14; Rev 6:8; 20:13-14.
36 Wolff, *Hosea*, 297.
37 How strong this conjunction of ᾅδης with personified θάνατος was can be seen from the textual history of 1 Cor 15:54–55 (NA[27], 470; cf. BDAG, *s.v.* ᾅδης).
38 Diettrich, 104.
39 Gunkel, *Aufsätze*, 183.
40 Even the Jesus of John's Gospel says, about the Son, to the heavenly Father: ἔδωκας αὐτῷ ἐξουσίαν πάσης σαρκός (John 17:2; cf. 5:27).
41 Georgi, 459.
42 In Abramowski's terminology the "I" is a *filius adoptivus*, but the redeemed Redeemer is *filius proprius*. "At the latter end there is to be no distinction between the true-born son and the adopted one" (see Abramowski, 57).
43 Contra Clarke, 51.
44 Cf. Pss 29:4 and 70:20 LXX; Wis 16:13; Rom 10:7; Heb 13:20; Payne Smith, 2:2648; BDAG, *s.v.* ἀνάγω, 1.
45 Frankenberg, 27; cf. BDAG, *s.v.* βάθος, 1.
46 Rahlfs, 2:93; Brenton, 750; Payne Smith, 2:2916–17; BDAG, *s.v.* κατώτατος.
47 LEH, *s.v.* κατώτατος; Lampe, 738. The influence of the LXX is made more likely since κατωτάτου and κατώτατα are translated in the Peshitta by ܬܚܬܝܬܐ and ܬܚܬܝ̈ܬܐ respectively (*OTSy*, pt. 2 fasc. 3, pp. 68 [Ps 63:10], 101 [Ps 86:13], 162 [Ps 139:15]). This argues against the "dependence of the Ode on the Syriac Psalm[s]" (Harris and Mingana, 2:365).
48 Payne Smith, 2:3063.
49 BDAG, *s.v.* στόμα, 1c, on ὄφις/δράκων in Rev 12:15, 16b; 16:13.

Num 16:32; Deut 11:6).[50] Anyone familiar with John 6:44 and 12:32 will be reminded by the verb ܢܓܕ (*ngad*), which recurs in *Ode* 33:4, of the eschatological use of ἕλκω.[51]

The vague term "enemies" in 5a is drawn from the context of these "Old Testament Psalms."[52] Resisting the temptation to interpret the plural of ἐχθρός/ܒܥܠܕܒܒܐ (*bᶜeldbābā*) as "Sheol" and "Death" (cf. 1 Cor 15:26), it is necessary, with Frankenberg, to look ahead to the ἔθνη in 8b (and, because of the repeated Pa. ܡܟܟ [*makkek*], also probably to the "mighty" of 8c), but without following him further to the equation "enemies" = "heathen" = "demons."[53] As will be seen at once in the exegesis of 6a-b and later that of 8a-c, the "enemies" and "peoples" derive mainly from that most influential Psalm 110 (109 LXX). Anyone who sees in the "sign" of 7a the "Christian sign of the Cross"[54] might think of τοὺς ἐχθροὺς τοῦ σταυροῦ τοῦ Χριστοῦ ("enemies of the cross of Christ") in Phil 3:18 and go even farther astray than Diettrich in his reference to Wis 16:16.[55] Since 8c has the same person speaking of "bringing low/humiliating,"[56] there is no reason to assimilate ܡܟܟܬ (*makkket*, "I humbled") to 10a and to read *makkekt* ("you humbled")[57] and even less to emend it to ܡܟܟ (*makkek*, "he humbled").[58] The use of the first person in 5a, in any case, fits best with the first person statement of 6a.

Before discussing the problems of 6a-b, it is necessary to take up for 5b what has been mentioned in an earlier excursus (Excursus 25). Bauer's remark, "*justify* in the sense of *leading to victory* as in 1 Tim 3:16,"[59] is relevant to the image of "enemies" in this passage, the only one to use the Pa. ܙܕܩ (*zaddeq*). But the connection with the term "grace," on the one hand (see above on 2b), and the declaration of faith that follows, on the other (see below on 6a), makes it necessary to pay more attention to the Pauline concept of soteriological "justification" by divine χάρις (Rom 3:24; cf. Gal 2:21) and human πίστις (Rom 3:22, 26, 28, 30; Gal 2:16).[60]

If γάρ/ܓܝܪ (*gēr*) in 6a, unlike that in 2a, is intended to do more than emphasize the preceding word, the particle may be "used causally."[61] In that case, the loan-word ܗܝܡܢ (*haymen*),[62] which, with following ܒ (*b*-), corresponds to πιστεύειν εἰς ("believe in"),[63] gives a basis to the whole of the preceding statement 5a-b (cf. the statements of faith in 28:3 and 34:6). Because the redeemed speaker believed in the "Messiah/Anointed One of the Lord," he was justified (5b) and was able also to humble his foes (5a; see on stanza IV below). Although the redeemed Redeemer, identical with the Κύριος Χριστός, has himself been justified (17:2, 16; cf. 25:11-12) and can even be linked to "faith" (28:3; cf. 8:11, also perhaps 39:13 and 41:1), the first person statement of 6a can only be attributed to the messianic Redeemer and Son (cf. 41:11-15), if there was a credible Christian, Gnostic, or Jewish tradition that *before* his exaltation in dogma and kerygma he had believed, in hope,[64] in a χριστὸς κυρίου ("Messiah/Anointed One of the Lord")[65] who was distinct from all possible

---

50 See BDAG, *s.v.* στόμα, 3: "of the earth in which a fissure is opened."

51 Payne Smith, 2:2276; BDAG, *s.v.* ἕλκω, 2: "to draw."

52 Gunkel, *Aufsätze*, 183.

53 Frankenberg, 56–57.

54 E.g., Harnack, 62; to the contrary, Spitta, 284.

55 Diettrich, 104.

56 See Payne Smith, 2:2100–2101; BDAG, *s.v.* ταπεινόω.

57 Contra Schultheß, 255.

58 Contra Diettrich, 104.

59 Bauer, 610; see Excursus 25, with more references.

60 See Karl Kertelge, "δικαιόω," *EWNT* 1 (1980) 799–804, esp. 802; *EDNT* 2:331–33, esp. 332.

61 Lattke, "Wörter," 289 = idem, *Bedeutung*, 4:138.

62 Brockelmann, *Grammatik* §180.D.

63 Payne Smith, 1:232; see Rudolf Bultmann, "πιστεύω, πίστις, κτλ.," *ThWNT* 6 (1959) 203–4, 211, 224; *TDNT* 6:203–4, 210, 222–23.

64 On the connection between "hope" and "belief," see Bultmann, "πιστεύω, πίστις, κτλ.," *ThWNT* 6:207–8; *TDNT* 6:207–8; Artur Weiser, "πιστεύω, πίστις, κτλ.," *ThWNT* 6 (1959) 195–96; *TDNT* 6:194–95.

65 On the combination χριστὸς κυρίου and its origins and relationships, see Ernst von Dobschütz, "ΚΥΡΙΟΣ ΙΗΣΟΥΣ," *ZNW* 30 (1931) 116; Franz Hesse, "χρίω, χριστός, κτλ.," *ThWNT* 9 (1973) 492–94; *TDNT* 9:502–4; Adam Simon van der Woude, "χρίω, χριστός, κτλ.," *ThWNT* 9 (1973) 500; *TDNT* 9:509; Marinus de Jonge, "χρίω, χριστός, κτλ.," *ThWNT* 9 (1973) 504–7; *TDNT* 9:513–15; Walter Grundmann, "χρίω, χριστός, κτλ.," *ThWNT* 9 (1973) 524–27; *TDNT* 9:532–35; Martin Karrer, *Der Gesalbte: Die Grundlagen des Christustitels* (FRLANT 151; Göttingen: Vandenhoeck & Ruprecht, 1991) 55, 240, 254–67, 312; Gerd Theißen and Annette Merz, *The Historical Jesus: A*

ψευδόχριστοι ("false Christs"; cf. Mark 13:22 and Matt 24:24). The sources, however, offer no direct or indirect support for this supposition.[66] So here, in the mouth of this nonmessianic speaker, the Christian "title Christ and Lord"[67] is clearly seen amalgamating with the language of the LXX and the "Kyrios religion," which, in its milieu, superseded the "YHWH religion."[68]

Verse 6b shows that Psalm 110 (109 LXX) has left traces also in the *Odes of Solomon*: *Εἶπεν ὁ κύριος τῷ κυρίῳ μου Κάθου ἐκ δεξιῶν μου, ἕως ἂν θῶ τοὺς ἐχθρούς σου ὑποπόδιον τῶν ποδῶν σου* ("The Lord said to my Lord, Sit thou on my right hand, until I make thine enemies thy footstool" [Ps 109:1 LXX]).[69] So both the personal pronoun αὐτός/ܗܘ (third masculine singular), in the contraction ܗܘܝܘ (*hūyū*),[70] and the predicate noun "Lord" refer to the "Anointed/Messiah" in 6a.[71] There would not be much sense, after 6a, in again bestowing this title on the almighty "Lord" (of the world, humanity, even Jesus Christ) even though it is grammatically possible. The particle ܕ (*d-*), used as a conjunction[72] and corresponding to ὅτι, makes it impossible to interpret the impersonal phrase ܐܬܚܙܝ ܠܝ (*ʾetḥzī lī*) as equivalent to ἐφάνη/ὤφθη μοι.[73] The expression corresponds either to ἔδοξέν μοι[74] or to a simple ἀνέβλεψα or ἔβλεψα (cf. John 9:11, 15).[75]

■ **7-9** Both Syriac manuscripts treat 7a-b[76] as a single line, which brings out the *parallelismus membrorum* of 7-8a more clearly than the editorial emendation allows. But, since 8b-9b with their "alternating chiastic pattern" depend on 8a,[77] the editorial decision to show 7 as a bicolon and thus to bring out the internal parallelism of "sign" and "light" seems only logical.[78]

The H reading ܠܗ (*leh* = "to him") in 7a cannot be correct; it was questioned already by Harris in his *editio princeps* of 1909.[79] But whom does the speaking "I," who remains the same before and after stanza IV, intend as the subject of the verbs in 7a-8a and the referent of the third masculine singular possessive suffixes to the

Comprehensive Guide (Minneapolis: Fortress Press, 1996) 531–40, 564, ET of *Der historische Jesus: Ein Lehrbuch* (Göttingen: Vandenhoeck & Ruprecht, 1996) 462–69, 526–27; Stefan Schreiber, *Gesalbter und König: Titel und Konzeptionen der königlichen Gesalbtenerwartung in frühjüdischen und urchristlichen Schriften* (BZNW 105; Berlin/New York: de Gruyter, 2000) 161–90.

66 Schreiber, too, considers that the idea that "Jesus hoped for a Messiah is less than likely" (letter dated October 24, 2001).

67 Abramowski, 53.

68 Von Dobschütz, "*ΚΥΡΙΟΣ ΙΗΣΟΥΣ*," 99.

69 Rahlfs, 2:124; cf. Matt 22:44; Mark 12:36; Luke 20:42-43; Acts 2:34-35; 1 Cor 15:25; Heb 1:3, 13.

70 Nöldeke §38.

71 Abramowski, 53. By the time the *Odes of Solomon* were written, the "titles" *Κύριος* and *Χριστός* had already been transferred to Jesus. In this, Psalm 110 (109 LXX) acted as a bridge: "For his disciples Jesus was never a secondary god or a divine hero to be worshiped in addition to God. That is what is unique about the Christian creed; Jesus is placed by the side of God, without any fear that this will violate the monotheism to which the Christians adhere as firmly as the Jews. The bridge is formed by Psalm 110, which Jesus himself quoted" (von Dobschütz, "*ΚΥΡΙΟΣ ΙΗΣΟΥΣ*," 113–14 and 116, referring to Acts 2:36).

72 In 1 Tim 1:17, μόνῳ θεῷ is translated by ܕܗܘܝܘ ܚܕ ܐܠܗܐ (*d-hūyū ḥad ʾallāhā* [*NTSy* on this passage]). In that case, the ܕ is a relative particle (Payne Smith, 1:980). So neither Franzmann's translation nor her grammatical and syntactical analysis can be supported (see Franzmann, 218–20).

73 Contra Franzmann, 219: "Lord" as "subj[ect] of ܐܬܚܙܝ." That distinguishes this passage from those which use ὤφθη/ὤπται + dative (Judg 13:10; Matt 17:3; Acts 7:2) or ἐφάνη + dative (Matt 1:20; Mark 16:9; Luke 1:11). In all these cases, there is a personal subject agreeing with the Ethpe. ܐܬܚܙܝ (*ʾetḥzī*; see Payne Smith, 1:1234).

74 Frankenberg, 27; BDAG, *s.v.* δοκέω, 2b.

75 Harris and Mingana, 2:363: "I saw that He was the Lord." There is hardly any difference between ἀνέβλεψα and ἔβλεψα because of the "total loss of force of ἀνα: *again*" (BDAG, *s.v.* ἀναβλέπω, 2aβ).

76 See Lattke, *Bedeutung*, 1:160–61.

77 Franzmann, 220.

78 Franzmann's inclusion of 6b in the first strophe of stanza IV is as incomprehensible as her abscission of 8b-9b (as a "second strophe") from 8a (see Franzmann, 220).

79 Harris, 129.

various nouns in 7a-8a and 9a-b? Following on from 6b in stanza III, one might suppose that in this dualistic mythic narrative of salvation[80] the Kyrios Christos has taken the place of the divine "Lord" and "Most High." But that would still not answer the question of who is meant by the possessive suffixes. Thus, the problem of stanza IV would only be made more complicated by undertaking to distinguish the subject of the verbs in 7a-8a from the referent, whether that is a common or a proper noun, of the suffixes (which represent the pronoun αὐτοῦ in 𝔊). The main indication that the "sign," "light," "word," and "power" are *God*'s comes from the phrase ῥάβδος δυνάμεως ("rod of power"), which originated in Ps 109:2a LXX (see 8a below). This, then, opens up the possibility that the "word" of 9a and 10a might be the personified "Logos."[81] Harnack's authoritative pronouncement that the "sign," as in 27:2 and 42:1, is "the Christian sign of the Cross," and that passages like 23:12 and 39:7 are "not comparable,"[82] can still be seen to influence Bauer[83] and leads Pierre to connect it with "light."[84] But if the idea is not τὸ σημεῖον τοῦ υἱοῦ τοῦ ἀνθρώπου ("the sign of the Son of man") of Matt 24:30 nor "especially . . . to consider the sign of the cross,"[85] neither should the parallelism of 7a and 7b delude one into importing the much later Manichaean concept of the "Cross of Light."[86] Connolly gives the most likely explanation for 7a,[87] even if his "additional connections" of "sign" with "wood" and "signpost" are not convincing.[88] Connolly singles out "sign" and "way" in 39:7 and 39:13, on the one hand, and "way" and "tracks" of light in 7:13-14, on the other (cf. also 22:11). So the "sign" of 29:7a is finally the "way" leading to *gnōsis*, which is "shown" and revealed, in this case, not by the Kyrios Christos (24:1, 13) but by the Most High Lord.[89]

The verb and its object in 7a are parallel to the verb and its object in 7b. In 17:5a the redeemed Redeemer himself was led by the thought of Truth, but this verse of *Ode* 29 is even closer to the first person statement of 38:1b ("Truth led me"), especially since the "light of Truth" is mentioned in 38:1a (see also the exaltation by or in the light in 21:6a). The Pe. of ܕܒܪ (*dḇar*) corresponds not to the aorist of ἄγω[90] but to that of ὁδηγέω.[91] This puts even more weight on the idea of "way" already noted (cf. the "tracks of his light" on the "way" to "*gnōsis*" in 7:13-14).

80 The description "narrative of salvation" (Lattke, *Oden*, 67) can be used only from the perspective of the first-person speaker; for his foes, the "peoples," conversely, it is a tale of metaphorical disaster. It is impossible to reconstruct a historical basis for these events, which are partly taken from Psalm 110 (109 LXX).

81 Harris and Mingana, 2:364–65. They show that 8a "is certainly based on Psalm cix. (cx.) 2, and Christ should be the speaker," yet only a little farther on they properly deny "that Christ is the speaker," which leads to the conclusion "that the 110th Psalm could be used to express the experience of a believer in Christ as well as of Christ Himself."

It is most unlikely that "Christ Himself" "appeared" to the "poet" or "singer" in a vision (contra Gunkel, *Aufsätze*, 183). Gunkel's reference to 2 Cor 10:4-5 correctly identifies the subject of stanza IV as God's "spiritual rule over the world." Unlike the human wars, which continue into the third millennium as bloody contests between inimical powers that define themselves as good and their adversaries as evil, the humbling subjection and the victory to be won are, here as in 2 Cor 10:3, not meant κατὰ σάρκα.

82 Harnack, 62.

83 Bauer, 610: "sign of the Christ."

84 Pierre, 149: "Le 'signe' en est le mystère de la lumineuse élévation sur la croix."

85 Contra Gunkel, *Aufsätze*, 184.

86 On this term, see Gottfried Nebe, "Jesus, der Gekreuzigte, der am Holz hängt–Das Lichtkreuz: Einige Beobachtungen und strukturelle Überlegungen zur Wirkungsgeschichte von Kreuz und Kreuzigung Jesu von der Bibel zum westlichen Manichäismus," in Michael Becker and Wolfgang Fenske, eds., *Das Ende der Tage und die Gegenwart des Heils: Begegnungen mit dem Neuen Testament und seiner Umwelt: Festschrift für Heinz-Wolfgang Kuhn zum 65. Geburtstag* (AGJU 44; Leiden: Brill, 1999) 265–79. Even Bousset, who discusses "some obscure passages in the *Odes of Solomon*" in connection with the "celestial Cross of Light" (see Wilhelm Bousset, "Platons Weltseele und das Kreuz Christi," *ZNW* 14 [1913] 284), does not cite 29:7 as a parallel for 27:2 and 42:1.

87 Connolly, "Odes," 303–5.

88 Kittel, 134; cf. 111.

89 On the Pa. ܚܘܝ (*ḥawwī*) and its possible Greek equivalents, see commentary on 24:13a.

90 Contra Frankenberg, 27.

91 Payne Smith, 1:811; BDAG, *s.v.* ὁδηγέω; cf. the

The common verb "to give," which already appeared in 2a and is used in a similar context in 22:4 ("he gave me authority"), has as its object here the ῥάβδος δυνάμεως ("rod of power") borrowed from Ps 109:2a LXX.[92] Greßmann considers this expression so central to *Ode* 29 that he gives the whole Ode the title "The Sceptre of Power."[93] It is difficult to conjecture why the uncommon ܚܝܠܬܢܘܬܐ (*ḥayltānūtā*) was preferred to ܥܘܫܢܐ (*ʿušnā*) or ܚܝܠܐ (*ḥaylā*) as the translation of δύναμις. Perhaps it is due to the plethora of terms of power in stanza IV and the poetic need to avoid repeating them.[94]

Excursus 29: "Power," "Might," and "Strength" in the *Odes of Solomon*

The translation of the Syriac terms for "power" is difficult because especially ܚܝܠܐ (*ḥaylā* [seven times in the singular, twice in the plural]) and ܥܘܫܢܐ (*ʿušnā* [three times]) have overlapping areas of meaning.[95] This especially affects their correspondence to δύναμις and ἰσχύς. The Coptic ϭομ (*com*) can correspond to either Syriac noun (6:17 and 25:6) and is used to translate the Greek δύναμις, ἰσχύς, and κράτος,[96] to list only the most important equivalents.[97] The third Syriac noun ܫܘܠܛܢܐ (*šulṭānā* [twice]) presents less of a problem, since the Greek loanword ἐξουσία, which is used in 22:4 ℭ ("authority over bonds"), is likely to have been used in 4:2a as well ("no power" over God's "holy place"), although κράτος cannot be completely ruled out (cf. 1 Tim 6:16; Heb 2:14).[98] The term ἐξουσία/ܫܘܠܛܢܐ does not occur in the *Odes of Solomon*, whether in the singular or the plural, in the sense "of transcendent rulers and functionaries: powers of the spirit world."[99] In both passages where the plural ܚܝ̈ܠܐ (*ḥaylē*) occurs, it refers to celestial powers ("hosts") (4:8a; 16:14), not to *miraculous* δυνάμεις.[100] The singular ܚܝܠܐ (*ḥaylā*) occurs once as a parallel to "work," meaning the "power" of the creative "thoughts" (8:18), which corresponds to δύναμις: "deed of power."[101] Whether 6:17 refers to a particular theological "strength" is not clearly illuminated even by the parallel term "light."[102] In all other cases, ܚܝܠܐ refers to the Lord and Most High, even when the "power" is upon the seal of the heavenly letter (23:9b).[103] The phrase δύναμις ὑψίστου (Luke 1:35) lies behind 32:3a ("holy power of the Most High") and also probably played a part in shaping the statement of salvation in 18:2a (see below on the Ethpa. of ܥܫܢ [*ʿšen*]). The decisive "victory" will be won with

quotation of Ps 85:11a LXX in Harris and Mingana, 2:364: ὁδήγησόν με, Κύριε, τῇ ὁδῷ σου.

92 On ῥάβδος/ܚܘܛܪܐ (*ḥuṭrā*), see BDAG, *s.v.* ῥάβδος; Payne Smith, 1:1249; on δύναμις/ܚܝܠܬܢܘܬܐ (*ḥayltānūtā*), see BDAG, *s.v.* δύναμις; Payne Smith, 1:1262. In contrast to ܚܝܠܐ (*ḥaylā*), the feminine ܚܝܠܬܢܘܬܐ (*ḥayltānūtā*) is rare and does not occur in the Syriac NT. The fact that Ps 110:2a uses ܚܘܛܪܐ ܕܥܘܫܢܐ (*ḥuṭrā d-ʿušnā*) (*OTSy*, pt. 2 fasc. 3, p. 135) suggests that the translator did not use the *Pšīṭtā* (see Harris and Mingana, 2:363–64), but made his own translation from the LXX.

93 Greßmann, 463. He interprets the "sign" of 7a as "the royal seal" and the "scepter of his power" as "the royal scepter." In doing so, he brings to mind—intentionally or otherwise—the phrase ῥάβδος τῆς βασιλείας σου ("scepter of thy kingdom") of Ps 44:7b LXX quoted in Heb 1:8 (Rahlfs, 2:47; Brenton, 724; cf. NA[27], p. 564, on *v.l.* αὐτοῦ). His reference to *T. Levi* 8:4 (in addition to Ps 109:2 LXX) is justified to the extent that the "staff" is the object of "to give" (see Robert H. Charles, *The Greek Versions of the Testaments of the Twelve Patriarchs* [Oxford: Clarendon, 1908; 3rd ed., repr., Darmstadt: Wissenschaftliche Buchgesellschaft, 1966] 43: ἔδωκέ μοι ῥάβδον; Jürgen Becker, *Die Testamente der zwölf Patriarchen* [JSHRZ 3.1; Gütersloh: Mohn, 1974] 52).

94 If this was true already for 𝔊, it is likely that in addition to δύναμις (8a) there would have been synonyms like δυναστεία and ἰσχύς (8c and 9b).

95 Payne Smith, 1:1258, 2:3004.

96 Crum, 815–16.

97 BDAG, *s.vv.* δύναμις, ἰσχύς, κράτος. *Ode* 5:8c is peculiar to ℭ ("and they have been defeated, although they have power"). And in 5:7c, the Syriac and Coptic versions differ radically.

98 In addition to the three roots already listed for Syriac terms of "power," there is the use of ܐܚܕ (*ʾeḥad*) and the related term ܐܘܚܕܢܐ (*ʾuḥdānā*) in some passages; cf. 5:6b and 7:16a ("seize," "possess") as well as 19:10c ("great power"). On the *hapax legomenon* ܡܨܐ (*mṣē*), corresponding to δυνάμενος, see 14:10 ("sufficient" ["equal to"]).

99 See BDAG, *s.v.* ἐξουσία, 5b; Payne Smith, 2:4179.

100 BDAG, *s.v.* δύναμις, 3; Payne Smith, 1:1258.

101 BDAG, *s.v.* δύναμις, 3.

102 See commentary on that passage for a discussion of the text-critical and text-historical problems it presents.

103 This "seal" was "stronger" (ܡܝܬܪ [*myattar*]) than those for whom "it was not lawful" to break it (23:9a). The adjective ܫܠܝܛܐ (*šallīṭā*), derived from the root *šlṭ*, corresponds here idiomatically to ἐξῆν (Payne Smith, 2:4181).

the Lord's "power" (29:9b; see below).[104] The "power of the Lord" is associated with raging rivers (39:1a; see below on the *hapax legomenon* ܥܫܝܢܐ), an image whose difficulty is not merely syntactic, since the mention of the "name of the Most High" (39:8a) raises the question who this "Lord" actually is.

Despite the existence of the Coptic text, it is not possible to determine whether the *hapax legomenon* ܚܝܠܬܢܐ (*ḥayltānā*) in 25:10a corresponds to δυνατός or ἰσχυρός.[105] Of importance is that the speaker represents himself as being "strong" or "powerful" by or in God's "truth." There is a similar problem connected with the passive participle of the Pa. ܚܝܠ (*ḥayyel*), which occurs only in 16:4a ("I am strengthened in his hymns"); it corresponds more probably to a passive form of ἐνδυναμόω[106] than to any form of ἐνισχύω.[107] Leaving aside for the moment the two occurrences of the uncommon term ܚܝܠܬܢܘܬܐ (*ḥayltānūtā*), the next term is the Ethpa. ܐܬܚܝܠ (*ʾetḥayyal*), which can represent the Greek verbs already mentioned and also the passive of κραταιόω.[108] The imperative of salvation in 9:5c runs, "be strong and be redeemed by his grace."[109] In *Ode* 10 the Redeemer is made to utter two parallel terms of metaphorical conflict, ܐܬܚܝܠܬ (*ʾetḥayylet*) and ܐܬܥܫܢܬ (*ʾetʿaššnet*): "I was made mighty and strengthened" (10:4a).[110]

This was the first of the three passages to use the Ethpa. of ܥܫܢ (*ʿšen*). The other two have also already been mentioned in discussing ܚܝܠܐ (see on δύναμις ὑψίστου above). The first speaks of "strengthening" the "members" (18:2a), and the other of the "strengthening" of the eternal and personified "truth" (32:3a). The only occurrence of ܥܫܝܢܐ (*ʿaššīnā*) has also been mentioned, where the connection of "raging rivers" with the "power of the Lord" (39:1a) still awaits closer study. The masculine ܥܘܫܢܐ (*ʿušnā*) in 29:8a may carry a negative connotation of δυναστεία.[111] In the positive connotations of the "power" of God's word (16:7) or his helping "strength" (25:6), the Greek original or equivalent is more probably ἰσχύς or δύναμις.

Turning to the abstract noun ܚܝܠܬܢܘܬܐ (*ḥayltānūtā*), which, to distinguish it from ܚܝܠܐ (*ḥaylā*), could be translated by the more recondite term "powerfulness," means a return to 29:8a. Already in 7:25a, it seems likely that 𝔊 used δύναμις (parallel to χάρις in 7:25b). The use of Ps 109:2a LXX (ῥάβδος δυνάμεως ["rod of power"]) in *Ode* 29 transforms this likelihood to a near certainty. Assuming that 𝔊 used three different terms of power (as 𝔖 does) in 29:8a-9b, it is possible to construct the following chart of possibilities and—in square brackets—of probabilities.

	𝔖	Possible equivalents	𝔊
8a	ܚܝܠܬܢܘܬܐ (*ḥayltānūtā*)	δύναμις, ἰσχύς, δυναστεία	δύναμις (from Ps 109:2a LXX)
8c	ܥܘܫܢܐ (*ʿušnā*)	δύναμις, ἰσχύς, δυναστεία*	[δυναστεία]
9b	ܚܝܠܐ (*ḥaylā*)	δύναμις, ἰσχύς	[ἰσχύς]

* The term μέγεθος is also possible (Payne Smith, 2:3004), but does not fit as well as the others.

Since there are really only two possibilities for 9b, and the first can be excluded because δύναμις was almost certainly used in 8a, ἰσχύς is the only likely word. This leaves δυναστεία for 8c, the negative connotation of which fits the sense of the clause and makes a contrast with the transcendent and luminous "power" of the Lord and Most High.

The two chiastic bicola 8b-c and 9a-b are both dependent on 8a; as martial utterances they threaten eschatological destruction but do not encourage wars between human beings in the name of God or Allah. The syntax of the verbs corresponds to a construction beginning with ἵνα + subjunctive and continuing with infinitives,[112] so there is no reason to correct the imperfect of the Shaph. of ܥܒܕ (*ʿbad*), used only in 8a, which is connected to the conjunction ܕ (*d-*), "because of the following infinitives."[113] If the sponsors for the verb and its object, in addition to Ps 109:6a LXX (κρινεῖ ἐν τοῖς

104 The key word "victory" is a reminder of another term of power, namely, the "right hand" of the Lord (cf. 18:7a, but also 8:6a; 14:4a; 22:7a; 25:2a, 9a; see also Excursus 27).
105 Payne Smith, 1:1262; Crum, 816; BDAG, *s.vv.* δυνατός, ἰσχυρός.
106 BDAG, *s.v.* ἐνδυναμόω, 2b.
107 BDAG, *s.v.* ἐνισχύω, 1; Payne Smith, 1:1260.
108 BDAG, *s.v.* κραταιόω; Payne Smith, 1:1260.
109 For other possible translations, see commentary on *Ode* 9:5c.
110 See commentary on *Ode* 10:4a.
111 Payne Smith, 2:3004; Lampe, *s.v.* δυναστεία: "tyranny, oppressive rule."
112 See BDF and BDR §§388–90.
113 Contra Diettrich, 104: ܠܡܫܥܒܕܘ (*la-mšaʿbādū*).

ἔθνεσιν, "He shall judge among the nations"),[114] were Ps 32:10b LXX (ἀθετεῖ δὲ λογισμοὺς λαῶν, "he brings to nought also the reasonings of the peoples")[115] or even—as in 1 Cor 15:15, 27—Ps 8:7b (πάντα ὑπέταξας ὑποκάτω τῶν ποδῶν αὐτοῦ, "thou hast put all things under his feet"),[116] then, instead of a form of καταδουλόω,[117] it would be preferable to use a form of ὑποτάσσω,[118] while the term "peoples" can stand for ἔθνη or λαοί.[119] Neither of these Greek terms, both of which may be translated by ܥܡܡܐ (*ʿammē*), carries any connotation of "Gentiles," whether here or in 10:5a.[120] What the "thoughts" of these generalized "adversaries" were is not explained (see Excursus 9).

The infinitive of the Pa. ܡܟܟ (*makkek*) connects 8c to 5a. In the first, the "enemies" were humbled (see Ps 109:1b LXX: τοὺς ἐχθρούς σου, "your enemies"), and here the eminent speaking "I" is to "hold down"[121] the tyrannical "power" of those who flaunt themselves *coram Dei et publico* as heroes or Titans.[122] Frankenberg does not offer a retroversion, but catches the sense of it with his ὕβριν τῶν δυνατῶν[123] (on δυναστεία as the possible original of ܥܘܫܢܐ [*ʿušnā*], see Excursus 29 above).

The mythological, apocalyptic terms "war" and "victory" in 9a-b are reminiscent of 9:6, 9, 12, of which Harnack remarked: "These are no earthly wars."[124] Although the infinitive of the Pe. ܥܒܕ (*ʿbad*) with the direct object ܩܪܒܐ (*qrābā*)[125] could correspond, in a transferred sense, to στρατεύεσθαι (cf. 1 Pet 2:11),[126] the *Vorlage* of 9a is more likely to have been ποιεῖν/ποιῆσαι πόλεμον.[127] The possible allusion to the wars in Revelation inverts matters so that the speaking "I" is found on God's side (cf. Rev 11:7; 12:17; 13:7; 19:19). The armament, however, is not swords and weapons but the ܡܠܬܐ (*melltā*) of the Lord and Most High, which on this earth is found only in human language (see Excursus 12). The parallelism between the term "word" and those denoting "power" in 8a and 9b (see Excursus 29 above) shows that the emphasis is on the dynamic and soteriological, not the noetic,[128] aspect of the word of God. And since it is quite uncertain whether 𝔖 had λόγος or ῥῆμα, it is also not clear "that the Word in our Ode is to have a capital letter: in the Syriac it is *Melletha*, and not in this case *Pethgama*; that is the word which finally takes its place in Syriac to express the Logos."[129]

The outcome of the exploits undertaken with the metaphorical rod of rulership (8a), derived from Psalm

114 Rahlfs, 2:124; Brenton, 767.

115 Rahlfs, 2:31; Brenton, 716. This Psalm is also used elsewhere in the *Odes of Solomon*. Its v. 10 as a whole demonstrates the interchangeability of ἔθνη and λαοί (both represented in the Peshitta by ܥܡܡܐ, *OTSy*, pt. 2 fasc. 3, p. 33). Although Harris and Mingana also remark on the identical Syriac wording ܡܚܫܒܬܐ ܕܥܡܡܐ (see 2:364), they say cautiously: "We cannot be quite sure about the dependence of the Ode on the Syriac Psalm from the coincidences, which appear to be natural" (2:365).

116 Rahlfs, 2:6; Brenton, 702.

117 Frankenberg, 27: καταδουλῶσαι; BDAG, *s.v.* καταδουλόω.

118 BDAG, *s.v.* ὑποτάσσω, 1a: "to subject"; cf. Heb 2:5, 8; Payne Smith, 2:2771.

119 See BDAG, *s.vv.* ἔθνος, λαός; Payne Smith, 2:2904.

120 Contra Charlesworth, 113. This removes the foundation for his remark: "This verse with its pejorative attitude towards the Gentiles is further evidence that the Odes are Palestinian and late first-century."

121 BDAG, *s.v.* ταπεινόω.

122 On the *hapax legomenon gabbārā*, a "forma vocis ܓܒܪܐ intensiva," see Payne Smith, 1:645.

123 Frankenberg, 27.

124 Harnack, 38.

125 The reference to this rare combination in Payne Smith, 2:3726, needs to be corrected, since 1 Pet 2:11 does not have the plural ܩܪ̈ܒܐ but the singular ܩܪܒܐ (*NTSy* on this passage).

126 BDAG, *s.v.* στρατεύω, 2.

127 BDAG, *s.v.* πόλεμος, 1a.

128 Contra Diettrich, 105: "mental combat."

129 Harris and Mingana, 2:365. Their reference to the amplification "*by His Word*" in the Targum on Ps 110:1a ("the Lord said by his word . . .") gives no reason to reject the idea that Psalm 109 LXX was used in this Ode, but is "very interesting and important" for the doctrine of the Logos: "In the Targum the Word is represented by *Memra*; this is the first instance we have found of the appearance of the *Memra* in the history of the doctrine of the Logos."

109 LXX, is to be "victory" (9b). The expression ܙܟܘܬܐ ܠܡܣܒ (object *zākūṯā* + "sign of the infin[itive]"[130] + infinitive of ܢܣܒ [*nsaḇ*]) could correspond, as in 4 Macc 2:18, to ἀριστεῦσαι in a moral sense.[131] But it is more likely—not only because of the chiastically parallel structure of 9a-b—that 𝔊 had νῖκος/νίκην λαμβάνειν/λαβεῖν[132] (cf. 9:12; 18:7). The "power" (in 𝔊 probably ἰσχύς)[133] of the Lord and Most High, which is parallel to "word," again shows that finally the victory is God's, as the subsequent verses attest.

■ **10** The singular verb form ܗܘܐ (*hwā*) in 10b, whose subject must be the "enemy" in 10a, shows that the reading ܒܥܠܕܒ̈ܒܐ (*bʿeldḇāḇē*) in H is impossible.[134] It was probably only a premature attempt at agreement with the plural "my enemies" in 5a, which is also at the end of a line in H (p. 22b, line 7).[135] In spite of the use of the term ἐχθρός/ܒܥܠܕܒܒܐ (*bʿeldḇāḇā*)—borrowed from the LXX and especially from the Psalms—10a is not "a doublet of v. 5a."[136] That contradiction depends not on a "feeling for Semitic languages,"[137] but on the change of subject from the "I" to the "Lord" and the repetition of the instrumental "by his word" (see on 9a above). The Aph. of ܪܡܐ (*rmā*) does not mean "put to death" (1 Macc 3:11: ἀπέκτεινεν) but—in human terms of conflict—"to throw (down)" in the sense of "topple, overthrow."[138] The austere text, with its connections to "war" and images such as "Death" and "Sheol" (see on 4a-b above), lends itself to embellishment from the last book of the Bible (for suggestions, cf. the context of Rev 12:9, 13; 20:3, 14).

The defeated "enemy" of the speaker is described in 10b with an image familiar from the accounts of the ἀσεβεῖς ("ungodly") in the LXX (cf. Ps 1:4; 17:43 LXX; 34:5 LXX; Job 21:18; 27:20; Wis 5:14; Isa 29:5). At the same time, the comparison of the enemy with the ܥܘܪܐ (*ʿūrā*), which forms a semantic parallel with 18:11a,[139] is not a direct quotation of Ps 1:4b; Wis 5:14; or Job 21:18b, as can be seen from the following table.[140]

Table 7: The Ancestry of *Ode* 29:10b

Ps 1:4	ὡς χνοῦς, ὃν ἐκριπτεῖ ὁ ἄνεμος	ܐܝܟ ܥܘܪܐ ܕܕܪܝܐ ܪܘܚܐ
Job 21:18	ὥσπερ κονιορτός, ὃν ὑφείλατο λαῖλαψ	ܐܝܟ ܥܘܪܐ ܕܫܩܠܐ ܠܗ ܥܘܥܝܬܐ
Wis 5:14	ὡς φερόμενος χνοῦς, ὑπὸ ἀνέμου	ܐܝܟ ܚܠܐ ܕܫܩܠܐ ܪܘܚܐ
	καὶ ὡς πάχνη ὑπὸ λαίλαπος	ܘܐܝܟ ܥܘܪܐ ܕܫܩܠܐ ܥܠܥܠܐ
Is 29:5	ὡς χνοῦς φερόμενος	ܐܝܟ ܥܘܪܐ ܕܥܒܪ
Ode 29:10b		ܐܝܟ ܥܘܪܐ ܕܫܩܠܐ ܠܗ ܪܘܚܐ

130 Payne Smith, *Dictionary*, 233.

131 Brockelmann, *Lexicon*, 432; Rahlfs, 1:1160; Hans-Josef Klauck, *4. Makkabäerbuch* (JSHRZ 3.6; Gütersloh: Mohn, 1989) 699: "to gain victory over the passions."

132 BDAG, *s.vv.* νίκη, νῖκος; Payne Smith, 1:1160.

133 See the end of Excursus 29. Grammatically "his power" could refer to "word" in 9a and 10a only if ܡܠܬܐ were used as a masculine to stand for "the Logos" (Payne Smith, *Dictionary*, 275). In 𝔊, αὐτοῦ could refer to either λόγος or ῥῆμα (see BDAG, *s.v.* ἰσχύς: "τοῦ λόγου ἰ[σχύς] Orig[en], C[ontra] Cels[um] 1, 62, 71"). But the parallel structure of 9a-b strongly suggests that both the "word" and the "power" belong to God.

134 Franzmann, 219.

135 Charlesworth, *Manuscripts*, 71.

136 Contra Harnack, 62.

137 Diettrich, p. 105, with a misleading reference to Wis 18:15.

138 Harris and Mingana, 2:363 ("overthrew"); cf. Payne Smith, 2:3924–26; BDAG, *s.v.* βάλλω, 1; Frankenberg, 28: ἔβαλε.

139 Franzmann, 221.

140 Because of the correspondence between ܥܘܪܐ (*ʿūrā*) and χνοῦς, Isa 29:5 has been added. This passage also clearly influenced Frankenberg's retroversion (see above). The Greek quotations are taken from Rahlfs, 2:1, 306, 351, 602, and the Syriac ones from *OTSy*, pt. 2 fasc. 3, p. 1; pt. 2 fasc. 1a, p. 27; pt. 2 fasc. 5, p. 8; pt. 3 fasc. 1, p. 48.

Since λαῖλαψ cannot be translated by ܪܘܚܐ (*rūḥā*),[141] the final word in 10b cannot be referred to Job 21:18 (and probably not to γνόφος in Job 27:20 either), but derives either from Wis 5:14[142] or Ps 1:4.[143] That means that χνοῦς is to be preferred to κονιορτός as the probable original of ܥܘܪܐ (*ʿūrā*). The correspondence of ܐܟ ܥܘܪܐ ܕܫܩܠܐ ܠܗ (*ʾak ʿūrā d-šāqlā leh*) with the Syriac translation of Job 21:18b does not necessarily lead to the conclusion that the Greek of the Ode used the middle voice of ὑφαιρέω (cf. Job 27:20). It is important to inquire what verb took the place of ἐκρίπτω in Ps 1:4. Influenced by Wis 5:14, it might have been an active form of φέρω, perhaps ἤνεγκε.[144] More probably it was a form of αἴρω or λαμβάνω[145] with the relative pronoun ὅν as its object. In ܣ this pronoun is represented by ܕ (*d-*), and the object is emphasized by ܠܗ (*l-* + third masculine singular suffix).[146] If 𝔊 actually had ὃν ἔλαβε, then the ἔβαλε in 10a would constitute a play on words. Anti-Jewish polemic is not visible in this image, which is not interpreted further.[147]

■ **11** In the doxological "self-description" of 11a,[148] which might also be called an "indirect doxology,"[149] the "Most High," who is equated with the "Lord," makes an entrance in the poem, as he does at the end of *Ode* 28 (see Excursus 17). In contrast to 28:19b, and despite the causal action of the "Most High," it is his "slave" or "servant" who is placed in the spotlight. He is not Paul, the δοῦλος Χριστοῦ. The third person construction of 11b-c could, however, suggest the messianic παῖς (cf. Matt 12:18) and, by the ending of *Ode* 29, biblically identify the Messiah in 6a-b. But the changes from first to third person in Psalm 86 (85 LXX) demonstrate that there is nothing unusual in the masculine speaker's description of himself as the doubled object of "made great." This would only partly solve the problem raised in the introduction. The identity of the believer[150] in this Ode does not become clear even in 11b-c.

This speaking "I" for the third time uses the common verb "to give" (see 2b and 8a above), this time in connection with δόξα/ܬܫܒܘܚܬܐ (*tešbuḥtā*). As in 6:7a, where the "giving" of praise is reciprocal, and in 10:4b and 21:9b, this ambiguous term here means "praise" and not, as in 2a, "glory" (see Excursus 21).[151]

The cause of the praise is that the Most High has "made great" the praising "I."[152] The use of biblical quotations as the object of the Aph. of ܪܒ/ܐܪܒ (*ʾireḇ*), from a root related to ܪܒܐ and ܪܒ and corresponding to μεγαλύνω,[153] does not admit of a construction with a first singular objective suffix.[154] But the "I" is speaking of itself and not metaphorically of the elect and redeemed people of God (cf. Wis 19:22a: ἐμεγάλυνας τὸν λαόν σου καὶ ἐδόξασας, "you have exalted and glorified your people"). If this self-description in 11b-c is traced back only to Wis 9:5 (ἐγὼ δοῦλος σὸς

141 See BDAG, *s.v.* λαῖλαψ; Payne Smith, 1:1695–96, *s.v.* ܟܘܟܝܬܐ (*kōkīṯā*); 2:2880, *s.v.* ܥܠܥܠܐ (*ʿalʿālā*); 2:3851, *s.v.* ܪܘܚܐ (*rūḥā*).

142 Frankenberg, 28: ἐγένετο ὡς χνοῦς φερόμενος ὑπὸ ἀνέμου.

143 See Diettrich, 105.

144 Payne Smith, 2:4284; LSJ, *s.v.* φέρω.

145 Klein, *Wörterbuch*, 102; BDAG, *s.vv.* αἴρω, λαμβάνω; Payne Smith, 2:4283–85.

146 I am grateful to Sebastian Brock for the information that ܠܗ (*leh*) is to be taken as the object of the active feminine participle of the Pe. ܫܩܠ (*šqal*) (letter of November 26, 2001). It follows that ܥܘܪܐ (*ʿūrā*) is one of the relatively common nouns that can be of either gender. Since it cannot here be feminine (Payne Smith, 2:2841; Payne Smith, *Dictionary*, 407), it is treated as a masculine (see the [incomplete] list in Nöldeke §87). Whether the designation "f." should be used at all in Payne Smith may be worth investigating.

147 *Barn.* 11:6-7 is a "quotation of Ps 1:3-5" (Prostmeier, 422) in which 11:7 (= Ps 1:4-5) displays "a pinnacle of anti-Jewish polemic" (ibid., 424). But even there "the author does not explicate the images" (ibid.).

148 See Lattke, *Oden*, 67, 83, 88.

149 Franzmann, 221.

150 This characterization of the speaking "I" is nearer the mark, especially in view of 29:6, than Stenger's in his generally accurate description: "The speaker of this 1st person *Ode* is a pious person, not the Redeemer" (see Stenger, *Christushymnus*, 156).

151 How ambiguous this term is can be seen by comparing the doxologies in 16:20 ("Glory and honor to his name") and in 18:16 ("Glory and majesty to his name"). The doxology in 17:16 ("Glory to thee, our Head, Lord Messiah") refers to the redeemed Redeemer, not to the Most High.

152 Bauer, 611.

153 Payne Smith, 1:1628–29; BDAG, *s.v.* μεγαλύνω, 2.

154 See the note on the translation of 11b above.

καὶ υἱὸς τῆς παιδίσκης σου, "I thy servant and son of thine handmaid"),[155] the quotation from the prayer of Solomon provides another good reason why these originally anonymous *Odes* were early but erroneously attributed to Solomon.[156] But things are not quite that simple, for Psalm 85 LXX has already been recognized as an influence (see on 4a and 7b above). In that psalm it is *David* who describes himself as *δοῦλος* ("servant" [Ps 85:4a LXX]) and turns to God with the words: *κύριε ὁ θεός μου, . . . , δὸς τὸ κράτος σου τῷ παιδί σου καὶ σῶσον τὸν υἱὸν τῆς παιδίσκης σου* ("Lord my God, . . . , give thy strength to thy servant, and save the son of thine handmaid" [Ps 85:12a, 16b-c LXX]).[157] The switch from *δοῦλος* to *παῖς* raises the question which of these words was translated by ܥܒܕܐ (*ʿabḏā*) from the Greek of 11b.[158] Adding Ps 115:7b LXX (*ἐγὼ δοῦλος σὸς καὶ υἱὸς τῆς παιδίσκης σου*, "I am thy servant, and the son of thine handmaid")[159] makes it unnecessary to consider either David or Solomon in the context of this hymn of thanksgiving of one who has been redeemed.[160] Persons without biblical knowledge in ancient times would still be well acquainted with the concepts *δοῦλος (τοῦ) θεοῦ* or *θεῶν παῖδες*.[161]

That the *hapax legomenon* ܐܡܬܐ (*ʾamṯā*), "handmaid," in 11c does not represent *δούλη*, with its possible reference to Mary (cf. Luke 1:38, 48), but *παιδίσκη*,[162] is clear from the scripture passages discussed above. The term "son," which plays such a role in the *Odes of Solomon*,[163] is not here stressed. Since women can also be described as "God's female slaves,"[164] they have an equal claim to the space and benefits of total freedom. This argumentation is found neither in Gunkel[165] nor in Kraus.[166] As for Hans Hübner, one may say, as he himself does of the grasp of "the human being without God": "his 'grasp' is too limited."[167] "God's servant/slave," whether male or female, is not under any-thing or any-body and is "negatively" defined as a free person, and that—with or without Isaiah 53—altogether "in the soteriological sense" of liberation.[168]

155 Rahlfs, 2:357; Brenton, 63, in Appendix, whose translation differs from the NRSV ("serving girl" [*sic*]); see Georgi, 434.

156 See Pierre, 25–37.

157 Rahlfs, 2:94; Brenton, 750.

158 Payne Smith, 2:2772; BDAG, *s.vv.* *δοῦλος*, *παῖς*; cf. *OTSy*, pt. 2 fasc. 3, p. 101.

159 Rahlfs, 2:129; Brenton, 769.

160 Hebrew Psalm 116 is equivalent to Psalms 114–15 LXX.

161 BDAG, *s.vv.* *δοῦλος*, 2bβ; *παῖς*, 3bα. Codex N has a mark of division after 11b. My earlier translation, "for he made him great, his servant . . ." (Lattke, *Oden*, 182; cf. idem, *Bedeutung*, 1:161), is perhaps too literal but has the merit of bringing out that "the determination" by ܠ "is more emphatic when the Object Suffix . . . is added to the verb" (Nöldeke §288).

162 Should be added to Payne Smith, 1:248.

163 Abramowski, 52–62.

164 BDAG, *s.v.* *παιδίσκη*.

165 Hermann Gunkel, *Die Psalmen* (4th ed.; Göttingen: Vandenhoeck & Ruprecht, 1926 = 5th ed., 1968) 502.

166 Kraus, *Psalmen*, 599 ("relationship of obedience and dependence"), 797 ("the terminology of law"). Neither in Ps 86:16 (85:16 LXX) nor in Ps 116:16 (115:7 LXX) nor in *Ode* 29:11 is the phrase "the son of the handmaid" (ibid., 797), it is always, significantly, "the son of *thy/his* handmaid." So it is extremely questionable whether "the Psalmist"—or the speaking "I" of the *Ode*—used this "appellation" "to describe himself as the least of the slaves and servants" (ibid.). In fact, the analogy is given a dialectical twist in all three cases.

Nor is the anthropological key word "freedom" to be found in Hans-Joachim Kraus, *Theologie der Psalmen* (BKAT 15.3; Neukirchen-Vluyn: Neukirchener Verlag, 1979) 270, index. The freedom of Yahweh is connected to the idea of liberation: "The rule of Yahweh in Israel is the *Rule of the Liberator.* What the Bible says about God confirms that the God of Israel is the power of liberation" (ibid., 62). But §6, "Mankind before God" (ibid., 171–222), has nothing to say about total freedom responding dialectically to faith.

167 Hans Hübner, *Die Weisheit Salomons–Liber Sapientiae Salomonis* (ATDA 4; Göttingen: Vandenhoeck & Ruprecht, 1999) 125.

168 Hübner, 124.

30

Ode 30: The Living Spring of the Lord

(I) 1a Draw water for yourselves from the living spring of the Lord,
1b because it has been opened for you.
2a And come, all you thirsty, and take the drink
2b and rest beside the spring of the Lord,
3 because it is beautiful and clear/pure and gives rest to the soul.
(II) 4a For much more pleasant than honey is its water,
4b and the honeycomb of bees is not to be compared with it,
5a because it issues from the lips of the Lord,
5b and from the heart of the Lord [is] its name.
6a And it came unbounded and unseen,
6b and until it was placed in their midst they did not know it.
(III) 7 Blessed are those who drank from it and found rest by it.
Hallelujah.

Introduction

Ode 30 is preserved in two Syriac manuscripts.[1] Schille's labelling of *Ode* 30 as a "reveille" and a "song on the theme of Rev 22:17"[2] is as questionable as his reference to only two Mandaean texts, one from the baptismal ritual of the *Qolastā* and one from the first book of the "*Oxforder Sammlung* [Oxford Collection]."[3] The influence of Isa 55:1 (Οἱ διψῶντες, πορεύεσθε ἐφ᾽ ὕδωρ, "Ye that thirst, go to the water"),[4] which can be felt in Rev 22:17 and John 7:37 (cf. John 4:14 and Rev 21:6), does *not* transform the "spring of the Lord" into a "baptismal stream" nor the whole Ode into "an Invitatory to Baptism."[5]

In 1QH xvi (formerly viii).4-24, it is the "community that is portrayed as God's marvellous *plantation*"[6] (emphasis added), although the terms "watercourse," "living waters," and "wellspring of life" occur,[7] and the comparison quoted in *Barn.* 11:2 between κύριος ("the Lord") and πηγὴ ὕδατος ζωῆς ("fountain of water of life" [Jer 2:13; cf. Jer 17:13])[8] is not relevant here either, because *Ode* 30 speaks of the "spring *of* the Lord" (1a, 2b; cf. 5a-b).[9]

This raises the question whether the "Lord" is the Christian-Jewish God or the Kyrios Christos (in the early Christian or the Gnostic-Christian sense). If the latter were true, it would not be possible to follow Harnack[10] in accepting that "our Ode need not be a Christian one."[11] And in that case the *speaker* of this Christian ode could not be the redeeming Messiah. But if—as is more

1 Mss.: Codex H, 23a–b; Codex N, 150r (s). Ed./trans.: Charlesworth, 113–15; Franzmann, 222–24; Lattke, 3:21–32.
2 Schille, 97.
3 Lidzbarski, *Liturgien*, 26–27, 178.
4 Rahlfs, 2:640; Brenton, 890.
5 Bernard, 114.
6 Lohse, *Texte*, 289.
7 Maier, *Qumran-Essener*, 1:89–91; Vermes, 187. Charlesworth (p. 114) also refers to 1QH viii.14 as a parallel to 1a.
8 Rahlfs, 2:658; Brenton, 903; cf. Lake, 1:379 ("spring of life"), with Ehrman, 2:53 ("fountain of life").
9 Diettrich (p. 106) can support the reference to Jer 2:13 and 17:13 only by "taking the genitive 'of the Lord' as a *genitivus appositionis*." Justin in his *Dialogue* somewhat alters the wording of Jer 2:13 to speak of τὸ μὴ δύνασθαι ἀπὸ τῆς τοῦ θεοῦ ζώσης πηγῆς πιεῖν (140.1; Marcovich, *Dialogus*, 310–11; Goodspeed, 262): "you cannot drink of the living fountain of God" (ANF 1:269).
10 Harnack, 63.
11 Diettrich, 106.

likely—this metaphorical spring is God's, the term could still, in a Christian interpretation, stand for the Messiah. The speaker, the audience (1-2), and those receiving the benediction (7) as well as users and readers of this Ode would perceive an allusion to the Johannine Jesus, who never, in his ἐγώ εἰμι discourses,[12] identifies himself as πηγή, but does reveal himself as the *Messias* (John 4:25-26) and also as the giver of ὕδωρ ζῶν ("living water" [John 4:10-11]). "The living water that Jesus gives is a gift that transmits the ζωὴ αἰώνιος ['eternal life']. It becomes a πηγὴ ὕδατος ἁλλομένου εἰς ζωὴν αἰώνιον ['a spring of water welling up to eternal life'] (4:14b)."[13] It is a short step from Jesus' "spring" of "living water" to the complete identification of the revealer and redeemer (John 4:42) with the "living spring of the Lord" (*Ode* 30:1a). Anyone who finds this too speculative can begin instead with Ps 35:10 LXX (παρὰ σοὶ πηγὴ ζωῆς, "with thee is the fountain of life")[14] and move outward to "the related concepts in the Old Testament,"[15] with special reference to Isa 55:1, and including other verses in the Psalms and the Wisdom books, for "What we are certain of is the use by the Odist of the Sapiential books."[16]

Interpretation

■ **1-3** Turning once more to the introduction to this Ode, it must be considered at least possible that already in early Christianity the "spring" of God "the Lord" was understood as a metaphor for the divine son.[17] Bauer seems to have made this interpretation himself, comparing this "spring of life" with the "Redeemer who gives the water of life" (on John 7:38b),[18] although he contradicts it in his introduction and translation of *Ode* 30.[19] In the context of the *Odes* as a whole, however, and especially in view of 11:6-8a and considering the link between Matt 11:38 and *Ode* 30:2-3, it is advisable to avoid the christological interpretation and accept the whole Ode as proceeding from the mouth of the Redeemer.[20] For the exegesis, it is of only secondary importance whether Christ or some other person having authority over the assembly is thought of as the speaker.

It is likely that the *Odes of Solomon* were also used liturgically,[21] but the structure of 1a with "plural imperative and pronoun" is hardly "evidence of use in public worship."[22] More relevant is Pierre's remark that *Ode* 30, after so much negative imagery in the preceding Odes, is a moment of paradisal rest,[23] which means, in the first place, that the metaphorical water of the "spring of life" is to be taken as an image of "divine salvation."[24] The Pe. ܡܠܐ (*mlā*), "draw," used in this sense only here, in the first of the three imperative calls to salvation, corresponds not to πληρόω[25] but to the verb ἀντλέω[26] used with ὕδωρ ("water") as its object. Whether 𝔊 actually had the reflexive ὑμῖν[27] is hard to determine, since ܠܟܘܢ (*lḵōn*) is an idiomatic usage.[28] An influence from John 4:7 and 4:15 cannot be excluded, but the invitation of 1a sounds more like a paradisal realization of the promise of Isa 12:3 (καὶ ἀντλήσετε ὕδωρ . . . ἐκ τῶν πηγῶν τοῦ σωτηρίου, "Draw ye therefore water . . . out of the wells of salvation").[29] In *Ode* 11:6b 𝔊 the "water" comes ἀπὸ πηγῆς ζωῆς κυρίου ("from the spring of life of the Lord"), while here the "spring" is modified by the

12 Schweizer, *Ego eimi*.
13 Herbert Leroy, *Rätsel und Missverständnis: Ein Beitrag zur Formgeschichte des Johannesevangeliums* (BBB 30; Bonn: Hanstein, 1968) 96.
14 Rahlfs, 2:35; Brenton, 718.
15 Diettrich, 106.
16 Harris and Mingana, 2:369.
17 See Lampe, 1080.
18 Walter Bauer, *Das Johannesevangelium* (HNT 6; Tübingen: Mohr Siebeck, 1933), 114.
19 Bauer, 611.
20 For Wetter (*Sohn Gottes,* 56), Matt 11:25-30 and *Ode* 30:1-3 are among the "expressions, becoming more stereotypical over time, that are placed into the mouths of such saviors."
21 See Lattke, *Bedeutung,* 1:59, on the "Hallelujah" in the manuscripts.
22 Contra Charlesworth, 114.
23 Pierre, 151: "une sorte de pause édénique."
24 Greßmann, 463. Frankenberg (p. 92) considers this water the personified "word of God," while Diettrich (p. 106) understands it as the "greatest benefit in Wisdom Literature," that is, the "Wisdom" described as "Knowledge" or "Truth."
25 Payne Smith, 2:2117–18.
26 BDAG, *s.v.* ἀντλέω, 1.
27 Frankenberg, 28.
28 Nöldeke §223. Harris and Mingana's note on the "language of this verse" (2:366), which Bauer (p. 611) seems to accept, is not at all clear. The allegedly Aramaizing addition ܠܟܘܢ (*lḵōn*) is not to be found in the Peshitta of Isa 12:3 (see *OTSy*, pt. 3 fasc. 1, p. 22).
29 Rahlfs, 2:582; Brenton, 847. The short hymn of

adjective ܚܝܐ (*ḥayyā*).[30] This ζῶσα πηγή ("living spring") "is a spring, whose water bestows immortality" (cf. John 4:14),[31] which, therefore, cannot exist in this world. This image surpasses even the prayer to God the Lord of Ps 35:10a LXX: παρὰ σοὶ πηγὴ ζωῆς ("with thee is the fountain of life").[32]

The causal clause 1b, indicatively explaining 1a, alludes, by use of the Ethpe. ܐܬܦܬܚ (*ʾetptaḥ*), to the Pe. ܦܬܚ (*ptaḥ*) of 4:10b, "open thy abundant springs" (see Excursus 30 below). It is not possible to know whether 𝔊 used a theological passive of ἀνοίγω[33] or διανοίγω.[34] Just as it is possible to "open a jar of wine or oil" or "a book in scroll form,"[35] springs may also be opened and made accessible.

Although the twofold "invitation" of 2a is similar to the call to salvation of Isa 55:1a,[36] it seems to have escaped notice that the imperative of ܐܬܐ (*ʾetā*)[37] can hardly correspond to πορεύεσθε.[38] Since an imperative of ἔρχομαι is not the sole possibility (cf. John 7:37; Rev 22:17), (supplementary) influence from Matt 11:28 on 2-3 cannot be excluded: Δεῦτε πρός με πάντες . . . , κἀγὼ ἀναπαύσω ὑμᾶς ("Come to me, all . . . , and I will give you rest"; cf. Matt 25:34).[39] The emphatic plural of the participial adjective ܨܗܐ (*ṣhē*), however, comes not from Matt 5:6 but from Isa 55:1 (οἱ διψῶντες, "Ye that thirst")[40] and serves as a reminder of 6:11a.[41] How selectively the *Odes of Solomon* use biblical quotations is shown by the remainder of 2a. This invitation to "take"—or perhaps "receive"—the "drink" of metaphorical water from the spring conflates John 7:37 (πινέτω) and Rev 22:17 (λαβέτω) and may even take a polemical position against the "stumbling block" of the "doctrine of the Eucharist" in the editorial paragraph John 6:51b-58 (cf. esp. John 6:55b: τὸ αἷμά μου ἀληθής/ἀληθῶς ἐστιν πόσις, "my blood is drink indeed").[42] The Pe. ܢܣܒ (*nsab*) occurs in other soteriological contexts also (see 11:4; 31:7b; Excursus 41).

Diettrich's translation of the imperative of the Ethpe. ܐܬܬܢܝܚܘ (*ʾettnīḥ*) as "refresh yourselves"[43] is poetically appealing, but masks to some extent the Gnosticizing aspect of 2b (see Excursus 3).[44] In the usage of the *Odes of Solomon,* this verb, derived from ܢܘܚ, ܢܚ (*nāḥ*) and corresponding to (ἐπ)αναπαύομαι or καταπαύομαι or an intransitive καταπαύω,[45] underlines the paradisal character of the image, which bears a certain resemblance, accented by the use of the word "honey" in 4a,

thanksgiving, Isaiah 12 LXX, could easily have been the source of other terms in *Ode* 30: κύριος (Isa 12:1, 2 [twice], 4, 5), ὄνομα αὐτοῦ or ὄνομα κυρίου (Isa 12:4, 5), and ἐν μέσῳ (Isa 12:6), see on 5-6 below.

30 However, the "speaking water" (11:6a) of *Ode* 11 is also called "living" (11:7 𝔖) and "immortal" (11:7 𝔊). For a possible connection to *Gos. Thom.* log. 13.5, see Peter Nagel, "Die Neuübersetzung des Thomasevangeliums in der *Synopsis quattuor Evangeliorum* und in *Nag Hammadi Deutsch* Bd. 1," *ZNW* 95 (2004) 225.

31 BDAG, *s.v.* πηγή, 2.

32 Rahlfs, 2:35; Brenton, 718.

33 Frankenberg, 28: ἀνεῴχθη.

34 Payne Smith, 2:3338; BDAG, *s.vv.* ἀνοίγω, 3; διανοίγω, 1b; Klein, *Wörterbuch*, 86.

35 BDAG, *s.v.* ἀνοίγω, 3.

36 Bauer, 611; Lattke, *Oden*, 184.

37 A similar soteriological use of "come" is found in 20:7b: "come into his Paradise" (cf. the term "rest" in 20:8b).

38 This imperative cannot be derived from the Peshitta of Isa 55:1, since that uses the imperative of ܐܙܠ (*ʾezal*) (*OTSy*, pt. 3 fasc. 1, 99). The retroversion προσέρχεσθε (Frankenberg, 28) is somewhat free, but does take into account that ἔρχομαι normally corresponds to ܐܬܐ. It is most unlikely that ἐκπορεύομαι (Klein, *Wörterbuch*, 32) could have been the *Vorlage* for this ܐܬܐ, although it is used in the Sinaitic and Curetonian Syriac translations of Matt 3:5.

39 BDAG, *s.v.* δεῦτε: "come to me."

40 Rahlfs, 2:640; Brenton, 890.

41 Cf. 6:12: "drink from the Most High"; on 6:13a, "blessed," see 7 below.

42 Ernst Haenchen, *John 1: A Commentary on the Gospel of John, Chapters 1–9* (trans. Robert W. Funk; ed. Robert W. Funk and Ulrich Busse; Hermeneia; Philadelphia: Fortress Press, 1984) 294–303; ET of *Das Johannesevangelium: Ein Kommentar aus den nachgelassenen Manuskripten* (ed. by Ulrich Busse with a *Vorwort* by James M. Robinson; Tübingen: Mohr Siebeck, 1980) 326–36. That there is any influence from 1 Cor 10:4 is unlikely, even though πόμα and πόσις can be translated by the one Syriac term ܡܫܬܝܐ (*maštyā*); see Payne Smith, 2:4351; BDAG, *s.vv.* πόμα, πόσις.

43 Diettrich, 106.

44 The preposition ܥܠ (*ʿal*) represents ἐπί (Payne Smith, 2:2886; BDAG, *s.v.* ἐπί; Bauer, 611: "an"). Bauer remarks on his translation: "The preposition (*ʿal*) in Syriac does not refer to proximity in space, but should be taken to mean 'rest upon.'"

45 Payne Smith, 2:2311–12; BDAG, *s.vv.* ἀναπαύω, ἐπαναπαύω, καταπαύω.

to Fragment 19F (i.e., recto) of UBE (the "Unknown Berlin Gospel"): "[ ] it (fem.) gives milk; another one (fem.) gives honey. [As for you (pl.)], rest yourselves [by] the <spring> (π‹η›γή) of [the water] of life" (lines 2–6).[46]

Both Syriac manuscripts treat 3, the indicative clause giving the reason for 2, as a monocolon.[47] The "spring of the Lord" receives the predicate ܫܦܝܪ (*šappīr*) meaning "beautiful" in the sense of "useful" (cf. 7:2; 11:20).[48] Perhaps the translation of this term might even be "potable." The second adjective, ܢܩܕ (*nqeḏ*), is a *hapax legomenon* and also refers to the pure and clear water of the spring, without ritual flavor.[49] There is no reason to think that it corresponds to διαυγής.[50] Again, the participle of the Aph. ܐܢܝܚ (*ʾanīḥ*), "giving rest," with "soul"—or in fact "self"[51]—as its direct object, cannot represent καταθύμιος,[52] since this participle, which expresses a "continuing . . . Present,"[53] corresponds to a transitive form of ἀναπαύω or καταπαύω that, in 𝔊, would not necessarily have been a participle.[54] As in 6:15, the word ψυχή/ܢܦܫܐ (*napšā*) is not used for the immortal soul, so-called.[55] The anomalous singular accusative noun is used generically for the complete living and thirsting human being.[56]

■ **4-6** Franzmann divides the description of the spring, which is closely connected to 3, into two strophes (4, 5-6) and sees 4a-b as "the central focus of the Ode."[57] This is correct only insofar as the parallel bicolon 4, the second part of which Diettrich omits for no good reason,[58] is near to the exact center of the poem. In content, however, 3 and 5 are at least as important as 4.

There can be no doubt that the language of 4a-b was influenced by the following passages in the LXX, although their subject is not a spring but the word/law of God or a relationship to Wisdom personified (see Table 3):[59]

Ps 18:11b	*καὶ γλυκύτερα ὑπὲρ μέλι καὶ κηρίον.* "sweeter also than honey and the honeycomb."[60]

46 Charles W. Hedrick and Paul A. Mirecki, *Gospel of the Savior: A New Ancient Gospel* (California Classical Library; Santa Rosa, CA: Polebridge, 1999) 73, 19H (i.e., verso) [*sic*]; see also Hans-Martin Schenke, "Das sogenannte 'Unbekannte Berliner Evangelium' (UBE)," *ZAC* 2 (1998) 212. According to Schenke, the editors Hedrick and Mirecki confused the recto and verso of the manuscript. Schenke made his own translation of the "UBE" into German some years ago and distributed the draft among colleagues. His version of 19F is as follows: "[. . . one . . .] that gives milk; one that gives honey. As for you [. . .] find your rest beside the spring of living [water . . .]." I am grateful for Stephen Emmel's advice and help in this matter; see also Emmel's article "The Recently Published *Gospel of the Savior* ("Unbekanntes Berliner Evangelium"): Righting the Order of Pages and Events," *HTR* 95 (2002) 61. Nagel, who argues for a late date, does not mention 19F (i.e., recto); see Peter Nagel, "'Gespräche Jesu mit seinen Jüngern vor der Auferstehung': Zur Herkunft und Datierung des 'Unbekannten Berliner Evangeliums,'" *ZNW* 94 (2003) 248.

47 Bauer (p. 611) and Charlesworth (pp. 113–14) follow Harris and Mingana in dividing it into 3a-b (see Harris and Mingana, vol. 1, on this passage; 2:366). Franzmann counters this remarking: "However there seems to be a deliberate inclusio for 1-2 by the repetition of ܡܥܝܢܐ ܕܡܪܝܐ in 1a and 2b, in which case 3 would function as a summary monocolon for the stanza" (see Franzmann, 223).

48 BDAG, *s.v.* καλός, 2a; Frankenberg, 28: καλή ἐστιν.

49 Payne Smith, 2:2451; BDAG, *s.v.* καθαρός, 1.

50 This retroversion of Frankenberg's (p. 28) is the less convincing since he himself describes the water of the fountain of life as "pure" (p. 92).

51 Charlesworth, 114 and n. 4.

52 Contra Frankenberg, 28.

53 Nöldeke §269.

54 Payne Smith, 2:2312–13; BDAG, *s.vv.* ἀναπαύω, καταπαύω.

55 See Friedo Ricken, "Unsterblichkeit II," *HWP* 11 (2001) 277–80.

56 Diettrich (p. 106) again chooses the translation "refresh" for the verb, which is more suitable here than "refresh oneself" in 2b. It has not been possible to verify his reference to "Pslm. 35, 25 (Peš.)." A reference to Matt 11:29 (εὑρήσετε ἀνάπαυσιν ταῖς ψυχαῖς ὑμῶν) is more relevant.

57 Franzmann, 223–24.

58 Diettrich, 106–7.

59 Quotations from Rahlfs, 2:17, 136, 418.

60 Rahlfs, 2:17; Brenton, 708.

Ps 118:103b	ὑπὲρ μέλι καὶ κηρίον τῷ στόματί μου. "more so than honey and the honeycomb to my mouth!"[61]
Sir 24:20	τὸ γὰρ μνημόσυνόν μου ὑπὲρ τὸ μέλι γλυκύ, καὶ ἡ κληρονομία μου ὑπὲρ μέλιτος κηρίον. "For my memorial is sweeter than honey, and mine inheritance than the honeycomb."[62]

In comparison with these passages, neither 4a nor 4b lays undue weight on the proverbial sweetness of honey.[63] That is why, in place of γλυκύ(ς)/ܚܠܐ (*ḥlē*), the adjective ܒܣܝܡܐ (*bassīmā*) is used, which corresponds, in 𝔊, rather to a comparative form of χρηστός[64] than to the comparative or superlative of ἡδύς.[65] The *Vorlage* of the adverb ܣܓܝ (*saggī*), which qualifies the compound comparative adjective constructed with ܡܢ (*men*), could be πολλῷ ("dat[ive] of degree"), but might equally be the accusative πολύ.[66] This completes a possible reconstruction of the Greek of 4a as ὑπὲρ μέλι γὰρ πολλῷ/πολὺ χρηστότερον τὸ ὕδωρ αὐτῆς. The "water," of course, is the springwater of 1a, whose "pleasant" taste is emphasized by the comparison with honey. The double comparison of 40:1, where "honey" and the "honeycomb" occur together with the term "milk," forms a tenuous link to the traditional phrase "a land flowing with milk and honey."[67]

Excursus 30: "Honey" and "Milk" in the *Odes of Solomon*

Even today one may ask about "The Land Flowing with Milk and Honey": "So where's the milk? Where's the honey?"[68] Much more has been written with less humor about this proverbial "formulation."[69] *Ode* 4:10c is among the passages influenced by it, although there the reference is not to γῆ/ܐܪܥܐ (*ʾarʿā*) but to God's "abundant springs" (4:10b).[70] On the other hand, the paradisal term "earth/land" is not connected to "milk and honey" (11:12b, 16h, 18; 15:10).

The connection between "honey" and "milk" in the twofold comparison at the beginning of *Ode* 40 is much looser. The hope upon God (40:1c; cf. Ps 145:5b LXX) is somewhat strangely compared, on the one hand, to the "honey" dripping from the honeycomb (40:1a) and, on the other, to the "milk" flowing from the woman who loves her children (40:1b). Although N may have inserted participles alluding to the sweetness of the honey and the richness of the milk (40:3), the images of 40:1a-b are meant literally. The terms "honey," "honeycomb," "bee," used in describing the metaphorical spring in 30:4, will be discussed at the end of this excursus. All other passages use "milk" and also "to milk" and "breasts/bosom" metaphorically.

Quantitatively, *Ode* 19 occupies the central position with these transferred usages. The "cup of milk" drunk "in the sweetness of the Lord's kindness" is equated with the "Son" (19:1-2a). This "milk" was milked from the "Father" (19:2b), or, more exactly, from his full "breasts" (19:3a), and this was done by "the Spirit of holiness" (19:2a) who opened his "bosom" (19:4a) to milk him and "mixed the milk of

61 Rahlfs, 2:136; Brenton, 773 [corr.].

62 Rahlfs, 2:418; Brenton, 95, in Appendix.

63 Lutz Röhrich, *Lexikon der sprichwörtlichen Redensarten* (Herder Spektrum 4800; 5 vols.; Freiburg: Herder, 1994 [= 4th ed., 1991]; repr., 1999) 735–36.

64 Payne Smith, 1:551; Bauer and Aland, *s.v.* χρηστός, 1a: "angenehm [pleasant]"; BDAG, *s.v.* χρηστός, 2: "fine."

65 Frankenberg, 28: πολλῷ ἡδίω. But Frankenberg's retroversion can be supported to some degree by referring to Cant 2:14: ὅτι ἡ φωνή σου ἡδεῖα – ܡܛܠ ܕܩܠܟܝ ܒܣܝܡ (Rahlfs, 2:263; *OTSy*, pt. 2 fasc. 5, on this passage); cf. BDAG, s.v. ἡδύς: "pleasant."

66 BDAG, *s.v.* πολύ; cf. Payne Smith, 2:2520.

67 Röhrich, *Lexikon*, 1033, referring correctly to "Paradise or the Beyond." According to the concordance, the relevant passages are Exod 3:8, 17; 13:5; 33:3; Lev 20:24; Num 14:8; 16:13 [referring to Egypt], 14; Deut 6:3; 11:9; 26:9, 15; 27:3; 31:20; Jos 5:6; Jer 11:5; 32:22; Ezek 20:6, 15; Sir 46:8.

68 Jeremy Pascall, *God: The Ultimate Autobiography* (London: Ebury; North Ryde, NSW: Angus & Robertson, 1987) 112, 117.

69 Werner H. Schmidt, *Exodus*, vol. 1: *Exodus 1–6* (BKAT 2.1; Neukirchen-Vluyn: Neukirchener Verlag, 1988) 164–65.

70 Cant 4:11 ("honey and milk are under your tongue") and Sir 39:26 are also among the passages influenced by Exod 3:8, etc., though the second of them also lists necessities of life additional to ὕδωρ, γάλα, and μέλι (see Georg Sauer, *Jesus Sirach / Ben Sira* [ATDA 1; Göttingen: Vandenhoeck & Ruprecht, 2000] 274). Pierre also uses *Ode* 4:10 to introduce her much fuller discussion, "Du site liturgique paradisiaque à l'herméneutique des *Odes de Salomon*" (see Marie-Joseph Pierre, "Lait et miel,

the two breasts of the Father" (19:4b). This mixture, given to the world or the Aeon, is, however, intended only for receptive Gnostics (19:5).

In the simile of 14:1, "son" and "father" are used quite unmetaphorically and also untheologically, but the term "breasts" in 14:2 is an "image of fullness, fertility and a source of nourishment,"[71] and could therefore, in parallel with "my delight," be translated as "my sources of milk," even though the Ode does not actually deal either with milk or with springs.

The Revealer and Redeemer of *Ode* 8, who even presents himself, in relation to his "own ones," as their (co)-Creator, unlike the narrator of *Ode* 19:3-4, speaks of his "own breasts" (8:16b) from which, clearly, his "holy milk" flows (8:16c). In addition to their metaphorical character, both terms bear a soteriological meaning (cf. 8:16c: "to live by it").

The "milk," described as the "dew of the Lord" (35:5b) and given to the redeemed person by the "group of the Lord" (35:4a), belongs to the completely human image of the "child" and its "mother" (35:5a). The construction of that sentence with double accusative demands closer scrutiny.

Mention has already been made of the distant connection between 30:4a-b and 40:1a in the commentary on 30:4a. As in that comparison, "honey" and "honeycomb" are found in the same colon (see on 40:1 above); in *Ode* 30 "water" (4a) is to "spring" (4b) as "honey" (4a) is to "honeycomb of bees" (4b).

In parallelism with 4a, the living spring itself is compared in 4b to τὸ κηρίον/ܟܟܪܝܬܐ (*kakkārīṯā*).[72] The plural of μέλισσα/ܕܒܘܪܝܬܐ (*debbōrīṯā*), "bees," whose activity, with few exceptions (e.g., Democritus, Fragment 227)[73]—and, of course, excepting the negatives of its sting—was greatly admired "in the folklore, religion and mythology of antiquity,"[74] attracts as little attention here as it does in 40:1a.[75] The negated participle of the Ethpa. of ܦܚܡ (*pḥam*), which occurs only here, expresses the incomparability of the honeycomb and the spring,[76] which refers more to their abundance than their taste or their usefulness. Since the term ܠܗ (*leh* [*l-* + third masculine singular suffix]) corresponds to αὐτῇ (i.e., τῇ πηγῇ), so the *Vorlage* of the participle will have been either a passive form of συγκρίνω[77] or one of (παρα)-συμβάλλω.[78]

"Lips" and "heart" are often juxtaposed in the *Odes of Solomon* (see Excursuses 4 and 16). The exegesis of 5a may be furthered by a comparison with 11:6, where "speaking water" draws near to the "lips" of the redeemed speaker. In 5a the "living spring" (1a) issues from the χείλη/ܣܦܘܬܐ (*sep̄wāṯā*) of the Lord.[79] This statement bears a similarity to the self-praise of Wisdom personified in Sir 24:3a: Ἐγὼ ἀπὸ στόματος ὑψίστου ἐξῆλθον ("I came forth from the mouth of the Most High").[80] But that is not enough to make it "abundantly clear that the flowing stream of which the Ode speaks is the Knowledge of the Lord, as it has been equally recognized in Ode vi."[81]

The "heart of the Lord" in 5b, in a double metaphor, stands for his inner being.[82] But what is the meaning of the term ὄνομα/ܫܡܐ (*šmā*) in this clause, a term that Frankenberg described as "unintelligible"?[83] A simple solution would be to take the "name" of the spring—in the sense of "title," "category," or "reputation"[84]—as a given, referring to the description "spring of the Lord" (1a, 2b). The use of τὸ ὄνομα/ܫܡܐ might have been

ou la douceur du Verbe," *Apocrypha: Revue internationale des littératures apocryphes* 10 [1999] 168–76) and its partial reprint "Lait et miel dans les '*Odes de Salomon*'" (see Marie-Joseph Pierre, "L'eucharistie des «*Odes de Salomon*»," in *Nourriture et repas dans les milieux juifs et chrétiens de l'antiquité: Mélanges offerts au professeur Charles Perrot* (Lectio divina 178; Paris: Cerf, 1999) 246–54. That "milk and honey symbolize communion to the suavity of the Word of God" is perhaps not quite accurate (see Pierre, "Lait et miel," 139).

71 Lattke, *Oden*, 140.

72 BDAG, *s.v.* κηρίον: "wax, honey-comb"; Payne Smith, 1:1729–30.

73 *FVS* 2:190.

74 Gerhard Schrot, "Biene. Bienenzucht," *KP* 1 (1964) 899; cf. Röhrich, *Lexikon*, 191–92.

75 BDAG, *s.v.* μέλισσα; Payne Smith, 1:815; Brockelmann, *Lexicon*, 140, *s.v.* ܕܒܘܪܝܬܐ.

76 Payne Smith, 2:3082: *incomparabilis*.

77 BDAG, *s.v.* συγκρίνω, 2; Frankenberg, 28. Frankenberg's retroversion of "honeycomb of the bees" to the plural of ἐγκρίς (cf. LEH, *s.v.* ἐγκρίς: "a cake made with oil and honey") is too free.

78 LSJ and LEH, *s.vv.* παρασυμβάλλω, συμβάλλω.

79 Charlesworth emends the participle of ܢܦܩ, which H marks with a dot above (*nāp̄eq*), to *np̄aq* and reads "perfect" as in 6:8a (Charlesworth, 113–15). This is a consequence of his suggested solution for "its name" in 5b (see below).

80 Rahlfs, 2:417.

81 Contra Harris and Mingana, 2:368.

82 BDAG, *s.v.* καρδία, 2: "interior, center, heart."

83 Frankenberg, 42.

inspired by Isaiah 12 LXX (see on 1a above). Thus, the name of the transcendent "Lord" in its title would be sufficient to differentiate this metaphorical "spring" from others bearing different names (e.g., πηγὴ τοῦ Ἰακώβ in John 4:6).

If readers find this solution too simplistic, they have the choice between "a Syriac emendation," for example, ܫܦܥܗ (*šep̄ʿeh*),[85] and seeking the "error . . . in the Greek" (as does Frankenberg, who suggests τὸ νᾶμα αὐτοῦ for τὸ ὄνομα αὐτοῦ).[86] Even Harris and Mingana admit that "Frankenberg's emendation"—that is, "flow" or "stream" for "name"—is "an excellent case for the defenders of the hypothesis of a Greek original."[87] One might add that Cant 8:2 does not use γλυκασμός (Amos 9:13; Joel 3:18 [= 4:18 LXX]) but νᾶμα for עסיס. So it is possible that νᾶμα could occasionally have been translated as ܚܠܝܘܬܐ (*ḥalyūṯā*),[88] which would have brought in the sweetness of the honey after all.[89] But it is more likely that bilingual Greek-Syriac readers imagined the "flow of waters" (12:2a) when reading νᾶμα and would have used a term like ܪܕܝܐ (*reḏyā*) for the translation.[90]

Connolly makes two observations on the third bicolon of stanza II. First, he draws attention to the assonance of ἀόριστος καὶ ἀόρατος (or perhaps ἀορίστως καὶ ἀοράτως) in 6a "when the Syriac is translated into Greek."[91] And, second, he emphasizes several times that the peculiar expression[92] in 6b represents "an unsemitic idiom," εἰς τὸ μέσον τιθέναι or *in medio ponere*.[93] These two observations are again "cogent reasons for concluding not merely that the Syriac is a translation from Greek, but also that the Odes were composed in Greek."[94]

The use of the Pe. ܐܬܐ (*ʾeṯā*) in 6a makes a kind of reciprocal connection with the imperative "come" (see on 2a above). It is more likely that 𝔊 used ἦλθεν rather than ἔρχεται.[95] Considering the nonliteral usages of ἔρχομαι in the New Testament (cf., e.g., ἔ. εἰς φανερόν ["come to light"] in Mark 4:22 and Luke 8:17),[96] the idea of our spring coming should be no more problematic than the previous statements. The particle ܟܕ (*kaḏ*) "before the finite verb, and esp[ecially] before a participle or adjective, denotes present action or state."[97] As already mentioned, the negated participle of the Ethpe. of ܣܘܟ, ܣܟ (*sāḵ*), found only here, represents ἀόριστος for reasons of assonance,[98] although both ἄπειρος and ἀπερίγραπτος could also have served as *Vorlage*

84 BDAG, *s.v.* ὄνομα, 3 and 4; Payne Smith, 2:4199.

85 Harris and Mingana, 2:367: "its overflow"; see Payne Smith, 2:4271: *exundantio*; Brockelmann, *Lexicon*, 796: *abundantia*; cf. Deut 33:19a (πλοῦτος). Charlesworth's emendation (pp. 114–15: ܫܡܗ = *šammah*, "it named") is just as unconvincing as Franzmann's suggested ܫܕܐ = *šḏā* "it flowed" (p. 223).

86 Frankenberg, 42. His retroversion is not faultless. He takes the pronoun αὐτοῖς in 4b for the antecedent of τὰ ὕδατα in 4a, the verb in 5a to refer to the spring, the Lord as antecedent of αὐτοῦ in 5b, and the spring again as antecedent to ἀπ' αὐτῆς in 7 (see Frankenberg, 28, 92). His emendation τὸ νᾶμα αὐτοῦ is accepted by Greßmann (p. 464, but "*their* drink" is correct) and Omodeo (p. 117: "il suo fiotto"). Eileen Elizabeth Freeman's translation, "Its essence from the Lord's own heart" is purely fanciful (see Freeman, *The Holy Week Book* [San Jose, CA: Resource Publications, 1979] 181).

87 Harris and Mingana, 2:367.

88 See *OTSy*, pt. 2 fasc. 5, on Cant 8:2d.

89 See LSJ, *s.v.* νᾶμα: "ν. θυγατέρων ταύρων i.e. honey." In antique zoology it was believed that bees might be "generated in decaying cattle . . . or dead horses" (Gerhard Schrot, "Biene. Bienenzucht," *KP* 1 [1964] 898; see also LSJ, *s.v.* θυγάτηρ).

90 See Payne Smith, 2:3821; also Lampe, 897, *s.v.* νᾶμα.

91 Connolly, "Greek," 534–35.

92 Klijn (p. 304) points out, countering Lattke, *Bedeutung*, 1:163, that ܒܡܨܥܬܐ (*ba-mṣaʿṯā*) refers to the preceding verb.

93 Connolly, "Greek," 530; idem, review of Abbott in *JTS* 14 (1912–13) 316.

94 Connolly, "Greek," 530–31; see also supporting arguments in Harris and Mingana, 2:367.

95 Frankenberg, 28.

96 The verb is used in this nonliteral way to describe even the "spiritual coming of God" (BDAG, *s.v.* ἔρχομαι, 4bβ; cf. John 14:23).

97 Payne Smith, *Dictionary*, 204.

98 Connolly, "Greek," 535.

(cf. 12:5c).[99] The case of the parallel and also negated participle of the Ethpe. of ܚܙܐ (*ḥzā*) is clearer, since, as in 16:8a, there is no alternative to ἀόρατος.[100] All these predicative adjectives—or their corresponding adverbs—in 𝔖 are weighted with earlier philosophical and theological significations[101] that transfer to the metaphorical spring.[102]

Although Diettrich (following Harnack)[103] quite properly translates the Ethpe. of ܝܗܒ (*yab*), followed by the preposition ܒ (*b*-), as "to be placed,"[104] he puts too much emphasis on the *hapax legomenon* ܡܨܥܬܐ (*mṣaʿṯā*): "This is a very difficult expression, because one does not know whether it is intended for the middle between two sorts of persons (the pious and the godless) or between God and humankind."[105] Since the Greek διδόναι can be "equivalent to τιθέναι,"[106] Connolly's suggestion that this is a case of "the idiomatic non-local sense which attaches to εἰς τὸ μέσον τιθέναι, . . . namely 'to publish,' 'make known,' 'bring forward openly' . . ."[107] is easy to accept. So the whole expression can be translated as "be revealed."[108] Whether ܥܕܡܐ ܕ (*ʿḏammā ḏ*-) corresponded to ἄχρι, ἄχρι οὗ or ἕως (ἄν), used as a conjunction in 𝔖,[109] is as difficult to determine as the tense of δίδωμι or τίθημι, which is to some extent dependent on it (ἔλθῃ, the aorist subjunctive of ἔρχομαι, does not come under consideration).[110] The third person plural of the verb "to know" has no "subject" and, as in Greek, therefore has the "indefinite subject."[111] Since "spring" makes a most peculiar object for (ἐπι)γινώσκω/ܝܕܥ (*ʾiḏaʿ*), "know," it is worth considering whether the third masculine singular objective suffix may not rather refer to "name" in 5b. But the Greek text cannot be reconstructed with certainty. So it is impossible to decide whether the relative pronoun was αὐτήν (for "spring") or αὐτό (for "name," or perhaps for τὸ νᾶμα [see on 5b above]).

■ **7** In conformity with both Syriac manuscripts,[112] the final metaphorical benediction must be accepted as a monocolon[113] and not divided before the second verb into 7a–b.[114] The sense of this beatitude is related to the conclusion of *Ode* 12, while the wording is close to 6:13 taken in the context of 6:11-18 (cf. also 9:8 and 11:18).[115]

This benediction, which is not addressed to an audience and differs from the paradoxical beatitudes of the Sermon on the Mount (Matt 5:3-12; cf. Luke 6:20-26), is meant inclusively, in spite of the masculine possessive

99 Payne Smith, 2:2550–51; Lampe, *s.vv.* ἀόριστος, ἄπειρος, ἀπερίγραπτος; Frankenberg, 28.
100 Frankenberg, 28; Connolly, "Greek," 535; Payne Smith, 1:1234; BDAG (and Lampe), *s.v.* ἀόρατος. The participle in 16:8a is also an active form and "passive" only in its meaning (see commentary on 16:8a). This statement is the opposite of 5:14a (see commentary on 5:14a).
101 LSJ, *s.v.* ἀόρατος, ἀόριστος.
102 The "image of the river" in 6:8-10, to which Diettrich refers (p. 107), is of interest in the wider context but not specifically relevant.
103 Harnack, 63.
104 See Payne Smith, 1:1564, *s.v.* ܝܗܒ (*posuit, locavit*).
105 Diettrich, 107.
106 BDAG, *s.v.* δίδωμι, 6c; cf. τίθημι, 1bβ.
107 Connolly, "Greek," 531. This means that passages that speak of "giving" or "being given" (35:5b and 6:12) are not parallel to this idiomatic expression. On εἰς τὸ μέσον as "into the middle," see BDAG, *s.v.* μέσος, 1b. The phrase ἐν τῷ μέσῳ is grammatically possible but corresponds less well to the Syriac (BDAG, *s.v.* μέσος, 1b; Payne Smith, 2:2194–95).
108 Greßmann, 464.
109 Payne Smith, 2:2799; BDAG, *s.vv.* ἄχρι, ἕως.
110 Contra Frankenberg, 28.
111 BDF and BDR §130; Nöldeke §253. Since the Ethpe. of ܝܕܥ (*ʾiḏaʿ*) is used in the *Odes of Solomon* (see Excursus 7), Frankenberg's retroversion (p. 28) οὐ γιγνώσκεται is somewhat unlikely.
112 Here also it is true "that there are no variants between the Syriac manuscripts in this Ode," although Charlesworth (p. 115) finds it "surprising."
113 As, e.g., Diettrich, p. 107, does.
114 Contra Harris and Mingana, vol. 1, on this passage, 2:366; Charlesworth, p. 114; Franzmann, p. 222. Franzmann's (p. 223) reason that "[t]he division is made on the basis of the structure" is insufficient.
115 Klaus Beyer suggests as a translation: "Blessed are they who have drunk of it and been refreshed by it" (letter of October 31, 2002).

suffix of ܛܘܒܐ (*ṭūḇā*), as the Greek equivalent *μακάριοι οἱ κτλ.* would also have been.[116] Except for the beginning and the probable use of the participle *πιόντες*, the Greek wording of 7 is not as easily reconstructed as Frankenberg believes (*μακάριοι οἱ πιόντες ἀπ' αὐτῆς | καὶ ἐπ' αὐτῇ ἀναπαυσάμενοι*).[117] The preposition ܡܢ (*men*), for instance, with its third masculine singular suffix, can represent either *ἀπό* or *ἐκ*.[118] The "having drunk of it" forms a parallel to the sense of 11:7, especially since 11:12a speaks of being given rest (though only in 𝔖, not 𝔊; see on 3 above).

The imperative of salvation in 2b ("rest") is slightly varied by the Ethpe. of ܢܘܚ, ܢܚ (*nāḥ*), in that the equally soteriological perfect is associated not with ܥܠ (*ʿal*) but with the instrumental ܒ (*b*-). This preposition, with its third masculine singular suffix, cannot represent *ἐπ' αὐτῇ*,[119] but must be either *ἐν αὐτῇ* or the instrumental dative *αὐτῇ*, referring again to the "spring." This construction, with ܒ for ܥܠ, which Franzmann properly calls unexpected,[120] may have arisen because 𝔊 used a form of *ἐπαναπαύομαι*[121] followed by the relative *αὐτῇ* governed by the preposition *ἐπί* contained in the composite verb, which the Syriac translator(s) treated as an instrumental dative. Yet, however that came about, the juxtaposition of "rest" and "drink" places this passage in a set that combines the early Christian and Gnostic idea of salvation with other soteriological aspects (16:12; 28:3; 35:6; see Excursus 3).

116 Payne Smith, 1:1437; BDAG, *s.v.* *μακάριος*, 2a.

117 Frankenberg, 28.

118 BDAG, *s.v.* *πίνω*, 1.

119 Contra Frankenberg, 28.

120 "Given the link between 7 and 2-3, one would have expected ܥܠܘܗܝ in 7b rather than ܒܗ" (Franzmann, 224). But her reference to "ܢܘܚ . . . with ܒ in 35:6" is not relevant because there ܒ is not used instrumentally.

121 Payne Smith, 2:2311; BDAG, *s.v.* *ἐπαναπαύομαι*, 2. I have previously referred to these problems in reconstructing 𝔊: "[T]here is no way, especially where the Ethpe. occurs, to discover whether the Greek version used only a verb or had a combination of a noun like *ἀνάπαυσις* or *κατάπαυσις* with a verb meaning 'to find' or 'to enter into'" (see Excursus 3).

31

Ode 31: The Manifestation of the Justified Lord and His Redemptive Function

(I)
1a The abysses/primal deeps dissolved before the Lord,
1b and darkness was destroyed by his appearance.
2a Error went astray and perished/was lost from him,
2b and Contempt suffered[a] immobility
2c and sank down out of the truth of the Lord.

(II)
3a He opened his mouth and proclaimed grace and joy
3b and spoke a new hymn (of praise) to his name.
4a And he lifted up his voice to the Most High
4b and presented to him those children who were through him.
5a And his person was declared righteous,
5b because thus his holy Father had granted to him.

(III)
6 Go forth [you] who have been oppressed, and receive joy,
7a and inherit yourselves by grace
7b and take immortal life for yourselves!

(IV)
8a And they condemned me when I stood up/entered,
8b me, who was not guilty/had not been condemned.
9 And they divided[b] my spoils, although nothing was owed to them.

(V)
10a But I endured and was silent and remained calm,
10b that I might not be disturbed by them.
11a I, however, stood undisturbed like the firm rock,
11b that is lashed by the breakers[c] and endures.

(VI)
12a And I bore their bitterness out of humility,
12b in order that I might redeem my people and inherit it,
13a and lest I might make void the promises to the patriarchs,
13b that I had promised, the salvation of their seed.
Hallelujah.

a 2b ܢܣܒܬܗ̇ N; ܣܒܬܗ̇ H.
b 9 ܘܦܠܓܘ H; ܘܦܠܓ N.
c 11b ܡܢ ܓ̈ܠܠܐ H; ܡܢ ܡܚ̈ܘܬܐ ܓ̈ܠܠܐ N.

Introduction

Ode 31 is preserved in two Syriac manuscripts.[1] Blaszczak's researches[2] will disabuse anyone who believes, with Gunkel,[3] that this Ode is "not hard to understand." After more than twenty years of further work on the *Odes of Solomon*, Blaszczak's concluding remarks, "Because we are unable at this stage of our research to answer satisfactorily the questions posed by the peculiar changes of form and content, we are unable to address the problem of the *Sitz im Leben* of the poem in its final form,"[4] are still valid. The final form, which offers no text-critical problems, must be the starting point, although it is clearer than for many of the other Odes that *Ode* 31 is made up of separate parts, which do not all cohere satisfactorily. It is only with reference to Harnack's hypothesis of aggregation,[5] accepted, for instance, by Spitta,[6] that it is possible to agree with Gunkel that "this *Ode*," despite its division into two,[7] is "unitary."[8] In view of several noticeable breaks, it would also be possible to call it a three-part (stanzas I–II, III, IV–VI)[9] or even four-part (stanzas I, II, III, IV–VI) poem.[10] Kittel's verdict on these "transitions in form and content"[11] is that "here in particular it is very clear that the author disdains to hint at links that will make it easy for the reader or hearer to follow his thought."[12]

It is desirable to reach a preliminary conclusion about the identity of the "Lord" (1a, 2c), on the one hand, and of the masculine[13] speaking "I" (8-13), on the other, before proceeding to the detailed analysis. In the first place, it is "probable that the protagonist of the events reported in vss 3-5 is to be identified with 'the Lord' whose presence occasions the destruction described in vss 1-2."[14] And since the "Lord" is contrasted with the "Most High" (4a) and with his "Father" (5b), the speaking "I" of the address that begins at 6a[15] can be identified with the "Lord" and also with the "Son" par excellence.[16] The "sons" (4b), meant inclusively, will then be the recipients of the imperatives of salvation (6-7) and may also be the "people" (12b) who are to be redeemed and the "seed" (13b), although they may not consist of a sociologically identifiable "group of people."[17]

Harris and Mingana are justified in declaring that *Ode* 31 "is somewhat like the 28th Ode in that it contains a selection of statements from the 22nd Psalm."[18] They think it likely that "there are more loans from the Canonical Psalter to be traced,"[19] but, as will be seen, other biblical writings in addition to the Psalter influenced the composition of this Ode.

1 Mss.: Codex H, 23b–24a; Codex N, 150r (s). Ed./trans.: Charlesworth, 115–18; Franzmann, 225–30; Lattke, 3:33–57.

2 Blaszczak, 43–58.

3 Gunkel, *Aufsätze*, 176.

4 Blaszczak, 58.

5 Harnack, 63–64.

6 According to Spitta (p. 285), "1-2 are an independent unit, a short Ode like no. 32." But Spitta admits that the alleged "interpolator" makes 1-2 refer to the "Christ" of 3-14 and "his fight against the kingdom of darkness." Some of Spitta's references to Matt 5:2; 11:25, 28-29; 16:25; John 17:11-12; Rom 15:3, 8; Heb 2:13, on the one hand, and Isaiah 50, on the other, will be discussed later.

7 Gunkel states (p. 313): "This Ode consists of two parts: 1-5 and 6-11 [= 13], the second of which is spoken by Christ." A possible alternative division would be: "The two parts of the Ode are 1-7 and 8-13. Placing the inviting imperatives of salvation (6-7), however, is a problem" (Lattke, *Oden*, 185).

8 Gunkel, 314.

9 Schille (p. 43) divides *Ode* 31 into three, and classifies 1-5 as a hymn of the Redeemer, puts 6-7 among the aubades (p. 96), and transforms 8-13 into a baptismal hymn to place among the hymns of initiation (p. 65).

10 It is clear from Blaszczak's survey that he divides the Ode into four parts, finding the connection between 1-2 and 3-5 no clearer than that between 6-7 and 8-13 (see Blaszczak, 44–45).

11 Blaszczak, 45.

12 Kittel, 26.

13 In s, the masculine subject of 3a could grammatically be the "truth" of 2c (Diettrich, 109). But "the Old Testament interpretation" of the whole Ode ("one eschatological hymn from start to finish"!) is as unconvincing as the attempt to identify the speaking "I" of 6-13 with "truth personified" (ibid., 108). The verbs in 3a refer not only to the "Lord" as "a word found in v. 1" (ibid., 109) but also and particularly to the final word in 2c, and that is no "distortion."

14 Blaszczak, 45.

15 Richter calls this address a "hymn of the Redeemer" and ranks it with *Odes* 10, 22, 23, and 24 as an example "that occasionally the way of the Redeemer . . . can be described without expressly mentioning the Incarnation" (see Georg Richter, "Die Fleischwerdung des Logos im Johannesevangelium," *NovT* 13 [1971] 104–5 = idem, *Studien*, 167–68).

16 See Abramowski, 53–56.

17 Hans-Martin Schenke, "Einführung," *NHD* 1 (2001) 6, on the Sethian Gnostics.

18 Harris and Mingana, 2:371.

19 Ibid., 372.

Interpretation

■ **1-2** The mythological and dualistic image of 1a-b cannot be simply explained either by a reference to 24:5 and 24:7[20] or by a comparison with 4 Esdr 13:4, *liquiscet cera quando senserit ignem* ("the wax melts when it feels the fire");[21] cf. Mic 1:4; Jdt 16:15; *1 Enoch* 1:6. If the plural of ܬܗܘܡܐ (*thōmā* [תהום])[22] refers to constituents of the material world, as in Ps 21:15 LXX (ἡ καρδία μου ὡσεὶ κηρὸς τηκόμενος, "my heart . . . like melting wax")[23] or Ps 96:5 LXX (τὰ ὄρη ἐτάκησαν ὡσεὶ κηρὸς ἀπὸ προσώπου κυρίου, "The mountains melted like wax at the presence of the Lord"),[24] one might imagine the "deeps"[25] or "abysses"[26] as subterranean regions or submarine mountains that "melt away" before the Lord (cf. 17:9c). But "were dissolved," as a less deterministic and more powerful translation of the Ethpa. of ܦܫܪ (*pšar*), may be preferred.[27] It cannot be decided whether 1a refers to "primal deeps" (cf., in connection with Noah's Flood, 24:5, 7), or personified "abysses," or just "deeps" that dissolve. In this uncertainty Berger and Nord found it necessary to use linked terms: "The primal flood of the abysses perished before the Lord."[28]

The plural ܬܗܘ̈ܡܐ (*thōmē*) makes it impossible to take ἄβυσσος as meaning "place of the dead" and thus as a synonym of ᾅδης.[29] Nor is there an allusion to the chaos before God's mythological word of creation, when σκότος ἐπάνω τῆς ἀβύσσου ("darkness was over the deep" [Gen 1:2 LXX]).[30] Whether 𝔊 used οἱ ἄβυσσοι at all (cf. Ps 70:20 and 76:17 LXX; Sir 24:5)[31] or merely τὰ βάθη (cf. Amos 9:3)[32] is also quite uncertain; Blaszczak should have listed it among the insoluble problems of *Ode* 31. However, in contrast to the simple preposition ܡܢ (*men*) in 1b, 2a, 2c, 10b, and 11b, the translation of ܡܢ ܩܕܡ (*men qdām*) in 1a offers no difficulty.[33] The "Lord" is not "God Himself"[34] but the Kyrios Christos.[35]

The Ethpa. of ܚܒܠ (*ḥbal*) in 1b as a parallel to the verb of 1a confirms the translation suggested above. Eschatological annihilation corresponds to complete dissolution, and this is true also of non-*gnōsis* (7:21a) and the power of Death (15:2a; see Excursus 28).[36] The "darkness" (σκότος/ܚܫܘܟܐ [*ḥeššōkā*]) that is "destroyed" here is dualistically opposed to "light" (cf. 18:6; 21:3; Excursus 10). So it is easy to associate the *hapax legomenon* ܚܙܘܐ (*ḥezwā*) with the transfigured εἶδος τοῦ προσώπου of Luke 9:29.[37] Following the passive verb, the preposition ܡܢ (*men*) serves to define the "outward appearance" of the Lord as the grammatical agent;[38] the Greek equivalent of the ܡܢ remains elusive.[39]

Up to now it has escaped notice that the remaining lines of stanza I, which Harris and Mingana, following N in preference to H, print as a bicolon,[40] with their mysterious and puzzling[41] statements about the personified powers πλάνη/ܛܥܝܘܬܐ (*ṭāʿyūtā*) and ἐξουδένωσις/

20 Contra Diettrich, 108; Kittel, 114.

21 *BSV* 2:1962; Josef Schreiner, *Das 4. Buch Esra* (JSHRZ 5.4; Gütersloh: Mohn, 1981) 394; Bauer, 612; Blaszczak, 46.

22 Brockelmann, *Grammatik* §98 ("Flut [flood]"), p. 210* ("Abgrund [abyss]").

23 Rahlfs, 2:20; Brenton, 710.

24 Rahlfs, 2:105; Brenton, 757.

25 Like Gunkel, 312; Greßmann, 464.

26 Like Ungnad and Staerk, 31; Gunkel, *Aufsätze*, 175: "Abgründe."

27 Harris and Mingana, 2:369; Payne Smith, 2:3329. Considering the passive of τήκω as the possible Greek equivalent of ܐܬܦܫܪ (*ʾetpaššar*), one could translate it as "dissolve" (i.e., disintegrate) instead of "melt," with a sense of "the end of the world" (BDAG, *s.v.* τήκω). An alternative would be the passive of διαλύω (BDAG, *s.v.* διαλύω, 1: "break up, dissolve").

28 Berger and Nord, 963.

29 Payne Smith, 2:4394; BDAG, *s.vv.* ἄβυσσος, ᾅδης, 1.

30 Rahlfs, 1:1; Brenton, 1.

31 Frankenberg, 28; Tsakonas, 144; Fanourgakis, 166.

32 BDAG, *s.v.* βάθος, 1.

33 BDAG, *s.vv.* ἀπέναντι, ἐναντίον. That ἔμπροσθεν was the equivalent of this compound preposition is quite unlikely (contra Frankenberg, 28).

34 Contra Harnack, 63; Diettrich, 108.

35 Kittel, 114; Abramowski, 53; cf. Charles Perrot, "Kyrios/Herr," *RGG*[4] 4 (2001) 1922.

36 Payne Smith, 1:1176–77.

37 Payne Smith, 1:1234–35; BDAG, *s.v.* εἶδος, 1 (on the variant in D, see NA[27], p. 187), see also BDAG, *s.v.* ἰδέα, 1. Very similar mythologoumena can be found in 42:13b (πρόσωπον in the sense of "gaze") and 42:16b ("chains of darkness").

38 Nöldeke §249.D.

39 Payne Smith, 2:2156, 2159; BDAG, *s.vv.* ἀπό, ὑπό.

40 Harris and Mingana, vol. 1, on this passage. This decision may result from a massive emendation affecting 2b-c (ܚܫܒܬ ܠܗ ܐܬܒܠܗ ܘܛܥܝܬ). But their reason for this correction carries as little

ܫܝܛܘܬܐ (*šīṭūṯā*),[42] are imaginative variations on Ps 106:40 LXX: Ἐξεχύθη ἐξουδένωσις ἐπ᾽ ἄρχοντας [+ αὐτῶν A], *καὶ ἐπλάνησεν αὐτοὺς ἐν ἀβάτῳ καὶ οὐχ ὁδῷ* ("Contempt is poured upon their princes, and he causes them to wander in a desert and trackless land").[43] The term "error," which Schenke, in his translation of the *Gospel of Truth*, consistently renders "delusion,"[44] belongs to the established Gnosticizing vocabulary of the *Odes of Solomon* (see Excursus 38).[45] Charlesworth ranks the wordplay in the repetition of the same root at the beginning of 2a as the "best example of this type of repetition" and considers it "the work of a skilled Semitic poet."[46] But a similar statement could equally be made about a Greek poet who skillfully connects a passive form of πλανάω (not λανθάνω)[47] with the nominative πλάνη[48] and thus achieves a marked variation on the keyword ἐπλάνησεν of Ps 106:40 LXX. In his justifiable criticism of Harris and Mingana's translation of the second part of 2a,[49] Charlesworth stresses the use of ܡܢ (*men*) as "sign of the agent"[50] but overlooks the idiomatic use of the Pe. ܐܒܕ (*ʾeḇaḏ*) with this preposition: "Cum ܡܢ rei, *privatus est* aliqua re . . . Cum ܡܢ pers[onae], *amissum est* aliquid ab aliquo."[51] Since Ps 106:40 LXX is no help here, it must remain uncertain whether the statement referring to the Lord can be translated by "perished on account of Him"[52] or by what I consider the more idiomatic expression, "perished/was lost from him" (cf., e.g., linguistically Exod 30:38). The *Vorlage* for this latter suggestion would have been ἀπώλετο ἐξ αὐτοῦ[53] rather than ἀπώλετο ἀπ᾽ αὐτοῦ.[54]

conviction as their other remarks on v. 2 (Harris and Mingana, 2:370–71).

41 Even Frankenberg (p. 28) gives up and renders 2b as "και η μωρια . . . ." [*sic*]. Blaszczak (p. 47) also writes: "The question of the precise meanings of 'error' and 'contempt' remains unresolved."

42 Flemming here translates "foolishness" with the note, "for ܫܝܛܘܬܐ read ܫܛܝܘܬܐ" (see Harnack, 63). Gunkel (p. 313) accepts this emendation and claims: "The parallel verse makes this sense unassailable." Harris and Mingana (2:370) consider the revision "somewhat violent." Emerton (p. 721 n. 2) even asserts, erroneously, that N confirms the reading ܫܛܝܘܬܐ ("folly").

On the confusion between ܫܝܛܘܬܐ (*šīṭūṯā*) and ܫܛܝܘܬܐ (*šāṭyūṯā*), see Payne Smith, 2:4094–95 and 4131. The Hebrew term בוז (*būz*) is translated by ἐξουδένωσις in the LXX in Pss 30:19; 106:40; 118:22; 122:3-4. Only Job 12:21 has ἀτιμία (cf. LEH, *s.v.* ἀτιμία: "dishonour, disgrace"; Hatch and Redpath, 175–76, 500). But matters in the Peshitta are different. The translation of Ps 119:22 (*OTSy*, pt. 2 fasc. 3, p. 143) is completely idiosyncratic; Ps 31:19 and Job 12:21 (*OTSy*, pt. 2 fasc. 3, p. 31, and pt. 2 fasc. 1a, p. 16) use ܫܛܝܘܬܐ. Ps 107:40 has a somewhat far-fetched term (ܒܝܫܬܐ [*bīštā*], *OTSy*, pt. 2 fasc. 3, p. 131). Finally Ps 123:3-4 offers both ܫܝܛܘܬܐ (twice banished to the critical apparatus) and ܫܛܝܘܬܐ (twice in the text, *OTSy*, pt. 2 fasc. 3, 152).

43 Rahlfs, 2:121; Brenton, 765. Perhaps Job 12:21-25 was another sponsor (especially in view of the term σκότος in 12:22 and 12:25; Rahlfs, 2:291–92). The Peshitta has ܠܐ ܐܘܪܚܐ (*lā ʾurḥā*) in both Ps 107:40 and Job 12:24 (*OTSy*, pt. 2 fasc. 3, p. 131, and pt. 2 fasc. 1a, p. 16) in place of ܠܐ ܗܠܟܬܐ (*lā hlaḵṯā*) used in *Ode* 31:2b, which makes a Greek *Vorlage* more probable than a Syriac one. This is another argument for Greek as the original language of the *Odes of Solomon*.

44 Hans-Martin Schenke, "Evangelium Veritatis (NHC I,3/XII,2)," *NHD* 1 (2001) 32.

45 It is remarkable that Schenke, after his monograph of 1958 (1959) and despite referring to the *Odes of Solomon* as a "book of hymns" (see Hans-Martin Schenke, "Evangelium Veritatis [NHC I,3/XII,2]," *NHD* 1 [2001] 30, 32), makes no use of them in his most recent translation of the *Gospel of Truth* (ibid., 33–44). If there is "a relationship between the *Gospel of Truth* and the *Odes of Solomon*," it is probably because the *Odes of Solomon* influenced the "*Planē* [= Error] myth" in the *Gospel of Truth* (ibid., 32).

46 Charlesworth, *Reflections*, 151.

47 Contra Frankenberg, 28: ἔλαθεν.

48 Payne Smith, 1:1492 and 1:1494; BDAG, *s.vv.* πλανάω, 2cβ; πλάνη; cf. linguistically Jas 5:19-20.

49 Harris and Mingana, 2:369: "disappeared from Him"; cf. Greßmann, 464: "vanished before him."

50 Charlesworth, 117.

51 Payne Smith, 1:8. The entry on ܐܒܕ ܡܢ in Payne Smith, *Dictionary*, 2, is less detailed: "to be deprived of, miss, lose." My earlier translation (Lattke, *Bedeutung*, 163; idem, *Oden*, 185: "was robbed of it") was influenced by Diettrich's note on ܐܒܕ ܡܢ, "to be deprived of a person or thing" (Diettrich, 108, which even refers to Payne Smith, 1:8).

52 Charlesworth, 116; cf. Bauer, 612: "perished by Him;" Blaszczak, 43: "perished because of Him."

53 LSJ, *s.v.* ἀπόλλυμι; BDAG, *s.vv.* ἀπόλλυμι, 1b; ἐκ, 1.

54 Frankenberg, 28.

The discovery of N, which has the Pe. ܢܣܒ (*nsab̲*) in 2b as the verb with feminine objective suffix in place of the less appropriate ܝܗܒ ("gave"),[55] has solved a number of previous difficulties.[56] The Syriac construction with the suffix ܗ (*-āh*) is not "very harsh and ungrammatical"[57] but emphasizes the "means of indicating a *Definite Object*"[58]—in this case without the use of ܠ (*l-*). This object ܠܐ ܗܠܟܬܐ (*lā hlak̲t̲ā*), "not-going"[59] (i.e., "immobility"),[60] is like the phrase "non-*gnōsis*" (7:21a) and therefore probably represents ἀνοδία in analogy to ἄγνοια;[61] it is inspired by the ending of Ps 106:40 LXX (ἐν . . . οὐχ ὁδῷ).[62] The beginning of this same verse provided the personified subject ἐξουδένωσις/ܫܝܛܘܬܐ (*šīṭūṭā*), which, as previously discussed, does not need to be emended to ἀφροσύνη/ܫܛܝܘܬܐ (*šāṭyūṭā*). For the verb ܢܣܒ (*nsab̲*) and its probable Greek equivalent λαμβάνω, the dominant sense here is not an active taking[63] but the passive getting or receiving (see Excursus 41).[64]

Verse 2c, with a vocabulary reminiscent of 24:7-10,[65] is somewhat of a variation on the more difficult part of 2a (see above). So the preposition ܡܢ (*men*) should be translated as "from" or "out of" and not as "by"[66] or "before."[67] The Pe. ܛܒܥ (*ṭb̲aʿ*), used here intransitively, whose subject is the personified "contempt" of 2b, may be equivalent to the passive of βυθίζω[68] or καταποντίζω.[69] However, it could also correspond to δύνω,[70] which would lead to an ironic echo of the metaphorical "δῦναι ἀπὸ κόσμου = die" in Ignatius *Rom.* 2:2,[71] where the theological and mythological domain of the ἀλήθεια/ܫܪܪܐ (*šrārā*), "truth," of the Lord is in dualistic opposition to the "darkness" of the world (see Excursus 1), and "contempt" *cannot* come πρὸς θεόν ("to God," as in the continuation of Ignatius *Rom.* 2:2).[72]

■ **3-5** Franzmann makes a definite division between 4a and 4b within stanza II, but she also, without explanation, divides 3a into two and thus improves the poetic structure of 3a-4a in "four lines."[73] Although the connection between stanza I and the actions described

55 Even translating *yab̲* by "offered" (Harnack, 63) does not result in a meaningful version of this difficult passage. Comparing the two verbs in the *Esṭrangelā* script will show how easy it is to mistake one for the other (cf. Lattke, *Bedeutung*, 1:162: "visual mistake?").

56 See Gunkel, 313; Harris and Mingana, 2:370–71.

57 Harris and Mingana, 2:370, who therefore undertake an unnecessary emendation.

58 Nöldeke §288.A.

59 Harnack, 63: "Nicht-Gehen."

60 See Emerton, 721 n. 3.

61 See Franzmann, 227, who calls ܠܐ ܗܠܟܬܐ "translation Syriac from the Greek ἀνοδία."

62 Both the LXX and *OTSy*, pt. 2 fasc. 3, p. 131 (ܠܐ ܐܘܪܚܐ [*lā ʾurḥā*]), are literal translations of the Hebrew of Ps 107:40 (cf. *BHS*, p. 1191), which is picked up by Harnack (p. 63) with his alternative translation "not-way (Nicht-Weg)."

63 BDAG, *s.v.* λαμβάνω, 1.

64 BDAG, *s.v.* λαμβάνω, 2; Payne Smith, 2:2392. For this reason I have changed my previous translation "took" (Lattke, *Oden*, 185) to "suffered." Diettrich's translation (p. 108), "ignominy made it [viz., error] unable to walk," is impossible. Kittel mistakenly reads ܘܫܛܝܘܬܐ, "and foolishness," in both H and N (see Gerhard Kittel, "Eine zweite Handschrift der Oden Salomos," *ZNW* 14 [1913] 87). From this premise he constructs the following translation of 2b: "foolishness, it was seized by not being able to walk" = "an inability to walk took hold of foolishness." I cannot agree with the reason given for this translation: "The subject is ܠܐ ܗܠܟܬܐ, ܗ refers to the preceding object ܫܛܝܘܬܐ" (Kittel, "Handschrift," 87; see also idem, 114).

65 See Franzmann, 228. I cannot accept her suggestion "that 2b is an addition" because of the probable use of Ps 106:40 LXX as discussed above.

66 So, e.g., Harris and Mingana, 2:369; Charlesworth, 116; Blaszczak, 43; Franzmann, 226. Similarly Emerton (p. 721) says: "it sank because of the truth of the Lord."

67 Greßmann, 464; Bauer, 612. Berger and Nord's (p. 963) paraphrase of 2a-c is too free: "Error lost its way and perished before [the face of] the Lord, its lack of direction brought it into contempt and it vanished from God's reality into the gulf."

68 BDAG, *s.v.* βυθίζω: "to sink."

69 BDAG, *s.v.* καταποντίζω: "to drown."

70 Payne Smith, 1:1427.

71 BDAG, *s.v.* δύνω.

72 Ehrman, 1:272–73.

73 Franzmann, 228; see also Gunkel, 312; idem, *Aufsätze*, 175; Greßmann, 464; Pierre, 155. Franzmann (p. 228) remarks, correctly, "3a and 4a are linked by the word-pair ܪܘܡ ܘܠܐ – ܦܬܚ ܦܘܡܐ." But this remains true when 3 and 4 are treated as bicola.

here is somewhat loose, the subject of the main clauses in stanza II is always the "Lord"[74] not "Truth" personified.[75] Before proceeding with the exegesis of the three bicola (3a-b, 4a-b, 5a-b), which owes much to Blaszczak's observations, but must take issue with his translation and commentary,[76] the following excursus will discuss the two connected terms from 3a and 4a (see Excursuses 12 and 16).

Excursus 31: "Mouth" and "Voice" in the *Odes of Solomon*

In all the metaphors and theological anthropomorphisms, the term ܦܘܡܐ (*pummā*), which occurs seventeen times and corresponds to τὸ στόμα, is used in its literal sense.[77] This is true even where it is used of the "beaks" of doves (28:1b) or where, in parallel to the Realm of the Dead, Death is provided with the "maw" or "gullet" of a monster (cf. 29:4b).[78]

The term ܩܠܐ (*qālā*) occurs only eight times and in all but one case (7:17c)[79] is the equivalent of the ambiguous term ἡ φωνή,[80] the meaning of which can shade from "voice" into "sound" or "tone" in one direction (e.g., 24:2b) and "call" in another (e.g., 33:3a; 37:2b; 42:19a). Except for the one plural use (see above on 7:17c), ܩܠܐ is not used in a hymnic, liturgical, or musical sense.[81]

The statement of creation in 7:24a could be taken to mean that the Most High Lord endowed his creatures with "speech."[82] However, in 7:24b στόμα/ ܦܘܡܐ should be translated by "mouth," though "to open," the verb that is commonly used about this part of the body, is poetically transferred to the "voice" of the "mouth."[83] Elsewhere it is the "mouth" that is "opened" (8:4b; 36:7a) or which the speaker or the subject of the narrative "opens" (16:5a; 31:3a). These statements are often juxtaposed with the Pa. ܡܠܠ (*mallel*), since "speaking" is considered the most typical—though not the most beautiful (or even always the most intelligent)—action of the mouth.

The divine spirit may also use an opened mouth as a speaking tube (16:5a). Just as God the Lord directed the "mouth" of the redeemed Redeemer by his "word" (10:1a), the Redeemer will speak by the "mouths" of his supporters (42:6b). The "mouth" can let flow not only words but also the "truth" (12:2b). The statements about the "mouth" of God himself, in which there is neither falsehood nor death (18:8a), and the speaking "mouth of the Most High" (12:11a; cf. 26:10b), derived from Sir 24:3, have at their apex: "Because the mouth of the Lord is the true word, and the gate of his light" (12:3b-c).[84]

All that can be said of the difficult passage 21:8-9[85] is that "heart" and "lips" belong to the domain of the term "mouth" (see Excursus 4). The same can be said of the domain of "voice" (37:1b). This brings us to the final group of passages, containing the term ܩܠܐ (*qālā*), which is regularly combined with the verb "to hear" (24:2b; 27:2b; 42:19a).

The "voice" of the mouth has already been discussed (see on 7:24b above). The dove's "voice" or cooing "sound" has also been mentioned (see on 24:2b above). Who it was that in 33:3a stood on a high peak and let loose his "voice," that is, "cried out" or "shouted,"[86] will be considered in its place. It may be worth asking, especially about the metaphorical expression in 37:2b, but also about "hearing" the voice of the believers (42:19a), whether φωνή/ ܩܠܐ is meant for the "call" or "cry" as it arrives (cf. Mark 15:37). On the other hand, the "voice" in 37:1b and 31:4a is itself lifted up to the Most High by, in the one case, the speaking "I" and, in the other, the Lord.

74 Blaszczak, 45. This conclusion refers primarily to the connection between stanzas I and II. After his commentary on 5b Blaszczak (p. 51), with excessive circumspection, warns: "Nothing in the Ode up to this point, however, justifies identifying the figure with Christ."

75 Contra Diettrich, 109.

76 Blaszczak, 47–51.

77 BDAG, *s.v.* στόμα; see Payne Smith, 2:3063–64, especially on the many metaphors.

78 BDAG, *s.v.* στόμα, 1c.

79 Even here the connection to φωνή is preserved, for the two words of 5 correspond to πολύφωνος (see Excursus 26). Two *hapax legomena* come within the ambit of the present excursus, namely, the plural ܩܝܢܢ (*qīnān*), referring to the "tones" of the cithara in 14:8b, and the plural ܢܥܡܬܐ (*neʿmāṯā*) in 7:23b, which is parallel to "heart" and is translated as "voices."

80 BDAG, *s.v.* φωνή.

81 See Payne Smith, 2:3619; Michael Lattke, "Sind Ephraems *Madrāšē* Hymnen?" *OrChr* 73 (1989) 38–40 = idem, *Bedeutung*, 4:68–69.

82 BDAG, *s.v.* φωνή, 2a.

83 BDAG, *s.v.* ἀνοίγω, 5a.

84 See commentary on that passage.

85 See commentary on that passage.

86 See BDAG, *s.v.* ἀφίημι, 1b.

Although, according to Franzmann's analysis (see above in the introduction to stanza II), one would expect the raising of the "voice" (31:4a) to occur before the doxological moment in 31:3b, allowance can be made for poetic freedom, and the close connection between 31:4a ("he lifted up his voice") and 31:3a ("he opened his mouth")[87] can be noted, even without postulating a *parallelismus membrorum*, which even takes on a chiastic appearance, for 31:3-4a.[88] This connection of the related terms "mouth" and "voice" is not disturbed even if 3a and 4a are the parallel first lines of consecutive bicola.

The opening of the mouth, as discussed in detail in the excursus, is what enables the Lord, who will later issue imperative invitations to salvation (stanza III) and then tell of himself in narrative form (stanzas IV–VI), to "speak" at all. In 3a the transitive Pa. ܡܠܠ (*mallel*), which appears twice, is better translated as "proclaim,"[89] while the twin objects ܛܝܒܘܬܐ ܘܚܕܘܬܐ (*ṭaybūṯā ʾu-ḥaḏuṯā*) represent "exactly χάριν καὶ χαράν ["grace and joy"]" (see Excursuses 32 and 33).[90] These two terms of eschatological salvation will recur in reverse order (see on 6b-7a below).

The paired objects of λαλέω/ܡܠܠ (*mallel*), "proclaimed," in 3a refer to "God's gift or favor of salvation" and "the joy that comes from it,"[91] but the direct object of that same verb in 3b, "spoke," is a new ܬܫܒܘܚܬܐ (*tešbuḥtā*), "hymn (of praise)." Whether the Greek of this passage had δόξαν καινήν[92] or ὕμνον καινόν as in Isa 42:10 is here—and in 41:16b where the same expression is translated by Frankenberg as ἔπαινος καινός[93]—less important than the fact that the indirect object, corresponding to the Greek τῷ ὀνόματι αὐτοῦ, refers in anticipation to the Most High of 4a,[94] not, that is, to Christ's "own name."[95] To "speak praise" of the name of the transcendent deity bears a meaning similar to δοξάζειν τὸ ὄνομα in the LXX (Isa 42:10; Ps 85:9, 12; cf. Rev 15:4). Harris and Mingana, who in 3b concentrate on τὸ ὄνομά σου and ὑμνήσω σε in Ps 21:23 LXX and endeavor to make a link with Isa 8:18 (see below on 4b and 5b),[96] overlook the abundance of relevant terms in the previously cited verse Isa 42:10: Ὑμνήσατε τῷ κυρίῳ ὕμνον καινόν . . . δοξάζετε τὸ ὄνομα αὐτοῦ ("Sing a new hymn to the Lord . . . glorify his name").[97]

Although "mouth" and "voice" are so closely related, which results in the parallelism between 3a and 4a (see above), this second bicolon describes a new event, in which the language of prayer (4a) is associated with the language of the sacrificial rites of antiquity (4b).[98] That means that for 4a one should refer to the beginning of the prayer in Acts 4:24 (ἦραν φωνὴν πρὸς τὸν θεόν, "they lifted their voices to God") in order to reconstruct the Greek: ἦρε τὴν φωνὴν αὐτοῦ πρὸς τὸν ὕψιστον.[99]

Translators have unnecessarily complicated 4b by treating the emphatic plural of ܒܪܐ (*brā*) and the demonstrative pronoun ܗܢܘܢ (*hānnōn*) as *two* accusative objects of the Pa. of ܩܪܒ (*qreḇ*).[100] Since "those" predestined ones were "through him"[101] (cf. purely linguistically John 1:10: δι' αὐτοῦ ἐγένετο; and for meaning John

87 Blaszczak (p. 48) overlooks this connection when he writes with reference to Gunkel's structuring, "the clear and strong parallelism that his arrangement yields is a forceful argument in its favor."
88 Gunkel, 312.
89 Payne Smith, 2:2109; BDAG, *s.v.* λαλέω.
90 See Connolly, "Greek," 534–35, on this and "[s]imilar assonances."
91 Blaszczak, 49.
92 Frankenberg, 28.
93 Ibid., 35.
94 Diettrich, 109; Blaszczak, 48.
95 Contra Kittel, 107.
96 Harris and Mingana, 2:372.
97 Rahlfs, 2:623; Brenton, 877. It is also worth referring to ᾆσμα καινόν, especially its occurrence in Ps 39:4 LXX, where it is parallel to ὕμνος (cf. in the LXX Pss 32:3; 95:1; etc.).
98 Blaszczak (p. 49) does consider the possibility of a connection between 4a and 4b "so that it [viz., 4a] would refer to some aspect of the presentation."
99 Frankenberg, 28. Because of the prepositional phrase with πρός/ܠܘܬ (*lwāṯ*), 𝔊 is unlikely to have used ἐπαίρω (BDAG, *s.v.* ἐπαίρω, 1; cf. Luke 11:27; Acts 2:14; 14:11; 22:22). In Luke 17:13, ἦραν φωνήν is also followed by a petition (BDAG, *s.v.* αἴρω, 1b). On the Aph. of ܪܘܡ, ܪܡ (*rām*) and the emphatic participle of the Pa. ܡܪܝܡܐ (*mrayymā*), see Payne Smith, 2:3858 as well as Excursus 17. That the expression ܐܪܝܡ ܩܠܗ (*ʾarīm qāleh*) represents ἐφώνησεν in this passage is unlikely (Payne Smith, 2:3859; cf. BDAG, *s.v.* φωνέω).
100 Contra Bauer, 612; Lattke, *Oden*, 185.
101 Literally, "by his hands." N may have the singular "by his hand." Whose the "hand(s)" is/are cannot be finally determined. The statement may be one of direct creation or one referring to a creative agent and redeemer. Translating it as "those who

17), they have always been the "children" of the Most High (cf. τέκνα ϑεοῦ in John 1:12).[102] The occurrence of the term "people" later (12b) suggests a reference to the Qumran *Temple Scroll*. Similarities of terminology are as evident as radical differences of meaning: "You shall not eat any abominable thing, for you are a holy people to YHWH, your God. [Lacuna]. You are the sons of YHWH, your God" (11QT xlviii.15-17).[103] The Pa. ܩܪܒ (*qarreḇ*), followed by the dative preposition ܠ (*l*-), the suffix of which refers to the Most High of 4a, can represent προσάγω in the transitive sense of "bring (forward),"[104] but also προσφέρω with the accusative of the person ("bring someone . . . to someone").[105] Both Greek verbs can mean "to offer" as a "technical term of sacrificial procedure."[106]

It should be evident that the Greek loanword πρόσωπον/ܦܪܨܘܦܐ (*p̄arṣōp̄ā*) in 5a,[107] in spite of its probable derivation from Isa 50:7 LXX, cannot here be translated by "face" (see Excursus 8).[108] The subject of the Ethpa. of ܙܕܩ (*zḏaq*), "was declared righteous," which, as in 17:2a, corresponds to the theological passive[109] ἐδικαιώϑη (see Excursus 25), is "his person,"[110] that is, the Lord "himself."[111] Since the statement of salvation predicts the positive outcome of the hostilities that will be described in the subsequent first person narrative, "justify," as in 29:5b and 1 Tim 3:16, means "give victory to."[112]

The common word "to give/grant" supplies the theological cause for this righteous victory. Since the expression "holy Father" is derived from John 17:11 (πάτερ ἅγιε),[113] there is no need, as do

were in his hands" (Bauer, 612) skews the sense slightly toward preserving and protecting (cf. Harris and Mingana, 2:369, "the sons that were in His hands").

102 Beyer suggests: "Brought to him the children who were under his care" (Beyer, letter). Charlesworth's reference (p. 117) to John 17:1-9 is justifiable, but his translation of 4b ("And offered to Him those that had become sons through Him") is inaccurate (p. 116). This translation is based ultimately on Harris and Mingana's freer alternative translation (2:369), "those who had become children by His means," and was later imitated by Blaszczak (p. 43): "And he presented to Him those who had become sons through him." The lower-case "him" shows that Blaszczak is not referring to the Most High. In consequence he can rewrite the statement as "they have already been brought into the filial relationship with God" (p. 50).

103 Annette Steudel, ed., *Die Texte aus Qumran II: Hebräisch/Aramäisch und Deutsch mit masoretischer Punktation, Übersetzung, Einführung und Anmerkungen* (Darmstadt: Wissenschaftliche Buchgesellschaft, 2001) 101; Vermes, 145.

104 Payne Smith, 2:3722; BDAG, *s.v.* προσάγω, 1; Bauer, 612.

105 BDAG, *s.v.* προσφέρω, 1.

106 BDAG, *s.vv.* προσάγω, 1bβ; προσφέρω, 2a; Greßmann, 464. Harris and Mingana's reference (2:372) to the quotation of Isa 8:17-18 in Heb 2:12-13, "The Odist is not quoting Hebrews, but the sources of Hebrews in a collection of *Testimonia*," cannot be rejected out of hand. Indeed, the focus should be enlarged to take in the whole of Heb 2:10-14. This reveals a number of terms that appear also in stanza II: δι᾽ οὗ, υἱοί and παιδία, ὄνομα (from Ps 21:23 LXX), ἔδωκεν. Bultmann combines *Ode* 31:4 with various passages from *Odes* 10, 17, and 42 (see Bultmann, "Bedeutung," 119, 128 = idem, *Exegetica*, 75, 89). However, *Ode* 31 does not deal with any "freeing of prisoners" (Bultmann, "Bedeutung," 135 = idem, *Exegetica*, 93).

107 See Lattke, "Wörter," 298 = idem, *Bedeutung*, 4:146.

108 As by, e.g., Harris and Mingana, 2:369; Charlesworth, 116; Franzmann, 226.

109 Payne Smith, 1:1084; BDAG, *s.v.* δικαιόω. Berger and Nord's translation (p. 963), "God accepted him [i.e., his self] as righteous," is thus correct. A possible model could be ὁ δικαιώσας με in Isa 50:8 (Rahlfs, 2:635).

110 Bauer, 612; Emerton, 721.

111 Greßmann, 464. Blaszczak erroneously labels this Greco-Syriac idiom "meaningless" and inserts the preposition ܒ (*b*-) before the noun ܦܪܨܘܦܐ (*p̄arṣōp̄ā*). This enables him to translate it as "And he was justified in His presence" (see Blaszczak, 43, 50). The emendation is as superfluous as Gunkel's "'They' were declared righteous" (see Gunkel, 312, 313: "read ܦܪܨܘܦܗܘܢ" = "their person"). Gunkel later returned to the manuscript text: "And his actions were accepted" = "his person was justified" (idem, *Aufsätze*, 175).

112 Bauer, 610; cf. Bultmann, "Bedeutung," 128 = idem, *Exegetica*, 85; Arvedson, *Mysterium*, 40; Christ, *Sophia*, 71; Stenger, *Christushymnus*, 157.

113 Bultmann, *Gospel of John*, 502 (= *Das Evangelium*, 384). "The Father can be called 'holy' in his distinction from the world" (Ernst Haenchen, *John: A Commentary on the Gospel of John* [2 vols.; trans. Robert W. Funk; ed. Robert W. Funk and Ulrich Busse; Hermeneia; Philadelphia: Fortress Press, 1984] 2:153 [= *Johannesevangelium*, 505], on

Stölten[114] or Bauer,[115] to refer to the eleventh chapter of the Coptic-Gnostic *Untitled Text*,[116] which is later than the *Odes of Solomon* and, in spite of a few similarities, tends in a different direction. Gnostic supporters and (Jewish-Christian) opponents of John's Gospel would, by now, be identifying the Lord, who is not the Most High and Father, with the Johannine Jesus, who is called ὁ χριστὸς ὁ υἱὸς τοῦ θεοῦ ("the Christ, the Son of God") in John 20:31, and who should, of course, also be distinguished from the historical Jesus.

■ **6-7** There is no good reason to transform the tricolon of imperatives of salvation 6-7b into four lines by dividing 6 into 6a-b.[117] Even though "the placement of these verses and their lack of introduction are puzzling,"[118] it is clear that "the speaker" of 6-13 is meant to be "Christ."[119]

Starting at 8, this speaker will reveal his own troubles in a first-person narrative and then go on (12b-13b) to tell of his redeeming acts toward his "people." This people or the "children" mentioned earlier (4b) must be the "oppressed" ones (6) whom he is addressing and with whom many of those using and influenced by the *Odes of Solomon* will have identified. For Χριστιανοί[120] and *Christiani*[121] were oppressed not only by Jews and Romans but by some who should have been their brothers and sisters *in Christo,* except that they rated their (asserted) orthodoxy higher than their relationship.

The meaning of the first word of 6 is ambiguous and therefore contested.[122] Taking into account 42:17a, one might connect this imperative of the Pe. ܢܦܩ (*npaq*) with the coming forth of the "dead"[123] from "Death and Sheol."[124] So this invitation could be taken as a fulfillment of the promise of John 5:28-29.[125] But this does not agree with describing the hearers as "oppressed ones" (οἱ θλιβόμενοι), which is the most likely equivalent of the Syriac construction with ܗܢܘܢ ܕ (*hānnōn d-*) and the Ethpe. of ܐܠܨ (*ʾelaṣ*).[126] Indeed, in the context of oppression and persecution, it might be considered a world-renouncing "euphemism" for "dying" (cf. 1 Cor 5:10: ἐκ τοῦ κόσμου ἐξελθεῖν, "leave the world").[127] In that case, the imperative ἐξέλθατε/ܦܘܩܘ (*poq*)[128] would imply a—very un-Pauline—call to leave the afflictions of this life behind and move toward the "immortal life" (see 7b below), which does not exist in this world.[129] A notable characteristic of this Utopia is the soteriological χαρά/ܚܕܘܬܐ (*ḥaḏuṯā*) that was adumbrated already in 3a ("joy"; cf. 7:2; 15:1; 23:1) and is now to

John 17:11). On the (not merely) "Roman Catholic misuse" of this theological appellation, see Michael Lattke, "Heiligkeit III. Neues Testament," *TRE* 14 (1985) 704. In the *Odes of Solomon* comparisons may be made with the following passages: 10:4b ("glory of the Most High and of God my Father"), 23:18b ("Son of Truth from the Most High Father"), 41:9 ("Father of Truth"), and 41:13 ("Son of the Most High . . . in the *plērōma* of his Father").

114 Stölten, 50.

115 Bauer, 612.

116 Schmidt, Till, and Schenke, *Schriften*, 349–51, esp. 350 lines 9-15; cf. Schmidt and MacDermot, *Jeu*, 246–48, esp. 247 lines 1-6.

117 So, e.g., Harris and Mingana, 2:369; Bauer, 612; Charlesworth, 115; Emerton, 721; Blaszczak, 43; Franzmann, 225; Pierre, 155; Lattke, *Oden*, 186; correct are Ungnad and Staerk, 32; Frankenberg, 28; cf. Lattke, *Bedeutung*, 1:162–63.

118 Blaszczak, 52.

119 Kittel, 115; cf. Grese, *Corpus*, 178 n. 663: "Christ speaks through the singer."

120 BDAG, *s.v.* Χριστιανός.

121 See Helga Botermann, *Das Judenedikt des Kaisers Claudius: Römischer Staat und Christiani im 1. Jahrhundert* (*Hermes: Zeitschrift für klassische Philologie*, Einzelschriften 71; Stuttgart: Steiner, 1996) 141–88.

122 See Diettrich, 109.

123 Gunkel, 313; idem, *Aufsätze*, 176.

124 Connolly, "Odes," 302. Blaszczak's verdict (p. 52), "Scholars who see in vss 6-7 an allusion to Christ's call to those imprisoned in the underworld go far beyond the evidence afforded by this Ode," is sound.

125 See BDAG, *s.v.* ἐκπορεύομαι, 1c.

126 Payne Smith, 1:219; BDAG, *s.v.* θλίβω, 3. The phrase οἱ θλιβόμενοι is more likely than οἱ τεθλιμμένοι as the Greek equivalent (contra Frankenberg, 28). Reference to Matt 11:28 (most recently Berger and Nord, 963) has already been countered by Diettrich (p. 109). "The use of the 3rd person in the relative clause is un-Syriac (therefore Greek!); Nöldeke §350A" (Klaus Beyer in a letter). Also see 2 Cor 1:6; 4:8; 7:5; 1 Thess 3:4; 2 Thess 1:7.

127 BDAG, *s.v.* ἐξέρχομαι, 2.

128 Payne Smith, 2:2419–21.

129 Anyone dissatisfied by these extreme interpretations of the verb may find it simpler to interpret it as an invitation to leave the *massa perditionis*. Frankenberg's suggestion (p. 62) that 6-7 refer to "powers of the soul that are not yet aware of their freedom" is pure fantasy.

be "experienced." In view of the verb in 7b, it is likely that the verb corresponding to the synonymous Pa. of ܩܒܠ (*qbal*) in 6 was not λαμβάνω but δέχομαι.[130] In any case, it is the passive sense of either verb that is dominant, so that it might be translated as "allow yourselves to be given joy."[131]

Unlike in 3a, "grace"[132] in 7a is not precisely parallel to "joy." The term χάρις/ܛܝܒܘܬܐ (*ṭaybūtā*) is not, here, the direct object of the verb, but instead describes, with the use of διά/ܒܝܕ (*b-yad*), the means necessary to achieve the result of the imperative of salvation.[133] "Soul" does not mean an immortal *part* of the human beings who are addressed nor their "earthly life, life itself,"[134] but the people *themselves* in their personhood, who will now—*sola gratia* and in a sort of "reflexive relationship"[135]—"inherit," that is, "require" and "obtain" these *selves* as their "share" or their "possession."[136] The Pe. ܐܪܬ (*ʾireṯ*), which is also parallel to ܢܣܒ (*nsab*) in 23:19a (see on 7b below), should not be taken too literally. For the speaking "I" also declares that *he* is to redeem his people and "inherit it" (12b). The emphasis falls on "grace" with its echo of Pauline theology that excludes human autonomy. Since ܐܪܬ corresponds to κληρονομέω,[137] in both cases the Greek of 7a can be conjecturally reconstructed thus: καὶ κληρονομήσατε ἑαυτοὺς (or τὴν ψυχὴν ὑμῶν) διὰ (τῆς) χάριτος.[138]

Verse 7b is the high point of stanza III (see Table 1). Since a "life without death"[139] or ζωὴ ἀθάνατος can only be found with God, and such a ζωὴ ἐν ἀθανασίᾳ ("life in immortality"), possibly even without a resurrection of the dead, is among the δῶρα τοῦ θεοῦ ("gifts of God") according to *1 Clem.* 35:1-2,[140] the linking of this greatest "of the benefits of salvation present here and now"[141] with a transitive verb like λαμβάνω/ܢܣܒ (*nsab*), "take," whose active meaning is emphasized by ἑαυτοῖς/ܠܟܘܢ (*lḵōn*),[142] produces an almost unbearable paradox.[143] Again it is possible to reconstruct 𝔊: καὶ λάβετε ἑαυτοῖς ζωὴν ἀθάνατον.[144]

■ **8-9** Already in 28:17c, with its allusion to and revision of Ps 21:19b LXX, one could observe "a feature that unmistakably refers to the events of Christ's execution,"[145] so here there is no doubt that the speaking "I" is alluding to the Christian passion narratives and certain biblical passages incorporated in them. Yet there is no mention of crucifixion and resurrection.[146] Franzmann

130 Payne Smith, 2:3468; BDAG, *s.v.* δέχομαι; cf. Frankenberg, 28: δέχεσθε χαράν.

131 Berger and Nord, 963.

132 Diettrich (p. 109) takes "grace" to be a "personification" as in *Ode* 33. I cannot agree. His criticism of Harnack's (p. 63), and also Zahn's (p. 761), translation "by *his* grace," however, is valid.

133 See Payne Smith, 1:1547; BDAG, *s.v.* διά. Also cf. 6:6c; 15:8b; 25:4b; 29:5b; 41:3a.

134 BDAG, *s.v.* ψυχή, 1b.

135 BDAG, *s.v.* ψυχή, 2g; see Nöldeke §223.

136 BDAG, *s.v.* κληρονομέω, 2.

137 Payne Smith, 1:1634.

138 See Frankenberg, 28.

139 Bauer, 612.

140 Ehrman, 1:96–97; see Andreas Lindemann, *Die Clemensbriefe* (HNT 17; Tübingen: Mohr Siebeck, 1992) 108; Lona, 377–79; BDAG, *s.v.* ζωή; Lampe, 41–43, 593–96.

141 Otto Knoch, *Eigenart und Bedeutung der Eschatologie im theologischen Aufriß des ersten Clemensbriefes: Eine auslegungsgeschichtliche Untersuchung* (Theophaneia 17; Bonn: P. Hanstein, 1964) 320.

142 In this case the "preposition ܠ with a reflexive personal pronoun" is not a "*dativus ethicus*" (Nöldeke §224) but an actual "*reflexive*" (ibid. §223).

143 Since there may be a (not necessarily literary) connection between *1 Clem.* 35:2 and *Ode* 31:7b, it is worth quoting Knopf's commentary *in extenso*: "Hellenistic influence is also visible, it stands out in the composition of the first element ζωὴ ἐν ἀθανασίᾳ (cf. *Did.* 9:3). . . . Life in this context is the personal gift of salvation, which can be understood and experienced at the present time in the community as eternal life in which the individual partakes. For *1 Clement* this ἀθανασία probably depends in the first place on *gnōsis*, cf. 36:2 τῆς ἀθανάτου γνώσεως, and secondly, according to our sequence, on ἀλήθεια. This association is reminiscent of Johannine material, e.g. John 5:24, although the relationship is not literary, and Paul also knows of this present life. ζωὴ ἐν ἀθανασίᾳ, however, is a surprising phrase to find in *1 Clement*. Did the form of divine service go on to affect the exegesis of the gifts of salvation?" (see Rudolf Knopf, *Die Lehre der zwölf Apostel: Die zwei Clemensbriefe* [HNT, Ergänzungs-Band: Die Apostolischen Väter I; Tübingen: Mohr Siebeck, 1920] 104).

144 Frankenberg, 28.

145 Kittel, 110; see commentary on 28:17c.

146 See Labourt and Batiffol, 90.

correctly points to "the central position" of 8b.[147] But since she divides the monocolon 9, contrary to the manuscript evidence, into a bicolon,[148] she then finds it necessary to transform the manuscript tricolon into five lines by also dividing 8a.[149] Instead of merely noting the "inclusio for the stanza by the repetition of ܚܝܒ"[150] she could have drawn attention to the fact that the Syriac root occurs in each of the three lines. Whether "the paronomasia is intended"[151] or enforced by a Greek *Vorlage* cannot be decided.

This paronomasia in ܣ may have persuaded Connolly (with a reference to Nöldeke §347) to translate 8a-b as "and they made me a debtor to him [viz., Death] to whom I was not a debtor."[152] This proposition can be rebutted, since "generally the verb ܚܝܒ [i.e., the Pa. *ḥayyeḇ*] means 'to condemn' (as culprit)."[153] The particle ܘ (*ʾu-*) at the beginning of the first-person narrative is not a pointer to any loss of preceding material. But omitting this often superfluous conjunction[154] or, especially, translating the Pa. of ܚܝܒ, ܚܒ (*ḥāḇ*), with its third masculine plural objective suffix, as an impersonal construction[155] is inadvisable, in view of the suffix ܗܘܢ (*-hōn*) in 9 (as well as in 10b and 12b) and the literary allusion to quite specific "persecutors."[156] It is not really possible to decide whether 𝔊 used καταδικάζω[157] or the more usual κατακρίνω[158] for the Pa. ܚܝܒ (*ḥayyeḇ*). The second is the more likely, since it is found both in the Synoptic predictions of the passion (Matt 20:18; Mark 10:33) and in the Sanhedrin's death sentence (Mark 14:64). In the description of that scene, witnesses arose (Mark 14:57: ἀναστάντες) and the high priest stood up (Mark 14:60: ἀναστάς), so a transferring of the verb (ἀν-, ἐξαν-, ἐπαν-, παρ-)ίστημι/ܩܘܡ, ܩܡ (*qām*)[159] to the speaking "I" offers the simplest explanation for the puzzling subordinate clause in 8a (see also 11a below). The line is no more a statement of resurrection than of a rebellious uprising.

Verse 8b begins with a correlative demonstrative pronoun used, with weakened meaning,[160] as the accusative object that, together with the negated ܐܝܬܝ ܗܘܝܬ (*ʾīṯay-wēṯ*)[161] and the predicative passive participle of the Pa. ܚܝܒ (*ḥayyeḇ*),[162] stands in apposition to the objective suffix "me" in 8a, which in 𝔊 might have been . . . με . . . τὸν μὴ ὄντα ἔνοχον/κατάκριτον.[163] Since ἔνοχος occurs in Mark 14:64 as well as in Matt 26:66, it is more likely to have appeared here, although in an absolute sense κατάκριτος is more commonly used.[164]

In connection with the *hapax legomenon* ܦܠܓ (*palleḡ*)[165] in 9, there have been justifiably many references made to Ps 21:19a LXX and the use of this Psalm in the

147 Franzmann, 229.
148 As also Lattke, *Bedeutung*, 1:162–63.
149 Franzmann, 225–26.
150 Ibid., 229.
151 Charlesworth, 117.
152 Connolly, "Odes," 302.
153 Harris and Mingana, 2:371: "That in this sentence the meaning of the verb refers probably to 'a condemnation' is borne out by the Participle ܡܚܝܒܐ which is seldom found in the sense of a debtor in money."
154 At least here in *Ode* 31 it forms a connection between the quite different stanzas III and IV.
155 Diettrich, 110: "*man*."
156 Blaszczak, 52.
157 BDAG, *s.v.* καταδικάζω; Payne Smith, 1:1213.
158 BDAG, *s.v.* κατακρίνω; Frankenberg, 29: κατέκρινάν με.
159 On the possible equivalents, see Payne Smith, 2:3522–25; BDAG, *s.vv.* ἀνίστημι, 6; ἐξανίστημι, 3; ἐπανίστημι; παρίστημι, 2. Perhaps a "legal technical term" was intended (BDAG, *s.v.* παρίστημι, 2aα). If an intransitive passive of ἐγείρω was used, it would remind the reader of the appearance of prophets (BDAG, *s.v.* ἐγείρω, 12). Any form of καθίστημι does not come under consideration (contra Frankenberg, 29: ὅτε κατέστην).
160 Nöldeke §228.
161 Ibid. §303: "was."
162 That the emphatic participle here corresponds to κατακρίνων is unlikely (Payne Smith, 1:1214).
163 See Payne Smith, 1:1214; BDAG, *s.vv.* ἔνοχος, 2; κατάκριτος. Since the nominalized participle ὤν "can only be used when there are other adjuncts to the predicate" (BDF and BDR §413; μή in the present case), the use of ἀκατάκριτος is not possible (see BDAG, *s.v.* ἀκατάκριτος: "uncondemned"). Frankenberg's retroversion (p. 29), τὸν οὐδέν τι ὑπεύθυνον, is also astray (see LEH, *s.v.* ὑπεύθυνος: "subject to [τινι]").
164 See LSJ, *s.v.* κατάκριτος.
165 On this Pa. of ܦܠܓ (*plaḡ* and *pleḡ*), see Payne Smith, 2:3135–36. The singular ܦܠܓ (*palleḡ*) in N is pronounced in exactly the same way as the plural and correct reading in H. The Greek equivalent is more likely to be διαμερίζω than μερίζω (BDAG, *s.vv.* διαμερίζω, 2; μερίζω, 2a).

passion narratives (cf. Matt 27:35; Mark 15:24; Luke 23:34; John 19:24),[166] especially since v. 19b LXX of the Psalm has left its traces on *Ode* 28:17c. When Spitta remarks that it is "striking" that the object is not *τὰ ἱμάτια* and suspects "an incorrect translation by the Syrian,"[167] he—and not he alone—is overlooking the origin of the term *σκῦλα*/ܒܙܬܐ (*bezztā*)[168] in Isa 53:12a where the "Servant" of God *κληρονομήσει πολλοὺς καὶ τῶν ἰσχυρῶν μεριεῖ σκῦλα* ("shall inherit many, and he shall divide the spoils of the mighty").[169]

The speaking "I," "Christ," not only speaks of his *ἱμάτια*, but also claims for himself the "spoils"[170] promised to the Servant of God (*παῖς θεοῦ*) and thus identifies himself here, even before reaching stanzas V–VI, as a member of the front rank in the history of salvation, while simultaneously modifying the archetype. Since there was "nothing owed"[171] to those who seized these "spoils" that were under theological sanction, the particle ܟܕ (*kad*) must have an adversative meaning, like the Greek *καίτοι*,[172] rather than a simple concessive one. The following attempt at reconstructing the Greek of 9 as *(δια)μερίσαντο τὰ σκῦλα μου καίτοι μηδενὸς ὀφειλομένου αὐτοῖς γενομένου*, which differs from Frankenberg, is an attractive conjecture.[173]

■ **10-11** The following remarks refer to the last two stanzas of *Ode* 31, V (10-11) and VI (12-13), which are among the most important passages in the *Odes of Solomon* for the dating of the *Odes* and the determination of their original language.[174] Harris and Mingana already noted, referring especially to *Barn.* 5:5-7 and 14:4, that there was "a curious coincidence both in thought and in language" between the *Odes of Solomon* and the *Epistle of Barnabas*[175] in which the *Epistle of Barnabas* "appears again to have been influenced by the language of the Odes."[176]

It can be shown that the anonymous author of the *Epistle of Barnabas* knew the *Odes of Solomon*—or, to put it more cautiously, vv. 8-13 of *Ode* 31, which may have originated elsewhere[177]—in the Greek language; in other words, the *Epistle of Barnabas* depends on the *Odes of Solomon*, not vice versa. The "most difficult passage"[178] in the whole "treatise,"[179] *Barn.* 5:6-7, originates from the "prophets" (*οἱ προφῆται*) who "prophesied" about the "Lord" (*εἰς αὐτὸν ἐπροφήτευσαν*).[180] This passage contains, in addition to allusions to 1 Tim 3:16 and 2 Tim

166 Harris and Mingana, 2:372; Bauer, 612; Charlesworth, 117; Blaszczak, 52–53.
167 Spitta, 286.
168 Payne Smith, 1:502. The neuter *σκῦλον* is almost always used in the plural (BDAG, *s.v. σκῦλον*: "booty, spoils"). On the loss of consonantal doubling in the Syriac word ܒܙܬܐ, see Nöldeke §21.B.
169 Rahlfs, 2:639; Brenton, 889. Once this origin is recognized, it opens one's eyes to other influences from Isaiah 53 on *Ode* 31. The beginning of stanza II, "He opened his mouth . . ." (see 3a above), suddenly becomes an antithesis to the statement that the Servant *οὐκ ἀνοίγει τὸ στόμα αὐτοῦ* (Isa 53:7). On the whole of this text block in Deutero-Isaiah and its use in the NT, see Ernst Haag, "Knecht Gottes," *LThK*³ 6 (1997) 155–56. *1 Clem.* 16:3-14 is even richer in quotations from Isaiah 53 (and one from Psalm 21 LXX; see Lona, 232–33).
170 "The one who had been robbed of all possessions in this life is now to receive them back in abundance" (Westermann, *Jesaja*, 216). The continuation, Isa 53:12b-c, which has been far more influential christologically and soteriologically, has left far fewer traces in the *Odes of Solomon*.
171 Bauer, 612.
172 See BDAG, *s.v. καίτοι*; BDF and BDR §§425, 450.
173 See Payne Smith, 1:1213; BDAG, *s.v. ὀφείλω*, 2αα. Frankenberg (p. 29) seems to have Luke 11:22 in mind for the first half of 9 and his retroversion of the second half is also problematic: (*ἐμέρισαν*) *διεδίδοσαν τὰ σκῦλά μου | οὐδὲν ὀφείλοντος αὐτοῖς*. Linguistically, one may refer to Heb 4:3, where a similar construction follows a quotation from Scripture (on the use of *γίνομαι*, cf., e.g., Mark 4:35; Luke 23:8; Acts 28:6; on the "genitive absolute," see BDF and BDR §§417, 423). Diettrich (p. 110), with no real justification, considers 9 (his 7c-d) an "interpolation" and brackets the "stich."
174 See Introduction, sec. 4.2.5. What Prostmeier has to say about the "place of origin and destination" of the *Epistle of Barnabas* also applies in part to the *Odes of Solomon* (see Prostmeier, 119–30). In fact "the homeland of the *Odes of Solomon* is no less uncertain" than "that of Barnabas" (ibid., 124 n. 82).
175 Harris and Mingana, 2:49.
176 Ibid., 2:53.
177 See Blaszczak, 57.
178 Markus Vinzent, "Ertragen und Ausharren—die Lebenslehre des Barnabasbriefes," *ZNW* 86 (1995) 85.
179 Ehrman, 2:3.
180 Ibid., 2:26–27. *Barn.* 5:5 goes so far as to call Jesus

1:10,[181] the parallel to *Ode* 31:10-13.[182] So the reference to the prophets is one of the "anonymous citations" (cf. the reference to *Barn.* 11:9-10 in the commentary on *Ode* 11:16c).[183]

Since ὑπομένειν ("endure"), which dominates *Barn.* 5:1-12 (cf. *Barn.* 14:4) and is intended to point to "the Incarnation and Passion of Jesus,"[184] cannot be traced to a biblical prophecy, it is permissible to suggest *Ode* 31:10-11 as its literary source. This theory may be supported by the hypothesis that the phrase στερεὰ πέτρα, which comes from Isa 50:7 LXX (see on 11a below), led the author of *Barnabas* to compose his whole section about the "incarnation, work and sufferings of the Lord (5:1-14)"[185] on the model of *Ode* 31, ending with a summary of Isa 50:6-7.[186] It is less certain that the quotation from Isa 53:5 and 53:7, with the comparison ὡς ἀμνὸς ἄφωνος ("like a silent lamb" [*Barn.* 5:2]), was also prompted by *Ode* 31:10a (see below). The strange phrase λαὸς κληρονομίας ("people of the inheritance") in *Barn.* 14:4, on the other hand, was almost certainly inspired by *Ode* 31:12b, since soon after—and again with no discernible scriptural foundation—we read in *Barn.* 14:6: γέγραπται γάρ, πῶς αὐτῷ ὁ πατὴρ ἐντέλλεται, λυτρωσάμενον ἡμᾶς ἐκ τοῦ σκότους ἑτοιμάσαι ἑαυτῷ λαὸν ἅγιον ("For it is written how the Father commanded him to prepare for himself a holy people after he redeemed us from darkness").[187]

So it is more than likely that this "theological treatise,"[188] dated not much later than 130 C.E., used extracts, written in Greek, from the *Odes of Solomon* that were considered prophetic; thus *Barnabas* cannot be used to interpret stanzas V–VI, but the text of *Barnabas* can certainly be used to ascertain what the Greek equivalents were to the Syriac of the existing texts of the *Odes of Solomon*.

Without unduly emphasizing "the Odist's love of paronomasia" (as Charlesworth does in connection with his own "restoration" of 11a: ܒܝ ܡܩܘܐ ܢܟܠܠܐ),[189] it is possible to say of the Syriac *translation* of a Greek original that "10a and 11b form the inclusio for the stanza by the repetition of the Paiel of ܣܒܪ. The repetition of ܣܒܪ and ܩܘܡ provides a mirror pattern (A B B A) for the four lines."[190]

The particle ܕܝܢ (*dēn*) in 10a is used syntactically like δέ[191] and emphasizes the contrast between the "I" and the villains of stanza IV.[192] The *Vorlage* of the quadrilit-

"Lord of the entire world" (cf. 6:12), while *Barn.* 21:5 "ascribes the title to God the Father" (Vinzent, 83). In spite of Wengst's reference (p. 151) to *Ode* 31:12-13, Vinzent (pp. 83–92) ignores *Ode* 31 in his discussion of *Barn.* 5:6-7.

181 It is also necessary, however, to consider Prostmeier's verdict (p. 97): "All attempts to prove that *Barnabas* uses New Testament texts may be said to have failed." If this is true, the close relationship with the hymnic passages of the Pastoral Epistles must be explained in other ways (see Oberlinner, *Pastoralbriefe*, 1:162–69; 2:26, 37–44). Even more important is that then Rom 15:8 could not have had any direct influence either (see below on 13a).

182 Ehrman, 2:26–27; Wengst, 150; Lindemann and Paulsen, 36.

183 Prostmeier, 92. "On the basis of *Barn.* 1:5; 4:9a and 17:1-2, it is" for Prostmeier "unquestionable that the author, in *Barn.* 2–16, is not only quoting 'the Scriptures'. It is his declared intention to pass on all his lore. So traditions of all sorts are included in *Barn.* 2–16. On the one hand, there are quotations, some exact, others merely indicating the underlying thought, from Greek translations of the Bible, especially from Isaiah, the Psalms, and the Torah; on the other, quotations from extracanonical works, whose common denominator is their prophetic standing (*Barn.* 1:7-8; 2:4a; 3:6)" (Prostmeier, 89). To this should be added that everything *Barnabas* conveys "pertains" to "salvation" (17:1 [εἰς σωτηρίαν]; Ehrman, 2:74–75; cf. Lindemann and Paulsen, 68–69).

184 Vinzent, 88.

185 Prostmeier, 229–50.

186 See Wengst, 151.

187 Ehrman, 2:64–65; cf. Lindemann and Paulsen, 62; Wengst, 178. Wengst (p. 179) considers the introductory γέγραπται to be only an "anticipation of the quotations in verses 7-9." If Prostmeier had considered *Ode* 31 here (as well as at *Barn.* 5:6-7), he might not have declared (p. 470): "Γέγραπται is primarily connected to the introduction λέγει οὖν ὁ προφήτης in the quotation in v. 7a." In any case the terms "Father" and "darkness" form another link to this Ode (see on 1b and 5b above).

188 Lindemann and Paulsen, 23.

189 Charlesworth, 118.

190 Franzmann, 229.

191 Lattke, "Wörter," 288, 290 = idem, *Bedeutung*, 4:136, 138.

192 BDAG, *s.v.* δέ, 4.

eral verb ܣܝܒܪ (*saybar*), derived from ܣܒܪ (*sḇar*), cannot be ἀνέχομαι or πάσχω;[193] it must be ὑπομένω,[194] used in Heb 12:2 and particularly in *Barnabas* 5 (see above) to refer to the cross of Jesus. The torture of crucifixion is never mentioned in the Ode; it merely stands threateningly on the historical horizon of the landscape of mythological judgment in which "the endurance of the speaker is the major point."[195] Although the influence of Isaiah 53 on *Ode* 31 has already been demonstrated (see on 9a above), so that for "background for these verses Is. 53.7 comes immediately to mind,"[196] an influence by Isa 42:14 cannot be excluded.[197] Anyone ignorant of the Jewish prophets and the Christian passion narratives (cf., in addition to Matt 26:63 and Mark 14:61, the discussion of *Gos. Pet.* 4:10b by John Dominic Crossan)[198] could still be reminded, by the silence of the "I," emphasized by the poetic hendiadys "was silent" and "remained calm," of the example of Socrates "before a jury."[199] The exact equation between the Pe. ܫܬܩ (*šṯeq*), which appears only here, and the Pe. ܫܠܐ (*šlā*) or ܫܠܝ (*šlī*),[200] which stresses the silence even more, with the two corresponding Greek verbs σιγάω and σιωπάω is hardly possible and not actually necessary.[201] There is no need for such a counsel of despair as the too free retroversion of Frankenberg: ἐγὼ δὲ ὑπέμεινα διὰ σιωπῆς ἐπεχόμενος.[202]

The beginning of 10b, ܐܟ ܕܠܐ (*ʾaḵ d-lā*), corresponds to the Greek ἵνα μή.[203] The form of the Ethpe./Ettaph. of ܙܘܥ, ܙܥ (*zāʿ*) cannot be "a third person masculine singular perfect."[204] It is, in fact, a first person singular imperfect and corresponds to the Greek subjunctive. It can be compared to the quotation of Ps 15:8 LXX in Acts 2:25 (ἵνα μὴ σαλευθῶ, "that I may not be shaken").[205] But it is quite uncertain whether 𝔊 had σαλεύομαι since the verbs κινέομαι (with ἀκίνητος in 11a) or σείομαι and even ταράσσομαι could have been used. The third masculine plural suffix of the preposition ܡܢ (*men*), which here corresponds to ὑπό, refers to

193 Payne Smith, 2:2511; Nöldeke §181.

194 BDAG, *s.v.* ὑπομένω, 2: "endure."

195 Blaszczak, 53.

196 Ibid.

197 Labourt and Batiffol, 90. The adjective ἄφωνος (the Peshitta uses ܫܬܝܩ [*šattīq*], *OTSy*, pt. 3 fasc. 1, p. 97) in Isa 53:7 has left no verbal impression on 10a. Instead of the comparison ὡς πρόβατον or ὡς ἀμνός (Isa 53:7; cf. Acts 8:32), the people of the *Odes* preferred a comparison with the less defenseless "rock" (see on 11a below).

198 John Dominic Crossan, *The Cross That Spoke: The Origins of the Passion Narrative* (San Francisco: Harper & Row, 1988) 180.

199 BDAG, *s.v.* σιωπάω, 1; see Blaszczak, 53.

200 This Pe. may also be used to translate παύομαι and ἡσυχάζω. Neither of these verbs fits the image of the silent victim.

201 Payne Smith, 2:4163, 4356; BDAG, *s.vv.* σιγάω, σιωπάω.

202 Frankenberg, 29. Berger and Nord's translation of 10a (p. 963) is too good to be true: "But I was patient, kept silence and remained peaceful." Emerton (p. 721) hits the right note: "But I endured, and was silent and quiet."

203 Nöldeke §364.B: "that not." Quite often ἵνα μή is simply translated by ܕܠܐ (*d-lā*). A more elevated form would use the nominalized infinitive: "The construction with *verbs of hindering, ceasing* etc. with τοῦ μή and the infinitive . . . clearly becomes 'so that . . . not' [cf. Luke 4:42]" (BDF and BDR §400 [4]). In that case, τοῦ μὴ σαλευθῆναι ὑπ᾽ αὐτῶν could be accepted (Frankenberg, 29).

204 Contra Blaszczak, 53. This makes his translation (p. 43) of 10b, "Like one who was not troubled by them," untenable. On this mistranslation he then founds his comparison of 10b with *Gos. Pet.* 4:10 and—with support from George W. E. Nickelsburg (*Resurrection, Immortality, and Eternal Life in Intertestamental Judaism* [HTS 26; Cambridge, Mass.: Harvard University Press; London: Oxford University Press, 1972] 48–93) and Dieter Georgi ("Der vorpaulinische Hymnus Phil 2, 6-11," in Erich Dinkler, ed., *Zeit und Geschichte: Dankesgabe an Rudolf Bultmann zum 80. Geburtstag* [Tübingen: Mohr Siebeck, 1964] 270–75, esp. 272)—the tracing back of 8-10a to Wis 2:12-20 (see Blaszczak, 54–55). In conclusion he says (p. 55): "If, indeed, there is a docetic sense implied in Ode 31.10b, it can probably be traced back to the docetism which Georgi sees in the Wisdom tradition." As far as I can see, Georgi does later call the *Wisdom of Solomon* "a Gnostic work, . . . the oldest that we have" (see Georgi, "Hymnus," 394) but fails to use the key word "docetic" (ibid., 391–94, 407–17).

205 BDAG, *s.v.* σαλεύω, 2: "to disturb inwardly." This would suggest ἀσάλευτος (BDAG, *s.v.* ἀσάλευτος, 2: "unshakable, enduring") in 11a. However, this adjective is never translated by ܕܠܐ ܙܘܥܬܐ (*d-lā zawʿṯā*) in the New Testament, but either by ܠܐ ܡܬܬܙܝܥ (*lā mettzīʿ* [Acts 27:41]) or by ܕܠܐ ܡܬܙܝܥܐ (*d-lā meṯzīʿā* [Heb 12:28]).

those anonymous persons who, in 8a and 9a, passed judgment and showed themselves greedy for booty.

The image that follows in 11a-b to some extent validates Gunkel's statement: "In such descriptions of the passion of Christ there is a convergence of memories of the historical Jesus, the prophecy of the Suffering Servant of Isa 53 and—as Harris[206] has pointed out—influences from Greek philosophy: one of the sayings of Marcus Aurelius (*Med.* 4.49 [LCL 94–95]), about the promontory that is unmoved by the fury of the waves, is closely related."[207] But these references to Isaiah 53 and the archetypal "cliff"[208] are not sufficient, since the phrase ܟܐܦܐ ܫܪܝܪܬܐ (*kēpā šarrīrtā*) must be modeled on Isa 50:7, ἀλλὰ ἔθηκα τὸ πρόσωπόν μου ὡς στερεὰν πέτραν ("but I set my face as a solid rock").[209] According to the English translation of *Han som kommer* (1951), Mowinckel stresses the literary connections between Isa 50:4-11 and *Ode* 31 as one of the examples "in the history of religion of a central figure . . . being introduced as speaking in the first person in a cultic circle, even if he is no longer visibly present on earth."[210] The phrase under discussion does not refer to Peter, even though "firm rock" was to become "a recognised title applied not only to Christ but also to Peter"; "Here at least, as not always in the Odes, it is certain that Christ is the speaker."[211]

The Pe. ܩܐܡ, ܩܡ (*qām*) in 11a, "stood," which follows the "adversative particle" ἀλλά/ܐܠܐ (*ʾellā*),[212] links it to 8a (see above). The Syriac, with the phrase ܕܠܐ ܙܘܥܬܐ (*dlā zawʿṯā*), "undisturbed," creates a play on words that may not have existed in 𝔊.[213] The *Vorlage* of the negated noun could have been ἀκίνητος (cf. πέτρα ἀκίνητος in Ignatius *Pol.* 1:1)[214] or ἀμετακίνητος.[215] That ἀσάλευτος could not be excluded was already noted in discussing 10b. There are also the less common adverbs such as ἀπτοήτως or ἀφρικτί.[216] Even ἀδιάσειστος[217] or ἄσειστος[218] come under consideration, since they match well with σείομαι (see on 10b above).

The demonstrative significance of the pronoun ܗܝ (*hāy*) at the beginning of 11b, like that of ܗܘ (*hāw*) in 8a, is quite weak.[219] It is a safe assumption that the participle of the Ethpa. of ܢܓܕ (*ngad*), which occurs only here, contains a hidden and distancing allusion to the predictions of the passion in the New Testament (Mark 10:34; Matt 20:19; Luke 18:33; cf. Matt 23:34) that mention "flogging as a punishment decreed by the synagogue"[220]

206 Harris, 131.

207 Gunkel, 314. The text and translation of the traditional piece of Stoic wisdom from Marcus Aurelius are as follows: Ὅμοιον εἶναι τῇ ἄκρᾳ, ᾗ διηνεκῶς τὰ κύματα προσρήσσεται· ἡ δὲ ἕστηκε, καὶ περὶ αὐτὴν κοιμίζεται τὰ φλεγμήναντα τοῦ ὕδατος ("Be like a headland of rock on which the waves break incessantly; but it stands fast and around it the seething of the waters sinks to rest"). See Willy Theiler, ed. and trans., *Kaiser Marc Aurel, Wege zu sich selbst* (BAWGR; 2nd ed.; Zurich/Munich: Artemis, 1974) 94–95.

208 German: "Klippe." This is Wilhelm Capelle's translation of the term ἄκρα (see *Marc Aurel, Selbstbetrachtungen* [KTA 4; 8th ed.; Stuttgart: Kröner, 1953 = 12th ed., 1973] 47) meaning "the extreme end," especially "upwards, i.e., the tip, peak, height, precipice, promontory, castle" (Kaegi, 28).

209 Rahlfs, 2:635; Brenton, 886. The adjective in the phrase "solid rock" (11a, in 𝔊 στερεὰ πέτρα) shows that the phrase is not taken from the original Hebrew or from the Syriac translation. The description of the Servant of God in Isa 50:4-11 has left other traces in *Ode* 31 (see above). In the context of Isaiah 50 and the use of Isa 50:6-7 in *Barn.* 5:14, the translation "hard rock" (Lindemann and Paulsen, 39), referring to τὸ πρόσωπον, is preferable to "strong rock" (Prostmeier, 230). The rock in *Ode* 31 is "genuine" (Lattke, *Bedeutung*, 1:165) or "true" (idem, *Oden*, 186) because it is "the solid rock" (Klijn, 304; cf. the meaning "firm, secure" in Bultmann, "Untersuchungen," 160 = idem, *Exegetica*, 170).

210 Sigmund Mowinckel, *He That Cometh* (trans. G. W. Anderson; Oxford: Blackwell, 1956; Nashville/New York: Abingdon, n.d.) 253.

211 Murray, "Rock," 352.

212 BDAG, *s.v.* ἀλλά; Payne Smith, 1:192.

213 Payne Smith, 1:1109.

214 BDAG, *s.v.* ἀκίνητος, 1: "immovable."

215 Frankenberg, 29. He did not notice that ܟܐܦܐ ܫܪܝܪܬܐ (*kēpā šarrīrtā*) derives from Isa 50:7 and used ἑδραία for στερεά in his retroversion, perhaps thinking of 1 Cor 15:58, where ἑδραῖος is found together with ἀμετακίνητος.

216 LSJ, *s.vv.* ἀπτοήτως, ἀφρικτί.

217 LSJ, *s.v.* ἀδιάσειστος; Tsakonas, 144.

218 LSJ, *s.v.* ἄσειστος; Fanourgakis, 167.

219 Nöldeke §228.

220 Berger and Nord (p. 963) make the connection explicit in their translation: "I was lashed as by waves and stood firm."

and/or the report in the Johannine passion story of the "*verberatio*" executed according to Roman criminal law (John 19:1; cf. Matt 27:26; Mark 15:15).[221] It should, however, be noticed that Isa 50:6 already speaks of torture by the "scourges."[222] This, though, does not convert the plural of κῦμα/ܓܠܐ (*gallā*)[223] into a poetic metaphor;[224] the image is that of a rock among waves and breakers. That the solid and abiding rock also "endures" (feminine singular active participle of ܣܝܒܪ [*saybar*]) rounds off the image and once more brings out forcefully the "fortitude and tenacity" of the speaking "I" (see 10a above), on which *Barn.* 5:1-14 will expand.[225] So stanza V should not end with ἀσάλευτος in 𝔊.[226] The most likely ending is a paronomasiac *inclusio* by a form of ὑπομένω.[227]

■ **12-13** In this final tetracolon,[228] the self-portrait of the speaking "I," which may be called a passion narrative omitting the crucifixion (and resurrection),[229] reaches calmer waters and debouches into an unprecedented soteriological claim that salvation and inheritance are the fulfilment of God's promises transferred to the speaking "I."

Although there are several possible equivalents, the Pe. ܣܒܠ (*sḇal*), which occurs only in 12a, here represents the verb ἀναφέρω, taken from Isa 53:11-12 LXX, which is not easy to translate.[230] The term πικρία/ܡܪܝܪܘܬܐ (*marrīrūṯā*)[231] is probably, as in 29:15b, "inspired" by the influential v. 22 of Ps 68 LXX,[232] while ܡܟܝܟܘܬܐ (*makkīḵūṯā*), which replaces the "antithesis" of 28:15, is reminiscent of both Matt 11:29[233] and Phil 2:3.[234] Then, in view of 41:12, where the connection to Phil 2:8 is clearer, the Greek equivalent ταπεινοφροσύνη ("humility")[235] is to be preferred here to the synonymous πραότης.[236] The preposition ܡܛܠ (*meṭṭol*) corresponds to διά with accusative and gives the reason why the speaking "I" burdened himself with the cruel "bitterness" of his adversaries.[237]

221 Payne Smith, 2:2279; BDAG, *s.vv.* μαστιγόω, 1a; φραγελλόω.

222 Rahlfs, 2:635; Brenton, 886; see BDAG, *s.v.* μάστιξ, 1.

223 I have already discussed Charlesworth's emendation (pp. 117–18) in my edition of the *Odes* (Lattke, *Bedeutung*, 1:49 n. 1). Franzmann (p. 227) also prefers H: "N has ܓ̈ܠܠܐ ܟܐ̈ܦܐ. The copyist mistakenly read ܟܐܦܐ from the preceding line." On the plural ܓ̈ܠܠܐ in H (there is no *linea occultans*: Charlesworth, *Manuscripts*, 74 line 9), see Brockelmann, *Grammatik* §§74 n. 1, 114.

224 See Payne Smith, 1:714; BDAG, *s.v.* κῦμα.

225 See Vinzent, 82–93.

226 Contra Frankenberg, 29.

227 BDAG, *s.v.* ὑπομένω, 2.

228 In N 12a and 12b appear as monocola, but H subdivides both (Lattke, *Bedeutung*, 1:76). In neither case does the subdivision make sense, and already Diettrich (p. 110 n. 4) discarded them.

229 As in all the Gospels, the speaking "I" speaks as one who has already been proclaimed by the faithful as risen from the dead, not merely recalled to life by God.

230 BDAG, *s.v.* ἀναφέρω; Payne Smith, 2:2503. The translation would be easier if 𝔊 had used ἤνεγκον (Frankenberg, 29; BDAG, *s.v.* φέρω). The Hebrew verbs represented by it are "often rendered 'bear' or 'take away'" (BDAG, *s.v.* ἀναφέρω, 4). But here ἀναφέρω might rather, as in Heb 9:28, mean "take upon oneself."

231 BDAG, *s.v.* πικρία, 2: "bitterness, animosity."

232 Blaszczak, 56; and see already Harris and Mingana, 2:361, on this "companion Psalm" to Psalm 22 (21 LXX).

233 Spitta, 286.

234 See Franzmann, 214, 230. The word ܣܒܠ (*sḇal*) throws further light on the variants in 29:15b, where "the word for 'bearing' is . . . ܛܥܢ" (Harris and Mingana, 2:372). Instead of the suggestion that "the Odist has changed the word" (ibid., 2:372), it is more likely that somewhere in the tradition ܛܥܢܬ (N) was corrected to ܛܥܝܢܬ (H) to harmonize with 31:12a (see commentary on 28:15b).

235 BDAG, *s.v.* ταπεινοφροσύνη. Frankenberg's choice (p. 29) of ταπεινότης shows that he is acquainted with the "habits of thought of the Alexandrian exegetes" (p. 62) but also imports a later "academic vocabulary" (p. 63) into the *Odes of Solomon*, which originated in the first quarter of the second century (see Lampe, 1773–74). The term ταπείνωσις from Isa 53:8 LXX (BDAG, *s.v.* ταπείνωσις: "humiliation") had no influence here.

236 BDAG, *s.v.* πραότης: "gentleness, humility"; cf. Payne Smith, 2:2103.

237 BDAG, *s.vv.* διά, B2a: "out of;" πικρία, 2. Linguistically, reference can be made to Eph 2:4. "The suffering was endured because Jesus was humble and not 'for humility's sake' as Harris-Mingana translated" (Charlesworth, 118). The *Odes*, of course, never mention the name Jesus.

The conjunction ܡܛܠ ܕ (*meṭṭol d-*) at the beginning of 12b, which hardly differs from the ܕ (*d-*) of 13a, should not be translated as "because"[238] or "since."[239] It actually corresponds to ἵνα in "final sense" and expresses the soteriological "purpose."[240] In deciding on the exact meaning of the imperfect of the Pe. ܦܪܩ (*praq*), *Barn.* 14:4-6 comes into play.[241] There, too, it is said in v. 4: αὐτὸς δὲ ὁ κύριος ἡμῖν ἔδωκεν εἰς λαὸν κληρονομίας, δι' ἡμᾶς ὑπομείνας ("but the Lord himself gave it to us, as a people of the inheritance, by enduring suffering for us"); "to prepare for himself a holy people" (ἑτοιμάσαι ἑαυτῷ λαὸν ἅγιον) is the final goal of the redemption sanctioned by the γέγραπται ("it is written")[242] in *Barn.* 14:6. Now this recourse to the written word "finds support in *Barnabas*" (Prostmeier, referring specifically to *Barn.* 5:7; see introduction to stanzas V–VI above).[243] But some of the prophetic content of *Barn.* 5:6-7, as has been shown, originates in *Ode* 31. This is true not only of the verb ὑπομένω (*Barn.* 5:6, etc.; see on 10a and 11b above), but also the plural of πατήρ and the singular ἐπαγγελία ("promise"; see 13a below) and the term λαός that is found here (cf. *Barn.* 5:7; on *Ode* 10:6c, see commentary on that passage). Since both *Barn.* 5:7 and 14:4, 6 use the term λαός ("people"), originally applied to the children of Israel and later to the Christians, the other term ἔθνος cannot have been the original of ܥܡܐ (*ʿammā*).[244] The speaking "I" distances himself from John 18:35, where Pilate mentions τὸ ἔθνος τὸ σόν, referring exclusively to the Jews (cf. John 11:48-52; see on 4b above).

The objective suffix of the imperfect of ܐܝܬ (*ʾireṯ*)[245] in 12b refers to "my people." The term "inherit" was used already in 7a, and here also it corresponds to κληρονομέω, a term that turns up in *Barn.* 14:4-5 in the extraordinary phrase λαὸς κληρονομίας ("people of inheritance"),[246] while Christ is described as κληρονομῶν ("the heir"),[247] so Charlesworth's derivation of the "verb form" ܐܘܪܬܝܘܗܝ from the Aph. ܐܘܪܬܝ (*ʾartī*),[248] which Reinink[249] rejects and McNeil[250] defends with fairly weak arguments, is erroneous. This also eliminates what Blaszczak, following McNeil, has to say, that "the instruction which saves is centered on *mkykwth* [*sic*], the humility the speaker showed in his silent endurance of persecution."[251]

That there is a "literary connection" between 13a and *Barn.* 5:7 is probable,[252] but the wording of 13a depends on the Pauline utterance Rom 15:8, εἰς τὸ βεβαιῶσαι τὰς ἐπαγγελίας τῶν πατέρων ("in order to confirm the promises given to the patriarchs").[253] This can be said with some certainty since Paul already seems to allude to the traditions of the Servant of God by his

238 Contra Bauer, 612.

239 Contra Lattke, *Bedeutung*, 1:165; idem, *Oden*, 186.

240 BDAG, *s.v.* ἵνα, 1.

241 Cf. λυτρωσάμενος ("redeeming") or λυτρωσάμενον in *Barn.* 14:5-6 (Ehrman, 2:64–65). The disciples in the Emmaus story (Luke 24:21) say, among other things, of the prophet Jesus of Nazareth, who will shortly reveal himself as the Christ/Messiah, ἡμεῖς δὲ ἠλπίζομεν ὅτι αὐτός ἐστιν ὁ μέλλων λυτροῦσθαι τὸν Ἰσραήλ ("But we had hoped that he was the one to redeem Israel"). On the verb λυτρόω, see Payne Smith, 2:3293; BDAG, *s.v.* λυτρόω. This Lukan pericope is important not only for the use of the verb but also for the programmatic use of the prophets and all the Scriptures for τὰ περὶ ἑαυτοῦ ("the things concerning himself" [Luke 24:27]).

242 Ehrman, 2:64–65.

243 Prostmeier, 470.

244 BDAG, *s.vv.* ἔθνος, λαός; Payne Smith, 2:2904–5.

245 The doubling and hardening of the second radical in "verbs of this sort" (Nöldeke §175.A) occurs only in ܐܙܠ and ܐܬܐ.

246 BDAG, *s.v.* κληρονομία, 1.

247 Hans Windisch, *Der Barnabasbrief* (HNT, Ergänzungs-Band: Die Apostolischen Väter III; Tübingen: Mohr Siebeck, 1920) 379; BDAG, *s.v.* κληρονομέω, 1a.

248 Charlesworth, 118; idem, *Reflections*, 26: "and instruct it."

249 G. J. Reinink, review of Charlesworth in *JSJ* 5 (1974) 68.

250 McNeil, "Sufferings," 34–35; cf. Lattke, *Bedeutung*, 3:333.

251 Blaszczak, 56.

252 Windisch, *Barnabasbrief*, 328.

253 Although Prostmeier (p. 245) was referring to Rom 15:8 in relation to *Barn.* 5:7, his introductory note on models and quotations is relevant here: "All attempts to demonstrate that the *Letter of Barnabas* uses any of the books of the New Testament have proved fruitless. Certainly there are contacts, but they always end at the tradition of the school to which the author belonged" (ibid., 97). This tradition clearly included the Greek text of the *Odes of Solomon*, whose Syriac translation, therefore,

choice of the term διάκονος to describe Christ.[254] The positive use of βεβαιόω to announce the goal in that passage corresponds here to the negation, constructed with ܕܠܐ (*d-lā*) and the imperative of the Pa. ܣܪܩ (*sarreq*), of a verb with negative connotations, so that the whole becomes a declaration of salvation. Frankenberg's choice of καταργήσω to translate the verb[255] departs radically from the tradition of Syriac translation, which generally equates καταργέω, which is used with ἐπαγγελία among other terms, with the Pa. ܒܛܠ (*baṭṭel*; but cf. Rom 4:14 and Gal 3:17 for the meaning).[256] So the only possible original is κενόω,[257] unless the regular use of the Ethpa. ܐܣܬܪܩ (*ʾestarraq*) to translate the passive ματαιοῦμαι should suggest the use of ματαιόω.[258] The choice of the plural of ܫܘܕܝܐ (*šūdāyā*)—rather than the synonymous ܡܘܠܟܢܐ (*mulkānā*)[259]—to represent the ἐπαγγελίαι ("promises") from Rom 15:8 evidently arises from the desire to imitate the paronomasia that probably existed in 𝔊 (see on ἐπαγγέλλομαι in 13b below).[260] The relative particle ܕ (*d-*) and the addition of the preposition ܠܘܬ (*lwāṯ*) make it, pedantically, more obvious than in the Syriac translations of the Bible that the ἐπαγγελίαι τῶν πατέρων of Rom 15:8 were and are "promises *to* the forefathers."[261] The addition of the *status constructus* of ܪܫܐ (*rēšā*) to the plural of ܐܒܐ (*ʾaḇā*) also makes clear that the "fathers" of Rom 15:8 are the biblical patriarchs,[262] with Abraham as the "forefather," the first among them (cf. Rom 4:1).[263]

The correlative phrase at the beginning of 13b is weakened, like those in 8b and 11b;[264] it refers to the "promises"[265] of 13a but not to the "patriarchs."[266] Many translators and commentators display unease at the "blurring of the boundary between God the Father and Christ so that the latter says *he* made the promises to the patriarchs" [emphasis added].[267] Berger and Nord, for instance, simply import Rom 4:21 into this verse: "what God had promised."[268] However, the first person singular of ܐܫܬܘܕܝܬ (*ʾeštawdī*) does not correspond to ἐπήγγελται (Rom 4:21; Gal 3:19; cf. ἐπαγγειλάμενος ὁ θεός in Heb 6:13) but to ἐπήγγελμαι.[269] A glance at 1 John 2:25 is enough to dispel the unease: καὶ αὕτη ἐστὶν ἡ ἐπαγγελία ἣν αὐτὸς ἐπηγγείλατο ἡμῖν, τὴν ζωὴν τὴν αἰώνιον ("And this is what [literally: the promise] he has promised us, eternal life").[270] For αὐτός

preceded and was independent of the later traditions of translation into Syriac.

254 "That behind the use of the word διάκονος here is the thought of Christ, as the *ʿebed YHWH*, though not certain, would seem to be likely" (C. E. B. Cranfield, *A Critical and Exegetical Commentary on the Epistle to the Romans*, vol. 2: *Commentary on Romans IX–XVI and Essays* [ICC; Edinburgh: T&T Clark, 1979; repr., with corrections, 1981] 741).

255 Frankenberg, 29.

256 BDAG, *s.v.* καταργέω, 2; Payne Smith, 1:510.

257 BDAG, *s.v.* κενόω, 2: "render void."

258 BDAG, *s.v.* ματαιόω; see Payne Smith, 2:2748–49.

259 Payne Smith, 2:2141.

260 Paronomasia in 𝔖, therefore, does not of itself argue for Syriac as the original language of the *Odes of Solomon*.

261 BDAG, *s.v.* ἐπαγγελία, 1bα, with genitive "to denote the one(s) for whom the promise is intended."

262 See BDAG, *s.v.* πατριάρχης.

263 Payne Smith, 2:3900; BDAG, *s.v.* προπάτωρ. Cranfield remarks on οἱ πατέρες in Rom 9:5: "Paul no doubt means specially Abraham . . . , Isaac . . . , Jacob . . . and the twelve patriarchs, the sons of Jacob" (Cranfield, *Romans*, 2:464).

264 Nöldeke §228.

265 Translated literally, 13b runs as follows: "those: the salvation of their seed I had promised" (Klaus Beyer, letter of October 31, 2002).

266 Contra Harris and Mingana, 2:370; Charlesworth, 117. Harris and Mingana's explanation for their translation (2:370–71) "To whom I was promised" is unconvincing. Charlesworth (p. 118) accepts their translation and draws far-reaching conclusions: "This passage was probably composed by the early Christian community, by Christians who were Jews and saw in Jesus the Messiah who fulfilled the promises to them." Blaszczak (p. 125 n. 57) quite properly criticizes Charlesworth's translation of the "eshtaphal of *ydʿ*."

267 Kittel, 116; he finds no difficulty here: "Even though Diettrich objects [see Diettrich, 108], Christ has to be the subject of this statement. . . . Just as the exalted Christ is sometimes indistinguishable from God . . . here, conversely, the actions of God in the past are ascribed to Christ."

268 Berger and Nord, 963.

269 BDAG, *s.v.* ἐπαγγέλλομαι, 1; Payne Smith, 1:1551. The perfect active ἐπήγγελκα (Frankenberg, 29) could also have been used, but it is less usual than the middle voice and thus less likely (see LSJ, *s.v.* ἐπαγγέλλομαι).

270 NA^{27}, p. 618; Pierre (p. 157) also refers to this passage.

refers to the "son" of 2:24: "αὐτός can only mean Jesus Christ, not God."[271]

The object of the verb "to promise" would probably have been constructed in 𝔊 also with a play on words: εἰς λύτρωσιν τοῦ σπέρματος αὐτῶν.[272] The abundance of occurrences of λυτρόομαι in *Barnabas* 14 (see above)[273] strongly suggests that, in this passage, the Greek term represented by ܦܘܪܩܢܐ (*purqānā*), "salvation," was not σωτηρία (in spite of 11:3a and Ps 21:6 LXX: ἐσώθησαν) but λύτρωσις (see Excursus 5).[274] In a transferred sense, σπέρμα/ܙܪܥܐ (*zarʿā*) is not, of course, the "male seed or semen," but collectively the "posterity" of the patriarchs and especially "Abraham's spiritual descendants."[275] So the conclusion of *Ode* 31 sets its bounds far wider than Psalm 22 (21 LXX), which, like Isa 53:10, talks of "seed," in the extended sense of the σπέρμα Ἰακώβ ("seed of Jacob") and the σπέρμα Ἰσραήλ ("seed of Israel") in Ps 21:24 LXX and in the narrower sense of τὸ σπέρμα μου ("my seed") in Ps 21:31 LXX,[276] that is, of the "posterity of the one who was delivered."[277]

271 Rudolf Bultmann, *Die drei Johannesbriefe* (KEK, 14. Abt.; 7th ed.; Göttingen: Vandenhoeck & Ruprecht, 1967) 45–46 n. 6; similarly Rudolf Schnackenburg, *Die Johannesbriefe* (HThKNT 13.3; 3rd ed.; Freiburg: Herder, 1965) 160; Hans-Josef Klauck, *Der erste Johannesbrief* (EKKNT 23.1; Zurich/Braunschweig: Benziger; Neukirchen-Vluyn: Neukirchener Verlag, 1991) 165. Georg Strecker contents himself with a question mark: "Does αὐτός mean God or Christ?" (see *The Johannine Letters: A Commentary on 1, 2, and 3 John* [Hermeneia; Minneapolis: Fortress Press, 1996] 69 n. 49 = *Die Johannesbriefe* [KEK 14; Göttingen: Vandenhoeck & Ruprecht, 1989] 130 n. 41), while Johannes Beutler, surprisingly, does not raise the matter at all and only speaks of "the Christian promise" (see *Die Johannesbriefe* [RNT; Regensburg: Pustet, 2000] 75).

272 Frankenberg, 29. See 12b above; cf. Luke 1:55, 68.

273 See BDAG, *s.v.* λυτρόω, 2.

274 BDAG, *s.v.* λύτρωσις, 1; Payne Smith, 2:3295.

275 BDAG, *s.v.* σπέρμα, 1b and 2a.

276 Rahlfs, 2:20–21; Brenton, 710.

277 Kraus, *Psalmen*, 183; see his statement, p. 185: "Vom AT her aber bieten sich die urbildlichen, überindividuellen Aussagegehalte des 22. Psalms als 'prophetische' Elemente an, die auf eine Füllung und Erfüllung des weitausgespannten Rahmens hindeuten" ("From the Old Testament, however, the archetypical, more than individual claims of Psalm 22 offer 'prophetic' elements that point to a completion and fulfillment of a wide-ranging framework").

32

Ode 32: Joy, Light, and Word of the Blessed—and Truth Itself

1a The blessed have joy from their heart
1b and light from him who dwells in them
2 and the word from that Truth which was her (own) self.[a]
3a Because she [viz., Truth] became strong by the holy power of the Most High,
3b she is also unshakable for ever and ever.[b]
Hallelujah.

a 2 H: ܡܢ ܢܦܫܗ.
b 3b H: ܠܥܠܡ ܠܥܠܡܝܢ.

Introduction

Ode 32 is preserved in two Syriac manuscripts.[1] Abramowski, whose translation is all but indefensible,[2] calls *Ode* 32 a "didactic poem,"[3] while Schille, somewhat diffidently,[4] classes "this short hymn" among the "reveilles," but also places it by the side of *Ode* 34:1-6.[5] Spitta simply sidelines *Ode* 32 without discussion as "out and out Jewish,"[6] and thus outdoes Harnack, who counts it among the "main set" of "indeterminate Odes."[7] Diettrich's verdict is that our Ode stands "altogether in Old Testament territory,"[8] but Harris and Mingana stress the parallelism of "Word from the Truth" (2) with "True Word" (12:3b; cf. 12:1a) and conclude: "This Ode belongs to the group of Wisdom-Odes or Logos-Odes, and so does the one that immediately follows."[9] They do not even consider whether the pronoun in 3b can refer to "the Truth who is self-originate" in 2, which I believe to be the case. Franzmann, unnecessarily, divides the central monocolon into 2a-b, and on this self-constructed basis finds herself forced to accept the reading of H.[10] Her translation of 2b ("who was from himself") is untenable, because ܗܘ ܕ (*hāw d-*) is not a relative pronoun referring to ܫܪܪܐ (see below). Analogously, however, to her *correct* observation "that either 3b or 3a-b may function as an indirect doxology (if ref[erence] is to the Truth),"[11] one could describe the first half of *Ode* 32 as an indirect benediction,[12] which, at its peak in the middle of 2, transforms into didactic statements on "Truth" personified and ends doxologically. It is not actually necessary to interpret these last statements and the Joy–Light–Word "triad"[13] in a Gnostic sense, but this second shortest of the whole collection of *Odes* does sound like a quarry for later Gnostic tracts (cf., e.g., *Treatise on Resurrection*;[14] *Tripartite*

1 Mss.: Codex H, 24a–b; Codex N, 150r–150v (s). Ed./trans.: Charlesworth, 118–19; Franzmann, 231–32; Lattke, 3:59–65.
2 Especially in 2-3: "and the word of the truth, which comes out of his soul. For there grew strong in his power the Holy One of the Most High and is immovably the same in eternity of eternity" (Abramowski, 50). It is not clear whether "his soul" refers to the "giver" of whom Abramowski, in the context of his theses on the "Messiah of the *Odes of Solomon*," has this to say: "*Ode* 32 leads deeper into the problems of our collection, because it connects the gifts to the giver."
3 Abramowski, 50.
4 *Ode* 32 "refrains from summons. So its inclusion in this class is not quite certain" (Schille, 100). It is not true that either *Ode* 34 or *Ode* 32, in its totality, is a description of the blessed.
5 Schille, 100.
6 Spitta, 286.
7 Harnack, 78.
8 Diettrich, 111.
9 Harris and Mingana, 2:373.
10 Franzmann, 231.
11 Ibid., 232.
12 See Introduction, sec. 8.
13 Diettrich (p. 111) reinterprets "word" as a "prophetic word" and remarks: "Christians would surely have linked this triad to the Trinitarian formula"; this is pure speculation. Even in the New Testament, faith, hope, and love were not brought into relationship with the triad Father–Son–Spirit (cf. 1 Cor 13:13 with Matt 28:19).
14 Hans-Martin Schenke, "Der Brief an Rheginus (NHC I,4) (Die Abhandlung über die Auferstehung)," *NHD* 1 (2001) 50–51.

Tractate;[15] *Origin of the World*;[16] *Gospel of the Egyptians*[17]). As a title for the whole Ode, which does not need to be divided into stanzas or strophes,[18] Greßmann, with a clear grasp of essentials, chooses "Truth that Originates in Itself."[19] This does, however, shortchange the eschatological benefits "joy" and "light" of 1a-b.

Interpretation

The plural of ܛܘܒܢܐ (*ṭūbānā*), "blessed," with preceding preposition ܠ (*l-*), corresponds to the dative τοῖς μακαρίοις,[20] and Bauer correctly interprets it as "the redeemed."[21] There is no allusion to Matt 5:8 or to the Sermon on the Mount in general. Rather the first reference to be made is to the address of Grace personified in another of the *Odes:* "and through me you will be saved and will be blessed" (33:11a). If a biblical text influenced this poem, then the terms ὕψιστος ("Most High"), φῶς ("light"), καρδία ("heart"), and εὐφροσύνη ("joy, gladness") would make it necessary to consider Ps 96:9a and 11 LXX. But the soteriological emphasis would have shifted with τοῖς μακαρίοις taking the place of the datives τῷ δικαίῳ and τοῖς εὐθέσι.[22] This would also explain the peculiar placement of the dative at the beginning of 1a. The term ܚܕܘܬܐ (*ḥadutā*), of course, means the "joy of the blessed."[23] The condition that it must come "out of" or "from their heart" (cf. 28:7a, "My heart is joyful") lies in its nature as a kerygmatic gift, which links 1a to the "joy" "that was central to the preceding Ode (31:6)" (see Excursus 4).[24]

Excursus 32: "Joy" and "To Rejoice" in the *Odes of Solomon*

This excursus deals mainly with the term ܚܕܘܬܐ (*ḥadutā*), which occurs nine times, and the Pe. and Pa. from the same root, which are each used once, but it overlaps another excursus that includes the remark: "So words from the root *bsm* also express joy" (Excursus 14). So the passages using τρυφή/ܒܘܣܡܐ (*bussāmā*) and εὐφραίνομαι/ܐܬܒܣܡ (*ʾetbassam*) will also be briefly examined. This can be justified since ܚܕܘܬܐ in 32:1a may not represent χαρά[25] but the related word εὐφροσύνη.[26] Generally, however, it may be assumed that χαρά (cf. 11:16g, only in 𝔊) corresponds to ܚܕܘܬܐ.[27] At the same time it is quite possible that 7:17b was an exception and had ἀγαλλίασις instead.[28]

By comparison with the New Testament, it is very noticeable that the antonym "sorrow" (λυπή) does not occur. Nor is the "apparently paradoxical thought of joy in suffering"[29] to be found. "Pain," "oppression," and "suffering" are no longer real for the redeemed (cf. 21:4), and the imperative of salvation, 31:6, carries only quite vague memories of Paul's "paradox . . . of the eschatological mastering of the world."[30] Even more than in the Fourth Gospel (John 15:11; 16:20-24; 17:13; cf. 1 John 1:4 and 2 John 4), "joy" dominates the *Odes of Solomon* as a "state of fulfillment."[31] It is only metaphorically that

15 Hans-Martin Schenke, "Tractatus Tripartitus (NHC I,5)," *NHD* 1 (2001) 59; Peter Nagel, *Der Tractatus Tripartitus aus Nag Hammadi Codex I (Codex Jung)* (Studien und Texte zu Antike und Christentum 1; Tübingen: Mohr Siebeck, 1998) 24 no. 24.

16 Hans-Gebhard Bethge, "'Vom Ursprung der Welt' (NHC II,5)," *NHD* 1 (2001) 243.

17 Uwe-Karsten Plisch, "Das heilige Buch des großen unsichtbaren Geistes (NHC III,2; IV,2) ('Das ägyptische Evangelium')," *NHD* 1 (2001) 297.

18 Franzmann disrupts the close connection between 2 (2b according to her division of the central monocolon) and 3a-b when she says (p. 231): "The six lines of the Ode comprise one stanza of two strophes (1–2, 3)."

19 Greßmann, 465.

20 Frankenberg, 29.

21 Bauer, 613; see Payne Smith, 1:1439; BDAG, *s.v.* μακάριος.

22 See Rahlfs, 2:106.

23 Berger and Nord, 963.

24 Pierre, 158.

25 See Hans Conzelmann, "χαίρω, . . . , χάρις, κτλ.," *ThWNT* 9 (1973) 362: "Gnosis"; *TDNT* 9:371.

26 See Conzelmann, "χαίρω," *ThWNT* 9:356; *TDNT* 9:365; also BDAG, *s.v.* εὐφροσύνη.

27 Payne Smith, 1:1199; BDAG, *s.v.* χαρά.

28 BDAG, *s.v.* ἀγαλλίασις. In Luke 1:44 and Heb 1:9 ἀγαλλίασις is translated by ܚܕܘܬܐ (*NTSy* on these two passages). Where χαρά and ἀγαλλίασις occur together (Luke 1:14) it is the first term that is represented by ܚܕܘܬܐ.

29 Conzelmann, "χαίρω," *ThWNT* 9:358; *TDNT* 9:368.

30 Conzelmann, "χαίρω," *ThWNT* 9:360; *TDNT* 9:370. For Paul, "χαρά is maintained in *the face of* θλῖψις" [emphasis added] (see 2 Cor 6:2; 7:4-16; 8:2; 1 Thess 1:6).

31 Conzelmann, "χαίρω," *ThWNT* 9:361; *TDNT* 9:370.

"joy" appears as a "profane mood,"[32] once in contrast to the equally emotional "anger" (7:1a-b) and once as the response to the daily appearance of the sun (15:1a). In both cases, the comparison serves to show that the "Lord" himself is "*metonymically*" the "joy" of the redeemed speaker (7:2a; 15:1b).[33]

Even if the Greek of 7:17b used ἀγαλλίασις rather than χαρά (see above), this "joy" is the "festal joy" known from the Old Testament and also the "basic mood in mystery piety" of Hellenism.[34]

If, in this mythic paradise, a or *the* ποταμὸς χαρᾶς (11:16g) should flow, the whole landscaped Utopia will be characterized by God's τρυφή/ܒܘܣܡܐ (11:16b, 24b). This paradisal joy is expressed verbally (20:8a) by εὐφραίνομαι/ܐܬܒܣܡ (*ʾetbassam*). But that joy is not confined to paradise, as is shown by the image of 11:15 ("And my breath rejoiced in the sweet fragrance of the Lord [ꞩ]/My breath was gladdened by the fragrance of the Lord's kindness [𝔊]") and also—influenced by Ps 15:9a LXX—the statement of salvation in 28:2a ("my heart is delighted").

Except for the variant "joy of heart" in ℭ (on which see the commentary on 6:14b), the remaining passages use words derived from the Syriac root ܚܕܐ/ܚܕܝ.[35] The redeemed speaker uses the Pa. *ḥaddī* saying: "and I was glad (to) myself because Truth had gone with me" (38:15b). And the redeemed, as a group, link, by the Pe. *ḥḏā/ḥḏī*, their joy to a conglomerate of soteriological terms: "we rejoice in the Lord by his grace and life we receive by his Messiah" (41:3; on the variant reading of 3a in H, see the commentary on that passage). That the "joy" that belongs to the "saints" or the "elect" (23:1a; cf. 23:2a, 3a), like the "joy" that will be received, again together with "grace" and "life" (31:6b; cf. 31:7a-b), is finally—even without a *direct* "connection back to God"[36]—a gift of salvation is shown by the statement about the Lord, who is not the Most High and Father, in 31:3a (he "spoke grace and joy"). This is true also for 32:1a where the εὐφροσύνη/ܚܕܘܬܐ (*ḥaḏutā*), perhaps derived from Ps 96:11b LXX, comes from the hearts of the redeemed and blessed ones. It must be remembered that εὐφροσύνη could have been used instead of χαρά.[37]

As Ps 96:11b LXX stands behind 1a, so 1b is a variation on Ps 96:11a LXX (cf. Diettrich, who refers to Psalm 97 (96 LXX) and also to Ps 27:1, although Ps 26:1a LXX has φωτισμός, "light").[38] 2 Cor 4:1-6, with its use of the terms λόγος τοῦ θεοῦ ("God's word" [4:2]), ἀλήθεια ("truth" [4:2]), φωτισμός ("light" [4:4, 6]), φῶς ("light" [4:6]), and καρδία ("heart" [4:6]), could also have been involved in this shaping, but would, at least in Christian circles, have awakened a train of associations. So it is impossible to decide whether 𝔊 had φῶς or φωτισμός (see Excursus 10).[39] In ꞩ, ܢܘܗܪܐ (*nuhrā*) refers to God the Lord (10:1b) who makes his (God's) *life* dwell in the Redeemer (10:2a).[40] While it can metaphorically and transcendentally be said of God that φῶς οἰκῶν ἀπρόσιτον ("he dwells in inaccessible light" [1 Tim 6:16; cf. 1 John 1:5, 7]),[41] 2 Cor 6:16 complements this from Lev 26:12, where God says ἐνοικήσω ἐν αὐτοῖς ("I will dwell in/among them").[42] Both οἰκέω and ἐνοικέω are more often used of the indwelling of the divine πνεῦμα (Rom 8:9, 11; 1 Cor 3:16; 2 Tim 1:14) and this may also have been the case here if 𝔊 used a participial construction with the genitive like ἐκ τοῦ ἐν αὐτοῖς οἰκοῦντος/ἐνοικοῦντος.[43]

After N was found, the manuscript tradition no longer "leaves in doubt" whether the term in 2 is "the words" or "the word."[44] The abbreviation ܦܬܓ, found at the end of a line in H and expanded to ܦܬܓܡܐ (*peṯgāmā*) by Harris and Mingana,[45] should, in any case, have shown the two dots that point a plural if it

32 Conzelmann, "χαίρω," *ThWNT* 9:359; *TDNT* 9:369.
33 BDAG, *s.v.* χαρά, 2a.
34 Conzelmann, "χαίρω," *ThWNT* 9:352–54; *TDNT* 9:362–63.
35 Brockelmann, *Grammatik* §182.
36 Conzelmann, "χαίρω," *ThWNT* 9:356; *TDNT* 9:365–66, on Philo "in opposition of Stoicism."
37 Frankenberg, 29.
38 Diettrich, 111.
39 In 2 Cor 4:4 (τὸν φωτισμὸν τοῦ εὐαγγελίου, "the light of the gospel") and 4:6 (ἐκ σκότους φῶς, "light out of darkness"), both of the terms for light are represented in Syriac by ܢܘܗܪܐ (*nuhrā*, *NTSy* on this passage; see BDAG, *s.vv.* φῶς, φωτισμός).
40 The Aph. ܐܥܡܪ (*ʾaʿmar*) there, like the Pe. ܥܡܪ (*ʿmar*) here, is a *hapax legomenon*.
41 BDAG, *s.vv.* ἀπρόσιτος, φῶς; Oberlinner, *Pastoralbriefe*, 1:285, 300.
42 Hans Windisch, *Der zweite Korinterbrief* (repr. of 1924 edition, ed. by Georg Strecker; KEK; Göttingen: Vandenhoeck & Ruprecht, 1970) 216; Victor Paul Furnish, *II Corinthians: Translated with Introduction, Notes, and Commentary* (AB 32A; Garden City, N.Y.: Doubleday, 1984) 363, 374.
43 Frankenberg, 29; see BDAG, *s.vv.* ἐνοικέω, οἰκέω; Payne Smith, 2:2919: "Part. act." ܥܡܪ (*ʿāmar*).
44 Diettrich, 111; cf. Lattke, *Bedeutung*, 2:200 line 1.
45 Harris and Mingana, vol. 1, on this passage; 2:373.

had been one.[46] The actual variant in H is the repetition of ܡܢ (*men*), which serves to align it with 7:12c (ܡܢ ܢܦܫܗܘܢ ܗܘܘ)[47] and which Franzmann can only declare original and defend on the basis of her division of 2 into 2a-b.[48] The pronominal phrase ܗܘ̇ ܕ (*hāw d-*) in this case is not a simple relative pronoun but a true "correlative,"[49] in which the demonstrative pronoun "that," used "adjectivally," in spite of being "post-positioned," carries considerable weight.[50] For the final words of 2 distinguish "Truth" personified from all correctnesses and factualities on earth (cf. esp. 38:4b and Excursus 1). The idiomatically Syriac sentence construction[51] should not obscure the fact that the short and clumsy relative clause is an attempt to replicate the Greek καὶ ὁ λόγος (or τὸ ῥῆμα) ἀπὸ/ἐκ αὐτῆς τῆς ἀληθείας ("and the word of/from Truth herself").[52] So neither 𝔊 nor 𝔖 alludes to "the Word of truth."[53] Further, ܢܦܫܗ (*napšeh*) refers not to "word" but, like the subject of ܗܘܐ (*hwā*), to "truth."[54] On the one hand, this excludes the possibility that ἀλήθεια/ܫܪܪܐ (*šrārā*) denotes the Johannine Logos/Jesus (cf. John 1:1-18; 14:6; Excursus 12).[55] On the other hand, the "word" derived out of/from the "Truth" (cf. 7:7; 8:8a; 12:1a)—and perhaps interpreted in an early Gnostic fashion—is not identical with the "Son of Truth" (23:18b). That even "Truth herself" is not "self-originated" from the beginning,[56] although she *was* and *is* for all time (38:4b), is attested by the phrase "Father of Truth" (41:9a) and also expounded in the next bicolon of this Ode.

In opposition to various attempts to make the masculine subject of the Ethpa. of ܥܫܢ (*ʿšen*) in 3a and the likewise masculine personal pronoun is 3b refer to the "word" of 2,[57] it is necessary to state firmly, with Ungnad and Staerk, Bernard, Berger and Nord,[58] and others, that the subject both of the causal clause 3a and of the main clause 3b is "Truth" personified. This means that the conjunction ὅτι/ܡܛܠ ܕ (*meṭṭol d-*) again precedes the particle ܘ (*ʾu-*), which should therefore be translated

46 See Lattke, *Bedeutung*, 1:60–61.

47 The N reading is, in any case, the *lectio difficilior.* My query, whether the H reading, for the translation of which reference should be made to 2 Cor 3:5 (ἐξ ἑαυτῶν = "of [our] own strength"; BDAG, *s.v.* ἑαυτοῦ), might be a "dittography" (Lattke, *Bedeutung*, 1:164), has been disposed of by the explanation given above.

48 Franzmann, 231.

49 Nöldeke §236.A.

50 Ibid. §§226–28.

51 See ibid. §223: ܗܘ ܢܦܫܗ = "it/herself" (literally "himself"). But since "truth" is masculine in Syriac, αὐτὴ ἡ ἀλήθεια would have become ܗܘ ܫܪܪܐ (*hū šrārā*; cf. αὐτὸ τὸ πνεῦμα = ܗܝ ܪܘܚܐ in Rom 8:26), and the pronominal phrase replacing it ܗܘ ܢܦܫܗ (*hū napšeh*).

52 See BDAG, *s.v.* αὐτός; BDF and BDR §288; Payne Smith, 2:2431: "3) *ipse*, ܢܦܫܗ [*napšeh*], αὐτός." As the later Syriac translation of 3 John 12 shows (καὶ ὑπὸ αὐτῆς τῆς ἐκκλησίας καὶ τῆς ἀληθείας = ܘܡܢܗ̇ ܕܥܕܬܐ ܘܡܢܗ ܕܫܪܪܐ, "from the church itself and from the truth itself"), the Syriac of *Ode* 32:2 could have been ܘܡܠܬܐ ܡܢܗ ܕܫܪܪܐ (cf. *NTSy* on this passage; NA[27], p. 628, sy[ph.hmg] in the text-critical apparatus). Frankenberg's retroversion imports a partly alien (ἐκ τῆς ἀληθείας αὐτοφυοῦς) and partly anachronistic term into the text: καὶ λόγος ἐκ τῆς αὐτοαληθείας (Frankenberg, 29; cf. LSJ, *s.v.* αὐτοφυής; Lampe, *s.vv.* αὐτοαλήθεια, αὐτοφυής).

53 Contra Charlesworth (1973 only), 118. I cannot agree with Diettrich's explanation (p. 111) either that "what is probably meant is the word of inspiration, the prophetic word, for, according to Ode 31:10-11, this originates in the *Truth.*" The reference given is incorrect. However, there is a close connection between "truth" and "word" in the *Odes of Solomon* (cf. 8:8; 12:1, 3, 12).

54 Bauer, 613. Klaus Beyer, who takes no note of the H reading (see above), makes ܢܦܫܗ (*napšeh*) dependent on the "word": ". . . and that word from the truth, which is its soul (= the truth is the soul of the word), because it became strong . . . and is unshakable" (letter of October 31, 2002). This deprives the demonstrative pronoun ܗܘ̇ (*hāw*), which precedes the relative pronoun ܕ (*d-*), of import (Nöldeke §236.B). The term "soul" then denotes metaphorically the principle of life or vital power of the "word" (see Alexander Sand, "ψυχή," *EWNT* 3 [1983] 1198; *EDNT* 3:501).

55 BDAG, *s.v.* ἀλήθεια. Bernard (p. 116) takes up an extreme position finding "*words* from the Truth" [emphasis added] in 2 and referring to "Christ the Truth."

56 Contra Harnack, 64.

57 E.g., by Harris and Mingana, 2:373; Charlesworth, 118.

58 Ungnad and Staerk, 32; Bernard, 116; Berger and Nord, 964.

adverbially as "also."[59] If one wanted to emphasize the causal sense of 3a-b and link it more closely to 2, one would need to translate as follows: "For she became strong . . . , and she is unshakable."[60] As in 10:4, it is impossible to determine the Greek equivalent of the Ethpa. ܐܬܥܫܢ (*ʾeṯʿaššan*),[61] but the instrumental phrase in 3a sounds as if δύναμις ὑψίστου ("power of the Most High"; cf. Luke 1:35) had been expanded by the addition of the attribute ܩܕܝܫܐ (*qaddīšā*), "holy," that belongs to ܚܝܠܐ (*ḥaylā*), making the ἁγία δύναμις ("holy power") nearly synonymous with the πνεῦμα ἅγιον ("holy Spirit"; see Excursuses 17 and 29). God the Most High is holy, indeed thrice holy (cf. Rev 4:8; 6:10),[62] so his protological, supernatural power can be qualified by the same adjective.[63]

Diettrich's reference to the image of 31:10-11[64] is somewhat misleading, since the Syriac term ܕܠܐ ܙܘܥܙܥܐ (*d-lā zuʿzāʿā*) in 3b, "unshakable," which Frankenberg daringly translates as ἀσάλευτος,[65] is again a *hapax legomenon*.[66] The related root of the previous term ܕܠܐ ܙܘܥܬܐ (*d-lā zawʿṯā*) is not enough to postulate a connection between the two passages (see commentary on 31:11a). The phrase, which has been translated in various ingenious ways,[67] only acquires its specific nuance from the doxologically formulaic-sounding addition ܠܥܠܡ ܥܠܡܝܢ (*l-ʿālam ʿālmīn*), which most probably represents the Greek εἰς τοὺς αἰῶνας (τῶν αἰώνων)[68] and confers on Truth personified the predicate of eschatological permanence "for all eternity."[69]

59 BDAG, *s.v.* καί. Although Greßmann (p. 465) and Bauer (p. 613) agree with this explanation, they disrupt the link between 3a and 3b, making "truth" (feminine in German) the subject of 3a but "word" (neuter in German) that of 3b. This is illogical of Greßmann, who puts "Truth" as the dominant theme into his heading for *Ode* 32. Bauer's heading, on the other hand, refers to the "Word of Truth."

60 See BDF and BDR §456; BDAG, *s.v.* ὅτι.

61 Payne Smith, 2:3003–4; cf. Frankenberg, 13 (ὑπερίσχυσα) with p. 29 (ἐδυναμώθη).

62 BDAG, *s.vv.* ἅγιος, ὕψιστος.

63 See Michael Lattke, "Heiligkeit III. Neues Testament," *TRE* 14 (1985) 704–5.

64 Diettrich, 111.

65 Frankenberg, 29.

66 Payne Smith, 1:1109. Both ἀσάλευτος (Acts 27:41; Heb 12:28) and ἀμετακίνητος (1 Cor 15:58) are translated into Syriac with constructions using a negated participle (cf. *NTSy* on these passages).

67 Some examples are "unshakable" (Bernard, 116); "unperturbed" (Harris and Mingana, 2:373); "unshaken" (Charlesworth, 118); "unmoved" (Emerton, 722); "undisturbed" (Franzmann, 231); "inébranlable [= unshakable]" (Pierre, 159; Azar, 151); "unerschütterlich [= imperturbable]" (Ungnad and Staerk, 32; Greßmann, 465); "ohne Erschütterung [= without shaking]" (Bauer, 613).

68 It is unlikely that 𝔖 used only εἰς αἰῶνας (Frankenberg, 29). Comparing NA^{27} with *NTSy*, with the help of *CKNTG*, gives the following results: The singular εἰς τὸν αἰῶνα is translated by ܠܥܠܡ except in 1 Pet 1:25 (ܠܥܠܡܝܢ); the same is true of the genitive phrase εἰς τὸν αἰῶνα τοῦ αἰῶνος (Heb 1:8); the plural εἰς τοὺς αἰῶνας, except in Luke 1:33; Heb 13:8; and 1 Pet 5:11 (ܠܥܠܡ), and the extended phrase εἰς τοὺς αἰῶνας τῶν αἰώνων are both translated by ܠܥܠܡ ܥܠܡܝܢ.

69 BDAG, *s.v.* αἰών.

33

Ode 33: Dualistic Myths and the Address of the Perfect Virgin "Grace"

(I) 1a But Grace ran back/again/up and abandoned Corruption,
1b and she descended into him to bring him to nought.
(II) 2a And he destroyed [with] destruction before him
2b and corrupted all its contrivance.
3a And he stood on a high peak and sent out his voice
3b from the ends of the earth to its ends.
4a And he drew to him all those who obeyed him,
4b and he did not appear like the/an Evil One.
(III) 5a But the Perfect Virgin stood up,
5b proclaiming and crying out[a] and saying:
6a "Sons of men, turn back,
6b and their daughters, come[b],
7a and leave the ways of this Corruption
7b and draw near to me;
8a then I will enter into you
8b and bring you out from destruction
8c and make you wise in the ways of truth.
(IV) 9 You will not be corrupted or perish.
10a Listen to me and you will be saved!
10b For I proclaim among you the grace of God,
11a and by me you will be redeemed and will be blessed.
(V) 11b I am your judge.
12a And those who put me on shall not be oppressed/wronged,
12b but will gain incorruption in the new world.
(VI) 13a My elect, walk in me,
13b and I will make my ways known to those who seek me,
13c and cause them to trust in my name."
Hallelujah.

a 5b ܩܥܝܐ N; ܩܪܝܐ H.
b 6b ܬܐܝܝܢ corr.; ܬܐܝܢ N; ܬܝܢ H.

Introduction

This Ode, preserved in two Syriac manuscripts,[1] "makes use of typical themes from Hellenistic missionary sermons and calls to repentance."[2] The fact that the subject changes between 1b and 2a (and again between 4b and 5a) raises "great difficulties in comprehending it."[3] Even if one assumes that the Syriac translator completely misunderstood the text, and if one replaces φϑορά as the subject of stanza II by χάρις, one cannot convert

1 Mss.: Codex H, 24b–25b; Codex N, 150v (s). Ed./trans.: Charlesworth, 119–22; Franzmann, 233–39; Lattke, 3:67–90.

2 Bauer, 613, with references to sources and secondary literature; see esp. Norden, *Theos*, 5–7, 190, 198, and 294–95; Heinz Becker, *Die Reden des Johannesevangeliums und der Stil der gnostischen Offenbarungsrede* (ed. Rudolf Bultmann; FRLANT 68 = N.F. 50; Göttingen: Vandenhoeck & Ruprecht, 1956) 16–18; Dibelius, 283.

that "indigestible lump" altogether into something that "follows on and makes sense."[4] For reasons that will be discussed later, Bauer brushes aside the difficulties "in the text as it exists today: the 'He' [viz., of stanza II] must be the Redeemer, in whom She, the goodness or grace of God, descended."[5] But this solution carries its own problems, as Blaszczak has documented, remarking about 2-4 that the masculine noun ܚܒܠܐ (*ḥḇālā*) "as the subject makes far better sense than the convoluted explanations and solutions of despair posited by most commentators."[6] If this statement is accepted, stanza III becomes the beginning of the second part of the Ode, which has some links to stanzas I and II, which form the first part,[7] and it consists mainly of the "speech within the speech" (6-13).[8]

For Abramowski, *Ode* 33 is closely connected to Ode 38 as one of the few Odes that exhibit "mythological speculation" and which can therefore be assigned to a "particular form of Gnosticism."[9] In connection with Arvedson's judgments on the "Wisdom" derived from the pseudo-Solomonic Proverbs that "became *Gnosis*,"[10] it is important "not to overlook the fact that significant features of the Gnostic myth are absent" and that the Ode as a whole has "Jewish words and ideas woven into it."[11] That *Ode* 33 should "very probably" be interpreted Mariologically[12] can be excluded[13] together with any exegesis linking it to a *descensus ad inferos*.[14] Finally, it is highly unlikely "that we should see the perfect virgin-grace figure of Ode 33 as a reference to the Holy Spirit."[15]

Interpretation

■ **1** There is no reason to assume that the particle ܕܝܢ (*dēn*), "but," in 1a "shows that this Ode is an excerpt from a larger whole."[16] Neither this particle, which probably corresponds to δέ in 𝔊, nor the adverb ܬܘܒ (*tūḇ*), which can be used like πάλιν—or αὖτις[17]—for "again"

3 Kittel, 116.

4 Frankenberg, 42. Greßmann originally only altered the subject of 2a-b (see Hugo Greßmann, "Die Oden Salomos," *Internationale Wochenschrift für Wissenschaft, Kunst und Technik* 5 [1911] 7) but later made "Grace" personified the subject of the whole section 1-5 (Greßmann, 465). Thus, these verses become the prologue to the address in 6-13.

5 Bauer, 613.

6 Blaszczak, 65.

7 Franzmann, 236.

8 See Introduction, sec. 8.

9 Abramowski, 45, 62.

10 Arvedson, *Mysterium*, 171.

11 Ulrich Wilckens, *Weisheit und Torheit: Eine exegetisch-religionsgeschichtliche Untersuchung zu 1. Kor. 1 und 2* (BHTh 26; Tübingen: Mohr Siebeck, 1959) 138. "So, from the point of view of religious history, we are dealing with an important link in the connection between the Jewish and the Gnostic doctrine of Sophia" (ibid., 135).

12 José M. Bover, "La Mariología en las Odas de Salomon," *EstEcl* 10 (1931) 363.

13 According to Harnack (p. 65), "It has nothing to do with the Virgin Mary."

14 Contra Barnes, "Hymn Book," 62–63; Bernard, 117–18; Connolly, "Odes," 302; Clarke, 51; Kittel, 116–24.

15 Contra Blaszczak, 74. It is not clear whether Spitta, who equates the "Perfect Virgin" with "wisdom" and identifies her "neither with the Virgin Mary nor the Holy Spirit," is at all inclined to see her as the "congregation" (Spitta, 287). Johannes Haussleiter, citing an article by Gustav Wohlenberg (see Lattke, *Bedeutung*, 3:174) in a newspaper, writes, on *Ode* 33: "Whom, then, does the poet mean by the 'Perfect Virgin'? Harnack, who does not consider it a Christian *Ode* ([Harnack], p. 64), asks whether the Virgin is to be understood as the holy Spirit or the Wisdom of God (Prov. 8). But is not a reference to Eph 5:7 or Rev 21:19 more apposite? The holy Virgin without a blemish, the Bride of the Lamb, is the congregation of Jesus Christ, and by her ministry the exalted Lord calls the nations to repentance" (see Johannes Haussleiter, "Der judenchristliche Charakter der 'Oden Salomos,'" *Theologisches Literaturblatt* 31 [1910] 271). Zahn (p. 774) explains the address of the Perfect Virgin similarly: "It is not the congregation that speaks in these hymns, but the individual singer, sometimes as himself, at others in the name of God or of Christ, once [i.e., here] in the name of the Church."

16 Diettrich, 113. He supposes that *Ode* 33 "was somehow connected to *Ode* 31" (cf. 31:7a). The particle ܕܝܢ (*dēn*) can also be found at the beginning of *Ode* 17 and marking the beginnings of sections (cf. 20:7a; 23:11a; 28:15a).

17 Frankenberg, 29: cf. LSJ, *s.v.* αὖϑις.

or "back,"[18] makes *Ode* 33 begin "abruptly and unintelligibly."[19] The immediate introduction of the personified antagonists "Grace" and "Corruption"[20] is embedded in a mythological dynamic, described by the use of four verbs, of ascent and descent on the one part and abandoning and intending to annihilate on the other. The three latter verbs present no great difficulties, but the Pe. ܪܗܛ (*rheṭ*), together with its adverb ܬܘܒ (*tūḇ*), has caused some perplexity. The metaphorical idea that "Grace" was in motion is not more peculiar than the image in 2 Thess 3:1 (ἵνα ὁ λόγος τοῦ κυρίου τρέχῃ, "that the word of the Lord may speed on") or the "petition," "in expectation of the parousia," in *Did.* 10:6a (ἐλθέτω χάρις καὶ παρελθέτω ὁ κόσμος οὗτος, "May grace come and this world pass away").[21] If the adverb ܬܘܒ is translated as "back,"[22] and not as the contested "again,"[23] the possibility that 𝔊 used a verb like ἀνατρέχω[24] or παλινδρομέω[25] becomes a probability. If the more general synonym ἀναβαίνω had been used in 𝔊, 𝔖 could have been expected to use the Pe. ܣܠܩ (*sleq*) as the opposite of ܢܚܬ (*nḥeṯ*), and that without the contested adverb ܬܘܒ (cf. Rom 10:6-7; Eph 4:8-10).[26] In any case, "Grace" personified, who must not be directly equated with "Christ" (see Excursus 33 below),[27] disappeared. In answer to the question whither did she run, the most one could say, considering the first verb of 1b, is mythologically "upward."

The running back/again/up of "Grace" is made manifest, dualistically, in the second part of 1a.[28] What she did was to "leave" the personified "Corruption."[29]

18 BDAG, *s.v.* πάλιν, esp. on the use of δὲ πάλιν; Payne Smith, 2:4400.

19 Contra Harris and Mingana, 2:376.

20 In both manuscripts ܚܒܠܐ is pointed as *ḥḇālā* (1a, 7a, 12b). This point in ܚܒܠܐ does not mark the "hard" pronunciation or doubling of the ܒ, as noted, e.g., in Brockelmann (*Grammatik*, 165*: ܚܒܠܐ "Verderber"; ܚܒܠܐ "Verderben") or Brockelmann, *Lexicon* (p. 211: ܚܒܠܐ "perniciosus"); it is "a sign of a fuller, stronger pronunciation" (Nöldeke §6; cf. Judah Benzion Segal, *The Diacritical Point and the Accents in Syriac* [London Oriental Series 2; London et al.: Geoffrey Cumberlege & Oxford University Press, 1953] 39–40). However, this clearly attested "corruption" was emended to "corruptor" quite early, though that should have been pointed ܚܒܠܐ (*ḥabbālā*), according to the general usage for intensive forms in the manuscripts. Diettrich simply says (p. 113) that he prefers "corruptor." I do not quite see how "corruptor" is more "appropriate to the context" (Harris and Mingana, 2:375), but the difference between a personified "corruption" and a "corruptor," who is also masculine in Syriac, is not enormous (see Franzmann, 235). Charlesworth joins those who translate "the Corruptor" (p. 120; cf. Harris and Mingana, 2:374) but he emends *la-ḥḇālā* to *l-ḥabbālā* (1a and 7a) only in the corrected reprint (1977, p. 119).

21 Ehrman, 1:432–33; Kurt Niederwimmer, *The Didache: A Commentary* (Hermeneia; Minneapolis: Fortress Press, 1998) 161–64, ET of *Die Didache* (KAV 1; Göttingen: Vandenhoeck & Ruprecht, 1989) 202; cf. Huub van de Sandt and David Flusser, *The Didache: Its Jewish Sources and Its Place in Early Judaism and Christianity* (CRINT 3.5; Assen: Van Gorcum; Minneapolis: Fortress Press, 2002) 301.

22 Diettrich, 534; Zahn, 774.

23 "Wieder/wiederum": Harnack, 64; Ungnad and Staerk, 33; Greßmann, "Oden Salomos," 7; Bauer, 613; Lattke, *Bedeutung*, 1:165; idem, *Oden*, 189; "again": Harris and Mingana, 2:374; Charlesworth, 120; Blaszczak, 59, 64; Franzmann, 234.

24 LSJ, *s.v.* ἀνατρέχω: "return," "run up." In compound words the prefix ἄνα expresses two ideas, "motion upwards, . . . up, opp κατά" and "the notion of back, backwards" (LSJ, *s.v.* ἄνα). The noun ἀναδρομή means both "running up" and "running back," but at the same time is a metaphorical term for the ascent of the soul εἰς θεόν (LSJ, *s.v.* ἀναδρομή).

25 LSJ, *s.v.* παλινδρομέω: "run back again." To express adverbial "again" Syriac uses the idiomatic construction ܗܦܟ ܪܗܛ (Payne Smith, 2:3834; Payne Smith, *Dictionary*, 105). To be able to translate ܬܘܒ by "for her part" (see Beyer, *ATTM*, 722), one would need to find a suitable Greek equivalent.

26 Payne Smith, 2:2646; BDAG, *s.v.* ἀναβαίνω, 1aβ: "of any upward movement, ascend, go up εἰς . . . οὐρανόν." Note that χάρις is mentioned also in Eph 4:7. Even more important is that in both Rom 10:6-7 and Eph 4:8-10 ἀναβαίνω precedes καταβαίνω.

27 Contra Harris and Mingana, 2:376.

28 Franzmann's division of 1a-b into a "four-line stanza" is capricious and gives no help in understanding the verse (see Franzmann, 233, 234, 236).

29 BDAG, *s.v.* φθορά, 1, and also 5, where Germ. "Untergang" is translated as "destruction"; see Ungnad and Staerk, 33; Harris and Mingana, 2:374: "left," though their object is "the Corruptor" (see above).

The Pe. ܫܒܩ (*šḇaq*) corresponds to ἀφίημι,[30] which does not correspond to "to overtake"[31] or "to drive away."[32] Even "dismiss"[33] is not as accurate as "abandon."[34] The masculine ܚܒܠܐ (*ḥḇālā*), "Corruption," to which the suffixes[35] in 1b refer (and which will appear as the subject in stanza II), is here the direct object of the verb that has a feminine form only in Syriac; it probably represents Greek φθορά rather than διαφθορά.[36]

The mythological importance and poetic intention of the statements in 1a are subordinated to the monocolon 1b, which carries the main weight of the antithetical *parallelismus membrorum*.[37] The final verb, together with the three preceding verbs of motion, gives the appearance of a hostile engagement with retreat and attack. It is clear that the Pe. ܢܚܬ (*nḥeṯ*), "descended," corresponds to καταβαίνω.[38] The "indication of the place to which one goes or comes down," for which Greek generally uses εἰς,[39] can be expressed in Syriac not only by ܠ (*l-*) but also by ܒ (*b-*).[40] In the context of 1a-b the suffix of the preposition following the first verb in 1b, as well as the objective suffix of the last verb, refers to "Corruption" (1a)[41] and not to some figure, such as "Christ"[42] or "Messiah,"[43] who has not been—and will not be—mentioned in the Ode.[44] The descent of "Grace" could be seen as a reworking of the foretelling of the parousia in 1 Thess 4:16 (αὐτὸς ὁ κύριος . . . καταβήσεται ἀπ' οὐρανοῦ, "the Lord himself will descend from heaven"), but without interpreting "Grace" as "a cryptic designation of our Lord" to explain the change in subject from stanza I to II.[45] Given the structure of stanza I and the general content of *Ode* 33, it is not possible to make a connection with 42:12 and to interpret "Corruption" by reference to Ps 15:10 LXX[46] as "Hades"[47] or the "Underworld."[48] So καταβαίνω/ܢܚܬ (*nḥeṯ*) does not refer to "Christ's descent into hell."[49]

The ultimate goal of the renewed descent by "Grace" is described, with the subordinating conjunction ܐܝܟ ܕ (*ʾaḵ d-* = ἵνα) and the imperfect of the Pa. of ܣܪܩ (*sraq*), which corresponds to a subjunctive form of κενόω,[50] as finally to "render" "Corruption" "void" (see on 12b below) and "deprive" him of his success and the "effect" depicted in stanza II.[51] At first it will seem that "Corruption" has the power to devastate and is not recognized by his adherents as the "Evil One" (see on 4b below).

■ **2-4** The six verbs of stanza II, excluding the subordinate clause in 4a, all have as their subject the

30 Payne Smith, 2:4037–39; BDAG, *s.v.* ἀφίημι. Frankenberg (p. 29) offers ἀφῆκεν, but then erroneously inserts εἰς before the object τὴν φθοράν.

31 Greßmann, 465.

32 Bauer, 613; cf. Blaszczak, 59, 64: "expel."

33 Charlesworth, 120.

34 Franzmann, 234.

35 Schultheß (p. 255) correctly notes that "the suffix of ܒܗ" refers to ܚܒܠܐ (*ḥḇālā*). His emendation of ܫܒܩܬ for ܫܒܩܬ (*šeḇqaṯ*) "should be rejected" (Charlesworth, 121).

36 Payne Smith, 1:1179; BDAG, *s.vv.* διαφθορά, φθορά.

37 His translation "expelled corruption" in 1a enables Blaszczak to reason as follows: "We could understand vs 1b as an event which followed the action reported in vs 1a, or we could regard it as in more or less *synonymous* parallelism with vs 1a" [emphasis added] (see Blaszczak, 59, 61).

38 Frankenberg, 29: κατέβη.

39 BDAG, *s.v.* καταβαίνω, 1aδ.

40 Payne Smith, 2:2344.

41 Bauer, 613; Blaszczak, 65; Franzmann, 234; Pierre, 160.

42 Contra Zahn, 774.

43 Contra Spitta, 286; Ungnad and Staerk, 33.

44 Harnack (p. 64) gives a singular explanation for the translation of ܒܗ as "in him": "This, of course, means (God) the Lord." Diettrich's "with him" (p. 113) makes no sense at all.

45 Contra Barnes, "Hymn Book," 62.

46 BDAG, *s.v.* διαφθορά. Cf. Ps 29:10 LXX; Acts 2:27, 31; 13:34-37.

47 Barnes, "Hymn Book," 62–63.

48 Kittel, 117–18.

49 Contra Kittel, 124. The translation of ܢܚܬܬ (*neḥtaṯ*) as "she returned" (Lattke, *Bedeutung*, 1:165; idem, *Oden*, 189) describes what happened, but is much too free.

50 Payne Smith, 2:2748.

51 BDAG, *s.v.* κενόω, 2. Frankenberg's retroversion (p. 29) ἵνα αὐτὴν καταργήσῃ is unconvincing because καταργέω is generally translated with the Pa. of ܒܛܠ (*bṭel*); see Payne Smith, 1:510; BDAG, *s.v.* καταργέω, 2 and 3.

"Corruption" introduced in stanza I as the antagonist of "Grace." [52] Anyone attempting to emend the masculine verb forms and suffixes and make "Grace"[53] the subject of stanza II has the greatest problem with 4b. Even in 𝔊, where the fact that χάρις and φθορά are both feminine leaves room for some ambiguity, the defensive statement that "Grace"—or the "Redeemer"[54]—did not appear "evil" makes no sense, even if 4b and 5a are taken as "one sentence."[55]

One reason for the search for a subject other than ܚܒܠܐ (*ḥḇālā*) is the fact that 2a-b *apparently* has two opposing destructive powers, "Corruption" on the one side and "destruction," also masculine in Syriac (viz., ܐܒܕܢܐ [*ʾaḇdānā*]), on the other. The expression ܚܒܠ ܬܘܩܢܗ (*ḥḇal tuqqānā*)—"to devastate one's array, preparations, or possessions"[56]—can hardly refer, suicidally, to "Corruption" itself; so 2b probably developed under the compulsion of *parallelismus membrorum* without the author paying much attention to the literal sense of 2a, which is an idiomatic expression in both Syriac and Greek. One might say that the poetic spirit ran away with him. In any case 2b carries less weight than 2a. What 2b did was to give an opportunity to use the Pa. ܚܒܠ (*ḥabbel*), "the same root that is found in the name of grace's opponent."[57]

The translation of the idiomatic expression, similar to the Syriac *infinitivus absolutus*, in 2a by "he made utter destruction" catches the sense exactly.[58] But, in spite of the reference to Nöldeke,[59] this is not specifically "Semitic paronomasia."[60] What "should be noted" as a "Semitism"[61] is also a "peculiarity of Greek": "A substantive related to the verb by its etymology or its meaning can occur as an *inner object* to reinforce the sense of the verb."[62] So the original, or translation, of the Aph. of ܐܒܕ (*ʾeḇaḏ*) with the "abstract" ܐܒܕܢܐ (*ʾaḇdānā*), derived from the same root, as "the general object,"[63] would, in 𝔊, have consisted of a construction with ἀπόλλυμι and ἀπώλεια as inner object.[64] Whether the compound preposition ܡܢ ܩܕܡ (*men qḏām*), "before," whose third masculine singular suffix reflexively refers to the subject "Corruption," corresponds to ἀπέναντι or ἐναντίον[65] or even to ἔμπροσθεν[66] is difficult to decide and not very important.

One may assume that in 2b 𝔊 also, a verb like (δια-, κατα-)φθείρω would have been used to match φθορά.[67] The third masculine singular suffix of ܬܘܩܢܗ (*tuqqānā*), as has been shown, makes sense only if it refers to the reinforcing object in 1a, which is now treated as a direct object.[68] Thus, the "destruction" perpetrated by "Corruption" personified appears, quite misleadingly, as an independent power, whose preparations or provisions are ruined.[69] The equivalent for ܬܘܩܢܗ (*tuqqānā*), "contrivance," from the root *tqn*, could be (δια-, κατα-) σκευή or σκευασία,[70] but not κατάστασις and certainly

52 The masculine pronoun "he" refers to Corruption, which is of masculine gender in Syriac. "Grace" is feminine in Syriac and is represented by the feminine pronoun "she."

53 So, e.g., Greßmann, 465.

54 Bauer, 613.

55 Frankenberg, 42.

56 Harris and Mingana, 2:375.

57 Blaszczak, 65.

58 Harris and Mingana, 2:375; similarly Diettrich, 113.

59 Nöldeke §§295–98; Blaszczak, 127.

60 Charlesworth, 121 (1973, not in the edition of 1977).

61 Harris and Mingana, 2:375.

62 BDR §153 (cf. BDF §153, esp. [3]).

63 Nöldeke §298; Payne Smith, 1:8.

64 BDAG, *s.vv.* ἀπόλλυμι, ἀπώλεια; see Frankenberg, 29: καὶ ἀπώλεσε τὴν ἀπώλειαν.

65 BDAG, *s.vv.* ἀπέναντι, ἐναντίον.

66 Frankenberg, 29; BDAG, *s.v.* ἔμπροσθεν.

67 BDAG, *s.vv.* διαφθείρω, καταφθείρω, φθείρω; Payne Smith, 1:1175–76.

68 Harris and Mingana (2:374), emending the word "corruption" found in the manuscripts (see Harris, 132), refer this suffix to "Corruptor." Diettrich, who also emends "corruption" to "Corruptor," treats the text of 2a-b even more cavalierly and translates: "And he [the Corruptor] . . . corrupted his [God's] whole creation" (Diettrich, 133, with his own addenda).

69 That strict logic cannot always be applied to poetic freedom is seen from the parallelisms of ܚܒܠܐ (*ḥḇālā*) and ܐܒܕܢܐ (*ʾaḇdānā*) in 7a and 8b, on the one hand, and ܠܐ ܬܬܚܒܠܘܢ (*lā teṯḥabblūn*) and ܠܐ ܬܐܒܕܘܢ (*lā tēḇdūn*) in 9, on the other.

70 LSJ, *s.vv.* διασκευή, κατασκευή, σκευασία; Payne Smith, 2:4486–87.

not σύστημα.[71] Although Blaszczak obviously refers "his works" in 2b to the subject "corruption," he correctly interprets the intention of 2a-b: "The verse thus underlines the totally destructive and corrupting activity of the subject."[72]

The influence of the "Proverbs of Solomon"[73] is felt even before stanza III (see below) in the destructive action of "Corruption," which imitates the Sapiential Virgin "Grace" and is therefore especially deceptive.[74] In the same way that "the depiction of the foolish woman [viz., as 'contrasted with Wisdom personified'] lacks somewhat of originality,"[75] the baleful actions of "Corruption" will be overshadowed by the soteriological statements of the "Perfect Virgin," who comes next on the scene. Whether the verb of condition ܩܐܡ, ܩܡ (*qām*) in 3a, "stood," used ingressively, corresponded to a form of ἵστημι[76] can be left undecided. On the other hand, the preposition ܥܠ (*ʿal*) clearly has the same spatial meaning as ἐπί ("on").[77] In the rush of metaphor, the function of the "summit" or "peak" is merely to provide unrestricted audibility, the *hapax legomenon* ܪܡܐ (*rāmā*) being perhaps inspired by the adjective ὑψηλός in Prov 8:2 and 9:3 LXX.[78] But the term ܪܫܐ (*rēšā*), which occurs more often and may represent ἡ ἄκρα or τὸ ἄκρον (cf. Prov 8:2 LXX) as well as κεφαλή or κορυφή,[79] in any case introduces the image of a mythological mountain (see Excursus 23), and therefore a secondary influence from the temptation story in Matthew cannot be excluded (cf. εἰς ὄρος ὑψηλὸν λίαν, "to a very high mountain," in Matt 4:8). The second half of 3a uses ἀφίημι/ܫܒܩ (*šbaq*) in a fashion that differs from 1b and 7a (cf. Gen 45:2; Mark 15:37).[80] To "let go" or "send out" one's voice means to let it "resound"[81] or "ring out"[82] (cf. a further idiomatic construction using φωνή/ܩܠܐ [*qālā*] in 37:2b). That "Corruption" has a mouth with a "voice" (cf. 7:24; 31:3-4) is a further attribute of the personification.

After the image of the lofty peak, the second monocolon, 3b,[83] brings the third dimension into the mythological picture and makes clear that he can be heard everywhere. The repeated plural of the term ܣܘܦܐ (*sawpā*), which occurs only here, derives from τὰ ἔσχατα τῆς γῆς (cf. 26:7).[84] This is not a geographical concept but a description of the whole known world as a habitation of persons able to hear. They are now the target of the intended temptation by "Corruption" personified.

In dualistic imitation of the promise by the Johannine Jesus (John 12:32: πάντα[ς] ἑλκύσω πρὸς ἐμαυτόν, "I will draw all men to myself"; ܐܓܕ ܟܠ ܢܫ ܠܘܬܝ [*ʾegged kol nāš lwāṯ*]; cf. John 6:44), the devastating and loud-voiced "Corruption" drew all those who obeyed him to or toward himself. In 4a, unlike 29:4, this is not a liberation from Hades and Death (but cf. ܢܓܕܐ [*neḡdē*] in 38:8).[85] The verb "to draw," in fact, has a threatening undertone of "to mislead."[86] The Ethpe. of ܫܡܥ (*šmaʿ*) with preposition ܠ (*l-*) corresponds to the active verb ὑπακούω with dative of the person or thing. This "being obedient," which is far more than "to hear" or "listen to,"[87] is due, existentially speaking, to God alone[88] but can, by faith, be transferred to Christ (Heb 5:9), who, as

71 Contra Frankenberg, 29.
72 Blaszczak, 66.
73 Harris and Mingana, 2:376.
74 See Gerrit J. Reinink, review of Charlesworth in *JSJ* 5 (1974) 68; Blaszczak (p. 126) needs to be emended.
75 Plöger, 107, on Prov 9:13-18.
76 BDAG, *s.v.* ἵστημι; Payne Smith, 2:3522–25; Frankenberg, 29: ἔστη.
77 Payne Smith, 2:2886; BDAG, *s.v.* ἐπί, 1.
78 BDAG, *s.v.* ὑψηλός, 1: "high"; Payne Smith, 2:3861.
79 Payne Smith, 2:3899; LEH, *s.vv.* ἄκρον, κορυφή; BDAG, *s.v.* κεφαλή; Beyer, *ATTM*, 689.
80 Payne Smith, 2:4038; BDAG, *s.v.* ἀφίημι, 1b.
81 Diettrich, 113.
82 Ungnad and Staerk, 33.
83 Franzmann's unnecessary division of the monocola 3a and 3b into bicola only conceals the fact that the phrases in 3b "express merismus (= the whole land)" (see Franzmann, 236).
84 Payne Smith, 2:2578; BDAG, *s.v.* ἔσχατος, 1: "the ends of the earth."
85 Payne Smith, 2:2276–77.
86 BDAG, *s.v.* ἕλκω, 1.
87 Diettrich, 114; Blaszczak, 59.
88 BDAG, *s.v.* ὑπακούω, 1; cf. Payne Smith, 2:4215.

"the *redeemed Redeemer*,"[89] is the eschatological model of ὑπακοή (Heb 5:8; cf. Phil 2:8).

Corruption personified thus deceptively imitates Jesus Christ and indeed usurps divine authority and dominion, for which he is indirectly described in 4b as "evil" or "the Evil One."[90] This is the only way in which that negative statement can make sense.[91] Contrary to normal rules of syntax, the masculine ܒܝܫܐ (*bīšā*) in *status emphaticus*, which corresponds either to πονηρός or to the nominalized adjective ὁ πονηρός,[92] forms the predicate of the final clause.[93] The Ethpe. of ܚܙܐ (*ḥzā*) could, unusually, correspond to ὤφθη without a dative (cf. Luke 9:31),[94] but the use of ὡσ(εί)/ܐܝܟ (*ʾak*) suggests rather a form of φαίνομαι.[95] This ends the parabolic mythos of "Corruption," but it reverberates still in stanzas III (7a), IV (9a), and V (12b).

■ **5-8** For the antithetical use of the "adversative particle" ἀλλά/ܐܠܐ (*ʾellā*), reference to 11:8 and 31:11 is more relevant than to 4:9 and 11:23;[96] here it forms the "transition to someth[ing] different."[97] Verse 5a is not a syntactical continuation of 4b[98] but an independent statement, which—together with the participles in 5b—introduces the address that follows. Within the Ode, the "Perfect Virgin," making this one appearance, is the personified "Grace" of stanza I, who, after her "descent," which should not be confused with a "fall,"[99] now, like her brash and negative opponent, "stood up" (see 3a above). It is not necessary to imagine either a Gnostic "Virgin of Light"[100] or a "Goddess of Mercy" Χάρις.[101] The term παρθένος/ܒܬܘܠܬܐ (*btūltā*) was used in the ancient world for "female deities,"[102] so the appearance of the Virgin Grace would not have appeared as strange as it does now.[103] Since this Virgin sounds, in places, like Wisdom personified,[104] although she should not be "equated with the Wisdom of God,"[105] it is not possible to rule out the influence of Wis 9:6 LXX. In that case the Virgin Grace would be pronounced τελεία ("perfect") by the feminine singular passive participle of ܓܡܪ (*gmar*) in the emphatic state,[106] because her "wisdom [is] of God"; at any rate the *hapax legomenon* here is neither a "divine attribute" nor a philosophical term of worth.[107]

Comparisons with Matt 11:25-30 and Sirach 24[108] or even Sirach 51[109] are of less use in understanding stanzas III–VI[110] than the emphatic reference to Proverbs 8.[111] But even if Prov 9:1-6 and 1:20-26 are included, the terminological influence of these "Wisdom texts"[112] remains quite modest, as can be seen from Table 8.

89 Gräßer, 1:309.
90 Contra Frankenberg, 42.
91 Diettrich, 114; Blaszczak, 65.
92 BDAG, *s.v.* ὁ πονηρός, 1bβ: "the devil"; Payne Smith, 1:440.
93 Brockelmann, *Grammatik* §191g.
94 BDAG, *s.v.* ὁράω, 1d.
95 BDAG, *s.v.* φαίνομαι, 4: "appear as someth[ing], appear to be someth[ing]" with a "predicate nom[inative]"; Payne Smith, 1:1234; cf. Frankenberg, 29: οὐκ ἐφάνη.
96 Franzmann, 235.
97 BDAG, *s.v.* ἀλλά, 2.
98 Contra Frankenberg, 29, 42; Greßmann, 465; Wilckens, *Weisheit*, 136; Bauer, 613.
99 Colpe, "Gnosis," 572 and 596.
100 Greßmann, "Oden Salomos," 9–10; Norden, *Theos*, 198; Wetter, *Sohn Gottes*, 114.
101 Günther Bornkamm, *Mythos und Legende in den apokryphen Thomas-Akten: Beiträge zur Geschichte der Gnosis und zur Vorgeschichte des Manichäismus* (FRLANT 49 = N.F. 31; Göttingen: Vandenhoeck & Ruprecht, 1933) 92–93. On the symbolism of the church as a virgin (παρθένος) in *Hermas, Vis.* 23 (IV.2).1-2, see Brox, *Hirt*, 171–72. The Virgin of this Ode, however, is neither "the community of Jesus" (Henri Leclercq, "Odes de Salomon," *DACL* 12.2 [1936] 1909) nor the "*virgo casta*" of 2 Cor 11:2 (Joseph Conrad Plumpe, *Mater Ecclesia: An Inquiry into the Concept of the Church as Mother in Early Christianity* [Studies in Christian Antiquity 5; Washington, D.C.: Catholic University of America Press, 1943] 26 and 73). To interpret her as the "personification of the ideal of asceticism" (Vööbus, 282) passes all acceptable bounds of imaginative exegesis.
102 Gerhard Delling, "παρθένος," *ThWNT* 5 (1954) 826; *TDNT* 5:827–28.
103 See BDAG, *s.v.* παρθένος, a; Payne Smith, 1:624.
104 Harris and Mingana, 2:374; Wilckens, *Weisheit*, 138–39.
105 Contra Bauer, 613.
106 Payne Smith, 1:739; BDAG, *s.v.* τέλειος, 1.
107 Gerhard Delling, "τέλος, . . . , τελειότης, κτλ.," *ThWNT* 8 (1969) 68, 70–73; *TDNT* 8:68–72.
108 Norden, *Theos*, 293–95; Bousset, *Kyrios Christos*, 46; Dibelius, 283.
109 Arvedson, *Mysterium*, 7, etc.
110 Franzmann's structural analysis (pp. 236–39) can be supplemented, *formgeschichtlich*, by the division

Table 8: The Influence of Proverbs 1:20-26 and 8–9 LXX on *Ode* 33

Proverbs	Terms and statements	*Ode* 33
1:21a	ἐπ᾽ ἄκρων δὲ τειχέων κηρύσσεται	3a, 5b
1:21c	λέγει	5b
1:26a	τῇ ὑμετέρᾳ ἀπωλείᾳ	2a, 8b
8:1	σὺ τὴν σοφίαν κηρύξεις	5b
8:2a	ἐπὶ γὰρ τῶν ὑψηλῶν ἄκρων ἐστίν	3a
8:2b	ἕστηκεν	3a, 5a
8:4a	ὑμᾶς, ὦ ἄνθρωποι, παρακαλῶ	6a-b
8:4b	προΐεμαι ἐμὴν φωνὴν υἱοῖς ἀνθρώπων	3a, 6a-b
8:6a	εἰσακούσατέ μου	10a
8:7a	ἀλήθειαν	8c
8:12a	ἐγὼ ἡ σοφία	8c
8:20a	ἐν ὁδοῖς	7a, 8c
8:31b	ἐν υἱοῖς ἀνθρώπων	6a-b
(8:32)	+ μακάριοι οἱ ὁδούς μου φυλάσσοντες	8c, 10a, 13b
(8:33)	+ ἀκούσατε παιδείαν (A σοφίαν) καὶ σοφισθῆτε	8c, 10a-b
8:34a	μακάριος ἀνήρ, ὃς εἰσακούσεταί μου	10a, 11a
8:34b	καὶ ἄνθρωπος, ὃς τὰς ἐμὰς ὁδοὺς φυλάξει	8c, 13b
9:1a	ἡ σοφία	8c
9:3b	συγκαλοῦσα μετὰ ὑψηλοῦ κηρύγματος . . . λέγουσα	3a, 5b
9:5a	ἔλθατε	6b
9:6a	ζήσεσθε	11a

of the address into "paragraphs" (Becker, *Reden,* 18) or "elements" (Blaszczak, 62) as can be seen by placing them side by side in comparison:

Becker	Blaszczak
1. Invitation–Promise (6-9)	(a) Address and Imperatives (6-7)
	(b) Motives (8-9)
2. Invitation–Promise (10, 11a)	(a') Imperatives (10a)
3. Self-description–Promise (11b, 12)	(b') Motives (10b-12)
4. Invitation–Promise (13)	(a'') Imperative (13a)
	(b'') Motives (13b-c)

Blaszczak describes the motives as either "promises" (8-9, 11a, 12, 13b-c) or "'I' statements" (10b, 11b). Becker defines the stylistic element "promise" more specifically as "*promise of redemption.*"

111 Harris and Mingana, 2:376; Egon Brandenburger, *Fleisch und Geist: Paulus und die dualistische Weisheit* (WMANT 29; Neukirchen-Vluyn: Neukirchener Verlag, 1968) 214; on the "relationship God–Wisdom–World," see Max Küchler, "Gott und seine Weisheit in der Septuaginta (Ijob 28; Spr 8)," in Hans-Josef Klauck, ed., *Monotheismus und Christologie: Zur Gottesfrage im hellenistischen Judentum und im Urchristentum* (Quaestiones disputatae 138; Freiburg: Herder, 1992) 136–39.

112 Blaszczak, 67.

The verb κηρύσσω (Prov 1:21a; 8:1; cf. 9:3b), in any case, lies behind the participle of the Aph. ܐܟܪܙ (*ʾakrez*), which occurs only in 5b, and certainly justifies the term "propaganda" first used by Norden[113] for the address that follows.[114] The participle of ܐܡܪ (*ʾemar*) corresponds to a form of λέγω or εἶπον/εἶπα,[115] but the participle in the middle poses a problem in textual criticism. The term in Prov 9:3b (συγκαλοῦσα) seems at first to support ܩܪܝܐ (*qāryā*) in H.[116] The N reading, then, would be a scribal error (ܩܥܝܐ [*qāʿyā*] for ܩܪܝܐ), because the words look very similar. But κράζω can also be translated by ܩܪܐ (e.g., in Gal 4:6: πνεῦμα . . . κρᾶζον = ܪܘܚܐ . . . ܩܪܝܐ [*rūḥā* . . . *qāryā*]),[117] so the reading of N should be preferred as the *lectio difficilior*. Even so, there might have been a scribal error involved in H (ܩܪܝܐ for ܩܥܝܐ, perhaps even ܩ݁ܪܝܐ for ܩ݁ܥܝܐ, that is, with a point above as a mark of the participle). If, however, there was no scribal error or other correction to the manuscript, both readings can be explained as alternative translations of a form of κράζω,[118] which is again an argument for a Greek original.[119]

The idiomatic expressions "sons of men" and "daughters [of men]" in 6a-b refer simply to male and female human beings.[120] The influence of Prov 8:4 is clear (cf. Prov 8:31b). Since those addressed are not God's "children,"[121] neither Isa 43:6 nor Wis 9:7 served as a *Vorlage*, even though the term "judge" is found in the latter text (see 11b below). Of the two imperative verbs, which are respectively parallel to the imperatives in 7a and 7b (6a || 7a; 6b || 7b), the one in 6b ("come") could derive from Prov 9:5a (ἔλθατε).[122] Unlike in 30:2 (cf. Matt 11:28) 𝔊 here did not use δεῦτε[123] where the plural imperative of ܐܬܐ (*ʾeṯā*) is found. The equivalent of the masculine plural imperative, also meant inclusively, of the Ethpe. ܐܬܦܢܝ (*ʾeṯpnī*) is an imperative form of στρέφομαι[124] or ἐπιστρέφω/ἐπιστρέφομαι.[125] As Wilckens points out, "this call to turn back is typical of Wisdom homilies and indeed of Jewish Wisdom discourses in general."[126] John 7:37, to which Blaszczak refers in connection with the same quotation,[127] is not relevant.

Just as Grace personified left "Corruption" (1a), it is now necessary for men and women—not just now and then but forever—to leave the ways of *this* dualistic opponent (on ἀφίημι/ܫܒܩ [*šḇaq*] and φθορά/ܚܒܠܐ [*ḥḇālā*], see above).[128] The term ἡ ὁδός/ܐܘܪܚܐ (*ʾurḥā*), "way," in 7a—and also in 8c and 13b—comes from Prov 8:20 and 8:34, and is used elsewhere in that pseudo-Solomonic collection (Prov 2:12-16; 3:17; 4:11 LXX; see Excursus 15). In the same way that 7a makes the call to return in 6a more specific, 7b adds a more explicit sense to the invitation to "come" in 6b.[129] It is not possible to decide whether the Ethpa. of ܩܪܒ (*qreḇ*), followed by ܠܝ (*lī* = *l-* + first singular suffix), corresponds to intransitive προσάγω[130] or to προσεγγίζω[131] or προσέρχομαι

113 Norden, *Theos*, 3, etc.
114 BDAG, *s.v.* κηρύσσω, 2bβ; Payne Smith, 1:1817; Blaszczak, 61.
115 Cf. 11:18; 38:10; Prov 9:3b; and see Excursus 12.
116 See Payne Smith, 2:3713, *s.vv.* ܩܪܐ (*qrā*), ܩܪܝ (*qrī*); BDAG, *s.v.* συγκαλέω: "summon."
117 See NA[27] and *NTSy* on this passage.
118 Payne Smith, 2:3682, 3712; BDAG, *s.v.* κράζω, 2.
119 Frankenberg neatly avoids the problem by using only two participles instead of three (see Frankenberg, 29: κηρύττουσα καὶ κράζουσα).
120 Linguistically, Frankenberg (p. 29) is of course aware of this. But interpretatively he inserts "allegories . . . of a scholarly imagination" (p. 3) into the text: "Those whom she [viz., χάρις] addresses as children of men are the λογισμοὶ ἀνθρώπινοι as opposed to the λ. δαιμονιακοί who are unteachable" (p. 93).
121 BDAG, *s.v.* θυγάτηρ, 2.
122 Both manuscripts (N ܬܐܝܢ, H ܬܝܢ) need slight corrections. Frankenberg's retroversion (p. 29) of ܬܐܝܢ (*tāyēn*) as προσέλθατε cannot be justified.
123 BDAG, *s.v.* δεῦτε.
124 Payne Smith, 2:3167; BDAG, *s.v.* στρέφω, 1b and 5: passive "w[ith] act[ive] force" or "in act[ive] sense," reflexive m[eani]ng, "turn around," "change."
125 BDAG, *s.v.* ἐπιστρέφω, 1–4: "turn around," "turn back"; see Frankenberg, 29: ἐπιστρέψασθε.
126 Wilckens, *Weisheit*, 138: "Mahnrede."
127 Blaszczak, 68, 128.
128 It is quite possible that 𝔊 used two different verbs and that it had καταλείπετε here (Frankenberg, 29; cf. BDAG, *s.v.* καταλείπω, 2).
129 This parallelism (6a || 7a; 6b || 7b), already discussed, is the main reason for departing from the manuscripts and making a bicolon of 7 (Lattke, *Bedeutung*, 1:76; cf. already Harris and Mingana, vol. 1, on this passage; 2:374).
130 BDAG, *s.v.* προσάγω, 2.
131 BDAG, *s.v.* προσεγγίζω; Frankenberg, 29: προσεγγίσατέ μοι. Wilckens makes the daring assertion that "*Ode* 33:7b agrees word for word with Sir 51:23 [viz., ἐγγίσατε πρός με]" (*Weisheit*, 138 n. 5). In essence that is correct.

with dative of the person.[132] The last of these verbs was regularly used in antiquity "of approach to or entry into a deity's presence" (cf. 1 Pet 2:4 for this meaning).[133]

The use of the future tense in 8a-c, after the imperatives of 6-7, may be considered Semitic syntax.[134] But this cannot be used to argue for a Syriac original, since such "constructions" are already "common" in the New Testament, whose Greek is therefore also "under Semitic influence."[135] Thus, the particle καί/ܘ (*w-*) at the beginning of 8a should be translated as "then."[136] The references with which Blaszczak supports 8a in "its background in the image of Wisdom entering into men" (cf. Prov 2:10 and Wis 7:27)[137] can be supplemented by ones that use εἰσέρχομαι with εἴς τινα (Wis 1:4; 10:16).[138] In 𝔊, a construction like εἰσελεύσομαι ἐν ὑμῖν[139] is even more likely, since the *hapax legomenon* ܥܠ (*ʿal*)[140] is linked to the preposition ܒ (*b-*), whose second masculine plural suffix is meant inclusively (ܒܟܘܢ [*bk̲ōn*]).[141]

Although the Aph. of ܢܦܩ (*np̄aq*) appears in 42:16b, 8b does not allude to Hades. Here the term ܐܒܕܢܐ (*ʾab̲dānā*), derived from Prov 1:26a (ἀπώλεια, "destruction"), is—unlike the case in 2a (see above)—parallel to φθορά/ܚܒܠܐ (*ḥb̲ālā*) in 7a (see Excursus 28).[142] Whether the promise of salvation was expressed in 𝔊 by ἐκφέρω[143] or ἐξάγω[144] cannot be decided as certainly as Frankenberg would have it.[145]

The passage Prov 8:32-34 LXX acted as sponsor in the formulation of 8c.[146] Therefore it is not necessary to take refuge in such generalizations as: "That Wisdom makes her adherents wise (*Odes Sol.* 33:8) is an axiom of the Jewish Chokhmah."[147] The *hapax legomenon* Pa. ܚܟܡ (*ḥakkem*), "make wise," stems from σοφισθῆτε (Prov 8:33),[148] not from the synonymous verb διδάσκω.[149] The "ways of truth" (cf. "way of truth," *Ode* 11:3) are not, after all, the direct object (cf. Prov 8:20 rather than 8:32, 34). They are not—or at least not directly—related to Truth personified of *Ode* 38 (see Excursus 1), instead describing, in contrast to the "ways of this Corruption" (7a), that in which[150] and about which Grace "aims to make humankind wise."[151] The occurrence in Prov 8:7b of the antithetical χείλη ψευδῆ ("false lips") supports the dualistic opposition between ἀλήθεια/ܫܪܪܐ (*šrārā*) and "falsehood" (cf. 3:10; 18:6). In the end, the "ways of truth" are identical with "my ways" (see 13b below).[152]

■ **9-11a** "Verse 9 is also a promise."[153] Although the two negated imperfects of the introductory monocolon[154]

132 BDAG, *s.v.* προσέρχομαι.
133 BDAG, *s.v.* προσέρχομαι, 1b; the reference to 1 Pet 2:4 should be emended here and in Bauer and Aland.
134 See Beyer, *Syntax*, 238–55: "*Imperativ* + καί + *Futurum*."
135 Ibid., *Syntax*, 252.
136 Klaus Beyer, letter of October 31, 2002 (Germ. "so").
137 Blaszczak, 68.
138 BDAG, *s.v.* εἰσέρχομαι, 1bγ.
139 Frankenberg, 29, though he uses εἰσέρχομαι.
140 Payne Smith, 2:2874. The first radical of ܥܠ (*ʿal*) undergoes secondary doubling in the imperfect: ܘܐܥܘܠ (*w-eʿʿol*).
141 It is surprising that Charlesworth has not corrected his note on 8a ("There is a beautiful subtlety about this line in Syriac, which was probably intended by the Odist," etc. [Charlesworth, 1973, p. 122]) in the "corrected reprint" (1977, pp. xi and 122).
142 Blaszczak does not comment on this inconsistency in the use of ܐܒܕܢܐ (*ʾab̲dānā*), but rather glosses over it (see Blaszczak, 68, where 8b is confused with 9a).
143 BDAG, *s.v.* ἐκφέρω, 1–2.
144 BDAG, *s.v.* ἐξάγω, 1; cf. Payne Smith, 2:2423.
145 Frankenberg, 29: καὶ ἐκ τῆς ἀπωλείας ὑμᾶς ἐξάξω.
146 See already Harris and Mingana, 2:337.
147 Wilckens, *Weisheit*, 138–39; Blaszczak, 68.
148 Payne Smith, 1:1265; BDAG, *s.v.* σοφίζω, 1a.
149 Contra Frankenberg, 30: διδάξω ὑμᾶς τὰς ὁδοὺς τῆς ἀληθείας.
150 The translation "on the ways of truth" (Harnack, 65; Diettrich, 144) distorts the image (on the translation above, see Ungnad and Staerk, 33; Bauer, 614).
151 Lattke, *Oden*, 190 n. 11.
152 See Sebastian Brock, "The Two Ways and the Palestinian Targum," in Philip R. Davies and Richard T. White, eds., *A Tribute to Geza Vermes: Essays on Jewish and Christian Literature and History* (JSOTSup 100; Sheffield: JSOT Press, 1990) 148: "Plurality of ways."
153 Blaszczak, 62, 68. Greßmann (p. 466) links 9 to 8c and translates 9 in his own peculiar fashion, "that you will not be annihilated or destroyed."
154 I cannot agree with Franzmann's division (pp. 233–34) of 9 into 9a-b, 10a into 10a-b (making 10b into 10c), and 11a into 11a-b (making 11b into 11c). Her analyses remain valuable even if the manuscript verse divisions are retained (see pp. 237–38).

could be interpreted modally ("you shall not . . .")[155] or even prohibitively,[156] in this passage they correspond to the construction οὐ μή . . . οὐδέ/μηδέ (with future indicative) and are "the most decisive way of negativing someth[ing] in the future."[157] These two verbs allude to the destructive powers φθορά/ܚܒܠܐ (*ḥbālā*) and ἀπώλεια/ܐܒܕܢܐ (*ʾabdānā*), "Corruption" and "destruction" (see 1-2, 7a, 8b above), whose powerlessness, at least over the elect (see 13a below), is thus made clear. Since Greek manuscripts use φθείρω interchangeably with διαφθείρω (e.g., Rev 19:2)[158] and καταφθείρω (e.g., 2 Pet 2:12),[159] the future passive of any one of these verbs comes under consideration as the equivalent of the Ethpa. ܐܬܚܒܠ (*ʾetḥabbal*).[160] Without being negated, this verbal stem is used for the eschatological destruction of death and darkness (15:9a; 31:1b), which lends even greater force to this promise of salvation. The same is true of the parallel Pe. ܐܒܕ (*ʾebad*), which corresponds to the middle future of ἀπόλλυμι, if one takes note of uses without a negative (5:14a; 24:7b, 9a; 31:2a) and draws on parallels to the promise of salvation that is founded in the mythos of the redeemed Redeemer (9:7a; 28:16a; 42:10b).[161]

Verse 10a again exhibits Semitic syntax[162] and more or less influence from Proverbs 8 (cf. Prov 8:6a [εἰσακούσατέ μου], 8:33 [ἀκούσατε], and 8:34a [μακάριος ἀνήρ, ὃς εἰσακούσεταί μου] in Table 8 above). In view of the blessing later in stanza IV (see 11a below), this source is more likely than Sir 16:24 LXX (ἄκουσόν μου).[163] The Pe. ܫܡܥ (*šmaʿ*), with first singular objective suffix, corresponding to an imperative of (εἰσ)ακούω with genitive, verges on a call to "obey,"[164] but should rather be understood as an eschatological "listen (to)" (cf. 8:8a; 15:4b).[165] From the "summons . . . to live"[166] there is no linguistic path to the Ethpe. of ܦܪܩ (*praq*).[167] So the Greek translation or *Vorlage* would have used an imperative, either a passive form of σῴζω[168] (cf. Ps 32:16a LXX || Ps 33:16a Pesh., and also the passage 4 Macc 6:27 "dating back to the end of the first century C.E.")[169] or, more probably, a passive form of λυτρόω (cf. Sir 51:2b-f LXX, καὶ ἐλυτρώσω τὸ σῶμά μου ἐξ ἀπωλείας . . . ἐγένου βοηθὸς καὶ ἐλυτρώσω με, "and you have delivered me from destruction . . . you have been my helper and delivered me").[170]

In the bicolon 10b-11a, 10b primarily corresponds to and explains the first part of 10a, while 11a interprets the second part with a promise of salvation that employs the same verb and adds an indirect benediction. The problem in 10b is the fact that Grace personified appears not merely as an agent of salvation but as "speaking the grace of God," that is, "proclaiming" it (cf. 31:3a). This dilemma, in spite of an accurate translation,[171] persuades Blaszczak to make the linguistically impossible suggestion that "the grace of God" should

155 Harnack, 65; Diettrich, 114; Bauer, 614.

156 Harris and Mingana, 2:374; Charlesworth, 120; Franzmann, 234, 237; Lattke, *Bedeutung*, 1:167; cf. Nöldeke §266.

157 BDAG, *s.v.* μή, 4; cf. Frankenberg, 30: οὐ μὴ φθαρήσεσθε οὐδὲ ἀπολεῖσθε.

158 NA[27], p. 671.

159 NA[27], p. 611.

160 BDAG, *s.vv.* διαφθείρω, 2; καταφθείρω, 1–2; φθείρω, 2; Payne Smith, 1:1176.

161 See BDAG, *s.v.* ἀπόλλυμι, 1b; Payne Smith, 1:8.

162 However, in this case there are "two syndetic imperatives" (Beyer, *Syntax*, 243, 253). It is not "a hendiadys" (contra Blaszczak, 62).

163 Brandenburger (*Fleisch*, 214), therefore, is justified in saying on stanzas III–VI: "Even its fashioning as a Wisdom speech goes back to Prov 8."

164 BDAG, *s.vv.* ἀκούω, 4; εἰσακούω, 1; Payne Smith, 2:4214; cf. Charlesworth, 120: "Obey me."

165 Bauer, 614; Blaszczak, 58.

166 Plöger, 103–4, on Prov 9:6a; cf. ζήσεσθε in LXX (Rahlfs, 2:197).

167 For the *substance,* one need not avoid the idea of such an influence; in fact one might also refer to Sir 51:11a-b LXX, καὶ εἰσηκούσθη ἡ δέησίς μου· ἔσωσας γάρ με ἐξ ἀπωλείας (Rahlfs, 2:469). The first point is that "σῴζεσθαι is often used in the Sept[uagint] as the equivalent of the Hebr[ew] חָיָה" (George Herbert Box and William O. E. Oesterley, "The Book of Sirach," *APOT* 1:323 n., on Sir 3:1b). Later σῴζεσθαι is often represented by ܚܝܐ (*ḥyā*), as can be seen even in the *Odes of Solomon* (cf. 5:3b; 6:18b). In the present context one could refer especially to Wis 9:18c, καὶ τῇ σοφίᾳ ἐσώθησαν – ܘܒܚܟܡܬܐ ܚܝܘ (Rahlfs, 2:358; *OTSy*, pt. 2 fasc. 5, on this passage).

168 Payne Smith, 2:3294; BDAG, *s.v.* σῴζω, 2; Frankenberg, 30: ἀκούετέ μου καὶ σῴζεσθε.

169 Klauck, *4. Makkabäerbuch*, 669.

170 Rahlfs, 2:468–69; BDAG, *s.v.* λυτρόω, 2.

171 Blaszczak, 59.

be treated as a "self-identification . . . in apposition to the first person singular pronoun."[172] The solution can, again, be found in Proverbs 8. The reading of Prov 8:33 LXX in the Codex Alexandrinus (ἀκούσατε σοφίαν)[173] can lead to the conclusion that Wisdom personified (Prov 8:12; 9:1) herself teaches wisdom. Therefore Grace personified can also here "proclaim" the grace of God.[174]

Excursus 33: "Grace" and Other Syriac Words from the Same Root in the *Odes of Solomon*

In conformity with *Greek* "usage,"[175] it would be necessary to include in this excursus the terms χαίρω, χαρά, and of course χάρισμα (for these words, see Excursuses 32 and 37). In *Syriac*, the feminine ܛܝܒܘܬܐ (*taybūtā*), corresponding to χάρις (11:1b) and translated throughout as "grace,"[176] thus distinguishing it from ἀγαθωσύνη/ܛܒܘܬܐ (*ṭābūtā*) = "goodness,"[177] belongs to the root ܛܘܒ.[178] In addition to the principal term "grace," which occurs more than twenty times, the following words derive from the same root:

- The feminine "goodness," whose written form closely resembles "grace" (possibly a variant reading for "grace" in 20:9b N; certainly a variant in 29:2b H; referring to the "name of the Lord" in 41:5).
- The adjective ἀγαθός/ܛܒܐ (*ṭābā*), which occurs three times, attributively linked to "captivity" (10:3b; cf. Eph 4:8) and "works/changes" (11:20b ܣ/𝔊), and in the feminine singular emphatic state ܛܒܬܐ (*ṭabtā*) corresponding either to an objective ἀγαθόν or to the adjectival part of the compound verb ἀγαθοποιέω (28:12a).[179]
- The masculine ܛܘܒܐ (*ṭūbā*), which as a construct plural always carries a suffix and which corresponds to μακάριοι κτλ. (11:18a) or to "Heb[rew] אַשְׁרֵי *blessed* (is, are), Mt. v 3-11; Lk. vii 23; xii 43."[180] It occurs five times and refers to the "ministers of that drink" (6:13a; μακάριοι and διάκονοι in ℭ), the wearers of the crown that is equated with truth (9:8b), those "planted" in paradise (11:18a; μακάριοι in 𝔊), the Gnostics (12:13a)[181] and those who "have drunk" from the spring of the Lord (30:7).
- The plural of the adjective ܛܘܒܢܐ (*ṭūbānā*), which in a nominalized form describes "the blessed" (οἱ μακάριοι) as having "joy" (32:1a) and predicatively calls those who are to be saved "blessed" (33:11a).
- Finally, two *hapax legomena* from *Ode* 8: (1) the Pa. ܛܝܒ (*ṭayyeb*): "My own breasts I prepared for them" (8:16b); (2) the Ethpa. ܐܬܛܝܒ (*ʾeṭṭayyab*): "Peace was prepared for you" (8:7a).

172 Ibid., 69. That would make it necessary to place the pronoun at the beginning, preceding "grace," which must be considered a nominative (cf., e.g., ἐγώ/ܐܢܐ [*ʾenā*] in John 12:46; Rev 22:16; before a name 2 Cor 10:1; Gal 5:2; etc.), instead of enclitically after the participle of the Pa ܡܠܠ (*mallel*). Or else "ܐܝܟ without ܕ" would have been used (Nöldeke §264.C). If it corresponded to a Greek construction with οὖσα (BDAG, *s.v.* εἰμί, 2a), one would expect a construction with ܕ (*d-*) or ܟܕ (*kad*) in ܣ. I was myself persuaded by Blaszczak (p. 69) to alter my original translation of 1979 (Lattke, *Bedeutung*, 1:167) to the erroneous "for I speak among you as the grace of God" (Lattke, *Oden*, 190), in which the appositional interpretation of the "Perfect Virgin," in 5a, by Greßmann (p. 465) and Bauer (p. 613) also played a part.

173 Rahlfs, 2:197.

174 BDAG, *s.v.* λαλέω, 2b. On the sentence structure of 10b, cf. 1 Cor 2:6 (σοφίαν [viz., θεοῦ] δὲ λαλοῦμεν ἐν τοῖς τελείοις, "Yet among the mature we do impart wisdom"; ܚܟܡܬܐ ܕܝܢ ܡܡܠܠܝܢܢ ܒܓܡܝܪܐ [*ḥekmtā dēn mmallīn-nan bagmīrē*]).

175 Hans Conzelmann, "χαίρω, . . . , χάρις, κτλ.," *ThWNT* 9 (1973) 350, 363; *TDNT* 9:360, 373.

176 Wilckens follows Bauer's translation (pp. 613–14; and already Bauer, *Oden*, 65, 67) and speaks of "goodness" rather than "grace" as expressing the closeness "to the image of personal חכמה" (see Ulrich Wilckens, "σοφία, κτλ.," *ThWNT* 7 [1964] 510; *TDNT* 7:509; cf. already idem, *Weisheit*, 136).

177 Payne Smith, 1:1439; BDAG, *s.v.* ἀγαθωσύνη; William Jennings, *Lexicon to the Syriac New Testament (Peshitta) with Copious References, Dictions, Names of Persons and Places and Some Various Readings Found in the Curetonian, Sinaitic Palimpsest, Philoxenian & Other MSS* (rev. by Ulric Gantillon; Oxford: Clarendon, 1926; repr., 1962) 84: "goodness."

178 Lattke, *Bedeutung*, 2:106; cf. Brockelmann, *Lexicon*, 269–70. The important term ܛܝܒܘܬܐ (*taybūtā*) is included in Payne Smith, *Dictionary*, 171–72, but it has found no place in the *Thesaurus* (see Payne Smith, 1:1436–40) or in the *Supplement* (see Margoliouth, *Supplement*, 139).

179 See commentary on that passage.

180 Jennings and Gantillon, 85.

181 Although I refer to "Gnostics" in the context of 12:13 (see commentary on that passage), I do not consider the *Odes of Solomon* as a whole "a product of early Christian Gnosticism" (see Jörg Frey,

"Grace" occurs in the *Odes of Solomon* only in a theological sense.[182] The significance of this result emerges in considering the "differential developments in Hellenism."[183] By concentrating on the *"grace" of God*,[184] which was a subject of philosophical debate in late antiquity, all the "favors" of earthly "rulers"[185]—and theologically also the "favor of the gods"[186]—were given the cold shoulder. This "development" of χάρις "into a power"[187] occurs in the writings of Philo and the New Testament,[188] but the *Odes of Solomon* also play a part, and the Gnostic aspect of "hypostatizing"[189] is not confined to *Ode* 33. It is well known that hypostases were not the invention of those early "sectarians" who "arrogated to themselves the description of 'knowers' or 'those capable of knowing.'"[190]

About half of the passages to be categorized have "grace" as the object of a verb. The Lord's "grace" may or should be "put on" like a garment (4:6a; 20:7a); "received" soteriologically (5:3a; cf. 20:9b H and 23:2a-b); and "known" (23:4b N), "sung" (7:22a) and "manifested" (7:25b). The Lord himself "spread out" his "grace" (24:13b), "gave to me" according to his "grace" (29:2b N),[191] and "proclaimed" χάριν καὶ χαράν ("grace and joy" [31:3a]). Similarly the hypostatization of "Grace"[192]—as Perfect Virgin—"proclaims" the "grace of God" (33:10b).[193]

In the second group of passages, the "grace" of the Lord or Most High appears as mediator of salvation. In this guise, χάρις moves along a trajectory of "power"—via "gift" (cf. the two "charisma" passages 11:9b and 35:6a)—to "hypostasis."[194] Through her, new members are "added" (6:6c). In the putting off of corruption and putting on of incorruption, "by his grace" (15:8b) is parallel to "by his name" (15:8a). Salvation and justification are both "by his grace" (25:4b and 29:5b).[195] There are the corresponding imperatives of salvation, "be redeemed by his grace" (9:5c) and "take possession of your souls through grace" (31:7a). Soteriologically, "Grace" the mediator can be parallel to "Messiah/Christ" the mediator (41:3a-b). In 9:5c, "Grace" approached the meaning of a theologically utopian place of salvation, but a fuller discussion of whether, in the context of soteriological rest, the preposition ܒ (*b*-) should be taken

review of Lattke in *ThLZ* 127 [2002] 1052, who uses "*Gnosis*"). In fact, I have remarked several times that these poems "are an anonymous and—in later terms—apocryphal product of an era in which Judaism, Gnosticism, and Christianity still overlapped like three circles with different centres" (Lattke, *Oden*, 18; cf. idem, "Dating," 49 = idem, *Bedeutung*, 4:118).

182 With the general influence of the Septuagint on the *Odes* (and here especially the Wisdom literature) it is important to emphasize the remark that "χάρις is never a theological word in the LXX" (Conzelmann, "χαίρω," *ThWNT* 9:379; *TDNT* 9:385).

183 Conzelmann, "χαίρω," *ThWNT* 9:365; *TDNT* 9:375.

184 Conzelmann, "χαίρω," *ThWNT* 9:366; *TDNT* 9:376.

185 Conzelmann, "χαίρω," *ThWNT* 9:365; *TDNT* 9:375.

186 Conzelmann, "χαίρω," *ThWNT* 9:364; *TDNT* 9:374.

187 Conzelmann, "χαίρω," *ThWNT* 9:366; *TDNT* 9:376.

188 Conzelmann, "χαίρω," *ThWNT* 9:380–90; *TDNT* 9:389–99.

189 Conzelmann, "χαίρω," *ThWNT* 9:391–92; *TDNT* 9:401; Dibelius, *Pastoralbriefe*, 107.

190 Jens Holzhausen, "Gnostizismus, Gnosis, Gnostiker. Ein Beitrag zur antiken Terminologie," *JAC* 44 (2001) 73; see also Wilckens, "σοφία," *ThWNT* 7:508–10; *TDNT* 7:507–9: "A Wisdom Myth in Judaism."

191 This is the place to refer to one of the three "charisma" passages: "and according to his gift he gave to me" (15:7a). In both of the other passages, this term, which has a much less prominent role than in the New Testament (Klaus Berger, "χάρισμα," *EWNT* 3 [1983] 1103–5; *EDNT* 3:460–61; Conzelmann, "χαίρω," *ThWNT* 9:394–97; *TDNT* 9:403–6), is used instrumentally (11:9b; 35:6a).

192 Conzelmann, "χαίρω," *ThWNT* 9:392; *TDNT* 9:401. The remark by Berger and Nord (964), "The part played by the virgin called 'Grace' may help to solve a puzzle in the history of early Christian literature, namely the figure of Tabitha in the Coptic *Apocalypse of Elijah*. Her function as opponent of the arch-enemy corresponds exactly to that described here," is probably worth pursuing on the linguistic side as well. Their translation of 10b should be corrected (see above and cf. Emerton, 723).

193 According to this interpretation the passages 33:10a ("listen to me"), 33:12a ("those who put me on") and 33:13b ("those who seek me") also belong to this group.

194 Conzelmann, "χαίρω," *ThWNT* 9:391–92; *TDNT* 9:401.

195 Here too "grace is the opening of access to God in the larger sense precisely by God himself" (Klaus Berger, "χάρις," *EWNT* 3 [1983] 1098; *EDNT* 3:458). *Ode* 33:11a, of course, also belongs here ("by me you will be saved").

instrumentally or, in a transferred sense, spatially is reserved to the end of *Ode* 37.[196]

Three passages remain, in which "Grace" is the subject.[197] The crowning soteriological statement, 34:6a ("Grace was revealed for your salvation"),[198] could be considered to belong to the first group ("grace" as object of a verb) if, in place of the theological passive, the Lord himself had appeared as the active revealer of divine grace. The intensely metaphorical statement, 11:1b, does not fit into any part of the pattern. The growing or budding χάρις/ ܛܝܒܘܬܐ (*ṭaybūṯā*) "is not here identified with the blossom of 1a but leads its own metaphorical life as a theological power."[199] "Grace" personified is opposed, in 33:1a, to the equally personified "Corruption."[200] Later she appears as the Perfect Virgin, making a speech reminiscent of the hypostatized σοφία,[201] describes herself as proclaimer of the "grace of God" (33:10b), and emphasizes her attribute as mediator of salvation (33:11a).[202]

Verse 11a makes clear, in spite of any linguistic speculation, how the second of the syndetic imperatives in 10a should be interpreted.[203] The idiomatic expression "by me" (lit., "by my hands"), Greek δι᾿ ἐμοῦ,[204] refers primarily to the imperfect of the Ethpe. of ܦܪܩ (*praq*), the verb repeated from 10a. Here, too, it is more likely that 𝔊 used the future passive of λυτρόω.[205] The term πόθεν ("from what") referring to "being redeemed" is not found, in contrast to *Barn.* 14:7,[206] but can be deduced from the dualistic context of *Ode* 33 (cf. 14:5 in Excursus 5). Since the instrumental phrase "by me" is put into the mouth of the Virgin "Grace," it produces a statement similar to Ignatius *Phld.* 11:1 (λυτρωθείησαν ἐν τῇ χάριτι, "may . . . be redeemed by the grace").[207] The *matter* of the first promise of salvation by Grace personified derives from Prov 9:6a (see on ζήσεσθε above). The second promise of salvation—and the conclusion of stanza IV—is in a certain sense parallel to the first[208] but also expresses an ongoing consequence of this being saved, and the wording is influenced by Prov 8:32 and 34a LXX (μακάριοι/μακάριος). In spite of a similar construction in Rom 5:19,[209] there is no reason to retranslate the imperfect of ܗܘܐ (*hwā*) by κατασταθήσεσθε.[210] If ἔσεσθε seems insufficient (cf., e.g., Mark 13:13; Matt 10:22; 24:9; John 8:36), one might consider γενήσεσθε for the translation or *Vorlage* in this indirect benediction.[211]

196 *Ode* 37:4: "by the grace of God" (Lattke, *Bedeutung*, 1:171) or "in the grace of the Lord" (idem, *Oden*, 198)?

197 The number of these passages can be much increased if the self-description of the Virgin Grace as "judge" (33:11b) and the actions of the speaker in *Ode* 33 of "proclaiming" (5b), "entering" (8a), "bringing out of destruction" (8b), "making wise" (8c), and "making known" the ways (13c) are included.

198 "Under the auspices of God's sovereignty, which apocalyptic thinking strongly emphasised, grace is the substance of salvation in the larger sense" (Klaus Berger, "χάρις," *EWNT* 3 [1983] 1100; *EDNT* 3:459). This remark about the New Testament cannot be uncritically applied to the *Odes of Solomon*.

199 See commentary on that passage.

200 As far as I have been able to determine, the term φθορά (and διαφθορά also), which may be translated as "destruction, death," is, despite its "opposition to ἀθανασία" in *Corp. Herm.* 1:28 (Günther Harder, "φθείρω, φθορά, κτλ.," *ThWNT* 9 [1973] 95, 97; *TDNT* 9:94, 96), never personified in Hellenistic Judaism or early Christianity.

201 Wilckens, "σοφία," *ThWNT* 7:510; *TDNT* 7:509–10.

202 It is not convincing to point to 33:12a as proof that the "Virgin" is hypostatized "Truth" (Diettrich, 114 n. 2), because "Grace" can also be "put on" (see on 4:6a and 20:7a above).

203 Beyer, *Syntax*, 243, 253.

204 Payne Smith, 1:1548.

205 As Frankenberg does (p. 30: λυτρωθήσεσθε) after using σῴζεσθε in 10a.

206 See Prostmeier, 449, 471.

207 Lake, 1:250–51; cf. Fischer, 202, and Ehrman, 1:294–95; BDAG, *s.v.* λυτρόω, 2. If this Ignatian statement is softened in translation to "find pardon" (Fischer, 203) or "receive forgiveness" (Bauer and Paulsen, 88; Lindemann and Paulsen, 225), it makes a less drastic impression than Schoedel's translation: "But may those who dishonored them be redeemed by the grace of Jesus Christ" (Schoedel, *Ignatius*, 212; cf. similar translations in Lake, 1:251, and Ehrman, 1:295). But even Schoedel waters down his interpretation with a reference to the forgiveness of sins in Ignatius *Phld.* 8:1.

208 Blaszczak, 69; Franzmann, 238.

209 See BDAG, *s.v.* καθίστημι, 3: "Pass[ive] be made, become."

210 Frankenberg, 30, with correction.

211 See Excursus 33 above. It is clear from the two

■ **11b-12** Since "God himself" does not come into question as the speaker of stanzas V–VI, there is no "change of [grammatical] subject" in 11b.[212] So the self-description, which is unique in the *Odes of Solomon*—and is followed by an esoteric criterion (12aα) and a twofold verdict (12aβ-b)—still issues from the mouth of the Virgin Grace[213] and not from the "mouth of Truth personified."[214] Charlesworth notes correctly on the *hapax legomenon* ܕܝܵܢܐ (*dayyānā*): "Both manuscripts have a dot above the Yūdh, signifying that the noun is 'judge' and not 'judgement' [viz., ܕܝܢܐ (*dīnā*)]."[215] That Harris and Mingana[216] read *dīnkōn* "*ex errore*" is not actually correct.[217] Charlesworth, however, fails to correct this text-critical observation as well as his own erroneous pointing of ܕܝܵܢܟܘܢ as *daynākōn*.[218]

If "judge"—a masculine noun referring to a feminine speaker[219]—were considered meaningless in the context of stanza V, two different emendations would have to be seriously considered. The first is Barth's: "instead of ܕܝܢܟܘܢ ܐܢܐ ܐܝܬܝ [*dayyānkōn ʾenā ʾītay*] 'I am your judge' (H[arris], Fl[emming]) read ܕܝܠܟܘܢ [*dīlkōn*] 'I belong to *you*.' There is no question here of judgment."[220] Kittel points to 42:20c as "converse of this statement" (and cf. 8:20b and 24:6b), but he considers the manuscript reading "fully supported by the subsequent you shall 'not suffer injustice'."[221] Connolly objects to this and suggests a different emendation: "for ܕܝܢܟܘܢ 'your judge' . . . I would suggest as possible ܙܝܢܟܘܢ 'your armour,' which would suit very well the following 'and they that put me on' [12a]."[222] At first sight the term "armor" or "weapon(s)"—in 𝔊 either singular τὸ ὅπλον (cf., e.g., Wis 18:21; *Act. Paul* 8.23)[223] or plural τὰ ὅπλα[224]—is appealing, both for the imagery of being clothed (cf. esp. ἐνδυσώμεθα τὰ ὅπλα τοῦ φωτός, "Let us . . . put on the armor of light," in Rom 13:12) and for the undercurrent of combat that characterizes this Ode (see 1b and 2a-b above). On the other hand, it must be remembered that "grace" is often the object of the verb ܠܒܫ (*lbeš*) (see Table 2; Excursus 33).

So the statement of 12a fits well with the introductory "self-description" of 11b,[225] which may have influenced the equation of the "[feminine] judge (κριτής)" with the "Virgin of the Light (-παρθένος)" in *Pistis Sophia*, chap. 111.[226] If the metaphorical use of "to put on, to clothe oneself" in the sense of "being transformed into a new

passages John 8:33 and 8:36 that γενήσεσθε and ἔσεσθε are considered synonyms. The variant reading in MS. 1241 is an attempt to harmonize v. 36 with the text of v. 33 (cf. NA[27], p. 276). Whether that was copied from an earlier manuscript makes no difference here.

212 Contra Harnack, 65.

213 See Franzmann, 238, on the structure of stanzas V and VI.

214 Contra Diettrich, 114, whose reference to "24, 8f." [= 24:10–12] is no more convincing than his excision of 33:12b.

215 Charlesworth, 122.

216 Harris and Mingana, vol. 1, on this passage.

217 Charlesworth, 120. Harris and Mingana (2:376) note, on 11b: "We have punctuated the word [*dīnkōn*] 'your judgement'; the manuscript has [*dayyānkōn*] 'your judge', which suits better the context." To anticipate, in the continuation of this passage, Harris and Mingana consider Connolly's suggestion "appropriate" but Barth's "[l]ess probable." Frankenberg (p. 30) bases his retroversion on the reading ܕܝܢܐ (*dīnā*): ἐγώ εἰμι ἡ δίκη ὑμῶν.

218 Charlesworth, 119.

219 Even considering only the Johannine metaphorical ἐγώ εἰμι passages, it can be seen that there is no problem. In addition to masculine forms such as ἄρτος ("bread" [John 6:35]) and ποιμήν ("shepherd" [10:11]), the Johannine Jesus uses feminine forms such as θύρα ("door" [10:7]), ἀνάστασις ("resurrection" [11:25]), ζωή ("life" [11:25; 14:6]), ὁδός ("way" [14:6]), ἀλήθεια ("truth" [14:6]), and ἄμπελος ("vine" [15:1, 5]), and even the neuter φῶς ("light" [8:12]); cf. also Rev 22:13 and 16. That means that it is not necessary for the translator to paste a feminine ending onto "judge" (contra Lattke, *Oden*, 191; Berger and Nord, 965).

220 Barth, 264.

221 Kittel, 121, who refers to 12a and offers a different translation.

222 Richard Hugh Connolly, review of Kittel in *JTS* 15 (1913–14) 468.

223 Schmidt and Schubart, *Acta Pauli*, 58–59, without, however, reference to Ps 5:13b LXX.

224 BDAG, *s.v.* ὅπλον, 2; Payne Smith, 1:1103: ܙܝܢܐ (*zaynā*).

225 Kittel, 121; Norden, *Theos*, 190, 198; Becker, *Reden*, 17.

226 Schmidt, Till, and Schenke, *Schriften*, 185 line 5; Schmidt and MacDermot, *Pistis Sophia*, 285 line 17; cf. Bauer, 614; influence in the opposite direction is unlikely.

being"[227] comes aptly from the mouth of the Virgin Grace,[228] the Ethpe. of ܛܠܡ (*ṭlam*) with its connotation of unjust oppression—firmly negated in this verse[229]—explains in retrospect the claim of the Virgin Grace to jurisdiction as "judge" and "divider,"[230] which is a claim to divine authority.[231] In support of this interpretation, it is possible to cite, in addition to the "staggering parallel" in the *Odes of Solomon* themselves (4:6),[232] a statement of salvation that is easier to understand and would have been familiar to anyone knowing Ps 102:6 LXX: ποιῶν ἐλεημοσύνας ὁ κύριος καὶ κρίμα πᾶσι τοῖς ἀδικουμένοις ("The Lord executes mercy and judgment for all that are injured").[233] The Lord who executes judgment for all who are "wronged" and "oppressed"[234] is, after all, himself the supreme "Judge."

Although ἀλλά/ܐܠܐ (*ʾellā*) is grammatically an "adversative particle," 12b is not in "contrast" to 12aβ (cf. similar constructions in 11:23b-c; 12:6a; 18:8; 39:10).[235] Instead there is an almost synonymous parallelism between the "3rd masc[uline] pl[ural] imperf[ect] verbal expressions ܠܐ ܢܬܛܠܡܘܢ and ܢܗܘܘܢ . . . ܠܐ ܚܒܠܐ" (Franzmann, with an apt reference to 15:8, where ܛܠܡ and ܠܐ ܚܒܠܐ "are also associated"; cf. also 11:11-12a).[236] Frankenberg links his choice of κτήσονται[237] to the object τὸν καινὸν κόσμον τὸν ἄφθαρτον[238] because he was confused by the misprint ܠܥܠܡܐ (*l-ʿālmā*) for ܒܥܠܡܐ (*b-ʿālmā*), which had not been corrected even in the second edition of Harris's publication.[239] The object is, therefore, the term ἀφθαρσία/ܠܐ ܚܒܠܐ (*lā ḥbālā*; see Excursus 28), "incorruption,"[240] and thus dualistically opposes the "devastating power" φθορά/ܚܒܠܐ (*ḥbālā*), "Corruption," in 1a and 7a.[241] Of greater concern, however, is Frankenberg's choice of κόσμος rather than αἰών to represent ܥܠܡܐ (*ʿālmā*; see Excursus 22).[242] Theologically, the temporal-spatial "new world"—which may be neither temporal nor spatial—corresponds less to the καινὴ κτίσις ("new creation") of 2 Cor 5:17 and Gal 6:15 than to the coming "Aeon," the "age to come."[243]

227 Blaszczak, 71.

228 On ἐνδύομαι in Gal 3:27 and similar enlightening passages in the New Testament and its contemporary writings, see Hans Dieter Betz, *Galatians: A Commentary on Paul's Letter to the Churches in Galatia* (Hermeneia; Philadelphia: Fortress Press, 1979; 2nd printing 1984) 187–88.

229 Bauer's translation (p. 614) of the negated imperfect as "will not fall into disfavour" achieves (in German) a satisfactory paronomasia with "grace" (or "goodness") but fails to bring out the connotations "*oppressus est*" and "*injuria affectus est*" (Payne Smith, 1:1477). The Greek equivalent of the verb made positive by negation is likely to have been the future passive of ἀδικέω or ζημιόω (BDAG, *s.vv.* ἀδικέω, 1c and 2; ζημιόω, 1; Frankenberg, 30: ἀδικηθήσονται (ζημιωθήσονται).

230 BDAG, *s.v.* κρίσις [*sic*], 1aβ.

231 See BDAG, *s.v.* κριτής, 1aβ. Bernard's reference to John 5:27 and Matt 25:31-46 as parallels to the image of the judge (see Bernard, 118; cf. also John 9:39) has been picked up and overemphasized by Blaszczak (p. 70) with respect to the Johannine Jesus.

232 See commentary on that passage.

233 Rahlfs, 2:110; Brenton, 759; BDAG, *s.v.* κρίμα, 3; cf. *OTSy*, pt. 2 fasc. 3, p. 119: ܛܠܝܡ̈ܐ (*ṭlīmē*) = "oppressed" (Ps 103:6).

234 Payne Smith, *Dictionary*, 175, *s.v.* Ethpe. ܐܬܛܠܡ (*ʾeṭṭlem*).

235 BDAG, *s.v.* ἀλλά.

236 Franzmann, 238.

237 BDAG, *s.v.* κτάομαι; Payne Smith, 2:3651–52. 𝔊 could as well have used κερδαίνω (see BDAG, *s.v.* κερδαίνω: "to gain") as κτάομαι.

238 Frankenberg, 30.

239 Harris, 1909 and 1911, on this passage. This misprint is the basis for the difficulties of the early translators, e.g. Harris (p. 132), Flemming (Harnack, 65), and Labourt (Labourt and Batiffol, 32), and even some later ones, e.g., Greßmann (p. 466) and Tsakonas (p. 151). It also led to the unnecessary emendation ܕܠܐ ܚܒܠܐ for ܠܐ ܚܒܠܐ (Harnack, 65 [with erroneous ܐ<ܕ>]; Ungnad and Staerk, 33; Diettrich, 114; Greßmann, "Oden Salomos," 7).

240 BDAG, *s.v.* ἀφθαρσία; Harder, "φθείρω," *ThWNT* 9:97, 102, 104–6; *TDNT* 9:96, 101–2, 103–5; Payne Smith, 1:1179.

241 Berger and Nord, 964.

242 Frankenberg, 30.

243 BDAG, *s.v.* αἰών, 2b; cf. Richard Löwe, *Kosmos und Aion: Ein Beitrag zur heilsgeschichtlichen Dialektik des urchristlichen Weltverständnisses* (NTF, 3. Reihe, 5. Heft; Gütersloh: Mohn, 1935; repr., Münster: Antiquariat Th. Stenderhoff, 1983) 125–38: "Der Einbruch der neuen Weltzeit [The irruption of the new age]"; Blaszczak, 70: "the eschatological age of salvation."

The attribute *καινός*/ܚܕܬܐ (*ḥaṯā*) is apocalyptically "the epitome of the wholly different and miraculous thing which is brought by the time of salvation."[244] Since it is quite possible that the promise of salvation in this passage was crafted under the influence of *2 Bar.* 44:11-12, that section of Baruch's address, written in Hebrew (or Aramaic) and finally translated into Syriac from a Greek version, may be quoted in full:[245]

> For there is a time [ܙܒܢܐ] that does not pass away. And that period is coming which will remain forever [ܠܥܠܡ]; and there is the new world [ܥܠܡܐ ܚܕܬܐ] which does not carry back to corruption [ܚܒܠܐ] those who enter into its beginning, and which has no mercy on those who come into torment or those who are living in it, and it does not carry to perdition [ܐܒܕܢܐ].[246]

■ **13** The discourse that purports to come from the mouth of Grace personified (1a), in her guise as the "Perfect Virgin" (5a), now reaches its finale. The address[247] in 13a is directed to both male and female persons, although the masculine plural of the construct state of the passive participle of ܓܒܐ (*gḇā*) with its first singular possessive suffix has a more esoteric sound than the summons of 6a-b (cf. 8:20c). As in 23:1-4, the address is based on Wis 3:9 and 4:15.[248] This is plausibly shown, both by the fact that the key word *ἐκλεκτοί* ("elect"), which is interchangeable with *ὅσιοι* ("holy ones"), is used directly and that the phrase *οἱ πεποιθότες ἐπ᾽ αὐτῷ* ("Those who trust in him") of Wis 3:9a has also left traces in 13c.[249] In the imperative of salvation, 13a, the Pa. ܗܠܟ (*hallek̠*) is again used metaphorically: ܗܠܟܘ (*hallek̠*) = imperative "walk" (cf. 10:6b; 17:4c; 23:4a). Grace thus appears as a new "territory for settlement."[250] The ethics of it—as is generally true in the *Odes of Solomon*—carry no great weight.[251]

Semitic syntax can again be detected in the transition from 13a to 13b-c (see 8a and 10a above). According to form criticism, the imperative of salvation is followed by a double promise of salvation, in which the expressions "my ways" and "seek" derive from Prov 8:32-34 and Wis 6:12 (see Excursus 19).[252] The close connection with 23:4 is underlined by the Aph. imperfect of ܝܕܥ (*ʾiḏaʿ*), "I will make known," which cannot be equated with certainty, in 𝔊, to the future of *γνωρίζω*.[253] But, as Blaszczak points out, the "ways of truth" (8c) have here become

244 Johannes Behm, "*καινός, κτλ.*," *ThWNT* 3 (1938) 451; *TDNT* 3:449.

245 See *APOT* 2:503; Leonhard Rost, *Einleitung in die alttestamentlichen Apokryphen und Pseudepigraphen einschließlich der großen Qumran-Handschriften* (Heidelberg: Quelle & Meyer, 1971; 2nd ed., 1979) 95; Albertus F. J. Klijn, *Die syrische Baruch-Apokalypse* (JSHRZ 5.2; Gütersloh: Mohn, 1976) 108–12.

246 *OTP* 1:634. The translation of the Syriac text (*OTSy*, pt. 4 fasc. 3, on this passage), which can have influenced the *Odes of Solomon* only in their translation from Greek into Syriac, is by Klijn (see also Klijn, *Baruch-Apokalypse*, 149). The Greek original must have had *αἰών* where the Syriac uses ܥܠܡܐ (*ʿālmā*). *Ode* 44:15 also refers to the "coming world" (ܥܠܡܐ ܕܐܬܐ [*OTP* 1:645]). The term ܐܒܕܢܐ (*ʾaḇdānā*), which Klijn translates as "Untergang [perdition]," is the one for which I use "destruction" (2a, 8b), while I use "Corruption" for the synonymous ܚܒܠܐ (*ḥbālā*) (1a, 7a).

247 Franzmann's objection (p. 236) to Harris and Mingana's grammatically possible but contextually faulty translation of 13a, "My chosen ones have walked in me" (Harris and Mingana, 2:375), is justified. Charlesworth (p. 121) follows Harris and Mingana: "My elect ones have walked with me." Note that already Diettrich (p. 115) remarked: "Flemming incorrectly 'walked in me' [Harnack, 65]."

248 Rahlfs, 2:348, 350; see Georgi, 415.

249 See Emerton, *Wisdom*, 4: ܐܝܠܝܢ ܕܬܟܠܝܢ ܥܠܘܗܝ.

250 Rudolf Hoppe, *Epheserbrief, Kolosserbrief* (Stuttgarter kleiner Kommentar, Neues Testament 10; Stuttgart: Katholisches Bibelwerk, 1987) 124, on the Lord Jesus Christ in Col 2:6.

251 On Col 2:6, in contrast, see Ernst Lohmeyer, *Die Briefe an die Kolosser und an Philemon* (KEK 9.2; 12th ed.; Göttingen: Vandenhoeck & Ruprecht, 1961) 96–99; Eduard Lohse, *Colossians and Philemon: A Commentary on the Epistles to the Colossians and Philemon* (Hermeneia; Philadelphia: Fortress Press, 1971) 94, ET of *Die Briefe an die Kolosser und an Philemon* (KEK 9.2; Göttingen: Vandenhoeck & Ruprecht, 1968) 142; BDAG, *s.v.* *περιπατέω*, 2aδ. This distinction between 13a and Col 2:6 is not sufficiently stressed by Blaszczak. A connection between 13a and "the clothing imagery" in 12a, by which "some sort of union" is expressed (Blaszczak, 71), should not be too hastily set aside.

252 Blaszczak, 72; see Georgi, 421.

253 See Payne Smith, 1:1557; Klein, *Wörterbuch*, 55; Frankenberg, 30: *γνωρίσω*.

"my ways."[254] There is no difference between the "seekers" and "my elect" (cf. 42:5b), since ζητέω/ܒܥܐ (*bʿā*) is not used as an exhortation, unlike in, for example, Col 3:1.[255] What Georgi has to say about Wis 6:12-13 applies also here: "*Gratia praeveniens* to the utmost! The possibility of a problem with human freedom of will or moral responsibility does not occur."[256]

Blaszczak translates 13c in the same way as Charlesworth ("And I will promise them my name")[257] and consequently loses his way in a number of dead ends when he tries to answer his own question, "What is involved in the promise of her name to those who desire her?"[258] The admittedly difficult and rare use of the Aph. from the root ܬܟܠ (cf. 15:10c)[259] can be compared to ܐܬܟܠܬܟ ܥܠ ܟܣܝܬܐ (*ʾatkeltāk ʿal kasyātā*), but hidden behind the accurate translation "*tibi secreta promisi*"[260] is the literal meaning "I caused you to trust in . . . ."[261] The first singular imperfect ܐܬܟܠ (*ʾatkel*) in 13c is not derived from καταθαρσέω[262] but corresponds to the use of ἐπελπίζω in Ps 118:49 LXX: ἐπήλπισάς με ("thou hast made me hope").[263] So the Greek text of 13c could have been καὶ ἐπελπιῶ αὐτοὺς ἐπ' ὄνομά μου.[264] In S, the primary meaning of "allow to hope"[265] or "give hope"[266] carries an additional connotation of "to trust" from the basic meaning of the root, though both ἐλπίζω and ἐλπίς as well as πέποιθα and πεποίθησις belong within the scope of the root ܬܟܠ.[267] The use of the phrase "my elect" and "my name" to frame the stanza creates a certain parallel with the difficult passage 8:20c-21c.[268] Since "Grace" is itself a "power,"[269] the element of "might" and "power" in the "name"[270] of Grace, who is personified not merely as a Virgin, is also enhanced (see Excursus 39). Therefore, the elect can indeed put their trust in "her protection and help."[271]

254 Blaszczak, 72. This does not mean that the "Perfect Virgin" is to be identified as "Truth." In fact, 13b makes it clear how 8c should be interpreted.

255 See Lohse, *Colossians*, 132 (*German*, 193).

256 Georgi, 422; see Hübner, 85–86.

257 Charlesworth, 121. In his explanation of this translation (p. 122 n. 15), "The idea of *making* 'the chosen ones' to trust is poor theology, and inconsistent with the general tone of the Odes," Charlesworth turns his back on the rich theological content of the Syriac text.

258 Blaszczak, 60, 72.

259 Payne Smith, 2:4433: "*in Peal inus. . . . nisi in part.,*" i.e. ܬܟܝܠ (*tkīl*).

260 Payne Smith, 2:4433.

261 On the plural of ܟܣܝܐ (*kasyā*), see Payne Smith, 1:1780.

262 Contra Frankenberg, 30.

263 Rahlfs, 2:133; Brenton, 772; cf. *OTSy*, pt. 2 fasc. 3, p. 144: ܐܬܟܠܬܝܗܝ (*ʾatkeltāy*) with third masculine singular suffix referring to "thy servant."

264 Contra Frankenberg, 30: καὶ καταθρασύνω αὐτοὺς ἐπ' ὀνόματί μου. "The formula ἐ[πὶ] τῷ ὀνόματί τινος, used w[ith] many verbs" (BDAG, *s.v.* ἐπί, 17), corresponds to the Syriac preposition ܒ (*b*-).

265 Koehler and Baumgartner, 389, on Ps 119:49.

266 Friedrich Rehkopf, *Septuaginta-Vokabular* (Göttingen: Vandenhoeck & Ruprecht, 1989), 114. See LSJ, *s.v.* ἐπελπίζω: "buoy up with hope"; Rengstorf, 689: "to cause (someone) to hope"; only in *Ant.* 18.329 (Loeb 7:393): "led him to hope."

267 Payne Smith, 2:4433–34.

268 See commentary on that passage.

269 Hans Conzelmann, "χαίρω," *ThWNT* 9:366; *TDNT* 9:376.

270 Hans Bietenhard, "ὄνομα," *ThWNT* 5:243, etc.; *TDNT* 5:243, etc.

271 Blaszczak, 72. At the conclusion of his commentary, Blaszczak (p. 73) again emphasizes "that the figure in Ode 33 is never called 'wisdom.' The titles she does bear, perfect virgin and grace of God, however, might point to some common sources shared by both wisdom and gnostic literature." Christ, who does not display Blaszczak's (p. 74) caution, counts the *Odes of Solomon* among the sources of "Gnosticism" (see Christ, *Sophia*, 11). In his Tables 4 and 5, *Ode* 33 receives its own column, although "Sophia" has no role in the Ode (ibid., 158–63). So it is not surprising that only a small number of cells in these tables contain references to verses 3, 4, 6-8, 10, and 12-13 of *Ode* 33.

34 *Ode* 34: Authentic and Inauthentic (Above and Below)

(I) 1a There is no rough way,
1b where there is a simple heart,
1c nor a blow/wound
1d in upright thoughts,
2a nor a storm/wind gust
2b in the depth of clear thought.
3a Where the beautiful one is surrounded on all sides,
3b there is nothing in him that is divided.

(II) 4a The archetype of what is below
4b is that[a] which is above.
5a For everything is above,
5b and below is nothing,
5c but it seems to be, to those in whom there is no *gnōsis*.

(III) 6a Grace was revealed for your redemption;
6b believe and [you will] live and be redeemed.
Hallelujah.

a 4b ܗܿܘ ܗܘܐ H; ܗܘܐ N.

Introduction

Ode 34 is preserved in two Syriac manuscripts.[1] "The two short *Odes* 32 and 34 belong to the class of *didactic* pieces. The second one propounds objective facts of piety; the closing verse adds an exhortation to a group of persons. There are traces of Gnostic ideas in the doctrine of archetype ['Urbild'] and likeness ['Abbild']."[2] So the primary theme of this unique and beautifully constructed Ode, which Schille categorizes as an "address of revelation" with a concluding "call to reconciliation" or a "reveille,"[3] is not merely the "grace" of 6a.[4] In fact, the polemical fashion in which the unidentified speaking "I" distances itself from "those in whom there is no *gnōsis*" (5c), the statement of salvation of 6a, and the imperatives of salvation of 6b serve to illumine the didactic introduction in stanza I. That stanza does not propound mere objective "facts of piety" but states eschatological and paradoxical truths of faith and redemption.

The influence of Proverbs 8–9 that was demonstrated in the case of *Ode* 33 supports Joseph Amstutz's conjecture that the "link to the Scriptures," which Harris and Mingana failed to find,[5] does in fact exist.[6] In addition to the key words ἁπλῶς ("simply") and ὁδός ("way") in Prov 10:9 LXX, one may mention, for 1a-b, καρδία ("heart") in Prov 10:8. This reference is certainly more convincing than Brian McNeil's suggestion at 3a of an "allusion to Ps 125:2."[7]

1 Mss.: Codex H, 25a–25b; Codex N, 150ᵛ (s). Ed./trans.: Charlesworth, 122–23; Franzmann, 240–43; Lattke, 3:91–105.
2 Abramowski, 50.
3 Schille, 98–99.
4 Contra Siegfried Schulz, "Salomo-Oden," *RGG*³ 5 (1961) 1340.
5 Harris and Mingana, 2:379.
6 Amstutz, 131 n. 102.
7 Brian McNeil, review of Lattke, *Bedeutung*, vols. 1–2 in *Ostkirchliche Studien* 29 (1980) 194. He probably means Ps 125:4 (124:4 LXX): *ἀγάθυνον, κύριε, τοῖς ἀγαθοῖς καὶ τοῖς εὐθέσι τῇ καρδίᾳ* ("Do good, Lord, to them that are good and upright in heart"); cf. Rahlfs, 2:143; Brenton, 777. McNeil's suggestion refers to "the good man" and not to the *κύκλῳ*/ܟܪܝܟ (*krīḵ*).

Ode 34 forms a textual unit in spite of its clearly marked sections. Stanza III, therefore, is neither a Christian addendum by reason of its meaning,[8] nor a prosaic appendage because of its form.[9] And the uncontested "traces of Gnostic ideas" in stanza II do not allow the excision of 4a-5b as a "later interpolation."[10] Kittel considers it "probable" that there were "influences of Greek philosophy in these verses," but, referring to Frants Buhl,[11] accepts "these passages also as belonging to the context and mental world of the *Odes*."[12]

Interpretation

■ **1-3** The skillful structure of stanza I, as Franzmann,[13] disputing Kittel's conclusions,[14] analyzed it, can be visualized by the following diagram of the statements that reciprocally interpret and complement each other:[15]

1a/1b			A/B
	1c-d	C/D	
	2a-b	C'/D'	
3a/3b			A'/B'

In this chiasmus, the two core statements C/D and C'/D', in both of which Codex H omits the caesura (hence the editorial indentation of 1d and 2b), exhibit exceptional parallelism with each other and, in content, also with the introductory bicolon.[16] Formally, the parallelism of A/B and A'/B' could be represented by A B B' A'. Then the "rough way" would, with a double negative, be a metaphor for an indecisive movement hither and thither (1a, 3b). On the other hand, the complete—perhaps even theological—surroundedness of the "beautiful one" (i.e., the inclusively imagined beautiful person) is then an image of the simple heart (3a, 1b). But such an interpretation, audacious enough considering the meaning of ܩܫܝܬܐ (*qšīṯā*) in 1a, comes to grief because the "inner division" expressed by δίψυχος κτλ. as a "fearful wavering of the heart" can be shown, from the sources, to be the "opposite" of the singleness of καρδία ("heart") and διάνοια ("thought") expressed by ἁπλοῦς κτλ.[17] Before proceeding to detailed exegesis, we should note that all four of the statements of what Amstutz calls this "mini-Didache" contradict the psychological and social facts of this world and can, therefore, be true only *sola gratia* and *sola fide*.[18] So these soteriological statements refer not to the merely "pious," who are the "righteous redeemed,"[19] but—as Amstutz correctly notes—to the redeemed, who have knowledge and faith, in their "Gnosticizing attitude."[20]

The assonance that Charlesworth rather overemphasizes in 1a-b[21] can be observed also in 1c-d. In fact, a large number of Syriac words end in *-ā*, so that this cannot really be used to argue for a Syriac original.

8 Contra Spitta, 287.

9 Contra Grimme, 125.

10 Contra Diettrich, 115. He considers "the editor not a Christian but a mystic who interpreted our *Odes* in a pantheistic sense." This description is as imprecise as the alternatives offered to interpret 4a-5b ("theological speculation"/"ethical speculation"). Diettrich lays too much emphasis on the "ethical tenor of the Ode" and its author's "hortatory style."

11 Buhl sees in the *Odes of Solomon* an amalgam of Christianity, Judaism, Gnosticism, and mystery religions (see Frants Buhl, "Salomos Oder," *Teologisk tidsskrift for den danske folkekirke* 3. Række, 2 [1911] 126; cf. Lattke, *Bedeutung*, 3:88). "Greek philosophy" plays a very minor part in the *Odes of Solomon*: "The power that Platonism exerted in Gnostic circles is fully visible only in *Ode* 34" (Greßmann, "Oden Salomos," 10).

12 Kittel, 126.

13 Franzmann, 242–43.

14 Kittel, 125–26.

15 Verses 1c-d and 2a-b are monocola in H, but bicola in N.

16 Charlesworth (p. 122) and Emerton (p. 723), following Harris and Mingana (vol. 1, on this passage; 2:378), treat 1a-b as a monocolon, contrary to the manuscript evidence.

17 Amstutz, 131; cf. Oscar J. F. Seitz, "Antecedents and Signification of the Term δίψυχος," *JBL* 66 (1947) 215–17.

18 A certain similarity to the beatitudes in the Sermon on the Mount seems evident; see Michael Lattke, "Glückselig durch den Geist (Matthäus 5, 3)," in Cornelius Mayer et al., eds., *Nach den Anfängen fragen: Gerhard Dautzenberg zum 60. Geburtstag am 30. Januar 1994* (Gießener Schriften zur Theologie und Religionspädagogik des Fachbereichs Evangelische Theologie und Katholische Theologie und deren Didaktik der Justus-Liebig-Universität 8; Gießen: Selbstverlag, 1994) 364, 375–80.

19 Contra Amstutz, 131.

20 Amstutz, 131 n. 101.

21 Charlesworth, *Reflections*, 130, 159–60, 164.

Although this passage does not fit into the general pattern (see Excursus 15), it is relevant to refer to 22:7b, where the hand of God smooths the "way" for the faithful. It is likely that there, as here in 1a, the word ὁδός/ܐܘܪܚܐ (ʾurḥā) was used figuratively and—especially because of the attributive adjective—"w[ith] the picture prominently in mind."[22] The proper meaning of the *hapax legomenon* ܩܫܝܛܐ (*qšīṭā*, feminine passive participle in emphatic state of ܩܫܐ [*qšā*])[23] is not easy to determine. If it corresponds to σκληρά,[24] it would be a "hard way."[25] But if it corresponds to τραχεῖα, the sense would be closer to "rough, uneven."[26] The connotation "dangerous" can probably be excluded.[27]

The parallel terms "thoughts" (1d) and "thought" (2b) highlight the rational aspect of the central term of being, καρδία/ܠܒܐ (*lebbā*), in 1b (see Excursus 4). The masculine emphatic passive participle of ܦܫܛ (*pšaṭ*), which is used only here as an adjective in the sense of ἁπλῆ, can be translated as "simple" in the sense of unpretentious, sincere genuineness.[28] Such a "simple heart"[29] is a gift of grace and the opposite of the dark and deadly διπλοκαρδία (cf. *Did.* 5:1; *Barn.* 20:1).[30]

The introductory statement of salvation (1a-b) is expanded by two parallel didactic utterances. The *hapax legomenon* ܡܚܘܬܐ (*mḥōṯā*) in 1c, which should not be pointed as *maḥḥūṯā*,[31] means "a stroke"[32] and "probably presupposes πληγή in Greek."[33] It is less certain that "upright thoughts" represents the Greek λογισμοὶ εὐθεῖς (see Excursus 9).[34] The participial adjective ܬܪܝܨܐ (*trīṣā*) corresponds not only to εὐθύς,[35] but also, e.g., to ὀρθός.[36] Given the breadth of meaning of ܡܚܫܒܬܐ (*maḥšaḇtā*), it is quite possible that 𝔊 had two different words, corresponding to the plural in 1d and the singular in 2b.[37] More to the point than the conclusion that here and in the context only "good and heartfelt words" are used[38] is a recognition of the brutal fact that right thoughts can meet with naked force (cf., e.g., the Suffering Servant of Isaiah 53 in *1 Clement* 16). So the statement in 1c-d is again valid only soteriologically.

The same is true of 2a-b, where the metaphorical *hapax legomenon* ܥܠܥܠܐ (*ʿalʿālā*) may correspond equally to καταιγίς[39] and to λαῖλαψ.[40] In either case, the image is of a "sudden blast of wind" or a "fierce gust of wind" from above, that can do no psychic harm in the "depth" of the limpid or "illuminated thinking" of the redeemed.[41] The term τὸ βάθος/ܥܘܡܩܐ (*ʿumqā*) = "depth" in 2b is an allusion not to Hades or Death (29:4; 42:12) but to heart, mind (*nous*), and soul.[42] The adjective ܢܗܝܪܐ (*nahhīrā*),[43] "clear," which attributively qualifies "thought" (see on 1d above), can represent φωτεινός[44] or λαμπρός[45] or even ἱλαρός.[46] But even if this is an allusion to "gladness of the soul,"[47] it is seen not as an inborn predisposition but as a "gift of salvation."[48]

22 BDAG, *s.v.* ὁδός, 2.
23 Payne Smith, 2:3767.
24 Frankenberg, 30.
25 Bauer, 614; BDAG, *s.v.* σκληρός, 2.
26 BDAG, *s.v.* τραχύς.
27 Contra Lattke, *Oden*, 192.
28 See BDAG, *s.v.* ἁπλοῦς; Payne Smith, 2:3319.
29 Amstutz, 130; Harnack, 65.
30 Seitz, "Antecedents," 218; BDAG, *s.v.* διπλοκαρδία: "lit[erally] 'double-heartedness'"; Prostmeier, 555–61: "The way of blackness." Even if a "dependence of Ephrem on the Odes" could be demonstrated in the case of *Ode* 34:1 (Harris and Mingana, 2:24), it would not aid either the historical-critical interpretation or the determination of the original language of the *Odes*.
31 Contra Charlesworth, 122–23: "barrier."
32 Nöldeke §77.
33 Bauer, 614; see BDAG, *s.v.* πληγή, 1–3; Payne Smith, 2:2067.
34 Amstutz, 130 n. 95.
35 BDAG, *s.v.* εὐθύς, 2b.
36 Frankenberg, 30; see BDAG, *s.v.* ὀρθός, 2: "correct, true"; Payne Smith, 2:4510.
37 See Payne Smith, 1:1397: διαλογισμός, λογισμός, διανόημα, νόημα, ἐπίνοια, σύνεσις, κτλ.
38 Harnack, 65.
39 BDAG, *s.v.* καταιγίς; Frankenberg, 30.
40 BDAG, *s.v.* λαῖλαψ; Payne Smith, 2:2880.
41 Bauer, 614.
42 BDAG, *s.v.* βάθος, 2; Payne Smith, 2:2916.
43 Payne Smith, 2:2299.
44 Frankenberg, 30; BDAG, *s.v.* φωτεινός.
45 BDAG, *s.v.* λαμπρός. In this case the adjective would call up images of clear and transparent water, through which one can see the deeps.
46 Greßmann, 466: "in the depths of a cheerful mind."
47 Greßmann, "Oden Salomos," 11.
48 Amstutz, 131 n. 96: "Illumination" like "knowledge" is a "gift of salvation" (with references).

The translation of 3a has, in the course of research on the *Odes*, given rise to a good many imaginative conjectures, as shown by this selection (including some suggested emendations):

> "Who is everywhere surrounded by excellence" (Harnack, 65 [Flemming, ܐܝܪ̈ܐ for ܐܝܟܐ]).
>
> "Who is everywhere surrounded by beauty" (Kittel, 125–26 [ܐܝܪ̈ܐ for ܐܝܟܐ]).
>
> "*He, who* is surrounded on all sides by beauty" (Barth, 264 [ܐܝܢܐ for ܐܝܟܐ]).
>
> "The one who is surrounded on every side by open country" (Harris and Mingana, 2:378 [ܐܝܢܐ for ܐܝܟܐ]).
>
> "Where one is surrounded on every side by pleasing country" (Charlesworth, 1973, p. 123).[49]
>
> "ὅπου περίκειται πανταχόθεν τὰ κρείσσονα" (Frankenberg, 30).
>
> "Where the beautiful (is) enclosed (?, surrounding?) from wherever" (Lattke, *Bedeutung*, 1:167).[50]
>
> "There where beautiful country is all around" (Bauer, 614; cf. Paulsen, *Studien*, 159).[51]
>
> "Where a person is surrounded by beautiful country" (Berger and Nord, 965).

Already in his review of Kittel's (1914) book, Connolly describes that translation of 3a—and thus a number of similar translations of this line—as "quite impossible."[52]

> The masc[uline] ܫܦܝܪܐ [*šappīrā*] cannot mean "the beautiful": that would at least require the fem[inine]. The meaning is not τὸ καλόν, but ὁ καλός (ἀνήρ). The above translation further necessitates emending ܐܝܟܐ [*ʾaykā*] to ܐܝܢܐ (not ܐܝܪ̈ܐ), and is even so inaccurate, since "with" is not expressed in the Syr[iac] and cannot be supplied. By translating literally we get a sense that is in perfect accord with the context: "Where the good (man) is surrounded on all sides, there is in him nothing divided." It has only to be observed that ܦܠܝܓ [*plīg*] "divided" frequently means divided in mind, doubtful, hesitating; so that the second clause may well mean "he is nothing dismayed."

Four more recent attempts at translation may serve to illustrate Connolly's important but often overlooked remark:

> "Where the man who is virtuous is surrounded on every side" (Emerton, 723).
>
> "Where the beautiful one surrounds from every place" (Franzmann, 240).[53]
>
> "Où atourne de partout le Beau" (Where the beautiful man is surrounded from all sides) (Pierre, 165).
>
> "Wo umschlossen (ist) von überall her der Schöne" (Where the beautiful man is enclosed on every side) (Lattke, *Oden*, 192).
>
> "Quand le vertueux est entouré de toute part" (When the virtuous man is surrounded from all sides) (Azar, 154).

The emphatic masculine form ܫܦܝܪܐ (*šappīrā*), then, is the subject of 3a ("the beautiful one") and most probably corresponds to the nominalized adjective καλός,[54] in all its ancient breadth of meaning. As a "mark of honor"[55] it sounds a paradisial note in the *Odes of Solomon* (cf. 11:20) and sums up in eschatological and soteriological fashion

---

49 Charlesworth later puts the preposition "by" in square brackets, but maintains that "the verse is lucid as it stands" (Charlesworth, 1977, p. 123 and n. 2).

50 Criticizing this first attempt of mine, McNeil remarked: "*špyrʾ* can also be understood in a personal sense: 'the good man' . . ." (see Brian McNeil, review of Lattke, *Bedeutung*, vols. 1–2 in *Ostkirchliche Studien* 29 [1980] 194; see also idem, "The *Odes of Solomon* and the Scriptures," *OrChr* 67 [1983] 120). In fact, that is how the word *must* be understood. Klijn's emendation, "Where that which is beautiful is surrounded from all sides," is heading in the right direction (see Klijn, 304).

51 Amstutz (pp. 130–31) took over this translation and expanded it with the phrase "psychic landscape."

52 Richard Hugh Connolly, review of Kittel in *JTS* 15 (1913–14) 468.

53 Franzmann prefers the active sense of ܟܪܝܟ (*krīḵ*), which is an unlikely one in this case.

54 BDAG, *s.v.* καλός; Payne Smith, 2:4275–76.

55 Kaegi, 450.

all the previous descriptions of the redeemed person. The term ܐܝܟܐ ܕ (ʾaykā ḏ-) corresponds to ὅπου, a particle denoting "a position in space, *where*,"[56] while the prepositional phrase ܡܢ ܟܠ ܐܬܪ (*men kol ʾaṯar*), "on all sides," corresponds either to πανταχόθεν[57] or to πάντοθεν.[58] Because of the use of the particle ܡܢ (*men*) the passive participle of ܟܪܟ (*kraḵ*) has to be translated by a passive form ("surrounded"),[59] but is still reminiscent—especially in its meaning—of its active and theological use in 22:6 ("and in every place thy name surrounded me"). The Greek equivalent would have been either περιεχόμενος or περικεκυκλωμένος.[60] Anyone aware of the Hellenistic definition of divine transcendence as "enclosing, not enclosed"[61] would be reminded in this passive description of the "beautiful one" of his/her integrity but also of the essential limitation even of a redeemed person *coram deo*.

The stress falls, as can be seen from the explanation in 3b, which is linked to the subject of 3a by the preposition ܒ (*b*-) with a personal suffix,[62] on the non-disunity parallel to the "simple heart" of 1b. Although 𝔊—whether as *Vorlage* or as translation—might have used μεμερισμένον[63] or διαμεμερισμένον[64] as the equivalent of the passive participle of ܦܠܓ (*plaḡ/pleḡ*), the neuter form of the more technical adjective δίψυχος ("double-minded") has to be given preference,[65] unless the expression was simply οὐκ ἔστι διψυχία.[66] This uncertainty demonstrates that, up to the end of stanza I, there has not yet been any clear indication that the Ode was originally written in Greek.

■ **4-5** This stanza is among the most difficult passages in the *Odes of Solomon*. Deleting 4a-b as marginalia[67] or excising 4a-5b as a "later editorial addition"[68] is taking the easy way out. And positing "mystical speculation" as the basis of 4a-5c,[69] or regarding 4a-b as "definition" of the *analogia entis et existentis*[70] means not giving sufficient weight to the hyperbole of 5a-b, which, together with 4a-b, forms a chiasmus of the pattern A B B' A'.[71] Because of the chiastic structures in stanza I (1-3) and the first part of stanza II (4a-5b),[72] 4a cannot be interpreted as the explanation of ܦܠܝܓ (*plīḡ*) in 3b ("... divided, the archetype of what is below"), while 4b is referred to the masculine person of 3a-b ("he is what is above")[73]—whom McNeil, alluding to 41:15a, even interprets christologically.[74]

56 BDAG, *s.v.* ὅπου, 1; Payne Smith, 1:148.
57 Frankenberg, 30; BDAG, *s.v.* πανταχόθεν.
58 Franzmann, 241, referring to *3 Macc.* 4:2 (and elsewhere); BDAG, *s.v.* πάντοθεν; Payne Smith, 1:426.
59 Payne Smith, 1:1823; contra Franzmann, 240–41.
60 BDAG, *s.vv.* περιέχω, 1; περικυκλόω.
61 William R. Schoedel, "Enclosing, not Enclosed: The Early Christian Doctrine of God," in William R. Schoedel and Robert L. Wilken, eds., *Early Christian Literature and the Classical Intellectual Tradition: In honorem Robert M. Grant* (ThH 54; Paris: Beauchesne, 1979) 76; see also Helmut Köster, "τόπος," *ThWNT* 8 (1969) 201; *TDNT* 8:201; Judith Hartenstein, "Eugnostos (NHC III,3; V,1) und die Weisheit Jesu Christi (NHC III,4; BG 3)," *NHD* 1 (2001) 340–41 (e.g., *Eugnostos* 96.1-3).
62 The masculine ܒܗ (*beh*) is meant inclusively.
63 Frankenberg, 30; BDAG, *s.v.* μερίζω, 1b.
64 BDAG, *s.v.* διαμερίζω, 3: "be divided."
65 BDAG, *s.v.* δίψυχος; Payne Smith, 2:3135; Seitz, "Antecedents," 211–16.
66 See Amstutz, 131; BDAG, *s.v.* διψυχία: "indecision, doubt."
67 Frankenberg, 42.
68 Diettrich, 115.
69 Harnack, 66.
70 Adam, *Psalmen des Thomas*, 67.
71 Franzmann, 243.
72 Verse 4a-b is a bicolon in both manuscripts. Verse 5a-b is a bicolon in N, but a monocolon in H without even a mark of division at the end. However, H has a small space before 5c.
73 Kittel, 126. Revising his original translation (Greßmann, "Oden Salomos," 10: "The archetype of what is below is what is above"; see below on ܕܡܘܬܐ), Greßmann (p. 466) is clearly guided by Kittel's reasoning and translates in a similar way: "... division, the image of what is below. He is that which is above; ...." Emerton (p. 723) has the following: "... discordant, / The likeness of what is beneath. / He is what is above; ...." However, in a footnote he writes: "Or attaching verse 4a to 4b instead of 3b, read 'Is he who'." I think that the translation of ܗܘܝܘ (*hūyū* [Nöldeke §312.C]) as "He is," which would make the remainder of 4b into a description of a celestial being like Philo's Logos (see H. Meinhardt, "Idee," *HWP* 4 [1976] 62), though possible in principle, is excluded in view of 5a.
74 McNeil, 135.

Three problems arise in this dualism[75] of "below" and "above." First is determining the tradition to which 4a-b and especially the terms "below" and "above" belong. Second, especially in view of the term ܕܡܘܬܐ (*dmūṯā*), "archetype," one would have expected "a reversed statement,"[76] if this term, whose exact meaning remains to be determined, should be taken "concretely as an image."[77] Third, the apparent contradiction between 4a-b and 5a-b needs to be resolved, since the "radical equation: the lower world = nothingness"[78] even persuaded Greßmann to make emphatic remarks on "Monism."[79]

The terms ܠܥܠ (*l-ʿel*) and ܠܬܚܬ (*l-taḥt*) in 5a-b correspond to ἄνω ("above") and κάτω ("below").[80] As is clear from the omission of ܗܘ (*hāw*) in N (4b), the adverbs, prefixed by the particle ܕ (*d-*), are equivalent in 4a-b to τὰ ἄνω and τὰ κάτω (cf. John 8:23) and therefore refer respectively to "heaven" and "this world."[81] Whether Moses Bār Kēphā was aware of the didactic saying of 4a-b[82] is not very important.[83] More important is Connolly's exposition:[84]

> Now Moses Bār Kēphā (saec. ix) in his Exposition of the Jacobite Liturgy (Brit. Mus. MS Add. 21210 fol. 51 *b*), after explaining that the deacons with their fans represent the cherubim and seraphim, adds:
>
> ܐܡܪܝܢ ܓܝܪ ܕܕܡܘܬܐ ܕܠܥܠ ܐܝܬܝܗܘܢ ܗܠܝܢ ܕܠܬܚܬ.
>
> "For they say: The likeness of what is above are those things that are below." It is obvious that there is some close connection between these two sayings and at first I took it for granted that Bār Kēphā was merely quoting in a loose way from the Ode. I now feel some hesitation about this conclusion. Bār Kēphā's quotation formula, "they say", rather suggests some philosophical dictum than an immediate quotation from such a book as the Odes; and in Ode xxxiv the Odist is himself definitely philosophizing; the passage cited above continues: "for everything is above, and what is below is nothing, but is imagined by those in whom there is no knowledge." It has occurred to me that the Odist may here be quoting as well as Bār Kēphā. If any evidence could be produced in confirmation of this suspicion, it might throw a flood of light on many questions which have arisen out of our Syriac text of the Odes.

75 Charlesworth calls this dualism "modified cosmic dualism of two worlds" (see Charlesworth, *Reflections*, 225) and remarks about 4a-5c: "Like John, the cosmic dualism of two worlds is modified because the 'world above' is so vastly superior" (ibid., 207). In both 5a and 5b he inserts a "from": "from above" and "from below" (also in Charlesworth, 123).

76 Harnack, 66: "Like the things above are those below." Cf., e.g., Gen 1:26-27.

77 Jervell, *Imago Dei*, 167, who has the "Semitic-speaking Gnosis" in his sights.

78 Funk, *Jakobus*, 131, with reference to *Gos. Truth* [NHC I,*3*] 17,23-25. This reference goes back to Schenke, *Herkunft*, 26. In his final, and radically different, translation of the *Gospel of Truth* (see Schenke, "Evangelium Veritatis," 30, 32) he refers only quite generally to the *Odes of Solomon*.

79 Greßmann, "Oden Salomos," 10–11. Bernard (p. 119) goes even further, finding in 4-5 the "common language of all Idealists from Plato to Bishop Berkeley" and discovering "Berkeleian Idealism." Real "Monism," of course, is not to be found in Gnosticism; at most there is "Dualism with a Monistic background" (Rudolph, *Gnosis*, 66).

80 Payne Smith, 2:2888, 4422.

81 BDAG, *s.vv.* ἄνω, 1; κάτω, 1.

82 Harris and Mingana, 2:29, 379.

83 I agree with van Unnik, who, noting "a reversed order of thoughts," says: "I myself fail to see any parallel between the passage of the Odes and that of Moses" (see Willem C. van Unnik, "A Note on *Ode of Solomon* xxxiv 4," *JTS* 37 (1936) 174 = van Unnik, 4). Odo Casel provides the context of this alleged quotation: "The rank of deacons is the order of the angels; for they perform the duties of the cherubim and seraphim whose wings cover the altar; not fanning away flies, but to prevent the approach of any forbidden thing. For it is said: The image of what is above are the things below" (see Odo Casel, "Literaturbericht [on Abramowski et al.]," *Archiv für Liturgiewissenschaft* 1 [1950] 298). Both might have remarked that "among the Rabbis" a "large measure of parallelism is maintained between what is and takes place above and what is and takes place below" (Büchsel, "ἄνω," *ThWNT* 1:376–37; *TDNT* 1:376–77).

84 Connolly, "Greek," 537–38.

Harnack had already, without explanation, included a passage from *Act. Phil.* 34,[85] but van Unnik begins by calling attention to *Testamentum Domini* 1.28:[86]

> He being the Christ who was crucified, by whom the things that were on the left hand were placed on the right hand, and *those which were beneath as those which were above*, and those which were behind as those which were before, when He rose from the dead, and trod down Sheol, and by death slew Death, &c.

To this he adds—like Casel, later on[87]—"a striking parallel in the *Acts of Peter* 38 (Mart. Petri 9)."[88]

> Peter is crucified and then expounds the Mystery of the Cross. He says that by his sin the first man has made everything the opposite to what it ought to be; then he goes on: *περὶ ὧν ὁ Κύριος ἐν μυστηρίῳ λέγει: ἐὰν μὴ ποιήσατε τὰ δεξιὰ ὡς τὰ ἀριστερὰ καὶ τὰ ἀριστερὰ ὡς τὰ δεξιὰ καὶ τὰ ἄνω ὡς τὰ κάτω καὶ τὰ ὀπίσω ὡς τὰ ἔμπροσθεν, οὐ μὴ ἐπιγνῶτε τὴν βασιλείαν.*

From this van Unnik deduces that there may have been an "old Christian agraphon," "a kind of Scripture text," "upon which both the author of the Ode and the writer of the *Acts of Peter* and the *Test. Domini* have built."[89] McNeil is also of the opinion that "the language of the odist is reminiscent of a logion of Jesus in a number of second-century texts."[90] However, all these passages—in contrast to this Ode—deal, in more or less detail, with either the overcoming or the unity of opposites, as can be seen from the following summary:

2 Clem. 12:2		without/within		male/female	
Gos. Thom. 22		without/within	above/below	male/female	
Gos. Eg. Frg.	two/one	‹without/within›		male/female*	
Gos. Phil. 69		without/within	above/below†		
Act. Pet. 38		right/left	above/below		behind/before
Test. Dom. 1.28		left/right	above/below		behind/before
Act. Phil. 34		left/right	above/below‡		

* This fragment of the apocryphal *Gospel of the Egyptians* is published as no. 3 in *NTApo*[2] (1924) 58 (with emendation); no. 1f in *NTApo*[3-4] 1 (1959 and 1968) 110–11, *NTApo*[5] 1 (1987) 175–76, and *NTApoc*, 1:210–11.

† In reverse order: above/below; without/within.

‡ In reverse order: above/below; left/right.

85 Harnack, 66. Bernard (p. 119) also prints the Greek text of "*Acta Philippi* 140 (34)," but he firmly rejects Harnack's comparison: "But our Odist is hardly so fantastic as this. What he says is that the Ideal is the archetype of the Real."

86 Van Unnik, "Note," 174 = van Unnik, 4; cf. Ignatius Ephraem Rahmani II, ed. and trans., *Testamentum Domini Nostri Jesu Christi* (Mainz: Kirchheim, 1899; repr., Hildesheim: Olms, 1968) 65.

87 Odo Casel, "Literaturbericht [on Abramowski et al.]," *Archiv für Liturgiewissenschaft* 1 (1950) 298.

88 Van Unnik, "Note," 175 = van Unnik, 5.

89 Ibid.

90 McNeil, 98, who fails to credit Harnack, saying: "The link between the language of Ode 34 and the agraphon of Jesus was first suggested by W. C. van Unnik, who interpreted the contrast between the things below and the things above in the light of Platonism. It seems to me preferable to make the link in the light of the second-century Christian concern for oneness, which is discussed in the Appendix to this Chapter" (ibid., 102; cf. *Ode* 41:15a).

In the search for the origin of this "philosophical dictum,"[91] the most important thing is an accurate translation of the abstract feminine noun ܕܡܘܬܐ (*dmūṯā*). Greßmann was the first to suggest "Urbild [archetype],"[92] which Bauer[93] accepted. Van Unnik also, in his search for parallels, says that "instead of 'likeness'[94] we should rather say 'the pattern,' as this brings out better the sort of platonic 'idea' the author seems to have had in mind."[95] The thoroughly eclectic Middle Platonist Albinus compiled, in the second century C.E., "an epitome of all the schools of thought in the exegesis of Plato"[96] in which he gives the following definition (*Didaskalikos* IX = H[ermanni ed.] 163, lines 14-17):

> *Ἔστι δὲ ἡ ἰδέα ὡς μὲν πρὸς θεὸν νόησις αὐτοῦ, ὡς δὲ πρὸς ἡμᾶς νοητὸν πρῶτον, ὡς δὲ πρὸς τὴν ὕλην μέτρον, ὡς δὲ πρὸς τὸν αἰσθητὸν κόσμον παράδειγμα, ὡς δὲ πρὸς αὑτὴν ἐξεταζομένη οὐσία.*[97]

The Idea, in relation to God is his thought, in relation to us it is the primary thinkable, in relation to matter it is measure, in relation to the cosmos perceptible by the senses it is the exemplar, in relation to itself it proves to be being.[98]

A little further on (H[ermanni ed.] 163, lines 23-24), with only a slight change, he refers again to the term under discussion:

> *Ὁρίζονται δὲ τὴν ἰδέαν παράδειγμα τῶν κατὰ φύσιν αἰώνιον.*
>
> *The Idea* is defined as the everlasting *exemplar of that which agrees with nature.*[99]

So the protological statement 4a-b derives from this tradition of Middle Platonism, which traces back to the first century C.E.,[100] although 𝔖 may not have used παράδειγμα. Other terms such as τύπος or ὑπόδειγμα could also be represented by ܕܡܘܬܐ (*dmūṯā*),[101] but terms such as εἶδος, εἰκών, μορφή, ὁμοίωμα, ὁμοίωσις (as in Gen 1:26) or ὁμοιότης can now be excluded.[102] In any case, ܕܡܘܬܐ here means "exemplar," "model," "archetype," or "prototype," not "copy," "image," "form," nor yet "likeness"[103] or "semblance."[104] As "what is below" stands for the "cosmos perceptible by the senses," so "what is above" takes the place of the elevated philosophical term "Idea."

91 Connolly, "Greek," 538.
92 Greßmann, "Oden Salomos," 10.
93 Bauer, 614.
94 Harris and Mingana, 2:378.
95 Van Unnik, "Note," 172 = van Unnik, 3.
96 Paul Kroh, *Lexikon der antiken Autoren* (KTA 366; Stuttgart: Kröner, 1972) 21.
97 John Whittaker, ed., and Pierre Louis, trans., *Alcinoos, Enseignement des doctrines de Platon* (Collection des universités de France, Association G. Budé; Paris: Les Belles Lettres, 1990) 20; cf. Willy Theiler, *Die Vorbereitung des Neuplatonismus* (Berlin/Zurich: Weidmann, 1934; repr., 1964) 9.
98 After Hans Meinhardt, "Idee," *HWP* 4 (1976) 61; see Eduard Zeller, *Die Philosophie der Griechen in ihrer geschichtlichen Entwicklung*, 3. Teil, 1. Abt.: *Die nacharistotelische Philosophie*, Erste Hälfte (ed. Eduard Wellmann; 5th ed.; Leipzig: Reisland, 1923; repr., 6th ed.; Darmstadt: Wissenschaftliche Buchgesellschaft, 1963) 835, 842–45.
99 Text and translation: Whittaker and Louis, 21; see also Reginald E. Witt, *Albinus and the History of Middle Platonism* (London: Cambridge University Press, 1937; repr., Amsterdam: Hakkert, 1971) 70–74; Jens Halfwassen, "Alkinoos," *MLAA* (1997) 26–27.
100 See Karl Praechter, *Friedrich Ueberwegs Grundriss der Geschichte der Philosophie*, vol. 1: *Die Philosophie des Altertums* (Basel/Stuttgart: Schwabe, 1967) 524–56.
101 BDAG, *s.vv.* τύπος, ὑπόδειγμα; Payne Smith, 1:914.
102 See Brockelmann, *Lexicon*, 156–57; Lattke, *Bedeutung*, 1:169; idem, *Oden*, 192.
103 Charlesworth, 123; McNeil, 98; Franzmann, 240. The *Odes of Solomon*, of course, are "not platonic" (Charlesworth, 123). This correct observation, however, does not prevent them from having absorbed popular philosophical traditions. For Plato and Platonic philosophy παράδειγμα "denotes" the "*archetype* of its likenesses in an *ontological* sense" in the "context of the philosophy of ideas" (Thomas Rentsch, "Paradigma," *HWP* 7 [1989] 74; cf., e.g., Hermann Diels, *Doxographi Graeci* [4th ed.; Berlin: de Gruyter, 1965] 308, 334, 447, 567, 653). Philo also "speaks of the unembodied and godlike paradigmata of the corporeal world" (Thomas Rentsch, "Paradigma," *HWP* 7 [1989] 76; cf. H. Meinhardt, "Idee," *HWP* 4 [1976] 62).
104 Pierre, 166.

If this finding were extended to 5a-b, the logical and ontological conclusion would be that "all" (in 𝔊 either τὸ πᾶν or τὰ πάντα) is the archetype of "nothingness" (in 𝔊 either οὐδέν ἐστιν or οὐκ ἔστι τι). But this is not a cosmic and philosophical dictum; it is an eschatological and soteriological statement in the form[105] of popular science, which confronts us with a radical Gnostic application of the following tradition (attributed to Aristotle):[106]

> *εἶναι δὲ λέγει δύο κόσμους | τὸν ἄνω καὶ τὸν κάτω, καὶ τὸν μὲν ἄνω ἄφθαρτον, τὸν δὲ κάτω φθαρτόν.*
>
> He says also that there are two worlds, that above and that below; the one above is imperishable, but the one below is perishable.

Comparing this—to repeat the description—hyperbolic statement with Paul's exposition in 1 Cor 15:51-57, one might call it a dualistic modification of the primitive Christian teaching on resurrection. In the setting of the *Odes of Solomon,* this statement, which even Berger and Nord qualify with the adverb "really,"[107] goes far beyond the other passages in which ܟܠ (*kol*) or ܟܠܡܕܡ (*kol meddem*) occurs[108] or which mention "ascent" (35:7; 38:1) or the "heights" (17:7; 21:1; 22:1; 23:5; 36:1-2; cf. 29:3).[109]

Going a step further and asking where the strange use of the terms "all" and "nothing" may have originated, it is Albinus again who provides the answer, in his discussion of the connection of τὸ ἄνω and τὸ κάτω with the terms "heavy" and "light," where he makes the polemical statement in *Didaskalikos* XX (H[ermanni ed.] 175, lines 14–15): οὐδὲν γὰρ εἶναι τὸ μὲν ἄνω τὸ δὲ κάτω ("for there is neither above nor below").[110] So the extravagant dual equation (world above = all; world below = nothing)[111] may be a partial counterpolemic rescuing τὸ ἄνω from οὐδέν and leaving only τὸ κάτω to destruction.

Verse 5c may be "a rather clumsy addition to this stanza,"[112] but this adversative conclusion, referring to 5b, sheds some hermeneutic light on the totality of stanza II. Only Gnostics perceive that in the last days, which have already begun, the dualism of "above" and "below" will be overcome by the dissolution of everything "below"—which had originally been formed on the pattern of what is "above"—into "nothingness." The Manichaeans later, and perhaps already the Gnostics of the *Gospel of Truth,*[113] would have agreed at once with this opinion or mythological statement. But here there is also the relatively unmythological[114] statement that it "seems" (participle of the Ethpe. of ܣܒܪ [*sḇar*], corresponding to the impersonal use of δοκεῖ)[115] to the non-Gnostics as though something remains "below."

105 Drijvers might also have referred to *Ode* 34 for his somewhat exaggerated statement: "The *Odes of Solomon* are deeply considered didactic poems" (see Drijvers, "Salomoschriften," 732).

106 Undoubtedly a simplification; see Hermann Diels, *Doxographi Graeci* (4th ed.; Berlin: de Gruyter, 1965) 592, lines 13-14; on Aristotle himself, see Walther Kranz, *Kosmos* (Archiv für Begriffsgeschichte 2, part 1; Bonn: Bouvier, 1955) 54–58; Wolfgang Scheffel, *Aspekte der platonischen Kosmologie: Untersuchungen zum Dialog "Timaios"* (Philosophia antiqua 29; Leiden: Brill, 1976) 3–15.

107 Berger and Nord, 965: "eigentlich."

108 Cf. 4:14-15; 6:3; 7:16; 11:22; 12:13; 16:18; 17:10; 22:11; 23:19.

109 What Schweizer means by "the gods . . . of the *Odes of Solomon*" (see Schweizer, *Ego eimi,* 130) remains obscure. *Ode* 34:5 is said to be "completely different" from the "claim of one who takes other gods seriously but places himself as the only true one in their stead" as expressed in the Johannine "I am" (ibid., 131). On the "theory of the two worlds" in Christian Platonism, see Andrew Louth, "Plato/Platonismus III. Christlicher Platonismus," *TRE* 26 (1996) 704–6.

110 Text and translation: Whittaker and Louis, 43.

111 See Funk, *Jakobus,* 131.

112 Franzmann, 243.

113 Karl-Wolfgang Tröger, who counts the *Odes of Solomon* among the sources of Gnosticism (*Die Gnosis: Heilslehre und Ketzerglaube* [Herder Spektrum 4953; Freiburg: Herder, 2001] 25, 69), illustrates the "concept of salvation" of the Gnostics by a passage from the *Gospel of Truth:* "Therefore, if one has knowledge, he is from above. If he is called, he hears, he answers, and he turns to him who is calling him, and ascends to him. . . . He who is to have knowledge in this manner knows where he comes from and where he is going" (*Gos. Truth* 22,2-15 [*NHLE,* 42]; cf. Tröger, *Gnosis,* 31). Gnostic "universal eschatology" begins with "the separation of what

The demarcation between Gnostics and non-Gnostics, achieved by revelation and salvation, is here again linked to a summons,[116] as will be seen at the end of the Ode.

■ **6** After the Gnosticizing disputation with philosophical tradition in stanza II, "the language of the New Testament" and "the doctrine of salvation by faith and grace"[117] make an appearance. This "reference to the redemption" is not "*added* by a Christian quill" [emphasis added].[118] It is typical of the *Odes of Solomon* that so-called orthodoxy is mingled with and more or less subordinated to "heresy."[119]

If the Ethpe. of ܓܠܐ (*glā*), and consequently the expected passive of ἀποκαλύπτω in 𝔊,[120] is not simply a theological passive, the verb of 6a, like that of 23:18a, could be translated as "to reveal oneself."[121] This would create a strong link to "Grace" personified of *Ode* 33 and the statements of salvation in that Ode. But there is nothing that hints at such a link, so this "crowning soteriological statement" (see Excursus 33) must be left with a general allusion to parallels like 9:5c or 33:10-11a. The New Testament speaks of the "coming" as well as the "revelation" of faith (cf. πίστις in Gal 3:23-26), but here the imperative "believe" is relegated to the next line (see below on 6b and Excursus 34), and the "revealing" of χάρις/ܛܝܒܘܬܐ (*ṭaybūṯā*) forms a didactic statement of salvation. The object of this "*doctrine of grace*," which can probably be traced back earlier even than Basilides,[122] as stated by the construction with εἰς/ܠ (*l-*)—and "by the change from the report style to a direct address to a 2nd masc[uline] pl[ural] group"[123]—is "your redemption" meant inclusively (see Excursus 5).

The indicative of salvation in 6a is followed by the absolute imperative of salvation ܗܝܡܢ (*haymen*) in 6b, to which are coupled two further imperatives used in place of the future tense.[124] This additional example of Semitic syntax still does not necessitate a Syriac original (see above on 33:8 and 33:10). Before discussing the two verbs "live" and "be redeemed," used here synonymously, it is time to locate the "quadriliteral" Paiel of ܐܡܢ (*ʾeman*)/ܗܡܢ (*hmen*) among its fellow derivatives.[125]

Excursus 34: "Belief" and "Believe" in the *Odes of Solomon*

In comparison with the "frequency with which the words πιστεύω and πίστις occur in the New Testament,"[126] the terms under discussion play a

is mixed, the division between light and darkness" (Tröger, *Gnosis*, 47).

114 So far Charlesworth (p. 123) is right to say: "One should not read gnostic [*sic*] mythology back into these verses." However, I will continue to translate ܝܕܥܬܐ (*ʾidaʿtā*) as "*gnōsis*," especially here (Lattke, *Oden*, 192; see Excursus 7), in spite of Frey's criticism (see Jörg Frey, review of Lattke in *ThLZ* 127 [2002] 1053), most of which I accept. For even if the term "knowledge" is influenced by the Platonizing use of the term γνῶσις—cf., e.g., the tradition in Albinus, *Didaskalikos* II (H[ermanni ed.] 152, lines 31-32): τοῦ μὲν ϑεωρητικοῦ [βίου] τὸ κεφάλαιον ἐν τῇ γνώσει τῆς ἀληϑείας κεῖται (Whittaker and Louis, 2), or *Didaskalikos* III (H[ermanni ed.] 153, lines 28-29): καλεῖται δὲ ἡ μὲν τῶν ὄντων γνῶσις ϑεωρητική (Whittaker and Louis, 3; on Plutarch (ca. 110 C.E.), see Jens Holzhausen, "Gnostizismus, Gnosis, Gnostiker. Ein Beitrag zur antiken Terminologie," *JAC* 44 (2001) 59)—the *Odes of Solomon* are dealing not with an ontological recognition of truth but with a quite specific *gnōsis* of salvation (Paulsen, *Studien*, 160).

115 Payne Smith, 2:2510; BDAG, *s.v.* δοκέω, 2b.

116 Schille, 99.

117 Harris and Mingana, 2:379.

118 Contra Spitta, 287.

119 Walter Bauer, *Orthodoxy and Heresy in Earliest Christianity* (translated by a team from the Philadelphia Seminar on Christian Origins; ed. Robert A. Kraft and Gerhard Krodel; Philadelphia: Fortress Press, 1971), ET of *Rechtgläubigkeit und Ketzerei im ältesten Christentum* (2nd ed., ed. Georg Strecker; BHTh 10; Tübingen: Mohr Siebeck, 1964) *passim*.

120 Payne Smith, 1:717–18.

121 Bauer and Aland, *s.v.* ἀποκαλύπτω, 1; cf. BDAG, *s.v.* ἀποκαλύπτω, a.

122 See Wolf-Dieter Hauschild, "Gnade IV. Dogmengeschichtlich (*Alte Kirche bis Reformationszeit*)," *TRE* 13 (1984) 477.

123 Franzmann, 243.

124 Beyer, *Syntax*, 243, 253. Greßmann (p. 466) had already recognized these imperatives as Semitic syntax: "Believe and you will live and be redeemed" (see also Rudolf Bultmann, "πιστεύω," *ThWNT* 6:181; *TDNT* 6:181). That means that the translations of Bauer (p. 615) and Berger and Nord (p. 965) are incorrect, as are my earlier ones (Lattke, *Bedeutung*, 1:169; idem, *Oden*, 192).

125 See Nöldeke §§180–81; Brockelmann, *Lexicon*, 175; Payne Smith, 1:231–38.

126 Klaus Haacker, "Glaube II. Altes und Neues Testament," *TRE* 13 (1984) 289.

quantitatively minor part in the *Odes of Solomon.*[127] Qualitatively, also, they can hardly be said to play a "key part,"[128] yet "belief" and "believe" are as "highly prized" here as among later "Gnostics."[129]

The Paiel ܗܝܡܢ (*haymen*), corresponding to the Greek active πιστεύω, occurs four times;[130] there are also six occurrences of various participles,[131] which correspond to forms of πιστεύω or represent the singular (28:3b) as well as the plural of πιστός, as can be seen from 11:22c 𝔊.[132] Since H does not have 42:19b, it is N alone that attests to seven occurrences of the feminine ܗܝܡܢܘܬܐ (*haymānūṯā*), which corresponds to the "nomen actionis" πίστις,[133] used in the sense of the "faithfulness" of God (4:5a).[134] The single occurrence of the Ethpaial ܐܬܗܝܡܢ (*ʾeṯhayman*) would have been represented in 𝔊 by the passive πιστεύομαί τι,[135] as the Coptic construction ⲦⲀⲚϩⲞⲨⲦ with preposition ⲉ- shows.[136] But this passage about the "ministers" to whom the "water" of God was "entrusted" (6:13) does not fit into the framework of the other statements of faith.

The first passage in which 𝔊 probably had πίστις fits just as badly: "For one hour of thy faithfulness / is more than all days and years" (4:5; cf. Ps 83:11a LXX). The strengthened singer of 16:4b has absolute "faith," where the prepositional expression, ܒܗ (*beh*), at the end of the verse, referring to God the Lord, has more the sense of "by him" than "in him." "Faith" occurs twice more in this absolute sense. Raging rivers can be crossed "in faith" (39:5), which sounds nearly as confiding as the Synoptic faith that can move mountains (cf. Matt 17:20 parr.; 1 Cor 13:2).[137] What "their faith" in 42:19b N means is shown by the cry of the dead for deliverance and salvation immediately before (42:15-18). For the reciprocal statement 8:11 ("keep my faith, you who are kept by it"), it has already been demonstrated that the direct object πίστιν μου/ܗܝܡܢܘܬܝ (*haymānūṯ*) does not mean "faith in me."[138] The parallelism between the terms "faith" (8:11) and "*gnōsis*" (8:12) may be noted in passing. In 39:13b there is a question whether the expression the "path of his faith," referring to the Lord Christ (39:11b), is an objective genitive (faith in him) or a subjective genitive (his own faith); but that is hardly relevant in 41:1b. For either the "truth of his faith" means the "truth of faith" in God the Lord,[139] or it is another example of the "faithfulness" of God: the "truth of his faithfulness/trustworthiness" (see on 4:5 above).

The passive participle ܡܗܝܡܢ (*mhayman*) in 28:3b clearly alludes to the Jewish description of God as πιστός. The "power of faith" as the "power of God"[140] is ultimately based on the faithfulness and credibility of God himself. This passage will be dealt with after the other participles have been discussed. The Greek term πιστός, which can be used as both a noun and an adjective, occurs twice in reference to believers and the faithful. In 11:22c 𝔊, it corresponds, as an attribute of the δοῦλοι ("servants"), to the plural active participle ܡܗܝܡܢܐ (*mhaymnē* [cf. 11:22b 𝔖]). In 22:7b ℭ it is a foreign word used as a noun, where 𝔖 has a construction using the plural active participle ܡܗܝܡܢܝܢ (*mhaymnīn*) with ܒܟ (*bāḵ*), which probably represents εἰς together with a participle of πιστεύω (see on 28:3b below). So a similar construction may be thought likely in 42:9b ("those who believe in me"), although there the first singular suffix of ܒ (*b-*) does not refer to God but to the redeemed Redeemer. In 4:3c it must remain doubtful whether the second masculine singular suffix to ܡܗܝܡܢܐ (*mhaymnē*) ("Thou gavest thy heart, Lord, to thy believers") represents the Greek τοῖς πιστοῖς or a participle of πιστεύω with a personal

127 The term האמין, which occurs in some fundamental statements in the Old Testament (Haacker, "Glaube II," 278–88) is "almost without exception expressed by πιστεύειν in the LXX" (Bultmann, "πιστεύω," *ThWNT* 6:197; *TDNT* 6:197).
128 Thomas Söding, "Glaube, Glauben III. Biblisch-theologisch: 3. *Neues Testament*," *LThK*³ 4 (1995) 670, referring to the New Testament.
129 Stuart George Hall, "Glaube IV. Alte Kirche," *TRE* 13 (1984) 306.
130 BDAG, *s.v.* πιστεύω; Payne Smith, 1:232.
131 Payne Smith, 1:232–33.
132 BDAG, *s.v.* πιστός.
133 Gerhard Barth, "πίστις, πιστεύω," *EWNT* 3 (1983) 219; *EDNT* 3:92–93; Haacker, "Glaube II," 280; Payne Smith, 1:238; BDAG, *s.v.* πίστις.
134 BDAG, *s.v.* πίστις, 1a.
135 BDAG, *s.v.* πιστεύω, 3.
136 See Crum, 421–22; Payne Smith, 1:238.
137 Thomas Söding, "Glaube, Glauben III. Biblisch-theologisch: 3. *Neues Testament*," *LThK*³ 4 (1995) 670.
138 See commentary on this passage.
139 BDAG, *s.v.* πίστις.
140 Ebeling, 96 = idem, *Wort und Glaube* (3rd ed.; Tübingen: Mohr Siebeck, 1967) 239.

pronoun—perhaps even with the addition of the preposition εἰς.

The final group of passages to be considered includes a return to 28:3a-b, "I had faith; therefore I was at rest, / because he is faithful in whom I had faith" (cf. Heb 4:3). The addition of ܒ (*b-*) in 28:3b sheds light on the absolute use of ܗܝܡܢ (*haymen*) in 28:3a. "There is nothing against putting this concentrated and partly didactic statement of salvation into the mouth of Christ, who now, as one regenerate and exalted by God's power, speaks of his own relationship to God."[141] However, in 29:6a it is the redeemed but nonmessianic speaker who, referring to the term "grace" (29:5b), says: "For I believed in the Messiah/ Anointed One of the Lord / and I considered that he is the Lord" (29:6a-b). Neither here nor elsewhere can this "faith" or "believing" be equated with a "new obedience," as Käsemann, following Peterson, interprets it in "Pauline theology."[142]

The only absolute imperative of "believe" is found in the Ode under discussion (34:6b). Even in the New Testament, πιστεύω—unlike πίστις—is used only very rarely "in absolute fashion"; the command μόνον πίστευε (Mark 5:36; cf. Luke 8:50) "is directed," on the one hand, "against fear (μὴ φοβοῦ, . . .)" and is aimed, on the other, toward wholeness, a redemption of what is ("ein Ganzwerden, ein Heilwerden der Existenz").[143]

Since 5c alludes to those who have *gnōsis*, it may be assumed that the imperative of salvation "believe" in 6b is addressed only to those who understand the soteriological revelation of grace in 6a and can connect to all that was said in stanzas I and II (cf. John 6:69; 1 John 4:16). The objective of this understanding in faith is expressed by the synonymous verbs ζῶ/ܚܝܐ (*ḥyā*) and σῴζομαι/ܐܬܦܪܩ (*ʾetpreq*), "live" and "be redeemed," which further underpin the objective of 6a (see Table 1; Excursus 5). Both verbs occur elsewhere as a "word-pair" (cf. 17:14a-b; 38:16a),[144] just as closely connected as "grace" and "live" or "be redeemed/saved" (cf. 5:3 𝔖 and ℭ; 9:5c; 33:10-11a).

141 See the commentary on that passage and its continuation.

142 Barbara Nichtweiß, *Erik Peterson: Neue Sicht auf Leben und Werk* (2nd ed.; Freiburg et al.: Herder, 1994) 227–28.

143 Ebeling, 95, 103, 110 = idem, *Wort und Glaube* (3rd ed.; Tübingen: Mohr Siebeck, 1967) 238, 247, 253; cf. Haacker, "Glaube II," 293.

144 Franzmann, 243.

35

Ode 35: Address of One Who Has Been Redeemed

(I)
1a The rain of the Lord overshadowed me with gentleness[a],
1b and he set a cloud of peace above my head,
2a which guarded me at all times
2b and[b] became salvation for me.

(II)
3a Everything was shaken[c] and agitated with fear,
3b and there went forth from them smoke and judgment.

(III)
4a But I was tranquil by/in the Lord's group,
4b and it was more than a shade/shelter to me[d]
4c and more than a foundation.
5a And like a child by its mother I was carried,
5b and it [viz., the group] gave me for milk the dew of the Lord.
6a And I grew up by his gift
6b and found rest in his *plērōma*.

(IV)
7a And I stretched out my hands in the ascent of myself [my soul],
7b and I erected myself towards the Most High[e],
7c and I was moved toward him.
Hallelujah.

a 1a ܒܢܝܚܘܬܐ N; ܒܢܝܚܬܐ H.
b 2b ܘܦܘܪܩܢܐ N; ܒܦܘܪܩܢܐ H.
c 3a ܐܬܬܙܝܥ ܟܠ H; ܐܬܬܙܝܥܘ ܟܠܡܕܡ N.
d 4b ܡܢ ܛܠܠܐ ܗܘܐ ܠܝ H; ܡܢ ܗܘܐ ܠܝ ܛܠܐ N.
e 7b ܡܪܝܡܐ N; ܡܪܝܐ corrected to ܡܪܝܡܐ in H.

Introduction

Ode 35 is preserved in two Syriac manuscripts.[1] At first glance Spitta seems to be right: "There is no sign of Christianity in the lovely 35th Ode."[2] But even if neither *Ode* 35 nor *Ode* 36 can be classified as a "baptismal hymn,"[3] a closer examination must take note of the following: "We shall see that the 36th Ode is probably spoken in the name of Christ; and if so, that should carry the 35th Ode to the same conclusion."[4] So it will be necessary to investigate whether "this initially baffling *Ode*"[5] really belongs among "the *Odes* where the answer to the question," Is it Jewish or Christian? "is of no consequence."[6] According to Diettrich, it is "certain" that *Ode* 35 is "an eschatological hymn."[7] Two points can be made about this: first, this first-person utterance is no hymn;[8] and, second, the soteriological eschatology is not a "description of the great final catastrophe" or the "cosmic overthrow of the final days as prophesied by Joel."[9] In view of the Gnostic key word "ascent"[10]

1 Mss.: Codex H, 25b–26a; Codex N, 150ᵛ (ꜱ). Ed./trans.: Charlesworth, 124–26; Franzmann, 244–47; Lattke, 3:107–24.
2 Spitta, 287.
3 Contra Schille (p. 64), who understands "redemption . . . as rebirth"; Bernard, 120–22.
4 Harris and Mingana, 2:382. Their arguments on "Isaiah in the Syriac version and in the Targum" and "dependence of the Odist on the Targum" are not enough to justify their decision to question this idea a few lines further down: "But this does not seem to be likely, nor a very defensible position" (pp. 382–83).
5 Gunkel, 319.
6 Harnack, 78. This question is independent of whether the "I" is any redeemed person or whether "he would be recognised as Christ from a Christian perspective" (ibid., 86). Harnack denies the latter.
7 Diettrich, 116.
8 Lattke, *Hymnus*, 251–53; idem, *Bedeutung*, 4:107–10.
9 Diettrich, 116–17.
10 Tröger, *Gnosis*, 31. The passage that Tröger quotes, *Gos. Truth* 22,2-20 (see on *Ode* 34:5c above), also contains the statement: "He receives rest" (Schenke, *Herkunft*, 38; see on 6b below).

and the associated term ܢܦܫܐ (*napšā*) in 7a, one might suggest titles like "The Ascent of the Soul"[11] or "The Passage to Heaven of the Soul."[12] But, as will appear in due course, the masculine speaker (4a, 5a) does not mean by "soul" an (immortal) part of his being: he is speaking reflexively of himself.[13] Pierre is perhaps a little too emphatic about "the link between this Ode and the previous one."[14]

Interpretation

■ **1-2** The imagery of stanza I owes most to the text of Isaiah in the LXX. There is no need to revert to the Targum to explain the poetic medley of terms.[15] Nor is a reference to 1 Cor 10:1-2—and thus to the "sacrament of baptism"[16]—any help in finding the key to the "skewed image" of 1a[17] or any of the other images of this Ode. The background of this disjointed *parallelismus membrorum* in 1a-b[18] is not found in the stories of the "cloud" in Exod 40:34-38,[19] but in the expressions σκιάσει νεφέλη (". . . shall a cloud overshadow") and εἰς σκιάν ("for a shadow") in Isa 4:5-6.[20] The image of the rain (ὑετός/ܡܛܪܐ [*meṭrā*]) in Isa 4:6 may have inspired the search for a more suitable term for 1a parallel to "cloud" in 1b. The singular ܪܣܝܣܐ (*rsīsā*), which also is used as a parallel to ܛܠܐ (*ṭallā*),[21] cannot here mean "drop" (cf. the plural ܪ̈ܣܝܣܐ [*rsīsē*] in 4:10).[22] The peculiar use of the seemingly abstract singular term[23] is most easily explained by the assumption that 𝔊 used the term νιφετός.[24] The "Lord" here, as in 4a, is the "Most High" of 7b.[25] This removes one important argument for denying the identification of the speaking "I" with Christ (cf. *Ode* 36). Emphasizing the protective character of the drizzle from the cloud, N puts the prepositional phrase ܒܢܝܚܘܬܐ (*b-nīḥūtā*) in front of the Aph. ܐܛܠ (*ʾaṭṭel*), which occurs only here (see below), a phrase that corresponds to either the adverb πράως/πραέως[26] or the prepositional phrase ἐν πραότητι.[27] Within the Syriac tradition,

11 Greßmann, 466; see also Gunkel, 319.

12 Bauer, 615; see also Rudolph, *Gnosis*, 240. Except for Rudolph, who emphasizes only "the present fact of redemption," the other authors (Bauer, 615; Greßmann, 466; Gunkel, 319–20) all employ the term "Verzückung [rapture]," which is hardly warranted by the imagery and context. Harnack (p. 86) describes the speaker as a "prophet who is also a mystic"; cf. Omodeo, 117–18.

13 Later Gnostics also did not always use the term "psyche/soul," with its multiple meanings, to refer to the "self" (see Tröger, *Gnosis*, 30–31).

14 Pierre, 167.

15 Contra Harris and Mingana, 2:382–83.

16 Greßmann, 466.

17 Bauer, 615.

18 Franzmann, 246, with reference to 5:5 as "antithesis of 1b."

19 Contra BDAG, *s.v.* ἐπισκιάζω, 2.

20 Rahlfs, 2:571; Brenton, 839; cf. LEH, *s.vv.* σκιά, σκιάζω.

21 Payne Smith, 2:3938. If the "plays on words" (Abramowski, 48) were really as important as Harris and Mingana make them in their argument for a Syriac original (see Harris and Mingana, 2:169, 380–81), one might have expected ܛܠܗ ܕܡܛܪܐ (see 5b below) in place of ܪܣܝܣܗ ܕܡܛܪܐ in 1a. This would also support the Greek term δρόσος in Frankenberg's problematic retroversion (p. 30), as well as the translation "cloud of dew" (Gunkel, 318), "rain of dew" (Greßmann, 466; Bauer, 615) or just "dew" (Harris and Mingana, 2:380; Emerton, 723, who, however, suggests "shower" as an alternative).

22 As Ungnad and Staerk (p. 34) point out, although they suggest "mist."

23 Cf. the translation "sprinkle," "sprinkling" in Lattke, *Bedeutung*, 1:169; idem, *Oden*, 193. Whether "sprinkling" in Charlesworth (p. 124) and Franzmann (p. 244, with ܐܛܠ in place of ܡܛܠ) is meant literally is not clear. Pierre's "drizzle," however, is unambiguous (see Pierre, 167: "bruine").

24 LSJ, *s.v.* νιφετός: "rain." As can be seen from Deut 32:2 (νιφετός together with ὑετός, δρόσος, and ὄμβρος), this term, which occurs in the plural in Dan 3:68a LXX, could have been translated by the plural of ܪܣܝܣܐ (see Rahlfs, 2:346; *OTSy*, pt. 1 fasc. 2, on this passage). It is perhaps the parallelism of "rain" and "cloud" that prevented this.

25 Diettrich (p. 117) deletes the ܕ of ܕܡܛܪܐ and makes the "Lord" the subject of 1a, but his arguments are insufficient.

26 LSJ, *s.v.* πράως. Greßman suspects "an adverb in 𝔊" (in a note referring to Gunkel's translation "invigorating" = "in invigoration" [see Gunkel, 318–19]) but makes no concrete suggestion.

27 BDAG, *s.v.* πραΰτης.

ܢܝܚܘܬܐ was corrected to ܢܝܚܬܐ (*nyāḥtā*) (as found in H) to assimilate it to 6b (see Excursus 3).[28] Suggested by the key words σκιάζω and σκιά (Isa 4:5-6, see above) and possibly reinforced by the occurrence of νεφέλη ("cloud") and ἐπισκιάζω ("overshadow") in the New Testament report of the Transfiguration (Matt 17:5), the *hapax legomenon* ܐܛܠ (Aph. *ʾaṭṭel*) with preposition ܥܠ (*ʿal*) + first singular suffix appears at the end of 1a. This causative does not relate to ܛܠܐ/ܛܐܠܐ (*ṭallā*) = "dew"[29] and therefore cannot mean "destillavit," as Brockelmann suggests with reference to *Ode* 35:1.[30] It is in fact derived from the root of ܛܠܠܐ (*ṭellālā*) = "shadow," which does not occur in the Pe.;[31] together with ܥܠ (*ʿal*) it corresponds not only to σκεπάζω (Wis 5:16) and κατασκιάζω (Heb 9:5; cf. συσκιάζω/σκιάζω in Exod 25:20; 37:9 LXX) but especially to ἐπισκιάζω (Matt 17:5; Mark 9:7; Luke 9:34). The Syriac verb might therefore be translated by "cover"[32] or "overspread,"[33] but the parallelism of 1a and 1b gives preference to "overshadow."[34]

The subject of 1b is not the "rain,"[35] though it is masculine in Syriac, but the "Lord" of 1a. This impairs the grammatical parallelism but does not strain the weather imagery. So the Aph. of ܐܩܝܡ, ܩܡ (*qām*), which contains the subject, is the equivalent of a transitive use of ἵστημι.[36] Unlike the "cloud of dew" (36:7; cf. νεφέλη δρόσου in Isa 18:4), the lovely metaphor of a "cloud of peace" is only partly biblical (cf. νεφέλη in Isa 4:5; νεφέλη φωτεινή in Matt 17:5).[37] Since the genitive of ܫܠܡܐ (*šlāmā*) that qualifies this metaphorical "cloud" was εἰρήνης in 𝔊, with or without a definite article (cf. 36:8),[38] the image of this "protecting cloud"[39] would carry, over and above its general sense of a "gift of God," associations not merely of "well-being" but especially of "peace" as a messianic "gift of salvation."[40] Without necessarily referring to the childhood narrative in Matthew (cf. ἐπάνω ["over"], Matt 2:9), the compound preposition ܠܥܠ ܡܢ (*l-ʿel men*) means merely "above."[41] The term κεφαλή/ܪܫܐ (*rēšā*), taken together with 3a-b,

28 Frankenberg (p. 30) bases his retroversion, κατ᾽ ἀνάπαυσιν, on the reading in H. But ܢܝܚܬܐ is only rarely used for ἀνάπαυσις. Generally ܢܝܚܐ (*nyāḥā*) is used for ἀνάπαυσις, while ܢܝܚܬܐ (*nyāḥtā*)—at least in earlier times—represents κατάπαυσις (Payne Smith, 2:2315–17; BDAG, *s.vv.* ἀνάπαυσις, κατάπαυσις; see Hatch and Redpath, 80–81, 741). I consider the N reading to be the *lectio difficilior* (as does Charlesworth, 124–25; contra Harris and Mingana, vol. 1, on this passage; 2:380). Since ܢܝܚܐ (*nyāḥā*) is used for "rest" in all other passages (3:5; 25:12; 26:3; 37:4) and ܢܝܚܬܐ (*nyāḥtā*) is a *hapax legomenon*, it is more likely that the technical term would have been used here. The reading in N is not such a technical term (cf. 14:6; 20:8; 26:12; 35:1) and would probably be better translated by "gentleness" (Emerton, 723) or "mildness" (Lattke, *Bedeutung*, 1:169: "Sanftheit") than by "rest" (Franzmann, 244; Lattke, *Oden*, 193: "Ruhe"). How Bauer (p. 615) came by the translation "as a gift" ("als Gabe") is totally obscure.

29 Contra Frankenberg, 43; Diettrich, 117.

30 Brockelmann, *Lexicon*, 275. This means that the sequence of entries in the concordance (Lattke, *Bedeutung*, 2:106–7) must be revised to insert the four occurrences of ܛܠܐ (ܛܐܠܐ) between ܛܠܠܐ and ܛܠܠܐ.

31 Payne Smith, 1:1469; Payne Smith, *Dictionary*, 174; Beyer, *ATTM*, 590. Harris and Mingana state, correctly, "The verb ܐܛܠ is commonly derived from 'shadow' and means 'to overshadow.'" But their translation of ܪܣܣܐ as "dew" leads them to suggest: "Here the Odist seems to derive it from ܛܠܐ" (see Harris and Mingana, 2:380). I cannot agree with this conclusion.

32 Lattke, *Bedeutung*, 1:169.

33 Lattke, *Oden*, 193; Bauer and Aland, *s.v.* κατασκιάζω ("bedecken"); BDAG, *s.v.* σκεπάζω, 1,

34 BDAG, *s.v.* ἐπισκιάζω, 1. "To give shade" = "beschatten" (Gunkel, 318; Ungnad and Staerk, 34; Bauer, 615; Klaus Beyer (letter of November 13, 2002) would also be possible instead of "overshadow."

35 Contra Harris and Mingana, 2:380; Charlesworth, 124.

36 Payne Smith, 2:3527; BDAG, *s.v.* ἵστημι, A1; see Frankenberg, 30: ἔστησε.

37 The idea of rapture in connection with a "cloud" (Acts 1:9; 1 Thess 4:17; BDAG, *s.v.* νεφέλη) comes into play only in the context of this Ode and *Ode* 36 as a whole. On the correspondence of ܥܢܢܐ (*ʿnānā*) and νεφέλη, see Payne Smith, 2:2924.

38 Payne Smith, 2:4189.

39 Gunkel, 319.

40 BDAG, *s.v.* εἰρήνη.

41 BDAG, *s.v.* ἐπάνω, 1b; Payne Smith, 2:2888.

might suggest a link with the beginning of *Ode* 24,[42] but the prominence of the terms "head" and "gentleness" seems rather to link 35:1a-b to 20:8 (see Excursus 23). If the speaker is meant to be Christ, this "cloud of peace" over his "head" would be a gentle opposite to the brutality recorded in the passion narrative (cf. Matt 27:29-30).[43]

The feminine forms of the perfect ܗܘܐ (*hwā*) show that the bicolon 2a-b, which follows the relative particle ܕ (*d*-),[44] refers to the "cloud" rather than directly to the "Lord." As in 14:4 the temporal phrase ܒܟܠܙܒܢ (*b-ḵol zḇan*) may represent either ἀεί[45] or διὰ παντός.[46] The wording may have been suggested by the occurrence of ἡμέρας ("by day") and νυκτός ("by night") in Isa 4:5.[47] That there are various possible Greek verbs equivalent to the participle of the Pa. ܢܛܪ (*naṭṭar*)[48] was mentioned already in connection with 18:7. Since the passage here also treats of "God's care,"[49] Psalm 91 (90 LXX) may also have had an influence, as it can be shown to have had elsewhere (cf. Ps 90:11 LXX in Luke 4:10). The key word "peace" might suggest a reference to Phil 4:7.[50] But τηρέω[51] and compounds such as παρατηρέω[52] or συντηρέω[53] are also possible. The wording of 𝔊 is unknown.

That the wording of 2b is based on the Bible, κύριος καὶ ἐγένετό μοι εἰς σωτηρίαν (Isa 12:2; cf. Exod 15:2 and Ps 117:14 LXX), can be stated with more confidence. As in 28:10, so here εἰς/ܠ (*l*-) is omitted, but should perhaps be added (see Excursus 5). Although "dew" is mentioned later (5b), σωτηρία/ܦܘܪܩܢܐ (*purqānā*) = "salvation" is connected only indirectly, if at all, to ἴαμα = "healing" in Isa 26:19. Frankenberg, in his retroversion,[54] adheres to the reading of H, which already Greßmann had characterized as "meaningless,"[55] a verdict borne out by the text of N. Even though the speaking "I" of *Ode* 35 does not speak of his role as redeemer (as in, e.g., *Odes* 17 and 42) the statement of salvation in 2b would suitably come from such a redeemed Redeemer (cf. 17:7; 21:2; 28:10). This means that it is necessary to keep open the possibility that not only *Ode* 36 but already *Ode* 35 was "spoken in the name of Christ."[56]

■ **3** This bicolon is not in the first person, unlike the rest of the Ode, and "semantically . . . stands in antithesis to stanzas 1 and 3 ."[57] Stanza II contains no mention of "demons."[58] It may be concerned with apocalyptic "signs of the end of time,"[59] but the key to the verbs of 3a, as well as the two *hapax legomena* "smoke" and "judgment," will be found, not in Diettrich's references (Jer 51:29; Ps 2:5; Joel 3:3; 4:2; Amos 4:10) but again in the LXX text of Isaiah. Prophecies of judgment and salvation are mingled and to some extent subverted, resulting in a contrast with the peaceful statement of salvation of 2b (cf. Isa 12:2; etc.) and a threatening presence in the wings for the eschatological rest of stanza III.

The image of judgment in Isaiah 13 LXX, heralding the ἡμέρα κυρίου (13:6, 9, 13), "day of the Lord," and stressing the ὅλος κτλ. (13:5, 9, 11) and the πᾶς κτλ. (13:7, 10), "whole" and "all, every," yielded the paired statements . . . πᾶσα ψυχὴ ἀνθρώπου δειλιάσει | καὶ ταραχθήσονται οἱ πρεσβεῖς . . . (13:7-8).[60] This most probably gave rise to the Greek *Vorlage* of the Syriac text: πάντα ἐταράχθη καὶ ἐδειλίασαν.[61] This is the only

42 Personal communication from Franzmann.
43 Michael Lattke, "κεφαλή," *EWNT* 2 (1981) 706; *EDNT*, 2:286.
44 Franzmann's criticism (p. 245) of Charlesworth's (p. 124) and Lattke's (*Bedeutung*, 1:169) translations is justified, which demands corrections to entries for ܕ (*d*-) in the concordance (*Bedeutung*, 2:68 [relative pronoun]; 2:73 [conjunction]).
45 BDAG, *s.v.* ἀεί, 1; Payne Smith, 1:1077.
46 BDAG, *s.v.* διά, A2a; see Frankenberg, pp. 16, 30: διάπαντος.
47 See BDAG, *s.v.* ἡμέρα, 1a, on these regularly juxtaposed genitives of "time."
48 Payne Smith, 2:2355.
49 BDAG, *s.v.* διαφυλάσσω: "guard, protect."
50 Bernard, 120; see BDAG, *s.v.* φρουρέω, 3.
51 BDAG, *s.v.* τηρέω, 2.
52 Frankenberg, 30.
53 BDAG, *s.v.* συντηρέω, 1: "protect, defend," "preserve" from "harm or ruin."
54 Frankenberg, 30: ἐν σωτηρίῳ for expected ἐν σωτηρίᾳ.
55 In Gunkel, 319: "for ܒ [*b*-] read ܘ [ʾ*u*-]."
56 Harris and Mingana, 2:382.
57 Franzmann, 246.
58 Contra Gunkel, 319; Frankenberg, 95; Greßmann, 466.
59 Diettrich, 117.
60 Rahlfs, 2:583; Brenton, 848: ". . . every soul of man shall be dismayed. The elders shall be troubled" (ET based on an earlier LXX edition). The Syriac text of Isa 13:7-8 had no influence on *Ode* 35:3a (cf. *OTSy*, pt. 3 fasc. 1, p. 23).
61 BDAG, *s.v.* δειλιάω, ταράσσω, 2. Without knowing

possible explanation for the H reading, with a singular verb preceding ܟܠ, for which the translation of πάντα/ܟܠ (*kol*) by "universe"[62] seems somewhat exaggerated.[63] At some point in the Syriac tradition, the verb was harmonized with the plural of the second verb—perhaps also under the influence of the plural suffix in 3b—resulting in the reading of N, which contrasts so sharply with 5:13a and which can hardly be based any longer on πάντες ἐταράχθησαν.[64] It is necessary now only to show that the two verbs taken from Isa 13:7-8 LXX were translated severally by the Ethpe. of ܙܘܥ, ܙܥ (*zāʿ*)[65] and the Ethpe. of ܪܗܒ (*rheb*). The uncommon use of the first Ethpe. for the passive of ταράσσω would remind later readers of ἐσείσθη in Matt 21:10 (Jesus' entry into Jerusalem: "all the city was stirred") and Matt 27:51 (occurrences connected with the death of Jesus: "the earth shook") and especially draw their attention to the birth story in Matthew, where King Herod ἐταράχθη ("was troubled, frightened") "and all Jerusalem with him" (Matt 2:3; cf. 14:26).[66] The second Ethpe., ܐܬܪܗܒܘ (*ʾeṯrheb*, third *plural* perfect!), is a *hapax legomenon* in the *Odes of Solomon* and, in general, is used to translate the passive of θορυβέω,[67] but several passages can be cited where it is used as a synonym for φοβέω κτλ./ܕܚܠ (*dḥel*), and is thus equivalent to δειλιάω (e.g., Deut 1:21).[68]

Verse 3b returns to Isa 4:4-5 (see on stanza I above), with the key words κρίσις (= מִשְׁפָּט/ܕܝܢܐ [*dīnā*], "judgment") and καπνός (= עָשָׁן/ܬܢܢܐ [*tennānā*], "smoke"), which refer to the "judgment" of the Lord and his coming to Mount Zion in Jerusalem. So there is no reason to interfere in the mysterious text, as does Greßmann,[69] with the "slight change" of ܕܝܢܐ to ܪܝܚܐ (*rēḥā*), placing "stench" next to "smoke."[70] There is no problem about the origin or meaning of either *hapax legomenon*,[71] but the Greek *Vorlage* of the Pe. ܢܦܩ (*npaq*), followed by the preposition ܡܢ (*men*), cannot be finally ascertained.[72] The retroversion ἐξεπορεύθη αὐτῶν[73] is at best only one possibility of many. It is more probable that ἀπ' αὐτῶν corresponded to ܡܢܗܘܢ (*mennhōn*), "from them" (cf. linguistically Matt 24:27), so that the image is not one of noxious emanations coming out of the insides of persons or powers.[74] More important is an explanation why "smoke" and "judgment" "went forth from" the beings alluded to in 3a. If the two terms taken from Isa 4:4-5 spoke of *personal* actions inimical to God,[75] they would not really fit the imagery of 3b. If, however, they refer to *God*'s appearance and the shock of his judgment, then the ones who are agitated in the terror of the end of time are merely material to demonstrate the supremacy that brings such disaster on them (cf. for the sense Rom 1:18-32).[76]

■ **4-6** Not everything in stanza III can be understood as readily as the image in 5a and the first half of 5b, which is common to the whole world. To decide on the subjects

the origin of his retroversion, Frankenberg's (p. 30) version ἐσαλεύθη πᾶν καὶ ἐταράχθησαν can only be described as fantasy.

62 Diettrich, 117: "*All.*"

63 See BDAG, *s.v.* πᾶς, 4dβ.

64 According to Klaus Beyer, the plural reading of N "is strange, but should not be dismissed out of hand"; he feels that "there is something wrong" with the whole v. 3 (Beyer, letter of November 13, 2002; on "ܟܠ in the Constr[uct] St[ate]" followed by a plural, see Nöldeke §218). Even if the more difficult reading of N should be the earlier, the exegesis would not be radically altered.

65 Payne Smith, 1:1106; passives of κινέω; πτύρω, σαλεύω, σείω, and ταράσσω were translated by ܐܬܬܙܝܥ (*ʾettzīʿ*).

66 BDAG, *s.v.* ταράσσω, 2; cf. NA[27] and *NTSy* on these passages.

67 BDAG, *s.v.* θορυβέω, 2.

68 See Rahlfs, 1:285; *OTSy*, pt. 1 fasc. 2, on this passage; Payne Smith, 2:3827; BDAG, *s.v.* δειλιάω: "be cowardly, fearful," "be afraid"; on connotations in antiquity, see Spicq, 1:200–202.

69 Greßmann in Gunkel, 319; cf. Greßmann, 466. Gunkel (pp. 318–19) then converts "smoke" and "stench" into "smoke" and "fumes," with reference to later traditions.

70 Bauer, 615.

71 Payne Smith, 1:843, 2:4464; BDAG, *s.vv.* καπνός, κρίσις.

72 See Payne Smith, 2:2419–21.

73 Frankenberg, 30.

74 See BDAG, *s.v.* ἐξέρχομαι, 1aβב.

75 E.g., Gunkel, 319; Greßmann, 466.

76 Berger and Nord's free translation (p. 965) catches this meaning exactly: "Smoke came from them as from the execution of a verdict."

of 4b-c and 5b it is necessary to consider the whole stanza. The masculine suffixes in 6a-b refer directly to the "Lord" of 5b and indirectly to the same "Lord" in 4a (and thus also in 1a-b). The "dew of the Lord" is not the subject of 5b,[77] but is placed in apposition[78] to the object "milk,"[79] so the masculine subject contained in the verb "to give" cannot be the "Lord."[80] Therefore this subject, like that of 4b-c, must be the loanword τάγμα,[81] which is masculine in Syriac. If ܒܛܓܡܗ (*b-ṭeḡmeh*) really *must* "be emended" to ܒܦܬܓܡܗ (*b-peṯḡāmeh*)[82] and thus read as "by/in the word of the Lord" (4a),[83] then the masculine ܦܬܓܡܐ (*peṯḡāmā*) would make good metaphorical sense as the subject of 4b-c, but not as subject of 5b. For the subject the "word of the Lord" would clash with the "dew of the Lord" in apposition to the object, just as the "Lord," which a number of commentators want to make the subject (see above), does. So there is no need to consider a change to the manuscript text of 4a—which does not make the interpretation of the difficult text of stanza III any easier.[84]

Because of the contrast with stanza II, the introductory particle ܘ (*w-*), preceding the emphasized ܐܢܐ (*ʾenā*), in 4a should be translated as "but" rather than "and."[85] In 𝔊, κἀγώ will have corresponded to ܘܐܢܐ.[86] Franzmann's observation that "6b and 4a form the inclusio for the stanza"[87] can receive further support from the semantic relationship between the *hapax legomenon* ܫܠܐ (*šlē*) in 4a and the verb in 6b derived from the root ܢܘܚ. As in 1 Tim 2:2, the passive participle of ܫܠܐ (*šlā*) could correspond to ἤρεμος.[88] But a form of ἡσυχάζω can also be considered (cf. 1 Thess 4:11 and the connection with φιλαδελφία ["love of brother/sister"] in 4:9-10).[89] Other verbs may also come under consideration,[90] so there is no need to accept Frankenberg's suggestion unquestioningly,[91] although ἀθόρυβος makes a clear contrast with stanza II.[92] Later in the passage the context will define "tranquil" more closely. The immediately following prepositional expression, which carries both an instrumental and a local meaning, does not help with a better understanding of ܫܠܐ (*šlē*). It is most likely that 𝔊 also had τάγμα,[93] not πρόσταγμα or σύνταγμα.[94] The word τάγμα does not carry any military connotation here,[95] nor does it refer to "angelic orders."[96] Translations like "order,"[97] "commandment,"[98]

77 As, e.g., in Harnack, 66; Ungnad and Staerk, 34; Diettrich, 118; Frankenberg, 30; Bernard, 120.

78 Franzmann (p. 247) divides 5b into a parallel bicolon 5b-c, "5c being in apposition with ܚܠܒܐ in 5b." There is no actual mark of division in H or N.

79 Harris and Mingana, 2:380; Bauer, 615.

80 Contra Harris and Mingana, 2:380; Charlesworth, 124; Franzmann, 245.

81 Bauer (p. 615) translates the loanword τάγμα with the masculine "Auftrag"; it never becomes clear whether he refers the "he" in 4b and 5b to this "task of the Lord" or to the "Lord" himself.

82 Diettrich, 118; Labourt and Batiffol, 33.

83 Frankenberg (pp. 30, 43) refers for his retroversion ῥήματι κυρίου to Julius Wellhausen. This is probably an error substituting W [Wellhausen] for D [Diettrich]. His reference to *GGA* 1910, no. 10, is likewise incorrect (ibid., p. 1). Greßmann's translation (p. 466) "in the word of the Lord" is perhaps based on the note by Harris and Mingana (2:381): "The elimination of the letter ܦ is possibly due to a slip of the copyist."

84 Charlesworth's conjecture (p. 125) "that the Odist chose ܛܓܡܐ [*sic*] because it immediately invokes in the reader ܦܬܓܡܐ, which only in the Odes, as far as the author knows, represents the divine Logos," does not address the problem.

85 Greßmann, 466; see Klaus Beyer, "Woran erkennt man, daß ein griechischer Text aus dem Hebräischen oder Aramäischen übersetzt ist?" in M. Macuch et al., eds., חכמות בנתה ביתה*: Studia Semitica necnon Iranica Rudolpho Macuch septuagenario ab amicis et discipulis dedicata* (Wiesbaden: Harrassowitz, 1989) 26.

86 Frankenberg, 30; see BDAG, *s.v.* κἀγώ, 2: "but I."

87 Franzmann, 247.

88 BDAG, *s.v.* ἤρεμος: "quiet, tranquil"; the translation for ἡσύχιος in that passage is the verbal adjective ܢܝܚܐ (*nīḥā*; cf. NA[27] and *NTSy* on the passage).

89 BDAG, *s.v.* ἡσυχάζω, 2.

90 See Payne Smith, 2:4164.

91 Frankenberg, 30.

92 See LSJ, *s.v.* ἀθόρυβος: "unperturbed."

93 Lattke, "Wörter," 299–300 = idem, *Bedeutung*, 4:148.

94 See Payne Smith, 2:4388.

95 LSJ, *s.v.* τάγμα: "ordinance, command."

96 Lampe, 1371.

97 "Befehl" (Gunkel, 318; Diettrich, 118 n. 1).

98 Bernard, 120.

"ranks,"[99] "task,"[100] "legion,"[101] or "company"[102] do not convey much meaning in the context of stanza III. The term here has, to begin with, the sense of a "group"[103] or "community"[104] that includes the speaking "I," which is then—similarly to Paul's "church of God,"[105] or the expression "people of God"[106]—theologically qualified by the genitive of κύριος/ܡܪܝܐ (*māryā*), "Lord," and thus distinguished from any earthly society.[107] So there is no reason, so far, to exclude Christ as the speaker of stanza III (see above).

In H, the bicolon 4b-c seems to offer no problems, but in N the text of 4b is clearly in confusion.[108] Franzmann's explanation, "N has ܡܢ ܗܘܐ ܠ ܛܐܠܐ, confusing the order of the elements in the sentence,"[109] is too facile. The reading of N, which Burkitt, unfortunately, merely lists,[110] is obviously "inferior,"[111] even "meaningless."[112] It also problematizes the text of H, which must now be interpreted, and without recourse to the earlier hypothesis of a "marginal note,"[113] even though Geo Widengren considered it "quite possible."[114]

Even if ܛܐܠܐ/ܛܠܐ (*ṭallā*) is assumed to be the "original reading" in 4b as well as in 5b,[115] "dew" and "foundation" would be related to each other as above and below.[116] Why it is *necessary* for "either 'shade' or 'foundation' to be corrupt" in the "parallelism" of 4b-c and for κρηπίς as the "protective wall" providing "shade" in an oriental manner to be suggested in place of "foundation"[117] is incomprehensible. One should rather derive the *hapax legomenon* ܛܠܠܐ (*ṭellālā*) from the key word σκιά (see on 1a above),[118] which is a synonym of σκέπη,[119] in Isa 4:6. The shade cast from above by a tree or a roof—"as a protection from heat"[120]—is outdone by the defense offered by the "Lord's group" (4a), expressed by the adverb of quality ܝܬܝܪ (*yattīr*), which occurs twice here and nowhere else, together with the preposition ܡܢ (*men*), which "introduces the comparison."[121]

What is meant by the second term of the comparison ܫܬܐܣܬܐ (*šeṯestā*), in 4c, used in synthetic *parallelismus membrorum* with 4b, is easier to determine than its Greek equivalent.[122] If Greßmann's suggestion of κρηπίς should be correct (see above), then the term would have the same sense as ἑδραίωμα (cf. 1 Tim 3:15, referring to the house or congregation/church of God),[123] ἔρεισμα,[124] or θεμέλιος,[125] namely, "foundation" in

99 Harris and Mingana, 2:380.
100 "Auftrag" (Bauer, 615).
101 Charlesworth, 124; Emerton, 724.
102 Franzmann, 245.
103 Josephus uses the term τάγμα ("group"; BDAG, *s.v.* τάγμα, 1b) as a synonym of αἵρεσις ("sect"; BDAG, *s.v.* αἵρεσις, 1) to describe the Essenes and the Sadducees, which can be translated by "order," "association," or "fraternity" (Josephus *Bell.* 2.122, 143, 160, 164 [LCL 2:368–71, 376–77, 384–87]; see Otto Michel and Otto Bauernfeind, eds., *Flavius Josephus, De Bello Judaico – Der Jüdische Krieg*, vol. 1: *Buch I–III* [2nd ed.; Munich: Kösel; Darmstadt: Wissenschaftliche Buchgesellschaft, 1962] 205, 209, 213, 215).
104 Klaus Beyer, letter of November 13, 2002.
105 BDAG, *s.v.* ἐκκλησία, 3c.
106 BDAG, *s.v.* λαός, 4.
107 Whether there was ever a (Jewish, primitive Christian, or Gnostic) sect that described itself sociologically as *serech* or "τάγμα of the Lord" is doubtful (on 1QS ii.20-26, and other passages in the Dead Sea Scrolls, see Michel and Bauernfeind, 436 n. 67; Maier, *Qumran-Essener*, 3:303, *s.v.* "Rang").
108 See already Lattke, *Bedeutung*, 1:43–44.
109 Franzmann, 245.
110 Burkitt, 379.
111 Grimme, "Handschrift," 493.
112 Gerhard Kittel, "Eine zweite Handschrift der Oden Salomos," *ZNW* 14 (1913) 88.
113 Lattke, *Bedeutung*, 1:44.
114 Geo Widengren, review of Lattke, *Bedeutung*, vols. 1–2 and 1a, in *TRev* 78 (1982) 15.
115 Ibid.
116 Even though Franzmann (p. 246) mentions objects and makes the "Lord" the subject of 4b-c, she points out correctly that the two nouns "express merismus—'shade' above and 'foundation' below."
117 Greßmann in Gunkel, 319.
118 Payne Smith, 1:1469; BDAG, *s.v.* σκιά, 1: "shade or shelter."
119 BDAG, *s.v.* σκέπη: "shade . . . suggesting protection or security."
120 LSJ, *s.v.* σκιά.
121 Brockelmann, *Grammatik* §§200, 204; on possible Greek equivalents, see Payne Smith, 1:1650–51.
122 Payne Smith, 2:4348, where θεμελιον [*sic*] should be corrected to θεμέλιος.
123 BDAG, *s.v.* ἑδραίωμα: "that which provides a firm base for someth[ing]."
124 LEH, *s.v.* ἔρεισμα: "support."
125 BDAG, *s.v.* θεμέλιος, 2: "foundation."

the sense of "basis" and "support" from below[126]–not from the side like a buttress.[127] Together these images in 4b-c are a partial explanation of the soteriological tranquillity of 4a. Further explanations and illustrations come in the next bicolon, whose use of two more terms derived from roots containing the consonants ܛ and ܠ has given rise to many claims for a Syriac original.[128] However "clever" and "pleasing" the poetic use of the Syriac words ܛܠܠܐ (*ṭellālā*), ܛܠܝܐ (*ṭalyā*), and ܛܠܐ (*ṭallā*) may be,[129] it can just as well be ascribed to the translation, since there are in fact–and in normal use–no real alternatives to these equivalents for "shade" (σκιά as in Isa 4:6 or σκέπη), "child" (see on 5a below) or "dew" (δρόσος).

In the metaphorical comparison of 5a, the most likely equivalent for ܛܠܝܐ (*ṭalyā*) is παιδίον,[130] which would remind those acquainted with the childhood narrative in Matthew of the "child" and his "mother" (cf. Matt 2:11, 13-14, 20-21). A connotation of ὡς παιδίον ("like a child") from Isa 53:2, though that would later be translated by ܐܝܟ ܝܠܘܕܐ (*ʾak yallūdā*),[131] would bring to mind the Suffering Servant of God. But it is not unthinkable that 𝔊 had βρέφος[132] (normally translated by ܥܘܠܐ [*ʿūlā*] or ܝܠܘܕܐ [*yallūdā*]) or even νήπιος.[133] That the μήτηρ/ܐܡܐ (*ʾemmā*) is no longer pregnant is shown by the Ethpe. of ܛܥܢ (*ṭʿen*), which occurs only here and expresses being "carried" with care.[134] Frankenberg's retroversion of the masculine participle of ܐܬܛܥܢ (*ʾeṭṭʿen*) by ἠνέχθην,[135] rather than ἐβαστάχθην, has its points.[136] However, it is impossible to attain linguistic certainty, since there is no literary model for 5a.

For the first half of the image in 5b also, which has nothing to do with the "milk of the Lord,"[137] there is no model from the Bible or elsewhere. The expected subject of the common verb "to give" (used in similar ways in 19:5 and 38:12; cf. 6:12) would be "mother," since the primal liquid nourishment "appears" "only when a mother and her baby are joined together."[138] The "milk" becomes metaphorical, in the first place, because the "group" of 4a takes the place of the mother (see on τάγμα above). At the same time, "a kind of double level metaphor"[139] comes into being, because γάλα/ܚܠܒܐ (*ḥalbā*)–quite unlike the passages 8:16 or 19:1-4[140]–moves into the background, and the emphasis falls on the "dew of the Lord" in apposition to it. The search for an "adequate explanation . . . of the Divine dew" turns up both Isa 26:19 LXX, ἡ γὰρ δρόσος ἡ παρὰ σοῦ ἴαμα αὐτοῖς ἐστιν ("for the dew from thee is healing to them"),[141] and Hos 14:6 LXX, where the Lord says: ἔσομαι ὡς δρόσος τῷ Ισραηλ ("I will be as dew to Israel").[142] The phrase ὡς νεφέλη δρόσου ("as a cloud of dew"), used eschatologically, taken from Isa 18:4 LXX, can be found in the background of the next Ode (36:7a). The genitive of κύριος/ܡܪܝܐ (*māryā*), "Lord," relating to the metaphorical "dew,"[143] which is linked to that other liquid "milk," wrenches the term out of its conventional context of "comfort and refreshment"[144] and proclaims it theologically to be the eschatological food, but without making it a "sacrament" of ascension.[145]

The bicolon 6a-b in no sense "continues the motif of motherhood."[146] For the term ܡܘܗܒܬܐ (*mawhabtā*), "gift," which corresponds either to δόμα[147] or to

126 Kaegi, 514.
127 Ibid., 334.
128 See, as a starting point, Harris and Mingana, 2:169, 381–83; Emerton, "Problems," 376–77.
129 Charlesworth, 125; idem, *Reflections*, 130, 160; he even includes the Ethpe. of ܛܥܢ (*ṭʿen*).
130 BDAG, *s.v.* παιδίον, 1.
131 Rahlfs, 2:639; *OTSy*, pt. 3 fasc. 1, p. 97.
132 Frankenberg, 30; BDAG, *s.v.* βρέφος, 2.
133 BAGD, *s.v.* νήπιος, 1; Payne Smith, 1:1472.
134 Payne Smith, 1:1499.
135 Frankenberg, 30; cf. BDAG and LSJ, *s.v.* φέρω.
136 Payne Smith, 1:1499; BDAG and LSJ, *s.v.* βαστάζω.
137 Contra Bauer, 615; Franzmann, 247.
138 Bauer, 615, with reference to 40:1b.
139 Franzmann, 247.
140 See BDAG, *s.v.* γάλα, "milk"; Payne Smith, 1:1273.
141 Rahlfs, 2:599; Brenton, 860; Harris and Mingana, 2:382.
142 Rahlfs, 2:501; Brenton, 1080; cf. ܛܠܐ (*ṭallā*) in *OTSy*, pt. 3 fasc. 4, on this passage; Payne Smith, 1:1471.
143 Payne Smith, 1:1471; LSJ, *s.v.* δρόσος. In the parts where Latin was spoken, also, the term *ros* was applied to any dripping "moisture" and, at least since Cicero, was poetically paired with *vitalis* as "milk from the breasts" (Georges, 2:2409; cf. the later *lacteus ros* in Minucius Felix *Octavius* 18.2; Bernhard Kytzler, *M. Minucius Felix, Octavius* [Ger.–Lat.; Munich: Kösel, 1965] 104–5).
144 Lampe, 388.
145 Contra Gunkel, 320.
146 Contra Franzmann, 247.
147 Frankenberg, 30; BDAG, *s.v.* δόμα, "gift."

χάρισμα (see Excursus 37),[148] does not refer back to the metaphorical "milk." Whether the instrumental phrase at the end of 6a refers, in addition to the divine "Lord," to the complete apposition "dew of the Lord" as a "divine essence,"[149] must be questioned in the light of such passages as 11:9b (χάρισμα in 𝔊) or 15:7a. Following on from the images of 5a-b, it must be considered possible that the *hapax legomenon* ܐܬܪܒܝܬ (*ʾetrabbī*, Ethpa. of ܪܒܐ [*rbā*]),[150] "I grew up," contains allusions to the childhood narrative—in this case from Luke or an oral tradition; cf. Luke 1:80 and 2:40 (παιδίον ηὔξανεν, "the child grew"), in the second passage expanded by χάρις θεοῦ, "favor of God"; 2:52 (Ἰησοῦς προέκοπτεν . . . χάριτι παρὰ θεῷ καὶ ἀνθρώποις, "Jesus increased . . . in favor with God and man"); 4:16 (ἦν [ἀνα]τεθραμμένος, "he had been brought up").[151] The periphrastic passive of (ἀνα)τρέφω is translated by ܐܬܪܒܝ (*ʾetrabbī*),[152] while both ηὔξανεν and προέκοπτεν appear in Syriac as ܪܒܐ ܗܘܐ (*rābē-wā*). Exactly how this passage appeared in 𝔊 is nearly impossible to determine, especially with regard to the use of αὐξάνω.[153] Frankenberg's retroversion ηὐξήθην[154] finds some support in the passage 1 Pet 2:2, although the imagery of that verse is only distantly related to *Ode* 35:5a-6a: ὡς ἀρτιγέννητα βρέφη τὸ λογικὸν ἄδολον γάλα ἐπιποθήσατε, ἵνα ἐν αὐτῷ αὐξηθῆτε (ܬܬܪܒܘܢ [*tetrabbōn*]) εἰς σωτηρίαν ("Like newborn infants, long for the pure, spiritual milk, so that by it you may grow into salvation").[155]

It is only in 𝔖 that 6b forms "an inclusio for the first three stanzas with 1a by the repetition of the root ܢܘܚ."[156] A similar observation could be true of 𝔊 if, in addition to κατ᾽ ἀνάπαυσιν in 1a (see above), 6b had employed ἀνεπαυσάμην,[157] both of which are extremely doubtful. For, besides an intransitive καταπαύω[158] and the middle voice of ἀναπαύω,[159] the Ethpe. of ܢܘܚ, ܢܚ (*nāḥ*), "found rest," can also represent, for example, the passive of παρακαλέω (cf. Luke 16:25, where Abraham in paradise says of the beggar Lazarus lying in his bosom: παρακαλεῖται/ܡܬܬܢܝܚ [*mettnīḥ*], "he is comforted").[160] A euphemistic use of τελευτάω probably does not need to be considered because of the prepositional phrase that follows (see Excursus 3).[161] After Excursus 35, the exact meaning of the verb of 6b will be examined again, with reference to parallels in meaning.

Excursus 35: "Plērōma," "Fullness," "Fill," "Fulfill," and "Full" in the *Odes of Solomon*

All the terms to be discussed are derived from the root ܡܠܐ.[162] Four of them are *hapax legomena* and will be dealt with first. The Pa. ܡܠܝ (*mallī*) states that the bright day and the dark night "complete" the indescribable beauty of God (16:17b). As in almost all these cases, it is necessary to decide, in the course of the commentary, what equivalent Greek word was

148 BDAG, *s.v.* χάρισμα, "gift" etc.; Payne Smith, 1:1567.
149 Widengren, 15.
150 Payne Smith, 2:3791.
151 See NA[27] and *NTSy* on these passages.
152 BDAG, *s.vv.* ἀνατρέφω, a: "be nourished"; τρέφω, 2: "Pass[ive] grow up."
153 BDAG, *s.v.* αὐξάνω; cf. προκόπτω.
154 Frankenberg, 30.
155 NA[27], p. 600; *NTSy* on this passage; cf. Lattke, "Bildersprache," 105 = idem, *Bedeutung*, 4:32; Brox, *Petrusbrief*, 91–92.
156 Franzmann, 247.
157 Frankenberg, 30.
158 BDAG, *s.v.* καταπαύω, 3: "rest."
159 BDAG, *s.v.* ἀναπαύω, 3b; cf. ἐπαναπαύομαι, 1–2. The reference in BDAG at ἀναπαύω, 3b, to "Ox 654 (= ASyn 187, 20//GTh 2), 8f: [ἀναπα]ήσεται; cp. GHb 187, 17," where the middle voice of ἀναπαύω is allegedly used absolutely for the "goal of gnosticism [*sic*]," should be revised, since it is not clear whether the term in *P. Oxy.* 654.8-9 is ἀναπαήσεται or ἐπαναπαήσεται, i.e., ἐπαναπαύσεται (see Harold W. Attridge, "Appendix: The Greek Fragments [of the Gospel according to Thomas]," in B. Layton, ed., *Nag Hammadi Codex II,2-7 together with XIII,2*, Brit. Lib. Or.4926[1] and P.Oxy. 1, 654, 655*, vol. 1: *Gospel according to Thomas, Gospel according to Philip, Hypostasis of the Archons, and Indexes* [NHS 20; Leiden: Brill, 1989] 113).
160 BDAG, *s.v.* παρακαλέω, 4.
161 BDAG, *s.v.* τελευτάω: "to die"; Payne Smith, 2:2311–12.
162 Payne Smith, 2:2117–30.

used in the *Vorlage* or translation. That 𝔊 did not use φράζω[163] in the verse under discussion needs to be emphasized because of Frankenberg's fanciful retroversion.[164] In place of the simple πληρόω[165] or the composite ἀναπληρόω,[166] one might even consider the doubly composite ἀνταναπληρόω, meaning "to complete" in *reciprocal* or *complementary* fashion.[167] In the grotesque image of the father's breasts filled with milk (19:3a), the Ethpe. ܐܬܡܠܝ (*ʾeṯmlī*) corresponds to a passive form of (ἐμ)πίμπλημι or πληρόω.[168] The sense of the verb, which in this image is used quite literally, is as clear as the meaning of the adverb ܡܫܡܠܝܐܝܬ (*mšamlyāʾīṯ*), which must correspond to τελείως, referring to the tablet that the "finger of God altogether" covered with writing (23:21b).[169] The related term ܡܫܡܠܝܘܬܐ (*mšamlyūṯā*) should perhaps be translated "perfection" to differentiate it from the more dominant ܫܘܡܠܝܐ (*šumlāyā*): "and he anointed me from his perfection" (36:6a).[170] This should be the meaning assigned to the "fullness"[171] of the Most High in this passage.

The Pe. ܡܠܐ (*mlā*) in its five occurrences, added to the one of the passive participle ܡܠܐ (*mlē*) (11:23c ["everything is filled with fruit"]; 𝔊 merely has καρποφορεῖ), is used very diversely. One may assume that the Coptic word ⲙⲉϩ (*meh*) in 1:5a ("Your fruits are full . . .") and 1:5b ("full of your salvation") is equivalent to the Syriac ܡܠܐ (*mlē*). But whether, and where, 𝔊 used μεστοί[172] or πλήρεις[173] is not easily decided; indeed, instead of the second term, one may need to consider πεπληρωμένοι with the dative, not the genitive.[174]

In one of the five cases, the Pe. ܡܠܐ (*mlā*) means "to flood" (6:10), where ℭ uses ⲁⲙⲁϩⲧⲉ (*amahte*) in a different sense. Again in connection with water, the Syriac verb is used totally differently in 30:1a, where 𝔊 will have had ἀντλέω.[175] Since ܡܠܐ can also mean "to become full,"[176] the growth of the root in 38:18b should be described by a *passive* form of (ἐμ)πίμπλημι[177] or πληρόω[178] or perhaps by some other verb. The term ἐπλήρωσεν is attested in 11:2c ("[the Most High] filled me with his love"), but the last passage to be considered, which has been emended in the commentary, may not have had ἐπλήρωσεν in 𝔊: "The word of truth filled me" (12:1a).[179] Frankenberg may, after all, have been right to suggest ἐνέπλησε.[180]

The term ܫܘܡܠܝܐ (*šumlāyā*) occurs twelve times, and we will admit at once that the general equation of the term with *plērōma* is "anything but uncontroversial."[181] Neither *Ode* 11 𝔊 nor the Coptic quotations from the *Odes of Solomon* (1; 5; 6; 22; 25) have the Greek term πλήρωμα, which is attested as a Gnostic *terminus technicus*[182] only somewhat later than our date for the *Odes of Solomon* (first quarter of the second century C.E.), but it can be assumed that πλήρωμα was the term most often used in the Greek text and that τελειότης ("perfection, completeness"), or τελείωσις ("perfection," "fulfilment of a promise"), is less likely.[183] Delling's introductory remarks are very relevant to the problems of translating early or pre-Gnostic uses of ܫܘܡܠܝܐ (*šumlāyā*), when he says, about the term πλήρωμα, that there is a scholarly "tendency to use the general term 'fulness' or to leave the term untranslated."[184]

163 BDAG, *s.v.* φράζω: "explain, interpret."
164 Frankenberg, 18.
165 See commentary on that passage.
166 BDAG, *s.v.* ἀναπληρόω: "make complete."
167 Gerhard Delling, "πλήρης," *ThWNT* 6 (1959) 305; *TDNT* 6:307; but on Col 1:24, see BDAG, *s.v.* ἀνταναπληρόω.
168 Payne Smith, 2:2121; BDAG, *s.vv.* ἐμπί(μ)πλημι, 1; πίμπλημι, 1a; πληρόω, 1a.
169 Payne Smith, 2:2129; BDAG, *s.v.* τελείως: "fully, perfectly, completely, altogether."
170 Payne Smith, 2:2119; cf. BDAG, *s.v.* τελειότης.
171 Lattke, *Oden*, 196.
172 BDAG, *s.v.* μεστός.
173 BDAG, *s.v.* πλήρης.
174 Delling, "πλήρης," *ThWNT* 6:289 n. 22; *TDNT* 6:290 n. 22.
175 BDAG, *s.v.* ἀντλέω: "draw" water.
176 Payne Smith, 2:2118.
177 Contra Frankenberg, 33: ἔπλησε.
178 See LSJ, *s.v.* πληρόω: "becoming full."
179 See commentary on that passage.
180 Frankenberg, 14; see BDAG, *s.v.* ἐμπί(μ)πλημι, 1: "fill"; also πίμπλημι, 1: "fill, fulfill," e.g., "of a pers[on's] inner life"; on both verbs and their dominant meanings, see Gerhard Delling, "πίμπλημι, ἐμπίμπλημι, πλησμονή," *ThWNT* 6 (1959) 128–30; *TDNT* 6:129–30; the meaning "satisfy, satiate," often found for the compound verb, does not occur in the *Odes of Solomon*.
181 See Jörg Frey, review of Lattke in *ThLZ* 127 (2002) 1053, on "Gnosis."
182 BDAG, *s.v.* πλήρωμα, 3b; Lampe, 1095; see Delling, "πλήρης," *ThWNT* 6:299; *TDNT* 6:300.
183 Payne Smith, 2:2128; BDAG, *s.vv.* τελειότης, τελείωσις.
184 Delling, "πλήρης," *ThWNT* 6:297; *TDNT* 6:298.

Beginning with the less technical passages: in 9:4c ("and imperishable is *your plērōma*/fullness")[185] it could be τελειότης or τελείωσις as the "perfection"[186] parallel to eternal life. One of these terms is not so easy to imagine in the address to God in 18:8b ("but the *plērōma* is thy will") or in the soteriological statement of 19:5b ("those who receive [it, i.e. the mixture] are in the *plērōma* of the right [hand]"). At the hymnological climax of 26:7 ("*his* is the *plērōma*"), the question whether it is God or his works that are "perfect" has already been discussed in the exegesis.[187]

God's own "fullness" or "perfection" is found in 17:7b in a Gnosticizing context ("the Most High in his complete *plērōma*"). If the petition in 18:5 ("do not withhold thy *plērōma* from me") lies on the line of development of Col 2:9 and Eph 3:19, it throws a different light on 18:8b (see above). The "Father of knowledge" (7:7) is, in 7:11b, called the "*plērōma* of the Aeons and their Father."[188] The rather mythological statement in 7:13a-b ("toward *gnōsis* he laid out his way . . . and brought it over the whole *plērōma*") brings out the spatial character of this "fullness." In the expression "the perfection of his *gnōsis*" (23:4c), the nouns are soteriological complements, on the one hand, to the Lord's own knowledge (23:4a) and on the other to the *plērōma* of the Most High (see on 17:7b above). Whether the term πλήρωμα, in the statement of 41:13 about the "son of the Most High" ("he appeared in the *plērōma* of his Father"), is taken and adapted from Col 1:19 and John 1:16 will be discussed in its place.[189] The parallelism between the "height of the Lord" (36:2a) and "his *plērōma*/fullness and his glory" (36:2b) certainly has a mythological-spatial resonance. It should also be noted, in the same Ode (see on 36:6a below), that there is a distinction between ܫܘܡܠܝܐ (*šumlāyā*) and ܡܫܡܠܝܘܬܐ (*mšamlyūṯā*). If only for this reason, it is quite unlikely that 𝔊 used τελειότης in both cases.[190] This means that in 36:2b it is all but certain that πλήρωμα was used for a divine "perfection of being";[191] but in 35:6b the association with the soteriological concept of "rest, to find rest" argues rather for a Gnosticizing use of the term "*plērōma*." This leads back to a short discussion of the ending of stanza III of *Ode* 35.

The question mark that Greßmann puts after τελείωσις (= "perfection"), which he suggests as the equivalent of ܫܘܡܠܝܐ (*šumlāyā*) in 6b, is justified.[192] Whether he links his sacramental suggestion "consecration" to τελειότης[193] is not addressed by Gunkel in his translation, "I . . . found refreshment in his 'consecration.'"[194] The verb must be translated as "to find rest,"[195] which brings out the eschatological and also soteriological nature of the statement that forms the connection to stanza IV (cf., e.g., *2 Clem.* 5:5: ἀνάπαυσις τῆς μελλούσης βασιλείας καὶ ζωῆς αἰωνίου, "a rest in the coming kingdom and eternal life").[196] Whether the tradition of Eph 1:23 lies behind the term πλήρωμα/ܫܘܡܠܝܐ (*šumlāyā*) is hard to determine. What is clear is that God's "fullness" is not here equated with τὸ σῶμα Χριστοῦ ("the body of Christ") or ἐκκλησία ("church"), which means that it is still possible to identify the speaking "I" with "Christ." The best interpretation of 6b can be found in the Coptic-Gnostic *Gospel of Truth* (NHC I,*3*), which, in addition to "the Church's scripture, including many of the Pauline epistles, the Synoptic Gospels, the Gospel of John, Hebrews and Revelation,"[197] probably also

185 Emphasis added. As a supplement to Delling's thorough account ("πλήρης," *ThWNT* 6:297–304; *TDNT* 6:298–305), one may list the following senses for πλήρωμα: "totality," "completion, perfection," "fulfilment" (as, e.g., the Old Testament by the New), "whole body," "company, total number of persons" (e.g., in connection with the angels or the church), "plenitude, fullness, divine perfection" (theologically, see Eph 1:20-23), "Gnost[ic], of totality of aeons, whole of divine sphere" (Lampe, 1094–95).

186 See Gerhard Delling, "τέλος, . . . , τελειότης, κτλ.," *ThWNT* 8 (1969) 79, 86; *TDNT* 8:78, 85.

187 See commentary on that passage.

188 See commentary on that passage.

189 In the meanwhile, see Delling, "πλήρης," *ThWNT* 6:301–2; *TDNT* 6:303–4.

190 Contra Frankenberg, 31.

191 See Delling, "πλήρης," *ThWNT* 6:299, 302; *TDNT* 6:300–301, 304, although in n. 14 he leans toward Frankenberg.

192 Gunkel, 319.

193 Like Frankenberg, 30.

194 Greßmann's own later translation of 6b is "I . . . found refreshment in his perfection" (see Greßmann, 467). Bauer (p. 615) retains "perfection."

195 Bauer, 615.

196 Ehrman, 1:172–73; see additional references in Käsemann, *Wandering People*, 137–39 = *Gottesvolk*, 85–86, and Schenke, *Herkunft*, 38.

197 Harold W. Attridge and George W. MacRae, "The Gospel of Truth. [NHC] I,*3*:16.31–43.24," in H. W. Attridge, ed., *Nag Hammadi Codex I (The Jung Codex): Introductions, Texts, Translations, Indices* (NHS 22; Leiden: Brill, 1985) 80–81.

assimilated the *Odes of Solomon*. For there, in 41,13-14, in the section on the "purpose for which Jesus was sent into the World" (40,30–41,35), it says: "and his [viz., the Son's] proper place of rest is his [viz., the Father's] *plērōma* (πλήρωμα)."[198]

■ **7** This short finale does not refer to "the early cruciform position for praying"[199] and indeed does not contain any "liturgical overtones."[200] There is certainly no trace of "a peculiar baptismal rite."[201] If 35:7a-c and 27:1-3 (and also 42:1-2) interpret each other, the "spreading out of the hands" (in addition to 37:1, see 21:1 and Excursus 27) has a far more specific meaning than merely "the identifying sign of the believer," and the "ascent" is more than the "ascension" of the "soul."[202] For the speaking "I" means its complete *self*, as the three verbs, with their rising pattern of actions, clearly show. McNeil thinks that 35:7 is spoken "either *ex ore odistae* or *ex ore Christi*."[203] A third possibility might be some member of the "group/association" mentioned in 4a, who has already used the key word "salvation" in 2b and spoken in 6b of eschatological "rest."[204] What is important is that again Christ as the speaker cannot be categorically excluded, as Charlesworth, for instance, does.[205]

Anyone who finds an allusion to the crucifixion in the first part of 7a (cf. John 21:18: ἐκτενεῖς τὰς χεῖράς σου, "you will stretch out your hands"; ܬܦܫܘܛ ܐܝܕܝܟ [*tepšoṭ ʾiḏayk*])[206] will find nothing further in the remainder of 7. The *hapax legomenon* ܣܘܠܩܐ (*sullāqā*), in the immediately following prepositional phrase, means that ἐκπετάννυμι as well as ἐκτείνω[207] must be considered as an equivalent of the Pe. ܦܫܛ (*pšaṭ*),[208] but without reference to Isa 65:2 (cf. Rom 10:21). So the "stretching out of the hands" is not so much a "gesture of prayer"[209] as "an imploring gesture,"[210] which is now explained by the mythologoumenon[211] of the "ascent to heaven."[212] For one may assume that 𝔊 used ἀνάλημψις as the term for "ascension," as in Luke 9:51 (cf. ἀναλαμβάνω in Mark 16:19; Acts 1:2, 11, 22; 1 Tim 3:16).[213] In contrast

198 Schenke, *Herkunft*, 55. The well-preserved Coptic text, with an English translation, runs as follows ⲁⲩⲱ ⲡⲉϥⲙⲁ ⲛⲙ̄ⲧⲁⲛ ⲡ̄ⲙⲓⲛ ⲙ̄ⲙⲁϥ ⲡⲉ ⲡⲉϥⲡⲗⲏⲣⲱⲙⲁ, "And his own resting-place is his pleroma [*sic*]" (Attridge and MacRae, "Gospel of Truth," 114–15). A number of annotations deal with the ambiguous term "*plērōma*" and also the term "rest" (Attridge and MacRae, "Gospel of Truth," 40 [on 16,35]; 64 [on 22,12]; and 130 [on 41,13-14]). In the final version of his translation of *Gos. Truth* 41,13-14 Schenke prefers "fullness" to "*plērōma*" for the term πλήρωμα (see Schenke, "Evangelium Veritatis," 43; on the spatial aspect, see Craig A. Evans, "The Meaning of πλήρωμα in Nag Hammadi," *Bib* 65 [1984] 260–61).

199 Contra Charlesworth, 125.

200 Contra Franzmann, 247.

201 Daniel Plooij, "The Attitude of the Outspread Hands ('Orante') in Early Christian Literature and Art," *ExpT* 23 (1911–12) 202; see Lattke, *Bedeutung*, 3:142.

202 Contra Diettrich, 118 nn. 4–5.

203 Brian McNeil, "A Liturgical Source in Acts of Peter 38," *VC* 33 (1979) 343.

204 Franzmann ("Man of Rest," 420) calls it "no more than speculation" that "the idea of rest is so important for the work that the odist, or final redactor of the Odes (if there was more than one author), or a later copyist may well have considered 'Solomon' to be a fitting pseudonym for the work." Drijvers ("Salomoschriften," 732) goes further than that, saying: "The odist is Christlike, living in a state of 'rest'. That is the link to Solomon 'who shall be a man of rest' and 'son of God' (1 Chr 22:9-10)."

205 Charlesworth, 126.

206 NA[27], p. 319; *NTSy*, on this passage; BDAG, *s.v.* ἐκτείνω, 1: "Of one who is crucified."

207 Frankenberg, 31.

208 Payne Smith, 2:3318.

209 Bauer, 615.

210 BDAG, *s.v.* ἐκπετάννυμι.

211 On μυθολογέω ("tell mythic tales") we have the remark—centuries before Rudolf Bultmann—of Plutarch *Is. Os.* 11 (355 B [LCL 5:28–29]), "you must not think that any of these tales actually happened in the manner in which they are related." See Herwig Görgemanns, ed., *Plutarch, Drei religionsphilosophische Schriften: Über den Aberglauben; Über die späte Strafe der Gottheit; Über Isis und Osiris* (Sammlung Tusculum; Düsseldorf/Zurich: Artemis & Winkler, 2003) 152–53.

212 On the use of ܒ (*b-*), see BDAG, *s.v.* ἐν, 2b and 5b.

213 BDAG, *s.v.* ἀνάλημψις. The sense of "death, decease" is not relevant here. McNeil remarks, on 35:7: "We are never told explicitly in the Odes that the Saviour died" (see McNeil, "Sufferings," 32). "In Lk. 9:51 ἀνάλημψις thus refers to the death of Jesus. . . . Possibly it also refers to the taking up, or taking back, to God which begins with death and which is completed with the Lucan ascension" (Gerhard Delling, "λαμβάνω, ἀναλαμβάνω, ἀνάλημψις, κτλ.," *ThWNT* 4 [1942] 9; *TDNT* 4:9).

to the use of the Aph. of ܣܠܩ (*sleq*) in 22:1 and 29:4, the term ܣܘܠܩܐ (*sullāqā*), derived from the same root, which is used specifically for Christ's ascent into heaven,[214] does not evoke an image of the "deeps" or "Sheol."[215] The term ܢܦܫܐ (*nap̄šā*), "soul," in the genitive, with first singular possessive suffix, does not make a contrast with σῶμα/ܦܓܪܐ (*pagrā*), "body," instead expressing the "reflexive relationship," as ψυχή does.[216] But it is not certain that τῆς ψυχῆς μου[217] was used in 𝔊. If we exclude the reflexive pronoun ἐμαυτοῦ, which, when used with a preposition (e.g., ἀπό, ἐξ, περί, ὑπέρ) or in the accusative with a transitive verb, often corresponds to ܢܦܫ (*nap̄š*),[218] a different possibility becomes a probability. For constructions such as Rom 14:5 (ἐν τῷ ἰδίῳ νοΐ, "in his own mind"), 1 Cor 9:7 (ἰδίοις ὀψωνίοις, "at his own expense"), or Gal 6:5 (τὸ ἴδιον φορτίον, "her/his own load") suggest that the second half of 7a—with a strong argument for a Greek original—corresponds, without the addition of the personal pronoun μου, to the prepositional phrase ἐν τῇ ἰδίᾳ ἀναλήμψει[219] = "in/at my own ascension."[220]

That the stretching out of the (arms and) hands in 7a would have been a vertical rather than a horizontal gesture (cf. 27:1a)[221] is supported by 7b.[222] The *hapax legomenon* ܐܬܬܪܨ (*ʾettarraṣ*, Ethpa. of ܬܪܨ [*traṣ*]), used reflexively, "I erected myself,"[223] reinforces the link with 27:3 and 42:2. Both passages use ܬܪܝܨܐ (*trīṣā*) as an adjective or as a noun. Since an active form of κατευθύνω does not come under consideration,[224] the choice of a Greek equivalent for the Syriac verb is between a passive form of ὀρθόω[225] and the reflexive passive of ἀνορθόω.[226] As in some earlier cases (see on 2a, 3b, 5a, 6a above), it is impossible to decide. What is clear is that the building or standing up of the speaking "I" was directed toward the transcendental "Most High" (see Excursus 17).

There are three reasons for rejecting the generally accepted reading of ܐܬܦܪܩܬ in 7c as the Ethpe. *ʾeṯparqeṯ* ("I was redeemed"). In the first place, both Syriac manuscripts have a point above the ܬ in the "preformative" ܐܬ.[227] Second, the speaking "I" has already spoken of being "saved" in 2b. And, third, the construction of Ethpe. first singular with ܠܘܬܗ (*lwāṯeh* = πρὸς αὐτόν, "toward him," i.e., the Most High; cf. John 1:1-2) would sound as peculiar as ἐσώθην πρὸς αὐτόν[228] and would also fit badly with the actions described by the other two verbs. So it is most likely that this is the Ethpa. of ܦܪܩ (*praq*).[229] Although, again, the exact verb used in 𝔊 cannot be determined, the passive aorist of κινέω[230] may be suggested with a linguistic reference to Jer 10:4 LXX.[231]

---

214 Payne Smith, 2:2649.

215 Neither the concept "Sheol" nor that of "death" can properly be imported here. It is certainly not "obvious that the answer to the question, 'Whence was he lifted up?', must be, 'From Sheol'. Does not this imply 'death'?" (McNeil, "Sufferings," 32). At most one might agree with Bertram's "ascension from the Cross" (see Georg Bertram, "Die Himmelfahrt Jesu vom Kreuz aus und der Glaube an seine Auferstehung," in Karl Ludwig Schmidt, ed., *Festgabe für Adolf Deissmann zum 60. Geburtstag 7. Nov. 1926* [Tübingen: Mohr Siebeck, 1927] 187–217), that is, if it can be shown that there is an allusion to the cross in this Ode.

216 BDAG, *s.v.* ψυχή, 2g; cf. Payne Smith, 2:2431.

217 Frankenberg, 31.

218 Cf. *NTSy* with the passages cited in BDAG, *s.v.* ἐμαυτοῦ.

219 See BDAG, *s.v.* ἴδιος, 2; BDF and BDR §286.

220 See Pierre, 170: "en ma propre montée," although she unnecessarily mentions "auto-crucifixion."

221 See commentary on that passage.

222 A further study of H (Charlesworth, *Manuscripts*, 78, line 7) enables me to correct the erroneous statement that ܡܪܝܡܐ (also found in N) was changed to ܡܪܝܐ "Lord," as in 1a, 4a, and 5b, by striking out a letter (Lattke, *Bedeutung*, 1:168; idem, *Oden*, 194 n. 13). It is more likely that the misspelling ܡܪܝܐ (*māryā*) for ܡܪܝܡܐ (*mrayymā*) was immediately rectified.

223 Payne Smith, 2:4509: *se erexit*.

224 Contra Frankenberg, 31: κατεύθυνα.

225 BDAG, *s.v.* ὀρθόω; Payne Smith, 2:4509: ὠρθώθη.

226 BDAG, *s.v.* ἀνορθόω, 2; Payne Smith, 2:4509: ἀνωρθώθη.

227 See Segal, *Point*, 18. This point is found also in 9:12 (only H) and 38:16 (H and N). In 17:4 H, on the other hand, the point is above the ܦ and probably denotes a "hard" pronunciation (Brockelmann, *Grammatik* §10).

228 Frankenberg, 31.

229 Payne Smith, 2:3294: *amotus est, dislocatus est*. The change from Ethpe. (Lattke, *Bedeutung*, 1:168–69) to Ethpa. (Lattke, *Oden*, 194) should also be recorded in the concordance (Lattke, *Bedeutung*, 2:158).

230 See LSJ, *s.v.* κινέω, B2: "to be moved."

231 Rahlfs, 2:673; Payne Smith, 2:3294.

There are good reasons for identifying the speaker of *Ode* 35 with the exalted Christ, and 7a-c should take its place in early Christian works[232] beside the New Testament writings that describe the ascension of the Lord Jesus Christ in various mythological ways and with diverse honorifics: Mark 16:19 (*ἀνελήμφθη εἰς τὸν οὐρανόν*, "he was taken up into heaven"), Luke 9:51 (*τῆς ἀναλήμψεως αὐτοῦ*, "of his ascension"), Luke 24:51 (*ἀνεφέρετο εἰς τὸν οὐρανόν*, "he was carried up into heaven"), John 6:62 (*τὸν υἱὸν τοῦ ἀνθρώπου ἀναβαίνοντα*, "the Son of man ascending"), John 20:17 (*ἀναβαίνω πρὸς τὸν πατέρα μου*, "I am ascending to my Father"), Acts 1:2 (*ἀνελήμφθη*, "he was taken up"), Acts 1:9 (*ἐπήρθη*, "he was lifted up"), Acts 1:11 (*ἀναλημφθεὶς ἀφ' ὑμῶν εἰς τὸν οὐρανόν*, "he was taken up from you into heaven"), Acts 1:22 (*ἀνελήμφθη ἀφ' ἡμῶν*, "he was taken up from us"), 1 Tim 3:16 (*ἀνελήμφθη ἐν δόξῃ*, "taken up in glory"), 1 Pet 3:22 (*πορευθεὶς εἰς οὐρανόν*, "he has gone into heaven"); cf. Eph 4:8-10 and Heb 4:14.

The conclusion of *Ode* 35 could have found a place in Rick Strelan's excellent essay on Acts 1:9-11,[233] which, showing that *νεφέλη* is an "element . . . with revelatory and ascent significance,"[234] may even cast some light on the "cloud of peace" at the beginning in 1b.

232 Cf. Lattke, *Bedeutung*, 4:189–225.

233 Rick Strelan, *Strange Acts: Studies in the Cultural World of the Acts of the Apostles* (BZNW 126; Berlin/New York: de Gruyter, 2004) 33–49: "Up, Up, and Away?"

234 Ibid., 36–38.

36

Ode 36: Address of the Exalted One

(I) 1a The Spirit of the Lord rested upon me[a],
1b and she lifted me up to the height[b]
2a and set me on my feet in the height of the Lord
2b before his *plērōma*/fullness and his glory.
(II) 2c While I gave praise by the composition of his odes,
3a she [viz., the Spirit] brought me forth before the face of the Lord.
3b And although I was a (son of) man, I was called the Shining One, the Son of God,
4a while I was glorious among the glorious[c]
4b and was great among the great.
(III) 5a For according to the greatness of the Most High, so she made me,
5b and according to his renewal he renewed me.
(IV) 6a And he anointed me from his perfection,
6b and I was/became one of those beside/near to him.
7a And my mouth was opened like a cloud of dew,
7b and my heart gushed forth a flood[d] of righteousness.
8a And my access [i.e., being brought near] was in peace,
8b and I was established in the spirit of the plan of salvation.
Hallelujah.

a 1a ܥܠ (H* and N) corrected to ܥܠܝ H.
b 1b ܠܪܘܡܐ N; ܠܡܪܘܡܐ H.
c 4a ܒܡܫܒ̈ܚܐ N; ܒܡܫܒ̈ܚܢܐ H.
d 7b ܠܒܝ ܡܒܘܥܬܐ N; ܠܒܝ ܐܝܟ ܡܒܘܥܬܐ H.

Introduction

Ode 36 is preserved in two Syriac manuscripts.[1] Although this Ode is closely related to the preceding one,[2] it is not permissible to treat these two first-person discourses, which are hardly "baptismal hymns,"[3] merely as fragments and melt them down to make a new whole.[4] Abramowski lists *Odes* 35 and 36 among "the *Odes* in which the human being, as *filius adoptivus* [emphasis added], undergoes an alteration toward God."[5] *Ode* 35 could already have been uttered by the Lord (Jesus) Christ, redeemed and ascended to the Most High, but *Ode* 36 shows even more marked messianic traits,[6] beginning already before v. 3.[7] After all, 1-2b

1 Mss.: Codex H, 26a–b; Codex N, 150ᵛ (ܣ). Ed./trans.: Charlesworth, 126–28; Franzmann, 248–52; Lattke, 3:125–40.
2 Pierre, 171.
3 Bernard, 121; Schille, 64.
4 Contra Grimme, 123; cf. Lattke, *Bedeutung*, 3:103.
5 Abramowski, 57.
6 Contra Kittel, 127–30.
7 Harris and Mingana, 2:384: "Christ speaks"; similarly Charlesworth, 127. Gunkel originally strongly identified "Christ"—even "Jesus"—with the speaking "I" (see Gunkel, 300–302), but in later years he distanced himself from that first impression and was inclined "to attribute" the "hymn" to the person of "the human poet" (Gunkel, *Aufsätze*, 184–85).

(stanza I)[8] and 2c (beginning of stanza II) are uttered by the same masculine speaking "I," who should not be identified with the poet (odist). Diettrich's prodigious exclusions of alleged interpolations, which far outdo Harnack and Spitta,[9] end with a final *reductio ad absurdum* in the following statement: "What the singer of 1, 2 and 4 has to say, after the manner of an apocalypse (cf. especially the *Book of Enoch*), in the original Ode, about his sojourn in Heaven, must have been so shocking to later readers that it had to be replaced by the innocuous passages 3 and 5-8."[10] It would have been interesting to hear more about this shocking material, but the manuscripts have transmitted the only available text of the Ode, in which the terms "Lord" and "Most High," as in *Ode* 35, refer to the transcendent God (cf. "son of God" in 3b).[11] In 3 and 5-8 neither 3b nor 6a is innocuous, as will be shown.

Interpretation

■ **1-2b** In almost all translations of 1a, the ambivalent verb form ܐܬܬܢܝܚܬ is read as Ethpe. first person singular perfect (*ʾettnīḥet*), which the following prepositional expression in H* and N seems to make obvious: "I rested on the Spirit of the Lord." Blaszczak emends ܥܠ (*ʿal*) to ܥܠܝ (*ʿlay*) and reads ܐܬܬܢܝܚܬ as the Ethpa. third person feminine singular perfect (*ʾettnīḥat*) and translates: "The Spirit of the Lord rested on/upon me."[12] This emendation, first suggested orally by John Strugnell (Harvard), which would transform ܪܘܚܗ ܕܡܪܝܐ (*rūḥeh d-māryā*) into a post-positioned subject, has now been confirmed by the discovery of a so far unnoticed correction of ܥܠ (*ʿal*) to ܥܠܝ (*ʿlay*) in H.[13] This throws new light on the opening of *Ode* 36, where the strange reading of H* and N reduced Greßmann to a despairing suggestion of καθίζεσθαι in an allegedly misunderstood original[14] and inspired Gunkel to an idiosyncratic comparison of the Spirit to "the wings of an enormous bird,"[15] while Frankenberg describes his own retroversion (ἀνεπαυσάμην ἐπὶ πνεύματι τοῦ κυρίου) as meaning "spiritual recreation,"[16] but for Zahn the Ode (including the *lectio recepta* for 1a) "does not pose any particular difficulties."[17]

The new *varia lectio* in H corresponds to a Greek original, founded on a fusion of Isa 11:2 LXX (ἀναπαύσεται ἐπ' αὐτὸν πνεῦμα τοῦ θεοῦ, "the Spirit of God shall rest upon him"; cf. 1 Pet 4:14)[18] and the even more christologically influential Isa 61:1 LXX (πνεῦμα κυρίου ἐπ' ἐμέ, "the Spirit of the Lord is upon me").[19] So the *Vorlage* of the Ethpe., identical with the Ettaph., of ܢܘܚ, ܢܚ (*nāḥ*) will have been the middle voice of ἀναπαύω[20] rather than the compound ἐπαναπαύομαι (cf. Num 11:25-26 and 2 Kgs 2:15, both using ἐπί and πνεῦμα).[21] Only ἐπ' ἐμέ can be considered equivalent to ܥܠܝ (*ʿlay*)

8 In codex H, unlike N, there is no mark of division between 2b and 2c. Franzmann (pp. 248–50) unnecessarily divides 2a into 2a-b, but correctly recognizes 2c (her 2d) as the beginning of stanza II.

9 Harnack, 66–67; Spitta, 287–88.

10 Diettrich, 119.

11 The subdivision of the unusually long line 3b into 3b-c (Harris and Mingana, vol. 1, on this passage; Charlesworth, 126), or even into 3b-d (Franzmann, 248), is capricious and not supported by either manuscript.

12 Blaszczak, 9, 11.

13 See Michael Lattke, "Eine übersehene Textvariante in den Oden Salomos (OdSal 36,1a)," *ZAC* 8 (2004) 346–49.

14 Greßmann in Gunkel, 299; cf. Greßmann, 467.

15 Gunkel, 300; idem, *Aufsätze*, 185.

16 Frankenberg, 31, 97: "geistige Erquickung."

17 Zahn, 699. At the same time, Zahn does count *Ode* 36 with *Odes* 10 and 28 among "the poems in which the Savior speaks of himself."

18 Blaszczak, 11.

19 Rahlfs, 2:581, 648; Brenton, 846, 896. Cf. in the New Testament Matt 5:3 (on which see Michael Lattke, "Glückselig durch den Geist (Matthäus 5,3)" in Cornelius Mayer et al., eds., *Nach den Anfängen fragen: Gerhard Dautzenberg zum 60. Geburtstag am 30. Januar 1994* [Gießener Schriften zur Theologie und Religionspädagogik des Fachbereichs Evangelische Theologie und Katholische Theologie und deren Didaktik der Justus-Liebig-Universität 8; Gießen: Selbstverlag, 1994] 375–80); Matt 11:5; Luke 4:18-19; Acts 4:27; 10:38 (on all these passages, see Ferdinand Hahn, *Theologie des Neuen Testaments* [2 vols.; Tübingen: Mohr Siebeck, 2002] 1:530, 2:236). The continuation of Isa 61:1 LXX (οὗ εἵνεκεν ἔχρισέν με) will later have a decisive part to play (see on 6a below).

20 BDAG, *s.v.* ἀναπαύω, 4, with preposition [ἐπί] "*rest upon*"; Frankenberg, 31: ἀνεπαυσάμην.

21 Payne Smith, 2:2311; BDAG, *s.v.* ἐπαναπαύομαι, 1.

in this passage.[22] Although the imagery of the *Odes of Solomon* can be subversive and grotesque,[23] the following excursus will show that the corrected reading of H can hold its place in the generality of those related images, that is, the Spirit rested on the speaking "I" and not *vice versa* (cf. esp. 28:1c).

Excursus 36: "Spirit" and "Wind" in the *Odes of Solomon*

Unlike the New Testament, in which πνεῦμα is a common term,[24] the *Odes of Solomon* employ πνεῦμα/ܪܘܚܐ (*rūḥā*) very sparingly. One must remember, also, that "[i]n spite of Stoicism, πνεῦμα has only slight and secondary significance in Greek thought as a whole. This is in contrast to its leading role in the NT."[25] In reference to the "development of the pneumatic self of Gnosticism,"[26] the only possible relevant passage would be *Ode* 28:6-7.[27] As a whole, the *Odes*, with respect to the few aspects of the term that occur there, stand with the Old Testament,[28] whose statements, especially about God's πνεῦμα/רוּחַ (*ruaḥ*), were as influential in antique Judaism[29] as in early Christianity.[30]

It is perhaps worth noting that the verbal noun πνεῦμα is neuter, while the term ܪܘܚܐ (*rūḥā*), derived from ܪܘܚ, ܪܚ (*rāḥ*), is treated in the *Odes of Solomon* as a feminine.[31] Jacob Kremer's words of warning must be taken into consideration: "In determining the sense of π[νεῦμα] one must remember that the usual tr[anslation] *spirit* (Germ[an] *Geist*) often erects a barrier to understanding, since in English one often associates 'spirit' with an insubstantial being (a 'ghost') or with understanding or reason (νοῦς). In addition π[νεῦμα] is not seldom conceived under the influence of church doctrine as a 'person.'"[32]

In two of the nineteen cases where ܪܘܚܐ (*rūḥā*) occurs, the Greek equivalent could have been ἄνεμος (6:1a; 29:10b). But in the first occurrence, where the "wind" that blows through the cithara is compared to the speaking "Spirit of the Lord" (6:2a), 𝔊 too may have had a play on the word πνεῦμα. The second quite clearly refers to the chaff blown away by the "wind" (ἄνεμος) of Ps 1:4 and Wis 5:14.

The exultant speaking "I" of *Ode* 40 speaks of its "spirit" in parallel with its "soul" (4b-c), not as a distinct part of itself but as the total of its "inner life" (cf. Luke 1:46-47).[33] The only occurrence of the plural of ܪܘܚܐ, in 6:7b (ܪܘܚܬܢ [*rūḥāṯan*], "our spirits"), comes about because 6:7a has "he gave *us*" (see on 6:7b below). Rom 8:16 is one example of how, instead of using a plural, a plural suffix can be attached to the singular (τῷ πνεύματι ἡμῶν/ܠܪܘܚܢ [*l-rūḥan*]).[34] Whether the term ܪܘܚܐ linked to the

22 BDAG, *s.v.* ἐπί, 14bβ; Payne Smith, 2:2886. I think it most possible that older Syriac manuscripts—which have unfortunately not survived—of the *Odes of Solomon* also had ܥܠܝ (*ʿlay*). In the *Estrangela* script, the difference between ܥܠܝ and ܥܠ is hardly visible. The erroneous ܥܠ (in H* and N) for ܥܠܝ seems to have two main causes: first, the ambivalence of ܐܬܬܢܝܚܬ; and, second, the fact that the subject was post-positioned in the original Syriac (and now in H as emended).

23 See Lattke, "Bildersprache," 100–108 = idem, *Bedeutung*, 24–35.

24 Eduard Schweizer, "πνεῦμα (D–F) κτλ.," *ThWNT* 6 (1959) 394–449; *TDNT* 6:396–451.

25 Hermann Martin Kleinknecht, "πνεῦμα. A. πνεῦμα im Griechischen," *ThWNT* 6 (1959) 355; "πνεῦμα in the Greek World," *TDNT* 6:357.

26 Schweizer, "πνεῦμα," *ThWNT* 6:387–94; *TDNT* 6:389–96.

27 The reference "O Sal 26, 6 f" (Schweizer, "πνεῦμα," *ThWNT* 6:391 n. 364; *TDNT* 6:393 n. 364) must be corrected.

28 Friedrich Baumgärtel, "πνεῦμα. B. Geist im Alten Testament (+ C.I.1)," *ThWNT* 6 (1959) 360–66; "Spirit in the OT," *TDNT* 6:362–67.

29 Werner Bieder, "πνεῦμα. C.I.2–II.2. Geist im Judentum," *ThWNT* 6 (1959) 367–70; "Spirit in Judaism," *TDNT* 6:368–72; Erik Sjöberg, "πνεῦμα. C.III. רוּחַ im palästinischen Judentum," *ThWNT* 6 (1959) 375, 379–86; "רוּחַ in Palestinian Judaism," *TDNT* 6:377, 381–88; Schweizer, "πνεῦμα," *ThWNT* 6:387–90; *TDNT* 6:389–92.

30 BDAG, *s.v.* πνεῦμα; Lampe, 1097–104.

31 That means that the following statements are not true for the *Odes of Solomon*: "plerumque f. nisi quum Spiritum Sanctum significat" (Payne Smith, 2:3850); "usually fem. except when used of the Holy Spirit" (Payne Smith, *Dictionary*, 533); "f. interdum m. pl." (Brockelmann, *Lexicon*, 718, but cf. Nöldeke §87).

32 Jacob Kremer, "πνεῦμα," *EWNT* 3 (1983) 282; *EDNT* 3:118.

33 BDAG, *s.v.* πνεῦμα, 3b.

34 See NA[27], p. 423; *NTSy*, on this passage.

genitive in the phrase "spirit of the plan of salvation" (36:8b) metaphorically serves to emphasize the second part, as, for example, in Isa 11:2 ("spirit of wisdom" etc.),[35] or is only used to describe the Spirit of God more clearly,[36] will be discussed in its place.

Next in the examination of the remaining passages come two beautiful images that deal with the (holy) "Spirit" of God the Lord and Most High. In exchange for the mythological "garments of skin" (cf. Gen 3:21), the speaking "I" receives a "covering" of God's "Spirit" (25:8a ܣ; for ℭ, see the commentary on that passage). And, in a simile, the "wings of doves over their nestlings" (28:1a) are likened by the speaking "I" to the "wings of the Spirit" over his heart—that is, over him (28:1c; cf. Luke 1:35). Further on in that same Ode, it is even said that the "Spirit"—again used in the absolute—is "within me" (28:7a) and, because it comes from "immortal life," is itself "life" or "alive" (28:6-7).

The "Spirit of the Lord" teaches without falsehood (3:10a) and is able to "speak" indirectly (6:2a; 16:5a) but is also the object of "hymns" (13:2b) and is praised as the "holy Spirit" (see below) by "our spirits" (6:7b; see above). The "cithara of your holy Spirit" (14:8a) also belongs to this hymnic context. It is by his "holy Spirit" (*τῷ ἁγίῳ πνεύματι αὐτοῦ* in 𝔊) that the Most High performs the circumcision of the speaking "I" (11:2a). Two passages mention the "Father" and the "Son"; one (23:22b) also has the "holy Spirit," and the other speaks of that "Spirit of holiness" (19:2c; cf. 19:4a) that can perform the most extravagant feats. These passages are influenced by Matt 28:19, later the "point of departure for the doctrine of the Trinity," and similar "triadic formulations" in the New Testament (cf. 2 Cor 13:13).[37]

Neither the relatively few passages that use "Spirit" in the *Odes of Solomon* nor the far more numerous and differentiated biblical and extrabiblical statements about the "Spirit" of God the Lord and Most High provide a space into which to fit the reading of 36:1a H* and N ("I rested on the Spirit of the Lord").[38] On the other hand, the corrected reading of H ("the Spirit of the Lord rested on me") makes excellent sense and acts as an introduction to the subsequent actions of this "spiritual power" in 36:1-5.

In the New Testament, Isa 61:1 LXX is used of Jesus of Nazareth as the Christ of God (Acts 4:27; 10:38), and its use is even attributed to him (Luke 4:18) as the good news;[39] in this verse—as later in 6a—the interest is limited to the opening words of the prophetic passage and the immediate connection between that passage and the exaltation of the speaking "I." There are certain points of contact between *Ode* 36:1a-b and frgs. 2–3 of the *Gospel of the Hebrews*,[40] such as the Holy Spirit resting on Christ the Lord or the Holy Spirit, named as his mother, removing the Savior to the top of a high mountain. But it is more probable that already from 1b the Ode comes under the literary influence of another prophetic passage in the LXX (cf. esp. Ezek 2:2, *ἦλθεν ἐπ' ἐμὲ πνεῦμα καὶ ἀνέλαβέν με καὶ ἐξῆρέν με καὶ ἔστησέν με ἐπὶ τοὺς πόδας μου*, "the Spirit came upon me, and took me up, and raised me, and set me on my feet"; similarly Ezek 3:24; *ἀνέλαβέν με*, "took me up"; see also Ezek 3:12, 14; 8:3; 11:1).[41] That does not mean that *ἀνέλαβέν με* is the only possible equivalent for the Aph. of ܪܘܡ, ܪܡ (*rām*) with first singular objective suffix.[42] Other verbs, such as *αἴρω*[43] and *ὑψόω*, can also come under consideration.[44] However, the subsequent use of ܒܪ ܐܢܫܐ (H)/ܒܪܢܫܐ (N) in 3b[45] rather suggests the direct influence of that prophetic work, where, from Ezek 2:1, the address *υἱὲ ἀνθρώπου* is regularly used,[46] and not a dependence on the Gospel of John, in which

35 See Payne Smith, 2:3852.
36 BDAG, *s.v.* *πνεῦμα*, 5e.
37 Kremer, "*πνεῦμα*," *EWNT* 3 (1983) 291; *EDNT* 3:122.
38 The only possibility is to make reference to 26:10a and, in analogy to the resting "with the Most High," translate: "I rested/found rest *with* the Spirit of the Lord."
39 It must be remembered that Jesus, in all four Gospels, speaks and acts as the Christ (Messiah) awakened and/or exalted by God. So his words and deeds are often styled as the fulfillment of promises/prophecies or expectations.
40 Philipp Vielhauer and Georg Strecker, "Judenchristliche Evangelien," *NTApo* (5th ed., 1987) 1:146; "Jewish-Christian Gospels," *NTApoc*, 1:177.
41 Bauer, 616; Rahlfs, 2:772–84; Brenton, 981–89.
42 BDAG, *s.v.* *ἀναλαμβάνω*, 1.
43 Frankenberg, 31 (*καὶ εἰς ὕψος με ἦρε*).
44 Cf. John 3:14; 8:28; 12:32, 34; Payne Smith, 2:3858.
45 Both spellings are pronounced *bar nāšā* and mean "(single) human being."
46 Zimmerli, *Ezechiel*, 70: "Menschensohn [Son of man]."

the phrase ὁ υἱὸς τοῦ ἀνθρώπου is always translated by the Syriac ܒܪܗ ܕܐܢܫܐ (*breh d-nāšā*).[47]

N uses ܪܘܡܐ (*rawmā*) twice (1b and 2a), but H, perhaps deliberately, differentiates between the common term ܡܪܘܡܐ (*mrawmā*) for "height" (1b; cf. 10:5 [plural]; 17:7; 21:1; 22:1; 23:5) and the more theological ܪܘܡܐ for the "*Lord's* height" (2a; cf. the more significant use of the plural in 26:7). These related terms belong to the same root as the Aph. in 1b,[48] and can both be used to translate τὰ ὑψηλά[49] as well as τὸ ὕψος,[50] which in the *Odes of Solomon*, as already in the New Testament, transcends heaven or the heavens in the same way as God is called ὕψιστος (see Excursus 17). The topic has nothing to do with "a *visionary* being caught up into heaven" [emphasis added].[51]

In 2a the influence of Ezek 2:2 and 3:24, adumbrated in 1b, becomes unmistakable. Similar literary influence can be discerned in Dan 8:18.[52] Diettrich gives his imagination free rein, observing of these and similar passages, "the seer is so overwhelmed by all he has seen that the Spirit . . . has to plant his feet on the ground."[53] "Above . . . , i.e. in Heaven, he [viz., Christ] stands on his own feet," claims Gunkel, disregarding the actual wording, and adds in gratuitous explanation that "it is not done to sit down in God's presence."[54] That the literary—not to say *formgeschichtlich*—influence of Ezek 2:2 (ἔστησέν με ἐπὶ τοὺς πόδας μου) is sufficient for the exegesis is shown by the phrase "glory of the Lord" (δόξα κυρίου), which influenced the wording of the second half of the bicolon 2a-b.

The preposition ܩܕܡ (*qdām*), with which 2b begins, is clearly meant "exclusively spatially" (cf. 1 *Enoch* 40:1; etc.).[55] This, by itself, already provides the ܫܘܡܠܝܐ (*šūmlāyā* [πλήρωμα in 𝔊]), *plērōma*, in its divine "fullness of being" and "fullness of essence"[56] with a mythospatial dimension (see Excursus 35),[57] which carries over to the parallel term δόξα/ܬܫܒܘܚܬܐ (*tešbuḥtā*), "glory" (see Excursus 21).

■ **2c-4** Verse 2c is the beginning of stanza II,[58] not the end of I.[59] The link that Franzmann detects between stanzas I and II by the "repetition of the root ܫܒܚ"[60] is valid only for 𝔖, since the active participle of Pa. ܫܒܚ (*šabbaḥ*) in 2c corresponds not only to δοξάζω but also to a number of other verbs of praising and singing.[61] And even 4a in 𝔖 is not "an exact repetition of 2c with the exception of the obj[ect] of ܒ."[62] As will be seen later, ܡܫܒܚ (*mšabbaḥ*) in 4a is the *passive* participle. Here in 2c the identical Syriac form makes sense only in the active voice, since the speaking "I" alludes, with "his odes," to the ܙܡܝܪܬܐ (*zmīrātā*) "to and about the Lord" (see Excursus 26). These are not the *Odes of Solomon* as such, but generally songs of praise for "worship in heaven."[63] The term ܬܘܩܢܐ (*tuqqānā*), which in this passage is not a theological term of creation but simply means "*formatio, fabricatio, constructio*"[64] and is defined by the genitive phrase that follows, might lead one to conclude that "the speaker identifies himself as one who composes, not merely recites odes."[65] But one must always be careful not to identify the speaking "I" with the author of the *Odes of Solomon* ("the Odist") or with the prophetic "cult leader" of an eschatological "congregation."[66] It is, of course, remarkable that the direct object of praising—or

47 Payne Smith, 1:582.
48 See Payne Smith, 2:3860, 3864.
49 BDAG, *s.v.* ὑψηλός, 1.
50 BDAG, *s.v.* ὕψος, 1b.
51 Contra Diettrich, 119, who refers to *1 Enoch* 39:3; Spitta (p. 287) similarly refers to *1 Enoch* 70:1-2 and 71:5, 15, 17.
52 See Eissfeldt, §71.8.
53 Diettrich, 120.
54 Gunkel, 300.
55 Diettrich, 120.
56 Delling, "πλήρης," *ThWNT* 6:299, 302; *TDNT* 6:300, 303.
57 Contra Blaszczak, 12.
58 Kittel, "Handschrift," 88; Greßmann, 467; Franzmann, 248–50.
59 Contra Harris and Mingana, 2:383; Bauer, 616; Charlesworth, 127; Blaszczak, 12.
60 Franzmann, 250.
61 Payne Smith, 2:4024.
62 Franzmann (p. 250), following her own division, should have referred to 2d; instead she reverts to the normal division of 2 into 2a-c.
63 BDAG, *s.v.* ᾠδή.
64 Payne Smith, 2:4487.
65 Blaszczak, 12.
66 Contra David E. Aune, *The Cultic Setting of Realized Eschatology in Early Christianity* (NovTSup 28; Leiden: Brill, 1972) 179–83.

glorification—is absent, but there are other examples of such a lack in the *Odes of Solomon* (cf. 21:7 and see Excursus 21). In particular, after the multifaceted particle ܟܕ (*kaḏ*), the participle with enclitic personal pronoun ܐܢܐ (*-nā*) "denote[s] a contemporary condition in the past."[67] In the main clause that now follows, the speaking "I" describes what he experienced in that mythological past.

The mythological occurrence in 3a should not, in spite of the feminine form of ܐܝܠܕ (*ʾileḏ*) with first singular objective suffix,[68] which is due to the antecedent ܪܘܚܐ (*rūḥā*), be reduced to a metaphorical giving birth (cf. Matt 1:20). In the case of the neuter πνεῦμα (the implied subject in 𝔊), the verb could not be τίκτω;[69] only γεννάω in the sense of "beget" or "bear" is suitable.[70] Instead of "Rebirth by the Spirit in Heaven before the Most High" (Bauer's title for the Ode),[71] one should perhaps speak of a "transbirth" (Gunkel, with a reference to the "Mysteries of Mithras")[72] or simply of "renewal before the face of the Lord."[73] The meaning of this becomes clear in the central part of stanza II and in III (see on 3b and 5a-b below). That the plural ܐܦܐ (*ʾappē*), "face," corresponds to the singular πρόσωπον seems definite (see Excursus 8).[74] What the preposition was in 𝔊 is not as immediately obvious. However, ἀπὸ προσώπου τινός, meaning "away from someone" (cf. Rev 6:16; 12:14; 20:11), makes no sense here, and that leaves only πρὸ προσώπου τινός, "before someone,"[75] which may stand under the influence of Isa 62:11 LXX.[76]

There is no need to give the repetition of ܟܕ (*kaḏ*) in 3b much poetic weight; it is consequent on the use of ܐܝܬܝ (*ʾīṯay* = *ʾīṯ* with first singular possessive suffix) instead of a participle.[77] This is another case of a "contemporary condition in the past,"[78] where 𝔊 would merely have used ὤν. But since the sense of this central statement of stanza II has a certain paradoxical quality, ܟܕ might be translated by "although" in place of "while" or "during";[79] in other words, it could have a slightly "adversative sense."[80] But it must not be interpreted as "an emphatic contradiction of the various assertions of Christ's pre-existence" (Kittel, with somewhat dogmatic references to 31:13 and 41:15).[81] At any rate, 3b does not speak against the possibility of identifying the speaking "I" with Christ. Blaszczak's assertion, following Hengel,[82] that "[i]t will become evident . . . that the speaker regards himself as having been made one of the heavenly or angelic beings,"[83] is not convincing (cf. 42:15b, where the messianic phrase "Son of God" recurs, and esp. 41:13, "Son of the Most High"). In spite of Brock's[84] and Reinink's[85] criticisms, Charlesworth stands by his unorthodox translation of ܟܕ as "because"[86] and insists that "the Son of Man is a Christological title in the Odes, and its linguistic form [*bar nāšā*] suggests that the Odes may be a late first-century composition."[87] On this

67 Nöldeke §275.
68 "No Syriac grammar has yet ventured to transcribe this form (i.e., ܝܠܕܬܢ). If one follows the method of pointing" used by Nöldeke §187, "it must be written" as follows: *ʾiledṯan* (Klaus Beyer, letter of November 13, 2002).
69 BDAG, *s.v.* τίκτω, 1.
70 BDAG, *s.v.* γεννάω, 1–2; Payne Smith, 1:1593; cf. Frankenberg, 31: ἐγέννησέ με.
71 Bauer, 616.
72 Gunkel, 300.
73 Blaszczak, 12.
74 Payne Smith, 1:278–80.
75 BDAG, *s.v.* πρόσωπον, 1bβℶ.
76 See Payne Smith, 2:3492.
77 See Nöldeke §§199, 305.
78 Ibid. §275.
79 See, e.g., Greßmann, 467.
80 Blaszczak, 13.
81 Kittel, 127.
82 Martin Hengel, *The Son of God: The Origin of Christology and the History of Jewish-Hellenistic Religion* (trans. John Bowden; Philadelphia: Fortress Press, 1976) 42.
83 Blaszczak, 13.
84 "In the important passage at 36:3 I very much doubt, despite Charlesworth's long note, whether *barnāšā* can at all legitimately be translated as 'the Son of Man'. His whole argument is in danger of circularity here" (Sebastian Brock, review of Charlesworth [1973] in *JBL* 93 [1974] 624). Franzmann (pp. 249–50), too, criticizes Charlesworth and refers, pertinently, to Mark 2:27-28. Charlesworth still defends his untenable translation of 3b (see Charlesworth, *Reflections*, 152).
85 Gerrit J. Reinink, review of Charlesworth in *Vox theologica: Interacademiaal theologische tijdschrift* 44 (1975) 305.
86 Charlesworth, 1977, 127; idem, *Reflections*, 152.
87 Charlesworth, 128. Although Aune accepts Charlesworth's translation, he does not agree with the early date for the *Odes of Solomon*. He suggests

point it is necessary to emphasize as strongly as possible that ܒܪ ܐܢܫܐ (H) and ܒܪܢܫܐ (N)[88] mean quite simply "a man," ἄνθρωπος,[89] or υἱὸς ἀνθρώπου as in Ps 8:5b LXX (quoted in Heb 2:6) and Dan 7:13 and elsewhere.[90] That the speaking "I" should refer to himself as a "human being, man" is not really surprising in the light of Rom 5:15 (τοῦ ἑνὸς ἀνθρώπου Ἰησοῦ Χριστοῦ) or 1 Tim 2:5 (ἄνθρωπος Χριστὸς Ἰησοῦς).[91] The two titles ܢܗܝܪܐ (*nahhīrā*) and ܒܪܗ ܕܐܠܗܐ (*breh d-allāhā*) in apposition to it are contrasted with the non-christological term "man." The second, "Son of God," in the tradition of Rom 1:3-4[92] and also, to some extent, by the application of Ps 2:7, is the well-known primitive *Christian* "messianic title";[93] the first, as a noun, may correspond to φωστήρ[94] (cf. the plural "stars in the world" in Phil 2:15, where it is parallel to τέκνα θεοῦ, "children of God") or equally to φῶς, "light."[95] A simple Φῶς in 𝔊[96] would, of course, have reminded the reader immediately of the Johannine Jesus, to whom "light" as the commonly accepted attribute of God is applied.[97] However, in that case 𝔖 would have been more likely to use ܢܘܗܪܐ (*nuhrā*) as equivalent. So one must assume that 𝔊 had φωτεινός, "shining,"[98] either as a predicate noun or as a pre-positioned attribute of "Son of God."[99] Erik Peterson's comparison to ὁ φαίνων "in the Hamburg papyrus of the Acts of Paul"[100] is less attractive than Bauer's reference to a didactic statement of the Poimandres:[101] ὁ δὲ ἐκ Νοὸς φωτεινὸς Λόγος υἱὸς θεοῦ, "the radiant Logos from the Spirit is the Son of God."[102] That is not a claim of a direct literary dependence of the *Odes of Solomon* on the Jewish-Platonic treatise of the Alexandrian Hermetics. It is, however, possible that the quotation was influenced by a "long tradition of Hellenistic interpretation of the Bible" or even that the "author of CH I," a "contemporary of Valentinus,"[103] may actually have known the *Odes of Solomon*, which cannot, as a whole, be described as either orthodox Christian or Gnostic.[104] The defining verb in 3b, Ethpa. ܐܫܬܡܗ (*ʾeštammah*),

"c. 125 C.E." (see David E. Aune, "Christian Prophecy and the Messianic Status of Jesus," in James H. Charlesworth, ed., *The Messiah: Developments in Earliest Judaism and Christianity. The First Princeton Symposium on Judaism and Christian Origins* [Minneapolis: Fortress Press, 1992] 417).

88 See Lattke, *Bedeutung*, 1:49 n. 12. Transcription of both: *bar nāšā*.

89 Payne Smith, 1:582; Payne Smith, *Dictionary*, 53; Frankenberg, 31.

90 Rahlfs, 2:6, 2:914; cf. Klaus Beyer, "אֱנָשׁ *ʾnāš I–III," *ThWAT* 9, Lief. 1 (2001) 61 [ET not available yet]; Michael Goulder, "Psalm 8 and the Son of Man," *NTS* 48 (2002) 18–19, 24–25. Heb 2:6 follows the Septuagint text of Ps 8:5, making ἄνθρωπος parallel to υἱὸς ἀνθρώπου. In the Peshitta, the Syriac term ܒܪܢܫܐ corresponds to the phrase υἱὸς ἀνθρώπου (Ps 8:5b; *OTSy*, pt. 2 fasc. 3, p. 7), while the expression ܒܪܗ ܕܐܢܫܐ (Heb 2:6; *NTSy*, on this passage) brings in the christological sense of Son of Man (which could be added in Goulder, 25). There is still quite a distance from the *Odes of Solomon* to the Gnostic theories on "man" and "son of man" (see, e.g., Judith Hartenstein, "Eugnostos [NHC III,3; V,1] und die Weisheit Jesu Christi [NHC III,4; BG 3]," *NHD* 1 [2001] 355–57, 365). Peel's reference to *Ode* 36:3 for *Treat. Res.* 44,21-26 is also doubtful (see Peel, *Rheginos*, 60).

91 See BDAG, *s.v.* ἄνθρωπος, 1d.

92 See Eduard Lohse, *Der Brief an die Römer* (KEK 4; Göttingen: Vandenhoeck & Ruprecht, 2003) 64–66.

93 BDAG, *s.v.* υἱός, 2dβ (ὁ υἱὸς τοῦ θεοῦ, υἱὸς θεοῦ).

94 BDAG, *s.v.* φωστήρ, 2: "splendor, radiance."

95 Payne Smith, 2:2300.

96 Bousset, *Kyrios Christos*, 174; see also Charlesworth, 127; idem, *Reflections*, 152.

97 BDAG, *s.v.* φῶς, 1bα; cf. *Paralip. Jer.* 6:9 (12); 11:3; 11:13 (14), and on that Berndt Schaller, *Paralipomena Jeremiou* (JSHRZ 1.8; Gütersloh: Gütersloher Verlagshaus, 1998) 732, 748, 752.

98 Bauer, 616; BDAG, *s.v.* φωτεινός.

99 Lattke, *Bedeutung*, 1:171.

100 Peterson, *Studien*, 206; see also Schmidt and Schubart, *Acta Pauli*, 34 (p. 3, lines 31 and 36 of the papyrus).

101 Bauer, 616.

102 *Corp. Herm.* 1:6: Nock and Festugière, 1:8; Richard Reitzenstein, *Poimandres: Studien zur griechisch-ägyptischen und frühchristlichen Literatur* (Leipzig, 1904; repr., Darmstadt: Wissenschaftliche Buchgesellschaft, 1966) 329; Colpe and Holzhausen, 12.

103 Jens Holzhausen, *Der "Mythos vom Menschen" im hellenistischen Ägypten: Eine Studie zum "Poimandres" (= CH I) zu Valentin und dem gnostischen Mythos* (Theophaneia 33; Bodenheim: Athenäum–Hain–Hanstein, 1994) 69 and 70 n. 268.

104 The term φῶς occurs more than ten times in the first treatise of the so-called *Corpus Hermeticum*, but φωτεινός is a *hapax legomenon* (Dieter Georgi and John Strugnell, *Concordance to the* Corpus Hermeticum. *Tractate One: The* Poimandres [Concordances to Patristic and Late Classical Texts,

derived from ܫܡܐ (*šmā*), occurs only here and corresponds to a passive form of ὀνομάζω: "'be named' in the sense *be known*."[105]

The reading of 4a-b in H may be translated as follows: "while I praised among those who give praise, I [was] also great among the great."[106] It is advisable, however, to follow N, which, by omitting the mark of division, emphasizes the connection between the parallel self-descriptions. On account of this parallelism, Barth translates both ܡܫܒܚ (*mšabbaḥ*) and ܡܫܒܚܐ (*mšabbḥē*)[107] by the passive participle: "While I was being praised among those being praised."[108] N thus not only makes a differentiation between 4a and 2c, but also shifts the statement as a whole, by the repetition of the particle ܟܕ (*kaḏ*), into simultaneity with 3b. That the repeated ܒ (*b-*) is used as a means of expressing the superlative[109] is grammatically possible[110] but not compelling or recommended. Whether 𝔊 used the same term in each case for the singulars and plurals ܡܫܒܚ (*mšabbaḥ*)/ܡܫܒܚܐ (*mšabbḥē*) and ܪܒ (*rab*)/ܪܘܪܒܢܐ (*rawrḇānē*), perhaps, for example, ἔνδοξος and μέγας, cannot be determined with certainty.[111] If the speaking "I" means to describe himself as an angelic being[112] ἔνδοξος would have to be taken to mean "glorious, splendid,"[113] and for 4b it would be necessary to consider the term ἄρχων, in spite of its negative connotation.[114] Probably the exalted one, named the "Son of God," is just reflecting on his christological renown[115] and the greatness bestowed on him by God (see on 5a below) among all those with claim to "rank and worth" in the antique pantheon.[116]

■ **5** This bicolon, which H perhaps divides into a tricolon by a mark of division after ܡܪܝܡܐ (*mrayymā*), follows on from the wording of 4b and supplements 3b with another explanation of the "rebirth" reported in 3a.[117] What Harris and Mingana call a "very slight change" is more like a large incision in the text of 5b, which appears the less necessary since "the obscurity of such a phrase as the Divine newness" is nowhere to be found.[118] For Charlesworth, 5a-b is the end of an extended specimen of Syriac "repetition," which he classes as one of the three forms of "paronomasia."[119] Such repetition of related roots can be found also in 𝔊; here the equivalent term to ܪܒܘܬܐ (*rabbūṯā*)[120] could have been μεγαλειότης,[121] μεγαλωσύνη,[122] or μέγεθος,[123] linking with μέγας in 4b. It is quite possible that "the Syrian misinterpreted" the "subject" of the Pe. ܥܒܕ (*ʿbaḏ*)

Vol. 0, Preliminary Issue; Cambridge, MA: Boston Theological Institute, 1971] 26).

105 BDAG, *s.v.* ὀνομάζω, 3; see Payne Smith, 2:4201–2. Correct ܐܫܬܡܐ to ܐܫܬܡܗ in Lattke 3:134.

106 Lattke, *Oden*, 196; on the formation of *nomina agentis* from participles by the suffix *ān*, see Nöldeke §130. But even in H it is not completely certain whether ܡܫܒܚ (*mšabbaḥ*) is in the active or the passive voice, so it could also be "I was praised" (= "glorious") instead of "I praised."

107 Since Barth was only aware of H, he must have silently emended ܡܫܒܚܢܐ (*mšabbḥānē*) to ܡܫܒܚܐ (*mšabbḥē*), a correction confirmed by N.

108 Barth, 265; similarly Kittel, "Handschrift," 88; cf. Kittel, 128 n. 2.

109 Harris and Mingana, 2:384; Charlesworth, 127; partly also Franzmann, 249.

110 See Robinson and Brockington, 49.

111 See Payne Smith, 2:4024 and 2:3783–84.

112 Blaszczak, 13; on the description of Christ as ἄγγελος, post-New Testament, see BDAG, *s.v.* ἄγγελος, 2a; and Lampe, 10.

113 BDAG, *s.v.* ἔνδοξος, 2.

114 BDAG, *s.v.* ἄρχων, 1; Lampe, 241.

115 See BDAG, *s.v.* ἔνδοξος, 1.

116 Bauer and Aland, *s.v.* μέγας, 2b; see BDAG, *s.v.* μέγας, 4a; on the still undecided question of Titus 2:13, see Oberlinner, *Pastoralbriefe*, 3:136–37.

117 Kittel, 128. I cannot agree with Franzmann's division of 5a-b into four lines, that is, 5a-d. Her demonstration that there is "some connection between stanzas 2 [II] and 3 [III] by the repetition of the root ܪܒ" (Franzmann, 251) may lead one to consider whether 5a should not, with the causative particle ܓܝܪ (*gēr*), be more closely linked to 4b (Lattke, "Wörter," 289–90 = idem, *Bedeutung*, 4:138).

118 Harris and Mingana, 2:385. It may be emphasized here, already, that the *hapax legomenon* ܚܘܕܬܐ (*ḥuddāṯā*) in 5b, which must not be confused with the similar ܚܛܘܬܐ (*ḥaṭūṯā*), should not be translated as "newness" (contra Harris and Mingana, 2:384; Charlesworth, 127), and so it does not correspond to καινότης (Peel, *Rheginos*, 92; cf. Payne Smith, 1:1208; BDAG, *s.v.* καινότης).

119 Charlesworth, *Reflections*, 148–50.

120 Payne Smith, 2:3787.

121 BDAG, *s.v.* μεγαλειότης, 1.

122 BDAG, *s.v.* μεγαλωσύνη.

123 BDAG, *s.v.* μέγεθος, 2.

with its first singular objective suffix,[124] and that it was not "the Most High."[125] For in 𝔊 ἐποίησέν με could refer equally to the feminine Spirit (neuter in Greek, feminine in Syriac) and to the masculine Most High. However, the actions of the ܪܘܚܐ (*rūḥā*) in 1-2 and 3a argue in favor of the feminine subject in 5a, although the other occurrences of the term of creation, ποιέω/ܥܒܕ (*ʿbad*), in the *Odes of Solomon* would tend to suggest a masculine subject.[126] In two of the passages (15:7 and 29:3 taken together with 29:2) ܐܝܟ (*ʾak*) occurs, as here in 5a and 5b, together with the phrase ܪܒܘܬ ܝܐܝܘܬܗ (*rabbūt yāʾyūteh*), which corresponds to μεγαλοπρέπεια ("majesty") and refers to the Lord. Since it is the redeemed Redeemer who speaks in both those passages, the speaking "I" here, most probably, is also not merely a "human singer."[127] That the expression used here is the "greatness of the Most High" instead of the "greatness of the Lord" follows from the mythological situation of *Ode* 36 (see above on "height"/"height of the Lord" in 1b-2a). Is it really "not at all clear in what sense the speaker was made"—by "the Spirit"—"according to the greatness of the Most High"?[128] Harris and Mingana already referred to the Epistle to the Hebrews in connection with 6a,[129] and a glance at that will help in understanding the self-portrait of the exalted human being called the "Son of God." As the "Son" (Jesus) who sits ἐν δεξιᾷ τῆς μεγαλωσύνης ἐν ὑψηλοῖς ("at the right hand of the Majesty on high") and has become κρείττων τῶν ἀγγέλων ("superior to angels") can be compared to the υἱός of Ps 2:7 LXX (Heb 1:3-5; cf. 2:5-9), so the speaking "I" is more than merely an "angelic being."[130]

The parallelism between 5a and 5b is impaired, first, because ܗܟܢܐ (*hākannā*) is not repeated in 5b (𝔊 is also likely to have used οὕτως only once)[131] and, second, because there is a change of subject.[132] Although there is certainly no "change of speaker,"[133] the subject "the Most High" (= "the Lord" [1a, 2a, 3a] = "God" [3b]), which has to be supplied, casts some anticipatory light on 6a at the beginning of stanza IV. The change of subject thus links stanza III firmly to IV.[134] But 5b is closer to 5a than to 6a both in form and meaning. In spite of the difficulties in reconstructing the Greek of 5b, one can begin by assuming that the terms ܚܘܕܬܐ (*ḥuddāṯā*) and the Pa. ܚܕܬ (*ḥaddeṯ*), which derive from the same root, would have corresponded to a similar play on words from the same root ("renewal" and "renew"), perhaps ἐγκαινισμός[135] and ἐγκαινίζω (as is 11:11),[136] or—as Frankenberg also considers more probable[137]—ἀνακαίνωσις and ἀνακαινίζω/ἀνακαινόω.[138] Any combination of these terms will reflect the poetic characteristics, which Charlesworth aims to demonstrate for the Syriac version, drawing far-reaching conclusions from them for the original language and date of composition of the Syriac *Odes*.[139] The "renewal" of the Most High is, of

124 See the note on the transcription of ܐܝܠܕܬܢ in 3a (*ʾiledṯan*) above.
125 Frankenberg, 43; see also Kittel, 128–29 n. 4.
126 Cf. 4:15; 7:9, 12; 12:10; 15:7; 29:2.
127 Kittel, 128.
128 Blaszczak, 14.
129 Harris and Mingana, 2:385.
130 Blaszczak, 13–14.
131 See Payne Smith, 1:1006–7.
132 The subject of 5b could be feminine, like that of 5a ("she" = "the Spirit"), if the letter ܬ were single. That would necessitate emending ܚܕܬܢ (*ḥaddṯan*) to ܚܕܬ‹ܬ›ܢ and transcribing it by *ḥaddet‹t›an* (Klaus Beyer, letter of November 13, 2002).
133 Contra Blaszczak, 14.
134 See Matthias Delcor, "Le vocabulaire juridique, cultuel et mystique de l' 'initiation' dans la secte de Qumrân," in Hans Bardtke, ed., *Qumran-Probleme: Vorträge des Leipziger Symposions über Qumran-Probleme vom 9. bis 14. Oktober 1961* (SSA 42; Berlin: Akademie-Verlag, 1963) 122.
135 Lampe, 399.
136 BDAG, *s.v.* ἐγκαινίζω, 1; Lampe, 399.
137 Frankenberg, 31.
138 BDAG, *s.vv.* ἀνακαινίζω, ἀνακαινόω, ἀνακαίνωσις; cf. Payne Smith, 1:1208.
139 Charlesworth, *Reflections*, 150, 163–64. As this footnote to 5b shows, Charlesworth will try anything to support his contention of a Syriac original for the *Odes*: "The transition from the 3fs. to the 3ms. is subtle in Syriac, because the third radical of 'he renewed', a Taw, is similar to the preceding suffixes of the 3fs. perfect, also a Taw" (see Charlesworth, 128).

course, not a "renewal by which God continually renews himself"[140] but "a renewal effected by the Most High himself" and therefore anything but "obscure."[141] For, in addition to the parallels cited in the exegesis of 5a (see esp. 15:7 and 29:2-3), it is pertinent to refer to 17:4, in which the redeemed Redeemer "received the face and likeness of a new *persona*."[142]

■ **6-8** The terms and images in stanza IV tumble about so bewilderingly that a number of matters toward the end of the Ode are left blurred. Even the unmistakable origin of certain phrases and ideas from Isaiah or Ephesians becomes obscure rather than gaining lucidity from the intertextuality. Or, to put it another way, this self-description of the exalted one makes idiosyncratic use of Jewish and Christian sources. Some of the difficulties are resolved if stanza IV is not taken simply as a logical continuation of what has hitherto been a celestial self-description, but as a new beginning—on earth as it were—and therefore a variation of stanzas I–III.

Although Coptic-Gnostic writings deal with a divine "anointing" of the Son,[143] 6a-b is not concerned with the "Gnostic mythos."[144] Harris and Mingana already noted the quotation from Ps 44:8b LXX in Heb 1:9 (ἔχρισέν σε ὁ θεός, "God has anointed you"),[145] but it is more probable that the *hapax legomenon* ܡܫܚ (*mšaḥ*) with first singular objective suffix originates in Isa 61:1 LXX (ἔχρισέν με, "anointed me").[146] As in the New Testament, where χρίω is used "in a Christological context," so here the "*actual performance* of anointing is not visualised";[147] what is intended is "an anointing by God" in a figurative sense.[148] The subject, the "Most High," which can be supplied from 5a-b, is transcendentally identical with "God" (3b) and the "Lord" (1a, 2a, 3a). In answer to the question *what was used* to anoint the speaking "I," a reference to the dative phrase πνεύματι ἁγίῳ καὶ δυνάμει ("with the Holy Spirit and with power") in Acts 10:38 lies nearer to hand than one to the accusative phrase ἔλαιον ἀγαλλιάσεως ("the oil of gladness") in Heb 1:9.[149] In any case, the need for such an answer is displaced by the revelation in 6a of the *origin* of this metaphorical anointing, expressed by the preposition ܡܢ (*men*) and the *hapax legomenon* ܡܫܡܠܝܘܬܐ (*mšamlyūṯā*), with third masculine singular possessive suffix, which is distinct from the Lord's "*plērōma*/fullness" in 2b and corresponds to the τελειότης ("perfection") of the Most High (see Excursus 35).[150] Among persons in Hellenistic times, it was commonplace to think "of God" as τέλειος ("perfect").[151] The "anointing of perfection" can be considered in some sense identical with the "rebirth" of 3a and the "renewal" of 5b.[152] In Christian circles, however, mention of anointing must have called up associations with the name or title "Messiah/Christ,"[153] which occurs seven times in the *Odes of Solomon*.[154] Taken with the quotation of Isa 61:1 and his

140 Contra Gunkel, 186.
141 Blaszczak, 14 and n. 21 (p. 105).
142 See commentary on this passage. Although Kittel (p. 129) notes 17:4 and mentions "renewal into a celestial being" and "renewal into a divine being," he considers that, on the whole, the person referred to is merely "a believer."
143 Michael Waldstein, "Das Apokryphon des Johannes (NHC II,1; III,1; IV,1 und BG 2)," *NHD* 1 (2001) 110 (6,23-26 in NHC II,*1*, and parr. in NHC III,*1*; IV,*1*; *BG* 2); Hans-Martin Schenke, "Das Evangelium nach Philippus (NHC II,3)," *NHD* 1 (2001) 206 (no. 95a = 74,12-18); and see idem, *Das Philippus-Evangelium (Nag-Hammadi-Codex II,3)* (TU 143; Berlin: Akademie-Verlag, 1997) 445–47.
144 Contra Käsemann, *Wandering People*, 138 = *Gottesvolk*, 85.
145 Harris and Mingana, 2:385.
146 Gunkel, 301. The use of the next section of Isa 61:1 LXX (πνεῦμα κυρίου ἐπ᾽ ἐμέ) as the basis of 1a supports the idea that this is a new beginning.
147 Peter Pilhofer, "Wer salbt den Messias? Zum Streit um die Christologie im ersten Jahrhundert des jüdisch-christlichen Dialogs," in Dietrich-Alex Koch and Hermann Lichtenberger, eds., *Begegnungen zwischen Christentum und Judentum in Antike und Mittelalter: Festschrift für Heinz Schreckenberg* (Schriften des Institutum Judaicum Delitzschianum 1; Göttingen: Vandenhoeck & Ruprecht, 1993) 335 n. 4.
148 BDAG, *s.v.* χρίω, b; cf. Payne Smith, 2:2235.
149 Contra Harris and Mingana, 2:385. The extensive conclusions that they draw from their tinkering with the text about "the name of Solomon attached to the Odes" can thus be put to rest (see Lattke, *Oden*, 196).
150 Payne Smith, 2:2129; BDAG, *s.v.* τελειότης.
151 See BDAG, *s.v.* τέλειος, 4b.
152 Kittel, 128.
153 BDAG, *s.v.* Χριστός; see Payne Smith, 2:2241, on the passive participle ܡܫܝܚܐ (*mšīḥā*).
154 See Lattke, "Messias-Stellen," 439–40 = idem, *Bedeutung*, 4:101–2.

self-description as the "Son of God" (3b), 6a strongly suggests that the speaking "I" is none other than the Lord (Jesus) Christ.

The *exact* meaning of the term ܩܪܝܒܐ (*qarrīḇā*) in 6b, which was used already in a similar way in 21:7 in the context of 21:6-9, is difficult to determine.[155] The third masculine singular possessive suffix, referring to the Most High and corresponding to αὐτοῦ, means that οἱ παρόντες ("those . . . present") would not make sense in 𝔊.[156] Similarly, οἱ ἐγγύς ("those who are near") followed by αὐτοῦ is hard to imagine syntactically,[157] so a direct influence from Eph 2:17 or Isa 57:19 LXX can probably be excluded. The participle of πλησιάζω with dative of the person is also unsuitable,[158] so the choice lies between οἱ πλησίον αὐτοῦ[159] and οἱ πάρεδροι αὐτοῦ.[160] Since the plural ܩܪܝܒܐ (*qarrīḇē*) does not here primarily refer to "believers" or "fellow humans" and does not bear the same meaning as in Ignatius *Pol.* 6:1, πάρεδροι might wake associations, on the one hand, with ideas from antiquity of "transcendent beings as πάρεδροι τοῦ μεγάλου θεοῦ"[161] and, on the other, at least indirectly, with Ps 109:1 LXX.[162] Insofar as the anointed and speaking "I" is only *one* (εἷς in 𝔊) of those "near," he "enters the circle of the majestic beings who surround the highest throne as their equal."[163] At the same time, as Christian "Son of God" he is *greater* than a Jewish "archangel."[164] For in the *Odes of Solomon* the "Messiah" is not only the exclusive "Son of the Most High" (42:13, 15) but also, like God himself, the "Lord."[165]

Even if the repetition of ܐܟ (*ʾaḵ*) in H reflects the original, Franzmann's division of the central bicolon of stanza IV into four lines is capricious and unnecessary.[166] Bauer's remark on 6a, "the anointing enables him to proclaim,"[167] gives the solution to the image in 7a-b. His reference to Isa 61:1-2 is the more relevant since this schematic message of good news embodies God's righteousness, and the key word δικαιοσύνη occurs three times in Isa 61 LXX (61:3, 8, 11). So 7 is not primarily about "inspiration,"[168] "praise," or "prophecy."[169] The image of 7a, "like a cloud of dew," comes from Isa 18:4 (ὡς νεφέλη δρόσου), although neither the original prophetic context[170] nor the biblical and early Christian metaphors of clouds[171] contribute anything

155 Payne Smith, 2:3727.
156 BDAG, *s.v.* πάρειμι, 1a.
157 BDAG, *s.v.* ἐγγύς, 3.
158 Contra Frankenberg, 31; see LSJ, *s.v.* πλησιάζω, II2: "consort, associate with."
159 BDAG, *s.v.* πλησίον, 2: "the one who is near or close by."
160 BDAG, *s.v.* πάρεδρος: "sitting beside."
161 BDAG, *s.v.* πάρεδρος; cf. *PGrM*, 4:1347; Preisendanz, 1:118–19: *"Beisitzer des großen Gottes."*
162 On the acceptance of Κάθου ἐκ δεξιῶν μου ("Sit thou on my right") in the New Testament, see BDAG, *s.v.* δεξιός, 1b; Lukas Bormann, "Ps 110 im Dialog mit dem Neuen Testament," in Dieter Sänger, ed., *Heiligkeit und Herrschaft: Intertextuelle Studien zu Heiligkeitsvorstellungen und zu Psalm 110* (Biblisch-Theologische Studien 55; Neukirchen-Vluyn: Neukirchener Verlag, 2003) 197–98.
163 Gunkel, *Aufsätze*, 185, taken *cum grano salis.*
164 Ibid. Contradicting his previous opinion (Gunkel, 300–330), he says that the "human being" in *Ode* 36 is "*a* son of God" and "an anointed one, *like* the Christ" [emphases added in the quotations]. That is why he can be equated with one of the "archangels:" "he has . . . now become an archangel!" (Gunkel, *Aufsätze*, 185).
165 Cf. 17:16; 24:1a (N); 29:6a-b; 39:11b. James D. G. Dunn's remarks on Acts 2:36 and other Lukan sayings should also be considered here: "Jesus had been given lordship by the Lord God . . . but as derived from the Lord God it was in effect an expression of God's lordship. . . . Christ can be Lord, at the centre of both scripture and faith, without in any sense challenging the lordship of God" (see Dunn, "*ΚΥΡΙΟΣ* in Acts," in Christof Landmesser, Hans-Joachim Eckstein, and Hermann Lichtenberger, eds., *Jesus Christus als die Mitte der Schrift: Studien zur Hermeneutik des Evangeliums* [Berlin/New York: de Gruyter, 1997] 378).
166 Franzmann, 248–51. I consider the text represented by N to be nearer to the original translation from 𝔊. The repetition of the comparative particle ܐܟ (*ʾaḵ*), corresponding to ὡς in 7b (H), is intended to underline the already existing parallelism of 7a-b.
167 Bauer, 616.
168 Gunkel, 301.
169 Blaszczak, 14. Blaszczak takes insufficient notice of the new beginning in stanza IV, saying: "This verse seems to describe what occurred after the speaker entered the divine presence and became an angelic being."
170 See Hans Wildberger, *Jesaja*, vol. 2: *Jesaja 13–27* (BKAT 10.2; Neukirchen-Vluyn: Neukirchener Verlag, 1978) 691.
171 See BDAG, *s.v.* νεφέλη; Lampe, 906–7.

illuminating. Perhaps the simplest explanation for this strange comparison of the mouth opening with the literary "cloud of dew" lies in the fact that there was already mention of a "cloud of peace" in 35:1 and of the "dew of the Lord" in 35:5.[172] As in 8:4b, and in contrast to the active use of ܦܬܚ (*ptaḥ*) in 31:3a, the Ethpe. ܐܬܦܬܚ (*ʾetptaḥ*) here in 7a corresponds, as a "theological passive" (see Excursus 31),[173] to the intransitive use of ἀνοίγω (cf. linguistically 1 Cor 16:9).[174]

The main emphasis of 7a-b lies on the last word of 7b (see above, and also Excursus 25 on δικαιοσύνη/ܙܕܝܩܘܬܐ [*zaddīqūṯā*]). The "heart" of the speaking "I" is parallel to his "mouth" (see Excursus 4). The interpretation of the paronomasiac image in 7b is made difficult because, unlike στόμα/ܦܘܡܐ (*pummā*) and καρδία/ܠܒܐ (*lebbā*), the Greek equivalent of the Pe. ܓܣܐ (*gsā*) and the related *hapax legomenon* ܓܐܣܝܬܐ (*gāsīṯā*) cannot be determined with any certainty.[175] More likely than Frankenberg's erudite ἀναβλύζω and ἀναβρασμός[176] would be the pairing of ἐρεύγομαι[177] and ἔρευξις[178] or ἔρευγμα.[179] The term ܓܣܐ (*gsā*) is used in a similarly transitive fashion in two other passages (16:2c; 40:2a-b), though there "what comes forth from his [viz., the speaker's] mouth may well be praise."[180] A connection between 7a-b and 1QH xvi.16 (previously viii.16) is unlikely.[181]

The final bicolon, 8a-b, like 6a-b, is characterized by "loose parallelism."[182] Only in ܣ does the *hapax legomenon* ܩܘܪܒܐ (*qurrāḇā*) link back to the last word of 6b, where 𝔊 would have used προσαγωγή ("a way of approach, *access*").[183] This Pauline and deutero-Pauline term (cf. Rom 5:2; Eph 2:18; 3:12) is now applied by the speaking "I" not to the believers redeemed by Jesus Christ but to himself as the exclusively anointed one, as a summary of the total process of his exaltation.[184] The eschatological key word εἰρήνη/ܫܠܡܐ (*šlāmā*), which connects the end of *Ode* 36 to the beginning of *Ode* 35 (cf. "peace" in 10:2), is also derived from the Pauline tradition (cf. Rom 5:1; Eph 2:14-15, 17) but needs less "Christologization" than the preceding term.

With the word πνεῦμα/ܪܘܚܐ (*rūḥā*) in 8b, the speaking "I" comes back to the beginning of his address, but now lays the stress more on the qualifier in the genitive (see Excursus 36 above).[185] This genitive of ܡܕܒܪܢܘܬܐ (*mḏabbrānūṯā*) corresponds to the genitive of οἰκονομία, which is another term from the Pauline tradition and historical influence, used in part somewhat subversively.[186] Diettrich's idea that the "spirit of guidance"—or more accurately of the divine "plan of salvation" and "arrangements for redemption of humans"[187]—presupposes "a specifically Christian mode of thought" is correct (cf. Ignatius *Eph.* 18:2 and 20:1).[188] That is why Connolly's opinion that "the Odist here presents us with the πνεῦμα ἡγεμονικόν of the LXX"[189] is not acceptable, although his criticism of Harris and Mingana's translation of the phrase as "Spirit of Providence"[190] is as justified as his conviction that the verb στηρίζω, found in Ps 50:14b LXX (although here it would be in the passive, as in 11:5a [ἐστηρίχθην]), is "a natural equivalent" of the Ethpa. ܐܫܬܪܪ (*ʾeštarrar*), which is used also in 38:16 and 40:5. However, in looking for other possible equivalents,[191] one also comes across the pas-

172 See Harris and Mingana, 2:382.
173 See commentary on 8:4b; Payne Smith, 2:3338.
174 Aland and Bauer, *s.v.* ἀνοίγω, 2: "to open, . . . to be opened"; BDAG, *s.v.* ἀνοίγω, 6–7.
175 See Payne Smith, 1:757; Brockelmann, *Lexicon*, 126: "fons" only "OS 36,7."
176 Frankenberg, 31; LSJ, *s.vv.* ἀναβλύζω, ἀναβρασμός.
177 BDAG, *s.v.* ἐρεύγομαι: "orig[inally] 'belch', then . . . utter, proclaim."
178 LSJ, *s.v.* ἔρευξις: "eructation."
179 Lampe, 547: "belching."
180 Blaszczak, 106 n. 24 (to p. 14).
181 Contra Carmignac, "Auteur," 82; see Maier, *Qumran-Essener*, 1:90.
182 Blaszczak, 15; see also Franzmann, 251.
183 Payne Smith, 2:3725; BDAG, *s.v.* προσαγωγή.
184 Blaszczak (p. 15) comes to a similar conclusion.
185 Blaszczak (p. 15) disagrees.
186 Cf. Eph 1:10; 3:2, 9; Col 1:25. Whether the *Odes of Solomon* should be included in the history of the extra–New Testament influence of St. Paul (Samuel Vollenweider, "Paulus," *RGG*[4] 6 [2003] 1058–63: "Wirkungsgeschichte") is a matter for future consideration.
187 BDAG, *s.v.* οἰκονομία, 2b; Payne Smith, 1:817–18.
188 Diettrich, 120.
189 Richard Hugh Connolly, review of Harris and Mingana in *JTS* 22 (1920–21) 81.
190 Harris and Mingana, 2:384; also Charlesworth, 127.
191 Payne Smith, 2:4299–300.

sives of *βεβαιόω*[192] and *στερεόω*.[193] This eschatological fixing or establishment, not so much *by* the Spirit[194] as *in* the Spirit of God's redemptive arrangements, still does not contradict the identification of the speaking "I" with the exalted Christ. It could, therefore, be described as a christological establishment or confirmation.

192 BDAG, *s.v.* *βεβαιόω*, 1–2.

193 BDAG, *s.v.* *στερεόω*, 1–2; see also Frankenberg, 31: *ἐστερεώθην*.

194 Blaszczak, 9, 15.

37

Ode 37: Address of One Who Is Redeemed (on the Cross?)

1a I stretched out my hands toward the Lord[a],
1b and toward the Most High I lifted up my voice,
2a and I spoke with the lips of my heart.
2b And he heard me when my voice reached him.
3a His word came to me,
3b that gave me the fruits of my labors
4 and gave me rest in the grace of the Lord.
Hallelujah.

a 1a ܡܪܝܐ N; ܡܪܝ H.

Introduction

Ode 37 is preserved in two Syriac manuscripts.[1] This skillfully constructed first-person address, one of the shortest of the *Odes* (cf. 13; 27; 32), is neither a "baptismal hymn"[2] nor a "hymn of thanksgiving."[3] There is no reason to divide 2b into 2b-c.[4] The mention of the "Lord" (1a, 4) forms an *inclusio* for *Ode* 37, in which, as in the two preceding *Odes*, he is equated with the transcendental "Most High" (1b). A rigorous scrutiny of the subjects of its verbs[5] reveals the underlying structure. The redeemed speaker describes his own actions in the first three lines (1a, 1b, 2a), and in the last three he speaks of the "word" of the Lord, the Most High, in its relationship to him (3a, 3b, 4). The central colon concerns the hearing by the Lord, the Most High, and the success of the goal-oriented actions of the speaking "I" (2b). So the form is not two bicola with a concluding "three-part stich" (1a-b; 2a-b; 3-4)[6] nor yet "three paired cola with a final colon."[7]

The key term of the whole Ode is the plural of ܥܡܠܐ (*ʿamlā*) in 3b, which cannot refer to "words of prayer,"[8] because prayer has not actually been mentioned and the "reaching out of the hands upward" is not, here or in the "parallel passages" (21:1; 27:1; 35:7; 42:1), primarily a "gesture of prayer."[9] Diettrich's question, "Is 'labors' here already used of the ascetic life, as in later Syriac usage, or does it merely mean the normal toil of daily living?" also points in the wrong direction.[10] For, on the one hand, it is necessary to take account of the close connection between *Odes* 35, 36, and 37,[11] and, on the other, there is the "interpretation of the 'Cross-event' . . . as an ascension" to be considered.[12]

Again the question arises as to the identity of the speaking "I."[13] Is it any redeemed person speaking with a touch of Old Testament "piety of suffering,"[14] or, more specifically, is it a Christian follower of Paul, perhaps even Paul himself?[15] Or is it not more likely that there is a subtle allusion to the Crucified and that the exalted

1 Mss.: Codex H, 20b; Codex N, 150[v] (ܣ). Ed./trans.: Charlesworth, 129; Franzmann, 253–54; Lattke, 3:141–47.
2 Contra Schille, 65. Bernard (p. 122), in a note on 4 refers to "baptismal rest" and on 1a he refers to 21:1. In a detailed note on 21:1, he shows the connection between "outstretching of the hands" and "baptismal rest" (p. 90), which, however, is not relevant to the *Odes of Solomon*.
3 Contra Greßmann, 467; Bauer, 617.
4 Contra Franzmann, 253–54.
5 All the verbs of *Ode* 37 are in the perfect. Why Berger and Nord (p. 966) translated them in the present is inexplicable.
6 Contra Diettrich, 121.
7 Contra Schille, 65.
8 Contra Greßmann, 467.
9 Contra Spitta, 260, who is still completely under Harnack's (pp. 67, 90) influence here, classifying *Ode* 37 as "purely Jewish" (see Spitta, 288).
10 The comparison with "Ode 27 (42:1-3)" does nothing to make it "possible . . . that we are moving in the mental world of the Essenes and Therapeutae" (Diettrich, 121).
11 Pierre, 167–76.
12 See commentary on 27:1.
13 Abramowski, 59.
14 Friedrich Hauck, "κόπος, κοπιάω," *ThWNT* 3 (1938) 827; *TDNT* 3:829.
15 Hauck, "κόπος," *ThWNT* 3:828–29; *TDNT* 3:829–30.

Christ himself is made the speaker? It may be true that *Ode* 37 played a part in the attribution of the whole collection to Solomon. But that "this Ode might be labelled an Ode of Solomon in a historical sense, without any need to introduce Christ as Solomon,"[16] is most unlikely.

Interpretation

■ **1-2a** The Pe. ܦܫܛ (*pšaṭ*) in 1a may correspond to a form of ἐκπετάννυμι, "spread/hold out,"[17] though without alluding to Isa 65:2 LXX (cf. Rom 10:21). More probably, however, 𝔊 had ἐξέτεινα τὰς χεῖράς μου πρὸς τὸν κύριον, which would make a slight allusion to John 21:18, the "stretching out of the hands" of the "crucified,"[18] but also—not least because of the parallel verb in 1b—would specify it as an extension *upward* (see Excursus 27).[19]

Verses 1b and 1a are "parallel with chiasmus" (AB || B'A').[20] Because line 2a will complete the tricolon, it is not permissible to import the term "mouth" from such passages as 7:28 and 31:3-4 and to interpret the "voice" of the speaking "I" as the voice of his *mouth*. In any case ܩܠܐ (*qālā*) here corresponds to φωνή, "voice,"[21] so the second statement of the speaking "I" could be subversive in the sense that the φωνὴ μεγάλη of the Crucified (Mark 15:37; Matt 27:50; Luke 23:46) becomes too soft for the public to hear. The paronomasia or "subtlety to the repetition of the root ܪܘܡ in 1[b]"[22] is present only in 𝔖, since the equivalent of the Aph. ܐܪܝܡ (*ʾarīm*) was probably not ὑψόω[23] but either αἴρω[24] or ἐπαίρω.[25] The decibel level is of no importance, as can be seen from the next line.

The singular image of the innermost "lips of the heart" bears no relation to the mystic "prayer of Jesus" or "prayer of the heart," in which "the understanding and the emotions of the heart" join together.[26] It must be understood in the context of the other occurrences of "heart" and "lips" in the *Odes of Solomon*.[27] As in 11:6, the Pa. ܡܠܠ (*mallel*) is equivalent to λαλέω.[28] Whether the preposition ἐν was placed before χείλεσι is not as important as the possibility that Ps 21:8b LXX (ἐλάλησαν ἐν χείλεσιν, "they spoke with *their* lips")[29] is here being used subversively. Psalm 22 (21 LXX) plays a part in the passion narratives (Mark 15:34; Matt 27:46) and also elsewhere in the *Odes of Solomon* and in early Christian writings (cf. *1 Clem.* 16:16).[30] *What* the speaking "I" said is not reported.

■ **2b** Already in the New Testament there is great reluctance to "ascrib[e] 'hearing' to God Himself."[31] If *Ode* 37 really refers to the Crucified, it will be necessary to include it in the list of early texts influenced by Matt 27:46 ("Jesus' cry of dereliction") and to consider the following: "This Word from the Cross posed difficulties for a belief in Christ's divinity."[32] The modern idea of the "absence of God"[33] is not relevant to 2b, since the "voice," mentioned in 1b, of the speaking "I" "came"[34] to the hearing of the Lord, the Most High, that is, "reached him."[35] In contrast to the Pe. ܫܡܥ (*šmaʿ*), which certainly corresponds to ἀκούω, "hear,"[36] it is not certain that the Pe. ܢܦܠ (*npal*) followed by the preposition ܠܘܬ (*lwāṯ*) represents a form of πίπτω, "to fall."[37] It is also quite possible that the expression of simultane-

16 Harris and Mingana, 2:389.
17 BDAG, *s.v.* ἐκπετάννυμι: "an imploring gesture."
18 BDAG, *s.v.* ἐκτείνω, 1.
19 See Payne Smith, 2:3318. Frankenberg still had only the H text, which says "to my Lord" instead of "to the Lord." He also omits the suffix to "hands" in his retroversion: ἐξέτεινα τὰς χεῖρας πρὸς τὸν κύριόν μου (see Frankenberg, 31).
20 Franzmann, 253.
21 Payne Smith, 2:3618; BDAG, *s.v.* φωνή, 2.
22 Franzmann, 254.
23 Contra Frankenberg, 31: ὕψωσα.
24 BDAG, *s.v.* αἴρω, 1b.
25 BDAG, *s.v.* ἐπαίρω, 1: "raise one's voice"; cf. Payne Smith, 2:3859. The Syriac verb of 1b is also used in 21:1a: "I raised my arms on high"; see commentary on that verse.
26 Amos Pichler, "Jesusgebet, Jesusmystik," *LThK*³ 5 (1996) 846.
27 Cf. 8:1; 12:2; 16:2; 20:4; 21:8; 30:5; 40:2; 42:14; and see Excursuses 4 and 16.
28 Also Frankenberg, 31: καὶ ἐλάλησα χείλεσι τῆς καρδίας μου.
29 Rahlfs, 2:20; Brenton, 709.
30 BDAG, *s.v.* χεῖλος, 1.
31 Gerhard Kittel, "ἀκούω, κτλ.," *ThWNT* 1 (1933) 222; *TDNT* 1:221.
32 Luz, *Matthäus*, 4:335.
33 Ibid., 4:340–42.
34 Ungnad and Staerk, 35.
35 Klaus Beyer, letter of November 13, 2002. Literally, "when my voice fell to/near him."
36 Payne Smith, 2:4214; BDAG, *s.v.* ἀκούω.
37 See Payne Smith, 2:2411–12; BDAG, *s.v.* πίπτω;

ity (ܟܕ [*kad*], "when," etc.) was represented in 𝔊 by ὡς ἐγένετο ἡ φωνή μου εἰς/πρὸς αὐτόν (cf. linguistically Luke 1:44).[38]

■ **3-4** It is not really possible to reconstruct the Greek of 3a. For ܦܬܓܡܐ (*petḡāmā*), which is, not only in the *Odes of Solomon*, interchangeable with ܡܠܬܐ (*melltā*), is used primarily "to translate λόγος and ῥῆμα" (see Excursus 12).[39] The Pe. ܐܬܐ (*ʾetā*), corresponding to ἔρχομαι, "come," with the reciprocally constructed preposition ܠܘܬܝ (*lwāt*; here with first singular suffix; cf. the third masculine singular suffix in 2b), comes near to personifying the "word" of the Lord, the Most High; although, compared to the mythological "coming of God" in John 14:23, it is not quite as astounding.[40]

The two last lines refer to 3a by use of the relative particle ܕ (*d*-).[41] The parallelism of 3b and 4[42] is based mainly on the actually redundant repetition of ܝܗܒ ܠܝ (*yab lī*), "gave me," which most probably represents two different verbs in 𝔊.[43] Either 3b or 4 might, however, have used a form of χαρίζομαι.[44] The remainder of 3b can be discussed after the excursus.

Excursus 37: "To Give, Grant" and "Gift (of Grace)" in the *Odes of Solomon*

Given the number of occurrences of ܝܗܒ (*yab*), including idiomatic phrases, in the *Odes of Solomon*, the use of this verb, whose imperfect is replaced by ܢܬܠ (*nettel*), is both uncomplicated and intensely theological.[45] In some thirty passages that use "give," to which another five must be added in which the regular Ethpe. ܐܬܝܗܒ (*ʾetīheb*) occurs,[46] more than two-thirds must be counted as theological, since the subject—or, for the passive, the instigator—is God the Lord, who may also be seen as the Most High or the Father. With few exceptions these passages can also be described as soteriological, since the *direct* objects—for the passive, the subjects (6:6c, 12; 15:10c; 30:6b [see below])—are often items or means of salvation: "thy heart, Lord, to thy believers" (4:3c); "us thy fellowship" (4:9a); "justice" (5:3a ℭ);[47] "us his praise for his name" (6:7a); "from the Most High the drink" (6:12); "a mouth to his creation" (7:24a); "life" (15:10c); "me the way" (17:8a); "me power over bonds" (22:4); "them energy for life" (22:10b); "me the rod of his powerfulness" (29:8a); "us (only in H) of his praises" (41:4b).

This listing has included also some of the *indirect* objects, which must, of course, be determined individually in context, but can be generally summarized as follows: "to me" (preponderant at thirteen times);[48] "to him" (7:12; 31:5); "to us" (4:9; 6:6, 7; 41:4 [H]; see also 14:9c); "to you" (9:2, 10); "to them" (6:12 [ℭ]; 22:10 [ℭ]; 24:6; 38:12); "to all" (15:10); "to the believers" (4:3); "to the creation" (7:24); "to the aeons" (12:4); "to the world" (19:5).[49] In some passages there is no indirect object (4:13; 17:12; 24:9b; 30:6).

In addition to the direct objects (for the passive, subjects) of this soteriological sort, there is quite a collection of other objects (or subjects) of "to give" and "to grant": "your/my soul," that is, your/my self (9:2); "it [viz., the word]" (12:4a); "our petitions" (14:9c); "him [viz., the Lord] for food" (24:6a); "the word," that is, the password or answer (24:9b); "praise" (29:11a); "wine to drink" (38:12b). Without *any* grammatical object is the summarizing assertion made to God: "For what thou gavest, thou gavest freely" (4:13a-b).

The commentary on 4:13 referred to "gift" or "gift of grace." This leads to the discussion of the

Frankenberg, 31: καὶ ἤκουσέ μου τῆς φωνῆς παρ' αὐτῷ πιπτούσης.

38 See Payne Smith, 2:1918; BDAG, *s.v.* γίνομαι.

39 See Payne Smith, 2:2110–12, 3335–36; BDAG, *s.vv.* λόγος, ῥῆμα. With the use of ܡܠܠ (*mallel*) in 2a, it appears that someone passed up an excuse for paronomasia, either in the Syriac original or in the translation from the Greek, both here and in 42:14b-c.

40 See Payne Smith, 1:414; BDAG, *s.v.* ἔρχομαι, 4bβ.

41 The entries for ܕ in the concordance should be corrected: Lattke, *Bedeutung*, 2:68 (relative pronoun); 2:74 (conjunction).

42 Franzmann, 254.

43 Frankenberg, 31: ἔδωκέν μοι … καὶ παρέστησέ μοι.

44 BDAG, *s.v.* χαρίζομαι, 1. For the wording, cf. Rom 8:32; Gal 3:18; Phil 2:9.

45 See Payne Smith, 1:1564–68.

46 Brockelmann, *Grammatik* §175 n. 2.

47 ℭ always uses the verb ϯ (*ti*) for "to give" (5:3; 6:12, 17; 22:4, 10). The Greek *Vorlage* of 5:3 ℭ is likely to have used χάριν (not κρίσιν), which agrees better with the Syriac text of 5:3: "Freely I received thy grace" (see commentary on *Ode* 5 stanza I).

48 See 5:3; 7:10; 9:2; 10:2; 14:9; 15:7; 17:8; 22:4; 29:2, 8; 35:5; 37:3, 4.

49 Two passages that differ from the others are 6:17 ("They gave strength to their coming [openness in ℭ] and light to their eyes") and 29:11 ("I gave praise to the Most High"); see BDAG, *s.v.* δίδωμι, 3. On the variant reading of H in 31:2b, see the commentary on that passage.

term ܡܘܗܒܬܐ (*mawhaḇṯā*), which occurs three times altogether, once as the direct equivalent of χάρισμα: ἐπλούτησα ἐν χαρίσματι αὐτοῦ (11:9b).[50] The New Testament translators always use ܡܘܗܒܬܐ and ܡܘܗ̈ܒܬܐ (*mawhḇāṯā*) for the singular and plural of χάρισμα. This is true also for the twelve occurrences of δωρεά[51] in the New Testament and even for the less common terms δόμα[52] and δώρημα.[53] That means that it is not possible to be sure that in the other two passages 𝔊 also used χάρισμα: "according to his gracious gift he gave to me" (15:7a); "I grew up by his gift" (35:6a).

The first of the passages just cited makes a return to the theological and soteriological uses of ܝܗܒ (*yaḇ*) and ܐܬܝܗܒ (*ʾeṯīheḇ*). One may assume that in most of the passages—already discussed or still awaiting discussion—equivalent forms of δίδωμι would have been used in 𝔊.[54] But there are other verbs, for example, δωρέομαι[55] and χαρίζομαι,[56] which also come under consideration in certain cases. *Ode* 15:7a is one of four passages where the *direct* object can be deduced from the context. The statement of the redeemed one in 29:2b, "according to his grace he also gave to me," is very close to 15:7a. Not quite as closely related, though, are the two occurrences of ܢܬܠ (*nettel*), "And according to the multitude of thy mercies / so thou wilt *grant* me. / And hasten to *grant* our petitions" (14:9a-b and 9c). In 31:5b "granted" refers to the justification of the Lord by his Father (31:5a).

The use of "to grant" changes radically when the emphasis falls on the dependent clause (see 7:10b, 12a; 10:2b). In 6:6c, "were given" means "were added" because the Ethpe. refers to "new members of the movement."[57] And in 30:6b, the Ethpe. followed by the preposition ܒ (*b-*) probably corresponds to τιθέναι: "until it [viz., the spring of the Lord] was set."[58]

Finally, four quite different passages remain to be discussed, in the order of their appearance, in which the "giving" of eschatological gifts is done by four different subjects, which can be called theological only in the broadest sense. "Righteousness" is so far personified that she can "take" and "give" the crown of truth (9:10; see Excursus 41). The redeemed Redeemer proclaims: "I gave my knowledge without jealousy" (17:12a). The holy Spirit "gave the mixture" of the milk from the two breasts of the Father "to the world" (19:5a). This mixture should not be mistaken for "the dew of the Lord," which is compared to "milk," that was "given" to the speaking "I" by the community (35:5b). And here in *Ode* 37 it is the "word" of the Lord, the Most High, that "gave me the fruits of my labors" and—in parallel with it—"rest in the grace of the Lord" (37:3b-4).[59]

It is now possible to return to 3b, where the key term of the whole Ode is the direct object of "to give." The metaphorical expression "fruits" poses no problems, since the plural can also be taken in the sense of yield (see Excursus 11).[60] The *hapax legomenon* ܥܡܠܐ (*ʿamlā*), on the other hand, which is also in the plural,[61] is much more difficult to interpret; it cannot refer to "words of prayer,"[62] nor to lifting up the voice (1b), nor the speaking with the lips of the heart (2a). If the "labors"—in 𝔊 the genitive plural of κόπος[63] or πόνος[64]—referred to any actions mentioned in the text of this Ode, it would be the stretching out of the hands (1a) interpreted as an indication of suffering. But since this stretching out expresses a movement toward the Most High (cf. 35:7 and the reference to the Ascension in *Ode* 27) rather than a painful dislocation of the limbs, the mention of "labors" or "pains" seems to me an allusion to the passion of (Jesus) Christ as a whole, probably linked to the "travail" of the Suffering Servant of God (Isa 53:11 LXX: ἀπὸ τοῦ πόνου τῆς ψυχῆς αὐτοῦ [cf. ἐν πόνῳ in v. 4]; *1 Clem.* 16:3, 12).[65]

Anyone who considers this interpretation too bold will have to find another explanation for that cryptic

50 See Payne Smith, 1:1567; BDAG, *s.v.* χάρισμα.
51 BDAG, *s.v.* δωρεά: "gift, bounty" of God.
52 BDAG, *s.v.* δόμα: "gift" (four times).
53 BDAG, *s.v.* δώρημα: "gift, present" (twice).
54 See BDAG, *s.v.* δίδωμι; Friedrich Büchsel, "δίδωμι, κτλ.," *ThWNT* 2 (1935) 168; *TDNT* 2:166, unfortunately is quite inadequate, despite Gerhard Kittel's foreword.
55 BDAG, *s.v.* δωρέομαι: "present, bestow."
56 BDAG, *s.v.* χαρίζομαι, 1: "to give freely as a favor, give graciously."
57 See commentary on that passage.
58 See commentary on that passage.
59 The statement of 37:3a-b is the "reverse" of 10:2b (he "granted me to speak the fruit of his peace") rather than of 8:1-2 and 14:6-7 (Gemünden, *Vegetationsmetaphorik*, 402 n. 164).
60 See BAGD, *s.v.* καρπός, 1b: "result, outcome, product."
61 See Payne Smith, 2:2913.
62 Greßmann, 467.
63 BDAG, *s.v.* κόπος, 1–2.
64 BDAG, *s.v.* πόνος, 1–2; Frankenberg, 31.
65 Rahlfs, 2:639; Brenton, 889: "from the travail of

term. In addition to κόπος and πόνος (see above), ܥܡܠܐ (*ʿamlā*) can also be used for μόχθος, but, since an allusion to Isa 61:8 LXX (δώσω τὸν μόχθον αὐτῶν δικαίοις, "I will give their labor to the just")[66] is quite unlikely,[67] one might think of "exertions" or "hardships" undergone, as in Paul's lists of his sufferings.[68] More generally, κόπος could be a reminder of "the actions of Wisdom on the model of the historical Psalms of the Old Testament": ἀπέδωκεν ὁσίοις μισθὸν κόπων αὐτῶν, "She gave to holy people the reward of their labors" (Wis 10:17 NRSV).[69] Even less illuminating is Diettrich's reference to the many occurrences of μόχθος in the commonplace wisdom of the Preacher.[70]

The complete phrase "fruits of my labors" is parallel to "rest" in 4, but at the same time ἀνάπαυσις/ܢܝܚܐ (*nyāḥā*) is in sharp contrast to the painful "labors" of 3b (see Excursus 3). "Homeland"[71] is not a suitable translation of the term "rest," which forms part of the Christian Gnostic vocabulary belonging to the complex of "realized eschatology."[72] The preposition ܒ (*b-*) does not have to correspond to ἐν in 𝔊.[73] But *even if* ἐν had been used, the phrase as a whole could still have been intended instrumentally.[74] Since it was the word of the Lord, the Most High, however, that gave the eschatological rest to the speaker, who had endured such labors, the expression "in the grace of the Lord" denotes the specific and powerful sphere of the total event of salvation (cf. for the wording 2 Cor 1:12).[75]

his soul." In view of *Hermas, Sim.* 105(IX.28):4 ("fruit" of martyrdom) and Ignatius *Smyrn.* 1:2 (the passion of Jesus Christ as the "fruit" from which we "come"), the meaning of the plural of "fruit" becomes still clearer (see Ehrman, 1:297, 2:455; BDAG, *s.v.* καρπός, 1b).

66 Rahlfs, 2:648; Brenton, 896.

67 See BDAG, *s.v.* μόχθος: "labor, exertion."

68 See Michael Wolter, "Leiden III. Neues Testament," *TRE* 20 (1990) 680–82.

69 Rahlfs, 2:360; Georgi, 436, 439.

70 Diettrich, 121. Cf. Qoh 1:3; 2:10-11, 18-22, 24; 3:13; 4:4, 6, 8-9; 5:14, 17-18; 6:7; 8:15; 9:9; 10:15.

71 Berger and Nord, 966: "Heimat."

72 Peel, *Rheginos*, 54, 140–43. If Wray had included *Ode* 37 in her conspectus, her definition of "rest" as "present inner-peace and tranquility as a result of trusting in Christ (*Odes of Solomon*)" (*Rest,* 32) would have been different (see ibid., 26–27, 32).

73 See Frankenberg, 31: χάριτι τοῦ κυρίου, "by the grace of the Lord."

74 See BDAG, *s.v.* ἐν, 5b.

75 On ἐν χάριτι θεοῦ, "in God's grace," see Rudolf Bultmann, *Der zweite Brief an die Korinther* (KEK, Sonderband; ed. Erich Dinkler; Göttingen: Vandenhoeck & Ruprecht, 1976) 37–39.

38

Ode 38: The Redeemed I and the Address of Truth Personified

(I) 1a I went up into the light of Truth as into a chariot.
1b And Truth led me and made me come
2a and allowed me to cross over empty chasms[a] and rifts
2b and saved me from cliffs and waves.
3a And she was/became for me a haven[b] of salvation
3b and set me on the step[c] to [lit. of] immortal life.
4a And she went with me, gave me rest, and did not let me go astray,
4b because she was and is[d] Truth.
(II) 5a And there was no danger for me,
5b since I walked with her.
5c And I did not stray in/because of anything,
5d because I obeyed her.
(III) 6a For Error fled[e] before her
6b and did not meet her.
7a But Truth went on the straight way,
7b and all that I did not know she showed me,
8a all the drugs/poisons of Error
8b and the blows/scourges that are believed[f] to be the sweetness of Death.
9a And I saw the Archcorruptor (corruptor of all),
9b while the Bride who brings corruption was being adorned[g]
9c and the Bridegroom who is corrupting and corrupted.
(IV) 10a And I asked Truth: "Who are these?"
10b And she said to me: "This is the Deceiver and Error,
11a and they imitate the Beloved and his Bride,
11b and they lead the world astray and corrupt it.
(V) 12a And they invite the many to the wedding feast,
12b and give them to drink the wine of their intoxication,
13a so that they vomit up their knowledges and their thoughts,
13b and make them[h] foolish/senseless,
14a and then they throw them out/abandon them.
(VI) 14b But they go about
14c raving[i] and corrupting/corrupted.
14d As there is no heart in them
14e they do not seek it."
(VII) 15a But *I* became wise, since I did

a 2a ܦܫܝܩܬܐ ܣܪܝܩܐ N; ܦܫܝܩܬܐ H.
b 3a ܠܠܡܐܢܐ N; ܠܡܐܢܐ H.
c 3b ܕܪܓܐ N; ܕܪ̈ܓܐ H.
d 4b ܘܗܘܝܘ N; ܗܘ H.
e 6a ܥܪܩܐ ܗܘܬ N; ܥܪܩܐ ܠܗ̇ H.
f 8b ܡܣܬܒܪܝܢ N; ܡܣܒܪܝܢ H.
g 9b ܟܕ ܡܬܨܒܬܐ ܗܘܬ ܟܠܬܐ ܕܡܚܒܠܢܝܬܐ N; ܟܕ ܡܬܨܒܬܐ ܟܠܬܐ ܕܡܚܒܠܬܢܝܬܐ H.
h 13b ܠܗܘܢ H; ܠܗܝܢ N.
i 14c ܦܩܪܝܢ N; ܦܩܕܝܢ H.

not fall into the hands of the Deceivers[k].
15b And I was glad for myself because Truth had gone with me.
16a Then I was established/firmly fixed and revived and was redeemed,
16b and my foundations were laid by the hand of the Lord,
16c because *he* planted me.
(VIII) 17a For *he* set the root
17b and watered, fixed, and blessed it,
17c and its fruits are for ever.[l]
(IX) 18a It went deep, grew upward, and spread out,[m]
18b and became full and large.
(X) 19a And the Lord alone was glorified/praised
19b by his planting and by his cultivation,
20a by his care and by the blessing of his lips,
20b by the beautiful planting of his right [hand]
21a and by the existence of his planting —
21b and by the understanding of his mind.
Hallelujah.

k 15a ܡܛܥܝ̈ܢܐ N; ܡܛܥܝܢܐ H (?); see Lattke, *Bedeutung*, 1:50, 70.
l 17c ܠܥܠܡܝܢ N; ܠܥܠܡ H.
m 18a ܐܥܡܩ ܘܣܠܩ ܘܐܬܦܬܝ N; ܥܡܩ ܘܐܣܩ ܘܦܬܝ H.

Introduction

Ode 38 is preserved in two Syriac manuscripts.[1] Even for those who accept the interpretation of *Ode* 38 as "the oldest anti-Manichaean document known so far" and the late dating that entails,[2] this "description of redemption"[3] is still "full of difficulties"[4] from beginning to end as well as "very obscure."[5] Although this long Ode, filled with images, contains "mythological speculations" and—in the context of antique Judaism—can be called "Christian Gnostic,"[6] it must not be classified as Valentinian. The explanation for the parallels between the *Odes of Solomon* (and especially *Ode* 38) and the *Gospel of Truth*, demonstrated by Robert M. Grant[7]

1 Mss.: Codex H, 26b–28a; Codex N, 150ᵛ–51ʳ (ܣ). Ed./trans.: Charlesworth, 129–34; Franzmann, 255–64; Lattke, 3:149–88.

2 Drijvers, "Odes," 129–30. Luise Abramowski's rejection of Drijvers's theory is based not only on his "preference for keeping the *Odes* and Ephraem as close together as possible" (see L. Abramowski, "Sprache," 84–88; see also eadem, review of Han J. W. Drijvers, *Studies in Early Syriac Christianity* [CStS 198; London: Variorum Reprints, 1984] in *JTS* n.s. 38 [1987] 218) but also on a remark by Harris and Mingana on the corruptors and deceivers of *Ode* 38: "If it were not for the fact that antiquity has been established for the Odes . . . we would be tempted to regard the attack on the heretical teachers who make men mad, as a conventional Patristic attack on Mani and his followers the Manichaeans" (see Harris and Mingana, 2:395).

3 Reitzenstein, *Das iranische Erlösungsmysterium*, 91. Rudolph pertinently quotes the beginning of *Ode* 38 as a description of the "presence of salvation" (see Rudolph, *Gnosis*, 240).

4 Harris and Mingana, 2:394.

5 Murray, *Symbols*, 133.

6 Abramowski, 45.

7 Robert M. Grant, "Notes on Gnosis," *VC* 11 (1957) 150–51. He later distanced himself from his claim "that the Odes are Valentinian" (idem, *Gnosticism and Early Christianity* [2nd ed.; New York: Columbia University Press, 1966] 134): "What the Odes have in common with the Gospel of Truth is a

and Schenke,[8] is that "the author of the *Gospel of Truth* belongs to the same milieu in which this collection of lyrics has its roots."[9] A number of the terms and images used in *Ode* 38 can be found among the building blocks of later Gnostic mythology.[10]

As a whole, *Ode* 38 is neither "an Apocalypse in verse"[11] nor a member of the class of "hymns of initiation."[12] Schille is, however, right to divide the Ode into two parts,[13] which Franzmann refined by noting that the first "sub-ode" (1-16, not 1-15 as Schille has it) is linked to the second by 16c "as a deliberate bridging verse."[14] One might even claim that the linking of the first-person address (1-16), including a didactic reply by Truth personified (10b-14a or even 10b-14e), with the second part of the Ode, in the third person (17-21),[15] begins with the theological passive and mention of the divine "Lord" in 16b.

The "I" of this Ode is, in the first place, an eminent redeemed person who is led and established by Truth personified (stanzas I and VII). This redeemed one, who has become wise, is not described as a "believer."[16] Drijvers also falls into some confusion, since, according to his somewhat questionable interpretation, "the redeemed believer . . . has become in a sense identical with Christ," and yet "the Light of Truth undoubtedly denotes Christ."[17] But the "I" distinguishes himself from the "light of Truth" (1a) and is, in the first part, subordinate to "Truth" as much as to the "Lord" who plants him (16b-c). In the second part, it is only the necessary "root" (17a), not the "fruits" (17c), much less the whole "plantation" (19-21), that can be equated to the "I" of the first part—who has, in any case, disappeared from the scene. One question that will arise is whether the "root" or the "shoot" stands for the "Messiah."[18] If that were so, the identity of the speaking "I" would be certain in the unity of two parts. At all events, it is doubtful that the "I" is merely Abramowski's "human being," the "*filius adoptivus*," who "experiences a turning toward God."[19] For the connection between the redeemed Redeemer of the *Odes of Solomon* (e.g., in 17:4-5) and the speaking "I" of this Ode in his relationship with "Truth" (e.g., 38:4-5, 15-16) must raise the question whether the "I" is the redeemed "Son of Truth" (23:18) and thus—as in *Odes* 35, 36, and 37—the Kyrios Christos, whose redemptive activity is not mentioned in this Ode, a lack that will be supplied in the Odes that follow.

Greßmann[20] describes Gunkel's commentary[21] as "fundamental." This judgment must be subject to some reservations, since Gunkel employs the terms "soul," "singer," "seer," and "poet" indiscriminately for the *masculine* "I" (see ܡܗܠܟ ܗܘܝܬ [*mhallek̲-wēt̲*] in 5b).[22] His headline style description of the subject of the Ode as "Ascent of the Soul to Heaven" has unfortunately taken root in subsequent work.[23] Whether there is, in fact, any notion of an "ascension" will be seen in due course.[24]

Interpretation

■ **1-4** The term "light" has no further part to play in *Ode* 38. One might refer to 29:7b ("and led me by his light"), but the use of ܢܘܗܪܐ (*nuhrā*) here in 1a is unique. As was pointed out already at 18:6, where the term

speculative Jewish Christianity which comes close to Gnosticism but is not fully Gnostic."

8 Schenke, *Herkunft*, 26–27, 34, 38.

9 Schenke, "Evangelium Veritatis," 32.

10 Franzmann has collected a large number of Gnostic parallels, especially to *Ode* 38 (Franzmann, "Background"), that are mainly evidence of the influence of the *Odes of Solomon* on later writers.

11 James Rendel Harris, "The Odes of Solomon and the Apocalypse of Peter," *ExpT* 42 (1930–31) 22.

12 Schille, 76.

13 Ibid., 78.

14 Franzmann, 260. This negates Schille's theory of two originally independent Odes (see Schille, 78). Diettrich's hypothesis of a revision, in which he removes more than half of *Ode* 38 in order to interpret 1-2 and 9-14 as "originally an apocalypse" (see Diettrich, 121) is, quite reasonably, rejected by Kittel (pp. 17, 130–32).

15 This part, though less Gnostically mythological, is also didactic (on the "intensely mythological didactic poems *Odes* 33 and 38," see Abramowski, 32).

16 Contra Drijvers, "Odes," 121.

17 Drijvers, "Odes," 121–22.

18 See BDAG, *s.v.* ῥίζα, 2.

19 Abramowski, 57.

20 Greßmann, 468.

21 Gunkel, 315–18.

22 Ibid., 316–18.

23 Apart from Greßmann, 468, see, e.g., Bultmann, "Bedeutung," 133 = idem, *Exegetica*, 91; idem, "Untersuchungen," 161 = idem, *Exegetica*, 172 ("Chariot of Truth"!); Rudolph, *Gnosis*, 240.

24 Abramowski, 58.

ܢܗܝܪܐ (*nahhīrā*), which also corresponds to φῶς, is, in dualistic fashion, *directly* parallel to ܫܪܪܐ (*šrārā*), "light" and "truth" are often to be found contextually linked in the *Odes of Solomon*.[25] So it is easy to see how the terms φῶς and ἀλήθεια, taken from Ps 42:3 LXX–not from "John's Gospel"[26]–were combined in poetic freedom into the phrase "light of truth" (see on 1b below).[27] This genitive pairing is not meant for "the good ship Light of Truth,"[28] nor is "light" a "philosophical metaphor for the intelligibility of being and truth."[29] Before returning to the many occurrences of the term "truth" in *Ode* 38 (see on 1b below; and see Excursus 1), it is necessary to determine the exact meaning of the Pe. ܣܠܩ (*sleq*). The first point that can be made is that the preposition ܠ (*l-*) that follows it corresponds to εἰς, although that may not be so when it recurs before the term "chariot," where that is compared to the metaphorical "light," or to the complete phrase "light of truth."[30] Since the *Vorlage* of the *hapax legomenon* ܡܪܟܒܬܐ (*markabtā*) is not a supposedly "misunderstood ὄχημα of a Greek text"[31] but probably ἅρμα,[32] the links that come to mind are τὸ ἅρμα τοῦ θεοῦ μυριοπλάσιον ("The chariots of God are ten thousand fold") in Ps 67:18a LXX[33] and also the memory that was strongly present in both Jewish history and early Christianity of "the story of the crossing of the Red Sea."[34] So the divine chariot of light, which has very little connection with the prophet's ὅρασις τοῦ ἅρματος (Ezek 43:3),[35] may be looked upon as a positive counter to the pharaonic chariots of war (cf. Exod 14:6-28; 15:4, 19). The accepted interpretation, with few exceptions,[36] of ܣܠܩ (*sleq*) + ܠ (*l-*) as the equivalent of ἀναβαίνω εἰς, "to go up, ascend," that is, as an "upward movement,"[37] is hardly supported by the remainder of the Ode. Even though ἀναβαίνω εἰς is occasionally used of embarking on "ships,"[38] it is notable that ἐμβαίνω εἰς[39] is commonly found as a variant reading, once even ἐπιβαίνω εἰς (Acts 21:6).[40] Whether 𝔊 used ἀναβαίνω or ἐμβαίνω cannot be determined. The

25 Cf. 12:1-3; 15:2-4; 25:7-10; 32:1-2; 41:14-16; and see Excursus 10.

26 Contra Drijvers, "Odes," 122.

27 See Harris and Mingana, 2:148–49, 394–95.

28 Harris, "Thirty-Eighth Ode," 30.

29 Werner Beierwaltes, "Licht," *HWP* 5 (1980) 282. Stölten (p. 53) already has a parallel to 1a: "Parmenides rides in a horse-drawn chariot to the light, and there receives a revelation of (from) the truth." If, in the vocative phrase τέκνα φωτὸς ἀληθείας (Ignatius *Phld.* 2:1; cf. Eph 5:8), ἀληθείας is *not* in apposition to φωτός (the Armenian version reads "children of light *and* truth" [see Fischer, 139, 194]) that would argue for a link between Ignatius of Antioch and the *Odes of Solomon*. This is the more likely as there are points of agreement between Ignatius *Phld.* 2-3 and *Ode* 38 (e.g., "plantation of the Father"; see on 16-21 below). It is strange that neither Paulsen (*Studien*, 31, etc.) nor Schoedel (*Ignatius*, 147, etc.) refers to *Ode* 38:1a, because, in view of this verse, one cannot claim that the phrase φῶς ἀληθείας is "peculiar to Ignatius" (Bauer and Paulsen [p. 81], referring to Ps 42:3 LXX). Accepting the traditional early date for the Ignatian epistles (see Georg Schöllgen, "Die Ignatianen als pseudepigraphisches Briefcorpus: Anmerkung zu den Thesen von Reinhard M. Hübner," *ZAC* 2 [1998] 16, 25) and also assuming that their author knew the *Odes of Solomon*, one can set the date for the origin of the latter near the beginning of the second century C.E. (see. Lattke, "Dating," 57 = idem, *Bedeutung*, 4:129; idem, *Oden*, 33). The expression "light of truth" in the Coptic *Gospel of Truth* 36,10-11 (Schenke, "Evangelium Veritatis," 41; Attridge and MacRae, "Gospel of Truth," 108–9) can also, perhaps, be traced to the first verse of *Ode* 38, although Schenke (*Herkunft*, 51) makes no reference to it. In general, however, "light of truth" is a favorite didactic expression, whose use in documents issued by the Vatican probably derives rather from the later church fathers.

30 On ܐܝܟ ܕ (*ʾak d-*), see Nöldeke §364.C.

31 Contra Harris and Mingana, 2:394.

32 Payne Smith, 2:3917; BDAG, *s.v.* ἅρμα; cf. Kittel's "doubts" (pp. 17–18) about the exegesis of the "*Ode* as a Noachian hymn" by Harris ("Thirty-Eighth Ode"; and idem, "Two Flood-Hymns").

33 Rahlfs, 2:69; Brenton, 736.

34 Drijvers, "Odes," 122.

35 Contra Diettrich, 123: "the throne of God likened to a chariot as in Ezek 1."

36 E.g., Wellhausen, 637; Lattke, *Bedeutung*, 1:173; idem, *Oden*, 199.

37 BDAG, *s.v.* ἀναβαίνω, 1a.

38 Cf. Jonah 1:3; Matt 14:32; Mark 6:51; Luke 8:22; John 6:24; Acts 21:6 and see BDAG, *s.v.* ἀναβαίνω, 1aα.

39 BDAG, *s.v.* ἐμβαίνω.

40 Omitted from BDAG, *s.v.* ἐπιβαίνω, 1. On these variants, see Rahlfs, 2:526; NA^{27} on the relevant passages.

important point is that there is not the "slightest indication" of any "ascension . . . of the soul to the heights of heaven" or "driving up in the chariot."[41] As one may embark on a ship, so one can also enter a sedan chair or get into, that is, mount, a chariot.[42]

These clarifications lead us to Greßmann's retroversion of 1a; in his opinion, "the *Odes* were originally written in Greek."[43] Criticizing Frankenberg, Greßmann expounds the text of 1a: "ἀνέβην εἰς τὸ φῶς τῆς ἀληθείας ὡς ἐφ' ἅρμα . . . (viz., καθήμενος ['seated'], I prefer the accusative), Fr[ankenberg, p. 31: . . . ὡς ἐφ' ἅρματος] translates correctly but then makes mistaken links; as the next verse shows ὡς ἐφ' ἅρμα τῆς ἀληθείας belong together."[44] Already in Gunkel's article,[45] his friend Greßmann remarks: "The translator probably misunderstood the original Greek."[46] But the two scholars go well beyond the linguistic aspect when their theory of an "ascent of the soul to heaven" leads them to abridge and distort their own retroversion: "I rose up to the light as if in the chariot of truth."[47] For the metaphorical, theological term "light," like the other metaphorical term "chariot"—with or without the addition of καθήμενος (cf. Acts 8:28)[48]—describes "not the goal, but the means."[49]

After this introduction (1a), which should not be divided into a bicolon,[50] 1b lays bare the origin of the terms "truth" and "light." Both of them, as well as the two synonymous verbs in 1b, are taken from Ps 42:3 LXX: . . . τὸ φῶς σου καὶ τὴν ἀλήθειάν σου· αὐτά με ὡδήγησαν καὶ ἤγαγόν με . . . (". . . thy light and thy truth: they have led me and brought me . . .").[51] The term "light" disappears after this, but "truth" becomes more distinctly personified. Where the Psalm treats the two theological terms equally, in the Ode "Truth" alone "takes the lead."[52] The omission of the two directional prepositions (εἰς both times in Ps 42:3 LXX) leaves the sense of ὁδηγέω/ܕܒܪ (*dbar*)[53] basically untouched (cf. esp. 17:5 but also 29:7), but weakens the Aph. of ܐܬܐ (*ʾetā*), corresponding to ἄγω,[54] as can be seen in some translations that are either too literal or too free: "brought me";[55] "caused me to come";[56] "caused me to arrive."[57] The proper meaningful translations[58]—such as the one above in this work ("made me come")—are usually based on the Greek model.

Ode 38:2a-b "is parallel with chiasmus."[59] The four nouns, three of them *hapax legomena*, are not related in any way to the "lower heavens."[60] They are "perils . . . described according to human experience on land (2a) and water (2b)."[61] For this reason—and also because of the use, later, of the loanword λιμήν (3a)—ܓܠܠܐ in 2b is not to be read as *glālē* ("valleys")[62] but as *gallē* ("waves").

The Aph. of ܥܒܪ (*ʿbar*) in 2a alludes to the miraculous dry-shod passage of the Red Sea during the exodus from Egypt,[63] "a very common symbol for the journey

41 Contra Kittel, 17, 131.
42 See LSJ, *s.v.* ἐμβαίνω.
43 Hugo Greßmann, "Referate [on Harris, Frankenberg, and Grimme]," *Deutsche Literaturzeitung* 32 (1911) 2900: "Decisive are" for this verdict "those cases where the Syriac gives evidence for an involution ['verschränkte Wortstellung'] that would have been idiomatic in Greek."
44 Ibid.
45 Gunkel, 316. Gunkel is here quoting unpublished philological notes by Hans Greßmann.
46 Gunkel, 299. The preposition ἐπί that he postulates would normally be translated into Syriac by ܥܠ (*ʿal*). But there are instances where ἀναβαίνω ἐπί is translated by ܣܠܩ (*sleq*) + ܠ (*l-*) (e.g., Luke 5:19; see NA[27] and *NTSy* on this passage).
47 Greßmann, 468; similarly Gunkel, 315.
48 BDAG, *s.v.* κάθημαι.
49 Kittel, 131.
50 Contra Franzmann, 255, 260.
51 Rahlfs, 2:44; Brenton, 723.
52 Diettrich, 123. Instead of calling on "angelic beings" (Diettrich, 123 n. 1) one might equally invoke the "supernatural" and "divine" Sophia, of whom it is said ὁδηγήσει με (Wis 9:11; cf. Georgi, 434–35).
53 BDAG, *s.v.* ὁδηγέω, 2; Payne Smith, 1:811–12. The objective suffix of the Syriac corresponds to the enclitic με in Ps 42:3 LXX. Frankenberg (p. 32) failed to notice this in his retroversion (ἡγεῖτο μοι).
54 BDAG, *s.v.* ἄγω, 1b; Payne Smith, 1:417.
55 Harris and Mingana, 2:390; Emerton, 725; Franzmann, 257; Ungnad and Staerk, 35: "brachte mich."
56 Charlesworth, 131.
57 Lattke, *Oden*, 199: "ließ mich ankommen."
58 E.g., Greßmann, 468; Bauer, 617.
59 Franzmann, 260.
60 Gunkel, 317.
61 Bauer, 617.
62 Contra Gunkel, 315; Kittel, 17: "Täler"; Harris and Mingana, 2:392; Charlesworth, 129, 131.

... from danger to salvation."[64] Charlesworth and Franzmann consider, because of the parallelism of 2a and 2b, that the passive participle of ܣܪܩ (*sraq*), which basically means "empty,"[65] is a later addition [to N],[66] while Kittel has an equally plausible explanation for the disappearance [from H] of the redundant description of the "chasms": "ܣܪܝܩܐ [*srīqē*] could easily be missed out, being followed by the very similar ܣܕܩܐ [*sedqē*]."[67] There can be no doubt that ܦܚܬܐ (*peḥtē*) corresponds to χάσματα,[68] and ܣܕܩܐ (*sedqē*) may go back to σχίσματα[69] or—but less probably—to ῥήγματα.[70] The sense of αἵρεσις (cf. Gal 5:20), which led to the later use of ܣܕܩܐ (*sedqā*) for the Manichaean sect,[71] can be excluded here.

As a noun, ܫܩܝܦܐ (*šqīpā*) is either a "steep slope or bank"[72] or a "rock"[73] in the sea close to the shore. Both meanings agree with the plural of ܓܠܐ (*gallā*) in 2b, which here is not a metaphor for any "false teachers" (as in Jude 13),[74] but means the actual danger from "waves,"[75] making an association with Exod 15:8c LXX (τὰ κύματα ἐν μέσῳ τῆς θαλάσσης, "the waves ... in the midst of the sea")[76] and another, slighter, allusion to the deliverance of the Israelites. The use of the Pe. ܦܪܩ (*praq*)—and the related noun ܦܘܪܩܢܐ (*purqānā*) in 3a—may be partly due to the influence of this well-known story of deliverance; cf. in the LXX Exod 14:30 (ἐρρύσατο κύριος, "the Lord delivered"); 15:2 (ἐγένετό μοι εἰς σωτηρίαν, "was to me ... for salvation"); 15:13 (ὡδήγησας ... τὸν λαόν σου τοῦτον, ὃν ἐλυτρώσω, "Thou hast guided ... this thy people whom thou hast redeemed").[77] Whether 𝔊 used λυτρόω ἀπό/ἐκ,[78] ῥύομαι ἀπό/ἐκ,[79] or the more paronomastically and soteriologically loaded σῴζω ἀπό/ἐκ[80] cannot be finally determined (see Excursus 5).[81]

There is no need to stress the loanword λιμήν[82] in the calmer imagery of 3a. The Greek term, which occurs only here in the *Odes of Solomon*, is not simply an image in its own right (as, e.g., in Ignatius *Smyrn.* 11:3 and Ignatius *Pol.* 2:3). Its connection to Exod 15:2 LXX (see above) is closer than that to Ps 106:30b LXX (ὡδήγησεν αὐτοὺς ἐπὶ λιμένα θελήματος αὐτῶν, "he guides them to their desired haven").[83] It is not "a quotation from Psalm cvii. 30,"[84] and even calling it a "[clear] reference to the 107th Psalm"[85] is still, in my opinion, putting it too strongly. The complete genitive phrase, ܠܡܐܢܐ ܕܦܘܪܩܢܐ (*lmēnā d-purqānā*), which in N is constructed with εἰς/ܠ (*l-*) (cf. 11:3a, 8a), is linked directly to the "extremely metaphorical language" of the little "missionary address" *Corp. Herm.* 7.[86] For in the early Gnostic vocabulary of that tractate one finds the phrases λαμπρὸν φῶς ("bright/shining light" [7:2]) and κάλλος τῆς ἀληθείας ("beauty of truth" [7:3]), and, especially, the expression ὁ τῆς σωτηρίας λιμήν ("haven of salvation"), both in the plural (7:1) and in the singular (7:2),

63 Cf. Ps 77:13a LXX and Wis 10:18 (διήγαγεν αὐτούς); see Payne Smith, 2:2785; LEH, *s.v.* διάγω.
64 Drijvers, "Odes," 122.
65 Widengren, 17; Payne Smith, 2:2747; BDAG, *s.v.* κενός, 1.
66 Charlesworth, 133; Franzmann, 259.
67 Kittel, "Handschrift," 89.
68 Payne Smith, 2:3086; BDAG and LSJ, *s.v.* χάσμα: "chasm."
69 LSJ, *s.v.* σχίσμα: "cleft."
70 BDAG, *s.v.* ῥῆγμα: "collapse," used, e.g., of "damage by water" about "a break in a dam on the Nile."
71 Payne Smith, 2:2531.
72 BDAG, *s.v.* κρημνός.
73 BDAG, *s.v.* πέτρα, 1; Payne Smith, 2:4296.
74 Anton Vögtle, *Der Judasbrief / Der 2. Petrusbrief* (EKKNT 22; Solothurn/Düsseldorf: Benziger; Neukirchen-Vluyn: Neukirchener Verlag, 1994) 69; Henning Paulsen, *Der Zweite Petrusbrief und der Judasbrief* (KEK 12.2; Göttingen: Vandenhoeck & Ruprecht, 1992) 72.
75 Payne Smith, 1:714; BDAG, *s.v.* κῦμα.
76 Rahlfs, 1:111; Brenton, 89–90.
77 Rahlfs, 1:111–13; Brenton, 89–90.
78 BDAG, *s.v.* λυτρόω, 2.
79 BDAG, *s.v.* ῥύομαι.
80 BDAG, *s.v.* σῴζω, 1.
81 See Payne Smith, 2:3293.
82 BDAG, *s.v.* λιμήν.
83 Rahlfs, 2:120; Brenton, 765.
84 Harris and Mingana, 2:148.
85 Ibid., 2:394–95.
86 Colpe and Holzhausen, 72–75; cf. *Corp. Herm.* 1:26-29, and see Reitzenstein, *Poimandres,* 336–37, on this passage.

which remains uncommon even in later works.[87] Given the other subjects (e.g., drunkenness, ignorance, death, evildoing, inattention) with which this pamphlet "On the Ignorance of God" (ἡ περὶ τοῦ θεοῦ ἀγνωσία) as the "greatest evil" (μέγιστον κακόν) deals,[88] it is quite possible that its author, who was steeped in Hellenistic and Jewish traditions, was acquainted with the Ode under discussion.[89] Anyone aware of the metaphorical use of λιμήν in the works of the Alexandrian philosopher of religion Philo[90] would find no difficulty in the image of the "haven of redemption/salvation" in connection with "truth."[91]

Gunkel's exegesis of 3b, limited to the reading ܕܪ̈ܥܐ (*drāʿē*) of H, converts the "eternal life" (ζωὴ αἰώνιος) into something "like a highest Aeon," which can receive the soul or the singer "like a child laid in its mother's arms."[92] Grimme still considers the then recently discovered reading ܕܪܓܐ (*dargā*) of N "inferior."[93] But the *hapax legomenon* ܕܪܓܐ is to be preferred, as Kittel and Charlesworth do;[94] it corresponds to ἀναβαθμίς,[95] ἀναβαθμός,[96] or κλιμακτήρ,[97] a metaphorical "step" up toward the "immortal life" (ζωὴ ἀθάνατος in 𝔖; see Table 1).[98] The "setting" or "placing"—𝔖 would probably have used (ἐφ)ίστημι ἐπί where ܣ has ܣܡܬܢܝ, ܣܡ (*sām*)[99]—is the only raising up the speaking "I" experiences in the whole Ode.

Unlike the "walking" of the redeemed one/redeemed Redeemer (cf. 15:6 and esp. 17:5) in the first line of the bicolon 4a-b, which should not be converted into a tricolon by dividing 4a,[100] it is Truth personified who "went" with the speaking "I."[101] This companionship is both calming and protective. The two verbs, ܐܢܝܚ (*ʾanīḥ*, Aph. of ܢܘܚ, ܢܚ [*nāḥ*]) and ܐܛܥܐ (*ʾeṭʿē*, Pe. 1st singular imperfect of ܛܥܐ [*ṭʿā*]), express basic concepts of the *Odes of Solomon*: the first one has already been discussed (see Excursus 3), and the second is the subject of this excursus.

Excursus 38: "Erring/Error," "To Err," and "To Lead into Error" in the *Odes of Solomon*

Ode 38 contains more than half of the passages under consideration, as well as all four of the terms that are derived from the same root.[102] Except for one reading in N (28:15b, while H has "I endured"), where the Pe. ܛܥܐ (*ṭʿā*) corresponds to a form of ἐπιλανθάνομαι,[103] all the Greek equivalents of the Syriac terms belong to the "group πλαν-":[104] πλανάω,[105] πλανάομαι,[106] ἡ πλάνη,[107] and ὁ πλάνος.[108]

87 Nock and Festugière, 1:81–82; Bauer, 618; see also Lampe, 803.

88 According to Reizenstein, "the title" of this "prophetic sermon, which not even the manuscripts attribute to Hermes," is as "ill-chosen" as possible (see *Poimandres,* 194).

89 See Colpe and Holzhausen, 72–74. See also Nock on Festugière's hypothesis: "In the end it is poetic imagery, rather like that in the *Odes of Solomon*" (Nock and Festugière, 1:80).

90 He uses λιμήν metaphorically in only five of its thirty-three occurrences (see Mayer, *Index*, 174; Peder Borgen, Kåre Fuglseth, and Roald Skarsten, *The Philo Index: A Complete Greek Word Index to the Writings of Philo of Alexandria* [Grand Rapids/Cambridge, U.K.: Eerdmans; Leiden: Brill, 2000] 206). Cf. *Sacr. AC* 90; *Rev. div. her.* 305; *Fug.* 50; *Som.* 2.225; *Spec. leg.* 4.201.

91 On σωτηρία/ܦܘܪܩܢܐ [*purqānā*], cf. esp. 7:16; 15:6; 17:2; 21:2; 28:10; 35:2; see also Excursus 5.

92 Gunkel, 317.

93 Grimme, "Handschrift," 493, with erroneous pointing ܕܪ̈ܓܐ (*dargē*); see Franzmann (pp. 255, 257, 259), "on the basis of the similarity in concept with 28:5d [*sic,* for 5b]").

94 Kittel, "Handschrift," 89; Charlesworth, 130–31. However, Kittel's hypothesis that "H correctly preserved the plural pointing," and that it should read ܕܪ̈ܓܐ (*dargē*): "in the footsteps," instead of ܕܪܓܐ (*dargā*), is invalid.

95 LEH, *s.v.* ἀναβαθμίς.

96 BDAG, *s.v.* ἀναβαθμός.

97 LEH, *s.v.* κλιμακτήρ; Payne Smith, 1:944–45.

98 Frankenberg, 32: ζωὴ ἀθάνατος.

99 Payne Smith, 2:2556; LEH, *s.v.* ἐφίστημι; BDAG, *s.v.* ἵστημι, A1.

100 Contra Franzmann, 255, 261.

101 On ܐܙܠ (*ʾezal*) + ܥܡ (*ʿam*) + first singular objective suffix, see Payne Smith, 1:107; BDAG, *s.v.* πορεύω, 1: πορεύομαι + σύν τινι.

102 See Payne Smith, 1:1492–94.

103 BDAG, *s.v.* ἐπιλανθάνομαι, 1: "to forget."

104 Herbert Braun, "πλανάω, κτλ.," *ThWNT* 6 (1959) 231; *TDNT* 6:229.

105 BDAG, *s.v.* πλανάω, 1: "lead astray, mislead, deceive."

106 BDAG, *s.v.* πλανάω, 2c: "go astray, be deluded."

107 BDAG, *s.v.* πλάνη: "error, deception."

108 BDAG, *s.v.* πλάνος, b: "deceiver, impostor." It is unlikely that ἀπατάω, generally employed for the fall of Adam and Eve (Braun, "πλανάω," *ThWNT* 6:249; *TDNT* 6:248; BDAG, *s.v.* ἀπατάω,

The "dualism of πλάνη and ἀλήθεια," found outside the New Testament as well as within it,[109] is striking not only in *Ode* 38 but also in the context of the other passages (again except for 28:15). The connection between Going and the Way is not made quite as clearly (see Excursus 15). Comparing the role played by "Error (*Planē*)" in the *Gospel of Truth*[110] with the totality of the *Odes of Solomon,* it is not possible to find in them a "rule of Mistress 'Error' over the world (myth of *Planē*)."[111] It is true, however, that "in the *Odes of Solomon* Error . . . is a personified power opposed to God."[112] That the personification is not as thoroughgoing as in the *Gospel of Truth,* where "the term recalls elements of the myth of the fall of Sophia,"[113] is shown by the two passages 15:6a and 18:14b, where ܛܥܝܘܬܐ (*ṭāʿyūṯā*) "is not"—at least not completely—"personified."[114] The first passages to be considered are those with the feminine πλάνη/ ܛܥܝܘܬܐ.

The first person statement of 15:6, "I forsook the way of error and went to him / and received salvation from him,"[115] conforms to the soteriology of the *Odes of Solomon*. In the next passage, "error" (18:10a) is parallel to "nothingness" (18:9a) and linked to "to know" (ܝܕܥ [*ʾiḏaʿ*], four times in 9-10): "And thou knowest not error / because neither does it know/acknowledge thee" (18:10a-b). The "Gnostics" of 18:13-15 (ܝܕܥ [*ʾiḏaʿ*] also occurs twice in 13a) "laughed at those who were walking in error" (14b). In 31:2a "Error went astray and perished/was lost from him" (on the Pe. ܛܥܐ [*ṭʿā*], see below; on the Pe. ܐܒܕ [*ʾeḇaḏ*], see Excursus 28 and, particularly, the commentary on this verse). In *Ode* 38 "Error fled" from Truth (6a), who shows the speaking "I" "all the drugs/poisons of Error" (8a) and unmasks the mythological "Beloved" (= "Bridegroom" [9c]) and "Bride" (9b, 11a) as the "Deceiver" and "Error" (10b). Whether these bridal images represent a "pair of ungodly aeons"[116] will be considered below.[117]

This exhausts the list of seven occurrences of "error." It has also partly covered the uses of the masculine πλάνος/ܡܛܥܝܢܐ (*maṭʿyānā*), the plural of which describes both members of the bridal pair—and perhaps others as well—as "deceivers," "seducers," or "impostors" (38:15a). The one Aph. of ܛܥܐ (*ṭʿā*) says of the two, the "Deceiver" and "Error," that they "lead the world astray" and "corrupt it" (11b).

So "leading astray" is as characteristic of "Error" as her own "going astray" (see on 31:2a above). The remaining passages in which the Pe. ܛܥܐ is used do not refer to Error personified or to the Deceiver, who is himself a personification, but to the speaking "I" of *Odes* 17 and 38 and are always preceded by a negation. The statements in these two passages are very similar and to some extent complementary, as can be seen in this comparison.

17:5a-b	The thought of Truth led me, and I followed it and did not go astray.
38:1b, 4a, 5b-c	And Truth led me and made me come. And she went with me, . . . and did not let me go astray, . . . since I walked with her . . . And I did not stray . . . .

The obvious link between these passages brings up the final question, whether the redeemed "I" of *Ode* 38 can, or even must, be identified with the redeemed Redeemer of *Ode* 17.

To return for a moment to 4a, the imperfect of ܛܥܐ (*ṭʿā*) with ܕ (*d-*) used as a conjunction depends on the negated

1: "deceive, mislead"), was used, even though Frankenberg (p. 32) has it in 38:11. In 31:2, equally, there is no reason for him to prefer λανθάνω to πλανάομαι (ibid., 28: ἔλαθεν ἡ πλάνη).

109 Braun, "πλανάω," *ThWNT* 6:246; *TDNT* 6:245.

110 See the references in Attridge, *Nag Hammadi Codex I,* 1:395 and the comments by Attridge and MacRae, "Gospel of Truth," 42–44.

111 Schenke, "Evangelium Veritatis," 32.

112 Schenke, *Herkunft*, 26, quoting 18:10; 31:1-2; 38:6-14; cf. Braun, "πλανάω," *ThWNT* 6:241; *TDNT* 6:240.

113 Attridge and MacRae, "Gospel of Truth," 44.

114 Schenke, *Herkunft*, 26 n. 2. In the *Gospel of Truth* also "the term is used to refer both to a cosmic force or power, as here, and to a characteristic of the human condition, as at 31.25, 32.35" (Attridge and MacRae, "Gospel of Truth," 43–44 on 17,14-15).

115 See Braun, "πλανάω," *ThWNT* 6:241; *TDNT* 6:240; he interprets the "way of error" as the "sphere of corruptibility and mortality."

116 Braun, "πλανάω," *ThWNT* 6:240; *TDNT* 6:239.

117 "Error" is not really "split into a male and female being" (Schenke, *Herkunft*, 26; he also alludes to an "ascent of the soul to heaven"). For the feminine "Error" is paired with the masculine "Deceiver" (ibid., 27). Later it will be necessary to clarify the relationship between this "Deceiver" and the "Corruptor of corruption" in 9a.

Pe. ܫܒܩ (*šḇaq*). This verb does not, here, mean "to leave" (as in 15:6 and elsewhere),[118] but corresponds to ἀφίημι with accusative and infinitive, "to let," "tolerate" (cf. linguistically, e.g., Mark 1:34).[119]

Since ܡܛܠ ܕ (*meṭṭol d-*) is only rarely used to represent a causal or explanatory γάρ (e.g., Mark 6:52b),[120] the causal conjunction in 4b 𝔊 was probably ἐπεί,[121] or—more likely still—the equally causal conjunction ὅτι.[122] As the conclusion of stanza I and thus of all the statements 1b-4a, 4b must have a subordinating function. But this subordination might be "often very loose . . . , so that it must be translated 'for.'"[123] The construction with ܐܝܬ (*ʾīṯ*) + third masculine singular suffix + ܗܘܐ (enclitic *-wā*) and the addition of the copula ܗܘܝܘ (*hūyū* = *hū* + *hū*), appended by the use of ܘ (*w-* or *ʾu-*), forms a most emphatic statement of the past and present being and power of Truth personified.[124] Whether 𝔊 had, in addition to ἦν and καί ἐστιν (with the predicate noun ἡ ἀλήθεια), αὐτή in the subject is hard to decide.

■ **5** The parallelisms between 5a and 5c and between 5b and 5d are much more visible when the manuscript bicolon[125] is divided into a tetracolon.[126] The "danger," expressed by the Greek loanword κίνδυνος in 5a, is, in the first place, a summary of all the perils listed in stanza I (2a-b). Indirectly—and anticipating 39:8b, where the Greek loanword recurs—there may be another hint at "the crossing of the Red Sea."[127] A Greek original can be dimly seen behind the Syriac construction of 5a, but it was not καὶ οὐκ ὑπῆρχέ μοι κίνδυνος;[128] it could have been either γέγονε or ἐγένετο linked to the personal pronoun standing for the subject of 5b-d (cf. linguistically Rom 11:25 or Luke 19:9).[129]

If 5b is based on a participial construction in 𝔊,[130] the particle ܕ (*d-*) should be interpreted not as a conjunction[131] but as a sort of relative pronoun.[132] Then 5b would have to be translated: "I, who walked with her."[133] But, considering the parallelism with 5d ("because"), it seems preferable to assume, at least for 𝔖, a loosely causal connection,[134] which does not mean that 𝔊 must also have used a causal conjunction such as ὅτι.[135] The lack of precision in 𝔖 does little damage to the first person statement, which affirms that freedom from danger is intimately connected with the metaphorically existential walking with Truth personified (cf. linguistically John 6:66; and see Excursus 15).[136]

118 Contra Lattke, *Oden*, 199.

119 BDAG, *s.v.* ἀφίημι, 5a; see Payne Smith, 2:4038; Frankenberg, 32: οὐκ ἀφῆκέ με πλανᾶσθαι.

120 BDAG, *s.v.* γάρ, 1–2; Payne Smith, 2:2076.

121 Frankenberg, 32. Frankenberg's retroversion still depends only on the ܗܘ (*hū*) in H, which I consider inferior, although Grimme ("Handschrift," 493–94) and Emerton (p. 726) prefer it over the N reading, ܘܗܘܝܘ (*ʾu-hūyū*), that Frankenberg did not know; see Nöldeke §312.C.

122 BDAG, *s.v.* ὅτι, 4a; Payne Smith, 2:2077.

123 BDF and BDR §456; see Lattke, *Oden*, 199.

124 Cf. esp. 32:2, and also 8:8; 9:8; 12:1-3, 13; 17:7; 18:6; 23:18; 24:10, 12; 31:2; 41:9.

125 There may have been a mark of division in N after the word ܩܝܢܕܢܘܣ (later corrected to ܩܝܢܕܘܢܘܣ). This variously spelled word for "danger" is the second Greek loanword in *Ode* 38; λιμήν in 3a is the first (cf. Lattke, "Wörter," 291–93 = idem, *Bedeutung*, 4:140–41).

126 Lattke, *Bedeutung*, 1:172–73; see also Franzmann, 261.

127 Drijvers, "Odes," 122.

128 Frankenberg, 32; see BDAG, *s.v.* ὑπάρχω, 2.

129 The phrase γέγονε ἐμοί τι is frequently used in the sense "someth[ing] has come to me = I have someth[ing]" (BDAG, *s.v.* γίνομαι, 4bγ).

130 See Frankenberg, 32: μετ᾽ αὐτῆς περιπατοῦντι.

131 Lattke, *Bedeutung*, 2:74.

132 Ibid., 2:68.

133 Suggested by Klaus Beyer, letter of November 13, 2002.

134 Nöldeke §366.B.

135 A Greek construction of 5a-b with a dative participle may be the reason why the Syriac translator originally wrote 5a-b without a mark of division, which later caused 5c-d, by parallelism, also to be transformed into a monocolon.

136 BDAG, *s.v.* περιπατέω, 1c. The interpretation of "Truth" as "psychopompos" (see Lampe, *s.v.* ψυχοπομπός) by Quasten ("Hirte," 397–400, with references to *Ode* 38 and John 14:6) fails because, first, there is no "soul's journey to heaven" in the Ode; second, the Truth of *Ode* 38 does not derive from John 14:6; and, third, there is a reciprocity of leading and accompanying by Truth, on the one hand (38:1, 4, 15), and following and walking with her by the speaking "I," on the other (17:5; 38:5).

In connection with the "journey of the soul to heaven," allusion is occasionally made (e.g., by Gunkel [p. 316 n. 1, etc.] and Bauer [p. 617 n. 2, etc.]) to Albrecht Dieterich, *Eine Mithrasliturgie* (2nd ed.; Leipzig/Berlin: Teubner, 1910) 235–36 [cf. 1st ed. 1903, 179]), who discusses works by

Parallel to 5a, and also linking back to 4a (see Excursus 38), the speaking "I" affirms in 5c that he did not go astray.[137] This metaphorical remark carries no hint of sheep.[138] The preposition ܒ (*b*-), which precedes the nominalized term ܡܕܡ (*meddem*),[139] can be used locatively or instrumentally; it may represent ἐν/ἐπί (cf. linguistically Heb 11:38), but if 𝔊 used the simple dative τινί, there may have been no equivalent for the Syriac word.

Verse 5d gives a reason for the statement of salvation in 5c, which is a rare occurrence. This concerns attentive obedience in faith in the widest sense, surpassing even the ἀληθείᾳ πείθεσθαι ("obeying the truth") of Gal 5:7 and the ὑπακοὴ τῆς ἀληθείας ("obedience to the truth") of 1 Pet 1:22, which is the verso of the gift of freedom.[140] For the Ethpe. of ܫܡܥ (*šma*ᶜ) must correspond to ὑπακούω, "obey."[141] This causal statement might argue against the identification of the redeemed speaking "I" with the Kyrios Christos, if there were not a number of early Christologoumena, which are not limited to the "cross" or "atonement" and yet speak of the obedience of the Son and human being Jesus Christ.[142] In the *Odes of Solomon,* these early sayings, especially in connection with the passage under consideration, need to be linked to the recognition that the "Son of Truth" descends from the Most High Father (23:18), who is himself, in a messianic context, described as the "Father of Truth" (41:9). This shows how the cauldron of the history of dogma is still simmering.

■ **6-9** What follows, especially in stanzas III–V, "is very difficult to explain."[143] The alternative "real experience"–"allegory"[144]–is illusory, since the pair of "Bride" and "Groom" is interpreted allegorically in stanza IV, though without any real clarification. What can be established about stanza III is that the language is mythological and metaphorical.[145] To decide whether what is described relates to "real experience" or "real heretics,"[146] it is necessary first to see whether any historical allusions are likely and whether what is being described is in any sense "the false church."[147] For ease of interpretation, it will be best first to sort out the hodgepodge of images in stanzas III and IV (and cf. 15b in stanza VII). The protagonists are the personified powers "Truth" (Ἀλήθεια) and "Error" (Πλάνη). "Death" (8b, in 𝔊 ὁ Θάνατος) is parallel to "Error."[148] Since there are only two images in the allegorical explanation 10a-11b–which are then probably aggregated in 15b as the plural "Deceivers"–the negative side of the dualism yields the following feminine–masculine pairings:[149]

Wilhelm Anz and Wilhelm Bousset among others. However, there is nothing really enlightening on *Ode* 38 to be found, either in what Dieterich called the "Liturgy of Mithras" or in his "still unsurpassed commentary" (Hans Dieter Betz, *Gottesbegegnung und Menschwerdung: Zur religionsgeschichtlichen und theologischen Bedeutung der 'Mithrasliturgie' [PGM IV.475–820]* [Hans-Lietzmann-Vorlesungen 6; Berlin/New York: de Gruyter, 2001] 2). The term ἀλήθεια, for instance, does not occur in the liturgy at all, and the verb ἀναβαίνω is used in a very different sense from that of *Ode* 38:1 (cf. Dieterich, *Eine Mithrasliturgie,* 238).

137 Frankenberg, 32: οὐκ ἐπλανήθην.

138 Cf. Ps 118:176 LXX; Isa 53:6; 1 Pet 2:25; *1 Clem.* 16:6; and see BDAG, *s.v.* πλανάω, 2b.

139 Nöldeke §219: "something."

140 Brox, *Petrusbrief,* 86; see BDAG, *s.v.* ὑπακοή, 1b.

141 Payne Smith, 2:4215; BDAG, *s.v.* ὑπακούω, 1.

142 Cf. Phil 2:8b; Käsemann, *Romans,* 157 (German, 149) on Rom 5:19; Gräßer, 1:305–8, on Heb 5:8.

143 Harris and Mingana, 2:394.

144 Ibid.

145 Lattke, *Oden,* 75.

146 Harris and Mingana, 2:394, referring to the situation in Antiochia; on Ignatius *Trall.* 6:2, see below.

147 See Drijvers, "Odes," 127. Drijvers omits any mention of Harris and Mingana's discussion of Ignatius *Trall.* 6:2, etc. (Harris and Mingana, 2:40–49) because that would undermine his hypothesis.

148 A close reading of the *Gospel of Truth* (Schenke, *Herkunft,* 33–57; cf. *NHLE,* 40–51) for the two dominant terms (especially in *Gos. Truth* 26,19-36) and some of the others found in *Ode* 38, such as "root" (17,30; 28,16; 41,17), "way" (18,20), "wise" (19,26), "death" (20,29; etc.), "rest" (22,12; etc.), "drunkenness" (22,17), "many" (22,20), "sweetness" (24,9; see also 31,20; 33,33; 41,3; 42,8), "blows" (29,16), "light of truth" (36,11-12), and "plantings" (36,36), did not yield much for the interpretation of this Ode. What the texts have in common is the Gnostic milieu saturated with Jewish and early Christian traditions.

149 Schlier, *Christus,* 69–70.

FEMININE	MASCULINE
Error (8a)[150]	Death (8b)
	Archcorruptor (9a)[151] [= the Devil?]
Bride (9b)	Groom (9c)
Error (10b)	Deceiver (10b)
Bride (11a)	Beloved (11a)

Although "truth" will not and must not flee before "falsehood" (cf. 18:6), here in 6a the antagonist "Error" "fled" from "Truth." The Pe. ܥܪܩ (*ʿraq*), which is also used of apostates (23:20), is often found in a construction with ܠ (*l-*) (which may explain the nonsense reading ܠܗ [*lāh*] in H),[152] but also commonly with the preposition ܡܢ (*men*), corresponding to ἀπό. Whether 𝔊 had φεύγω (as in Jas 4:7; Rev 9:6)[153] or ἀποφεύγω with genitive (not accusative, as Frankenberg, knowing only H, reconstructed it)[154] can no longer be determined.

If 6b describes, in a *parallelismus membrorum*, the results of her flight, then Error cannot "meet" Truth any longer.[155] In an inimical sense, these two largely interchangeable Greek verbs[156] can also mean "to encounter, oppose."[157] That would make the negated statement, constructed with ܠܗ (*leh*), of 6b more or less synonymous with 6a.

By the use of the ill-chosen μετέρχομαι[158] with accusative of εὐθεῖα ὁδός (see Excursus 15),[159] Frankenberg was probably attempting to make a clear link between the related but differing statements 7a and 4a.[160] But the Greek of these two lines did not use aorist forms of (μετ)έρχομαι, but different forms of πορεύομαι (most probably ἐπορεύθην and ἐπορευόμην).[161] The only question is what the following phrase, ܒܐܘܪܚܐ (*b-urḥā*), "on the way," represents: ἐν τῇ ὁδῷ (cf. Luke 9:57), τῇ ὁδῷ (cf. Acts 14:16; Jude 11; *1 Clem.* 12:4), τὴν ὁδόν (cf. Acts 8:39), or perhaps κατὰ τὴν ὁδόν (cf. Acts 8:36). The subject here is simply the straight and direct way on or along which Truth personified "went" (cf. the somewhat different uses in 11:3b ["way of truth," opposite to 15:6, "way of error"] and 33:8c ["ways of truth," opposite to 33:7, "ways of corruption"]). The use of ܬܪܝܨܐ (*trīṣā*), "upright," in 27:3 and 42:2 is not related to its occurrence here in 7a (= "straight"). 𝔊 might have employed ὀρθός (see, e.g., *Hermas, Man.* 35 [VI.1]:2)[162] here in place of the more usual adjective εὐθύς. That both "way" and its positive attribute are meant metaphorically is obvious.

It is unusual that the active participle of ܝܕܥ (*ʾidaʿ*) is followed in 7b by ܗܘܝܬ (*-wēṯ*) + objective ܠܗ (*leh*) (see Excursus 7). The stress is neither on the ignorance of the speaking "I" (in 𝔊 οὐκ ᾔδειν)[163] nor on the exaggerated "everything,"[164] but on the ending, which must not be detached,[165] of 7b and its adumbration of the "mysterious utterances" that follow.[166] Given the many possible Greek equivalents, it is not easy to determine the exact nuance of the Pa. ܚܘܝ (*ḥawwī*).[167] The term δείκνυμι, for instance, would bring to mind some of the "apocalyptic visions" (cf. Rev 1:1; etc.).[168] In any case, the image is of something "hidden,"[169] of "[s]ecrets" to be revealed.[170] These secrets are then described, somewhat long-windedly, but not really laid bare to the uninitiated. This has led to more than normally intrusive attempts at emendation of a passage that is already full of variant readings. These variants in 8b-9b demonstrate that even

150 This term, which is feminine in Syriac, will be linked later with the "Bride" (10b-11a).
151 Lit., "corruptor of corruption." Klaus Beyer suggests "cause of corruption" (letter of November 13, 2002).
152 See Kittel, "Handschrift," 89.
153 BDAG, *s.v.* φεύγω, 1.
154 Frankenberg, 32; see BDAG, *s.v.* ἀποφεύγω, 1; Payne Smith, 2:2997.
155 On the *hapax legomenon* ܐܪܥ (*ʾeraʿ*), see Payne Smith, 1:396; BDAG, *s.v.* ἀπαντάω or ὑπαντάω—in either case + τινί.
156 See Michael Lattke, "ἀπαντάω, ἀπάντησις," *EWNT* 1 (1980) 275; *EDNT* 1:115.
157 BDAG, *s.v.* ὑπαντάω, b.
158 LSJ, *s.v.* μετέρχομαι.
159 See BDAG, *s.v.* εὐθύς, 1: "straight."
160 Frankenberg, 32.
161 See Nöldeke §277; BDAG, *s.v.* πορεύω, 1; Payne Smith, 1:106–7.
162 BDAG, *s.v.* ὀρθός, 1b.
163 See BDAG, *s.v.* οἶδα, 1b.
164 Nöldeke §219.
165 Contra Franzmann, 255, 257, 261.
166 Gunkel, 317.
167 See Payne Smith, 1:1208–9; Klein, *Wörterbuch*, 47.
168 BDAG, *s.v.* δείκνυμι, 1.
169 BDAG, *s.v.* ἀναδείκνυμι, 1.
170 See BDAG, *s.v.* δηλόω, 1; and Frankenberg, 32: ἐδήλωσέν μοι.

the users in antiquity and the copyists in the Middle Ages found the text difficult.

That the plural of the *hapax legomenon* ܣܡ̈ܐ (*sammā*) in 8a corresponds to φάρμακα is clear.[171] So, in consideration of the term "Death" in 8b, one might suggest the θανάσιμον φάρμακον, "the deadly poison" of a "heretical sect" among Christians (Ignatius *Trall.* 6:1-2).[172] But that would be prematurely to decide to interpret the subsequent words and images as allusions to some "sect" of the period. The translation "herbs of error"[173] for the genitive phrase is rather feeble, since the reference is ironically diluted *sensu bono* to simples or "remed[ies]."[174] Roughly halfway between "poison" and "medicine" is the sense "magic potion."[175]

Even the *translation* of 8b[176] "is very difficult."[177] Whether the construction is a case of "involution"[178] or "ellipsis,"[179] the terms ܢܓ̈ܕܐ (*negdē*) and ܕܡܘܬܐ (*d-mawtā*) "naturally belong together."[180] Emending ܢܓ̈ܕܐ to ܥܩ̈ܪܐ (*ʿeqqārē*), "blows" to "roots,"[181] is as unnecessary as Schultheß's emendation of ܕܚܠܝܘܬܐ (*d-ḥalyūtā*) to ܕܚܝܠܘܬܐ (*dḥīlūtā*, without the conjunction ܕ [*d-*]).[182] Both Syriac manuscripts witness to ܚܠܝܘܬܐ (*ḥalyūtā*), translated as "sweetness,"[183] which must be retained. H has the active participle of ܣܒܪ (*sbar*), while N uses a passive form, about which Kittel remarks: "Attempts to translate the participle in H were always unsatisfactory; now, at last, the meaning of this form is certain."[184] Frankenberg, working with H, was forced to torment his "linguistic conscience."[185] If he had known N, his remark, "The established term ܕܚܠܝܘܬܐ is correct, but the other words, from ܗܘܝܢ to ܗܝ, are the comment of a reader on ܢܓ̈ܕܐ, which has slipped from the margin into the text and been inserted between the words ܘܠܢܓ̈ܕܐ ܕܡܘܬܐ that really belong together!" [*sic*], might have been a little less measured. What, however, is necessary to make sense of the text as it stands? It is not quite certain that the Greek *Vorlage* of 8b used the plural of πληγή (but cf. 34:1; 2 Cor 6:5; Rev 9:18; etc.),[186] because the *hapax legomenon* ܢܓܕܐ (*negdā*) can also be used to represent μάστιξ (e.g., Heb 11:36).[187] Thus, it can mean deadly flagellations but also in a transferred sense the "Egyptian plagues" (*1 Clem.* 17:5).[188] In any case, it is more than "temptations."[189] As Pierre makes clear by capitalizing "Death,"[190] θάνατος/ܡܘܬܐ (*mawtā*) is the personified power Death parallel to Error (cf. 15:9a; 42:11b).[191] Those who view the "blows/scourges of Death" as the "sweetness of Death"[192] in the first place find themselves in opposition to the Jewish understanding that "death" is πικρός (1 Kgdms 15:32; cf. Eccl 7:26).[193] One step further leads to Wis 1:16,[194] where the "ungodly summoned death," "considering him a friend."[195] What must be firmly understood is that 8b expresses a contrary opinion and that it is—under the influence of "Error"—a perverted one. For the speaking "I" and his guide

171 Payne Smith, 2:2652; BDAG, *s.v.* φάρμακον, 1.
172 Fischer, 176–77; Bauer and Paulsen, 61; BDAG, *s.vv.* αἵρεσις, 1b; θανάσιμος.
173 Barth, 264.
174 BDAG, *s.v.* φάρμακον, 3.
175 BDAG, *s.v.* φάρμακον, 2; cf. Rev 9:21, where it is parallel to "murders."
176 Lit., "and the blows, of which it is thought that they are the sweetness of death."
177 Lattke, *Oden*, 200, where n. 13 needs some revision.
178 Nöldeke §379; Charlesworth, 133.
179 Nöldeke §382.
180 Greßmann, "Referate," 2900; on the "correlative," see Nöldeke §236.B.
181 Barth, 264.
182 Schultheß, 256: "object of dread," "terror," taken up as φοβερόν by Greßmann, "Referate," 2900; Payne Smith, 1:864.
183 Kittel, "Handschrift," 89; Charlesworth, 132; Payne Smith, 1:1281; BDAG, *s.v.* γλυκύτης.
184 Kittel, "Handschrift," 89.
185 Frankenberg, 43.
186 Greßmann, "Referate," 2900, following Frankenberg, 32; BDAG, πληγή, 1–3.
187 Payne Smith, 2:2279.
188 BDAG, *s.v.* μάστιξ, 2.
189 Contra Bauer, *Oden*, 70; Bauer, 618.
190 Pierre, 179: "Mort."
191 BDAG, *s.v.* θάνατος, 1e; Payne Smith, 2:2057.
192 On the active ܣܒܪܝܢ (*sābrīn*) in H, see Payne Smith, 2:2509–10, with many Greek equivalents; on the more apposite passive ܣܒܝܪܝܢ (*sbīrīn*) in N, see Payne Smith, 2:2510.
193 See Thomas Krüger, *Kohelet (Prediger)* (BKAT 19 [Sonderband]; Neukirchen-Vluyn: Neukirchener Verlag, 2000) 265–68; more references in Wilhelm Michaelis, "πικρός, κτλ.," *ThWNT* 6 (1959) 122–23; *TDNT* 6:122–24.
194 See already Kittel, "Handschrift," 89 n. 2, "on the subject."
195 "The expression, to think death a friend, is a disparaging allusion to the Greco-Hellenistic playing

"Truth" (feminine in 𝔊), Death is and always will be an enemy (cf. 1 Cor 15:26).

It is now necessary to return to consider Ignatius *Trall.* 6:1-2. Harris and Mingana devote only a little space to their exegesis of "sweetness": "If we take ܚܠܝܘܬܐ in the sense of 'juice of fruits, liquor', we may see in it an underlying Greek *οἰνόμελι* like the corresponding ܚܘܠܝܐ (*ḥulyā*). This sense would be in harmony with the rest of the Ode which deals with intoxication."[196] This remark is based on a more extensive discussion in their introduction,[197] which Virginia Corwin partly accepts[198] and to which Paulsen devotes serious consideration in a discussion of "similar traditional connections."[199] But Schoedel, in his commentary on Ignatius *Trall.* 6:2, is very critical: "A connection here between Ignatius and *Odes Sol.* 38.8 . . . is not likely. Ignatius' language is closer to the popular metaphor."[200] Since Bauer and Paulsen actually quote *Ode* 38:7-8 as an "especially notable" parallel,[201] it is necessary to take a closer look at the difficult passage Ignatius *Trall.* 6:1-2.

> 1. . . . *ἀλλοτρίας δὲ βοτάνης ἀπέχεσθε, ἥτις ἐστὶν αἵρεσις· 2. οἳ ἑαυτοῖς παρεμπλέκουσιν Ἰησοῦν Χριστὸν καταξιοπιστευόμενοι, ὥσπερ θανάσιμον φάρμακον διδόντες μετὰ οἰνομέλιτος, ὅπερ ὁ ἀγνοῶν ἡδέως λαμβάνει ἐν ἡδονῇ κακῇ τὸ ἀποθανεῖν* [emphases added].[202]

> 1. . . . abstain from a foreign plant, which is heresy. 2. Even though such persons seem to be trustworthy, they mingle Jesus Christ with themselves, as if giving a *deadly drug* mixed with *honeyed wine*, which the unsuspecting gladly takes with evil pleasure, but then *dies*.[203]

That neither the Ode nor the epistle quotes the other is obvious at first glance. This leaves the probability of an allusion, where "it is easier to argue that Ignatius knew the *Odes* than the converse."[204] What can be said about that? One can agree completely with the last remark. But the "drugs/poisons of Error" in *Ode* 38 are not immediately connected to "sweetness" or to "death." Nor is the abstract "sweetness" the same as the concrete "mead." On the other hand, the text of Ignatius contains no mention of either the "blows/scourges of Death" or the "sweetness of Death." "Similar images" to those of Ignatius *Trall.* 6:2, "borrowed from the language of medicine," were also "commonly used by other writers in the Early Church."[205] So Schoedel is to be preferred over Harris and Mingana.

The last two words of 9a ("I saw") should not be placed at the beginning of 9b, in spite of the punctuation in both manuscripts.[206] By following H and N,[207] one would provide the verb "to show" (7b) with another object, but leave the verb "to see"—corresponding to

with the idea of death as a positive power (a path to eternal fame or to becoming a hero; death as a friend or liberator)—especially in poetry and philosophy" (Georgi, 406, note on Wis 1:16).

Reference must also be made, at least cursorily, to the tradition enshrined in Rev 9:6, where the author "drops out of the role of seer" (Bousset, *Offenbarung*, 299; cf. Kraft, *Offenbarung*, 141): "And in those days people will seek death but will not find it; they will long to die, but death will flee from them" (cf. Heinz Giesen, *Die Offenbarung des Johannes* [RNT; Regensburg: Pustet, 1997] 218). *Ode* 38 may similarly be alluding to the plagues of Egypt in Exodus.

196 Harris and Mingana, 2:393; see Brockelmann, *Lexicon*, 234.

197 Harris and Mingana, 2:40–49, esp. 42: "*a quotation*" or "*the equivalent of a quotation.*"

198 Virginia Corwin, *St. Ignatius and Christianity in Antioch* (Yale Publications in Religion 1; New Haven: Yale University Press, 1960) 72–75.

199 Paulsen, *Studien*, 31.

200 Schoedel, *Ignatius*, 147.

201 Bauer and Paulsen, 61.

202 Fischer, 176; Lindemann and Paulsen, 202.

203 Ehrman, 200–203; see Lake, 216–19; Bauer and Paulsen, 61; Lindemann and Paulsen, 203.

204 Corwin, *St. Ignatius and Christianity*, 75; cf. Harris and Mingana, 2:43.

205 As Bauer and Paulsen admit (p. 61).

206 Lattke, *Bedeutung*, 1:76–77; see already Harris and Mingana, vol. 1, on this passage; 2:391; Bauer, 618.

207 Wellhausen, 637; Kittel, "Handschrift," 89; Charlesworth, 130; Franzmann, 255, 259, 261–62.

"to show"–which governs the remainder of stanza III, without a direct object. What the speaking "I" "saw"[208] "offers some difficulty."[209] Wellhausen places a question mark after his literal translation "corruptor of corruption,"[210] while Gunkel transforms the singular term into its plural ܡܚܒܠܢܐ (*mḥabblānē*) and identifies the "corruptors of corruption" (i.e., "the corruptors whose being is corruption") with the images of the "Bride and Groom" interpreted as "demons," whom he sees as a Gnostic "pairing of Aeons opposed to God."[211] This passage, which Barth calls "confused" and "incomprehensible,"[212] needs to be considered more coolly and without "omitting the last word" of 9c, a gratuitous interference in a text made difficult enough already by the variants found especially in 9b.

Linguistically, the idiom in 9a, which cannot be simply (re)translated as ὀλεθρευτὴς τῆς διαφθορᾶς,[213] Διαφθορεὺς τῆς διαφθορᾶς,[214] or φθορεὺς τῆς φθορᾶς,[215] is "a kind of superlative" in Syriac.[216] Ungnad and Staerk consider "the corruptor of corruption" as "the corruptor who brings about corruption."[217] Klaus Beyer calls him "the one who brings (about) [nothing but] corruption."[218] If 𝔊 had used a similar "figura etymologica" (cf. esp. 1 John 5:16),[219] it might have been an expression like ὁ τὸν ὄλεθρον ὀλεθρεύων (cf. Exod 12:23 LXX).[220] Other possibilities would be ὁ τὴν διαφθορὰν διαφθείρων,[221] ὁ τὴν φθορὰν (δια)-φθείρων,[222] or an individual Greek word that has so far not been identified.

Objectively this Archcorruptor is the parallel to "Death" personified[223] and may even be "the Devil."[224] For there is a close connection between "Death" and "the Devil," both in the history of religion and in mythology. That he "tempts" is one of the characteristics of the Devil.[225] I believe that this diabolical and deadly corruptor or destroyer will reappear in the text in the guise of the "Bridegroom" (9c) and the "Deceiver" (10b).

The image in 9b of the adorning of the Bride poses no difficulty. The Ethpa. of ܨܒܬܐ (*ṣeḇtā* = κόσμος) corresponds to a passive form of κοσμέω (cf. linguistically νύμφη κεκοσμημένη in Rev 21:2)[226] or καλλωπίζω.[227] "Bride"[228] and "Groom"[229] are shown negatively, in contrast to the lovely image of 42:7b-9. The conjunction ܟܕ (*kaḏ*), which refers to 9b-c, "denotes present action or state"[230] and links the context of this demonic spectacle to the perspective of the seeing and speaking "I." The

208 For possible Greek equivalents of ܚܙܐ (*ḥzā*), see Payne Smith, 1:1233; Klein, *Wörterbuch*, 47.

209 Harris and Mingana, 2:393. Charlesworth vocalizes ܚܒܠܐ (*ḥḇālā*) incorrectly and, in spite of his reference to Bauer, translates ܡܚܒܠܢܐ (*mḥabblānā*) as "corrupting" (see Charlesworth, 130–34; cf. Bauer, 618).

210 Wellhausen, 637.

211 Gunkel, 317.

212 Barth, 265.

213 Frankenberg, 32.

214 Tsakonas, 164, 168.

215 Fanourgakis, 170.

216 Bauer, 618: something like "Allverderber [omnicorruptor]"; "Erzverderber [Archcorruptor]" in Diettrich, 124; Kittel, "Handschrift," 89; Lattke, *Oden*, 200.

217 Ungnad and Staerk, 36.

218 Klaus Beyer, letter of February 11, 2004, referring to ܡܩܛܠ ܩܛܠܐ (*meqṭal qeṭlā*); Nöldeke §298.

219 BDR §153; cf. BDF §153; BDAG, *s.v.* ἁμαρτάνω, c.

220 See Payne Smith, 1:1179–80; BDAG, *s.vv.* ὄλεθρος, 1; ὀλοθρεύω.

221 BDAG, *s.vv.* διαφθείρω, 2; διαφθορά.

222 BDAG, *s.vv.* φθείρω, 2; φθορά, 1.

223 Rudolf Bultmann, "θάνατος, κτλ.," *ThWNT* 3 (1938) 14; *TDNT* 3:14.

224 Spitta, 288. To a certain extent one can agree with Spitta that there is "no reason" for placing the presumably Christian Devil beside the "bride" and "groom." Unfortunately, there is no way to remove him from the extravagant and obscure text. A reference to "concepts like those of *4 Macc.* 18:7-8," which led to "a misunderstanding of the originally quite clear image in the *Ode*," gives no help in comprehending it (on the "exhortation of the Maccabean mother" in 4 Macc. 18:6-19, see Klauck, *4. Makkabäerbuch*, 754).

225 Otto Böcher, "Teufel III. Neues Testament," *TRE* 33 (2002) 119; cf. Braun, "πλανάω," *ThWNT* 6:247–49; *TDNT* 6:246–48.

226 BDAG, *s.v.* κοσμέω, 2αα.

227 BDAG, *s.v.* καλλωπίζω; Payne Smith, 2:3361.

228 Payne Smith, 1:1733; BDAG, *s.v.* νύμφη, 1.

229 Payne Smith, 1:1411; BDAG, *s.v.* νυμφίος.

230 Payne Smith, *Dictionary*, 204.

omission of the enclitic ܗܘܬ (*-wāṯ*) in H after the participle of ܐܣܛܒܒܬ (*ʾesṭabbaṯ*) is of less significance than the passive reading ܡܬܚܒܠܐ (*meṯḥabblā*), which describes the Bride as "corrupted." The active voice, ܡܚܒܠܐ (*mḥabblā*) in N, is to be preferred, since it accords better with the explanation in stanza IV.[231]

On the other hand, it is said of the Bridegroom[232] in 9c that he is both "corrupting" and "corrupted."[233] This description is a very faint echo of the "Stoic and neo-Platonic proverb about the deceived deceiver."[234] Barth's exclusion of ܘܡܬܚܒܠ (*ʾu-meṯḥabbal*)[235] does as little justice to the text as this paraphrase: "The Bride is debauched and the Groom is both debaucher and debauchee."[236] The Bridegroom, who represents "Death" and "the Devil," is not only "corrupting," like his Bride (and thus "the Deceiver"; see 10b and 11b below), but also "corrupted," either by the power of his mythological Bride ("Error"; see 10b below) or by his wickedness and rebellion against God. However, this description hardly leads to the conclusion that the figures in 9b-c are metaphors for "Antichrist and Heresy."[237]

■ **10-11** As "show" (7b) corresponds to "see" (9a), so, in reverse order, does "ask" (10a) to "say" (10b). Using the Pe. ܫܐܠ (*šel*),[238] which occurs only in 10a and represents ἐρωτάω followed by τινά,[239] the speaking "I" puts his question to Truth personified, asking to be enlightened about the mythologically negative figures of the "Archcorruptor"/"Bridegroom," and "Bride" that appeared in 9. The question consists of the interrogative pronoun ܡܢ (*man*) with third masculine plural enclitic personal pronoun and the plural demonstrative pronoun, and is introduced by the facultative particle ܕ (*d-*) as a quasi-direct address.[240]

Since 10b contains the beginning of the answer, which carries through at least as far as the end of stanza V, the Pe. ܐܡܪ (*ʾemar*) may be translated by "answer" as appropriately as by "say,"[241] but it should not be back-translated by ἀποκρίνομαι.[242] The masculine singular demonstrative pronoun, with enclitic third masculine singular personal pronoun for the copula, refers, strictly grammatically, to ܡܛܥܝܢܐ (*maṭʿyānā* = πλάνος, "Deceiver"), but in idiomatic Syriac usage—just as in Greek—also includes ܛܥܝܘܬܐ (*ṭāʿyūṯā* = πλάνη, "Error"; on the two personifications, see Excursus 38 above).[243]

Verse 11a is only a reference back to 9b-c. The term replacing "Bridegroom," ܚܒܝܒܐ (*ḥabbīḇā*), can represent ἀγαπητός as well as ἠγαπημένος or ἀγαπώμενος.[244] There is no more of an allusion to the "Lord" of Hos 2:19-20[245] than to "Christ" the "Lamb" of Rev 19:7, 9.[246] Since a bridegroom (νυμφίος) is loved (ἀγαπώμενος) by his bride (νύμφη), he can simply be described as "the beloved"; this is a universal idiom, understood by readers of any age, not limited to interpreters of the Song of Songs such as Gregory of Nyssa at the end of

231 See Payne Smith, 1:1176.
232 The participle "adorned" should have been repeated here in the masculine for the Groom (Klaus Beyer, letter of November 13, 2002). The expression "the bride, who brings corruption" (for "is corrupting") is also due to Beyer.
233 See again, Payne Smith, 1:1176.
234 Braun, "πλανάω," *ThWNT* 6:232, 250; *TDNT* 6:230, 249, on 2 Tim 3:13; cf. Dibelius, *Pastoralbriefe*, 89; Oberlinner, *Pastoralbriefe*, 2:142.
235 Barth, 265.
236 Gunkel, 317.
237 Contra Burkitt, 385.
238 See Beyer, *ATTM*, 105 n. 1.
239 Payne Smith, 2:4004; BDAG, *s.v.* ἐρωτάω, 1.
240 See Nöldeke §367; the particle is not found in the answer that follows. Franzmann's subdivision of 10a, 10b, and 11b (pp. 255, 257) is arbitrary and not really justified by her analysis (ibid., 262).
241 BDAG, *s.v.* εἶπον, 1b and 2.
242 Contra Frankenberg, 32; see Payne Smith, 1:243, and εἶπα in 11:18 𝔊.
243 See Nöldeke §322; BDF and BDR §§131–35.
244 Payne Smith, 1:1170; BDAG, *s.vv.* ἀγαπάω, ἀγαπητός.
245 Diettrich, 124.
246 Connolly, "Odes," 306. The very free translation of *Ode* 38 by Berger and Nord (p. 967) reaches something of a climax in 11a: "They are only imitating the Messiah, the Beloved, and his Bride" (cf. Rev 19:7; 21:9).

the fourth century.[247] In spite of his theory of "a male and female Antichrist," Connolly accurately remarks that "the Syriac verb ܐܬܕܡܝ followed by the preposition ܒ regularly means 'to imitate', as may be seen from most of the N. T. passages in which the Peshitta translates *μιμοῦμαι* or *μιμητής*. The Greek word was without doubt *μιμοῦνται*."[248]

The description of the wedding feast befitting this bridal pair, which has no connection with the cultic "wedding of Wisdom,"[249] is postponed to stanza V. Meanwhile, 11b harks back to 9a-c and describes the negative activity and its effects with two synonymous participles, the one of the Aph. ܐܛܥܝ (*ʾaṭʿī*) and the other of the Pa. ܚܒܠ (*ḥabbel*). The first verb, found only here, expresses the cheating and deception intrinsic to both the Deceiver and Error (see Excursus 38 above); the second, which occurs elsewhere, summarizes everything said of the Archcorruptor/Bridegroom and his Bride (see Excursus 28). 𝔊 will have used *τὸν κόσμον* rather than *τὸν αἰῶνα* (see Excursus 22). "World" refers to the many in 12a who represent "humankind" or "the world of man."[250] In a search for linguistic and substantive parallels, passages dealing with the "Devil" (e.g., Rev 12:9: *ὁ πλανῶν τὴν οἰκουμένην ὅλην*, "the deceiver of the whole world") are likely to be more productive than those in which the "Antichrist," as *κοσμοπλάνος* ("world-deceiver"), is found performing "signs and wonders" (*Did.* 16:4).[251] This supports the interpretation of the "Archcorruptor" (9a) as the "Devil." What is missing in both the parallel passages quoted is the duality of Deceiver and Error and the macabre bridal couple who represent them.[252]

■ **12-14a** That the speech of Truth personified, which begins in 10b, may extend past the end of stanza V to include VI has already been mentioned (see above).[253] The theme of stanza VI and the fact that the first person address only resumes in stanza VII make this all but certain, regardless of the subject of 14b (see below on 14a and 14b).

Since stanzas IV and V are so closely connected, the "drinking party" of 12a,[254] which depicts a perverted and demonic "wedding," would have been called in 𝔊, "w[ith] no difference in m[eani]ng," either *γάμος* in the singular or *γάμοι* in the plural.[255] The actual "marriage"[256] of the Bridegroom/Deceiver and the Bride/Error carries no weight, as the *hapax legomenon* ܡܫܬܘܬܐ (*meštūtā*), from the root ܫܬܐ (*štā*), makes linguistically clear.[257] Since *καλέω*/ܩܪܐ (*qrā*) is part of the technical vocabulary of weddings, the active participle Pe. ܩܪܝܢ (*qārēn* = *καλοῦσιν* in 𝔊) is translated by "invite" rather than "call."[258] Whether ܣܓܝܐܐ (*saggīyē*) merely means "many . . . people" or is used with an esoteric "connotation of disapproval" as *hoi polloi*, "the many,"[259] cannot

247 See Franz Dünzl, *Gregor von Nyssa, In Canticum Canticorum homiliae – Homilien zum Hohenlied* (FontChr 16.1–3; Freiburg: Herder, 1994) 368–69 on Cant 3:1-4.

248 Connolly, "Odes," 306; also Frankenberg, 32; on the Ethpa. *ʾeddammī*, see Payne Smith, 1:913; BDAG, *s.v.* *μιμέομαι*, with accusative of the person or thing.

249 Contra Arvedson, *Mysterium*, 102 n. 6.

250 See commentary on 10:4a; 19:5a.

251 See Ehrman, 1:443; Wengst, 88–91; Niederwimmer, 261–62; BDAG, *s.v.* *κοσμοπλανής*.

252 Unlike Drijvers, I do not have "the impression that the Odist is perverting Manichaean statements about their own church" (see Drijvers, "Odes," 127). His bold assertion that *Ode* 33 "refers to the same opponent, also called the Corruptor," leads Drijvers to the conclusion that "*Ode of Solomon* 33 . . . should, therefore, be considered a second instance of polemics with the Manichaean church" (ibid., 127 n. 29). If Drijvers were right, it would be necessary to consider the *Odes of Solomon* to be indirect sources for Manichaeism, but no trace of that can be found in Franzmann's book (see Majella Franzmann, *Jesus in the Manichaean Writings* [London/New York: T&T Clark/Continuum, 2003] 157–68 [Index]).

253 See Lattke, *Oden*, 75, 201.

254 Bauer, 619. Whether this is "meant to be the infernal wedding feast" held in "the supernatural world, where the demonic pair is in its element" (Bauer, 619 n. 1) can be left undecided. Gunkel (p. 318), who is the source of Bauer's suggestion, aims to separate the "impious wedding" from the positive idea "that the Beloved and his Bride are also united in marriage." But there is only one pair in question.

255 BDAG, *s.v.* *γάμος*, 1.

256 BDAG, *s.v.* *γάμος*, 2.

257 Payne Smith, 2:4350.

258 BDAG, *s.v.* *καλέω*, 2; Payne Smith, 2:3713; Bauer, 619; Lattke, *Oden*, 201.

259 BDAG, *s.v.* *πολύς*, 2aβℵ; cf. Payne Smith, 2:2518.

really be decided either by appeal to the grammar or by retrospective consideration of the "world" in 11b.

The hosts make their many guests drunk—that is the gruesome quintessence of 12b (see Excursus 37). 𝔊 will have used δίδωμι followed by the infinitive of πίνω (+ αὐτοῖς, of course) and the accusative of οἶνος.[260] This intoxication—in spite of linguistic similarities—is the diametrical opposite of the drinking and drunkenness in 11:7-8a. In that passage μέθη corresponds to ܪܘܝܘܬܐ (*rawwāyūṯā*), but here the term could have been the plural μέθαι.[261] In that case, the image, taking the *hapax legomenon* ܚܡܪܐ (*ḥamrā*) literally together with the following genitive, would not be merely of "hard liquor"[262] or the "wine of their intoxication,"[263] but comprehensively the wine of their carousing.[264]

The apparently "pointless change of [grammatical] subject"[265] in 13a is intended as a sign of the importance of the following statement and a preparation for 13b; "and" here means "(so) that."[266] The Aph. ܐܬܝܒ (*ʾaṯīḇ*), which occurs also in 42:11, does not, then, mean "to rehash"[267] or "to make spit out"[268] but "to vomit up"—or quite plainly—"to spew."[269] The exact meaning of the plurals of ܚܟܡܬܐ (*ḥeḵmṯā*) and ܡܕܥܐ (*maddʿā*), which form the direct object, can only be guessed at, since it is not even clear whether these two terms, which are found elsewhere only in the singular, have a negative or a positive sense (see Excursus 7). In any case, the first plural does not represent τὴν σοφίαν.[270] The plural of σοφία occurs very rarely,[271] so one might rather consider the plural of ἐπιστήμη as equivalent to *scientiae*.[272] The synonymous second half of the object is more likely to correspond to the plural of νόημα (cf. τὰ νοήματα ["thoughts"] in 2 Cor 3:14 and 4:4)[273] than to the plural of φρήν.[274] At the end of *Ode* 38, ܡܕܥܐ (*maddʿā*) recurs in the singular (see below). If this is accepted as approximating the Greek original, the translation "their wisdoms and their understandings"[275] must be emended to "their knowledges and their thoughts" (see above). That, however, is not yet the last word on this subject. Bauer's reference to *Corp. Herm.* 7:1 is not completely applicable because neither that passage nor this Ode is concerned with the "wine of ἀγνωσία," "which they cannot endure and must spit out."[276] The Hermetic tractate is concerned with a drunkenness (μεθύοντες) caused by drinking the undiluted *dogma* of ignorance (τὸν τῆς ἀγνωσίας ἄκρατον λόγον ἐκπιόντες). The demand ἐμεῖτε—"spit it out"—refers to this "dogma of ignorance" (on the relationship between *Corp. Herm.* 7 and *Ode* 38 as a whole, see on 3a above).[277]

Verse 13b is not just a consequence of 12b; it is also the result of 13a. The hosts intend to have their guests appear "without sense."[278] Here, too, it would be interesting to know what the predicate was in the double accusative that followed ποιέω, "make."[279] Syriac normally translates ἄφρων by the *status constructus* of ܚܣܝܪܐ (*ḥassīrā*), so the predicative ܕܠܐ ܪܥܝܢܐ (*d-lā reʿyānā*) most probably corresponds to ἀνοήτους (cf. Titus 3:3) and not to ἀφρόνας.[280] There is no great difference in mean-

260 Contra Frankenberg, 32, who suppresses πιεῖν; see BDAG, *s.vv.* δίδωμι, 1; πίνω, 1; Payne Smith, 2:4349.
261 See BDAG, *s.v.* μέθη, on Gal 5:21: "drinking bouts"; Payne Smith, 2:3841.
262 Gunkel, 316.
263 Bauer, 619.
264 See BDAG, *s.v.* οἶνος, 1.
265 Diettrich, 124 n. 8.
266 In Semitic languages a simple "and" is commonly used for "so that" (Klaus Beyer, letter of November 13, 2002; see already Greßmann, 468; and Bauer, 619).
267 Diettrich, 124: "vorkauen."
268 Lattke, *Oden*, 201 n. 19.
269 Berger and Nord, 967; Payne Smith, 2:4399; LSJ, *s.v.* ἐξεμέω.
270 Contra Frankenberg, 32; Greßmann, 468.
271 LSJ, BDAG, *s.v.* σοφία.
272 Payne Smith, 1:1267; cf. LSJ, *s.v.* ἐπιστήμη; Georges, 2:2527–28.
273 BDAG, *s.v.* νόημα, 1a.
274 Contra Frankenberg, 32: τὰς φρένας; see BDAG, *s.v.* φρήν: "thinking, understanding."
275 Lattke, *Oden*, 201.
276 Bauer, 619 n. 2; Lattke, *Oden*, 201 n. 20.
277 Colpe and Holzhausen, 74; Nock and Festugière, 1:81.
278 Klijn, 304.
279 BDAG, *s.v.* ποιέω, 2hβ; on ܥܒܕ (*ʿḇad*), see Payne Smith, 2:2765–69.
280 Contra Frankenberg, 32; see BDAG, *s.vv.* ἀνόητος, ἄφρων: "foolish"; LEH, *s.v.* ἀνόητος: "senseless"; Payne Smith, 2:3946–47.

ing between these two possibilities (cf. also 28:14).[281] To prefer the grammatically incorrect and inferior reading ܠܗܝܢ (*lhēn*) of N to the masculine ܠܗܘܢ (*lhōn*) of H is to import a totally anachronistic "political correctness" into the manuscript tradition.[282]

The interpretation and translation of 14a will decide, at least in part, who is the subject of 14b and thus of stanza VI as a whole (see below). Since it can be taken for granted that the active participle of ܫܒܩ (*šḇaq*) corresponds to a present form of ἀφίημι,[283] the gist of the conclusion of stanza V, using the *hapax legomenon* ܗܝܕܝܢ (*hāydēn* = τότε),[284] can be translated in two ways: either "they [viz., the hosts] dismissed them [viz., the guests],"[285] or "they left them to lie there."[286]

Examples of the first interpretation include Bauer's translation "then they let them go."[287] Lattke's is more drastic—"then they throw them out"[288]—but it belongs to this group just as much as Berger and Nord's "After that they are thrown out."[289] The verb translated as "to throw out" means "to dismiss, send away, disown,"[290] but here reminds one of the term "bouncer."

Examples of the second interpretation include "and then they leave them";[291] "and after that they leave them";[292] "And then they leave them";[293] "Then they abandon them;"[294] "after that they leave them."[295]

In the second case, which goes at least as well with befuddled drunkenness as the first one, the guests cannot even reel, which rather predetermines the subject of the following stanza. But even on the first interpretation, the despicably treated and thoroughly inebriated guests would have great difficulty going around and seeking anything. The final decision as to the subject of 14b-e must rest on the interpretation of these two bicola.[296]

■ **14b-e** "The Party's Over" (Nat King Cole), though not the address of Truth personified with its extravagant metaphors. But who is the subject of this finale, reminiscent of 28:13-14, which may represent no more than three lines of 𝔊?[297] The answer to the question is left unclear or ambiguous in many of the translations; Franzmann, however, explains her placing of the separation of stanza VI "semantically by the change of focus from the Deceiver and Error to the group of those who have been corrupted (the new 3rd masc[uline] pl[ural] subj[ect])."[298] The commentary on 14a has already established that it would be very difficult to envisage the

281 Charlesworth originally translated 13b as: "And prepare for them nonsense" (1973, p. 132). Later he gives the correct version: "And make them senseless" (1977, p. 132). That ought to have entailed correcting the explanation for the original translation (p. 134 n. 19). He does not alter his erroneous translation of 13a ("So they cause them to vomit up . . ."); see on 13a above.

282 See the correct evaluation by Grimme, "Handschrift," 494; also Kittel, "Handschrift," 89; Franzmann, 259; Emerton, 726 n. 10, on 13b is far astray.

283 Payne Smith, 2:4037–39.

284 Payne Smith, 1:1002; BDAG, *s.v.* τότε, 2: "then."

285 Gunkel, 316; Greßmann, 468.

286 See BDAG, *s.v.* ἀφίημι, 3b: "give up, abandon."

287 Bauer, 619: "dann lassen sie sie laufen."

288 Lattke, 3:170: "und werfen sie dann hinaus"; cf. Lattke, *Bedeutung*, 1:175; idem, *Oden*, 201.

289 Berger and Nord, 967: "Danach werden sie wieder hinausgeworfen."

290 Klaus Beyer, letter of November 13, 2002.

291 Harnack, 68: "und darnach lassen sie sie."

292 Ungnad and Staerk, 36: "und darauf verlassen sie sie."

293 Harris and Mingana, 2:391.

294 Charlesworth, 132; Emerton, 726; Franzmann, 258.

295 Pierre, 181: "or ça les laissent."

296 Whether the "Wedding of the Corruptor" [*sic*] "is depicted as a perversion of the sacrament of the bridal chamber (cf. *Ode* 42,8–9)" (Klauck, *Herrenmahl*, 214) can be examined later. Of course one can say that in these images "wine is viewed negatively," but I cannot share Klauck's further "conjecture, that the images have a connection to Gnostic rites, especially the eucharist with water."

297 There is no mark of division in H between 14b and 14c, but it is possible that there is one in N (cf. Lattke, *Bedeutung*, 1:76, 174–75). The Greek text of 14b-c was certainly more compact than the Syriac, quite possibly only a monocolon.

298 Franzmann, 263. Logically she should then have exploited the possibility of translating the second participle in 14c by "corrupted" instead of "corrupting" (ibid., 258).

abandoned or ejected guests as the subject of 14b-e. On the other hand, the context of these four lines, which should not be reduced by omitting 14d,[299] suggests not a new subject but rather a continuation of the evildoings of Error/Bride and Deceiver/Groom. The proliferating plural participles (14b-c and e), one of which has a linguistic connection to the corrupt and corrupting nature of this strange couple (14c; see 9a-c, 11b above), still refer, I think, to the plural subject of 11a-14a. The use of the participles indicating duration in 11a-14a also argues against Diettrich's assertion of the "introduction of a new subject."[300]

Instead of retreating to the bridal bed, as would be expected in a nonallegorical image, the two seducers continue their depravity. The emphatically prepositioned third masculine plural personal pronoun, followed by ܕܝܢ (*dēn*), in 14b corresponds to οἳ δέ, οἱ δέ, or αὐτοὶ δέ (cf. linguistically Mark 15:23; John 5:11; Job 37:12 LXX). Whether 𝔊 also had καί at the beginning can no more be decided here than in other passages (cf., e.g., 18:15a). More important is ascertaining the meaning of the Ethpe. of ܟܪܟ (*krak*).[301] Frankenberg's choice of the uncommon verb ῥεμβάζω[302] can only be called exotic,[303] even though a glimmering connection—limited to 𝔊—can be seen with ῥεμβασμὸς ἐπιθυμίας in Wis 4:12b, the "wandering of concupiscence" describing a sort of "orgiastic staggering."[304] Since there is no indication of place or of the area traversed, it is hardly likely that περιάγω[305] would have been used intransitively. The same goes for intransitive διοδεύω[306] and περικυκλόω.[307] This leaves three possible equivalents, all more or less synonymous ("go about"). In cases in which διέρχομαι[308] or περιέρχομαι[309] is used in an absolute sense, the Syriac will use ܐܬܟܪܟ (*ʾetkrek*).[310]

The reading ܦܩܕܝܢ (*pāqdīn*) of H in 14c had already been emended to ܦܩܪܝܢ (*pāqrīn*) by Harris,[311] a correction that was confirmed by N.[312] Both participles in 14c depend on ܟܕ (*kad*) "describing a synchronous

299 Contra Diettrich, 125.
300 Diettrich, 125 n. 2.
301 See Payne Smith, 1:1824. The unusual use of the masculine plural participle of ܗܘܐ (*hwā*) followed by ܡܬܟܪܟܝܢ (*metkarkīn*) can only be explained by its forced linking to the preceding participles (Klaus Beyer, per telephone). An examination of all the occurrences of ܗܘܝܢ (*hāwēn*) in the *NTSy* (see Kiraz, 3905–6) yielded the following: Generally the participle is found in the combination ܗܘܝܢ ܗܘܘ (*hāwēn-waw*) corresponding to ἦσαν; the passages where this is not true (Matt 23:30; Luke 17:17; Acts 7:14; Rom 5:19; 1 Cor 10:18; 1 Pet 4:12) are all exceptional in some way.
302 Lampe, 1215.
303 Frankenberg, 32: ῥεμβάζονται.
304 Georgi, 414.
305 BDAG, *s.v.* περιάγω, 2: "go around."
306 BDAG, *s.v.* διοδεύω, 2: "go about."
307 LSJ, *s.v.* περικυκλόω: "go round."
308 BDAG, *s.v.* διέρχομαι, 1a.
309 BDAG, *s.v.* περιέρχομαι, 1. The term διαπορεύομαι (Job 1:7; 2:2 LXX) is synonymous at least with the second of these verbs. It is interesting that "Satan" appears in both verses, although his "role" "especially in the Book of Job is not unambiguous" (Kirsten Nielsen, "Teufel II. Altes Testament," *TRE* 33 [2002] 116).
310 Cf. Acts 8:4, 40; 19:13. In these passages the *NTSy* twice uses ܡܬܟܪܟܝܢ ܗܘܘ (*metkarkīn-waw*) and once ܡܬܟܪܟ ܗܘܐ (*metkrek-wā*). It would be good to know how περινοστέω (LSJ and Lampe, *s.v.* περινοστέω) and συμπερινοστέω (LSJ, *s.v.* συμπερινοστέω) were translated into Syriac. These are the verbs Justin uses to describe the vagrant pair Simon and Helena (*Apol. Maior* 26.3; Goodspeed, 43; Marcovich, *Apologiae*, 70; ANF 1:171; see also Stephen Haar, *Simon Magus: The First Gnostic?* [BZNW 119; Berlin/New York: de Gruyter, 2003] 124). Without referring to that passage, Harris (p. 136) writes about *Ode* 38: "There are some things which suggest Simon Magus and his Helena, who went about to mislead the faithful. It is, however, useless to try and define the situation more closely."
311 Harris, on this passage.
312 "H has mistakenly written ܕ for ܪ" (Franzmann, 259); see Grimme, "Handschrift," 493: "ܦܩܪܝܢ [emendation proposed by] Nestle." The ܦܩܕܝܢ in H does not mean "seeking" (contra Harnack, 68; Kittel, "Handschrift," 89) but rather something like "commanding" (see Lattke, *Bedeutung*, 1:175; idem, *Oden*, 201; Payne Smith, 2:3212).

condition" in the mythological "past" of the narrative.[313] The first belongs to the Pe. ܦܩܪ (*pqar*) and brings to mind, in the first place, the "mad dogs" of 28:13a and, in the second, the "itinerant preachers" called κύνες λυσσῶντες ("raving dogs") in Ignatius *Eph.* 7:1.[314] The second participle belongs to the Pa. ܚܒܠ (*ḥabbel*) and may be either active or passive;[315] it connects, as already mentioned, to the overall description of the Bridegroom/Deceiver and the Bride/Error (see above and Excursus 28). That 𝔊 did not have ἄνοοι[316] is certain. Probably it, like 𝔖, used a participle, but nothing more can be ascertained.

A somewhat chiastic structure (A B B' A') is achieved by placing the subordinate clause 14d, with the repeated particle ܟܕ (*kad*), at the beginning of the second bicolon of stanza VI.[317] The meaning of ܟܕ here wavers between "although" and "while."[318] Verse 14d is not meant to relate to 14e as a causal clause. Frankenberg mistakes ܠܝܬ ܒܗܘܢ (*layt bhōn*)[319] for ܠܝܬ ܠܗܘܢ (*layt lhōn*), reconstructing the original of 14d as οὐκ ἔχοντες καρδίαν.[320] We can also exclude ἀκάρδιος,[321] even though this adjective expresses exactly—in 𝔊 probably with a genitive absolute—what is meant in the parallelism with 14c (it would probably have been οὐ/μὴ οὔσης/ὑπαρχούσης ἐν αὐτοῖς καρδίας or a similar construction with μηδεμίας καρδίας).[322] Clearly, ܠܒܐ (*lebbā*) represents καρδία (see Excursus 4). What is difficult is the determination of its exact place on the line from "organ of thought"[323] via moral arbiter to center of emotion.[324] Here "it might show the lack of empathy displayed by the Seducer and his Bride toward their victims."[325] Without putting undue weight on the moral aspect, one might say that the Deceivers and Corruptors of this world (11b) lack a personal center, which leaves them hollow and inhuman.

The rather abrupt ending of this harsh and grotesque answer from Truth points out that the heartless Deceivers are not (and cannot be) aware of their hollowness, and thus do not seek for a personal center. In the context of this somber passage, that can hardly be called "nonsensical."[326] A final active participle is used in 14e,[327] but this, for the first time since 11a, is strongly negated. This negation is meant to emphasize the mythological fact that the Bride/Error and her Groom/Deceiver are the negative opposites of Wisdom personified and also of the at least partially enlightened speaking "I." For the first time since his question in 10a, this speaker breaks his silence.[328]

313 See Nöldeke §275.

314 Ehrman, 1:226–27; see also Fischer, 146; Bauer and Paulsen, 33; Payne Smith, 2:3223; BDAG, *s.v.* λυσσάω.

315 Payne Smith, 1:1176.

316 Contra Frankenberg, 32; see LSJ, *s.v.* ἄνοος.

317 From 14d onward Charlesworth (pp. 130–33) deviates from the conventional numbering of the verses of *Ode* 38. He should have begun his duplicate numbering with "15 (14c)" (he follows H in not dividing 14b into 14b-c) rather than at "16 (15)" and on to "22 (21)." In his translation, unfortunately, he omits the duplicate numbering (pp. 132–33).

318 See Payne Smith, *Dictionary*, 204.

319 Cf., e.g., John 8:44 in NA[27] and *NTSy*: οὐκ ἔστιν ἀλήθεια ἐν αὐτῷ – ܫܪܪܐ ܠܝܬ ܒܗ (*šrārā layt beh*).

320 Frankenberg, 32.

321 See LEH, *s.v.* ἀκάρδιος: "heartless," "senseless."

322 In most cases a Greek genitive absolute is represented by ܟܕ (*kad*) etc., as is shown by an examination of such passages in the New Testament.

323 As in the Old Testament, the heart is also the organ of thought = "brain" (Klaus Beyer, letter of November 13, 2002).

324 See BDAG, *s.v.* καρδία, *passim;* Payne Smith, 2:1877.

325 Diettrich, 125 n. 1.

326 Contra Diettrich, 125 n. 2.

327 On the Pe. ܒܥܐ [*bʿā*] and its possible Greek equivalents, see Excursus 19.

328 On mature consideration, Klaus Beyer "would refer" 14b-e "to the deceived and not the deceivers. The term *hennōn* in 14b marks the change of subject" (Beyer, letter of February 26, 2004). However, the subject of 14b-e is ambiguous, and therefore the emphatic placing of *hennōn*—after ܠܗܘܢ (*lhōn*) has appeared three times as the object, in 12b, 13b, and 14a—could also be interpreted as resuming the subject of 11-14a. Beyer's suggested translation contrasts 14b-e with 15-16a: "[14b] *They* [= the deserted ones] then go [= wander] around, [14c] demented and corrupted [passive participle of the Pa.]. [14d] Lacking understanding [14e] they, indeed, no longer desire it [= they no longer miss it]. [15a] But *I* have become wise (in contrast to the aforementioned persons), so that (because) I did not fall into the hands of the deceivers (as they did). [15b] And I was glad of myself, because Truth accompanied me. [16a] And I was established and lived and became free."

■ **15-16** There is no compelling reason to divide the manuscript bicolon 15a-b into a tetracolon, although the length of the lines has sometimes led to such a suggestion.[329] Whether 𝔊 also emphasized the return of the speaking "I" by the use of ἐγώ is difficult to tell. If it did, 15a will have begun *Καὶ ἐγώ* or *Ἐγὼ δέ* or even *Καὶ ἐγὼ δέ*.[330] The speaking "I" is not making a contrast with 13a by the use of the Ethpa. of ܚܟܡ (*ḥkam*), which is unlikely to represent ἐσωφρονίσθην.[331] Although 14b-e forms part of the speech of Truth personified, the structure of *Ode* 38 produces a certain opposition to the subjects of the previous groups of lines, regardless of the identity of each subject (see above). The sense of what the speaking "I" is saying can be shown even more clearly by comparison with 24:10-12, where there is mention of a lack of truth and wisdom. Linguistically a reference to Prov 8:33 (σοφίσθητε)[332] or 27:11 LXX (σοφὸς γίνου), "be(come) wise," in other words, to the passive of σοφίζω[333] or the juxtaposition of γίνομαι (or ἐγενόμην) with σοφός,[334] will suffice.[335] The explanation for this wisdom is the fact that the speaking "I" did not fall into the hands (i.e., the power) of the antagonists of Truth personified, who are described in stanzas III–VI.[336] The *Vorlage* of the Pe. ܢܦܠ (*npal*) is more probably ἐμπίπτω than merely πίπτω.[337] Franzmann prefers the singular ܡܛܥܝܢܐ (*maṭʿyānā*) and makes a connection with the "Deceiver" of 10b.[338] But, quite apart from the fact that the plural points were probably added in H,[339] the plural reading "fits" "very well, since a pair of demons is involved."[340] So the speaker, in contrast to the many, did not fall εἰς χεῖρας τῶν πλάνων, "into the hands of the Deceivers" (see Excursus 38 above).[341]

The form ܚܕܝܬ (both manuscripts have a point above)[342] in 15b is the Pe. *ḥdīt*, not the Pa. *ḥaddīt*.[343] The most likely equivalent of the Pe. ܚܕܐ (*ḥdā*), ܚܕܝ (*ḥdī*) is χαίρω.[344] The ܠ (*l-*) that follows cannot here stand for the preposition ἐπί. The reflexive ܠܢܦܫ (*l-napš*) does not stand for κατ᾽ἐμαυτόν[345] and makes as little sense when taken as an explicit "to me (myself)"[346] as does "about myself." This reflexive use of the preposition—as of ܠܝ (*lī*) in 42:6a—is probably meant as a kind of "dativus ethicus,"[347] which would not have had an equivalent in 𝔊. The causal conjunction ܡܛܠ ܕ (*meṭṭol d-*), "because," does not differ in meaning from the "simple ܕ" in 15a.[348] The Pe. ܐܙܠ (*ʾezal*) followed by the preposition ܥܡ (*ʿam*) + first singular suffix has already appeared in 4a (see above πορεύομαι + σύν τινι). In both cases, the phrase, in 𝔖 as well as in 𝔊, means "to accompany."[349] "Truth" is mentioned for the last time, which, only in 𝔖, forms a link to the following bicolon "by the terrace pattern of the repetition of the root ܫܪ."[350]

With 11:5a (ἐστηρίχθην) as an example, one might agree that the Ethpe. ܐܫܬܪܪ (*ʾeštarrar*) in 16a,

329 Lattke, *Bedeutung*, 1:174–75; Franzmann, 256, 258, 263; Lattke, *Oden*, 202.

330 On the word order in Syriac "verbal sentences," see Nöldeke §324.

331 Contra Frankenberg, 32; see BDAG, *s.v.* σωφρονίζω.

332 Rahlfs, 2:197, critical apparatus.

333 BDAG, *s.v.* σοφίζω, 1a.

334 BDAG, *s.vv.* γίνομαι, 5b; σοφός, 2a.

335 One who hears the voice of Christ here can make connections with the "Wisdom of Christ" in the New Testament and the Pauline Christ as θεοῦ σοφία in 1 Cor 1:24 (see BDAG, *s.v.* σοφία, 1bβ).

336 The conjunction ܕ (*d-*) cannot here have a final meaning (Nöldeke §258.B). Translating it as "since" (Nöldeke §366.B) merely serves to differentiate it from the synonymous conjunction "because" in 15b and 16c (see below).

337 BDAG, *s.vv.* ἐμπίπτω, 2; πίπτω, 1a; Payne Smith, 2:2411–12.

338 Franzmann, 259.

339 See Charlesworth, *Manuscripts*, 82 line 1.

340 Kittel, "Handschrift," 89.

341 See Frankenberg, 32, who, knowing only the faulty *editio princeps*, of course uses τοῦ πλάνου; Charlesworth (*Reflections*, 208–9), in his table on "dualism between Truth and Error" in *Ode* 38, only contrasts "the Deceivers" with "Truth." But the speaking "I" is also part of this contrast. I consider that "The Beloved and his Bride" (11a) belong on the side of "Error" not of "Truth."

342 See Segal, *Point*, 17–18.

343 Contra Harris and Mingana, vol. 1, on this passage; Charlesworth, 130; Lattke, *Oden*, 265.

344 Payne Smith, 1:1198; BDAG, *s.v.* χαίρω; Frankenberg, 32: ἐχάρην.

345 Contra Frankenberg, 32.

346 Nöldeke §223.

347 Ibid., §224.

348 Ibid., §§358–60.

349 See BDAG, *s.v.* πορεύω, 1.

350 Franzmann, 263.

corresponding to the passive of στηρίζω,[351] means, as in 36:8b, to "establish in a christological sense" (see commentary on that verse) or, in a Pauline sense, represents "a soteriological and eschatological establishing in legal language."[352] However, στηρίζω is not the only possibility; the passive of βεβαιόω[353] must also be considered. Additionally the reader of the Syriac text would have had another association with the Ethpa. of ܫܪ (*šar*) in connection with the terms for roots and planting, which occur in the following verses. Since Homer (*Od.* 13.163)[354] ῥιζόω has been used metaphorically.[355] This usage is to be found, for example, in Jer 12:2 (ἐρριζώθησαν; cf. "periphr. Hex." ܐܫܬܪܪܘ ܥܩܪܝܗܘܢ).[356] Col 2:7 and Eph 3:17 have ἐρριζωμένοι.[357] The Syriac translations of these two passages use various terms and forms derived from the root ܫܪ, both with and without the term ܥܩܪܐ (*ʿeqqārā*), "root."[358] For the remainder of 16a, one can first of all make reference to 8:22, where it is said of the Revealer and Redeemer that he "lives" and "was saved."[359] Here the *Vorlage* of the Pe. ܚܝܐ (*ḥyā*) was either ἀναζάω or ζάω/ζῶ (see Table 1).[360] This statement of salvation by the speaking "I" can be generally applied to the "transcendent . . . life of a child of God,"[361] but it is important to note that the Kyrios Christos in the New Testament also (ἀν)έζησεν, "lived (again)" (Rom 14:9; cf. Rev 2:8) and ζῇ ἐκ δυνάμεως θεοῦ, "lives by the power of God" (2 Cor 13:4; cf. John 5:26; 6:57). The Greek equivalent of the Ethpe. of ܦܪܩ (*praq*) remains unknown. This reflexive is uncommon in the New Testament, but may occur as a translation of the passive of λυτρόω (1 Pet 1:18),[362] ῥύομαι (Luke 1:74),[363] and σῴζω (Eph 2:8).[364] Such a christological utterance is not to be found in the New Testament,[365] but it occurs in a number of passages in the *Odes of Solomon* (cf. 7:16a; 8:22e; 15:6-9; 17:2-4; see also Excursus 5). So there is no reason why the speaker of *Ode* 38 should not be distinguished from the generality of the redeemed as the

351 BDAG, *s.v.* στηρίζω, 2.

352 Erich Dinkler, "Die Taufterminologie in 2 Kor. i 21 f," in *Neotestamentica et Patristica: Eine Freundesgabe, Herrn Professor Dr. Oscar Cullmann zu seinem 60. Geburtstag überreicht* (NovTSup 6; Leiden: Brill, 1962) 178 = idem, *Signum*, 104; see Payne Smith, 2:4300: "jur. *ratus, validus factus est.*" The construction with ܘ (*w-*) and ܕܝܢ (*dēn*) is just as excessive as 14b. Frankenberg (p. 32) omits the text of 16a.

353 BDAG, *s.v.* βεβαιόω, 2.

354 Helmut van Thiel, ed., *Homeri Odyssea* (Bibliotheca Weidmanniana I; Hildesheim/Zurich/New York: Olms, 1991) 179.

355 LSJ, *s.v.* ῥιζόω: "plant, fix firmly."

356 Payne Smith, 2:4299.

357 BDAG, *s.v.* ῥιζόω: "pass[ive] be/become firmly rooted/fixed."

358 See Barbara Aland and Andreas Juckel, eds., *Das Neue Testament in syrischer Überlieferung II: Die paulinischen Briefe* (3 vols.; ANTT 14, 23, 32; Berlin/New York: de Gruyter, 1991–2002) 2:285, 414.

359 See commentary on that passage.

360 BDAG, *s.vv.* ἀναζάω, 1b; ζάω, 1aє and 2; Payne Smith, 1:1251–52.

361 BDAG, *s.v.* ζάω, 2.

362 BDAG, *s.v.* λυτρόω, 1b: "be ransomed."

363 BDAG, *s.v.* ῥύομαι: "be rescued from someone's power."

364 BDAG, *s.v.* σῴζω, 2b: "be saved, attain salvation." Note that the passive of σῴζω is normally translated by a term derived from the root ܚܝܐ (*ḥyā*). This is true even of Rom 8:24, where ἐσώθημεν is translated by ܐܬܦܪܩܢ only in the late Harklean version (see Aland and Juckel, *Briefe*, 1:187). How often the active of σῴζω is translated by a word derived from the root ܚܝܐ (*ḥyā*) is a subject worthy of investigation. 1 Cor 1:21 (εὐδόκησεν ὁ θεὸς . . . σῶσαι τοὺς πιστεύοντας, "it pleased God/God decided . . . to save those who believe"), as a high point, would be a good place to start, since, in the widest sense, the Jesus Christ of the New Testament might also be reckoned among the believers, as can be seen from the debate about the πίστις Ἰησοῦ Χριστοῦ, which is still under way (BDAG, *s.v.* πίστις, 2b; on the passage quoted from 1 Corinthians, see Aland and Juckel, *Briefe*, 1:285).

365 On the contrary, cf. Mark 15:30-31; Matt 27:40, 42, 49; Luke 23:35, 37, 39; John 12:27.

redeemed Redeemer and perhaps even identified with the Messiah/Christ of the *Odes of Solomon* (cf. esp. 41:11-16).

The plural of ܫܬܐܣܬܐ (*šeṯesṯā*) in 16b corresponds to the plural of τὸ θεμέλιον[366] or the plural of ὁ θεμέλιος.[367] In either case, there is a close connection with the "image of planting"[368] that follows. But the metaphorical sense of "foundation" directs attention also to "Christ" as the "foundation of the Christian church or congregation."[369] The Ethpa. of ܣܘܡ, ܣܡ (*sām*),[370] corresponding to the passive of τίθημι, points ahead to 17a.[371] The remainder of 16b does not mean "on account of the Lord's hand"[372] or "upon the hand of the Lord"[373] but "by the hand of the Lord" or simply "by the Lord,"[374] "by the Lord's action."[375] So the preposition ܥܠ (*ʿal*) is here equivalent to ܒ (*b*-), as is shown by passages where διὰ χειρός ([τῶν] χειρῶν) τινος occurs.[376] It must be noted that the actions are no longer those of Truth personified but those of the divine Lord, who is also the subject of the final line of this stanza.

As the "I" of *Ode* 38 was emphasized by the wording of 15a, so the third masculine singular pronoun in 16c (probably αὐτός in 𝔊) focuses attention on the Lord. The causal conjunction (it will have been ὅτι in 𝔊 as in 15b) refers to 16a as well as to 16b. Compared to the "juxtaposition of building and planting" in 1 Cor 3:6-17,[377] the stress at the end of stanza VII and especially in stanzas VIII–IX lies exclusively on the planting. There is no mention, however, of "believers" as individual "plants of Christ."[378] It was not, primarily, the church that was planted (cf. φυτεία πατρός in Ignatius *Trall.* 11:1 and *Phld.* 3:1; note already Matt 15:13), but the preeminent speaking "I," who was led/accompanied by Truth. This passage is thus not parallel to 11:18-21. The Pe. ܢܨܒ (*nṣaḇ*), which can represent φυτεύω[379] and also καταφυτεύω,[380] draws the attention of anyone with biblical knowledge to Israel as the vine transplanted from Egypt (Ps 80 [79 LXX]:9-16),[381] while at the same time expanding it. The speaking "I" makes his final appearance, including himself by the use of the first singular objective suffix, but is to be identified as the "root" in stanzas VIII–IX.[382]

■ **17** The second part of *Ode* 38 (stanzas VIII–X), which is not a treatise on agri- or horticulture, is firmly linked to the first part by the resonance of 17a with the finale of that section. The third masculine singular pronoun, referring to God the Lord, is placed right at the beginning, emphasized even more strongly than was the case in 16c. So there is no change of subject between the end of stanza VII and the beginning of VIII. The particle ܓܝܪ (*gēr*), like the Greek γάρ, is explanatory[383] and connects the being planted of the speaking "I" with the setting of the root by the self-same Lord. One must agree with Franzmann that *Ode* 38:17-19 "can be linked with *Acta Thomae* only in a very broad sense and certainly not as providing traces of the lost parable [of Jesus] which Bauckham proposes to elicit from *Acta Thomae* 146."[384] Bauckham considers the first three verbs of 17a-b to be "a possible relic of the parable which has not been

366 Frankenberg, 32, though he adds a question mark; cf. *Hermas, Sim.* 98 (IX.21):2; Ehrman, 2:440–41.

367 Payne Smith, 2:4348; LSJ and BDAG, *s.v.* θεμέλιος, 2.

368 Gemünden, *Vegetationsmetaphorik*, 384–85.

369 BDAG, *s.v.* θεμέλιος, 2b. Cf. 1 Cor 3:11; *Hermas, Sim.* 91 (IX.14):6.

370 The reading of H (ܐܬܬܣܝܡܬ), which Franzmann notes (p. 259) and which Charlesworth even prefers (p. 131), is merely a variant of ܐܬܬܣܡܬ (see Brockelmann, *Grammatik*, 126; Nöldeke §§50.B, 158.C, 168).

371 BDAG, *s.v.* τίθημι, 1a: "lay"; Payne Smith, 2:2560 (n.b. φυτεύειν, line 9 from the bottom).

372 Contra Charlesworth, 132.

373 Contra Franzmann, 258.

374 Harris and Mingana, 2:392.

375 Bauer, 619: "durch den Herrn"; cf. Payne Smith, 1:1549: *per* = διὰ χειρός.

376 BDAG, *s.v.* χείρ, 2a.

377 Bauer, 619 n. 4; see also Vielhauer, *Oikodome*, 46.

378 Contra Hans-Werner Bartsch, *Gnostisches Gut und Gemeindetradition bei Ignatius von Antiochien* (BFCThM 44; Gütersloh: "Der Rufer" Evangelischer Verlag, 1940) 28.

379 BDAG, *s.v.* φυτεύω.

380 LEH, *s.v.* καταφυτεύω; cf. Payne Smith, 2:2435–36.

381 Kraus, *Psalmen*, 558–59.

382 After the various allusions to the exodus from Egypt in the first part of *Ode* 38, this may be taken as another, though vaguer, one. Whether that was intentional is not clear.

383 BDAG, *s.v.* γάρ, 2.

384 Majella Franzmann, "The Parable of the Vine in *Odes of Solomon* 38.17-19? A Response to Richard Bauckham," *NTS* 35 (1989) 608.

preserved in *Acts of Thomas* 146."[385] This theory is not as likely as the idea (referring to the vine of Ps 80:9-16 [cf. Isa 60:21; 61:3] and despite the fact that "[t]he plant is not said to be a vine") "that the odist was in fact thinking of a vine."[386] Actually the species of plant is not important. If it were, it would have been named, for example, if a clearer allusion to John 15:1-8 had been intended.

As the verbs τίθημι/ܣܝܡ, ܣܡ (*sām*) can express the laying of a foundation (see 16b above),[387] they can also be used to describe the setting of a root. That this refers to the *planting out* of a seedling is shown by the parallel between φυτεύει ἄμπελον and ܣܡ ܟܪܡܐ (*sām karmā*) in the "Syriac Geoponica" 12.7.[388] Although this passage is not an explicit allegory, the term ῥίζα/ܥܩܪܐ (*ʿeqqārā*)—as a *pars pro toto* of a plant (whether a vine or not), and quite unlike 11:16-17 in the context of 11:16-23[389]—refers to one person only, which helps to characterize the speaking "I" of the first part more clearly. There can, in my opinion, be no doubt that the choice of the biblical term "root," instead of the metaphorical "vine" (ἄμπελος/ܓܦܬܐ [*gpettā*]), is meant for the Christos/"Messiah" who is called ῥίζα τοῦ Ἰεσσαί (Rom 15:12; cf. Isa 11:10 LXX) or ῥίζα Δαυίδ (Rev 5:5; cf. Sir 47:22).[390] In the last chapter of the New Testament, it is *Jesus* himself who says: ἐγώ εἰμι ἡ ῥίζα καὶ τὸ γένος Δαυίδ, "I am the root and the descendant of David" (Rev 22:16).[391] Isaiah 53 LXX, in which the Suffering Servant of God is compared to a ῥίζα ἐν γῇ διψώσῃ, "root in dry land" (53:2), is also applied to the κύριος Ἰησοῦς Χριστός, "Lord Jesus Christ" (see *1 Clem.* 16:1-14, esp. 2-3).

The first two verbs of 17b are not metaphors but part of the image of planting out. The Aph. from the root ܫܩܐ (i.e., ܐܫܩܝ [*ʾašqī*]),[392] which is not used in the Pe., is a *hapax legomenon* but corresponds to ποτίζω in the part of *Ode* 11 that is preserved only in 𝔊.[393] However, there is no connection between the content of 11:16g (much less 11:6a-b) and 38:17b.[394] This holds good also for the Aph. of ܬܩܢ (*tqen*), which in 11:5b is the equivalent of συγκαθίζω. The Greek equivalent in the present case cannot be determined.[395] If the plant under consideration is a seedling with a well-developed root system,[396] which can be expected to become a "free standing, treelike vine,"[397] the "fixing" may describe both the careful placing of the root into the hole dug for it and the "training of the vine by a support (*cum pedimento*)."[398] There is no evidence that the Pa. ܒܪܟ (*barrek*) does not here mean εὐλογέω.[399] Generally, a gardener, having finished a task, will, at most, speak encouragingly to the plants.[400] "The blessing of the plant," therefore, is "appropriate to the Lord but scarcely to a human vinedresser."[401]

Thus, 17c also surpasses anything human and finite, bringing up, by the use of the plural of καρπός/ܦܐܪܐ (*pērā*), the parable of the vine, related by the Johannine Jesus (John 15:2, 4-5, 8, 16), although one might have expected "branches" rather than eternal "fruits" (see Excursus 22).[402] But τὸ κλῆμα, "branch," is nothing more than ὁ τῆς ἀμπέλου κλάδος, "branch of the vine,"[403] so it is quite permissible to point out the close connection of κλάδοι and καρποί (cf. 1:2, 5). Therefore the "fruits" of the personified root are, as in John 15, meant for "persons" redeemed and belonging to the

385 Richard Bauckham, "The Parable of the Vine: Rediscovering a Lost Parable of Jesus," *NTS* 33 (1987) 89.
386 Ibid., 88–89.
387 BDAG, *s.v.* τίθημι, 1a; Payne Smith, 2:2556–57.
388 Payne Smith, 2:2557; see Anton Baumstark, *Geschichte der syrischen Literatur mit Ausschluß der christlich-palästinensischen Texte* (Bonn: Marcus & Weber, 1922; repr., Berlin: de Gruyter, 1968) 171.
389 Contra Franzmann, "Parable," 607–8.
390 BDAG, s.v. ῥίζα, 2: "shoot, scion."
391 See Christian Maurer, "ῥίζα, κτλ.," *ThWNT* 6 (1959) 990; *TDNT* 6:989; Ferdinand Hahn, *Christologische Hoheitstitel: Ihre Geschichte im frühen Christentum* (UTB 1873; 5th ed.; Göttingen: Vandenhoeck & Ruprecht, 1995) 248–49.
392 Payne Smith, 2:4281.
393 BDAG, *s.v.* ποτίζω, 1c.
394 Contra Franzmann, "Parable," 607–8.
395 See Payne Smith, 2:4484–86.
396 See *MEL* 25:134, *s.v.* "Weinbau."
397 Galling, 33.
398 Kai Ruffing, "Wein II. Klassische Antike. A. Weinbau. B. Weinhandel," *DNP* 12/2 (2002) 430–31.
399 Cf. 28:4a and the line of 11:22 found only in 𝔊; also "blessing" in 20a below. See Payne Smith, 1:611; BDAG, *s.v.* εὐλογέω, 2b.
400 Irmtraud Petersson (personal communication).
401 Bauckham, "Parable," 89.
402 BDAG, *s.v.* καρπός, 1αα.
403 BDAG, *s.vv.* κλάδος, κλῆμα; Johannes Behm, "κλῆμα," *ThWNT* 3 (1938) 756; *TDNT* 3:757.

Messiah (See Excursus 11).[404] Though these receive no further mention, stanza IX will return to the root. The reading ܠܥܠܡܝܢ (*l-ʿālmīn* = εἰς τοὺς αἰῶνας) is preferred on the basis of the general comparison of H and N.[405] H has the singular ܠܥܠܡ (*l-ʿālam* = εἰς τὸν αἰῶνα). Unlike the use in 14b, ܗܘܝܢ (*hāwēn*) here corresponds to εἰσίν (as in 1 Cor 10:18, although the Harklean translation has ܐܝܬܝܗܘܢ [*ʾīṯayhōn*], which makes no difference in the meaning).[406]

■ **18** Since the subject of 17c already was no longer the "Lord," the change "from the action of the Lord to the action by the plant/root" in 18a is considerably moderated.[407] All five stages of growth of the "root" in 18a-b are consonant with the development of a healthy vine from the carefully planted root. Grimme[408] takes no notice of the crucial difference between H and N in 18a, while Kittel, for no convincing reason, "prefers H," though keeping open "the possibility that both traditions have been corrupted."[409] The most convincing explanation of the difference must start from the presumption that an at least partially ambiguous Greek text gave rise to two different Syriac translations. Added to this is the near synonymity of the Pa. and Aph. of the Syriac roots ܥܡܩ and ܦܬܐ/ܦܬܝ (see below). To anticipate, I believe that 18a 𝔊 ran as follows: ἐβάθυνε καὶ ἀνέβη καὶ ἐπλατύνθη, with the subject ῥίζα implied. Neither 18a nor 18b should be interpreted allegorically.

That the vine root needs to penetrate deep into the soil was known to the ancients. The verb βαθύνω, used transitively, means "make deep" and, intransitively, "go down deep"; in Luke 6:48, for instance, both are possible.[410] In H—as in the passage from Luke in the *NTSy*—the Pa. ܥܡܩ (*ʿammeq*) is used for ἐβάθυνε in the intransitive sense (cf. Jer 49:8, 30).[411] N, on the other hand, uses the Aph. ܐܥܡܩ (*ʾaʿmeq*), which can have the same meaning as the Pa.,[412] but here also has the intransitive meaning of βαθύνω.

Once the root has firmly fixed the plant in the soil, the vigorous stem of the vine can grow upward—or, as H puts it, the root allows it to grow upward. That the verb ἀναβαίνω, used of "vines" and other "plants,"[413] may be translated by the Aph. ܐܣܩ (*ʾasseq*), as in H,[414] can be seen, linguistically in, e.g., Wis 19:12 (ἀνέβη = ܐܣܩܬ [*ʾasseqt*]).[415] N logically uses ܣܠܩ (*sleq*).[416]

According to the tending it receives and its habit of growth, the branches and tendrils of the vine spread out.[417] The passive of πλατύνω means "[become] broad, . . . enlarged,"[418] in N represented by the Aph. ܐܦܬܝ (*ʾap̄tī*),[419] which must here have an intransitive sense ("spread out widely").[420] H uses the Pa. ܦܬܝ (*pattī*), which can have the same transitive meaning as the Aph.[421] As a transitive verb, though, it ought to have a direct object.

In 18b, H and N are back in agreement, with no ambiguity about the subject. The vine is now in full

404 See Lattke, *Einheit*, 187. The phrase ἁγία ἄμπελος Δαυίδ in *Did.* 9:2 "is probably a metaphor for salvation itself" (Niederwimmer, 183), but the interpretation of "vine" in the *Syriac Apocalypse of Baruch* is closer to the image of the Ode. The "vine" in *2 Bar.* 36–40 is not directly a metaphor "for the Messiah" (Johannes Behm, "ἄμπελος," *ThWNT* 1 [1933] 346; *TDNT* 1:342).

405 See Lattke, *Bedeutung*, 1:66–70.

406 See Nöldeke §§199, 305; Aland and Juckel, *Briefe*, 1:397.

407 Franzmann, 264.

408 Grimme, "Handschrift."

409 Kittel, "Handschrift," 89–90. Kittel, following Schultheß (p. 256), clearly considers the "Lord" the subject of 18a: "he made it grow in depth and height and breadth" (H); "he made it grow into the depth and he grew upwards and he spread wide" (N), and thus proposes "a clumsy change of subject." Flemming's translation of 18a anticipates the still-unknown reading of N: "it penetrated deep down, grew upwards and spread out" (Harnack, 68).

410 BDAG, *s.v.* βαθύνω.

411 Brockelmann, *Lexicon*, 531: *penitus penetravit*.

412 Payne Smith, 2:2916: *profundum fecit*.

413 BDAG, *s.v.* ἀναβαίνω, 1b: "come up."

414 Payne Smith, 2:2648: *ascendere fecit*.

415 Rahlfs, 2:376; Emerton, *Wisdom*, 37.

416 Payne Smith, 2:2646: *ascendit*.

417 See the illustrations in Kai Ruffing, "Wein II. Klassische Antike. A. Weinbau. B. Weinhandel," *DNP* 12/2 (2002) 430.

418 BDAG, *s.v.* πλατύνω.

419 Payne Smith, 2:3334.

420 Payne Smith, *Dictionary*, 469.

421 Payne Smith, 2:3333: *dilatavit*.

leaf and bearing clusters of grapes (cf. linguistically Phil 1:11). The *Vorlage* of the intransitive Pe. ܡܠܐ (*mlā*), which means "to be full,"[422] may have been ἐπλήσθη (cf. Ps 79:10 LXX),[423] or ἐπληρώθη (cf. Ps 103:24 LXX).[424] The two verbs were used interchangeably in the textual history of the New Testament (cf. Luke 2:21; Acts 7:30).

The Ethpalp. of ܪܒ (*rab*), corresponding to the passive of μεγαλύνω (cf. linguistically 2 Cor 10:15),[425] can be taken as the summary of the growth of the whole plant. So 𝔊 was not ἔπλησε καὶ ηὐξήθη,[426] but—factoring in the necessary uncertainty—ἐπληρώθη/ἐπλήσθη καὶ ἐμεγαλύνθη. Taking stanza IX as a whole, the only similarity between the full vine and any hypothetical group of persons would be the (fruitful) growth of that group. The christological parable of the "vine" as "tree of life" (John 15:1-8)[427] would have to be revised as follows: "I am the root"—"you are the vine." It is hardly "possible that the author" of stanza IX "has the Pauline texts [viz., of 1 Cor 3:6 and 10] in mind."[428] Even if *Ode* 38 did not refer to the vine, which has always been cultivated around the Mediterranean and especially in Syria,[429] but to some other tree or plant, the texts Drijvers draws on from the "Manichaean Psalm-Book" are not "exact parallels,"[430] whether to verses 16c-18b, already discussed, or to the hymnic poem that follows.

■ **19-21** The closing doxological poem[431] is only in part "a scriptural commentary based on Isa 60:21; 61:3; Ps 80:15."[432] Although ܢܨܒܬܐ (*neṣbṯā*) occurs three times, in 19b, 20b, and 21a, it should not mislead one to suppose that the "planting" is the theme of stanza X. The term, of course, is the link with the divine actions of planting (16c-17b) and the description of the rooted and fruit-bearing plant (17c–18b), but it is only the instrument of the hymnic glorification of the Lord, with its rather Gnostic culmination in 21b. Terms such as "blessing" (20a; cf. "to bless" in 17b) and "right [hand]" (20b; cf. "hand" in 16b) are additional links to the preceding material. But not all the nouns of "the careless imagery"[433] correspond exactly to the action verbs used earlier. The preposition ܒ (*b-*), which occurs seven times in 19b-21b, has instrumental meaning. Whether 𝔊 used a simple dative throughout, or perhaps a compound construction of ἐν (+ dative) or διά (+ genitive) in the corresponding cases, cannot be determined. Unlike 11:16-24, this is not a "divine plantation in heaven" or a "tree of Paradise."[434]

All six lines of stanza X are governed by the one verb in 19a, the *hapax legomenon* ܐܫܬܒܚ (*ʾeštabbaḥ*, Ethpa., from the root ܫܒܚ, which does not occur as a Pe.; see Excursus 21), "was glorified." Since it is unlikely that this verb corresponds here to a passive form of ὑμνέω, the original must have been either δοξάσθη or ἐνδοξάσθη.[435] If this "planting" is a metaphor for the totality of the congregation, including the basic root of its beginning, then it can be linked to the Johannine "glorification of the Father by the Son" (John 13:31-32; 14:13; 17:1, 4) and "by his own" (John 15:8).[436] Only God the Lord is worthy of being glorified with honor and praise,

422 Payne Smith, *Dictionary*, 273; Brockelmann, *Lexicon*, 388; Payne Smith, 2:2118: *plenus fuit*.
423 BDAG, *s.v.* πίμπλημι, 1aα.
424 BDAG, *s.v.* πληρόω, 5.
425 Payne Smith, 2:3783; BDAG, *s.v.* μεγαλύνω, 1: "increase, grow"; see Aland and Juckel, *Briefe*, 2:147.
426 Contra Frankenberg, 33; his translation of 18a is also rather free.
427 See Schweizer, *Ego eimi*, 37–41, 166.
428 Contra Massaux, *Influence*, 72, who refers, not uncritically, to Harris and Mingana, 2:124.
429 See the map in Kai Ruffing, "Wein II. Klassische Antike. A. Weinbau. B. Weinhandel," *DNP* 12/2 (2002) 425.
430 Drijvers, "Odes," 128.
431 There are formally similar passages elsewhere in the *Odes of Solomon* (cf. 12:4; 19:10-11; 26:5-7). Franzmann (p. 264) calls stanza X "a kind of litany, an extended indirect doxology to conclude the Ode." She may have correctly identified a mark of division in N after ܒܢܨܒܬܗ in 20a.
432 Bauckham "Parable," 89.
433 Frankenberg, 43.
434 Contra Gunkel, 318.
435 Payne Smith, 2:4024–25; BDAG, *s.vv.* δοξάζω, 2; ἐνδοξάζομαι.
436 See BDAG, *s.v.* δοξάζω, 2. The passage John 21:19, referring to "martyrdom," is not relevant; in any case it occurs in the postscript to the Fourth Gospel (see Michael Lattke, "Joh 20, 30f als Buchschluß," *ZNW* 78 [1987]). There are other images of Christ and the church, for example, the head and members in 17:15-16 (see Michael Lattke, "κεφαλή," *EWNT* 2 [1981] 706; *EDNT* 2:286). In Ignatius *Trall.* 11:1-2 the image of the "planting of the Father" (φυτεία πατρός) is linked with that of the "head" (κεφαλή) and its "limbs" (μέλη

which at once demotes all so-called gods (cf. already Exod 22:19 and Judg 10:16 LXX) and all human beings arrogating lordship to themselves. The stress here is not on the uniqueness of God[437] and its acclamation[438] but on the fact that he alone is the Kyrios to be worshiped. For there can be no doubt that the compound expression ܒܠܚܘܕܘܗܝ (*ba-lḥōḏaw*), also poetically ܗܘ ܠܚܘܕܘܗܝ (*hū lḥōḏaw* = *ille solus*),[439] corresponds to the Greek adjective *μόνος*, "alone." The adverbial use of the neuter *μόνον* would have been translated ܒܠܚܘܕ (*ba-lḥōḏ*).[440] In early Christian writings, *μόνος κύριος* does not occur at all.[441] It is also surprising that *μόνος* occurs so rarely in the LXX in connection with *θεός* and/or *κύριος*.[442]

As with the phrase *φυτεία πατρός*, "planting of the Father," in Ignatius *Trall.* 11:1 and *Phld.* 3:1, the chain of connections runs through Matt 15:13 (cf. John 15:2) to Isa 61:3 (cf. Isa 60:21).[443] This makes it difficult to decide whether the Greek equivalent of ܢܨܒܬܐ (*neṣbṯā*) was *φυτεία* (as in Matt 15:13)[444] or *φύτευμα* (as in Isa 60:21; 61:3 LXX).[445] The second possibility is the more likely one, since the term *δόξα* plays a large part in the context of Isa 60:19 to Isa 61:3.[446] The noun ܦܘܠܚܢܐ

αὐτοῦ); cf. Lake, 1:222–23, with Ehrman, 1:266–67 ("parts"). This context includes "the first mention in Christian literature" of the "image of the Tree of the Cross" (Fischer, 179 n. 42). The identification of the "plant" with the odist by Harris and Mingana (2:394) is somewhat inaccurate.

437 See BDAG, *s.v.* *εἷς*, 2.

438 See Erik Peterson, *Εἷς θεός: Epigraphische, formgeschichtliche und religionsgeschichtliche Untersuchungen* (FRLANT 41 = N.F. 24; Göttingen: Vandenhoeck & Ruprecht, 1926) *passim*.

439 Payne Smith, 2:1924.

440 Occasionally a Syriac text will even use ܒܠܚܘܕ (*ba-lḥōḏ*) where the Greek has *μόνος* (e.g., Rev 15:4 *μόνος* [*εἶ*] *ὅσιος*, and similar passages).

441 See the sparse theological passages using *μόνος* cited in BDAG, *s.v.* *μόνος*, 1aδ, and in Kraft, *Clavis*, 298.

442 Hatch and Redpath, 933–34. In the two passages already cited *κύριος μόνος* is contrasted with other gods (Exod 22:19; Judg 10:16). The following summary takes no notice of varying word order or of the presence of the definite article. The pairing *κύριος μόνος* is found by itself in a very small number of cases (Neh 9:6 [= Ezra 19:6]; Sir 18:2; Isa 2:11, 17). *1 Esdras* (= *3 Ezra*) 8:25, *Εὐλογητὸς μόνος ὁ κύριος* ("blessed [be] the only Lord God"), is especially noted because it was known and used by early Christian authors (Karl-Friedrich Pohlmann, *3. Esra-Buch* [JSHRZ 1.5; Gütersloh: Mohn, 1980] 380, 413). The pairing *θεὸς μόνος* is just as rare (4 Kgdms 19:15; Ps 85:10b; Isa 37:16, 20; 2 Macc 7:37; *4 Macc.* 5:24 [on this passage, cf. Exod 3:14 and Klauck, *4. Makkabäerbuch,* 712 n. c, on v. 24). But some of these passages have *κύριος* in the immediate context (Ps 85:11a; Isa 37:16, 20). This is also the case (Ps 82:19a) where God is acknowledged as *μόνος ὕψιστος ἐπὶ πᾶσαν τὴν γῆν* (Ps 82:19b; similar statements of sovereignty are found in 4 Kgdms 19:15; Isa 37:16, 20; Dan 3:45b). The term *μόνος* is explicitly combined with both *κύριος and θεός* only twice (3 Kgdms 18:37 [A and a few other Christian manuscripts]; Dan 3:45a).

443 *Ode* 38 should have been cited in the section on "Saint Matthew" (Massaux, *Influence*, 63–66). The reference to "planting" in Qumran as "description of their community" (Lohse, *Texte*, 281; cf. Lattke, *Oden*, 203) can now be amplified by additional texts as identified by Håkan Ulfgard: 4Q 415–418; 1QS viii.5; xi.8; 1QH[a] vi(xiv).15; viii(xvi).6; CD i.7-8 (see Håkan Ulfgard, "The Branch in the Last Days: Observations on the New Covenant before and after the Messiah," in Timothy H. Lim, ed., *The Dead Sea Scrolls in Their Historical Context* [Edinburgh: T&T Clark, 2000] 235). These passages and their parallels "in para-biblical literature such as *1 Enoch* and *Jubilees* (*1 Enoch* 10:16; 84:6; 93:5 and 10; *Jub.* 1:16; 16:26; 21:24; 36:6)" derive from "Isa 61:3" (ibid., 235, with more references; see also Michael Lattke, review of Timothy H. Lim, ed., *The Dead Sea Scrolls in Their Historical Context* [Edinburgh: T&T Clark, 2000] in *BO* 60 [2003] 185). I cannot detect any direct connection between any of these passages and *Ode* 38.

444 BDAG, *s.v.* *φυτεία*.

445 LEH, *s.v.* *φύτευμα*; Payne Smith, 2:2436. Frankenberg (p. 33), who occasionally overdoes things, first uses the term *φύτευσις* (19b), which is synonymous with *φυτεία*, and then *φυτεία* (20b-21a), a term that was later used to mean "church" (see Lampe, 1503).

446 See Rahlfs, 2:648.

(*pulḥānā*), derived from ܦܠܚ (*plaḥ*),[447] which means "*labor*" in its widest sense (cf. 16:6 [ἐργασία?]),[448] might, as in 16:2, represent διακονία (cf. linguistically 2 Cor 9:12). However, the specifically agricultural term γεωργία[449] is a better match. This term would lead back to consideration of the divine "vinedresser" in John 15:1 (ὁ πατήρ μου ὁ γεωργός ἐστιν), and, indirectly, of the "Christian congregation as God's field" in 1 Cor 3:9.[450]

To determine the exact meaning of the *hapax legomenon* ܝܨܝܦܘܬܐ (*yaṣṣīp̄ūṯā*), it is necessary to decide which of its equivalents best accords with the "blessing" in the same line, 20a.[451] Two appropriate possibilities come immediately to mind, namely, ἐπιμέλεια[452] and πρόνοια.[453] Other terms of less likelihood would be ἀκρίβεια,[454] κηδεμονία,[455] and σπουδή.[456] On the other hand, it is quite clear that the term ܒܘܪܟܬܐ (*burkṯā*), which refers back to the Pa. ܒܪܟ (*barreḵ*) in 17a, represents εὐλογία (cf. esp. Heb 6:7).[457] Among the *Odes of Solomon*, reference can be made to 30:5a, where the living spring of the Lord "issues from the lips of the Lord" (see Excursus 16). This alone is reason enough why it would not be "better if, instead of ܕܣܦܘܬܗ [*d-sep̄wāṯeh* = τῶν χειλέων αὐτοῦ, 'from his lips'], it read ܕܣܘܟܬܗ [*d-sawkāṯeh* = τῶν κλάδων αὐτοῦ, 'from his branches']."[458]

In 20b, the "planting" is not merely described as "beautiful" or "good,"[459] but, with an unmistakable allusion to Ps 79:16 LXX (ἣν ἐφύτευσεν ἡ δεξιά σου, "which thy right hand has planted"),[460] it is again equated to a vine. In *4 Esdr.* 3:6, which also depends on this psalm verse, "the Garden of Eden was planted by God's right hand,"[461] but this planting is neither in the antediluvian paradise nor in the *iucunditatis paradisus*, "the paradise of delight" (*4 Esdr.* 7:36; cf. *Odes Sol.* 11:24).[462] The "right hand" is also connected with aspects of salvation (25:2) and exaltation (25:9; see Excursus 27).

The suggestion, first made by Schultheß,[463] that in 21a the *hapax legomenon* ܫܟܝܚܘܬܐ (*šḵīḥūṯā*), meaning *existentia* = τὸ ὑπάρχον,[464] should be replaced by the equally unusual term ܫܒܝܚܘܬܐ (*šḇīḥūṯā*) "should be rejected because the difficult reading is usually the more original, and because the parallelism in the following line is not improved."[465] Frankenberg, in accepting this conjecture, as do various others,[466] and rendering

447 If two aspirated letters of the *b g d k p t* group occur in succession, the first retains its plosive pronunciation as in *wa-b-p̄ulḥāneh* in 19b (Klaus Beyer, letter of November 13, 2002; see Nöldeke §26.B). This rule can also be seen in *wa-b-ḇurkṯā* (20a) and *d-ṯarʿīṯeh* (21b).

448 Payne Smith, 2:3150.

449 LSJ, *s.v.* γεωργία: "of vineyards and orchards"; Lampe, 314: "cultivation," later also used theologically of "God's care"; see Payne Smith, 2:3150: *cultura agrorum*.

450 BDAG, *s.vv.* γεώργιον, γεωργός, 2.

451 Payne Smith, 1:1618.

452 Frankenberg, 33; BDAG, *s.v.* ἐπιμέλεια: "care, attention."

453 BDAG, *s.v.* πρόνοια: "foresight, providence."

454 BDAG, *s.v.* ἀκρίβεια: "exactness."

455 LEH, *s.v.* κηδεμονία: "care."

456 BDAG, *s.v.* σπουδή, 2: "diligence."

457 Payne Smith, 1:614; BDAG, *s.v.* εὐλογία, 3: "blessing."

458 Contra Frankenberg, 43; see Payne Smith, 2:2694; BDAG, *s.v.* χεῖλος, 1.

459 Payne Smith, 1:1533; BDAG, *s.v.* καλός.

460 Rahlfs, 2:88; Brenton, 747.

461 Michael E. Stone, *Fourth Ezra: A Commentary on the Book of Fourth Ezra* (ed. Frank Moore Cross; Hermeneia; Minneapolis: Fortress Press, 1990) 68.

462 *BSV*, 2:1945; Klaus Berger, Gabriele Fassbeck, and Heiner Reinhard, *Synopse des Vierten Buches Esra und der Syrischen Baruch-Apokalypse* (Texte und Arbeiten zum neutestamentlichen Zeitalter 8; Tübingen/Basel: Francke, 1992) 63; Josef Schreiner, *Das 4. Buch Esra* (JSHRZ 5.4; Gütersloh: Mohn, 1981) 347. As we have seen in 38:16a, "firmly fixed" can mean "rooted" (cf. Rahlfs, 2:483: ἡ φυτεία αὐτῶν ἐρριζωμένη εἰς τὸν αἰῶνα).

463 Schultheß, 256.

464 Payne Smith, 2:4150; BDAG, *s.v.* ὑπάρχω, 1; Lampe, 1435.

465 Charlesworth, 134.

466 Gunkel (p. 316) follows Schultheß and translates the term by "magnificence" (as do Greßmann [p. 469] and Bauer [p. 619]). Diettrich (p. 126) describes the text as "meaningless" and accepts another of Schultheß's suggestions, "glory." Harris and Mingana consider the text of H and N a misspelling and insert the emendation into the text of their edition (vol. 1, on this passage) and translate it as "splendour" (2:392; this should be corrected in Lattke, *Oden*, 203 n. 33, although already there

it by τὸ κάλλος,[467] reflects Schultheß's hypothesis.[468] Anyone who likes can try to find a better match than ἐνδοξασμός, εὔκλεια, or τὸ περιφανές for this term in its sense of *magnificentia eius*.[469] Until then, the term used in H and N, which is at least as difficult, will have to do, only it should not be translated as "discovery"[470] as "a synonym for 'understanding' (in 21b)."[471] Since the next and final line is also somewhat "abstract,"[472] 21a can be considered a summary of the preceding details that could have been increased to almost any extent, which might then be translated as follows: "and in *total* by the existence of his planting."

That the Gnosticizing term ܡܕܥܐ (*maddʿā*) in 21b should correspond to τὸ νόημα[473] is even less likely than that ܬܪܥܝܬܐ (*tarʿīṯā*) might equate with ἡ βουλή.[474] The Greek text is quite simply unknown (see Excursuses 7 and 9).[475] It is not even clear whether this at first glance quite abrupt final line concerns God's mythological "insight" into his own "understanding"[476] or the redeeming "recognition of his mind."[477] On closer examination, however, the ending of this "complex and beautiful Ode"[478] does not seem nearly so abrupt, if one considers the parallel passages that use the term ܬܪܥܝܬܐ (*tarʿīṯā* [= *t.*]), a term that in any case applies to God. Two passages in particular attract notice, in which the synonymous term ܡܚܫܒܬܐ (*maḥšaḇṯā* [= *m.*]) also appears, as it does in 12:4d-e. In the one, following the "thought" (*m.*) of the Lord about his Christ/Messiah (9:3b), the protological "mind" (*t.*) of the Lord, the Most High, who is also called God and Father, turns eschatologically to the "eternal life" of the audience (9:4b and 9:5b). In the other, the Gnostics with *their* "thoughts" (plural of *m.*) are said to have always been in or by the "mind of the Most High" (*t.*; 18:13b-14a). This second parallel is all the more relevant, since its context dualistically opposes the terms "error" and "truth" (18:14b-15a) that play such an important part in *Ode* 38.[479] What originally seemed totally obscure has now become much less incomprehensible.

the meaning "existence" in place of "discovery" is mentioned in connection with the manuscript text).

467 Frankenberg, 33, 43; also Fanourgakis, 171.

468 Schultheß, 256: "glory, magnificence."

469 See Payne Smith, 2:4025.

470 Barth (p. 265) corrects this translation to "existence," but then offers a new text-critical suggestion: "Such a colourless abstract term cannot be considered a parallel to 'beautiful.' It should be replaced by a more substantial word such as ܒܫܘܦܪܐ ܕܢܨܒܬܗ 'by the beauty of his planting.'" I cannot agree with such an interference with the manuscript text.

471 See Harnack, 69.

472 Franzmann, 264.

473 BDAG, *s.v.* νόημα, 1–2.

474 Frankenberg, 33; BDAG, *s.v.* βουλή, 1–2.

475 See Payne Smith, 1:1560; 2:3948–49.

476 See Bauer, 619; Harris and Mingana, 2:392: "thought of His mind."

477 See Gunkel, 316; Charlesworth, 133: "understanding of His mind."

478 Charlesworth, "Wisdom Texts," 334. I agree completely with the first adjective. What Charlesworth has to say of this *Ode* is true for many of the others: "It would take an entire book to capture all its traditions and subtleties."

479 Charlesworth remarks, in reference to *Ode* 38, "how the personification, and even hypostatization, of Wisdom seems to help shape the presentation of 'Truth,' who—not which—is able to lead the Odist and to walk with him" (see Charlesworth, "Wisdom Texts," 333). Now, the speaking "I," as has been seen, is not identical with the "Odist." Charlesworth finds "no obvious answer" to his own question "why the Odist chose Truth over Wisdom" (ibid., 335), except the general one deriving from the title of the "international seminar on Qumran and Wisdom," namely: "The Odes of Solomon are part of the evolution of the Jewish Wisdom literature" (ibid., 349). Since the theory does not exclude "intertextuality" between the *Odes of Solomon* and other "biblical writings" or the influence of "apocalypticism"/"eschatology" and—following Georgi (pp. 394–95)—contact with "early Gnostic" traditions, one can agree with Charlesworth on the "Wisdom elements and traditions within the *Odes*" (Charlesworth, "Wisdom Texts," 332 and *passim*). In answer to his question above, one must consider the fact that the term "Truth" matches the Gnosticizing mythological term "Error" better than "Wisdom" would.

39

Ode 39: Parable about the Power of God and the Kyrios Christos

(I) **1a** **Raging rivers, the power of the Lord,**
1b **that turn head downward those who despise him**
2 **and entangle their steps and destroy their fords**
3 **and seize their bodies and ruin their souls,**
4 **for they are more sudden than lightnings[a] and faster.**
(II) **5** **But those who cross them in faith will not be disturbed,**
6 **and those who walk in them without blemish will not be perturbed.**
7a **For the Lord is a sign on/in them [the rivers],**
7b **and the sign is the way of those who cross in the name of the Lord.**
(III) **8a** **Put on, therefore, the name of the Most High and know him;**
8b **then you shall cross without danger[b]**
8c **while the rivers will be obedient to you.**
(IV) **9a** **The Lord bridged them by his Word/Logos,**
9b **and he [the Logos] went and crossed them on foot.**
(V) **10a** **And his footprints remained on the waters and were not destroyed,**
10b **but they were like wood that is truly fixed.**
11a **And on this side and on that the waves rose up,**
11b **but the footprints of our anointed Lord [Lord Messiah] stand firm**
12 **and are not blotted out nor destroyed.**
(VI) **13a** **And a way has been established for those who cross after him,**
13b **and for those who follow the walk of his faith and revere his name.**
Hallelujah.

a 4 ܒܪ̈ܩܐ N; ܒܪܩܐ H.
b 8b ܡܚܝܕܘܬܗ H; ܡܚܝܕܝܬܗ N.

Introduction

Ode 39 is preserved in two Syriac manuscripts.[1] "I" or "we" is not to be found in this Ode, whose mythological imagery and enigmatic details have given rise to some ingenious interpretations. Right in the middle—in a form that Schille[2] describes as a "reveille"—there is a Gnosticizing imperative of salvation (8a) followed by a promise of salvation (8b-c), in which the narrator addresses a group as "you," and, as a consequence, Rudolf Abramowski[3] counts *Ode* 39 as a "song of the

1 Mss.: Codex H, 28a–29a; Codex N, 151r (s). Ed./trans.: Charlesworth, 134–37; Franzmann, 265–69; Lattke, 3:189–211.
2 Schille, 98.
3 Abramowski, 51.

congregation." This central tricolon[4] concludes the first part, in which the "Lord" is equated to the "Most High" (1a, 7a-b, 8b) and which, therefore, deals with the "might of God" or the "power of God."[5] If one does not exclude 11b and 12 as a "Christian addition"[6] or consider the "Messiah" in 11b as an "interpolation,"[7] then 9 "begins" "a new section, which, as Harnack partly recognized, differs from what precedes it."[8] The difficulty is that in the second part the "Lord" is identical with the "Anointed" (11b, 13a-b; cf. 9b). This early Christian confusion or blending of terms, which extends even to the term "name" (7b, 13b), will be discussed later (see Excursus 39 below). "Rivers" are only indirectly mentioned in this second part (9a-b), being replaced by "water" and its "waves" (10a, 11a). The biblical miracles or passages that form the basis of these two—perhaps originally separate—parts will need to be investigated. It is also necessary to examine whether this Ode bears "especially clear marks of a Greek original."[9]

Interpretation

■ **1-4** After the allusions to the exodus from Egypt[10] found in *Ode* 38, it is likely that the "crossing of the Red Sea" is also behind this Ode.[11] Already Wellhausen comments on *Ode* 39: "The Crossing of the Red Sea (so popular among the Mandaeans) is the basis, the trial by water for the Egyptians and the Israelites, for the scorners and the believers."[12] Even Harris and Mingana's remark that this Ode is "like a little sermon" on such texts as Isa 43:3 and Ps 77:20[13] comes around to the "miraculous overcoming of the threatening danger of the Sea of Reeds,"[14] the "miracle of the Sea"[15] in the history of salvation. To that extent Harnack's remark,[16] directed against Harris,[17] is unjustified, and his comparison of the "great river" with the "tribunal of the Lord" is inaccurate. Frankenberg's equation of the "*δύναμις* of God" with the "manifold *πειρασμοί* of this life" is too shallow.[18] Since this Ode has nothing to say about

4 Franzmann (p. 265) changes this tricolon into a tetracolon. She also makes bicola of the manuscript monocola 2-6 and tricola of the bicola 7a-b, 10a-b, and 13a-b.

5 Frankenberg, 100; Abramowski, 55.

6 So Diettrich, 126, 128.

7 So Harnack, 70.

8 Spitta, 288.

9 Greßmann, "Referate," 2900. According to Greßmann, the following verses are "Greek, not Semitic": 1b (*καταφέρειν ἐπὶ κεφαλήν*), 4 (*ὀξύτεροι*), 8a (*οὖν*), 8b (*ἄνευ κινδύνου*), 8c (*πειθομένων*), and 11b (*δέ*). Charlesworth's reference (p. 137) to an article by Henri Del Medico, who has elsewhere been accused of "mythomania" (André Dupont-Sommer, *Die essenischen Schriften vom Toten Meer* [trans. Walter M. Müller; Tübingen: Mohr Siebeck, 1960] 444), is limited to the assertion "that a fourth-century Aramaic silver amulet was dependent upon *Ode* 39," which adds nothing to the interpretation of the Ode. What he does not mention is that Del Medico concludes, from his questionable comparison of lines 4-9 of the amulet with the text of *Ode* 39, that "we can be sure that the *Odes of Solomon* derive from a Greek original"; his inferences about "the age of Ode 39, from the discovery of this fourth-century text," are, since the publication of Ode 11 𝔊, no longer "of the greatest importance" (see Henri E. Del Medico, "La Lamelle Virolleaud," *Annuaire de l'institut de philologie et d'histoire orientales et slaves* 9 [1949] 189; cf. 186–87). See further the entry by Franzmann in Lattke, *Bedeutung*, 3:228.

10 "The attempt to interpret the exodus from Egypt allegorically and eschatologically can be traced as far back as the Alexandrian hermeneutics. Egypt and its fleshpots are the image of physical and sensual existence; the exodus is the flight from this hylic to the spiritual world, with the Red Sea as the boundary between these two worlds, in which the wicked perish while only the believers cross it. The after-effects of these ideas can still be found in the Mandaic writings" (Mark Lidzbarski, *Das Johannesbuch der Mandäer: Einleitung, Übersetzung, Kommentar* [Gießen: Töpelmann, 1915] XXI). Similar after-effects are found also here and in other "Gnostic circles."

11 Bauer, 620. Also cf. in the LXX Exod 7:19; 8:1; 14:15-31; 15:1-10; Pss 65:6; 76:16-20; 77:11-16; Wis 10:15-21; Isa 19:1-10; 37:25; 43:2, 16-17; 51:10.

12 Wellhausen, 638.

13 Harris and Mingana, 2:397.

14 Karl Elliger, *Deuterojesaja*, vol. 1: *Jesaja 40,1–45,7* (BKAT 11.1; Neukirchen-Vluyn: Neukirchener Verlag, 1978) 294.

15 Kraus, *Psalmen*, 533.

16 Harnack, 69: "Isa 43:2 is different."

17 Harris [1st ed.], 137.

18 Frankenberg, 100; and that equation is further diluted by the remark: "It may be more properly understood as life itself, which is often compared to a stormy sea that must be crossed" (p. 101).

the "way of the soul to the netherworld across wide waters,"[19] there is no need for learned disquisitions on the "Greek Isles of the Blessed" and the Babylonian "Epic of Gilgamesh," much less quotations from Schiller's poem "Sehnsucht [Longing]."[20] Gunkel, whose ideas will be discussed again later (see on 10-12 below), considers the Ode "a bizarre unity,"[21] but his exegesis, which even includes elements of German mythology, is even more bizarre than the images and metaphors in the text, which must now be discussed more soberly.

The first point is that the term "sea"[22] does not occur in *Ode* 39, which instead speaks of "rivers" (1-9) and "water" (10a). In pursuing the literary ancestry of the plural of ܢܗܪܐ (*nahrā*), which is not used in the same way as in 23:14, and which, like ποταμοί, can also mean "canals,"[23] the LXX passages previously cited about the exodus repeatedly offer ποταμός,[24] so that the "rivers" of Isa 43:2 are not, perhaps, used for "Babylonian local colour."[25] It is, of course, possible that the whole of the predicate[26] of 1a, "raging rivers," can be traced back to συναγωγὴ ὕδατος (Isa 19:6; 37:25 LXX), but a Greek phrase like ποταμοὶ ἰσχυροί[27] is much more likely (cf. ἐν ὕδατι ἰσχυρῷ, "in the mighty water," in Isa 43:16 LXX).[28] So the *hapax legomenon* ܥܫܝܢܐ (*ʿaššīnā*) does not here correspond to δυνατός or πολύς (cf. Wis 10:18 in Greek and Syriac), but to the adjective ἰσχυρός used in connection with wind and water.[29] The subject of 1a is the phrase "power of the Lord," referring to God, which, in the light of Exodus 14–15, makes a contrast with the δύναμις of the Egyptian pharaoh (Exod 14:28; 15:4). The term τὸ κράτος can be excluded as the equivalent here of ܚܝܠܐ (*ḥaylā*),[30] so only δύναμις[31] and ἰσχύς come under consideration (cf. Exod 9:16 [where A uses δύναμιν; cf. Rom 9:17]; 15:6, 13, etc.; see also Excursus 29).[32] There might even have been paronomasia in 𝔊 (. . . ἰσχυροὶ ἡ ἰσχύς . . .). If the narrating poet had been aiming for variety, the Greek of the incongruous opening might have been ποταμοὶ ἰσχυροί ἡ δύναμις (τοῦ) κυρίου. These metaphorical "flowing waters," indeterminate as to place and course, whose Lord is "the creator of all,"[33] are now, as the armed forces of God, the subject of 1b-4. Since the "danger from ποταμοί" (cf. 2 Cor 11:26)[34] was clear to all dwellers around the Mediterranean and in Mesopotamia, hearers or readers needed no explanation of the descriptions that follow.

19 Contra Gunkel, *Aufsätze*, 177.
20 Gunkel, *Aufsätze*, 178.
21 Ibid., 179.
22 Cf., of the previously listed LXX passages, Exod 14:16, 21-23, 26-29; 15:1, 4, 10, 19-20; Ps 76:20; 77:13; Wis 10:18; Isa 19:5.
23 But "canals" (διώρυχες or διώρυγες) are also distinguished from "rivers" (ποταμοί); cf. in LXX Exod 7:19; 8:1; Sir 24:30-31; Isa 19:6; 27:12; 33:21. In one of these passages (Isa 19:6) and in Isa 37:25 LXX the phrase συναγωγὴ ὕδατος ("reservoir [gathering]/pool of water") is rendered, rather surprisingly, by ܢܗܪܘܬܐ ܥܫܝܢܐ (*nahrawwāṯā ʿaššīnē*) in the Peshitta (Rahlfs, 2:590, 616; Brenton, 853, 871; *OTSy*, pt. 3 fasc. 1, pp. 32, 65). This συναγωγὴ ὕδατος should not be confused with the συναγωγαὶ ([ὑδάτων] = ὠκεανὸς ἀπέραντος, "boundless ocean") in *1 Clem.* 20:6, 8 (Ehrman, 1:72–73; Lindemann and Paulsen, 104–5; cf. BDAG, *s.v.* ὠκεανός).
24 Cf. Exod 7:19; 8:1; Pss 65:6; 77:16; Isa 19:5-8.
25 Karl Elliger, *Deuterojesaja*, vol. 1: *Jesaja 40,1–45,7* (BKAT 11.1; Neukirchen-Vluyn: Neukirchener Verlag, 1978) 274 (Targum), 294.
26 William R. Newbold emends ܚܝܠܗ (*ḥayleh*) to ܚܝ̈ܠܐ (*ḥaylē*), an "emph[atic] pl[ural] without pron[ominal] suff[ix]" ("The Descent of Christ in the Odes of Solomon," *JBL* 31 [1912] 188 n. 45), but, even without this emendation, the predicate noun is not "power" but "rivers."
27 Frankenberg, 33.
28 Rahlfs, 2:625; Brenton, 878; cf. *OTSy*, pt. 3 fasc. 1, p. 78.
29 Payne Smith, 2:3005; BDAG, *s.v.* ἰσχυρός, 2: e.g., "violent." Of the many adjectives found with ποταμός (LSJ, *s.v.*), one could also consider δεινός (BDAG, *s.v.*: "fearful, terrible") and λάβρος (LEH, *s.v.*: "violent, impetuous").
30 Contra Frankenberg, 33.
31 BDAG, *s.v.* δύναμις.
32 BDAG, *s.v.* ἰσχύς; Payne Smith, 1:1258.
33 Karl Heinrich Rengstorf, "ποταμός, κτλ.," *ThWNT* 6 (1959) 598; *TDNT* 6:598.
34 Rengstorf, "ποταμός," *ThWNT* 6:603; *TDNT* 6:603.

Verse 1b views those who "despise" God[35] from the perspective of the believing and redeemed ones of stanzas II–VI. The *hapax legomenon* ܒܣܪ (*bassar*), followed by the preposition ܥܠ (*ʿal*), derives from καταφρονέω τινός.[36] So the Pa. participle following the "correlative"[37] corresponded to the Greek object τοὺς καταφρονοῦντας αὐτοῦ. The subject "rivers" is contained in the participle of the Aph. of ܐܬܐ (*ʾeṯā*), "bring down."[38] The preposition ܒܬܪ (*bāṯar*) + ܪܝܫܐ (*rēšā*) means "head downwards,"[39] representing ἐπὶ κεφαλὴν.[40] So 1b 𝔊 can be reconstructed, without difficulty, as follows: καὶ τοὺς καταφρονοῦντας αὐτοῦ καταφέρουσιν ἐπὶ κεφαλήν.[41] The first punitive action of the waters can be interpreted as depicting the drowning of the Egyptians, which is drastic enough in the original.[42] At the same time, the tale of disaster in 1b contains a generalization that even precedes the origin of the *Odes of Solomon*.

The next four punitive actions by the mighty rivers are each described in a synthetic *parallelismus membrorum* (2-3). "The word-pair ܗܠܟ – ܥܒܪ occurs also in 5-6, 9b, 13a-b."[43] The plural of the term ܗܠܟܬܐ (*hlakṯā*), "steps," which Charlesworth vocalizes wrongly,[44] and which is repeated in a positive sense in 13b ("walk"),[45] corresponds to διαβήματα, thus making a linguistic connection with the verb διαβαίνω (cf. Isa 43:2 LXX; Heb 11:29)[46] used in the description of the crossing of the Red Sea. The next *hapax legomenon*, ܥܪܩܠ (*ʿarqel*), "entangle," is the Par. of the root ܥܩܠ.[47] Frankenberg suggests κωλύουσι, but then brings it into question with the alternative ἐμπεδῶσι;[48] he might also have offered συμπεδῶσι or συμποδίζουσι for the participle (cf. Ps 77:31 LXX).[49] The Pa. ܣܪܚ (*sarraḥ*) is also a *hapax legomenon*, corresponding to ἀφανίζω.[50] The object of this verb is the plural of ܡܥܒܪܬܐ (*maʿbarṯā*), another *hapax legomenon* (but cf. the Pe. ܥܒܪ [*ʿḇar*] in 5, 7b, 8b, 9b, 13a) that corresponds to διάβασις (cf. Isa 51:10 LXX).[51] This is at least an indirect reminder of the "act of salvation at the Sea of Reeds."[52]

The parallelism of the punitive actions in 3 is even more marked than in 2, because "body and soul"—like the expression "flesh and blood"—describes the whole of a human being, though the same is true for each of the terms σῶμα/ܦܓܪܐ (*pagrā*) and ψυχή/ܢܦܫܐ (*napšā*) by itself (cf. 2 Macc 15:30).[53] The two verbs used as participles, the Pe. ܚܛܦ (*ḥṭap̄*) and the Pa. ܚܒܠ (*ḥabbel*), "seize" and "ruin," are also in parallel. The first one corresponds to ἁρπάζω,[54] while the second translates διαφθείρω,[55] καταφθείρω,[56] or even plain φθείρω (see Excursus 28).[57] Since the compound verb διαφθείρω appears at least in a loose connection with the exodus out of Egypt (Ps 77:45 LXX), it is probably the one that should be given preference. The other compound may be more generally associated with God's judgment in

35 The masculine suffix of the preposition ܥܠ (*ʿal*) may refer either to "the power" or "the Lord." In 𝔊 αὐτοῦ (see below) would refer to κύριος.
36 Payne Smith, 1:552; BDAG, *s.v.* καταφρονέω, 1.
37 Nöldeke §236.
38 Payne Smith, 1:415–16; BDAG, *s.v.* καταφέρω, 1.
39 Payne Smith, *Dictionary*, 57; cf. Payne Smith, 1:626–27.
40 LSJ, *s.v.* κεφαλή, 1d.
41 Frankenberg, 33; cf. Greßmann "Referate," 2900.
42 Cf. Exod 14:26-28, 30; 15:1, 4-5, 10, 19, 21; Wis 10:19.
43 Franzmann, 268, on 2 (2a-b in H).
44 Charlesworth, 135.
45 Payne Smith, 1:1015.
46 BDAG, *s.v.* διαβαίνω.
47 Payne Smith, 2:2964, where "Parʾel" and "Ethparʾal" should be corrected.
48 Frankenberg, 33; Kaegi, 267; cf. BDAG, *s.v.* ἐμποδίζω: "hinder."
49 LSJ, *s.vv.* συμπεδάω, συμποδίζω; LEH, *s.v.* συμποδίζω.
50 Payne Smith, 2:2734; BDAG, *s.v.* ἀφανίζω: properly "render invisible or unrecognisable," but also "destroy, ruin."
51 Payne Smith, 2:2789; LEH, *s.v.* διάβασις: "crossing over, passage."
52 Westermann, *Jesaja*, 196.
53 Payne Smith, 2:2430–31, 3033; BDAG, *s.vv.* σῶμα, ψυχή; Eduard Schweizer, "σῶμα, κτλ.," *ThWNT* 7 (1964) 1040, 1044, 1047, 1049, 1053; *TDNT* 7:1042, 1047, 1050, 1051, 1056; idem, "ψυχή, κτλ. D," *ThWNT* 9 (1973) 645; *TDNT* 9:645–46.
54 Payne Smith, 1:1247–48; BDAG, *s.v.* ἁρπάζω, 2.
55 BDAG, *s.v.* διαφθείρω.
56 BDAG, *s.v.* καταφθείρω.
57 BDAG, *s.v.* φθείρω; Payne Smith, 1:1176.

the world, and that may be what Harnack was thinking of (cf. Isa 24:1a LXX: κύριος καταφθείρει τὴν οἰκουμένην, "the Lord is about to lay waste the world").[58]

Lightning can be a "[t]ype of the greatest speed,"[59] so the statement of 4 that these mythological rivers surpass the ܒܪ̈ܩܐ (*barqē*), "lightnings,"[60] enhances the danger of the threatening streams. The statement of this surpassing is constructed with the preposition ܡܢ (*men*) and two synonymous adjectives, the first of which corresponds to the comparative of ὀξύς, "sharper" (Hab 1:8 LXX).[61] If the people of the *Odes of Solomon* were as familiar with the Homeric epics as modern scholars, the retroversion of the *hapax legomenon* ܩܠܝܠܐ (*qallīlā*), "faster," by the comparative adjective θάττονες[62] would be acceptable (cf. θάσσονας in *Iliad* 13.819). It is, however, much more likely that the comparative of κοῦφος formed the ending of stanza I in 𝔊.[63] I think the key word "lightnings" derives from one of the texts about the exodus listed above, Ps 76:19b LXX: ἔφαναν αἱ ἀστραπαί σου τῇ οἰκουμένῃ ("thy lightnings appeared to the world").[64] The terms ὁδός ("way") and ἴχνη ("footprints") from the following verse of the psalm will play a decisive part later in *Ode* 39 (see stanzas II and V below).

■ **5-7** A passage from the LXX (Isa 43:2) may aptly illuminate the difference between stanzas I and II, where the κύριος ὁ θεός ("the Lord God") tells Israel: ἐὰν διαβαίνῃς δι᾽ ὕδατος, μετὰ σοῦ εἰμι, καὶ ποταμοὶ οὐ συγκλύσουσίν σε ("if thou pass through water, I am with thee; and the rivers shall not overflow thee").[65] The believers of stanza II are *not* overflowed, that is, overcome, by the dangerous rivers (see stanza I above). The participle of the Pe. ܥܒܪ (*ʿbar*), "cross," used in the first monocolon with an accusative object—not as in 7b—which follows the demonstrative correlative, found also in 6, translates οἱ δὲ διαβαίνοντες αὐτούς (cf. Heb 11:29).[66] The term πίστις/ܗܝܡܢܘܬܐ (*haymānūtā*), "faith," qualifying the crossing of the rivers, is belief and trust in God the Lord (see Excursus 34, and see on 13b below). This is the first indication of the "Christianity of the Ode" (cf. πίστει in Heb 11:29).[67] Because the meanings of the Ethpe. of ܙܘܥ, ܙܥ (*zāʿ*), "be disturbed," and the Ethpe./Ethpa. of ܕܠܚ (*dlaḥ*), "be perturbed," which occurs only in 6, largely overlap,[68] it is clear that the negated verbs at the ends of 5 and 6 are synonyms.[69] One of them probably corresponds to ταραχθήσονται (cf. Ps 76:17c LXX: ἐταράχθησαν ἄβυσσοι, "the depths were troubled"), the other one either to σαλευθήσονται (cf. Ps 76:19c LXX: ἐσαλεύθη . . . ἡ γῆ, "the earth trembled") or to φοβηθήσονται (cf. Ps 76:17b LXX: . . . ὕδατα καὶ ἐφοβήθησαν, "the waters . . . feared").[70] It is not possible to match them up more exactly.[71]

The participle of the Pa. ܗܠܟ (*hallek*) in 6, "walk," also comes out of the exodus narrative: οἱ δὲ υἱοὶ Ισραηλ ἐπορεύθησαν διὰ ξηρᾶς ἐν μέσῳ τῆς θαλάσσης ("But the children of Israel walked through dry land in the midst of the sea" [Exod 14:29; 15:19]; see on 9b below, and see Excursus 15).[72] In contrast to Heb 11:29 (see above), there is no mention of dry land or of the sea, since the topic is still the rivers that divide, to which the prepositional expression ܒܗܘܢ (*bhōn*), "in them," refers. Parallel to the "power of the faith that can move mountains (of water) (cf. Mark 11:23 parr.)"[73] is

58 Harnack, 69; Rahlfs, 2:596; Brenton, 857.

59 BDAG, *s.v.* ἀστραπή, 1.

60 H has the singular ܒܪܩܐ (*barqā*), which does not change the meaning of 4. "Lightning" is also a *hapax legomenon* in the *Odes of Solomon* (cf. Payne Smith, 1:619).

61 BDAG, *s.v.* ὀξύς, 1; on the *hapax legomenon* ܚܪܝܦܐ (*ḥarrīpā*), see Payne Smith, 1:1380; Greßmann, "Referate," 2900; Frankenberg, 33: ὀξύτεροι.

62 Frankenberg, 33; LSJ, *s.v.* ταχύς, C.

63 LEH, *s.v.* κοῦφος; Payne Smith, 2:3616. Cf. linguistically Isa 19:1 and 30:16 LXX.

64 Rahlfs, 2:82; Brenton, 743–44.

65 Rahlfs, 2:624; Brenton, 878; cf. LSJ, *s.v.* συγκλάζω.

66 Frankenberg, 33; Payne Smith, 2:2783; BDAG *s.v.* διαβαίνω.

67 Kittel, 133, on the "anointed one" of 11b; cf. Gräßer, 3:179–80, on Heb 11:29.

68 In my concordance (Lattke, *Bedeutung*, 2:76), I used "Ethp." to leave open the possibility of Ethpe. or Ethpa.; I have now decided on the latter.

69 Payne Smith, 1:906–7.

70 Rahlfs, 2:82; Brenton, 743–44.

71 BDAG, *s.vv.* σαλεύω, ταράσσω, φοβέω. I cannot share Frankenberg's philological certainty. He decides on σαλευθήσονται in 5 and φοβηθήσονται in 6. Instead of his οἱ βαδίζοντες ἐν αὐτοῖς ἄμωμοι in 6 (Frankenberg, 33), I should prefer οἱ πορευόμενοι ἐν αὐτοῖς ἄμωμοι in 𝔊.

72 Rahlfs, 1:111–12; Brenton, 90.

73 Gräßer, 3:180.

the qualification ܕܠܐ ܡܘܡܐ (*d-lā mūmā*), "without blemish," corresponding to ἄμωμος, which here too "must not be narrowly moralised" (cf. linguistically Ps 14:2 and other passages in the LXX).[74]

If the term "sign" (σημεῖον/ܐܬܐ [ʾāṯā])[75] is not considered a polemical allusion to "God's 'signs' in Egypt" (Exod 3:12, etc.),[76] then 7a-b is a new and very complex concept, which links to the key word ὁδός ("way"), familiar from the exodus narratives (Ps 76:20 LXX; Wis 10:17b), but first invests God the Lord with the predicate noun "sign." The almost syllogistic sequence (Lord = sign = way)[77] makes sense only if ܒܗܘܢ (*bhōn*) refers, as in 6, to the "water" of the rivers.[78] Whether 𝔊 used ἐν or ἐπί is difficult to decide (cf. linguistically, e.g., Matt 14:8, 11; Mark 6:25, 28). However, the distinction between ܒ (*b-*) here and ܥܠ (*ʿal*) in 10a suggests that both in 6 and in 7a the phrase was ἐν αὐτοῖς.[79] Since the enclitic third masculine singular personal pronoun at the end of 7a does not necessarily correspond to the copula in 𝔊, it is comparatively simple to reconstruct the Greek text as follows: ὅτι σημεῖον ἐν αὐτοῖς (ἐστιν) ὁ κύριος.[80]

Diettrich is quite right that the participle ܗܘܝܐ (*hāwyā*) "does not sound Syriac."[81] This does not, however, justify his drastic emendation of 7b; in fact it suggests that 𝔊 used an explanatory copula, which Emerton translates as "becomes."[82] Verse 7b, then, can also be easily reconstructed: καὶ τὸ σημεῖόν ἐστιν ἡ ὁδὸς τῶν ἐν ὀνόματι (τοῦ) κυρίου διαβαινόντων.[83] So the "Lord" himself is transformed into the "way"[84] of the believers who in his name cross the rivers. Before Frankenberg's almost correct retroversion is examined linguistically and, in the light of the Exodus passages, also according to the history of biblical tradition, it is necessary to consider the over-elaborate Syriac prepositional phrase "in the name of the Lord" in connection with related expressions.

Excursus 39: "Name" in the *Odes of Solomon*

The Syriac term ܫܡܐ (*šmā*), related to the Hebrew שם (*šem*), always corresponds to ὄνομα as well as to ⲢⲀⲚ in one passage (22:6b).[85] Of the twenty-one occurrences, one refers to the "name" of the "spring of the Lord" (30:5b, where νᾶμα was suggested in

74 See commentary on 13:4; see also BDAG, *s.v.* ἄμωμος, 2a; Payne Smith, 2:2037.

75 Diettrich's reading (p. 127 n. 1) of ܐܬܐ as *ʾeṯā* is not only merely linguistically impossible (because of the copula) but exegetically quite untenable: "For the Lord comes in them [i.e., the streams of water]." On the "sign," see Payne Smith, 1:412–13; BDAG, *s.v.* σημεῖον; Karl Heinrich Rengstorf, "σημεῖον, κτλ.," *ThWNT* 7 (1964) 199–268; *TDNT* 7:200–269.

76 Rengstorf, "σημεῖον," *ThWNT* 7:221; *TDNT* 7:222–23; Hatch and Redpath, p. 1263.

77 See Paul Thom, "Syllogismus; Syllogistik," *HWP* 10 (1998) 687.

78 Greßmann, "Referate," 2900; Connolly, "Odes," 303; Kittel, 134; Emerton, 727; contra Bauer, 620, and Lattke, *Oden*, 204.

79 Contra Frankenberg, 33; Greßmann, "Referate," 2900; Kittel, 134.

80 Greßmann and Kittel accept the emendation of Frankenberg, whose explanation of his retroversion (p. 33: ἐπεὶ ἐπ᾽αὐτοῖς τὸ σημεῖον τοῦ κυρίου) is rather facile and takes no account of the copula: "ܗܘܝܐ by itself is somewhat harsh, read rather ܕܗܘܝܐ" (idem, p. 43, misprint ܕܗܘܝܐ). Greßmann ("Referate," 2900), attempting to recreate the "Greek original," should have realized that σημεῖον without the article is a predicate noun and that it is ὁ κύριος that is the subject of 7a (see BDF and BDR §273). Kittel, following Greßmann's revised reconstruction (ὅτι τὸ σημεῖον ἐπ᾽αὐτοῖς τοῦ κυρίου ἐστίν) translates it "[for] on them is the sign of the Lord" (Kittel, 134). Whether this "demonstrates" the "identity" of the "signs" with the "footprints" (see on 10-11 below) will have to be considered. Connolly must be treated with similar skepticism, although his translation, "for a *sign* on them is the Lord" ("Odes," 303), shows that he has recognized "sign" as a predicate noun. Emerton's translation (p. 727), "Because the Lord is a sign in them," is unambiguous.

81 Diettrich, 127.

82 Emerton, 728.

83 See Frankenberg, 33, in which ἔσται may not be a misprint.

84 My reference to John 14:5-6 (Lattke, *Oden*, 204 n. 4; see Excursus 15) can be justified, since the equivalence of a divine being with the "way" can be traced in other texts as well. And the Johannine Jesus also says in John 10:30: ἐγὼ καὶ ὁ πατήρ ἕν ἐσμεν ("I and the Father are one"). The Most High Lord (see on 8a below), especially, can be metaphorically called the "way" because the "Anointed One" also bears the title "Lord" (see on 11b below).

85 See Payne Smith, 2:4199; BDAG, *s.v.* ὄνομα; Crum, 297–98. At this point the texts of ℭ and of N are

place of ὄνομα). Most of the other occurrences refer to the "name" of God the Lord and Most High or the Father. In a few cases it is not quite clear whose name is meant (8:21; 18:1; 25:11; 41:5, 16). In two of the passages where "my name" is mentioned (8:21; 18:1; 33:13; 42:20), it is possible to identify the speaking "I" more precisely. In the first, the mythic virgin "Grace" allows her elect to trust in her name (33:13c).[86] In the other, the redeemed Redeemer set his name on the head of the redeemed persons (42:20).

Philosophical or religio-historical speculations on the "manifold names of God" and the "namelessness of God" have left no traces in the *Odes of Solomon*.[87] The specific usage "the name of Yahweh"[88] and, above all, the use of "שֵׁם יהוה as an alternative for Yahweh"[89] belong to the far past, but the influence of the LXX can be seen in the "formulaic ἐν τῷ ὀνόματι," which "is unusual in classical Greek."[90] Philo's distinction between the "names ϑεός and κύριος in the Greek Bible"[91] as denoting distinct "powers of God" is also irrelevant, since the terms ϑεός/ܐܠܗܐ (*ʾallāhā*), "God," and κύριος/ܡܪܝܐ (*māryā*), "Lord," are used interchangeably for the "Most High" and the "Father," but especially because "the Lord," the absolutely dominant name of God, has already in New Testament usage been transferred to "Christ's being and actions": "because the essence of the Most High is in it, because the name of Lord belongs to both God and Jesus Christ, it is the name above all names, i.e., beings (cf. Eph 1:21; Phil 2:9–11)."[92] New Testament influence on the *Odes of Solomon* is visible, on the one hand, quite generally in the use of "prepositional combinations" that "show wide Semitic influence" on Greek usage[93] and, on the other, in two specific passages.[94] Themes from the Lord's Prayer appear in 14:5 (cf. Matt 6:9-13),[95] while 23:22 "unites the name of the Father, the Son and the Holy Spirit" (cf. Matt 28:19).[96]

The use of ܠܫܡܗ (*la-šmeh*), "to his name," in three final doxologies confers on the name of God three different hymnic terms, derived from the language of the Psalms (16:20; 18:16; 20:10). Some other passages are also more or less doxological (6:7; 31:3; 39:13). The last of these shows that the Lord Christ receives the same honor as the Most High God and Lord. This also partially elucidates the beginning of *Ode* 18: "My heart was lifted up by the love of the Most High . . . that I might glorify him through my name" (18:1a-b).[97]

The statement of the speaking "I" of *Ode* 8, that "they [my elect] will not separate themselves from my name, because it is with them" (8:21b-c; cf. 42:20a), is related to the previous passage. How closely the name of God and the name of the Revealer are associated[98] can be seen in the mention of the "name of your Father" at the end of the same *Ode* (8:23).

close: "Your name was around me" and "surrounded me." According to H, the name of the Lord was "blessed" (on this scribal error, see the commentary on that passage).

86 Bearing in mind the close connection between the metaphorical "way" and the "name" of the Lord, the Most High (39:7-8), one may remark that the redeemed Redeemer in 33:13b will make known *his* "ways."

87 See Hans Bietenhard, "ὄνομα, κτλ.," *ThWNT* 5 (1954) 248–51, 264; *TDNT* 5:248–52, 264–65.

88 Bietenhard, "ὄνομα," *ThWNT* 5:254–61; *TDNT* 5:255–58.

89 Bietenhard, "ὄνομα," *ThWNT* 5:257, 260; *TDNT* 5:257, 260.

90 Bietenhard, "ὄνομα," *ThWNT* 5:262; *TDNT* 5:262.

91 Bietenhard, "ὄνομα," *ThWNT* 5:264; *TDNT* 5:265.

92 Bietenhard, "ὄνομα," *ThWNT* 5:272; *TDNT* 5:273. Samuel Vollenweider describes Phil 2:9-11 as the "germ cell for all praise of Christ" (see Vollenweider, *Horizonte neutestamentlicher Christologie: Studien zu Paulus und zur frühchristlichen Theologie* [WUNT 144; Tübingen: Mohr Siebeck, 2002] 294). This second principal part is the "counterpoise of the total text" Phil 2:6-11 and the "mythical logos of foundation of the Christ cult," which "proclaims *the universal reign of the Kyrios Jesus Christ*" (ibid., 305; see also Larry W. Hurtado, *Lord Jesus Christ: Devotion to Jesus in Earliest Christianity* [Grand Rapids/Cambridge, U.K.: Eerdmans, 2003] 146–49).

93 Bietenhard, "ὄνομα," *ThWNT* 5:270; *TDNT* 5:271.

94 Bietenhard, "ὄνομα," *ThWNT* 5:274–75; *TDNT* 5:275–76.

95 Bietenhard, "ὄνομα," *ThWNT* 5:275; *TDNT* 5:276.

96 Bietenhard, "ὄνομα," *ThWNT* 5:274; *TDNT* 5:274: "Only through this link with the name of the Son and Holy Ghost does the name of Father acquire its fulness. The common name (ὄνομα occurs only once) also expresses the unity of being." What Bietenhard has to say about the "baptismal formula" in connection with εἰς τὸ ὄνομα is hardly relevant to ܠܫܡܗ (*la-šmeh*) in the *Odes of Solomon* (cf. 6:7; 8:23; 16:20; 18:16; 20:10; 31:3; 39:13).

97 See commentary on that passage. The Ethpa. ܐܫܬܡܗ (*ʾeštammah*), derived from ܫܡܐ (*šmā*), occurs only once, in 36:3b: "And although I was a (son of) man, I was called the Shining One, the Son of God" (see Payne Smith, 2:4201–2).

98 Bietenhard, "ὄνομα," *ThWNT* 5:270–79; *TDNT* 5:271–80.

As equally soteriological as this conclusion is the parallel placing of the two theological expressions of power, "by his name" and "by his grace" (15:8). Whether the operative giving of life by the Redeemer (cf. 41:11-15) "by the truth of his name" (41:16a) is done in the "name of (God) the Lord" (41:5a) or in the "name" of his Messiah (cf. 41:3, 15) will be thoroughly discussed in the commentary on that most important Ode. That will also be the place to return to the problem of 25:11b, found only in S, "I became the Lord's by the name of the Lord" (cf. 29:6a-b).

Just as complex as the use of "Lord" in these two passages is the use of "Lord" as "sign" and "way," on the one hand, and in the formulaic "in the name of the Lord," on the other (39:7a-b). There can be no doubt that the "Lord," in contrast to 11b, stands for the "Most High," whose "name" the believers are to put on and know (39:8).[99] Thus we come back to the reconstructed text of 39:7b.

Since the term "sign" has occurred already in 7a, σημεῖον/ܐܬܐ (*ʾāṯā*) in 7b, "as something well known or as that which alone merits the designation (the only thing to be considered)," takes the definite article.[100] The same is true for the (miraculous) "way" of the "exodus narrative,"[101] which occurs *here* for the first time, but is well known from Ps 76:14, 20 LXX and Wis 10:17. This is not an allusion to, or reminiscence of, the "way to *gnōsis*" and its "tracks of light" (7:13-14).[102] The correlative ܗܢܘܢ ܕ (*hannōn d-*) is as clumsy as that in 5-6[103] and can be similarly interpreted. The genitive qualifying ὁδός/ܐܘܪܚܐ (*ʾurḥā*), "way," without a direct object,[104] corresponds to τῶν διαβαινόντων ("of those who cross"), taking up, in part, οἱ διαβαίνοντες αὐτούς in 5. For (τῇ) πίστει/ܒܗܝܡܢܘܬܐ (*b-haymānūṯā*), "in faith," this verse has ἐν (τῇ) ὀνόματι (τοῦ) κυρίου/ܒܫܡܗ ܕܡܪܝܐ (*ba-šmeh d-māryā*), "in the name of the Lord," meaning "while calling on the name of the Lord,"[105] where "calling upon" God's name invokes his "power" and "presence" without any use of magic.[106] The two prepositional phrases in 5 and 7b interpret each other, showing that a profound faith can lay claim to God's power and actualize it.

■ **8** The literary unity of stanza III "is indicated by the shift to the second pl[ural] imper[ative] in 8."[107] Although κίνδυνος[108] is "a loanword in common use,"[109] previously established criteria support agreement with Frankenberg and Greßmann, who suggest that the Greek original of 8b-c used ἄνευ κινδύνου and—as a genitive absolute—τῶν ποταμῶν ὑμῖν πειθομένων.[110] The exact form of verbs and other details are, naturally, not quite certain.

This uncertainty is found at once in the question whether the compound ܗܟܝܠ (*hāḵēl*) in 8a, "then," translates the "inferential particle" ἄρα[111] or corresponds more loosely to οὖν.[112] On the other hand, the imperative of the Pe. ܠܒܫ (*lḇeš*), "put on," almost certainly represents the metaphorically used middle voice of ἐνδύω.[113] If the imperative was not ἐνδύεσθε but the more probable ἐνδύσασθε,[114] then links to the Pauline imagery are even easier to make.[115] The "image" here is also "bold":[116] "to *don* the name, i.e., to shelter under

99 See Table 2. Since in 15:8a-b "by his name" and "by his grace" are parallel, and since "grace" is in other passages the object of the metaphorical verb "to put on, don, dress oneself" (4:6a; 20:7a), the shock of 39:8a is diminished.
100 BDF and BDR §273.
101 See Georgi, 439: "motif of the ways."
102 Contra Connolly, "Odes," 304.
103 See Nöldeke §236.
104 See LSJ, *s.v.* διαβαίνω: "abs[olute] (θάλασσαν or ποταμόν being omitted), cross over."
105 See BDAG, *s.v.* ὄνομα, 1dγɔ.
106 Bietenhard, "ὄνομα," *ThWNT* 5:270; *TDNT* 5:271.
107 Franzmann, 268, although she unnecessarily divides 8a into 8a-b.
108 On different spellings of ܩܝܢܕܘܢܘܣ (*qīndūnos*), see Payne Smith, 2:3605 (see also 1:1724). In N it was corrected in 38:5 (Lattke, *Bedeutung*, 1:50) but not here.
109 Abramowski, "Sprache," 85.
110 Frankenberg, 33; Greßmann, "Referate," 2900; see also Lattke, "Wörter," 291–92 = idem, *Bedeutung*, 4:140.
111 BDAG, *s.v.* ἄρα, 1–2.
112 Frankenberg, 33; BDAG, *s.v.* οὖν, 1–2; see also Payne Smith, 1:1006.
113 Payne Smith, 2:1887; BDAG, *s.v.* ἐνδύω, 2b. It is possible, but not likely, that ἐπενδύομαι was used (BDAG, *s.v.* ἐπενδύομαι; cf. 2 Cor 5:2, 4).
114 Frankenberg, 33.
115 Werner Straub, *Die Bildersprache des Apostels Paulus* (Tübingen: Mohr Siebeck, 1937) 24–25; cf. esp. Rom 13:14.
116 Bauer and Aland; and BDAG, *s.v.* ἐνδύω, 2b.

the protecting name."[117] If the metaphorical expression were to refer to the Lord Christ (see below), one might refer to the "name borne by followers of Jesus Christ."[118] But this bold metaphor is even more significant, since, following the usage of the LXX (especially the Psalms)—and only implicitly polemicizing against *Ζεὺς ὕψιστος* or any other *ϑεὸς ὕψιστος*[119]—it refers to the name of the "Most High,"[120] thus putting out of doubt the identity of the "Lord" of stanzas I–II. For the Most High "in the *Odes* is always the Father."[121] Important as the first imperative of 8a is, the second is its equal. This second imperative, with its third masculine singular objective suffix, is vocalized differently but equally erroneously by Harris and Mingana[122] and Charlesworth.[123] Whether this imperative of the Pe. ܝܕܥ (*ʾida*ʿ), "know," in 𝔊 was (*ἐπι*)*γινώσκετε* (cf. Gal 3:7)[124] or *γνῶτε/ἐπιγνῶτε*[125] is not as important as the decision whether the accusative object was *τὸ ὄνομα*, "the name" (therefore *αὐτό*), or the "Most High" (and thus *αὐτόν*). If the verb, which is Gnostically tinged in the *Odes of Solomon*, derives from the anti-Egyptian exodus narrative (cf. in the LXX Exod 14:4, 18; Isa 19:21), it would argue for the second possibility, which would only require the substitution of *ὕψιστος* for *κύριος*.

The Pe. ܥܒܪ (*ʿbar*), "cross," occurs for a third time in 8b (see 5 and 7b above). Its imperfect corresponds to the future tense of *διαβαίνω*.[126] "This sequence of imperative-future, taken literally, makes no sense ... suggesting that the logical relationship is more complicated."[127] Therefore, the *καί*/ܘ (*ʾu*-) should not be translated as "and"[128] but as an inferential "then, so."[129] In place of *ἄνευ κινδύνου* ("without danger"; see above), 𝔊 could, of course, have used the predicative *ἀκίνδυνοι* (cf. linguistically Ps 14:2a LXX: *πορευόμενος ἄμωμος*, "He that walks blameless")[130] or the adverb *ἀκινδύνως*.[131]

The concurrent circumstance in 8c, introduced by ܟܕ (*kad*), "while"—that the raging rivers "obey" those who cross them safely[132]—has, as immediate cause, the protection by the name of the Most High (8a), but is, finally, due also to the soteriological recognizing and knowing and to all that has been noted about "faith" and "the way" in stanza II. Frankenberg's retroversion, with genitive absolute + dative of the person, *τῶν ποταμῶν ὑμῖν πειϑομένων*, can be accepted.[133]

■ **9** The second part of *Ode* 39 (9b-13b) begins halfway through this bicolon, artistically attached to the end of the first part. Verse 9a allows the Most High Lord a final mythological action, but in 9b the "Logos" as "the independent personified expression of God" becomes active.[134] This is the only way in which the three metaphorical verbs of 9a-b can be understood as "a logical progression of action."[135] Following Harnack,[136] Spitta observes "that the two halves of this verse do not really

117 Bauer, 620 n. 5. That this metaphorical expression was well understood is clear from a passage in the Pseudo-Clementine *Homilies*: *μόνον μοι τὸ ὄνομα τοῦτο μὴ ἔχειν χάρισαι· εὐλαβοῦμαι γὰρ τὸ τῆς ἀρχῆς ἐνδύσασϑαι ὄνομα*, "Only grant me not to have this name; for I am afraid of assuming the name of the rulership" (*Hom.* 3.63.2; Bernhard Rehm and Georg Strecker, *Die Pseudoklementinen*, vol. 1: *Homilien* [GCS; 3rd ed.; Berlin: Akademie-Verlag, 1992] 79; ANF 8:250; cf. Peterson, *Studien,* 297 n. 48).

118 BDAG, *s.v.* *ὄνομα*, 1d*β*.

119 BDAG, *s.v.* *ὕψιστος*, 2.

120 Frankenberg's retroversion (p. 33) should really have used *τὸ ὄνομα τοῦ ὑψίστου* rather than *ὄνομα τοῦ κυρίου*. On "putting on the name of God," see Alois Kehl, "Gewand (der Seele)," *RAC* 10 (1978) 972–73.

121 Kittel, 47. This statement is correct in itself, but does not agree with what Kittel (p. 133) had to say on "the Lord" (as "God") in discussing the first part of *Ode* 39. Cf. 9:5; 12:4, 11; 23:18; 31:4; 41:13.

122 Harris and Mingana, vol. 1, on this passage.

123 Charlesworth, 135.

124 BDAG, *s.v.* *γινώσκω*, 1b.

125 Frankenberg, 33; see BDAG, *s.v.* *ἐπιγινώσκω*, 1b.

126 Frankenberg, 33: *διαβήσεσϑε*.

127 Beyer, *Syntax*, 240–41.

128 Contra Bauer, 620; Lattke, *Oden*, 204.

129 Greßmann, 204.

130 Rahlfs, 2:11; Brenton, 705.

131 LSJ, *s.v.* *ἀκινδύνως*.

132 See Lattke, "Wörter," 295–96 = idem, *Bedeutung*, 4:144; BDAG, *s.v.* *πείϑω*, 3b.

133 Frankenberg, 33.

134 BDAG, *s.v.* *λόγος*, 3, with a lengthy bibliography.

135 Franzmann, 269.

136 Harnack, 69.

fit together—that is, if one takes it that the Lord bridged the waters by his creative word and by walking over them on foot."[137] He overcomes this "disharmony" by recognizing "that the word is in fact the Logos" (cf. 41:11-16a; John 1:1-14).[138] The incarnate "Word" of God the Lord thus becomes, to quote Heb 12:2, ἀρχηγὸς πίστεως ("pioneer of faith"; see on 13b below), preparing the way for his faithful followers.

The literary basis of 9b onward is still the exodus narrative, but the *hapax legomenon* ܓܫܪ (*gšar*), "bridged," at the beginning of 9a, which represents a form of γεφυρόω, comes either from an unknown Judeo-Christian expansion of the passage through the Red Sea or from the inventiveness of the people of the *Odes of Solomon*.[139] The accusative object αὐτούς/ܐܢܘܢ (*ʾennōn*), used twice, clearly refers to the "rivers" of 1-8.

Since ܡܠܬܐ (*melltā*), when translating ὁ λόγος in its christological sense, is considered masculine (cf. John 1:1; etc.),[140] the two verbs ܗܠܟ (*hallek*, "walk"; see 6 above) and ܥܒܪ (*ʿbar*, "cross"; see 5, 7b, 8b above), both of which have occurred previously, appear in the third person *masculine* singular, impossible to duplicate in Greek. The Pa., derived from Exod 14:29 and 15:19 LXX and therefore corresponding to πορεύομαι—not περιπατέω (cf. Matt 14:25, 29)[141]—is omitted by Frankenberg,[142] while Fanourgakis includes it in a participle: καὶ διέβη αὐτοὺς <u>πορευόμενος</u> ἐν ποδί.[143] There is no reason why 𝔊 could not equally have had καὶ ἐπορεύθη καὶ διέβη αὐτοὺς ποδί. Rather surprisingly, the verb διαβαίνω/ܥܒܪ (*ʿbar*), again taken from Isa 43:2 LXX, is now, in anticipation of the "footprints" in 10-12,[144] linked to another key word from "Israel's *Kultusgeschichte*" that "re-enacted the miraculous crossing of the sea on the bank of Jordan."[145] The word in question is ποδί ("on foot") in Ps 65:6b LXX.[146] The theological statement in Job 9:8b LXX (περιπατῶν ὡς ἐπ' ἐδάφους ἐπὶ θαλάσσης, "walks on the sea as on firm ground"),[147] which Gnilka connects with "Jesus' walking on the water,"[148] has had no influence, either here or in later passages. So the speculation, shared also by Charlesworth and Massaux,[149] about an allusion to "Christ walking on the water" or a "connection with the pericope of Jesus and Peter walking on the water" can only be considered, not proven.[150] Although Harris at first happily accepted a possible allusion to "our Lord's walking on the sea of Galilee,"[151] he later distanced himself from this idea in view of "parallel expressions in the Old Testament"—which he, unfortunately, left unspecified.[152]

■ **10-12** The key to this unmistakable Christologizing of the exodus narratives is not to be found in "the description in the Book of Joshua of the passage of the Jordan" (cf. Josh 3:15, 17 LXX); nor is it typologically a story of "a greater Leader, who leads to the true

137 Spitta, 289. Even if the "Lord" of 9a was already interpreted as "the Christ" (Kittel, 133), who first bridges the rivers by his word of power and then crosses them himself, the two parts of the bicolon would still not agree properly.

138 Spitta, 289.

139 See Payne Smith, 1:795; LSJ, *s.v.* γεφυρόω: "throw a bridge over"; Frankenberg, 33; Tsakonas, 171; Fanourgakis, 172; the last three all use ἐγεφύρωσεν. Except for the doubtful reading γεφυροῦν in 2 Macc 12:13, this verb is not found in the Bible (Adolf Kamphausen, "Das zweite Buch der Makkabäer," *APAT* 1 [1900] 110; James Moffatt, "The Second Book of Maccabees," *APOT* 1 [1913] 148: "For γεφυροῦν [om. V, Syr., &c.] read γεφύραις [55, Vg. = *firmum pontibus*]"; Christian Habicht, *2. Makkabäerbuch* [JSHRZ 1.3; Gütersloh: Mohn, 1976] 262: "here left untranslated"). Josephus uses it three times (Karl Heinrich Rengstorf, ed., *A Complete Concordance to Flavius Josephus* [Study Edition in 2 vols.; Leiden: Brill, 2002] 357). Since the noun ܓܫܪܐ (Payne Smith, 1:796) is used to translate γέφυρα (in the LXX only in Isa 37:25) the *Vorlage* of ܓܫܪ (*gšar*) can only be ἐγεφύρωσεν, which makes unnecessary the suggestion of ἔζευξεν as an alternative (Frankenberg, 33).

140 Payne Smith, 2:2111.

141 Contra Tsakonas, 171.

142 Frankenberg, 33.

143 Fanourgakis, 172 [emphasis added].

144 Kittel, 133; contra Grimme, 124.

145 Kraus, *Psalmen*, 457.

146 Rahlfs, 2:66; Brenton, 735; BDAG, *s.v.* πούς, 1; Payne Smith, 2:3811: *pedibus*.

147 Rahlfs, 2:286; Brenton, 672.

148 Joachim Gnilka, *Das Evangelium nach Markus*, vol 1: *Mk 1–8,26* (EKKNT 2.1; Zurich: Benziger; Neukirchen-Vluyn: Neukirchener Verlag, 1978) 269, on Mark 6:48-49; cf. Matt 14:25-26, 29.

149 Charlesworth, 137; Massaux, *Influence*, 79.

150 Contra Spitta, 289.

151 Harris, 137.

152 Harris and Mingana, 2:397.

Land of Promise *through the baptismal waters*" [emphasis added].[153] The images of stanza V may run into one another, but they are quite defined and even unique in their ancient context of tales of gods and heroes "making a path in the sea."[154] What is not quite definite, again, is the exact meaning of the verbs and of some other words.

Following on from the expression "on foot" (9b), the plural of the feminine ܥܩܒܬܐ (*ʿeqḇṯā*), in 10a and 11b, does not mean "tracks of light" (7:14; 10:6) but "footprints."[155] These tracks are not "the footsteps . . . of God,"[156] but, as it were, the actual, and, in contrast with the Docetism of *Act. John* chap. 93, the visible tracks of the incarnate Logos (see on 9a-b above), the Kyrios Christos (see on 11b below).[157] The term itself, despite the fanciful embellishments to the image,[158] is still derived from the exodus narratives, in which it is said of God in Ps 76:20c LXX: τὰ ἴχνη σου οὐ γνωσθήσονται ("thy footsteps cannot be known").[159] As so often in the traditions of the exodus, there is mention of the "water(s)." The water[160] of this Ode is not that of the "sea" (16:10) but of the "rivers" of part 1. The "footprints" are not identical with the "sign" of 7a-b,[161] but they form a christological parallel to that theological term. The link between the terms "sign" and "footprints" is drawn even closer, in what Kittel recognized as the "connection between the two parts of the *Ode*,"[162] by the term "way" (7b, 13a). The quotation from Psalm 76 LXX (Psalm 77 MT), which, in its negation, is "of special significance,"[163] has here been transposed into the affirmative. One could, therefore, say that the *theologia negativa* of the Old Testament has been complemented by a similarly metaphorical *christologia positiva*. There can be little doubt that the feminine plural of the predicative adjective ܩܝܡܐ (*qayyāmā*) represents a verbal construction in 𝔊, either a finite form or a participle of (δια)μένω or of ἵστημι used intransitively.[164] In a construction with a participle, of course, there would not be a second καί ("and") before the final verb. The negated Ethpa. of ܚܒܠ (*ḥḇal*), "were not destroyed," should not be (back-)translated by ἄφθαρτα (see Excursus 28).[165]

Since the aspect of 10a is the past, ܐܝܬܝܗܝܢ (*ʾīṯayhēn*), following the adversative particle ἀλλά/ܐܠܐ (*ʾellā* = "but"), in 10b must be translated as "were."[166] Diettrich's view is topsy-turvy when he says: "The Lord made the rivers of water so solid that the footsteps remained

153 Contra Bernard, 127.

154 Adela Yarbro Collins, "Rulers, Divine Men, and Walking on the Water (Mark 6:45-52)" in Lukas Bormann et al., eds., *Religious Propaganda and Missionary Competition in the New Testament World: Essays Honoring Dieter Georgi* (NovTSup 74; Leiden: Brill, 1994) 211–23, esp. 214.

155 Payne Smith, 2:2960; BDAG, *s.v.* ἴχνος, 1.

156 Contra Harnack, 69 n. 9.

157 Pierre (p. 187) also refers to *Act. John* chap. 93 (9 [Iames]), which runs ἐβουλόμην δὲ πολλάκις σὺν αὐτῷ βαδίζων ἴχνος αὐτοῦ ἐπὶ τῆς γῆς ἰδεῖν εἰ φαίνεται· ἑώρων γὰρ αὐτὸν ἀπὸ τῆς γῆς ἑαυτὸν ἐφαίροντα· καὶ οὐδέποτε εἶδον , "And I often wished, as I walked with him, to see if his footprint appeared on the ground—for I saw him raising himself from the earth—and I never saw it" (*AAAp* 2.1:197; *NTApo*$^{3-5}$ 2:165; *NTApoc* 2:181). There is no mention of any "water of life" (Bernhard Kötting, "Fuß," *RAC* 8 [1972] 739).

158 Gunkel, unfortunately, does not reveal the provenance of the legend (*Zaubermärchen*) from which the image derives and which he retells so thrillingly: "The great magician builds a marvelous bridge across the water because his footprints do not vanish in the water but remain 'like piles driven into the ground'—this metaphor must have originated near some great river where pile dwellings existed" (see Gunkel, *Aufsätze*, 178). Gunkel's conviction that this reflects "the well-known biblical story of Jesus walking on the water" is one I cannot share. His reference to "St. Hyacinthus of Krakow," who leaves indelible tracks on the water of a river, is, at best, an illustration of this idea from *Ode* 39.

159 Rahlfs, 2:82; Brenton, 744.

160 In 𝔊, ὕδωρ or ὕδατα; see BDAG, *s.v.* ὕδωρ, 1; Payne Smith, 2:2080.

161 Contra Connolly, "Odes," 303–4; Kittel, 134.

162 Kittel, 134.

163 Kraus, *Psalmen*, 533.

164 BDAG, *s.vv.* διαμένω, ἵστημι, μένω; Payne Smith, 2:3532–33. Diettrich's translation (p. 128), "remained," is better than "remain" (contra Frankenberg, 33: διαμένει). However, the addition of ܗܘܝ (*-way*) is unnecessary. For a construction with a finite verb one might suggest the pluperfect of ἵστημι (cf. the perfect in 2 Tim 2:19). The adjective ܩܝܡܐ (*qayyāmā*) means "lasting" (Payne Smith, 2:3532: *permanens, durans*).

165 Contra Frankenberg, 33; Fanourgakis, 172.

166 See Bauer, 620; Nöldeke §305.

imprinted in the water."[167] That is why he continually emphasizes the "solidity of the water." But the simile introduced into the image by ὡς/ܐܟ (*ʾak*), "like," depicts the footprints "standing in the water like piles driven in"[168] and making "a kind of bridge."[169] The term ξύλον/ܩܝܣܐ (*qaysā*), "wood," which is used very differently in 27:3 and 42:2, is in no sense, directly or indirectly, the beam of the "cross"[170] to which Pierre alludes, with mention of "the Valentinian teaching of the cross."[171] Whether the participle of the Aph. of ܬܩܢ (*tqen*), "fixed," corresponded to a form of στηρίζω[172] is impossible to decide, in view of the number of other possible equivalents.[173] It would be possible, in view of 11:5a, to posit a play on words with the adverb of στερεός,[174] except that a nontechnical use of ἀληθῶς—or even ἐν ἀληθείᾳ[175]—as an equivalent of the prepositional phrase ܒܫܪܪܐ (*ba-šrārā*), "truly," is more likely and more obvious.[176]

The plural of ܓܠܠܐ (*gallā*) in 11a, "waves," is not derived from Matt 14:24 (ὑπὸ τῶν κυμάτων, "by the waves"),[177] nor is it in any sense a parallel to *Ode* 31:10b. It can be traced back to Exod 15:8c (ἐπάγη τὰ κύματα ἐν μέσῳ τῆς θαλάσσης, "the waves were congealed in the midst of the sea"),[178] just as the image as a whole is adapted from that of the miraculous walls of water of the exodus.[179] The place of "on the right hand" and "on the left" is taken by an expression that also denotes "on both sides."[180] The participle of the Ethpe. of ܪܘܡ, ܪܡ (*rām*), "rose up," which is not used elsewhere in this sense, with suffixed ܗܘܘ (*-waw*), corresponds, in 𝔖 also, to "a form expressing continuance or repetition in past times."[181] Whether this was a passive form of ἐπαίρω[182] or some more elaborate construction,[183] the verb of 11a speaks of the mythological past.[184]

In 11b, the remaining and standing firm of the "footprints" (see on 10a above) moves into the narrative and kerygmatic present and is also clearly interpreted christologically, without referring to "a specific occurrence in the life of Christ."[185] The term ܡܫܝܚܐ (*mšīḥā*), in fact, stands for "ὁ Χριστός," and, therefore, "our Lord" designates the Exalted One, who is identified by the same expression in primitive Christianity.[186] By the time the *Odes of Solomon* were composed, early in the second century, using κύριος (ἡμῶν) for ὁ Ἰησοῦς, Χριστός, or Ἰησοῦς Χριστός no longer posed any problem.[187] In addition, the use of "Lord" (= God) and "our Lord" (=

167 Diettrich, 128.
168 Harnack, 69.
169 Labourt and Batiffol, 36.
170 BDAG, *s.v.* ξύλον, 2c; see Payne Smith, 2:3606.
171 Pierre, 187; see also Charlesworth, 137 n. 11.
172 Frankenberg, 33: ἐστηριγμένον; BDAG, *s.v.* στηρίζω, 1.
173 Payne Smith, 2:4485–86.
174 Frankenberg, 33: στερεῶς.
175 BDAG, *s.v.* ἀλήθεια, 3.
176 Payne Smith, 2:4304; BDAG, *s.v.* ἀληθῶς, a; cf. Lattke, *Oden*, 205, where the translation of 10-12 needs revising. How dangerous an overdogmatic retroversion can be is shown by *Ode* 11:5a. Frankenberg (p. 13) represents the Syriac genitive phrase ܫܘܥܐ ܕܫܪܪܐ (*šūʿā da-šrārā*) by πέτρα τῆς ἀληθείας. When the Greek text of this Ode came to light many years later the equivalent of the Syriac expression was found to be, in a biblical set phrase, στερεὰ πέτρα (see BDAG, *s.v.* στερεός, 1; see also the commentary on that passage).
177 See BDAG, *s.v.* κῦμα; Payne Smith, 1:714.
178 Rahlfs, 1:111; Brenton, 89–90.
179 Cf. in the LXX, after Ps 77:13b (ἔστησεν ὕδατα ὡσεὶ ἀσκόν, "he made the waters to stand as in a bottle") and Exod 15:8b (ἐπάγη ὡσεὶ τεῖχος τὰ ὕδατα, "the waters were congealed as a wall"), esp. Exod 14:21-22 and 14:29 (. . . ἐσχίσθη τὸ ὕδωρ . . . καὶ τὸ ὕδωρ αὐτοῖς τεῖχος ἐκ δεξιῶν καὶ τεῖχος ἐξ εὐωνύμων, ". . . the water was divided . . . and the water of it was a wall on the right and a wall on the left"); Rahlfs, 1:110–11; 2:83; Brenton, 89, 744.
180 BDAG, *s.v.* ἐντεῦθεν (or possibly ἔνθεν); Payne Smith, 1:1656.
181 Nöldeke §277; cf. BDF and BDR §318.
182 Payne Smith, 2:3857; BDAG, *s.v.* ἐπαίρω.
183 Frankenberg, 33: ἐπαναστάντα ἤρθη.
184 Ungnad and Staerk, 37; Diettrich, 128; contra Greßmann, 469; Bauer, 620.
185 Frankenberg, 101.
186 Schultheß, 256; see BDAG, *s.v.* μαράνα θά ("Lord, come!"), on μαρὰν ἀθά (ܡܪܢ ܐܬܐ [*māran ʾāṯā*] = "our Lord has come") in 1 Cor 16:22; Aland and Juckel, *Briefe*, 1:498, 598. I cannot agree with Schultheß's other textual criticisms of *Ode* 39:8-13, for not all the verbs in this section are "in the present tense," and it is not "based" on Matt 14:25-33. His contention that "our Lord" could not refer to God is unsustainable in view of various passages in the LXX and also in the NT (cf. Pss 8:2, 10; 134:5; 146:5; Ps. Sol. 10:5; Rev 11:15; *OTSy*, pt. 2 fasc. 3, pp. 6–7, 158, 170).
187 BDAG, *s.v.* κύριος; see, e.g., James D. G. Dunn,

Christ = the Logos) serves as another subtle connection between the two parts of the Ode.

The second participle in the monocolon 12, which Harris and Mingana and Charlesworth divide into a bicolon,[188] returns to the Ethpe. of ܚܒܠ (*ḥbal*) in 10a, "destroyed," but the image of the first participle is suited more to dry land than to water. Determining the exact sense of the Ethpe. of ܥܛܐ (*ʿṭā*), "blotted out," is as difficult here as for the N reading of 23:20b.[189] But even here the meaning is clear enough, and the remaining verbs in stanza V attest to it.[190] This heavy emphasis on the permanence of the metaphorical "footprints" might lead a person who remembered Isa 43:17 LXX or examined a collection of exodus narratives (cf. Exod 14:28) to consider it an antithesis of the extinguishing (ἐσβέσθησαν) of the "mighty" Egyptian "multitude" (ὄχλος ἰσχυρός).[191]

■ **13** In the first place, this bicolon, which concludes the second part of the Ode, is not a tricolon,[192] and, in the second, it is not merely "a kind of summary of important themes in the Ode."[193] The vocabulary, which has already been used in the first part, serves to connect this christological section to the previous one, so that the complete Ode appears in the form of a diptych. It also serves to gather up similar statements from the first part and focus them on "our Lord" (11b) and his followers and worshipers. This exalted Kyrios Christos is not merely a "guide of souls."[194] The "sufferings of Jesus" and "sufferings of his followers" that McNeil discerns[195] are more applicable to the "theology of the passion" of 1 Pet 2:21-25.[196] Since all three third person masculine singular possessive suffixes (αὐτοῦ each time in 𝔊) refer to the "Lord Christ" and not to God, it is necessary to insert a somewhat overdue summary (cf. the remarks on the "Lord" in the commentary to *Ode* 1).

Table 9: "Lord" Used of God and the Christ/Messiah in the *Odes of Solomon*

Following Dunn's example,* this table lists all passages where the word "Lord" occurs, explicitly, in the singular (for the only plural see 28:13). The context of these passages is likely to include associated statements (see, e.g., *Ode* 40). The expanded titles of the columns are as follows:

1. Occurrence of κύριος.
2. Occurrence of ϫⲟⲉⲓⲥ (*čoïs*).
3. Occurrence of ܡܪܝܐ (*māryā*).
4. Terms connected by the genitive (e.g., Spirit *of the Lord*; except: Exultation *over the Lord*).
5. Occurrence of "my Lord."
6. Occurrence of "our Lord."

* Dunn, pp. 368–72.

"ΚΥΡΙΟΣ in Acts," in Christof Landmesser, Hans-Joachim Eckstein, and Hermann Lichtenberger, eds., *Jesus Christus als die Mitte der Schrift: Studien zur Hermeneutik des Evangeliums* (BZNW 86; Berlin/New York: de Gruyter, 1997) 363–78, esp. 369–72.

188 Harris and Mingana, vol. 1, on this passage, 2:396; Charlesworth, 135–36.

189 Payne Smith, 2:2857; see Frankenberg, 33: οὐκ ἐξαλείφεται. Frankenberg (pp. 23, 41) reads ܐܬܥܛܝܘ (*ʾetʿṭīw*) in 23:20b as well and gives ἐξηλείφθησαν as his reconstruction of the Greek *Vorlage* (see BDAG, *s.v.* ἐξαλείφω, 1–2).

190 See commentary on 23:20.

191 Rahlfs, 2:625; Brenton, 878.

192 Contra Harris and Mingana, vol. 1, on this passage; 2:396; Charlesworth, 135–36.

193 Franzmann, 269, who would really like to divide the "tricolon" into a tetracolon.

194 Contra Quasten, "Hirte," 396 ("Psychopompos"). See Lampe, 1554, *s.v.* ψυχοπομπός.

195 Brian McNeil, "Suffering and Martyrdom in the Odes of Solomon," in William Horbury and Brian McNeil, eds., *Suffering and Martyrdom in the New Testament: Studies Presented to Geoffrey M. Styler* (Cambridge: Cambridge University Press, 1981) 137.

196 See Karl Hermann Schelkle, *Die Petrusbriefe. Der Judasbrief* (HThKNT 13.2; 2nd ed.; Freiburg/Basel/Vienna: Herder, 1964) 82; Leonhard Goppelt, *Der Erste Petrusbrief* (ed. by Ferdinand Hahn; 1st ed. of this *Neubearbeitung*; KEK 12.1; 8th ed.; Göttingen: Vandenhoeck & Ruprecht, 1978) 198–212.

Table 9: "Lord" Used of God and the Christ/Messiah in the *Odes of Solomon* (*Cont.*)

7. "Lord" used of God (the Most High, Father).
8. "Lord" used of Christ/Messiah, sometimes + ܡܫܝܚܐ (*mšīḥā*); see also 9:3b and 41:15a.
9. "Lord" used of God *or* Christ/Messiah.

Ode	1. 𝔊	2. ℭ	3. 𝔖	4. . . . of the Lord	5. my	6. our	7. God	8. Christ	9. ?
1:1		x							x
3:3			x				x		
3:6			x				x		
3:10			x	Spirit . . .			x		
4:3			x				x		
4:15			x				x		
5:1		x	x				x		
5:10		x	x				x		
5:11			x				x†		
5:15			x				x		
6:2			x	Spirit . . .			x		
6:3			x				x		
6:6			x				x		
6:18		x	x				x		
7:2			x				x		
7:3			x				x		
7:17			x	Coming . . .			x		
7:19			x				x		
7:21			x	*Gnōsis* . . .			x		
7:22			x	Grace . . .			x		
7:23			x	Sublimity . . .			x		
8:1			x	Exultation . . .			x		
8:2			x				x		
8:6			x	Right hand . . .			x		
8:22			x	Love . . .			x		
9:3			x	Word . . .			x		
9:4			x	Will . . .			x		
9:11			x	Covenant . . .			x		
10:1			x				x		
11:1			x				x‡		
11:6	x		x	Spring . . .			x		
11:11	x		x				x		
11:13	x		x				x		
11:15	x		x	Kindness/ Fragrance . . .			x		
11:16	x		x	Delight/Joy . . .			x		
11:17	x		x				x		
11:18	x		x				x		

† ℭ omits the term "Lord." Instead, in reference to the "Lord" (5:10), it says: "For thou art my God, my Savior" (5:11a).

‡ 𝔊 uses θεός, not κύριος.

Table 9: "Lord" Used of God and the Christ/Messiah in the *Odes of Solomon* (*Cont.*)

Ode	1. 𝔊	2. ℭ	3. 𝔖	4. . . . of the Lord	5. my	6. our	7. God	8. Christ	9. ?
12:3			x	Mouth . . .			x		
12:13			x				x		
13:1			x				x		
14:1			x				x		
14:3			x				x		
14:4			x		x		x		
14:6			x				x		
14:8			x				x		
15:1			x				x		
15:10			x	Land . . .			x		
16:1			x	Psalm . . .			x		
16:3			x				x		
16:5			x	Glory . . .			x		
16:8			x	Word . . .			x		
16:18			x				x		
17:2			x		x		x		
17:16			x					x ܡܫܝܚܐ	
18:3			x				x		
18:4			x				x		
19:1			x	Kindness . . .			x		
20:1			x	Priest . . .			x		
20:4			x	Offering . . .			x		
20:7			x	Grace . . .			x		
21:1			x	Compassion . . .			x		
21:5			x	Thought . . .			x		
21:9			x	Exultation . . .			x		
23:4a			x	*Gnōsis* . . . (N)			x§		
23:4b			x	Grace . . . (N)			x		
24:1			x	Head . . . (N)		x		x ܡܫܝܚܐ	
24:5			x					x	
24:7			x	Submersion . . .				x	
24:10			x					x	
24:13			x					x	
25:11			x	Name . . .					x
26:1			x				x		
26:8			x	Odes . . .			x		
26:11			x	Ode . . .			x		
27:1			x		x		x		
29:1			x				x		
29:6a			x	Messiah . . .			x	(ܡܫܝܚܐ)	
29:6b			x					x	
29:10			x				x		

§ H has ܡܪܝܡܐ (*mrayymā*) in place of ܡܪܝܐ (*māryā*).

Table 9: "Lord" Used of God and the Christ/Messiah in the *Odes of Solomon* (*Cont.*)

Ode	1. 𝔊	2. ℭ	3. 𝔖	4. . . . of the Lord	5. my	6. our	7. God	8. Christ	9. ?
30:1			x	Spring . . .			x		
30:2			x	Spring . . .			x		
30:5a			x	Lips . . .			x		
30:5b			x	Heart . . .			x		
31:1			x					x	
31:2			x	Truth . . .				x	
35:1			x	Rain . . .			x		
35:4			x	Group . . .			x		
35:5			x	Dew . . .			x		
36:1			x	Spirit . . .			x		
36:2			x	Height . . .			x		
36:3			x	Face . . .			x		
37:1			x		x		x		
37:4			x	Grace . . .			x		
38:16			x	Hand . . .			x		
38:19			x				x		
39:1			x	Power . . .			x		
39:7a			x				x		
39:7b			x	Name . . .			x		
39:9			x				x		
39:11			x			x		x ܡܫܝܚܐ	
40:2			x	Praise(s) . . .			x		
41:1			x				x		
41:3a			x	(Grace . . .)			x		
41:3b				(Messiah . . .)			x	(ܡܫܝܚܐ)‖	
41:5			x	Name . . .			x		
41:7			x	Exultation . . .			x		
41:16			x				x		
42:1			x		x		x		

‖ 41.3 reads in N: "We rejoice in the Lord by his grace, and life we receive by his Messiah/Anointed One."

The previous images, with all their allusions to the "crossing of the Red Sea,"[197] now fade away and give place to what really concerns these more or less esoteric followers of the Kyrios Christos. The "way" laid down by the legendary footprints in 10-12, is, in spite of the use of the same term ὁδός/ܐܘܪܚܐ (*ʾurḥā*), not identical with the "way" mentioned in the hyperbolic language of 7a-b (God the Lord = the sign = the way).[198] It is a completely new, christological way, which, however, is not equated with the Logos and anointed Lord, thus distinguishing

197 Bauer, 620. The reservations I expressed about Bauer (Lattke, *Oden*, 204 n. 1) have turned out to be groundless in the course of my closer examination of *Ode* 39.

198 See Lattke, "Bildersprache," 101 = idem, *Bedeutung*, 4:26.

the image of 13a from that of John 14:6. The use of the Ethpe. of ܣܘܡ, ܣܡ (*sām*), "established," corresponding to ἐτέθη,[199] is close to that in 38:16b ("foundations were laid"), but 7:14a and 10:6a ("tracks of light were set") are not parallel to it. There is a *true* parallel in the use of the active Pe. ܣܡ (*sām*), in the context of one of these passages: "For toward *gnōsis* he [viz., the Father] laid out his way" (7:13a; cf. 7:13b and 14b). The elaborate correlative, as elsewhere in *Ode* 39 (see 1b and 5-7 above), hints at a more elegant Greek construction with participle, which in this case used the dative τοῖς διαβαίνουσιν ("for those who cross"). This is the final echo of the key verb διαβαίνω/ܥܒܪ (*ʿbar*) derived from the exodus tradition (see 5, 7b, 8b, 9b above). But even this verb receives a new coloration by being associated with a key word taken from the New Testament language of discipleship. For the preposition ܒܬܪ (*bāṯar*)—with the suffix referring to the Kyrios Christos, that is, "after him"—does not correspond in any sense to μετ' αὐτόν.[200] This preposition of place corresponds instead to the improper, Hebraistic, preposition ὀπίσω + genitive, which is used in the sense "be an adherent/follower" with verbs of going (ἀπέρχομαι, ἔρχομαι, πορεύομαι) and even with ἀκολουθέω.[201]

Only one correlative (see 5-6 above), with a repeated *nota dativi* ܠ (*l-*), adds two more verbs in the Pe. form, the *hapax legomenon* ܫܠܡ (*šlem*), "follow," and ܣܓܕ (*sgeḏ*), "revere," which in 11:17 corresponds to προσκυνέω (cf., e.g., Deut 6:13 LXX in Matt 4:10 and Luke 4:8), but is also sometimes used to translate σέβομαι.[202] The verb λατρεύω (cf. *1 Clem.* 45:7), suggested by Frankenberg,[203] would agree better with the Pe. ܦܠܚ (*plaḥ*),[204] as can be seen in the exhortation in Deut 6:13, which immediately follows Deut 6:4, "Hear, O Israel." This passage, in spite of the mention of the "name" of God and the preceding allusion to the bringing up out of Egypt, is not the background of *Ode* 39. Although the "name" (Matt 28:19) plays hardly any part in the context of Matt 28:9 and 28:17 (see also Luke 24:52), the occurrence of προσκυνέω (+ accusative or dative) in these passages moves them into the immediate background of the worship transferred from God to the resurrected and exalted One.[205] Of an actual "proskynesis," which, although Philo of Alexandria already exposed it as a "barbarian custom" (*Leg. Gaj.* 116),[206] is still practiced in some governing and ecclesiastical circles, there is no sign at the end of *Ode* 39. Such a "gesture of worship"[207] would not be fitting for those who are "free," upon whose proud heads the redeemed Redeemer and Son of God has placed his own "name" (cf. 42:15-20; see also Excursus 39 above).

The central section of this final line, which appears unduly long only in 𝔖, would be far less difficult if only the possessive suffix were attached to the term ܗܠܟܬܐ (*hlakṯā*), "walk," and ܗܝܡܢܘܬܐ (*haymānūṯā*), "faith," linking back to 5, were to disappear. This genitive of "faith" with its suffix (in 𝔊 τῆς πίστεως αὐτοῦ) raises the question whether it means the belief of the Kyrios Christos himself or the belief in him of his followers (see Excursus 34). If the latter should be the case, then the metaphorical "pace" or "walk" must be derived from that of preceding fellow believers. Independent of this, there is also the question whether ܗܠܟܬܐ (*hlakṯā*) actually corresponds to ἀναστροφή.[208] The term πορεία would seem a more obvious *Vorlage* (cf. linguistically Ps 67:25 LXX)[209] or διάβημα again (see 2 above).[210] Frankenberg's retroversion of the participle of ܫܠܡ (*šlem*), "follow," with its subsequent preposition ܠ (*l-*), by the participle of σπουδάζω (+ accusative) is also farfetched.[211] A participle of ἐπακολουθέω in the dative is

199 BDAG, *s.v.* τίθημι, 4.
200 Contra Frankenberg, 33; cf. BDAG, *s.v.* μετά, B1.
201 BDAG, *s.v.* ὀπίσω, 2a; cf. Payne Smith, 1:625–26.
202 BDAG, *s.v.* σέβω, 1b: "worship"; Payne Smith, 2:2522.
203 Frankenberg, 33.
204 Payne Smith, 2:3148.
205 See BDAG, *s.v.* προσκυνέω, bε, with additional messianic references.
206 Heinrich Greeven, "προσκυνέω, προσκυνητής," *ThWNT* 6 (1959) 763; *TDNT* 6:762–63.
207 Wolfgang Fauth, "Proskynesis," *KP* 4 (1972) 1189.
208 Frankenberg, 33; BDAG, *s.v.* ἀναστροφή.
209 BDAG, *s.v.* πορεία, 1.
210 BDAG, *s.v.* διάβημα; Payne Smith, 1:1015.
211 Frankenberg, 333; see BDAG, *s.v.* σπουδάζω, 1.

possible, though without reference to 1 Pet 2:21,[212] but, in general, one would expect *στοιχέω* (cf. Rom 4:12) or *συστοιχέω* as *Vorlage*.[213] The meaning of the Syriac verb is "agree to"[214] or "adhere to."[215] The Greek might, in addition to "following," have carried the military connotation of holding formation.[216]

Returning now to the genitive phrase "of his faith" (see above), at first sight and in light of 8:11 and 28:3, the subjective sense should be preferred. Even if the Kyrios Christos of the *Odes of Solomon* is never named as Jesus, it is still possible to refer to the "wandering people of God"[217] whose members look *εἰς τὸν τῆς πίστεως ἀρχηγὸν καὶ τελειωτὴν Ἰησοῦν* ("to Jesus the pioneer and perfecter of our faith" [Heb 12:2]).[218] The reason why most biblical scholars are disinclined to consider the subjective interpretation of the *πίστις Ἰησοῦ Χριστοῦ*[219] is that throughout the New Testament Jesus (the) Christ appears as already the Lord and Son of God. While the unfinished debate on this can be left to New Testament scholars, here follows an outline of the logic for the interpretation of it in *Ode* 39. Starting with the absolute and general use of "faith" (see 5 above), the path leads via christological specificity (9b-12) to the personal faith of the Kyrios Christos (13b) and thus indirectly to the faith implicit in discipleship and veneration not only of God the Lord but also of "our anointed Lord" (11b; cf. 42:9b). One of the marks of distinction between these two *κύριοι* ("Lords")[220] is exactly the belief in the God of the Lord (Jesus) Christ who is identical with the redeemed Redeemer of the *Odes of Solomon*.

212 BDAG, *s.v.* ἐπακολουθέω, 1.
213 BDAG, *s.vv.* *στοιχέω*, *συστοιχέω*; Payne Smith, 2:4183–84.
214 Harris and Mingana, 2:396; see already Harnack, 70; Diettrich, 128: "zustimmen."
215 Harris, 136.
216 BDAG, *s.v.* *συστοιχέω*: "stand in the same line."
217 See Käsemann, *Wandering People*.
218 BDAG, *s.vv.* *ἀρχηγος*, 3; *ἀφοράω*, 1: "fix one's eyes;" *τελειωτής*.
219 Cf. Rom 3:22, 26; Gal 2:16, 20; 3:22; Eph 3:12; Phil 3:9.
220 BDAG, *s.v.* *κύριος*, 2b.

40

Ode 40: Hope, Hymns, and Redemption

(I) 1a As honey drips from the honey-comb of bees,
1b and milk flows from the woman who loves her children,
1c so also my hope is on thee, my God.
(II) 2a As a spring gushes out its water,
2b so my heart gushes out praises[a] of the Lord,
2c and my lips bring forth a hymn to him.
(III) 3a And my tongue is sweet in his anthems,
3b and my limbs are fat/lush[b] in his odes[c],
4a and my face[d] rejoices in exultation over him,
4b and my spirit exults in love of him,
4c and my soul shines by/in him.
(IV) 5a And fear[e] shall trust in him,
5b and redemption will be made firm by him.
6a And its [i.e., redemption's] gain is eternal life,
6b and those who receive it [i.e., life] are imperishable.
Hallelujah.

a 2b ܬܫܒܚ̈ܬܗ N; ܬܫܒܘܚܬܗ H.
b 3a-b H omits ܐܝܟ ܒܚܒܝ̈ܒܘܗܝ ܘܗܕܡܝ ܗܕܝ̈ܪ.
c 3b ܒܙܡܝܪ̈ܬܗ N; ܙܡܝܪ̈ܬܗ[[ܒ]] H (see Lattke, *Bedeutung*, 1:50, 62, 68).
d 4a ܐܦ̈ܝ H; ܐܦܝ N.
e 5a ܘܕܚܠܬܐ N; ܘܕܚ̈ܠܬܐ H.

Introduction

Ode 40 is preserved in two Syriac manuscripts.[1] If Diettrich had known N, his verdict, "This Ode offers no problems," would have been different.[2] Text-critically *Ode* 40 is one of the most difficult in the whole collection. The substance of this relatively short poem is "a wonderful summary of the ruling ideas of the *Odes*."[3] The lack of any overtly "Christian resonance," however, does not give a licence to call *Ode* 40 a "purely Jewish" poem and, after excluding those sections of the *Odes* that are "purely Christian in origin" (among them *Odes* 41 and 42), to label it "an ending without peer."[4]

The unidentified speaking "I" is not necessarily one of the "two sons" whom Rudolf Abramowski contrasts with the congregation.[5] Anyone, woman or man, can be imagined speaking this poem with its wealth of images and metaphors. And the speaker is not merely the soul thirsting for God "in Bernardine fashion"[6] nor yet the soul rejoicing in the Lord.[7] The *whole person* speaks in confidence of salvation and, with a self-description that can portray anyone, employs three inward and four outward aspects (2-4: heart, spirit, soul; lips, tongue, limbs, face) and expands its personal hope (1c) into more general statements of salvation (5-6).

"God," addressed only in 1c, is identical with the "Lord" of 2b, the referent of the much-used third masculine singular suffix (2b-5b; see Table 9). *Ode* 40 could, therefore, be *ex ore Christi*, but this purely theoretical possibility should be opposed even more strongly than

1 Mss.: Codex H, 29a–b; Codex N, 151ʳ (s). Ed./trans.: Charlesworth, 137–39; Franzmann, 270–73; Lattke, 3:213–23.
2 Diettrich, 128.
3 Spitta, 269.
4 Spitta, 268–69, 289.
5 Abramowski, 52–62, esp. 59.
6 Harnack, 70, contradicting Harris, 137.
7 Harnack, agreeing with Spitta, 269.

in the case of *Ode* 21, which is parallel to *Ode* 40 "in many of its expressions."[8]

Interpretation

■ **1** In spite of the "near illegibility at the beginning of *Ode* 40" in N,[9] the Syriac text does not seem to have any variants in stanza I. It is, however, possible that 1c harbors a lacuna, like that in 3a-b in H (see below), and that this derives from a faulty Greek *Vorlage*. For the simile, expressed by ὡς/ܐܝܟ ܕ (*ʾak̲ d-*) and οὕτως/ܗܟܢܐ (*hāk̲annā*), "as" and "so," is not just "ambiguous";[10] it is lame, not at all "a figure of speech to heighten and illuminate the basic concord of the associated spheres."[11] The hope that is directed toward or rests on[12] God is not comparable to honey and/or milk (see Excursus 30). So Engelbrecht's suggestion, "It may mean that the hope of the Odist flows toward God like honey and milk," is wide of the mark.[13] For it to make sense, there would have to be some mention of the impatient expectation of the baby, which stimulates the letting down of milk in the mother or wet-nurse.[14]

The image of 1a is more difficult to restore, since it makes no mention of the larvae and drones that live on honey.[15] In contrast to 30:4, where the "honey" and "honeycomb of bees" are compared with the still sweeter water of the living spring of the Lord (cf. 30:1-3), this passage has the Pe. ܢܛܦ (*nṭap̄*), "drips." The active participle of this *hapax legomenon* corresponds either to στάζει[16] or to an intransitive use of ἀποστάζει (cf. the transitive use in Cant 4:11a LXX).[17]

The second part of the image in 1b has some similarities with 35:5, but, except for the term γάλα/ܚܠܒܐ (*ḥalb̲ā*), "milk," which they share, the differences are equally notable.[18] The participle of the Pe. ܪܕܐ (*rd̲ā*), "flows," could easily represent πηγάζεται,[19] although an active present like ῥέει is more likely in 𝔊.[20] It is also possible that the inclusive expression qualifying the *hapax legomenon* ܐܢܬܬܐ (*ʾattt̲ā*), "woman," can be traced back to the composite term φιλότεκνος ("loving one's children"), which was used especially in reference to women and mothers (cf. Titus 2:4).[21] So the following linguistic elements in 𝔊 can be considered fairly well established: *τὸ μέλι ἀπὸ τοῦ (μελισσῶν) κηρίου καὶ γάλα ἀπὸ γυναικὸς φιλοτέκνου*.[22] The paired images cannot be described as a metaphor for the Gnostic "revelation as a life giving and nourishing power"[23] any more than they can be listed among Klauck's "metaphors bearing a religious character."[24] Even Engelbrecht admits that "the content is not clearly eucharistic."[25]

Like 5:10, as Bernard notes,[26] the statement in 1c is based on the language of the Psalms. Again one should draw attention to Ps 145:5b LXX: *ἡ ἐλπὶς αὐτοῦ ἐπὶ κύριον τὸν θεὸν αὐτοῦ* ("whose hope is in the Lord his

8 See Harris and Mingana, 2:322, 399.
9 Lattke, *Bedeutung*, 1:41 n. 3.
10 Engelbrecht, "God's Milk," 516.
11 Gero von Wilpert, *Sachwörterbuch der Literatur* (KTA 231; 5th ed.; Stuttgart: Kröner, 1969) 820; cf. Lattke, "Bildersprache," 101–2 = idem, *Bedeutung*, 4:26–28.
12 Since 1c is lacking a verb, the supplementation of the enclitic ܗܘ (*hū*) is left to individual taste.
13 Engelbrecht, "God's Milk," 516.
14 Both this reflex and that to secrete milk can be called into play by preparing to nurse a child or even by the hunger cry of a baby. Information supplied by my daughter Birgit Schickinger.
15 *MEL*, 4:151–53; 12:248.
16 BDAG, *s.v.* στάζω, 2; Payne Smith, 2:2350.
17 LSJ, *s.v.* ἀποστάζω; Frankenberg, 33. In the transcription, the first *d* of *d-d̲ebbōryāt̲ā* (30:4b; 40:1a) retains its plosive quality (Klaus Beyer, letter of November 13, 2002; cf. Nöldeke §26.B). It may be considered possible that the metaphors of Cant 4:11a-b LXX influenced the imagery of *Ode* 40: *κηρίον ἀποστάζουσιν χείλη σου, νύμφη, μέλι καὶ γάλα ὑπὸ τὴν γλῶσσάν σου* ("Thy lips drop honeycomb, my spouse: honey and milk are under thy tongue" [Rahlfs, 2:265; Brenton, 832]).
18 See Lattke, "Bildersprache," 105 = idem, *Bedeutung*, 4:31.
19 Frankenberg, 33; see LSJ, *s.v.* πηγάζω: *πηγάζοντες μαστοί*.
20 Payne Smith, 2:3818; BDAG, *s.v.* ῥέω; see Fanourgakis, 172.
21 BDAG, *s.vv.* γυνή, 2; φιλότεκνος; Payne Smith, 1:287, 578; 2:3880.
22 Frankenberg, 33, who, as a classical scholar, prefers ἀπὸ τῶν κηρίων, but omits the bees completely.
23 Otto Betz, *Offenbarung und Schriftforschung in der Qumransekte* (WUNT 6; Tübingen: Mohr Siebeck, 1960) 117.
24 Klauck, *Herrenmahl*, 213–14.
25 Engelbrecht, "God's Milk," 516.
26 Bernard, 128.

God").[27] Even more relevant is a passage from Ps 61:8b LXX: *καὶ ἡ ἐλπίς μου ἐπὶ τῷ θεῷ* ("and my hope is in God").[28] The theological emphasis of stanza I rests on this final existential statement, which, after 1a-b, is indeed "unusual,"[29] since the noun "hope" is rare in comparison with the New Testament (cf. only 5:2; 29:1) and the verb "to hope" occurs only once (42:5).

■ **2** Unlike the previous, skewed, comparison,[30] this one, which uses the same particles of comparison,[31] succeeds. The active participle of Pe. ܓܣܐ (*gsā*), "gushes out" (there is no variant ܪܓܣܐ),[32] is the *tertium comparationis*.[33] The final line, 2c, no longer depends on ܗܟܢܐ (*hāḵannā*), "so."[34] With "hymn," it picks up an important word from 2b (for the textual criticism, see below), but its main function is as a link to stanza III.

Because of the verb in 2a-b, it is necessary to refer at once to Ps 118:171a LXX, since this verse has also influenced the shaping of the comparison here: *ἐξερεύξαιντο* (*-ξονται* A, *-ξαντο* S) *τὰ χείλη μου ὕμνον* ("Let my lips utter a hymn"); cf. also *ἡ καρδία μου* ("my heart") in Ps 118:161b and Ps 44:2a LXX: *ἐξηρεύξατο ἡ καρδία μου λόγον ἀγαθόν* ("My heart has uttered [*eructavit*] a good matter").[35] In place of the verb *ἐξερεύγομαι*, used both literally and metaphorically,[36] one might consider *ἐρεύγομαι* without a prefix to be the original of ܓܣܐ (*gsā*) (cf. 16:2 and 36:7).[37] However, there is no reason to alternate between *ἀναβλύζει*[38] and *ἐρεύγεται*.[39] "Spring" and "water" are often linked (e.g., 30:4).[40] The masculine ܡܒܘܥܐ (*mabbūʿā*), "spring," derived from ܢܒܥ (*nḇaʿ*), to which the suffix of ܡܝܐ (*mayyā*) refers, "its water," is used in its literal sense only here in 2a and in 26:13a.[41] The variant reading ܬܫܒܚܬܗ (*tešbḥāṯeh*) in 2b, "praises," which is preferable, suggests that 𝔊 also used the plural of *ὕδωρ*.[42] In 12:2, a similar comparison used "water."[43]

Two other points in 2b are more important than the textual criticism. On the one hand, there is the term *ὕμνος*/ܬܫܒܘܚܬܐ (*tešbuḥtā*), whether singular (H) or plural (N), which has its source in 2a and therefore in Ps 118:171a LXX (see above).[44] On the other hand, the third masculine singular suffix represents the objective genitive *τοῦ κυρίου* ("of the Lord" = "for/to the Lord"), which is corroborated by ܠܗ (*leh*) in 2c, "to him," and that is decisive for the interpretation of the final word forms in 3a-4b (see below). The term *καρδία*/ܠܒܐ (*lebbā*), "heart," as the center of the human being, may owe something to Ps 44:2a LXX (see above), but is used elsewhere in the *Odes of Solomon* in a similar way[45] and is often parallel to "lips."[46] That the "Lord" is the "God" of 1c has already been established.

The origin of *χείλη*/ܣܦܘܬܐ (*sep̄wāṯā*) and *ὕμνος*/ܬܫܒܘܚܬܐ (*tešbuḥtā*), "lips" and "hymn," in the verses of the psalm quoted above can hardly be doubted (see Excursuses 16 and 21), but there are so many possible

27 Rahlfs, 2:160; Brenton, 785.
28 Rahlfs, 2:63; Brenton, 733.
29 Franzmann, 272.
30 Even Bauer's attempt (p. 621) at a plausible interpretation, "As the honeycomb and the milk of the nursing mother overflow, so the hope of the faithful overflows in torrential abundance towards God," does not succeed. Greßmann (p. 470) substitutes "praise" for "hope," which enables him to connect stanzas I and II and say: "Rejoicing flows from him like honey from the honeycomb, like water from the spring."
31 BDAG, *s.vv.* *οὕτως*, *ὡς*.
32 Contra Charlesworth, 138; cf. N, 151ʳ lines 14 and 15 (Lattke, *Bedeutung*, 2:201).
33 Gero von Wilpert, *Sachwörterbuch der Literatur* (KTA 231; 5th ed.; Stuttgart: Kröner, 1969) 771, 820.
34 Contra Franzmann, 272.
35 Rahlfs, 2:46, 140–41; Brenton, 724, 775. The intertextuality of these two LXX Psalms and *Ode* 40 is quite plain since, in addition to "lips" and "heart," the terms "tongue" (Pss 44:2c; 118:172a) and "soul" (Ps 118:167a, 175a) also occur (see on stanza III below; perhaps *σωτήριον* ["salvation"] in Ps 118:174a has also influenced 5b in stanza IV).
36 LSJ and LEH, *s.v.* *ἐξερεύγομαι*.
37 BDAG, *s.v.* *ἐρεύγομαι*; Payne Smith, 1:757.
38 See LSJ, *s.v.* *ἀναβλύζω*.
39 Contra Frankenberg, 34.
40 See BDAG, *s.v.* *πηγή*, 1a: "springs of water."
41 Payne Smith, 2:2272.
42 Franzmann (p. 271) chooses the H reading ܬܫܒܘܚܬܗ (*tešbuḥteh*): "The choice for the sing[ular] as in H is based on the parallelism of 2b with 2c where the sing[ular] appears." I think she overemphasizes the parallelism (see above).
43 Payne Smith, 2:2080; BDAG, *s.v.* *ὕδωρ*.
44 Since Frankenberg (p. 34) did not notice this dependence, he artistically varied the terms *δόξα* (2b) and *ἔπαινος* (2c).
45 Cf. 18:1; 21:8; 26:4; 36:7; 41:6.
46 Cf. 8:1; 16:2; 20:4; 21:8; 30:5; 37:2; and see Excursus 4.

equivalents that the connotation of the Aph. of ܢܦܩ (*npaq*) in 2c, "bring forth," cannot be certainly determined.[47] The term ἐκβάλλω used metaphorically—with both indirect and direct objects—is an obvious possibility.[48] But one cannot rule out the possibility that the Syriac participle could have meant προφέρει.[49] The "hymn" is not *Ode* 40 itself, although this Ode is one of those that have "great significance in the hymnody expressed in and forming the background of the *Odes of Solomon*."[50]

■ **3-4** If the Syriac text of H had been all that survived, the remnants of 3a-b would follow on from 2c as "and my tongue his odes," in 𝔊 καὶ ἡ γλῶσσά μου τὰς ᾠδὰς αὐτοῦ (on the implied verb, see above).[51] The fuller text of N is not an expansion of this short text, as can be seen from the erasure of ܒ (*b-*) before ܙܡܝܪܬܗ (*zmīrāṯeh*) in H.[52] This must "have been an omission in codex H."[53] Willey corrected the misprint ܥܢܝܢܘܗܝ in Burkitt's collation[54] to ܥܢܝܢܘܗܝ (*ʿenyānaw*, "his anthems"),[55] but Grimme made bad worse by his emendation ܪܢܝܢܘܗܝ.[56] His unnecessary, indeed preposterous, emendation of the "mutilated words" in N by ܒܚܝܠܐ ܕ (*b-ḥaylā ḏ-*) was unfortunately taken up by Kittel[57] and thus made its way into Greßmann's translation: "My limbs are expanded by the power of the odes concerning him."[58]

Following "heart" (2b) and "lips" (2c), 3a-4c mentions five more parts of the speaking "I." The first two of these, the "tongue" as the organ of speech and song (3a) and the "limbs" denoting the whole body (3b), are described by participles that refer back to characteristics of "honey" (1a) and "milk" (1b). Verse 3a could just as easily have used the synonymous "mouth" as the *hapax legomenon* ܠܫܢܐ (*leššānā*), "tongue."[59] How holistically γλῶσσα could be used is shown by the quotation of Ps 15:9 LXX in Acts 2:26.[60] The adjectival passive participle of the Pe. ܚܠܐ (*ḥlī*) is also a *hapax legomenon* and corresponds to γλυκεῖα ("sweet").[61] And here the difficulties begin.

The exact translation of the preposition ܒ (*b-*) is made more difficult by the fact that the Greek (original) is not available. It is translated as "in" (3a-4b), but it could also be translated by the instrumental preposition "by" (cf. 4c). On the other hand, ܒܗ (*beh*) in 4c could be translated by a locative preposition used in a transferred sense ("in him"). The third masculine singular suffix used at the end of each line of stanza III poses the next set of problems. The first four occurrences of this suffix, referring to God the Lord, correspond to αὐτοῦ (3a-4b), and the last to αὐτῷ (4c, with or without ἐν). The first three are objective genitives (see on 2b-c above); in 4b, however, αὐτοῦ could also be subjective. The parallelism of 4a and 4b suggests a preference for the objective interpretation, although that is no help in resolving the ambiguity in 4c (see below). A third problem lies in the

47 Payne Smith, 2:2422–24.
48 Frankenberg, 34; see LSJ, *s.v.* ἐκβάλλω; BDAG, *s.v.* ἐκβάλλω, 2: "send out."
49 See LSJ and BDAG, *s.v.* προφέρω: "bring forth/out."
50 Lattke, *Hymnus*, 253. Also cf. 6:1-7; 7:17-25; 13:2; 14:7-8; 16:1-7; 21:7-9; 26; 36:2-4; 37; 41:1-7.
51 Frankenberg, 34.
52 Lattke, *Bedeutung*, 1:62.
53 Ibid., 1:68.
54 Burkitt, 380.
55 Duncan Willey, "The Odes and Psalms of Solomon," *JTS* 14 (1912–13) 294.
56 Grimme, "Handschrift," 495. However, Grimme's translation of this word with preceding preposition ܒ (*b-*) as "in his discourses" follows Burkitt's English translation "with his colloquies" (see Burkitt, 385). Kittel accepts this contradiction without comment (see Kittel, "Handschrift," 90). As we shall see, neither "discourses" nor "colloquies" is an accurate translation for this word, which occurs only in N.
57 Kittel, "Handschrift," 90.
58 Greßmann, 470. Bauer's translation (p. 621) is similar (see Bauer, *Oden*, 75). But his particular emendation, ܒܚܠܝܘܬܐ ܕ (*b-ḥalyūtā ḏ-*), picking up the key word "sweet," should be translated as "my limbs are expanded *by the sweetness* of his songs" (cf. 19:1).
59 Payne Smith, 2:1973; BDAG, *s.v.* γλῶσσα, 1a.
60 On this Old Testament passage, which has been christologically ransacked, see Gunkel, *Psalmen*, 50–54; Kraus, *Psalmen*, 124–27.
61 Payne Smith, 1:1281; BDAG, *s.v.* γλυκύς.

interpretation of the other participles (3b-4c), which may, like that in 3a, all represent adjectives. These questions will all have to be considered in their proper place.

The fourth problem is found already in 3a, where the *hapax legomenon* ܥܢܝܢܐ (*ʿenyānā*), "anthem, antiphon," cannot mean ὁμιλία, ἀσχολία, or διατριβή.[62] More appropriate would be ἀπόκρισις, ὑπακοή, or ὑπόψαλμα in a liturgical sense.[63] However, ἀντίφωνον as a noun plays a not inconsiderable part as early as Book 19 (ὅσα περὶ ἁρμονίας) of Aristotle's *Problemata physica* (918b30; 921a8),[64] so the liturgical term ἀντίφωνα as equivalent for the plural ܥܢܝ̈ܢܐ (*ʿenyānē*) would not be anachronistic.[65]

"Limbs" and "heart" (2b) are parallel terms in other contexts also (26:4). In 3b, however, it is the plural of μέλος/ܗܕܡܐ (*haddāmā*) that is directly parallel to "tongue" (see Excursus 18)[66] while the plural of ᾠδή/ܙܡܝܪܬܐ (*zmīrtā*), "odes," is parallel to the musical terms "antiphons" and "hymns" (cf. 36:2 and Excursus 26). The active participle of the Pe. ܕܗܢ (*dhan*), "fat/lush," shares in the basic meaning "to grow fat" (cf. 20:9c)[67] and alludes to the "fat content" of breast milk.[68] Whether 𝔊 had a passive form of πιαίνω (cf. Isa 58:11 LXX)[69] or the poetic adjective πῖος[70] cannot be determined. For the meaning, reference can be made to Ps 62:6 LXX, where στέαρ ("marrow") and πιότης ("fatness") are used in a hymnic context together with soul, lips, and mouth.[71]

The active participle of the Pe. ܪܘܙ (*rwaz*) in 4a, "rejoices," might, as in 11:12b, correspond to a participle of γελάω. But there are many other possibilities.[72] One of them is the adjective φαιδρός, which is also used elsewhere to describe πρόσωπον ("face"; see Excursus 8).[73] Frankenberg equates ܕܝܨܐ (*dyāṣā*), "exultation," here and in 21:9, with ἀγαλλίασις.[74] But both ἀγαλλίαμα and εὐφροσύνη should also be considered.[75]

The use of the active participle of ܕܘܨ, ܕܨ (*dāṣ*) in 4b, "exults," creates a wordplay in ܨ (see 4a above)[76] that should not be blurred by the use of the verb σκιρτάω, which is here—unlike in 28:2—quite unsuitable.[77] The immediate choice is between ἀγαλλιάομαι[78] and εὐφραίνομαι,[79] but again the use of an adjective like εὔφραντός cannot be excluded.[80] The linguistic situation in 4a-b 𝔊 becomes more or less complex as one does or does not suppose paronomasia in that language also. The Greek equivalents of ܪܘܚܐ (*rūḥā*) and ܚܘܒܐ (*ḥubbā*), "spirit" and "love," pose far fewer difficulties. At the same time, "spirit" must not be taken as "the incorporeal *part* of the human being,"[81] but as one *aspect* of the complete person (cf. the anthropological plural of πνεῦμα in 6:7).[82] On "love," as was discussed above, the parallelism of 4a and 4b suggests that the probable Greek phrase, ἐν τῇ ἀγάπῃ αὐτοῦ, should be interpreted objectively.[83]

62 Payne Smith, 2:2929.
63 Lampe, 198, 1433, 1465.
64 "This, the most interesting and also most difficult book of the *Problemata*" contains statements about τὸ ἀντίφωνον that have given rise to reams of musicological theory; see Hellmut Flashar, *Aristoteles, Problemata physica* (Aristoteles Werke in deutscher Übersetzung 19; Darmstadt: Wissenschaftliche Buchgesellschaft, 1975; Lizenzausgabe des Akademie-Verlages Berlin [1962]) 160, 165, 595, 610–11, and see LSJ, *s.v.* ἀντίφωνος, III.
65 Payne Smith, 2:2930; Lampe, 160: "antiphon."
66 Payne Smith, 1:975; BDAG, *s.v.* μέλος, 1.
67 Payne Smith, 1:826–27. Kittel's faulty reference "20a" refers to *Ode* 20:9c: "you will be fat" = "you will prosper" (see Kittel, "Handschrift," 90 n. 1).
68 *MEL*, 16:671.
69 LEH, *s.v.* πιαίνω.
70 LSJ, *s.v.* πῖος.
71 Rahlfs, 2:63; Brenton, 734; see LEH, *s.vv.* πιότης, στέαρ.
72 See Payne Smith, 2:3845.
73 LSJ, *s.v.* φαιδρός: "beaming with joy, bright, cheerful." The smudged reading ܐܦ in N can be "left out of consideration" (Kittel, "Handschrift," 90).
74 Frankenberg, 22, 34.
75 LEH, *s.vv.* ἀγαλλίαμα, εὐφροσύνη; BDAG, *s.v.* εὐφροσύνη; cf. Payne Smith, 1:847.
76 Payne Smith, 1:845.
77 Cf. BDAG, *s.v.* σκιρτάω: "leap"; Frankenberg, 26, 34: σκιρτᾷ.
78 BDAG and LEH, *s.v.* ἀγαλλιάομαι.
79 BDAG and LEH, *s.v.* εὐφραίνομαι.
80 LSJ, *s.v.* εὐφραντός.
81 Payne Smith, 2:3851: "*Pars* hominis incorporealis" (emphasis added).
82 See BDAG, *s.v.* πνεῦμα, 3a.
83 See BDAG, *s.v.* ἀγάπη, 1bβ: "love toward God"; Payne Smith, 1:1171.

"Soul" in 4c is, again, not an (immortal) part but an aspect of the whole (cf. 3:5a-b: "I" = "my soul"). That it is ψυχή/ܢܦܫܐ (*napšā*)—and not πρόσωπον/ܐܦܐ (*ʾappē*), "face," as in 41:6—that is linked to the active participle of the Pe. ܢܗܪ (*nhar*), "shines," shows clearly how interchangeable these anthropological terms are.[84] If 𝔊 did not use a verb form like (ἐκ)λάμπεται[85] as the equivalent of ܢܗܪܐ (*nāhrā*), it might have had an adjective like ἔκλαμπρος or λαμπρός,[86] whose Syriac equivalent would normally have been ܢܗܝܪܐ (*nahhīrā*).[87] The influence of the preceding participles would have dictated the translation found here.[88] The sense is clear enough, and that leaves only the referent of the last little word in stanza III to be considered. "Love" is a masculine noun in Syriac, so ܒܗ (*beh*) could refer to it (i.e., "by it" or "in it"). However, if ἀγάπη αὐτοῦ in 4b is an objective genitive (i.e., "love of him"), this suggestion does not really suffice. So the Greek was probably not ἐν αὐτῇ but ἐν αὐτῷ, referring to God the Lord.

■ **5-6** Although Frankenberg was still unaware of N, he placed a question mark after his retroversion (ὁ φοβούμενος) of the word ܕܚܠܐ, which in H is marked by a point above it as the masculine singular active participle *dāḥlā*.[89] In N, which was discovered only a little later, the word ܕܚܠܐ has a point below it, marking the vocalization as *deḥlā*,[90] a circumstance not noted by Burkitt, Charlesworth, or Lattke.[91] This unusual masculine noun in 5a, like the Aramaic feminine דחלה, means "fear"[92] and is to be preferred for its parallelism with the abstract noun in 5b.[93] In comparison with its feminine synonym ܕܚܠܬܐ (*deḥltā*), which is the term normally used to translate φόβος,[94] this *hapax legomenon* is rare in other Syriac texts also; it will be appropriate to examine it, together with the Pe. ܕܚܠ (*dḥel*) and some other Syriac roots.

Excursus 40: "To Fear," "To Be Frightened," "To Flee," and "To Be Terrified" in the *Odes of Solomon*

The Ethpe. of ܪܗܒ (*rheb*) in 35:3a ("agitated with fear")[95] is mentioned in this miscellaneous excursus because of its semantic relationship to the other verbs.[96] It is preceded in the same verse by the often-used Ethpe. of ܙܘܥ, ܙܥ (*zāʿ*): "Everything was shaken."[97] In the remaining passages, ܐܬܙܝܥ (*ʾettzīʿ*) is commonly negated,[98] giving it a positive meaning, as is the case also in the single occurrence of the Pe.: "And I did not tremble" (7:5a). *Ode* 22:10a is an exception, since the participle "motionless" refers to the "dead bones" (22:9a). The endurance and silence of the condemned is the result of his determination not to be "disturbed" by his persecutors (31:10b).[99] Those who cross raging rivers in faith "will not be disturbed" (39:5).[100] The unshakability of the redeemed one (5:12b), contrasted with the "disturbance" of everything else (5:13a), is due to the fearlessness of his hope in and by the Lord: "I shall not fear" (5:10b and 5:11b, where ℭ has ⲣ ϩⲟⲧⲉ [*ʾr-hote*] for the first ܕܚܠ [*dḥel*]).[101]

84 See BDAG, *s.v.* ψυχή; Payne Smith, 2:2431.
85 BDAG, *s.vv.* ἐκλάμπω, λάμπω; see Frankenberg, 34.
86 BDAG, *s.v.* λαμπρός; LEH, *s.vv.* ἔκλαμπρος, λαμπρός.
87 Payne Smith, 2:2299.
88 Payne Smith, 2:2297.
89 Frankenberg, 34.
90 Harris and Mingana, vol. 1, on this passage.
91 Burkitt, 380; Charlesworth, 137; Lattke, *Bedeutung*, 1:178; but cf. idem, *Oden*, 207.
92 Beyer, *ATTM*, 548; see Brockelmann, *Lexicon*, 148–49.
93 Franzmann, 271.
94 Payne Smith, 1:864; BDAG, *s.v.* φόβος.
95 The Saph. ܣܪܗܒ (*sarheb*), derived from the same root, in 14:9c is a *hapax legomenon* and outside the semantic purview of this excursus (Payne Smith, 2:3828).
96 See Payne Smith, *Dictionary*, 531: "to be disquieted, agitated with fear, to be afraid."
97 See Payne Smith, *Dictionary*, 113: "to be moved, agitated in mind or body, in a good or bad sense." The Aph. from this verb, meaning "to disturb" (23:13a), is also a *hapax legomenon*.
98 The derived phrase ܕܠܐ ܙܘܥܙܥܐ (*d-lā zuʿzāʿā*) occurs only once in reference to the hypostasis of "Wisdom," and means "unshakable" (32:3b).
99 Another derived phrase, ܕܠܐ ܙܘܥܬܐ (*d-lā zawʿtā*), is put into the mouth of the condemned one: "I, however, stood undisturbed like the firm rock" (31:11a).
100 In parallel to this there is the only occurrence of the Ethpe. of ܕܠܚ (*dlaḥ*) meaning "to be perturbed" (39:6). The key word "faith" will be considered later, in the exegesis of 40:5.
101 Crum, 721a: "be afraid." There is no Coptic equivalent to 5:11b.

The final passage that uses the Ethpe. of ܙܘܥ, ܙܥ (*zāʿ*) draws an even closer parallel with the Pe. ܕܚܠ (*dḥel*): "And the inhabitants were afraid, / and the sojourners were disturbed" (24:3a-b). That leaves just three passages with the verb ܕܚܠ. In the first of these, one might be tempted to treat "to fear" and "to flee" as parallels. But that is not the case: in the first part, it is the personified letter that "escaped" from the hostile fingers of the human hands that pursued it (23:8a), while in the second the scene has shifted, and the statement that "they were afraid of it [viz., the letter] and of the seal which was upon it" (23:8b) can be taken quite impersonally. When the apostates flee in 23:20, the Pe. ܥܪܩ (*ʿraq*) has no more connotation of fear or fright than in other contexts (18:6; 25:1; 38:6). Conversely, the adversaries who were afraid in 25:11 are not described as fleeing. That 40:5a H uses the active participle of ܕܚܠ (*dḥel*) is quite surprising, since the form ܕܚܠܐ (*daḥḥīlā*) would have served just as well.[102] It may be that after all the preceding participles, ܕܚܠܐ was also considered a participle and therefore was vocalized as such. N, on the other hand, preserved the uncommon masculine noun "fear,"[103] the context of which will now be discussed.

The logic behind 5a-b is similar to that of Luke 8:50 (cf. Mark 5:34, 36): *Μὴ φοβοῦ, μόνον πίστευσον, καὶ σωθήσεται* ("Do not fear. Only believe, and she will be saved"). Thus faith enters indirectly. Those who trust in God have no more fear. Verse 5a has no connection with the *φόβος θεοῦ* ("fear of God") of, for example, Ps 35:2 LXX in Rom 3:18 (cf. 2 Cor 7:1) or the *φόβος τοῦ κυρίου* ("fear of the Lord") of, for example, Acts 9:31. On the contrary, the "fear" or "terror" of this world is banished because the persons in such existential circumstances rely on God the Lord. The Ethpe. from the root ܬܟܠ occurs only here, but the Pe. participle ܬܟܝܠܐ (*tkīlā*), which means "trusting," is found in significant statements of salvation (15:10; 23:2); ܢܬܬܟܠ (*nettkel*), "shall trust," may correspond to ἐλπίσει[104] or—and this is more probable—to the second perfect of πείθω.[105] Generally it is found in a construction with ܥܠ (*ʿal*), but it can, as here, also be used with ܒ (*b-*).[106] Both of these prepositions are, after all, very common.[107]

After "fear" has joined with "trust," God's "salvation" comes to pass and "is set fast by him."[108] It is too daring to attempt a reconstruction of the Greek of 5b. Even Frankenberg leaves room for ambiguity: *ἡ σωτηρία ἐν αὐτῷ στερεωθήσεται (στηριχθήσεται)*.[109] In view of 6a, it is not impossible that ܦܘܪܩܢܐ (*purqānā*) here represents *σωτηρία* and means the "salvation, w[ith] focus on transcendent aspects."[110] This salvation begins in the present and will be perfected in the future, becoming the opposite of *θάνατος* (cf. 2 Cor 7:10). However, both *ἀπολύτρωσις*[111] and *λύτρωσις*[112] must be considered the possible equivalent or *Vorlage*. Indeed, it is possible that *σωτήριον* might have been borrowed from Ps 118:174 LXX.[113] As for the Ethpa. of ܫܪ (*šar*), "made firm," there are soteriological parallels in 36:8 and 38:16 as well as the equation with the passive of *στηρίζω* in 11:5.[114] In addition to this, the passive of *στερεόω*[115] and the passive of *βεβαιόω* must be considered possible *Vorlagen* (cf. Heb 2:3).[116]

Charles's emendation of ܝܘܬܪܢܗ (*yutrāneh*) to ܝܘܪܬܢܗ (*yurtāneh* = *κλῆρος/κληρονομία αὐτοῦ*),[117] though

102 Payne Smith, 1:864.
103 Brockelmann, *Lexicon*, 148: *timor*.
104 BDAG, *s.v.* ἐλπίζω, 1c.
105 See Frankenberg, 34: ἐπ' αὐτῷ πέποιθε. With only a dative, this perfect with present meaning has nearly the sense of "believe in" in the NT and LXX (BDAG, *s.v.* πείθω, 2a).
106 Payne Smith, 2:4433; Payne Smith, *Dictionary*, 612.
107 See Beyer, *ATTM*, 526–28, 655–56.
108 Bultmann, "Untersuchungen," 160 = idem, *Exegetica*, 170 n. 100.
109 Frankenberg, 34.
110 BDAG, *s.v.* σωτηρία, 2 (cf. the original Germ. "d[as] Heil, das die wahre Gottesverehrung verleiht" [Bauer and Aland, *s.v.* σωτηρία, 2]). This term is most often translated by Syriac ܚܝܐ (*ḥayyē*) (Payne Smith, 1:1254). Since this important soteriological term occurs in 6a, where it certainly corresponds to ζωή, it could not also be used in 5b.
111 Klein, *Wörterbuch*, 85, 108, needs correction.
112 BDAG, *s.vv.* ἀπολύτρωσις, λύτρωσις; Payne Smith, 2:3295.
113 See LEH, *s.v.* σωτήριον; BDAG, *s.v.* σωτήριος, b: "deliverance," "in our lit[erature] of Messianic salvation and the one who mediates it."
114 See BDAG, *s.v.* στηρίζω.
115 BDAG, *s.v.* στερεόω.
116 BDAG, *s.v.* βεβαιόω; Payne Smith, 2:4299–300; Aland and Juckel, *Briefe*, 3:259. On the "salvation" that "was declared at first by the Lord" and "was attested to us by those who heard him" (Heb 2:3), see Gräßer, 1:98–107.
117 Robert Henry Charles, "A Church Hymnal of the

Greßmann and Harris accepted it,[118] must be rejected, if only because of the "consensus between N and H."[119] The *hapax legomenon*, which is clearly attested in 6a, stands for κέρδος or ὠφέλεια,[120] and should not be translated as "surplus";[121] it refers neither to the Lord nor to the fear or the one who fears.[122] It means, in fact, the eschatological "gain" or "profit" of the "redemption" fixed and assured by God in 5b. The legal analogy that might have been drawn with "properly guaranteed security"[123] is transcendentally dynamited because there is no "life without death" in this world.[124]

Less abstract than the preceding statements 5a-6a is the conclusion in 6b, which in a terrace pattern links to ζωή/ܚܝܐ (*ḥayyē*), "life," and, by adding *-ān* to make a noun of the Pa. ܩܒܠ (*qabbel*), "receive," describes the recipients of divine life as ἄφθαρτοι.[125] This eschatological statement can be explained by referring to NHC I,*4* where "the author definitely echoes the language of I Cor. 15.53-54."[126] In fact a reference to Paul's own letters should suffice: *Οὕτως καὶ ἡ ἀνάστασις τῶν νεκρῶν. σπείρεται ἐν φθορᾷ, ἐγείρεται ἐν ἀφθαρσίᾳ* ("So it is with the resurrection of the dead. What is sown is perishable, what is raised is imperishable" [1 Cor 15:42]; see Excursus 28).[127] The plural of the *hapax legomenon* ܡܩܒܠܢܐ (*mqabblānā*) cannot here be translated as "guests."[128] Instead of "accept,"[129] the right shade of meaning is given by "receive," as in 41:3b.[130] 𝔊 would have used a nominalized participle with an accusative object, either *οἱ (ἀπο)δεχόμενοι αὐτήν*[131] or *οἱ ὑποδεχόμενοι αὐτήν* (see Excursus 41).[132]

First Century," *Times Literary Supplement* No. 430 (April 7, 1910) 124.

118 Greßmann, "Referate," 2900; Harris, 137.

119 Kittel, "Handschrift," 90.

120 BDAG, *s.vv.* κέρδος, ὠφέλεια; Payne Smith, 1:1650.

121 Contra Ungnad and Staerk, 38; Harnack, 70; Diettrich, 129; Kittel, "Handschrift," 90.

122 Contra Harris and Mingana, 2:398; Charlesworth, 138. Franzmann (p. 271) has "fear" in 5a and "gain" in 6a, but it is not clear to whom "his gain" refers.

123 See BDAG, *s.v.* βεβαιόω, 1.

124 Bauer, 621. Also cf. 10:2; 15:10; 28:6; 31:7; 38:3; and Table 1.

125 BDAG, *s.v.* ἄφθαρτος. Frankenberg's retroversion (p. 34) of ܕܠܐ ܚܒܠܐ (*d-lā ḥbālā*), "imperishable," as χωρὶς φθορᾶς is too literal.

126 Peel, *Rheginos*, 94, on the passage *Treat. Res.* 48,38–49,4.

127 See Payne Smith, 1:1179; Schrage, *1 Korinther*, 4:293–96; Aland and Juckel, *Briefe*, 1:478–79.

128 Harnack, 70; see Payne Smith, 2:3475; BDAG, *s.v.* ξένος, 2c. Even "those who participate in it [viz., immortal life]" is not an adequate translation (Harris, 137; Harris and Mingana, 2:398). Franzmann's translation of 6b (p. 271), "and the incorrupted receive it," is grammatically impossible.

129 As, for example, in Ungnad and Staerk, 38; Diettrich, 129.

130 Bauer, 621–22; cf. Charlesworth, 138, 140.

131 BDAG, *s.vv.* ἀποδέχομαι, 1; δέχομαι, 1.

132 Frankenberg, 34; BDAG, *s.v.* ὑποδέχομαι; Payne Smith, 2:3475.

41

Ode 41: Call to Rejoice, First-Person Address by the Son, and Christological Poem

(I) 1a Let us praise[a] the Lord, all his children,
1b and accept[b] the truth of his faith.
2a And with him his children will be known/acknowledged;
2b therefore let us sing in his love!

(II) 3a We rejoice[c] in the Lord by his grace,
3b and life we receive by his Messiah/Anointed One.
4a For a great day has shone upon us,
4b and wonderful is he who gave[d] of his praises.

(III) 5a So we will all league together on the name of the Lord,
5b and we will honor him in his goodness.
6a And may our faces shine in his light,
6b and our hearts shall/will meditate on his love by night and by day.
7 Let us exult out of the exultation over the Lord!

(IV) 8a They will be amazed, all those who see me,
8b because I am of another race.
9a For the Father of Truth remembered me,
9b he who gained/possessed me from the beginning.
10a For his wealth begat me
10b and the thought of his heart.

(V) 11a And his Word (Logos) is with us in all our way:
11b The Savior who gives life and does not reject our souls,
12 the man who was humbled and exalted by his own righteousness.
13 The Son of the Most High has appeared in the *plērōma* of his Father,
14 and the light dawned from that Word that was in him from the beginning.
15a The Christ/Messiah in truth is one,
15b and he was known/acknowledged from the foundation of the world,
16a that he might give life to souls forever by the truth of his name.

(VI) 16b A new hymn to the Lord from those who love him.
Hallelujah.

a 1a ܢܫܒܚ N; ܢܫܒܚܘܗܝ H.
b 1b ܘܢܩܒܠ N; ܘܢܩܒܠܘܗܝ H.
c 3a ܚܕܝܢ N; ܚܝܝܢ H.
d 4b H adds "us."

Introduction

Ode 41 is preserved in two Syriac manuscripts.[1] Although this Ode, which Everett Ferguson[2] includes in his annotated collection of sources, is a "cento,"[3] "it is necessary to attempt to find the unity of the *Ode*."[4] The division into three parts is shown formally already by the change from a section in the first person plural (1-7) to a shorter one in the first person singular (8-10) to a didactic and very important poem in the third person masculine singular (11-16a), followed by an "indirect doxology" (16b)[5] in the third person plural that is strongly influenced by the vocabulary of the Psalms and harks back, in its content, to the beginning of the Ode. The final monocolon[6] is not a later addition and is no more prosaic than many other lines in the Ode.[7]

Diettrich's attempt "to support Harnack's arguments from content by formal ones" and, by emending the "plural suffixes" of 11a to "singular suffixes," to excise 8a-11a as a six-part Jewish-Essene "fragment,"[8] must be taken as both arbitrary and unsuccessful. *Ode* 41 is of "purely Christian origin."[9] The only question is whether the "I" of 8-10 is one of the children of 1a;[10] or the "Messiah/Christ" explicitly named in 3b and 15a as the "Redeemer."[11]

For Schille, 11-16 is one of the "triumphal hymns of the cross,"[12] a subset of the "hymns of the Redeemer."[13] This classification is more acceptable than that of 3-6 as a "hymn of baptism."[14] Diettrich's remarks on "Syriac liturgies"[15] may have persuaded Rudolf Abramowski to call the whole of *Ode* 41 a "liturgy."[16] In 1-7 he even senses "the distinct rhythm of a Syriac original,"[17] while he has to make a "somewhat radical back-translation" to put 11-16a into its proper "form."[18] The first assertion is based on the "elimination of two minor additions" in 5a and 6b and is governed by a certain discomfort at the "assumption of a Greek original."[19] Later, in his discussion of the "two sons,"[20] Abramowski describes the christological "conclusion" of the Ode (11-16a) as a "hymn of the congregation,"[21] of a "congregation" having the same "enthusiasm that can be heard in the songs and prayers of its individual members."[22]

Having reconsidered the division between 2a (end of stanza I) and 2b (beginning of stanza II) by Franzmann and Lattke,[23] which is based on a circular argument

1 Mss.: Codex H, pp. 29b–30a; Codex N, 151r (s). Ed./trans.: Charlesworth, 139–43; Franzmann, 274–80; Lattke, 3:225–47.

2 Everett Ferguson, *Early Christians Speak: Faith and Life in the First Three Centuries* (3rd ed.; Abilene, Tex.: ACU Press, 1999) 148.

3 Harnack, 70.

4 Kittel, 27.

5 Lattke, *Oden*, 208, where the Ode is erroneously divided into two sections, 1-7 and 8-16a.

6 Contra Lattke, *Bedeutung*, 1:76, 180–81.

7 Contra Grimme, 125.

8 Diettrich, 130–31; cf. idem, "Liedersammlung," 534.

9 Spitta, 268, although one need not agree with him in everything.

10 Bernard, 129: "the baptized Christian rejoicing in his new birth"; Kittel, 27, 136; Greßmann, 470: one who "leads the congregation in prayer."

11 Spitta, 268; Labourt and Batiffol, 110; Charles Bruston, *Les plus anciens cantiques chrétiens: Traduits sur la seconde édition du texte syriaque avec une introduction et des notes* (Geneva: Jeheber; Paris: Fischbacher, 1912) 441; Bauer, 621. Verses 8-10 may even be editorially headed "Christ speaks" (e.g., Harris and Mingana, 2:400; Charlesworth, 141; Everett Ferguson, *Early Christians Speak: Faith and Life in the First Three Centuries* [3rd ed.; Abilene, Tex.: ACU Press, 1999] 148).

12 Schille, 43–45.

13 Ibid., 37.

14 Ibid., 60, 63; see already Bernard, 129.

15 Diettrich, 130.

16 Abramowski, 48.

17 Ibid., 48–49.

18 Ibid., 49.

19 Ibid., 48. The contradiction in Abramowski's judgment of 1-7 and 11-16a is resolved by this reference (p. 49): "Harris and Mingana's assumption that it originated in a bilingual Syriac-Greek area, so that the question of the original language remains open and is not felt to be a problem, is one that most strongly recommends itself" (see Harris and Mingana, 2:138–75, esp. 165). I will keep a sharp lookout for evidence of a Syriac original of 1-7 in what follows.

20 Abramowski, 52–62.

21 Ibid., 57.

22 Ibid., 61, again on 1-7.

23 Franzmann, 274–77; Lattke, *Oden*, 208.

derived from the readings of H in 1a-b, I will treat 2b as part of stanza I. The readings of N in 1a-b fit best with the text of 2b and are to be preferred. In any case, the reading of N in 1a is the *lectio difficilior* in the context of the exordium.

Interpretation

■ **1-2** Having decided in favor of the N readings for 1a-b (see above), I can now describe the structure of stanza I. It is framed by the first person plural summons to praise and song (1a, 2b; see Excursuses 21 and 26). Between them is another invitation (1b), where an alleged variant, ܢܣܒܘܢ ("they should gather"), in H does not exist.[24] This invitation, in which the "we" is identical with "all his children" (1a), is followed by a promise of future salvation in the third person plural: in 2a "it is intimated that by receiving the truth of His faith the sons of God will be recognized by Him."[25]

The "Lord" of *Ode* 41 (1a, 3a, 5a, 7, and 16b) is God, the "Father of Truth" (9a) and "Most High" (13), who is distinct from his "children/sons" (1a, 2a) as well as from his "Christ/Messiah" (3b, 15a), his "son" par excellence (13 in the context of 11-16a; see Table 9). Even if the plural of ܝܠܘܕܐ (*yallūdā*), which occurs only in 1a, did *not* represent νήπιοι[26] but τέκνα or παιδία,[27] νήπιοι would still have to be inserted into Käsemann's verdict: "There is no difference between υἱοί, τέκνα, and παιδία."[28] The Pa. ܫܒܚ (*šabbaḥ*), from the same root as ܬܫܒܘܚܬܐ (*tešbuḥtā*) in 4b and 16b, in parallel to "sing" (2b) and "exult" (7), probably here means to "praise" rather than to "glorify." So it corresponds not to δοξάζω[29] but to αἰνέω or—even more likely—to ὑμνέω.[30]

The key word "faith" in 1b should not be attached directly to the term "children" in 1a, which would introduce the misleading concept of ܝܠܘܕܐ ܒܗܝܡܢܘܬܐ (*yallūdē b-haymānūtā* = νεόφυτοι) into the text (cf. *Acta Andreae et Matthiae* 32).[31] Before discussing the phrase "the truth of his faith," an excursus will consider the Pe. ܢܣܒ (*nsab*) and the Pa. ܩܒܠ (*qabbel*).

Excursus 41: "Take," "Accept," and "Receive" in the *Odes of Solomon*

Like λαμβάνω with some of its compounds,[32] ܢܣܒ (*nsab*) covers the whole spectrum of meanings from "take"/"grasp" (active) via "accept"/"take up" to "receive"/"obtain" (passive). When ܩܒܠ (*qabbel*) corresponds to δέχομαι or any of its compounds,[33] the active connotation is generally absent. The reactive and passive senses of δέχομαι and λαμβάνω "become easily interchangeable."[34] Sometimes δέχομαι can even mean "take" or "grasp,"[35] and it is then translated by ܩܒܠ (*qabbel*) as well as by ܢܣܒ (*nsab*) (e.g. Luke 16:6-7; 22:17). On the whole, ܩܒܠ (*qabbel*) covers both the Greek verbs and a number of their compounds,[36] while ܢܣܒ (*nsab*) equates to λαμβάνω

24 This reading, still found in Burkitt (p. 380), is based on a misprint in Harris's edition (1909 and 1911, on this passage). In his personal copy of the second edition, which belonged to Tony Brown and is now in the possession of Majella Franzmann, Harris corrected both the misprint and the translation in his own hand. The reading ܢܣܒܘܢ in H is quite certain (see Charlesworth, *Manuscripts*, 85 line 5). This renders nugatory the text-critical expositions of Schultheß, 256; Frankenberg, 43; and Kittel, "Handschrift," 90.

25 Harris and Mingana, 2:401.

26 BDAG, *s.v.* νήπιος.

27 Payne Smith, 1:1596.

28 Käsemann, *Wandering People,* 148 n. 178 = *Gottesvolk*, 93 n. 10; he uses this quotation of *Ode* 41:1-2a as evidence for his contention that the "redeemed" become "sons of God" "primarily by becoming sons or children of the Redeemer" (*Wandering People,* 148; *Gottesvolk,* 92), which is not immediately relevant here. The term νήπιοι would not stand in opposition to τέλειοι, unlike Heb 5:13-14 (cf. BDAG, *s.v.* τέλειος, 2b). "Children/sons" is probably not meant to include all God's creatures, but only the redeemed or to be redeemed people of the *Odes of Solomon*.

29 Frankenberg, 34.

30 Payne Smith, 2:4023–24.

31 *AAAp* 2.1:114 line 15; William Wright, *Apocryphal Acts of the Apostles* (ed. from Syriac manuscripts in the British Museum and other libraries with English translations and notes; London, 1871; repr., Amsterdam: Philo, 1968) ܩܒܗ; Lampe, 905: "newly converted."

32 Gerhard Delling, "λαμβάνω, ἀναλαμβάνω, ἀνάλημψις, κτλ.," *ThWNT* 4 (1942) 5–16; *TDNT* 4:5–15.

33 Walter Grundmann, "δέχομαι, κτλ.," *ThWNT* 2 (1935) 49–59; *TDNT* 2:50–59.

34 Grundmann "δέχομαι," *ThWNT* 2:49; *TDNT* 2:50.

35 BDAG, *s.v.* δέχομαι, 2.

36 Payne Smith, 2:3468–69.

κτλ., but can also be used to translate such verbs as αἴρω and κομίζομαι.[37]

In the *Odes of Solomon*, ܩܒܠ (*qabbel*) occurs ten times and in some passages is expressly used as a synonym of ܢܣܒ (*nsab̲*), as witnessed by the context of 9:5-7 and 31:6-7. That "giving" as opposite or antecedent to "taking/receiving" is found only in connection with ܢܣܒ (*nsab̲*) is probably accidental.[38] The root ܢܣܒ occurs only twenty times, all in the Pe., while a number of words derived from the other root ܩܒܠ are also used, namely, in addition to ܠܘܩܒܠ (*luqb̲al* = ⲟⲩⲃⲉ in ℭ)[39] and ܣܩܘܒܠܐ/ܣܩܘܒܠܝܐ (*saqqub̲lā/ saqqub̲lāyā*),[40] the two *hapax legomena* ܩܘܒܠܐ (*qubbālā*) and ܡܩܒܠܢܐ (*mqabblānā*). The first of them is used for the reciprocal "reception" of the bright day and the dark night (16:17), while the plural of the second characterizes "those who receive" eternal life (40:6b).

Next come the more or less passive uses of ܩܒܠ (*qabbel*). "Asking" and "receiving" belong together (7:10b), as they do in the New Testament (cf. Matt 7:8 and Luke 11:10, although both those passages use λαμβάνει/ܢܣܒ [*nāseb̲*]). One can "receive" the knowledge of the Most High (8:8b) and also his mind (9:5b). The redeemed will "receive" of the kindness and grace of the Lord in paradise (20:9b). The invitation to "receive" joy (31:6b) gives the verb a slight bias toward the more active "accept." Those who "received" the blessing of the redeemed Redeemer live in consequence of it (17:14a). This Redeemer is the Head and Kyrios Christos (17:15-16) through whom the speakers of 41:1-7 also "receive" life (3b). Compared to the soteriological heights of these statements, the Pa. ܩܒܠ (*qabbel*) used in 23:11a is of no importance: "A wheel received it [viz., the letter]." The image of 11:14b is concerned only with the dew, as can be seen from the use of ἐδροσίσθη in 𝔊: "my face received the dew [= was bedewed]." In 18:7b, it is quite uncertain whether the verb has a passive meaning: "thou [viz., the Lord] wilt collect from every place."

The important objects of ܩܒܠ have so far been "*gnōsis*" (8:8), "mind" (9:5), "blessing" (17:14), "joy" (31:6), and "life" (41:3), to which can be added the following objects of ܢܣܒ (*nsab̲*): "grace" (5:3a; 23:2b), "a wreath" (9:10), "salvation" (15:6b), "the mixture" (19:5b), "drink" (30:2a), and "truth" (41:1b; see below).[41] The partial synonymity of the two Syriac verbs is emphasized by the fact that "*gnōsis*" and "life" also appear as objects of the more frequently used ܢܣܒ (11:4 [in 𝔊 ἔλαβον] and 31:7b). The term ܢܣܒ also occurs in the sense of "take away" (4:13d [object: gifts]; 14:3b [object: kindness]) as does the Coptic verb ϥⲓ (*fi*) in 25:9b (object: sickness); the Syriac of that passage is: "thou didst cause infirmity to pass from me." In a positive sense, ܢܣܒ is altogether active in 9:10 (see above), 22:9a (where ϫⲓ [*či*] is used also in the active sense, unlike in 6:14 ℭ), 23:7b ("take" beside "snatch"), and probably in 31:7b also (see above). The objects "dead bones" (22:9) and "the letter" (23:7; see on 23:11a above) differ somewhat from those more commonly found. A more passive tendency cannot be excluded in the following passages: 7:4a ("that I might receive him"; although it is parallel to 4b, "that I might put him on"), 17:4b ("I received the face and figure of a new person"), 23:19a (the Son of Truth "inherited everything and took possession" from the Most High Father; on "inherit," cf. 31:7a), and 30:2a ("take the drink"). The term ܢܣܒ (*nsab̲*) is unmistakably passive—in spite of having a direct object—in 5:3a ("freely I received thy grace"), 9:7b (without a direct object), 11:4 ("I received his understanding"), 15:6b ("received salvation"), 23:2b ("receive it [grace]"), and 31:2b ("Contempt suffered immobility").

Ode 41:1b would seem to belong to this last group. But, because of the construction with the modal imperfect (as in 41:1a and 41:2b), "receive" is not as good a translation as "accept" for the Syriac verb, which may correspond to the Greek λαμβάνω.[42]

The direct object of ܢܣܒ (*nessab̲*) is not the individual term ἀλήθεια/ܫܪܪܐ (*šrārā*), "truth," which will recur

37 Payne Smith, 2:2392; see also BDAG, *s.vv.* αἴρω; κομίζομαι; λαμβάνω.

38 In 5:3a, the Coptic text has "thou hast given" in place of the Syriac "I received." In 9:10, "gave" follows "took"; the object of both verbs is the "wreath."

39 See the concordance, *s.v.* "against" (6:5; 8:19; 25:3, 11).

40 See the concordance, *s.v.* "against:" "opposing, adversary, standing in the way" (6:5; 23:14[N] and 23:14[H]).

41 The idiomatic expressions in 19:6b ("conceive") and 29:9b ("take the victory") can be left to one side.

42 BDAG, *s.v.* λαμβάνω, 4 and 7; see also Tsakonas, 178; Fanourgakis, 173.

later, but the whole genitive phrase of 1b (see Excursuses 1 and 34). In fact, the main emphasis is on the term πίστις/ܗܝܡܢܘܬܐ (*haymānūṯā*), "faith," with its third masculine singular suffix referring to God the Lord in 1a, which corresponds to αὐτοῦ. That does not answer the question whether this is God's own "faithfulness" (cf., e.g., *Pss. Sol.* 8:28 [ἡ πίστις σου]; 14:1 [πιστὸς κύριος τοῖς ἀγαπῶσιν ἐν ἀληθείᾳ]; Rom 3:3 [πίστις τοῦ θεοῦ])[43] as in 4:5, or whether, as in 16:4, it is an objective "faith"—or "trust"—in the Lord (cf. Mark 11:22 [πίστις θεοῦ]).[44] The "truth" of the "body of faith" that "acc[ording] to God's will, is to be believed"[45] is not under consideration here any more than the ecclesiastical πίστις ἀληθείας ("belief in the truth") in 2 Thess 2:13, following on from οἱ μὴ πιστεύσαντες τῇ ἀληθείᾳ ("[all] who did not believe the truth") in 2:12.[46]

The suffix of ܠܘܬ (*lwāṯ*) in 2a[47] also refers to God the Lord and not to the Revealer (as, e.g., in John 10:14).[48] The Ethpe. of ܝܕܥ (*ʾiḏaʿ*), "to be acknowledged," bears the connotation of "to be chosen" perhaps even more emphatically than in 15b (see Excursus 7).[49] The passage closest in meaning to this, apart from 6:6b-c, is the statement referring to the people of God in *Ps. Sol.* 17:27c: γνώσεται γὰρ αὐτοὺς ὅτι πάντες υἱοὶ θεοῦ εἰσιν αὐτῶν ("For he shall know [i.e., acknowledge] them, that they are all the sons [i.e., children] of their God."[50] In this pseudepigraphical psalm, which is "of the greatest importance for the Messianology (Christology) of early Judaism and the New Testament,"[51] the plural of υἱός is meant inclusively, as here in 2a.[52]

As has been noted earlier, 2b, as the direct consequence of 2a, belongs to stanza I, forming a parallel frame with 1a. In spite of its close relationship to 16:3 (in the context of 16:2-4), it is not certain whether ἀγάπη αὐτοῦ/ܚܘܒܗ (*ḥubbeh*) is the "love" *by* or *for* the Lord (cf. 6:2; 7:19; 40:4; and see Excursus 2). This question will recur in 6b. In any case one can agree with Frankenberg's retroversion, διὰ τοῦτο ᾄδωμεν ἐν τῇ ἀγάπῃ αὐτοῦ (see Excursus 26).[53]

■ **3-4** There are some problems in these two bicola, on the one hand, caused by variant readings in 3a and 4b, and, on the other, concerned with the meanings of some important terms and in part with the question of the original language of the *Odes*. If one limits the text to the readings of H,[54] 3a and 3b collide unacceptably. For the plural of the adjective ܚܝܐ (*ḥayyā*), used as a verb, with its enclitic first plural pronoun,[55] has the same meaning as the longer expression "we receive life" in 3b. In the Greek original or translation from the Syriac, it would be slightly different, for ζῶμεν could have been parallel to a suitable verb of receiving (see Excursus 41 above) that had σωτηρίαν or σωτήριον as direct object (cf., e.g., 2 Tim 2:10 and Heb 1:14 or Luke 3:6). But that

43 BDAG, *s.v.* πίστις, 1a.

44 BDAG, *s.v.* πίστις, 2a; cf. Payne Smith, 1:238.

45 BDAG, *s.v.* πίστις, 3, on πίστις θεοῦ in Ignatius *Eph.* 16:2.

46 See Wolfgang Trilling, *Der zweite Brief an die Thessalonicher* (EKKNT 14; Zurich: Benziger; Neukirchen-Vluyn: Neukirchener Verlag, 1980) 113, 121–22. Connecting 1b to 18:15 (and 31:2) could be justified only if, in addition to the "sense of firmness," there were a stronger emphasis on "truth" as the "sphere of God" (Bultmann, "Untersuchungen," 159–61 = idem, *Exegetica*, 170–72). In that case, one might go a step further and inquire whether there is an allusion to John 1:17 and 14:6 (see BDAG, *s.v.* ἀλήθεια, 2b).

47 The variant reading "ܠܘܬ (1 m.)" in N does not exist (contra Harris and Mingana, vol. 1, on this passage). Charlesworth points out this error, but then accepts the translation of ܠܘܬܗ (*lwāṯeh*) as "by Him" (Harris and Mingana, 2:399; Charlesworth, 140–41). One can thus quote his own criticism of Mar Yosip against him: "He must have blindly copied Harris-Mingana's translation at this point" (Charlesworth, 141 n. 1). The prepositional expression ܠܘܬܗ (see Payne Smith, 2:1918: *apud, chez*) does not represent ὑπ᾽ αὐτῷ (cf. 1 Cor 8:3; Gal 4:9) but either παρ᾽ αὐτῷ (Frankenberg, 34; BDAG, *s.v.* παρά) or πρὸς αὐτόν (BDAG, *s.v.* πρός) and should be translated into English as "with/near/beside him" rather than "to him" (contra Emerton, 729; Franzmann, 275).

48 Contra Harnack, 71; Bultmann, "Bedeutung," 117–18 = idem, *Exegetica*, 73–74.

49 See BDAG, *s.v.* γινώσκω, 7.

50 Rahlfs, 2:487; Holm-Nielsen, 103 and note b; see also *OTP* 2:667.

51 Lattke, "Salomoschriften," 807.

52 Lit., "his sons." The inclusive term "children" (1a) is synonymous with "sons" (cf. 31:4; 40:1).

53 Frankenberg, 34; BDAG, *s.v.* ᾄδω; Payne Smith, 1:1136.

54 Harris and Mingana, vol. 1, on this passage; Charlesworth, 139; Franzmann, 274.

55 Payne Smith, 1:1253.

ܚܝܐ (*ḥayyē*) here corresponds to ζωήν as object is really most uncertain.[56] If these speculations about 𝔊 should be correct, they could be supported by reference to passages where "live" and "be redeemed" occur together (17:14a-b; 34:6; 38:16a).

The relationship of words, or perhaps only of meaning, between 3a and 3b, however, does not guarantee that "H's variant is better in light of Odes 5:3 and 31:7."[57] The variant in N (ܚܕܝܢܢ [*ḥāḏēn-nan*]), in the first place, follows on better from 2b in stanza I. Second, the participle of the Pe. ܚܕܐ/ܚܕܝ (*ḥḏā/ḥḏī*), which can mean ἀγαλλιάω (cf. Luke 1:47; Hab 3:18; Isa 61:10 LXX),[58] εὐφραίνομαι,[59] or χαίρω,[60] does not clash with the statement in 3b. And third, as Franzmann herself noted,[61] "joy" in 23:1-2 and 31:6-7 forms "a word-pair" with "grace" (cf. also 7:2, 17; 15:1; 32:1; Excursus 32). Since the prepositional expression ܒܡܪܝܐ (*b-māryā*), "in the Lord," corresponding to ἐν κυρίῳ, refers to God the Lord, such passages as Phil 3:1; 4:4; and 4:10 cannot be adduced directly for the explication of 3a. For in these and many other Pauline sayings containing ἐν κυρίῳ, κύριος is the Lord Jesus.[62] The "joy" of the apostle and the recipients of his letters is thus based on "their shared connection with Christ."[63] This description could be modified, with a backward glance at 2a-b, to depict a joyful connection with God, which is complemented, somewhat inflatedly, by the instrumental phrase (ἐν) χάριτι αὐτοῦ/ܒܛܝܒܘܬܗ (*b-ṭaybūṯeh*), "by his grace."[64]

Verse 3b has, as parallel to the phrase just discussed, another instrumental prepositional expression ἐν (τῷ) Χριστῷ αὐτοῦ/ܒܡܫܝܚܗ (*ba-mšīḥeh*), "by his Messiah/ Anointed One," which is not completely equivalent to the common (deutero-)Pauline expression ἐν Χριστῷ.[65] For the "Anointed of the Lord," reference must naturally be made to *Ps. Sol.* 18:7 (cf. also *Pss. Sol.* 17:32; 18:5).[66] In the Ode things are even clearer, since the Christ/ Messiah, who shatters the narrow bounds of politics, is expressly distinguished, by the use of the third masculine singular suffix, from God the Lord (cf. 9:3; 29:6).[67] There are other passages in which—as in the *Psalms of Solomon*—the Christ/Messiah is himself called "Lord" (17:16; 24:1[N]; 29:6; 39:11; see Table 9). The remainder of 3b has already been discussed above. Specific traces of a Syriac "original"[68] have not yet come to light.

Using the post-positioned particle ܓܝܪ (*gēr*),[69] where Greek γάρ would also be placed second or third,[70] 4a expresses the main reason for joy and redemption/ life and thus bears more than a "little relation to the verses preceding" 4a-b.[71] The Aph. of ܢܗܪ (*nhar*) is less ambiguous here than in 11:14a;[72] its subject[73] is not to be

56 Payne Smith, 1:1254.

57 Charlesworth, 141 n. 6, with additional reference to 7:22, 26; 23:4; 31:3.

58 BDAG, *s.v.* ἀγαλλιάω.

59 BDAG, *s.v.* εὐφραίνω, 2.

60 BDAG, *s.v.* χαίρω, 1; see also Payne Smith, 1:1198–99.

61 Franzmann, 276.

62 Joseph A. Fitzmyer, "κύριος, κτλ.," *EWNT* 2 (1981) 817–18; *EDNT* 2:330.

63 Joachim Gnilka, *Der Philipperbrief* (HThKNT 10.3; Freiburg: Herder, 1968; 4th ed., 1987) 173.

64 Cf. 6:6; 23:2, 4[N]; 31:7; 37:4; see also Excursus 33. 𝔊 could also have used διὰ τῆς χάριτος αὐτοῦ in place of ἐν χάριτι αὐτοῦ or χάριτι αὐτοῦ (see BDAG, *s.v.* χάρις; linguistically, cf., e.g., Acts 15:11).

65 Ferdinand Hahn, "Χριστός, κτλ.," *EWNT* 3 (1983) 1157–60; *EDNT* 3:482–84. Although not impossible, it is less likely in this case that 𝔊 had διὰ (τοῦ) Χριστοῦ αὐτοῦ (see BDAG, *s.v.* Χριστός).

66 See Holm-Nielsen, 104, 108; Lattke, "Psalms," 856.

67 Lattke, "Messias-Stellen," 442 = idem, *Bedeutung*, 4:103.

68 Abramowski, 49.

69 Which should be added in Lattke, "Wörter," 290 = idem, *Bedeutung*, 4:138.

70 Contra Frankenberg, 34: ὅτι.

71 Contra Franzmann, 278.

72 Harris and Mingana, 2:268, 401.

73 The subject of 4a is not the "Lord" (Greßmann, 470) but the "great day" (Bauer, 622; Harris and Mingana, 2:399). In 11:14a, however, the question whether ܐܢܗܪ (*ʾanhar*) is intended as a third masculine singular transitive (Greßmann, 448; Bauer, 591; see the commentary on that verse in this work) or a third feminine plural intransitive (Harris and Mingana, 2:266: "My eyes were enlightened") is still undecided. For the intransitive sense, in both passages, the possible Greek equivalents would be λάμπω (BDAG, *s.v.*), φαίνω (BDAG, *s.v.*), or perhaps φωτίζω (BDAG, *s.v.*; see also Payne Smith, 2:2298–99).

equated with the day of baptism,[74] the "Day of Atonement,"[75] or even the great day of the "Last Judgment."[76] Although it would be erroneous to speak of "the *fact* of Easter," Diettrich's decision "for Easter" is closer to the point.[77] In a broader sense, however, the great day may be the epiphany of the Redeemer (see below and cf. 2 Tim 1:10).[78] The key word "wonderful" in 4b makes possible a further explanation of the expression *ἡμέρα μεγάλη*/ܝܘܡܐ ܪܒܐ (*yawmā rabbā*), "great day." It has escaped Harris and Mingana[79] and also Bauer[80] that the bicolon 41:4a-b, like 11:5a,[81] could be a "missing link" between Ps 117:23-24 LXX and *Barn.* 6:4, where we read, in the second proof from Scripture for the "resurrection of the Lord" or the total "Christ event": *Αὕτη ἐστὶν ἡ ἡμέρα ἡ μεγάλη καὶ θαυμαστή, ἣν ἐποίησεν ὁ κύριος* ("This is the great and wonderful day which the Lord has made").[82] This rather later statement cannot, however, be retroactively incorporated into the *Odes of Solomon* to cancel the distinction just made between the "day" and the "Lord."[83]

Although Bultmann did not yet know of the existence of N and its alleged omission of ܠܢ (*lan*) in 4b, Charlesworth bases his preference for the H text on the following quotation from Bultmann's review,[84] which, in any case, is relevant to the whole of the we-passage 1-7: "The singer is not a solitary individual. He is singing for a like-minded congregation."[85] But ܠܢ could equally be a (dittographic) addition in H (see 4a above), especially since the common word "to give" demands an indirect object (cf. linguistically Matt 25:8). The construction with the preposition ܡܢ (*men*) in place of a direct object speaks for a Greek *Vorlage* with *δίδωμι ἔκ τινος*.[86] If 𝔊 had *ὁ διδούς*, it would be possible to read ܝܗܒ as the participle *yāheḇ*.[87] However, both manuscripts have a dot *under* the verb,[88] so it should probably be *yaḇ*. The plural of ܬܫܒܚܬܐ (*tešbuḥtā*) cannot be interpreted as any sort of powerful "angelic beings"[89] or as "glories."[90] Like 40:2b the meaning is "praises" of the Lord, and thus, perhaps, "the ability . . . to praise him."[91] Whether one accepts this further explanation or not, among the Greek equivalents are the genitives *ὕμνων* (cf. Eph 5:19; Col 3:16), *αἰνέσεων*, *ᾀσμάτων*, and even *ᾠδῶν* (see Excursus 21).[92] In place of Bauer's interpretation, one might ask whether the congregation was taught the celestial "songs of praise" of the "angels," an idea that would resonate with the enthusiasm manifested in 3a

74 Bernard, 78–79, on 15:3; 129, on 41:4 and 41:6: "baptismal illumination."

75 On *μεγάλη ἡμέρα*, see BDAG, *s.v.* *ἡμέρα*, 2d; *Kerygma Petri*, 2: Erich Klostermann, *Apocrypha I: Reste des Petrusevangeliums, der Petrusapokalypse und des Kerygma Petri* (KlT 3; Bonn: Marcus & Weber, 1903) 15 line 11.

76 BDAG, *s.v.* *ἡμέρα*, 4bβ.

77 Diettrich, 131.

78 See BDAG, *s.v.* *ἐπιφάνεια*, 1. Charlesworth (p. 142) rejects Leclercq's equation of the great day with the day of resurrection and says: "The Odist, however, is probably referring to the incarnation."

79 Harris and Mingana, 1:49–53.

80 Bauer, 622.

81 See commentary on that passage.

82 Lake, 1:358–59; Lindemann and Paulsen, 38–39; see also Ehrman, 2:30–31; and Prostmeier, 251–55.

83 Contra Greßmann, 470. Franzmann distinguishes between "a great day" and "he who gave," but speculates, in the same vein as Greßmann's translation, that "[i]t may be that the 3rd sing[ular] masc[uline] subj[ect]s (the great day, the amazing one) are to be interpreted synonymously (cf. 7:23; 15:1-2)" (see Franzmann, 275, 278).

84 Rudolf Bultmann, "Ein jüdisch-christliches Psalmbuch aus dem ersten Jahrhundert," *MPTh* 7 (1910) 26.

85 Charlesworth, 142 n. 8, where "et" should be corrected to "er."

86 BDAG, *s.v.* *δίδωμι*, 1; Payne Smith, 1:1565. Frankenberg's retroversion with *μετέδωκεν* is less likely, to say nothing of the singular *τῆς δόξης αὐτοῦ* (Frankenberg, 34; cf. Diettrich, 130: "of his glory").

87 See Bauer, 622: "who gives us."

88 See Brockelmann, *Grammatik* §5.

89 BDAG, *s.v.* *δόξα*, 4.

90 Contra Kittel, 136.

91 Bauer, 622. Emerton (p. 729) and Franzmann (p. 275) correctly differentiate their translations—"of his praises," "from his praises"—from that of Harris and Mingana (2:399) and Charlesworth (p. 140), "of His glory," which is based on an interference with the text.

92 See Payne Smith, 2:4028.

(cf. *Protev.* 15:3).[93] It has already been noted that the *hapax legomenon* ܬܡܝܗܐ (*tmīhā*), "wonderful," belongs to the vocabulary of the Psalms and is probably quoted directly from Ps 117:23 LXX.[94]

■ **5-7** The five imperfects of 5-7 take up again the "pointing to the future" or "modal coloring" of the four verbs in 1-2, which does not make translation any easier.[95] The lack of intertextuality, except for 6b, means that it is hard to draw conclusions about the vocabulary of any biblical models. As for the poetic structure of stanza III, this five-section conclusion to the first part of *Ode* 41 "has a unique position."[96] For it is the extra monocolon, 7, that is the true conclusion, and it has similarities with 2b (the conclusion of stanza I) and 4b (the conclusion of stanza II), but it does not form "a parallel bicolon with an inserted tricolon" with 5a[97] nor yet an *inclusio* with 2b.[98] In spite of the discrete character of each of these five lines, 5a-b and 6a-b should be treated as bicola, which is more clearly expressed, by the "word-pair ܐܦ̈ܐ - ܠܒܐ" in the second pair of lines, than in the first.[99]

As in 39:8a, 5a uses ܗܟܠ (*hāḵēl*), "so," to draw the conclusion from the messianic promise of salvation in stanza II. The expression ܟܠܢ ܐܟܚܕܐ (*kullan ʾaḵḥdā*), "all together," corresponding to πάντες ὁμοῦ, connects the oathbound congregation to the children of God in stanza I (1a, 2a) and at the same time separates them from all the others of 8a, that is, the ones in the second part of the Ode.[100] The Ethpe. of ܫܘܐ (*šwā*), "to league," is a *hapax legomenon* meaning "with . . . ܥܠ of the object"–and in this case without any negative connotation of conspiracy[101]–"to be of the same opinion, to agree, make an agreement."[102] This harmonious association[103] will and must be founded on the mighty name of the Lord, "Lord" here and in 7 still meaning God, and ܥܠ (*ʿal*), unlike its use in 33:13c, corresponding to περί rather than to ἐπί (cf. linguistically Matt 18:19; and see Excursus 39).[104]

Both the objective suffix of the *hapax legomenon* ܝܩܪ (Pa. *yaqqar*), "to honor," and the possessive suffix of ܛܒܘܬܐ (*ṭāḇūṯā*), "goodness," refer to God the Lord, not to his name. The *Vorlage* of the verb in 5b is most likely to have been τιμάω (cf. John 5:23; 8:49),[105] and God's "goodness" would have been expressed in 𝔊 by ἀγαθότης (cf. Wis 7:26; 12:22) or ἀγαθωσύνη (cf. *Barn.* 2:9).[106]

In 6a, unlike 40:4c, the Pe. ܢܗܪ (*nhar*), "shine," forms part of the vocabulary of transfiguration, which is, after all, not limited to Jesus (compare Matt 13:43 [ἐκλάμψουσιν] to Matt 17:2 [ἔλαμψεν]; see Excursus 8). This also makes a connection with the Aph. in 4a, which may not have been as clearly paronomastic in 𝔊.[107] However, 𝔊 could have used ἐπιφώσκω[108] and φῶς as "the element and sphere of the divine" forming a play on words contained within 6a (see Excursus 10).[109] In place of "in his light,"[110] the prepositional expression ܒܢܘܗܪܗ (*b-nuhreh*) could equally be translated as "by his light," thus placing stress on the instrumental aspect.[111] With a look forward to 14 in the third part of *Ode* 41–and perhaps another backward to 3b–readers would then be even more definitely reminded of the Johannine Jesus.[112]

93 BDAG, *s.v.* ὕμνος; see Oscar Cullman, "Kindheitsevangelien," *NTApo*[5] 1 (1987) 344; "Infancy Gospels," *NTApoc* 1:432.
94 See Payne Smith, 2:4456; BDAG, *s.v.* θαυμαστός.
95 See Nöldeke §266.
96 Diettrich, 130.
97 Contra Franzmann, 278.
98 Contra Lattke, *Oden*, 79.
99 Franzmann, 278, who also notes the "strikingly similar vocabulary" in 40:4.
100 See BDAG, *s.v.* ὁμοῦ, 2; Payne Smith, 1:147, 1195.
101 Payne Smith, 2:4079; LSJ, *s.v.* συμφωνέω, II 8.
102 Payne Smith, *Dictionary*, 562.
103 See Diettrich, 131; Bauer, 622.
104 Contra Frankenberg, 34; see BDAG, *s.vv.* περί, 1a; συμφωνέω, 3.
105 BDAG, *s.v.* τιμάω; Payne Smith, 1:1623.
106 BDAG, *s.vv.* ἀγαθότης, ἀγαθωσύνη; Payne Smith, 1:1439.
107 See Payne Smith, 2:2297; BDAG, *s.vv.* ἐκλάμπω, λάμπω.
108 BDAG, *s.v.* ἐπιφώσκω.
109 BDAG, *s.v.* φῶς, 1b; see Payne Smith, 2:2301.
110 Bauer, 622.
111 Diettrich, 131.
112 See John 1:4-5, 7-9; 3:19, 21; 8:12; 9:5; 12:35-36, 46; cf. Luke 2:32.

Anyone who in Hellenistic times was versed in the Psalms would recognize the description of the righteous believer in Ps 1:2b LXX: *ἐν τῷ νόμῳ αὐτοῦ* (= *κυρίου*) *μελετήσει ἡμέρας καὶ νυκτός* ("and in his law will he meditate day and night").[113] The Syriac translation[114] corresponds to the Hebrew[115] as well as to the Greek text and also displays similarities to 6b. Charlesworth quotes the first half of Harris and Mingana's conclusion, "we may possibly be justified in inferring an actual dependence of the Ode upon the *Syriac* Psalm,"[116] but omits their caution, "though the translation is a natural one and the ideas simple."[117] Apart from the important differences ("love" instead of "law," "our hearts" instead of "he," the sequence of "night" and "day"), it is the minor ones that argue *against* a direct influence of the Syriac Psalm on the Ode, namely, the repetition of the preposition ܒ (*b-*) before "night" and "day," which is the common usage in the *NTSy* for translations of *ἡμέρας καὶ νυκτός*, *νυκτὸς καὶ ἡμέρας* and *νύκτα καὶ ἡμέραν* (except Acts 9:24).[118] The change in sequence of the temporal terms has nothing to do with the beginning of "divine service in the evening,"[119] since it is already much commoner in the New Testament and the Apostolic Fathers than in the LXX.[120]

It is indeed "interesting to note the substitution of Love for Law."[121] The total avoidance of the Jewish term *νόμος*[122] in the *Odes of Solomon* is still "significant"[123] even if the psalm verse in question is read in (a translation of) Buber's German translation: "[O the happiness of the man who . . . enjoys HIS *direction*] murmuring about his *direction* by day and night!"[124] Because of the model that is both used and altered, the expression ܒܚܘܒܗ (*b-ḥubbeh*), which has already occurred in 2b and which again corresponds to *ἐν τῇ ἀγάπῃ αὐτοῦ*,[125] should not here be translated as "in His love"[126] but as "about his love"[127] or "on his love."[128] Otherwise the Ethpa. of ܗܓܐ (*hgā*), "meditate," would correspond to *μελετάω* used absolutely.[129] The subject of 6b is an improper plural of *καρδία*/ܠܒܐ (*lebbā*), as can be seen by comparison with other passages (7:23; 8:1; 32:1; Excursus 4). The "love" of the Lord, the Most High, is mentioned elsewhere in connection with the heart as the rational "symbol of the inner person" (16:2; 18:1).[130]

Frankenberg obeys the rules of his own retroversion

113 Rahlfs, 2:1; Brenton, 699.
114 *OTSy*, pt. 2 fasc. 3, p. 1: ܒܢܡܘܣܗ ܢܬܗܓܐ ܐܝܡܡܐ ܘܠܠܝܐ (*b-nāmōseh neṯhaggē ʾimāmā ʾu-lēlyā*).
115 *BHS*, 1087.
116 Charlesworth, 142.
117 Harris and Mingana, 2:403.
118 See citations in BDAG, *s.v.* *ἡμέρα*, 1a.
119 Contra Diettrich, 131 n. 1.
120 Hatch and Redpath, 954–56; Kraft, *Clavis*, 305.
121 Harris and Mingana, 2:403.
122 Payne Smith, 2:2383–84.
123 Charlesworth, 142.
124 Martin Buber, *Die Schriftwerke: Verdeutscht* (new ed.; Cologne/Olten: Hegner, 1962) 9 [emphasis added]. Harris and Mingana (2:403) draw far-reaching conclusions from the fact that the author of the *Odes of Solomon* ("the Odist") not only does not mention the law—or the Torah (Georg Steins, "Tora," *LThK*³ 10 [2001] 110–12)—but "that he substitutes for it as well as avoids it. This single consideration is of such weight that we may be sure *he is neither a Jew nor a Jewish proselyte*." Charlesworth (p. 142) both criticizes and amplifies this verdict: "This statement, however, is ambiguous, and may lead to the assumption that . . . the Odist . . . must have been a Gentile. . . . The meaning is that he is not a Jew who rejected Christianity, but a Jew who was converted to Christianity: a Jewish Christian" (see Emerton, 684, and James H. Charlesworth, "Solomon, Odes of," *The Anchor Bible Dictionary* [ed. David Noel Freedman; 6 vols.; New York: Doubleday, 1992] 6:114). Whether 6b can really be used to identify the author is debatable in view of the part that the "love of God" plays already in the Old Testament (see Thomas Söding, "Liebe III. Biblisch-theologisch," *LThK*³ 6 [1997] 910; on the aspect 'love' in the Old Testament "concept of law," see Gottfried Quell, "[*δίκη, κτλ.*] Der Rechtsgedanke im AT," *ThWNT* 2 [1935] 177 no 3; "The Concept of Law in the OT," *TDNT* 2:175 n. 3).
125 Frankenberg, 34.
126 E.g., Greßmann, 470; Bauer, 622; Lattke, *Oden*, 209: "in seiner Liebe"; Harris and Mingana, 2:399; Charlesworth, 140.
127 Ungnad and Staerk, 38: "über seine Liebe."
128 Franzmann, 275.
129 Payne Smith, 1:966; BDAG, *s.v.* *μελετάω*, 3.
130 See Schroer and Staubli, *Körpersymbolik*, 46.

of 40:4a-b, reconstructing the joyful ending, 7, by σκιρτήσωμεν ἀγαλλιάσει τοῦ κυρίου,[131] which unfortunately destroys the paronomasia. A glance at Luke 1:44 will show that this scholarly hypothesis is not at all certain.[132] More important than determining the exact Greek wording is the recognition that this is an objective genitive, that is, "exultation over the Lord" (cf. 8:1; 21:9; and esp. 23:4, "for the exultation over him").[133] The preposition ܡܢ (*men*), which Diettrich already rendered idiomatically as "with,"[134] might here, as in 4b, be an indication of participation not so much in "worship in heaven"[135] as in the "joy of the last time."[136]

■ **8-10** This second part of *Ode* 41 consists of three bicola spoken in the first person singular, but its grammatical subject in 8a is not equivalent to the "we" of the previous section, and in 9-10 it is the "Father of Truth," identical with God the Lord. So only 8b is fully in the first person singular. "The words that this individual uses of himself, can, finally, be the utterance only of the Redeemer, who has already been mentioned in v. 3."[137] Even if the parts of stanza IV have very different sources, they are also clearly connected to other statements in the *Odes of Solomon*, which prohibits the separation of 8-10 "as an interpolated fragment"[138] or a "Jewish fragment."[139]

There is no real difference between the Ethpa. of ܕܡܪ (*dmar*) in 8a, which has already appeared in 28:8 ("were amazed"), and the Pe. ܬܡܗ (*tmah*), spoken by the redeemed Redeemer in 17:6. How similar those two verses are to the bicolon under discussion is shown in this comparison:[140]

17:6 And all who saw me were amazed,
and I seemed to them like a stranger (ξένος).
28:8 They were amazed, those who saw me,
because I [viz., the (redeemed) Redeemer] was persecuted.
41:8 They will be amazed, all those who see me,
because I am of another race (γένος).

While it is uncertain whether θαυμάζω was used in all three cases,[141] the origin of the more or less spiritual amazement of all who saw the speaking "I" is much clearer. A check on the usage of (ἐκ)θαμβέω, (ἐκ)θαυμάζω, and ἐκπλήσσω in the christological tradition of the Synoptic Gospels demonstrates that these verbs—and occasionally ἐξίστημι as well (Matt 12:23; Mark 6:51)—depict the amazement, ranging from incomprehension through alarm to outright rejection, of sympathizers and opponents at the Jesus who speaks so strangely and does miraculous deeds (on the verb ܚܙܐ [*ḥzā*], "see," cf. 17:6 and 28:8).[142]

It is remarkable that 8b and 17:6b each use a Greek *hapax legomenon*.[143] The totally different ancestry and affinity of the speaking "I," intended above all to transcend Davidic descent (cf. Rev 22:16),[144] is clarified in the subsequent verses.[145]

The influence of Ps 8:5, which Goulder asserts in connection with the unsolved problem of the "Son of Man" in the New Testament,[146] is felt also in 9a. Since the term υἱὸς ἀνθρώπου/ܒܪܢܫܐ (*barnāšā*)[147] is synonymous with ἄνθρωπος/ܓܒܪܐ (*gaḇrā*), which will occur later (see on

131 Frankenberg, 34.
132 See *NTSy*, on this passage.
133 Bauer, 622.
134 Diettrich, 131: "with joy in the Lord."
135 BDAG, *s.v.* ᾠδή.
136 Rudolf Bultmann, "ἀγαλλιάομαι, ἀγαλλίασις," *ThWNT* 1 (1933) 19; *TDNT* 1:20; idem, "εὐφραίνω, εὐφροσύνη," *ThWNT* 2 (1935) 771; *TDNT* 2:773; on the meaning and possible equivalents of the Syriac preposition, see Payne Smith, 2:2154–57.
137 Bauer, 621.
138 Harnack, 71.
139 Diettrich, 129.
140 Harris and Mingana, 2:402; Franzmann, 30–31.
141 As Frankenberg (pp. 18, 26, 34) does, varying between active and deponent forms.
142 See Payne Smith, 1:921, 2:4456; BDAG, *s.vv.* ἐκθαμβέω, ἐκθαυμάζω, ἐκπλήσσω, ἐξίστημι, 2b, θαμβέω, θαυμάζω.
143 See Lattke, "Wörter," 290, 294 = idem, *Bedeutung*, 4:138–39, 142–43. Elsewhere the word for "strange(r)" is not ܐܟܣܢܝܐ (ξένος) but the Syriac ܢܘܟܪܝܐ (*nukrāyā*); see Franzmann, "Strangers," 30–31 ("The Lord and the Odist as strangers"). That the word ܓܢܣܐ (γένος) is used here does not automatically suggest a Greek original.
144 BDAG, *s.v.* γένος, 1.
145 Wayne A. Meeks's reference to the "quasi-gnostic Ode of Solomon" 41:8 as an expression "of the pride in uniqueness" is not quite justified, since Tertullian posits "a third race" in relation to the church (see Meeks, "Image of the Androgyne," 167).
146 Michael Goulder, "Psalm 8 and the Son of Man," *NTS* 48 (2002) 24–25; on Heb 2:5-8, see Otto Michel, "μιμνήσκομαι, κτλ.," *ThWNT* 4 (1942) 680; *TDNT* 4:676.
147 It is christologically significant that υἱὸς ἀνθρώπου

12 below), the well-known text of Ps 8:5a can be quoted here: מָה־אֱנוֹשׁ כִּי־תִזְכְּרֶנּוּ—ܡܢܘ ܓܒܪܐ ܕܐܬܕܟܪܬܝܗܝ (*mānaw gaḇrā ḏ-eddkertāy*)—*τί(ς) ἐστιν ἄνθρωπος, ὅτι μιμνῄσκῃ αὐτοῦ* ("What [who] is man, that thou art mindful of him?").[148] The speaker transfers this verse—and thus the relevant parts of Ps 8:5-7 (cf. Ps 109:1 LXX)—to himself. In doing so, he uses a completely new name for God, "Father of Truth," the complement of "Son of Truth" (23:18; cf. 11:4; 31:5; see on 13 below on "Son of the Most High"), which may derive from John 4:23-24 (cf. John 14:6; 17:17). Stölten calls this appellation "Valentinian,"[149] and Wengst, in a note on *2 Clem.* 3:1, says that "the designation of God as the 'Father of Truth' in *non-apocryphal* early Christian writings occurs only here and in *2 Clem.* 20:5" [emphasis added].[150] Karl Paul Donfried, to whom Wengst refers, places *Ode* 41:9 among passages "in the gnostic literature of the second century."[151] Like Völker,[152] he draws attention to "Heracleon's commentary on John,"[153] which raises the question whether the *Odes of Solomon* could have influenced this early Gnostic commentary.[154]

Verse 9b is even more difficult than 23:3c, where the elect are described in a rhetorical question as those "who gained" the love of God "from the beginning," and therefore it is theirs.[155] The declaration of preexistence, ܡܢ ܒܪܫܝܬ (*men b-rēšīṯ*), found in both passages, will be further clarified in the third part of *Ode* 41 (see on 14 and 15b below). The Pe. ܩܢܐ (*qnā*), "gain/possess," with its first person singular objective suffix, which probably does *not* correspond to *ἔσχέν με*,[156] reminds some readers of Ps 73:2a LXX, a verse in which *μνήσθητι* ("Remember") also occurs (see on 9a above).[157] The speaking "I," however, claims to be older than God's *συναγωγή* ("congregation").[158] There is an unmistakable echo of Prov 8:22-25 LXX (cf. *Ode* 7:8; John 1:1-2; Col 1:17).

The term *ὁ πλοῦτος*/ܥܘܬܪܐ (*ʿuṯrā*), which in 11:16b refers to paradise, means "wealth" or "abundance."[159] Here in 10a this masculine noun *may* "as progenitor ... have been partly personified,"[160] but it is still a long way from the Mandaic "uthras."[161] The term is more closely allied to Pauline usage (e.g., Phil 4:19; Rom 11:33), whose theological and christological influence is shown, for instance, in the phrase *πλοῦτος τῆς δόξης* ("riches of the glory") in Col 1:27 (cf. Eph 1:18; 3:16). The Pe. ܐܝܠܕ (*ʾileḏ*), "begat," with its first singular objective suffix is, even more clearly than in 36:3, equivalent to a form of *γεννάω*.[162] This linguistic connection with *Ode* 36[163] confirms the hypothesis about the speaker of stanza IV, about whom there will be more information in the next section of *Ode* 41.

The phrase in 10b is parallel to the subject of 10a, as the second subject of the same verb, thus casting more doubt on the personification of ܥܘܬܪܐ (*ʿuṯrā*).[164] The

(Ps 8:5 LXX) is normally represented by ܒܪܗ ܕܐܢܫܐ (*breh d-nāšā*) in the Syriac tradition of Heb 2:6 (Aland and Juckel, *Briefe*, 3:260–61).

148 See *BHS*, 1092; *OTSy*, pt. 2 fasc. 3, pp. 6–7; Rahlfs, 2:6; Brenton, 702.

149 Stölten, 55.

150 Wengst, 243; BDAG, *s.v.* ἀλήθεια, 2b.

151 Karl Paul Donfried, *The Setting of Second Clement in Early Christianity* (NovTSup 38; Leiden: Brill, 1974) 111.

152 Völker, *Quellen*, 74.

153 Donfried, *Setting*, 112.

154 See Werner Foerster, *Von Valentin zu Herakleon: Untersuchungen über die Quellen und die Entwicklung der valentinianischen Gnosis* (BZNW 7; Gießen: Töpelmann, 1928) 18–20. Origen quotes Heracleon as describing God as ὁ πατὴρ τῆς ἀληθείας (Alan E. Brooke, *The Fragments of Heracleon: Newly Edited from the MSS. with an Introduction and Notes* [TextsS 1.4; Cambridge: Cambridge University Press, 1891; repr., Nendeln/Liechtenstein: Kraus Reprint, 1967] 71 lines 9–10) and also uses the expression himself (*Cels.* 8.12 and 8.76).

155 See commentary on that passage.

156 BDAG, *s.v.* ἔχω, 2a.

157 Rahlfs, 2:78; Brenton, 741.

158 See Payne Smith, 2:3651–52; BDAG, *s.v.* κτάομαι, 1 and 3; Frankenberg, 34: ὃς ἐκτήσατό με ἀπ' ἀρχῆς.

159 BDAG, *s.v.* πλοῦτος, 2; Payne Smith, 2:3012.

160 Bauer, 622.

161 Drower and Macuch, 347; Schweizer, *Ego eimi*, 56–57 n. 93.

162 Payne Smith, 1:1593; BDAG, *s.v.* γεννάω, 1b; Frankenberg, 34: ἐγέννησε.

163 Should be added on p. 279 of Franzmann.

164 See above on Bauer, 622.

term ܡܚܫܒܬܐ (*maḥšabṯā*), "thought," which also occurs in 16:19b, shows how entirely καρδία/ܠܒܐ (*lebbā*), "heart," was considered to be the organ of thought (cf. 6b; see Excursus 9). The parallel term ܡܠܬܐ (*melltā*), "word," which begins the third part, has occurred already in 16:19a (11a ["Word"]; cf. 14).

■ **11-16a** If the third part of *Ode* 41 had made its way into the New Testament, there would hardly be a voice raised in objection. However, New Testament scholars would, as in the case of the related "Psalms of Christ,"[165] start a controversy whether this short poem in the third person should be called a "hymn"[166] or an "encomium."[167] Here we will attempt, building on earlier work,[168] to interpret the didactic statements of salvation of stanza V as far as possible within the framework of the *Odes* themselves.[169] Some of the problems in this amalgam of Christology, soteriology, and theology will necessitate reference to the New Testament. Whether it will be necessary to consult the texts from the Dead Sea, the letters of Ignatius, or New Testament Apocrypha will be considered especially in connection with the exegesis of 15a.

In connection with the numbering of 11a-16a, the transformation of the manuscript monocola 12-14 into three bicola by Harris and Mingana[170] and Charlesworth[171] should be resisted. Franzmann associates herself with this segmentation and even goes further, changing 11b into 11b-c, which leads to problems and contradictions in the "division into strophes."[172] One must, however, agree with her that "11a functions as the introduction to the new section, which focusses on the central character of the Word," and that "15a in the pres[ent] tense makes an abrupt break in the narration in the past tense which continues thereafter in 15b."[173]

In a link to stanza IV, the suffix of ܡܠܬܐ (*melltā*) in 11a refers to the divine "Father of Truth" (9a). If it were not that in stanza V also the "Father" (13) and the preexistent "Word" (14, clearly in the feminine gender)[174]

165 Martin Hengel, "Das Christuslied im frühesten Gottesdienst," in Walter Baier et al., eds., *Weisheit Gottes – Weisheit der Welt: Festschrift für Joseph Kardinal Ratzinger zum 60. Geburtstag* (St. Ottilien: EOS, 1987) 393–404.

166 Abramowski, 57. The generic name in 16b can be translated as "hymn," "song," or simply "praise." Abramowski's retroversion (p. 49) is notable for its use of participles and may be reproduced in full as a prolegomenon to the exegesis that follows. It is possible that 15a-b was actually a monocolon in 𝔊.

11a *ὁ λόγος αὐτοῦ μεθ' ἡμῶν ἐστιν ἐν ὅλῃ τῇ ὁδῷ ἡμῶν·*
11b *ὁ σωτὴρ ὁ ζῳοποιῶν καὶ οὐκ ἀθετῶν τὰς ἡμῶν ψυχάς,*
12 *ὁ ἀνὴρ ὁ ταπεινωθεὶς καὶ ὑψωθεὶς ἐν τῇ δικαιοσύνῃ αὐτοῦ,*
13 *ὁ υἱὸς τοῦ ὑψίστου ὁ ἐπιφανῶν ἐν τῇ τελειότητι τοῦ πατρός,*
14 *τὸ φῶς τὸ ἀνατεῖλαν ἐκ τοῦ λόγου ὃς ἐξ ἀρχῆς ἐν αὐτῷ ἦν,*
15a-b *ὁ χριστὸς ὃς ἐν ἀληθείᾳ εἷς καὶ γνωστός ἐστι πρὸ καταβολῆς κόσμου*
16a *ὃς ζῳοποιήσει τὰς ψυχὰς εἰς αἰῶνας ἐν τῇ ἀληθείᾳ τοῦ ὀνόματος αὐτοῦ.*

167 Klaus Berger, *Formgeschichte des Neuen Testaments* (Heidelberg: Quelle & Meyer, 1984) 240, etc., on Phil 2:6-11; see also Lattke, *Hymnus*, 233. Charlesworth (pp. 142–43) reverses the point when he remarks on 12: "There is a striking similarity between this verse and Phil 2:8-9. In fact Phil 2:6-9 reads very much like an Ode." His partly reflexive translation of 12 is taken up by Robert Winterhalter, who even surpasses it by substituting "because of his right-mindedness" (see Robert Winterhalter, *The Odes of Solomon: Original Christianity Revealed* [St. Paul: Llewellyn, 1985] 254) for "because of His own righteousness."

168 Lattke, "Messias-Stellen," 442–45 = idem, *Bedeutung*, 4:104–6.

169 See Excursuses 1, 5, 7, 10, 12, 15, 17, 20, 22, 24, 25, 35, and 39; see also Table 1.

170 Harris and Mingana, vol. 1, on this passage; 2:400.

171 Charlesworth, 140–41. The discrepancy in Charlesworth's numbering of 15-16 can be traced to the fact that Harris and Mingana had 15a-b and 16a-b in their edition (vol. 1, on this passage) but 15a-c and 16 in their translation (2:400). I am following the manuscript division of 15a-16a and will also treat 16b as a monocolon (contra Lattke, *Bedeutung*, 1:180–81).

172 Franzmann, 279–80.

173 Ibid., 279.

174 See Emerton, 729–30 ("Word").

are mentioned, one might agree with Bauer that "it [i.e., the powerful word] never occurs in the sense of *Logos* (as in John 1:1)."[175] His judgment about exactly this unique passage in the *Odes of Solomon*, which because of the "appositions that follow" must "in any event be brought into connection with the tradition of the Logos prologue of John's Gospel,"[176] can really only refer to the *later* christological use of ܡܠܬܐ (*melltā*) in the masculine gender as the equivalent of ὁ Λόγος.[177] But even the Diatessaron and Aphraates still consider *melltā* feminine.[178] Instead of referring to the "Targum on Gen xxxv. 3" for "His Word"[179] in connection with ܥܡܢ (*ʿamman*), "with us," attention should be directed to the interpretation of Emmanuel as μεθʼ ἡμῶν ὁ θεός ("God with us") in Matt 1:23 (cf. Isa 7:14; 8:8, 10 LXX), while the suffix of the preposition ܥܡ (*ʿam*) refers to the "we" of the first part (1-7). The term ὁδός/ܐܘܪܚܐ (*ʾurḥā*), used metaphorically, means not merely "way" of life[180] but way of salvation to *eternal* life (cf. Acts 16:17)[181] with a Gnostic mythological tinge in the *Odes of Solomon*.[182]

As in the case of 5:11 ℭ and 42:18b, one can assume that ܦܪܘܩܐ (*pārōqā*), "Savior," in 11b corresponds not to the uncommon term ὁ ῥυόμενος (cf. Isa 59:20 LXX in Rom 11:26)[183] but to the Hellenistic title ὁ σωτήρ.[184] In the New Testament, where σωτήρ is often represented by ܡܚܝܢܐ (*maḥḥyānā*),[185] as also in early Christian writings in general, this title may be, under the influence of the LXX, used theologically, but even more often it is given as an attribute in manifold ways to Jesus the Lord and Christ. Here the "Savior"[186] is described by two verb phrases, the first of which will be taken up in 16a, while the second negates any negation of the first. Especially because of 16a, one must assume that the direct object at the end of 11b is governed by both the Aph. participles (cf. Jas 1:21; 1 Pet 1:9; *Mart. Pol.* 19:2). If 𝔊 used σῴζων (cf. Luke 9:56)[187] rather than ζῳοποιῶν,[188] there would have been rather a lovely play on words with the title σωτήρ. The "we" of this Ode, unlike the rejected of 24:12, express their confidence in salvation; the Redeemer will not "reject" them (in 𝔊 more likely οὐκ ἀθετῶν[189] than ἐξουθενῶν).[190] The expression "our souls" simply means "us"[191] or "ourselves."[192]

The parallelism of 11b and 12, which is somewhat obscured in Franzmann,[193] shows that the prepositional expression in 12, "by his own righteousness," refers to both verbs, "was humbled and was exalted." The ܘ (*w-*), therefore, is not adversative.[194] The translation of the preposition ܒ (*b-*) is difficult, as so often. What makes it worse is that it is uncertain whether 𝔊 used ἐν or just the instrumental dative τῇ δικαιοσύνῃ αὐτοῦ.[195] Even assuming the use of the preposition ἐν,[196] there is still the question whether this was in the transferred local sense "to denote a state of being"[197] or was meant

175 Bauer, 622.
176 Lattke, "Messias-Stellen," 443 = idem, *Bedeutung*, 4:105; see also Dodd, *Interpretation*, 272–73.
177 Payne Smith, 2:2111; BDAG, *s.v.* λόγος, 3.
178 Murray, *Symbols*, 71–72, on John 1:14; see Peter Bruns, trans., *Aphrahat, Unterweisungen* (2 vols.; FontChr 5.1–2; Freiburg: Herder, 1991) 1:200, on *Demonstrationes* 6.10.
179 Harris and Mingana, 2:402.
180 Wilhelm Michaelis, "ὁδός, κτλ.," *ThWNT* 5 (1954) 88–95; *TDNT* 5:84–91.
181 Strelan, *Acts*, 115.
182 Cf. 7:13; 24:13; 39:7, 13; see also Käsemann, *Wandering People*, 87–96, esp. 90–91 = *Gottesvolk*, 52–58, esp. 56.
183 BDAG, *s.v.* ῥύομαι.
184 BDAG, *s.v.* σωτήρ, b; Payne Smith, 2:3295.
185 See Payne Smith, 1:1257.
186 Greßmann, 471: "Heiland."
187 BDAG, *s.v.* σῴζω, 3; Payne Smith, 1:1252.
188 Frankenberg, 35; BDAG, *s.v.* ζῳοποιέω, 1a.
189 BDAG, *s.v.* ἀθετέω, 2.
190 BDAG, *s.v.* ἐξουθενέω; contra Frankenberg, p. 35; for other possible equivalents, see Payne Smith, 2:2638.
191 Berger and Nord, 970: "uns."
192 Charlesworth, 141.
193 Franzmann, 279.
194 Contra Charlesworth, 141.
195 See Payne Smith, 1:1085; BDAG, *s.v.* δικαιοσύνη. It is noteworthy that 𝔖 used ܙܕܝܩܘܬܐ (*zaddīqūtā*) and not the feminine ܟܐܢܘܬܐ (Payne Smith, 1:1663), which is the translation for δικαιοσύνη favored by the Peshitta.
196 Frankenberg, 35; Abramowski, 49; Fanourgakis, 173. Tsakonas (pp. 177, 184) uses the preposition διά, which leads the reader astray: "Τὸ «διὰ τῆς δικαιοσύνης Του» μαρτυρεῖ μᾶλλον εἰς τὴν διὰ θανάτου ταπείνωσιν." This interpretation goes with Charlesworth's translation of 12 (a-b): "The Man who humbled Himself, / But was exalted because of His own righteousness" (see Charlesworth, 141).
197 Bauer and Aland, *s.v.* ἐν, 4d; see BDAG, *s.v.* ἐν, 2b.

instrumentally.[198] Additionally, the term ܕܝܠܗ (*dīleh*), "his own," is used "to give more prominence to the possessor"[199] and thus refers unambiguously to the subject of 12, while in 𝔊 the word ΑΥΤΟΥ could have been equivocal.[200] For as αὐτοῦ—as against αὑτοῦ = ἑαυτοῦ[201]—the pronoun could refer to the "Father," which could shift the meaning from "His own righteousness"[202] to God's righteousness as one of his characteristics (cf., e.g., Rom 3:21-26).[203] Considering the *Syriac* text of this Ode, reference to the other passages with ܙܕܝܩܘܬܐ (*zaddīqūṯā*), "righteousness" (8:21a and 36:7b) is less helpful than drawing on the soteriological use of the Pa. ܙܕܩ (*zaddeq*) in 29:5 and the Ethpa. ܐܙܕܕܩ (*ʾezdaddaq*) in 17:2a and 31:5a. This brings us back to "the victory (ἐδικαιώθη) of Jesus" in 1 Tim 3:16: "Again, as shown by the passive verb, it is God who acts. He 'justifies' Jesus."[204] The theological passive appears in the passage under discussion both in ܐܬܡܟܟ (*ʾeṯmakkak*), "was humbled," and in ܐܬܬܪܝܡ (*ʾettrīm*), "was exalted," although it would be incorrect to read into it the total self-abasement μέχρι θανάτου, θανάτου δὲ σταυροῦ of Phil 2:8 ("unto death, even death on a cross"). The main thing is the incarnation of the Redeemer, which the Father himself brought about (cf. Phil 2:7), and his subsequent exaltation. Therefore, it is quite possible that ܓܒܪܐ (*gaḇrā*), "man," here represents not ἀνήρ (as, e.g., in Acts 17:31, where it is also associated with ἐν δικαιοσύνῃ, "in righteousness") but ἄνθρωπος (as, e.g., in Heb 2:6, quoting Ps 8:5 LXX; see on 9a above).[205] Whether 𝔊 poetically used passive participles of ταπεινόω and ὑψόω,[206] or in a relative clause ἐταπεινώθη καὶ ὑψώθη,[207] is unknown.[208]

In a more narrative style, and connecting to the second verb of 12, a new christological title comes into play in 13,[209] namely, υἱὸς ὑψίστου, familiar from Luke 1:32 (cf. *Protev.* 11:3).[210] "Son of the Most High" occurs only once in the *Odes of Solomon*, compared to "Son of God" twice (36:3; 42:15), but it is parallel to "Son of Truth from the Father, the Most High" (23:18b; cf. 3:6b-7c). The "Most High" is the "Father" himself (cf. 7:11b; 31:5b; 41:9a), whose ܫܘܡܠܝܐ (*šumlāyā*), "*plērōma*"—especially following the exaltation of the divine man/person in 12—may be meant in a more localized mythological sense than could be inferred from a combination of the retroversions of Frankenberg and Rudolf Abramowski.[211] The term here bears no relationship to the πλήρωμα ("fullness") of John 1:16 or Col 1:19; 2:9 (in contrast, cf. 7:11, 13; 17:7b; 36:2b). As in 7:12a and 23:18a, ܐܬܚܙܝ (*ʾeṯḥzī*), "appeared," corresponds to ἐφάνη[212] and not to the loaded ὁ ἐπιφανῶν,[213] the more so as there is nothing in this verse about Jesus' "appearance on earth."[214] Even though ܐܬܚܙܝ cannot here represent ὤφθη, the relationship with the meaning of ὤφθη ἀγγέλοις ("seen by angels") in 1 Tim 3:16 cannot be missed: "The exalted Christ appears visibly before the members of the celestial sphere in his sovereign power."[215]

Verse 14 again comes closer to John 1. The divine "light" was mentioned already in 6a (cf. John 1:4-5). The Pe. ܕܢܚ (*dnaḥ*), "dawned," corresponds either to λάμπω (cf. Isa 9:1 LXX)[216] or to intransitive ἀνατέλλω,[217] though without alluding to the epiphany in the "Hellenistic ruler cult."[218] The compound preposition

198 BDAG, *s.v.* ἐν, 5b.
199 Nöldeke §225.
200 See Payne Smith, 1:881–82.
201 BDAG, *s.v.* ἑαυτοῦ, 1.
202 Charlesworth, 141.
203 BDAG, *s.v.* δικαιοσύνη, 2.
204 Roloff, 205.
205 See Payne Smith, 1:644; BDAG, *s.vv.* ἀνήρ, 3b; ἄνθρωπος, 1b; Käsemann, *Wandering People*, 101–17, esp. 107 = *Gottesvolk*, 61–71, esp. 65.
206 Abramowski, 49.
207 Frankenberg, 35.
208 See Payne Smith, 2:2101, 3857; BDAG, *s.vv.* ταπεινόω, ὑψόω.
209 Franzmann, 279.
210 See Michel Testuz, *Papyrus Bodmer V: Nativité de Marie* (Cologny-Genève: Bibliothèque Bodmer, 1958) 76.
211 Frankenberg, 35; and Abramowski, 49: ἐν τῇ τελειότητι τοῦ πατρὸς αὐτοῦ.
212 See commentary on 23:18a; Frankenberg, 35.
213 Contra Abramowski, 49; see BDAG, *s.v.* ἐπιφαίνω.
214 BDAG, *s.v.* ἐπιφάνεια, 1a.
215 Roloff, 206; see also Oberlinner, *Pastoralbriefe*, 1:166–67.
216 BDAG, *s.v.* λάμπω ("shine forth").
217 Payne Smith, 1:926.
218 BDAG, *s.v.* ἀνατέλλω, 2a; see also BDAG, *s.v.* ἐπιλάμπω.

ܡܢ ܩܕܝܡ (*men qdīm*), "from the beginning," following the feminine expression ܡܠܬܐ ܗܝ ܕ (*melltā hāy d-*), "that Word that," does not here mean πρότερον[219] but ἀπ'/ἐξ ἀρχῆς[220] and refers to the ἐν ἀρχῇ ("in the beginning") of John 1:1-2.[221] Instead of the twice-repeated πρὸς τὸν θεόν ("with God") of the prologue to John, the Ode has ἐν αὐτῷ/ܒܗ (*beh*), "in him," which must refer to the "Father" in 13 (cf. John 1:14, 18). In spite of the different terminology, this verse also deals with the preexistence of the Logos.[222]

If 15a could be treated as a gloss (in 𝔊 perhaps εἷς [ἐστιν] ἀληθῶς/ἐν ἀληθείᾳ Χριστός; cf. Ignatius *Magn.* 7:2), the subject of 15b-16a would refer to the "light" of 14 (cf. the terms φῶς and ζωή in John 1:4-5). That would explain the abrupt change of style as well as the (defensive?) polemic of this "confessional statement."[223] But, whether early or late, marginal note or not, this acclamation, reminiscent of 1 Cor 8:6 and Eph 4:5,[224] although it mentions neither κύριος nor Ἰησοῦς,[225] must be treated as part of the text. First, it should be noted that both (ὁ) Χριστός/ܡܫܝܚܐ (*mšīḥā*), "(the) Christ/Messiah," and the nominalized εἷς/ܚܕ (*ḥad*), "one," can be either subject or predicate noun (cf., in reference to Christ, Matt 23:8; 23:10).[226] "The one" as subject would be the one and only Savior and Son of 11b-13, who is now declared the one true and actual Messiah.[227] But if the Christos of 3b—used as a title and not as a name or *cognomen* of Jesus—in further apposition to the "Word" of 11a and 14, is the subject of 15a, then the predicate noun emphasizes his "unity"[228] and uniqueness,[229] without necessarily opposing "the division between a celestial Christ and a terrestrial Jesus."[230] With a reference back to 9-10 as preparation for 15a, one may quote Drijvers: "There are therefore not two Messiahs, an eternal Word and a Son of the Most High, who appeared on earth, but these two are one. These concepts . . . are not opposed to the Jewish ideas of the Qumran community as Carmignac[231] and Charlesworth[232] suppose, but are the *forerunners* of the christological disputes of the fourth century."[233] Without following McNeil in his connection of the "*polymorphia* of Jesus" in *Act. John* 87–102 with the themes of *Ode* 41:8-16, it is still possible to accept his verdict that "I would not agree with Drijvers that this is a polemic against docetism."[234] Returning to the enigmatic passage Ignatius *Magn.* 7:1-2, one must, despite all the

219 BDAG, *s.v.* πρότερος, 1b.
220 BDAG, *s.v.* ἀρχή, 1b.
221 See Theobald, *Fleischwerdung*, 220.
222 See Harris and Mingana, 2:402.
223 Franzmann, 279.
224 Schnackenburg, *Epheser*, 168.
225 Contra Grimme, 131.
226 Contra Lattke, "Messias-Stellen," 444 = idem, *Bedeutung*, 4:106.
227 See BDAG, *s.v.* ὑπάρχω 1, on *Act. Paul* "1, 18" in the Hamburg Papyrus; Schmidt and Schubart, *Acta Pauli*, 24.
228 Harnack, 71.
229 BDAG, *s.v.* εἷς, 2b.
230 See Bauer, 621; Lampe, 1531. "The Logos, Christ, the Son and the Redeemer are one and the same" (Schenke, *Herkunft*, 28). It may be pertinent in this connection to call to mind Paul's question in 1 Cor 1:13: μεμέρισται ὁ Χριστός; ("Is Christ divided?"); on the ecclesiological implications, see Schrage, *1 Korinther*, 1:152–53.
231 Carmignac, "Auteur," 80–81.
232 Charlesworth, 143.
233 Drijvers, "Polemik," 53; see Lampe, 1532. My emphasis and emendations in this quotation are from Drijvers, with whose late date ("no earlier than ca. 200 C.E.) I agree as little as with his translation of 15b-16a (Drijvers, "Polemik," 52, 54). To those "ideas of the Qumran community" not relevant to the *Odes of Solomon*, it is now necessary to add Kenneth Atkinson's conclusion: "Because the Branch of David is also called the 'Messiah of Righteousness' (משיח הצדק) in 4Q252, this figure in 4Q174 is certainly a Davidic Messiah. 4Q174's exposition of 2 Sam 7:14 therefore demonstrates that the title 'Son of God' is an additional epithet for the Davidic Messiah" (see Kenneth Atkinson, "On the Herodian Origin of Militant Davidic Messianism at Qumran: New Light from *Psalm of Solomon* 17," *JBL* 118 [1999] 457 ["epitaph" corrected to "epithet"]; German translations of the texts will be found in Maier, *Qumran-Essener*, 2:104, 198; cf. idem, 1:3 [CD xx.1] and 1:191 [1QS ix.11]).
234 McNeil, 134; cf. idem, "Le Christ," 198–200. The reference to *Ode* 34:3-5 for the exegesis of 41:15a (in the context of 41:11-16a) is not really helpful (contra McNeil, 98–102, 133–35; idem, "Le Christ," 201).

problems of dating, take seriously Harris and Mingana's considered judgement: "This passage may be taken as a comment upon the sentence in the Ode, which it actually reproduces (without the adverb 'truly')."[235] Whether 𝔊 had ἀληθῶς or ἐν (τῇ) ἀληθείᾳ or even ἐπ' ἀληθείας[236] is unknown.[237] What is important is that the term "truth" again plays a great part in this Ode (1b, 9a, 15a, 16a) and that it is generally found in proximity to the knowledge of salvation (e.g., 8:12; 12:13b) and to the mythological "above" of the "Most High" (e.g., 8:8; 17:7; 18:15; 23:18). So the translation of ܒܫܪܪܐ (*ba-šrārā*) as "truly" (20:9c; 39:10b) might be too feeble for this verse.

In 15b "Christ's preexistence is roundly asserted."[238] The reference to John 17:5 also accords with the sense of this line, although in that verse neither πρὸ καταβολῆς κόσμου (John 17:24; Eph 1:4; 1 Pet 1:20)[239] nor ἀπὸ καταβολῆς κόσμου (Matt 13:35; 25:34; Luke 11:50; Heb 4:3; 9:26; Rev 13:8; 17:8)[240] is to be found. For one of these protological expressions is, except for the use of the theological passive (see 2a), the basis for the statement in 15b, which, according to Connolly, is "almost conclusive evidence" that "our present Syriac text is a translation from Greek."[241] The Ethpe. of ܝܕܥ (*ʾidaʿ*), "was known/acknowledged," which is more likely to correspond to ἐγνώσθη[242] than to γνωστός ἐστι,[243] is a term of theological election (cf. 1 Cor 8:3; Gal 4:9).[244] Although the Pe. belonging to this Ethpe. is used in Gnosticizing parallels (cf. 7:7-9; 8:8-14; 17:7), this passage does not deal with "Gnosis" in its proper sense.[245]

The conjunction ἵνα/ܕ (*d-*), "that,"[246] with which 16a begins expresses the soteriological intention of the christological election. The Aph. of ܚܝܐ (*ḥyā*), "give life," has already occurred in 11b (and cf. 3b). The plural "souls"—here, unlike 11b, without a personal suffix—means "living creatures,"[247] that is, breathing "humans"[248] or, in a more modern expression, "persons."[249] It makes no difference whether ܠܥܠܡ (*la-ʿālam*), "forever," represents εἰς αἰῶνας or εἰς αἰῶνα.[250] The decision, however, whether ὄνομα/ܫܡܐ (*šmā*), "name," refers to God the Lord (as in 5a) or to Christ the Redeemer of 11b-15b, is of great importance. Although the general usage in the *Odes of Solomon* of the term "name"—and also of "truth"—offers no unambiguous answer, the context of 16a supports the latter.[251] In that case, it is worth pointing out that ὄνομα means not only "name" but also "title."[252] The final occurrence of the

235 Harris and Mingana, 2:48; see also Lake, 1:202–3; Fischer, 166–67; Ehrman, 1:246–49. It is surprising that Schlier, in his chapter on "Christ and the ἕνωσις of the Church" (see Schlier, *Untersuchungen*, 97–102), discusses Ignatius *Magn.* 7:2 (p. 99) and considers that "it is necessary to stipulate the unity and union of God and Christ" (p. 101) without ever mentioning *Ode* 41 (see Lattke, *Bedeutung*, 3:202).

236 BDAG, *s.vv.* ἀλήθεια, 3; ἀληθῶς, a.

237 See Bultmann, "Untersuchungen," 160 = idem, *Exegetica*, 170.

238 Harnack, 71.

239 Already noted by Clarke, 52; Rudolf Bultmann, "Bekenntnis- und Liedfragmente im ersten Petrusbrief," in *Conjectanea Neotestamentica XI in honorem Antonii Fridrichsen sexagenarii* (ConNT 11; Lund/Copenhagen: 1947) 10–12 = idem, *Exegetica*, 293–95.

240 See BDAG, *s.v.* καταβολή ("before/from the foundation of the world").

241 Richard Hugh Connolly, review of Abbott in *JTS* 14 (1912–13) 315; on the plural of ܬܪܡܝܬܐ (*tarmīṯā*), see Payne Smith, 2:3928. Both manuscripts have the plural ܬܪܡܝܬܐ (*tarmyāṯā*), "foundations" (see Harris and Mingana, vol. 1, on this passage; 2:401; Charlesworth, *Manuscripts*, 86 line 12). This voids Kittel's text-critical remarks (see Kittel, "Handschrift," 90–91).

242 Frankenberg, 35.

243 Abramowski, 49.

244 BDAG, *s.v.* γινώσκω, 7; cf. the passive of προγινώσκω in 1 Pet 1:20 and on it BDAG, *s.v.* προγινώσκω, 2; and Leonhard Goppelt, *Der Erste Petrusbrief* (ed. by Ferdinand Hahn; 1st ed. of this *Neubearbeitung*; KEK 12.1; 8th ed.; Göttingen: Vandenhoeck & Ruprecht, 1978) 124.

245 Jens Holzhausen, "Gnosis/Gnostizismus," *MLAA* (1997) 278.

246 Verse 16a in 𝔊 could not have begun with the relative pronoun ὅς (contra Abramowski, 49).

247 Bauer and Aland, *s.v.* ψυχή, 2.

248 Berger and Nord, 970; see also Schroer and Staubli, *Körpersymbolik*, 61–73.

249 BDAG, *s.v.* ψυχή, 3; Charlesworth, 141.

250 BDAG, *s.v.* αἰών, 1b; Payne Smith, 2:2899.

251 Bousset, *Kyrios Christos*, 244; McNeil, 135.

252 See BDAG, *s.v.* ὄνομα, esp. 3.

term "truth" in this little poem casts a ray of light backward on 15a, which no longer seems so abrupt.

■ **16b** Verse 16b is neither a prosaic addition[253] nor "a description, either of the total Ode or of some final section of it."[254] Rather than a "doxology" in the strict sense,[255] it should be called an "indirect doxology,"[256] thus drawing attention to the differences between it and other doxologies.[257] Although "Lord" sometimes also refers to the Christ/Messiah (cf. 17:16), here, as in the whole of *Ode* 41, κύριος/ܡܪܝܐ (*māryā*) means God, the Most High and Father (of Truth) (1a, 3a, 5a, 7, 9a, 13). It is something of a paradox that the qualification καινός/ܚܕܬܐ (*ḥdattā*), "new," of the hymnic term ܬܫܒܘܚܬܐ (*tešbuḥtā*), used also in 4b, should derive from a formulaic usage in the Bible (cf. ὕμνος καινός ["new hymn"] in Isa 42:10 [and Jdt 16:13][258] and ᾠδὴ καινή ["new song"] in Ps 143:9 LXX [also Rev 5:9 and 14:3], but esp. ᾆσμα καινόν ["new song"] in the LXX: Pss 32:3; 39:4; 95:1; 97:1; 149:1).[259] Frankenberg's suggestion, ἔπαινος καινός ("new praise"),[260] stays within the realm of possibility (cf., e.g., linguistically Rom 2:29 and 13:3),[261] but, like δόξα καινή, it can be excluded in this context. So there is no direct connection between the ending of *Ode* 41 and εἰς δόξαν θεοῦ πατρός ("to the glory of God the Father") in the "singular triumph" of Phil 2:11.[262] The most likely influence on this passage—perhaps differing from 31:3b—is Isa 42:10 LXX: Ὑμνήσατε τῷ κυρίῳ (θεῷ S*L) ὕμνον καινόν ("Sing a new hymn to the Lord [God]").[263] How far from universal the sense of 16a is, becomes again very clear in the last words of 16b. For that it is necessary to consider not only the similarly esoteric love between the redeemed Redeemer and his own in 42:4 (cf. 42:20) but also the reciprocal use of the noun "love" (cf. 8:1, 13; 16:3; 23:3; 40:4) especially in *Ode* 41 itself (see on 2b and 6b above). This "mutual love . . . suggests the Gospel of John, without actually being a proper parallel."[264] The possibility of an influence by Pauline theology, also, cannot be excluded (cf. Rom 8:28; 1 Cor 2:9; 8:3).[265] It is true that this "formulaic language of primitive Christianity," which was even applied to the Lord Jesus Christ (Eph 6:24), traces back to a "self-description of pious Jews."[266] The Greek original of 16b can now, with the help of Frankenberg's retroversion,[267] be reconstructed as follows:

ὕμνος καινὸς τῷ κυρίῳ ἀπὸ τῶν ἀγαπώντων αὐτόν.

253 Contra Grimme, 25; cf. Lattke, *Bedeutung*, 3:104.

254 Contra Franzmann, 280, who, however, is right in pointing to the use of the root ܫܒܚ at the beginning of 1a.

255 Harris and Mingana, 2:400; Charlesworth, 141.

256 Lattke, *Oden*, 79, 83; see Introduction, sec. 8.3.

257 Cf. 11:24; 16:20; 17:16; 18:16; 20:10.

258 Even in the "song" or "hymn" of Judith (Jdt 16:1-17; Rahlfs, 1:999–1001), 16:13a is so formulaic that Zenger's remarks on "new" sound exaggerated (see Erich Zenger, *Das Buch Judit* [JSHRZ 1.6; Gütersloh: Mohn, 1981] 516–21, esp. 519).

259 BDAG, *s.v.* καινός, 2; Payne Smith, 1:1207. Arvedson's statement, "Again and again it is emphasised that the believer wants to praise Yahweh with a 'new' song. That means, that he does not use stock formulae, but a song only now inspired by God," is not really justifiable in relation to these Old Testament passages or to *Ode* 41:16b (see Arvedson, *Mysterium*, 19).

260 Frankenberg, 35. It is probably an oversight that Frankenberg does not translate the dative ܠܡܪܝܐ (*l-māryā*); therefore, τῷ κυρίῳ should be added. See BDAG, *s.v.* ἔπαινος, 1b.

261 But see Aland and Juckel, *Briefe*, 1:112, 246.

262 Ernst Lohmeyer, *Kyrios Jesus: Eine Untersuchung zu Phil. 2, 5-11* (SHAW.PH 1927/28, 4. Abh.; Heidelberg: Winter, 1928; 2nd ed.; repr., Darmstadt: Wissenschaftliche Buchgesellschaft, 1961) 62–89, esp. 66, 85, 88.

263 Rahlfs, 2:623; Brenton, 877; see Tsakonas, 177; Fanourgakis, 174; contra Greßmann, 471: "new song"; Bauer, 612, 623 ("new praise"), who alludes to the Psalms listed above.

264 Lattke, *Einheit*, 60; on the Aph. ܐܚܒ (*ʾaḥḥeb*), see Payne Smith, 1:1169.

265 BDAG, *s.v.* ἀγαπάω, 1aβ. In all three passages, the Syriac tradition dominantly uses the Aph. ܐܚܒ (*ʾaḥḥeb*). Only in 1 Cor 2:9 do the participles vary between ܪܚܡܝܢ and ܡܚܒܝܢ (Aland and Juckel, *Briefe*, 1:190, 301–2, 365; on the synonymity of these two roots in the *Odes of Solomon*, see Excursus 2).

266 Dibelius, *Jakobus*, 120, on Jas 1:12; 2:5.

267 Frankenberg, 35.

42

Ode 42: Mythological Address of the Exalted and Redeemed Redeemer

(I) 1a I stretched out my hands and drew near to my Lord,
1b because the spreading out of my hands is his sign,
2a and my stretching [up] is the straight wood,
2b that was hung upon the way of the upright one.

(II) 3aα I became/was useless/unnecessary to those
3aβ who knew/acknowledged me,
3bα because I will hide myself from those[a]
3bβ who did not hold fast to me,
4 and I will be with those who love me.

(III) 5a All my persecutors died.
5b And those who proclaimed me sought me,
5c because I am living.
6a And I stood (up/there) and am with them
6b and will speak by their mouths.
7a For they rejected those who persecute them.

(IV) 7b And I laid on them the yoke of my love.
8a Like the arm of the bridegroom on the bride,
8b so my yoke is on those who know/acknowledge me.
9a And like the bridal tent, pitched in the house of the bridal pair,
9b so my love is over those who believe in me.

(V) 10a I was not rejected, although I seemed [to be],
10b and I did not perish, although they thought [it] of me.

(VI) 11a The realm of the dead [Sheol] saw me and became wretched,
11b and Death vomited me up and many with me.

(VII) 12a I became/was vinegar and bitterness[b] to him [i.e., Death],
12b and I descended with(in) him as far as his lowest depth[c].
13a And he let feet and head go limp,
13b because he could[d] not endure my presence.

(VIII) 14a And I made a congregation of living ones among his [i.e., Death's] dead,
14b and I spoke to them[e] with living lips,
14c that my [the redeemed Redeemer's] word should not cease.

(IX) 15a And those who had died ran to me
15b and cried out and said: "Have pity on us, Son of God!

a 3aβ-bα Omitted in H (haplography).
b 12a ܘܡܪ̈ܪܬܐ N; ܘܡܪܪܬܐ H.
c 12b Lit., ". . . insofar as depth was in him."
d 13b ܐܫܟܚ N; ܐܫܟܚܘ H.
e 14b ܠܘܬܗܘܢ N; ܥܡܗܘܢ H.

16a And deal with us according to thy kindness,
16b and bring us out from the chains of darkness.
17a And open the gate for us, that we may come out to thee,
17b for we see that our death does not come near thee.
18a May we also be saved with thee,
18b because thou art our Savior."
(X) 19a And I heard their voice
19b and took their faith to heart[f].
20a And I set[g] my name upon their head,
20b because they are free,
20c and they are mine.
Hallelujah.[h]

f 19b "and . . . heart" omitted in H (haplography).
g 20a ܘܣܡܬ N; ܘܣܡܠܬ H (scribal error).
h 20c Text of *Ps. Sol.* 1 follows. Heading in H: ܙܡܝܪܬܐ ܕܡ ܘܬܠܬ ("*Ode*" 43); in N: ܕܡܓ ("Nr." 43).

Introduction

Ode 42 is preserved in two Syriac manuscripts.[1] For this Ode, as for *Odes* 17, 22, and 24, there exists what might be called a commentary by August Vogl.[2] The editor, Brian McNeil, explains: "This study forms part of the projected dissertation, 'Christus und Scheol' [Christ and Sheol], a study of the treatment in earliest Syriac literature of the descent of Christ to Hades, which was left unfinished at P. Vogl's untimely death in 1972."[3] The new "division into verses," which Vogl bases, with small justification, on the manuscript "markings" in H, creates nothing but confusion.[4] His equally new "arrangement of strophes" gives him a "thematic sequence" and makes the "text somewhat more comprehensible."[5] Franzmann's division into stanzas, however, is to be preferred, although stanzas VI and VII could perhaps be joined. Franzmann herself says about 12-13: "This stanza flows easily from stanza 6 [i.e., VI] since the image of the 'I' as vinegar/bitterness descending into the deeps of Sheol/Death provides the background for the description in 11b of Death's vomiting up the 'I.'"[6]

Interpretation

■ **1-2** Since the beginning of the last Ode has already been considered together with *Ode* 27,[7] a short summary of the exegesis of stanza I will suffice.

The speaker of 1-2 is identical with the "I" who speaks the remainder of the Ode, with the exception

1 Mss: Codex H, 30a–31b; Codex N, 151ʳ (ܣ). Ed./trans.: Charlesworth, 143–48; Franzmann, 281–89; Lattke, 3:249–80.
2 Vogl, 69–74.
3 Ibid., 75, editor's notes; see also August Vogl, "Allein—Mit grosser Menge: Ein Motiv des Abstiegs in den Scheol bei den alten Syrern," ed. Brian McNeil, *OrChrP* 45 (1979) 171–77.
4 Vogl, 69–71.
5 Ibid., 71. This makes it possible to use Vogl's "thematic sequence" as a preliminary list of contents: "Christ speaks (i) of his undertaking on the cross (as a signpost on the way for the upright person, who loves him); (ii) of the 'persecutors'; (iii) of his presence after his apparent destruction; (iv) of his confrontation with Sheol and Death; (v) of the gathering of life; (vi) of the plea of the dead; (vii) of the granting of the plea." Some of the details here will be criticized later.
6 Franzmann, 287.
7 The translation of *Ode* 27 is repeated here:

   1 I stretched out my hands and hallowed my Lord,
   2 because the spreading out of my hands is his sign,
   3 and my stretching [up] is the wood, which is upright/correct.

of the passage in the first person plural beginning at 15b and ending at 18b. So, in spite of all the difficulties "concerning meaning and composition,"[8] the much discussed question is not "undecided, whether it is a first person song of Christ's descent into hell or a song of initiation."[9] The speaking "I," by his use of the term "wood," draws attention to his cross as the sign of God's salvation, but lays no more weight on it than on his resurrection.[10] There may even be some incipient polemics against the cross; in any case, "the concept of the crucifixion is diverted."[11] The proposition that the "Son of God" and "Savior" (15b, 18b) here interprets the crucifixion event as his "ascension into heaven" must be kept firmly in mind (cf. 35:7a, "ascent").[12]

The short *Ode* 27 was revised and expanded[13] to serve as the introduction to *Ode* 42, which is more than merely "Jesus' Triumph in Hades."[14] "The most difficult"[15] part is indeed the phrase ܐܘܪܚܗ ܕܬܪܝܨܐ (*ʾurḥeh da-ṯrīṣā*) in 42:2b.[16] For an alternative to the earlier interpretation, there is Connolly's suggestion: "The expression ܐܘܪܚܗ ܕܬܪܝܨܐ is to be compared with ܩܝܣܐ ܕܬܪܝܨ in xxvii 3: as in the latter passage the meaning is 'the wood *that is* straight' (i.e., here upright), so in the former the meaning is 'His way *that is* straight' (cp. xxxviii 7)."[17] In that case, "his way" would be parallel to "his sign" (cf. 39:7) and refer not to the "upright one"[18] but to God the Lord.[19]

■ **3-4** What the speaking "I" of stanza II, who is identical with the "Son of God" (15b) and the "Savior" (18b), has to say in this section, which is only loosely

8 Harnack, 72.

9 Schille, 79, who without "closer analysis" generally prefers the latter; cf. Kittel, 139–41, who assigns only 1-2 to "the singer," hearing the words of the "crucified and risen one" from 3a onward. Heinz-Wolfgang Kuhn, without using the term "singer," distinguishes two first-person speakers: "Except for the writings from Nag Hammadi, the only example in our era is the *Odes of Solomon*. In them, whose 'Gnosticism' is debated, *the believer* says that the spreading out of the hands to pray corresponds to the 'extended wood,' the 'sign' of the Lord (27:2-3 par. 42:1-2)" (Kuhn, "Kreuz II: Neues Testament und frühe Kirche (bis vor Justin)," *TRE* 19 [1990] 722 [emphasis added]). I do not consider either the stress on "prayer" or the christological interpretation of "Lord" to be correct.

10 Contra James H. Charlesworth, "Les Odes de Salomon et les manuscrits de la mer Morte," *RB* 77 (1970) 549; idem, "Odes of Solomon," *IDBSup* (1976) 638; Schulz, col. 1340; on the "ambivalence of the wood" and the "mystery of the wood," see Wolfgang Speyer, "Holz," *RAC* 16 (1994) 109–11, 115; on the theological "symbolism of the cross," see Aloys (Alois) Grillmeier, *Der Logos am Kreuz: Zur christologischen Symbolik der älteren Kreuzigungsdarstellung* (Munich: Hueber, 1956) 67–80; see also already Johannes Lindblom, "Altchristliche Kreuzessymbolik: Einige Bemerkungen zu einer Stelle der Bell'schen Papyrusedition von 1924," *Studia orientalia* [Societas Orientalis Fennica] 1 (1925) 104.

11 Abramowski, 64.

12 On the New Testament idea of "Jesus going up into the sky with arms outstretched," see Strelan, *Acts*, 33.

13 This opinion, which Kittel (p. 139 n. 3), for example, does not share, is, I believe, supported by the observation that 42:2a-b is a monocolon in both Syriac manuscripts (see Lattke, *Bedeutung*, 1:76). So the shorter text of 27:3 must have been augmented, though it was not divided into a bicolon in the manuscripts. All the same, it has been justly treated as a bicolon since Harris and Mingana's edition (Harris and Mingana, vol. 1, on this passage; 2:403; Charlesworth, 143, 145; Franzmann, 281–82; Pierre, 195).

14 Stroker, *Sayings*, 158–59.

15 Kittel, 140 n. 2.

16 Which could also be translated: "that was hung upon his way, which is right."

17 Richard Hugh Connolly, review of Kittel in *JTS* 15 (1913–14) 468.

18 Vogl, 71.

19 The entries in the concordance (Lattke, *Bedeutung*, 2:69, 2:72) would have to be revised accordingly. Vogl's assertion (pp. 72–73) that "because of the 3rd person suffix" the only possible translation is "the way of the upright one" is incorrect. The singular term ܬܪܝܨܐ (*trīṣā*) can be either the masculine emphatic state or the feminine absolute state of the word. In the first case, it is a nominalized participial adjective to which the suffix refers. In the second, however, the adjective *must* refer predicatively to the feminine emphatic ܐܘܪܚܐ (*ʾurḥā*), as noted by Connolly (review of Kittel in *JTS* 15 [1913–14] 468).

connected to the introduction fashioned out of *Ode* 27, is, except for the monocolon 4, "not easy"[20] to explain. From the text-critical point of view, H can hardly be said to have "the better reading" in 3.[21] However, the text was rather less complicated before the discovery of N.[22] This leads Grimme to describe the "value of the addition of N," compared to H, as "very problematical" and to reject the so-called addition as "a gloss that had made its way into the text."[23] But, according to the principles of textual criticism,[24] one should adhere to the conclusion that the H text is due to haplography caused by homoioteleuton.[25] "The cause is clearly *parablepsis* facilitated by the same word, ܠܗܢܘܢ."[26] Charlesworth's ingenious suggestion that the manuscript from which N was copied, after the first ܠܗܢܘܢ (*l-hānnōn*), "to those," had ܕܠܐ ܝܕܥܝܢ ܠܝ (*d-lā yāḏʿīn lī*), "who do not know me," not ܕܝܕܥܝܢ ܠܝ (*d-yāḏʿīn lī*), "who know me," would still leave it easy to understand the omission in H.[27] What would be more difficult to understand is how "the negative particle (viz. ܠܐ [*lā*]) has dropped out of N,"[28] especially since the reference to ܕܝܕܥܝܢ ܠܝ (*d-yāḏʿīn lī*) in 8b supports the contention that "the verb ܝܕܥ should be interpreted positively in this Ode."[29] So it becomes necessary, one way or another, to find the sense of the longer and more difficult text of 3a-b in N. The problems include the phrase ܕܠܐ ܚܫܚܘ (*d-lā ḥāšḥū*) in 3aα[30] and the negated participle of the Pe. ܐܚܕ (*ʾeḥaḏ*) in 3bβ, as well as the syntax of 3-4. For "there is a semantically disturbing change in tense from the past in 3a to the future followed by past in 3b and the future followed by pres[ent] (part[iciple]) in 4."[31] It is useful to make a note of clear parallels (||) and oppositions(↔): "know" (3aβ) || "love" (4); "hide" (3bα) ↔ "be with" (4). This raises the question whether "useless" or "without utility" is a

20 Vogl, 73.

21 Contra Brian McNeil, review of Lattke, *Bedeutung*, vols. 1–2, in *Ostkirchliche Studien* 29 (1980) 194. McNeil has some justification for saying: "At 42:3, something is wrong in the text, as neither MS. H nor MS. N gives a reading that makes perfect sense."

22 In H, 3 is a monocolon, in N a bicolon. Some samples of interpretations that predate the discovery of N: "This is the beginning of the originally Jewish-Essene *Ode* in which Truth personified speaks" (Diettrich, "Liedersammlung," 536). Diettrich repeats this unjustifiable assertion in a later work (Diettrich, 134) and refers to Isa 3:10 LXX (δύσχρηστος ἡμῖν ἐστιν, "he is burdensome to us") for the problematic phrase "useless." Zahn (p. 695) translates monocolon 3 in H: "I became useless to those who did not take hold (take possession) of me." He explains in a note: "In any case the contrast between those who rejected the Messiah and gained nothing from his appearance and those who believed in him and were abundantly blessed is quite clear." Spitta (p. 263) suggests: "He is of use to those who take hold of him—not, that is, to his enemies, who, here, do not want to take hold of him (cf. the opposite in 5:6), but to those who endeavor to live in loving unity with him." Hans Heinrich Schaeder in his Aramaistic deliberations on κατέλαβεν in John 1:5 still refers to the text of H for *Ode* 42:3-4 (see Schaeder, "Der 'Mensch' im Prolog des IV. Evangeliums," in Reitzenstein and Schaeder, *Studien*, 312–13; and see Bauer, *Johannesevangelium*, 15).

23 Grimme, "Handschrift," 495.

24 While "the maxim: lectio difficilior lectio potior ('the more difficult reading is the more probable reading')" is valid here, the rule "lectio brevior lectio potior ('the shorter reading is the more probable reading')," as so often, is not applicable (see Kurt and Barbara Aland, *The Text of the New Testament: An Introduction to the Critical Editions and to the Theory and Practice of Modern Textual Criticism* [trans. Erroll F. Rhodes; 2nd ed.; Grand Rapids: Eerdmans; Leiden: Brill, 1989] 281).

25 Lattke, *Bedeutung*, 1:68.

26 Charlesworth, 146 n. 7.

27 The cause of the omission, then, would not be "homoioteleuton" but "homoioarcton" (Kurt and Barbara Aland, *Text of the New Testament*, 285). Fanourgakis (p. 174) and Berger and Nord (p. 970) accept Charlesworth's suggestion and bring 3a into parallel with 3b.

28 Charlesworth, 146 n. 8.

29 Franzmann, 184.

30 Lit., "useless," but here in the sense of "not needed."

31 Franzmann, 285. Kittel's historicizing flattening does not do justice to the syntax of 3-4: "I was concealed from the disciples so that they could not lay hold on me and profit from me—but I will be (now in a spiritual sense) with those who love me" (see Kittel, "Handschrift," 91). His preceding statement, "The speaker is Christ," is correct.

satisfactory translation of the phrase ܕܠܐ ܚܫܚܘ (*d-lā ḥāšḥū*).[32] Whether this Syriac phrase represents ἀχρεῖος or ἄχρηστος[33] or perhaps even ἄνευ χρείας, it suffers from the same vagueness and breadth of meaning as χράομαι and χρεία.[34] The speaking "I" became or was "useless,"[35] or without "use," "utility," or "necessity,"[36] for those of his own who knew him to the extent that they no longer needed him in his concealment (see Excursus 7).[37] With her reference to *Gos. Truth* 19,15-16, on the one hand, and *Ap. Jas.* 11,11-17, on the other, Pierre may have illuminated some part of this text: "Those who have *gnōsis* ('they who know me'), therefore, are not in need."[38]

The final statement of 3a is not in opposition to the close connection between the Redeemer and his own (see below 4 and 7b-9, esp. 8b), but is simply the logical consequence of the causally constructed announcement in 3b. This puts the negated passive participle of ܐܚܕ (*ʾeḥad*) in 3bβ, "not holding fast," in its transitive sense,[39] in opposition to "know/acknowledge" (3aβ) and "love" (4). It might even be referring to the "persecutors"[40] of stanza III (cf. 5:6), but is more probably here intended only for the "non-adherents."[41] 𝔊 would probably have used a form of κρατέω (cf. Col 2:19)[42] rather than one of ἐπιλαμβάνομαι[43] or συλλαμβάνομαι.[44] The *hapax legomenon* ܐܬܛܫܝ (*ʾeṭṭaššī*) in 3bα, the Ethpa. of ܛܫܐ (*ṭšā*) or ܛܫܝ (*ṭšī*), may be an allusion to the end of John 12:27-36: Ἰησοῦς . . . ἐκρύβη ἀπ᾽ αὐτῶν ("Jesus . . . hid himself from them").[45]

In 4 there is no feminine textual variant ܕܚܒܝܢ.[46] The

32 Connolly, "Odes," 305 n. 1; Emerton, 730; Bauer, 623. Harnack (p. 72) had already described the translation "without utility" as "obscure." Bauer (p. 623) tries to make some sense of it by translating the second part of 3a as "for those, who (merely) know me."

33 BDAG, *s.vv.* ἀχρεῖος, 1; ἄχρηστος.

34 See LSJ and BDAG, *s.vv.* χράομαι, χρεία; Payne Smith, 1:1399–400.

35 Menge and Güthling, 128.

36 Ibid., 750–51.

37 In my translation, "unnecessary," I assumed that the sense *necessitas* could be transferred from ܚܫܚܬܐ (*ḥšaḥṯā*) to ܚܫܚܘܬܐ (*ḥāšḥūṯā*) (Lattke, *Bedeutung*, 1:181; cf. Brockelmann, *Lexicon*, 262). Harris and Mingana (2:407) may be right in their remark: "The writer is working on the 88th Psalm as a description of the descent into Hades." Cf. Ps 87:4-13 LXX (Rahlfs, 2:94–95; Brenton, 751), especially vv. 4b (καὶ ἡ ζωή μου τῷ ᾅδῃ ἤγγισεν, "and my life has drawn nigh to Hades"), 9a (ἐμάκρυνας τοὺς γνωστούς μου ἀπ᾽ ἐμοῦ, "Thou hast removed my acquaintance far from me"), 10c (διεπέτασα πρὸς σὲ τὰς χεῖράς μου, "I spread forth my hands to thee"); but also Isa 65:2 and *Odes* 27:1 and 42:1a. It is doubtful, though, whether the reference to ἀβοήθητος ("without help") in Ps 87:5b LXX puts "the key in the lock" (Harris and Mingana, 2:407–8). The remainder of their commentary (2:408–9) is more relevant to the later influence of *Ode* 42 than to its exegesis.

38 Pierre, 195; cf. Francis E. Williams, "The Apocryphon of James. [NHC] I,2:1.1–16.30," in Attridge, *Nag Hammadi Codex I*, 1:44–45; 2:27.

39 Payne Smith, 1:117; Nöldeke §280. "The participial form ܐܚܝܕܝܢ ܗܘܘ [*ʾaḥīḏīn-waw*] expresses the continued action of holding on to" (Connolly, "Odes," 305 n. 2). I cannot share his confidence that 42:1-2 can be used to interpret 42:3 (p. 305). Kittel ("Handschrift," 91 n. 2) also prefers "translation in the active voice" of the "participial form." His criticism of Connolly's translation, however, is unfounded.

40 "The negative meaning of the verb in this context is similar to its usage in Jn 7:44 and 10:39" (Franzmann, 284).

41 Kittel, "Handschrift," 91.

42 BDAG, *s.v.* κρατέω, 6a: "hold fast to."

43 BDAG, *s.v.* ἐπιλαμβάνομαι, 1 and 4.

44 BDAG, *s.v.* συλλαμβάνω, 1b. There is no need to take shelter under the middle voice of ἀντέχω (BDAG, *s.v.* ἀντέχω, 1; contra Frankenberg, 35). "The translation of ܐܚܕ by 'possess' (Charlesworth 1977) is ambiguous, an obvious attempt to mollify the difficulty with the text" (Franzmann, 284).

45 See Payne Smith, 1:1530; BDAG, *s.v.* κρύπτω, 1a. Greßmann (p. 471) evens out the syntax ("for I am hidden"), while Bauer (p. 623) tries "should" for "will" ("because I should hide myself"). That is a possible translation of the imperfect, but sheds no light into the obscurity of the text.

46 Contra Charlesworth, 144, 147 n. 9; cf. the ـܝܢ (*-īn*)-endings on that same page of H in Charlesworth, *Manuscripts*, 87 lines 5, 9, 12–13.

contrast between 3b and 4 may justify the translation of ܘ (*w*-) as "but."[47] It may be, on the other hand, that, after the tortuous and obscure statements of 3a-b, this conclusion is no longer dependent on the conjunction ܡܛܠ ܕ (*meṭṭol d*-), "because," but is a simple promise of salvation, which in 𝔊 would have been καὶ γενήσομαι πρὸς τοὺς με ἀγαπῶντας (cf. *Ode* 3 and 41:16; see Excursus 2).[48] The vocabulary of 4 is reminiscent both of the Fourth Gospel (cf. John 8:42; 14:15, 21, 23, 28) and of the formulaic "blessing" of Eph 6:23-24.[49]

■ **5-7a** Since stanza III is also part of the address of the "exalted Christ,"[50] it might occur to the reader to use 5a to date it. This would mean considering the Jews of John 5:16 (cf. 1 Thess 2:15) as well as the representatives of the "cosmos" of John 15:19, and in addition such persons as that Jew of the Diaspora Παῦλος (Σαῦλος, Σαούλ [שאול]), who persecuted the Lord Jesus and his followers.[51] However, the mythic tinge of all the passages in which words from the root *rdp* appear (cf. 5:4; 23:20; 28:8; 42:7) precludes such a historical application.[52] Instead of speaking of his *own* death, the speaking "I" sweepingly announces that all his nonadherents (see 3bβ above),[53] those who persecuted *him* as they persecuted all who proclaimed him, are "dead" (see 7a below).[54] In 𝔊, the persecutors could have been called διώκοντες, ἐκδιώκοντες, or καταδιώκοντες, which would have reminded anyone who knew the LXX of the vocabulary of the Psalms.[55]

The Pa. ܣܒܪ (*sabbar*)[56] in 5b can be derived either from the root *sbr*[57] or from the term ܣܒܪܬܐ (*sḇarṯā*), formed by metathesis (= Greek ἀγγελία, εὐαγγέλιον), meaning "he preached the gospel."[58] "The translation 'proclaimed' should be favored here because of the kerygmatic statements that follow."[59] As in 33:13b, the Pe. ܒܥܐ (*bʿā*) corresponds to the Greek verb ζητέω (see Excursus 19).[60]

Greater stress is laid on the explanatory self-description in 5c, which, in N, is logically detached from 5b.[61] The adjective ܚܝܐ (*ḥayyā*), "living," with its enclitic personal pronoun, can, of course, be translated by the verb "I live" (see Table 1).[62] In any case, it expresses, as the opposite of 5a, "the idea of eternal life."[63] In view of "hell and death" in 11a-b, one might conclude that "this really seems to be an allusion" to Rev 1:18.[64]

Whether the Pe. ܩܘܡ, ܩܡ (*qām*) in 6a, "I stood," "refers to the resurrection of Jesus Christ"[65] has been debated since Harnack declared: "6a should not be taken as an actual resurrection."[66] All the same, Zahn, who points to the use of ܩܡ in statements about the "resurrection of Jesus,"[67] asks: "What other form of arising could there

---

47 Harris and Mingana, 2:404; Bauer, 624: "aber."

48 Frankenberg, 35; BDAG, *s.v.* ἀγαπάω, 1aβℶ; Payne Smith, 1:1169.

49 See Schlier, *Epheser*, 309–12, esp. 311.

50 As Diettrich (p. 134) correctly observes, among his many unsupported expositions and annotations (pp. 132–36).

51 Cf. Acts 9:4-5; 22:7-8; 26:14-15; Gal 1:13-14; Phil 3:5-6; 1 Tim 1:13.

52 Cf., e.g., passages in *Pistis Sophia* (Schmidt, Till, and Schenke, *Schriften*, 391, *s.v.* διωγμός, διώκειν, διωκτής).

53 Wellhausen, 638; Greßmann, 471.

54 These deceased persecutors are not identical with the dead mentioned later in 14a and 15a.

55 See Hatch and Redpath, 338, 423, 730; Albrecht Oepke, "διώκω," *ThWNT* 2 (1935) 232; *TDNT* 2:229; C. Frevel "רָדַף *rāḏap*," *ThWAT* 7 (1993) 369–72; *TDOT* 13:348–51.

56 It might mean "who trusted in me" (Emerton, 730).

57 Brockelmann, *Lexicon*, 456; Payne Smith, 2:2510.

58 Brockelmann, *Lexicon*, 457; see also Brockelmann, *Grammatik* §38, and p. 185*. Harris and Mingana (2:404) translate it as ". . . who proclaimed *about* me." As the Syriac translation of εὐαγγελιζόμενοι τὸν κύριον Ἰησοῦν ("preaching the Lord Jesus") in Acts 11:20 shows, the preposition I have emphasized is superfluous.

59 Vogl, 73.

60 Frankenberg, 30, 35.

61 See Lattke, *Bedeutung*, 1:76; Franzmann, 281–82.

62 Payne Smith, *Dictionary*, 138.

63 Spitta, 264; cf. Mark 16:11; John 14:19; Rom 14:9; Rev 1:18; 2:8.

64 Spitta, 264–65.

65 Charlesworth, 147.

66 Harnack, 72.

67 In his excellent inventory of the "polysemy" of the "resurrection of the dead," Jacob Kremer says on "resurrection or raising up": "The 'resurrection' of one who is dead is, for Jews, always the work of God (cf. Rom 4:17; 2 Kgs 5:7); therefore the noun ἀνάστασις, like the verbs ἀνίστημι and ἐγείρω (even when used intransitively as in the forms ἀνέστη and ἠγέρθη = 'he arose'), always describe an act of God" (in Gisbert Greshake and Kremer, *Resurrectio mortuorum: Zum theologischen Verständnis der leiblichen Auferstehung* [2nd ed.; Darmstadt:

be?"[68] In the first place, one must remember that the exalted one has just said: "I live."[69] The Syriac syntax of 6a-b (past–present–future) should not mislead the reader to find a new beginning, that is, a new statement of resurrection that looks to the past.[70] For in 𝔊, the participle ἀναστάς (cf. Mark 16:9) might have expressed, in traditional fashion, only the condition that made 5c possible: "an eternal standing before God."[71] It is also possible, however, that ܩܐܡܬ (*qāmet*) with the ethical dative ܠܝ (*lī*)[72] does not represent ἀναστάς or ἀνέστην at all,[73] but a participle of ἵστημι, either στάς or ἑστώς (cf. John 20:14; Acts 7:55-56).[74] In that case, "the emphasis [is] less on 'standing' than on 'being, existing.'"[75] However the first part of 6a was intended or is understood, the main weight falls on the statement of salvation of the second part, with its reminiscence of Matt 28:20 (ἐγὼ μεθ' ὑμῶν εἰμι, "I am with you"; cf. Acts 18:10).[76] Charlesworth did not need to remove his reference to 4,[77] since the prepositions ܥܡ (*ʿam*) and ܠܘܬ (*lwāt*) are sometimes interchangeable (see below on 14b in H and N; cf. similar statements with ܥܡ in 8:21c and 41:11a).

The co-optation of 6b for the occurrence of prophecy in early Christianity[78] has been validly criticized by Hill: "the verse in question from Ode 42 does not specifically refer to prophets but to believers in general."[79] As can be seen from 8:4, the singular of στόμα/ܦܘܡܐ (*pummā*), "mouth," would do just as well here as the plural. That there are a number of "mouths"[80] is made clear by the plural suffix (see Excursuses 12 and 31).

In 7a, in contrast to the plural of ܪܕܘܦܐ (*rādōpā*) in 5a but with no difference in meaning, there is a participle of the Pe. ܪܕܦ (*rdap̄*), "persecute." If this is an allusion to John 15:20, there is, again, no point in speculating about an actual historical episode of persecution. The exact meaning of the Aph. of ܣܠܐ (*slā*) is even more difficult to determine than was the case in 41:11b. Frankenberg was quite right to put a question mark after

Wissenschaftliche Buchgesellschaft, 1992] 8–15, listing all important passages in the New Testament). Even ἐγήγερται ("he was raised") in 1 Cor 15:12 is translated by ܩܡ (*qām*).

68 Zahn, 695 n. 2; Spitta (p. 264) is even more laconic: "But why not?"

69 Vogl, 73 on 5c.

70 I do not understand how Charlesworth (p. 145) came to begin 6a with "Then."

71 Walter Grundmann, "Stehen und Fallen im qumrānischen und neutestamentlichen Schrifttum," in Hans Bardtke, ed., *Qumran-Probleme: Vorträge des Leipziger Symposions über Qumran-Probleme vom 9. bis 14. Oktober 1961* (SSA 42; Berlin: Akademie-Verlag, 1963) 148. Franzmann (pp. 281–82, 286) divides 6a into 6a-b (so that 6b becomes 6c) to claim that "[t]he verbs ܩܘܡ and ܚܝܐ combine to form a delayed antithesis to ܡܝܬ in 5a."

72 Nöldeke §224. This would invalidate previous remarks on this preposition (Lattke, *Oden*, 213 n. 3).

73 Frankenberg, 35.

74 See Strelan, *Acts*, 150–51. In that case, the "standing" of the exalted one might allude to the "standing at the right hand of God" (Acts 7:55-56).

75 BDAG, *s.v.* ἵστημι, 2.

76 Massaux (*Influence*, 65) asks: "Is it possible to see here a reference to the text of the first gospel?" His answer softens this idea somewhat: "But it may also be the simple application of a traditional theme in the description of martyrdom, Christ speaking through the mouth of those who are persecuted; the following verse of the ode speaks indeed of persecution" (pp. 65–66). Vogl's reference (p. 73) to Burkitt is not impaired by his remarks about the "direct speech" in Matt 28:20 and the "indirect [speech] here" (his reference to "Burkitt 273" should be corrected). Burkitt (p. 373) remarks that "the Syriac version may be accepted as a very faithful rendering of the original Greek of the Odes. . . . The Odes in Syriac are a creditable piece of work, but their language is a very different thing from the graceful and flexible tongue in which the Acts of Judas Thomas and the Dialogue on Fate are written." And in a note he draws attention to the difference between ܐܢܐ ܥܡܟܘܢ ܐܢܐ of Matt 28:20 in the Peshitta and ܐܝܬܝ ܥܡܗܘܢ (*ʾīṯay ʿammhōn*) in *Ode* 42:6.

77 Charlesworth, 1973 (not 1977), 147 n. 11.

78 By, e.g., Gunkel, *Aufsätze*, 173; Philipp Vielhauer and Georg Strecker, "Einleitung [zu: C. Apokalypsen und Verwandtes]," *NTApo*⁵ 2 (1989) 514; "Introduction [to: Apocalypses and Related Subjects]," *NTApoc* 2:567.

79 David Hill, "On the Evidence for the Creative Role of Christian Prophets," *NTS* 20 (1974) 265; see also idem, *New Testament Prophecy* (London: Marshall, Morgan & Scott, 1979) 161–67.

80 Lattke, *Oden*, 213: "Münder."

ἐβδελύξαντο.[81] Up to now, the verb has generally been translated as "despised."[82] 𝔊 would have had ἀτιμάζω or ἐξουθενέω for that.[83] But Zahn already had suspected "a translation of ἀκυροῦν" here (cf. Mark 7:13; Gal 3:17).[84] Although "annihilate" may be too strong,[85] the possible equivalents include, besides ἀκυρόω and ἀθετέω (cf. 41:11), ἀποδοκιμάζω (see 10a below) in the sense of "reject."[86] Because of the *inclusio* between 5a and 7a, it forms part of stanza III, but the liberation from the oppressive persecutors achieved by the Redeemer provides the necessary basis for understanding the next stanza.

■ **7b-9** The *inclusio* of stanza III by "persecutors" corresponds to that of IV by "love." A second reason for following Franzmann's division into stanzas[87] rather than Vogl's "gathering into strophes"[88] is the fact that stanza IV disrupts the connection between 7a and 10.[89] Even so, stanza IV is not a poetic intrusion but firmly rooted in the preceding text (cf. 3a with 8b; 4 with 7b and 9b).

Verse 7b introduces the two similes in 8-9. The metaphorical ζυγός/ܢܝܪܐ (*nīrā*), "yoke," is not meant for a "burden";[90] the qualifying genitive (in 𝔊 τῆς ἀγάπης μου, "of my love"; cf. John 15:9-10 and also Rom 8:35; 2 Cor 5:14; Eph 3:19),[91] as in *Did.* 6:2 ("yoke of the Lord") and *1 Clem.* 16:17 ("yoke of his grace")[92]—and without any irony[93]—transmutes it positively.[94] Bernard suggests: "There may be here a veiled allusion to the easy yoke of Christ (Matt. xi 29) which the neophyte takes upon him in baptism."[95] There is, however, not even an indirect mention of baptism, and any connection with Matt 11:29-30[96] must also be questioned: "But no clue in the context allows us to determine with certainty that the author of the ode had the Matthean text in mind."[97] The Aph. of ܪܡܐ (*rmā*), followed by the preposition ܥܠ (*ʿal*), which occurs four times in stanza IV (7b, 8a, 8b, 9b), "will correspond to the Greek βάλλειν, which means not only *to throw* but also *to lay*."[98]

81 Frankenberg, 35; see Payne Smith, 2:2638; BDAG, *s.v.* βδελύσσομαι.

82 Flemming in Harnack, 72; Wellhausen, 638; Bauer, 624; Lattke, *Oden*, 213 (all: "verachteten"); cf. Harris and Mingana, 2:404.

83 See BDAG, *s.vv.* ἀτιμάζω, ἐξουθενέω.

84 Zahn, 695; BDAG, *s.v.* ἀκυρόω: "make void" as a "legal t[echnical] t[erm]."

85 See Spitta, 264.

86 BDAG, *s.v.* ἀποδοκιμάζω, b; Charlesworth, 145; Emerton, 730; Franzmann, 282; Ungnad and Staerk, 39: "verwerfen"; Pierre, 196: "rebuter."

87 Franzmann, 281, 283, 286.

88 Vogl, 69–71.

89 As Harnack (p. 73) realized; he becomes quite agitated and exclaims: "how abrupt verse 7 is! and how unexpected are 'the yoke of love' and 'those who believe in me.'"

90 BDAG, *s.v.* ζυγός, 1; see also Payne Smith, 2:2366.

91 Käsemann, rather curiously, lists *Ode* 42:7-9 among the parallels that he uses for the "interpretation of the agapē as aeon" and the "connection between pistis and agapē" (see Käsemann, *Leib*, 152–53).

92 Lona's remark (p. 234), "the phrase ὑπὸ τὸν ζυγὸν τῆς χάριτος is unique in early Christian writings," is correct. But he fails to cite *Ode* 42:7.

93 See Hadumod Bußmann, *Lexikon der Sprachwissenschaft* (KTA 452; Stuttgart: Kröner, 1983) 221.

94 Lindemann's comment (p. 64) on *1 Clem.* 16:17 is also relevant here: "Perhaps the Jewish concept of the 'yoke' of the Kingdom of heaven or of the Torah is behind this expression" (see Michael Lattke, "Zur jüdischen Vorgeschichte des synoptischen Begriffs der 'Königsherrschaft Gottes,'" in Peter Fiedler and Dieter Zeller, eds., *Gegenwart und kommendes Reich: Schülergabe Anton Vögtle zum 65. Geburtstag* [SBB; Stuttgart: Katholisches Bibelwerk, 1975] 24; idem, "On the Jewish Background of the Synoptic Concept 'The Kingdom of God,'" trans. M. Rutter, in Bruce Chilton, ed., *The Kingdom of God in the Teaching of Jesus* [Issues in Religion and Theology 5; Philadelphia: Fortress; London: SPCK, 1984] 87). But the "metaphor of the yoke" is quite widespread: "The believer in Isis also bears 'the yoke of religion' (*ministerii iugum*, Apuleius *Metam.* 11.15.5)" (Bauer, 624 n. 3). Felix Christ (*Sophia*, 108) suspects influence from "Sir 6 and 51" as examples of the "yoke that Wisdom imposes and herself is."

95 Bernard, 130.

96 Bauer, 624; Lattke, *Oden*, 213.

97 Massaux, *Influence*, 66.

98 Bauer, 624; see Payne Smith, 2:3924–25; BDAG, *s.vv.* βάλλω, 2; ἐπιβάλλω, 1b; Frankenberg, 35: ἐπέβαλον ἐπ᾽ αὐτούς. Arvedson (*Mysterium*, 177) concludes from his interpretation of Hos 11:4 "that the drawing with ropes and cords represents a marriage custom and the imposition of the yoke images the actual act of love." He continues: "This image can be found being put into practice in

It is rather extravagant to use the "so-called 4Q*Sapiential Work C* (4Q424) Frag. 3,4–5" in explaining the stylistic figure of comparison ("like . . . so"),[99] which is quite common in the *Odes of Solomon*, in order to demonstrate an influence of the "Qumran Wisdom texts" on "the *Odes* . . . within Early Judaism."[100] The terms in 8a and 9a are meant literally, the first describing a universal amatory gesture[101] and the second traditional Jewish marriage customs. "Bridegroom" and "Bride" are therefore not metaphors for "Christ" and "the church."[102] And the metaphorical "union of God and humanity as bridegroom and bride" with the "image of the wedding and the bridal chamber" so popular "among Gnostics" does not come under consideration either.[103] Since 8a has no verb, it is easy to deduce the Greek wording: ὡς/ὥσπερ ὁ βραχίων τοῦ νυμφίου ἐπὶ τῆς νύμφης.[104]

The first "apodosis" of the "comparison,"[105] beginning with οὕτως/ܗܟܢܐ (*hākannā*), "so," picks up only the term "yoke" from 7b, but implies the complete paradoxical expression "the yoke of my love." At the same time, 8b reverts to 3a and, as it were, explodes the comparison by the use of the plural participle of ܝܕܥ (*ʾidaʿ*), "know" (cf. the similar change from plural to singular in 28:1a-c). Here too it is easy to reconstruct the Greek: οὕτως ὁ ζυγός μου ἐπὶ τῶν με γιγνωσκόντων (see Excursus 7).[106]

The question marks that Frankenberg inserted in his retroversion of 9a into Greek mark difficulties, which can also be seen from the following translations of the *hapax legomenon* ܓܢܘܢܐ (*gnōnā*): "couch,"[107] "bridal couch,"[108] "wedding couch,"[109] "wedding bower,"[110] "four-poster,"[111] "bridal bower,"[112] "bridal feast,"[113] "bed,"[114] "bridal bed,"[115] "bridal chamber."[116] As the passive participle of the Pe. ܡܬܚ (*mtaḥ*), "pitched,"[117] also found in 16:11 ("he stretched out")—and especially the preposition ܥܠ (*ʿal*) in 9b—suggest, the image is of something *above* the bridal pair: "the nuptial tent,"[118] "the canopy,"[119] "the wedding tent (*chuppāh*)."[120] 𝔊 would hardly

Odes Sol. 42." Wolff's critical commentary (*Hosea*, 258–59) has demolished any such interpretation.

99 Lattke, "Bildersprache," 101–2 = idem, *Bedeutung*, 4:26–28.

100 Contra Charlesworth, "Wisdom Texts," 348–49.

101 The gesture of 8a is beautifully illustrated by the oil painting *The Lovers* by Pablo Picasso (National Gallery of Art, Washington, D.C.). McNeil even detects echoes of Cant 2:6 and 8:3 in this passage (see McNeil, "Martyrdom," 141; cf. Gillis Gerleman, *Ruth • Das Hohelied* [BKAT 18; Neukirchen-Vluyn: Neukirchener Verlag, 1965] 119–20; illustration 94 in Othmar Keel, *Deine Blicke sind Tauben: Zur Metaphorik des Hohen Liedes* [SBS 114, 115; Stuttgart: Katholisches Bibelwerk, 1984] 173).

102 Contra Bernard, 131. Engelbert Krebs, too, finds the "image of the church as virgin" in *Ode* 42 (see Krebs, *Der Logos als Heiland im ersten Jahrhundert: Ein religions- und dogmengeschichtlicher Beitrag zur Erlösungslehre; Mit einem Anhang, Poimandres und Johannes: Kritisches Referat über Reitzensteins religionsgeschichtliche Logosstudien* [Freiburger theologische Studien 2; Freiburg: Herder, 1910] 65); his criticism (pp. 65–67) of Harnack is overstated. The use of the terms "bride" and "bridegroom" in 38:9-11 is not comparable.

103 Contra Bauer, 624 n. 6; Lattke, "Bildersprache," 103 = idem, *Bedeutung*, 29. The sentence above is quoted, almost word for word, from Gunkel, *Aufsätze*, 174. Franzmann is right not to draw on *Ode* 42 in her discussion of the Gnostic "bridal chamber" (see Majella Franzmann, "The Concept of Rebirth as the Christ and the Initiatory Rituals of the Bridal Chamber in the *Gospel of Philip*," *Antichthon* 30 [1996] 37–48).

104 See Frankenberg, 35; Payne Smith, 1:953, 1411, 1733; BDAG, *s.vv.* βραχίων; νύμφη, 1; νυμφίος.

105 BDAG, *s.v.* ὥσπερ, a.

106 Frankenberg, 35.

107 Harris and Mingana, 2:404.

108 Flemming in Harnack, 73; Diettrich, 135: "Brautlager."

109 Ungnad and Staerk, 39: "Hochzeitslager."

110 Wellhausen, 638–39: "Hochzeitslaube."

111 Greßmann, 472; Arvedson, *Mysterium*, 177: "Himmelsbett."

112 Bauer, 624: "Brautlaube."

113 Charlesworth, 145.

114 Emerton, 731.

115 Franzmann, 283.

116 Lattke, *Bedeutung*, 1:183; idem, *Oden*, 213: "Brautgemach."

117 See Payne Smith, 2:2247: *extensus*.

118 Labourt and Batiffol, 37: "la tente de fiançailles."

119 Pierre, 196: "le dais."

120 Josef Schmid, "Brautgemach," *RAC* 2 (1954) 525; Lattke, *Oden*, 213 n. 6; Berger and Nord, 971: "das Hochzeitszelt." Schmid (col. 526 [with slight correction]) explains: "Later, and even today, *chuppāh* is the term for a baldachin under which the marriage ceremony takes place." See Gesenius, 249; Koehler and Baumgartner, 325; Marcus Jastrow,

have used *κοίτη*;[121] *νυμφών* would be the word that first came to mind.[122] But it is just as likely that 𝔊 would have used *παστός* (cf. Ps 18:6 LXX)[123] and in that very sense of "bridal canopy or curtain (freq. used loosely as a symbol of marriage)."[124] The phrase made up of the inclusively intended plural of ܚܬܢܐ (*ḥatnā*)[125] and ܒܝܬ (*bēṯ*) is a sort of "locative": "in the house of the bridal pair."[126]

Verse 9b finally shows where the stress lies in the simile "the yoke of my love" (7b; cf. 17:12; Excursus 2). There is a reciprocity in the love of his own (4) and the love of the exalted one spread over them like a wedding canopy,[127] which is reminiscent of John's Gospel.[128] "To know" (8b) and "to believe in" are not opposites but parallel and complementary terms (cf. 8:10-13 and Excursus 34). Further on (19b) there will be specific mention of the faith of those who are liberated from the "chains of darkness" (16b).

■ **10** If we knew the Greek (original) of stanza V, it would be easier to determine the exact meaning of the four Syriac verbs. The first verb of 10a connects to 7a at the end of stanza III, so that stanza V—unlike stanza VI—is not yet part of the introduction to stanza VII.[129] The only thing that is clear, to start with, in the synonymous parallelism of 10a and 10b, is that the speaking "I" denies something negative concerning him,[130] contrary, on the one hand, to general opinion (or appearances) and, on the other, to the (generalized) views of unspecified persons. After that the questions begin.

Does the subject of the Pe. ܪܢܐ (*rnā*), which occurs only here (10b: "they thought") and is more likely to represent *φρονέω* + *περί/ὑπέρ* than *φροντίζω*,[131] stand for the persecutors of stanza III or the adherents—marked by their acknowledgment, faith, hope, and love—of the speaking "I"? Does the Ethpe. of ܣܒܪ (*sḇar*) in 10a, "I seemed," which is used differently in 17:6b and 34:5c, represent a form of *δοκέω*,[132] *λογίζομαι*,[133] *οἴομαι*,[134] or *νομίζω*?[135] Is the negated Ethpe. of ܣܠܐ (*slā*), "I was not rejected," intended to correct the predictions of

A Dictionary of the Targumim, the Talmud Babli and Yerushalmi, and the Midrashic Literature (New York: Judaica Press, 1989) 437.

121 Contra Frankenberg, 35; see LEH, *s.v.* *κοίτη*.

122 BDAG, *s.v.* *νυμφών*, 2; see also Str-B, 1:500. Billerbeck's remark on Matt 9:15, "The days of Messiah considered a wedding feast," is not relevant here (Str-B, 1:517; on Jewish marriage customs, see ibid., 1:500–517 and also 2:372–99).

123 Rahlfs, 2:17; Brenton, 708: "chamber."

124 LSJRevSup, *s.v.* *παστός*.

125 Labourt corrects this plural (Labourt and Batiffol, 37), since the "wedding tent . . . was set up in the house of the bridegroom" (Josef Schmid, "Brautgemach," *RAC* 2 [1954] 525). Harris and Mingana (2:407) justifiably consider the correction unnecessary.

126 Klaus Beyer, letter of November 13, 2002: The preposition ܒ is not left out before "any other word beginning with *b*." See Payne Smith, 1:478; Payne Smith, *Dictionary*, 43. So with "adverbially used" ܒܝܬ (*bēṯ*) = "in the house of, *i.e.* in the place of" (Nöldeke §156). Charlesworth's remark (p. 147 n. 14), "The preposition Bēth has assimilated with the Bēth of 'house,'" is invalid. Further, ܒܝܬ would not be "due to haplological ellipsis of a syllable" from ܒܒܝܬ (Brockelmann, *Grammatik* §70; Lattke, *Bedeutung*, 1:182; Franzmann, 286; Lattke, *Oden*, 213 n. 7).

127 It is probably fortuitous that the stretching of the bridal tent (9a) and the "spreading out" of the hands (1b) employ words from the same Syriac root. McNeil does not notice the simile but finds a deeper meaning: "The 'spreading-forth' of Christ on the Cross (42.1-2) made possible his spreading-forth of the bridal-chamber of his love for those who believe in him" (see McNeil, "Martyrdom," 140).

128 Cf. Lattke, *Einheit*, 22–24, 60–62.

129 Contra Franzmann, 286.

130 The only thing that is unambiguous in meaning—not necessarily in its Greek wording—is the repeated ܐܦܢ (*ʾāp̄-en*), "although." I think *κἄν* is more likely in 𝔊 than *καίπερ* (contra Frankenberg, 35; see Payne Smith, 1:327; BDAG, *s.vv.* *καίπερ*; *κἄν*, 2).

131 Contra Frankenberg, 35; see BDAG, *s.vv.* *φρονέω*, 1; *φροντίζω*; Payne Smith, 2:3935–36.

132 BDAG, *s.v.* *δοκέω*, 2; see Fanourgakis, 174: *εἰ καὶ οὕτως ἔδοξα αὐτοῖς*.

133 BDAG, *s.v.* *λογίζομαι*, 1b; see Tsakonas, 187: *ἂν καὶ ἐλογίσθην οὕτως*.

134 BDAG, *s.v.* *οἴομαι*; see Frankenberg, 35: *καίπερ ᾠήθησαν*.

135 BDAG, *s.v.* *νομίζω*, 2; see Kaegi, 608: "supposed to be, seen to be" in the passive; Payne Smith, 2:2510.

the passion in the Synoptic Gospels (Mark 8:31; 9:12; Luke 9:22)?[136] Or is it not, more probably, a case of the theological passive: "that he has not experienced ... any *repulsa* by God"?[137] Does the equally negated Pe. ܐܒܕ (*ʾeḇaḏ*), "I did not perish," corresponding to a form of ἀπόλλυμι (see Excursus 28),[138] import "a docetic nuance"?[139] Do these two negations justify such verdicts as "The Christ asserts his impassibility" and "renewed denial of the death of the Christ"?[140] Is it possible, in view of 17:7-10 and 28:8-18, in spite of possible "references to the cross" (cf. 27; 35:7; 41:1-2), to agree with McNeil: "In conclusion, there is no evidence to suggest that the odist thought the Saviour had died, and there are two explicit passages in Odes 28 and 42 which deny his death"?[141] Finally, is it possible to apply the Christian-Gnostic "Docetism"[142] of *2 Treat. Seth*, "For one who is persecuted and appears to die but does not in reality, cf. *The Second Treatise of the Great Seth* 55,9–56,19,"[143] to the elucidation of *Ode* 42:10?

First, and with explicit reference to the commentary on 28:8-9 and 28:16-18, it is necessary to affirm that the "passion of the Gnostic revealer," which is "merely illusory,"[144] is worlds apart from the first person statements of the exalted Christ of this Ode, which predates both "orthodoxy" and the "universal church." Although there is no emphasis on the lethal torture of the σταυρὸς τοῦ Χριστοῦ ("cross of Christ" [1 Cor 1:17]; cf. Gal 6:12-14; Phil 2:8) or on the Crucified in his suffering (cf., in addition to the passion narratives of the Synoptic Gospels, 1 Cor 2:2 and Gal 3:1), neither stanza I nor stanza V denies the death of the speaking "I." So the worst of which one can accuse the *Odes of Solomon*—perhaps with more reason than the Fourth Gospel—is an "unreflected Docetism."[145] In order to preserve the attractive notion of the *Salvator salvatus,*[146] it is necessary—as in the case of the New Testament and other early Christian works—to define him in two ways. In the first place, he is the Redeemer who, in spite of having died, is kerygmatically and theologically "rescued once and for all from the clutches of Death."[147] In the second place, he is the *exalted* Savior, the *Salvator exaltatus.*[148]

The speaking "I" of stanza V is not one of the mortals "that go down to the pit" (Ps 87:5a LXX); he was exalted on the cross and now himself, as one *not* rejected by God and *not* having perished once and for all, mythologically makes his way into the realm of Death, "Hades" (cf. Ps 87:4b LXX).[149] And what follows are indeed "images of extraordinary size and beauty."[150]

■ **11** This bicolon, constructed in parallel, changes the scene in two senses. First, the mythology of stanzas VI–X[151] does not follow logically from stanzas II–V. Stanza VI is to some extent a new beginning (although also introduced by stanza I), describing the confrontation between the one exalted on the cross and the

136 Spitta, 264: "the one rejected by the Jews has become beloved by his adherents."
137 Zahn, 696 n. 2; see also Diettrich, 135; Gunkel, *Aufsätze*, 174: "Christ [appeared] rejected by God."
138 Frankenberg, 35: οὐδὲ ἀπωλόμην (middle aorist 2; BDAG, *s.v.* ἀπόλλυμι, 1b).
139 Charlesworth, 147 n. 17.
140 Labourt and Batiffol, 92.
141 McNeil, "Sufferings," 33.
142 Silvia Pellegrini, "Der zweite Logos des großen Seth (NHC VII,2)," *NHD* 2 (2003) 577.
143 As Franzmann does (pp. 286–87).
144 Silvia Pellegrini, "Der zweite Logos des großen Seth (NHC VII,2)," *NHD* 2 (2003) 577, 583 on *2 Treat. Seth* 55,18-20; cf. Gregory Riley, "NHC VII,*2*: Second Treatise of the Great Seth," in Birger A. Pearson, ed., *Nag Hammadi Codex VII* (NHMS 30; Leiden: Brill, 1996) 135–36, 162–63.
145 Käsemann, *Testament,* 66 (= *Wille*, 62); see still Labourt and Batiffol, 94–98.
146 So Adam, *Psalmen des Thomas*, 34 and 44, on 8:22, etc.; see also Colpe, *Schule*, 180–81.
147 Gisbert Greshake and Jacob Kremer, *Resurrectio mortuorum: Zum theologischen Verständnis der leiblichen Auferstehung* (2nd ed.; Darmstadt: Wissenschaftliche Buchgesellschaft, 1992) 10.
148 Cf. the Vulgate translation of ὑψόω; see Excursuses 5 and 17.
149 Rahlfs, 2:94; Brenton, 751.
150 Kittel, 138.
151 Stanzas VI–VIII and X are quoted by Samuel Vollenweider to support the thesis that Christ exerts his redeeming power throughout the universe even in the deeps of hell (see Arnold Benz and Vollenweider, *Würfelt Gott? Ein ausserirdisches Gespräch zwischen Physik und Theologie* [Düsseldorf: Patmos, 2000] 251–52).

almost hendyadic personifications "Sheol" ("the realm of Death"/"netherworld") and "Death." Since there is no mention of a tomb (cf., e.g., Matt 27:60-61 with the terms μνημεῖον and τάφος) or of a burial (cf., e.g., ἐτάφη, "he was buried," in 1 Cor 15:4), one might suggest that the Redeemer's ascension to heaven from the cross[152] balances his descent to hell from the cross.[153] Whether the realm of the dead can "see" only one who has really died and is still considered to be dead is a meaningless question for a text as early as this, just as it is for the passages 1 Pet 3:18-22 and 4:6,[154] and even for the statement "He descended into hell" in the later Apostles' Creed.[155]

Second, stanza VI is, in a sense, a summary of the narratives that follow. That means that it is not necessary to accept Harnack's deletion of the second part of 11b as a Christian addition (cf. Matt 27:52-53).[156] The words "and many with me" bear "no relationship"[157] to the statement in 12a but anticipate the dead mentioned and liberated in 14-20. Those, whose petitions come later (15b-18) and are heard (19), whom the Redeemer can count as liberated among his own (20), are quite distinct from the adherents mentioned in stanzas II–IV (or even II–V).

Ernst Koch, referring to *Odes Sol.* 17, 22, and 42 among his sources, remarks: "*Ode* 42:11-20 points to extensive mythological associations."[158] These associations have "analogies in the religious history . . . of the milieu surrounding the Old Testament and the New Testament," extending from "Sumer and Babylon" and the "Egyptian belief in the after-life" to the "descent [*catabasis*] of the heroes (Theseus, Hercules, Orpheus)" in the Greco-Roman era.[159] Since the "interrogation of the New Testament produces no exegetical starting point in any of its passages (i.e., 1 Pet 3:19-20; 4:6; Eph 4:8-10) for the development of the concept of the descent into hell"[160] *Ode* 42 should have been mentioned in the first section of Koch's article, because this Ode

152 See commentary on *Ode* 27.

153 Reitzenstein's remark on a "text of the Kantaeans, a sect standing between the Manichaeans and the Mandaeans"—"The 'descent into hell' is actually an ascent into heaven"—is not relevant here (see Reitzenstein, *Das mandäische Buch*, 28–30). Later he claims that *Odes* 17 and 42 "are quite comparable to Mandaean and Manichaean texts" (p. 31 n. 3; p. 32 n. 1). That the earlier *Odes of Solomon* influenced the later Mandaean and Manichaean writings would be hard to deny. On the word and idea of "Höllenfahrt [journey to hell]," see Colpe, who declares "Christ's journey to hell" to be the "true journey to hell" (Carsten Colpe, "Höllenfahrt," *RAC* 15 [1991] 1016–17). On the ambiguity of "descent" and "ascent" in the history of religion, see Alois Grillmeier, "Höllenabstieg Christi, Höllenfahrt Christi," *LThK*² 5 (1960) 451.

154 Alois Grillmeier, "Höllenabstieg Christi, Höllenfahrt Christi," *LThK*² 5 (1960) 452–53.

155 Carl Clemen, *'Niedergefahren zu den Toten': Ein Beitrag zur Würdigung des Apostolikums* (Gießen: Töpelmann, 1900). It is amazing that Christ's *descensus ad inferos* or *ad inferna* (viz., *loca*) plays such a minor part in the ancient creeds (see Heinrich Denzinger, *Kompendium der Glaubensbekenntnisse und kirchlichen Lehrentscheidungen* [ed. Peter Hünermann; 37th ed.; Freiburg: Herder, 1991] 1698, *s.v.* "Unterwelt [netherworld]": "Hinabstieg Christi in die Unterwelt"). Although in the Orthodox and Eastern churches the "descent into hell (or rather 'into Hades') is unknown as an 'article of faith,'" yet "the motif has a central place in liturgy, hymnography, homiletics and iconography" (Peter Plank, "Höllenabstieg Christi, Höllenfahrt Christi. IV. Ostkirchlich," *LThK*³ 5 [1996] 239). In the Anaphora of St. Basil, for instance, it is said: "*by the cross* [emphasis added] he descended into Hades, in order to fill everything with himself, and he loosed the pains of death" (ibid., 239).

156 Harnack, 73.

157 Diettrich, 135.

158 Ernst Koch, "Höllenfahrt Christi," *TRE* 15 (1986) 456–57: "Die Hadesfahrt Christi als Bestandteil altkirchlichen Erlösungsglaubens [Christ's descent into Hades as an element in the faith in salvation of the early church]."

159 Alois Grillmeier, "Höllenabstieg Christi, Höllenfahrt Christi," *LThK*² 5 (1960) 450–52; cf. Gunkel, 304, who refers especially to later Mandaean writings.

160 Ernst Koch, "Höllenfahrt Christi," *TRE* 15 (1986) 455; contra Werner Bieder, "Höllenfahrt Christi," *EKL* 2 (1958 = ²1962) 195.

offers more of the "earliest perceptible traces" pointing to "the first half of the second century" than all the others put together.[161]

The Syriac feminine noun ܫܝܘܠ (*šyōl*), "Sheol," undoubtedly corresponds to the Greek masculine noun ᾅδης, so in this next excursus the latter term will be used, because it carries less baggage than the word "hell." In order to bring out the parallelism with "Death" personified and to avoid its original Greek meaning of "the name of the god of the underworld,"[162] the English equivalent used will be "realm of the dead."

Excursus 42: "Hades" as the Realm of the Dead in the *Odes of Solomon*

The Syriac word ܫܝܘܠ (*šyōl*) is taken from the Hebrew Bible in which *šᵉʾôl* is used as both "a masculine and a feminine noun" as the name of "the underground realm of the dead."[163] That the LXX, almost without exception, translates שאול by ᾅδης[164] is one of those Hellenistic phenomena that can have at least three consequences. In the first place, the images of Hades may more or less coincide (e.g., the underworld, darkness, gates, even its use as a personification). In the second place, Hebrew and Semitic characteristics may spread to the Greek (e.g., parallelisms, details, theological aspects). And in the third place, Greek mythology can influence the mental perception of the culture (e.g., Hades/Pluto as a god, the hell-hound Cerberus, Persephone/Kore).[165] One can take for granted a long evolutionary history and possibly radical changes in meaning for each word.[166] Because the Hebrew loanword survived in Syriac,[167] the evolutionary lines from the Old Testament were

161 Koch gives this section the title: "The origins of the concept in early Christianity" (see Ernst Koch, "Höllenfahrt Christi," *TRE* 15 [1986] 455–56). Neither Bo Reicke nor Otto Böcher even mentions the *Odes of Solomon* (see Reicke, "Höllenfahrt Christi I. Neutestamentlich und dogmengeschichtlich," *RGG*³ 3 [1959] 408–10; Böcher, "Höllenfahrt Jesu Christi I. Neues Testament," *RGG*⁴ 3 [2000] 1855–56). Johannes Weiß, commenting on Luke 23:43, emphasizes that "Jesus never went to Hades" (see Weiß, "Höllenfahrt im NT," *RGG* 3 [1912] 83). For Georg Bertram ("Höllenfahrt: II. Höllenfahrt Christi," *RGG*² 2 [1928] 1969–70), *Ode* 42 is one of the more or less universalizing and more or less moralizing sources from the "post New Testament era" for "Christ's descent into hell," which the sixteen-year-old Goethe made the subject of a poem and on which Harnack concludes: "In the churches of today it is no more than a dried-up relic, but *then* [viz., before Marcion] it was not only *a*, but almost *the* principal part in the proclamation of the Redeemer" since "it is only in descending into the netherworld" that the Redeemer finds "the multitudes in need of salvation." See Adolf Harnack, *Marcion: Das Evangelium vom fremden Gott. Eine Monographie zur Geschichte der Grundlegung der katholischen Kirche. Neue Studien zu Marcion* (TU 45 [+ 44,4]; 2nd ed.; Darmstadt: Wissenschaftliche Buchgesellschaft, 1960) 130 and n. 1.

162 Hertha Sauer, "Hades," *KP* 2 (1967) 903; see also Jan N. Bremmer, "Hades," *DNP* 5 (1998) 51.

163 Str-B, 4:1016, in the excursus on this term (pp. 1016–29), the "Gehinnom" (pp. 1029–118) and the threefold "paradise" (pp. 1118–65); on the Old Testament "concept of the world," see Manfred Oeming, "Welt/Weltanschauung/Weltbild IV/2. Altes Testament," *TRE* 35 (2003) 572–78, esp. illustrations 1–6.

164 Similarly "ᾅδης has become the name for the realm of the dead in Hellenistic Judaism, in a number of pseudepigrapha and in the New Testament (Matt 11:23; 16:18; Luke 10:15; 16:23; Acts 2:27, 31; 1 Cor 15:55(?); Rev 1:18; 6:8; 20:13; 20:14)" (Str-B, 4:1016). It should be noted that in the New Testament there is a "sharp distinction between ᾅδης and γέεννα" (Joachim Jeremias, "γέεννα," *ThWNT* 1 [1933] 655; *TDNT* 1:658).

165 Jan N. Bremmer, "Hades," *DNP* 5 (1998) 51–52. Aphrodite herself is said "to have gone down to Hades" (εἰς ᾅδου καταβαίνειν) in order to ransom Adonis/Tammûz from Persephone, the wife of Hades (Aristides *Apology* 11.3 [SC 470, pp. 218–19, 276–77; cf. Goodspeed, 14] should be added to Vinciane Pirenne-Delforge, "Aphrodite," *DNP* 1 [1996] 842, *s.v.* "Mythen"). The descent in itself poses no difficulties for the contemporaries of the *Odes of Solomon*. It is only the impotence of the goddess that is targeted.

166 See Str-B, 4:1016–29; Joachim Jeremias, "ᾅδης," *ThWNT* 1 (1933) 147–49; *TDNT* 1:147–49; Ludwig Wächter, "שְׁאוֹל *šᵉʾôl*," *ThWAT* 7 (1993) 903–10; *TDOT* 14:241–48; Martin P. Nilsson, *Geschichte der griechischen Religion* (2 vols.; HAW 5.2.1–2; 3rd ed.; Munich: Beck, 1967–76) 1:875, *s.v.* "Hades"; 1:889, *s.v.* "Unterwelt"; 2:737, *s.v.* "Hades"; 2:746, *s.v.* "Unterweltsglaube."

167 Payne Smith, 2:4009.

more clearly preserved. But bilingual Syria was quite aware of the blending of שאול/ܫܝܘܠ (*šyōl*) and ᾅδης.[168]

In the *Odes of Solomon,* the term ܫܝܘܠ (*šyōl*) = ᾅδης occurs only three times and each time parallel to ܡܘܬܐ (*mawtā*) = θάνατος. To simplify the following summary the three passages can be quoted as follows:

15:9 Death was annihilated before my face
and the realm of the dead [Sheol]
destroyed by my word.
29:4 And he caused me to ascend from the
depths of Sheol,
and from the mouth of Death he drew me.
42:11 The realm of the dead [Sheol] saw me and
became ill,
and Death vomited me up and many with
me.

The term "death," not always as a personification, occurs far more often and in many other contexts (see Table 1).

In 15:9a-b, where the redeemed Redeemer also is speaking, and 42:11a-b, the terms "Death" and "realm of the dead" could just as easily have been reversed. Touching the career of the speaking "I" in the history of salvation, it should be noted that the statements of 15:9 already proclaim the final victory (to which Paul,[169] for instance, looked forward), while here in 42:11 the personifications of "Hades" and "Death" still appear in their original positions. Their ultimate fate is not mentioned. The connection between these two passages is reinforced by the key word ܦܪܨܘܦܐ (*parṣōpā* [πρόσωπον]), "face," which is found also in 42:13 (where it means "presence").

In the mythological imagery of 29:4a-b, the terms are not so easily interchangeable: the "deeps" would not qualify "Death" as appropriately as they do the "realm of the dead." But since the "realm of the dead" also has an "insatiable maw" (cf. Isa 5:14; Prov 1:12),[170] and 42:12b mentions the "depth" of death (but see on stanza VII below), the exchange is still not unthinkable. In *Ode* 29, however, the speaking "I" is not the redeemed Redeemer but a redeemed believer in Christ.

Ode 29:4 is even less of a *descensus* text than 15:9. Whether 17:8b-11 and 22:1-5 could be considered as such has already been discussed in the commentary on those passages. The only indisputable testimony in the *Odes of Solomon* for the descent into Hades as place and realm of the dead is 42:11-20. Given the connection between *Odes* 41 and 42, it can also be assumed that it is the descent of Christ that is meant.[171]

168 Hans Dieter Betz describes what Lucian of Samosata in the second century C.E. has to say on the "topography of Hades" and on the "judgment of the underworld." "Lucian abstains from the task of describing the details, since everyone knows them anyway." See Betz, *Lukian von Samosata und das Neue Testament: Religionsgeschichtliche und paränetische Parallelen. Ein Beitrag zum Corpus Hellenisticum Novi Testamenti* (TU 76 = V. Reihe, Bd. 21; Berlin: Akademie-Verlag, 1961) 81–89, esp. 82 n. 1.

169 The passage 1 Cor 15:53-55 bristles with text-critical problems (hence the question mark in the Billerbeck quotation [Str-B, 4:1016] above). The important point in the current context is the fact that the terms ᾅδης and θάνατος occur in parallel in v. 55, instead of a repetition of θάνατος (NA^{27}, on this passage; see Aland and Juckel, *Briefe*, 1:491, 597).

170 Str-B, 4:1016.

171 Hans Windisch says of *Ode* 42:11-20 that of all the known variants of the "mythos of CHRIST'S DESCENT INTO HELL . . . of the second century and later," it is "the most affecting" (see Windisch, *Die Katholischen Briefe* [HNT 15; 2nd ed.; Tübingen: Mohr Siebeck, 1930] 71). *Ode* 42, of course, also plays a part in Josef Kroll's account of the "*Descensus* in Early Christianity" (Kroll, *Hölle*, 1–125, esp. 41–44). His treatment is more informative about the influence of the *Ode* on later thought than helpful for the explication of the text (see ibid., Index, 561, *s.v.* "Oden Salomos," though some of the page numbers are inaccurate). Kroll's polemic against Carl Schmidt (see Schmidt and Wajnberg, *Gespräche*, 453–576: "Der Descensus ad inferos in der alten Kirche [The *Descensus ad inferos* in the Early Church]") and his partisanship for Bousset (Bousset, *Gnosis*, 255–60; idem, *Kyrios Christos*, 26–33) are not altogether justified. Schmidt correctly identifies 42:11-20 as the "principal passage" in the *Odes of Solomon*, songs that "cannot easily be fitted into the framework of this Christian literary form [*Eidos*]" (Schmidt and Wajnberg, *Gespräche*, 560–64). As an expert on the *Pistis Sophia,* he declares: "For my part, I accept their [viz., the *Odes of Solomon*] Christian character as fact; in particular the *Odes* have no connection with *heretical* Gnosticism. . . . Christ's descent into Hades, especially, argues against their Gnostic character" (p. 561, emphasis added). Whether the descent into Hades is "a favorite motif in the *Odes of Solomon*" (pp. 564–67, esp. on *Odes* 17:8b-15 and 22) is a different question. On the concept of the "underworld" in

There is no variant reading in 11a.[172] The Pe. ܚܙܐ (*ḥzā*), "saw," is used metaphorically with the realm of the dead personified as its subject (cf. 17:6a; 28:8a; 41:8a). The other two verbs of 11a-b are more violent. Since the pointing of ܐܬܕܘܝܬ in N does not resolve the ambiguity,[173] this passive/reflexive form of ܕܘܐ (*dwā*), which occurs only here, may be read either as the Ethpe. *ʾeddawyaṯ*[174] or as the Ethpa. *ʾeddawwyaṯ*.[175] The translation "was shattered"[176] is not as good here as "was made miserable,"[177] "was grieved,"[178] or "was in distress."[179] In connection with the Ethpa., Brockelmann refers to Ps 35:14.[180] The verb in Ps 34:14 LXX, σκυθρωπάζω, is also the one that best fits here.[181] The realm of death felt nauseous, and "everything took on a greenish-yellow hue."[182]

As in 29:4b, Death personified, who is parallel to the realm of the dead,[183] clearly has a "maw" in 11b.[184] The Aph. ܐܬܝܒ (*ʾaṯīḇ*), which has occurred already in 38:13 as a consequence of intoxication, expresses the vomiting or spewing up.[185] Since at the time of the composition of the *Odes of Solomon* the theologoumenon the "power of God over the underworld" was undisputed among Jews and Christians,[186] one may suspect the use of a vocabulary associated with being raised from the dead, and may refer for the meaning either to Jonah 2:3-11[187] or to Rev 20:13.[188] Here in stanza VI, the vomiting up is a consequence of seeing and becoming nauseated.[189] If stanza VII, which is closely connected to VI, is drawn on for the explanation, its images will serve as adequate reasons for Death's spontaneous reaction.[190] The plural of ܣܓܝܐܐ (*saggīyā*) does not stand for the proverbial *hoi polloi* (as in 23:19b; 25:5a; 38:12a) but for the indefinable total of the redeemed described in stanzas VIII–X.[191]

Gnostic writings, see the indexes of Schmidt, Till, and Schenke, *Schriften*, 421, and *NHD* 2:913, *s.v.* "Unterwelt."

172 Contra Charlesworth, 144; cf. Lattke, *Bedeutung*, 1:58; 3:316; Sebastian P. Brock, review of Charlesworth in *BSOAS* 38 (1975) 142.

173 See Segal, *Point*, 17–18.

174 Payne Smith, 1:825; Payne Smith, *Dictionary*, 84; Diettrich, 135.

175 Brockelmann, *Lexicon*, 143.

176 Charlesworth, 145; Franzmann, 283.

177 Harris, 139.

178 Emerton, 731.

179 Harris and Mingana, 2:404; see LSJ and BDAG, *s.v.* ταλαιπωρέω, and BDAG, *s.v.* ταλαίπωρος (= *dāwyā* in Rom 7:24).

180 Brockelmann, *Lexicon*, 143: *debilitatus est.*

181 LSJ, *s.v.* σκυθρωπάζω: "to be of a sad colour"; LEH, *s.v.* σκυθρωπάζω: "to look angry or sullen, to be of a sad countenance"; cf. BDAG on the adjective σκυθρωπός: "pert[aining] to having a look suggestive of gloom or sadness, sad, gloomy, sullen, dark."

182 *MEL*, 31:1093. Zahn's imagery can hardly be reconciled with the "puking" in 11b: "Hell (Sheol)" reacted "like a wild animal when the trainer enters its cage" (Zahn, 696).

183 BDAG, *s.vv.* ᾅδης, θάνατος; cf. Ludwig Wächter, "שְׁאוֹל *šᵉʾôl*," *ThWAT* 7 (1993) 906; *TDOT* 14:245.

184 See Diettrich, 135.

185 Payne Smith, 2:4399; see also LSJ, *s.v.* ἐξεμέω.

186 Wächter, "שְׁאוֹל *šᵉʾôl*," *ThWAT* 7:901, 910; *TDOT* 14:239, 248.

187 Rick Strelan, in conversation. The ecclesiastical importance of Jonah 2:3-10 (cf. Wächter, "שְׁאוֹל *šᵉʾôl*," *ThWAT* 7:909; *TDOT* 14:247) is emphasized by the fact that the Προσευχὴ Ιωνα ("Prayer of Jonas") was included in the Odes of the Septuagint (Rahlfs, 2:173–74; cf. Brenton, 1095). Jonah 2:11 LXX, which says of the fish ἐξέβαλεν τὸν Ιωναν ("it cast up Jonas") is, naturally, omitted (see Rahlfs, 2:528; Brenton, 1095). The theme is, after all, "God's immense providence; it forces the fish to vomit up Jonah. . . . The word קִיא occurs in the Old Testament only in images arousing disgust . . . and corresponds to the coarse verb 'to puke'" (Hans Walter Wolff, *Dodekapropheton 3: Obadja und Jona* [BKAT 14.3; Neukirchen-Vluyn: Neukirchener Verlag, 1977] 114).

188 See Jeremias, "ᾅδης," *ThWNT* 1:149; *TDNT* 1:149.

189 See Ungnad Staerk, 40.

190 Spitta (p. 265), quoting A. Blaurer's hymn for Ascension Day ("Rejoice in rapture, faithful Christians," verse 3 line 3: "so that sin, death and hell become powerless and empty"), summarizes the connection between stanzas VI and VII as follows: "So Christ has weakened Hell and Death and thus prevented them from detaining him and the dead" (cf. Rev 1:18).

191 Vogl has made an excellent compilation of the Syriac texts that exhibit the formula "alone—with a great company" in reference to "the motifs of descent and ascent" (see August Vogl, "Allein—Mit grosser Menge: Ein Motiv des Abstiegs in den Scheol bei den alten Syrern," ed. Brian McNeil, *OrChrP* 45 [1979] 172, 174–77). It is not unlikely that *Ode* 42 influenced this tradition. It is intriguing that Cyril of Jerusalem in the fourth century equates the "descent into Hades" with the "descent into death" (ibid., 175).

■ **12-13** The close connection between stanzas VI and VII that Franzmann[192] stresses is shown, first, by the occurrence of seeing and/or πρόσωπον in 11a and 13b. Second, 12a and 13a add further details to the nausea of 11a. And, third, the descent in 12b is the necessary precondition for *all* that happened in stanza VI.

The *hapax legomenon* ܚܠܐ (*ḥallā*), "vinegar," and the term ܡܪܪܐ (*mrārā*), "bitterness,"[193] normally used in the plural (as here in N), in 12a correspond to the sense of οἶνος/ὄξος and χολή of the Matthean passion (Matt 27:34; cf. Ps 68:22 LXX) and to the English phrase "gall and wormwood."[194] The allusion in the terminology to the sufferings of Jesus, however, is, at best, subversive. The first term, here, does not mean "sour wine" but "wine vinegar."[195] The second does not correspond to χολή, "gall,"[196] but most probably to πικρία[197] in its literal sense and denotes the "bitter taste" that the speaking "I" made Death experience.[198]

Does 12b include Death as well as the realm of the dead? For H, this question can be answered in the affirmative, since the plural ܐܫܟܚ (*ʾeškaḥ*) in 13b does not "refer to the feet and head"[199] but can only refer to the two powers "Death and Sheol."[200] So, in the case of H, one could follow Schultheß in "correcting" ܒܗ (*beh*) to ܒܗ̇ (*bāh*), which would refer to the feminine noun "Sheol."[201] But, even though 29:4a mentions "the deeps of the realm of the dead [Sheol]" (see Excursus 42 above; cf. Prov 9:18),[202] there are several reasons why, in 12b, the singular ܥܘܡܩܐ (*ʿumqā*), "depth,"[203] corresponding to τὸ βάθος, must refer to Death.[204] In the first place, the masculine Syriac noun "Death" (11b) is unambiguously the subject of 13a and b. In the second place, the suffix of ܠܗ (*leh*) in 12a, "to him," and ܥܡܗ (*ʿammeh*) in 12b, "with(in) him," probably[205] refers to this masculine noun. Third, even in 14a there is still reference to "his [viz., Death's] dead." So the reading in 12b is most probably ܒܗ (*beh*) and not ܒܗ̇ (*bāh*). The ambiguity is not so much due to a "love for *double entendre*"[206] as to the fact that the Greek prepositional phrase ἐν αὐτῷ can refer either to ᾅδης ("Hades") or to θάνατος ("Death"): καὶ κατέβην μετ' αὐτοῦ ἐφ' ὅσον βάθος ἦν ἐν αὐτῷ.[207] But even μετ' αὐτοῦ (or the less likely σὺν αὐτῷ) in 12b, the dative αὐτῷ following ἐγενόμην in 12a, and the genitive αὐτοῦ in 14a (see below) are all ambiguous, and so are the Greek verbs in 13a-b.

The actual difficulty in 12b, namely, the exact meaning of the preposition ܥܡ (*ʿam*), has not yet been considered, a difficulty that is clearly illustrated by the translations "with him/it,"[208] "mit ihm,"[209] "avec elle/lui."[210] Greßmann is an exception, recognizing that ܥܡܗ

192 Franzmann, 287.
193 In 11:21, the singular ܡܪܪܐ (*mrārā*) is expressly equated with the nominalized Greek adjective πικρόν (BDAG, *s.v.* πικρός). It looks as if H uses the singular in this verse also.
194 German "Gift und Galle"; Zahn, 696 n. 5; Kroll, *Hymnodik*, 78; Greßmann, 472.
195 BDAG, *s.v.* ὄξος; Payne Smith, 1:1272.
196 Contra Frankenberg, 35.
197 Payne Smith, 2:2203.
198 See BDAG, *s.v.* πικρία, 1.
199 Contra Vogl, 74.
200 Vogl, 74.
201 Schultheß, 257; see also Labourt and Batiffol, 38.
202 On Prov 9:18, see Ludwig Wächter, "שְׁאוֹל *šᵉʾôl*," *ThWAT* 7:904; *TDOT* 14:241–42.
203 This singular is found also in the Syriac of Prov 9:18 (*OTSy*, pt. 2 fasc. 5, on this passage), where the LXX also has the singular in the phrase πέτευρον ᾅδου ("snare of hell") in place of the Hebrew plural עִמְקֵי שְׁאוֹל (Rahlfs, 2:198; Brenton, 796; *BHS*, 1287).
204 See Payne Smith, 2:2916–17; BDAG, *s.v.* βάθος, 1.
205 But only probably. The three suffixes in 12a-b are not pointed and could thus also be feminine (that is, *lāh*, *ʿammāh*, *bāh*). In that case, 12a-b would refer to the realm of the dead (like 11a), and 13a-b to Death (like 11b). However, that would be unusual in these two Syriac manuscripts, in which the third feminine singular suffix of these prepositions is almost always signaled by a point above (see Lattke, *Bedeutung*, 1:42, 72; exceptions in N are 8:11 [*bāh* without point]; 7:21 [*lāh* twice without point]).
206 Charlesworth, 147.
207 Apart from some doubt about the word order, this was the Greek of 12b (contra Frankenberg, 35). In view of Matt 25:40 and 25:45, I consider ἐφ' ὅσον more probable than καθ' ὅσον as the *Vorlage* of ܐܝܟܢܐ ܕ (*kmā d-*); see Payne Smith, 2:1980; Payne Smith, *Dictionary*, 216: "as much," "as far," "as long"; BDAG, *s.v.* ἐπί, 13.
208 In various translations, from Harris (p. 139) to Franzmann (p. 283).
209 Equivalent in English to "with him." In various translations, from Harnack (p. 73) to Lattke (*Oden*, 214).
210 Equivalent in English to "with her/him." In various translations, from Labourt and Batiffol (p. 38) to Pierre (p. 197).

(ʿ*ammeh*) corresponds to μετ' αὐτοῦ,[211] but then translating too freely: "I descended after him, to the deeps of the abyss."[212] The particle "with" therefore has here the connotation of "in the midst of."[213] In this case there is no sense of accompanying.[214] Both in ܣ and 𝔊, it can be seen that the language of mythos has reached its uttermost bounds.

The stress of 12b lies on the Pe. ܢܚܬ (*nḥeṯ*), "descend," which corresponds to καταβαίνω,[215] a verb that, since its use in Num 16:30 LXX (καταβήσονται ζῶντες εἰς ᾅδου, "they shall go down alive into Hades"; cf. Num 16:33 LXX),[216] is used also of God's "punishment by death" (cf. *1 Clem.* 51:4).[217] In *Ode* 42, the descent is that of an active and paramount Christ, not from heaven above (cf. John 6:38; 1 Thess 4:16) but from the cross.[218] Thus, the language of the mythos makes ironic allusion to the mocking and derision suffered by the Crucified (Mark 15:29-32; Matt 27:39-42). Werner Bieder, who interprets Christ "here as a *hunter*,"[219] sees this "coming down" just as fancifully as a "*Descensus* after the *Descensus*, as it were, into the lowest and furtherest hiding-places of the netherworld."[220] However, the assumption of a simple descent will suffice. For, on the one hand, it is true of Death personified what Gisela Kittel has to say in the course of her remarks on "Sheol" and "Hades":[221] "In any case the realm of the dead is in the deeps and even—as the opposite of heaven—at the lowest point of the spatially imagined world" (cf. Amos 9:2; Ps 139:8; Job 11:8). On the other hand, this "peculiar reality" in mythology is marked by metaphorical "depth,"[222] which can also be attributed to concepts such as the heart, sleep, or dreams. This shows that Diettrich's emendation of ʿ*umqā* ("depth") to ʿ*ummāqā* ("descend") is neither necessary nor helpful.[223]

In the image of 13a, the words πόδες/ܪ̈ܓܠܐ (*reḡlē*)[224] and κεφαλή/ܪܫܐ (*rēšā*), "feet" and "head,"[225] are meant literally as "the physical extremities of the body."[226] So now Death personified is provided, in addition to its "maw" (29:4b), with "feet" (= "legs"?) and a "head."[227] But there is no more stress on these parts of the body than in the Homeric phrase "from head to foot" (*Il.* 23.169).[228] That the *hapax legomenon* ܐܪܦܝ (ʾ*arpī*), the Aph. of ܪܦܐ (*rp̄ā*), expresses the opposite of muscular tonus ("let [it] go limp"),[229] is more perspicuous than Frankenberg's suggested Greek equivalent ἀνῆκε (cf. Isa 35:3 LXX: χεῖρες ἀνειμέναι, "relaxed hands").[230]

211 Greßmann, "Referate," 2900.
212 Greßmann, 472.
213 BDAG, *s.v.* μετά, A1; on the meanings of the Syriac preposition, see Beyer, *ATTM*, 659–60.
214 Contra Zahn, 696 n. 6.
215 Payne Smith, 2:2343–44; BDAG, *s.v.* καταβαίνω.
216 Rahlfs, 1:244; Brenton, 198.
217 See Lona, 545; Lake, 1:96–97; Ehrman, 1:126–27; *OTSy*, pt. 1 fasc. 2, on this passage.
218 In the *Ascension of Isaiah*, "the actual *Descensus* is the downward movement of the multiform Christ *from the seventh heaven* throughout all the lower regions *to the Earth*" (Bieder, *Höllenfahrt*, 166–67 [emphasis added]). Darrell Hannah questions the alleged Docetism of this work and thus parenthetically also considers the *Odes of Solomon* (see Hannah, "*Ascension of Isaiah*," 184–85).
219 Bieder, *Höllenfahrt*, 197; he is clearly following Greßmann's translation (p. 472) when he remarks: "'After him' makes for a much clearer image than 'with him.'"
220 Bieder, *Höllenfahrt*, 197.
221 Gisela Kittel, "Das leere Grab als Zeichen für das überwundene Totenreich," *ZThK* 96 (1999) 463–66, esp. 464. Her numerous references to Psalm 88 (pp. 464–66) are completely relevant, but they should not lead one to infer that the author or speaker of *Ode* 42 "is working on the 88th Psalm as a description of the descent into Hades" (Harris and Mingana, 2:407).
222 Gisela Kittel, "Das leere Grab," 465.
223 Diettrich, 135 n. 7; see Payne Smith, 2:2917; Brockelmann, *Lexicon*, 532.
224 There is no need to suppose that this plural is a euphemism for the genitals (see Stefan Schorch, *Euphemismen in der Hebräischen Bibel* [Orientalia biblica et Christiana 12; Wiesbaden: Harrassowitz, 2000] 194–96; Konrad Weiß, "πούς," *ThWNT* 6 (1959) 626; *TDNT* 6:627). How many feet or legs the monster Death has is not stated.
225 In contrast to Cerberus with its many—usually three—heads (Christine Walde, "Kerberos," *DNP* 6 [1999] 440), Death personified (at least here) has only one.
226 Franzmann, 287.
227 BDAG, *s.vv.* πούς, 1; κεφαλή, 1a; Payne Smith, 2:3810, 3899.
228 Helmut van Thiel, *Homeri Ilias* (Bibliotheca Weidmanniana II; Hildesheim/Zurich/New York: Olms, 1996) 443 (ἐς πόδας ἐκ κεφαλῆς). The case is different in 1 Cor 12:21, where the terms "head" and "feet" (as well as other parts of the body) in

Before the discovery of N confirmed the singular ܐܫܟܚ (ʾeškaḥ) in 13b, which Schultheß had already suggested,[231] there were, between 1910 and 1912, sometimes quite wild ideas expressed on the subject of the plural ܐܫܟܚܘ (also pronounced ʾeškaḥ), which have now been overtaken and need not be further discussed.[232] The subject of 13b is Death personified. Verse 13b provides the reason for the adjacent 13a and also for 11a earlier. Unlike the endurance of the "I" of 31:10a, where again ܣܝܒܪ (*saybar*), "endure," probably corresponds to ὑπο-μένω,[233] Death could not endure the πρόσωπον of the Redeemer who has come down. The Greek loanword does not stand for his "countenance" or his "person" in a subjective sense but rather for his objective "presence" or "appearance."[234] The "Redeemer descending" into Death, equated with the netherworld, "is a threat and an affliction for Death personified."[235]

■ **14** Without necessarily interpreting 17:14 as forming part of a *descensus* text, it is still possible to agree with Connolly that the content of that verse parallels 42:14a.[236] It does not, however, describe "the *foundation* of the *underground ecclesia*."[237] For, first, stanzas VIII and X must be closely linked.[238] And, second, the *hapax legomenon* ܟܢܘܫܬܐ (*knūštā*), "congregation," most probably does not represent ἐκκλησία but συναγωγή.[239] Its pairing with the plural of ܚܝܐ (*ḥayyā*),[240] in the emphatic state, "living ones," does not necessarily conceal an attack on the Jews, like that in the slander of the "Jews as 'the Synagogue of Satan'" in Rev 2:9.[241] The Pe. ܥܒܕ (*ʿḇad*), "make," which recurs in 16a ("deal"), has a breadth of meaning similar to ποιέω and is often used for creation or re-creation.[242] So "his dead"[243] can be seen as an allusion to the νεκροί ("dead") of Rom 6:13 (cf. Rom 4:17; 10:7; 11:15; Eph 5:14). With or without the article, νεκροί can mean "all the dead, all those who are in the underworld."[244] The "congregation of the living" is a fraction of these, the ones who believe in and are set free by (19-20) the "Son of God" (15b) and "Savior" (18b).

Verse 14b explains the preceding statement of salvation more precisely, resulting in a parallelism between 14a and b.[245] The inclusively intended suffix of ܠܘܬ (*lwāṯ*), "to,"[246] then, refers to the dead of 14a (cf. 15a at the beginning of stanza IX). Although the deceased here are not the same *dramatis personae* as those in stanzas II–IV, there are connections, of both vocabulary and

their literal sense are used by Paul in his polemic against the over- or underestimation of the "members of the body of Christ" (Schrage, *1 Korinther*, 3:204–42, esp. 221–25).

229 Brockelmann, *Lexicon*, 741.

230 Frankenberg, 35; Rahlfs, 2:611; Brenton, 869; see Payne Smith, 2:3961; BDAG, *s.v.* ἀνίημι.

231 Schultheß, 257.

232 E.g., by Zahn, 697; Diettrich, 136; idem, "Liedersammlung," 536; and Frankenberg, 44; cf. Vogl, 74.

233 Payne Smith, 2:2511; BDAG, *s.v.* ὑπομένω, 2; Frankenberg, 29, 35.

234 BDAG, *s.v.* πρόσωπον, 2 and 4.

235 Lattke, "Wörter," 298 = idem, *Bedeutung*, 4:147.

236 Connolly, "Odes," 299.

237 Contra Bieder, *Höllenfahrt*, 179.

238 Murray, *Symbols*, 61, laying a proper stress on "freedom."

239 See Dibelius, *Jakobus*, 165–67, on Jas 2:2. Unfortunately, Murray has nothing to say on this question (see Murray, *Symbols*, 18, 61). In the Syriac translation of Prov 5:14, ܟܢܘܫܬܐ (*knūštā*) still stands for קהל/ἐκκλησία and ܥܕܬܐ (*ʿētā*) for עדה/συναγωγή (*OTSy*, pt. 2 fasc. 5, on this passage; see Wolfgang Schrage, "συναγωγή, κτλ.," *ThWNT* 7 (1964) 803; *TDNT* 7:802), but in the New Testament ἐκκλησία is generally translated by ܥܕܬܐ (exceptions are Acts 7:38: ܟܢܘܫܬܐ; Acts 19:32 and 19:40[41]: ܟܢܫܐ [*kenšā*]; Acts 19:39 and 2 Cor 11:28: ܟܢܘܫܝܐ [*knūšyā*]; see Kiraz, 1461–70). Since συνέδριον ("council") as equivalent to ܟܢܘܫܬܐ can be eliminated, συναγωγή becomes the only choice (Payne Smith, 1:1773; BDAG, *s.v.* συναγωγή, 3b and 4).

240 Vogl's statistical justification of his grammatically possible translation, "*Assembly of Life*" (Vogl, 74), is as unconvincing as Zahn's rationalistic one (Zahn, 697).

241 Heinz Giesen, *Die Offenbarung des Johannes* (RNT; Regensburg: Pustet, 1997) 108; see pp. 132–34 on Rev 3:9.

242 Payne Smith, 2:2765–66; BDAG, *s.v.* ποιέω.

243 In ܣ, these are clearly the dead of Death personified. One must remember, however, the possible ambiguity of ܓ (see on 12b above).

244 BDAG, *s.v.* νεκρός, B1; see also Payne Smith, 2:2055–56.

245 Franzmann, 288.

246 The H reading ܥܡܗܘܢ (*ʿammhōn*), "with them," may be an assimilation to 6a (see above on the interchangeability of the two prepositions).

meaning, between 14b and 5c-6b. The organs of speech χείλη/ܣܦܘ̈ܬܐ (*sep̄wātā*) are qualified by the equally plural attribute ܚ̈ܝܬܐ (*ḥayyāṯā*), "living," not because these "lips" produce an unending flow of words (cf. the phrase "living = running water")[247] but because they give life and eschatologically enable the Redeemer to awaken the dead (see Excursus 16). However one may interpret 1 Pet 3:19-20 and 4:6,[248] in *Ode* 42 there is what can be described as "Christ's preaching in Hades." Its universalism is, however, confuted because only a portion of the dead joined the assembly of the living. There is no mention of judgment.

The conjunction ܡܛܠ ܕ (*meṭṭol d-*), "that," in 14c is used finally rather than causally.[249] That "14c refers to 14b" is clear.[250] But this closing utterance can be a "confessional statement" only if it is interpreted corroboratively.[251] As a statement of the objective, with negated imperfect of ܗܘܐ (*hwā*) + participle of ܒܛܠ (*bṭel*), "should not cease," it serves to delineate the imperfect "pointing to the future, even though the principal clause may lie in the past."[252] With this statement, the speaking "I" places added emphasis on his mythic address "with living lips." Although he does not mention the content of his sermon, he wishes his life-giving word the success it deserves. Whether 𝔊 had ἵνα μὴ ἀργῇ[253] or perhaps ἵνα μὴ παύ(σ)ηται[254] is unknown.[255] A glance at 15:9b shows that ܡܠܬܐ (*melltā*) could easily have replaced ܦܬܓܡܐ (*peṯgāmā*), "word" (see Excursus 12). Since both terms are used to translate λόγος as well as ῥῆμα, Frankenberg ought to have put a question mark after ὁ λόγος here also.[256]

■ **15-18** The realm of the dead is still the scene of the mythos (see Excursus 42 above). This statement, however, is true only because the four bicola[257] of stanza IX, with their "speech within the speech,"[258] which interrupts the first person address of the Redeemer, are firmly integrated into the context of stanzas VI–X. Outside this *descensus* narrative, one might not get further than "the idea of the salvation of the members" of the σῶμα Χριστοῦ (cf. 10:1-6; 17:8b-11).[259]

The subject of 15a is those of the dead who became the "congregation of the living" (see 14a above).[260] Since there is "no substantive antecedent," the Pe. ܪܗܛ (*rheṭ*), "run," corresponding to τρέχω (ἔδραμον), is followed by the correlative ܗܢܘܢ ܕ (*hānnōn d-*) + ܡܝܬ (*mīṯ*), "those who had died."[261] 𝔊 probably used οἱ τεθνηκότες and not ἀποθάνοντες.[262] How the "deceased"[263] could be able to move and speak is, in spite of the statement in 1 Bar 2:17 that is "only comprehensible against a Hebrew background,"[264] as futile a question here as it would be about all the doings of the dead in Lucian's

247 BDAG, *s.v.* ὕδωρ, 1.

248 See Goppelt, *Der Erste Petrusbrief*, 246–55, 275–78; on its later influence, see Heinz-Jürgen Vogels, *Christi Abstieg ins Totenreich und das Läuterungsgericht an den Toten: Eine bibeltheologisch-dogmatische Untersuchung zum Glaubensartikel „descendit ad inferos"* (Freiburger theologische Studien 102; Freiburg/Basel/Vienna: Herder, 1976) 183–235; on Vogels's monograph and other "treatments" of the "*descensus* tradition," see Harold W. Attridge, "Liberating Death's Captives: Reconsideration of an Early Christian Myth," in J. E. Goehring et al., eds., *Gnosticism & the Early Christian World: In Honor of James M. Robinson* (Sonoma, Calif.: Polebridge, 1990) 103–15.

249 Contra Bauer, 625; see Payne Smith, 2:2077: "*cum futuro* ἵνα" otherwise ὅτι.

250 Franzmann, 288.

251 Ibid., 283, 288.

252 Nöldeke §§267, 300.

253 Frankenberg, 36; see BDAG, *s.v.* ἀργέω.

254 BDAG, *s.v.* παύω, 2: middle voice παύομαι.

255 See Payne Smith, 1:509.

256 Frankenberg, 17 and 36.

257 Franzmann (p. 288), who rejects Charlesworth's division of 17a (see Charlesworth, 144, 146) because "there is no basis for this in N or H," can be criticized in the same way for dividing 15b into 15b-c at the point where direct speech begins.

258 Introduction, sec. 8.

259 Pokorný, *Epheserbrief*, 39.

260 The perfect tense in 14a looks forward. The redemption is still in progress and is only concluded in stanza X.

261 Nöldeke §236; BDAG, *s.v.* τρέχω, 1; Payne Smith, 2:3833.

262 Contra Frankenberg, 36.

263 Bauer and Aland, and BDAG, *s.v.* θνῄσκω, 1; see also Payne Smith, 2:2055.

264 Antonius H. J. Gunneweg, *Das Buch Baruch* (JSHRZ 3.2; Gütersloh: Mohn, 1975) 165–81, here 174. In 1 Bar 2:17, it is said in part: ὅτι οὐχ οἱ τεθνηκότες ἐν τῷ ᾅδῃ, ὧν ἐλήμφθη τὸ πνεῦμα αὐτῶν ἀπὸ τῶν σπλάγχνων αὐτῶν, δώσουσιν δόξαν καὶ δικαίωμα τῷ κυρίῳ, "for the dead in Hades, whose spirit has been taken out of their entrails, will give unto the Lord neither praise nor righteousness" (Rahlfs, 2:751; Brenton, pt. 2 [Apocrypha], p. 123,

thirty Νεκρικοὶ διάλογοι.[265] The preposition ܠܘܬ (*lwāṯ*) will be considered later (see on 17a below).

The introduction to the embedded petition (15b) uses two verbs that appear also in the introduction to the address of the Perfect Virgin (33:5b). In fact there are a number of interesting parallels to *Ode* 42 in the context of that address (cf. 33:6-13). The speech of the deceased here is, as it were, an answer to the word of the Redeemer (see 14b-c above), even though 14b and 15b use different verbs of speaking (see Excursus 12). The "Son of God" whom they address is the Exalted One (cf. 36:3b), who is still soteriologically in demand even in the nethermost regions of Death. Even so, given that the gate is closed (17a) and that the Redeemer himself is alive (17b; cf. 5c and 14b), one can logically ask whether he is addressed as one who has already been vomited up by Death (11b). This question will recur when we consider 18a. The Greek of the imperative of the Pe. ܚܢ (*ḥan*), with objective suffix, "have pity on us," can be restored as ἐλέησον ἡμᾶς,[266] which immediately reveals connections to passages in the New Testament in which the Synoptic Jesus, as υἱὸς Δαυίδ, "Son of David," is begged for miraculous help.[267] But in all those passages, and also in Luke 16:24, where the rich man (Dives) calls across the "unbridgeable" gulf of Hades to beg Father Abraham for help,[268] ἐλέησον is translated into Syriac by words derived from the root *rḥm*.[269] Since ἱλάσκομαι can hardly be considered the original or translation (cf. Luke 18:13: ἱλάσθητί μοι, "be merciful to me" = ܚܘܢܝܢ [*ḥonayn*]),[270] the only possibility left is οἰκτίρω.[271] So it is at least possible that 𝔊 had οἰκτίρησον ἡμᾶς.[272]

The term ποιέω/ܥܒܕ (*ʿbaḏ*) has already been discussed in 14a, and the use of the preposition ܥܡ (*ʿam*), "with," in 16a corresponds exactly to that of μετά with ποιέω (cf. linguistically Acts 14:27; 15:4).[273] The term χρηστότης/ܒܣܝܡܘܬܐ (*bassīmūṯā*), "kindness," which is usually used in a theological sense, is here employed christologically (see Excursus 14).[274]

The Aph. of ܢܦܩ (*npaq*) in 16b, "bring out," makes connection with 33:8b, although there is no mention of Hades in that passage. Linguistically, one may refer to Isa 42:7 LXX (quoted in *Barn.* 14:7): ἀνοῖξαι ὀφθαλμοὺς τυφλῶν, ἐξαγαγεῖν ἐκ δεσμῶν δεδεμένους καὶ ἐξ οἴκου φυλακῆς καθημένους ἐν σκότει ("to open the eyes of the blind, to bring the bound and them that sit in darkness out of bonds and the prison-house").[275]

slightly changed; Gunneweg, 174). Whether one can say of *Ode* 42 that "Christ speaks of his bringing the *souls* out of Sheol" (Murray, "Rock," 357 [emphasis added]) is debatable.

265 Karl Mras, *Die Hauptwerke des Lukian* (OG/Ger.; Munich: Heimeran, 1954; 2nd ed., 1980) 162–281: "Totengespräche [Conversations with the Dead]."

266 Frankenberg, 36.

267 Matt 9:27; 15:22; 20:30-31; Mark 10:47-48; Luke 18:38-39; cf. Matt 17:45 and Luke 17:13.

268 See BDAG, *s.v.* χάσμα, on Luke 16:26.

269 This is true of most of the other passages in the New Testament in which ἐλεέω occurs (BDAG, *s.v.* ἐλεέω). Exceptions are Matt 18:33 (Pe. ܚܢ [*ḥan*] twice); Rom 11:30; 1 Cor 7:25; 1 Tim 1:13 (Ethpe. ܐܬܚܢܢ [*ʾeṯḥnen*] in all cases); see Payne Smith, 1:1314; on 1 Tim 1:13, see Aland and Juckel, *Briefe*, 3:126.

270 BDAG, *s.v.* ἱλάσκομαι, 1.

271 BDAG, *s.v.* οἰκτίρω; Payne Smith, 1:1314. In primitive Christian writings οἰκτίρω occurs only in Rom 9:15. This quotation from Exod 33:19 LXX is of interest, because οἰκτίρω there is parallel to ἐλεέω. Tracing the sequences of the Hebrew, Greek, and Syriac traditions, one finds the following interchanges among the roots: חנן - ἐλεέω - ܪܚܡ (*rḥm*), on the one hand, and רחם - οἰκτίρω - ܚܢ (*ḥn*), on the other. On the whole, ἐλεέω is used in the LXX more often to translate חנן than רחם, while for the rarer verb οἰκτίρω the proportion is closer to 50/50.

272 In Ps 4:2, οἰκτίρησόν με translates חנני (*BHS*, 1088; Rahlfs, 2:3). The Peshitta has ܪܚܡ ܥܠ (*OTSy*, pt. 2 fasc. 3, p. 3), but the so-called Syriac Hexapla has ܚܘܢܝܢ (Payne Smith, 1:1314).

273 BDAG, *s.v.* μετά, 2aγℶ. Syriac would have used ܠ (*l-*) in the translation of ποίησον ἡμῖν (Frankenberg, 36).

274 See BDAG, *s.v.* χρηστότης: "goodness, kindness, generosity."

275 Rahlfs, 2:622; Brenton, 877; see also Prostmeier, 449, 471. The words emphasized in the quotation are found also in *Ode* 42:16b-17a. In *Barn.* 14:7 the quotation is followed by γινώσκομεν οὖν, πόθεν ἐλυτρώθημεν ("We know then whence we have been redeemed" [Lake, 1:392–93]; cf. Ehrman, 2:66–67; translations of Lake and Ehrman differ from Brenton's translation of Isa 42:7 LXX). In view of 18a (see below) one could reasonably ask whether *Ode* 42 might have sponsored the choice of the quotation.

Since σκότος/ܚܫܘܟܐ (*ḥeššōkā*), "darkness," is not used here in a primarily dualistic sense, unlike 18:6 and 21:3 (cf. 11:19), but as part of the standard description of Hades/Sheol,[276] any reference to the "statement of Pistis Sophia in the hymnic interpretation of *Ode* 25:1" and other passages in the Coptic of the Gnostic *Pistis Sophia* is misleading.[277] In 17:4a, 11, and 22:4 there is mention of "chains" or "bonds" but not of "darkness." So Poirier's linking of these passages to 42:16a-b is questionable.[278] The Greek of 16b can now, with the aid of Frankenberg, be reconstructed as follows: ἐξάγε ἡμᾶς ἐκ τῶν δεσμῶν τοῦ σκότους.[279]

Although the ancients generally spoke of the "doors," "gates," or "portals" of the realm of the dead[280] even "when only one gate is meant,"[281] the plural πύλαι is interchangeable with the singular πύλη to denote the "steel entry door" of Hades.[282] Whether 17a is thinking of one leaf (θύρα) of the door or of the πύλη as a two-leaved portal is difficult to determine.[283] Since this passage is still "purely petitionary prayer,"[284] *Ode* 42:15b-17a can hardly be used as evidence for miraculous openings of doors in antiquity. When the Son of God is besought to "open the gate"[285] (cf. ἀνοίγειν in one of the texts cited by Betz), the question arises: Will this be from the outside/above or from within? The conjunctional[286] clause that follows fairly definitely locates the Redeemer before the door, that is, outside Hades, especially with the use of the preposition ܠܘܬ (*lwāt*), "to." The contradiction with the use of the same preposition in 15a that this entails has not perturbed either the authors/editors or the copyists of the *Odes*. Otherwise ܥܡܟ (*ʿammāk*), "with thee," could perhaps have been used here as fittingly as in 18a (cf. the variants in 14b). In 𝔖, the use of the imperfect of the Pe. ܢܦܩ (*npaq*), "come out," produces a paronomasia with the beginning of 16b. Franzmann even calls it an "inclusio."[287] If 𝔊 did not have ἐξέρχομαι πρός,[288] but the passive of ἐξάγω,[289] that would also have made a paronomasia.

The problems of the next statement that interrupts the petitions are described by Franzmann ("15c" = the second half of 15b).[290]

> 17b is semantically ambiguous and its specific function thereby unclear. If one interprets that the "I" is not affected adversely by the death state of the "we", then 17b functions as a summary for 15c-17a; that is, 17b presents the reason for the possibility of making the petitions to the "I". If 17b is taken more literally as meaning that the death state of the "we" prevents them from approaching the "I", then 17b functions more as a summary for 16b-17a; that is, it presents the reason for the opening and bringing forth actions of the "I."

276 H. D. Betz, *Lukian,* 81. Gisela Kittel, "Das leere Grab," 464.

277 Contra Lattke, *Oden*, 215; Poirier, "Descensus," 198.

278 Poirier, "Descensus," 198. On the "comic strip" in *Trim. Prot.* 41,2-15, Gesine Schenke remarks: "Attributes of hell are transferred into the sphere of the Demiurge, giving a bird's-eye view of the earthly heaven, the earthly world and the netherworld together" (see Gesine Schenke, *Die dreigestaltige Protennoia [Nag-Hammadi-Codex XIII]* [TU 132; Berlin: Akademie-Verlag, 1984] 122–24).

279 Frankenberg, 36; see BDAG, *s.v.* ἐξάγω, 2: "free from bonds."

280 See Joachim Jeremias, "πύλη, πυλών," *ThWNT* 6 (1959) 923–24; *TDNT* 6:924–25, on Matt 16:18.

281 BDAG, *s.v.* ᾅδης, 1.

282 H. D. Betz, *Lukian,* 82 and n. 4. Rodin's *Door of Hell* (*La Porte de l'Enfer*) has, naturally, two leaves. English generally refers to the piece as the *Gates of Hell*, but this unfinished masterpiece is also described as a "gate" (as in Dante's *Divine Comedy*: "Per me . . . porta" [*Inferno,* canto 3, 1–11]; see Erwin Laaths, ed., *Dante, La Vita Nuova, La Divina Commedia – Das Neue Leben, Die Göttliche Komödie* [Sonderausgabe der Tempel-Klassiker; Wiesbaden: Vollmer, n.d.] 71).

283 See Joachim Jeremias, "θύρα," *ThWNT* 3 (1938) 173 n. 4; *TDNT* 3:173; BDAG, *s.vv.* θύρα, 1a; πύλη, a; Payne Smith, 2:4505.

284 Weinreich, *Wunder*, 443.

285 Bieder's remark (*Höllenfahrt*, 180), "from the plea to open the door one can conclude that, alongside the idea of the monster, there is also the *idea of a castle*," is rather fanciful.

286 In the concordance in Lattke, *Bedeutung*, vol. 2, the references to 42:17 must be moved from p. 69 to p. 74. The particle ܕ (*d-*) is used as a conjunction in both 42:17a and 42:17b.

287 Franzmann, 288.

288 See BDAG, *s.v.* ἐξέρχομαι, 1aα; Frankenberg, 36.

289 See LSJ and BDAG, *s.v.* ἐξάγω, 1; Payne Smith, 2:2420.

290 Franzmann, 288.

But if the particle γάρ/ܓܝܪ (gēr) does not have any "real explanatory function,"[291] there would have to be a full stop at the end of 17a, and 17b would be attached even more firmly to 18a-b: "For we see that our death does not come near thee; may we also be saved. . . ." Whatever the case, the vocabulary of 17b makes a number of connections with other parts of *Ode* 42. The participle of the Pe. ܚܙܐ (ḥzā), "see," which may here correspond to a form of *either* βλέπω *or* εἶδον,[292] connects to 11a. The key word θάνατος/ܡܘܬܐ (*mawtā*), "death," connects 17b to 11b and also to 14a and 15a, even to 5a. Its content also connects it to the theological and christological purport of 18:8a and 28:17a (see Table 1). The Ethpa. of ܩܪܒ (*qreb*), "come near," finally, poetically integrates the distinctive statement, that is, the one that differs from *Ode* 27, in 1a into the total text of *Ode* 42.

At first sight, 18a is "the final petition for the stanza."[293] But, in contrast to 15b-17a, there is no imperative, so the expression of confidence in salvation in the imperfect is perhaps just a future indicative: "We too will be saved with thee."[294] The form corresponding to the Ethpe. of ܦܪܩ (*praq*), "be saved," will have been a passive of λυτρόω (cf. *Barn.* 14:7 [see on 16b above])[295] or of σῴζω.[296] That this idea of being redeemed permeates the whole collection of the *Odes* is clear (cf. esp. 8:22e; 33:10a, 11a; 34:6b);[297] it is even applied to the Redeemer himself (cf. 17:4c and again 8:22e; Excursus 5). So the question arises whether 18a with its emphasis on "we also" and especially in connection with the prepositional phrase ܥܡܟ (*ʿammāḵ*), "with thee," refers, at least implicitly, to the *Salvator salvandus/salvatus*. Whether 𝔊 had μετὰ σοῦ[298] or σὺν σοί is not clear.[299] In the first case, one might refer to Luke 22:43 and John 17:24.[300] In the second, there would be even more emphasis on the "future communion with Christ" (cf. 2 Cor 4:14; 13:4; 1 Thess 4:17; 5:10; Col 2:13; 3:3-4; also Rom 6:8 [συζήσομεν/-σωμεν αὐτῷ/τῷ Χριστῷ]; Eph 2:5 [συνεζωοποίησεν τῷ Χριστῷ]; 2:6 [συνήγειρεν κτλ.]).[301]

In the final causal section (18b, using ὅτι in 𝔊), the personal pronoun σύ/ܐܢܬ (*ʾat*), "thou,"[302] is emphasized as strongly as the personal pronoun ἡμεῖς/ܚܢܢ (*ḥnan*), "we," in the middle of 18a. The chiastic paronomasia "by the repetition of ܦܪܩ at the beginning of 18a and at the conclusion of 18b"[303] may be peculiar to 𝔖 (see on the verb of 18a above). Since σωτήρ ("Savior") can be assumed to be the equivalent of ܦܪܘܩܐ (*pārōqā*) here, just as much as in 41:11b (cf. 5:11 ℭ), it is possible to reconstruct the Greek of 18b: ὅτι σὺ εἶ ὁ σωτὴρ (λυτρωτὴς?) ἡμῶν.[304]

■ **19-20** After the interruption of his first-person address (15b-18b), the Son of God and Redeemer resumes, first giving his own reaction to the speech within the speech and then the final vindication (cf. 18b)[305] of his redeemed. Even though "the conclusion of

291 Lattke, "Wörter," 289–90 = idem, *Bedeutung*, 4:138.
292 BDAG, *s.vv.* βλέπω, εἶδον; Payne Smith, 1:1233.
293 Franzmann, 289.
294 Lattke, *Oden*, 215 n. 19.
295 BDAG, *s.v.* λυτρόω, 2.
296 BDAG, *s.v.* σῴζω, 2–3; Payne Smith, 2:3294; Frankenberg, 36: σωθείημεν.
297 Alegre, "Salvación," *passim*.
298 Frankenberg, 36.
299 "This distinction, however, had already disappeared by the classical period, and the choice of σ[ύν] or μ[ετά] usually became a matter of style" (Winfried Elliger, "σύν," *EWNT* 3 [1983] 697; *EDNT* 3:291).
300 Walter Radl, "μετά," *EWNT* 2 (1981) 1018; *EDNT* 2:413.
301 Elliger, "σύν," *EWNT* 3:698; *EDNT* 3:291.
302 The reference to 4:9 was accidentally omitted from the concordance, Lattke, *Bedeutung*, 2:52, *s.v.* ܐܢܬ.
303 Franzmann, 289.
304 Similar to Frankenberg, 36. The distinction between ὁ Σωτὴρ in 41:11 and ὁ Λυτρωτής in 42:18 made by Tsakonas (pp. 177, 188) and Fanourgakis (pp. 173, 175, ὁ λυτρωτής) is quite arbitrary. It is not until later that λυτρωτής comes to be more often used christologically (Lampe, 816). In the LXX, λυτρωτής occurs twice of God as "Savior" (Ps 18:15; 77:35). In the New Testament, it is a *hapax legomenon* (Acts 7:35; BDAG, *s.v.* λυτρωτής) describing Moses as the "Redeemer/Savior" sent by God (Gerhard Schneider, *Die Apostelgeschichte*, vol. 1: *Einleitung, Kommentar zu Kap. 1,1–8,40* [HThKNT 5.1; Freiburg: Herder, 1980] 462).
305 Franzmann's references (p. 289) to 13b and 18b are more relevant than that to 14c. Her description of the statements of salvation in 20b and 20c as "confessional statements" does not convince me.

unexpected grandeur"[306] invites generalizations on the subjects "faith" and "freedom" (cf. 10:3), according to the understanding of early Christianity,[307] the hermeneutics demand attention first within the mythological framework of the *descensus*. In expanding the soteriological exegesis past *Ode* 42, one should not immediately turn to the souls converted in Hades described by Origen (*Cels.* 2.43),[308] but, noting that the last sentence[309] is identical with 8:20b, consider it in connection with 8:10-23.

The emphasized and pre-positioned personal pronoun ἐγώ/ܐܢܐ (*ʾenā*), "I," in 19a carries much more weight than the enclitic in 5c and continues the sequence of "we" and "thou" in 18a-b. Although the preceding text is largely composed of petitionary prayers, the retroversion of the Pe. ܫܡܥ (*šmaʿ*), "hear," by εἰσακούω is less appropriate than the simple ἀκούω.[310] The object ܩܠܐ (*qālā*), "voice," formally refers to the crying out and saying of 15b. As the variant readings of Luke 1:42 show so well, the equivalent of ܩܠܐ could be κραυγή as well as φωνή.[311] However, κραυγή is most often translated by ܩܥܬܐ (*qʿāṯā*),[312] which makes φωνή[313] the likelier term. Whether the Greek construction with ἀκούω used the accusative τὴν φωνήν or the genitive τῆς φωνῆς cannot be determined.[314]

H omits 19b for much the same reason that it omits 3a-b (see above).[315] "The reading of N handsomely rounds off the conclusion of the *Ode*."[316] The idiomatic expression "take to heart" is ultimately derived from the Hebrew,[317] but is here, as in Luke 1:66, a "Septuagintism."[318] The object (τὴν) πίστιν αὐτῶν/ܗܝܡܢܘܬܗܘܢ (*haymānūṯhōn*)[319] refers primarily to the "faith" of the liberated, redeemed, and simultaneously ejected dead (cf. 11b, 14a, 15-18), but also forms a link outside *Ode* 42 (see 9b above) with 8:11 (see Excursus 34).

In connection with 20a, Gschwind legitimately refers to 8:20-21 (cf. 33:13).[320] This is not a "blessing" (as in 17:14 or 28:4) or a "laying on of hands," but a vigorous "taking possession":[321] "As the property of Christ they [viz., the redeemed dead] henceforth bear his name" (see Excursus 39).[322] Harris's early translation ("my name I sealed upon their heads"),[323] although it was

306 Harnack, 73. His phrase "free men" accords with the vocabulary of the early twentieth century. Cf. Vogl, 74: "sons of the free, free persons."

307 See Heinrich Schlier, "ἐλεύθερος, κτλ.," *ThWNT* 2 (1935) 484–500; *TDNT* 2:487–502; Ernst Käsemann, *Der Ruf der Freiheit* (5th ed.; Tübingen: Mohr Siebeck, 1972); Michael Lattke, "Ten Theses on Christian Freedom or Are You Afraid of Christian Freedom?" *Colloquium* 25 (1993) 37–38.

308 Contra Lattke, *Oden*, 215 n. 20.

309 H makes a monocolon of 42:20b-c (Harris and Mingana, vol. 1, on this passage; 2:405; Charlesworth, 144, 146), while N divides 20b from 20c (Lattke, *Bedeutung*, 1:184–85; Franzmann, 282–83).

310 Contra Frankenberg, 36; see Payne Smith, 2:4214; BDAG, *s.vv.* ἀκούω, εἰσακούω. The term printed as εζηκουσα in Frankenberg (p. 36) is probably meant for εἰσήκουσα.

311 See NA[27], p. 153; *NTSy*, on this passage; Payne Smith, 2:3618–19.

312 BDAG, *s.v.* κραυγή; Payne Smith, 2:3682.

313 BDAG, *s.v.* φωνή: "voice," "call," "cry."

314 BDAG, *s.v.* ἀκούω. The hearing by the Most High (37:2b) can be connected to the hearing by the Redeemer by a symbolic chain such as is characteristic of the Fourth Gospel (see Lattke, *Einheit*, 24–26: "Kettenartige Abbildhaftigkeit"). But, while in John 5:25 and 5:28 it is the dead in their tombs who hear the voice of the Son of God, here it is the Son of God who hears the voice of his people in Hades.

315 See Charlesworth, 148 n. 24. Franzmann (p. 284) agrees. I cannot trace the misreading she finds in Lattke, *Bedeutung*, vol. 2 (but see the text-critical note on ܘܣܡܬ in Lattke, *Bedeutung*, 1:184).

316 Grimme, "Handschrift," 495. I cannot accept Grimme's retroversion of 19b (idem, "Handschrift," 496: ואשים בלבי את־אמונתם) as the original Hebrew.

317 Payne Smith, 2:1878; Brockelmann, *Lexicon*, 470; Payne Smith, *Dictionary*, 233.

318 Schürmann, *Lukasevangelium*, 83 n. 19; see BDF and BDR §4; BDAG, *s.v.* τίθημι, 1bε. Since Brock does not list the *Odes of Solomon* among the works written in Syriac (see Sebastian Brock, "Syrien VI.2: Syrische Christliche Literatur," *RGG*[4] 7 [2004] 2003–4) he clearly considers them a "translation into Syriac" (col. 2005).

319 In spite of the masculine suffixes and other terms in masculine forms (see above on "free men" in Harnack, 73) the characters in stanza X (apart from the speaking "I") are intended inclusively.

320 Gschwind, *Niederfahrt*, 233.

321 Ibid.

322 Bieder, *Höllenfahrt*, 180.

323 Harris, 140.

later corrected ("I set my name upon their heads"),[324] introduced the Gnostic "idea of sealing" into the discussion.[325] If κεφαλή/ܪܫܐ (*rēšā*), "head," were not used in the prepositional phrase (see Excursus 23), one might consider it a conferring of names, as in Mark 3:16-17.[326] But that is grammatically impossible. The spiritualized "idea of the magic name, brought down by the Redeemer from on high"[327] does not belong here either. If the "head"—one for each of the many—(cf. 8:4b) stands in each case for the complete person,[328] who all now bear the name of their Redeemer (cf. Acts 9:15), then one might consider it a "baptism,"[329] in a sense, and speculate that the "motif of baptism,"[330] which later appears alongside the "preaching in Hades" and "liberation,"[331] might have originated in *Ode* 42.[332] There is some uncertainty in the Greek of 20a concerning the verb ("set") and the possible repetition of the preposition ἐπί.[333] Whether the opening words of 19b and 20a in 𝔊 were identical, as they are in 𝔖 (ܘܣܡܬ [ʾu-sāmeṯ]), cannot be determined either. The parallel of the theological sense between this passage and that of *Ps. Sol.* 9:9, where the "election" is linked to the "laying" of the name "on us" (i.e., the "House of Israel"),[334] argues for the use of τίθημι + ἐπί.[335]

In connection with 20b, reference must be made to John 8:36: ἐὰν (οὖν) ὁ υἱὸς ὑμᾶς ἐλευθερώσῃ, ὄντως ἐλεύθεροι ἔσεσθε/ἐστε/γενήσεσθε ("So if the Son makes you free, you will be free indeed").[336] The plural of ἐλεύθερος[337] there is as inclusive as the plural of ܒܪ ܚܐܪܐ (*bar ḥērē*), "free."[338] But, just as one must take care not to blend the statement of the Johannine Jesus with similar Pauline statements,[339] one must not separate the *hapax legomenon* under consideration completely from the *descensus* matrix. The "free" are first of all those who have been "freed" from the realm of the dead and the power of Death.[340] That means that a reference to Philo's "Essenes" and "Therapeutae" is quite irrelevant.[341]

The last clause, 42:20c, which is identical to 8:20b, together with 42:20b, gives the reason for 42:19a-20a. Liberation and the rule of (the) Christ are the two sides of the coin, and therefore akin to the Pauline dialectic of ἐλευθερία ("freedom") and εἶναι τοῦ Χριστοῦ ("belong to Christ").[342] But it is only the "elect" (8:20c) whom the exalted and redeemed Redeemer forms into the "congregation of the living" (see 14a above). Just as the statement of 15:9 shatters Pauline eschatology (cf. on that passage 1 Cor 15:26, 54), so here, in the

324 Harris and Mingana, 2:405.

325 Gunkel, 304–5; idem, *Aufsätze*, 175; Zahn, 697 n. 2; Stölten, 57. Bernard's conjecture points in a very different direction: "Is this a cryptic way of expressing the story of the *Descensus*, 'Et extendens dominus manum suam *fecit signum crucis* super Adam et super omnes sanctos suos'?" (see Bernard, 131, on Harris's translation of 20a).

326 See BDAG, *s.v.* ὄνομα, 1b: "ἐπιθεῖναι ὄν[ομά] τινι w[ith] acc[usative] of the name."

327 Bultmann, "Bedeutung," 108 = idem, *Exegetica*, 64 n. 16, on John 17:6, 11, 26 and *Ode* 42:19-20 among others.

328 Michael Lattke, "κεφαλή," *EWNT* 2 (1981) 705; *EDNT* 2:285.

329 BDAG, *s.v.* ὄνομα, 1dβ.

330 Alois Grillmeier, "Höllenabstieg Christi, Höllenfahrt Christi," *LThK*² 5 (1960) 455.

331 Georg Bertram, "Höllenfahrt: II. Höllenfahrt Christi," *RGG*² 2 (1928) 1968–69.

332 See Bernard, 131.

333 See BDAG, *s.vv.* ἐπιτίθημι, τίθημι.

334 Rahlfs, 2:481; see also Holm-Nielsen, 84; Lattke, "Salomoschriften," 807.

335 Trafton, 1:99 (n. 47 is not to be found); 2:38–39 (vv. 17-18).

336 NA[27], 276.

337 BDAG, *s.v.* ἐλεύθερος, 2.

338 Payne Smith, *Dictionary*, 53. Charlesworth's note that this construction (see Payne Smith, 1:587) "also means 'nobles', 'princes'" (see Charlesworth, 148 n. 26) goes well beyond the context of *liberation* from Hades.

339 Contra Schlier, "ἐλεύθερος," *ThWNT* 2:493–95; *TDNT* 2:497–98.

340 Bultmann, "Bedeutung," 135 = idem, *Exegetica*, 93, where 49 must be corrected to 42.

341 Contra Diettrich, 136 n. 3; idem, "Liedersammlung," 536 n. 57.

342 It would be even better to include the Κύριος-ship of God and Jesus Christ in this dialectic (see Joseph A. Fitzmyer, "κύριος, κτλ.," *EWNT* 2 [1981] 815-20; *EDNT* 2:329–31).

less than universal bringing back from the dead, there is no more waiting until *ζῳοποιηθήσονται . . . οἱ τοῦ Χριστοῦ ἐν τῇ παρουσίᾳ αὐτοῦ* ("at his coming those who belong to Christ . . . shall be made alive" [1 Cor 15:22-23]).[343] The "apocalyptic tradition of a messianic interregnum"[344] of which Paul makes use, and also his own "expectation of the *parousia*"[345] were far in the past by the time *Ode* 42 was composed.[346]

343 Schrage, *1 Korinther*, 4:150–231, esp. 161–69.

344 Ibid., 4:154.

345 Ibid., 4:169 n. 754. Cf. 1 Thess 2:19; 3:13; 4:15; 5:23. This comparison with Paul gives me an opportunity to emphasize the fact that there are at least as many parallels between the Pauline epistles and the *Odes of Solomon* as between the *Odes* and the more often quoted Gospel of John (see, e.g., Friedrich Spitta, "Die Oden Salomos und das Neue Testament," *MPTh* 7 [1910] 94–99). To conclude from that that Paul "knew the text of the *Odes*" (ibid., 99), however, inverts the matter.

346 From his "impression that our poet was closer to Ignatius than to John," Heinrich Boehmer concludes, with explicit reference to *Ode* 42, that he too "certainly" should be considered "a Christian from Asia Minor" (see Heinrich Boehmer, "Die Oden Salomos, I–IV," *Kirchliche Rundschau für die evangelischen Gemeinden Rheinlands und Westfalens* 25 [1910] 269–70). However, with a date for the Greek original "between 115 and 140 C.E.," this placing in ecclesiastical history is qualified: "That does not mean that he lived and worked in Asia Minor. He might, like Ignatius, have been active in Antioch or some other Syrian congregation" (ibid., 270). Abramowski (pp. 64–65) finds "certain lines of division between the *Odes* and related Gnostic works" and emphasizes the "linkage" with Ignatius: "It seems that Ignatius and the *Odes* not only interpret each other in a certain number of expressions, but that they have a common ground that is clearly recognizable in both. From that grew these two splendid blossoms of patristic literature, the Ignatian epistles with a tinge of the universal church, the *Odes* with a Gnostic one."

Concordance to the English Translation of the *Odes of Solomon*

The following words are omitted: articles, particles, pronouns, most conjunctions, prepositions, "something, anything" (ܡܕܡ [*meddem*]), "is" (ܐܝܬ [*ʾīt*]), "is not" (ܠܝܬ [*layt*]), "not" (ܠܐ [*lā*]) and "to be" (ܗܘܐ [*hwā*]). These words, some of which occur very frequently, as well as prefixes and suffixes will be found in the complete concordance in Lattke, *Bedeutung*, vol. 2. The reason for the numerous "*See*" references is that the Syriac words that belong to the same root are collected in one place and follow the sequence found in the *Thesaurus Syriacus* of Payne Smith and the *Lexicon Syriacum* of Brockelmann. The foreign words are cited in the order Greek, Coptic, Latin, Syriac, as appropriate. The Greek and Hebrew words found in the Syriac text are put in square brackets after the transcription of the Syriac. A "*see also*" after some words draws attention to important related entries. Where there is a possibility of confusion, verbs are distinguished by "to" or "(*v.*)."

abandon: *See* leave
abide, remain: ܩܘܝ (*qawwī*) 8:22; 14:6; 24:9; 26:11
abide: *See* stand up
able: ܡܨܐ (*mṣē*) 14:10
able, be: *See* find
above: ܠܥܠ (*l-ʿel*) 11:12; 34:4, 5; 35:1 (+ ܡܢ [*men*]: over)
abundant: *See* rich, be
abysses, primal deeps: ܬܗܘܡܐ (*thōmē* [תְּהוֹם]) 24:5, 7; 31:1
accept: *See* take
access: *See* draw near
according to: *See* like
according to . . . so: *See* like
acknowledge: *See* know
acquire: *See* gain (*v.*)
add: *See* give
adorned, be: ܐܨܛܒܬ (*ʾeṣṭabbaṭ*) 38:9
adversary: ἀντίδικος, ܒܥܠܕܝܢܐ (*bʿeldīnā*) 22:3; *see also* enemy; judgment
adversary: *See* against
aeon, eternity, world, ages, eternal, ever, for ever and ever: αἰών, ⲉⲛⲉϩ (*eneh*), ܥܠܡܐ (*ʿālmā*) 6:18; 7:11; 8:23; 9:4, 8; 10:4, 6(*bis*); 11:22, 24; 12:4, 8; 16:19; 19:5; 20:3; 22:11; 23:22(*bis*); 25:12(*bis*); 32:3(*bis*); 33:12; 38:11, 17; 41:15, 16
affliction: *See* oppress
afraid, be, to fear: ⲣ̄-ϩⲟⲧⲉ (*ʿr-hote*), ܕܚܠ (*dḥel*) 5:10, 11; 23:8; 24:3; 25:11; 40:5(H); *see also* agitated with fear
  fear: ܕܚܠܐ (*deḥlā*) 40:5(N)
after: *See* place
again, also, back, no more: ܬܘܒ (*tūḇ*) 9:7; 25:3; 33:1
  vomit up: ܐܬܝܒ (*ʾaṯīḇ*) 38:13; 42:11
again: *See* now
against: ⲟⲩⲃⲉ (*ube-*), ܠܘܩܒܠ (*luqḇal*) 6:5; 8:19; 25:3, 11
  receive, collect: ܩܒܠ (*qabbel*) 7:10; 8:8; 9:5; 11:14; 17:14; 18:7; 20:9; 23:11; 31:6; 41:3
  reception: ܩܘܒܠܐ (*qubbālā*) 16:17
  those who receive: ܡܩܒܠܢܐ (*mqabblānē*) 40:6
  opposing, adversary, standing in the way: ܣܩܘܒܠܐ (*saqquḇlā*) 6:5; 23:14(N); ܣܩܘܒܠܝܐ (*saqquḇlāyā*) 23:14(H)
ages: *See* aeon
agitated with fear, be: ܐܬܪܗܒ (*ʾeṯrheḇ*) 35:3
  hasten: ܣܪܗܒ (*sarheḇ*) 14:9
air: ἀήρ, ܐܐܪ (*ʾāʾar*) 5:5
alien: *See* stranger
alive: *See* live (*v.*)
all: *See* totality
alone: *See* one
also: *See* again
although: *See* if
always, at all times, continually: ܒܟܠ ܙܒܢ (*b-ḵol zḇan*) 13:4; 14:1, 4; 35:2
always: *See* totality
amazed, be: ܬܡܗ (*tmah*) 17:6
  wonderful: ܬܡܝܗܐ (*tmīhā*) 41:4
amazed, be: *See* wonder
angels: *See* archangels
anger: ܚܡܬܐ (*ḥemṯā*) 7:1
annihilated, be: *See* corruption
anoint: *See* Messiah
Anointed One: *See* Messiah
another: *See* end
anthem: ܥܢܝܢܐ (*ʿenyānā*) 40:3(N)
anything that lives: *See* soul
apostates: *See* turn away from
apparent: *See* lay bare
appear: *See* see (*v.*)
appearance: *See* form
archangels: ܪܒܝ ܡܠܐܟܐ (*rabbay malaḵē*) 4:8; *see also* great
Archcorruptor: *See* corruptor
archetype: *See* form
area: *See* place
arise against: *See* stand up
arm: ܕܪܥܐ (*drāʿā*) 21:1; 38:3(H); 42:8
around: κύκλῳ 11:16
around, surrounded by: ܟܪܝܟ (*krīḵ*) 22:6; 34:3
  go about: ܐܬܟܪܟ (*ʾeṯkreḵ*) 38:14
arrogant, be: *See* high
arrow: ܓܐܪܐ (*gērā*) 23:6
as . . . so: *See* like
ascend, cause to: *See* go up into
ascent: *See* go up into
ashamed, be: ܒܗܬ (*bheṯ*) 8:17; 9:7; 29:1

carry away: ܫܩܠ (*šqal*) 29:10
cast away, drop: ῥίπτω, ܫܕܐ (*šḏā*) 11:10a, 10b; 18:4(N); 21:2
pour out, discharge, shoot with force: ܐܫܬܕܝ (*ʾeštḏī*) 19:3; 23:6
cast down: *See* join (*v.*)
cast lots: ܢܦܣ (*np̄as*) 28:17
cast off: *See* leave
catch, receive: *infirmo*, ܓܘܦ, ܓܦ (*gāp̄*) 19:6
catch: *See* take
cease*, be calm: ܫܠܝ (*šlī*) 26:3*; 31:10
tranquil: ܫܠܐ (*šlē*) 35:4
silence: ܫܠܝܐ (*šelyā*) 8:4
cease, to stop: ܒܛܠ (*bṭel*) 4:4; 16:13; 23:19(N); 42:1
lie fallow: ἀργέω, ܒܛܝܠܐ (*baṭṭīlā*) 11:23
be destroyed, cease*: ܐܬܒܛܠ (*ʾeṯbaṭṭal*) 15:9; 23:19(H)*
chaff: *See* spray
chains: *See* bind
change (*v.*), transform, pervert: ܫܚܠܦ (*šaḥlep̄*) 4:1a, 1b; 17:13; 28:14
be changed: ܐܫܬܚܠܦ (*ʾeštaḥlap̄*) 4:3
change (*v.*): *See* turn
changed, be: μεταλάσσω 11:21
chariot: ܡܪܟܒܬܐ (*markaḇtā*) 38:1
chasm: ܦܚܬܐ (*peḥtā*) 38:2
child (foetus): *fetus*, ܒܛܢܐ (*baṭnā*) 19:6
child: ܛܠܝܐ (*ṭalyā*) 35:5
child: *See* son
children: *See* give birth
choose: ܓܒܐ (*gḇā*) 22:8
elect: ܓܒܝܐ (*gaḇyā*) 4:8; 8:20; 23:2, 3; 33:13
choose: *See* will (*v.*)
Christ: *See* Messiah
circumcise: περιτέμνω, ܓܙܪ (*gzar*) 11:2
circumcision: περιτομή, ܓܙܘܪܬܐ (*gzūrtā*) 11:3
be circumcised: περιτέμνομαι, ܐܬܓܙܪ (*ʾeṯgzar*) 11:1
circumcision: *See* circumcise
cithara: ܩܝܬܪܐ (*qīṯārā* [κιθάρα]) 6:1; 7:17; 14:8; 26:3
clear, pure: ܢܩܕ (*nqeḏ*) 30:3
clear: *See* light
cleverly devise: *See* wisdom
cliffs: ܫܩܝܦܐ (*šqīpē*) 38:2
clothe oneself: *See* put on
cloud: ⲕⲗⲟⲟⲗⲉ (*kloole*), ܥܢܢܐ (*ʿnānā*) 5:5; 35:1; 36:7
collect: *See* against
come, spread: ⲉⲓ (*i*), ܐܬܐ (*ʾeṯā*) 5:4, 7; 6:8, 10; 7:21; 10:3; 18:12; 20:7; 23:11, 16; 30:2, 6; 33:6; 37:3
coming: [παρουσία], ܡܐܬܝܬܐ (*mēṯīṯā*) 6:17; 7:17
to make come, bring, carry, turn*: ⲉⲓⲛⲉ (*ine*), ܐܝܬܝ (*ʾaytī*) 6:8, 10; 7:13; 8:2; 16:16; 22:11; 38:1; 39:1*
come forth: *See* go out
come out: *See* go out
coming: *See* come
command (*v.*): ܦܩܕ (*pqaḏ*) 38:14(H)
decree: ܦܘܩܕܢܐ (*puqdānā*) 23:17

compare: ܐܬܦܚܡ (*ʾetpaḥḥam*) 30:4
compassion, mercy: ⲛⲁ (*na*) 25:8; ܚܢܢܐ (*ḥnānā*) 7:10; 21:1, 2
have compassion, mercy, pity: ܚܢ (*ḥan*) 7:5, 10; 42:15
compassion: *See* love (*v.*)
complete: *See* fill; totality
completion: *See* follow
composition: *See* preparation
conception: ܒܛܢܐ (*baṭnā*) 19:6
condemn: *See* sins
condemned: *See* oppression; sins
confess, give thanks, praise, thank: ⲟⲩⲱⲛϩ [ⲉⲃⲟⲗ] (*wōnᵉh* [*ebol*]), ܐܘܕܝ (*ʾawdī*) 5:1; 7:25; 10:5; 21:7; *see also* glory
confessors: ܡܘܕܝܢܐ (*mawdyānē*) 12:4
confession/thanksgiving: ܬܘܕܝܬܐ (*tawdīṯā*) 26:6
promises: ܫܘܕܝܐ (*šūḏāyē*) 31:13
to promise: ܐܫܬܘܕܝ (*ʾeštawdī*) 4:11; 31:13
confession: *See* confess
confessors: *See* confess
congregation: ܟܢܘܫܬܐ (*knūštā*) 42:14
gather: ܟܢܫ (*kanneš*) 22:2
be gathered: ܐܬܟܢܫ (*ʾeṯkannaš*) 10:5; 17:14; 23:17
consolation: *See* entreat
construction: ⲕⲏⲧ (*kēt*) 6:9
build: ⲕⲱⲧ (*kōt*), ܒܢܐ (*bnā*) 22:12
contempt: ܫܝܛܘܬܐ (*šīṭūṯā*) 31:2; *see also* target of contempt
be despised: [ϫⲓ] ⲥⲱϣ ([*či*] *sōš*), ܐܬܬܫܝܛ (*ʾettšīṭ*) 8:5; 25:5
continually: *See* totality; always
contrivance: *See* preparation
coo: *See* sing
correct: *See* upright
corrupt (*v.*): *See* corruption
corrupted, be: *See* corruption
corruption, perishability, destruction: ⲧⲁⲕⲟ (*tako*), ܚܒܠܐ (*ḥḇālā*) 15:8b; 22:11; 33:1, 7; 38:9
imperishable, imperishably: ܕܠܐ ܚܒܠܐ (*d-lā ḥḇālā*) 7:11; 8:23; 9:4; 11:12; 17:2; 21:5; 22:11; 28:5; 40:6
imperishability, incorruption, indestructibility: ἀφθαρσία, ⲙⲛ̄ⲧⲁⲧⲧⲁⲕⲟ (*mᵉnt-at-tako*), ܠܐ ܚܒܠܐ (*lā ḥḇālā*) 11:12; 15:8a; 22:11; 33:12
to corrupt, destroy, be destructive: ⲧⲁⲕⲟ (*tako*), ܚܒܠ (*ḥabbel*) 22:7; 24:8; 28:14; 33:2; 38:9b(N), 9c, 11, 14; 39:3
be corrupted, destroyed, annihilated: ܐܬܚܒܠ (*ʾeṯḥabbal*) 7:21; 15:9; 31:1; 33:9; 38:9b(H), 9c; 39:10, 12
corruptor: ܡܚܒܠܢܐ (*mḥabblānā*) 38:9
destruction: ܚܘܒܠܐ (*ḥubbālā*) 24:8
corruptor: *See* corruption
counsel: *See* sense
countenance: *See* face
course: *See* go; run
covenant: *See* stand up

draw back: ܢܛܦ (*nṭap̄*) 4:13
draw back: *See* take
draw near: ἐγγίζω, ܩܪܒ (*qreḇ*) 11:6
  war: ܩܪܒܐ (*qrāḇā*) 8:7; 9:6, 9; 29:9
  sacrifice: ܩܘܪܒܢܐ (*qurbānā*) 20:2, 4
  offer, present, sacrifice: ܩܪܒ (*qarreḇ*) 7:22; 20:2, 5; 31:4
  be offered, draw near: ܐܬܩܪܒ (*ʾeṯqarraḇ*) 19:1; 33:7; 42:1, 17
  access: ܩܘܪܒܐ (*qurrāḇā*) 36:8
  near (to), neighbor, related: ܩܪܝܒܐ (*qarrīḇā*) 6:15; 7:19; 20:6; 21:7; 36:6
drink: *See* drink (*v.*)
drink (*v.*): πίνω, ⲥⲱ (*sō*), ܫܬܐ (*šṯā* [*ʾeštī*]) 6:11; 8:16; 11:7; 19:1; 30:7; 38:12
  drink: ⲥⲱ (*sō*), ܡܫܬܝܐ (*maštyā*) 6:12, 13; 30:2
  wedding feast: ܡܫܬܘܬܐ (*meštūṯā*) 38:12
drip (*v.*): ܢܛܦ (*nṭap̄*) 40:1
drip (*v.*): *See* flow (*v.*)
drop: *See* cast away
droplets: *See* sprinkle
drugs, poisons: ܣܡ̈ܡܢܐ (*sammānē*) 38:8
drunk, become: μεθύσκομαι, ܪܘܐ (*rwā*), ܪܘܝ (*rwī*) 11:7
  drunkenness, intoxication: μέθη, ܪܘܝܘܬܐ (*rawwāyūṯā*) 11:8; 38:12
drunkenness: *See* drunk, become
dry: ϣⲟⲩⲱⲟⲩ (*šwōw*) 1:3; 6:11
due, be: *See* sins
dwell: ܥܡܪ (*ʿmar*) 32:1; *see also* loose (settle*)
  dwelling-place: ⲙⲁⲛ̄ϣⲱⲡⲉ (*ma-ʿn-šōpe*), ܒܝܬ ܡܥܡܪܐ (*bēṯ maʿmrā*) 22:12
  cause to dwell: ܐܥܡܪ (*ʾaʿmar*) 10:2
  inhabitant: ܥܡܘܪܐ (*ʿāmōrā*) 24:3
dwelling-place [tabernacle]: ܡܫܟܢܐ (*mašknā*) 12:12
dwelling-place: *See* dwell; house

ear: ܐܕܢܐ (*ʾeḏnā*) 9:1; 15:4; 16:9
earth, land*: γῆ, (χαμαί), ⲕⲁϩ (*kah*), ܐܪܥܐ (*ʾarʿā*) 6:10, 11; 7:20; 11:10, 12, 13, 16f, 16h, 18, 21; 15:10; 16:10*, 16; 33:3
east: *See* dawn (*v.*)
elect: *See* choose
emanation: ἀπόρροια 6:8; *see also* rivulet
embrace: ܥܦܩ (*ʿp̄aq*) 28:6(N)
end: ܚܪܬܐ (*ḥarṯā*) 4:12; 7:14; 14:4; 26:7; τέλος, ܚܪܝܬܐ (*ḥrāyṯā*) 6:4; 11:4; *see also* follow (end)
  another, other: ܐܚܪܢܐ (*ḥrēnā*) 4:1; 41:8
end: ܣܘܦܐ (*sawp̄ā*) 33:3(*bis*)
end: *See* follow
endure: ܣܝܒܪ (*saybar*) 31:10, 11; 42:13
enemy: ϫⲁϫⲉ (*čače*), ܒܥܠܕܒܒܐ (*bʿeldḇāḇā*) 22:3; 29:5, 10
  adversary: ἀντίδικος, ܒܥܠܕܝܢܐ (*bʿeldīnā*) 22:3
enemy: *See* adversary
energy: *See* do
enough, be: ܣܦܩ (*sp̄aq*) 26:12
  for no reason, uselessly: ܣܦܝܩܐܝܬ (*sp̄īqāʾīṯ*) 19:3, 8
entangle: ܥܪܩܠ (*ʿarqel*) 39:2
enter in: ܥܠ (*ʿal*) 33:8
  bring in: ܐܥܠ (*ʾaʿʿel*) 7:1
entirely: *See* fill
entreat, seek, require: ܒܥܐ (*bʿā*) 7:10; 8:22; 15:1; 19:9; 20:6; 24:5; 26:13; 28:17, 18; 33:13; 38:14; 42:5
  consolation: ܒܥܘܬܐ (*bāʿūṯā*) 17:12
  desirable: ܡܬܒܥܐ (*meṯbʿē*) 19:3
entrusted, be: *See* believe in
envy: *See* jealousy
erect oneself: *See* upright
error: *See* go astray
escape, flee: ⲡⲱⲧ (*pōt*), ܥܪܩ (*ʿraq*) 18:6; 23:8, 20; 25:1; 38:6
establish: *See* lay; stand up; truth
eternal: αἰώνιος 11:16
eternal: *See* aeon
eternity: *See* aeon
every: *See* totality
everybody: *See* totality
everyone: *See* totality; human being
everyone, everybody: ܟܠ ܐܢܫ (*kol nāš*) 6:18; 28:12
everything: *See* totality
evil, (the) Evil One: ϩⲟⲟⲩ (*how*), ܒܝܫܐ (*bīšā*) 14:5; 18:7; 22:7; 33:4
  malicious: κακῶς, ܒܝܫܐܝܬ (*bīšāʾīṯ*) 5:9
  uselessness, wickedness: πονηρία, ܒܝܫܘܬܐ (*bīšūṯā*) 11:21
Evil One: *See* evil
exalt: *See* high
except: *See* if
existence: *See* find
expectation: ܣܘܟܝܐ (*sukkāyā*) 12:7
experience (*v.*): *See* learn
expire: *See* breathe; go out; target of contempt
explanation: ܡܦܫܩܢܘܬܐ (*mp̄aššqānūṯā*) 12:11
extinguished, be: *See* quenched, be
exult, leap: ܕܘܨ, ܕܨ (*dāṣ*) 28:2a, 2b; 40:4; 41:7
  exultation: ܕܝܨܐ (*dyāṣā*) 8:1; 21:9; 23:4; 40:4; 41:7
exult: *See* high
exultation: *See* exult
eye: ὀφθαλμός, ⲃⲁⲗ (*bal*), ܥܝܢܐ (*ʿaynā*) 5:5; 6:17; 11:14; 13:1; 14:1a, 1b; 15:3; 16:9; 25:5a, 5b

face, countenance, person, presence: πρόσωπον, ϩⲟ (*ho*), ܦܪܨܘܦܐ (*parṣōp̄ā* [πρόσωπον]) 8:15; 11:14; 15:9; 17:4; 22:11; 25:4; 31:5; 42:13
face: πρόσωπον, ܐܦ̈ܐ (*ʾappē*) 6:10; 8:14; 11:13; 13:2, 3; 15:2; 16:16; 17:4; 21:6, 9; 36:3; 40:4; 41:6
faith: *See* believe in
faithful: *See* believe in
faithfulness: *See* believe in
fall, reach*: ϩⲉ (*he*), ܢܦܠ (*np̄al*) 5:4, 5, 9; 6:16; 9:6; 12:6; 18:2; 37:2*; 38:15
fall on: *See* turn
fallow: *See* cease
falsehood: ܕܓܠܘܬܐ (*daggālūṯā*) 3:10; 18:6, 8
far: *See* become far from

be given, offered, added, placed: ϯ (*ti*), ܐܬܝܗܒ (*ʾetiheb*) 6:6, 12; 15:10; 24:6; 30:6
give birth, bear, bring forth, beget: ܐܝܠܕ (*ʾiled*) 19:6, 7, 10a, 10b; 24:5; 36:3; 41:10
origin: ܐܝܠܝܕܘܬܐ (*ʾilīdūtā*) 28:16
children: ܝܠܘܕܐ (*yallūdē*) 41:1
give life: *See* live
give rest: *See* rest
give thanks: *See* confess
give up: *See* leave
glad, be: *See* joy
gladdened, be: *See* sweet
glorify: *See* glory
glory: δόξα, ܫܘܒܚܐ (*šubḥā*) 11:24
glorified: ܫܒܝܚܐ (*šbīḥā*) 17:7(N)
praise, glorify: ܫܒܚ (*šabbaḥ*) 6:7; 7:19, 24; 14:8; 17:7(H); 18:1; 21:7; 26:4; 36:2, 4(*bis*[N]); 41:1
glory, praise, hymn: δόξα, ܬܫܒܘܚܬܐ (*tešbuḥtā*) 6:7; 10:4; 11:17; 12:4; 13:2; 14:5; 16:1, 2, 4, 5, 20; 17:16; 18:16; 20:9a, 9c, 10; 21:9; 26:1, 5; 29:2, 11; 31:3; 36:2; 40:2b, 2c; 41:4, 16
praised [ones]: ܡܫܒܚܢܐ (*mšabbḥānē*) 36:4(H)
be glorified: ܐܫܬܒܚ (*ʾeštabbaḥ*) 38:19
glow (*v.*): ܪܬܚ (*rtaḥ*) 17:9
gnōsis: *See* know
go, blow*, walk: ܗܠܟ (*hallek*) 6:1*; 7:14; 10:6; 17:4; 18:14; 20:9; 23:4; 33:13; 38:5; 39:6, 9
course, steps*, walk: ܗܠܟܬܐ (*hlaktā*) 12:5; 17:8*; 31:2 (ἀνοδία[?], "immobility"); 39:2*, 13
go, follow*, attack**: ܐܙܠ (*ʾezal*) 7:18; 8:21; 15:6; 17:5, 11; 23:10*; 28:13**; 38:4, 7, 15
go about: *See* around
go astray, stray, wander, forget: ܛܥܐ (*ṭʿā*) 17:5; 28:15(N); 31:2; 38:4, 5
error: ܛܥܝܘܬܐ (*ṭāʿyūtā*) 15:6; 18:10, 14; 31:2; 38:6, 8, 10
lead astray: ܐܛܥܝ (*ʾaṭʿī*) 38:11
deceiver: ܡܛܥܝܢܐ (*maṭʿyānā*) 38:10, 15
go forth: *See* go out
go out, come out, go forth, come forth, flow from, expire, issue forth: ⲉⲓ [ⲉⲃⲟⲗ] (*i* [*ebol*]), ܢܦܩ (*npaq*) 6:8, 15; 7:17; 28:6(H); 30:5; 31:6; 35:3; 42:17
bring forth, bring out: ܐܦܩ (*ʾappeq*) 33:8; 40:2; 42:16
go up into, grow upward, rise: ܣܠܩ (*sleq*) 15:10; 38:1, 18(N)
ascent: ܣܘܠܩܐ (*sullāqā*) 35:7
bring up, cause to ascend, lead up: ⲉⲓⲛⲉ ⲉϩⲣⲁⲓ (*ine ehraï*), ܐܣܩ (*ʾasseq*) 22:1; 29:4; 38:18(H)
goaded, be: ܐܙܕܩܬ (*ʾezdqet*) 12:10
goal: *See* follow
God: θεός, ⲛⲟⲩⲧⲉ (*nute*), ܐܠܗܐ (*ʾallāhā*) 4:1, 14; 5:1, 11; 9:5; 10:4; 11:9, 24; 16:17; 17:1; 18:8; 23:21; 25:1; 33:10; 36:3; 40:1; 42:15; *see also* Father; Lord; Most High
good: ἀγαθός, ܛܒܐ (*ṭābā*) 10:3; 11:20; 28:12
goodness, (grace?): ܛܒܘܬܐ (*ṭābūtā*) 20:9(N?); 29:2(H); 41:5
blessed: μακάριος, ܛܘܒܐ (*ṭūbā*) 6:13; 9:8; 11:18; 12:13; 30:7; ܛܘܒܢܐ (*ṭūbānā*) 32:1; 33:11
grace: χάρις, ܛܝܒܘܬܐ (*taybūtā*) 4:6; 5:3; 6:6; 7:22, 25; 9:5; 11:1; 15:8; 20:7, 9(H); 23:2, 4(N); 24:13; 25:4; 29:2(N), 5; 31:3, 7; 33:1, 10; 34:6; 37:4; 41:3
prepare: ܛܝܒ (*ṭayyeb*) 8:16
be prepared: ܐܬܛܝܒ (*ʾeṭṭayyab*) 8:7
goodness: *See* good; sweet
governance: *See* lead to
grace: *See* good
gracious gift: *See* give
grant: *See* give
grave: τάφος, ܩܒܪܐ (*qabrā*) 22:8
great, arch(angel)*: ⲛⲟϭ (*noc*), ܪܒܐ (*rabbā*) 4:8*; 6:8; 18:12; 23:21; 36:4(*bis*); 41:4
greatness, magnificence*, majesty*, sublimity*: ܪܒܘܬܐ (*rabbūtā*) 7:3, 23*; 15:7*; 18:16*; 19:11; 29:3*; 36:5
become large: ܐܬܪܘܪܒ (*ʾetrawrab*) 38:18; *see also* grow up; increase
great: *See* grow; grow up; increase
great power: *See* take hold of
great price: *See* honor
greatness: *See* great
grief: *See* feel grief
group: ܬܓܡܐ (*teḡmā* [τάγμα]) 35:4
grow: ܣܓܝ (*sḡī*), ܣܓܐ (*sḡā*) 8:1
multitude: ܣܘܓܐ (*soḡā*) 14:9; 16:7; 23:14
great, generous, many, much more: πολύς, ⲙⲏⲏϣⲉ (*mēēše*), *multus*, ܣܓܝܐܐ (*saggīyā*) 7:10, 17; 11:23; 19:7, 10; 23:7, 15, 19; 25:5; 30:4; 38:12; 42:11
increase: ܐܣܓܝ (*ʾasgī*) 6:6; 8:22 (adverbial "much"); 12:3
grow: *See* sprout
grow up: ܐܬܪܒܝ (*ʾetrabbī*) 35:6; *see also* great; increase
grow up: *See* sprout
grow upward: *See* go up into
grown naturally: *See* sprout
growth: *See* sprout
guard: *See* keep
guide: *See* lead (*v.*)
guilty: *See* sins
gush forth, bring up: ܓܣܐ (*gsā*) 16:2; 36:7; 40:2a, 2b
flood: ܓܣܝܬܐ (*gāsītā*) 36:7

hallelujah: ἀλληλουϊά, ܗܠܠܘܝܐ (*hallēlūyā*) 3–42 (*finis*)
hallow: *See* holiness
hand: ϭⲓϫ (*cič*), ܐܝܕܐ (*ʾidā*), generally in the idiom, "by (the hand[s])," 12:11, 13; 15:5, 8; 16:6; 17:4; 18:1; 22:5, 7; 23:7; 26:3; 27:1, 2; 31:4, 7; 33:11; 35:7; 37:1; 38:15, 16; 42:1a, 1b; *see also* right; stretch out the hand
handmaid: ܐܡܬܐ (*ʾamtā*) 29:11
hang: ܬܠܐ (*tlā*) 3:2
be hung: ܐܬܬܠܝ (*ʾettlī*) 42:2
harmony: ܫܘܝܘܬܐ (*šawyūtā*) 12:9, 10

interpreter: *See* interpret
intoxication: *See* drunk, become
inundate: *See* fill
invite: *See* read
iron: ܦܪܙܠܐ (*parzlā*) 17:9a, 9b
irrationality: ἀλογιστία 11:8; *see also* knowledge
irritated, be: ܐܬܥܝܛ (*ʾeṯʿayyaṭ*) 23:20(H)
issue forth: *See* go out

jealousy: *See* zealous, be
jealousy: ܚܣܡܐ (*ḥsāmā*) 3:6
  without jealousy, without envy: ܕܠܐ ܚܣܡܐ (*d-lā ḥsāmā*) 7:3; 11:6; 15:6; 17:12; 20:7; 23:4; *see also* ἀφθονία in 11:6 𝔊
join (*v.*): ܪܡܐ (*rmā*) 22:2
  foundation: ܬܪܡܝܬܐ (*tarmyāṯā* [Plural of *tarmīṯā*]) 41:15
  cast down, lay: ܐܪܡܝ (*ʾarmī*) 29:10; 42:7
join (oneself to): ܐܬܢܩܦ (*ʾeṯnaqqap̄*) 3:8
joy: χαρά 11:16; ⲟⲩⲣⲟⲧ (*urot*) 6:14; ܚܕܘܬܐ (*ḥaḏuṯā* [sic]) 7:1, 2, 17; 15:1a, 1b; 23:1; 31:3, 6; 32:1; *see also* sweet
  be glad, rejoice: ܚܕܐ (*ḥḏā*), ܚܕܝ (*ḥḏī*) 38:15; 41:3
judge: ܕܝܢܐ (*dayyānā*) 33:11
judgment: ܕܝܢܐ (*dīnā*) 35:3; *see also* adversary
justice: ϩⲁⲡ (*hap*) 5:3
justify: ܙܕܩ (*zaddeq*) 29:5
  righteousness: δικαιοσύνη, ܙܕܝܩܘܬܐ (*zaddīqūṯā*) 8:5, 21; 9:10; 20:4; 25:10; 36:7; 41:12
  be justified, declared righteous: ⲧⲙⲁⲓⲟ (*tmayo*), ܐܙܕܕܩ (*ʾezdaddaq*) 17:2; 25:12; 31:5

keep: ܢܛܪ (*nṭar*) 8:10, 11, 22
  guard, protect: ܢܛܪ (*naṭṭar*) 18:7; 19:11; 35:2
  be kept: ܐܬܢܛܪ (*ʾeṯnaṭṭar*) 8:10, 11
kidneys/reins: νέφροι, ܟܘܠܝܬܐ (*kulyāṯā*) 11:2; 20:5
kindness: *See* sweet
kingdom: *See* kingship
kingship, kingdom: ܡܠܟܘܬܐ (*malkūṯā*) 18:3; 22:12; 23:12
  reign as king: ܐܡܠܟ (*ʾamleḵ*) 23:22
kiss (*v.*): ܢܫܩ (*nšaq*) 28:6
know, recognise, acknowledge, perceive, understand: ܝܕܥ (*ʾiḏaʿ*) 3:3, 10, 11; 4:7a, 7b; 7:9; 8:9, 12(*bis*), 14; 9:7; 12:6, 10, 13; 16:13; 17:7; 18:9a, 9b, 10a, 10b, 13a(*bis*); 19:5; 23:4, 10; 24:14; 26:12; 30:6; 38:7; 39:8; 42:3, 8; ⲥⲟⲟⲩⲛ (*sowᵉn*), ܐܫܬܘܕܥ (*ʾeštawdaʿ*) 6:18; 7:12; 12:13; 24:14; 28:16(N)
  knowledge, *gnōsis*, understanding, ignorance: σύνεσις, ܝܕܥܬܐ (*ʾiḏaʿṯā*) 6:6; 7:7(*bis*), 13, 21a, 21b, 23; 8:8, 12; 11:4, 8 (*see also* irrationality); 12:3; 15:5; 17:12; 18:11; 23:4a, c; 28:13; 34:5
  mind, *gnōsis*, understanding, thought: ܡܕܥܐ (*maddʿā*) 8:20; 17:7; 38:13, 21
  be acknowledged, be known: ܐܬܝܕܥ (*ʾeṯiḏaʿ*) 6:6; 7:16; 15:10; 41:2, 15
  let (it) be known, make known: ܐܘܕܥ (*ʾawdaʿ*) 7:3; 33:13
knowledge: *See* know
knowledges: *See* wisdom
known, make: *See* show

labor: ܥܡܠܐ (*ʿamlā*) 37:3
labor: *See* service
labor, be in: ܚܒܠ (*ḥabbel*) 19:7
laborers: οἱ ἐργαζόμενοι, ܦܥܠܐ (*pāʿlē*) 11:20
lack: *See* lack (*v.*)
lack (*v.*): ܚܣܪ (*ḥsar*) 24:11
  having need, lack: ܚܣܝܪܐ (*ḥassīrā*) 4:9b, 9c; 18:4; 24:9
  without stint: ܕܠܐ ܚܘܣܪܢܐ (*d-lā ḥusrānā*) 15:10
  deprive: ܐܚܣܪ (*ʾaḥsar*) 20:6
lamp: ϩⲏⲃⲥ (*hēbᵉs*), ܫܪܓܐ (*šrāḡā*) 25:7
land: *See* earth
large: *See* grow up
large, become: *See* great
lashed, be: *See* draw (*v.*)
laugh: ܓܚܟ (*gḥaḵ*, *gḥeḵ*) 18:14
laugh, rejoice: γελάω, ܪܘܙ (*rwaz*) 11:12, 16; 40:4
lay, put, set, remove, bring (it) over, to place, establish, take to heart*: ⲕⲱ (*kō*), ܣܐܡ, ܣܡ (*sām*) 4:1; 7:13, 14; 8:20; 9:8, 11; 18:7; 20:8; 25:7; 38:3, 17; 42:19*, 20
  treasury: ܣܝܡܬܐ (*sīmṯā*) 16:15a, 15b
  be established, be laid, be made fast: ܐܬܬܣܝܡ (*ʾettsīm*) 10:6; 28:5; 38:16; 39:13
lay: *See* join (*v.*)
lay bare: γυμνόω, ܓܠܐ (*glā*) 11:2
  apparent, manifest: ܓܠܐ (*glē*), ܓܠܝܐ (*galyā*) 4:12, 14; 16:8
  become manifest, be revealed: ܐܬܓܠܝ (*ʾeṯglī*) 23:18; 34:6
lead: ⲧⲁϩⲧ (*tahᵉt*), ܐܒܪܐ (*ʾaḇārā*) 25:5
lead (*v.*): ܕܒܪ (*dḇar*) 17:5; 29:7; 38:1
  bees: ܕܒܘܪܝܬܐ (*debbōryāṯā*) 30:4; 40:1
  guide: ܡܕܒܪܢܐ (*mḏabbrānā*) 14:4
  governance, plan of salvation: ܡܕܒܪܢܘܬܐ (*mḏabbrānūṯā*) 23:12; 36:8
lead astray: *See* go astray
lead away: *See* bring
lead down: *See* descend
lead up: *See* go up into
league, to: *See* harmony
lean on, trust in: ܐܣܬܡܟ (*ʾestammaḵ*) 20:8
leap: *See* exult
learn, experience (*v.*): ܝܠܦ (*ʾilep̄*) 7:6; 13:2; *see also* teach
leave, abandon, cast off, forsake, give up*, let go, send out: ἀφίημι (*see also* ἐκτρέπω in 11:18 𝔊), ⲕⲱ (*kō*), ܫܒܩ (*šḇaq*) 5:2; 11:8, 10; 15:6; 17:11; 24:4*; 33:1, 3, 7; 38:4, 14
left (side): ϩⲃⲟⲩⲣ (*hbur*), ܣܡܠܐ (*semmālā*) 25:7
less than: ܒܨܝܪܐ ܡܢ (*bṣīrā men*) 4:3
let (it) go limp: ܐܪܦܝ (*ʾarpī*) 42:13
let go: *See* leave
letter: ܐܓܪܬܐ (*ʾeggarṯā*) 23:5, 7, 10, 17, 21
level (*v.*): *See* harmony
liberated, be: *See* loose

middle: *See* midst
midst: ⲙⲏⲧⲉ (*mēte*), ܡܨܥܬܐ (*mṣaʿṯā*) 30:6
  those in the middle: *see also* ⲙⲏⲧⲉ (*mēte*); ܡܨܥܝܬܐ (*meṣʿāyāṯā*) 22:2
midwife: *See* live (*v.*)
mightier: *See* gain
mighty: *See* man; power
milk: ܚܠܒܐ (*ḥalḇā*) 4:10; 8:16; 19:1, 3, 4; 35:5; 40:1
  to milk: ܚܠܒ (*ḥlaḇ*) 19:2
  be milked: ܐܬܚܠܒ (*ʾeṯḥleḇ*) 19:2
milk (*v.*): *See* milk
mind: *See* know; sense; thought
minister: διάκονος, ܡܫܡܫܢܐ (*mšammšānā*) 6:13
mirror: *See* see (*v.*)
mix: ܡܙܓ (*mzaḡ*) 19:4
  be united: ܐܬܡܙܓ (*ʾeṯmzeḡ*) 3:7
mixture: ܚܘܠܛܢܐ (*ḥulṭānā*) 19:5
more than: *See* gain
Most High: *See* high
mother: *mater*, ܐܡܐ (*ʾemmā*) 19:7; 28:2; 35:5
motionless: *See* tremble
mouth, beak*: ܦܘܡܐ (*pummā*) 7:24a, 24b; 8:4; 10:1; 12:2, 3, 11; 16:5; 18:8; 21:8; 26:10; 28:1(*bis*)*; 29:4; 31:3; 36:7; 42:6
move: *See* tremble
moved, be: *See* redeem
mow down: ܚܨܕ (*ḥṣaḏ*) 23:13
much more: *See* grow (*v.*)
multitude: *See* grow (*v.*)
mystery: ܪܐܙܐ (*rāzā*) 8:10

nakedness: ܦܘܪܣܝܐ (*pursāyā*) 20:6
name: ⲣⲁⲛ (*ran*), ܫܡܐ (*šmā*) 6:7; 8:21, 23; 14:5; 15:8; 16:20; 18:1, 16; 20:10; 22:6; 23:22; 25:11; 30:5; 31:3; 33:13; 39:7, 8, 13; 41:5, 16; 42:20
  be called: ܐܫܬܡܗ (*ʾeštammah*) 36:3
narration: *See* narrator
narrator: ܡܬܢܝܢܐ (*mṯannyānā*) 12:4
  description, narration: ܬܘܢܝܐ (*tunnāyā*) 12:5a, 5b
nature: ܟܝܢܐ (*kyānā*) 7:6
near: *See* draw near
need: *See* lack (*v.*)
needs: *See* useless
neighbor: *See* draw near
nestlings: ܦܪܘܓܐ (*parrūḡē*) 28:1a, 1b
never: ܠܐ ܡܬܘܡ (*lā mṯōm*) 4:4; 12:6
new: ܚܕܬܐ (*ḥaṯā*) 17:4; 31:3; 33:12; 41:16
  renew: ἐγκαινίζω, ܚܕܬ (*ḥaddeṯ*) 11:11; 36:5
  renewal: ܚܘܕܬܐ (*ḥuddāṯā*) 36:5
  be renewed: ⲣ̄ ⲃⲣ̄ⲣⲉ (*ᵉr bᵉrre*), ܐܬܚܕܬ (*ʾeṯḥaddaṯ*) 22:11
night: ܠܠܝܐ (*lēlyā*) 16:15, 16; 41:6 ("by night")
no one: ܠܐ ܐܢܫ (*lā nāš*) 4:1; *see also* human being
north: ܓܪܒܝܐ (*garbyā*) 26:6
nourish: ܬܪܣܝ (*tarsī*) 16:2
now, again: ܡܟܠ (*mekkēl*) 4:13; 8:5

obey: ܐܬܛܦܝܣ (*ʾeṭṭpīs* [πεῖσαι]) 8:19; 39:8
obey: *See* hear
obtain: *See* gain (*v.*)
ode: *See* sing
offer: *See* draw near; give
offspring, seed: σπέρμα, ܙܪܥܐ (*zarʿā*) 22:5; 31:13
  to sow: ܙܪܥ (*zraʿ*) 17:13
older: ܩܫܝܫܐ (*qaššīšā*) 4:3; 28:17
on this side, on that side: ܡܟܐ (*mekkā*) 39:11(*bis*)
once: ܒܙܒܢ (*ba-zḇan*) 8:3
one: ܚܕܐ (*ḥḏā*) 4:5; 12:8(*bis*), 12:9(*bis*); 16:17(*bis*); 28:9; 36:6; 41:15
  alone, one: ܒܠܚܘܕ (*ba-lḥōḏ*) 23:1; 38:19
open: *See* vain ones
open (*v.*): ܦܬܚ (*pṯaḥ*) 4:10; 7:24; 8:1(*bis*); 9:1; 10:1; 13:1; 14:8; 16:5; 17:8; 19:4; 31:3; 42:17
  opening: ܦܬܚܐ (*pṯāḥā*) 17:10
  be opened: ܐܬܦܬܚ (*ʾeṯpṯaḥ*) 8:4; 24:5; 30:1; 36:7
opening: *See* open (*v.*)
openness: παρρησία 6:17
opposing: *See* against
oppress: ܐܠܨ (*ʾelaṣ*) 20:5b, 5c
  affliction: ܐܘܠܨܢܐ (*ʾulṣānā*) 21:4
  be oppressed: ܐܬܐܠܨ (*ʾeṯeleṣ*) 31:6
oppressed, be: *See* oppress; oppression
oppression: ܛܠܘܡܝܐ (*ṭlumyā*) 28:10
  be condemned, oppressed, rejected, wronged: ܐܬܛܠܡ (*ʾeṭṭlem*) 4:6; 33:12
origin: *See* give birth
other: *See* end
over: *See* above
overflow: *See* gain; spring
overshadow: *See* shade
overthrow: πατάσσω, ܣܚܒ (*saḥḥeḇ*) 22:5

pain: *See* feel grief, feel pain
paradise: παράδεισος, ܦܪܕܝܣܐ (*pardaysā* [παράδεισος]) 11:16, 18, 23, 24; 20:7
paralysed: *See* loose
parched: ϣⲟⲟⲩⲉ (*šowe*), ܝܒܝܫܐ (*yabbīšā*) 6:14
pass before, through: *See* cross (*v.*)
pass from: *See* turn
pass, cause to: *See* cross (*v.*)
password: *See* word
patriarchs: *See* head
peace: *See* follow
peak: *See* head
people: ܥܡܐ (*ʿammā*) 10:5, 6; 23:15(N); 29:8; 31:12
perceive: ܐܣܬܟܠ (*ʾestakkal*) 8:15
perceive: *See* know
perfect: ܓܡܝܪܐ (*gmīrā*) 33:5
perfection: *See* fill
perish, be destroyed, lost: ܐܒܕ (*ʾeḇaḏ*) 5:14; 9:7; 24:7, 9; 28:9, 16; 31:2; 33:9; 42:10
  destruction: ܐܒܕܢܐ (*ʾaḇdānā*) 28:5; 33:2, 8
  destroy: ϥⲱⲧⲉ ⲉⲃⲟⲗ (*fōte ebol*), ܐܘܒܕ (*ʾawbeḏ*) 6:3; 22:5; 24:10; 28:18; 33:2
perishability: *See* corruption
persecute: ⲡⲱⲧ ⲛ̄ⲥⲁ (*pōt ᵉnsa*), ܪܕܦ (*rḏap̄*)

redemption, salvation: σωτηρία, ⲛⲟⲩϩⲙ (*nuhᵉm*), ܦܘܪܩܢܐ (*purqānā*) 5:11 (*see also* savior [σωτήρ]); 7:16; 11:3; 15:6; 17:2; 18:7; 19:11; 21:2; 25:2; 28:10; 31:13; 34:6; 35:2; 38:3; 40:5
be redeemed, be saved: ⲛⲟⲩϩⲙ (*nuhᵉm*), ܐܬܦܪܩ (*ʾetpreq*) 5:3; 6:18; 8:22; 9:5, 12; 10:6; 14:5; 17:4, 14; 26:9; 33:10, 11; 34:6; 38:16; 42:18
be moved: ܐܬܦܪܩ (*ʾetparraq*) 35:7
redeemed ones: *See* redeem
redemption: *See* redeem
regret: ܬܘܬܐ (*twāṯā*) 4:11
to regret: ܐܬܘܝ (*ʾeṯwī*) 4:11
reign as king: *See* kingdom
reins: *See* kidneys
reject: *See* target of contempt
rejected, be: *See* target of contempt; oppression
rejoice: *See* joy; laugh; sweet
related: *See* draw near
release (*v.*): *See* loose
remain: *See* abide; stand up
remember: ܐܬܕܟܪ (*ʾeddkar*) 41:9
remembrance, memorial, memory: μνεία, ܕܘܟܪܢܐ (*dukrānā*) 11:22; 28:17, 18
remembrance: *See* remember
remnant: λεῖμμα, ܫܪܟܢܐ (*šarkānā*) 11:22
remove: *See* high; lay; separate (*v.*)
renew: *See* new
renewal: *See* new
require: *See* entreat
rescued, be: ⲛⲟⲩϩⲙ (*nuhᵉm*), ܐܬܦܠܛ (*ʾeṯpallaṭ*) 25:1
resemble: *See* form
rest, gentleness*: ܢܝܚܘܬܐ (*nīḥūṯā*) 14:6; 20:8; 26:12; 35:1(N)*; ⲙ̄ⲧⲟⲛ (*ᵉmton*), ܢܝܚܐ (*nyāḥā*) 3:5; 25:12*; 26:3; 37:4; ܢܝܚܬܐ (*nyāḥtā*) 35:1(H)
give rest, revive, be pleased: ⲕⲧⲟ (*kᵉto*), ܐܢܝܚ (*ʾanīḥ*) 6:14; 7:15; 11:12 (*see also* recall to life); 30:3; 38:4
to rest, find rest: ܐܬܬܢܝܚ (*ʾettnīḥ*) 16:12; 26:10, 12; 28:3; 30:2, 7; 35:6; 36:1
rest (*v.*): *See* rest
restrain, dam up, withhold: κωλύω, ⲁⲙⲁϩⲧⲉ (*amahte*), ܟܠܐ (*klā*) 6:9a, 9b; 18:5; 25:3
restraints: ܟܠܝܢܐ (*kelyānē*) 6:9
unhindered: ܕܠܐ ܟܠܝܢܐ (*d-lā ḵelyānā*) 7:1
restraints: *See* restrain
return, turn back: ἐκτρέπω, ܐܬܦܢܝ (*ʾeṯpnī*) 11:9; 33:6
bring back: ܐܦܢܝ (*ʾapnī*) 10:3
revealed, be: *See* lay bare
revere: *See* worship (*v.*)
revive: *See* rest
rich, be/become: πλουτέω, ܥܬܪ (*ʿṯar*) 9:5; 11:9
riches, wealth, fullness: πλοῦτος, ܥܘܬܪܐ (*ʿuṯrā*) 11:16; 41:10; ⲙⲛ̄ⲧⲣⲙ̄ⲙⲁⲟ (*mᵉnt-rᵉmmao*) 22:12
abundant: ܥܬܝܪܐ (*ʿattīrā*) 4:10; 26:13
riches: *See* rich
rift: ܣܕܩܐ (*seḏqā*) 38:2
right, right hand, right side: ⲟⲩⲛⲁⲙ (*unam*), ܝܡܝܢܐ (*yammīnā*) 8:6, 20; 14:4; 18:7; 19:5; 22:7; 25:2, 7, 9; 28:15; 38:20
south: ܬܝܡܢܐ (*taymnā*) 26:6
righteous, be declared: *See* justify
righteousness: *See* justify
ripe: ϫⲏⲕ (*čēk*) 1:5
rise: *See* go up into; stand up
rise up: *See* high
rise (*v.*): *See* dawn (*v.*)
river: ποταμός 11:16; ⲓⲉⲣⲟ (*yero*), ܢܗܪܐ (*nahrā*) 6:8; 23:14; 26:13; 39:1, 8
rivulet: ܬܦܐ (*tappā*) 6:8; *see also* emanation
rock: πέτρα, ܫܘܥܐ (*šūʿā*) 11:5
rock, stone: ܟܐܦܐ (*kēpā*) 9:9; 22:12; 31:11a, 11b(N)
rod (sceptre): ܚܘܛܪܐ (*ḥuṭrā*) 29:8
root: ῥίζα 11:16; ⲛⲟⲩⲛⲉ (*nune*), ܥܩܪܐ (*ʿeqqārā*) 22:5; 38:17
uproot: ܥܩܪ (*ʿqar*) 23:15
rough: ܩܫܝܬܐ (*qšīṯā*) 34:1
run, rush*: τρέχω, ܪܗܛ (*rheṭ*) 11:3; 12:11; 16:13; 23:7*, 16; 33:1; 42:15
course: ܪܗܛܐ (*rehṭā*) 7:1a, 1b, 2; 16:13
rush: *See* run

sacrifice: ܕܒܚܬܐ (*debḥṯā*) 7:10(?); *see also* being
sacrifice: *See* draw near
sacrifice (*v.*): *See* draw near
saint: *See* holiness
salvation: *See* plan of salvation; redeem
salvation: ⲟⲩϫⲁⲓ (*učaï*) 1:5
sanctuary: *See* holiness
sand: ϣⲱ (*šō*) 6:11
save: *See* redeem
savior: *See* redeem
say, speak: εἶπα, ܐܡܪ (*ʾemar*) 8:9; 11:18; 33:5; 38:10; 42:15; *see also* word
scatter: ϫⲱⲱⲣⲉ ⲉⲃⲟⲗ (*čōōre ebol*), ܒܕܪ (*baddar*) 10:5; 22:3
sceptre: *See* rod
scheme: *See* sense
scheme (*v.*): ϣⲟϫⲛⲉ (*šočne*) 5:7
scourges: *See* draw (*v.*)
scroll: *See* head
sea: ܝܡܐ (*yammā*) 16:10; 18:11
seal: ܚܬܡܐ (*ḥāṭmā*) 4:7; 23:8, 9a, 9b; *see also* sink down
search: ܒܨܐ (*bṣā*) 16:8
see, behold: θεάομαι 11:16; ⲛⲁⲩ (*naw*), ܚܙܐ (*ḥzā*) 5:4, 6; 7:5, 19; 9:12; 13:1; 15:3; 16:9; 17:6; 23:10; 25:3; 28:8; 38:9; 41:8; 42:11, 17
appearance: ܚܙܘܐ (*ḥezwā*) 31:1
seers: ܚܙܝܐ (*ḥazzāyē*) 7:18
mirror: ܡܚܙܝܬܐ (*maḥzīṯā*) 13:1
appear, be seen, what is seen, be manifest, seem: φαίνομαι, ⲟⲩⲱⲛϩ [ⲉⲃⲟⲗ] (*wōnᵉh* [*ebol*]), ܐܬܚܙܝ (*ʾeṯḥzī*) 5:14; 7:12, 18; 11:1; 16:8; 17:10; 18:11; 23:18; 25:3; 28:9; 29:6; 30:6; 33:4; 41:13
seed: *See* offspring
seek: *See* entreat
seem: *See* see (*v.*); suppose

ܩܡ (*qām*) 6:5; 8:3, 19; 12:6(*bis*); 16:13; 18:3; 25:3; 26:12; 31:8, 11; 33:3, 5; 42:6
covenant: ܩܝܡܐ (*qyāmā*) 9:11
standing firmly, firm: ܩܝܡܐ (*qayyāmā*) 5:13; 39:10, 11
stand upright: ܐܬܩܝܡ (*ʾetqayyam*) 8:3
set upright, awaken, establish, raise, stand upright: ⲧⲁϩⲟ ⲉⲣⲁⲧ⸗ (*taho erat⸗*), ܐܩܝܡ (*ʾaqīm*) 6:14, 16; 15:2; 16:12; 22:5; 35:1; 36:2
stand upright: *See* stand up
standing in the way: *See* against
stars: ܟܘܟ̈ܒܐ (*kawkbē*) 16:11
steering: ܓܪܪܐ (*grārā*) 16:1
step: ܕܪܓܐ (*dargā*) 38:3(N)
steps: *See* go, blow*
still (*v.*): *See* loose
stink: ܣܪܝܘܬܐ (*saryūtā*) 18:11
stint: *See* lack (*v.*)
stone: *See* rock
stop: *See* cease; stand up
storm [wind gust]: ܥܠܥܠܐ (*ʿalʿālā*) 34:2
straight: *See* upright
straighten: *See* upright
stranger, alien: ܐܟܣܢܝܐ (*ʾaksnāyā* [ξένος]) 17:6; ܢܘܟܪܝܐ (*nukrāyā*) 3:6; 6:3; 20:6
stray: *See* go astray
strength: *See* power
strengthen: *See* power
stretch out: ܦܫܛ (*pšaṭ*) 27:1; 35:7; 37:1; 42:1
simple, upright: ܦܫܝܛܐ (*pšīṭā*) 34:1b; 42:2a
stretching up, simplicity: ܦܫܝܛܘܬܐ (*pšīṭūtā*) 7:3; 27:3; 42:2
stretch out: *See* pitch
stretch out the hand: ܐܘܫܛ (*ʾawšeṭ*) 14:4
stretch over: † ϩⲓ- (*ti hi-*), ܩܪܡ (*qram*) + ܥܠ (*ʿal*) 22:9
stretching up: *See* stretch out
string: ܡܢܬܐ (*menntā*) 6:1
strip off: *See* take off
strong: *See* power
subdue: *See* do
subject, be: *See* do
sublimity: *See* great; beautiful
submerged, be: *See* sink down
submersion: *See* sink down
sudden: ܚܪܝܦܐ (*ḥarrīpā*) 39:4
swiftness, sharpness: ܚܪܝܦܘܬܐ (*ḥarrīpūtā*) 12:5
suffer: *See* take
sufferings: ܚ̈ܫܐ (*ḥaššē*) 21:4
sun, Helios: ἥλιος, ܫܡܫܐ (*šemšā*) 11:13; 15:1, 2; 16:15, 16
suppose, think: ܣܒܪ (*sbar*) 7:12; 18:12; 28:9; 38:8
hope: ἐλπίς, ܣܒܪܐ (*sabrā*) 5:2, 10; 29:1; 40:1
seem: ܐܣܬܒܪ (*ʾestbar*) 7:4; 17:6; 34:5; 42:10
trust in: ܣܒܪ (*sabbar*) 42:5(?); *see also* proclaim
supremely: *See* gain
surround: ⲕⲱⲧⲉ (*kōte*) 22:6; ܚܕܪ (*ḥdar*) 28:13
surrounded by: *See* around
swallowed up, be: ܐܬܒܠܥ (*ʾetblaʿ*) 28:9
sweet: ܚܠܝܐ (*ḥalyā*) 40:3
sweetness: ܚܠܝܘܬܐ (*ḥalyūtā*) 19:1; 28:15; 38:8
sweet, pleasant: ܒܣܝܡܐ (*bassīmā*) 11:15; 30:4
benevolence, goodness, kindness: χρηστότης, [χρηστός]*, ܒܣܝܡܘܬܐ (*bassīmūtā*) 7:3; 11:15, 21; 14:3; 17:7; 19:1, 11; 20:9; 25:12*; 42:16
delight: τρυφή, ܒܘܣܡܐ (*bussāmā*) 11:16, 24
be gladdened, be delighted, rejoice: εὐφραίνομαι, ܐܬܒܣܡ (*ʾetbassam*) 11:15; 20:8; 28:2
sweetness: *See* sweet
swiftness: *See* fast; sudden
sword: ܣܦܣܪܐ (*sapsērā* [σαμψήρα]) 28:4

tablet: ܦܢܩܝܬܐ (*penqītā* [πινακίδιον, πίναξ]) 23:21
take, accept, receive, take hold, catch, draw back, take away*, suffer**: ϥⲓ (*fi*) 22:2; 25:9; λαμβάνω, ϫⲓ (*či*), *accipio*, ܢܣܒ (*nsab*) 4:13; 5:3; 6:14; 7:4; 9:7, 10; 11:4; 14:3*; 15:6; 17:4; 19:5, 6; 22:9; 23:2, 7, 19; 29:9; 30:2; 31:2**, 7; 41:1
take away: *See* loose; take
take captive: ܫܒܐ (*šbā*) 10:3, 4
captivity: ܫܒܝܬܐ (*šbītā*) 10:3
take hold: *See* take
take hold of, seize, hold, possess, hold fast, hold back, take possession of, shut: ⲁⲙⲁϩⲧⲉ (*amahte*), ܐܚܕ (*ʾeḥad*) 4:8; 5:6; 6:10, 15; 7:16; 17:8, 10, 11; 18:7; 28:15; 42:3
great power: ܐܘܚܕܢܐ ܣܓܝܐܐ (*ʾuḥdānā saggīyā*) 19:10
take off, put off, strip off: ἀποδύομαι, ܫܠܚ (*šlaḥ*) 11:10; 15:8; 21:3
take possession of: *See* take hold of
take to heart: *See* lay
target of contempt: ܣܘܠܢܐ (*sulānā* [sic]) 28:11; *see also* contempt
be despised, rejected: ⲛⲟⲩϫⲉ [ⲉⲃⲟⲗ] (*nuče* [*ebol*]), ܐܣܬܠܝ (*ʾestlī*) 24:12; 25:5; 42:10
expire, reject: ⲛⲟⲩϫⲉ (*nuče*), ܐܣܠܝ (*ʾaslī*) 6:15; 41:11; 42:7
teach: ܐܠܦ (*ʾallep*) 3:10; 14:7; *see also* learn
teach: ⲧⲥⲁⲃⲟ (*tsabo*) 22:2; ܐܪܬܝ (*ʾartī*) 31:12(?); *see also* inherit
teacher: ܡܢܟܦܢܐ (*mnakkpānā*) 12:4
temple: ⲣⲡⲉ (*rpe*), ܗܝܟܠܐ (*hayklā*) 6:8
thank, give thanks, thanksgiving: *See* confess
then: *See* therefore
thence, there: ܬܡܢ (*tammān*) 17:8; 22:6
there: *See* thence
therefore, then, so: ܗܟܝܠ (*hākēl*) 6:13; 8:19; 39:8; 41:5
think: ܪܢܐ (*rnā*) 42:10
think: *See* suppose
think of: *See* thought
thirst: ⲉⲓⲃⲉ (*ibe*), ܨܗܝܐ (*ṣahyā*) 6:11
thirsty (ones): ܨ̈ܗܝܐ (*ṣhayyā*) 6:11; 30:2
thirsty (ones): *See* thirst

Editions and translations of the *Odes of Solomon*

Azar, Éphrem
Les Odes de Salomon (Paris: Cerf, 1996).
Bauer, Walter
Die Oden Salomos (KlT 64; Berlin: de Gruyter, 1933).
Idem
"Die Oden Salomos," *NTApo*[3-4] 2 ([3]1964 = [4]1971) 576–625.
Bernard, John Henry
The Odes of Solomon (TextsS 8.3; Cambridge: Cambridge University Press, 1912; repr., Nendeln/Liechtenstein: Kraus Reprint, 1967).
Beskow, Per, and Sten Hidal
Salomos oden: Den äldsta kristna sångboken översatt och kommenterad (Stockholm: Proprius, 1980).
Bruston, Charles
Les plus anciens cantiques chrétiens: Traduits sur la seconde édition du texte syriaque avec une introduction et des notes (Geneva: Jeheber; Paris: Fischbacher, 1912).
Charlesworth, James H., ed. and trans.
The Odes of Solomon (Oxford: Clarendon, 1973; rev. repr., SBLTT 13; SBLPS 7; Missoula, Mont.: Scholars Press, 1977).
Diettrich, Gustav
Die Oden Salomos unter Berücksichtigung der überlieferten Stichengliederung (Neue Studien zur Geschichte der Theologie und der Kirche 9; Berlin: Trowitzsch, 1911; repr., Aalen: Scientia, 1973).
Emerton, J. A.
"The Odes of Solomon," in H. F. D. Sparks, ed., *The Apocryphal Old Testament* (Oxford: Clarendon, 1984) 683–731.
Erbetta, Mario
"Le Odi di Salomone (II SEC.)," in idem, ed., *Gli Apocrifi del Nuovo Testamento* I/1 (Turin: Marietti, 1975) 608–58.
Fanourgakis, Vassilios [Basileios] D.
Αἱ Ὠδαὶ Σολομῶντος: Συμβολὴ εἰς τὴν ἔρευναν τῆς ὑμνογραφίας τῆς ἀρχαϊκῆς ἐκκλησίας (Analekta Blatadon [Vlatadon] 29; Thessaloniki: Patriarchal Institute for Patristic Studies, 1979).
Frankenberg, Wilhelm
Das Verständnis der Oden Salomos (BZAW 21; Gießen: Töpelmann, 1911).
Franzmann, Majella
The Odes of Solomon: An Analysis of the Poetical Structure and Form (NTOA 20; Fribourg: Academic Press; Göttingen: Vandenhoeck & Ruprecht, 1991).
Greßmann, Hugo
"Die Oden Salomos," *NTApo*[2] (1924) 437–72.
Grimme, Hubert
Die Oden Salomos syrisch-hebräisch-deutsch: Ein kritischer Versuch (Heidelberg: Winter, 1911).
Harnack, Adolf
Ein jüdisch-christliches Psalmbuch aus dem ersten Jahrhundert [The Odes . . . of Solomon, now first published from the Syriac version by J. Rendel Harris, 1909]. Aus dem Syrischen übersetzt von Johannes Flemming (TU 35.4; Leipzig: Hinrichs, 1910).
Harris, J. Rendel
The Odes and Psalms of Solomon, Now First Published from the Syriac Version (Cambridge: Cambridge University Press, 1909; 2nd ed., revised and enlarged, with facsimile, 1911).
Idem and Alphonse Mingana
The Odes and Psalms of Solomon (2 vols.; Manchester: Manchester University Press, 1916–20).
Labourt, Jean, and Pierre Batiffol
Les Odes de Salomon: Une œuvre chrétienne des environs de l'an 100–120 (Paris: Gabalda, 1911).
Lattke, Michael
Oden Salomos (FontChr 19; Freiburg et al.: Herder, 1995).
Idem
Oden Salomos: Text, Übersetzung, Kommentar (3 vols.; NTOA 41.1–3; Fribourg: Academic Press; Göttingen: Vandenhoeck & Ruprecht, 1999–2005).
Münter, Fridericus [Friedrich] C. C. H.
Odae Gnosticae Salomoni tributae: Thebaice et Latine, praefatione et adnotationibus philologicis illustratae (Copenhagen: Schultz, 1812).
Onuki, Takashi
"Solomon no shoka [Odes of Solomon]," in Sasagu Arai, ed., *Seishyo Gaiten Giten* [*Biblical Apocrypha and Pseudepigrapha*], Hoi [supplementary vol.] 2 (Tokyo: Kyobunkwan, 1982) 277–390, 497–557.
Peral, Antonio, and Xavier Alegre
"Odas de Salomon," in Alejandro Díez Macho, ed., with the collaboration of Maria Angeles Navarro, Alfonso de la Fuente, and Antonio Piñero, *Apócrifos del Antiguo Testamento* (3 vols.; Madrid: Ediciones Cristiandad, 1982) 3:59–100.
Pierre, Marie-Joseph
"Odes de Salomon," in François Bovon and Pierre Geoltrain, eds., *Écrits apocryphes chrétiens* (2 vols.; Bibliothèque de la Pléiade; Paris: Gallimard, 1997, 2005) 1:671–743.
Idem
Les Odes de Salomon: Texte présenté et traduit avec la collaboration de Jean-Marie Martin (Apocryphes 4; Turnhout: Brepols, 1994).

Ryle, Herbert Edward, and Montague Rhodes James, eds.
Ψαλμοὶ Σολομῶντος: Psalms of the Pharisees, commonly called the Psalms of Solomon. The text newly revised from all the MSS (Cambridge: Cambridge University Press, 1891) 155–61.
Testuz, Michel, ed.
Papyrus Bodmer X–XII (Cologny-Genève: Bibliothèque Bodmer, 1959).
Tondelli, Leone
Le Odi di Salomone: Cantici cristiani degli inizi del II secolo. Versione dal siriaco, introduzione e note (Preface by Angelo Mercati; Rome: Ferrari, 1914).
Tsakonas, Basileios G.
Αἱ Ὠδαὶ Σολομῶντος (Εἰσαγωγή – Κείμενον – Ἑρμηνεία) (repr. from: *Θεολογία* [*Theologia*] 44 [1973] 389–416, 583–605; 45 [1974] 129–49, 309–46, 511–58, 608–46).
Ungnad, Arthur, and Willy Staerk
Die Oden Salomos (KlT 64; Bonn: Marcus & Weber, 1910).
Westerman Holstijn, H. J. E.
Oden van Salomo: Zangen van rust in den Heere. Een bundel lyriek uit de tweede eeuw uit het Grieksch vertaald en metrisch bewerkt (Zutphen: Ruys, [1942]).
Woide, Charles Godfrey
Appendix ad editionem Novi Testamenti Graeci e codice MS. Alexandrino (Oxford: Clarendon, 1799) 148–51.

Other Ancient Literature

Aland, Barbara, and Andreas Juckel, eds.
Das Neue Testament in syrischer Überlieferung II: Die paulinischen Briefe (3 vols.; ANTT 14, 23, 32; Berlin/New York: de Gruyter, 1991–2002).
Allberry, C. R. C., ed.
A Manichaean Psalm-Book, with a contribution by Hugo Ibscher (Manichaean Manuscripts in the Chester Beatty Collection, 2, pt. 2; Stuttgart: Kohlhammer, 1938).
Attridge, Harold W.
"Appendix: The Greek Fragments [of the Gospel According to Thomas]," in Bentley Layton, ed., *Nag Hammadi Codex II,2–7 Together with XIII,2*, Brit. Lib. Or.4926(1) and P.Oxy. 1, 654, 655*, vol. 1: *Gospel According to Thomas, Gospel According to Philip, Hypostasis of the Archons, and Indexes* (NHS 20; Leiden: Brill, 1989) 95–128.
Idem, ed.
Nag Hammadi Codex I (The Jung Codex) (2 vols.; NHS 22, 23; Leiden: Brill, 1985).
Idem, and George W. MacRae
"The Gospel of Truth. [NHC] I,*3*:16.31–43.24," in Harold W. Attridge, ed., *Nag Hammadi Codex I (The Jung Codex)* (2 vols.; NHS 22, 23; Leiden: Brill, 1985) 1:55–117; 2:39–135.
Idem, and Elaine H. Pagels
"The Tripartite Tractate. [NHC] I,*5*:51.1–138.27," in Harold W. Attridge, ed., *Nag Hammadi Codex I (The Jung Codex)* (2 vols.; NHS 22, 23; Leiden: Brill, 1985) 1:159–337; 2:217–497.
Becker, Jürgen
Die Testamente der zwölf Patriarchen (JSHRZ 3.1; Gütersloh: Mohn, 1974).
Berger, Klaus
Das Buch der Jubiläen (JSHRZ 2.3; Gütersloh: Mohn, 1981),
Bethge, Hans-Gebhard
"'Vom Ursprung der Welt' (NHC II,5)," *NHD* 1 (2001) 235–62.
Betz, Hans Dieter, ed.
The Greek Magical Papyri in Translation, Including the Demotic Spells (2nd ed.; Chicago/London: University of Chicago Press, 1986).
Beyer, Klaus
Die aramäischen Texte vom Toten Meer samt den Inschriften aus Palästina, dem Testament Levis aus der Kairoer Genisa, der Fastenrolle und den alten talmudischen Zitaten (2 vols.; Göttingen: Vandenhoeck & Ruprecht, 1984–2004).
Idem
Die aramäischen Texte vom Toten Meer samt den Inschriften aus Palästina, dem Testament Levis aus der Kairoer Genisa, der Fastenrolle und den alten talmudischen Zitaten: Ergänzungsband (Göttingen: Vandenhoeck & Ruprecht, 1994).
Bonwetsch, Nathanael
Texte zur Geschichte des Montanismus (KlT 129; Bonn: Marcus & Weber, 1914).
Bovon, François, and Pierre Geoltrain, eds.
Écrits apocryphes chrétiens (2 vols.; Bibliothèque de la Pléiade; Paris: Gallimard, 1997, 2005).
Brock, Sebastian P.
"The Psalms of Solomon," in H. F. D. Sparks, ed., *The Apocryphal Old Testament* (Oxford: Clarendon, 1984) 649–82.
Brooke, A. E.
The Fragments of Heracleon: Newly edited from the MSS. with an introduction and notes (TextsS 1.4; Cambridge: Cambridge University Press, 1891; repr., Nendeln/Liechtenstein: Kraus Reprint, 1967).
Brox, Norbert
Der Hirt des Hermas (KAV 7; Göttingen: Vandenhoeck & Ruprecht, 1991).
Idem
Irenäus von Lyon, Epideixis, Adversus haereses – Darlegung der apostolischen Verkündigung, Gegen die Häresien (5 vols.; FontChr 8.1–5; Freiburg: Herder, 1993–2001).
Bruns, Peter
Aphrahat, Unterweisungen (2 vols.; FontChr 5.1–2; Freiburg: Herder, 1991).
Burchard, Christoph
Joseph und Aseneth (JSHRZ 2.4; Gütersloh: Mohn, 1983).

Buschmann, Gerd
Das Martyrium des Polykarp (KAV 6; Göttingen: Vandenhoeck & Ruprecht, 1998).

Capelle, Wilhelm
Marc Aurel, Selbstbetrachtungen (KTA 4; 8th ed.; Stuttgart: Kröner, 1953 = 12th ed., 1973).

Charles, Robert Henry
The Greek Versions of the Testaments of the Twelve Patriarchs (Oxford: Clarendon, 1908; repr. [3rd ed.]; Darmstadt: Wissenschaftliche Buchgesellschaft, 1966).

Colpe, Carsten, and Jens Holzhausen, eds.
Das Corpus Hermeticum Deutsch (Stuttgart-Bad Cannstatt: Frommann-Holzboog, 1997).

Denis, Albert-Marie, ed.
Apocalypsis Henochi Graece, ed. M. Black (PVTG 3; Leiden: Brill, 1970) 45–246.

Diels, Hermann
Doxographi Graeci (4th ed.; Berlin: de Gruyter, 1965).

Dieterich, Albrecht
Eine Mithrasliturgie (2nd ed.; Leipzig/Berlin: Teubner, 1910).

Dünzl, Franz
Gregor von Nyssa, In Canticum Canticorum homiliae – Homilien zum Hohenlied (3 vols.; FontChr 16.1–3; Freiburg: Herder, 1994).

Ehrman, Bart D., ed. and trans.
The Apostolic Fathers (2 vols.; LCL 24–25; Cambridge, Mass./London: Harvard University Press, 2003).

Eigler, Gunther, ed.
Platon Werke in 8 Bänden (OG/Ger.; 8 vols.; Darmstadt: Wissenschaftliche Buchgesellschaft, 1971–83).

Elliger, Winfried
Dion Chrysostomos, Sämtliche Reden (BAWGR; Zurich/Stuttgart: Artemis, 1967).

Emmel, Stephen, ed.
Nag Hammadi Codex III,5: The Dialogue of the Savior (NHS 26; Leiden: Brill, 1984).

Ferreira, Johan
The Hymn of the Pearl: The Syriac and Greek Texts with Introduction, Translations, and Notes (Early Christian Studies 3; Sydney: St Pauls Publications, 2002).

Fischer, Joseph A.
Die Apostolischen Väter (Munich: Kösel, 1956; 9th ed.; Darmstadt: Wissenschaftliche Buchgesellschaft, 1986).

Flashar, Hellmut
Aristoteles, Problemata physica (Aristoteles Werke in deutscher Übersetzung 19; Darmstadt: Wissenschaftliche Buchgesellschaft, 1975; Lizenzausgabe des Akademie-Verlages Berlin [1962]).

Funk, Wolf-Peter
Die zweite Apokalypse des Jakobus aus Nag-Hammadi-Codex V (TU 119; Berlin: Akademie-Verlag, 1976).

Gebhardt, Oscar von, ed.
Ψαλμοὶ Σολομῶντος: Die Psalmen Salomo's zum ersten Male mit Benutzung der Athoshandschriften und des Codex Casanatensis herausgegeben (TU 13.2; Leipzig, Hinrichs, 1895).

Georgi, Dieter
Weisheit Salomos (JSHRZ 3.4; Gütersloh: Mohn, 1980).

Goodspeed, Edgar J., ed.
Die ältesten Apologeten: Texte mit kurzen Einleitungen (Göttingen: Vandenhoeck & Ruprecht, 1914; repr., 1984).

Görgemanns, Herwig, ed.
Plutarch, Drei religionsphilosophische Schriften: Über den Aberglauben; Über die späte Strafe der Gottheit; Über Isis und Osiris (Sammlung Tusculum; Düsseldorf/Zurich: Artemis & Winkler, 2003).

Grant, Robert McQueen, ed. and trans.
Theophilus of Antioch, Ad Autolycum (OECT; Oxford: Clarendon, 1970).

Gunneweg, Antonius H. J.
Das Buch Baruch (JSHRZ 3.2; Gütersloh: Mohn, 1975) 165–81.

Guyot, Peter, trans., and Richard Klein, intr.
Gregor der Wundertäter, Oratio prosphonetica ac panegyrica in Origenem – Dankrede an Origenes. With appendix: *Origenis epistula ad Gregorium Thaumaturgum* (FontChr 24; Freiburg: Herder, 1996).

Habicht, Christian
2. Makkabäerbuch (JSHRZ 1.3; Gütersloh: Mohn, 1976).

Harris, J. Rendel, and J. Armitage Robinson
The Apology of Aristides (TextsS 1.1; 2nd ed.; Cambridge: Cambridge University Press, 1893; repr., Nendeln/Liechtenstein: Kraus Reprint, 1967).

Hartenstein, Judith
"Eugnostos (NHC III,3; V,1) und die Weisheit Jesu Christi (NHC III,4; BG 3)," *NHD* 1 (2001) 323–79.

Hedrick, Charles W., and Paul A. Mirecki
Gospel of the Savior: A New Ancient Gospel (California Classical Library; Santa Rosa, Calif.: Polebridge, 1999).

Holl, Karl, ed.
Epiphanius I: Ancoratus und Panarion haer. 1–33 (GCS 25; Leipzig: Hinrichs, 1915).

Idem, ed.
Epiphanius II: Panarion haer. 34–64 (ed. Jürgen Dummer; GCS; 2nd ed.; Berlin: Akademie-Verlag 1980).

Holm-Nielsen, Svend
Die Psalmen Salomos (JSHRZ 4.2; Gütersloh: Mohn, 1977).

Hübner, Hans
Die Weisheit Salomons – Liber Sapientiae Salomonis (ATDA 4; Göttingen: Vandenhoeck & Ruprecht, 1999).
James, Montague Rhodes
The Apocryphal New Testament (Oxford: Clarendon, 1924; repr. and corr., 1953; many reprints).
Janssen, Enno
Testament Abrahams (JSHRZ 3.2: Gütersloh: Mohn, 1975) 193–256.
Klauck, Hans-Josef
4. Makkabäerbuch (JSHRZ 3.6; Gütersloh: Mohn, 1989).
Klostermann, Erich
Apocrypha I: Reste des Petrusevangeliums, der Petrusapokalypse und des Kerygma Petri (KIT 3; Bonn: Marcus & Weber, 1903).
Idem
Apocrypha II: Evangelien (KIT 8; Bonn: Marcus & Weber, 1904).
Kytzler, Bernhard
M. Minucius Felix, Octavius (Ger.–Lat.; Munich: Kösel, 1965).
Lake, Kirsopp, ed. and trans.
The Apostolic Fathers (2 vols., LCL 24–25; Cambridge, Mass.: Harvard University Press; London: Heinemann, 1913; repr., 1976–77).
Layton, Bentley, ed.
The Gnostic Scriptures: A New Translation with Annotations and Introductions (Garden City, N.Y.: Doubleday, 1987).
Idem, ed.
Nag Hammadi Codex II,2-7 Together with XIII,2, Brit. Lib. Or.4926(1) and P.Oxy. 1, 654, 655*, vol. 1: *Gospel According to Thomas, Gospel According to Philip, Hypostasis of the Archons, and Indexes* (NHS 20; Leiden: Brill, 1989).
Lidzbarski, Mark
Das Johannesbuch der Mandäer: Einleitung, Übersetzung, Kommentar (Gießen: Töpelmann, 1915).
Idem
Mandäische Liturgien (Abhandlungen der königlichen Gesellschaft der Wissenschaften zu Göttingen, Philosophisch-historische Klasse, N.F. 17.1; Berlin, 1920; repr., Göttingen: Vandenhoeck & Ruprecht, 1970).
Lindemann, Andreas, and Henning Paulsen, eds.
Die Apostolischen Väter (Tübingen: Mohr Siebeck, 1992).
Lona, Horacio E.
Der erste Clemensbrief (KAV 2; Göttingen: Vandenhoeck & Ruprecht, 1998).
Long, Herbert S., ed.
Diogenis Laertii vitae philosophorum (2 vols.; Oxford: Clarendon, 1964 = 1966).
MacRae, George W.
"The Apocalypse of Adam," in Douglas M. Parrott, ed., *Nag Hammadi Codices V, 2-5 and VI with Papyrus Berolinensis 8502, 1 and 4* (NHS 11; Leiden: Brill, 1979).
Marcovich, Miroslav
Iustini Martyris Apologiae pro Christianis (PTS 38; Berlin/New York: de Gruyter, 1994; repr., 2005).
Idem
Iustini Martyris Dialogus cum Tryphone (PTS 47; Berlin/New York: de Gruyter, 1997; repr., 2005).
Merk, Otto, and Martin Meiser
Das Leben Adams und Evas (JSHRZ 2.5; Gütersloh: Mohn, 1998).
Michel, Otto, and Otto Bauernfeind, eds.
Flavius Josephus, De Bello Judaico – Der Jüdische Krieg, vol. 1: *Buch I–III* (2nd ed.; Munich: Kösel; Darmstadt: Wissenschaftliche Buchgesellschaft, 1962).
Nagel, Peter
Die Thomaspsalmen des koptisch-manichäischen Psalmenbuches (Quellen: Ausgewählte Texte aus der Geschichte der christlichen Kirche N.F. 1; Berlin: Evangelische Verlagsanstalt, 1980).
Idem
Der Tractatus Tripartitus aus Nag Hammadi Codex I (Codex Jung) (Studien und Texte zu Antike und Christentum 1; Tübingen: Mohr Siebeck, 1998).
Nock, Arthur Darby, and André-Jean Festugière, eds.
Corpus Hermeticum (4 vols.; Paris: Belles Lettres, 1946–54; repr., 1972–73).
Peel, Malcolm Lee
The Epistle to Rheginos: A Valentinian Letter on the Resurrection (New Testament Library; London: SCM, 1969).
Idem
"NHC I,*4*: The Treatise on the Resurrection," in Harold W. Attridge, ed., *Nag Hammadi Codex I (The Jung Codex)*, vol. 1: *Introductions, Texts, Translations, Indices* (NHS 22; Leiden: Brill, 1985) 123-57.
Pellegrini, Silvia
"Der zweite Logos des großen Seth (NHC VII,2)," *NHD* 2 (2003) 569–90.
Petermann, Julius Heinrich, ed., and Moritz Gotthilf Schwartze, trans.
Pistis Sophia: Opus gnosticum Valentino adiudicatum e codice manuscripto coptico Londinensi (Berlin: Dümmler, 1851–53).
Pohlmann, Karl-Friedrich
3. Esra-Buch (JSHRZ 1.5; Gütersloh: Mohn, 1980).
Pötscher, Walter
Porphyrios, Πρὸς Μαρκέλλαν (Philosophia antiqua 15; Leiden: Brill, 1969).
Preisendanz, Karl, ed. and trans.
Papyri graecae magicae – Die griechischen Zauberpapyri (2 vols.; ed. Albert Henrichs; 2nd ed.; Stuttgart: Teubner, 1973–74).
Preysing, Konrad, trans.
Des heiligen Hippolytus von Rom Widerlegung aller

Häresien (Philosophumena) (BKV 40; Munich/Kempten: Kösel & Pustet, 1922).
Quispel, Gilles
Ptolémée, Lettre à Flora: Analyse, texte critique, traduction, commentaire et index grec (SC, série annexe de textes non chrétiens, 24 *bis*; 2nd ed.; Paris: Cerf, 1966).
Rahlfs, Alfred, ed.
Septuaginta. Id est Vetus Testamentum graece iuxta LXX interpretes (2 vols.; Stuttgart: Württembergische Bibelanstalt, 1935 = 8th ed., 1965; many reprints).
Idem
Psalmi cum Odis (VTG 10; 3rd ed.; Göttingen: Vandenhoeck & Ruprecht, 1979).
Rahmani, Ignatius Ephraem, II, ed. and trans.
Testamentum Domini Nostri Jesu Christi (Mainz: Kirchheim, 1899; repr., Hildesheim: Olms, 1968).
Rehm, Bernhard, and Georg Strecker
Die Pseudoklementinen, vol. 1: *Homilien* (GCS; 3rd ed.; Berlin: Akademie-Verlag, 1992).
Riley, Gregory
"NHC VII,*2*: Second Treatise of the Great Seth," in Birger A. Pearson, ed., *Nag Hammadi Codex VII* (NHMS 30; Leiden: Brill, 1996) 129–99.
Rosenbach, Manfred, ed.
L. Annaeus Seneca, Ad Lucilium epistulae morales I–LXIX – An Lucilius, Briefe über Ethik 1–69 (Darmstadt: Wissenschaftliche Buchgesellschaft, 1974).
Roussel, Petrus, ed.
Inscriptiones Deli (*IG* 11.4; Berlin: Reimer, 1914).
Santos Otero, Aurelio de
"Jüngere Apostelakten," *NTApo*[5] 2 (1989) 381–438; "Later Acts of the Apostles," *NTApoc*, 2:426–82.
Sauer, Georg
Jesus Sirach (Ben Sira) (JSHRZ 3.5; Gütersloh: Mohn, 1981).
Schäferdiek, Knut
"Johannesakten," *NTApo*[5] 2 (1989) 138–90; "The Acts of John," *NTApoc*, 2:152–209.
Schaller, Berndt
Paralipomena Jeremiou (JSHRZ 1.8; Gütersloh: Gütersloher Verlagshaus, 1998).
Schenke, Gesine
Die dreigestaltige Protennoia (Nag-Hammadi-Codex XIII) (TU 132; Berlin: Akademie-Verlag, 1984).
Schenke, Hans-Martin
Das Philippus-Evangelium (Nag-Hammadi-Codex II,3) (TU 143; Berlin: Akademie-Verlag, 1997).
Idem
"'Der Brief an Rheginus' (NHC I,4) (Die Abhandlung über die Auferstehung)," *NHD* 1 (2001) 45–52.
Idem
"'Evangelium Veritatis' (NHC I,3/XII,2)," *NHD* 1 (2001) 27–44.
Idem
"'Tractatus Tripartitus' (NHC I,5)," *NHD* 1 (2001) 53–93.
Idem
"'Das Evangelium nach Philippus' (NHC II,3)," *NHD* 1 (2001) 183–213.
Schmidt, Carl, ed.
Pistis Sophia: Neu herausgegeben mit Einleitung nebst griechischem und koptischem Wort- und Namensregister (Coptica 2; Copenhagen: Nordisk Forlag, 1925).
Idem, ed., and Violet MacDermot, trans.
The Books of Jeu and the Untitled Text in the Bruce Codex (NHS 13; Leiden: Brill, 1978).
Idem, ed., and Violet MacDermot, trans.
Pistis Sophia (NHS 9; Leiden: Brill, 1978).
Idem, and Wilhelm Schubart, eds.
ΠΡΑΞΕΙΣ ΠΑΥΛΟΥ – Acta Pauli: Nach dem Papyrus der Hamburger Staats- und Universitäts-Bibliothek (Veröffentlichungen aus der Hamburger Staats- und Universitäts-Bibliothek, Neue Folge der Veröffentlichungen aus der Hamburger Stadtbibliothek 2; Glückstadt/Hamburg: Augustin, 1936).
Idem, Walter C. Till, and Hans-Martin Schenke, eds.
Koptisch-gnostische Schriften, vol. 1: *Die Pistis Sophia. Die beiden Bücher des Jeû. Unbekanntes altgnostisches Werk* (GCS; 4th ed.; Berlin: Akademie-Verlag, 1981).
Idem, and Isaak Wajnberg
Gespräche Jesu mit seinen Jüngern nach der Auferstehung: Ein katholisch-apostolisches Sendschreiben des 2. Jahrhunderts (Leipzig, 1919; repr., Hildesheim: Olms, 1967).
Schneemelcher, Wilhelm
"Das Kerygma Petri," *NTApo*[5] 2 (1989) 34–41; "The Kerygma Petri," *NTApoc*, 2:34–41.
Schreiner, Josef
Das 4. Buch Esra (JSHRZ 5.4; Gütersloh: Mohn, 1981).
Snell, Bruno, ed.
Heraklit, Fragmente (OG/Ger.; 6th ed.; Munich: Heimeran, 1976).
Sparks, H. F. D., ed.
The Apocryphal Old Testament (Oxford: Clarendon, 1984).
Stählin, Otto
Des Clemens von Alexandreia ausgewählte Schriften (5 vols.; BKV 7, 8, 17, 19, 20; Munich: Kösel-Pustet, 1934–38).
Idem, ed.
Clemens Alexandrinus, vol. 1: *Protrepticus und Paedagogus*; 3rd ed. by Ursula Treu (GCS; Berlin: Akademie-Verlag, 1972).
Idem, ed.
Clemens Alexandrinus, vol. 2: *Stromata I–VI*; 4th ed. with supplements by Ursula Treu (GCS; Berlin: Akademie-Verlag, 1985).
Idem
Clemens Alexandrinus, vol. 3: *Stromata VI–VII, Excerpta ex Theodoto, etc.*; 2nd ed. by Ludwig Früchtel and Ursula Treu (GCS; Berlin: Akademie-Verlag, 1970).

Steudel, Annette, ed.
Die Texte aus Qumran, vol. 2: *Hebräisch/Aramäisch und Deutsch mit masoretischer Punktation, Übersetzung, Einführung und Anmerkungen* (Darmstadt: Wissenschaftliche Buchgesellschaft, 2001).

Testuz, Michel, ed.
Papyrus Bodmer V: Nativité de Marie (Cologny-Genève: Bibliothèque Bodmer, 1958).

Tromp, Johannes
The Assumption of Moses: A Critical Edition with Commentary (SVTP 10; Leiden: Brill, 1993).

Uhlig, Siegbert
Das äthiopische Henochbuch (JSHRZ 5.6; Gütersloh: Mohn, 1984).

Ulrich, Jörg
Phoebadius, Contra Arianos – Streitschrift gegen die Arianer (FontChr 38; Freiburg: Herder, 1999).

Vermes, Geza
The Dead Sea Scrolls in English (3rd ed.; London: Penguin Books, 1987; repr., 1990).

Viteau, Joseph, and François Martin
Les Psaumes de Salomon: Introduction, texte grec et traduction, avec les principales variantes de la version Syriaque (Documents pour l'étude de la Bible; Paris: Letouzey et Ané, 1911).

Wendland, Paul, ed.
Hippolytus Werke, vol. 3: *Refutatio omnium haeresium* (GCS 26; Leipzig: Hinrichs, 1916; repr., Hildesheim/New York: Olms, 1977).

Wengst, Klaus
Didache (Apostellehre), Barnabasbrief, Zweiter Klemensbrief, Schrift an Diognet (Schriften des Urchristentums 2; Darmstadt: Wissenschaftliche Buchgesellschaft, 1984).

Whittaker, John, ed., and Pierre Louis, trans.
Alcinoos, Enseignement des doctrines de Platon (Collection des universités de France, Association G. Budé; Paris: Les Belles Lettres, 1990).

Williams, Francis E.
"The Apocryphon of James. [NHC] I,*2*:1.1–16.30," in Harold W. Attridge, ed., *Nag Hammadi Codex I (The Jung Codex)* (2 vols.; NHS 22, 23; Leiden: Brill, 1985) 1:13–53; 2:7–37.

Wright, William
Apocryphal Acts of the Apostles (ed. from Syriac Manuscripts in the British Museum and other libraries with English translations and notes; London, 1871; repr., Amsterdam: Philo, 1968).

Zenger, Erich
Das Buch Judit (JSHRZ 1.6; Gütersloh: Mohn, 1981).

Studies

Abbott, Edwin A.
The Fourfold Gospel: The Beginning (Diatessarica 10, Section 2; Cambridge: Cambridge University Press, 1914).

Idem
Light on the Gospel from an Ancient Poet (Diatessarica 9; Cambridge: Cambridge University Press, 1912).

Idem, and Richard Hugh Connolly
"The Original Language of the Odes of Solomon," *JTS* 15 (1913–14) 44–47.

Abramowski, Luise
"Sprache und Abfassungszeit der Oden Salomos," *OrChr* 68 (1984) 80–90.

Abramowski, Rudolf
"Der Christus der Salomooden," *ZNW* 35 (1936) 44–69.

Adam, Alfred
Die Psalmen des Thomas und das Perlenlied als Zeugnisse vorchristlicher Gnosis (BZNW 24; Berlin: de Gruyter, 1959).

Idem
"Die ursprüngliche Sprache der Salomo-Oden," *ZNW* 52 (1961) 141–56.

Idem, and Christoph Burchard
Antike Berichte über die Essener (KIT 182; 2nd ed.; Berlin: de Gruyter, 1972).

Aland, Barbara
"Welche Rolle spielen Textkritik und Textgeschichte für das Verständnis des Neuen Testaments? Frühe Leserperspektiven," *NTS* 52 (2006) 303–18.

Alegre, Xavier
"El concepto de salvación en las Odas de Salomon: Contribución al estudio de una soteriología gnostizante y sus posibles relaciones con el cuarto evangelio" (Dr. theol. diss., Münster University, 1977).

Amstutz, Joseph
ΑΠΛΟΤΗΣ: Eine begriffsgeschichtliche Studie zum jüdisch-christlichen Griechisch (Theophaneia 19; Bonn: Hanstein, 1968).

Arnold-Döben, Victoria
Die Bildersprache der Gnosis (AMRG 13; Cologne: Brill, 1986).

Eadem
Die Bildersprache des Manichäismus (AMRG 3; Cologne: Brill, 1978).

Eadem
"Die Symbolik des Baumes im Manichäismus," *Symbolon: Jahrbuch für Symbolforschung* N.F. 5 (1980) 9–29.

Arvedson, Tomas
Das Mysterium Christi: Eine Studie zu Mt 11.25–30 (Arbeiten und Mitteilungen aus dem neutestamentlichen Seminar zu Uppsala 7; Uppsala: Wretmans, 1937).

Attridge, Harold W.
"Liberating Death's Captives: Reconsideration of an Early Christian Myth," in J. E. Goehring et al., eds., *Gnosticism & the Early Christian World: In Honor of James M. Robinson* (Sonoma, Calif.: Polebridge, 1990) 103–15.

Aune, David Edward
"Christian Prophecy and the Messianic Status of Jesus," in James H. Charlesworth, ed., *The Messiah: Developments in Earliest Judaism and Christianity. The First Princeton Symposium on Judaism and Christian Origins* (Minneapolis: Fortress, 1992) 404–22.

Idem
"The *Odes of Solomon* and Early Christian Prophecy," *NTS* 28 (1982) 435–60.

Aytoun, Robert Alexander
"The Mysteries of Baptism by Moses bar Kepha Compared with the *Odes of Solomon*," *Exp*, 8th Ser., 1 (1911) 338–58.

Baarda, Tjitze
"'Het uitbreiden van mijn handen is Zijn teken': Enkele notities bij de gebedshouding in de Oden van Salomo," in *Loven en geloven: Opstellen . . . aangeboden aan Nic. H. Ridderbos* (Amsterdam: Ton Bolland, 1975) 245–59.

Baars, Willem
"A Note on Ode of Solomon xi 14," *VT* 12 (1962) 196.

Idem
"Psalms of Solomon," in *OTSy*, pt. 4 fasc. 6 (1972).

Bacon, B[enjamin] W[isner]
"The Odes of the Lord's Rest," *Exp* 8th Ser., 1 (1911) 193–209.

Barnes, W. E.
"An Ancient Christian Hymn Book," *Exp* 7th Ser., 10 (1910) 52–63.

Idem
"The Text of the Odes of Solomon," *JTS* 11 (1909–10) 573–75.

Barth, Jakob
"Zur Textkritik der syrischen Oden Salomos," *RevSém* 19 (1911) 261–65.

Batiffol, Pierre
"Les Odes de Salomon," *RB* 8 (1911) 21–59, 161–97.

Bauckham, Richard
"The Parable of the Vine: Rediscovering a Lost Parable of Jesus," *NTS* 33 (1987) 84–101.

Bauer, Walter
Das Johannesevangelium (HNT 6; Tübingen: Mohr Siebeck, 1933).

Idem
Rechtgläubigkeit und Ketzerei im ältesten Christentum (ed. Georg Strecker; BHTh 10; 2nd ed.; Tübingen: Mohr Siebeck, 1964), ET *Orthodoxy and Heresy in Earliest Christianity* (ed. Robert A. Kraft and Gerhard Krodel; Philadelphia: Fortress, 1971).

Idem, and Kurt Aland, eds.
Walter Bauer, *Griechisch-deutsches Wörterbuch zu den Schriften des Neuen Testaments und der frühchristlichen Literatur* (eds. Kurt Aland and Barbara Aland; 6th ed.; Berlin/New York: de Gruyter, 1988).

Idem, and Henning Paulsen
Die Briefe des Ignatius von Antiochia und der Brief des Polykarp von Smyrna (HNT 18: Die Apostolischen Väter 2; 2nd ed.; Tübingen: Mohr Siebeck, 1985).

Baumgartner, Walter
"Das trennende Schwert in Oden Salomos 28,4," in Walter Baumgartner, ed., *Festschrift Alfred Bertholet zum achtzigsten Geburtstag* (Tübingen: Mohr Siebeck, 1950) 50–57.

Baumstark, Anton
Geschichte der syrischen Literatur mit Ausschluß der christlich-palästinensischen Texte (Bonn: Marcus & Weber, 1922; repr., Berlin: de Gruyter, 1968).

Baus, Karl
Der Kranz in Antike und Christentum: Eine religionsgeschichtliche Untersuchung mit besonderer Berücksichtigung Tertullians. Mit 23 Abbildungen auf 16 Tafeln (Theophaneia 2; Bonn: Hanstein, 1940; repr., 1965).

Beck, Edmund
"Das Bild vom Spiegel bei Ephräm," *OrChrP* 19 (1953) 5–24.

Becker, Heinz
Die Reden des Johannesevangeliums und der Stil der gnostischen Offenbarungsrede (ed. Rudolf Bultmann; FRLANT 68 = N.F. 50; Göttingen: Vandenhoeck & Ruprecht, 1956).

Beer, Georg
"Pseudepigraphen des AT.s," *RE* 24 (1913) 375–79.

Idem
"Salomo-Oden," PW, 2. Reihe, 1.2 (1920) 1999–2001.

Begrich, Joachim
"Der Text der Psalmen Salomos," *ZNW* 38 (1939) 131–64.

Berger, Klaus
Formgeschichte des Neuen Testaments (Heidelberg: Quelle & Meyer, 1984).

Idem, and Christiane Nord
Das Neue Testament und frühchristliche Schriften (Frankfurt am Main/Leipzig: Insel, 1999).

Bertholet, Alfred
Die Macht der Schrift in Glauben und Aberglauben (Abhandlungen der Deutschen Akademie der Wissenschaften zu Berlin, Philologisch-historische Klasse, Jahrgang 1948, Nr. 1; Berlin: Akademie-Verlag, 1949).

Bertram, Georg
"Die Himmelfahrt Jesu vom Kreuz aus und der Glaube an seine Auferstehung," in Karl Ludwig Schmidt, ed., *Festgabe für Adolf Deissmann zum 60. Geburtstag 7. Nov. 1926* (Tübingen: Mohr Siebeck, 1927) 187–217.

Betz, Hans Dieter
Gottesbegegnung und Menschwerdung: Zur religionsgeschichtlichen und theologischen Bedeutung der 'Mithrasliturgie' (PGM IV.475–820) (Hans-

Lietzmann-Vorlesungen 6; Berlin/New York: de Gruyter, 2001).
Idem
Lukian von Samosata und das Neue Testament: Religionsgeschichtliche und paränetische Parallelen. Ein Beitrag zum Corpus Hellenisticum Novi Testamenti (TU 76 = V. Reihe, Bd. 21; Berlin: Akademie-Verlag, 1961).
Betz, Johannes
"Die Eucharistie als Gottes Milch in frühchristlicher Sicht," *ZKTh* 106 (1984) 1–26, 167–85.
Betz, Otto
Offenbarung und Schriftforschung in der Qumransekte (WUNT 6; Tübingen: Mohr Siebeck, 1960).
Idem
Der Paraklet: Fürsprecher im häretischen Spätjudentum, im Johannes-Evangelium und in neu gefundenen gnostischen Schriften (AGSU 2; Leiden: Brill, 1963).
Beyer, Klaus
Semitische Syntax im Neuen Testament, vol. 1: *Satzlehre, Teil 1* (SUNT 1; 2nd ed.; Göttingen: Vandenhoeck & Ruprecht, 1968).
Idem
"Woran erkennt man, daß ein griechischer Text aus dem Hebräischen oder Aramäischen übersetzt ist?" in M. Macuch et al., eds., *חכמות בנתה ביתה: Studia Semitica necnon Iranica Rudolpho Macuch septuagenario ab amicis et discipulis dedicata* (Wiesbaden: Harrassowitz, 1989) 21–31.
Bieder, Werner
Die Vorstellung von der Höllenfahrt Jesu Christi: Beitrag zur Entstehungsgeschichte der Vorstellung vom sog. Descensus ad inferos (AThANT 19; Zurich: Zwingli, 1949).
Blaszczak, Gerald R.
A Formcritical Study of Selected Odes of Solomon (HSM 36; Atlanta: Scholars Press, 1985).
Böcher, Otto
"Höllenfahrt Jesu Christi I. Neues Testament," *RGG*[4] 3 (2000) 1855–56.
Boehmer, Heinrich
"Die Oden Salomos, I–IV," *Kirchliche Rundschau für die evangelischen Gemeinden Rheinlands und Westfalens* 25 (1910) 215–19, 238–43, 266–70, 297–301.
Boll, Franz, Carl Bezold, and Wilhelm Gundel
Sternglaube und Sterndeutung: Die Geschichte und das Wesen der Astrologie (Mit einem bibliographischen Anhang von Hans Georg Gundel; 7th ed.; Darmstadt: Wissenschaftliche Buchgesellschaft, 1977).
Bousset, Wilhelm
Hauptprobleme der Gnosis (Göttingen: Vandenhoeck & Ruprecht, 1907; repr., 1973).
Idem
Kyrios Christos: A History of the Belief in Christ from the Beginnings of Christianity to Irenaeus (Nashville/New York: Abingdon, 1970), ET of *Kyrios Christos: Geschichte des Christusglaubens von den Anfängen des Christentums bis Irenaeus* (2nd ed.; Göttingen: Vandenhoeck & Ruprecht, 1921; 5th repr., 1965).
Bover, José M.
"La Mariología en las Odas de Salomon," *EstEcl* 10 (1931) 349–63.
Bovon, François
New Testament Traditions and Apocryphal Narratives (PTMS 36; Allison Park, Pa.: Pickwick Publications, 1995).
Brandenburger, Egon
Fleisch und Geist: Paulus und die dualistische Weisheit (WMANT 29; Neukirchen-Vluyn: Neukirchener Verlag, 1968).
Braun, Herbert
"Entscheidende Motive in den Berichten über die Taufe Jesu von Markus bis Justin," *ZThK* 50 (1953) 39–43.
Brenton, Sir Lancelot Charles Lee
The Septuagint with Apocrypha: Greek and English (London: Samuel Bagster & Sons, 1851; repr., Peabody, Mass: Hendrickson, 1986; 2nd printing 1987).
Brock, Sebastian P.
"Bibelübersetzungen I. Die alten Übersetzungen des Alten und Neuen Testaments. [Sections] 1.1, 2, 3.2, 4.1, 5.2, 7.2, 8.2, 9.2, 10.2, 11.2," *TRE* 6 (1980) 161, 163–72, 177–78, 181–89, 199–200, 204–5, 206–7, 209–11, 213, 215–16.
Idem
"The Gates/Bars of Sheol Revisited," in William L. Petersen, Johan S. Vos and Henk J. de Jonge, eds., *Sayings of Jesus: Canonical and Non-Canonical. Essays in Honour of Tjitze Baarda* (NovTSup 89; Leiden: Brill, 1997) 7–24.
Idem
The Holy Spirit in the Syrian Baptismal Tradition (Syrian Churches Series 9; Poona: Anita Printers, 1979).
Idem
"The Odes of Solomon," in Emil Schürer, *The History of the Jewish People in the Age of Jesus Christ (175 B.C. – A.D. 135)* (rev. and ed. by Geza Vermes et al.; 4 vols.; Edinburgh: T&T Clark, 1973–87) 3.2:787–89.
Idem
Syriac Perspectives on Late Antiquity (CStS 199; London: Variorum Reprints, 1984).
Idem
Syriac Studies: A Classified Bibliography (1960–1990) (Kaslik, Lebanon: Parole de l'Orient, 1996).
Idem
"Syrien VI.2: Syrische Christliche Literatur," *RGG*[4] 7 (2004) 2002–5.
Idem
"The Two Ways and the Palestinian Targum," in Philip R. Davies and Richard T. White, eds., *A Tribute to Geza Vermes: Essays on Jewish and*

Christian Literature and History (JSOTSup 100; Sheffield: JSOT Press, 1990) 139–52.

Brockelmann, Carl
Grundriss der vergleichenden Grammatik der semitischen Sprachen (2 vols.; Berlin: Reuther & Reichard, 1908–13; repr., Hildesheim: Olms, 1982).

Idem
Lexicon Syriacum (2nd ed.; Halle, 1928; repr., Hildesheim: Olms, 1966).

Idem
Syrische Grammatik mit Paradigmen, Literatur, Chrestomathie und Glossar (Porta linguarum orientalium 5; 6th ed.; Leipzig: Harrassowitz, 1951).

Brox, Norbert
Der erste Petrusbrief (EKKNT 21; Zurich: Benziger; Neukirchen-Vluyn: Neukirchener Verlag, 1979).

Bruston, Charles
"Les plus anciens cantiques chrétiens: Les Odes de Salomon," *RThPh* 44 (1911) 465–97.

Idem
"Rectifications à la traduction des plus anciens cantiques chrétiens I–II," *Revue de théologie et des questions religieuses* 21 (1912) 440–42, 536–37.

Idem
"Rectifications à la traduction des plus anciens cantiques chrétiens III–XII," *Revue de théologie et des questions religieuses* 22 (1913) 54–64, 367–75.

Büchler, A.
"A Study of Ode XI," *Abstract of Proceedings for the Year 1911–1912, Society of Historical Theology* (Oxford, 1912) 20–26.

Buck, Fidelis
"Are the 'Ascension of Isaiah' and the 'Odes of Solomon' Witnesses to an Early Cult of Mary?" in *De primordiis cultus mariani 4: Acta Congressus Mariologici-Mariani in Lusitania anno 1967 celebrati, ed. C. Balić OFM* (Rome: Pontificia Academia Mariana, 1970) 371–99.

Buhl, Frants
"Salomos Oder," *Teologisk tidsskrift for den danske folkekirke*, 3. Række, 2 (1911) 97–128.

Bultmann, Rudolf
"Die Bedeutung der neuerschlossenen mandäischen und manichäischen Quellen für das Verständnis des Johannesevangeliums," *ZNW* 24 (1925) 100–46; repr. in idem, *Exegetica*, 55–104.

Idem
"Bekenntnis- und Liedfragmente im ersten Petrusbrief," *Conjectanea Neotestamentica XI in honorem Antonii Fridrichsen sexagenarii* (ConNT 11; Lund/Copenhagen, 1947) 1–14; repr. in idem, *Exegetica*, 285–97.

Idem
"Δικαιοσύνη θεοῦ," *JBL* 83 (1964) 12–16.

Idem
Die drei Johannesbriefe (KEK, 14. Abt.; Göttingen: 7th ed.; Vandenhoeck & Ruprecht, 1967), ET *Johannine Epistles: A Commentary on the Johannine Epistles* (trans. R. Philip O'Hara with Lane C. McGaughy and Robert Funk; ed. Robert W. Funk; Hermeneia; Philadelphia: Fortress, 1973).

Idem
Exegetica: Aufsätze zur Erforschung des Neuen Testaments (ed. Erich Dinkler; Tübingen: Mohr Siebeck, 1967).

Idem
Die Geschichte der synoptischen Tradition (2nd ed., 1931; "Nachwort" by Gerd Theissen; FRLANT 29 = N.F. 12; 10th ed.; Göttingen: Vandenhoeck & Ruprecht, 1995), ET *History of the Synoptic Tradition* (trans. John Marsh; New York: Harper & Row, 1968).

Idem
The Gospel of John: A Commentary (ed. G. R. Beasley-Murray; trans R. W. N. Hoare and J. K. Riches; Philadelphia: Westminster, 1971), ET of *Das Evangelium des Johannes* (KEK, 2. Abt.; Göttingen: Vandenhoeck & Ruprecht, 1941; repr., 1964; *Ergänzungsheft*: Neubearbeitung 1957).

Idem
"Ein jüdisch-christliches Psalmbuch aus dem ersten Jahrhundert," *MPTh* 7 (1910) 23–29.

Idem
"Untersuchungen zum Johannesevangelium (Teil A. Ἀλήθεια)," *ZNW* 27 (1928) 113–63; repr. in idem, *Exegetica*, 124–73.

Burkitt, F. C.
"A New MS of the Odes of Solomon," *JTS* 13 (1911–12) 372–85.

Cameron, Peter
"The Crux in Ode of Solomon 19:6: A New Solution," *JTS* n.s. 42 (1991) 588–96.

Idem
"The 'Sanctuary' in the Fourth *Ode of Solomon*," in William Horbury, ed., *Templum amicitiae: Essays on the Second Temple presented to Ernst Bammel* (JSNTSup 48; Sheffield: JSOT Press, 1991) 450–63.

Carmignac, Jean
"Les affinités qumrâniennes de la onzième Ode de Salomon," *RevQ* 3 (1961) 71–102.

Idem
"Un Qumrânien converti au Christianisme: l'auteur des Odes de Salomon," in Hans Bardtke, ed., *Qumran-Probleme: Vorträge des Leipziger Symposions über Qumran-Probleme vom 9. bis 14. Oktober 1961* (SSA 42; Berlin: Akademie-Verlag, 1963) 75–108.

Idem
"Recherches sur la langue originelle des Odes de Salomon," *RevQ* 4 (1963) 429–32.

Charles, Robert Henry
"A Church Hymnal of the First Century," *Times Literary Supplement* No. 430 (April 7, 1910) 124.

Charlesworth, James H.
Critical Reflections on the Odes of Solomon, vol. 1: *Literary Setting, Textual Studies, Gnosticism, the*

Dead Sea Scrolls and the Gospel of John (JSPSup 22; Sheffield: Sheffield Academic Press, 1998).

Idem
"Haplography and Philology: A Study of *Ode of Solomon* 16:8," *NTS* 25 (1978–79) 221–27.

Idem
"Les Odes de Salomon et les manuscrits de la mer Morte," *RB* 77 (1970) 522–49.

Idem
"Odes of Solomon," *DNTB* (2000) 749–52.

Idem
"Odes of Solomon," *IDBSup* (1976) 637–38.

Idem
"The *Odes of Solomon* and the Jewish Wisdom Texts," in Charlotte Hempel, Armin Lange, and Hermann Lichtenberger, eds., *The Wisdom Texts from Qumran and the Development of Sapiential Thought* (BEThL 159; Leuven: Peeters, 2001) 323–49.

Idem
"Odes of Solomon (Late First to Early-Second Century A.D.): A New Translation and Introduction," *OTP* 2:725–71.

Idem, ed.
Papyri and Leather Manuscripts of the Odes of Solomon (Dickerson Series of Facsimiles of Manuscripts Important for Christian Origins 1; Durham, NC: International Center for the Study of Ancient Near Eastern Civilizations and Christian Origins, Duke University, 1981).

Idem
"Paronomasia and Assonance in the Syriac Text of the *Odes of Solomon*," *Semitics* 1 (1970) 12–26. Rev. repr. in *Reflection*, 1:147–65.

Idem
"Solomon, Odes of," in David Noel Freedman, ed., *The Anchor Bible Dictionary* (6 vols.; New York: Doubleday, 1992) 6:114–15.

Idem, and Craig A. Evans, eds.
The Pseudepigrapha and Early Biblical Interpretation (JSPSup 14; Studies in Scripture in Early Judaism and Christianity 2; Sheffield: Sheffield Academic Press, 1993).

Chilton, Bruce
"God as 'Father' in the Targumim, in Non-Canonical Literatures of Early Judaism and Primitive Christianity, and in Matthew," in James H. Charlesworth and Craig A. Evans, eds., *The Pseudepigrapha and Early Biblical Interpretation* (JSPSup 14; Studies in Scripture in Early Judaism and Christianity 2; Sheffield: Sheffield Academic Press, 1993) 151–69.

Christ, Felix
Jesus Sophia: Die Sophia-Christologie bei den Synoptikern (AThANT 57; Zurich: Zwingli, 1970).

Clarke, William Kemp Lowther
"The First Epistle of St Peter and the Odes of Solomon," *JTS* 15 (1913–14) 47–52.

Clemen, Carl
'Niedergefahren zu den Toten': Ein Beitrag zur Würdigung des Apostolikums (Gießen: Töpelmann, 1900).

Collins, Adela Yarbro
"Rulers, Divine Men, and Walking on the Water (Mark 6:45–52)," in L. Bormann et al., eds., *Religious Propaganda and Missionary Competition in the New Testament World: Essays Honoring Dieter Georgi* (NovTSup 74; Leiden: Brill, 1994) 207–27.

Colpe, Carsten
"Die Christologie der Oden Salomos im Zusammenhang von Gnosis und Synkretismus," ed. Michael Lattke, in Julia Männchen, ed., with Torsten Reiprich, *Mein Haus wird ein Bethaus für alle Völker genannt werden (Jes 56,7): Judentum seit der Zeit des Zweiten Tempels in Geschichte, Literatur und Kult: Festschrift für Thomas Willi zum 65. Geburtstag* (Neukirchen-Vluyn: Neukirchener Verlag, 2007) 39–52.

Idem
"Gnosis II (Gnostizismus)," *RAC* 11 (1981) 537–659.

Idem
"Heidnische, jüdische und christliche Überlieferung in den Schriften aus Nag Hammadi X," *JAC* 25 (1982) 65–101.

Idem
Die religionsgeschichtliche Schule: Darstellung und Kritik ihres Bildes vom gnostischen Erlösermythus (FRLANT 78 = N.F. 60; Göttingen: Vandenhoeck & Ruprecht, 1961).

Idem, and Wilhelm Schmidt-Biggemann, eds.
Das Böse: Eine historische Phänomenologie des Unerklärlichen (Suhrkamp Taschenbuch Wissenschaft 1078; Frankfurt am Main: Suhrkamp, 1993).

Connolly, Richard Hugh
"Greek the Original Language of the Odes of Solomon," *JTS* 14 (1912–13) 530–38.

Idem
"The Odes and Psalms of Solomon: An Amends," *JTS* 22 (1920–21) 159–60.

Idem
"The Odes of Solomon: Jewish or Christian?" *JTS* 13 (1911–12) 298–309.

Conybeare, F[rederick] C[ornwallis]
"Note on the Odes of Solomon," *ZNW* 14 (1913) 96.

Idem
"The *Odes of Solomon* Montanist," *ZNW* 12 (1911) 70–75.

Conzelmann, Hans
"Die Mutter der Weisheit," in Erich Dinkler, ed., *Zeit und Geschichte: Dankesgabe an Rudolf Bultmann zum 80. Geburtstag* (Tübingen: Mohr Siebeck, 1964) 225–34.

Corwin, Virginia
St. Ignatius and Christianity in Antioch (Yale Publications in Religion 1; New Haven: Yale University Press, 1960).
Crossan, John Dominic
The Cross That Spoke: The Origins of the Passion Narrative (San Francisco: Harper & Row, 1988).
Crum, Walter E.
A Coptic Dictionary (Oxford: Clarendon, 1939; repr., 1962, 1972).
Daniélou, Jean
Théologie du judéo-christianisme (Tournai: Desclée, 1958).
Deissmann, Adolf
Licht vom Osten: Das Neue Testament und die neuentdeckten Texte der hellenistisch-römischen Welt (4th ed.; Tübingen: Mohr Siebeck, 1923), ET *Light from the Ancient East: The New Testament Illustrated by Recently Discovered Texts of the Graeco-Roman World* (trans. Lionel R. M. Strachan; New York: Harper, 1927).
Delcor, Matthias
"Le vocabulaire juridique, cultuel et mystique de l' 'initiation' dans la secte de Qumrân," in Hans Bardtke, ed., *Qumran-Probleme: Vorträge des Leipziger Symposions über Qumran-Probleme vom 9. bis 14. Oktober 1961* (SSA 42; Berlin: Akademie-Verlag, 1963) 109–34.
Delius, Walter, and Hans-Udo Rosenbaum
Texte zur Geschichte der Marienverehrung und Marienverkündigung in der Alten Kirche (KlT 178; 2nd ed.; Berlin/New York: de Gruyter, 1973).
Del Medico, H. E.
"La Lamelle Virolleaud," *Annuaire de l'institut de philologie et d'histoire orientales et slaves* 9 (1949) 179–92.
Dibelius, Martin
Aufsätze zur Apostelgeschichte (ed. Heinrich Greeven; 4th ed.; Göttingen: Vandenhoeck & Ruprecht, 1961).
Idem
Botschaft und Geschichte: Gesammelte Aufsätze, vol. 2: *Zum Urchristentum und zur hellenistischen Religionsgeschichte* (ed. Günther Bornkamm and Heinz Kraft; Tübingen: Mohr Siebeck, 1956).
Idem
Der Brief des Jakobus (KEK 15; ed. Heinrich Greeven; 11th ed.; Göttingen: Vandenhoeck & Ruprecht, 1964).
Idem
"Ἐπίγνωσις ἀληθείας," in *Neutestamentliche Studien Georg Heinrici zu seinem 70. Geburtstag (14. März 1914)* (Leipzig: Hinrichs, 1914) 178–89.
Idem
Die Formgeschichte des Evangeliums (2nd repr. of the 3rd ed.; with *Nachtrag* by Gerhard Iber; ed. Günther Bornkamm; 5th ed.; Tübingen: Mohr Siebeck, 1966).
Idem
Die Isisweihe bei Apuleius und verwandte Initiations-Riten (SHAW.PH 1917, 4. Abh.; Heidelberg: Winter, 1917).
Idem
Die Pastoralbriefe (HNT 13; ed. Hans Conzelmann; 4th ed.; Tübingen: Mohr Siebeck, 1966).
Diekamp, Franz, ed.
Doctrina patrum de incarnatione verbi (ed. E. Chrysos, with corrections and additions of B. Phanourgakis; 2nd ed.; Münster: Aschendorff, 1981).
Dieterich, Albrecht
Nekyia: Beiträge zur Erklärung der neuentdeckten Petrusapokalypse (3rd ed.; Darmstadt: Wissenschaftliche Buchgesellschaft, 1969 = 2nd ed., Leipzig/Berlin: Teubner, 1913).
Diettrich, Gustav
"Eine jüdisch-christliche Liedersammlung (aus dem apostolischen Zeitalter)," in *Die Reformation: Deutsche evangelische Kirchenzeitung für die Gemeinde* 9 (1910) 306–10, 370–76, 513–18, 533–36.
Dinkler, Erich
"Jesu Wort vom Kreuztragen," in Walther Eltester, ed., *Neutestamentliche Studien für Rudolf Bultmann zu seinem siebzigsten Geburtstag am 20. August 1954* (BZNW 21; Berlin: Töpelmann, 1954) 110–29 = idem, *Signum*, 77–98.
Idem
Signum crucis: Aufsätze zum Neuen Testament und zur Christlichen Archäologie (Tübingen: Mohr Siebeck, 1967).
Idem
"Die Taufterminologie in 2 Kor. i 21 f," in *Neotestamentica et Patristica: Eine Freundesgabe, Herrn Professor Dr. Oscar Cullmann zu seinem 60. Geburtstag überreicht* (NovTSup 6; Leiden: Brill, 1962) 173–91 = idem, *Signum*, 99–117.
Idem
"Zur Geschichte des Kreuzsymbols," *ZThK* 48 (1951) 148–72 = idem, *Signum*, 1–25.
Dobschütz, Ernst von
"*ΚΥΡΙΟΣ ΙΗΣΟΥΣ*," *ZNW* 30 (1931) 97–123.
Dodd, Charles Harold
The Interpretation of the Fourth Gospel (Cambridge: Cambridge University Press, 1953; 1st paperback ed., 1968).
Dölger, Franz Joseph
Sol Salutis: Gebet und Gesang im christlichen Altertum. Mit besonderer Rücksicht auf die Ostung in Gebet und Liturgie (Liturgiegeschichtliche Forschungen 4/5; 2nd ed.; Münster: Aschendorff, 1925).
Idem
Sphragis: Eine altchristliche Taufbezeichnung in ihren Beziehungen zur profanen und religiösen Kultur des

Altertums (Studien zur Geschichte und Kultur des Altertums 5.3–4; Paderborn: Schöningh, 1911).

Dörrie, Heinrich
"Was ist 'spätantiker Platonismus'? Überlegungen zur Grenzziehung zwischen Platonismus und Christentum," *ThR* N.F. 36 (1971) 285–302.

Drijvers, H. J. W.
"Early Syriac Christianity: Some Recent Publications," *VC* 50 (1996) 159–77.

Idem
"Kerygma und Logos in den Oden Salomos dargestellt am Beispiel der 23. Ode," in Adolf Martin Ritter, ed., *Kerygma und Logos: Beiträge zu den geistesgeschichtlichen Beziehungen zwischen Antike und Christentum. Festschrift für Carl Andresen zum 70. Geburtstag* (Göttingen: Vandenhoeck & Ruprecht, 1979) 153–72.

Idem
"The 19th Ode of Solomon: Its Interpretation and Place in Syrian Christianity," *JTS* n.s. 31 (1980) 337–55.

Idem
"Die Oden Salomos und die Polemik mit den Markioniten im syrischen Christentum," in *Symposium Syriacum 1976 célebré du 13 au 17 septembre 1976 au Centre Culturel "Les Fontaines" de Chantilly (France)* (OrChrA 205; Rome: Pontificium Institutum Orientalium Studiorum, 1978) 39–55.

Idem
"Odes of Solomon and Psalms of Mani: Christians and Manichaeans in Third-Century Syria," in Roelof van den Broek and Maarten J. Vermaseren, eds., *Studies in Gnosticism and Hellenistic Religions presented to G. Quispel on the Occasion of his 65th Birthday* (EPRO 91; Leiden: Brill, 1981) 117–30.

Idem
"Salomo/Salomoschriften III. Sapientia Salomonis, Psalmen Salomos und Oden Salomos," *TRE* 29 (1998) 730–32.

Idem
"Solomon as Teacher: Early Syriac Didactic Poetry," in H. J. W. Drijvers, R. Lavenant, C. Molenberg, and G. J. Reinink, eds., *IV Symposium Syriacum 1984: Literary Genres in Syriac Literature (Groningen–Oosterhesselen 10-12 September)* (OrChrA 229; Rome: Pontificium Institutum Studiorum Orientalium, 1987) 123–34.

Idem
East of Antioch: Studies in Early Syriac Christianity (CStS 198; London: Variorum reprints, 1984).

Driver, Godfrey R.
"Notes on Two Passages in the *Odes of Solomon*," *JTS* n.s. 25 (1974) 434–37.

Drower, Ethel Stefana, and Rudolf Macuch
A Mandaic Dictionary (Oxford: Clarendon, 1963).

Duensing, Hugo
"Zur vierundzwanzigsten der Oden Salomos," *ZNW* 12 (1911) 86–87.

Dunn, James D. G.
"*ΚΥΡΙΟΣ* in Acts," in Christof Landmesser, Hans-Joachim Eckstein, and Hermann Lichtenberger, eds., *Jesus Christus als die Mitte der Schrift: Studien zur Hermeneutik des Evangeliums* (BZNW 86; Berlin/New York: de Gruyter, 1997) 363–78.

Ebeling, Gerhard
"Jesus und Glaube," *ZThK* 55 (1958) 64–110.

Ehrhardt, Arnold
"Christianity before the Apostles' Creed," *HTR* 55 (1962) 73–119.

Eissfeldt, Otto
The Old Testament: An Introduction including the Apocrypha and Pseudepigrapha, and Also the Works of Similar Type from Qumran. The History of the Formation of the Old Testament (trans. Peter R. Ackroyd; Oxford: Blackwell, 1974).

Emerton, J. A.
"Notes on Some Passages in the Odes of Solomon," *JTS* n.s. 28 (1977) 507–19.

Idem
"Some Problems of Text and Language in the Odes of Solomon," *JTS* n.s. 18 (1967) 372–406.

Idem, and Robert P. Gordon
"A Problem in the Odes of Solomon xxiii. 20," *JTS* n.s. 32 (1981) 443–47.

Emmel, Stephen
"The Recently Published *Gospel of the Savior* ("Unbekanntes Berliner Evangelium"): Righting the Order of Pages and Events," *HTR* 95 (2002) 45–72.

Engelbrecht, Edward
"God's Milk: An Orthodox Confession of the Eucharist," *JECS* 7 (1999) 509–26.

Evans, Craig A.
"The Meaning of πλήρωμα in Nag Hammadi," *Bib* 65 (1984) 259–65.

Fabbri, E. E.
"El enigma de la 24ª Oda de Salomón," *Ciencia y fe* 16 (1960) 383–98.

Idem
"El símbolo de la leche en las Odas de Salomón," *Ciencia y fe* 17 (1961) 273–87.

Idem
"El tema del Cristo vivificante en las Odas de Salomón," *Ciencia y fe* 14 (1958) 483–97.

Fauth, Wolfgang
Helios megistos: Zur synkretistischen Theologie der Spätantike (Religions in the Graeco-Roman world 125; Leiden: Brill, 1995).

Ferguson, Everett
"Spiritual Circumcision in Early Christianity," *SJT* 41 (1988) 485–97.

Foerster, Werner
Von Valentin zu Herakleon: Untersuchungen über die Quellen und die Entwicklung der valentinianischen Gnosis (BZNW 7; Gießen: Töpelmann, 1928).

Fossum, Jarl E.
The Image of the Invisible God: Essays on the Influence of Jewish Mysticism on Early Christology (NTOA 30; Fribourg: Academic Press; Göttingen: Vandenhoeck & Ruprecht, 1995).

Franzmann, Majella
"Background and Parallels of the Imagery of the Coptic, Greek and Syriac *Odes of Solomon*," Unpublished manuscript resulting from an Australian Research Council research project (University of Queensland, 1990).

Eadem
"The Odes of Solomon, Man of Rest," *OrChrP* 51 (1985) 408–21.

Eadem
"The Parable of the Vine in *Odes of Solomon* 38. 17–19? A Response to Richard Bauckham," *NTS* 35 (1989) 604–8.

Eadem
"Portrait of a Poet: Reflections on 'the Poet' in the *Odes of Solomon*," in Edgar W. Conrad and Edward G. Newing, eds., *Perspectives on Language and Text: Essays and Poems in Honor of F. I. Andersen's Sixtieth Birthday July 28, 1985* (Winona Lake, Ind.: Eisenbrauns, 1987) 315–26.

Eadem
"Strangers from Above: An Investigation of the Motif of Strangeness in the Odes of Solomon and Some Gnostic Texts," *Mus* 103 (1990) 27–41.

Eadem
"A Study of the Odes of Solomon with Reference to the French Scholarship 1909–1980," in Michael Lattke, *Die Oden Salomos in ihrer Bedeutung für Neues Testament und Gnosis* (5 vols.; OBO 25.1/1a–4; Fribourg: Academic Press; Göttingen: Vandenhoeck & Ruprecht, 1979–98) 3:371–425 and passim.

Eadem
"The Wheel in Proverbs xx 26 and Ode of Solomon xxiii 11–16," *VT* 41 (1991) 121–23.

Eadem
"'Wipe the harlotry from your faces': A Brief Note on Ode of Solomon 13,3," *ZNW* 77 (1986) 282–83.

Fries, Samuel Andreas
"Die *Oden Salomos*: Montanistische Lieder aus dem 2. Jahrhundert," *ZNW* 12 (1911) 108–25.

Galling, Kurt, ed.
Biblisches Reallexikon (HAT, Erste Reihe 1; 2nd ed.; Tübingen: Mohr Siebeck, 1977).

Gemünden, Petra von
Vegetationsmetaphorik im Neuen Testament und seiner Umwelt: Eine Bildfelduntersuchung (NTOA 18; Fribourg: Academic Press; Göttingen: Vandenhoeck & Ruprecht, 1993).

Georges, Karl Ernst
Ausführliches Lateinisch-Deutsches Handwörterbuch (ed. Heinrich Georges; 2 vols.; 14th ed.; Hannover: Hahnsche Buchhandlung, 1976).

Gerleman, Gillis
Ruth • Das Hohelied (BKAT 18; Neukirchen-Vluyn: Neukirchener Verlag, 1965).

Gero, Stephen
"The Spirit as a Dove at the Baptism of Jesus," *NovT* 18 (1976) 17–35.

Gesenius, Wilhelm
Hebräisches und aramäisches Handwörterbuch über das Alte Testament (ed. Frants Buhl; 17th ed.; Berlin: Springer, 1915; repr., 1962).

Giesel, Helmut
Studien zur Symbolik der Musikinstrumente im Schrifttum der alten und mittelalterlichen Kirche (von den Anfängen bis zum 13. Jahrhundert) (Kölner Beiträge zur Musikforschung 94; Regensburg: Bosse, 1978).

Goppelt, Leonhard
Christentum und Judentum im ersten und zweiten Jahrhundert: Ein Aufriß der Urgeschichte der Kirche (BFCTh 55; Gütersloh: Mohn, 1954).

Idem
Der Erste Petrusbrief (ed. Ferdinand Hahn; 1st ed. of this *Neuarbeitung*; KEK 12.1; 8th ed.; Göttingen: Vandenhoeck & Ruprecht, 1978).

Graf, Georg
"Der vom Himmel gefallene Brief," *Zeitschrift für Semitistik und verwandte Gebiete* 6 (1928) 10–23.

Grant, Robert McQueen
Gnosticism and Early Christianity (2nd ed.; New York: Columbia University Press, 1966).

Idem
"The Mystery of Marriage in the *Gospel of Philip*," *VC* 15 (1961) 129–40.

Idem
"Notes on Gnosis," *VC* 11 (1957) 145–51.

Gräßer, Erich
An die Hebräer (3 vols.; EKKNT 17.1–3; Zurich: Benziger; Neukirchen-Vluyn: Neukirchener Verlag, 1990–97).

Grese, William C.
Corpus Hermeticum XIII and Early Christian Literature (SCHNT 5; Leiden: Brill, 1979).

Greßmann, Hugo
"Die Oden Salomos," *Die Christliche Welt: Evangelisches Gemeindeblatt für Gebildete aller Stände* 25 (1911) 633–35, 650–52, 674–77, 703–5.

Idem
"Die Oden Salomos," *Deutsche Literaturzeitung* 32 (1911) 1349–56.

Idem
"Die Oden Salomos," *Internationale Wochenschrift für Wissenschaft, Kunst und Technik* 5 (1911) 1–20.

Idem
"Ode Salomos 23," SPAW.PH (1923) 616–24.
Idem
"Referate [on Harris, Frankenberg, and Grimme]," *Deutsche Literaturzeitung* 32 (1911) 2896–902.
Idem
"Die Sage von der Taufe Jesu und die vorderasiatische Taubengöttin," *ARW* 20 (1920–21) 1–40, 323–59.
Grillmeier, Aloys (Alois)
Der Logos am Kreuz: Zur christologischen Symbolik der älteren Kreuzigungsdarstellung (Munich: Hueber, 1956).
Grimme, Hubert
"Die 19. Ode Salomos," *ThGl* 3 (1911) 11–18.
Idem
"Zu den Oden Salomos," *TRev* 10 (1911) 601–05.
Idem
"Zur Handschrift N der Oden Salomos," *OLZ* 15 (1912) 492–96.
Gschwind, Karl
Die Niederfahrt Christi in die Unterwelt: Ein Beitrag zur Exegese des Neuen Testamentes und zur Geschichte des Taufsymbols (NTAbh 2.3–5; Münster: Aschendorff, 1911).
Gunkel, Hermann
Das Märchen im Alten Testament (Religionsgeschichtliche Volksbücher für die deutsche christliche Gegenwart, II. Reihe, 23./26. Heft; Tübingen: Mohr Siebeck, 1921).
Idem
"Die Oden Salomos," *ZNW* 11 (1910) 291–328.
Idem
Die Psalmen (4th ed.; Göttingen: Vandenhoeck & Ruprecht, 1926 = 5th ed., 1968).
Idem
Reden und Aufsätze (Göttingen: Vandenhoeck & Ruprecht, 1913), esp. 163–92 ("Die Oden Salomos," first publ. in *Deutsche Rundschau* 39 [1913] 25–47).
Idem
"Salomo-Oden," *RGG*[1] 5 (1913) 226–30.
Idem
"Salomo-Oden," *RGG*[2] 5 (1931) 87–90.
Idem, and Joachim Begrich
Einleitung in die Psalmen: Die Gattungen der religiösen Lyrik Israels (Göttingen: Vandenhoeck & Ruprecht, 1933; 3rd ed., 1975; 4th ed., 1985 [mit einem Stellenregister von Walter Beyerlin]), ET: *Introduction to the Psalms: The Genres of the Religious Lyric of Israel* (trans. James M. Nogalski; Macon, Ga.: Mercer University Press, 1998).
Haenchen, Ernst
John: A Commentary on the Gospel of John (2 vols.; trans. Robert W. Funk; ed. Robert W. Funk and Ulrich Busse; Hermeneia; Philadelphia: Fortress, 1984), ET of *Das Johannesevangelium: Ein Kommentar aus den nachgelassenen Manuskripten* (ed. by Ulrich Busse with a *Vorwort* by James M. Robinson; Tübingen: Mohr Siebeck, 1980).
Hahn, Ferdinand
Christologische Hoheitstitel: Ihre Geschichte im frühen Christentum (UTB 1873; 5th ed.; Göttingen: Vandenhoeck & Ruprecht, 1995), ET *Titles of Jesus in Christology: Their History in Early Christianity* (New York: World; London: Lutterworth, 1969).
Idem
Theologie des Neuen Testaments (2 vols.; Tübingen: Mohr Siebeck, 2002).
Hanig, Roman
"Christus als 'wahrer Salomo' in der frühen Kirche," *ZNW* 84 (1993) 111–34.
Hannah, Darrell D.
"The *Ascension of Isaiah* and Docetic Christology," *VC* 53 (1999) 165–96.
Harnack, Adolf
Über das gnostische Buch Pistis Sophia. Brod und Wasser. Die eucharistischen Elemente bei Justin. Zwei Untersuchungen (TU 7.2; Leipzig: Hinrichs, 1891).
Harris, J. Rendel
"The Odes of Solomon and the Apocalypse of Peter," *ExpT* 42 (1930/31) 21–23.
Idem
"The Thirty-eighth Ode of Solomon," *Exp* 8th Ser., 2 (1911) 28–37.
Idem
"Two Flood-Hymns of the Early Church," *Exp* 8th Ser., 2 (1911) 405–17.
Hatch, Edwin, and Henry A. Redpath
A Concordance to the Septuagint and the Other Greek Versions of the Old Testament (Including the Apocryphal Books) (2 vols.; Oxford: Clarendon, 1897; repr., Graz: Akademische Druck- und Verlagsanstalt, 1954).
Haussleiter, Johannes
"Der judenchristliche Charakter der 'Oden Salomos,'" *Theologisches Literaturblatt* 31 (1910) 265–76.
Hegermann, Harald
Die Vorstellung vom Schöpfungsmittler im hellenistischen Judentum und Urchristentum (TU 82; Berlin: Akademie-Verlag, 1961).
Heitmüller, Wilhelm
"*ΣΦΡΑΓΙΣ*," in *Neutestamentliche Studien Georg Heinrici zu seinem 70. Geburtstag (14. März 1914)* (Leipzig: Hinrichs, 1914) 40–59.
Helderman, Jan
Die Anapausis im Evangelium Veritatis: Eine vergleichende Untersuchung des valentinianisch-gnostischen Heilsgutes der Ruhe im Evangelium Veritatis und in anderen Schriften der Nag Hammadi-Bibliothek (NHS 18; Leiden: Brill, 1984).
Hengel, Martin
"Das Christuslied im frühesten Gottesdienst," in Walter Baier et al., eds., *Weisheit Gottes – Weisheit*

der Welt: Festschrift für Joseph Kardinal Ratzinger zum 60. Geburtstag (St. Ottilien: EOS, 1987) 357–404.
Idem
Judentum und Hellenismus. Studien zu ihrer Begegnung unter besonderer Berücksichtigung Palästinas bis zur Mitte des 2. Jh. v. Chr. (WUNT 10; Tübingen: Mohr Siebeck, 1969).
Idem
The Son of God: The Origin of Christology and the History of Jewish-Hellenistic Religion (trans. John Bowden; Philadelphia: Fortress, 1976).
Hess, Hamilton
"Salvation Motifs in the Odes of Solomon," *StPatr* 20 (1989) 182–90.
Hilgenfeld, Adolf
Die Ketzergeschichte des Urchristentums urkundlich dargestellt (Leipzig: Fues, 1884; repr., Darmstadt: Wissenschaftliche Buchgesellschaft, 1966).
Hill, David
New Testament Prophecy (London: Marshall, Morgan & Scott, 1979).
Idem
"On the Evidence for the Creative Role of Christian Prophets," *NTS* 20 (1974) 262–74.
Hofius, Otfried
Katapausis: Die Vorstellung vom endzeitlichen Ruheort im Hebräerbrief (WUNT 11; Tübingen: Mohr Siebeck, 1970).
Hofmann, Karl-Martin
Philema hagion (BFCTh 38; Gütersloh: "Der Rufer" Evangelischer Verlag, 1938).
Holzhausen, Jens
Der 'Mythos vom Menschen' im hellenistischen Ägypten: Eine Studie zum "Poimandres" (= CH I) zu Valentin und dem gnostischen Mythos (Theophaneia 33; Bodenheim: Athenäum–Hain–Hanstein, 1994).
Horst, Pieter Willem van der
"'The Finger of God': Miscellaneous Notes on Luke 11:20 and Its *Umwelt*," in William L. Petersen, Johan S. Vos and Henk J. de Jonge, eds., *Sayings of Jesus: Canonical and Non-Canonical. Essays in Honour of Tjitze Baarda* (NovTSup 89; Leiden: Brill, 1997) 89–103.
Idem
"Sarah's Seminal Emission: Hebrews 11:11 in the Light of Ancient Embryology," in David L. Balch et al., eds., *Greeks, Romans, and Christians: Essays in Honor of Abraham J. Malherbe* (Minneapolis: Fortress, 1990) 287–302.
Hugedé, Norbert
La métaphore du miroir dans les Epîtres de saint Paul aux Corinthiens (Bibliothèque théologique; Neuchâtel/Paris: Delachaux et Niestlé, 1957).
Jervell, Jacob
Die Apostelgeschichte (KEK 3; Göttingen: Vandenhoeck & Ruprecht, 1998).
Idem
Imago Dei: Gen 1,26 f. im Spätjudentum, in der Gnosis und in den paulinischen Briefen (FRLANT 76 = N.F. 58; Göttingen: Vandenhoeck & Ruprecht, 1960).
Jonas, Hans
Gnosis und spätantiker Geist, vol. 1: *Die mythologische Gnosis. Mit einer Einleitung: Zur Geschichte und Methodologie der Forschung* (3rd ed.; Göttingen: Vandenhoeck & Ruprecht, 1964).
Joosten, Jan
"*Odes de Salomon* 7,3a: Observations sur un hellénisme dans le texte syriaque," *ZNW* 89 (1998) 134–35.
Idem
"West Aramaic Elements in the Old Syriac and Peshitta Gospels," *JBL* 110 (1991) 271–89.
Jüngel, Eberhard
Gottes Sein ist im Werden: Verantwortliche Rede vom Sein Gottes bei Karl Barth. Eine Paraphrase (2nd ed.; Tübingen: Mohr Siebeck, 1967).
Idem
"Thesen zum Verhältnis von Existenz, Wesen und Eigenschaften Gottes," *ZThK* 96 (1999) 000–00.
Kaegi, Adolf
Benselers griechisch-deutsches Schulwörterbuch (12th ed.; Leipzig/Berlin: Teubner, 1904).
Karrer, Martin
Der Gesalbte: Die Grundlagen des Christustitels (FRLANT 151; Göttingen: Vandenhoeck & Ruprecht, 1991).
Käsemann, Ernst
Commentary on Romans (London: SCM, 1980), ET of *An die Römer* (HNT 8a; 4th ed.; Tübingen: Mohr Siebeck, 1980).
Idem
"Gottesgerechtigkeit bei Paulus," *ZThK* 58 (1961) 367–78.
Idem
Leib und Leib Christi: Eine Untersuchung zur paulinischen Begrifflichkeit (BHTh 9; Tübingen: Mohr Siebeck, 1933).
Idem
Der Ruf der Freiheit (5th ed.; Tübingen: Mohr Siebeck, 1972).
Idem
The Testament of Jesus According to John 17 (trans. Gerhard Krodel; Philadelphia: Fortress, 1968), ET of *Jesu letzter Wille nach Johannes 17* (3rd ed.; Tübingen: Mohr Siebeck, 1971).
Idem
The Wandering People of God: An Investigation of the Letter to the Hebrews (trans. Roy A. Harrisville and Irving L. Sandberg; Minneapolis: Augsburg, 1984), ET of *Das wandernde Gottesvolk: Eine Untersuchung zum Hebräerbrief* (FRLANT 55 = N.F. 37; Göttingen: Vandenhoeck & Ruprecht, 1939 = 4th ed., 1961).

Keel, Othmar
Deine Blicke sind Tauben: Zur Metaphorik des Hohen Liedes (SBS 114/115; Stuttgart: Katholisches Bibelwerk, 1984).

Kiraz, George Anton
A Computer-Generated Concordance to the Syriac New Testament according to the British and Foreign Bible Society's Edition (6 vols.; Leiden: Brill, 1993).

Kittel, Gerhard
"Eine zweite Handschrift der Oden Salomos," *ZNW* 14 (1913) 79–93.

Idem
Die Oden Salomos – überarbeitet oder einheitlich? (Beiträge zur Wissenschaft vom Alten Testament 16; Leipzig: Hinrichs, 1914).

Kittel, Gisela
"Das leere Grab als Zeichen für das überwundene Totenreich," *ZThK* 96 (1999) 458–79.

Klauck, Hans-Josef
Herrenmahl und hellenistischer Kult: Eine religionsgeschichtliche Untersuchung zum ersten Korintherbrief (NTAbh N.F. 15; Münster: Aschendorff, 1982).

Klein, Otto
Syrisch-griechisches Wörterbuch zu den vier kanonischen Evangelien nebst einleitenden Untersuchungen (BZAW 28; Gießen: Töpelmann, 1916).

Kleinert, Paul
"Zur religionsgeschichtlichen Stellung der Oden Salomos," *ThStK* 84 (1911) 569–611.

Klijn, Albertus Frederick Johannes
Review of Lattke, *Bedeutung*, vols. 1–2, in *VC* 34 (1980) 302–4.

Idem
Review of Testuz in *NedThT* 14 (1959–60) 447–48.

Kluge, Friedrich
Etymologisches Wörterbuch der deutschen Sprache (ed. Elmar Seebold; 22nd ed.; Berlin/New York: de Gruyter, 1989).

Köbert, Raimund
"Ode Salomons 20,6 und Sir 33,31," *Bib* 58 (1977) 529–30.

Koehler, Ludwig, and Walter Baumgartner
Hebräisches und aramäisches Lexikon zum Alten Testament (ed. Walter Baumgartner, Johann Jakob Stamm, and Benedikt Hartmann; 5 vols.; Leiden: Brill, 1967–95).

Kraft, Heinrich
Clavis patrum apostolicorum (Darmstadt: Wissenschaftliche Buchgesellschaft, 1963).

Idem
Die Offenbarung des Johannes (HNT 16a; Tübingen: Mohr Siebeck, 1974).

Kragerud, Alv
Die Hymnen der Pistis Sophia (Oslo: Universitetsforlaget, 1967).

Kranz, Walther
Kosmos (Archiv für Begriffsgeschichte 2, pt. 1; Bonn: Bouvier, 1955).

Kraus, Hans-Joachim
Psalmen (2 vols.; BKAT 15.1–2; Neukirchen-Vluyn: Neukirchener Verlag, 1961 = 3rd ed., 1966).

Idem
Theologie der Psalmen (BKAT 15.3; Neukirchen-Vluyn: Neukirchener Verlag, 1979).

Krebs, Engelbert
Der Logos als Heiland im ersten Jahrhundert: Ein religions- und dogmengeschichtlicher Beitrag zur Erlösungslehre. Mit einem Anhang: Poimandres und Johannes. Kritisches Referat über Reitzensteins religionsgeschichtliche Logosstudien (Freiburger theologische Studien 2; Freiburg: Herder, 1910).

Kroll, Josef
Die christliche Hymnodik bis zu Klemens von Alexandreia (1921; 2nd ed.; Libelli 240; Darmstadt: Wissenschaftliche Buchgesellschaft, 1968).

Idem
Gott und die Hölle: Der Mythos vom Descensuskampfe (Studien der Bibliothek Warburg 20; Leipzig/Berlin: Teubner, 1932; repr., Darmstadt: Wissenschaftliche Buchgesellschaft, 1963).

Kruse, Heinz
"Die 24. Ode Salomos," *OrChr* 74 (1990) 25–43.

Küchler, Max
"Gott und seine Weisheit in der Septuaginta (Ijob 28; Spr 8)," in Hans-Josef Klauck, ed., *Monotheismus und Christologie: Zur Gottesfrage im hellenistischen Judentum und im Urchristentum* (Quaestiones disputatae 138; Freiburg: Herder, 1992) 118–43, 218–25.

Idem
"'Niemand verändert Deinen heiligen Ort . . .' Zum antik-jüdischen Hintergrund der erste[n] Stanza von Od Sal 4," in Pauline Allen, Majella Franzmann, and Rick Strelan, eds., *"I Sowed Fruits into Hearts" (Odes Sol. 17:13): Festschrift for Professor Michael Lattke* (Early Christian Studies 12; Strathfield, NSW: St Pauls, 2007) 107–15.

Lagrand, James
"How Was the Virgin Mary 'Like a Man' (ܐܝܟ ܓܒܪܐ)? A Note on Mt. i 18b and Related Syriac Christian Texts," *NovT* 22 (1980) 97–107.

Lambdin, Thomas O.
Introduction to Sahidic Coptic (Macon, Ga.: Mercer University Press, 1983).

Lampe, Geoffrey William Hugo
A Patristic Greek Lexicon (Oxford: Clarendon, 1961; repr., 1976).

Lattke, Michael
"Die Bedeutung der apokryphen *Salomo-Oden* für die neutestamentliche Wissenschaft," in Peter Slater and Donald Wiebe, eds., *Traditions in Contact and Change: Selected Proceedings of the XIVth Congress of the International Association for the History of Religions (Winnipeg, Man., August 15–20, 1980)* (Studies in Religion 3; Waterloo, ON: Wilfrid Laurier University Press, 1983) 267–83, 704–7, repr. and corr. in Lattke, *Bedeutung*, 4:49–66.

Idem
"Bestandsaufnahme frühchristlicher Literaturgeschichte," in idem, *Bedeutung*, 4:189–209.

Idem
"Dating the *Odes of Solomon*," *Antichthon* 27 (1993) 45–59.

Idem
Einheit im Wort: Die spezifische Bedeutung von ἀγάπη, ἀγαπᾶν und φιλεῖν im Johannesevangelium (SANT 41; Munich: Kösel, 1975).

Idem
"Entwicklungslinien frühchristlicher Literaturgeschichte," in idem, *Bedeutung*, 4:210–25.

Idem
"Forschungsgeschichtliche Bibliographie 1985–1997 mit Ergänzungen bis 1984," in idem, *Bedeutung*, 4:233–53.

Idem
"Die griechischen Wörter im syrischen Text der *Oden Salomos*," in *A Festschrift for Dr. Sebastian P. Brock* (special issue *ARAM Periodical* 5:1–2; Leuven: Peeters, 1993) 285–302.

Idem
Hymnus: Materialien zu einer Geschichte der antiken Hymnologie (NTOA 19; Fribourg: Academic Press; Göttingen: Vandenhoeck & Ruprecht, 1991).

Idem
"Die Messias-Stellen der *Oden Salomos*," in Ciliers Breytenbach and Henning Paulsen, eds., *Anfänge der Christologie: Festschrift für Ferdinand Hahn zum 65. Geburtstag* (Göttingen: Vandenhoeck & Ruprecht, 1991) 429–45.

Idem
"Oden Salomos," *LThK*³ 7 (1998) 972–73.

Idem
"Die Oden Salomos: Einleitungsfragen und Forschungsgeschichte," *ZNW* 98 (2007) 277–307.

Idem
Die Oden Salomos in ihrer Bedeutung für Neues Testament und Gnosis (5 vols.; OBO 25.1/1a–4; Fribourg: Academic Press; Göttingen: Vandenhoeck & Ruprecht, 1979–98).

Idem
"On the Jewish Background of the Synoptic Concept 'The Kingdom of God'" (trans. M. Rutter), in Bruce Chilton, ed., *The Kingdom of God in the Teaching of Jesus* (Issues in Religion and Theology 5; Philadelphia: Fortress; London: SPCK, 1984) 72–91.

Idem
"Psalms of Solomon," *DNTB* (2000) 853–57.

Idem
"Salomo-Ode 13 im Spiegel-Bild der Werke von Ephraem Syrus," *Mus* 102 (1989) 255–66.

Idem
"Salomoschriften I–III: Weisheit Salomos, Psalmen Salomos, Oden Salomos," *RGG*⁴ 7 (2004) 805–9.

Idem
"Sammlung durchs Wort: Erlöser, Erlösung und Erlöste im Johannesevangelium," *BK* 30 (1975) 118–22.

Idem
"Sind Ephraems *Madrāšē* Hymnen?" *OrChr* 73 (1989) 38–43.

Idem
"Titel, Überschriften und Unterschriften der sogenannten *Oden* und *Psalmen Salomos*," in Hans-Gebhard Bethge, Stephen Emmel, Karen L. King, and Imke Schletterer, eds., *For the Children, Perfect Instruction: Studies in Honor of Hans-Martin Schenke on the Occasion of the Berliner Arbeitskreis für koptisch-gnostische Schriften's Thirtieth Year* (Leiden/Boston: Brill, 2002) 439–47.

Idem
"Eine übersehene Textvariante in den Oden Salomos (OdSal 36,1a)," *ZAC* 8 (2004) 346–49. Online: http://eprint.uq.edu.au/archive/00001360/

Idem
"Wie alt ist die Allegorie, daß Christus (Messias) der wahre Salomo sei? Eine wissenschaftliche Anfrage," *ZNW* 82 (1991) 279.

Idem
"Zur Bildersprache der Oden Salomos," *Symbolon: Jahrbuch für Symbolforschung* N.F. 6 (1982) 95–110.

Idem
"Zur jüdischen Vorgeschichte des synoptischen Begriffs der 'Königsherrschaft Gottes,'" in Peter Fiedler and Dieter Zeller, eds., *Gegenwart und kommendes Reich: Schülergabe Anton Vögtle zum 65. Geburtstag* (SBB; Stuttgart: Katholisches Bibelwerk, 1975) 9–25.

Leclercq, Henri
"Odes de Salomon," *DACL* 12.2 (1936) 1903–21.

Le Déaut, Roger
"Le thème de la circoncision du coeur (Dt. xxx 6; Jér. iv 4) dans les versions anciennes (LXX et Targum) et à Qumrân," in *Congress Volume: Vienna* 1980 (VTSup 32; Leiden: Brill, 1981).

Leisegang, Hans
Die Gnosis (KTA 32; Leipzig: Kröner, 1924; 5th ed., Stuttgart: Kröner, 1985).

Leroy, Herbert
Rätsel und Missverständnis: Ein Beitrag zur Formgeschichte des Johannesevangeliums (BBB 30; Bonn: Hanstein, 1968).

Lewy, Hans
Sobria ebrietas: Untersuchungen zur Geschichte der antiken Mystik (BZNW 9; Gießen: Töpelmann, 1929).

Lindblom, Johannes
"Altchristliche Kreuzessymbolik: Einige Bemerkungen zu einer Stelle der Bell'schen Papyrusedition von 1924," *Studia orientalia* [Societas Orientalis Fennica] 1 (1925) 102–13.

Idem
Om lifvets idé hos Paulus och Johannes samt i de s.k. Salomos oden (UUÅ 1910; Uppsala: Lundquist, 1911; cf. Ger. trans.: *Das ewige Leben: Eine Studie über die Entstehung der religiösen Lebensidee im Neuen Testament* (Leipzig: Harrassowitz, 1914).

Lohmeyer, Ernst
Vom göttlichen Wohlgeruch (SHAW.PH 1919, 9. Abh.; Heidelberg: Winter, 1919).

Lohse, Eduard, ed.
Die Texte aus Qumran: Hebräisch und deutsch mit masoretischer Punktation, Übersetzung, Einführung und Anmerkungen (Darmstadt: Wissenschaftliche Buchgesellschaft, 1964).

Loisy, Alfred
"La mention du temple dans les Odes de Salomon," *ZNW* 12 (1911) 126–30.

Löwe, Richard
Kosmos und Aion: Ein Beitrag zur heilsgeschichtlichen Dialektik des urchristlichen Weltverständnisses (NTF, 3. Reihe, 5. Heft; Gütersloh: Mohn, 1935 = Münster: Antiquariat Th. Stenderhoff, 1983).

Luz, Ulrich
Das Evangelium nach Matthäus (4 vols.; EKKNT 1.1–4; Zurich/Düsseldorf: Benziger; Neukirchen-Vluyn: Neukirchener Verlag, 1985–2002).

Maas, Martha
"Kithara," *The New Grove Dictionary of Music and Musicians* (2nd ed.; Washington, D.C.: Grove's Dictionaries of Music, 2001) 13:638–40.

MacRae, George W.
"Sleep and Awakening in Gnostic Texts," in Ugo Bianchi, ed., *Le origini dello gnosticismo: Colloquio di Messina, 13–18 Aprile 1966* (Leiden: Brill, 1967; repr., 1970) 496–507.

Margoliouth, Jessie Payne
Supplement to the Thesaurus Syriacus of R. Payne Smith (Oxford: Clarendon, 1927; repr., Hildesheim/New York: Olms, 1981).

Martikainen, Jouko
Gerechtigkeit und Güte Gottes: Studien zur Theologie von Ephraem dem Syrer und Philoxenos von Mabbug (Göttinger Orientforschungen, I. Reihe: Syriaca 20; Wiesbaden: Harrassowitz, 1981).

MarYosip, Michael
The Oldest Christian Hymn-Book (Temple, Tex.: M. MarYosip, 1948).

Massaux, Édouard
The Influence of the Gospel of Saint Matthew on Christian Literature before Saint Irenaeus, vol. 2: *The Later Christian Writings* (trans. Norman J. Belval and Suzanne Hecht; ed., with introduction and addenda, Arthur J. Bellinzoni; New Gospel Studies 5.2; Leuven: Peeters; Macon, Ga.: Mercer University Press, 1992).

Mayer, Günter
Index Philoneus (Berlin/New York: de Gruyter, 1974).

McNeil, Brian
"Le Christ en vérité est Un," *Irénikon* 51, no. 2 (1978) 198–202.

Idem
"A Liturgical Source in Acts of Peter 38," *VC* 33 (1979) 342–46.

Idem
"The *Odes of Solomon* and the Scriptures," *OrChr* 67 (1983) 104–22.

Idem
"The Odes of Solomon and the Sufferings of Christ," in *Symposium Syriacum 1976 célebré du 13 au 17 septembre 1976 au Centre Culturel "Les Fontaines" de Chantilly (France)* (OrChrA 205; Rome: Pontificium Institutum Orientalium Studiorum, 1978) 31–38.

Idem
"The Provenance of the Odes of Solomon: A Study in Jewish and Christian Symbolism" (Ph.D. diss.; Cambridge, 1977–78).

Idem
"The Spirit and the Church in Syriac Theology," *ITQ* 49 (1982) 91–97.

Idem
"Suffering and Martyrdom in the Odes of Solomon," in William Horbury and Brian McNeil, eds., *Suffering and Martyrdom in the New Testament: Studies Presented to Geoffrey M. Styler* (Cambridge: University Press, 1981) 136–42.

Meeks, Wayne A.
"The Image of the Androgyne: Some Uses of a Symbol in Earliest Christianity," *HR* 13 (1973) 165–208.

Idem, ed.
Zur Soziologie des Urchristentums: Ausgewählte Beiträge zum frühchristlichen Gemeinschaftsleben in seiner gesellschaftlichen Umwelt (ThBü 62; Munich: Kaiser, 1979).

Menge, Hermann, and Otto Güthling
Enzyklopädisches Wörterbuch der griechischen und deutschen Sprache, vol. 1: *Griechisch-Deutsch* (17th ed.; Berlin-Schöneberg: Langenscheidt, 1962).

Miranda, Juan Peter
Der Vater, der mich gesandt hat: Religionsgeschichtliche Untersuchungen zu den johanneischen Sendungsformeln: Zugleich ein Beitrag zur johanneischen Christologie und Ekklesiologie (Europäische Hochschulschriften, Reihe 23: Theologie 7; Bern/Frankfurt: P. Lang, 1972).

Morawe, Günter
"Vergleich des Aufbaus der Danklieder und hymnischen Bekenntnislieder (1 QH) von Qumran mit dem Aufbau der Psalmen im Alten

Testament und im Spätjudentum," *RevQ* 4 (1963) 323–56.
Muraoka, Takamitsu
Classical Syriac: A Basic Grammar with a Chrestomathy (With a Select Bibliography Compiled by S. P. Brock; Porta linguarum orientalium n.s. 19; Wiesbaden: Harrassowitz, 1997).
Murray, Robert
"The Rock and the House on the Rock: A Chapter in the Ecclesiological Symbolism of Aphraates and Ephrem," *OrChrP* 30 (1964) 315–62.
Idem
Symbols of Church and Kingdom: A Study in Early Syriac Tradition (London/New York: Cambridge University Press, 1975).
Mußner, Franz
Christus, das All und die Kirche: Studien zur Theologie des Epheserbriefes (Trierer theologische Studien 5; Trier: Paulinus, 1955 = 2nd ed., 1968).
Idem
ΖΩΗ: Die Anschauung vom "Leben" im vierten Evangelium, unter Berücksichtigung der Johannesbriefe: Ein Beitrag zur biblischen Theologie (Münchener theologische Studien, Historische Abteilung 5; Munich: Zink, 1952).
Nagel, Peter
"'Gespräche Jesu mit seinen Jüngern vor der Auferstehung': Zur Herkunft und Datierung des 'Unbekannten Berliner Evangeliums,'" *ZNW* 94 (2003) 215–57.
Idem
"Die Neuübersetzung des Thomasevangeliums in der *Synopsis quattuor Evangeliorum* und in *Nag Hammadi Deutsch* Bd. 1," *ZNW* 95 (2004) 209–57.
Nebe, Gottfried
"Jesus, der Gekreuzigte, der am Holz hängt – Das Lichtkreuz: Einige Beobachtungen und strukturelle Überlegungen zur Wirkungsgeschichte von Kreuz und Kreuzigung Jesu von der Bibel zum westlichen Manichäismus," in Michael Becker and Wolfgang Fenske, eds., *Das Ende der Tage und die Gegenwart des Heils: Begegnungen mit dem Neuen Testament und seiner Umwelt: Festschrift für Heinz-Wolfgang Kuhn zum 65. Geburtstag* (AGJU 44; Leiden: Brill, 1999) 245–79.
Newbold, William R.
"Bardaisan and the Odes of Solomon," *JBL* 30 (1911) 161–204.
Idem
"The Descent of Christ in the Odes of Solomon," *JBL* 31 (1912) 168–209.
Niederwimmer, Kurt
The Didache: A Commentary (trans. Linda M. Maloney; Hermeneia; Minneapolis: Fortress, 1998), ET of *Die Didache* (KAV 1; Göttingen: Vandenhoeck & Ruprecht, 1989).
Nöldeke, Theodor
Compendious Syriac Grammar (trans. Peter D. Daniels; Winona Lake, Ind.: Eisenbrauns, 2001).
Norden, Eduard
Agnostos Theos: Untersuchungen zur Formengeschichte religiöser Rede (4th ed.; Darmstadt: Wissenschaftliche Buchgesellschaft, 1956).
Oberlinner, Lorenz
Die Pastoralbriefe (3 vols.; HThKNT 11.2.1–3; Freiburg: Herder, 1994–96).
Omodeo, Adolfo
"Le Odi di Salomone," *ParPass* 1 (1946) 84–118.
Onuki, Takashi
Gemeinde und Welt im Johannesevangelium: Ein Beitrag zur Frage nach der theologischen und pragmatischen Funktion des johanneischen "Dualismus" (WMANT 56; Neukirchen-Vluyn: Neukirchener Verlag, 1984).
Paulsen, Henning
"Das Kerygma Petri und die urchristliche Apologetik," *ZKG* 88 (1977) 1–37.
Idem
Studien zur Theologie des Ignatius von Antiochien (Forschungen zur Kirchen- und Dogmengeschichte 29; Göttingen: Vandenhoeck & Ruprecht, 1978).
Idem
Der Zweite Petrusbrief und der Judasbrief (KEK 12.2; Göttingen: Vandenhoeck & Ruprecht, 1992).
Payne Smith (Margoliouth), Jessie, ed.
A Compendious Syriac Dictionary (Oxford: Clarendon Press, 1903; repr., 1957, 1967).
Payne Smith, R., ed.
Thesaurus Syriacus (2 vols.; Oxford: Clarendon, 1879–1901; repr., Hildesheim/New York: Olms, 1981).
Percy, Ernst Olof
Untersuchungen über den Ursprung der johanneischen Theologie: Zugleich ein Beitrag zur Frage nach der Entstehung des Gnostizismus (Lund: Håkan Ohlssons Buchdruckerei, 1939).
Peterson, Erik
Εἷς ϑεός: Epigraphische, formgeschichtliche und religionsgeschichtliche Untersuchungen (FRLANT 41 = N.F. 24; Göttingen: Vandenhoeck & Ruprecht, 1926).
Idem
Frühkirche, Judentum und Gnosis: Studien und Untersuchungen (Freiburg: Herder, 1959).
Pétrement, Simone
A Separate God: The Christian Origins of Gnosticism (trans. Carol Harrison; London: Darton, Longman & Todd, 1991), ET of *Le Dieu séparé: Les origines du gnosticisme* (Paris: Cerf, 1984).
Philonenko, Marc
"Conjecture sur un verset de la onzième Ode de Salomon," *ZNW* 53 (1962) 264.
Pierce, Mark
"Themes in the 'Odes of Solomon' and Other Early Christian Writings and Their Baptismal Character," *Ephemerides liturgicae* 98 (1984) 35–59.

Pierre, Marie-Joseph
"L'eucharistie des '*Odes de Salomon*,'" in *Nourriture et repas dans les milieux juifs et chrétiens de l'antiquité: Mélanges offerts au professeur Charles Perrot* (LD 178; Paris: Cerf, 1999) 241–54.
Idem
"Lait et miel, ou la douceur du Verbe," *Apocrypha: Revue internationale des littératures apocryphes* 10 (1999) 139–76.
Pilhofer, Peter
"Wer salbt den Messias? Zum Streit um die Christologie im ersten Jahrhundert des jüdisch-christlichen Dialogs," in Dietrich-Alex Koch and Hermann Lichtenberger, eds., *Begegnungen zwischen Christentum und Judentum in Antike und Mittelalter: Festschrift für Heinz Schreckenberg* (Schriften des Institutum Judaicum Delitzschianum 1; Göttingen: Vandenhoeck & Ruprecht, 1993) 335–45.
Plöger, Otto
Sprüche Salomos (Proverbia) (BKAT 17; Neukirchen-Vluyn: Neukirchener Verlag, 1984).
Plooij, Daniel
"The Attitude of the Outspread Hands ('Orante') in Early Christian Literature and Art," *ExpT* 23 (1911–12) 199–203, 265–69.
Idem
"De Boom der Bitterheid," *Theologisch tijdschrift* 46 (1911–12) 294–303.
Idem
"Der Descensus ad inferos in Aphrahat und den Oden Salomos," *ZNW* 14 (1913) 222–31.
Plumpe, Joseph Conrad
Mater Ecclesia: An Inquiry into the Concept of the Church as Mother in Early Christianity (Studies in Christian Antiquity 5; Washington, D.C.: Catholic University of America Press, 1943).
Poirier, Paul-Hubert
"La *Prôtennoia Trimorphe* (NH XIII,1) et le vocabulaire du *Descensus ad inferos*," *Mus* 96 (1983) 193–204.
Pokorný, Petr
Der Brief des Paulus an die Epheser (ThHKNT 10.2; Leipzig: Evangelische Verlagsanstalt, 1992).
Idem
Der Epheserbrief und die Gnosis: Die Bedeutung des Haupt-Glieder-Gedankens in der entstehenden Kirche (Berlin: Evangelische Verlagsanstalt, 1965).
Idem
"Epheserbrief und gnostische Mysterien," *ZNW* 53 (1962) 160–94.
Praechter, Karl
Friedrich Ueberwegs Grundriss der Geschichte der Philosophie, vol. 1: *Die Philosophie des Altertums* (Basel/Stuttgart: Schwabe, 1967).
Preuschen, Erwin
"Ein Übersetzungsfehler in den Oden Salomos," *ZNW* 16 (1915) 233–35.
Prostmeier, Ferdinand R.
Der Barnabasbrief (KAV 8; Göttingen: Vandenhoeck & Ruprecht, 1999).
Quasten, Johannes
"Der gute Hirte in frühchristlicher Totenliturgie und Grabeskunst," in *Miscellanea G. Mercati*, vol. 1: *Bibbia – Letteratura cristiana antica* (Studi e testi 121; Vatican City: Biblioteca Apostolica Vaticana, 1946) 373–406.
Idem
Patrology, vol. 1: *The Beginnings of Patristic Literature* (Utrecht/Antwerp: Spectrum, 1950; repr., 1966).
Quispel, Gilles
Makarius, das Thomasevangelium und das Lied von der Perle (NovTSup 15; Leiden: Brill, 1967).
Rebell, Walter
Neutestamentliche Apokrypen und Apostolische Väter (Munich: Kaiser, 1992).
Reitzenstein, Richard
Die hellenistischen Mysterienreligionen nach ihren Grundgedanken und Wirkungen (3rd ed.; Leipzig: Teubner, 1927; repr., Darmstadt: Wissenschaftliche Buchgesellschaft, 1966).
Idem
Historia Monachorum und Historia Lausiaca: Eine Studie zur Geschichte des Mönchtums und der frühchristlichen Begriffe Gnostiker und Pneumatiker (FRLANT 24; Göttingen: Vandenhoeck & Ruprecht, 1916).
Idem
Das iranische Erlösungsmysterium: Religionsgeschichtliche Untersuchungen (Bonn: Marcus & Weber, 1921).
Idem
Das mandäische Buch des Herrn der Größe und die Evangelienüberlieferung (SHAW.PH 1919, 12. Abh.; Heidelberg: Winter, 1919).
Idem
Poimandres: Studien zur griechisch-ägyptischen und frühchristlichen Literatur (Leipzig, 1904; repr., Darmstadt: Wissenschaftliche Buchgesellschaft, 1966).
Idem
"Weltuntergangsvorstellungen: Eine Studie zur vergleichenden Religionsgeschichte," *Kyrkohistorisk årsskrift* 24 (1924; Uppsala/Stockholm, 1925) 129–212.
Idem, and Hans Heinrich Schaeder
Studien zum antiken Synkretismus aus Iran und Griechenland (Studien der Bibliothek Warburg 7; Leipzig/Berlin: Teubner, 1926; repr., Darmstadt: Wissenschaftliche Buchgesellschaft, 1965).
Rengstorf, Karl Heinrich, ed.
A Complete Concordance to Flavius Josephus (Study edition in 2 vols.; Leiden: Brill, 2002).
Richter, Georg
"Die Fleischwerdung des Logos im

Johannesevangelium," *NovT* 13 (1971) 81–126; 14 (1972) 257–76.
Idem
Studien zum Johannesevangelium (ed. Josef Hainz; BU 13; Regensburg: Pustet, 1977).
Richter, Siegfried
Exegetisch-literarkritische Untersuchungen von Herakleidespsalmen des koptisch-manichäischen Psalmenbuches (Arbeiten zum spätantiken und koptischen Ägypten 5; Altenberge: Oros, 1994).
Robinson, Theodore H., and Leonard Herbert Brockington
Paradigms and Exercises in Syriac Grammar (4th ed.; Oxford: Clarendon, 1962; repr., 1978).
Röhrich, Lutz
Lexikon der sprichwörtlichen Redensarten (Herder Spektrum 4800; 5 vols.; Freiburg: Herder, 1994 [= 4th ed., 1991]; repr., 1999).
Roloff, Jürgen
Der erste Brief an Timotheus (EKKNT 15; Zurich: Benziger; Neukirchen-Vluyn: Neukirchener Verlag, 1988).
Rost, Leonhard
Einleitung in die alttestamentlichen Apokryphen und Pseudepigraphen einschließlich der großen Qumran-Handschriften (Heidelberg: Quelle & Meyer, 1971 = 2nd ed., 1979).
Rudolph, Kurt
Die Gnosis: Wesen und Geschichte einer spätantiken Religion (UTB 1577; 3rd ed.; Göttingen: Vandenhoeck & Ruprecht, 1990).
Idem
Die Mandäer, vol. 2: *Der Kult* (FRLANT 75 = N.F. 57; Göttingen: Vandenhoeck & Ruprecht, 1961).
Idem
"War der Verfasser der *Oden Salomos* ein 'Qumran-Christ'? Ein Beitrag zur Diskussion um die Anfänge der Gnosis," *RevQ* 4 (1964) 523–55.
Ryssel, Victor
"Die Sprüche Jesus', des Sohnes Sirachs," *APAT* 1 (1900 = 1962) 230–475.
Sanders, Jack Thomas
The New Testament Christological Hymns: Their Historical Religious Background (SNTSMS 15; Cambridge: Cambridge University Press, 1971).
Sandt, Huub van de, and David Flusser
The Didache: Its Jewish Sources and Its Place in Early Judaism and Christianity (CRINT 3.5; Assen: Van Gorcum; Minneapolis: Fortress, 2002).
Schaeder, Hans Heinrich
"Der 'Mensch' im Prolog des IV. Evangeliums," in Richard Reitzenstein and Hans Heinrich Schaeder, *Studien zum antiken Synkretismus aus Iran und Griechenland* (Studien der Bibliothek Warburg 7; Leipzig/Berlin: Teubner, 1926; repr. Darmstadt: Wissenschaftliche Buchgesellschaft, 1965) 306–41.
Idem
"Zur manichäischen Urmenschlehre," in Richard Reitzenstein and Hans Heinrich Schaeder, *Studien zum antiken Synkretismus aus Iran und Griechenland* (Studien der Bibliothek Warburg 7; Leipzig/Berlin: Teubner, 1926; repr., Darmstadt: Wissenschaftliche Buchgesellschaft, 1965) 240–305.
Scheffel, Wolfgang
Aspekte der platonischen Kosmologie: Untersuchungen zum Dialog "Timaios" (Philosophia antiqua 29; Leiden: Brill, 1976).
Schenke, Hans-Martin
Der Gott 'Mensch' in der Gnosis: Ein religionsgeschichtlicher Beitrag zur Diskussion über die paulinische Anschauung von der Kirche als Leib Christi (Göttingen: Vandenhoeck & Ruprecht, 1962).
Idem
Die Herkunft des sogenannten Evangelium Veritatis (Göttingen: Vandenhoeck & Ruprecht, 1959).
Idem
"Das sogenannte 'Unbekannte Berliner Evangelium' (UBE)," *ZAC* 2 (1998) 199–213.
Schille, Gottfried
Frühchristliche Hymnen (Berlin: Evangelische Verlagsanstalt, 1965).
Schlier, Heinrich
Der Brief an die Epheser (Düsseldorf: Patmos, 1957; 5th ed., 1965; 7th ed., 1971).
Idem
Der Brief an die Galater (KEK 7; 4th ed.; Göttingen: Vandenhoeck & Ruprecht, 1965).
Idem
Christus und die Kirche im Epheserbrief (BHTh 6; Tübingen: Mohr Siebeck, 1930).
Idem
Religionsgeschichtliche Untersuchungen zu den Ignatiusbriefen (BZNW 8; Gießen: Töpelmann, 1929).
Idem
"Zur Mandäerfrage," *ThR* N.F. 5 (1933) 1–34, 69–92.
Schnackenburg, Rudolf
Der Brief an die Epheser (EKKNT 10; Zurich: Benziger; Neukirchen-Vluyn: Neukirchener Verlag, 1982).
Idem
The Gospel According to St. John (3 vols.; London: Burns & Oates; New York: Herder & Herder, 1968), ET of *Das Johannesevangelium* (4 vols.; HThKNT 4.1–4; Freiburg: Herder, 1965–84).
Idem
Die Johannesbriefe (HThKNT 13.3; 3rd ed.; Freiburg: Herder, 1965).
Schoedel, William R.
"Enclosing, Not Enclosed: The Early Christian Doctrine of God," in William R. Schoedel and Robert L. Wilken, eds., *Early Christian Literature and the Classical Intellectual Tradition: In Honorem Robert M. Grant* (ThH 54; Paris: Beauchesne, 1979) 75–86.

Idem
Ignatius of Antioch: A Commentary on the Letters of Ignatius of Antioch (Hermeneia; Philadelphia: Fortress, 1985).

Idem
"Some Readings in the Greek Ode of Solomon (Ode XI)," *JTS* n.s. 33 (1982) 175–82.

Schöllgen, Georg
"Die Ignatianen als pseudepigraphisches Briefcorpus: Anmerkung zu den Thesen von Reinhard M. Hübner," *ZAC* 2 (1998) 16–25.

Schottroff, Luise
Der Glaubende und die feindliche Welt: Beobachtungen zum gnostischen Dualismus und seiner Bedeutung für Paulus und das Johannesevangelium (WMANT 37; Neukirchen-Vluyn: Neukirchener Verlag, 1970).

Schrage, Wolfgang
Der erste Brief an die Korinther (4 vols.; EKKNT 7.1–4; Zurich/Düsseldorf: Benziger; Neukirchen-Vluyn: Neukirchener Verlag, 1991–2001).

Schreiber, Stefan
Gesalbter und König: Titel und Konzeptionen der königlichen Gesalbtenerwartung in frühjüdischen und urchristlichen Schriften (BZNW 105; Berlin/New York: de Gruyter, 2000).

Schroer, Silvia, and Thomas Staubli
Die Körpersymbolik der Bibel (Darmstadt: Wissenschaftliche Buchgesellschaft, 1998).

Schultheß, Friedrich
"Textkritische Bemerkungen zu den syrischen Oden Salomos," *ZNW* 11 (1910) 249–58.

Schulz, Siegfried
Q: Die Spruchquelle der Evangelisten (Zurich: Theologischer Verlag, 1972).

Idem
"Salomo-Oden," *RGG*³ 5 (1961) 1339–42.

Schulze, Winfried
"Der Fragebogen," *Forschung & Lehre* 6 (Bonn: Deutscher Hochschulverband, 1999) 616.

Schürmann, Heinz
Das Lukasevangelium (2 vols.; HThKNT 3.1–2; Freiburg: Herder, 1969–94).

Schweizer, Eduard
Der Brief an die Kolosser (EKKNT 12; Zurich: Benziger; Neukirchen-Vluyn: Neukirchener Verlag, 1976).

Idem
Ego eimi: Die religionsgeschichtliche Herkunft und theologische Bedeutung der johanneischen Bildreden, zugleich ein Beitrag zur Quellenfrage des vierten Evangeliums (FRLANT 56 = N.F. 38; Göttingen: Vandenhoeck & Ruprecht, 1939; 2nd ed., 1965).

Segal, Judah Benzion
The Diacritical Point and the Accents in Syriac (London Oriental Series 2; London et al.: Geoffrey Cumberlege & Oxford University Press, 1953).

Seitz, Oscar J. F.
"Antecedents and Signification of the Term δίψυχος," *JBL* 66 (1947) 211–19.

Siegert, Folker
Nag-Hammadi-Register: Wörterbuch zur Erfassung der Begriffe in koptisch-gnostischen Schriften von Nag-Hammadi mit einem deutschen Index (WUNT 26; Tübingen: Mohr Siebeck, 1982).

Slee, H. M.
"A Note on the Sixteenth *Ode of Solomon*," *JTS* 15 (1913–14) 454.

Smith, Jonathan Z.
"Geburt in verkehrter oder richtiger Lage?" in Wayne A. Meeks, ed., *Zur Soziologie des Urchristentums: Ausgewählte Beiträge zum frühchristlichen Gemeinschaftsleben in seiner gesellschaftlichen Umwelt* (ThBü 62; Munich: Kaiser, 1979) 284–309.

Smith, Preserved
"The Disciples of John and the Odes of Solomon," *The Monist: A Quarterly Magazine Devoted to the Philosophy of Science* 25 (1915) 161–99.

Speyer, Wolfgang
Frühes Christentum im antiken Strahlungsfeld: Ausgewählte Aufsätze (Tübingen: Mohr Siebeck, 1989).

Idem
"Das Weiblich-Mütterliche im christlichen Gottesbild," *Kairos* N.F. 24 (1982) 151–55.

Spicq, Ceslas
Notes de lexicographie néo-testamentaire (3 vols.; OBO 22.1–3; Fribourg: Academic Press; Göttingen: Vandenhoeck & Ruprecht, 1978–82).

Spitta, Friedrich
"Die Oden Salomos," *Monatsschrift für Gottesdienst und kirchliche Kunst* 15 (1910) 245–49, 273–78.

Idem
"Die Oden Salomos und das Neue Testament," *MPTh* 7 (1910) 91–101.

Idem
"Zum Verständnis der Oden Salomos," *ZNW* 11 (1910) 193–203, 259–90.

Sprengling, Martin
"Bardesanes and the *Odes of Solomon*," *AJT* 15 (1911) 459–61.

Staerk, Willy
"Kritische Bemerkungen zu den Oden Salomos," *ZWTh* N.S. 17 (1910) 289–306.

Steidle, Basilius
"Die Oden Salomons," *Benediktinische Monatsschrift zur Pflege religiösen und geistigen Lebens* 24 (1948) 242. [241: Der Herr meine Sonne. 15. Ode Salomons.]

Stenger, Werner
Der Christushymnus 1 Tim 3,16: Eine strukturanalytische Untersuchung (Regensburger Studien zur Theologie 6; Frankfurt/Main: P. Lang; Bern: H. Lang, 1977).

Stölten, Willy
"Gnostische Parallelen zu den Oden Salomos," *ZNW* 13 (1912) 29–58.
Strecker, Georg
Die Johannesbriefe (KEK 14; Göttingen: Vandenhoeck & Ruprecht, 1989).
Strelan, Rick
Paul, Artemis, and the Jews in Ephesus (BZNW 80; Berlin/New York: de Gruyter, 1996).
Idem
Strange Acts: Studies in the Cultural World of the Acts of the Apostles (BZNW 126; Berlin/New York: de Gruyter, 2004).
Stroker, William D.
Extracanonical Sayings of Jesus (SBL, Resources for Biblical Study 18; Atlanta: Scholars Press, 1989).
Stübe, Rudolf
Der Himmelsbrief: Ein Beitrag zur allgemeinen Religionsgeschichte (Tübingen: Mohr Siebeck, 1918).
Sühling, Friedrich
Die Taube als religiöses Symbol im christlichen Altertum (RQSup 24; Freiburg im Breisgau: Herder, 1930).
Theiler, Willy
Die Vorbereitung des Neuplatonismus (Berlin/Zurich: Weidmann, 1934; repr., 1964).
Theobald, Michael
Die Fleischwerdung des Logos: Studien zum Verhältnis des Johannesprologs zum Corpus des Evangeliums und zu 1 Joh (NTAbh N.F. 20; Münster: Aschendorff, 1988).
Till, Walter C.
Koptische Grammatik (Saïdischer Dialekt) mit Bibliographie, Lesestücken und Wörterverzeichnissen (Lehrbücher für das Studium der orientalischen und afrikanischen Sprachen 1; 4th ed.; Leipzig: VEB Verlag Enzyklopädie, 1970).
Tondelli, Leone
"I Salmi e le Odi di Salomone," *Enciclopedia italiana di scienze, lettere ed arti* 30 (1936) 550–51.
Tosato, Angelo
"Il battesimo di Gesù e le *Odi di Salomone*," *BeO* 18 (1976) 261–69.
Idem
"Gesù e gli zeloti alla luce delle *Odi di Salomone*," *BeO* 19 (1977) 145–53.
Trafton, Joseph L.
The Syriac Version of the Psalms of Solomon: A Critical Evaluation (with a supplement: *The Psalms of Solomon: Syriac and Greek Texts*; SBLSCS 11; Atlanta: Scholars Press, 1985).
Tröger, Karl-Wolfgang
Die Gnosis: Heilslehre und Ketzerglaube (Herder Spektrum 4953; Freiburg: Herder, 2001).
Ulfgard, Håkan
"The Branch in the Last Days: Observations on the New Covenant before and after the Messiah," in Timothy H. Lim, ed., *The Dead Sea Scrolls in Their Historical Context* (Edinburgh: T&T Clark, 2000) 233–47.
Unnik, W. C. van
"De ἀφθονία van God in de oudchristelijke literatuur," *Mededelingen der Koninklijke Nederlandse Akademie van Wetenschappen, Afdeling Letterkunde,* n.s. 36, no. 2 (1973) 3–55.
Idem
"A Note on *Ode of Solomon* xxxiv 4," *JTS* 37 (1936) 172–75.
Idem
Sparsa Collecta, vol. 3 (NovTSup 31; Leiden: Brill, 1983).
Urner-Astholz, Hildegard
"Spiegel und Spiegelbild," in Erich Dinkler, ed., *Zeit und Geschichte: Dankesgabe an Rudolf Bultmann zum 80. Geburtstag* (Tübingen: Mohr Siebeck, 1964) 643–70.
Vielhauer, Philipp
Aufsätze zum Neuen Testament, vol. 1 (ThBü 31; Munich: Kaiser, 1965).
Idem
Oikodome: Aufsätze zum Neuen Testament, vol. 2 (ed. Günter Klein; ThBü 65; Munich: Kaiser, 1979).
Vinzent, Markus
"Ertragen und Ausharren – die Lebenslehre des Barnabasbriefes," *ZNW* 86 (1995) 74–93.
Vogels, Heinz-Jürgen
Christi Abstieg ins Totenreich und das Läuterungsgericht an den Toten: Eine bibeltheologisch-dogmatische Untersuchung zum Glaubensartikel "descendit ad inferos" (Freiburger theologische Studien 102; Freiburg/Basel/Vienna: Herder, 1976).
Vogl, August
"Allein—Mit grosser Menge: Ein Motiv des Abstiegs in den Scheol bei den alten Syrern," ed. Brian McNeil, *OrChrP* 45 (1979) 171–77.
Idem
"Oden Salomos 17, 22, 24, 42: Übersetzung und Kommentar," ed. Brian McNeil, *OrChr* 62 (1978) 60–76.
Völker, Walther
Quellen zur Geschichte der christlichen Gnosis (SAQ, N.F. 5; Tübingen: Mohr Siebeck, 1932).
Vollenweider, Samuel
Horizonte neutestamentlicher Christologie: Studien zu Paulus und zur frühchristlichen Theologie (WUNT 144; Tübingen: Mohr Siebeck, 2002).
Vööbus, Arthur
"Neues Licht zur Frage der Originalsprache der Oden Salomos," *Mus* 75 (1962) 275–90.
Wagner, Andreas, ed.
"Der Lobaufruf im israelitischen Hymnus als indirekter Sprechakt," in idem, ed., *Studien zur hebräischen Grammatik* (OBO 156; Fribourg:

Academic Press; Göttingen: Vandenhoeck & Ruprecht, 1997) 143–54.
Weinreich, Otto
Gebet und Wunder: Zwei Abhandlungen zur Religions- und Literaturgeschichte (originally in *Genethliakon* [Tübinger Beiträge zur Altertumswissenschaft 5; Stuttgart: Kohlhammer, 1929], 169–464; repr., Darmstadt: Wissenschaftliche Buchgesellschaft, 1968).
Weiß, Johannes
Der erste Korintherbrief (KEK 5; 9th ed.; Göttingen: Vandenhoeck & Ruprecht, 1910; repr., 1970).
Wellhausen, Julius
Review of Harris and Harnack in *GGA* 172 (1910) 629–42.
Wensinck, A. J.
"De Oden van Salomo: Een oudchristelijk psalmboek," *Theologische studiën* 29 (1911) 1–60.
Westendorf, Wolfhart
Koptisches Handwörterbuch (Heidelberg: Winter, 1977).
Westermann, *Claus*
Das Buch Jesaja: Kapitel 40–66 (ATD 19; 3rd ed.; Göttingen: Vandenhoeck & Ruprecht, 1976).
Idem
Genesis (2 vols.; BKAT 1.1–2; Neukirchen-Vluyn: Neukirchener Verlag, 1974–81).
Wetter, Gillis Petersson
"Der Sohn Gottes": Eine Untersuchung über den Charakter und die Tendenz des Johannes-Evangeliums. Zugleich ein Beitrag zur Kenntnis der Heilandsgestalten der Antike (FRLANT 26 = N.F. 9. Göttingen: Vandenhoeck & Ruprecht, 1916).
Widengren, Geo
Review of Lattke, *Bedeutung*, vols. 1–2 and 1a, in *TRev* 78 (1982) 16–20.
Wilckens, Ulrich
Weisheit und Torheit: Eine exegetisch-religionsgeschichtliche Untersuchung zu 1. Kor. 1 und 2 (BHTh 26; Tübingen: Mohr Siebeck, 1959).
Willey, Duncan
"The Odes and Psalms of Solomon," *JTS* 14 (1912–13) 293–98.
Windisch, Hans
Der Barnabasbrief (HNT, Ergänzungs-Band: Die Apostolischen Väter III; Tübingen: Mohr Siebeck, 1920).
Winterhalter, Robert
The Odes of Solomon: Original Christianity Revealed (St. Paul: Llewellyn, 1985).
Wolff, Hans Walter
Dodekapropheton 1: Hosea (BKAT 14.1; 2nd ed.; Neukirchen-Vluyn: Neukirchener Verlag, 1965).
Worrell, W. H.
"The Odes of Solomon and the Pistis Sophia," *JTS* 13 (1911–12) 29–46.
Wray, Judith Hoch
Rest as a Theological Metaphor in the Epistle to the Hebrews and the Gospel of Truth: Early Christian Homiletics of Rest (SBLDS 166; Atlanta: Scholars Press, 1998).
Zahn, Theodor
Geschichte des neutestamentlichen Kanons, vol. 2: *Urkunden und Belege zum ersten und dritten Band. Erste Hälfte* (Erlangen/Leipzig: Deichert, 1890; repr., Hildesheim/New York, Olms, 1975).
Idem
"Die Oden Salomos," *NKZ* 21 (1910) 667–701, 747–77.
Zehnder, Markus
"Zentrale Aspekte der Semantik der hebräischen Weg-Lexeme," in Andreas Wagner, ed., *Studien zur hebräischen Grammatik* (OBO 156; Fribourg: Academic Press; Göttingen: Vandenhoeck & Ruprecht, 1997) 155–70.
Zeller, Eduard
Die Philosophie der Griechen in ihrer geschichtlichen Entwicklung, 3. Teil, 1. Abt.: *Die nacharistotelische Philosophie* (ed. Eduard Wellmann; 5th ed.; Leipzig: Reisland, 1923; repr. [6th ed.]; Darmstadt: Wissenschaftliche Buchgesellschaft, 1963).
Ziegler, Joseph
Dulcedo Dei: Ein Beitrag zur Theologie der griechischen und lateinischen Bibel (AtAbh 13.2; Münster: Aschendorff, 1937).
Zimmerli, Walther
Ezechiel (2 vols.; BKAT 13.1–2; Neukirchen-Vluyn: Neukirchener Verlag, 1969).
Zintzen, Clemens, ed.
Der Mittelplatonismus (Wege der Forschung 70; Darmstadt: Wissenschaftliche Buchgesellschaft, 1981).

1. Passages

a / Old Testament and Apocrypha

Exodus (*continued*)
37:9 LXX 480
40:34-38 479

Leviticus
6:9 LXX 49
26:12 445

Numbers
11:25-26 493
14:8 419[67]
16:13 419[67]
16:14 419[67]
16:30 405, 598
16:32 406
16:33 598
20:8-11 159
23:19 59

Deuteronomy
1:21 482
4:11 LXX 66[58]
5:19 66[58]
5:22 66[58]
6:3 419[67]
6:4 555
6:14 LXX 555
9:10 339
10:16 155, 157[57]
11:6 406
11:8-17 58
11:9 58, 419[67]
11:11 58
11:12 158
11:14 58
11:17 58
26:9 419[67]
26:15 419[67]
27:3 419[67]
30:6 155, 157[57]
31:20 419[67]
32:2 58, 479[24]
33:19a 421[85]

Joshua
3:15 LXX 548
3:17 LXX 548
5:6 419[67]

Judges
10:16 LXX 536
13:10 407[73]

1 Samuel (1 Kgdms LXX)
15:11 59
15:29 59
15:32 521

2 Samuel (2 Kgdms LXX)
7:14 579[233]
12:25 6
22:12 67
22:25 288

1 Kings (3 Kgdms LXX)
5:12 6
9:3 51
19:10 349[129]
19:14 349[129]

2 Kings (4 Kgdms LXX)
2:15 493
5:7 587[67]
9:30 194

1 Chronicles
22:9-10 6, 489[204]
22:9 370

2 Chronicles
7:16 51

Nehemiah
1:5 280

Esther
8:16 328[48]

Job
1:7 LXX 528[309]
2:2 LXX 528[309]
9:8b LXX 548
10:10 LXX 272
11:8 598
12:21-25 427[43]
12:21 427[42]
12:24 427[43]
21:18 412–13
27:20 412–13
33:28 303
37:12 LXX 528

Psalms
1–9 Common Numbering
1:2b 573
1:3-5 413[147]
1:4 263[169], 412–13, 494
2:3a 237
2:4 LXX 266[220]
2:5 481
2:7 498, 500
4:2 601[272]
5:13b LXX 462[223]
7:1 65[46]
7:10 156[49]
7:17 67, 334
8:2 267[234],
8:4 222[77]
8:5-6 404
8:5-7 575
8:5 498, 574–75, 578
8:6 232, 297
8:7 222[77], 411
8:10 550[186]
9:8 LXX 375
9:14b LXX 245[164]
9:16 67

Masoretic Numbering 11–146
16:9 (15:9 LXX) 387, 445
16:20 545
18:12 (17:12 LXX) 67
18:16 545
19:1-2 178
19:4-5 181
19:4 181[95]
20:10 545
22 (21 LXX) 397, 425, 439[232], 442, 506
22:10-11 280
25:7 204
27:1 (26:1 LXX) 72, 445
27:5 (26:5 LXX) 158[76]
30 (29 LXX) 299–300, 301[36]
30:2a 299
30:3 241
30:7b 73
30:11-13 299
31:16 65[46]

Greek (LXX) Numbering 10–145

Wisdom of Solomon (*continued*)
8:8c 246
8:16 302
9:5 413, 456
9:6 454
9:7 456
9:11 238, 514[52]
9:15 118
9:18 458[167]
10:7 154
10:15-21 540[11]
10:16 457
10:17 509, 544, 546
10:18 514[63], 541
10:19 542[42]
12:5 122
12:22 572
16:13 214, 241, 405
16:16 406
16:21 271
17:16c 400
18:4 55
18:15 412[137]
18:21 462
19:12 534
19:22a 413

b / Old Testament Pseudepigrapha

1 Enoch
1:6 426
2:1 227[159]
9:4 178
10:16 536[443]
24:3–25:7 165[181]
32:3-6 165[181]
39:3 496[51]
40:1 496
41:5-8 229
69:20 230[200]
69:25 230[200]
70:1-2 496[51]
71:5 496[51]
71:15 496[51]
71:17 496[51]
84:6 536[443]
93:5 536[443]
93:10 536[443]
96:6 160[92]

2 Enoch
8:1-8 165[181]

2 Baruch
36–40 534[404]
44:11-12 464

Apocalypse of Adam
83:7-8 66

Apocalypse of Moses
20:1 294

Ascension of Isaiah
1:7 38, 222[69]
10:24-31 352[182]
11:2-22 277

Assumption of Moses
1:14 60[130]

Joseph and Aseneth
8:10 258
8:11 116[53]
12:1 381[38]

Jubilees
1:16 536[443]
1:23 156
3:9 165[181]
3:12 165[181]
3:15-35 165[181]
10:5ff. 202[70]
16:26 536[443]
19:28 202[70]
21:24 536[443]
23:29 202[70]
36:6 536[443]

Paralipomena Jeremiou
6:9 498[97]
6:12 498[97]
11:3 498[97]
11:13 498[97]
11:14 498[97]

Psalms of Solomon
5:1 113
5:2 40
8:18 137[79]
8:28 569
9:9 605
10:1 550[186]
10:5 550[186]
14:1 388, 569
14:3-4 173[321]
14:3 165[183], 167
14:4 173[321]
15:3 51[52], 220[43, 44]
16:6-13 4
17:10 388
17:27c 569
17:32 344, 570
18:5 133, 344, 570
18:7 133, 344, 570

Testament of the Twelve Patriarchs
Testament of Judah
26:1 64

Testament of Levi
8:4 409[93]

Testament of Abraham
I 397[160]
A XI 294
XVI 397[160]

c / Dead Sea Scrolls and Related Texts

1QH
i.7-8 100
i.8 171
i.20 171
i.28 220[44]
ix.26-27 99[100]
viii.14 415[7]
x.9 171
xi.7-18 (prev. iii.7-18) 349
xvi.4-20 (prev. viii.4-20) 165[181]
xvi.4-24 (prev. viii.4-24) 415
xvi.16 (prev. viii.16) 503

1QH[a]
vi(xiv).15 536[443]
viii(xvi).6 536[443]

1QpHab
xi.13 156

d / Other Jewish Literature

e / New Testament

John (*continued*)
1:1-14 99, 223, 548
1:1-18 326, 446
1:1 60, 184[149], 231, 548, 577
1:3 122
1:4-5 183, 572[112], 578–79
1:4 142, 178[35], 392
1:5 146, 178[35], 253, 258, 585[22]
1:7-9 142, 178[35], 572[112]
1:9 183
1:10 231, 274, 322, 430
1:11-12 275[102]
1:11 102
1:12-13 282
1:12 97[70], 274, 431
1:13 282
1:14 95, 184[149], 188, 577[178], 579
1:15 399
1:16-17 354[209]
1:16 488, 578
1:17 117, 354[209], 355[212], 569[46]
1:18 187, 273, 391, 579
1:20 63[11]
1:22 353
1:23 317[104], 342[13]
1:30 399
1:32 346
1:37-39 331
1:41 251, 343
3:14 495[44]
3:16 104, 144[49], 178, 274
3:16b 136
3:19 142, 572[112]
3:19a 178[35]
3:20 107[208]
3:21 572[112]
3:27 102[136]
3:29 91[21], 394[117]
3:33 55
3:35 144[49]
4:6 421
4:7 416
4:10-11 161, 416
4:10 87[111]
4:14 415–17
4:15 416
4:18 344[49]
4:21 8
4:23-24 575
4:24 392
4:25-26 416
4:25 251, 343
4:32 350
4:34 350
4:42 416
5:11 528
5:16 393, 587
5:18 399
5:20 393
5:21 163, 280[179]
5:23 572
5:24 157[57], 327, 433[143]
5:25 249, 604[314]
5:26 391–92, 531
5:27 405[40], 463[231]
5:28-29 432
5:28 318, 319[125], 604[314]
5:34 293
5:36 104
6:24 513[38]
6:27 55, 350
6:35 462[219]
6:38 598
6:44 406, 453
6:51b-58 417
6:55 350, 417
6:57 531
6:62 491
6:63 392
6:66 518
6:69 477
7:1 399
7:3 87[111]
7:6 394[117]
7:8 394[117]
7:28 398[184]
7:30 349[129]
7:34 399
7:37 415, 417, 456
7:38 161, 377[101], 416
7:44 586[40]
8:12 142, 146, 266, 301[39], 462[219], 572[112]
8:12a 178[35]
8:17 394[117]
8:23 240, 471
8:28 203, 495[44]
8:31 352
8:32 188
8:33 462[211]
8:36 461, 462[211], 605
8:40 176
8:42 587
8:44 529[319]
8:45-46 176
8:46 144
8:49 572
8:54 243[133]
8:57-58 398[184]
9:5 142, 178[35], 572[112]
9:11 407
9:15 407
9:22 63[11]
9:39 463[231]
10:3 102
10:4 102
10:7 462[219]
10:9 246
10:11 462[219]
10:12 102
10:14 121, 569
10:24 130[11], 396
10:30 544[84]
10:39 349[129], 586[40]
11:9 127
11:25 44, 462[219]
11:31 319[125]
11:41 63[16]
11:44 121, 237
11:48-42 440
11:52 144, 249, 260[110], 336[169]
12:17 319[125]
12:27-36 586
12:27 130[11], 531[365]
12:28 243[133]
12:32 336[169], 406, 453, 495[44]
12:34 495[44]
12:35-36 178[35], 572[112]
12:35 146, 266
12:46 142, 178[35], 301[39], 352, 459[172], 572[112]

13:1 102
13:23 391
13:31-32 535
13:31 243[133]
14:2-3 49, 168
14:5-6 212, 544[84]
14:6 117, 159[79], 354, 446, 462[219], 518[136], 555, 569[46], 575
14:7 188
14:13 535
14:15 587
14:16 92
14:17 45, 188
14:19 587[63]
14:21 587
14:23 421[96], 507, 587
14:26 45, 92
14:27 135
14:28 91[21], 587
15:1-8 533, 535
15:1-11 33
15:1 462[219], 537
15:2 533, 536
15:4-5 533
15:4-6 352
15:5 462[219]
15:6 33[34]
15:7 68
15:8 533, 535
15:9-10 127, 352, 589
15:11 91[21], 444
15:16 533
15:18-19 107[208]
15:18 395
15:19 587
15:20 395[137], 588
15:23-25 395
15:26 45, 92
16:7 92, 176
16:20-24 444
16:20 91[21]
16:21 281, 349[132]
16:22 91[21]
16:24 91[21]
16:33 143
17 430–31
17:1-9 431[102]
17:1 144[49], 243[133], 535
17:2 405[40]
17:3 188
17:4 182, 243[133], 535
17:5 580
17:6 102, 605[327]
17:9 128
17:11-12 125[166], 425[6]
17:11 128, 431, 605[327]
17:13 91[21], 444
17:14 107[208]
17:17 117, 575
17:24 580, 603
17:26 605[327]
18:22 353
18:35 440
19:1 439
19:9 353
19:23 399
19:24 435
19:28-30 397[162]
19:42 319[125]
20:11 319[125]
20:14 588
20:17 491
20:28 358
20:29 145
20:31 432
21:18 381[39], 489, 506
21:19 535[436]

Acts
1:2 489, 491
1:8 336[169]
1:9-11 491
1:9 480[37], 491
1:11 489, 491
1:22 489, 491
2:11 222[68]
2:14 430[99]
2:17-21 109
2:26 560
2:27 355, 365, 451[46], 594[164]
2:31 451[46], 594[164]
2:33 364
2:34-35 407[69]
2:36 407[71], 502[165]
2:39 336[169]
4:24 225[113], 226, 430
4:27 493[19], 495
5:12 315[67]
5:19 244
5:23 244
5:30 383
7:2 407[73]
7:6 347
7:14 528[301]
7:22 313[31]
7:30 535
7:35 603[304]
7:38 599[239]
7:48 105[174]
7:50 222[77]
7:53 336[169]
7:55-56 588
8:4 528[310]
8:23 314
8:28 514
8:32 183, 437[197]
8:36 520
8:39 520
8:40 528[310]
9:4-5 587[51]
9:14 50
9:15 605
9:24 573
9:31 563
10:36 135
10:38 344[44], 493[19], 495, 501
10:39 383
11:20 587[58]
12:10 244
13:5 344[49]
13:22 130
13:34-37 451[46]
13:35 355, 365
14:3 315[67]
14:11 430[99]
14:16 520
14:27 601
15:4 601
15:11 570[64]
16:9 316
16:14 113
16:17 105[174], 577
16:26-27 244
17:23 105
17:25 57
17:30 108[213], 263

13:1 292[79]
13:2 336[169]
13:3 581
13:12 258, 462
13:14 53
14:4 256
14:5 490
14:6 63[16]
14:9 531, 587[63]
14:22 60
15:3 425[6]
15:8 9, 425[6], 436[181], 440–41
15:9 63[15]
15:12 533
15:15 404[27]
15:29 249
16:4 63[16], 569
16:18 250
16:20 315[65]
16:26 336[169]

1 Corinthians
1:4 63[16], 404[27]
1:9 388[42]
1:13 579[230]
1:14 63[16]
1:17-18 382[51]
1:17 592
1:18 394
1:21 531[364]
1:24 354, 530[335]
1:25 354[209]
2:1 118
2:2 382[51], 592
2:4 282
2:5 382[51]
2:6-14 188
2:6 321[163], 459[174]
2:9-10 223
2:9 224, 581
2:10 223–24
3:2 263, 270[20]
3:6-17 532
3:6 535
3:9 537
3:10 404[27], 535
3:11 322, 532[369]
3:16 445
3:17 316
3:19 162[130], 321[163]
3:20 264
4:3 263
4:7b 136[73]
4:9 354[209]
5:5 389[62]
5:9 13
5:10 321[163], 432
6:15 250[249]
6:17 41, 44
7:25 601[269]
7:31 321[163]
8:3 569[47], 580–81
8:6 60, 80[50], 122, 230–31, 579
9:2 55
9:7 218, 490
9:25 30, 34
10:1-2 479
10:4 159, 417[42]
10:9-10 352
10:13 388[42]
10:18 528[301], 534
11:25 270[25]
11:33 141[14]
12:3 250
12:8 99, 354
12:12-31 257
12:12 302
12:21 598[228]
12:24 257
12:27 250[249]
13:2 476
13:3 64
13:8 182
13:12 191[12]
13:13 182, 443[13]
14:2 222
14:4 243[136]
14:7 203
14:8 389
14:18 63[16]
14:26 109[222]
14:37-38 45[52]
15:4 593
15:12 588[67]
15:15 411
15:22-23 606
15:22 163
15:23 86[100]
15:24 50[28], 56
15:25 407[69]
15:26 213–14, 405–6, 522, 605
15:27 411
15:34 108[213]
15:35-54 363[104]
15:42 213, 391, 564
15:43 364
15:44 302
15:50 391[77]
15:51-57 474
15:52 391
15:53-54 564
15:53-55 195, 213, 595[169]
15:53 53–54, 213[101], 391[77]
15:54-55 405[37]
15:54 213, 259, 391[77], 393, 605
15:55 214, 594[164]
15:58 320, 438[215], 447[66]
16:9 503
16:17 86[100]
16:21 394[117]
16:22 550[186]

2 Corinthians
1:6 432[126]
1:7 256
1:8 277[131]
1:12 509
1:18 388[42]
1:22 55
1:23 130[11]
2:14-16 164[171]
2:15 394
3:1 336[167]
3:5 376, 446[47]
3:14 526
3:17a 392[89]
3:18 191[12]
4:1-6 445
4:2 445
4:3 394
4:4 191[12], 445, 526
4:6 191[12], 210, 445
4:8 432[126]
4:13 388[38]
4:14 603

2 Corinthians (*continued*)
5:1-4 363[104]
5:1 118[68], 255[29]
5:2 319, 546[113]
5:4 118[68], 213, 277[131], 393, 546[113]
5:14 589
5:16 118[67], 262
5:17 463
6:2 316
6:5 521
6:7 361
6:14–7:1 301[39]
6:14 301[39]
6:16 445
6:18 105
6:41 53
7:1 563
7:5 432[126]
7:6-7 86[100]
7:8 354[209]
7:10 157[60], 563
7:14 354[209]
8:1 404[27]
8:2 94[44]
8:4 279
8:9 327
8:24 282
9:11 94[44]
9:12 537
9:13 94[44]
10:1 459[172]
10:2 266[222]
10:5 117
10:15 535
11:2 395, 454[101]
11:16 264[192]
11:26 541
11:28 599[239]
12:2-4 166
12:4 165[183]
12:15 130[11]
13:4 364, 531, 603
13:13 269, 339, 495

Galatians
1:13-14 587[51]
1:15 404[27]
2:6 238[59]
2:16 387[34], 406, 556[219]
2:20 387[34], 556[219]
2:21 399, 406
3:1 382[51], 592
3:7 547
3:9 388
3:13 383
3:17 441, 589
3:18 507[44]
3:19 441
3:22 387[34], 556[219]
3:23-26 475
3:23 108
3:25 108
3:26 41
3:27 53, 463[228]
4:4-7 41
4:4 95, 104, 144[49]
4:6 456
4:8-9 262
4:9 569[47], 580
4:27 281
5:2 459[172]
5:7 519
5:20 515
6:1 400
6:5 490
6:12-14 592
6:15 463

Ephesians
1:4 580
1:6 38
1:9-11 282
1:10 278, 503[186]
1:13 55, 116, 176
1:14 305
1:16 63[16]
1:17 99[95], 117
1:18 86[99], 575
1:19 283
1:20-23 488[185]
1:21 50[29], 56, 545
1:22-23 250[250]
1:23 488
2:2 266[222], 321[163]
2:4 439[237]
2:5 280[179], 359, 603
2:6 159, 603
2:7 164[171]
2:8 359, 531
2:14-15 503
2:14-16 336[169]
2:14-18 310
2:14 135
2:17 135, 502–3
2:18 503
2:19 39, 323
2:22 323
3:2 404[27], 503[186]
3:4 158[69]
3:7-8 404[27]
3:9 278, 503[186]
3:12 387[34], 503, 556[219]
3:16 575
3:17 531
3:19 258, 488, 589
4:3 143
4:4-6 269
4:5 579
4:7 450[26]
4:8-10 143, 450, 491, 593
4:8 143, 212[87], 459
4:9 143
5:
4:15 250[250], 335, 344
4:16 249
4:17 266[222]
4:18 108[213], 154
4:21 116
4:22-24 363[104]
4:24 53, 195, 213
4:25 176, 250[249]
4:30 55
4:31 397
5:2 101[123], 164[171]
5:6-14 208
5:7 449[15]
5:8 147, 301[39], 513[29]
5:9 138
5:13 224[101]
5:14 114, 208, 599
5:19 5, 13, 109[222], 221, 371, 571
5:20 63[16]
5:23 250[250]
5:30 250[249]
6:23-24 587
6:24 391, 581

Titus
1:2 44
2:4 558
2:13 499[116]
3:3 526
3:4 164[171]

Philemon
4 63[16]

Hebrews
1:2 122, 232
1:3-5 500
1:3 191[12], 283, 407[69]
1:8 409[93], 447[68]
1:9 344[44], 444[28], 501
1:10 222[77]
1:13 407[69]
1:14 569
2:3 563
2:5-8 574[146]
2:5-9 500
2:5 411[118]
2:6 498, 575[147], 578
2:7 232, 297
2:9 232, 297
2:10-14 431[106]
2:10 118, 201[51]
2:12-13 431[106]
2:13 425[6]
2:14 409
2:17 40[32]
3–4 38
3:14 31
4:3 387, 435[173], 477, 580
4:4 39
4:12-13 181[100]
4:12 223
4:14 304, 491
5:8 454
5:9 453
5:13-14 567[28]
5:13 366[137]
6:7 249, 537
6:13-18 59
6:13 441
6:14 388
7:26 355, 365
8:3 141[14]
9:5 480
9:24 359[39]
9:26 100[123], 351[162], 580
9:28 141[14], 439[230]
10:7 334[143]
10:12 100[123]
10:22-24 64
10:23 388[42]
11:11 388[42]
11:29 542–43
11:36 521
11:38 519
12:2 118, 201[51], 387, 437, 548, 556
12:9-11 142
12:11 142
12:18 66[58], 146
12:28 320, 437[205], 447[66]
13:8 447[68]
13:15 51[52], 63[11], 220[44]
13:17 124, 130[11]
13:20 312, 405

James
1:5 94[44]
1:8 116
1:10-11 154
1:12 34, 235[27], 581[266]
1:18 176
1:21 577
2:2 599[239]
2:5 581[266]
3:6 332[116]
3:15 329
3:17-18 142
3:18 248[224]
4:7 520
5:7 86[100]
5:19-20 427[48]
5:19 238[70]
5:20 212

1 Peter
1:2-3 117
1:3 100
1:7 232, 297
1:9 577
1:14 108[213]
1:18 531
1:20 580
1:22 519
1:24 154
1:25 447[68]
2:2 270[20], 486
2:4-8 322
2:4 457
2:5 286
2:11 411
2:15 108[213]
2:21-25 551
2:21 556
2:25 519[138]
3:18-19 381[33]
3:18-22 593
3:19-20 593, 600
3:20-21 350[134]
3:22 56, 491
4:6 248[220], 319[129], 593, 600
4:12 528[301]
4:14 493
4:19 388[42]
5:4 33
5:11 447[68]

2 Peter
1:4 97
1:13 255[29]
1:16 86[100]
1:17 232, 267[235], 297
2:2 157[60], 158[62]
2:4 146, 312[27]
2:5-7 350[134]
2:6 282
2:10 305[81]
2:12 458
2:17 146
3:4 86[100]
3:10-12 322[174]
3:12 86[100]

1 John
1:3 394[117]
1:4 91[21], 444
1:5 304[66], 445
1:7 304[66]
1:7b 178
1:9 63[11], 388[42]
2:1 92
2:8 258[91]

2:11	86[99], 266
2:21	259[100]
2:23	63[11]
2:25	441
2:28	86[100]
3:6	327[32]
3:10	316
4:2-3	63[11]
4:9	104
4:15	63[11]
4:16	327, 477
4:19	37
5:16	523
5:18	327[32]
5:20	215

2 John

4	444
7	63[11]

3 John

12	446[51]

Jude

8	305[81]
9	314
11	520
12	144[57]
13	515

Revelation

1:1	520
1:6	286
1:13	272
1:18	587, 594[164], 596[190]
2:7	45[52], 165[183]
2:8	531, 587[63]
2:9	599
2:10	34
2:11	45[52]
2:17	45[52]
2:23	156[49]
2:29	45[52]
3:5	63[11], 138
3:6	45[52]
3:9	599[241]
3:13	45[52]
3:22	45[52]
4:1	245[162]
4:8	447
4:9	232, 297
4:11	232, 297
5:1-3	330
5:2	331
5:3	330
5:5	331, 533
5:9	581
5:10	286
6:8	405[35], 594[164]
6:10	447
6:16	497
7:17	172, 397
9:1-2	350[134]
9:6	520, 522[195]
9:18	521
9:21	521[175]
10:7	118
11:7	411
11:15	339, 550[186]
11:17	63[16]
12:1-5	276
12:2	277
12:3-10	314
12:3	315, 334
12:7	315
12:9	315, 412, 525
12:10	315
12:12	331
12:13	412
12:14	497
12:16a	405
12:17	411
13:1	334
13:6	331
13:7	411
13:8	580
14:3	581
14:5	261[132]
14:15-16	333
15:4	355, 365, 430, 536[440]
16:5	355, 365
16:15	293
17:3	334
17:8	580
18:14	130[11]
19:2	458
19:7	524
19:9	524
19:13	184[149]
19:19	411
20:1-3	350[134]
20:2	314
20:3	412
20:6	286
20:10	350[134]
20:11	497
20:13-14	405[35]
20:13	594[164], 596
20:14	412, 594[164]
21:2	523
21:6	83, 160[91], 415
21:9	524[246]
21:19	449[15]
22:1-2	83, 167
22:2	167[217]
22:13	462[219]
22:15	396
22:16	459[172], 462[219], 533, 574
22:17	415, 417

f / Early Christian Literature and Ancient Church

1 Clement

4:12	312
5:4	49
5:7	49
12:4	520
14:3	271
16	468
16:1-14	533
16:2-3	533
16:3-14	435
16:3	508
16:6	519[138]
16:12	508
16:16	506
16:17	589
17:5	521
18:2	204
20:6	541[23]
20:8	541[23]
27:3	304
27:6	304
33:2-7	225
35:1-2	433
35:3	102[134]

20:1 468
21:5 436[180]

Epistle to Diognetus
3:3 162[130]
3:4 57
5:16-17 395
6:5 117
7:4 202[78]
9:6 215
12:1 165

Ephrem the Syrian
Madrasha de Paradiso
7:21 6

Eusebius
Theophania
i. 35. 5 260[112]

Gospel of the Hebrews
frgs 2–3 495
frg 3 276[123]
frg 4b 376[91]
frg 5 276[123]

Gospel of Peter
4:10 437
8 170

Gospel of Philip
53.3-4 39
59,4-6 392[86]
63,35-36 392[86]
69 472
84,10-13 177[19]

Gospel of Thomas (NHC II,*2*)
1 376[87]
2 376[91]
13.5 417[30]
17 224
22 472
53 156

Gospel of Truth
(NHC I,*3* + XII,*2*)
16,35 489[198]
17,14-15 517[114]
17,23-25 471[78]
17,30 519[148]
18,20 519[148]
19,15-16 586
19,26 519[148]
19,35–20,24 138
20,25-27 383[69]
20,29 519[148]
21,3-5 138
22,2-15 474[113]
22,2-20 478[10]
22,12 489[198], 519[148]
22,17 519[148]
22,20 519[148]
22,38–32,1 138
24,9-11 270[20]
24,9 519[148]
26,19-36 519[148]
26,28–27,7 178[35]
28,16 519[148]
29,16 519[148]
31,20 519[148]
31,25 517[114]
32,35 517[114]
33,33 519[148]
36,10-11 513[29]
36,11-12 519[148]
36,35-39 168
36,36 519[148]
37,25–38,4 103[144]
38,29-32 73[124]
40,30–41,35 489
41,3 519[148]
41,13-14 489
41,17 519[148]
42,8 519[148]
42,26-28 73[124]

Gregory Thaumaturgos
Panegyricum in Originem
119 192[17]
142 192[17]

Shepherd of Hermas 53
Mandates
28 (III).1 45, 261
35 (VI.1).2 520
Similitudes
68 30[13]
79 158[69]
89 (IX.12).2 230
91 (IX.14).6 532[369]
96 (IX.19).2 177
98 (IX.21).2 532[366]
105 (IX.28).4 509[65]
Visions
3 (I.3).4 226
23 (IV.2).1-2 454[101]
23 (IV.2).4 202[67]

Heracleon
Frg. 20 8

Hippolytus
Elenchos
7.30.1 396
Refutatio omnium haeresium
5.8.45 283[238]

Ignatius
Ephesians
4:1 77
4:2 250[249]
7:1 396, 529
14:2 327[32]
16:2 569[45]
17:1 164[171], 264
18:2 503
19:3 108[217], 321
20:1 503
Magnesians
7:1-2 579
7:2 579, 580[235]
8:2 115[36]
10:2 164[171]
14 164
Philadelphians
1:2 77
2–3 513[29]
2:1 513[29]
3:1 532, 536
8:1 247[209], 314, 461[207]
9:2 106
11:1 461
Polycarp
1:1 438
2:3 515
6:1 502
Romans
2:2 428
6:2 142
7:2 83[72], 87[111], 110[240], 159[90], 161

2. Greek Words

3. Subjects

4. Authors

In the design of the visual aspects of *Hermeneia*, consideration has been given to relating the form to the content by symbolic means.

The letters of the logotype *Hermeneia* are a fusion of forms alluding simultaneously to the letter forms of Hebrew (dotted vowel markings) and Greek (geometric round shapes). In their modern treatment they remind us of the electronic age, the vantage point from which this investigation of the past begins.

The Lion of Judah used as visual identification for the series is based on the Seal of Shema. The version for *Hermeneia* is again a fusion of Hebrew calligraphic forms, especially the legs of the lion, and Greek elements characterized by the geometric. In the sequence of arcs, which can be understood as scroll-like images, the first is the lion's mouth. It is reasserted and accelerated in the whorl and returns in the aggressively arched tail: tradition is passed from one age to the next, rediscovered and re-formed.

> "Who is worthy to open the scroll and break
> its seals. . . ."
>
> Then one of the elders said to me
> "weep not; lo, the Lion of the tribe of David,
> the Root of David, has conquered,
> so that he can open the scroll
> and its seven seals."
>
> Rev. 5:2, 5

To celebrate the signal achievement in biblical scholarship which Hermeneia represents, the entire series by its color will constitute a signal on the theologian's bookshelf: the Old Testament will be bound in yellow and the New Testament in red, traceable to a commonly used color coding for synagogue and church in medieval painting; in pure color terms, varying degrees of intensity of the warm segment of the color spectrum. The colors interpenetrate when the binding color for the Old Testament is used to imprint volumes from the New and vice versa.

Wherever possible, a photograph of the oldest extant manuscript, or a historically significant document pertaining to the biblical sources, will be displayed on the end papers of each volume to give a feel for the tangible reality and beauty of the source material.

The title-page motifs are expressive derivations from the Hermeneia logotype, repeated seven times to form a matrix and debossed on the cover of each volume. These sifted-out elements are in their exact positions within the parent matrix.

The type has been set with unjustified right margins to preserve the internal consistency of word spacing. This is a major factor in both legibility and aesthetic quality; the resultant uneven line endings are only slight impairments to legibility by comparison. In this respect the type resembles the handwritten manuscripts where the quality of the calligraphic writing is dependent on establishing and holding to integral spacing patterns.

All of the type faces in common use today have been designed between 1500 C.E. and the present. For the biblical text a face was chosen which does not date the text arbitrarily, but rather is uncompromisingly modern and unembellished, giving it a universal feel. The type style is Univers by Adrian Frutiger.

The expository texts and footnotes are set in Baskerville, chosen for its compatibility with the many brief Greek and Hebrew insertions. The double-column format and the shorter line length facilitate speed reading and the wide margins to the left of footnotes provide for the scholar's own notations.

Kenneth Hiebert

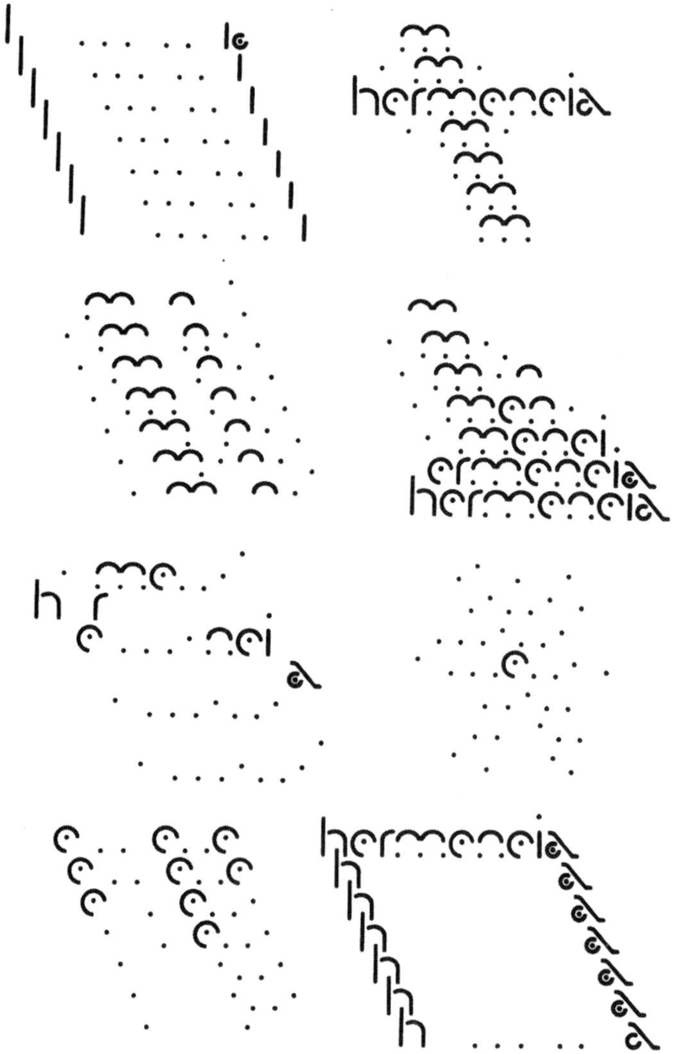

Category of biblical writing,
key symbolic characteristic,
and volumes so identified.

1
Law
(boundaries described)
- Genesis
- Exodus
- Leviticus
- Numbers
- Deuteronomy

2
History
(trek through time and space)
- Joshua
- Judges
- Ruth
- 1 Samuel
- 2 Samuel
- 1 Kings
- 2 Kings
- 1 Chronicles
- 2 Chronicles
- Ezra
- Nehemiah
- Esther

3
Poetry
(lyric emotional expression)
- Job
- Psalms
- Proverbs
- Ecclesiastes
- Song of Songs

4
Prophets
(inspired seers)
- Isaiah
- Jeremiah
- Lamentations
- Ezekiel
- Daniel
- Hosea
- Joel
- Amos
- Obadiah
- Jonah
- Micah
- Nahum
- Habakkuk
- Zephaniah
- Haggai
- Zechariah
- Malachi

5
New Testament Narrative
(focus on One)
- Matthew
- Mark
- Luke
- John
- Acts

6
Epistles
(directed instruction)
- Romans
- 1 Corinthians
- 2 Corinthians
- Galatians
- Ephesians
- Philippians
- Colossians
- 1 Thessalonians
- 2 Thessalonians
- 1 Timothy
- 2 Timothy
- Titus
- Philemon
- Hebrews
- James
- 1 Peter
- 2 Peter
- 1 John
- 2 John
- 3 John
- Jude

7
Apocalypse
(vision of the future)
- Revelation

8
Extracanonical Writings
(peripheral records)